SOMETHING ABOUT THE AUTHOR®

Something about
the Author *was named
an "Outstanding
Reference Source,"
the highest honor given
by the American
Library Association
Reference and Adult
Services Division.*

ISSN 0276-816X

something
ABOUT the
AUThor®

**Facts and Pictures about Authors
and Illustrators of Books for Young People**

volume 141

GALE®

THOMSON

™

GALE

Detroit • New York • San Diego • San Francisco • Cleveland • New Haven, Conn. • Waterville, Maine • London • Munich

Something about the Author, Volume 141

Project Editor
Scot Peacock

Editorial
Katy Balcer, Shavon Burden, Sara Constantakis, Anna Marie Dahn, Alana Joli Foster, Natalie Fulkerson, Arlene M. Johnson, Michelle Kazensky, Julie Keppen, Joshua Kondek, Thomas McMahon, Jenai A. Mynatt, Judith L. Pyko, Mary Ruby, Lemma Shomali, Susan Strickland, Maikue Vang, Tracey Watson, Thomas Wiloch, Emiene Shija Wright

Research
Michelle Campbell, Barbara McNeil, Tamara C. Nott, Gary J. Oudersluys, Tracie A. Richardson, Cheryl L. Warnock

Permissions
Margaret Chamberlain

Imaging and Multimedia
Dean Dauphinais, Robert Duncan, Leitha Etheridge-Sims, Mary K. Grimes, Lezlie Light, Dan Newell, David G. Oblender, Christine O'Bryan, Kelly A. Quin, Luke Rademacher

Manufacturing
Stacy L. Melson

LIBRARY OF CONGRESS CATALOG CARD NUMBER 72-27107

ISBN 0-7876-5213-X
ISSN 0276-816X

Printed in the United States of America
10 9 8 7 6 5 4 3 2 1

Contents

Authors in Forthcoming Volumes vii
Introduction ix
SATA Product Advisory Board xi
Acknowledgments xiii
Illustrations Index 215
Author Index 241

A

Agarwal, Deepa 1947- 1

Anholt, Laurence 1959- 2

B

Beresford, Elisabeth 1926- 8

Borden, Louise (Walker) 1949- 13

Autobiography Feature 16

Bottone, Frank G., Jr. 1969- 28

Brian, Janeen (Paulette) 1948- 29

Brown, Dee (Alexander) 1908-2002

Obituary Notice 33

Byalick, Marcia 1947- 34

C

Canales, Viola 1957- 36

Carey, Bonnie

See Marshall, Bonnie C. 108

Casey, Tina 1959- 36

Curlee, Lynn 1947- 38

D

Derrickson, Jim 1959- 41

Duncan, Lois 1934- 42

Autobiography Feature 47

E-F

Easton, Kelly 1960- 59

Erdrich, Louise 1954- 61

Erickson, Jon 1948- 69

Fuqua, Jonathon Scott 1966- 73

G-H

George, Sally

See Orr, Wendy 125

Giambastiani, Kurt R. A. 1958- 75

Gilman, Phoebe 1940-2002

Obituary Notice 76

Hawkins, (Helena Ann) Quail 1905-2002

Obituary Notice 76

Hazell, Rebecca (Eileen) 1947- 77

Hermes, Patricia 1936- 79

Hines, Anna Grossnickle 1946- 85

Hyde, Catherine Ryan 1955- 90

J-K

Jackson, Melanie 1956- 93

Janover, Caroline (Davis) 1943- 94

Johnson, Stephen T. 1964- 96

Kerry, Lois

See Duncan, Lois 42

L

Landau, Elaine 1948- 98

Lawrinson, Julia 1969- 105

Louise, Heidi

See Erdrich, Louise 61

M

Markusen, Bruce (Stanley Rodriguez) 1965- . 107

Marshall, Bonnie C. 1941- 108

McPherson, James M(unro) 1936- 111

N-O

Nelson, Robin Laura 1971- 120

Nicolson, Cynthia Pratt 1949- 123

North, Milou

See Erdrich, Louise 61

Orr, Wendy 1953- 125

Orwin, Joanna 1944- 129

P

Peretti, Frank E. 1951- 131

Pluckrose, Henry (Arthur) 1931- 134

R

Reynolds, Marilynn 1940- 143

Rhynes, Martha E. 1939- 147

Rounds, Glen (Harold) 1906-2002

Obituary Notice 148

S

Sanders, Nancy I. 1960- 150

Scheeder, Louis 1946- 152

Schwarz, (Silvia Tessa) Viviane 1977- 153

Scoltock, Jack 1942- 154

Sherrard, Valerie (Anne) 1957- 155

Sill, Cathryn 1953- 156

Simmons, Andra 1939- 158

Smith, Derek 1943- 158

Stafford, Liliana 1950- 160

Stephens, Rebecca 1961- 162

Stewart, Gail B. 1949- 162

Sullivan, Kathryn A. 1954- 166

T-U

Tipene, Tim 1972- 167

Unzner, Christa 1958- 167

Unzner-Fischer, Christa

See Unzner, Christa 167

V

Vande Velde, Vivian 1951- 171

Van Leeuwen, Jean 1937- 176

Autobiography Feature 183

W

Wallace, Ian 1950- 196

Wallace, Nancy Elizabeth 1948- 202

Y-Z

Yaccarino, Dan 1965- 207

Zebra, A.

See Scoltock, Jack 154

Authors in Forthcoming Volumes

Below are some of the authors and illustrators that will be featured in upcoming volumes of *SATA*. These include new entries on the swiftly rising stars of the field, as well as completely revised and updated entries (indicated with *) on some of the most notable and best-loved creators of books for children.

*Judy Blume: Since she published her first book in 1969, Blume has become one of the most popular and controversial authors for children. Her books for younger children, such as *Tales of a Fourth Grade Nothing, Blubber,* and *Otherwise Known as Sheila the Great,* deal with problems of sibling rivalry, establishing self-confidence, and social ostracism. Books for older readers, such as *Are You There God? It's Me, Margaret, Deenie,* and *Just as Long as We're Together* consider matters of divorce, friendship, family breakups, and sexual development. In 2002 Blume published *Double Fudge.*

*Raymond Chang: Chemistry professor Chang has written several highly praised chemistry textbooks for college students, but he also draws on his memories growing up in China in the books he has coauthored for children. Together with his wife, Margaret Scrogin Chang, Chang has written *In the Eye of War,* a novel for children about a Chinese family living in occupied Shanghai. Also with his wife, he has created the texts for several picture books based on traditional Chinese tales, among them *The Cricket Warrior* and *The Beggar's Magic.*

Joan Dash: Dash is a prizewinning author of biographies for young adults. Her early works, including *A Life of One's Own: Three Gifted Women and the Men They Married, Summoned to Jerusalem: The Life of Henrietta Szold,* and *The Triumph of Discovery: Women Scientists Who Won the Nobel Prize,* are part of the growing movement to bring to light the achievements of notable women in history. In 2001 Dash received the *Boston Globe/Horn Book* Award for Nonfiction and a Sibert Honor Book citation for *The Longitude Prize.*

Rick Geary: Geary is a prominent cartoonist whose drawings have appeared in such well-known publications as the *New York Times* and the *Los Angeles Times* as well as *National Lampoon* and *Mad* magazine. He has earned a following among young adults with his graphic novels, notably his contributions to the "Treasury of Victorian Murder" series. In 2002 Geary illustrated Patricia Lakin's book *Harry Houdini: Escape Artist.*

*Mordecai Gerstein: Gerstein worked for many years in animation, but since the early 1980s, he has devoted his time to children's books. He is the author and illustrator of more than thirty books for young readers, including picture books, chapter books, and novels. Illustrating the work of other writers, especially that of Elizabeth Levy, he has over two dozen more book credits. *What Charlie Heard,* a 2002 publication, earned a Parents' Choice Award and an American Library Association notable book citation.

Kathy Kacer: Canadian author Kacer's novel *The Secret of Gabi's Dresser* is a first-person fictionalized account of Kacer's mother's escape from the Nazis in Slovakia during World War II. That work was followed by *Clara's War,* which offers another view of the Holocaust and the effect of the Nazi plan for the Jews on a family in Czechoslovakia. In 2003 Kacer published *The Night Spies.*

*Jill Murphy: Murphy's "Worst Witch" books, about a young British schoolgirl and her trials and tribulations at a school for witches, include *The Worst Witch, The Worst Witch Strikes Back, A Bad Spell for Worst Witch,* and *The Worst Witch at Sea.* In addition to this popular series, Murphy has also written and illustrated several warm and humorous picture books featuring the Larges, a family of pachyderms, two titles about the Bear family, and a duet of books about a loveable little monster named Marlon. Recipient of several Kate Greenaway Award nominations for her illustrations, Murphy published the self-illustrated title *All for One* in 2002.

*Stephanie S. Tolan: The author of over twenty novels for children and young adults as well as several musical plays, Tolan often writes of children who are, in some way or another, special if not exceptional. Among her award-winning titles are *Welcome to the Ark, Ordinary Miracles,* and *Flight of the Raven.* Tolan's 2002 work *Surviving the Applewhites* was named a Newbery Honor Book.

*Bjarne Reuter: Danish author Reuter is one of that country's most beloved children's writers, creator of almost sixty titles, only four of which have been translated into English. Winner of the prestigious Mildred Batchelder Award in 1990 for the translated edition of his children's novel *Buster's World,* Reuter was also a recipient of an Academy Award for the script of the film *Pelle the Conqueror.*

Vladimir Vagin: Vagin is a Russian-born illustrator of children's books whose detailed artwork reflects the influences of his heritage. He has teamed up with prominent authors such as Frank Asch, Katherine Paterson, and Jane Yolen in award-winning and highly commended fable-like picture books and retellings, and has also illustrated his own retellings of folktales and popular stories, including *The Nutcracker Ballet, Peter and the Wolf,* and *The Twelve Days of Christmas.* Vagin illustrated Jane Yolen's *The Flying Witch,* published in 2003.

Introduction

Something about the Author (*SATA*) is an ongoing reference series that examines the lives and works of authors and illustrators of books for children. *SATA* includes not only well-known writers and artists but also less prominent individuals whose works are just coming to be recognized. This series is often the only readily available information source on emerging authors and illustrators. You'll find *SATA* informative and entertaining, whether you are a student, a librarian, an English teacher, a parent, or simply an adult who enjoys children's literature.

What's Inside SATA

SATA provides detailed information about authors and illustrators who span the full time range of children's literature, from early figures like John Newbery and L. Frank Baum to contemporary figures like Judy Blume and Richard Peck. Authors in the series represent primarily English-speaking countries, particularly the United States, Canada, and the United Kingdom. Also included, however, are authors from around the world whose works are available in English translation. The writings represented in *SATA* include those created intentionally for children and young adults as well as those written for a general audience and known to interest younger readers. These writings cover the entire spectrum of children's literature, including picture books, humor, folk and fairy tales, animal stories, mystery and adventure, science fiction and fantasy, historical fiction, poetry and nonsense verse, drama, biography, and nonfiction.

Obituaries are also included in *SATA* and are intended not only as death notices but also as concise overviews of people's lives and work. Additionally, each edition features newly revised and updated entries for a selection of *SATA* listees who remain of interest to today's readers and who have been active enough to require extensive revisions of their earlier biographies.

Autobiography Feature

Beginning with Volume 103, *SATA* features two or more specially commissioned autobiographical essays in each volume. These unique essays, averaging about ten thousand words in length and illustrated with an abundance of personal photos, present an entertaining and informative first-person perspective on the lives and careers of prominent authors and illustrators profiled in *SATA*.

Two Convenient Indexes

In response to suggestions from librarians, *SATA* indexes no longer appear in every volume but are included in alternate (odd-numbered) volumes of the series, beginning with Volume 57.

SATA continues to include two indexes that cumulate with each alternate volume: the Illustrations Index, arranged by the name of the illustrator, gives the number of the volume and page where the illustrator's work appears in the current volume as well as all preceding volumes in the series; the Author Index gives the number of the volume in which a person's biographical sketch, autobiographical essay, or obituary appears in the current volume as well as all preceding volumes in the series.

These indexes also include references to authors and illustrators who appear in Gale's *Yesterday's Authors of Books for Children, Children's Literature Review,* and *Something about the Author Autobiography Series.*

Easy-to-Use Entry Format

Whether you're already familiar with the *SATA* series or just getting acquainted, you will want to be aware of the kind of information that an entry provides. In every *SATA* entry the editors attempt to give as complete a picture of the person's life and work as possible. A typical entry in *SATA* includes the following clearly labeled information sections:

- *PERSONAL:* date and place of birth and death, parents' names and occupations, name of spouse, date of marriage, names of children, educational institutions attended, degrees received, religious and political affiliations, hobbies and other interests.

- *ADDRESSES:* complete home, office, electronic mail, and agent addresses, whenever available.

- *CAREER:* name of employer, position, and dates for each career post; art exhibitions; military service; memberships and offices held in professional and civic organizations.

- *AWARDS, HONORS:* literary and professional awards received.

- *WRITINGS:* title-by-title chronological bibliography of books written and/or illustrated, listed by genre when known; lists of other notable publications, such as plays, screenplays, and periodical contributions.

- *ADAPTATIONS:* a list of films, television programs, plays, CD-ROMs, recordings, and other media presentations that have been adapted from the author's work.

- *WORK IN PROGRESS:* description of projects in progress.

- *SIDELIGHTS:* a biographical portrait of the author or illustrator's development, either directly from the biographee—and often written specifically for the *SATA* entry—or gathered from diaries, letters, interviews, or other published sources.

- *BIOGRAPHICAL AND CRITICAL SOURCES:* cites sources quoted in "Sidelights" along with references for further reading.

- *EXTENSIVE ILLUSTRATIONS:* photographs, movie stills, book illustrations, and other interesting visual materials supplement the text.

How a SATA Entry Is Compiled

A *SATA* entry progresses through a series of steps. If the biographee is living, the *SATA* editors try to secure information directly from him or her through a questionnaire. From the information that the biographee supplies, the editors prepare an entry, filling in any essential missing details with research and/or telephone interviews. If possible, the author or illustrator is sent a copy of the entry to check for accuracy and completeness.

If the biographee is deceased or cannot be reached by questionnaire, the *SATA* editors examine a wide variety of published sources to gather information for an entry. Biographical and bibliographic sources are consulted, as are book reviews, feature articles, published interviews, and material sometimes obtained from the biographee's family, publishers, agent, or other associates.

Entries that have not been verified by the biographees or their representatives are marked with an asterisk (*).

Contact the Editor

We encourage our readers to examine the entire *SATA* series. Please write and tell us if we can make *SATA* even more helpful to you. Give your comments and suggestions to the editor:

BY MAIL: Editor, *Something about the Author,* The Gale Group, 27500 Drake Rd., Farmington Hills, MI 48331-3535.

BY TELEPHONE: (800) 877-GALE

BY FAX: (248) 699-8054

Something about the Author **Product Advisory Board**

The editors of *Something about the Author* are dedicated to maintaining a high standard of excellence by publishing comprehensive, accurate, and highly readable entries on a wide array of writers for children and young adults. In addition to the quality of the content, the editors take pride in the graphic design of the series, which is intended to be orderly yet inviting, allowing readers to utilize the pages of *SATA* easily and with efficiency. Despite the longevity of the *SATA* print series, and the success of its format, we are mindful that the vitality of a literary reference product is dependent on its ability to serve its users over time. As literature, and attitudes about literature, constantly evolve, so do the reference needs of students, teachers, scholars, journalists, researchers, and book club members. To be certain that we continue to keep pace with the expectations of our customers, the editors of *SATA* listen carefully to their comments regarding the value, utility, and quality of the series. Librarians, who have firsthand knowledge of the needs of library users, are a valuable resource for us. The *Something about the Author* Product Advisory Board, made up of school, public, and academic librarians, is a forum to promote focused feedback about *SATA* on a regular basis. The nine-member advisory board includes the following individuals, whom the editors wish to thank for sharing their expertise:

- **Eva M. Davis,** Youth Department Manager, Ann Arbor District Library, Ann Arbor, Michigan

- **Joan B. Eisenberg,** Lower School Librarian, Milton Academy, Milton, Massachusetts

- **Francisca Goldsmith,** Teen Services Librarian, Berkeley Public Library, Berkeley, California

- **Harriet Hagenbruch,** Curriculum Materials Center/Education Librarian, Axinn Library, Hofstra University, Hempstead, New York

- **Monica F. Irlbacher,** Young Adult Librarian, Middletown Thrall Library, Middletown, New York

- **Robyn Lupa,** Head of Children's Services, Jefferson County Public Library, Lakewood, Colorado

- **Eric Norton,** Head of Children's Services, McMillan Memorial Library, Wisconsin Rapids, Wisconsin

- **Victor L. Schill,** Assistant Branch Librarian/Children's Librarian, Harris County Public Library/Fairbanks Branch, Houston, Texas

- **Caryn Sipos,** Community Librarian, Three Creeks Community Library, Vancouver, Washington

Acknowledgments

Grateful acknowledgment is made to the following publishers, authors, and artists whose works appear in this volume.

ANHOLT, LAURENCE. From an illustration in *Leonardo and the Flying Boy,* by Laurence Anholt. Barron's, 2000. © 2000 Laurence Anholt. Reproduced by permission./ Anholt, Catherine, illustrator. From an illustration in *Sophie and the New Baby,* by Laurence Anholt. Albert Whitman and Company, 2000. Illustrations © 1995 by Catherine Anholt. Reproduced by permission./ Anholt, Laurence, photograph. © 2002 Laurence Anholt. Reproduced by permission.

BERESFORD, ELISABETH. Wallner, John, illustrator. From a jacket of *Curious Magic,* by Elisabeth Beresford. Copyright © 1980 by Elisabeth Beresford. Reproduced by permission of Dutton Children's Books, A division of Penguin Young Readers Group, A Member of Penguin Group (USA) Inc., 345 Hudson St., New York, NY 10014. All rights reserved./ Beresford, Elisabeth, photograph. AP/Wide World Photos. Reproduced by permission.

BORDEN, LOUISE (WALKER). Borden, Louise, seated in front of bookcase, photograph by Robert A. Flischel. Reproduced by permission./ All other photographs reproduced by permission of Louise Borden.

BOTTONE, FRANK G., JR. From a cover of *The Science of Life: Projects and Principles for Beginning Biologists,* by Frank G. Bottone, Jr. Chicago Review Press, 2001. Cover images © 2001 Photodisc. Reproduced by permission.

BRIAN, JANEEN (PAULETTE). King, Stephen Michael, illustrator. From an illustration in *Where Does Thursday Go?,* by Janeen Brian. Margaret Hamilton Books, a division of Scholastic Australia Pty Limited, 2001. Illustrations © 2001 by Stephen Michael King. Reproduced in the U.S. by permission of Clarion Books/Houghton Mifflin Company, in the U.K. by permission of Scholastic Australia Pty. Ltd./ Brian, Janeen Paulette, photograph. Reproduced by permission.

BYALICK, MARCIA. Byalick, Marcia, photograph by Jane Schweiger. Reproduced by permission of Marcia Byalick.

CASEY, TINA. Smythe, Theresa, illustrator. From an illustration in *The Runaway Valentine,* by Tina Casey. Albert Whitman & Company, 2001. Illustrations © 2001 by Theresa Smythe. Reproduced by permission.

CURLEE, LYNN. From an illustration in *Seven Wonders of the Ancient World,* by Lynn Curlee. Atheneum Books for Young Readers, 2002. Copyright © 2002 Lynn Curlee. Reproduced by permission of Atheneum Books for Young Readers, an imprint of Simon & Schuster Children's Publishing Division.

DUNCAN, LOIS. Duncan, Lois, standing on beach, photograph by Jennifer Bishop. Reproduced by permission./ Duncan, Lois, with her husband, Don Arquette, working in their office, photograph by Jennifer Bishop. Reproduced by permission./ All other photographs reproduced by permission of Lois Duncan.

EASTON, KELLY. Easton, Kelly, photograph by William Fridrich. Reproduced by permission of Kelly Easton.

ERDRICH, LOUISE. From an illustration in *The Birchbark House,* by Louise Erdrich. Hyperion Paperbacks for Children, 1999. © 1999 by Louise Erdrich. Reproduced by permission./ Johnson, Steve, and Lou Fancher, illustrators. From an illustration in *The Range Eternal,* by Louise Erdrich. Hyperion Books for Children, 2002. Illustrations © 2002 by Steve Johnson and Lou Fancher. Reproduced by permission./ Erdrich, Louise, photograph. © Jerry Bauer. Reproduced by permission.

ERICKSON, JON. From a photograph in *Quakes, Eruptions and Other Geologic Cataclysms,* by Jon Erickson. Facts on Files, Inc., 1994. Photo courtesy of USGS./ Eagle, Jeremy, and Dale Dyer, illustrators. From an illustration in *Lost Creatures of the Earth: Mass Extinction in the History of Life,* by Jon Erickson. Checkmark Books, 2001. Illustrations © 2001 by Facts on File. Reproduced by permission of Facts on File, Inc.

GIAMBASTIANI, KURT R. A. From a cover of *The Year the Cloud Fell: An Alternate History,* by Kurt R. A. Giambastiani, 2001. New American Library/Penguin Putnam. Reproduced by permission.

HAZELL, REBECCA (EILEEN). Cann, Helen, illustrator. From an illustration in *The Barefoot Book of Heroic Children,* retold by Rebecca Hazell. Barefoot Books, 2000. Illustrations © 2000 Helen Cann. Reproduced by permission.

HERMES, PATRICIA. Vojnar, Kamil, illustrator. From a jacket of *Cheat the Moon,* by Patricia Hermes. Little, Brown and Company, 1998. Reproduced by permission./ Harrington, Glenn, illustrator. From a cover by Elizabeth B. Parisi of *A Perfect Place: Joshua's Oregon Trail Diary, Book Two,* by Patricia Hermes. Scholastic, 2002. Illustration copyright © 2002 by Scholastic Inc. Reproduced by permission./ Hermes, Patricia, photograph by Capitol Photo. Reproduced by permission.

HINES, ANNA GROSSNICKLE. Sweet, Melissa, illustrator. From an illustration in *My Grandma Is Coming to Town,* by Anna Grossnickle Hines. Candlewick Press, 2003. Illustration copyright © 2003 by Melissa Sweet. Reproduced by permission of the publisher Candlewick Press, Inc., Cambridge, MA./ Hines, Anna Grossnickle, photograph by Nathan Snippen Stephens. Reproduced by permission of Anna Grossnickle Hines.

JANOVER, CAROLINE (DAVIS). Fremaux, Charlotte, illustrator. From an illustration in *How Many Days Until Tomorrow?* by Caroline Janover. Woodbine House, 2000. Reproduced by permission./ Janover, Caroline, photograph. Reproduced by permission.

JOHNSON, STEPHEN T. Johnson, Stephen T., illustrator. From an illustration in *Love as Strong as Ginger,* by Lenore Look. Atheneum Books for Young Readers, 1999. Illustrations © 1999 by Stephen T. Johnson. Reproduced by permission of Atheneum Books for Young Readers, an imprint of Simon & Schuster Children's Publishing Division.

LANDAU, ELAINE. Brown, Molly, photographer. From a photograph in *Heroine of the Titanic: The Real Unsinkable Molly Brown,* by Elaine Landau. Clarion Books, 2001. Photograph courtesy of the Colorado Historical Society. Reproduced by permission./ Lies, Brian, illustrator. From an illustration in *Popcorn!,* by Elaine Landau. Charlesbridge Publishing Inc., 2003. Illustration copyright © 2003 by Brian Lies. Reproduced by permission of Charlesbridge Publishing, Inc. All rights reserved./ Landau, Elaine, photograph. Reproduced by permission.

LAWRINSON, JULIA. Lawrinson, Julia, photograph by Shawn Salmon. Reproduced by permission of Julia Lawrinson.

MARKUSEN, BRUCE (STANLEY RODRIGUEZ). From a photograph in *Roberto Clemente: The Great One,* by Bruce Markusen. Sports Publishing LLC. Reproduced by permission of National Baseball Hall of Fame and Museum, Inc.

MARSHALL, BONNIE C. Halpern, Joel M., photographer. From a photograph in *Tales from the Heart of the Balkans,* retold by Bonnie C. Marshall. Libraries Unlimited, Inc., 2001. Reproduced by permission./ Marshall, Bonnie C., photograph. Reproduced by permission.

MCPHERSON, JAMES M(UNRO). Lynch, Kathleen, illustrator. From a cover of *For Cause and Comrades: Why Men Fought in the Civil War,* by James M. McPherson. Oxford University Press, Inc., 1997. Copyright © 1997 by James M. McPherson. Cover photograph by Archive Photos. Reproduced by permission of Oxford University Press, Inc./ Tran, David, illustrator. From a cover of *Drawn with the Sword: Reflections on the American Civil War,* by James M. McPherson. Oxford University Press, Inc., 1997. Copyright © 1996 by James M. McPherson. Reproduced by permission of Oxford University Press, Inc./ Hope, Captain James, artist. From a cover of *Crossroads of Freedom: Antietam,* by James M. McPherson. Thorndike Press, 2002. Cover illustration courtesy of Antietam National Battlefield. Reproduced by permission of Oxford University Press, Inc./ From an illustration in *Fields of Fury: The American Civil War,* by James M. McPherson. Atheneum Books for Young Readers, 2002. Illustration © Bettmann/Corbis. Reproduced by permission of Corbis./ McPherson, James M., photograph. Reproduced by permission.

NELSON, ROBIN LAURA. Stepanowicz, L. S., photographer. From a photograph in *A Rainy Day,* by Robin Nelson. Lerner Publications, 2002. Photo © L. S. Stephanowicz/Visuals Unlimited. Reproduced by permission.

NICHOLSON, CYNTHIA PRATT. Griggs, J. D., photographer. From a photograph in *Volcano!,* by Cynthia Pratt Nicolson. Kids Can Press Ltd., 2001. Photo courtesy of the USGS.

ORR, WENDY. Millard, Kerry, illustrator. From a jacket of *Nim's Island,* by Wendy Orr. Copyright © 1999 by Wendy Orr. Jacket illustration © 2001 by Kerry Millard. Reproduced in the U.S. by permission Alfred A. Knopf, an imprint of Random House Children's Books, a division of Random House, Inc., in the U.K. by permission of Allen & Unwin Pty Ltd./ Henshaw, Jacqui, illustrator. From a cover of *Peeling the Onion,* by Wendy Orr. Laurel-Leaf Books, 1999. Reproduced by permission of Random House Children's Books, a division of Random House, Inc./ Orr, Wendy, photograph by Albert Dodman. Reproduced by permission of Wendy Orr.

ORWIN, JOANNA. Orwin, Joanna, photograph. Reproduced by permission.

PERETTI, FRANK E. Fournet, Annette, photographer. From a jacket of *The Wounded Spirit,* by Frank Peretti. Word Publishing, 2000. © 2000 W Publishing, Nashville, Tennessee. All rights reserved.. Reproduced by permission./ Peretti, Frank E., photograph. AP/Wide World Photos. Reproduced by permission.

PLUCKROSE, HENRY (ARTHUR). From a cover of *Sorting,* by Henry Pluckrose. Children's Press, 1995. © 1994 Watts Books, London, New York, Sydney. Reproduced by permission./ From a photograph in *On the Farm,* by Henry Pluckrose. Franklin Watts, 1998. Photograph by JCB Landpower Ltd. Reproduced by permission./ Short, Michael, and Gavin Hellier, photographers. From a cover of *Czech Republic,* by Henry Pluckrose. Franklin Watts, 1999. © Franklin Watts 1999. Reproduced by permission./ From a photograph in *On the Move,* by Henry Pluckrose. Franklin Watts, 1999. Photograph by Zefa Visual Media Group. Reproduced by permission.

REYNOLDS, MARILYNN. McCallum, Stephen, illustrator. From an illustration in *Belle's Journey,* by Marilynn Reynolds. Orca Book Publishers, 1993. Illustrations © 1993 by Stephen McCallum. Reproduced by permission./ Kilby, Don, illustrator. From an illustration in *The Prairie Fire,* by Marilynn Reynolds. Orca Book Publishers, 1999. Illustrations © 1999 by Don Kilby. Reproduced by permission.

RHYNES, MARTHA E. Rhynes, Martha E., photograph. © 2003 Martha E. Rhynes. Reproduced by permission.

something ABOUT the AUThOR

AGARWAL, Deepa 1947-

Personal

Born December 23, 1947, in Almora, Uttranchal, India; daughter of Arthur (a doctor) and Nancy (a teacher; maiden name, Joshi) Rawat; married Dilip Agarwal (in business), March 29, 1972; children: Garima Agarwal Swarup, Sonali, Geetika Agarwal Sharma. *Ethnicity:* "Indian." *Education:* Allahabad University, M.A., 1969. *Hobbies and other interests:* Reading, classical music, traveling.

Addresses

Agent—c/o Author Mail, Scholastic India (Pvt.) Ltd., 29 Udyog Vihar, Phase-1, Gurgaon, 122 016 Haryana, India. *E-mail*—akdk@de13.vsnl.net.in.

Career

S.P.M. College, New Delhi, India, lecturer, 1969-72; writer.

Member

Indian Society of Authors (life member), Association of Writers and Illustrators for Children (life member), Society of Children's Book Writers and Illustrators, Lekhika Sangh (life member).

Awards, Honors

Book prizes, Children's Book Trust, 1987, for *A Capital Adventure,* 1991, for *The Toy Horse,* and 1997, for *The Walking Tree;* National Award for Children's Literature, Government of India, 1993, for *Ashok's New Friends;* short story prize, *Asian Age,* 1995, for "Cradle Song."

Writings

FOR CHILDREN

A Capital Adventure (mystery novel), Children's Book Trust (New Delhi, India), 1990.

Three Days To Disaster (mystery novel), Ratnasagar (New Delhi, India), 1990.

Traveller's Ghost (ghost story), HarperCollins (New Delhi, India), 1994.

Lippo Goes to the Park (picture book), Frank Educational Aids (Noida, India), 1994.

Squiggly Goes to School (picture book), Frank Educational Aids (Noida, India), 1994.

Everyday Tales (short stories), HarperCollins India (New Delhi, India), 1995.

The Hunt for the Miracle Herb (mystery novel), Penguin India (New Delhi, India), 1995.

Ghosts Everywhere (short stories), A'N'B Publishers (New Delhi, India), 1996.

Adventures in the Hills (short stories), A'N'B Publishers (New Delhi, India), 1996.

Folk Tales From India (retold folk tales), Macmillan India Limited (Chennai, India), 1997.

Myths and Legends From India (retold myths and legends), Macmillan India Limited (Chennai, India), 1997.

Animals and Birds in Myth and Legend (retold myths and legends), Macmillan India Limited (Chennai, India), 1997.

The Hilltop Mystery (novel), Vikas House (New Delhi, India), 1999.

Ashok's New Friends (picture book), Children's Book Trust (New Delhi, India), 1999.

The Walking Tree (picture book), National Book Trust (New Delhi, India), 1999.

Birju and the Flying Horse (picture book), Frank Educational Aids (Noida, India), 1994.

Lippo Goes to a Party (picture book), Frank Educational Aids (Noida, India), 2000.

Squiggly Goes for a Picnic (picture book), Frank Educational Aids (Noida, India), 2000.

Cheeko and the School Bag (picture book), Frank Educational Aids (Noida, India), 2000.

Flippi the Flying Pup (picture book), Frank Educational Aids (Noida, India), 2000.

What's Right What's Wrong (short stories), Save the Children Fund (New Delhi, India), 2001.

Anita and the Game of Shadows (fantasy novel), Scholastic India (Haryana, India), 2002.

Bamba and Pinky (picture book), Frank Educational Aids (Noida, India), 2002.

Flippi the Doggieangel (picture book), Frank Educational Aids (Noida, India), 2002.

Also author of *The Toy Horse.*

FOR ADULTS

Hyena and Other Short Stories (translated adult short story collection from Hindi), Ocean Books (New Delhi, India), 1998.

The Crusade (translated adult novel from Hindi), Ocean Books (New Delhi, India), 2001.

If the Earth Should Move (adult short story collection), Srishtis (New Delhi, India), 2002.

Contributor of articles, short stories, poetry, translations, and reviews to periodicals for both adults and children.

Work in Progress

A novel for adults; an adventure novel for children; research on the history of children's literature in India; research on trading communities on the Indo-Tibetan border; poetry collection for adults; short story collection for children.

Sidelights

Deepa Agarwal told *SATA*: "My primary motivation for writing is communication and a desire to inculcate the values of equality in both children and adults. My writing process depends on the work in question. I research the topic before getting down to writing, and revise a lot. I draw my themes from my immediate environment as well as my past experiences. The position of women and children in my country as well as the world at large has been a moving force in my writing. My earlier writing was more journalistic; now I concentrate mostly on my fiction and poetry."

ANHOLT, Laurence 1959-

Personal

Born August 4, 1959, in London, England; son of Gerald Simon (an artist) and Joan (a teacher; maiden name, Pickford) Anholt; married Catherine Hogarty (an illustrator and writer), July, 1984; children: Claire, Tom and Madeline (twins). *Education:* Attended Epsom School of Art and Design, 1976-77; Falmouth School of Art, B.A. (with honors), 1982; Royal Academy of Art, M.A., 1987.

Addresses

Agent—c/o Author Mail, Penguin Putnam, 375 Hudson St., New York, NY 10014. *E-mail*—info@anholt.co.uk.

Career

Self-employed carpenter/joiner, London, England, 1983-84; freelance writer and illustrator of children's books, 1987—; art teacher in secondary school, Oxford, England, 1988-89. Part-time education teacher at Swindon School of Art and West Dean College, 1990—.

Awards, Honors

Named one of the "*Independent on Sunday*'s Top 10 UK Children's Authors;" *What I Like* was named one of the Children's Book Foundation Books of the Year, 1991; Gold Smarties Award, 1999, for *Snow White and the Seven Aliens,* 2001, for *Chimp and Zee;* Kids' Club Network Award; Right Start Toy and Book Award (three titles); Oppenheim Toy Portfolio Gold Award Winner (twice); English Association Four to Eleven Awards (two titles); shortlisted for the Federation of Children's Book Awards (three titles), Sainsbury Baby Book Award, Experian Big 3 Book Prize, Nottinghamshire Children's Book Award, and U.S. Smithsonian Institute (highly recommended); Sheffield Children's Book Award; Blue Peter Book Award, BBC, for *Eco-Wolf and the Three Pigs.*

Writings

WITH WIFE, CATHERINE ANHOLT UNDER NAME LAURENCE ANHOLT; ILLUSTRATED BY CATHERINE ANHOLT, EXCEPT AS NOTED

What I Like, Putnam (New York, NY), 1991.

Going to Playgroup, Orchard Books (New York, NY), 1991.

Going to Playground, Orchard Books (New York, NY), 1992.

The Twins: Two by Two, Candlewick Press (Cambridge, MA), 1992.

The Forgotten Forest, self-illustrated, Sierra Book Club (San Francisco, CA), 1992.

Can You Guess?, Frances Lincoln, 1992.

All About You, Viking (New York, NY), 1992.

Kids, Candlewick Press (Cambridge, MA), 1992.

Tiddlers, Candlewick Press (Cambridge, MA), 1993.

Bear and Baby, Candlewick Press (Cambridge, MA), 1993.

Camille and the Sunflowers: A Story about Vincent van Gogh, self-illustrated, Barron's Educational (Hauppauge, NY), 1994.

The New Puppy, Artists and Writers Guild (New York, NY), 1995.

Bear Skates, Candlewick Press (Cambridge, MA), 1995.

Degas and the Little Dancer: A Story about Edgar Degas, self-illustrated, Barron's Educational (Hauppauge, NY), 1996.

Knee-High Norman, illustrated by Arthur Robins, Candlewick Press (Cambridge, MA), 1996.

The Magpie Song, illustrated by Dan Williams, Houghton Mifflin (Boston, MA), 1996.

Cinderboy, illustrated by Arthur Robins, Orchard (New York, NY), 1997.

Eco-Wolf and the Three Pigs, illustrated by Arthur Robins, Orchard (New York, NY), 1997.

Snow White and the Seven Aliens, illustrated by Arthur Robins, Orchard (New York, NY), 1998.

Picasso and the Girl with a Ponytail, self-illustrated, Barron's Educational (Hauppauge, NY), 1998.

Silly Jack and the Bean Stack, illustrated by Arthur Robins, Meadowbrook Press (Minnetonka, MN), 1999.

Summerhouse, illustrated by Lynne Russell, DK Publishers (New York, NY), 1999.

Billy and the Big New School, Whitman (Morton Grove, IL), 1999.

The Emperor's New Underwear, illustrated by Arthur Robins, Meadowbrook Press (Minnetonka, MN), 1999.

Stone Girl, Bone Girl: The Story of Mary Anning, illustrated by Sheila Moxley, Orchard (New York, NY), 1999.

Tina the Tiniest Girl, illustrated by Tony Ross, Orchard (New York, NY), 1999.

Little Red Riding Wolf, Simon & Schuster (New York, NY), 2000.

Ghostyshocks and the Three Scares, illustrated by Arthur Robins, Orchard (New York, NY), 2000.

Leonardo and the Flying Boy, self-illustrated, Barron's Educational (Hauppauge, NY), 2000.

I Like Me, I Like You, illustrated by Adriano Gon, DK Publishers (New York, NY), 2001.

The Child's Gift of Art, self-illustrated, Barron's Educational (Hauppauge, NY), 2002.

Jack and the Dream Sack, illustrated by Ross Collins, Bloomsbury Publishing (New York, NY), 2003.

The Magical Garden of Claude Monet, self-illustrated, Barron's Educational (Hauppauge, NY), 2003.

UNDER NAME OF COAUTHOR/ILLUSTRATOR, WIFE CATHERINE ANHOLT

Truffles' Day in Bed, Methuen (London, England), published in the U.S. as *Truffles Is Sick,* Little Brown (Boston, MA), 1987.

Truffles in Trouble, Joy Street Books (Boston, MA), 1987.

Chaos at Cold Custard Farm, Methuen (London, England), 1988.

When I Was a Baby, Joy Street Books (Boston, MA), 1988.

Tom's Rainbow Walk, Heinemann (London, England), 1989.

The Snow Fairy and the Spaceman, Dell (New York, NY), 1990.

Aren't You Lucky!, Little Brown (Boston, MA), 1990.

Laurence Anholt

Come Back, Jack!, Candlewick, Press (Cambridge, MA), 1994.

One, Two, Three, Count with Me, Viking (New York, NY), 1994.

What Makes Me Happy?, Candlewick Press (Cambridge, MA), 1995.

Sun, Snow, Stars, Sky, Viking (New York, NY), 1995.

Here Come the Babies, Candlewick Press (Cambridge, MA), 1995.

First Words and Pictures, Candlewick Press (Cambridge, MA), 1996.

A Kiss Like This, Barron's Educational (Hauppauge, NY), 1997.

Catherine and Laurence Anholt's Big Book of Families, Candlewick Press (Cambridge, MA), 1998.

Harry's Home, Farrar Straus Giroux (New York, NY), 2000.

Sophie and the New Baby, Whitman (Morton Grove, IL), 2000.

Chimp and Zee, Penguin Putnam (New York, NY), 2001.

Monkey Around with Chimp and Zee, Penguin Putnam (New York, NY), 2002.

Chimp and Zee's Noisy Book, Penguin Putnam (New York, NY), 2002.

Chimp and Zee and the Big Storm, Penguin Putnam (New York, NY), 2002.

Sidelights

Laurence Anholt is a British writer and illustrator for children, author of over fifty picture books in collaboration with his wife, illustrator Catherine Anholt, and others. Among his most popular team efforts with his wife is the "Chimp and Zee" series, winner of the prestigious Gold Smarties Award in 2001. Working with illustrator Arthur Robins, Anholt has also produced a number of humorous take-offs on the standard fairy tale repertoire, including *Silly Jack and the Bean Stack* and *The Emperor's New Underwear*. Anholt once told *SATA:* "Almost all the titles listed have been produced with my wife, Catherine. People are often confused about which one of us writes and which one illustrates. In general, Catherine does the illustration and I do the writing, but there are one or two exceptions, for example, *The Forgotten Forest,* which I illustrated and wrote, and *Good Days, Bad Days,* which was written and illustrated by Catherine. Just to make things more complicated, I did not use my name as a writer until 1991 because I was still primarily working as a teacher and wanted to keep the writing as a separate activity. Our titles published before this date are therefore in Catherine's name only."

Anholt's background contributes to his abilities as a children's book writer and illustrator. "I was born in London, but spent much of my childhood in Holland as my father's family is Dutch," the author told *SATA*. "My father has painted on and off for many years and for me it seemed only natural to follow in his footsteps. I spent eight years at art school and it was not until much later that I began writing seriously. I still spend a lot of time working on my painting and teach painting classes at Adult Education Centers."

In 1984, Anholt married illustrator and writer Catherine Hogarty. "Catherine and I have three children: Claire, and twins Tom and Madeline. All the ideas for our books come from our day-to-day experiences with the family and we often test ideas on the children to see how they respond. In fact one of our ... projects, *The Twins: Two by Two,* is really about our own twins."

Though his publishing career began in 1987 in joint projects under his wife's name, Anholt's first title under his own name was the 1991 *What I Like,* "one of the simplest books that we have worked on," the author recalled. "Again, the idea came from listening to our children talking. At first the idea seemed too simple and I had to resist the temptation to complicate it by adding a story or more text. However, in the end it is the simplicity which makes it direct and, in this country, the book was recently selected one of the Children's Book Foundation Books of the Year. I think this lesson on simplicity, or, more to the point, economy, is one of the hardest to learn, but it is there in much of the literature and art that I admire." Reviewing that title in *School Library Journal,* Virginia Opocensky praised the "cheerful watercolor cartoons and rhyming text" which lists likes and dislikes of a half-dozen children. *Booklist*'s Hazel Rochman also lauded the "strong and subtle" text.

Anholt's first solo effort, *The Forgotten Forest,* has an eco-message. The forests of the world have all but disappeared and only one small, fenced-in patch remains. When bulldozers come to knock the trees down to make way for new buildings, children gather to watch.

Young Zoro discovers that his teacher, Leonardo da Vinci, is building a flying machine in **Leonardo and the Flying Boy,** *written and illustrated by Anholt.*

However the crew changes their mind at the last moment, and knock down the fence instead, then begin planting new trees. Anna Biagioni Hart, writing in *School Library Journal,* thought the art was better than the text in this picture book, commending the colors that "wash the pages with good feeling," but finding ultimately that this "vague parable is not an effective piece of story-telling." A reviewer for *Junior Bookshelf,* however, enjoyed the "good surprise happy ending" of this "fable."

Anholt has also created a number of concept books, such as *One, Two, Three, Count with Me,* a blend of counting, size, days of the week, colors, and parts of the body. *Booklist*'s Rochman called this a "joyful concept book." *Sun, Snow, Stars, Sky* introduces the seasons, while *What Makes Me Happy?* deals with the emotions. Reviewing the latter title, *Horn Book*'s Margaret A. Bush thought it was "at once simple and beautifully conceived as both a celebration of daily life and a means of helping children to recognize and name their feelings." *Booklist*'s Rochman, reviewing the same title, noted that the Anholts "once again dramatize the small child's daily life."

New schools, puppies, and dogs take center stage in other books from Anholt. Fear of the new inspires the concept book *Billy and the Big New School,* a "poignant but reassuring treatment of the anxiety a child feels facing the first day at a new school," according to a contributor for *Publishers Weekly.* Fearful of his first day, Billy learns a lesson from a sparrow he rescues and then sets free. "Reading this story is a reassuring way to help children talk about their anxieties," wrote Rochman in a *Booklist* review. Elizabeth Bush, writing in *Bulletin of the Center for Children's Books,* felt that though "the bird analogy is a bit labored," still readers would "understand the metaphor and welcome the reassurance of the Anholt's gentle tale." Shelley Woods, reviewing the same title in *School Library Journal,* likewise felt the book would "disipate children's fears about starting school." Fear of leaving home is addressed in *Harry's Home,* in which the young urban dweller leaves his mother for the first time to visit his grandfather on a small farm. *Booklist*'s Rochman once again lauded the Anholt's work, noting that children would find satisfaction in this tale recognizing "their own discovery of differences." For Rochman, the "pleasure [of the book] is in the loving particulars of place." A reviewer for *Publishers Weekly* thought the Anholts "create warm picture postcards of both country and city life in this picture book about the meaning of home." And Miriam Lang Budin, writing in *School Library Journal,* called the same story a "very satisfying adventure ... [with] plenty of child appeal."

Stories of puppies and new babies have also won favorable critical response for Anholt. Young Anna has a passion for dogs in *The New Puppy,* but when her father gets her a puppy named Tess, she learns that having a puppy can also be a big responsibility. Tess makes a mess on the floor and chews Anna's slippers, but after scolding the animal, she hears it crying in the

Sophie excitedly waits for her new brother to be born, but her feelings change upon his arrival in Sophie and the New Baby, *a collaborative effort by Anholt and his wife, illustrator Catherine Anholt.*

middle of the night and comforts it. Leone McDermott, writing in *Booklist,* found that this "engaging story is gently instructive without preachiness," while Betsy Hearne, writing in *Bulletin of the Center for Children's Books,* concluded that "story and art share a traditional coziness with just enough mischief to keep things lively." With *Sophie and the New Baby,* the Anholts "synchronize the cycle of life with the rhythms of the seasons," according to a contributor for *Publishers Weekly.* Sophie's mood is as black as the winter storms when her little brother first arrives, but over the course of the year, she grows to love the new arrival. The same contributor felt that the author and illustrator "convincingly depict Sophie's maturation" in this "heartwarming" picture book. Martha Topol, reviewing the tale in *School Library Journal,* thought that the "changing of the seasons gives great supporting structure and expanded definition to the story."

Families are at the center of *Catherine and Laurence Anholt's Big Book of Families,* in which the collaborators celebrate domestic life in their "signature style," according to Rochman in a *Booklist* review: with "simple chanting verse and lots of small clear individual ink-and-watercolor scenarios." All sorts of families are pictured: small ones and sprawling extended ones; families at play and work. A reviewer for *Publishers Weekly* felt that the "rollicking and sweet" short poems of the collection "pays homage to families of various configurations and personalities."

Working solo, Anholt has also written several picture books about artists. His *Camille and the Sunflowers* tells a story of Vincent van Gogh's stay in the south of France. Partly based on real information, the tale concerns the family who helped the newcomer van Gogh out with their furniture and friendship; van Gogh in turn painted members of the family. Using his own artwork as well as reproductions of van Gogh's paintings, Anholt presents a "sad tale," according to Carolyn Jenks in *School Library Journal,* and one that can "provide a greater understanding of this gifted, troubled man." Sheila Holligan, reviewing the title in *School Librarian,* felt that the "pictures are equally as important as words in this delightful book." The painter and sculptor Edgar Degas is featured in *Degas and the Little Dancer,* a story that helps explain the statue of the same name. Anholt tells the story of the young ballerina who inspired Degas's work. Frances Ball, writing in *School Librarian,* felt that the book "provides a delightful introduction to seeing a stature rather than just looking at it." Pablo Picasso receives a similar treatment in *Picasso and the Girl with a Pony Tail,* "beautifully illustrated and engagingly told," according to Kit Spring in the *Observer.* And Leonardo da Vinci also comes under the Anholt scrutiny in *Leonardo and the Flying Boy,* a "cleverly executed and engaging account," as a reviewer for *Publishers Weekly* described the book. The same reviewer found this account a "fun-filled and accessible introduction." The story of young Zoro and how he worked with Leonardo on his flying machine, the book is an "attractive starting point for youngsters learning about Leonardo's work for the first time," according to *Booklist*'s Gillian Engberg.

A change of pace for Anholt is the 1999 *Stone Girl, Bone Girl,* the story of the young British fossil hunter, Mary Anning, who helped to advance dinosaur studies with her discovery of an ichthyosaur skeleton when she was just twelve years old. Janice M. Del Negro, writing in *Bulletin of the Center for Children's Books,* thought that Anholt "capably tells the early life story of the fossil-hunting Mary" in this picture book biography. *Booklist*'s Ilene Cooper found Mary Anning to be a "wonderfully fresh topic for a book," and concluded that the book "works well as biography and history . . . [and] is also a fine piece of storytelling."

One of Anholt's most popular creations, in collaboration with his wife, is the "Chimp and Zee" series. The stories recount the adventures of two mischievous monkeys and their mother, Mumkey. In the first outing, *Chimp and Zee,* the eponymous heroes are separated from Mumkey while shopping for bananas, but manage to end up back home. Reviewing that title in *School Library Journal,* Rachel Fox felt that "youngsters should enjoy the story and the oversized, action-packed pictures." A reviewer for *Publishers Weekly* also had praise for the book, noting that the Anholts "offer a decidedly old-fashioned but surely toddler-pleasing tale." The pair resume their adventures in *Monkey Around with Chimp and Zee* and *Chimp and Zee's Noisy Book.* Olga R. Kuharets, writing in *School Library Journal,* pointed out that "babies and toddlers can easily follow these rhythmic texts." And in *Chimp and Zee and the Big Storm,* the monkey siblings are tired of being inside, but going outside on a windy day they are soon swept away. Finally Mumkey is able to catch up to the twins and snag one of their tails with an umbrella. Once again, Chimp and Zee pleased the reviewers. Diane Foote, writing in *Booklist,* felt that the "livley images, bright colors, and recognizable mischief make this a cheerful read—rain or shine."

Anholt elaborated for *SATA* on the responsibilities inherent in becoming a children's book author: "When we work on a book we are always very aware of the responsibility that we have. Books are extremely influential. I was reminded of this recently when I bought an old children's anthology from a second-hand book store. It was a book I had loved as a child, but had not seen for more than twenty-five years. I was amazed to find how intimately I knew each story and illustration. I even found that my favorites and least favorites had remained the same. A young child enters into a book completely and, as they read and reread, it shapes the adult they become—and so the society they inhabit. I think it is essential, then, that children's writers and illustrators put a huge amount of care into what they say. I would like to think that our books help children to open their minds to issues of equality—gender and race—to environmental issues, but most of all I want children to get the message that books are fun—it is okay to enjoy yourself, there is plenty to be optimistic about, and the world is a good place to grow up in."

Biographical and Critical Sources

PERIODICALS

Booklist, September 1, 1991, Hazel Rochman, review of *What I Like,* p. 59; June 1, 1994, Hazel Rochman, review of *One, Two Three, Count with Me,* p. 1824; December 1, 1994, Hazel Rochman, review of *Camille and the Sunflowers,* p. 684; May 1, 1995, Hazel Rochman, review of *What Makes Me Happy?,* p. 1578; May 15, 1995, Janice Del Negro, review of *Sun, Snow, Stars, Sky,* p. 1650; August, 1995, Leone McDermott, review of *The New Puppy,* p. 1954; December 15, 1998, Hazel Rochman, review of *Catherine and Laurence Anholt's Big Book of Families,* p. 753; February 1, 1999, Ilene Cooper, review of *Stone Girl, Bone Girl,* p. 974; February 15, 1999, Susan Dove Lempke, review of *Summerhouse,* p. 1074; March 1, 1999, Hazel Rochman, review of *Billy and the Big New School,* p. 1218; May 1, 2000, Hazel Rochman, review of *Harry's Home,* p. 1675; September 15, 2000, Connie Fletcher, review of *Sophie and the New Baby,* p. 247; January 1, 2001, Gillian Engberg, review of *Leonardo and the Flying Boy,* p. 954; October 1, 2002, Diane Foote, review of *Chimp and Zee and the Big Storm,* p. 330.

Books for Keeps, November, 1992, review of *Going to the Playgroup,* p. 15; March, 1997, review of *Cinderboy* and *Daft Jack and the Bean Stack,* p. 22; July, 1999, review of *Picasso and the Girl with a Pony Tail,* p. 4.

Bulletin of the Center for Children's Books, July, 1995, Betsy Hearne, review of *The New Puppy,* p. 376; February, 1999, Janice M. Del Negro, review of *Stone Girl, Bone Girl,* p. 195; May, 1999, Elizabeth Bush, review of *Billy and the Big New School,* p. 307.

Horn Book, July-August, 1995, Margaret A. Bush, review of *What Makes Me Happy?,* p. 447.

Junior Bookshelf, April, 1992, review of *The Forgotten Forest,* pp. 55-56; February, 1995, review of *Camille and the Sunflowers,* p. 7; August, 1996, review of *Degas and the Little Dancer,* p. 145.

Kirkus Reviews, October 1, 2000, review of *Sophie and the New Baby,* p. 1418.

Magpies, November, 1992, Renya Spratt, review of *Going to the Playgroup,* p. 26.

New York Times Book Review, November 21, 1999, Natalie Angier, review of *Stone Girl, Bone Girl,* p. 31.

Observer (London, England), December 13, 1998, Kit Spring, review of *Picasso and the Girl with a Pony Tail,* p. 16.

Publishers Weekly, November 23, 1998, review of *Catherine and Laurence Anholt's Big Book of Families,* p. 65; February 8, 1999, review of *Billy and the Big New School,* p. 213; March 15, 1999, review of *Stone Girl, Bone Girl,* p. 58; May 8, 2000, review of *Harry's Home,* p. 220; October 30, 2000, review of *Sophie and the New Baby,* p. 74; November 6, 2000, review of *Leonardo and the Flying Boy,* p. 90; July 30, 2001, review of *Chimp and Zee,* p. 83; July 15, 2002, review of *Chimp and Zee and the Big Storm,* p. 75.

School Librarian, May, 1995, Sheila Holligan, review of *Camille and the Sunflowers,* p. 57; August, 1996, Frances Ball, review of *Degas and the Little Dancer,* p. 98.

School Library Journal, December, 1991, Virginia Opocensky, review of *What I Like,* p. 78; April, 1992, Anna Biagioni Hart, review of *The Forgotten Forest,* p. 86; February, 1995, Carolyn Jenks, review of *Camille and the Sunflowers,* p. 72; December, 1998, Maura Bresnahan, review of *Catherine and Laurence Anholt's Big Book of Families,* p. 99; March, 1999, Shelley Woods, review of *Billy and the Big New School,* p. 162; April, 2000, Miriam Lang Budin, review of *Harry's Home,* p. 90; November, 2000, Martha Topol, review of *Sophie and the New Baby,* p. 110; February, 2001, Miriam Lang Budin, review of *Leonardo and the Flying Boy,* p. 92; October, 2001, Rachel Fox, review of *Chimp and Zee,* p. 104; April, 2002, Olga R. Kuharets, review of *Chimp and Zee's Noisy Book,* p. 100; September, 2002, Heather E. Miller, review of *Chimp and Zee and the Big Storm,* p. 180.

OTHER

Catherine and Laurence Anholt Home Page, http://www.anholt.co.uk (May 22, 2003).

B

BERESFORD, Elisabeth 1926-

Personal

Born August 6, 1926, in Paris, France; citizenship, British; daughter of J. D. (a novelist) and Evelyn (Roskams) Beresford; married Maxwell Robertson (a sports commentator), 1949; children: Kate, Marcus. *Education:* Attended schools in Brighton, Sussex, England. *Hobbies and other interests:* Reading, photography, gardening, "and not working, if at all possible."

Addresses

Home—22 Little Street, Alderney, Channel Islands. *Agent*—Juvenilia, Avington, Winchester, Hampshire SO21 1DB, England.

Career

Writer; freelance journalist, beginning 1949; radio broadcaster. *Military service:* Women's Royal Naval Service, radio operator during World War II.

Awards, Honors

Member, Order of the British Empire.

Elisabeth Beresford

Writings

FOR CHILDREN

The Television Mystery, Parrish (London, England), 1957.
The Flying Doctor Mystery, Parrish (London, England), 1958.
Trouble at Tullington Castle, Parrish (London, England), 1958.
Cocky and the Missing Castle, illustrated by Jennifer Miles, Constable (London, England), 1959.
Gappy Goes West, Parrish (London, England), 1959.
The Tullington Film-Makers, Parrish (London, England), 1960.
Two Gold Dolphins, illustrated by Peggy Fortnum, Constable (London, England), 1961, new edition, illustrated

by Janina Domanska, Bobbs-Merrill (Indianapolis, IN), 1964.
Danger on the Old Pull 'n' Push, Parrish (London, England), 1962, White Lion, 1976.
Strange Hiding Place, Parrish (London, England), 1962.
Diana in Television, Collins (London, England), 1963.
The Missing Formula Mystery, Parrish (London, England), 1963.
The Mulberry Street Team, illustrated by Juliet Pannett, Friday Press (Penshurst, Kent, England), 1963.
Awkward Magic, illustrated by Judith Valpy, Hart-Davis (London, England), 1964, new edition, illustrated by Janina Domanska, published as *The Magic World,* Bobbs-Merrill (Indianapolis, IN), 1965, revised edi-

tion, illustrated by Cathy Wood, published as *Strange Magic,* Methuen (London, England), 1986.

The Flying Doctor to the Rescue, Parrish (London, England), 1964.

Holiday for Slippy, illustrated by Pat Williams, Friday Press (Penshurst, Kent, England), 1964.

Game, Set, and Match, Parrish (London, England), 1965.

Knights of the Cardboard Castle, illustrated by C. R. Evans, Methuen (London, England), 1965, revised edition, illustrated by Reginald Gray, 1976.

Travelling Magic, illustrated by Judith Valpy, Hart-Davis (London, England), 1965, published as *The Vanishing Garden,* Funk (New York, NY), 1967.

The Hidden Mill, illustrated by Margery Gill, Benn (London, England), 1965, Meredith Press (New York, NY), 1967.

Peter Climbs a Tree, illustrated by Margery Gill, Benn (London, England), 1966.

Fashion Girl, Collins (London, England), 1967.

The Black Mountain Mystery, Parrish (London, England), 1967.

Looking for a Friend, illustrated by Margery Gill, Benn (London, England), 1967.

More Adventure Stories (includes *The Mulberry Street Team*), Benn (London, England), 1967.

The Island Bus, illustrated by Robert Hodgson, Methuen (London, England), 1968, revised edition, illustrated by Gavin Rowe, 1977.

Sea-Green Magic, illustrated by Ann Tout, Hart-Davis (London, England), 1968.

David Goes Fishing, illustrated by Imre Hofbauer, Benn (London, England), 1969.

Gordon's Go-Kart, illustrated by Margery Gill, McGraw (New York, NY), 1970.

Stephen and the Shaggy Dog, illustrated by Robert Hales, Methuen (London, England), 1970.

Vanishing Magic, illustrated by Ann Tout, Hart-Davis (London, England), 1970.

Dangerous Magic, illustrated by Oliver Chadwick, Hart-Davis (London, England), 1972.

The Secret Railway, illustrated by James Hunt, Methuen (London, England), 1973.

Invisible Magic, illustrated by Reginald Gray, Hart-Davis (London, England), 1974.

Snuffle to the Rescue, illustrated by Gunvor Edwards, Kestrel (London, England), 1975.

Beginning to Read Storybook, Benn (London, England), 1977.

Toby's Luck, illustrated by Doreen Caldwell, Methuen (London, England), 1978.

Secret Magic, illustrated by Caroline Sharp, Hart-Davis (London, England), 1978.

The Happy Ghost, illustrated by Joanna Carey, Methuen (London, England), 1979.

The Treasure Hunters, illustrated by Joanna Carey, Elsevier Nelson (New York, NY), 1980.

Curious Magic, illustrated by Claire Upsdale-Jones, Elsevier Nelson (New York, NY), 1980.

The Four of Us, illustrated by Trevor Stubley, Hutchinson (London, England), 1981.

The Animals Nobody Wanted, illustrated by Joanna Carey, Methuen (London, England), 1982.

During his vacation on a small island off the coast of England, Andy experiences an enchanting adventure that involves magical curses, pirates, and a white witch. (Jacket illustration by John Wallner.)

(Adaptor) *Jack and the Magic Stove* (folktale), illustrated by Rita van Bilsen, Hutchinson (London, England), 1982.

The Tovers, illustrated by Geoffrey Beitz, Methuen (London, England), 1982.

The Adventures of Poon, illustrated by Dinah Shedden, Hutchinson (London, England), 1984.

The Mysterious Island, illustrated by Joanna Carey, Methuen (London, England), 1984.

One of the Family, illustrated by Barrie Thorpe, Hutchinson (London, England), 1985.

The Ghosts of Lupus Street School, Methuen (London, England), 1986.

Emily and the Haunted Castle, illustrated by Kate Rogers, Hutchinson (London, England), 1987.

Once upon a Time Stories, illustrated by Alice Englander, Methuen (London, England), 1987.

The Secret Room, illustrated by Michael Bragg, Methuen (London, England), 1987.

The Armada Adventure, Methuen (London, England), 1988.

The Island Railway, illustrated by Maggie Harrison, Hamish Hamilton (London, England), 1988.

Rose, Hutchinson (London, England), 1989.

Charlie's Ark, Methuen (London, England), 1989.

The Wooden Gun, Hippo (London, England), 1989.

Tim the Trumpet, Blackie (London, England), 1992.

Jamie and the Rola Polar Bear, illustrated by Janet Robertson, Blackie (London, England), 1993.

Lizzie's War, illustrated by James Mayhew, Simon & Schuster (London, England), 1993.

Rola Polar Bear and the Heatwave, illustrated by Janet Robertson, Blackie (London, England), 1994.

The Smallest Whale, illustrated by Susan Field, Orchard Books (London, England), 1996.

Lizzie's War, Part II, illustrated by James Mayhew, Simon & Schuster (London, England), 1996.

Island Treasure, illustrated by Gillian Hunt, Macdonald Young (Hove, England), 1998.

Pirate Gold, illustrated by Rhiannon Powell, Oxford University Press (Oxford, England), 2000.

Tommy in Trouble, illustrated by Rhiannon Powell, Oxford University Press (Oxford, England), 2000.

Tessa on TV, illustrated by Rhiannon Powell, Oxford University Press (Oxford, England), 2000.

Danny and the Dolphin, Ormer Hourse (Alderney, Channel Islands), 2003.

"THE WOMBLES" SERIES; FOR CHILDREN

The Wombles, illustrated by Margaret Gordon, Benn (London, England), 1968, Meredith Press (New York, NY), 1969.

The Wandering Wombles, illustrated by Oliver Chadwick, Benn (London, England), 1970.

The Invisible Womble and Other Stories, illustrated by Ivor Wood, Benn (London, England), 1973.

The Wombles in Danger, Benn (London, England), 1973.

The Wombles at Work, illustrated by Margaret Gordon, Benn (London, England), 1973, revised edition, illustrated by B. Leith, 1976.

The Wombles Go to the Seaside, World Distributors (London, England), 1974.

The Wombles Annual, 1975-1978 (four volumes), World Distributors (London, England), 1974-77.

The Wombles Book (includes *The Wombles* and *The Wandering Wombles*), Benn (London, England), 1975.

Tomsk and the Tired Tree, illustrated by Margaret Gordon, Benn (London, England), 1975.

Wellington and the Blue Balloon, illustrated by Margaret Gordon, Benn (London, England), 1975.

Orinoco Runs Away, illustrated by Margaret Gordon, Benn (London, England), 1975.

The Wombles Gift Book, illustrated by Margaret Gordon and Derek Collard, Benn (London, England), 1975.

The Snow Womble, illustrated by Margaret Gordon, Benn (London, England), 1975.

The Wombles Make a Clean Sweep, illustrated by Ivor Wood, Benn (London, England), 1975.

The Wombles to the Rescue, illustrated by Margaret Gordon, Benn (London, England), 1975.

Tobermory's Big Surprise, illustrated by Margaret Gordon, Benn (London, England), 1976.

Madame Cholet's Picnic Party, illustrated by Margaret Gordon, Benn (London, England), 1976.

Bungo Knows Best, illustrated by Margaret Gordon, Benn (London, England), 1976.

The Wombles of Wimbledon (includes *The Wombles at Work* and *The Wombles to the Rescue*), Benn (London, England), 1976.

The MacWomble's Pipe Band, illustrated by Margaret Gordon, Benn (London, England), 1976.

The Wombles Go round the World, illustrated by Margaret Gordon, Benn (London, England), 1976.

The World of the Wombles, illustrated by Edgar Hodges, World Distributors (London, England), 1976.

Wombling Free, illustrated by Edgar Hodges, Benn (London, England), 1978.

Also author of *The Wombles* (screenplay), 1971, sixty television scripts for *The Wombles* (series), 1973, fifty-two television scripts for *The Wombles* (second series, and *The Wombles* (play), first produced in London, England, 1974.

ADAPTOR; FROM "WOMBLES" TELEVISION SERIES

Camping and Cloudberries, Hodder Children's (London, England), 1997.

The Ghost of Wimbledon Common, Hodder Children's (London, England), 1998.

Tomsk to the Rescue, Hodder Children's (London, England), 1998.

Orinoco the Magnificent, Hodder Children's (London, England), 1998.

Shansi's Surprise, Hodder Children's (London, England), 1998.

Beautiful Boating Weather, Hodder Children's (London, England), 1999.

Deep Space Womble, Hodder Children's (London, England), 1999.

Buggy Trouble, Hodder Children's (London, England), 1999.

The Great Cake Mystery, Hodder Children's (London, England), 1999.

Bigfoot Womble, Hodder Children's (London, England), 1999.

Chaos on the Common, Hodder Children's (London, England), 1999.

The Great Womble Explorer, Hodder Children's (London, England), 1999.

The Wombles: Womble Winterland and Other Stories, Hodder Children's (London, England), 1999.

NOVELS; FOR ADULTS

Paradise Island, Hale (London, England), 1963.

Escape to Happiness, Hale (London, England), 1964, Norton (New York, NY), 1980.

Roses 'round the Door, Hale (London, England), 1964, Paperback Library (New York, NY), 1965.

Island of Shadows, Hale (London, England), 1966, Dell (New York, NY), 1980.

Veronica, Hale (London, England), 1967, Norton (New York, NY), 1980.

A Tropical Affair, Hale (London, England), 1967, published as *Tropical Affairs,* Dell (New York, NY), 1978.

Saturday's Child, Hale (London, England), 1968, published as *Echoes of Love,* Dell (New York, NY), 1979.

Love Remembered, Hale (London, England), 1970, Dell (New York, NY), 1978.

Love and the S. S. Beatrice, Hale (London, England), 1972, published as *Thunder of Her Heart,* Dell (New York, NY), 1978.

Pandora, Hale (London, England), 1974.

The Steadfast Lover, Hale (London, England), 1980.

The Silver Chain, Hale (London, England), 1980.

The Restless Heart, Valueback (New York, NY), 1982.

Flight to Happiness, Hale (London, England), 1983.

A Passionate Adventure, Hale (London, England), 1983.

OTHER

(With Nick Renton) *Road to Albutal* (play), produced in Edinburgh, Scotland, 1976.

(With Peter Spence) *Move On,* BBC Publications, 1978.

The Best of Friends (play), produced in the Channel Islands, 1982.

Also contributor of short stories to magazines.

Adaptations

The "Wombles" were featured on postage stamps in 2001.

Work in Progress

Katy Goes to War, Danny and the Dolphin, and *Ben and the Magic Chair,* children's books; research for an autobiography, *But Don't Tell Mother.*

Sidelights

Elisabeth Beresford has achieved her greatest success as a writer through the creation of the "Wombles," a small race of creatures that inhabit her "Wombles" series of books for children. In over twenty-five books, this hard-working, fun-loving family, who live by the motto "make good use of bad rubbish," uphold old-fashioned virtues and introduce children to the more modern value of conservation.

Beresford was born in Paris, France, where her father, novelist J. D. Beresford, was living at the time. She returned to England and was educated in British schools. "Having a novelist for a father and two brothers who were successful writers I was brought up in a world of books," Beresford once recalled, "so it seemed natural that I should become a writer too." She began working as a journalist and eventually became a radio and television reporter for the British Broadcasting Corporation, a job that took her from the Australian outback to the jungles of South America. "Which, of course, all make wonderful backgrounds for books," she explained. "I've also met some extraordinary and unusual people; from goldminers to royalty, from Dukes to derelicts."

Beresford's furry Wombles, creatures who live in burrows underneath the London suburb of Wimbledon, take their names from an atlas, are led by Great Uncle Bulgaria, and were introduced to young readers for the first time in 1969. As ardent collectors of things, words, and knowledge, Wombles are expert recyclers, intelli-

gent, and, as Ginger Brauer observed in *Library Journal,* "generally superior in virtues to [Humans] ... with whom they don't normally associate." In the many books that followed—from *The Wombles at Work* and *Wellington and the Blue Balloon* to *Wombling Free,* the crowning book of the series—Beresford's engaging characters go beyond merely illustrating moral tales about picking up garbage and conserving natural resources. Their inventiveness and positive approach to many of society's growing problems have drawn praise from critics, and the author's sprightly prose keeps young readers interested. With the Wombles, Beresford "has done more than graft human characters on to animals," noted Margery Fisher in *Growing Point.* Instead the author "has created a new race, as consistent and plausible as the hobbits of Tolkien, whose likeness to ourselves is only one aspect of their existence."

The illustrations for Beresford's "Wombles" books were inspired by the puppetry magic of Ivor Wood, who designed the marionette figures used in the popular television series *The Wombles.* The majority of the books in the series have depicted Wood's original puppet characters—like Bungo, Tomsk, and Wellington—in vivid illustrations by Margaret Gordon. The Wombles have become somewhat of a legend in children's literature. The stories have been translated into twenty languages and made into both films and two television series.

Beresford has written many other novels for children, including both fantasy and adventure. Beresford "shares in some degree the dilemma of [Arthur] Conan Doyle," commented Marcus Crouch in *St. James Guide to Children's Writers.* Explaining that Conan Doyle's character of Sherlock Holmes "hung around his neck like a dead weight," forcing him to continue writing fiction featuring that famous detective long after he wanted to, Crouch continued, "Beresford invented the Wombles.... There can be no doubt that, in writing these gently humorous tales, she is sharing with readers her own warm affection for these curious creatures. But, in achieving a run-away success with the Wombles, Beresford has distracted attention from her other, and not less important, writing."

The Animals Nobody Wanted is just one of Beresford's books of real-life adventure focusing on the concerns of young readers. Sharing the theme of conservation with the Wombles books, this 1982 novel tells about Rosa and Paul, who go on a seaside vacation and meet Granny Campbell, an old woman who lives in run-down Ballig Fort near the sea. Granny is dedicated to caring for the oil-soaked seabirds she finds near her door, as well as other sick animals that are gathered up by a local boy named Midge. Rosa and Paul bring their city-bred instincts for commerce to the aid of Granny and her animal hospital, gathering support from the nearby townspeople and getting funding for the woman's humanitarian efforts. "Elisabeth Beresford knows how to tell a good story and this one is nicely constructed [and] pleasantly readable," D. A. Young wrote in *Junior Bookshelf.*

In *The Adventures of Poon* Beresford portrays the problems of an average family in dealing with a disabled child. Poon is profoundly deaf; when she is taken by her social worker to a farm in the country to allow her mother a chance to rest, Poon tries to run away. It is then that her adventures begin: in her quest for independence she helps the police by discovering an important piece of evidence in a police investigation into cattle rustling, uncovers a flint axehead for a local archaeologist, and, along the way, learns to cope with her own sense of isolation from speaking people and accept and to enjoy her new surroundings. In a *School Librarian* review, Sheila Armstrong commented that the characters are "likeable and amusing" but not idealized, and added that Poon's adventures "are told with a lighthearted and sure touch."

Being uprooted and having to cope with a whole new set of people and circumstances is a situation that many children—not only those who are hearing-impaired or otherwise disabled—have to deal with sometime in their childhood, and it provides the subject of Beresford's 1988 novel *The Island Railway* as well. When Police Sergeant Stafford is transferred from a busy town to a small, scantily populated island off the English coast, his son Thomas is not thrilled. Grudgingly, he seeks the friendship of Matthew, whose father is a fisherman, and together the two boys explore the small island with the help of Matthew's dog. When they find an old engine and a pair of abandoned railcars left behind after a local quarry shut down years before, the boy's persistence inspires the entire community—including a cantankerous elderly neighbor who alone has the knowledge to get the old engine moving again—to help set up a railroad on the island. "Beresford always fills her tales with vigorously drawn characters and this new story is no exception," commented Fisher in *Growing Point.* "Here is a most believable group of people linked in an unusual enterprise."

In Beresford's books, the everyday world can often stray into the realm of the fantastic, often at the most unpredictable times. Quite ordinary children can suddenly find themselves experiencing quite extraordinary things. "One of the many wonderful things about children is that *they* still live in a world where anything is possible," Beresford commented, "and the words 'once upon a time' can make it all happen." In the author's "Magic" books that began in 1964 with the publication of *Awkward Magic,* she weaves a spell of various impossibilities. In this first novel, for example, Beresford's characters journey through time. On his first day of school vacation, Joe finds a stray dog cowering in the basement of the flat where he lives with his father's landlady. The dog, which is actually an ancient griffin, has been sent from Antiquity to recover a lost treasure. Along the way, Joe and the Griffin gain an ally in Grace, a young girl who lives in the mansion where the treasure is finally located. "Beresford has the happily offhand, confident way with magic with which Edith Nesbit conducted her tales," commented Fisher in her *Growing Point* review of the 1986 update, retitled *Strange Magic.* The critic added that "comic fantasy is one of the trickiest outlets for imagination, demanding discipline, moderation, lightness of touch and complete confidence, all of which Elisabeth Beresford certainly has."

In *Secret Magic,* Beresford showcases her skills in the story of two boys who run a vegetable stand in the local farmer's market for their great uncle. When they discover a scruffy-looking cat haunting the market, they first react as typical boys and try to shoo it away. The cat begins to speak in its own defense and turns out to be a 3,000-year-old Sphinx banished from his home for talkativeness. "Very well written indeed," B. Clark wrote in *Junior Bookshelf,* "this is first-class reading." *Curious Magic* repeats the time-travel motif as young Andy Jones comes to realize a striking similarity between the Mr. Dunk he knows as a neighbor on the island where he is spending his winter vacation, a Mr. Donkey from Roman days, and a Mr. Dunker from the Tudor period. The reason he knows so many people from ages past? His neighbor, the "white witch" Mrs. Tressida, and her niece Ella practice a form of magic that carries the three in and out of ages past to experience British history first-hand. *Curious Magic* "is warmed by humour and sharpened by the unexacting and intriguing shifts in time which Andy, a responsive but not over-emotional lad, takes in his stride," according to Fisher of *Growing Point.*

Although she has been a successful author for most of her adult life, Beresford is quick to note that it hasn't gotten any easier. "I hate typing the dreaded words 'Chapter One' as I find writing very hard work and will think up a dozen good reasons for *not* sitting down at the typewriter," she once confessed. "But one of the great bonuses is getting letters from children all over the world who sometimes just put 'The Wombles, England' on the envelope." "My pet peeve is the people who say, 'Of course I could write a book if I had the time,'" she once commented. "If I had a sunny day for every time that's been said to me I should live in a world of perpetual sunshine." Despite her professed difficulty with writing, Beresford's love of her craft has inspired many others—including her own children: daughter Kate has written several children's books and son Marcus is a sports journalist.

"Children (and adults) write to me from all over the world," Beresford explained, "and quite often they seem to know more about my books than I do. I particularly like listening to children, because—fortunately—they still go on believing that anything is possible and that all kinds of adventures are just around the next corner. And when I put something funny into a story and it makes me laugh I know it will make a lot of children laugh. And there's no better sound in the world than children laughing." Beresford mentioned that recent letters have come from as far away as Tasmania, Fiji, and Hungary.

The author once commented that some of her reasons for continuing to write are: "I feel lost if I don't—I always have. I am always getting new ideas. I am also supporting four foster children in the Third World, along with countless charities."

Biographical and Critical Sources

BOOKS

Twentieth-Century Romance and Historical Writers, 3rd edition, St. James Press (Detroit, MI), 1994.
Crouch, Marcus, *St. James Guide to Children's Writers,* 5th edition, St. James Press, Gale (Detroit, MI), 1999.

PERIODICALS

Booklist, March 15, 1978, p. 1185.
Growing Point, January, 1976, p. 2785; March, 1979, p. 3467; July, 1980, Margery Fisher, review of *Curious Magic,* p. 3716; July, 1981, p. 3910; July, 1986, Margery Fisher, review of *Strange Magic,* p. 4641; September, 1988, Margery Fisher, review of *The Island Railway,* p. 5026; July, 1989, p. 5096.
Horn Book, August, 1965, p. 390.
Junior Bookshelf, December, 1978, B. Clark, review of *Secret Magic,* p. 298; August, 1982, D. A. Young, review of *The Animals Nobody Wanted,* p. 138; December, 1988, p. 287; February, 1990, p. 34; April, 1994, p. 54.
Library Journal, March 15, 1970, article by Ginger Brauer, p. 1192.
Publishers Weekly, May 1, 1967, p. 56.
School Librarian, March, 1979, p. 34; December, 1982, p. 329; September, 1984, Sheila Armstrong, review of *The Adventures of Poon,* p. 233.
School Library Journal, May 15, 1967, pp. 55, 74; August, 1980, p. 60; March, 1981, p. 140.
Times Educational Supplement, August 7, 1987, p. 19.
Times Literary Supplement, June 6, 1968, p. 584; June 15, 1972, p. 684; April 6, 1973, p. 386; July 11, 1975, p. 763; December 5, 1975, p. 1446; August 19-25, 1988, p. 917.

*   *   *

BORDEN, Louise (Walker) 1949-

Personal

Born October 30, 1949, in Cincinnati, OH; daughter of William Lee (president of a sales distributorship) and Louise (Crutcher) Walker; married Peter A. Borden (president of a sales distributorship), September 4, 1971; children: Catherine, Ayars (daughter), Ted. *Education:* Denison University, B.A., 1971. *Politics:* Independent. *Religion:* Methodist. *Hobbies and other interests:* "Spending time with my family and friends, writing, reading, gardening, tennis, skiing, travel, summers in Leland, Michigan, and the Cincinnati Reds."

Addresses

Home—628 Myrtle Ave., Terrace Park, OH 45174.

Career

Meadowbrook School, Weston, MA, teaching assistant, 1971-73; Cincinnati Country Day School, Cincinnati, OH, pre-primary teacher, 1973-74; The Bookshelf (bookstore), Cincinnati, OH, co-owner, 1988-91; writer

and speaker. Served on the boards of Redeemer Nursery School, Cincinnati Children's Theater, and Hillsdale Alumni Association.

Member

Society of Children's Book Writers and Illustrators, Authors Guild, Ohio Council of Teachers of Language Arts.

Writings

Caps, Hats, Socks, and Mittens: A Book about the Four Seasons, illustrated by Lillian Hoban, Scholastic (New York, NY), 1989.
The Neighborhood Trucker, illustrated by Sandra Speidel, Scholastic (New York, NY), 1990.
The Watching Game, illustrated by Teri Weidner, Scholastic (New York, NY), 1991.
Albie the Lifeguard, illustrated by Elizabeth Sayles, Scholastic (New York, NY), 1993.
Just in Time for Christmas, illustrated by Ted Lewin, Scholastic (New York, NY), 1994.
(With Mary Kay Kroeger) *Paperboy,* illustrated by Ted Lewin, Clarion (New York, NY), 1996.
Thanksgiving Is . . . , illustrated by Steve Bjorkman, Scholastic (New York, NY), 1997.
The Little Ships: The Heroic Rescue at Dunkirk in World War II, illustrated by Michael Foreman, Margaret McElderry (New York, NY), 1997.
Good-bye, Charles Lindbergh: Based on a True Story, illustrated by Thomas B. Allen, Margaret McElderry (New York, NY), 1998.
Good Luck, Mrs. K.!, illustrated by Adam Gustavson, Margaret McElderry (New York, NY), 1999.
A. Lincoln and Me, illustrated by Ted Lewin, Scholastic (New York, NY), 1999.
Sleds on Boston Common: A Story from the American Revolution, illustrated by Robert Andrew Parker, Margaret McElderry (New York, NY), 2000.
The Day Eddie Met the Author, illustrated by Adam Gustavson, Margaret McElderry (New York, NY), 2001.
(With Mary Kay Kroeger) *Fly High!: The Story of Bessie Coleman,* illustrated by Teresa Flavin, Margaret McElderry (New York, NY), 2001.
America Is . . . , illustrated by Stacey Schuett, Margaret McElderry (New York, NY), 2002.
(With Trish Marx) *Touching the Sky: Flying Adventures of Wilbur and Orville Wright,* illustrated by Peter Fiore, Margaret McElderry (New York, NY), 2003.
Sea Clocks: The Story of Longitude, illustrated by Erik Blegvad, Margaret McElderry (New York, NY), 2004.

Contributor of poetry to *Christmas in the Stable,* Harcourt (New York, NY), 1990.

Work in Progress

The Greatest Skating Race, The A+ Custodian, The True Escape of Curious George—A Story about Margret and H.A. Rey, and *Across the Blue Pacific.*

Sidelights

A former school teacher, Louise Borden has written several books for young readers that take a gentle approach to childhood. A young boy realizes his dream of riding in his favorite truck in *The Neighborhood Trucker,* while in *The Little Ships: The Heroic Rescue at Dunkirk in World War II,* a fisherman's daughter helps come to the aid of Allied soldiers trapped on the beach at Dunkirk. Family traditions are the focus of *Just in Time for Christmas,* which a *Publishers Weekly* contributor described as "a poignant story, sparely and smoothly told." And a young boy has a once-in-a-lifetime encounter with an American hero in *Good-bye, Charles Lindbergh,* a picture book based on the real-life recollections of Harold Gilpin, who met the famed aviator when Lindbergh landed his plane in a field near Gilpin's Mississippi home. "More than just a retelling," asserted *Booklist* reviewer Shelle Rosenfeld, "the book explores the complex issues of age versus youth, modern technology versus the Old World, innocence versus experience." Rosenfeld added that *Good-bye, Charles Lindbergh* is "both an interesting glimpse back in time and a moving story of how the ordinary can suddenly become extraordinary."

Borden was born in Cincinnati, Ohio, in 1949. "Growing up, I had a grandmother who loved history," she recalled in an interview for Simon & Schuster. "In grade school, I enjoyed maps, geography, and fiction and nonfiction relating to history. I was fortunate enough to have several wonderful history teachers during my elementary and secondary school years who nourished that interest. Later, in college, I majored in history. The idea of ordinary people against the backdrop of historical events has always interested me much more than specific dates, facts, and issues." After graduating from college, Borden worked at teaching positions in Weston, Massachusetts, and in her hometown of Cincinnati, before indulging in a lifelong love of books and becoming co-owner of a bookstore, The Bookshelf, in 1988. Borden's first book, *Caps, Hats, Socks, and Mittens,* was published for Scholastic the following year. "The sound of language and the poet's voice have always fascinated me," she once explained, "and so I think that writing picture books was a natural step for me. The sound and rhythm that are inherent in good picture books are a continuing challenge—to craft a text that has its own natural voice, as well as a good story line."

Borden started work on *Caps, Hats, Socks, and Mittens: A Book about the Four Seasons* after her second child began primary school. Her work as an assistant first-grade teacher gave her a good sense of how to write a beginning reader in a way that would help students sound out new words. She sent the book to Scholastic and was pleasantly surprised when they sent back a contract for its publication. Borden was even more pleased when her editor at Scholastic chose artist Lillian Hoban to create the pictures. "Everyone always asks if authors are pleased with the illustration for their books. I cannot now think of my words as separate from Lillian Hoban's wonderful pictures," Borden explained.

The author's second book, *The Neighborhood Trucker,* is the story of Elliot Long, a little boy who loves to watch the trucks roll by his home. His favorite is a cement truck from Sardinia Concrete with the number forty-four painted on its side; it is driven by a truck driver named Slim. "The working title for the book was 'More Trucks Please,'" Borden noted. "I had never looked twice at trucks until our son Ted pulled me into their loud, noisy, exciting world. From an early age, Ted has had a passion for trucks—especially cement mixers. There really is a Sardinia Concrete several miles from our village, and there really is a Slim—a tall, thoughtful driver who shares a special friendship with Ted. The rest is fiction. And, as I tell children, Ted is not the main character in this book. I am. I am Elliot Long. That's what writers do. We pretend a lot. And we become other people." In a review of *The Neighborhood Trucker* for *Bulletin of the Center for Children's Books,* Roger Sutton called the story "a poetic . . . portrait of vocational obsession" and a "good bedtime choice for revved-up trucksters."

The Watching Game, Borden's next effort, describes a game played by four cousins when they visit their grandmother in the country. Each child tries to be the first to spot the fox in the woods and to put out their grandfather's hat so the fox will know it has been seen. *School Library Journal* contributor Patricia Pearl offered a favorable assessment of the book, noting that the story "emphasizes the significant themes of family love and respect for nature." *The Watching Game* actually began as a poem called "Granny's Fox." Borden explained, "There was no watching at all—just a boy who spotted a fox." The story took shape with the advice of Borden's editor. "In the first working drafts of the book I did not name the cousins or give them any characteristics. But names are very important to me. I choose them with care. I want children to remember my characters, to know that they are distinctive and have their own identities."

Borden creates another distinctive character in *Albie the Lifeguard.* In this story, a young boy realizes that his lack of skill as a swimmer will keep him off the local swim team. He decides instead to work lifeguard duty at his backyard swimming pool. By the end of the summer, he has gained the confidence to join his friends in swimming the entire lap-length of his town pool, in a story that "pays tribute to the natural ability of a child to recognize and respect his own timetable and abilities," according to *School Library Journal* contributor Liza Bliss. Also enthusiastic about the story, a *Publishers Weekly* reviewer found *Albie the Lifeguard* "a winning tale that indirectly and elegantly demonstrates the psyche's inventiveness."

The Little Ships is a fictionalized re-creation of an important historical event: the 1940 rescue of 300,000 Allied soldiers from the beach at Dunkirk, France, who were taken to safety in Dover, England, by hundreds of small boats captained by naval officers and brave English fishermen. The story is told from the point of view of an English girl who, dressed as a boy, joins her fisherman father in helping to transport the soldiers. Jon Scieszka, writing in the *New York Times Book Review,* maintained that *The Little Ships* "gives a personal, memorable character to what might otherwise be an abstract chapter of history." Scieszka also praised Borden for the tone of her storytelling, noting that her young heroine "describes her exhaustion, and the spectacle of more than 300,000 Allied troops fleeing from the beach to boats and back to England, in a spare and dramatic child's voice, wonderfully free of patriotic preaching or moralizing."

"Today many teachers are integrating various subjects of the curriculum in wonderful ways," Borden explained in discussing the use of historical fiction in the classroom in the Simon and Schuster publicity release. "For example, skills in social studies, reading, and language arts can all be taught in a holistic way through the use of good literature. Historical fiction—whether picture books or novels—is widely used to introduce topics in social studies and broaden students' knowledge of social and political history. I think if history is made accessible to young readers in interesting ways, they will discover just how rich it is, rather than viewing history as boring and dry."

Borden's *Good-bye, Charles Lindbergh* is another fictional recreation of an actual event. "I saw a 'Dear Abby' letter in my local paper with the name Lindbergh in the title," the author recalled in her interview. "[This] caught my eye because I admired Anne Morrow Lindbergh's writing. I read the letter from Harold Gilpin of Pine Bluff, Arkansas, that told of his meeting Charles Lindbergh near the Mississippi farm that Gilpin grew up on. I immediately pictured an image of a boy on his horse looking up into the sky to see a biplane. I thought that contrast was remarkable: the ordinary meeting the extraordinary. I filed the newspaper clipping but carried the image inside, hoping to someday find a way to write a book about a Mississippi boy meeting the nation's hero."

"A few years later, when I decided to write the book, I actually tracked down Harold Gilpin. We corresponded via phone and mail for several months, and in January 1995, I flew to Arkansas to meet the Gilpins in person. . . . I then drove 175 miles to Canton, Mississippi, so that I could get a feel for the setting of the book. I returned to Cincinnati, contacted the National Air and Space Museum, researched biplanes, read Anne Morrow Lindbergh's journals, listened to the taped interview of Harold Gilpin that I had made in Pine Bluff, and then began writing the story."

Borden later returned to the subject of flight in *Fly High!: The Story of Bessie Coleman.* This was her second collaboration with coauthor Mary Kay Kroeger. Coleman, who grew up picking cotton in Texas, later became the first African-American to earn a pilot's license. "The authors' flair for imparting history soars" in this book, Gay Lynn Van Vleck commented in a review for *School Library Journal.*

The picture book *Good Luck, Mrs. K!* is also based on a real-life experience. Told in the words of a nine-year-old narrator, the story centers on a favorite teacher who is hospitalized with cancer. "It is about an exceptional third-grade teacher and her class," the author noted. "Mrs. K. is a composite of the many wonderful teachers whom I have met during my school visits—this is my way to honor them. The story is also based on a teacher I knew, a great friend, who had cancer. Essentially, it's a book about the joy of teaching and learning."

In *The Day Eddie Met the Author* Borden drew on her experiences as a visiting author to write about a little boy who thinks very hard about what question to ask when a real live author comes to visit his school. He is crushed when he does not get a chance to ask his question during the assembly, but luckily he bumps into the author later and gets his answer. Lee Bock, who reviewed the book for *School Library Journal,* noted that not only is *The Day Eddie Met the Author* "enjoyable to read," but it is also "gently instructive" in helping to prepare children for author visits at their own schools.

"I think that I learned the craft of writing through osmosis, because long before I was a writer of books for children, I was a reader," Borden once explained. "And because reading has brought me so much pleasure—has given me most of what I have inside my head and inside my heart—it is a real thrill today to realize that maybe one of my books will hook a child into the same wonderfully rich world that I was drawn to at an early age."

Biographical and Critical Sources

PERIODICALS

Booklist, August, 1994, p. 22; March 1, 1997, p. 1162; February 1, 1998, Ilene Cooper, review of *Thanksgiving Is . . . ,* pp. 925-926; March 1, 1998, Shelle Rosenfeld, review of *Good-Bye, Charles Lindbergh: Based on a True Story,* p. 1129; July, 1999, Carolyn Phelan, review of *Good Luck, Mrs. K!,* p. 1942; November 15, 1999, Ilene Cooper, review of *A. Lincoln and Me,* p. 622; July, 2000, Kay Weisman, review of *Sleds on Boston Common,* p. 2028; February 15, 2001, Carolyn Phelan, review of *Fly High!: The Story of Bessie Coleman,* p. 1152; March 1, 2001, Ilene Cooper, review of *The Day Eddie Met the Author,* p. 1275.

Bulletin of the Center for Children's Books, December, 1990, Roger Sutton, review of *The Neighborhood Trucker,* p. 79; April, 1997, p. 276.

Horn Book, May-June, 1997, p. 302; November, 2000, Mary M. Burns, review of *Sleds on Boston Common,* p. 743.

Kirkus Reviews, April 1, 1997, p. 549; October 1, 1999, review of *A. Lincoln and Me,* pp. 1574-1575.

New York Times Book Review, May 18, 1997, John Scieszka, "War is Heck," p. 25; October 17, 1999, Perry Nodelman, review of *Good Luck, Mrs. K!,* p. 31.

Publishers Weekly, May 24, 1993, review of *Albie the Lifeguard,* p. 87; September 19, 1994, review of *Just in Time for Christmas,* p. 30; April 9, 1998, review of *Good-bye, Charles Lindbergh,* p. 78; May 17, 1999, review of *Good Luck, Mrs. K!,* p. 79; November 1, 1999, review of *A. Lincoln and Me,* p. 83; August 14, 2000, review of *Sleds on Boston Common,* p. 355; December 4, 2000, review of *Fly High!,* p. 73.

School Library Journal, October, 1990, p. 86; August, 1991, Patricia Pearl, review of *The Watching Game,* p. 142; June, 1993, Liza Bliss, review of *Albie the Lifeguard,* p. 70; March, 1998, Patricia Dole, review of *Good-bye, Charles Lindbergh,* p. 166; March, 1998, Gale W. Sherman, review of *Thanksgiving Is . . . ,* p. 192; May, 1999, Jackie Hechtkopf, review of *Good*

Luck, Mrs. K!, p. 86; October, 1999, Linda Greengrass, review of *A. Lincoln and Me,* p. 1942; December, 2000, Nancy Menaldi-Scanlan, review of *Sleds on Boston Common,* p. 97; January, 2001, Gay Lynne Van Vleck, review of *Fly High!,* p. 114; May, 2001, Lee Bock, review of *The Day Eddie Met the Author,* p. 110.

OTHER

A Conversation with Louise Borden, Author of "Good-bye, Charles Lindbergh" (publicity release), Simon & Schuster, 1998.

Louise Borden, http://www.louiseborden.com/ (October 19, 2001).

Autobiography Feature

Louise Borden

Writing

This is how it begins . . . writing. It begins with a pen in my hand, with memory as well as the present. Today, with winter sunlight on my shoulder and my hand casting a shadow on smooth paper, my creative vision is not to write a picture book text for children.

No, today it is something different, known and yet unknown, full of images and echoes.

I trust my writing instincts. They come from the heart. And like an artist, I have some rough sketches that surround me. Snippets of text. Names from my past. Family. Books. Teachers. Photographs. Friends and mentors. Places.

What is essential to me?

What can I leave out?

This is my process as a writer.

Perhaps I will begin the story by using white space. Yes . . . make a visual poem. I will begin with Louise Borden's style and listen to the sound of her life's words as I write them. This way has helped me to tell other stories.

A Home in Terrace Park, Ohio

The gray clapboard house that I live in
with my husband Pete
was built in 1940 . . .
the same year that an armada of little ships
rescued soldiers from the beaches of Dunkirk
and that two artists,
Margret and Hans Rey,
fled from Paris on bicycles,
carrying with them the original manuscript
for *Curious George.*

The floors creak in a few rooms of our house
and on our stairs,
and the maple trees and oaks in our yard
are beautiful and enduring
in each of the four seasons.
On blue sky days
I study their October leaves
and their bare February branches.

Whenever I think that our closets are too small,
and that our house looks unfancy and a bit outdated,
I remember the history that took place in 1940.
And I am glad that I live in a house built in a year
marked not only by war,
but also by courage
and the goodness of the human spirit.
It is a year that I have written about
in two of my books.

Recently,
an older man up the street told me
that he helped to lay the floors of our house
when he was young . . .
and that the builder was a Dutchman named Hans
who had served in the German trenches during World
    War I
before coming to America.
That is a story . . .
and now it is connected to the history of our house in
    Terrace Park
and to the history of my own life.
Hans.
Dutchman.
Such mysterious and unexplained echoes
resonate in books I have written.
I welcome these echoes.

They don't surprise me ...
I find them inevitable,
because I am a writer.

Terrace Park is a Cincinnati suburb.
Suburb.
What an awkward word for the end of a line.
Not meant for a poem.
Not a word that moves across the page like ... *vil-
    lage.*
Terrace Park is also a village
known for its many trees.
Early settlers came to this area in 1789
and built a station
near the banks of the Little Miami River,
so there is a long history to the place I now call
    home.
I like that sense of history,
and the stories that are layered through the years
of my old-fashioned neighborhood.

Distance.
Direction.
Weather and season.
Place.
Rivers and lakes and oceans.
To me,
these are important and interesting aspects of the
    world.
I want to share them with my readers.

Some Terrace Park families stow canoes in their back-
    yards
and fishing rods in their garages.
Some take walks on the village trails down by the
    river.
A few of our streets are named for colleges:
Yale ... Harvard ... Oxford ... Miami ...
    Michigan ...
and Denison, my alma mater.

Other streets are named for trees ...
like Elm and Poplar.
We live at 628 Myrtle
and we have a lot of myrtle
that grows in our yard.

I'm a gardener.
I love when our myrtle blooms in the spring
like an unspoken promise.
It is something I watch for each year,
the soft gleam of blue
among those shiny green leaves.
I tend my garden, and dig in the earth.
Some summers,
everything blooms.
Other summers ... well.

A garden mirrors writing,
and publishing.
It takes hard work ... patience ...
perseverance ... faith.
Sunshine and rain.

We moved into this house almost 22 years ago.
Our yard holds flashes of memories of our three
    children

Louise Borden

Cate (now a Spanish teacher),
Ayars (rhymes with bears),
and Ted (a college student, 6'5")
building snowmen ...
mixing mud pies ...
chasing lightning bugs,
kittens, and baby ducks ...
and heading off to school
at Terrace Park Elementary across the street.

I can stand in my kitchen,
look out the window,
and hear the bells ring each day:
for school to begin ...
for recess ...
for lunch ...
for dismissal.
The sound of those bells
is like having an extra set of clocks in our house.

Schools have been important places in my life.
And I suddenly realize
that I have been connected to one school or another
for most of my life.

I like that the word *SCHOOL*
is painted on the street near our driveway.
I like the closeness to classrooms and students,
to the adventure of learning,
and to this brick building
that dates back to 1913.
1913.

I love numbers and dates
and I picture the generations of children
who have walked through the front doors of Terrace
    Park School
including now,
our three grown children.
That's what writers do—
we imagine the lives of others,
and in doing so,
we can sometimes inhabit those lives
when we create the images and events of a story.

The artist Pierre Bonnard once wrote:
"Let it be felt that the painter was there."
I hope that this can be said
about the books I write for children.

Still Writing

Since we live on the corner of Myrtle and Marietta, I'm able to look out our front windows each morning and see the sixth-grade crossing guards, with their orange traffic belts, keeping younger children safe as they cross the streets. Most of the students ride their bikes to school, and many of them pass by my house. Every day, except in the summer, there are more than a hundred bicycles lined up outside of that 1913 building. Because of its size, our village has continued a few traditions from an earlier lifestyle: schoolchildren are allowed to go home for lunch if they choose.

I've spoken in over five hundred other schools, from Maine to Colorado to Seattle. But when I come home to Terrace Park from far away, I drive down Elm Avenue and see our neighborhood school with those bicycles lined up outside—or the lights shining out from the windows at night—and it's like a big heart, greeting me. My good friend, Mary Kay Kroeger, who has written two published books with me, teaches fourth grade in this school. I look for her classroom each time I drive by. It's an important touchstone in my life.

Our house is only a block from the village green, and I cross it each time I walk to our small post office to mail off a new manuscript to one of my editors. Rhonda, the postmistress, knows me by name. Over the years she has weighed and stamped many envelopes to publishers. Rhonda is a familiar face on my writing road. Last summer,

Terrace Park School

after I mailed back contracts to Houghton Mifflin for *The True Escape of Curious George—A Story about Margret and H. A. Rey,* I went home and celebrated the August afternoon by painting a tiny picture in my journal.

But now it is no longer summer. It is snowing outside my window as I write these words on a January day. Behind me, in my writing room, are bookshelves and two dozen notebooks, filled with pages of words, sketches, lists, and quotes on writing and art. I write about people, landscape, weather, process, writing and reading, my publishing life, mentors, and travel. I record the date and the time of day, and where I am when I am writing an entry. It is a familiar and known part of my writing life—to my family and my friends—a notebook on my desk, or carrying one with me on my travels. These pages have given me rich material to draw from when I write my books. The first time I wrote in a notebook was during a train trip to California when I was eleven years old. I also took my first pictures with a camera, something I often do now to record images that I want to write about. During that long ago train trip, I was paying attention to my world. I had the impulses of a writer, but I didn't yet know it.

Sometimes I'll see a neighbor at the post office who asks me: "*Are you still writing? Are you still doing those children's books?*" I realize that I spend hours alone—at my desk or traveling to schools far from Terrace Park. I talk to my editors on the phone or in their offices and discuss manuscripts, sketches, and final proofs. It is the life that I now live, the life of a working writer, a creative life that my husband Pete understands and encourages, and that our three children have grown up with. This is also the life of close friends and mentors in the children's book field: Cat Bowman Smith, George Ella Lyon, Johanna Hurwitz, Florence Heide, Trish Marx, and Pat Giff. We share a common experience at our desks or in schools.

But it's probably a mystery to others, and to my neighbors. They don't know firsthand the belief that one must have in oneself to remain focused and hopeful, despite rejections and the changing terrain in publishing. They cannot visualize the process. I must, in the end, have a passion for my subject, and I must be a risk-taker. I consider it a small miracle whenever one of my manuscripts is accepted, even though I have had many books published.

Picture books: so few words. Like a poem with white space. My job is to make the process look effortless to my readers. Which it is not. But it is the process that I love the most and always learn from. Creating something enduring from a blank sheet of paper.

"Yes, I'm still writing ... " I always answer with a smile to my Terrace Park neighbors in the post office. Rhonda calls an encouraging good-bye to me as I walk out the door.

*

"Searching memory might be compared to throwing the beam of a strong light, from your hilltop camp site, back over the road you traveled by day."

(Charles A. Lindbergh, *The Spirit of St. Louis,* 1953)

Leaves on the Family Tree

My mother's and father's families have old roots in America. Both of my parents' ancestors came from England, Ireland, and Scotland shortly before the American Revolution and settled on farms in Virginia and Maryland. Later they would migrate west.

On my father's side, my great-great-great-grandfather, Henry Walker, was born in 1799 and moved to Kentucky as a young man. There he bought property overlooking the Ohio River, across from Cincinnati, the city where I was born over a hundred years later. When I chose to use the name Henry for my main character in *Sleds on Boston Common,* published in the year 2000, that sturdy English name provided a small echo of someone in my own family during a long ago century. The early Walkers were a hardy breed of farmers and townsfolk to which the dates on the gravestones in our family plots attest. Many of them lived well into their eighties and nineties. They are all buried in northern Kentucky, a few miles from downtown Cincinnati.

But three of them died too soon in their lives, including my grandfather Walker, whose death left my grandmother a widow. She was to raise my father and his two brothers with fortitude and cheerfulness during the Great Depression. One of those brothers, Ted Walker, became a naval officer aboard a submarine that was lost in the Sea of Japan during WWII, and I have written about this uncle whom I never knew in a forthcoming book called *Across the Blue Pacific.*

As a kid, I remember going to Evergreen Cemetery every Christmas to hang wreaths on the Walker monument. It was usually a blustery cold day, and my two sisters and I would stamp our feet to keep warm while our parents and our grandmother, whom we affectionately called Bami, tied the wreaths with red ribbons. There was my grandfather's grave, and near it, Uncle Ted's, which fascinated us as children because it was the only one with a naval insignia. I sensed then, even as a child, that this memorial grave must be a special sadness in the life of my tall strong father, and Bami. The other grave my sisters and I whispered about belonged to an early Walker named Samuel who had died as a boy. According to family lore, he had drowned while swimming in the Ohio River. We couldn't imagine wading out into the great muddy currents that flowed south under Cincinnati's bridges. We shivered at the thought.

Bami was an independent woman, full of energy and opinions, and her water blue eyes never missed anything. My sisters and I adored her. There was nothing in the world that our wonderful grandmother couldn't sew. She had a gift for taking cloth and thread and turning it into something elegant and exquisite, or fun.

I remember the notorious speed with which Bami drove her white Oldsmobile and the many hours she spent with us. I recall sitting on the front seat of her car as she was backing out of a parking space near the dentist's office where my sister Margaret and I had just had our checkups. It was a warm spring day, and Bami had treated us to chocolate milkshakes to celebrate the few hours we were missing school. I was enjoying my first sip when for some reason my grandmother slammed on the brakes of her car with as much force as she usually used on the accelerator. The entire contents of my Dairy Queen cup came sloshing

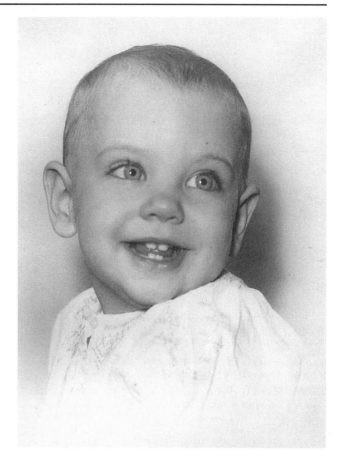

The author as a baby

down the front of my school uniform, and we had to speed home so I could change my clothes.

Bami was the grandmother who would arrive in our kitchen on a cold Saturday before Christmas and instruct the rest of the family on the art of making cream candy using a recipe that she had learned years earlier from my grandfather Walker. We made batch after batch and filled coffee cans, scrubbed and covered with holiday paper, with layers of the white ribboned pieces. Our teachers and neighbors received our gifts of homemade candy every year. I wrote about this candy in the book *Just in Time for Christmas.* That story doesn't take place in our Cincinnati kitchen, but on a Kentucky tobacco farm that my parents purchased at an auction when I was in high school ... a farm that had been owned by a Walker uncle decades earlier and where my father and his brothers spent time during their childhood.

My mother's family, the Bryans and the Crutchers, came from Nashville and carried the South and Tennessee's history in the family stories handed down to later generations. They had last names like McFerrin and McGavock, and among the women, there were a lot of Louises and Cynthias. *Cynthia Tennessee McGavock.* That was my great-great-grandmother's name, and she would marry a McFerrin, a staunch Methodist who served as a chaplain in the Confederate Army. After the Civil War, he became a bishop and wrote a book about his church. For years his portrait hung in my parents' dining room. I liked him immediately because he was sitting at a desk, holding a

Louise and Bami

quill pen in his hand. Our three children, though, found John McFerrin's picture foreboding. Ayars, whose middle name is McGavock, used to tell us that he reminded her of Count Dracula.

Shaw Avenue and Bayard Drive

There were already two Louises in my house when I was born: my mother and my grandmother Nana, who lived with us when I was growing up. So early on, I was given the name of Leezie. This is a name that my family still calls me. Years later, my niece was born and also named Louise. Then there were four of us at holiday gatherings with the same name. Sometimes my mail is addressed to Louisa, or Lousie, or Lewis, or Lois. Names and their pronunciations have always interested me, so writing about a teacher named Kempczinski was a natural thing for me to do, and now having an editor named Margaret McElderry seems wonderful and is an echo of my own "Mc" family names.

I was born on October 30, in 1949, just four years after WWII ended. My parents, Louise and Bill Walker, were part of the so-called "greatest generation." My father had served in the Pacific as a captain in the air force, doing weather reconnaissance. Three groomsmen in my parents' wedding in 1942 were to go off to war also, but not return. I was brought home from the hospital to a house at 3554 Shaw Avenue in Cincinnati. I lived in this house until I was six with my parents, Nana, my sisters Cindy (two years older) and Margaret (two years younger), Lula Johnson, an older housekeeper who worked for us, and our beloved black and white dog named Corky. Memories from this solid red brick house include walking five blocks to kindergarten at Hyde Park School, playing with my Ginny dolls on our front porch with Cindy and Marg, and eating so much watermelon at one backyard summer picnic that I threw up all night. I still carry a distrust of watermelon to this day. I formed a special friendship with Lula, who made the best yeast rolls in the world.

When I was in first grade, our family moved to a larger house, on Bayard Drive, and in the first sadness of my life,

Lula retired and moved away. I had lost my truest friend beyond the circle of my sisters. I remember addressing letters to send to Lula, telling her of our family news, until she died a few years later.

As a child growing up, I could never keep any of our relatives straight. But Nana, also a widow like Bami, sure could. Nana continued to live with us in the house on Bayard Drive, and she was as slow a driver as Bami was fast. Shifting the gears on her old blue Merc created a loud grinding commotion. Nana was the quietest family member at our dinner table and kept her opinions to herself. Unlike Bami, Nana was a college graduate, class of 1915, and a reader as well as a letter writer. It was this gentle grandmother, Louise Crutcher, who taught me about the joy of books and kindled my interest in history. A southerner, despite living in Cincinnati, Nana was strict about one thing: always my sisters and I had to answer her soft voice with either a polite "Yes, Ma'am" or a "No, Ma'am." Neither of my grandmothers lived to see me begin my publishing journey, but I carry their love and their voices with me, like a blue stone in my pocket.

Cincinnati is a river city. As a child, I pressed my face against the car window when our parents drove us across one of the bridges to Covington, Kentucky, to have Sunday dinner with Uncle Will Walker. I liked the view of the Ohio—mud brown in the spring and summer, and pewter blue in the winter and fall. I liked to see the long barges moving slowly up and down the river. I wondered where they had come from, and where they were headed. I liked the wide curves in the river. Which state owned that river, I wanted to know. Did it belong to Ohio, my home state, or to Kentucky, where my father's family had been born? I was fascinated by the fact that I could cross from one state to another in a matter of minutes.

Today as an adult, I still am intrigued by state borders and driving across Cincinnati's many bridges, especially the Suspension Bridge, nicknamed "the singing bridge" by my sister Cindy because it made our car tires hum. John Roebling designed our singing bridge in the 1860s as a model for his later more famous Brooklyn Bridge. In the Depression years, Bami's father worked as a toll collector on the Suspension Bridge, so I like to think that I inherited my affection for rivers and bridges from him. In October of 1999, the month that I turned fifty, I celebrated by walking across the singing bridge, and then a few days later the Brooklyn Bridge, and on my actual birthday, the Golden Gate Bridge.

Cincinnati is also a baseball town, so my childhood was woven inextricably with watching the Reds play at old Crosley Field. I had a Gus Bell glove when I was a kid, and Tony Perez is still one of my all-time baseball heroes (I used Perez as a last name in the book _Good Luck, Mrs. K!_). Besides the Ohio River, and the famed Big Red Machine, my city also is known for its hillsides. Most people think Ohio is flat—and parts of our state are. But not my hometown. Some of the streets seem as steep as those in San Francisco. The move to Bayard Drive meant living at the top of a Cincinnati hill. Our front yard even had a slope which we sledded on every winter. My sisters and I used to ride our bikes down, down our street, and then to the local dime store to buy candy bars or meet up with our friends. Coming home, we had to pedal _up_ Bayard. Pedaling slowly up my street may be where I learned perseverance, something all writers need when they are working alone at their desks.

Lotspeich Years

Now Cindy and Marg and I were attending a wonderful grade school called Lotspeich, where I made my closest childhood friend. Hathaway Gamble remains a gleam in my life even though she has lived miles away, in California, since college.

Lotspeich School is also where I became a lifelong reader, and Mrs. Bricker's first-grade classroom began that rich journey. I loved our school library and its shelves of books, especially the picture books by Edward Ardizzone that portrayed children on the coast of England and their daring adventures at sea. Little did I know that thirty years later I would write *The Little Ships* about an English fisherman and his daughter who lived in Deal, a setting that echoed Ardizzone's stories about Tim and Charlotte. Other favorites of mine as a Lotspeich reader were *The Wheel on the School* and *The Witch of Blackbird Pond* as well as biographies of famous Americans.

When I was in third grade, I wanted to be a composer. I was taking piano lessons from our music teacher at school, Miss Cornn. Her hair was as shiny black as the piano I practiced on, and she had a little fringe of bangs across her forehead. Miss Cornn filled our school with her love of music, and I connected with Miss Cornn because we shared a name. Her first name was Louise, just like mine.

As a third grader, I went to her music room once a week for my piano lessons after school. Miss Cornn had a bookcase, with glass doors, filled with books about music. One was a small red book: *The Story of One Hundred Great Composers,* with a page or two about each composer. *I* wanted to be a composer, so I often asked to look at the red book and page through it. I coveted that little book because I thought it would help me become what I wanted to be. I also loved it because it was *small,* just right for the size of my hands, and the book was red, and in the bookcase, it stood out from Miss Cornn's other music books.

During my piano lessons in third, fourth, and fifth grades, I often asked my teacher if I could have her red book to keep. Miss Cornn always smiled and told me, "I need that book for my teaching, but you can look at it anytime you want...." I gave up asking if I could have her little red book, but I still took my piano lessons and practiced my new skills at home on our black upright piano. I wasn't very good, and I had trouble reading music, but still, I loved running my fingers up and down the keys, trying to sound out songs. Music was a wonderful and rich world to me. Sitting alone at the piano in our living room on Bayard Drive, I could pretend that I was touching a part of that world with my own hands.

Meanwhile, being a student at Lotspeich seemed an adventure every day. Our class shared unique experiences together that included sled riding or skating during winter gym classes (the school had a good coasting hill and a creek), and putting on plays in a red barn that belonged to the school.

I remember the twins in my class, Rhoda and Ruth Allen, who appeared at one of my October birthday parties carrying a taffy kitten as a gift. I'm not sure that my mom was thrilled to have one more pet in the house, but it was my birthday. How could she refuse me such a gift? So Ladybug joined our dog Corky and my sister Margaret's pet duck, until she was run over in our street by a neighbor's car.

Although I was unaware of it at the time, many seeds of my writing life came from my six years at Lotspeich School. Our principal, Mr. Wuerfel, was a serious-faced educator who emphasized the arts and the outdoors, and who believed in the education of well-rounded students. I can picture in sharp focus the school assemblies that were held in the Lotspeich library and recall sitting on the floor by class and watching breathlessly as our principal carefully pulled a dead bird from the side pocket of his tweed jacket. It resembled a magic show, but Mr. Wuerfel's intent was to educate us in a very real way about the natural world. He would hold the still bird gently in the palm of his hand and teach us about its markings and habitat.

Once a year, the school held an assembly that we all looked forward to and that was an early catalyst to my future travels. A man named Ted Bumiller would arrive, set up a projector and screen, and show the students slides of his travels to countries in Europe. I recall sitting on the floor in the darkened gym, next to Hathaway and our friends, seeing images on that slide screen of faraway countries with people and customs that seemed marvelous to me. *I* wanted to go to those places ... to the Swiss Alps, to Holland, and to Sweden. But of course, I couldn't go. I was just a kid in grade school who had a lively imagination.

My parents took a subscription to *National Geographic* magazine, so I began to cut out the tourist information offers on the back pages of some issues and mailed away requests for free pictures and brochures. One by one, the long fat envelopes addressed to Leezie Walker arrived in our mailbox. They contained maps and pamphlets with glossy travel photos. I pored over them on rainy afternoons, dreaming that someday when I was grown up I could go to the places where Ted Bumiller had been. I laugh now when I realize that I had become an armchair traveler as early as fourth grade, and when I stand in a school gym, showing

The author's parents, Louise and Bill Walker

slides to students about my research travels to places in America and Europe, I sense the possibilities *I* am now sharing with children.

Besides teaching students about birds, Mr. Wuerfel's other passion was geography. Every sixth grader at my school was required to take a world regions course that our principal taught. Each week, Mr. Wuerfel appeared in our classroom armed with a stack of maps. We had to label in pencil the mountain ranges, rivers, oceans, countries, and capitals that we were to learn, and learn well, for no student was allowed to graduate from Lotspeich without mastering these map tests.

That school year of 1960-61 was an exciting time in current events. Hawaii and Alaska had recently gained statehood. I remember our *Weekly Reader* newspaper filled with articles about the changing borders of the world. Not only were new states being added to the U.S. map, but territories all over the world were gaining their independence and becoming nation states.

I loved studying maps and the geography that Mr. Wuerfel wanted us to carry into our futures: the Amazon River . . . the Kamchatka Peninsula . . . the Ural Mountains. These were words for places far away, places that were real. I loved the big world that Mr. Wuerfel's maps unfolded to me, and I wanted to transform those black-and-white papers into sheets of color, with squiggly lines for borders and blue for the oceans. That class was where I began a lifelong fascination for maps. Today studying maps is an important part of the research for my historical books (*Good-bye, Charles Lindbergh; The Little Ships; Sleds on Boston Common; Sea Clocks; Fly High!; The True Escape of Curious George;* etc.) I collect maps everywhere I travel, and a map of the world painted in a hallway in 1944 which I saw during a school visit is a strong visual element in *Across the Blue Pacific.*

Another interest of mine in grade school was art. I remember the wall of windows in Mrs. Briedenbach's classroom and sitting at tables that were covered with years of paint drippings, blobs of clay, and the project histories of other young Lotspeich artists. I loved everything that our art teacher showed us about color and shape and medium. I loved the process of *making.* Later in college, I took art classes as well as art history. Now thanks to my Minnesota friend and painting teacher Patty Hegman, in midlife I have returned to that fun I had in Mrs. Briedenbach's classroom by experimenting with canvas, watercolors, and sketches. I even own two easels. I have no plans to become an illustrator—I would need another lifetime to try to do that. But I enjoy standing on the edge of that world when I watch real artists create the design and pictures for my books. My continuing friendships with these professional illustrators are very meaningful to me, as well as my close association with Ann Bobco, the art director at McElderry Books.

At the end of sixth grade, our class graduated from Lotspeich, and we had an outdoor celebration with our teachers. I remember standing in the sunshine on that long ago June day. Miss Cornn came over and gave me a good-bye hug and then with a smile, she handed me the little red book, *The Story of One Hundred Great Composers,* from her classroom bookcase. What a thoughtful surprise! Inside the book my teacher had written: "To Leezie—with love and thanks for the fine musical experiences you gave to all

At Hillsdale School, 1966

of us." Well. I never gave *anyone* any fine musical experience. And I stopped taking piano lessons the next year since Miss Cornn only taught Lotspeich students. But I carried the red book home like a treasure, and I still have it on my bookshelf, more than forty years later. Miss Cornn was the best kind of teacher . . . she believed in me, and in what I could become. I didn't grow up to be a composer. Instead, I grew up to be a writer. But I like to think that my books are songs.

Hillsdale Uniforms

I was a lucky, lucky daughter. I grew up in a home with loving and active parents, and two fun sisters. We shared everything together—our school days, our friends, our dolls, and our family events. My parents and sisters were always there for me in my life, as steady anchors. I was one of the Walker girls. It seemed as if my parents had a thousand friends. These friends, and their children, also are part of the fabric of my childhood, adolescence, and adult years.

I left Lotspeich and Miss Cornn, and headed into a new academic experience, complete with a green tunic uniform. I attended an all-girls school, Hillsdale School, for grades seven through twelve. My sisters also went to Hillsdale, and my mother often told us that our uniforms made her life as the mother of three teenage daughters much easier.

I formed lifelong friendships with my classmates, including eight girls whom I now travel with once a year. We call ourselves the Eight Graces, and for the past fifteen years, we have spent an annual weekend together in places ranging from California to the West Indies. Old friends are a treasure, just like the red book given to me by Miss Cornn.

The thirty-two girls I graduated with from Hillsdale knew me long before I was a wife or a mother or a children's book writer. We studied together and grew up together. The class of 1967 was a mix of intellect, humor, wild times, and ordinary fun. I value those classmates, and the history that I share with each of them.

As a Hillsdale student, I had some fine history teachers who were to point me in the direction of my college major, beginning in seventh grade with Margaret Dunphy. I can still picture Miss Dunphy, seated at her desk, going through a stack of our assigned papers on China or Egypt (she taught world history). Behind her were windows that let in the afternoon sunlight and a view of Hillsdale's sports field, where in the fall we played field hockey. You could see the two goals from Miss Dunphy's room.

My teacher's white hair and elegant blue linen suits confirmed to me the dignity of her age: here indeed, was a *real lady*. And she wanted the uniformed girls she taught at Hillsdale to become ladies as well. Although I never actually *saw* Margaret Dunphy wearing white gloves, I had a strong suspicion that she owned several pairs, just as my grandmother Nana did. I'm sure Miss Dunphy's lecture style of teaching history would be considered outdated in today's classrooms, but for some reason I connected deeply to her kindness and to the subject she taught, and I like to think that she would be very pleased to read the historical books I have written.

During second semester of my eighth grade, the whole school of two hundred girls was convened during a special morning assembly. The announcement by the headmaster that my history teacher had been in a serious car accident came as a sudden shock, as was her death a week later. I had never known any grown-up in the circle of people in

The author with Margaret K. McElderry (center) and Ann Bobco

my life to die, except for Lula, but she had been far away at the time of her death. Miss Dunphy was in the here and now—in my classroom each day, correcting my papers. I sat in the back row for the rest of the year, out of sorts with the replacement teacher and missing Miss Dunphy's gracious presence. I'm not sure that students are ever quite aware of the positive impact of a teacher until they are far enough along in life to be able to turn around and point and say, yes, that was the one who led me into a subject more deeply. And when I was a Hillsdale student, little did I know that almost forty years later another Margaret with white hair and elegant suits would become a beloved part of my publishing life: the legendary editor Margaret K. McElderry.

Other teachers who remain etched in my Hillsdale memories: Roger Loud (U.S. history) and Margie Highlands (modern Europe). I loved their classes and their passionate discussions with students. Renée Lowther, who was my French teacher at Hillsdale, is now eighty years old. This past year, she gave me hours of help in translating H. A. Rey's work diaries. Our headmaster, Mr. Lovett, was a stern-faced and, to me, distant figure at our school. He signed my report cards and nodded to me curtly in the halls. He was busy with college admissions and running the school.

Most people my age clearly remember where they were on November 22, 1963, when John F. Kennedy was assassinated. I was sitting at my desk as a ninth grader when our homeroom teacher told our class the tragic news. Many years later, in 1996, my mother would die from cancer on that same date in November. Another clear and life-changing memory.

My world was small in the early 1960s—bounded by family and neighbors, holidays with cousins, school, and evenings watching TV after our homework was done. With no brothers, I found the world of boys to be somewhat of a mystery. The dances at Hillsdale plus a few other gatherings provided a few but inconclusive clues. Boys were the main topic of conversation at our lunch tables in the school cafeteria and the subject of notes passed from desk to desk during study hall. In my limited experience, dates were how girls socialized with boys. Two of the three boys I dated in high school both were named Pete. (Neither were the Pete I was later to marry.)

My mother and father must have had their moments, raising three girls, but I never stopped to notice. Life was busy in the house on Bayard Drive, the white uniform blouses were lined up neatly on hangers in the laundry room, and we daughters were always in motion with our friends from school. Our home life was traditional, in keeping with the times in which I grew up. My father put on his suit and tie and went off to the office every morning. My mother didn't work, but she drove a thousand carpools, played bridge on Tuesdays, and was the steadiest putter in any golf foursome. She could whip up dinner for fifty people at the drop of a hat. Louise Walker's energy was limitless, and I was glad that we shared the same name even though everyone but the principal called me Leezie. Mom lived to see my first six books published and was an encourager of everything that I ever tried to do. Both of my parents were positive and optimistic influences in my life, and they were later terrific grandparents to our three children.

Nana was still very much a part of our family, escaping the noise and clamor to read in her bedroom, located up a set of stairs that led to our third floor. Meanwhile, I loved all of it, our roomy house, my mother's parties, and even those green Hillsdale uniforms.

Flying ... and Leland

I can't write about my life without including two key influences. My father's eyesight had prevented him from becoming a pilot in WWII. But when I was thirteen, Dad earned the pilot's license he had always wanted, and I was the first of our family to fly with him one afternoon. I remember the tiny plane we were in, a red and white two-seater Cessna 150. I was excited and afraid, as my mother stood near the hangar, nervously waving good-bye. I had only been on a commercial plane once or twice. Here I was in something smaller than my mother's station wagon. But as the 150 climbed up into the afternoon sky and I looked down on the landscape below, I knew at once why my father loved flying. Dad was to own several small planes over the next twenty years, and many Cincinnati friends can recall memorable flights with Bill Walker as their pilot. Now my father is at the end of a long journey with Alzheimer's disease, and he doesn't understand when I show him the three books I have written about airplanes

Pete Borden, 1969

and famous aviators. But our times flying together are an enduring part of the love and admiration that I have for my dad. 2171 X ray and 2643 Sierra are Cessna plane numbers I'll never forget.

Another essential part of my life is the town of Leland, Michigan, where my family has vacationed during the summer for five generations. My parents, like my grandparents before them, spent time on Lake Leelanau during my childhood. Then in 1959, they built their own cottage and named it Tanglewood. Every June, we piled into my mother's car and traveled the five hundred miles north to a landscape of lakes, sand dunes, woods, and cherry orchards. My sisters and I grew up with a love of water because of our summers spent on Lake Leelanau and the Lake Michigan beaches close by.

For hours on end, we explored the shorelines with our friends in small boats or sailed from bay to bay in races. I often went out with my dad in the early evening to fish. As a child, I loved the quiet and the patience that fishermen must have, but I never learned to like the taste of fish, which is now a joke with Pete and our children. And at the height of middle age, at least once a summer I have to prove to our kids that I can still water-ski. I know that it's my chosen day when I walk around the side of the cottage and see an old wooden slalom ski, nicknamed *the Shark,* leaning against the screened porch. Each summer Pete and I look forward to spending time on the dock with our kids and catching up on their lives in Denver, Atlanta, and Ann Arbor.

Leelanau County is where I learned to snow ski, a winter sport that I still enjoy doing in Colorado where our daughter Cate lives. My parents raised their three daughters to enjoy many outdoor sports, and now our children are following those interests as well. Leland remains a vital place for all of us.

English Class and More Echoes

People often ask me now: "Did you always want to become a writer? Did you major in English or Journalism?" My writing skills evolved, in part, I believe, from my love of reading. I had grown up reading, and I think that I learned by osmosis how to put words together. I had good teachers along the way. One of them was Mr. Stanton, an earnest young man, who taught his English students to notice descriptive images, and he got me to think about my writing. I also had my required summer reading each summer and waded through tomes like *Lord Jim.* But of all those titles I read—some wonderful and some boring to a teenage girl—I do remember one very powerful book: *Cry, the Beloved Country,* by Alan Paton. I didn't understand all of the political and moral implications of the book, but I knew that here was a book that opened up another new world to me, far beyond my sheltered childhood in Ohio. Here were words that I would remember all my life: "There is a lovely road that runs from Ixopo into the hills. These hills are grass-covered and rolling and they are lovely beyond any singing of it." I was drawn in by language. From then on, I began to listen to the *sound* of writing.

During an assignment for my senior English class, I chose to study the poet Anne Morrow Lindbergh. Her poems held images of the sea, and of loss, and I admired the strong voice in her poetry. I was to continue to study her writings and journals as I grew older. More than thirty years after writing that English paper, my book *Good-bye, Charles Lindbergh* would unexpectedly begin a correspondence and writer's friendship with Anne's daughter, Reeve Lindbergh. One day, Reeve wrote to tell me of her mother's enjoyment when my book was read aloud to her and how she admired the illustrations of her husband Charles. It seemed a full circle to me, and another echo. In May 2002, Pete and I were invited by Reeve to her celebration at the National Air and Space Museum of the seventy-fifth anniversary of the New York to Paris flight, and we danced to music beneath the *Spirit of St. Louis* and the Wright Flyer ... something else I will remember all my life.

I worked on the Hillsdale yearbook staff—specifically on the layout of photos and blocks of text. I was not an artist, but again, I loved standing at the edge of that world. Today, when I am working on my picture books, I make a dummy of pages with my text. This brings me closer to the experience of bookmaking and also helps me determine the sequence and pace of the text.

One more Hillsdale echo: during a recent book research trip, I was seated at a table next to my sister Cindy in the Denver Public Library, paging through scrapbooks about the Tenth Mountain Division that trained in Leadville, Colorado, during WWII. Cindy pointed to a young private's letter written to his parents signed *Frank Lovett*.

"Look, Leez," she said. "Doesn't that look like *Mr. Lovett's* handwriting?" We peered at the letter closely, and I asked the librarian to add it to my list of copies. I took the letter home and then, upon my return to Cincinnati, I read through a school history of Hillsdale and learned that our headmaster, Francis Lovett, *did* serve with the Tenth Mountain Division. I had newfound respect for the man who had signed his signature on my report card all those years ago. Connections like these seem present in each book that I write. I look for them, and consider them as good luck omens when they appear.

College Studies

I remember arriving at Denison University on my first day as a freshman and helping my parents unload a few suitcases and boxes from our Ford station wagon. Certainly going to college in the fall of 1967 did not entail the incredible unloading ordeal that occurred when Pete and I took Cate and Ayars as first-year students to Miami University. I took no microwave. No computer. No phone or answering machine. No TV. Just my clothes, some framed pictures, apprehension, and courage. I had left my sister Margaret behind at home—still in high school. But since I was following my older sister to the same college, Cindy would be a few dorms away, my safety net. The beautiful, classic campus seemed huge to me after my small Hillsdale. Two thousand students! Now of course, when Pete and I visit our son Ted at the University of Michigan where he is studying economics, I realize how small Denison is. But what a strong liberal arts education I received—including taking creative writing—and I made lifelong friends during my four years in Granville, Ohio. One of my roommates, Sydney (Henderson) McCurdy, now lives in Connecticut. During many trips to New York for editorial meetings over the past sixteen years, I have often taken the train to Westport to visit Syd. How

The author's children: (left to right) Ted, Ayars, and Cate, summer 2001

wonderful to see my old Denison friend and to share my book world with her. In college I learned how to drink beer, and I had a fairly traditional college experience although my last two years were marked by the divisive and questioning times in our country with the war in Vietnam, the generation gap, and huge social change.

I met Peter Borden during the winter of my freshman year on a blind date. He was from Hillside, New Jersey, not far from Manhattan. Pete was two years ahead of me, in Cindy's class, and was a lanky, quiet varsity athlete and a leader on campus. He played goalie on the Denison men's soccer team and was an attack man in lacrosse, a sport I had never seen played until I arrived at Denison. For the next two years, until he graduated, my future husband walked me home from the library to my dorm along chapel walk, and I cheered for number nineteen and his teammates at every lacrosse game. This was the wonderful young man who several years later would take me to lunch at the top of the Pan Am Building in New York City on a March day after we had shopped for an engagement ring.

Now when I am hurrying along the streets of midtown Manhattan, headed to lunch with Margaret McElderry or en route to see proofs for a new book at Simon & Schuster, I look up, up at that tall same building. The words Pan Am are long gone, and it is now known as the Met Life to present-day New Yorkers. Little did I know in the spring of 1971 that my life would unfold in a way that would bring me back again and again to this vibrant city as a writer of children's books.

Besides falling in love at Denison, I also focused on the study of history. The department's staff was flamboyant and popular. Al Lever was a young energetic professor who served as my advisor until he was killed tragically in a motorcycle accident when I was a junior. When taking European and German history from Dr. Lever, I was moved by his compelling stories about his own father who had served in the German army during WWI. It was Al Lever who encouraged my studies, deepening my interest in the human element in history. One day months after his death, I walked into the Denison library, headed for my desk to work on a research project. In the lobby was a cart stacked high with some of Dr. Lever's books. He had died leaving no family, so the history department had given his books to the library—and then offered these remaining ones to students for a nominal amount. What a *gift,* I thought, to serve as a custodian for books that had been a meaningful part of my favorite professor's intellectual passion. I bought five of them, and I still have those books on our bookshelves in Terrace Park today.

I also was influenced by other history professors at Denison: John Huckaby and David Watson. Dr. Huckaby led a group of twenty students to Europe for six weeks the summer after my freshman year, a trip that was life-altering for me. I was able to visit places that I had only known through textbooks and maps. I was able to stand in museums and study the paintings that I had learned about in art history. Cindy was also on this same European program, and we bicycled together in Holland, an experience I was to use as firsthand research when writing the story of Margret and H. A. Rey's flight from Paris in 1940.

John Huckaby died while I was a student at Denison—quite suddenly. I couldn't believe that three history teachers, who had touched my academic life in lasting ways, died such unexpected deaths. Dr. Watson then became the faculty advisor for my year-long senior research (*The European Response to Hitler: Resistance Movements in WWII*), in which my focus was the ordinary citizen caught up in historical events. That year I served as

a fellow in the department, helping with classroom discussions and grading papers. Last summer when I received an Alumni Citation from my college in recognition of my work in children's books "which reflect honor upon Denison University" I felt that I was accepting the award on behalf of my remarkable professors.

After Denison

I married the quiet and romantic number nineteen, Peter Ayars Borden, on September 4, 1971, and we headed to New England to teach at private schools in the Boston area for two years. Pete taught history at Rivers Country Day School, and I worked as an assistant first-grade teacher at the Meadowbrook School, which was similar in many ways to Lotspeich. These years helped me enormously in learning to teach early reading skills and in how to connect with students. This classroom experience also enabled me to relate to the many grade levels I encounter during my author visits to schools. At Meadowbrook, I had a fine mentor, a veteran teacher named Bev Rogers, who appears in the dedication of *Thanksgiving Is . . . ,* and I loved the pond where our first graders enjoyed long skating recesses during winter. Another echo from my own school years at Lotspeich.

Our return to Cincinnati in 1973 brought new chapters: a year of teaching pre-primary students at Cincinnati Country Day School, buying our first house, and starting

Louise and Pete, Dover, England, May 2000

our family of three kids. Pete continued to teach history for several more years and then began working in the business world. Today he travels to other continents as part of his work and helps to coach a Terrace Park lacrosse team, but our shared interest in history has never ceased. All of my books have been possible because of my husband's constant support and encouragement.

For me, early parenting years were a blur of tricycles, diapers, swimming and ballet lessons, and continual laundry. I loved being at home with these healthy and loving children who grew up in the blink of an eye. I looked at life through a new lens—that of a mother. Cate and Ayars were both born in November, two years apart, and grew up in tandem, one a towhead and one a brunette, ahead of their brother Ted, who was born on Abraham Lincoln's birthday when Ayars was five. This connection to Lincoln balanced my southern roots, and Pete's mother was pleased since her grandfather, Peter B. Ayars, had fought for the Union side at Gettysburg.

During these years of soccer and baseball games, homework, and Halloween costumes, I was involved in our children's school world. At the same time, I was at my desk during spare minutes, taking steps toward my future publishing life. I remember walking outside early one morning in the spring of 1984 to pick up the *Cincinnati Enquirer* from our lawn. There on page A10 of the newspaper was my first published piece, a poem entitled "Opening Day," about the Cincinnati Reds. I sat on our front steps in my nightgown and savored the moment. The date was April 2—my mother's birthday.

Over ten years later, Camilla Warrick, a fine and well-known journalist who worked for both of the major newspapers in Cincinnati, became a Terrace Park neighbor and good friend of mine. Our conversations during walks around our village always centered on the creative process, voice, and various works-in-progress. Camilla's death from cancer in the summer of 2002 was a deep personal loss. It is something I find as difficult to write about as the sudden death of another friend, Linda Dodd, a teacher whose love of books and language arts always inspires me when I am working at my desk.

In 1986, while I was submitting manuscripts to publishers, I began working part-time in a small independent bookstore and then became one of four owners until 1991, when I turned my energies to writing full-time. Through my work at the Bookshelf, I learned about publishing from a different perspective, and I had three partners who were seasoned booksellers. They were good teachers as well. We have now all "retired" from the Bookshelf, but Janet, Ellie, and Jeanie are still in the circle of my closest friends.

I signed my first book contract in 1987 with Scholastic. At the time, I was recovering from a fall while ice-skating and had double plaster casts due to breaking both wrists, so my signature was a bit of a scrawl. *Caps, Hats, Socks, and Mittens* was published by Scholastic in 1989 and is still in print. My editor, Grace Maccarone, published six more of my manuscripts over the next ten years. The editors with whom I have worked have been profoundly important in my creative life. Grace published my first book, gave me confidence as a writer, and continues to be an encourager. Nina Ignatowicz, formerly at Clarion Books and now at Holt, edited the beautifully published *Paperboy,*

the first book that I wrote as a coauthor, with Mary Kay Kroeger. Nina's counsel and conversations helped me to focus my ideas and voice for future books, and gave Mary Kay and me the affirmation that we could collaborate successfully in a shared text. Amy Flynn (Houghton Mifflin), my editor for two forthcoming books, encouraged my perseverance and passion in finding the clues to Margret and Hans Rey's escape from Paris in 1940. Our continuing conversations about words, art, and children always lead me to new thinking about my writing.

Since 1995, I have worked on a dozen books with Margaret K. McElderry. Our paths first crossed at an American Booksellers Convention in 1991. I knew then of Margaret's reputation as a publisher, but I also immediately sensed her depth and her graciousness. After writing *The Little Ship*s, I sent it to Margaret, knowing that she would understand the heart of the book. Some of the twelve books Margaret has edited have been historical fiction. Others have been school stories or nonfiction. Margaret understands in just the right way my vision for each book, and she is an essential sounding board. My McElderry titles are elegantly published because of Margaret's care and creative collaboration with Emma Dryden, Ann Bobco, Sarah Nielsen, and the rest of the McElderry team. Whether I am sitting in her office at Simon & Schuster going over a manuscript set in wartime Holland, or in her book-lined living room on Washington Square discussing the creative process over a glass of wine, I always pinch myself, not sure if this publishing life is really an imagined dream.

Other scenes in this dream include attending Barbara Lucas' publishing workshops at Vassar College ... crossing the English Channel with Pete on the deck of a little ship ... signing a book contract with M. K. Kroeger ... walking through Macy's with Johanna Hurwitz, in deep conversation about our book lives ... observing inspiring teachers in Dublin City Schools and in other classrooms across Ohio ... standing on the prime meridian, zero degrees longitude ... sitting in Bob Parker's studio looking at book illustrations ... having phone calls with Ted and Betsy Lewin ... attending the Christophers ... being in Ypres, Belgium with Michael Foreman and Trish Marx ... meeting thousands of schoolchildren ... visiting John Harrison's grave with my guide and fellow writer, Maryann Macdonald ... forming friendships with national educators ... following the Reys' 1940 escape route from Paris ... sharing photos of that trip with Amy Flynn at Houghton Mifflin on a snowy October morning.

There are uncounted parts of this ongoing dream, and sometimes they reach beyond the imagination I use at my desk.

It is a Monday ... or a Tuesday
or a Friday morning before the school day begins.
It is still dark outside,
but the sun is beginning to rise
over the fields in the distance.
I have driven to this Ohio school down a country
    road,
and I'm miles away from my house in Terrace Park
as I walk through the front doors
that have just been unlocked by the custodian.

The hallwys are silent now
but they'll soon fill with the voices of strangers:
teachers and their kindergarten to sixth grade students.
There ahead of me in a case in the school lobby
is a display of my published books.
On nearby walls are welcome signs,
painted by the hands of children.
I stand alone in the quiet,
reading the words,
and then peer through the glass.
The jackets of my books
gleam in the bright light,
and in bold letters on each one is my name,
Louise Borden.

The many people who have touched my life
are not with me in this solitary moment.
Those who are still living are miles away,
beginning a morning in their own busy lives:
Pete and our three grown children,
my editors,
the illustrators, art designers, and printers,
librarians and research contacts,
friends and mentors,
and all the others along my life road.

I look at my picture books
and hear the echoes.
Then I walk up the hall ...
ready to share the dream
with young readers and writers.

BOTTONE, Frank G., Jr. 1969-

Personal

Born November 13, 1969, in Red Bank, NJ. *Education:* Virginia Wesleyan College, B.A., 1993; Old Dominion University, M.S., 1996.

Addresses

Home—112 Taylor Glen Drive, Morrisville, NC 27560. *E-mail*—bionotes@yahoo.com.

Career

University of North Carolina at Chapel Hill, Chapel Hill, NC, laboratory research specialist, 1997-2000; NIEHS (division of National Institutes of Health), Research Triangle Park, NC, biologist, 2000—. Freelance contributor to *Muscle and Fitness Magazine,* 2000—.

Member

AAAS.

Awards, Honors

Best Books for Children, *Smithsonian magazine,* 2001.

Writings

The Science of Life: Projects and Principles for Beginning Biologists, Chicago Review Press (Chicago, IL), 2001.

Contributor of scientific papers to the *Journal of Nutrition* and *Pediatric Research;* scientific abstracts published in *Society for Neuroscience,* and *American Journal of Respiratory and Critical Care Medicine;*

contributor to *Muscle and Fitness, Ambion's TechNotes,* and the *New Jersey Times.*

Work in Progress

Researching breast and colon cancer, and how NSAIDs inhibit cancer.

Sidelights

Frank G. Bottone, Jr., told *SATA:* "As a writer, I try to make complicated things seem more understandable after just one read. Where that becomes challenging is not talking down to your reader or coming across sounding like a textbook. My first project was an enormous overview of biology. I anticipate my next project focusing on a much more concentrated area of science, such as nutrition or cancer."

Frank G. Bottone, Jr. provides students with a hands-on introduction to each of the five biological kingdoms, bacteria, plants, animals, fungi, and protozoans, in his book *The Science of Life: Projects and Principles for Beginning Biologists.* With the guidance of his book, young scientists can conduct elucidating experiments using flowers or common spiders, they can grow a variety of bacteria and learn how to encourage or inhibit that growth, or they can learn how to grow fungi or carnivorous plants. Some experiments presented by Bottone are common to many science books for young people, noted Pamela Longbrake in *Book Report,* though others seem original to the author. Although the author's instructions are considered well written and easy to understand, many of the projects, whether for a classroom experiment or a science fair project, should be conducted with the help of an adult, contended Maren Ostergard in *School Library Journal.*

FRANK G. BOTTONE, JR.

Molecular biologist Frank G. Bottone, Jr. helps readers explore life from bacteria to plants and animals through twenty-five projects such as cloning a mushroom. (Cover photos by Photodisc.)

The book contains a chapter on safety precautions and a list of sources where hard-to-find ingredients for the experiments may be ordered. Furthermore, each experiment has variations for the beginning student and for the more advanced. These were all considered welcome features by reviewers. But it is Bottone's knowledge of how and when young scientists are likely to have trouble with each experiment, and his advice on how to avoid problems that are an outstanding feature of this science book, according to Longbrake. Ostergard was similarly impressed by *The Science of Life,* concluding that "the volume provides a thorough introduction to this area of science and would be useful in most collections."

Biographical and Critical Sources

PERIODICALS

Book Report, November, 2001, Pamela Longbrake, review of *The Science of Life,* p. 82.
School Library Journal, November, 2001, Maren Ostergard, review of *The Science of Life,* p. 171.

BRIAN, Janeen (Paulette) 1948-

Personal

Born March 13, 1948, in Adelaide, South Australia, Australia; daughter of Frederick Keith (a business manager) and Paulette Elsie (Allert) Colyer; married David Ridyard, 1968 (divorced, 1972); married Tony Brian, 1976 (divorced, 1978); partner of Jonathan Grant (a driving instructor); children: (first marriage) Natalie; (second marriage) Cassie. *Education:* Wattle Park Teachers' College, Adelaide, South Australia, Australia, Registered Primary Teacher Certificate, 1966. *Hobbies and other interests:* Keeping fit, yoga, travel, making mosaics, going to the theatre, film-going, reading and writing, gardening.

Addresses

Home—11 Short Ave., Glenelg East, South Australia, 5045 Australia. *E-mail*—janeenb@ozemail.com.au.

Career

Children's writer. Primary school teacher and librarian, South Australia, 1966-90; professional actor, Patch Theatre, South Australia, 1980-84.

Member

South Australian Children's Writers (EKIDNAS), South Australian Writers' Centre (board of management member, 2000-2001), Australian Society of Authors (ASA), CBC-Children's Book Council, Trees for Life, Patch Theatre.

Awards, Honors

Ian Maudie award for article, Fellowship of Australian Writers, 1987, for "The Dreaming of Dying"; third place in children's stories, Coolum and Interstate Writers' Association, 1991, for "Thistle" and highly commended, 1991, for "Emergency"; second place, Eaglehawk and Dahlia Festival Awards, 1996, for poem "Ward 5K"; Honour Book Award, CBC Book Awards, 1997, for *Pilawuk: When I Was Young;* winner, Calambeen Literary Award, children's short story, 1997, for "Pegasus"; CBC Notable Books, 1998, for *Rocky, Dog Star,* and *Duck Down;* highly commended, Equal Opportunities Award, 1999, for *Max Colwell: When I Was Young* and *Maria Donato: When I Was Young;* commended, Children's Peace Literature Award, 1999, for *Leaves for Mr. Walter,* highly commended, Midlands Literary Awards, 2000, for children's story, "Small Frog, Balong"; Honour Book Award, Early Childhood, CBC, 2002, for *Where Does Thursday Go?;* shortlisted, Crighton Award, 2002, for *Silly Galah!;* shortlisted, Wilderness Society Environmental Award, 2002.

Janeen Brian

Writings

CHILDREN'S SHORT FICTION

Tomorrow Is A Great Word, Era Publications (Flinders Park, South Australia, Australia), 1991.

Moving On, illustrated by Katharine Stafford, Era Publications (Flinders Park, South Australia, Australia), 1992.

The Ups and Downs of Desmond, illustrated by Jim Tsinganos, Era Publications (Flinders Park, South Australia, Australia), 1992.

The Charms of Thomas Filbett, illustrated by Annie McQueen, Era Publications (Flinders Park, South Australia, Australia), 1993.

Brolga, illustrated by Annie McQueen, Era Publications (Flinders Park, South Australia, Australia), 1994.

Winnie Whistlebritches, illustrated by Trevor Pye, Omnibus (Norwood, South Australia, Australia), 1994.

Dust in My Eyes, illustrated by Veronica Osborn, Era Publications (Flinders Park, South Australia, Australia), 1995.

Dragon Fire, illustrated by Pauline King, Wendy Pye, 1995.

The Kite Place, illustrated by Min Huang, Era Publications (Flinders Park, South Australia, Australia), 1996.

Circus Detective, illustrated by Tom Jellett, Era Publications (Flinders Park, South Australia, Australia), 1996.

Dog Star, illustrated by Ann James, Omnibus (Norwood, South Australia, Australia), 1997.

Duck Down, illustrated by Mike Johnson, Omnibus (Norwood, South Australia, Australia), 1997.

Rocky, illustrated by Harry Slaghekke, Omnibus (Norwood, South Australia, Australia), 1997.

In a Pickle, illustrated by Bettina Guthridge, Addison Wesley Longman (South Melbourne, Australia), 1998.

Alex and the Dragon, Macmillan (Sydney, New South Wales, Australia), 1999.

Time Wise, Macmillan (Sydney, New South Wales, Australia), 1999.

Wild Abbie!, illustrated by Rae Dale, Addison Wesley Longman (South Melbourne, Australia), 1999.

Fudge and the Pet Detectives, illustrated by Bettina Guthridge, Addison Wesley Longman (South Melbourne, Australia), 1999.

Tom and the Terrible Crankyshanks, illustrated by Bettina Guthridge, Addison Wesley Longman (South Melbourne, Australia), 1999.

The Adventures of Ramsden Plum, Barrie Publishing (Kew, Victoria, Australia), 1999.

Rats, Crispin Canoodle!, Barrie Publishing (Kew, Victoria, Australia), 2000.

Train Trouble, Pearson Education Australia (Frenchs Forest, New South Wales, Australia), 2000.

The Surprise Patch, Pearson Education Australia (Frenchs Forest, New South Wales, Australia), 2000.

What a Load of Rubbish, Pearson Education Australia (Frenchs Forest, New South Wales, Australia), 2000.

Sea Stars, Pearson Education Australia (Frenchs Forest, New South Wales, Australia), 2000.

What's in the River?, Omnibus (Norwood, South Australia, Australia), 2001.

What's Wrong, Aram?, Omnibus (Norwood, South Australia, Australia), 2001.

Pitch Black, Nelson Thomson Learning (Southbank, Victoria, Australia), 2002.

Party Time!, Penguin (Camberwell, Victoria, Australia), 2002.

CHILDREN'S NONFICTION

South Australia's Early Colonial Years, illustrated by Cait Wait, Hodder & Stoughton (Lane Cove, New South Wales, Australia), 1985.

Amazing Landforms, Era Publications (Flinders Park, South Australia, Australia), 1992.

Natural Disasters, Era Publications (Flinders Park, South Australia, Australia), 1992.

Rescues, Era Publications (Flinders Park, South Australia, Australia), 1992.

Making Masks, Era Publications (Flinders Park, South Australia, Australia), 1995.

Making Pop-Ups, Era Publications (Flinders Park, South Australia, Australia), 1995.

Pilawuk: When I Was Young, Era Publications (Flinders Park, South Australia, Australia), 1996.

Maria Donato: When I Was Young, Era Publications (Flinders Park, South Australia, Australia), 1996.

Max Colwell: When I Was Young, Era Publications (Flinders Park, South Australia, Australia), 1996.

Young Achievers, Era Publications (Flinders Park, South Australia, Australia), 1996.

Sausage Jam! (playscript), Longman/Pearson Education Australia (South Melbourne, Australia), 2002.

Theseus and the Minotaur (playscript), Longman/Pearson Education Australia (South Melbourne, Australia), 2002.

Brothers Grimm (biography), Pearson Education Australia (South Melbourne, Australia), 2003.

CHILDREN'S POETRY

Putrid Poems, Omnibus (Norwood, South Australia, Australia), 1985.

Petrifying Poems, Omnibus (Norwood, South Australia, Australia), 1986.

Vile Verse, Omnibus (Norwood, South Australia, Australia), 1988.

Four & Twenty Lamingtons, Omnibus (Norwood, South Australia, Australia), 1989.

Off the Planet, Omnibus (Norwood, South Australia, Australia), 1989.

Fractured Tales & Ruptured Rhymes, Omnibus (Norwood, South Australia, Australia), 1990.

Stay Loose, Mother Goose, Omnibus (Norwood, South Australia, Australia), 1990.

Christmas Crackers, Omnibus (Norwood, South Australia, Australia), 1990.

(With Gwen Pascoe) *There Was a Big Fish* (limericks), illustrated by Steven Woolman, Era Publications (Flinders Park, South Australia, Australia), 1992.

100 Australian Poems for Children, Random House (Milson's Point, New South Wales, Australia), 2002.

CHILDREN'S PICTURE BOOKS

My Sister Learns Ballet, illustrated by Jim Gully, Childerset (Melbourne, Australia), 1984, published as *Friends Learn Ballet,* Gareth Stevens (Milwaukee, WI), 1985.

Mr. Taddle's Hats, illustrated by Carol McLean-Carr, Era Publications (Flinders Park, South Australia, Australia), 1987.

Down They Rolled, illustrated by Jane Cheshire, Era Publications (Flinders Park, South Australia, Australia), 1987.

Andrea's Cubby, illustrated by Simone Kennedy, Era Publications (Flinders Park, South Australia, Australia), 1988.

Beach Pirates, illustrated by Annmarie Scott, JamRoll Press/UQP (Nundah, Queensland, Australia), 1993.

Thumpety-Rah!, illustrated by Maurizio Dotti, Wendy Pye (New Zealand), 1996.

Mr. Dallytap's Magic Coat, illustrated by Nathan Jurevicius, Era Publications (Flinders Park, South Australia, Australia), 1996.

The Letter-Box, illustrated by Deborah Baldassi, Era Publications (Flinders Park, South Australia, Australia), 1997.

Leaves for Mr. Walter, illustrated by David Cox, Margaret Hamilton (Sydney, New South Wales, Australia), 1998.

Silly Galah!, Omnibus (Norwood, South Australia, Australia), 2001.

Where Does Thursday Go?, illustrated by Stephen Michael King, Margaret Hamilton (Sydney, New South Wales, Australia), 2001.

Wishbone, ABC Books (Sydney, New South Wales, Australia), 2002.

Its and Bits of Nature, van Gastel Printing for South Australian Museum (Wingfield, South Australia, Australia), 2002.

The Tinderbox (retelling), Pearson Education Australia (South Melbourne, Australia), 2003.

Teddy Bears Picnic (playscript), Pearson Education Australia (South Melbourne, Australia), 2003.

Also the author of numerous short stories for children and adults; contributor to *Animal Scraps,* Omnibus/Scholastic (Norwood, South Australia, Australia), 2003; contributor to anthologies, including *Original Sin,* 1996, and *The Girl Who Married a Fly,* 1997; author of children's television scripts and plays; contributor of poems and articles to children's magazines including *School Magazine* and *Cricket,* and to adult publications such as *Prime Time, The Australian Woman's Weekly, Primary Education,* and *Australian House and Garden,* among others.

Work in Progress

The Horse That Could Fly, Thomas Nelson (Southbank, Victoria, Australia), 2004; *Pop-Up Fox,* Penguin Australia (Camberwell, Victoria, Australia), 2004. Also, two picture books, a novel, and a collection of animal poems.

Sidelights

Janeen Brian is an Australian author of over sixty works for children, including picture books, short story collections, non-fiction titles, short novels for young readers, and poetry anthologies; many of her works have not yet appeared in the United States. A versatile and prolific

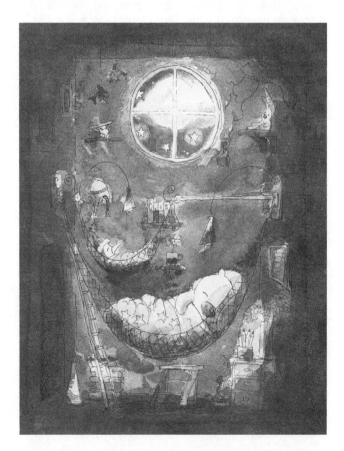

Friday is coming, so Bruno and Bert want to say goodbye to Thursday in Brian's **Where Does Thursday Go?,** *illustrated by Stephen Michael King.*

writer, Brian is the winner of the 2002 Honour Book Award in the Early Childhood category of the Children's Book Council for her picture book title, *Where Does Thursday Go?,* which has also been translated into four languages. Brian brings to her writing an intimate knowledge of the reading needs of children with over twenty years as a primary school teacher and librarian, as well as the mother of two children.

Born in Adelaide, South Australia, in 1948, Brian was one of three children. She has continued to make her home in the same vicinity, though she has also traveled internationally, in Britain, New Zealand, Bali, Singapore, Hong Kong, Canada, and for three months lived in a remote Indian village. As a child she developed an early love of reading, making up plays and stories, and creating things in general. Such projects included knitting and sewing, in addition to more literary efforts. Growing up near the ocean, Brian also developed a love for the sea in all its moods. Unfortunately for the young Brian, she also grew up with few books in the home, and with no school library to speak of she got her reading material by borrowing books from other children. "I wish I'd been a bit braver as a child," Brian noted on her author's Web site, "because once when I went to the small local library with a friend, my friend got such a telling off from the librarian because she'd brought a book back late, it stopped my going to the library (which I'd only just discovered) for many years." Brian's father was sick during much of her childhood, but he still found the energy to recite funny poems to her, some of which she committed to memory. She noted that she got her "love for the ridiculous" from such early verse exposure. The radio was another companion to her as a child, introducing her to the world of plays and stories.

Brian attended Adelaide's Brighton Primary School and High School; at the latter she enjoyed her English classes, especially the plays she read. While languages came easily for her, math and science were a different matter, requiring more effort. In 1966 she earned her teaching certificate from the Wattle Park Teachers' College in Adelaide and went to work as a primary school teacher and school librarian, a position she held from 1966 to 1990. In her first years of teaching, she started dabbling in writing; her first creation was a short story, "Little Blue Pig," which was rejected. She began writing more seriously and stubbornly at age thirty, attending a weekend seminar on writing and becoming determined to stick with it until she was published. To augment her teaching income, she wrote for a wide variety of markets, placing stories in magazines, writing jokes and greeting cards, and even running a personalized poem business for a time. Additionally, she was a part-time actor and voice-over presenter. Then in 1990 she decided to "take the plunge" into writing full time as she told *SATA.* "It was the best thing I could have done," Brian further explained. "To live from an income of writing is strong motivation to write."

One of her early titles, *Friends Learn Ballet,* was chosen for the "Growing Up" series from American publisher Gareth Stevens. Reviewing that picture book in *Reading Teacher,* Kathleen Naylor praised the manner in which the book "reinforces reading skills through the context of family values." Naylor also noted that the books in the series provide "enjoyable reading." Another title from Brian, *Beach Pirates,* was inspired by her own love of the Australian coast, and tells the story of one picnic at the beach. Frances Kelly, writing in *Emergency Librarian,* found that picture book to be a "delightful . . . treat for all ages."

More aquatic themes are presented in the gathering of limericks, *There Was a Big Fish,* dubbed a "lively collection" by Mandy Cheetham in *Magpies.* From poetry, Brian turns to short novels with *Moving On,* the story of three children in a fatherless family learning to deal with their mother's new and controlling friend. Patsy Jones, reviewing the easy-reader in *Magpies,* was of two minds about *Moving On,* noting that while Brian's text would not "intimidate the not-quite-confident reader," neither would it "convince them of the pleasures of reading." *Leaves for Mr. Walter,* on the other hand, is an award-winning title about the relationship between a crusty old man and an equally plucky young girl. Mr. Walter Buttress meets little Emilia one day when dumping leaves into her yard. After all, Mr. Walter Buttress reasons, it is only right the leaves go back in that yard, for that is where the gum tree is that has dropped all the foliage. Emilia is not put off by the old man, nor is she deterred when he threatens to build his fence higher if Emilia's father chooses to build her a tree house in the offending gum tree. "What unfolds is a delight," according to Cynthia Anthony, writing in *Magpies.* Emilia is able to break through the old man's rough exterior and find a place in his heart by acts of kindness such as carrying fallen leaves away on her bike. She soon discovers that the old man was once a carpenter, skills he ultimately uses to help build the tree house for the young girl. Anthony also noted that "this is a lovely book for children to read or be read to."

Books from Brian geared toward the beginning reader just setting out on his or her own appear in the "Solo" series. *What's in the River?* is a book "which puts a very satisfying spin on dealing with pollution," according to Margaret Phillips in *Magpies.* Focusing on a group of jungle animals who become increasingly disturbed by the things they find in the river, they decide to take such refuse back to the people living upstream who obviously misplaced the items. *What's Wrong, Aram?* again deals with animals, though this time with ones held in captivity and how they are changed by such an experience. Aram the elephant becomes bored by captivity, but is saved by the new zookeeper, Deb. "All the stories [in the series] will be enjoyed by readers," concluded Phillips in *Magpies.* Animals are at the center of the 2001 *Silly Galah!,* as well, but this time featured in eighteen one-stanza poems which are "sure to be a favorite," according to Phillips in *Magpies.* Each poem is accompanied with brief factual information about the animal, "combining fun with fact," as Phillips further remarked.

Of all the works by Brian to be published in the United States, the most popular has been the 2002 CBC Honour Book, *Where Does Thursday Go?*. Bruno the bear has had a great time at his birthday party, but now that the day is ending, he wonders where the time has gone so quickly. He in fact goes in search of Thursday with his friend, Bert, and at one point decides that the moon is Thursday because it reminds him of his round birthday cake. *Booklist*'s Carolyn Phelan found the book "gracefully written," while a reviewer for *Publishers Weekly* called it a "gentle tale." Kathleen Kelly MacMillan, reviewing the title in *School Library Journal,* concluded that *Where Does Thursday Go?* is a "perfect bedtime story."

Brian, who does workshops in schools much of the year in her native Australia, is an industrious professional with a regular schedule. Her writing day begins with a brisk walk, and by 8:30 she is at her desk in her home office. Writing first drafts with paper and pen, she revises her works on the computer. "I am very disciplined and determined as a person," Brian told *SATA.* "I can focus and concentrate and I think this has been one of my best attributes where writing is concerned." Brian concluded, "I write because I love it; because I can channel experiences into words; because I can play with language, and because I have a strong commitment to children and their reading. Writing for me is, and maybe always will be, *hard fun!*"

Biographical and Critical Sources

PERIODICALS

Booklist, March 1, 2002, Carolyn Phelan, review of *Where Does Thursday Go?,* p. 1139.
Emergency Librarian, March, 1994, Frances Kelly, review of *Beach Pirates,* p. 20.
Magpies, September, 1993, Mandy Cheetham, review of *There Was a Big Fish,* p. 38; July, 1994, Patsy Jones, review of *Moving On,* p. 29; May, 1998, Cynthia Anthony, review of *Leaves for Mr. Walter,* pp. 26-27; May, 2001, Margaret Phillips, review of *What's in the River?,* p. 29; November, 2001, Margaret Phillips, review of *Silly Galah!,* p. 28, and *What's Wrong, Aram?,* p. 29.
Publishers Weekly, January 28, 2002, review of *Where Does Thursday Go?,* p. 289.
Reading Teacher, May, 1986, Kathleen Naylor, review of *Friends Learn Ballet,* pp. 986-987.
School Library Journal, April, 2002, Kathleen Kelly MacMillan, review of *Where Does Thursday Go?,* p. 100.

OTHER

Janeen Brian Web site, http://www.janeenbrian.com/ (March 4, 2003).

BROWN, Dee (Alexander) 1908-2002

OBITUARY NOTICE—See index for *SATA* sketch: Born February 28, 1908, near Alberta, LA; died December 12, 2002, in Little Rock, AR. Librarian, historian, educator, and author. Brown was a noted expert on the American West whose writings helped readers see the United States' treatment of Native Americans from the native people's perspective. He received a bachelor's degree in library science from George Washington University in 1937, later going on to earn his master's from the University of Illinois in 1952. His first job was as a library assistant for the U.S. Department of Agriculture during the late 1930s, followed by a librarianship at the Beltsville Research Center in Maryland. During World War II, Brown served in the U.S. Army, returning home to become a technical librarian for the U.S. War Department in Aberdeen, Maryland. The remainder of his career was spent at the University of Illinois at Urbana-Champaign, where he was a librarian from 1948 to 1972, and a professor of library science from 1962 to 1975. Brown had been sympathetic to the plight of the American Indian since the time he was a boy growing up in Oklahoma, where he made many Native American friends and quickly learned that the Indians portrayed in theaters were not at all like the real people. The stories his grandmother told him about his great-grandfather, who was a friend to Davy Crockett, also sparked his interest in the Old West. Brown maintained this fascination for the history of the American West into adulthood, and while he worked as a librarian he spent his spare time researching and writing about this period. He discovered that European settlers committed many horrifying injustices against these native peoples, including mass slaughters, theft, repeated broken treaties, and unjust relocations of entire tribes. He published his findings in his many history books, the best known of which is *Bury My Heart at Wounded Knee: An Indian History of the American West* (1970). Brown also dispelled other myths about the West in such books as *The Gentle Tamers: Women of the Old Wild West* (1958), *The Westerners* (1974), and *Dee Brown's Civil War Anthology* (1998), publishing nineteen nonfiction books in all. He was also the author of nine Western novels, including *Wave High the Banner* (1942), *Kildeer Mountain* (1983), and his last, *The Way to Bright Star* (1998). His writings won several awards, as well, including the Best Western for Young People award in 1981 for *Hear that Lonesome Whistle Blow: Railroads in the West* and the Saddleman Award in 1984, both from the Western Writers of America.

OBITUARIES AND OTHER SOURCES:

BOOKS

Contemporary Authors Autobiography Series, Volume 6, Gale (Detroit, MI), 1988.
Contemporary Southern Writers, St. James (Detroit, MI), 1999.

PERIODICALS

Chicago Tribune, December 14, 2002, Section 2, p. 11.
Los Angeles Times, December 14, 2002, p. B20.

New York Times, December 14, 2002, p. B18.
Times (London, England), December 17, 2002, p. 28.
Washington Post, December 14, 2002, p. B6.

*   *   *

BYALICK, Marcia 1947-

Personal

Born April 9, 1947, in Brooklyn, NY; daughter of Al (a dry cleaner) and Mona (Goldsmith) Finkelstein; married Robert Byalick (a psychologist), November 22, 1967; children: Jennifer, Carrie. *Education:* Brooklyn College of the City University of New York, M.A., 1969. *Politics:* "Liberal Democrat." *Religion:* Jewish. *Hobbies and other interests:* Theater, exercise, "any excuse to get together with friends and family."

Addresses

Home and office—22 Lydia Ct., Albertson, NY 11507.

Career

Writer. Editor in chief, *Women's Record,* 1985-93. Columnist, feature writer, *Spotlight, Distinction,* 1996—. Hofstra University, C. W. Post writing teacher, 1993—. Journalist, Long Island section of the *New York Times.*

Awards, Honors

Eleven awards from Long Island Press Club, 1986-2002, for work as a columnist; Books for the Teen Age, New York Public Library, 1996, for *It's a Matter of Trust; Quit It* chosen as one of Bank Street College of Education's Best Children's Books of 2003.

Writings

FOR YOUNG ADULTS

Reel Life, 1993.
You Don't Have to Be Perfect to Be Excellent, 1993.
It's a Matter of Trust, Harcourt (Orlando, FL), 1995.
Quit It, Delacorte Press (New York, NY), 2002.

OTHER

(With Linda Saslow) *The Three Career Couple: Mastering the Art of Juggling Work, Home, and Family* (humorous self-help), Peterson's Press (Princeton, NJ), 1993.
(With Linda Saslow) *How Come I Feel So Disconnected If This Is Such a User Friendly World? Reconnecting with Your Family, Your Friends—and Your Life,* Peterson's Press (Princeton, NJ), 1995.
(With Ronald A. Ruden) *The Craving Brain: The Biobalance Approach to Controlling Addictions,* HarperCollins (New York, NY), 1997, second edition published as *The Craving Brain: A Bold New Approach to Breaking Free from drug Addiction, Overeating, Alcoholism, Gambling,* Perennial (New York, NY), 2000.

Marcia Byalick

Sidelights

"Acne, clothes and friends are not all today's teens are concerned with," Marcia Byalick once told interviewer Ramin P. Jaleshgari of the *New York Times.* Byalick's young adult novels draw upon this conviction by centering on characters with serious problems, realistically depicted. In her first young adult novel to be widely reviewed, *It's a Matter of Trust* the life of sixteen-year-old Erika Gershon is turned upside down when her father is indicted on racketeering charges. In addition to her feelings about her father, Erika must cope with the intrusion of the media upon her family, her friends' gossip, and the death of a beloved uncle. "Young readers will find a wealth of issues to discuss in this unsettling, thought-provoking novel," predicted *School Library Journal* contributor Jana R. Fine. Byalick further tests the fine-tuning on her readers' judgment when she causes her protagonist to cheat during a tennis match and then lie about it. Erika is also growing up during all this turmoil, and finds herself developing romantic feelings for her camp mate Greg. "YA girls will find much to like about Erika and her story of maturation," asserted *Voice of Youth Advocates* contributor Lucy Marx.

"My ultimate goal is to help teens become comfortable dealing with hard issues," Byalick told Jaleshgari. "Young people need to know that time always brings change. Through my writing I'd like to teach them that coping with those changes positively is always within their control." The "hard issue" young Carrie must deal with in Byalick's novel *Quit It* is Tourette's syndrome, and the involuntary twitches, tics, and throat-clearings which make her dream of disappearing into anonymity as she starts the seventh grade a mere illusion. Though Carrie has a difficult row to hoe, she has the enduring friendship of Clyde, who is bothered by obsessive compulsive disorder, but not by Carrie's twitching, and they both benefit from joining the Lunch Bunch, a support group, at school. A contributor to *Kirkus Reviews* praised Byalick's treatment of Tourette's within the framework of Carrie's story. "While [Byalick] doesn't skimp on any unpleasant details, she doesn't make it seem as if having the illness is the worst thing in the world either," this critic remarked.

Carrie's parents are in fact two people in the novel who are least able to cope with Carrie's problem honestly and in their efforts to put a brave face on their disappointment they hurt Carrie's feelings. Then, when Rebecca, a new girl at school, joins the Lunch Bunch and befriends Carrie, Byalick's protagonist is at first delighted, and then must reevaluate the relationship, for Rebecca is determined to come between Carrie and her old friend. "Carrie's voice is strong and the author tells a convinc-

ing story," asserted Linda B. Zeilstra in *School Library Journal.* Likewise, *Booklist* contributor Shelle Rosenfeld praised Byalick's protagonist and her informative, but not preachy, treatment of a neurological disorder rarely found in young adult literature: "Carrie is an engaging character, whose descriptive, first-person narrative balances a matter-of-fact tone with wry observations and lively commentary."

Biographical and Critical Sources

PERIODICALS

Booklist, October 1, 2002, Shelle Rosenfeld, review of *Quit It,* p. 324.

Bulletin of the Center for Children's Books, January, 1996, p. 156.

Kirkus Reviews, August 1, 2002, review of *Quit It,* p. 1123.

New York Times, January 21, 1996, interview with Ramin P. Jaleshgari, p. 14.

School Library Journal, December, 1995, Jana R. Fine, review of *It's a Matter of Trust,* p. 128; November, 2002, Linda B. Zeilstra, review of *Quit It,* p. 158.

Voice of Youth Advocates, February, 1996, Lucy Marx, review of *It's a Matter of Trust,* p. 368.

C

CANALES, Viola 1957-

Personal

Born April 21, 1957, in McAllen, TX; daughter of Antonio (a business owner) and Dora (a substitute teacher; maiden name, Casas) Canales. *Ethnicity:* "Latina (Hispanic)." *Education:* Harvard University, A.B. (cum laude), 1986, J.D., 1989. *Hobbies and other interests:* Painting, hiking.

Addresses

Home—665 Alvarado Row, Stanford, CA 94305. *Agent*—Andrea Brown, Andrea Brown Literary Agency, P.O. Box 429, El Granada, CA 94018-0429. *E-mail*—ViolaCanales@aol.com.

Career

O. Melveny & Myers (law firm), attorney in Los Angeles and San Francisco, CA, 1989-94; U.S. Small Business Administration, administrator for Region 9 (California, Nevada, Arizona, and Hawaii), 1994-2000; writer, 2000—; TEC International, vice president of emerging markets, 2003—. Texas Book Festival and Texas Center for the Book, member of New Voices of Texas Author Tour, 2002. City of Los Angeles, civil service commissioner, 1992-93; KQED-Radio, board member; United Farm Workers, community organizer. *Military service:* U.S. Army, 1981-85; served in Germany; became captain; received Commendation Medal with oak leaf cluster.

Writings

Orange Candy Slices and Other Secret Tales (young adult short stories), Arte Público Press (Houston, TX), 2001.

Work in Progress

A book of stories; a novel.

Biographical and Critical Sources

PERIODICALS

Palo Alto Weekly, January 2, 2002, Don Kazak, review of *Orange Candy Slices and Other Secret Tales.*
Voice of Youth Advocates, June, 2002, Leslie Carter, review of *Orange Candy Slices and Other Secret Tales.*

OTHER

Texas Book Festival, http://www.texasbookfestival.org/ (September 10, 2002).

* * *

CAREY, Bonnie
See MARSHALL, Bonnie C.

* * *

CASEY, Tina 1959-

Personal

Born March 7, 1959, in Philadelphia, PA; daughter of Henry Harrison (a medical educator and researcher) and Paula (an art educator; maiden name, Rosenblatt) Finck; married Edward Charles Casey (in sales), 1985; children: Thomas Henry, Paulina May. *Education:* Columbia University School of General Studies, B.A., 1985. *Politics:* Democrat. *Religion:* Jewish. *Hobbies and other interests:* Music, art.

Addresses

Home and office—93 Ashwood Avenue, Summit, NJ 07901.

Career

Author. New York City Department of Consumer Affairs, New York, NY, researcher, 1985-1987, Department of Environmental Protection, deputy director of public affairs, 1987-90. Freelance writer, 1990—, including public affairs materials for Overlook Hospital, Summit, NJ.

Board of directors, Summit (NJ) Junior Baseball League, 2001—.

Awards, Honors

Creating Extraordinary Beads from Ordinary Materials was included on the New York City Pubic Library's 1999 List of 1,000 Best Books for Teenagers and the 1999 summer reading list.

Writings

Creating Extraordinary Beads from Ordinary Materials (craft book), North Light Books (Cincinnati, OH), 1997.

Fabulous Fashion Doll Clothing You Can Make (craft book), North Light Books (Cincinnati, OH), 1999.

The Runaway Valentine (picture book), illustrated by Theresa Smythe, Albert Whitman (Morton Grove, IL), 2001.

Work in Progress

The Underground Gators, a picture book about alligators living in the New York City sewers, illustrated by Lynn Munsinger, for Dutton.

Sidelights

Tina Casey told *SATA:* "I started writing fiction in my mid-twenties, thinking I was a serious writer who wrote serious stories. But they were no fun to write and nobody wanted to publish them. Fortunately, it wasn't long before I had children and they quickly convinced me that my true destiny was to be a serious goof, and write funny tales for children. This is a great excuse to do all the stuff I loved when I was a kid, explore the woods behind school, dig for worms, play music and do art projects, watch movies that star talking animals, and go bike riding and horseback riding. It's all research!"

Tina Casey's first published picture book for children is *The Runaway Valentine.* In this story, illustrated with cut-paper illustrations by Theresa Smythe, a very fancy valentine who thinks too highly of himself brings about his own downfall, literally. This valentine, who actually plays twenty love songs with the push of a button, is so certain that everyone will want to buy him that he elbows his way to the front of the card rack and in so doing falls out of the rack and onto the floor. It's not long before he's out in the street, being used to scoop a marble out of a puddle, having a phone number scribbled on his back, and even being tucked into a shoe. When there's nothing much left but the glittery cardboard that was the foundation for all his glamour, a little girl picks him up and incorporates him into a handmade valentine she gives to her grandmother. Finally, his true value is recognized. For a contributor to *Publishers Weekly,* this valentine's ultimate vindication is one that

Leaving the card shop and setting out on his own, Victor the Valentine card becomes more and more tattered as he is picked up and used by one person after another on his journey. (From The Runaway Valentine, *written by Tina Casey and illustrated by Theresa Smythe.)*

all those who humbly make their own Valentine's Day cards may share.

Casey's first two books are also a celebration of the handmade. Her first, *Creating Extraordinary Beads from Ordinary Materials,* details how to make beads from such items as paper, yarn, cloth, and glue. "Casey's beads are often humorous items . . . and finished off with clear nail polish," remarked a contributor to *Library Journal.* And glue plays a vital role in Casey's second book, *Fabulous Fashion Doll Clothing You Can Make,* as what *Booklist* reviewer Barbara Jacobs dubbed "a one-trick pony with infinite adaptations." Here, Casey instructs readers how to make doll clothing of every kind—the book contains sixty-five full-color examples—using cloth scraps or castoff clothing and glue, instead of a sewing machine.

Casey offered the following advice for young writers: "An aspiring writer is really just a writer aspiring to get published. The only hard part is to keep on being a writer long enough for somebody to publish something. For me, that meant constantly writing new stories (not reworking one story) and sending them out, and only allowing myself five minutes on an egg timer to feel bad about a rejection slip. It's all worth it once you open that book and see yourself looking back from the inside flap."

Biographical and Critical Sources

PERIODICALS

Arts and Activities, October, 2000, Ivan E. Johnson, review of *Creating Extraordinary Beads from Ordinary Materials,* p. 12.

Booklist, April 1, 1999, Barbara Jacobs, review of *Fabulous Fashion Doll Clothing You Can Make,* p. 1377.

Kirkus Reviews, September 1, 2001, review of *The Runaway Valentine,* p. 1287.

Library Journal, October 15, 1997, Constance Ashmore Fairchild, review of *Creating Extraordinary Beads from Ordinary Materials,* p. 60.

Publishers Weekly, October 1, 2001, review of *The Runaway Valentine,* p. 61.

School Library Journal, November, 2001, Debbie Stewart, review of *The Runaway Valentine,* p. 112.

*   *   *

CURLEE, Lynn 1947-

Personal

Born October 9, 1947, in NC. *Education:* Attended College of William and Mary, 1965-67; University of North Carolina, B.A., 1969, M.A., 1971.

Addresses

Home and office—P.O. Box 699, Jamesport, NY 11947.

Career

Exhibiting gallery artist, 1973—; freelance writer, 1991—.

Writings

SELF-ILLUSTRATED, FOR CHILDREN

Ships of the Air, Houghton Mifflin (Boston, MA), 1996.

Into the Ice: The Story of Arctic Exploration, Houghton Mifflin (Boston, MA), 1998.

Rushmore, Scholastic (New York, NY), 1999.

Liberty, Scholastic (New York, NY), 2000.

The Brooklyn Bridge, Atheneum (New York, NY), 2001.

Seven Wonders of the Ancient World, Atheneum (New York, NY), 2002.

Capital, Atheneum (New York, NY), 2003.

The Parthenon, Atheneum (New York, NY), 2004.

OTHER

(Illustrator) Dennis Haseley, *Horses with Wings,* Harper-Collins (New York, NY), 1993.

Sidelights

Lynn Curlee is best known for writing and illustrating stunning picture books starring famous landmarks of the American landscape. His first two books, however, celebrated the wonders of early human flight. *Horses with Wings,* an account of a balloon escape from Paris during the Franco-Prussian War written by Dennis

Haseley, was illustrated by Curlee with acrylic paintings hailed by *Booklist* contributor Kay Weisman as "stunning." *Ships of the Air,* Curlee's second book but the first that he both wrote and illustrated, continues with the flight motif. It is a brief history of balloon and dirigible crafts. A *Kirkus Reviews* critic found that the book "delights as well as ... informs." Susan P. Bloom, writing in the *Horn Book* magazine, noted that *Ships of the Air* provides an account of the role hot-air balloons played in Arctic explorations of the 1920s, and perhaps whetted the author's appetite for tales of Arctic explorers. His next book, *Into the Ice: The Story of Arctic Exploration,* supplies "a readable and quite beautiful treatment of Arctic exploration," according to Carolyn Phelan in *Booklist.* Here, Curlee tells the story of human explorers who were compelled to travel to the frozen lands of the far North, and of the people who called that land home. "Curlee's stark acrylic paintings seem particularly sympathetic to his subject matter," remarked Bloom. Relying on a restricted palette of blues, grays, and white, the artist "creates the forbidding and formidable landscape of the North."

Rushmore, a tribute to the making of this famous tribute to United States presidents in South Dakota, is Curlee's first book on significant American architectural sites. John Gutzon de la Mothe Borglum, a sculptor of monumental ego and ambition, undertook the project in the 1920s to transform the Black Hills of South Dakota into a tourist attraction and homage to American presidents Washington, Lincoln, Jefferson, and Theodore Roosevelt. During the nearly two decades of production, workers on the site had to climb the equivalent of a forty-story building in order to get to work each day and the artist's gray and blue acrylic paintings ably provide readers with a sense of the project's scale, reviewers noted. "Curlee conveys the sensitivity in the faces of the giant chiseled sculpture while simultaneously demonstrating a sense of scale," remarked a contributor to *Publishers Weekly.* The text of the book covers the engineering as well as the artistic feat involved in creating the monument, and describes controversies over who ought to be depicted. *Booklist* reviewer Stephanie Zvirin complained that Curlee's paintings of Rushmore sacrifice feeling for accuracy, in their predominantly blue and gray overtones, however: "they make the monument seem cold and remote, rather than a warm, forceful testament to vision, hard work, and national pride." On the other hand, Mary M. Burns, writing in *Horn Book,* found Curlee's renderings of the monument to be more than realistic, "rather, they are an exultant view into the nature of art and, yes, patriotism."

Like *Rushmore, Liberty,* Curlee's next book, showcases a famous American monument through a scientific explanation of the mechanics of bringing the original vision to reality, anecdotes of its creation, and affecting illustrations, which one critic, Alicia Eames, writing in *School Library Journal,* described as "richly hued, stylized acrylic paintings, which are both compellingly dramatic and strikingly static." The Statue of Liberty was the brainchild of French intellectuals and artists, and was brought to fruition with the timely aid of American

In his self-illustrated work Seven Wonders of the Ancient World, *Lynn Curlee investigates these grand and mysterious achievements.*

newspaper magnate Pulitzer, in Curlee's historical overview. Here again, as in the earlier book, an unabashed patriotism infuses the artist's renderings of his subject. "Stunning, stylized portraits of the lady heighten Curlee's lucid, appreciative text," remarked a contributor to the *Horn Book* magazine. Likewise, a contributor to *Publishers Weekly* dubbed *Liberty,* "a reverent, absorbing homage to the world-renowned symbol of American freedom."

Curlee's next American landmark was the Brooklyn Bridge, which upon its completion in 1883 was by far the tallest human-made structure in its surroundings, and was the longest bridge in the world at the time. In his *Brooklyn Bridge,* Curlee details the engineering feats that went into the bridge's construction, but wraps it in the human drama of the Roebling family: John A., who conceived the vast structure but died just as it was begun, his son Washington, who took over the project

until ill health forced him into seclusion, and Washington's wife, Emily, who oversaw the day-to-day operation of construction after her husband fell ill. As in his earlier tributes to the Statue of Liberty and Mount Rushmore, *Brooklyn Bridge* features stunning illustrations that work on the emotions of the viewer. "The sweeping cityscape oil paintings of the bridge during sunset fireworks and glowing in the moonlight illustrate its majesty and pageantry," a contributor to *Publishers Weekly* attested.

The Brooklyn Bridge was once considered by some to be the eighth wonder of the world, and so it is only fitting that Curlee's next book was *Seven Wonders of the Ancient World.* The book provides a brief look at what the seven wonders of the ancient world, as deemed by the Greek poet Antipater of Sidon, would probably look like, as all but the Great Pyramid at Giza have long since disappeared. "The expanse of his ambitious subject does not allow the author to delve into the kinds of details allowed by his single-subject volumes, but he certainly whets readers' appetites," concluded a contributor to *Publishers Weekly*. Drawing upon contemporary accounts and modern archeology, Curlee creates a vision of what each might have looked like in its day, as well as an account of its destruction. Although *Booklist* contributor Ilene Cooper notes some flaws in the historical account, "there's no denying that this book is both fascinating and strongly executed," she concluded.

Biographical and Critical Sources

PERIODICALS

Booklist, November 15, 1993, Kay Weisman, review of *Horses with Wings,* p. 630-631; September 1, 1996; April, 1998, Carolyn Phelan, review of *Into the Ice,* p. 1316; March 1, 1999, Stephanie Zvirin, review of *Rushmore,* p. 1204; April 15, 2001, Randy Meyer, review of *Brooklyn Bridge,* p. 1548; December 1, 2001, Stephanie Zvirin, review of *Brooklyn Bridge,* p. 658; January 1, 2002, Ilene Cooper, review of *Seven Wonders of the Ancient World,* p. 850; January 1, 2003, Carolyn Phelan, review of *Capital,* p. 880.

Bulletin of the Center for Children's Books, October, 1996, pp. 53-55.

Childhood Education, Jeanie Burnett, review of *Brooklyn Bridge,* p. 171.

Horn Book, November-December, 1996, p. 757; May-June, 1998, Susan P. Bloom, review of *Into the Ice,* p. 357; March, 1999, Mary M. Burns, review of *Rushmore,* p. 221; May, 2000, review of *Liberty,* p. 330; July, 2001, review of *Brooklyn Bridge,* p. 470.

Kirkus Reviews, June 1, 1996, review of *Ships of the Air,* p. 821; January 1, 2002, review of *Seven Wonders of the Ancient World,* p. 43; December 1, 2002, review of *Capital,* p. 1766.

New York Times, December 7, 1998, Christopher Lehmann-Haupt, "Adventuring From a Child's Imagination to the Arctic," review of *Into the Ice.*

New York Times Book Review, May 20, 2001, Sam Swope, "Oz on the Hudson," review of *Brooklyn Bridge,* p. 30.

Publishers Weekly, September 13, 1993, pp. 132-137; February 15, 1999, review of *Rushmore,* p. 107; May 29, 2000, review of *Liberty,* p. 83; May 14, 2001, review of *Brooklyn Bridge,* p. 82; December 24, 2001, review of *Seven Wonders of the Ancient World,* p. 64; November 25, 2002, review of *Capital,* p. 65.

School Library Journal, December, 1993, pp. 88-89; May, 1998, Patricia Manning, review of *Into the Ice,* p. 152; March, 1999, Rosie Peasley, review of *Rushmore,* p. 191; May, 2000, Alicia Eames, review of *Liberty,* p. 180; May, 2001, Susan Lissim, review of *Brooklyn Bridge,* p. 162; March, 2002, Kathleen Baxter, "Castles in the Air: Inspire Readers with Personal Stories of Creative Vision," review of *Brooklyn Bridge,* p. 49; September, 2002, Mary Ann Carcish, review of *Seven Wonders of the Ancient World,* p. 242.*

D

DERRICKSON, Jim 1959-

Personal

Born September 30, 1959, in Falls Church, VA.

Addresses

Home—Willow Station, AK. *Agent*—c/o Author Mail, Scholastic, Inc., 557 Broadway, New York, NY 10012.

Career

Writer. Has worked as a construction laborer, 1980-86; a federal park police ranger and law enforcer, 1986-89; a performing songwriter, 1987-96; and farrier (horseshoer), 1991—.

Member

Alaska State Farrier's Association.

Awards, Honors

Teluride Troubador finalist, Teluride Guitar Picking finalist, "SIBL Project" Songwriting finalist.

Writings

FOR CHILDREN

Bomo and the Beef Snacks: A Story of Friendship and Promises along the Iditarod Trail, Scholastic (New York, NY), 2001.

Also author of music and lyrics for *Sing to Me,* produced by Paint Pony Publishers, 1997, and of several unpublished collections of songs. Contributor of short fiction and journalism to *Anvil* magazine.

Work in Progress

A "comic-tragic novel on surviving reality," a collection of "barnyard stories," a collection of poems, and four songwriting collections, as well as various short stories, children's story projects, and songwriting pieces. Research into animal communications.

Sidelights

Jim Derrickson told *SATA:* "I gave up creativity, considering it an impractical goal, while still finishing school, and pursued a number of vocations before I one day suddenly quit my job and started writing songs. Ever since, my day jobs have centered around allowing space to write. I cannot explain why the unused talent persisted, instead of being lost.

"*Bomo and the Beef Snacks: A Story of Friendship and Promises along the Iditarod Trail,* is about underlings and the survival of their solidarity amidst the increasing, commercially competitive atmosphere of the yearly Alaskan dog mushing race. *Bomo* will hopefully acquaint readers with the values of importance in dog mushing, as opposed to those that are not and yet prevalent, on the actual circuit.

"*Bomo* is published in French and English and distributed throughout Canada and in Alaska. It is my first children's book. I have been writing literary fiction for around ten years and some activist-related journalism; songwriting is my area of deepest devotion. One piece, 'Winter of Our Discontent,' based on the Steinbeck novel, has been placed in the SIBL project library of songs, a collection of contemporary and historic lyric songs inspired by literature and used in reading programs for the illiterate in various institutional systems.

"*Advice to Writers*—If one has the desire and has it for the right reasons, the capacity follows. Be clear about your message and never fear any form of 'writer block.' Surround any problematics with research and thinking; approach it from every angle. Then pause, and the inspiration will come."

Biographical and Critical Sources

PERIODICALS

Canadian Review of Materials, November 30, 2001, Ruth McMahon, review of *Bomo and the Beef Snacks: A Story of Friendship and Promises along the Iditarod Trail.*

Resource Links, December, 2001, Zoe Johnstone Guha, review of *Bomo and the Beef Snacks,* p. 4.

*   *   *

DUNCAN, Lois 1934-
(Lois Kerry)

Personal

Born Lois Duncan Steinmetz, April 28, 1934, in Philadelphia, PA; daughter of Joseph Janney (a magazine photographer) and Lois (a magazine photographer; maiden name, Foley) Steinmetz; married an attorney, 1953 (marriage ended, c. 1962); married Donald Wayne Arquette (an electrical engineer), July 15, 1965; children: (first marriage) Robin, Kerry, Brett; (second marriage) Donald Jr., Kaitlyn (deceased). *Education:* Attended Duke University, 1952-53; University of New Mexico, B.A. (cum laude), 1977.

Addresses

Agent—c/o Random House, Children's Books Division, 1540 Broadway, New York, NY 10030.

Career

Writer; magazine photographer; instructor in department of journalism, University of New Mexico, 1971-82. Lecturer at writers' conferences.

Member

Society of Children's Book Writers.

Awards, Honors

Three-time winner during high school years of *Seventeen* magazine's annual short story contest; Seventeenth Summer Literary Award, Dodd, Mead & Co., 1957, for *Debutante Hill;* Best Novel Award, National Press Women, 1966, for *Point of Violence;* Edgar Allan Poe Award runner-ups, Mystery Writers of America, 1967, for *Ransom,* 1969, for *They Never Came Home,* 1985, for *The Third Eye,* 1986, for *Locked in Time,* and 1989, for *The Twisted Window;* Zia Award, New Mexico Press Women, 1969, for *Major André: Brave Enemy;* grand prize winner, *Writer's Digest* Creative Writing Contest, 1970, for short story; Theta Sigma Phi Headliner Award, 1971; Best Books for Young Adults citations, American Library Association (ALA), 1976, for *Summer of Fear,* 1978, for *Killing Mr. Griffin,* 1981, for *Stranger with My Face,* 1982, for *Chapters: My Growth as a Writer,* and 1990, for *Don't Look behind You;* Best Books for

Children citations, *New York Times,* 1981, for *Stranger with My Face,* and 1988, for *Killing Mr. Griffin;* Ethical Culture School Book Award, Library of Congress' Best Books citation, and *English Teacher's Journal* and University of Iowa's Best Books of the Year for Young Adults citation, all 1981, and Best Novel Award, National League of American Pen Women, 1982, all for *Stranger with My Face;* Notable Children's Trade Book in the Field of Social Studies, National Council for Social Studies/Children's Book Council, 1982, for *Chapters: My Growth as a Writer;* Children's Books of the Year citation, Child Study Association of America, 1986, for *Locked in Time* and *The Third Eye;* Children's Book Award, National League of American Pen Women, 1987, for *Horses of Dreamland;* Margaret A. Edwards Award, 1991, *School Library Journal/*Young Adult Library Services Association, for body of work.

Duncan has also received numerous librarians', parents' and children's choice awards from the states of Alabama, Arizona, California, Colorado, Florida, Indiana, Iowa, Massachusetts, Nevada, New Mexico, Oklahoma, Tennessee, Texas, South Carolina, and Vermont, as well as from groups in England.

Writings

YOUNG ADULT NOVELS

Debutante Hill, Dodd (New York, NY), 1958.

(Under pseudonym Lois Kerry) *Love Song for Joyce,* Funk, 1958.

(Under pseudonym Lois Kerry) *A Promise for Joyce,* Funk, 1959.

The Middle Sister, Dodd (New York, NY), 1961.

Game of Danger, Dodd (New York, NY), 1962.

Season of the Two-Heart, Dodd (New York, NY), 1964.

Ransom, Doubleday (Garden City, NY), 1966, published as *Five Were Missing,* New American Library (New York, NY), 1972.

They Never Came Home, Doubleday (Garden City, NY), 1969.

I Know What You Did Last Summer, Little, Brown (Boston, MA), 1973.

Down a Dark Hall, Little, Brown (Boston, MA), 1974.

Summer of Fear, Little, Brown (Boston, MA), 1976.

Killing Mr. Griffin, Little, Brown (Boston, MA), 1978.

Daughters of Eve, Little, Brown (Boston, MA), 1979.

Stranger with My Face, Little, Brown (Boston, MA), 1981.

The Third Eye, Little, Brown (Boston, MA), 1984, published as *The Eyes of Karen Connors,* Hamish Hamilton (London, England), 1985.

Locked in Time, Little, Brown (Boston, MA), 1985.

The Twisted Window, Delacorte (New York, NY), 1987.

Don't Look behind You, Delacorte (New York, NY), 1989.

Gallows Hill, Delacorte (New York, NY), 1997.

FOR CHILDREN

The Littlest One in the Family, illustrated by Suzanne K. Larsen, Dodd (New York, NY), 1960.

Silly Mother, illustrated by Suzanne K. Larsen, Dial (New York, NY), 1962.

Giving Away Suzanne, illustrated by Leonard Weisgard, Dodd (New York, NY), 1963.

Hotel for Dogs, illustrated by Leonard Shortall, Houghton Mifflin (Boston, MA), 1971.

A Gift of Magic, illustrated by Arvis Stewart, Little, Brown (Boston, MA), 1971.

From Spring to Spring: Poems and Photographs, photographs by the author, Westminster, 1982.

The Terrible Tales of Happy Days School (poetry), illustrated by Friso Henstra, Little, Brown (Boston, MA), 1983.

Horses of Dreamland, illustrated by Donna Diamond, Little, Brown (Boston, MA), 1985.

Wonder Kid Meets the Evil Lunch Snatcher, illustrated by Margaret Sanfilippo, Little, Brown (Boston, MA), 1988.

The Birthday Moon (poetry), illustrated by Susan Davis, Viking (New York, NY), 1989.

Songs from Dreamland (poetry), illustrated by Kay Chorao, Knopf (New York, NY), 1989.

The Circus Comes Home: When the Greatest Show on Earth Rode the Rails, photographs by Joseph Janney Steinmetz, Delacorte (New York, NY), 1993.

The Magic of Spider Woman, illustrated by Shonto Begay, Scholastic (New York, NY), 1996.

The Longest Hair in the World, illustrated by Jon McIntosh, Bantam (New York, NY), 1999.

I Walk at Night, illustrated by Steve Johnson and Lou Fancher, Viking Penguin (New York, NY), 2000.

Song of the Circus, illustrated by Meg Cundiff, Philomel (New York, NY), 2001.

OTHER

Point of Violence (adult), Doubleday (New York, NY), 1966.

Major André: Brave Enemy (young adult nonfiction), illustrated by Tran Mawicke, Putnam (New York, NY), 1969.

Peggy (young adult nonfiction), Little, Brown (Boston, MA), 1970.

When the Bough Breaks (adult), Doubleday (New York, NY), 1974.

How to Write and Sell Your Personal Experiences (nonfiction), Writers Digest, 1979.

Chapters: My Growth as a Writer (autobiography), Little, Brown (Boston, MA), 1982.

A Visit with Lois Duncan (videotape), RDA Enterprises, 1985.

Dream Songs from Yesterday (cassette), RDA Enterprises, 1987.

Our Beautiful Day (cassette), RDA Enterprises, 1988.

The Story of Christmas (cassette), RDA Enterprises, 1989.

Who Killed My Daughter?: The True Story of a Mother's Search for Her Daughter's Murderer, Delacorte (New York, NY), 1992.

Psychics in Action (audio cassette series), Silver Moon Productions, 1993.

(With William Roll) *Psychic Connections: A Journey into the Mysterious World of Psi,* Delacorte (New York, NY), 1995.

(Editor) *Night Terrors: Stories of Shadow and Substance,* Simon & Schuster (New York, NY), 1996.

(Editor) *Trapped! Cages of Mind and Body,* Simon & Schuster (New York, NY), 1998.

(Editor) *On the Edge: Stories at the Brink,* Simon & Schuster (New York, NY), 2000.

Contributor of over five hundred articles and stories to periodicals, including *Good Housekeeping, Redbook, McCall's, Woman's Day, Writer, Reader's Digest, Ladies' Home Journal, Saturday Evening Post,* and *Writer's Digest.* Contributing editor, *Woman's Day.*

Adaptations

Summer of Fear was adapted as the television movie *Strangers in Our House,* NBC-TV, 1978; *Killing Mr. Griffin* was adapted as a television movie, NBC-TV, 1997; *I Know What You Did Last Summer* was adapted as a feature film, Mandalay, 1997; *Gallows Hill* was adapted as a television movie, NBC-TV, 1998; and *Ransom* was adapted as a television movie. Listening Library made cassettes of *Down a Dark Hall,* 1985, *Killing Mr. Griffin,* 1986, *Summer of Fear,* 1986, and *Stranger with My Face,* 1986; RDA Enterprises made cassettes of *Selling Personal Experiences to Magazines,* 1987, and *Songs from Dreamland,* 1987.

Work in Progress

A sequel to *Who Killed My Daughter?,* with working title *The Tally Keeper.*

Sidelights

Award-winning writer Lois Duncan's young adult novels of suspense and the supernatural have made her a favorite of adult critics and young readers alike. According to *Times Literary Supplement* reviewer Jennifer Moody, Duncan is "popular . . . not only with the soft underbelly of the literary world, the children's book reviewers, but with its most hardened carapace, the teenage library book borrower." Equally enthusiastic was critic Sarah Hayes, who observed in *Times Literary Supplement* that "Duncan understands the teenage world and its passionate concerns with matters as diverse as dress, death, romance, school, self-image, sex and problem parents." But Hayes added that, while other writers for young adults show life in a humorous, optimistic light, "Duncan suggests that life is neither as prosaic nor as straightforward as it seems at first."

In most of Duncan's books, her protagonists are usually high school students—most often young women—who find themselves suddenly confronted with a sinister threat to their "normal" existence. "It is a mark of Duncan's ability as a writer that the evils she describes are perfectly plausible and believable," noted an essayist in *St. James Guide to Young Adult Writers.* "As in her use of the occult, her use of warped human nature as a tool to move the plot along briskly never seems contrived or used solely for shock effect; it is integral to the story."

Born in Philadelphia, Pennsylvania in 1934, and raised in Sarasota, Florida, Duncan grew up in a creative household where her early efforts at writing were encouraged by her parents, noted photographers Joseph and Lois Steinmetz. She started writing stories for magazines as a pre-teen and progressed to book-length manuscripts as she matured. She enrolled in Duke University in 1952, but found it a difficult adjustment after the relaxed, creative environment in which she had been raised. She also grew frustrated with the lack of privacy in dormitory life, and decided to leave after one year to get married.

One of her first serious efforts at publication was a love story for teens, *Debutante Hill,* which Duncan wrote in between magazine articles as a way of passing the lonely hours as a young homemaker and mother while her first husband first served in the U.S. Air Force, and then enrolled in law school. She entered the book in Dodd, Mead and Company's Seventeenth Summer Literary Contest. The manuscript "was returned for revisions because in it a young man of twenty drank a beer," Duncan once observed. "I changed the beer to a Coke and resubmitted the manuscript. It won the contest, and the book was published." While Duncan considered the story "sweet and sticky ... pap," a reviewer for the *Christian Science Monitor* maintained that Duncan "writes exceptionally well, and has the happy ability to make a reader care what happens to her characters." Still, the prize—one thousand dollars and a book contract—did much to encourage the budding novelist, who, in 1958, suddenly found herself a published novelist at the age of twenty-four.

When her first marriage ended in divorce, Duncan returned to magazine writing to support her family. In 1962 she relocated to Albuquerque, New Mexico. She eventually got a teaching job at the University of New Mexico's department of journalism, and earned her master's degree. In 1965 she married engineer Don Arquette, and since "the financial pressure was off, I also felt free to turn back to my non-lucrative, but immeasurably enjoyable, hobby of writing teenage novels," she once recalled. Over the years young adult novels had changed, however, and Duncan found she was no longer constricted by many of the taboos of the 1950s. The result of this newfound freedom was 1966's *Ransom,* an adventure story of five teenagers kidnapped by a schoolbus driver. When Duncan's publisher refused to handle the book because it deviated from her former style, Doubleday took it on, and *Ransom* became a runner-up for the prestigious Edgar Allan Poe Award. It also received a healthy dose of critical praise, with reviewer Dorothy M. Broderick commenting in *New York Times Book Review* that the character of Glenn Kirtland, whose consistently selfish behavior endangers the whole group, "sets the book apart and makes it something more than another good mystery." *Ransom* established Duncan in a genre she would master to great success.

While teaching, studying, and raising her five children, Duncan continued to publish young adult suspense novels, such as *I Know What You Did Last Summer, Down a Dark Hall,* and *Summer of Fear.* Duncan's style remained consistent in its simplicity; as a writer for

Twentieth-Century Children's Writers observed, Duncan "places an individual or a group of normal, believable young people in what appears to be a prosaic setting such as a suburban neighborhood or an American high school; on the surface everything is as it should be, until Duncan introduces an element of surprise that gives the story an entirely new twist." These elements are often supernatural; *Summer of Fear* features a young witch who charms herself into an unsuspecting family, while *Down a Dark Hall* involves a girls' boarding school whose students are endangered by the malevolent ghosts of dead artists and writers.

In a similar fashion, *Stranger with My Face* details a young girl's struggle to avoid being possessed by her twin sister, who uses astral projection to take over others' bodies. While the novel's premise might be difficult to accept, "Duncan makes it possible and palatable by a deft twining of fantasy and reality, by giving depth to characters and relationships, and by writing with perception and vitality," stated Zena Sutherland of the *Bulletin of the Center for Children's Books.* This depth is typical of all of Duncan's mystic novels; as the writer for *Twentieth-Century Children's Writers* commented, "an element of the occult is an integral part of [Duncan's] fast-moving plot, but it is always believable because Duncan never carries her depiction of the supernatural into the sometimes goofy realms that a writer such as Stephen King does. Character and plot are always predominant; the books are first and foremost good mysteries made even more interesting for young readers by some aspect of the unusual."

Duncan doesn't rely solely on supernatural events to provide suspense, however. In *Killing Mr. Griffin,* a teenage boy guides a group of friends into kidnapping their strict high school teacher and intimidating him into giving less homework. The teacher dies when he misses his heart medication, and the students try to cover up their involvement. "Duncan breaks some new ground in a novel without sex, drugs or black leather jackets," commented Richard Peck in *New York Times Book Review.* "But the taboo she tampers with is far more potent and pervasive: the unleashed fury of the permissively reared against any assault on their egos and authority.... The value of the book lies in the twisted logic of the teenagers and how easily they can justify anything."

While Peck liked the beginning of *Killing Mr. Griffin,* he criticized the ending for descending "into unadulterated melodrama.... The book becomes an 'easy read' when it shouldn't." For her part, Duncan pointed to her readers to explain the style of her writing, noting that, to be read, her books have to be tailored to a generation of teens more familiar with television than novels. "Television has had an enormous effect upon youth books," she once stated. "Few of today's readers are patient enough to wade through slow paced, introductory chapters as I did at their ages to see if a book is eventually going to get interesting." Television "has conditioned its viewers to expect instant entertainment," the author continued, and because of this, "writers have been forced into utilizing all sorts of TV techniques to hold their readers' attention."

Perhaps one of Duncan's most well-known novels, *Daughters of Eve* features a dangerous leader: a faculty adviser who leads a high school girls' club into increasingly more violent acts in the name of feminism. The book's portrayal of a negative feminist element drew some strong remarks from critics. "It has an embittered tone of hatred that colors the characterization," suggested Zena Sutherland in her *Bulletin of the Center for Children's Books* review. Jan M. Goodman presented a similar assessment in *Interracial Books for Children Bulletin:* Duncan "clearly places a harsh value judgment on violent solutions, and ... she leaves the impression that fighting for women's rights leads to uncontrollable anger and senseless destruction.... The book's deceptive interpretation of feminism plus its dangerous stereotypes make it a harmful distortion of reality." But Natalie Babbitt found the work "refreshing" and liked the fact that "there are no lessons." In *New York Times Book Review,* Babbitt compared the novel to William Golding's *Lord of the Flies* and concluded that *Daughters of Eve* "is strongly evenhanded, for it lets us see that women can be as bloodthirsty as men ever were."

Even though she features extraordinary events in her books, "the things I have written about as fiction in suspense novels are no part of our everyday lives," Duncan once commented. This reassuring fact, however, was shattered in 1989 when her youngest daughter, Kaitlyn, was murdered in an incident that paralleled the plot of *Don't Look behind You,* a novel Duncan had published just a month before the crime took place. In the novel, the character April—who was based on Kaitlyn—is run down and killed by a hitman in a Camaro. "In July 1989," Duncan recalled, "Kait was chased down and shot to death by a hitman in a Camaro." This brutal crime would involve Duncan and her family in a police investigation similar to that described in *Killing Mr. Griffin,* and dealings with a psychic like the one described in Duncan's novel *The Third Eye.* While three men were arrested, none were charged with the murder.

Duncan shared her tragic experience with readers in *Who Killed My Daughter?,* which was published in 1992 in the hope that it might be read by someone with information on her daughter's murder. Through private investigators hired by the family, she learned that her daughter's boyfriend had been involved in an insurance fraud scam, and suspects that Kaitlyn learned of the scam and was planning to break up with him. As the facts became known, Duncan realized that other circumstances surrounding her daughter's murder paralleled the novel she had just published. "It was as if these things I'd written about as fiction became hideous reality," Duncan explained to interviewer Roger Sutton in *School Library Journal.*

Who Killed My Daughter?, Duncan's first work of nonfiction, was praised by numerous reviewers and was nominated for teen reading awards in nine states. According to *Kliatt* contributor Claire Rosser, readers "will find this tragedy all the more poignant simply because it is horrifyingly true." While Mary Jane Santos noted in her appraisal for *Voice of Youth Advocates* that readers might "get lost in the myriad of minutia" Duncan marshals in her effort to solve the crime—numerous transcripts and other factual evidence is presented in the book—the critic went on to add that "the strength and tenacity of Duncan is admirable."

Several years after the murder, Duncan and her husband moved to the West Coast to attempt to rebuild their life. Meanwhile, the coincidences between her daughter's murder and her own YA novel had led Duncan to contact Dr. William Roll, a director at the Psychical Research Foundation and an expert in Extra-Sensory Perception (ESP) who explained to Duncan that, as she told Sutton, "precognition is very much a proven reality, that it's also been proven that people who are creative individuals have much more psychical ability than others."

For several years Duncan focused on editing collections of suspenseful short fiction and penning books for younger readers, such as *The Circus Comes Home: When the Greatest Show on Earth Rode the Rails,* about the Ringling Brothers-Barnum & Bailey circus that wintered near Duncan's childhood home in Florida, and *The Magic of Spider Woman,* a retelling of a Navajo myth that a *Publishers Weekly* contributor praised for its "thoughtful message, grounded in well-chosen details and adeptly relayed through [Duncan's] personable storytelling." However, with 1997's *Gallows Hill,* Duncan returned to her characteristic suspense format, as protagonist Sarah, the new girl in town, attempts to gain popularity by starting a fortune-telling business. When her fortunes prove accurate and she becomes haunted by dreams of the Salem Witch Trials of the seventeenth century, Sarah's plan backfires, and soon she is looked on with suspicion by what a *Publishers Weekly* contributor described as "adults [who] are unsympathetic and clueless, allowing their teens to run rampant into the alluring arms" of an evil Sarah's supernatural ability seems to have unleashed. In *Voice of Youth Advocates* critic Delia A. Culberson praised Duncan's ability to meld historical fact with compelling fiction, dubbing *Gallows Hill* "an unusual and intriguing tale peopled with believable characters.... [that] illustrates how ignorance and bigotry can prevail against fairness and common sense."

In 1995 Duncan teamed with Dr. Roll to write *Psychic Connections: A Journey into the Mysterious World of Psi,* which provides teens with explanations of various types of psychic phenomenon—ghosts, telepathy, ESP, psychic healing—from a balanced perspective. Duncan shows how data and facts can be misconstrued, and she also explores how the psychic interviewing process works, relating such things to her own inconclusive experiences with the paranormal in the case of her daughter. *School Library Journal* contributor Cathy Chauvette found the book "compelling," while Nancy Glass Wright praised the work in *Voice of Youth Advocates* as "a comprehensive overview" that is "sometimes riveting." A more ambivalent reaction was experienced by *Bulletin for the Center of Children's Books* critic Deborah Stevenson, who viewed *Psychic Connections* as "successful neither as a collection of true mysterious tales nor as a science-based defense of a controversial subject."

Several of Duncan's books have found their way onto television, and one even appeared on movie screens in 1997. Pleased with television adaptations of *Summer of Fear* and *Killing Mr. Griffin,* Duncan was understandably excited when movie rights to *I Know What You Did Last Summer* were sold and production on the 1997 motion picture release began. However, she was dismayed by the film version, starring actress Jennifer Love Hewitt. "They made it into a slasher film," Duncan told Susan Schindehette in *People.* "And I don't think murder is funny."

Biographical and Critical Sources

BOOKS

Contemporary Literary Criticism, Volume 26, Gale (Detroit, MI), 1983.

Duncan, Lois, *Chapters: My Growth as a Writer,* Little, Brown (Boston, MA), 1982.

St. James Guide to Young Adult Writers, 2nd edition, St. James Press (Detroit, MI), 1999.

Something about the Author Autobiography Series, Volume 2, Gale (Detroit, MI), 1986.

Twentieth-Century Children's Writers, 3rd edition, edited by Tracy Chevalier, St. James Press (Detroit, MI), 1989.

PERIODICALS

Best Sellers, August, 1978, Hildagarde Gray, review of *Killing Mr. Griffin,* pp. 154-155.

Booklist, April 15, 1992, p. 1482; February 15, 1994, Ilene Cooper, review of *The Circus Comes Home,* p. 1078; June 1, 1995, Ilene Cooper, review of *Psychic Connections,* p. 1743; May 15, 1996, Stephanie Zvirin, review of *Night Terrors,* p. 1581; April 15, 1997, Ilene Cooper, review of *Gallows Hill,* p. 1420; July, 1998, Roger Leslie, review of *Trapped!,* p. 1873; February 15, 1999, Karen Harris, review of *Don't Look behind You,* p. 1984; February 1, 2000, Gillian Engberg, review of *I Walk at Night,* p. 1028; June 1, 2000, G. Engberg, review of *On the Edge,* p. 1882.

Bulletin of the Center for Children's Books, February, 1974; January, 1980, Zena Sutherland, review of *Daughter of Eve,* pp. 92-93; April, 1982, Zena Sutherland, review of *Stranger with My Face,* p. 146; July-August, 1987; September, 1995, Deborah Stevenson, review of *Psychic Connections,* pp. 12-13; July-August, 1998, p. 393.

Children's Book Review Service, spring, 1982, Leigh Dean, review of *Chapters: My Growth as a Writer,* p. 116.

Christian Science Monitor, February 5, 1959, "Widening Horizons: Debutante Hill," p. 11.

Horn Book, February, 1965, Ruth Hill Viguers, review of *Season of the Two-Heart,* p. 59; April, 1977, Ethel L. Heins, review of *Summer of Fear,* p. 167; February, 1982; November-December, 1993, Margaret A. Bush, review of *The Circus Comes Home,* p. 754; July-August, 1996, Elizabeth S. Watson, review of *The Magic of Spider Woman,* p. 470.

Interracial Books for Children Bulletin, Vol. 11, no. 6, 1980, Jan M. Goodman, review of *Daughters of Eve,* pp. 17-18.

Kirkus Reviews, September 1, 1973, review of *I Know What You Did Last Summer,* p. 972; January 1, 1982, review of *Stranger with My Face,* p. 11.

Kliatt, May, 1994, Claire Rosser, review of *Who Killed My Daughter?,* p. 26.

New York Times Book Review, June 5, 1966, Dorothy M. Broderick, review of *Ransom,* p. 42; June 8, 1969, Richard F. Shepard, review of *They Never Came Home,* p. 42; November 10, 1974, Gloria Levitas, "Haunts and Hunts," pp. 8, 10; March 6, 1977, Julia Whedon, "Witches and Werewolves," p. 29; April 30, 1978, Richard Peck, "Teaching Teacher a Lesson," p. 54; January 27, 1980, Natalie Babbitt, review of *Daughters of Eve,* p. 24; August 16, 1998, p. 14.

People, November 24, 1997, Susan Schindehette, "Who Killed My Daughter? An Eight-Year-Old Unsolved Slaying Still Plagues Writer Lois Duncan," p. 103.

Publishers Weekly, April 20, 1992, Maria Simpson, "'Who Killed My Daughter?' Lois Duncan (and Delacorte) Search for an Answer," p. 19; March 11, 1996, review of *The Magic of Spider Woman,* p. 64; March 17, 1997, review of *Gallows Hill,* p. 84; June 1, 1998, review of *Trapped!,* p. 48; January 10, 2000, review of *I Walk at Night,* p. 67; June 26, 2000, review of *On the Edge,* p. 76; September 18, 2000, review of *The Magic of Spider Woman,* p. 113; February 12, 2001, review of *The Longest Hair in the World,* p. 214.

School Library Journal, November, 1971, Peggy Sullivan, review of *A Gift of Magic,* p. 122; April, 1974, Linda Silver, review of *I Know What You Did Last Summer,* p. 64; September, 1979, Cyrisse Jaffee, review of *Daughters of Eve,* p. 155; November, 1981; July, 1989; June 1992, Roger Sutton, interview with Lois Duncan, pp. 20-24; August, 1992, p. 190; May, 1995, Cathy Chauvette, review of *Psychic Connections,* p. 125; May, 1997, Bruce Anne Shook, review of *Gallows Hill,* p. 132; March, 2000, review of *I Walk at Night,* p. 194.

Times Literary Supplement, March 26, 1982, Jennifer Moody, "The Onset of Maturity," p. 343; February 22, 1985, Anthony Horowitz, "Parent Problems," p. 214; January 29-February 4, 1988, Sarah Hayes, "Fatal Flaws," p. 119.

Voice of Youth Advocates, December, 1992, Mary Jane Santos, review of *Who Killed My Daughter?,* p. 304; August, 1995, Nancy Glass Wright, review of *Psychic Connections,* p. 181; April, 1997, Delia A. Culberson, review of *Gallows Hill,* p. 28.

Autobiography Feature

Lois Duncan

I can't remember a time when I did not think of myself as a writer. It's the only thing I ever wanted to be. When I was three years old I was dictating poems and stories to my parents, and as soon as I learned to print, I was writing them down myself. I shared a room with my younger brother, and at night I would lie in bed inventing tales to give him nightmares. I would pretend to be the "Moon Fairy," come to deliver the message that the moon was falling toward the earth.

"And what will happen to *me?*" Billy would ask in his quavering little voice.

"You'll be blown up into the sky," the Moon Fairy would tell him. "By the time you come down the world will be gone, and you'll just keep falling forever."

"With no breakfast?" poor Billy would scream hysterically. Eventually, our parents had the good sense to put us in separate rooms.

My first—and only—poetry recitation was given at age five, and it was a disaster. It was kindergarten show-and-tell time, and since I had forgotten to bring anything to show, I volunteered to recite a "made-up poem." It was a very dramatic ballad about a shipwreck.

My performance was greeted by a long silence, during which I waited patiently for the deluge of praise I was sure would come.

Instead my teacher said coldly, "You didn't make that up."

I was so surprised that I couldn't think of a thing to answer. I just stood there, staring at her.

"That's a well-known poem," my teacher said. "I've heard it many times. Go sit in the corner until you are ready to tell the truth."

I spent the rest of the day in the corner, and it was years before I trusted a teacher again.

Aside from tormenting Billy, I had few hobbies. A shy little girl, I was a bookworm and a dreamer. My parents, Joseph and Lois Steinmetz, were magazine photographers. They moved us from Philadelphia, Pennsylvania, soon after Billy was born, to settle us in Sarasota, Florida, from which they were in a good position to take photo assignments throughout the southeast United States and the Caribbean. They planned most of these trips for summer so Billy and I could go with them.

I grew up in Sarasota and spent a lot of time playing alone in the woods and on the beaches. I had a secret hideaway in the middle of a bamboo clump. I would bend the bamboo until I could straddle it, and then it would

Lois Duncan

spring up, and I would slide down into the hollow at its heart with green stalks all around me and leaves like lace against my face. I'd hide there and read.

Or I'd ride my bicycle. I would pedal for miles along the beach road with the wind blowing in my face and sun hot on my hair. There was a special point where I turned the bike off the road and walked it down a little path between the dunes. I parked it there and lay on my back in the sand and listened to the waves crash against the rocks and watched the clouds scud across the sky.

All of the thoughts that trickled through my mind during those long hours of dreaming found their way onto paper. I have today a whole drawerful of notebooks that I filled during those early years.

When I was ten, I submitted my first typed manuscript to *Ladies' Home Journal*. The story was about a little boy

The author, with brother Billy, celebrating her sixth birthday, 1940

who enjoyed playing in the woods with fairies until he became six years old and decided to stop believing. The story was returned rather quickly, but it was accompanied by a kind letter from the editor. He said that he appreciated my effort and that the story was a nice one, considering the age of the author, but that his particular publication was not currently in the market for fairy tales. The warmth of the letter cushioned its impact. I swallowed my disappointment and mailed the story off to another magazine. And I wrote another story and sent it to the *Journal.*

By the time that one came back, I had another ready to mail off, and so it continued. I now had a hobby, collecting rejection slips. It was painful, but exciting. Each day when other, better adjusted children were skipping rope and playing hopscotch and going over to play at each other's houses, I was rushing home to check the mail and see what stories had come back from what magazines.

My writing attempts became more and more ambitious. Tales of flaming romance, blood-spurting violence, pain and passion, lust and adventure flew back and forth to New York in a steady stream. My parents thought me cute and funny. My teachers thought me horrid and precocious. As for myself, I was proud. I—plump, bespeckled, and unimpressive as I might seem—was plunging ahead to advance my glamorous career.

Three years passed, and I accumulated so many rejection slips that my mother made me stop saving them.

Then, one day, I came home from school to find a strange man occupying the living-room sofa. He was a new neighbor who had just moved in down the beach from us, and he was a writer. His name was MacKinlay Kantor.

"Lois," my father said after introductions had been made, "why don't you show Mr. Kantor that story that just came back from the *Saturday Evening Post?*"

He did not have to ask me twice. What an opportunity! I rushed to get the story and stood expectantly at his elbow as Mr. Kantor scanned the pages.

"My dear," he said finally, "I hate to tell you, but this is trash."

"Mack!" my mother exclaimed. "Lois is only thirteen!"

"I don't care how old she is," said Mr. Kantor. "If she is trying to sell her stories, she's old enough to be told what's wrong with them. What kind of subject matter is this for a kid? Lois has never had a love affair or seen a man get murdered. Good writing comes from the heart, not off the top of the head."

He turned to me and added more gently, "Throw this stuff away, child, and go write a story about something you know about. Write something that rings true."

I was crushed. I was also challenged. Later that week I did write a story about a fat, shy little girl with braces and glasses who covered her insecurity by writing stories about imaginary adventures. I submitted it to a teen publication called *Calling All Girls,* and by return mail I received a check for twenty-five dollars.

It was the most incredible moment of my life.

From then on my fate was decided. I wrote what I knew about, and could hardly wait to rush home from school each day to fling myself at the typewriter. The pain and joy of adolescence poured onto page after page. My first kiss, my first heartbreak, both became subjects for stories. When I wasn't invited to Carol Johnson's slumber party, I wiped away my tears and wrote about it. When I lost the lead in the class play to Barbara Werner, I wrote a story in which I *got* the lead. I flooded the teen magazines with manuscripts, and despite the unpolished writing, the gut reality of the material carried them over the line, and a surprising number of them sold.

Now that I was being published I had a decision to make. My name was Lois Duncan Steinmetz, and I had been named after my mother. When my work appeared in print I didn't want everybody to think that Mother had written it.

We discussed the situation, and Mother wasn't too keen on the idea of changing her own name so it wouldn't be confused with mine. She suggested that I drop *Steinmetz* and use my first and middle names to write under. The idea pleased me. Duncan had been my grandmother's maiden name and it conjured up romantic visions of brightly kilted Scotsmen marching over rolling hills to the blare of bagpipes. So I wrote my editor and told her that I was going to publish under a pseudonym, *Lois Duncan.*

At sixteen I won second prize in *Seventeen* magazine's annual short-story contest. At seventeen I won third prize, and at eighteen I took first. My greatest triumph was the sale of my home economics report. I was the only girl in the class who flunked home ec. Lost in daydreams, I forgot to knot my thread and hemmed my skirt all semester long, working my way round and round the circle of material, drawing the thread smoothly along an endless path. When the end-of-the-year fashion show was held, I could not participate, but I wrote up the whole sad tale and sold it for fifty dollars. With that, I bought a skirt that was perfectly beautiful. Whenever people asked me where I got it, I told them, "Home Ec."

My parents had always taken it for granted that both my brother and I would go to college. Daddy had graduated from Princeton, and Mother from Smith. Education was a tradition in our family, and I moved automatically from high school into Duke University, just as I had moved from grammar school into junior high.

It was a total surprise to discover that I was out of place there.

It wasn't the classes that created the problem. Those I found interesting, especially the English and history. What I missed was my own space. At home I had had my own room and a tremendous amount of privacy. At Duke, all our time was scheduled. Not only were there classes, there were dorm meetings, campus meetings, and religious services. There was constant togetherness. Girls flowed in and out of each other's rooms as though they were common territory, and each person's phone calls and callers were announced over a loudspeaker, so even those, in a manner, were shared. We ate together, studied together, exercised together, and brushed our teeth standing in a row in front of a line of basins. If you were noncommunicative, two dozen well-meaning dorm mates asked anxiously what the matter was. If you closed yourself in your room for twenty minutes, people rapped on the door to find out if you were "all right in there."

Within weeks I was longing desperately for the ocean—the long stretch of empty beach, the whisper of waves and the cry of gulls—and solitude.

And I couldn't write! That was the most frustrating thing. Oh, I cranked out term papers at appropriate intervals, but I didn't consider that real writing. It wasn't communication, because no one got to read them except the graduate assistants who graded them. It seemed a waste of time and energy to spend days dredging up information and setting it on paper if nobody was going to publish it.

My own writing was impossible for me. My mind was numb, and my ears were ringing. In order to be creative, I needed time alone, and that was one thing college life did not provide. Neither did it provide freedom. I had thought somehow that leaving home would be a giant step toward independence, but I found myself under stricter chaperonage than my easygoing parents had ever provided.

When I went home at Christmas, I told my parents I thought one year of college might be all I wanted.

They regarded me blankly.

"But, if you drop out, what will you do?"

It was a question I could not answer. This was an era in which single women did not have their own apartments. They lived at home until they were married. Much as I loved my family, I had no desire to go back to being a child in their home. I wanted to be an adult in the adult world.

I returned to college, made the honor roll with my first semester grades, and started dating a senior prelaw student. Buzz was attractive, intelligent, and charming. He was also very persuasive, and I was at a point in life when I was vulnerable to persuasion. When he proposed, I said, "Yes." We were married in May, three weeks before his graduation and four days after my nineteenth birthday.

Our marriage lasted nine years. The first two, I was an air force wife, setting up housekeeping in one little service town after another. Our first daughter, Robin, was born in Seattle, Washington. When Buzz received his discharge from the service, he entered law school in St. Petersburg, Florida, and there our second daughter, Kerry, was born.

Back in school, in a class composed of mostly single young men, Buzz swung quickly into a single way of living. If he wasn't in the library studying, he was out playing tennis, or water-skiing, or chatting in bars, or attending parties. Since we couldn't afford a babysitter, I usually stayed home.

To fill the lonely hours, I began work on a novel. Since I was still so close to my own teen years, it seemed natural that this—my first long project—would be a teenage love story. Its title was *Debutante Hill,* and it was sweet and sticky and pap, but in the 1950s that's the kind of book teenagers read.

When it was finished, I dedicated the novel to my mother and entered the manuscript in the "Seventeenth Summer Literary Contest," sponsored by Dodd, Mead and Company. It was returned for revisions because in it a young man of twenty drank a beer.

"We can't judge this," the editor told me. "You can't mention liquor in a book for young people. Clean it up and resubmit it, and then we'll read it."

I changed the beer to a Coke and resubmitted the manuscript. It won the contest, and the book was published. When the first bound copy arrived in the mail, and I lifted it out of its wrappings and held it in my hands, I felt almost as thrilled as I had been when I'd first held my newborn babies.

Meanwhile, my marriage was rapidly fading into nothing. Buzz graduated from law school, passed the bar, and became a lawyer. From then on, he was so busy that I

Duncan's photographer parents, Joseph and Lois Steinmetz, in the Florida Keys on assignment for **Holiday** *magazine, 1949*

never saw him. For the next seven years I continued to write books and to raise our children—a little boy, Brett, had now joined the family—and to try to pretend to myself that I was happy.

What I wrote were romances, and they were pretty awful. I can't accept the total blame for this, however. Whenever I attempted something more interesting, publishers refused to accept it.

An example of this was my first attempt at an adventure novel. *Game of Danger* was the story of a girl and her brother, fourteen and twelve, who were engaged in a wild chase through New England in an effort to keep secret documents out of the hands of the "bad guys." Midway through the book, too exhausted to flee further, they stopped at an inn, rented a room, and slept for a couple of hours.

This chapter came back with exclamation marks in the margin.

"You have two people of opposite sexes sharing a room, and they're not married!"

"But they're brother and sister," I protested. "They're fully clothed, and they're lying on twin beds."

"That makes no difference," my editor said. "Librarians would never touch a book that included such a suggestive scene. You will have to have them rent separate rooms."

Since my characters had almost no money, I could not imagine their doing such a thing. Still, I didn't want to offend the nation's librarians. We finally reached a

The author in the backyard of her home in St. Petersburg, Florida, with daughters Robin and Kerry, 1956

compromise with an L-shaped alcove in which the boy could nap out of sight of his sister.

When I was twenty-seven, the inevitable happened—Buzz fell in love with somebody else. We were divorced, and I was devastated. Those were days when marriages were expected to last forever. I had never known a divorced person. In a desperate effort to start my life over, I took the children and moved to Albuquerque, New Mexico, where my brother (now called "Bill," not "Billy") was living.

I had a half-dozen books in print by this time, but they were far from best sellers. If I remember right, they were earning me about $2,000 a year. I knew I couldn't support myself and the children on my tiny royalty check, so for the first time in my life I went out to find a "real job."

With nothing to recommend me—no college degree, no business training, no work experience—I was no prize as an employee. I was hired at last by a small advertising agency to answer the telephone, run errands, and write occasional copy. My monthly salary was $275, which I hoped to supplement by writing articles and stories in the evenings.

That was wishful thinking. By the time I left work and picked up Brett at his nursery, collected the girls at their after-school baby-sitter's, came home and cooked dinner and spent some time with the children, got them bathed and bedded down, cleaned up the apartment, did the laundry and got things into order for the next day, I was too exhausted to write a letter to my parents, much less something suitable for publication. I sat like a zombie in front of the typewriter and often ended up asleep with my head on the keyboard.

Because of this I was constantly looking for extra ways to earn money. On my lunch hour I entered contests. One was sponsored by the Florida Development Commission and was for "happy snapshots taken on vacation in Florida." Another was for "the most frightening experience of your life in one hundred words or less."

One day I came home from work after an especially tiring day, gave the mail a quick once-over and, finding nothing there but bills and ads, tossed it into a heap on the coffee table. The following evening I picked it up again to give it a second look before throwing it away. There was a letter I had thought was an ad because it started "Dear Reader." Now I saw that it was not an ad at all.

"Dear Reader," it said. "It is my pleasant duty to inform you that your 'frightening experience' has won first prize in *True Story's* contest. Your check is enclosed."

Enclosed in what? Robin, whose job it was to take out the trash each day, had been conscientious. She had thrown away the envelope.

Our apartment was part of a huge, low-cost complex. There must have been fifty garbage cans lined up out back. The children and I got a flashlight and, starting at one end of the row, went rooting through all of them. Finally, halfway down about the fifteenth can, buried under somebody's leftover spaghetti, we found the envelope. Inside, there was a check for $500.

Five hundred dollars was almost twice what I was earning each month at the agency, and by working away from home I had the expenses of a nursery for Brett, an after-school sitter for the girls, commuting and panty hose for myself. I made my decision quickly. If there was this kind of money to be made by writing for the confessions, there was no sense spending my days writing advertising copy. One thing that made the decision easier was a phone call from the Florida Development Commission informing me that my "happy snapshot" had won first prize: a live, trained porpoise from Marineland, Florida. At my strangled gasp of horror (I had a vision of the thing arriving in a crate of salt water and having to be kept in the bathtub) I was offered a chance to sell the porpoise back to Marineland for $1,000.

With this nest egg to draw upon while I taught myself the craft of confession writing, I quit my job, went to the newsstand, and bought every confession magazine on the rack. By the time that I'd read each one from cover to cover, I had a pretty good idea of how these stories were put together. They were sensational dramas of sin and suffering, written in first person as though they were true, but since they bore no by-lines, it was obvious they were really fakes.

I decided that I'd had enough practice writing fiction to be able to do these, so from then on, every morning, I got up, brushed my teeth, and sat down at the typewriter to confess. I wrote a story a week. Not every one sold, but most did, and not one editor ever asked me if my stories were true.

Soon the kids and I were living better than we had since the divorce. I gave up our awful apartment and bought a house. The little girls took dancing lessons and piano lessons and ice skating lessons, while Brett went to a private kindergarten. We ate steak at least once a week and sometimes more often. I got very good and very fast. I could start a confession Monday and have the final draft completed and in the mail by Wednesday. Among the titles of the stories of mine that were published (anonymously, thank God!) during those busy years were "We Killed Our Baby," "I Made My Son a Daughter," and "Twenty-nine and Mother of Two, I Wanted an Affair with a Teenage Boy." I won't elaborate upon their contents.

After two years on this schedule, however, I began to run out of sins to write about. Glued to my typewriter, I had had no time for doing research. One day Bill, who worked for the government, took pity on me.

"Get a babysitter," he told me, "and I'll take you out to the base and introduce you to some of the bachelor types who work in missile design. They'll tell you about sins you never dreamed of."

That evening I met Don Arquette, the man to whom I'm now married.

Don and I knew each other two years before he proposed. Each time he was ready to pop the question, another confession story would come out and he would panic. The week he did ask me to marry him, *Personal Romances* published "I Carry That Dreadful Disease," and he almost reneged. On our wedding day, out came "Can He Bear to Touch Me on Our Wedding Night?" which made him think twice. But he did go through with the ceremony and adopted the children, and another stage of life began for us all.

Duncan with husband, Don Arquette, 1973

As an electrical engineer with a Master's degree, Don earned a good living, and it was no longer necessary for me to be the family provider. Don expected (and I guess I did also) that I would now settle back to being what I had been once before, a full-time housewife who spent her idle hours writing gentle novels.

But sweet romances now bored me. I had grown used to marathon writing, and I'm a creature of habit; I automatically jumped up in the morning and sat down to confess. Story followed story, until one day I wrote "One of My Babies Must Die," about the operation to separate our Siamese twins. This story brought in mail from all over the country from readers who wanted information about the operation and the doctor who had performed it. It was evident, even to me, that I had gone too far.

"Don't you think it's time to move on a little?" Don said. "Why don't you stop this confession writing and start writing articles for nice wholesome magazines like *Good Housekeeping* and *Ladies' Home Journal?*"

"I could never sell to those," I told him. "I tried the *Journal* back when I was first starting out. They're not like the confessions; they use true material, and they publish your by-line."

"Then write something true," Don said reasonably. "Hasn't anything interesting ever happened to you?"

"Well—," a thought occurred to me. "I *did* once win a trained porpoise in a contest."

To please him, I wrote a two-page featurette called "The Year I Won the Contest" and mailed it off to *Good Housekeeping.* Back came a check for three times the amount I was used to receiving for a sixteen-page confession story. I was incredulous. Somehow, during those years of sitting down every day and forcing out words, I had learned the professional way of telling a story, and those story-telling techniques could evidently be transferred over into other forms of writing. From then on, I continued to write regularly for the national women's magazines, and to this day I have never written another confession story.

Now that the financial pressure was off, I also felt free to turn back to my non-lucrative, but immeasurably enjoyable, hobby of writing teenage novels. I immediately discovered that something had happened in the time that I had been away. The world had changed, and so had the books that were considered acceptable reading for young people. No longer did any writer have to worry about getting a manuscript back because someone in it drank a beer. When I browsed the young adult section of our local library, I found books on alcoholism, drug use, social and racial problems, premarital sex, parental divorce, mental illness, and homosexuality.

Thus began a whole new period of my writing career. The first novel I wrote under the new set of ground rules was *Ransom,* an adventure story about teenagers kidnapped by their school bus driver. Dodd, Mead wouldn't publish that book ("It's not your style of writing," the editor told me), but it was accepted by Doubleday, who published it in 1966.

Ransom was more successful than anyone expected, and the Dodd, Mead editor was very unhappy. It was runner-up for the Edgar Allan Poe Award which is presented by the Mystery Writers of America for each year's best mysteries. Suddenly librarians, who hadn't known before that I existed, began to notice me, and when my next book, *They Never Came Home,* appeared, they stocked it. That book, too, was runner-up for the Edgar. It also was taken by the Junior Literary Guild.

Meanwhile, at home, both good and bad things were happening. On the good side, my marriage to Don was a happy one, and within the next several years I gave birth to two children, Don Jr. and Kate. On the bad side, I lost my mother, who was my dearest friend, and for a long time I was so numbed by grief that I couldn't function. Family crises brought me back into motion—Robin broke her leg skiing, Kerry almost cut her thumb off carving a Halloween pumpkin, Brett slammed the car door on one of his fingers—but still I couldn't set words on paper. I was totally drained of all creativity.

Finally I came to the realization that I had to force myself to get back to work. If I didn't break this block, I might never write again. The book I had been working on when Mother died had been a murder mystery. I took that manuscript now, and threw it in the trash can. There was no way that I could write about death, so I decided to do the opposite. I would write something light and humorous, aimed at a younger age group, and I would accept in advance the fact that it would not be publishable. It would simply serve as an exercise to get me moving.

The book was called *Hotel for Dogs,* and to my surprise, Houghton Muffin published it in 1971. It did quite well, and is still in print in paperback. For the next thirteen years, this book served as my token attempt at humor. Then, in 1983, I wrote *The Terrible Tales of Happy Days School* which was published by Little, Brown. Each of these books was reviewed as having been written by a "new author, not to be confused with the Lois Duncan who writes teenage suspense novels." Because I was not known as a writer of humor, nobody realized that the two Lois Duncans were the same person.

Graduating, at forty-three, from the University of New Mexico, cum laude, with a B.A. in English, 1977

Something else important happened in 1971. I was invited to teach a class in magazine writing at the University of New Mexico. The idea of doing this scared me to death. I wasn't a teacher, in fact, I wasn't even educated. I'd had only one year of college, and that had been long ago.

But Don, who knew how shy I was, thought the experience would be good for me.

"Give it a try," he said encouragingly. "What's there to lose?"

And so I became a lecturer for the journalism department, a position I held for eleven years. I also became a student. I had always regretted my decision to drop out of college, and being back on a university campus was exciting. I began by taking just one or two classes—a literature course here, a psychology class there—and then I signed up for a course in news photography. I did well in this, for having been raised by photojournalist parents, I had absorbed a lot about photography without even knowing it. Even before the class was over, I was submitting photos to magazines, and Don had converted our extra bathroom into a darkroom. This hobby has been a source of lasting pleasure. In 1982, I had a book of juvenile verse called *From Spring to Spring* published by the Westminster Press, and the poems were illustrated by my own photographs.

Going back to school in middle age was a strange experience. In some of my classes, my own students were my fellow classmates. I would be lecturing them one hour as "Professor Duncan," and the next they would be nudging me and saying, "Lois, can I borrow your notes?" In 1977, I finally graduated, cum laude, with a B.A. degree in English, and we celebrated the event with a family party.

On the day of my graduation I was too excited to think about anything else, so I spent the morning at my desk, writing about it. The result was an article, "A Graduate in the Family," which subsequently sold to *Good Housekeeping.* The check they sent me covered the cost of my whole tuition.

So, the years passed. I'm not a person who has had many great adventures; most of my life has been centered around my family. Little League games, dance recitals, amateur theater productions, camping trips, ski vacations, and visits to grandparents filled our days. Robin grew up and became a professional singer; Kerry grew up and became an actress and then a television newswoman; Brett became a sound engineer with a rock band. My lonely father remarried. His second wife, Louise Palmer, is a talented artist, and MacKinlay Kantor, who had by this time reaped the Pulitzer Prize for his novel *Andersonville,* was best man at their wedding.

Another nice thing happened to my father in his later years. In 1979, an archive of work by early studio photographers was created at the Carpenter Center for the Visual Arts at Harvard University. My parents' photographic work during the thirties and forties was suddenly "discovered," and, overnight, my father leapt to fame. He was given a one-man show at Harvard in 1982, and a collection of his photographs was published in a catalog titled *Killing Time.* The show was exhibited all around the country, and Daddy, now almost eighty, was heralded as "a social historian and an artist far ahead of his time."

My father accepted this notoriety with a complacent smile.

"I was just doing my job," he said, "and having fun."

For my own part, I continued, of course, to write books. I won't try to discuss them all in this short essay, but

The Arquette family, Albuquerque, New Mexico, 1974: seated, Don Sr. holding Don Jr., age six; Lois holding Kate, four; Robin, eighteen; standing, Kerry, sixteen; and Brett, thirteen

I will mention several that for one reason or another seem of special significance.

A Gift of Magic was my first book about psychic phenomena, and it was published by Little, Brown in 1971. During my year at Duke, back in 1952, the freshman class had served as subjects for ESP (extrasensory perception) experiments conducted by a Dr. Rhine. I became fascinated by the subject, and from that time on read everything about it that I could find. I decided that it would be fun to write a fiction story for eight-to-twelve-year-olds about a girl who had this gift, but it took me years to find someone willing to publish it. Every publisher I sent it to told me, "Kids aren't interested in things like that." I didn't agree with this, I thought young readers would love it. When *A Gift of Magic* did finally make it into print, I was proven right. The book did well and established me as a forerunner in a genre that has since become hugely popular.

Down a Dark Hall taught me about the newest in taboos for youth novels. With all the freedom we writers now had in choice of subject matter, I had assumed I could write about almost anything I wanted to. *Down a Dark Hall* was a strange sort of Gothic about a girl who went off to boarding school and discovered too late that the head mistress was a medium. Ghosts of long dead artists, writers, and composers came flocking back to invade the minds and bodies of the unfortunate students.

This book was returned for revisions, not because the plot was so wild, but because the ghosts in the story were male and the victims were female. Like an echo from the past—"Librarians won't touch a book in which a sister and brother share a hotel room,"—I was now told "Librarians won't touch a book that portrays women as the weaker sex." When I changed the ghost of a male poet into the ghost of Emily Brontë, the book was accepted.

With *Summer of Fear,* a book about an Albuquerque family that was being intimidated by witchcraft, I learned something about the crazy world of film making. Retitled "Stranger in Our House," this story was televised as an NBC Movie of the Week, starring Linda Blair.

Kerry, who at that time was living in Hollywood, auditioned and won a small part in the picture. She called me often to tell me what was going on.

"You know the little dog in the book?" she asked me.

"Of course, I know him," I said. "After all, I created him."

"You wouldn't recognize him now," Kerry said. "Linda Blair likes horses, so the dog is now a horse."

That meant that all the scenes I had placed around an Albuquerque swimming pool were now laid at a California riding stable, and the handsome lifeguard my heroine Rachel was in love with was now her riding instructor. When the movie appeared on television, there wasn't much about it that I recognized. Like most authors, I preferred the book.

Television has had an enormous effect upon youth books. Not only has it exposed young people to sophisticated subject matter at an early age, it has conditioned its viewers to expect instant entertainment. Few of today's readers are patient enough to wade through slow paced, introductory chapters as I did at their ages to see if a book is eventually going to get interesting. If their interest isn't caught immediately, they want to switch channels.

Because of this, writers have been forced into utilizing all sorts of TV techniques to hold their readers' attention. In *Killing Mr. Griffin,* I began with the sentence, "It was a wild, windy southwestern spring when the idea of killing Mr. Griffin occurred to them." I knew I was not going to have this man die until a third of the way into the book, and I was afraid that if I didn't give my readers an inkling that dramatic action lay ahead, they would not be willing to hang around that long.

With a family the size of ours, we've never had much room in which to spread out, and until recently my work area was a corner of the bedroom. This has now changed. As the older children left home, new rooms opened up, and I grabbed one of those for an office. I moved in my desk and filing cabinets, and then took a step into the Brave New Computer Age and replaced my ancient typewriter with a word processor.

This miraculous machine has made my work much easier. When writing *The Third Eye,* for instance, I originally envisioned the story as being laid in the autumn with high-school football games churning in the background and all the trees leafed out in gold. Then, a quarter of the way through, I realized that I was going to need to have a little girl drown in the Rio Grande. Since this is a river that runs fast and deep only in springtime, I would have to switch my autumn-based story to spring.

Formerly that simple change in season would have meant retyping sixty pages of manuscript. With the word processor, the changes took me ten minutes. All I had to do

The author in 1984

was go through the manuscript, locate the pages of description, and change gold leaves to green and football to softball. Then I scattered around a few daffodils. I pressed a button on the keyboard, and the printer went into action and ground out a nice, new, perfectly typed springtime manuscript.

I faced a similar situation with *Stranger with My Face.* In this book, I created a character named Jeff who was to be the love interest for my heroine, Laurie. I started out with Jeff a conventionally handsome teenage boy, and then, when I was partway into the novel, I got an idea for a way to make him more interesting. I decided to give him a scarred face. This meant going back through the early chapters of the book and changing every section in which Jeff's looks were referred to. It also meant altering his personality to reflect the emotional damage that the physical disfigurement had caused. With the help of the word processor, I was able to make these changes quickly and easily and could also insert a full-page flashback detailing the accident that had produced the scarring.

Most of the books I've written have been fiction. There are two, however, that were a real change of pace for me. *Chapters: My Growth as a Writer,* published by Little, Brown in 1982, is an autobiographical how-to for young people who want to become writers. Some of the material in this essay has been drawn from it. This book contains samples of the stories and poems I was writing at various ages and describes what was happening in my life at the time I wrote them. My book for adults, *How to Write and Sell Your Personal Experiences,* published by Writer's Digest Books in 1979, takes up chronologically where *Chapters* ends and incorporates much of what I taught at the university.

This past year I turned fifty years old. I spend so much of my time submerged in the minds of the teenage characters in my novels that it comes as a shock when I look in the mirror and find I have gray in my hair. Don Jr. is now seventeen, and Kate is fourteen. Kerry is married and is soon to make me a grandmother.

Fifty seems a nice age to be, but then, so has every other age. I've enjoyed my life, and I expect to continue enjoying it. I look forward to travel and leisure time with Don after his retirement—to watching my children's adult lives unfold—to spoiling my grandchildren.

People ask, "Are you going to keep writing?" They might as well ask if I plan to continue breathing. I expect to do both just as long as I possibly can. Like my father, I'm "doing my job and having fun."

I'm working right now on a book called *Locked in Time.* It's the story of a family who have stopped the process of aging and are stuck forever as they are, unable to grow and change.

I find that a horrible concept, but I think the book will be a good one. As with every new book I write, I'm excited about it.

(Portions of this essay are based in part on material from the author's books *How to Write and Sell Your Personal Experiences,* Writer's Digest Books, 1979, copyright by Lois Duncan, and *Chapters: My Growth as a Writer,* Little, Brown, 1982, copyright by Lois Duncan.)

POSTSCRIPT

Lois Duncan provided the following update to *SATA* in 2003:

When I read the autobiographical essay that I wrote almost twenty years ago I have the feeling that I'm reading something that was authored by another person—somebody I vaguely remember and for whom I feel empathy, but to whom I can't really relate. How complacent I was at that time, how unbearably smug! How delighted I was with my near-perfect life, and how supremely confident that it would continue to happily unwind along the course I had charted!

It did for a while, both personally and professionally. After *Locked in Time* was published, I signed a contract to write three more teenage suspense novels, pocketed a nice advance, and set to work with enthusiasm. Meanwhile, our married daughter, Kerry, produced Don's and my first grandchild, and our musician daughter, Robin, and I created a recording of original lullabies as a welcome-to-the-world gift for baby Erin. I wrote the lyrics and narrated the tape, and Robin composed the music and performed the vocals. *Songs from Dreamland* was published by Knopf as part of their series of "Book and Cassette Classics," and Robin and I were so thrilled by our overnight success as a mother-daughter songwriting team that we immediately produced a second tape of original songs for children called *Our Beautiful Day*. On that, we interacted with a precocious four-year-old named Adrienne Clark, whom Robin found by advertising in the newspaper for "a preschooler with personality who can carry a tune." (As an adult, Adrienne went on to become a professional singer.)

We had a lot of fun with that project, but there was a fly in the ointment. Although *Songs from Dreamland* got good reviews—"A delicately illustrated collection of 14 original lullabies and a sweetly sung cassette recording of the songs" (*School Library Journal*)—it had a very short lifetime. During the second printing, the book was accidentally packaged with somebody else's cassette about a pig and his barnyard buddies. Parents who received the book and cassette as a baby present would pop in the tape, anticipating songs that would sooth their babies to sleep and, instead, the poor children would be jolted into hysterics by a bombardment of earsplitting "oinks." Returns poured in, but the publisher's computer didn't understand why, it just knew the product was suddenly extremely unpopular. The publisher hurriedly yanked *Songs from Dreamland* off the market and wouldn't even consider *Our Beautiful Day*. (Robin now sells the CDs for both recordings from her personal web site.)

But my suspense novels were doing just fine. I was at the peak of my career, enjoying my work and chalking up young readers' awards in one state after another. I completed *The Twisted Window,* a plot-oriented story with more twists and turns than a corkscrew, and followed it up with *Don't Look behind You,* an adventure story about a family with a teenage daughter that was forced into the Federal Witness Protection Program.

One month after that book was published, our world blew apart.

The author with her first grandchild, Erin, 1987

I had based the personality of April, the teenage heroine of *Don't Look behind You,* on the personality of our youngest daughter, Kait. (She's referred to as "Kate" in the first of these essays, but changed the spelling of her name when she entered high school in order to appear more exotic.) In *Don't Look behind You,* April's family informed on an interstate drug operation, and April was chased by a hitman in a Camaro.

That book was published in June, 1989.

In July, 1989, our own Kait, eighteen, was chased down in her car and shot to death. A witness described the killer as a man in a Camaro.

On that soft summer night, the world as our family knew it was changed forever, for we lost, not only our beloved daughter and "baby sister," but also our naïve belief in the integrity of the American Justice System.

The police dubbed Kait's murder a "random drive-by shooting," and refused to investigate any other possibility, despite strong evidence that Kait was deliberately murdered because, like her counterpart April in *Don't Look behind You*, she was in a position to blow the whistle on organized crime. In Kait's case, the link to the interstate crime ring was a Vietnamese boyfriend, with whom she was breaking up on the weekend she was killed. We were later to learn, through private investigation, that the boyfriend and his friends were involved in criminal activities that appear to have been protected by a small group of rogue cops, one of whom may have orchestrated the cover-up of Kait's murder.

Overnight, subjects that I had once written about as fiction became hideous reality. Death threats to the rest of our family drove us out of our home, and we took refuge in a rented townhouse with a security system. It wasn't the Witness Protection Program, but it certainly felt like it. We turned for guidance to psychic detectives, like Karen in my

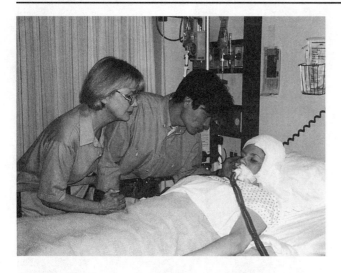

Photo taken during the film reenactment of the Kaitlyn Arquette homicide for Unsolved Mysteries *in 1992. Actors portray Lois; Kait's boyfriend, Dung Nguyen; and Kait as she lay in a coma after the shooting.*

novel, *The Third Eye,* and private investigators and forensic experts became such an everyday part of our lives that they began to seem like members of the family.

When the Albuquerque Police Department dropped off the unsolved case in 1991, I wrote a nonfiction book, *Who Killed My Daughter?,* to motivate informants and to keep the facts of Kait's case from becoming buried. Adrenaline kept me going until I completed work on the manuscript, and then my health gave out. I was leaning over to take a pan of chicken out of the oven, when I suddenly discovered that my left hand wouldn't close around the door handle. Then my left arm went limp and fell to my side. I tried to call out to the family, who were already gathered at the dinner table, but my face contorted and the words came out in a garble.

What I was trying to say was, "I think I've had a stroke!"

On the way to the hospital I got my speech back and dictated a living will.

Later that night I became able to move my arm and hand. As I lay in the hospital bed, clenching and reclenching my left fist in a frenzied effort to reassure myself that I could still do so, a nurse kept popping in to ask if I could swallow. I quickly realized that swallowing was some kind of test so, of course, my mouth dried up every time the nurse appeared in the doorway. In between her visits I manufactured saliva, which I surreptitiously stockpiled in the crevices of my mouth so that when she next materialized I could demonstrate my swallowing skills.

A myriad of tests revealed no overt cause for a stroke. Except for high blood pressure, which I had developed soon after the murder and which was being controlled by medication, I was in seemingly good health. I was lucky in that the only obvious after-effects of the stroke were that my smile was now lopsided and it was quite a long while before I could type with my left hand.

"There's no good reason for a nonsmoking, middle-aged woman who doesn't have a weight problem to suffer a stroke," one doctor said accusingly. "You are going to have to learn to cope better with everyday stress and to stop letting life's little problems become major issues for you."

I promised to try.

Who Killed My Daughter? hit the city of Albuquerque like a nuclear explosion. One bookstore, that had placed an order for one hundred copies, sold them all within hours and frantically wired the warehouse for another shipment. TV newscasts showed customers scrambling for the last copies on the shelves, and newspaper headlines screamed "Sloppy Police Work Frustrated Duncan" and "Mother Relentlessly Searches for the Awful Truth."

In April of 1992, I set off on a cross-country book tour that started in New York City and ended in Los Angeles. Beginning with *Good Morning, America, Larry King Live,* and *Unsolved Mysteries,* I appeared on radio and television shows from coast to coast to relate Kait's story and plead with informants to come forward. Eventually the cities began to blur in my mind until the day came when I woke up in the morning and had to call down to the desk to find out where I was. I did not use the deadbolts on the doors of my hotel rooms for fear I might have a second stroke and need medical attention in the night.

Fortunately, that didn't happen.

As soon as the tour was over, Don applied for early retirement from Sandia Laboratories and our family left Albuquerque for good. We had no preconceived destination; we just got in the car and drove east until the road ran out. Don and I now live on a sand dune on the Outer Banks of North Carolina, so I've ended up as I started—falling asleep at night to the roar of the surf and waking in the morning to the cries of sea gulls.

Who Killed My Daughter? and the subsequent publicity did stimulate tipsters, and our private investigators continued to develop new information implicating members of the Vietnamese crime ring. But the police had closed the unsolved case as a "random drive-by shooting" and refused to review any evidence that indicated otherwise. Since nobody in authority was willing to look at our new information, our oldest son, Brett, who by now had progressed from his days with a rock band to become a computer guru, created a "Kaitlyn Arquette" Web site. From then on, every time we received new information, we offered it to the police, and when they wouldn't look at it, we posted it on the Internet. The police weren't happy about that, but we liked to think that Kait's killers weren't happy about it either.

After Kait's death I was no longer motivated to write suspense novels. Creating a fictional mystery about a young woman in jeopardy, while our own horrendous true mystery remained unsolved, seemed like an impossible challenge. Yet, I still owed my publisher the final book from the three-book contract I had signed several years before the shooting. Although my editors were patient and sympathetic, as time continued to go by and I didn't produce the third novel, I could sense the unspoken question—"When is Lois Duncan going to get her act together?"

In 1997, I finally forced myself to write *Gallows Hill,* a story based on the theme of reincarnation. When I got that manuscript completed and shipped off to my publisher, I felt as if the weight of the world was off my shoulders. From here on out, I promised myself, I would write only what I wanted to write, which, for the time being at least, would not be mysteries. I knew there was something else waiting for me—something that I was meant to accomplish at this particular stage of life—but I didn't know what it was. So I passed the time editing short story anthologies and writing fanciful books for young children, while I waited for some sort of cosmic revelation that would turn me in the direction I was meant to go next.

I wasn't thinking about finances, although I certainly should have been. With the loss we had taken on the sale of our home back in Albuquerque and the depletion of our savings by years of private investigation, we were not in good shape. But, before things got really desperate, a miracle occurred, and I received an offer for the film rights to a novel that I had written back in the '70s. I had all but forgotten that *I Know What You Did Last Summer* existed, as it hadn't been very successful other than as a resource for remedial reading teachers who had discovered, to their surprise and mine also, that it worked well as a Hi-Lo (high interest, low reading level) book for special education classes.

Over the years, several of my novels had been filmed for television, but this was my first box office movie, and I was very excited. When the film was released, I bought my ticket and a box of popcorn and settled into my seat at the theater, eager to see my characters come to life on the Big Screen. I had laid the story in New Mexico, so I found it a bit disconcerting when the backdrop for the credits was a seascape. "Maybe it's a mountain lake?" I speculated. Then, an insane fisherman strode onto the screen. *Where in the world had he come from? He wasn't in my book. And what was he going to do with that ice hook he was carrying?*

Well, I soon found out. He was going to decapitate my characters. The shrieks from the audience were as frenzied as the screams from the mutilated actors, as blood spurted from severed necks, heads tumbled to the floor, and a swarm of crabs erupted from the gaping mouth of a corpse that was stashed in the trunk of my heroine's car. The climax came when my teenage heroine tried to hide in an ice bin on a fishing boat (that wasn't in my book) and dug into the ice cubes to uncover the heads of her two best friends. The first thing I did upon leaving the theater was phone Kerry and tell her not to let the grandchildren see the movie.

I Know What You Did Last Summer was a box office hit. My sudden notoriety as the author of the book upon which the atrocity was very loosely based led to a new surge of media attention. All of a sudden I was no longer "Lois Duncan, Unproductive Author," I was "Lois Duncan, Slasher Queen!" My publisher had new covers designed for my backlist, so they all looked like billboards for horror movies, and novels that had been published as far back as the '60s started selling like crazy to a generation of teenagers who assumed I was a brand new author. Everybody jumped onto the bandwagon. Psychic hotlines ran ads claiming, *"We Know What You'll Do Next Summer!"* Proctor and Gamble developed an ad for Tide

Detergent —*"I See What You Spilled Last Summer!"* In an interview for *People* magazine, I expressed my disgust with the horrible movie and stated that, as the mother of a murdered teenager, I saw nothing amusing about sensationalized violence. As I made that statement, I felt a bit hypocritical. There was no denying that the income from the movie was a lifesaver.

Now that I no longer had to feel guilty about not supplementing Don's retirement income by writing new novels, I suddenly realized what it was that I wanted to do in my Golden Years. Since *Who Killed My Daughter?* was published, I had been deluged with letters and e-mail from families of other murder victims who had reason to believe that their loved ones' homicides had not been honestly and thoroughly investigated by law enforcement. Many of those people had spent their life savings on private investigation but had nowhere to take their new information, because police refused to reopen cases that they had closed as "random shootings," accidents or suicides. Those families were as desperate as we were to prevent their loved one's cases from being forgotten, but, unlike us, they were not able to get a book published or attract the attention of the media.

So Don and I have created a "Real Crimes" Web site as a way to give those controversial cases public exposure. I write the case reports, based on phone interviews with the families, and Don links the allegations to documentation such as police reports, autopsy reports, crime scene photos and transcripts of depositions. Our "Real Crimes" site has become a valuable resource for investigative reporters and television shows, and, thanks to that media pressure, several cases have been solved and others have been reopened. We continue to pray that Kait's case will eventually be one of those.

As I predicted twenty years ago in the closure of my original essay, I have not stopped writing in my older years. I am continuing to use the gift God gave me, but in a much different way than I ever would have imagined. Without my being aware of it, each step I've taken in life seems to have led me to where I am now. From the years spent writing magazine articles, I learned how to conduct

The author and her husband writing up homicide cases and documenting evidence for their **"Real Crimes"** *Web site*

interviews and condense rambling personal stories into a tight, punchy format that researchers for television shows are willing to read. From the plotting of mystery novels, I developed an investigative thought process and the ability to make sense out of the senseless. And my lifetime of literary output, plus my unexpected and bizarre leap to fame as the author of *I Know What You Did Last Summer,* gave me a recognizable name that seems to cause people to take our "Real Crimes" cases seriously.

Ironically, the stories I'm now writing are once again mysteries—but then, at heart, all stories are mysteries, because readers don't know what the endings will be until they get there.

And life, itself, is the greatest mystery of all.

E–F

EASTON, Kelly 1960-

Personal

Born 1960; divorced; children: Isabelle Easton Spivack and Isaac Easton Spivack. *Education:* University of California—Irvine, B.A., 1985; University of California—San Diego, M.F.A., 1991.

Addresses

Agent—Jane Dystel Literary Management, One Union Square, New York, NY 10003. *E-mail*—Eastonspivack@ hotmail.com

Career

Kaiser Permanente, and Kaiser Permanente Hospice, San Diego, CA, consultant, 1990-93; University of North Carolina-Wilmington, Wilmington, NC, lecturer in English and creative writing, 1993-2000; University of Rhode Island, Kingston, RI, guest artist, fall 2000; Roger Williams University, Bristol, RI, adjunct professor of creative writing, 2002—.

Member

Society of Children's Writers and Illustrators.

Awards, Honors

North Carolina Writers' Network Fiction Competition, 1997, for "The Watcher of the Compound;" Robert Ruark 1997 Fiction Competition, honorable mention, for "Sentences;" Sojourner Fiction Competition, honorable mention, 1998, for "Air;" Golden Kite Honor Award, selected by the New York Public Library for the Books for the Teen Age, selected for the ALA list of Popular Paperbacks for Teens, all 2002, and Teen Readers BookSense Top Ten 76 List, 2003, all for *The Life History of a Star.*

Kelly Easton

Writings

FOR CHILDREN

The Life History of a Star, Simon & Schuster (New York, NY), 2001.
Trouble at Betts Pets, Candlewick Press (Cambridge, MA), 2002.
Canaries and Criminals: Trouble at Betts Pets, Candlewick Press (Cambridge, MA), 2003.
Above the Tightrope, Simon & Schuster (New York, NY), 2004.

PLAYS

Three Witches, Words and Music, 1991.
Ordinary Objects, first produced at The Greenwich Street
    Theater, 1991.
The Modern Heart and Housing, first produced in the
    Warren Theater, at the University of California—San
    Diego, 1990.
It Falls Like a Stone, first produced at the Virginia Woolf
    Conference at Bard College, 1995.

Author of a play, *Self Defense,* produced in the Warren
Theater, at the University of California—San Diego.
Contributor of short fiction to *Paterson Literary Review,
Sojourner, Blue Moon Review, Rio Grande Review,
Washington Square, Iris, Connecticut Review, Prairie
Hearts: An Anthology of Women Writing about the
Midwest, Frontiers,* and *Phoebe.*

Sidelights

The personal is interwoven with the political in Kelly
Easton's young adult novels. Her first, *The Life History
of a Star,* is a first-person narrative in the form of a
journal written by fourteen-year-old Kristin Folger
during the school year 1973-74. Her diaries are filled
with references to contemporary political upheavals,
including the Watergate scandal that eventually brought
down the presidency of Richard Nixon, and the kidnapping of Patricia Hearst, as well as television shows and
popular music of the time. They are also a place where
Kristin can express her mixed feelings about more
personal issues, such as her developing body, the
changes she sees in her friends, and the breakup of her
parents' marriage. Most troubling of all is Kristin's
brother David, who has lived like a ghost in the attic
since his return from the Vietnam War. "The format
makes this novel easy to read and it certainly allows
readers to get to know Kristin, who comes through as a
very real teen," remarked Toni D. Moore in *School
Library Journal.* "Anyone who reads this book will be
able to identify with her," critic Lisa Marx likewise
wrote in a review posted on *Teen Reads.* By novel's end,
Kristin's writing has helped her break through her own
defenses, allowing her to grieve her losses and move on,
observed Gillian Engberg in *Booklist.* The result is "an
uneven but affecting first novel."

The political aspect of *Trouble at Betts Pets,* Easton's
next novel, takes the form of a homeless woman, a
community garden, and the creeping gentrification of an
old urban neighborhood. Aaron Betts, the novel's fifth-
grade narrator, is a responsible twelve-year-old who
works in his parents' pet store, and worries about the
changes in his neighborhood as much as he frets over his
assignment to a stuck-up rich girl for math tutoring.
Then, when the survival of the family pet store is
threatened by a thief, Aaron leaps into action to solve the
mystery. "The protagonist is likable and believable, and
shows quite a bit of moral fiber throughout the book,"
asserted Sharon R. Pearce in *School Library Journal.*
While a contributor to *Publishers Weekly* felt that Easton
had attempted too many subplots to resolve any of them

satisfactorily, this critic also praised the author for
"moments of delicious sarcasm, insight and verve." For
Booklist reviewer Kathy Broderick, however, Easton's
novel "teaches the children—and readers—about life,
friendship, and loyalty."

Kelly Easton told *SATA:* "I fell in love with books after
reading the 'Oz' series, and knew that that was what I
wanted to do with my life. The other thing that I wanted
to be was a composer and a musician. My family was
quite poor, though, and I knew I wouldn't be able to
afford the necessary training. The only training you
really need to be a writer is to read read read, and then to
practice. It's a very democratic profession that way. I
was eight or nine when I read Baum's imaginative
series, but didn't get around to writing seriously until I
was thirty. By then I had been an actor, a dancer, a
police dispatcher, a waitress, and a student. My favorite
children's book is *Holes.* I also love the works of Zilpha
Keatly Snyder and Roald Dahl. All of these books have
in common a strong feeling for humanity and a concern
for how individuals can discover and express themselves
when the odds are against them. These are the subjects
about which I write.

"My happiest moments, as a writer, are when ideas flow,
and also when children write to me and have enjoyed my
books. The most common question children ask me is if
I ever owned a pet store because the narrator of Betts
Pets does. I haven't owned a pet store, but as a child I
wished I did. And I remembered how much I wanted a
pet raccoon, and my mother, wisely, wouldn't let me
have one. Raccoons do not make good pets. They're
mean and mischievous. Now, I have two dogs and a
turtle.

"Right now, I live on an island. It feels an ideal
metaphor for being a writer. That is, you are so much on
your own, but an island is rich with life, and abundant
with plants, animals, stones, shells, even people. And
writing is so much about just floating in your own mind.
I often get ideas when I'm walking around the island or
swimming in the ocean or bicycling. I also read a great
deal, which is the most important thing a writer can do. I
teach in universities, and enjoy how smart and talented
the students are. Aside from that, I love to cook and eat,
and above all, to play with my kids."

Biographical and Critical Sources

PERIODICALS

Booklist, April 15, 2001, Gillian Engberg, review of *The
    Life History of a Star,* p. 1545; September 1, 2002,
    Kathy Broderick, review of *Trouble at Betts Pets,*
    p. 123.
Childhood Education, spring, 2002, Sylvia Loh, review of
    The Life History of a Star, p. 173.
Publishers Weekly, March 19, 2001, review of *The Life
    History of a Star,* p. 101; April 15, 2002, review of
    Trouble at Betts Pets, p. 65.
School Library Journal, July, 2001, Toni D. Moore, review
    of *The Life History of a Star,* p. 106; April, 2002,

Sharon R. Pearce, review of *Trouble at Betts Pets,* p. 146.

OTHER

Teen Reads, http://www.teenreads.com/ (August 31, 2002), Lisa Marx, review of *The Life History of a Star.*
Washington Parent, http://www.washingtonparent.com/ (August 31, 2002), review of *The Life History of a Star.*

*   *   *

ERDRICH, Louise 1954-
(Heidi Louise, a joint pseudonym; Milou North, a joint pseudonym)

Personal

Name is pronounced "UR-drick"; born Karen Louise Erdrich, June 7, 1954, in Little Falls, MN; son of Ralph Louis (a teacher with the Bureau of Indian Affairs) and Rita Joanne (a teacher with the Bureau of Indian Affairs and a painter; maiden name, Gourneau) Erdrich; married Michael Anthony Dorris (a writer and professor of Native American Studies), October 10, 1981 (died, April 22, 1997); children: (adopted) Reynold Abel (deceased), Jeffery Sava, Madeline Hannah; (with Dorris) Persia Andromeda, Pallas Antigone, Aza Marion; (with a partner) Azure. *Education:* Dartmouth College, B.A., 1976; Johns Hopkins University, M.A., 1979. *Politics:* Democrat. *Religion:* "Anti-religion." *Hobbies and other interests:* "Playing chess with daughters and losing, playing piano badly, speaking terrible French"; also quilting, running, and drawing.

Addresses

Home—Kenwood, MN. *Office*—Birchbark Books, 2115 W. 21st St., Minneapolis, MN 55405. *E-mail*—birchbark books@yahoo.com

Career

Author, educator, journalist, and bookstore owner. North Dakota State Arts Council, visiting poet and teacher, 1977-78; Johns Hopkins University, Baltimore, MD, writing instructor, 1978-79; Boston Indian Council, Boston, MA, communications director and editor of newspaper the *Circle,* 1979-80; Charles-Merrill Co., textbook writer, 1980; founder and owner, Birchbark Books, Minneapolis, MN, 2000—. Worked variously as a beet weeder and hoer, a lifeguard, a waitress, a salesperson, a short-order cook, a library aide, a photograph developer, an aide in a psychiatric hospital, a teacher of poetry in prisons, a construction flag signaler, a researcher for a film on the Sioux for Mid-American Television, and the publications director of a small press; also has judged writing contests.

Louise Erdrich

Member

International Writers, Authors League of America, Turtle Mountain Band of Objibwa, Authors Guild, PEN (member of executive board, 1985-88).

Awards, Honors

Academy of Poets Prize, 1974; teaching fellow, Johns Hopkins University, 1978; writing fellowship, Mac-Dowell Colony, 1980; writing fellowship, Yadoo Colony, 1981; visiting fellowship, Dartmouth College, 1981; first prize, Nelson Algren Fiction Award, 1982, for "The World's Greatest Fisherman"; fellowship, National Endowment for the Arts, 1982; Pushcart Prize in Poetry, 1983; National Magazine Fiction Award, 1983 and 1987; Virginia McCormack Scully Prize, best book of the year dealing with Western Indians, 1984, National Critic Circles Award, best work of fiction, 1984, *Los Angeles Times* Award, Sue Kaufman Prize for Best First Fiction, American Academy and Institute of Arts and Letters, best novel, American Book Award, Before Columbus Foundation, and citation, Best Eleven Books of 1985, *New York Times Book Review,* all 1985, all for *Love Medicine;* Guggenheim fellowship, 1985-86; Best Books citation, *Publishers Weekly,* 1986, for *The Beet Queen;* first prize, O. Henry Award, 1987; Western Literary Association Award, 1992; National Magazine Award, *Harper's* magazine, 1993, for "A Woman's Work"; nomination, National Book Critics Circle Award, 1999, and World Fantasy Award, best novel, 1999, both for *The Antelope Wife;* Parents' Choice

Award, Parents' Choice Foundation, and finalist, National Book Award, both 1999, and Woodcraft Circle Writer of the Year Award, children's literature category, 2000, all for *The Birchbark House;* finalist, National Book Award, fiction category, and Ten Best Books of the Year citation, *Globe and Mail* (Toronto, Ontario, Canada), both 2001, Minnesota Book Award, Minnesota Humanities Commission, 2002, and Dublin Literary Award, Dublin City (Ireland) Trustees and Library System, 2003, all for *The Last Report on the Miracles at Little No Horse.* Erdrich also received the Minnesota Humanities Prize for Literature, Minnesota Humanities, 2002, for her body of work.

Writings

FOR CHILDREN

Imagination (writing textbook), Charles E. Merrill (Westerville, OH), 1980.

Grandmother's Pigeons (picture book), illustrated by Jim LaMarche, Hyperion Books for Children (New York, NY), 1996.

(Self-illustrated) *The Birchbark House* (historical fiction), Hyperion Books for Children (New York, NY), 1999.

The Range Eternal (picture book), illustrated by Steve Johnson and Lou Fancher, Hyperion Books for Children (New York, NY), 2002.

A seven-year-old Ojibwa girl living on an island in Lake Superior discovers her meeting with a stranger brings an invisible enemy—smallpox—to her people. (From The Birchbark House, *written and illustrated by Erdrich.)*

"NORTH DAKOTA" SERIES; ALSO CALLED THE "MATCHIMANTO" SERIES

Love Medicine, Holt, Rinehart & Winston (New York, NY), 1984, revised and enlarged edition, 1993.

The Beet Queen, Henry Holt (New York, NY), 1986.

Tracks, Henry Holt (New York, NY), 1988.

The Bingo Palace, HarperCollins (New York, NY), 1994.

Tales of Burning Love, HarperCollins (New York, NY), 1996.

The Antelope Wife, HarperFlamingo (New York, NY), 1998.

The Last Report on the Miracles at Little No Horse, HarperCollins (New York, NY), 2001.

The Master Butchers Singing Club, HarperCollins (New York, NY), 2002.

ADULT POETRY

Jacklight, Holt, Rinehart & Winston (New York, NY), 1984.

Baptism of Desire, Harper & Row (New York, NY), 1989.

Original Fire: Selected and New Poems, HarperCollins (New York, NY), 2003.

OTHER

The Blue Jay's Dance: A Birth Year (memoir), HarperCollins (New York, NY), 1985.

(With Michael Dorris) *The Crown of Columbus* (novel), HarperCollins (New York, NY), 1991.

(With Michael Dorris) *Route Two and Back* (travel essays), Lord John Press (Northridge, CA), 1991.

(Editor) *Best American Short Stories, 1993,* Houghton Mifflin (Boston, MA), 1993.

Books and Islands in Ojibwe Country, National Geographic (Washington, DC), 2003.

Contributor of introductions to *The Broken Cord: A Family's Ongoing Struggle with Fetal Alcohol Syndrome,* written by Michael Dorris, Harper & Row (New York, NY), 1989, published as *A Broken Cord: A Father's Story;* Collins (New York, NY), 1990; *A Link with the River,* written by Desmond Hogan, Farrar, Straus & Giroux (New York, NY), 1989; *The Falcon: A Narrative of the Captivity and Adventures of John Tanner,* written by John Tanner, Penguin Books (New York, NY), 1994; and *First Person, First Peoples: Native American College Graduates Tell Their Stories,* edited by Andrew Garrod and Colleen Larimore, Cornell University Press (Ithaca, NY), 1997. Contributor of poetry and short stories to numerous anthologies. Contributor to numerous magazines and newspapers, including *American Indian Quarterly, Atlantic Monthly, Georgia Review, Harper's, Kenyon Review, Ms., New Yorker, New York Times Book Review, Redbook* (with her sister Heidi Erdrich, under the joint pseudonym Heidi Louise), and *Woman* (with Michael Dorris, under the joint pseudonym Milou North). Erdrich's works have been translated into approximately fifteen languages, including Spanish. Under the name the Louise Erdrich Papers, a collection of the author's manuscripts is included in the Orin G. Libby Manuscript Collection, Chester Fritz Library, University of North Dakota, Grand Forks, ND.

Adaptations

The Crown of Columbus and *Love Medicine* have been optioned for film production; the latter also was optioned as a television serial. The sound recording *Louise Erdrich and Michael Dorris: Interview with Kay Bonetti* was released by American Audio Prose Library, 1986. *Louise Erdrich and Michael Dorris: Searching for a Native American Identity* was released on video by Bill Moyers Series: A World of Ideas, Public Broadcasting System, 1988. *Love Medicine/The Beet Queen* (excerpts read by the author) was released on audio cassette by American Audio Prose Library, 1987; *The Antelope Wife* was released as an audio cassette by Books on Tape, 1998; *The Last Report on the Miracles at Little No Horse* was released on audio cassette by Books on Tape, 2001; *The Birchbark House* was released on audio cassette by Audio Bookshelf, 2002.

Work in Progress

A book about Mustache Maude, a female cattle rancher in North Dakota.

Sidelights

A Native American author of picture books and historical fiction for children and of novels, poetry, short stories, and nonfiction for adults, Louise Erdrich is the creator of moving literature that has brought her both critical and popular acclaim. As a writer for adults, Erdrich—who is a member of the Turtle Island Mountain Band of Ojibwa (also known as Anishinaabe and Chippewa)—is best known as the author of a series of novels that is set in and around the fictional town of Argus, North Dakota. These works, which Erdrich called "one continuous novel" in an interview with Katie Bacon of the *Atlantic Monthly,* span the whole of the twentieth century, as well as the present. The series is known as the "North Dakota" saga, or the "Matchimanto" books, after the lake that flows near the reservation. They feature three generations of Ojibwa and their friends and neighbors, who are of Native descent, European descent, and a mixture of both. While describing how these characters experience the joys and sorrows of life while attempting to find their place in the world, Erdrich outlines the challenges faced by Native Americans in the United States, as well as how they surmount their situations with grace, courage, and humor. Erdrich also is respected for her poetry which, like her novels, centers around Native American subjects and themes.

Although she does not direct her "North Dakota" series to young people, Erdrich has found a readership among young adults, who are attracted to different aspects of the books, including: the teenage protagonists within the families that she describes, the quests for self-knowledge and community on which her characters embark, the supernatural elements that are part of their daily lives, the funny incidents that befall them, and to Erdrich's intriguing storytelling. Many of her books are studied in senior high schools and colleges. As a writer for children, Erdrich is the creator of two picture books, *Grandmother's Pigeons* and *The Range Eternal,* and a volume of historical fiction for middle-graders, *The Birchbark House.* The first volume of a projected series featuring an Ojibwa girl and her family, *The Birchbark House* has been described as the Native American version of the "Little House" series, popular stories of frontier life by Laura Ingalls Wilder.

Erdrich explores some fundamental issues in her books, such as the meaning of human existence and our relationships with God, with nature, with our ancestors, and with each other. In her "North Dakota" series, the author uses recurring characters and themes and Native American folklore and mythology to create stories of individuals who struggle with fate, with the patterns developed by their ancestors, and with their current circumstances. Her characters face poverty, broken marriages, alcoholism, alienation, racism, sexual abuse, and political and cultural exploitation. In addition, Erdrich addresses the tensions between traditional Ojibwa beliefs and the Christian religion, specifically that of the Roman Catholic Church. Despite the injustices that they face and their personal flaws, the characters demonstrate endurance, tenacity, ingenuity, and a highly developed sense of humor. They find strength in their native faith and customs, in the security of home, in visions and memories, and in the power of love.

Erdrich is well known for transforming Native American oral tradition, myth, and allegory into written literature. She tells her stories by using a lyrical, poetic style; strong imagery, and humor that ranges from broadly slapstick to darkly satiric. The author also is known for the unconventional format of her "North Dakota" books: Erdrich favors multiple narrators for her novels, each with his or her particular point of view, as well as cyclical, non-chronological time lines. She invites her readers to decipher plots, relationships, and meanings—in other words, to become co-creators of her books, much as if they were listening to and participating with a traditional Ojibwa storyteller. Erdrich has written her novels both alone and with her late husband Michael Dorris, who was an author and educator of Native American descent.

The couple developed a collaboration process in which they worked out plots together and edited each other's work; even though their individual stamps were on the books, the couple shared the formal authorship of only two of them. The first is the best-selling adult novel *The Crown of Columbus,* which describes how two Dartmouth professors, researching the voyage of Christopher Columbus in 1492, become involved in an adventure that changes their views about themselves and about the impact of Columbus's journey, especially on Native Americans. The second collaboration, *Route Two and Back,* is a collection of travel essays based on the couple's trek across North America to visit relatives.

Reviewers generally view Erdrich as author of extraordinary talent and genuine cultural significance. She is praised for bringing attention to Native American life and for influencing other authors of multicultural literature through her works, which are credited with being among the first to present an authentic portrayal of their subjects. Erdrich has been compared to writers such as Charles Dickens, Mark Twain, Nathaniel Hawthorne, Herman Melville, and, especially, William Faulkner (whose Yoknapatawpha County often is paralleled with Argus, North Dakota, by critics). She is acclaimed for her realistic characterizations and for her understanding of and compassion for her characters. In addition, several of Erdrich's works have achieved best-seller status.

Writing in *Newsday,* Dan Cryer commented that Erdrich's books "transform the lives of quite ordinary contemporary Native Americans ... and their white neighbors into extraordinary art." P. Jane Hanfen of *Dictionary of Literary Biography* noted that the author's cycle of novels "is an extraordinary achievement. She has paradoxically created a Chippewa experience in the context of the European American novelistic tradition. Yet, she bends that tradition within the scope of storytelling, overlapping temporal and narrative techniques. Complemented by her other writings, the novels comprise an already-significant career." Writing in *Reference Guide to American Literature,* Peter G. Beidler concluded, "Erdrich is likely to be an enduring voice in American fiction.... She has done what all writers dream but few accomplish: created a world of her own in which enough of the characters breathe that it does not matter that others remain lifeless. She brings to American literature a timely and honest authenticity about the multiple cultures in the United States, moves easily in both the dominant and a minority culture, and knows how to write with grace and force about what it is to be a woman in contemporary America."

Born Karen Louise Erdrich in Little Falls, Minnesota, the author grew up in Wahpeton, North Dakota, where both of her parents were teachers in a boarding school that was run by the Bureau of Indian Affairs. Later, Erdrich would use the town of Wahpeton as the model for Argus in her "North Dakota" tales. As are some of her characters, Erdrich is a "blood," or mixed-blood Indian. Her father Ralph—who, according to family legend, was born in a tornado—is of German-American descent, and her mother Rita is Objibwa and French-American. Rita Erdrich was raised on the Turtle Mountain Reservation, where her father, Pat Gourneau, was the tribal chairperson. Through her mother, Erdrich is related to Kaishpau Gourneau, who was the tribal chairperson of the Turtle Mountain Band of Ojibwa in 1882; she used a derivation of his first name as the surname for one of the main families in her "North Dakota" novels. As a girl, Erdrich spent much of her time at the reservation, which later would become the model for Little No Horse. She gave the attributes of her family members to several of her characters; for example, Nector and Marie Kashpaw, a couple who appear in a number of the "North Dakota" books, have some traits of her maternal grandparents. Erdrich credits her maternal grandmother with teaching her about the conflicts between Native and white cultures; her maternal grandfather, who practiced both the Ojibwa and Roman Catholic faiths, gave her a sense of both traditions. Her grandfather also influenced Louise with his stories about the Great Depression and his experiences in a labor organization, the International Workers of the World. Erdrich's paternal grandparents were German immigrants who ran a butcher shop in Little Falls, the town where she was born; later, butcher shops would feature prominently in Erdrich's poetry and in several of her novels.

The eldest of seven children, Erdrich was a shy child who liked to listen and observe. However, in first grade at the local Catholic school, she was lively enough to be put into the Naughty Box, the place where disobedient children were sent; in *The Beet Queen,* her character Dot Adare also is placed in the Naughty Box. Erdrich has noted that much of her love of language is due to the fact that she grew up without a television set and without seeing many movies. Consequently, she read a lot and listened to oral literature. For example, Erdrich has woven some of her mother's stories of life on the reservation into her works, especially in *Tracks.* Ralph Erdrich recited poetry from authors like Lord Byron and Robert Frost to Louise and her siblings. Their father also introduced the children to the plays of Shakespeare: Louise would listen frequently to a recording of *King*

A young girl sees visions of the past in the window of her mother's old-fashioned wood stove, and as a young mother teaches her son to do the same. (From The Range Eternal, *illustrated by Steve Johnson and Lou Fancher.)*

Lear—"It has always been my ground text," she told Mark Anthony Rolo of the *Progressive*—on a little record player that Ralph had bought with green stamps. Erdrich also read and enjoyed the "Little House" books by Laura Ingalls Wilder; later, she would create *The Birchbark House,* a story that presents the same setting and time period—the Midwest during the 1800s and 1900s—from a Native American perspective. As a young girl, Erdrich began to write and draw her own books. She once commented, "My father used to give me a nickel for every story I wrote, and my mother wove strips of construction paper together and stapled them into book covers. So at an early age I felt myself to be a published author earning substantial royalties." Erdrich added, "Mine were wonderful parents. They got me excited about reading and writing in a lasting way." The literary atmosphere of the Erdrich home also had its effect on Louise's sisters Heidi and Lise, who are authors of fiction and poetry; Louise and Heidi have collaborated on short stories for magazines under the pseudonym Heidi Louise.

In high school, Erdrich listened to folksinger Joan Baez, dressed in her father's Army clothes, and joined the cheerleading squad for the wrestling team at her high school. She also began to write poetry, recording her efforts in a series of journals. After graduating from high school, Erdrich received a scholarship to Dartmouth College in Hanover, New Hampshire, a school that was founded originally to educate young Indians. In 1972, she became a member of the first Dartmouth class to admit women. At Dartmouth, Erdrich majored in English and creative writing and had her first poems published in the school's literary magazines. In her junior year, Erdrich was cited for her literary excellence by Dartmouth professor A. B. Paulson. Another teacher who lauded Erdrich for her scholastic ability was Michael Dorris, the director of the Native American Studies department. Dorris, who was half Modoc Indian, had arrived at Dartmouth on the same day as Erdrich; later, she would take his class in anthropology. Dorris convinced Erdrich to take classes in the Native American studies program, which he had founded; until that time, she had not explored her heritage formally. In her senior year, Erdrich had some of her poems accepted for national publication by *Ms.* magazine.

After graduating from Dartmouth, Erdrich worked as a teacher and visiting poet in schools for the North Dakota State Arts Council. She also worked at a variety of minimum-wage jobs, several of which have been represented in her novels. In 1979, Erdrich received a fellowship to attend Johns Hopkins University in Baltimore, Maryland. At Johns Hopkins, Erdrich taught classes and worked on the poems that she submitted for her master's thesis, as well as on *Tracks,* which was then a novel in progress. Erdrich borrowed sections from this manuscript for her early novels before reworking *Tracks* as her third book. In 1979, Erdrich received her master's degree in creative writing from Johns Hopkins; shortly thereafter, she moved to Boston to become the communications director for and editor of the *Circle,* a

newspaper published by the Boston Indian Council. At around the same time, she produced her first published book, *Imagination,* a textbook on writing for children. Erdrich returned to Dartmouth as a visiting fellow in 1980. At Dartmouth, she reconnected with Michael Dorris, with whom she had been corresponding by letter; they were married in 1981. At the time of their marriage, Dorris, who was born in 1945, already had produced a book of nonfiction, *Native Americans: Five Hundred Years After,* and had worked as an educator in California and New Hampshire. In addition, as one of the first single men in the United States to be approved as an adoptive father, he had adopted three Native American children, Abel, Sava, and Madeline. Later, Dorris and Erdrich had three daughters of their own, Persia, Pallas, and Aza.

The literary partnership between Erdrich and Dorris began when the couple began writing romance stories for magazines under the pseudonym Milou North, which came from a combination of their first names and from the location of their New Hampshire home. The stories, several of which were published in *Redbook,* a domestic magazine for women, were especially popular in Great Britain, where they appeared in the periodical *Woman.* Shortly after their marriage, Dorris became Erdrich's agent, and encouraged his wife, who was writing short stories, to compete for the Nelson Algren Fiction Award. Just before the deadline for submission, Erdrich completed "The World's Greatest Fisherman," the story that would become the opening chapter of *Love Medicine.* In 1982, Erdrich won the Algren Award, which often is credited with launching her career as a writer. In 1984, Erdrich produced her first volume of poetry, *Jacklight.* The first volume in her "North Dakota" saga, *Love Medicine,* made its debut the following year.

Love Medicine is a collection of fourteen interrelated short stories that features characters and speakers from four Ojibwa families: the Kashpaws, the Lamartines, the Morrisseys, and the Pillagers. The novel opens in the 1980s, goes back to the 1930s, and then returns to the 1980s. Named for the Native belief in love potions, the book has seven narrators, some unnamed. According to D. J. R. Bruckner of the *New York Times,* these narrators "unfold a score of interleaved stories of love, mystery, death, adventure, tragedy, and hope." *Love Medicine* begins at a family gathering following the death of June Kashpaw, a prostitute who had left Little No Horse to move to the city. After a tryst with a white engineer, June decides to walk back to the reservation, but freezes to death on the way. At their gathering in remembrance of June, the characters introduce one another by sharing stories about her that reveal their history and beliefs. The story of Nector Kashpaw, a tribal chief, and his wife Marie Lazarre Kashpaw, who has opened her home to abandoned children, provide the main narrative thread. Nector and Marie have been having marital difficulties, mostly because of Nector's wandering eye. He has begun an affair with Lulu Lamartine, an attractive married woman who has had eight children by eight different men. In order to rekindle the passion between

Nector and Marie, their grandson Lipsha Morrissey is asked by his grandmother to prepare "love medicine," a potion that will be given to Nector without his knowledge. Lipsha, a well-meaning boy with budding talents as a healer, finds that he is missing a key ingredient for the potion: the heart of a wild male goose. Instead, he substitutes a frozen turkey heart from the neighborhood supermarket. While eating his dinner, Nector chokes to death on the turkey heart. After Nector's death, he appears as a ghost to Marie, Lulu, and Lipsha until the latter banishes him back to the spirit world. At the conclusion of the novel, Marie and Lulu unite and become tribal elders, and Lipsha also discovers the identity of his father, Gerry Nanapush, a trickster and activist for Native American rights who often is at odds with the police.

Love Medicine is considered among the most successful and most complex of Erdrich's books. It was praised for introducing a new voice in American fiction, a voice that departed from the then-current trend of minimalism by using oral discourse in written form to provide an expansive, resonant, and unique view of Native American life. Writing in *Best Sellers,* Jeanne Kinney noted of Erdrich, "At age thirty, by capturing the depth of spirit of the Native through her artistry, she leaps into the role of major American novelist on her first try." Thomas M. Disch of Chicago *Tribune Books* said, "While her peers were writing just those novels that the young are expected to write, chronicling their first dates and drug busts, Erdrich lighted out into the territory of Literature, working on a scale, and with an artistry, that simply dwarfs her contemporaries." D. J. R. Bruckner of the *New York Times* stated, "There are at least a dozen of the many vividly drawn people in [this novel] who will not leave the mind." Elaine Jahner of *Parabola* concluded that the "compulsive fascination" of *Love Medicine* comes from the fact that Erdrich "knows how to tell grand stories about characters whose intensity shatters banality and leaves us rethinking the whole matter of being human." In 1993, Erdrich produced an expanded version of *Love Medicine* that included four new stories as well as additions to the existing tales.

Subsequent novels in the "North Dakota" series continue the stories of the protagonists from *Love Medicine* while introducing new characters and amplifying the stories of others. *The Beet Queen,* which covers the years 1932 to 1972, introduces two fatherless white children, Karl and Mary Adare, who are abandoned by their mother Adelaide when she runs off with a circus stunt pilot; forty years later, Adelaide's granddaughter Dot repeats family history when she flies off with another stunt pilot. However, rather than abandoning her family and friends, Dot decides to return to Argus. The next novel, *Tracks,* is a prequel that takes place between 1912 and 1924. Considered one of the author's most powerful works as well as her personal favorite, the novel has two main narrators, Nanapush, an Ojibwa tribal leader who survived the consumption epidemic of 1912, and Pauline Puyat, a mixed-blood Ojibwa who is ashamed of the Indian side of her heritage. Pauline denies her native

traditions in order to become Sister Leopolda, a Catholic nun. Nanapush is being pressured by the white government to give up Native land. He also discovers Fleur Pillager, a young woman who is the last member of her family left alive. Fleur, a mystical woman with magical powers, will become an important figure in later works; she also becomes the mother of Lulu Lamartine, Nector's love interest from the first novel.

Lipsha Morrissey of *Love Medicine* is the primary narrator of Erdrich's fourth novel, *The Bingo Palace,* a work that is set in the mid-1990s. The illegitimate son of June Kashpaw and Gerry Nanapush, Lipsha has returned to Little No Horse from the city in search of the meaning of his life. While working at a bingo parlor owned by his uncle Lyman Lamartine, Lipsha falls in love with his uncle's girlfriend, the powwow dancer Shawnee Ray Toose. Lipsha embarks on a spiritual vision quest in order to impress Shawnee, but gets sprayed by a skunk. In contrast to the comic events of the novel is Lipsha's personal journey: he works to accept his dead mother, June Kashpaw, who had tried to drown him as an infant, and his father, Gerry Nanapush, who often has been absent from his life. Finally, June appears to him as a spirit and gives Lipsha a book of magic bingo tickets that allows him to get a car. Shawnee decides to go to college, thus leaving both Lipsha and Lyman. However, Lipsha has become a whole person; by understanding his background, accepting his parents, and attaining some belief in himself, he is able to perform two noble acts. First, Lipsha helps his father Gerry escape from the police, driving him to Canada in a stolen car. Neither father nor son realizes that the car contains a baby. Trapped in a blizzard after his father escapes, Lipsha stays in the car rather than abandoning the child. He wraps the infant in his coat and awaits the future.

Tales of Burning Love centers on the five ex-wives of Jack Mauser, a mixed-blood Objibwa who was married to June Kashpaw. After her death, Jack remarries four times before faking his death in a house fire. Unaware of his ruse, the four women attend Jack's funeral. Riding together in a car after the service, they are trapped in a blizzard. In order to stay alive during the night, they swap stories about Jack and build strong relationships with each other. With *The Antelope Wife,* Erdrich introduced a new set of characters—the Roy, Shawingo, and Whiteheart Bead families—to her saga. Set mainly in and near Minneapolis, the novel focuses on the spiritual bonds between humans and animals while using multiple narrators to define the links between generations. The title character, an Ojibwa girl, is rescued by a cavalry soldier during an attack. He raises the girl as his own, until her mother comes to claim her. After the girl loses her mother, she is raised by a herd of antelope. When she grows up, the girl marries Indian trader Klaus Shawano; now the Antelope Wife, she uses her mysterious powers to link together the white and Native sides of the three families. In *The Last Report on the Miracles at Little No Horse,* Erdrich refers back to Sister Leopolda, the nun who, as Pauline Puyat, was one of the narrators of *Tracks.* Spanning the years 1912 to 1996, the novel describes how another nun, Agnes DeWitt, is forced to leave the convent because of her passion for music. She becomes the common-law wife of a German farmer, who is murdered by a bandit. During a flood, Agnes is washed away; although she survives, she loses her memory. After the flood, Agnes finds the drowned body of a Catholic priest, Damien Modeste, who was on his way to minister to the people of Little No Horse. Agnes decides to switch clothes—and identities—with Modeste.

In *The Master Butchers Singing Club,* Fidelis Waldvogel, a trained sniper with a beautiful singing voice, makes his way from Germany to America shortly after the end of World War I. Landing in Argus, he prospers as a butcher and forms a singing club with the best vocalists in the town. Fidelis is joined by his wife Eva and her young son—a boy who was fathered by Waldvogel's best friend, a man who had died in combat before his son was born. The Waldvogels meet Delphine Watza, a woman who runs a traveling circus show. Delphine befriends Eva, and acts as her nurse through her death from cancer. Delphine also falls in love with Fidelis. The novel takes the characters and their descendants through many changes, both to themselves and to their town. In assessing Erdrich's epic series as a whole, Jean Strouse of the *New York Times Book Review* commented, "Louise Erdrich has been populating a specific place—the Chippewa Indian reservation and its North Dakota-Minnesota surround—with characters as strong and original, as funny and tough, as furious and vivid as any who have recently graced the American literary landscape. Her sure sense of the way people think and talk keeps it hard to remember she is making them all up, and her lithe, athletic prose makes wildly improbable events seem as natural as the weather." Writing in *Booklist,* Bill Ott concluded, "It's high time to acknowledge that Erdrich's ongoing sequence of novels about Native American life on an Ojibwe reservation in North Dakota over the last century stands at the pinnacle of recent American fiction."

In addition to her works for adults, Erdrich has received acclaim as the author of picture books and historical fiction for children. Her first picture book, *Grandmother's Pigeons,* is a story that, like her books for adults, blends fantasy and reality. During a family vacation, Grandmother—a woman who trained kicking mules and skied the Continental Divide—announces that she always has wanted to see Greenland. To the amazement of her two grandchildren, the young narrator and her younger brother, Grandmother sails away on the back of an accommodating porpoise. A year after Grandmother's disappearance, the saddened family feel that they finally are ready to clean out her room. They find a twig nest that contains three eggs: the eggs hatch into passenger pigeons, a species that has been extinct since 1914. When the media and the scientific community find out what has happened, they descend on the family. Finally, the children decide to release the birds. Before doing so, they tie a message to Grandmother on the leg of one of the pigeons. The story ends with a letter from Grand-

mother, who promises to return home. Writing in *Booklist,* Ilene Cooper noted, "Children reside in the world of magic realism, and this offering by adult books author Louise Erdrich will both tantalize them and make them feel utterly at home.... Besides the sense of the unexpected that permeates every page is the freshness of the language.... The writing is never over children's heads.... Like the pigeons, this is a rare bird—a book that evokes wonder, in both its meanings." Harriett Fargnoli of *School Library Journal* called *Grandmother's Pigeons* "a moving paen to a mysterious grandmother and a fantasy as well," before concluding that the book is "a small gem, a bit of a puzzle, and a delight to pore over and ponder." Nancy Caldwell Sorel of the *New York Times Book Review* commented, "We know Louise Erdrich as a writer of luminous poetry and fiction and a perceptive observer of the natural world, so we expect *Grandmother's Pigeons* to excel both in style and history. In fact, it soars. Never mind that a few words will have to be explained to a young child the first (and perhaps second) time around; this is a book for many times around."

Erdrich's second picture book is *The Range Eternal,* a reminiscence about growing up in the Turtle Mountains of North Dakota. In this work, a little Ojibwa girl lives with her family in a home that is heated by the Range Eternal, a cast-iron, wood-burning stove with its brand name emblazoned on its front. The girl is both warmed and comforted by the Range Eternal: at night, she lays by it and feels protected from the Windigo, the ice-monster that she imagines is lurking beside the house. The Range Eternal also provides a source for imaginative play. As the girl stares into the flames, she sees another kind of range—the one where the deer, the eagle, the buffalo, the fox, and the wolf all live, and where she herself has played. When electricity comes to Turtle Mountain, the Range Eternal is taken away and replaced by an electric range. After the girl grows up, she becomes a married woman with a small son of her own. The woman finds a Range Eternal in an antique store, brings it home, and teaches her son to enter the pictures that the flames make, just as she did as a child. A reviewer in *Publishers Weekly* observed, "Erdrich skillfully weaves family memories into a poignant and lyrical story of home and hearth. The symbolism may be more moving to adults, but the theme of family and reservation will resonate with children." Noting the "sensitive yet down-to-earth tone of the text," Carolyn Phelan of *Booklist* stated, "The most memorable part of the story is Erdrich's clearly conceived, detail-studded depiction of the child's life." Writing in *School Library Journal,* Susan Oliver concluded by calling *The Range Eternal* an "evocative glimpse into the past."

The first of a projected series of stories for children, *The Birchbark House* was inspired by Erdrich's efforts to retrace the history of her family. The cycle of stories begins in the mid-1800s and is projected to conclude a century later. Divided into four seasons, during which the Ojibwa characters move to find food and shelter, *The Birchbark House* chronicles the year 1847 in the life of an Ojibwa girl, seven-year-old Omakayas, who lives on Madeline Island on Lake Superior. A brave and kind child, Omakayas is a survivor. As a baby, she alone escaped the smallpox epidemic that decimated her people. Omakayas was rescued by Old Tallow, a strong and solitary woman who brought the infant to live with an Ojibwa family on the island. Now, as an adopted child with no knowledge of her past, Omakayas enjoys life within her tightly-knit community. However, things change when a French "voyageur" comes to spend the night in the village. Thin and feverish, the man dies shortly after his arrival—he has brought smallpox to Madeline Island. In the subsequent epidemic, Omakayas again is spared from the disease. She nurses her loved ones, most of whom survive; however, Omakayas loses her beloved baby brother to smallpox. Old Tallow helps Omakayas to regain her strength through both food and story. She tells the girl about her past and helps her to understand life and death as well as her role in society. Finally, Omakayas realizes that she will become a healer of her community. Weaving Ojibwa words and customs into her text, Erdrich illustrated *The Birchbark House* with small, detailed portraits in pencil that she drew from photographs.

Writing about *The Birchbark House* in *Booklist,* Hazel Rochman asked, "Why are there so few good children's books about the people displaced by the little house in the big woods?.... Erdrich makes us imagine what it was like for an Ojibwa Indian child when the chimooko-man (non-Indian white people) were opening up the land.... Little House readers will discover a new world, a different version of a story they thought they knew." Writing on her *Children's Literature Site,* Carol Hurst commented that *The Birchbark House* "is what many of us have been seeking for many years, a good story through which the Native American culture during the Westward Expansion of the United States is realistically and sympathetically portrayed.... It's the good story and strong characterizations that lift what could have been earnest and dull into the realm of good literature. If you are introducing children of any culture to that period of United States history or just looking for a good book to share, you will want this book to begin to balance the picture." A reviewer in *Publishers Weekly* noted, "Universal themes and situations are woven together with historical facts to create a story as enlightening as it is entertaining." Writing in *Contemporary Novelists,* a critic projected that the series of novels beginning with *The Birchbark House* "promises to be an important, fruitful addition to the historical novel genre for children." In an interview with Hazel Rochman of *Booklist,* Erdrich commented, "These are the people who are mentioned in passing in travelers' journals, people who impressed or somehow surprised the non-Indian travelers. I feel very lucky to have a chance to bring them to life, into the present, somehow, to draw a connection."

After the death of her husband, Erdrich moved from New Hampshire to Minneapolis, which is close to her parents in North Dakota. In 2000, she added another

profession to those of writer and educator: bookstore owner. When the author and her daughters discovered an abandoned storefront in the Kenwood neighborhood of Minneapolis, they saw its potential and opened Birchbark Books. The store, an independent, nonprofit venture that specializes in Native Americana, includes Native literature, music, and art and also serves as a community resource and gathering place, offering readings, craft demonstrations, and Ojibwa language classes, among other services. At the age of forty-six, Erdrich became a mother for the fourth time: she had a daughter, Azure, with an Ojibwa man whose identity she prefers to keep to herself. In assessing her work as an author, Erdrich told William Swanson of *MPLS-St. Paul Magazine,* "I think of it as a huge tangle, a huge knot. Sometimes I grab a piece of the string and I work on straightening it out." Erdrich noted that her characters "have come to me—I haven't chosen them. They do seem to have a life of their own.... They come and they speak to me." She told Karen Olson of *Book,* "These are the people who came and talked to me way back when. And they keep talking to me, so I have to keep writing about them. I don't have a real choice about it. It's not like I can say, 'Now, I'm finished,' because they come back, and they have another story to tell."

Biographical and Critical Sources

BOOKS

Beidler, Peter G., and Guy Barton, *A Reader's Guide to the Novels of Louise Erdrich,* University of Missouri Press (Columbia, MO), 1999.

Chaikin, Allan, and Nancy Feyl Chaikin, editors, *Conversations with Louise Erdrich and Michael Dorris,* University Press of Mississippi (Jackson, MS), 1994.

Contemporary Literary Criticism, Gale (Detroit, MI), Volume 39: Yearbook 1985, 1986; Volume 54, 1989; Volume 120, 1999.

Contemporary Novelists, 7th edition, edited by Neil Schlager and Josh Lauer, St. James Press (Detroit, MI), 2001.

Dictionary of Literary Biography, Gale (Detroit, MI), Volume 152: *American Novelists Since World War II,* 1995; Volume 175: *Native American Writers of the United States,* 1997; Volume 206: *Twentieth-Century American Western Writers,* 1997.

Reference Guide to American Literature, 4th edition, edited by Thomas Riggs, St. James Press (Detroit, MI), 2000.

PERIODICALS

Atlantic Monthly, January 17, 2001, Katie Bacon, "An Emissary of the In-Between World."

Best Sellers, December, 1984, Jeanne Kinney, review of *Love Medicine,* pp. 324-325.

Book, May, 2001, Karen Olson, "The Complicated Life of Louise Erdrich," p. 32.

Booklist, May 1, 1996, Ilene Cooper, review of *Grandmother's Pigeons,* p. 1502; April 1, 1999, Hazel Rochman, "Little House on the Lake," and review of *The Birchbark House,* p. 1427; February 15, 2001, Bill Ott, review of *The Last Report on the Miracles at Little*

No Horse, p. 1085; October 1, 2002, Carolyn Phelan, review of *The Range Eternal,* p. 334.

MPLS—St. Paul Magazine, April, 2001, William Swanson, "Louise Erdrich Hears Voices," p. 74.

Newsday, November 30, 1986, Dan Cryer, "A Novel Arrangement," pp. 19-23.

New York Times, December 20, 1984, D. J. R. Bruckner, review of *Love Medicine,* p. C21.

New York Times Book Review, October 2, 1988, Jean Strouse, "In the Heart of the Heartland," pp. 1, 41-42; November 10, 1996, Nancy Caldwell Sorel, review of *Grandmother's Pigeons,* p. 49.

Parabola, May, 1985, Elaine Jahner, review of *Love Medicine,* pp. 96, 98, 100.

Progressive, April, 2002, Mark Anthony Rolo, interview with Louise Erdrich, p. 36.

Publishers Weekly, January 14, 2002, review of *The Birchbark House* (audio book), p. 26; September 9, 2002, review of *The Range Eternal,* p. 67.

School Library Journal, July, 1996, Harriett Fargnoli, review of *Grandmother's Pigeons,* p. 59; October, 2002, Susan Oliver, review of *The Range Eternal,* p. 104.

Tribune-Books (Chicago), September 4, 1988, Thomas M. Disch, "Enthralling Tale: Louise Erdrich's World of Love and Survival," pp. 1, 6.

OTHER

Birchbark Books Web site, http://www.birchbarkbooks.com/ (March 4, 2003).

Carol Hurst's Children's Literature Site, http://www.carolhurst.com/ (November, 1999), Carol Hurst, review of *The Birchbark House.**

*   *   *

ERICKSON, Jon 1948-

Personal

Born April 3, 1948, in Fosston, MN; son of Stuert (with the FAA) and Hazel (Peterson) Erickson. *Education:* University of Arkansas, M.S.

Addresses

Home—2051 K Road, Fruita, CO 81521.

Career

Geologist and writer.

Writings

"DISCOVERING EARTH SCIENCE" SERIES

The Mysterious Oceans, TAB Books (Blue Ridge Summit, PA), 1988.

Violent Storms, TAB Books (Blue Ridge Summit, PA), 1988.

Volcanoes and Earthquakes, TAB Books (Blue Ridge Summit, PA), 1988.

Exploring Earth from Space, TAB Books (Blue Ridge Summit, PA), 1989.

The Living Earth: The Coevolution of the Planet and Life, TAB Books (Blue Ridge Summit, PA), 1989.

Greenhouse Earth; Tomorrow's Disaster Today, TAB Books (Blue Ridge Summit, PA), 1990.

Ice Ages: Past and Future, TAB Books (Blue Ridge Summit, PA), 1990.

Dying Planet: The Extinction of Species, TAB Books (Blue Ridge Summit, PA), 1991.

Target Earth!: Asteroid Collisions Past and Future, TAB Books (Blue Ridge Summit, PA), 1991.

World out of Balance: Our Polluted Planet, TAB Books (Blue Ridge Summit, PA), 1992.

"THE LIVING EARTH" SERIES

An Introduction to Fossils and Minerals: Seeking Clues to the Earth's Past, Facts on File (New York, NY), 1992, revised edition, 2000.

Plate Tectonics: Unraveling the Mysteries of the Earth, Facts on File (New York, NY), 1992, revised edition, 2001.

Rock Formations and Unusual Geologic Structures: Exploring the Earth's Surface, Facts on File (New York, NY), 1993, revised edition, 2001.

Quakes, Eruptions and Other Geologic Cataclysms: Revealing the Earth's Hazards, Facts on File (New York, NY), 1994, revised edition, 2001.

Marine Geology: Undersea Landforms and Life Forms, Facts on File (New York, NY), 1996, revised edition, 2002.

Making of the Earth: Geologic Forces that Shape our Planet, Facts on File (New York, NY), 2000.

Lost Creatures of the Earth: Mass Extinction in the History of Life, Facts on File (New York, NY), 2002.

Environmental Geology: Facing the Challenge of Our Changing Earth, Facts on File (New York, NY), 2002.

Historical Geology: Understanding Our Planet's Past, Facts on File (New York, NY), 2002.

Asteroids, Comets and Meteorites: Cosmic Invaders of the Earth, Facts on File (New York, NY), 2002.

"THE CHANGING EARTH" SERIES

Craters, Caverns and Canyons: Delving Beneath the Earth's Surface, Facts on File (New York, NY), 1993.

The Human Volcano: Population Growth as Geologic Force, Facts on File (New York, NY), 1995.

A History of Life on Earth: Understanding Our Planet's Past, Facts on File (New York, NY), 1995.

Glacial Geology: How Ice Shapes the Land, Facts on File (New York, NY), 1996.

Sidelights

Author Jon Erickson has blended a professional interest in geology and related topics with a penchant for writing with "signature clarity and liveliness," according to *Booklist's* Donna Seaman. The result is two dozen books in the earth sciences for junior high and high school readers in three different series: "Discovering Earth Science," "The Changing Earth," and "The Living Earth." Erickson's books entertain as well as inform, and have been commended by reviewers for their reader-friendly prose as well as their scholarly approach. He has written on topics from the environment—such as the population explosion and the greenhouse effect—to the formation of the earth and plate tectonics.

Born in 1948, in Fosston, Minnesota, Erickson earned his master's degree in natural science and geology at the University of Arkansas, and began writing for young readers in 1988 with his first title in the "Discovering Earth Science" series. His *The Mysterious Oceans* was a "timely" book, according to a *Kliatt* reviewer, who further praised Erickson's description of the history, biology, and chemistry of the world's oceans in "clear, nontechnical terms." Topics from ocean pollution and over-fishing to the influence of oceans on weather are covered in the title. Writing in *Voice of Youth Advocates*, Linda Palter praised this series starter as a "well-written and interesting science book." Erickson takes a look at climate and weather in another series title, *Violent Storms*, "nearly an encyclopedic treatment of the subject," as Mick Tuccillo noted in *Voice of Youth Advocates*. Tuccillo further remarked that Erickson does

more than merely look at bad weather; his book also focuses on good and not-so-good weather, on the folklore of weather, and even on "nuclear winter." Tuccillo praised Erickson's "clear and concise" narrative, tempering "scientific fact with a graceful literary technique." A reviewer for *Times Educational Supplement* also called the same title "readable and well illustrated."

Erickson also explored topics from volcanoes to the future of the earth in this first series. His *Volcanoes and Earthquakes* is an "excellent general text for anyone with a basic understanding of geology," according to *Booklist*'s George R. Hampton. With *Exploring Earth from Space*, Erickson chronicles our attempts at a better understanding of this planet's geology by a study of the geology of other planets and by a view of planet Earth from space. Carole Mann, writing in *Book Report*, found this to be a "browsable volume [that] demonstrates a thorough exploration of the geological uses of space." *Dying Planet*, on the other hand, offers a very different view of this planet. As Jon Kartman noted in a *Booklist* review, "We view Earth as the planet of life, but perhaps

Jon Erickson explains the causes and environmental effects of geological hazards such as volcanoes, landslides, dust storms, and meteor showers in **Quakes, Eruptions and Other Geologic Cataclysms.** *(Photo courtesy of the USGS.)*

it's more accurately seen as the planet of death." Erickson's book takes a look at five major periods of extinction in Earth's history; in these periods half or more of the species alive died out. Kartman called Erickson's book both "sobering and frightening." The author details causes of such extinctions, from meteors hitting Earth to volcanism on the planet. Most sobering of all is Erickson's contention that we are entering another period of extinction now, spurred on by man's tampering with the biological balance. Frances Bradburn, reviewing the same title in *Wilson Library Bulletin,* praised Erickson's use of "fascinating detail."

Erickson further explores climatic change on this planet in *Greenhouse Earth* and *Ice Ages.* In the former book he gives a "useful" overview of the subject of global warming, according to Susan Hamilton, writing in *Appraisal: Science Books for Young People.* In *Ice Ages* he traces historical periods as well as makes forecasts of ice ages to come, discussing how ice not only shaped the landscape but also determined climate and biological changes. *Booklist*'s Hampton commended Erickson for making complex topics and interrelationships "easy to grasp." *Target Earth!* examines the geological record for asteroid collisions with Earth and speaks of the possibility of such future occurrences. Janet Hofstetter, reviewing this title in *Book Report,* was less than enthused, finding the author's account to be full of "gloom and doom," and also questioning some of the science. In *World out of Balance* Erickson "makes a strong case for cleaning up the planet by presenting well-documented evidence of pollution and its consequences," according to *Kliatt*'s Sue E. Budin. The same critic concluded that although some of his arguments are "a bit simplistic and one-sided," Erickson makes a "compelling case for humankind to clean up its act." Other reviewers, however, including L. H. Stevenson in *Choice,* found that Erickson's "passion for environmental protection" leads to "scientific integrity [being] severely compromised." Herbert J. Mason, writing in *Science Books and Films,* also complained that a "great deal of technical information [is presented] in the form of generalizations without specific supporting documentation."

For Facts on File publishers, Erickson has created two series, or actually one that has evolved into the other. The early books in what was called "The Changing Earth" series mostly were later revised for a second series, "The Living Earth." Again, Erickson surveys a wide variety of topics in earth sciences, beginning with *An Introduction to Fossils and Minerals,* a book that presents "interesting and important information on earth's history in less than 300 pages," according to Lori D. Kranz, writing in *American Reference Books Annual.* Kranz also praised Erickson's "clear and interesting" writing. This 1992 title was revised in the year 2000 to incorporate new discoveries in earth sciences which could help to shed some light on the history of our planet. The same format was maintained, however, from its original edition, a format that holds true for all titles in the series. The books, all around 200 pages, are divided into ten chapters, beginning with a history of the

Erickson's **Lost Creatures of the Earth,** *illustrated by Jeremy Eagle and Dale Dyer, explains the mass extinction of species such as the giant ground sloth.*

topic, and proceeding to various more specialized aspects of that topic. Included also are charts, maps, illustrations, and tables, as well as a glossary, and bibliography of articles from periodicals found in most general use libraries. A hallmark of all the books in the series is Erickson's "well-developed expository prose style that is especially appropriate for making complex scientific principles understandable to a layperson," as Sally Kramer noted in a *RQ* review of a book in the "Changing Earth" series, *Craters, Caverns and Canyons.*

Plate Tectonics, the second title in the series, deals not only with such mechanics at work on our planet, but on other bodies in the solar system, as well. Claudia Moore, writing in *School Library Journal,* found that title "quite comprehensive" yet "appropriate for ninth-grade students." Kartman, writing in *Booklist,* praised both early titles for their mixture of illustrations and "clear, straightforward prose [that] make them a wellspring of information." More basic geological concepts are presented in *Rock Formations and Unusual Geologic Structures,* a book that is, on the whole, "refreshingly clear," and one that will "entertain the reader with the wonders of the rock world," according to C. J. Casella, writing in *Choice.* Erickson expands on this topic in *Craters, Caverns and Canyons,* a title which hardly does justice to the "broad scope of the book," as Donald R. Coates noted in *Science Books and Films.* Here Erickson tackles subjects from petrology to geomorphology, employing what *Booklist*'s Donna Seaman referred to as "crisp descriptions" along the way. Coates dubbed the book "quitre authoritative and readable," while a reviewer for *Book Report* called his approach in the same title and others in the series "unique" and written in "reader friendly fashion."

Further titles deal with topics from population explosion to earthquakes and the oceans. *The Human Volcano* focuses on population growth and ensuing environmental degradation, a major concern for Erickson. M. Evans, writing in *Choice,* found the work "interesting—albeit academically superficial," while Lane Jennings, writing for *Futurist,* thought the book was "written in a style that young people as well as adult readers can enjoy." In his *Quakes, Eruptions and Other Geologic Cataclysms,* Erickson "masterfully presents" the mechanisms of such earth-shaping events, according to *Booklist*'s Hampton. "A work of wide appeal," added T. L. T. Grose in *Choice.* And a reviewer for *School Library Journal* also praised the title, calling it an "excellent geological resource."

With the 244 pages of *A History of Life on Earth,* Erickson "covers billions of years of the Earth's geological and biological history," according to Dino Vretos in *School Library Journal.* Vretos went on to commend the writer for making the processes involved in such a history "understandable and plausible." Marilyn Brien, writing in *Voice of Youth Advocates,* found that Erickson's book "contains a wealth of information on historical geography and paleontology." The author's *Marine Geology* takes readers closer to the Earth's core in an "instructive and useful book," according to Seaman in *Booklist.* Claudia Moore, writing in *School Library Journal,* found the same title provided a "much-needed, but seldom seen, link between usually isolated disciplines of geology, oceanography, and biology." *Glacial Geology* serves the same function for the sculpting power of ice. It is, as J. T. Andrews wrote in *Choice,* a "broad treatment of episodes of glaciation within the context of earth history."

Further titles in "The Living Earth" series include *Making of the Earth* and *Lost Creatures of the Earth,* from 2000 and 2002 respectively. Seaman called the former title a "well-illustrated overview of geomorphology" in a *Booklist* review, and added that Erickson "vividly explain[s]" forces from mountain building to volcanoes and tectonics. *Lost Creatures of the Earth* is a "scholarly work," as Patricia Manning noted in *School Library Journal.* Erickson examines mass extinction in the history of life on Earth, a title similar to his earlier *Dying Planet.* Manning also lauded the author's "readable" text and the "vast amount of factual material" presented, hallmarks of all his work.

Biographical and Critical Sources

PERIODICALS

American Reference Books Annual, 2001, Lori D. Kranz, review of *An Introduction to Fossils and Minerals,* p. 703.

Appraisal: Science Books for Young People, winter, 1991, Susan Hamilton, review of *Greenhouse Earth,* pp. 14-15; winter, 1992, Charlotte A. Pavelko, review of *Dying Planet,* pp. 23-24; fall, 1996, Sarah Helman, review of *Glacial Geology,* p. 42.

Booklist, January 1, 1989, George R. Hampton, review of *Volcanoes and Earthquakes* and *Violent Storms,* pp. 736-737; October 1, 1990, George Hampton, review of *Ice Ages,* pp. 235-236; June 1, 1991, Jon Kartman, review of *Dying Planet,* p. 1848; April 15, 1992, Jon Kartman, review of *An Introduction to Fossils and Minerals* and *Plate Tectonics,* p. 1490; May 1, 1993, Donna Seaman, review of *Craters, Caverns and Canyons,* p. 1556; August, 1994, George Hampton, review of *Quakes, Eruptions and Other Geologic Cataclysms,* p. 2008; December 1, 1995, Donna Seaman, review of *Marine Geology,* p. 596; December 1, 2000, Donna Seaman, review of *Making of the Earth,* p. 683.

Book Report, January, 1990, Carol Mann, review of *Exploring Earth from Space,* p. 62; September, 1991, Janet Hofstetter, review of *Target Earth!,* p. 54; January, 1993, Liz Hunter, review of *An Introduction to Fossils and Minerals,* p. 59; December, 1993, review of *Craters, Caverns and Canyons.*

Choice, January, 1991, D. J. Ives, review of *Ice Ages,* p. 798; October, 1992, L. H. Stevenson, review of *World Out of Balance,* p. 320; December, 1993, C. J. Casella, review of *Rock Formations and Unusual Geologic Structures,* p. 633; January, 1995, T. L. T. Grose, review of *Quakes, Eruptions and Other Geologic Cataclysms,* p. 818; September, 1995, M. Evans, review of *The Human Volcano,* p. 148; September, 1996, J. T. Andrews, review of *Glacial Geology,* p. 158; November, 1996, J. T. Andrews, review of *Marine Geology,* p. 487.

Futurist, July-August, 1995, Lane Jennings, review of *The Human Volcano,* p. 63.

Horn Book Guide, fall, 1991, Daniel Brabander, review of *Target Earth!,* p. 295; spring, 1996, Danielle J. Ford, review of *A History of Life on Earth,* p. 105.

Kliatt, January, 1989, review of *The Mysterious Oceans,* p. 56; November, 1992, Sue E. Budin, review of *World Out of Balance,* p. 42.

RQ, winter, 1993, Sally Kramer, review of *Craters, Caverns and Canyons,* pp. 281-282.

School Library Journal, March, 1993, Claudia Moore, review of *An Introduction to Fossils and Minerals* and *Plate Tectonics,* pp. 240-241; November, 1994, review of *Quakes, Eruptions and Geologic Cataclysms,* p. 146; May, 1996, Dino Vretos, review of *A History of Life on Earth,* pp. 150-151; July, 1996, Claudia Moore, review of *Glacial Geology* and *Marine Geology,* p. 109; August, 2002, Patricia Manning, review of *Lost Creatures of the Earth,* p. 137.

Science Activities, winter, 1994, John W. McLure, review of *Craters, Caverns and Canyons,* p. 41.

Science Books and Films, May, 1992, Herbert J. Mason, review of *World Out of Balance,* p. 107; November, 1993, Donald R. Coates, review of *Craters, Caverns and Canyons;* August, 1995, Kathleen Human, review of *The Human Volcano,* p. 170.

Times Educational Supplement, March 24, 1989, review of *Violent Storms,* p. 36.

Voice of Youth Advocates, February, 1989, Linda Palter, review of *The Mysterious Oceans,* p. 300; April, 1989, Mick Tuccillo, review of *Violent Storms,* pp. 55-56; February, 1996, Marilyn Brien, review of *A History of Life on Earth,* pp. 392-393.

Wilson Library Bulletin, November, 1991, Frances Bradburn, review of *Dying Planet,* pp. 94-95.

FUQUA, Jonathon Scott 1966-

Personal

Born March 26, 1966, in Frankfurt, Germany; son of William Claiborne and Mary Cary (a psychologist; maiden name, Monet; present surname, Johnston) Fuqua; married Julie Ann Lauffenburger (an art conservator), September 18, 1993; children: Calla Grace. *Education:* College of William and Mary, graduated, 1990. *Politics:* Democrat. *Religion:* Episcopalian. *Hobbies and other interests:* Running, history, travel, hiking, reading.

Addresses

Home and office—2209 Lake Ave., Baltimore, MD 21213. *Agent*—Robbie Anna Hare, Goldfarb and Associates, 1501 M St., Suite 1150, Washington, DC 20005. *E-mail*—jonathon_fuqua@yahoo.com.

Career

Center of Marine Biotechnology, Baltimore, MD, naturalist artist and writer, 1991-93; Baltimore City Life Museums, Baltimore, MD, coordinator of special projects, 1993-96; writer, 1996—. Seminar leader and speaker at middle schools, high schools, colleges, and universities.

Awards, Honors

Three fiction awards from Maryland State Arts Council, beginning 1993; Editor's Choice Award, *Booklist,* citation among "best books of the year," *School Library Journal* and *Library Journal,* citation among "best books for the teen age," New York Public Library, all 1999, and Alex Award, 2000, all for *The Reappearance of Sam Webber.*

Writings

The American Rowhouse Classic Designs (illustrations), Stemmer House (Owings Mills, MD), 1997.
The Reappearance of Sam Webber (young adult novel), Bancroft Press (Baltimore, MD), 1999.
Darby (young adult novel), Candlewick Press (Cambridge, MA), 2002.
Catie & Josephine, Houghton Mifflin (Boston, MA), 2003.
The Willoughby Spit Wonder, Candlewick Press (Cambridge, MA), 2004.

Author, illustrator, and director of the multimedia educational series *The Treasure of the Chesapeake,* published by Sea Grant College; author and illustrator of a children's book, *B & O: America's Railroad,* for B & O Railroad Museum. Contributor to *In the Shadow of Edgar Allan Poe,* Vertigo Comics; contributor of illustrations to the "Core Knowledge Series" of textbooks. Contributor to *Baltimore Sun.*

Sidelights

Jonathon Scott Fuqua told *SATA:* "I was born in Germany, and my family relocated eleven times before I was fourteen years old. New schools and situations were a constant fixture in my life until, on my fourteenth birthday, my mother put a stop to our travels and settled us in her family's home in Norfolk, Virginia. Except for art classes, I had, to that point, never enjoyed school. I was embarrassed that I couldn't memorize simple math formulas and that I spelled so poorly. Even though I was actually a pretty good student, it was always a struggle for me.

"After high school, I attended the College of William and Mary in Williamsburg, Virginia, where I began concentrating on art and art history. During my sophomore year, however, I took an adolescent literature course. Entranced by the language and subject matter, and despite my poor spelling, I tested into a fiction-writing class, where I began scratching out a succession of half-decent autobiographical short stories.

"About that time, a series of tests indicated that I was dyslexic. In a way, I was relieved by the news—to know that it wasn't laziness or stupidity that made school so hard. From then on, my writing really gained confidence and momentum.

"After earning my bachelor's degree, I moved to Charlottesville, Virginia, where I penned movie reviews at a small-town paper called the *Charlottesville Observer.* I also illustrated portions of E. D. Hirsche's critically acclaimed 'Core Knowledge Series' of textbooks. And in the hours between assignments, I wrote constantly.

"A year later, I knew that I had met my future wife, and I moved to Baltimore to be near her. I took a part-time position as a naturalist writer and artist at the Center of Marine Biotechnology. Working hand in hand with scientists, I illustrated specimens, diagramed laboratory techniques, and wrote, illustrated, and directed the multimedia educational series, 'The Treasure of the Chesapeake,' eventually published by the Sea Grant College. All the while, I continued to write, and in 1993 I received a Maryland State Arts Council fiction-writing award for outstanding literary achievement.

"That same year, I switched jobs and took a position at the Baltimore City Life Museums. I was responsible for conducting oral history interviews with a vast spectrum of individuals, including well-known personalities and working-class Baltimoreans. My subject matter extended from the civil rights movement to block-busting, from suburbanization and the fast-food industry to the development of gas stations and Baltimore's jazz scene. The wide variety of research enabled me to write many historical dramas, as well as a large production for the Maryland Science Center, 'Coffee and Comets and the Starlight Diner.' All of that historical research began seeping into my fiction writing, expanding my interests and my subject matter.

"Upon leaving the Baltimore City Life Museums in 1996, I painted a series of postcards and book covers, wrote and illustrated a children's book, *B & O: America's Railroad,* and had a book of illustrations, *American Rowhouse Classic Designs,* published. I also completed a manuscript titled 'In the Faded Light of Baltimore,' about a boy thrust into an unfamiliar world. That story would become *The Reappearance of Sam Webber.*

"*Sam Webber* was purchased by tiny Bancroft Press in the summer of 1997 and finally hit bookstores in the spring of 1999. Since then, it has received numerous honors and a good deal of critical recognition.

"In the spring of 2002 my second novel, *Darby,* came out. I couldn't be happier with it. Candlewick Press really took a strong interest in it immediately and helped me hone the book with incredible precision. Based very, very loosely on a series of oral history interviews I conducted in Marlboro County, South Carolina, *Darby* has a wonderful sound, feel, and cadence. The story deals with an aspect of southern history that has been somewhat lost, and Darby's character was a joy to see through and write from.

"Right now, I continue to write and learn, and my work is maturing and changing appropriately."

G–H

GEORGE, Sally
See ORR, Wendy

*   *   *

GIAMBASTIANI, Kurt R. A. 1958-

Personal

Name is pronounced *Jeeahm-bahs-tee-AH-nee*; born December 4, 1958; son of Ronald Achilles Giambastiani (a lithographer) and Dellores Dymond; married Ilene Fay Schoenfeld, July 30, 1983. *Education:* San Francisco State University, 1976-78; Rubin Academy of Music, 1978-79. *Politics:* "Reluctant Democrat." *Religion:* Jewish.

Addresses

Home—16034 Burke Ave. N., Shoreline, WA 98133. *Agent*—Eleanor Wood, Spectrum Literary Agency, 320 Central Park West, Ste. 1-D, New York, NY 10025. *E-mail*—kurtrag@earthlink.net.

Career

Author. Worked as a teller and head teller in banks in Greenbrae, Mill Valley, and San Luis Obispo, CA, 1980-85; and as an analyst and programmer for information technology and insurance companies in Seattle and Bellevue, WA, 1985—.

Writings

SHORT STORIES

Bio-Dome, Alexandria Digital Entertainment, 1998.
Veiled Glimpses, Alexandria Digital Entertainment, 1998.
Supplanter, Alexandria Digital Entertainment, 1998.
Sum of the Angles, Alexandria Digital Entertainment, 1998.
Still Falling, Alexandria Digital Entertainment, 1998.
Spencer's Peace, Alexandria Digital Entertainment, 1998.

In this work of alternate history, a young Cheyenne woman believes the son of U.S. President George Armstrong Custer, captured after his experimental dirigible falls from the sky, has been sent to save them from eighty years of conflict with the government.

"FALLEN CLOUD" SAGA

The Year the Cloud Fell: An Alternate History, Onyx (New York, NY), 2001.
The Spirit of Thunder: An Alternate History, ROC (New York, NY), 2002.
Shadow of the Storm: An Alternate History, ROC (New York, NY), 2003.

Contributor to *Oceans of the Mind, MZB's Fantasy Magazine, Talebones, Tomorrow, Year 2000, Dragon Magazine, Air Fish, Midnight Zoo, Science Fiction Review,* and *Vision.*

Work in Progress

Cry of the Wind: An Alternate History, book 4 in Fallen Cloud Saga, due in 2004; *Khamsin, a Modern Fantasy of the Middle East* (suspense); *Rootbound* (mainstream), and *The Ploughman Chronicles* (fantasy). Research on cathedral building in the tenth century, the necropolis of Alexandria, and the conscious mind.

Sidelights

Kurt R. A. Giambastiani once commented: "My first artistic endeavors were musical, playing viola and violin in symphonies and quartets, and in them I experienced firsthand the reciprocal and interactive joy of creative performance. I tend, therefore, to bring that same view to my writing. For me, writing is not a solitary activity that I achieve alone in a room with pen and paper; writing is a performance, albeit a greatly extended one. Thus, my relationship with my readers is very important to me. I listen to what they say, through letters and e-mails. I'm not talking about critics and reviewers here; they're not talking to me and, in general, there's no pleasing them. I'm talking about everyday readers, the people who buy my books. Many of them take the time to write me a note to tell me what their favorite parts were and what they hope to see in the future. And I listen to them. I'm writing, after all, for their enjoyment.

"I want to create a story that grips my readers and carries them forward through the plot. The best way to do that is with good characterizations. I strive to create characters that my readers care about, and in order to care about someone, you first must understand them. That's why I work so hard to make my characters comprehensible, especially the antagonists. My editors will tell you that I always argue strongest to keep those sections that explain a character's background or motivation. Stories, after all, are about people. Stories tell us about ourselves, about what we're good at, and what we still need to work on. Stories tell us about being human. Whether they're set in Iron Age Egypt or on a twenty-fourth-century colony on Mars, stories are about us, or they're about nothing at all."

Biographical and Critical Sources

PERIODICALS

Booklist, February 1, 2003, Roland Green, review of *Shadow of the Storm,* p. 979.
Kliatt, July, 2001, Gail E. Roberts, review of *The Year the Cloud Fell,* p. 26.

*   *   *

GILMAN, Phoebe 1940-2002

OBITUARY NOTICE—See index for *SATA* sketch: Born April 4, 1940, in New York, NY; died of leukemia August 29, 2002, in Toronto, Ontario, Canada. Educator and author. Gilman was a popular author and illustrator of children's picture books and was best known for her series character Jillian Jiggs. In love with art and illustration since she was a child, Gilman studied at the Art Students' League and Hunter College in New York during the late 1950s. She then moved to Israel, where she lived for four years and continued her studies at the Bezalel Academy in Jerusalem. Instead of returning to the United States, she next moved to Toronto and taught at the Ontario College of Art and Design from 1975 to 1990. Gilman did not try her hand at children's books until later in life, publishing her first picture book, *The Balloon Tree,* in 1984. Her popular character Jillian appeared in her next book, 1988's *Jillian Jiggs.* Jillian would appear in four more books, the last of which was *Jillian Jiggs and the Great Big Snow* (2002). Some of her other books include *Something from Nothing* (1990) and *The Gypsy Princess* (1995). At the time of her death Gilman was working on a manuscript for another children's book, *The Blue Hippopotamus,* and had just completed a short autobiography.

OBITUARIES AND OTHER SOURCES:

BOOKS

Writers Directory, 17th edition, St. James Press (Detroit, MI), 2002.

PERIODICALS

Quill & Quire (Toronto, Ontario, Canada), October, 2002, p. 11.
Toronto Star, October 21, 2002.

*   *   *

HAWKINS, (Helena Ann) Quail 1905-2002

OBITUARY NOTICE—See index for *SATA* sketch: Born March 29, 1905, in Spokane, WA; died August 16, 2002, in Pacific Grove, CA. Bookseller and author. Hawkins was an expert in children's literature who also wrote books for children and young adults. Although she attended the University of California at Berkeley in 1927, she did not receive a degree, instead working as a bookseller during the 1920s. She was also briefly on the staff of *Publishers Weekly* before joining Sather Gate

Bookshop in 1931. Starting as a salesperson there, she eventually became head of the adult and juvenile departments. From 1954 to 1961 she worked in sales for the University of California Press before returning to Sather Gate Bookshop as a consultant on library services and book fairs. Hawkins enjoyed visiting schools and libraries and promoting children's literature; she also encouraged now-famous authors, such as Ursula K. LeGuin and Beverly Cleary, to pursue writing careers. Among her own books are *A Puppy for Keeps* (1943), *The Aunt-Sitter* (1958), and her retelling of *Androcles and the Lion* (1970). In 1963, Hawkins also wrote the material on children's literature for the *Encyclopedia Britannica.*

OBITUARIES AND OTHER SOURCES:

BOOKS

Ward, Martha E., and others, *Authors of Books for Young People,* Scarecrow Press (Metuchen, NJ), 1990.

PERIODICALS

Los Angeles Times, August 29, 2002, p. B15.
New York Times, August 27, 2002, p. C13.
San Francisco Chronicle, August 30, 2002, p. A27.

*   *   *

HAZELL, Rebecca (Eileen) 1947-

Personal

Born July 23, 1947, in Austin, TX; daughter of Donovan Verloe Geppert (an electronics engineer) and Doris Geppert Knotts (a technical editor); married Mark Stephan Hazell (vice president of a real estate investment trust company), May 20, 1972; children: Elisabeth Olive Aloka, Stephan Harrison Ananda. *Education:* University of California—Santa Cruz, B.A. (cum laude), 1969. *Politics:* Liberal. *Religion:* Buddhist.

Addresses

Home—2710 Swaine St., Halifax, Nova Scotia B3L 3R5, Canada. *E-mail*—mbhazell@hfx.eastlink.ca.

Career

Writer and illustrator.

Awards, Honors

Notable New Book selection, International Jugendbibliothek, 1997, for *The Barefoot Book of Heroes;* Honor Title, Storytelling World Awards, 2001, for *Heroic Children.*

Writings

(And illustrator) *The Barefoot Book of Heroines: Great Women from Many Times and Places,* Barefoot Books (London, England), 1996, published as *Heroines: Great Women through the Ages,* Abbeville Press (New York, NY), 1996.

(And illustrator) *The Barefoot Book of Heroes, Great Men from Many Times and Places,* Barefoot Books (London, England), 1997, published as *Heroes: Great Men through the Ages,* Abbeville Press (New York, NY), 1997.

The Barefoot Book of Heroic Children, illustrated by Helen Cann, Barefoot Books (London, England), 2000, second edition, Barefoot Books (New York, NY), 2002.

(And illustrator) *Women Writers* ("Women in the Arts" series), Abbeville Press (New York, NY), 2002.

Hazell's work has been translated into Greek and Korean.

Work in Progress

Two more books about women in the arts; a novel for adults, in trilogy form, set in the thirteenth century.

Sidelights

Rebecca Hazell is an author and illustrator of several books for young readers that provide role models embodying courage and compassion. Written in a "you are there" format, Hazell's *The Barefoot Book of Heroines: Great Women from Many Times and Places* and its two companion volumes cover the spectrum of human history from ancient Greece through modern times in presenting the lives of notable folk of many cultures, among them Socrates, Benjamin Franklin, William Shakespeare, Anne Frank, Marie Curie, and Martin Luther King, Jr. Hazell has also developed a second three-volume series called "Women in the Arts" which focuses on creative women working as writers and in other formats.

As a young girl, Hazell first fell under the power of a book when her mother let her borrow a treasured copy of *Richard Halliburton's Complete Book of Marvels,* which Hazell described to *SATA* as "an imaginary trip around the world, led by the author, himself a famous world traveler." She credits her interest in world history—as well as her love of travel—as stemming from reading Halliburton's work. She was also fascinated by Andrew Lang's classic "colored" fairy books, such as the *Lilac Fairy Book* and the *Olive Fairy Book.* In addition, illustrators such as Arthur Rackham, Kay Nielsen, and Edmund Dulac captured Hazell's young imagination.

Hazell's first serious writing was undertaken in junior high school, when she signed on as journalist and staff artist for her school's newspaper. In high school and the first two years of college she took honors English classes and focused on writing poetry supplemented by the occasional short story. While attending the University of California—Santa Cruz, her classes were driven by her curiosity about the world, and history became her passion. "What always fascinated me were three themes," she explained to *SATA:* "spirituality; myth, legend, and fairy tales; and the marvelous nature of this world.... I took every class I could in world history, from Japan to the African nations, plus classes in

Rebecca Hazell writes of twelve courageous children who overcame disabilities and prejudices to become heroes, as in the story of David and Goliath. (From The Barefoot Book of Heroic Children, *illustrated by Helen Cann.)*

Oriental religions; at the end, when I *had* to declare a major in order to graduate, I totaled up my credits and voila! Russian and Chinese history won."

After graduating from college in 1969, Hazell toyed with clerical and sales jobs before settling down as a writer of educational filmstrips while also developing designs for needlepoint that she sold to high-end decorating stores. However, she did not find what she was doing to be ultimately satisfying. "What I really wanted to do was to share my vision of the world as an amazing place, full of amazing stories.... A practicing Buddhist by then, I created a coloring book for the children of our community: biographies expressing the vision that there are heroic and fascinating people everywhere, in every culture on Earth. It was quite a local hit." Encouraged to find a publisher for her work, Hazell prepared a book proposal and sent it off to England's Barefoot Books. The idea was accepted, and Hazell's publishing career was born.

The Barefoot Book of Heroines, followed by *The Barefoot Book of Heroes, Great Men from Many Times and Places* and *The Barefoot Book of Heroic Children* were Hazell's first three published works and were released in the United States as well as in England. Consisting of biographies and short stories focusing on the men, women, and children who have given of themselves and their time in an effort to improve their own corner of the world, Hazell's three-book series involves readers in the lives of her subjects, using first-person narrative. Praising *The Barefoot Book of Heroines* in *Resource Links,* reviewer Judy Davies noted that Hazell's effort is "set apart from other books on the topic of heroism by the author's clearly defined purpose and her ability to combine thorough research with exceptional design and illustrations." Reviewing the same book in *Shambhala Sun,* reviewer Laurie Fisher Huck cited "a respect for fearlessness and the power of compassion" as characteristics distinguishing Hazell's heroines, noting: "I was surprised by stories I'd never heard before and tickled by the author's ability to make an experience live for the reader." Calling *The Barefoot Book of Heroic Children* "an enjoyable collection" that can "help foster better communication and relationships among ethnic groups in our multicultural society," *MultiCultural Review* contributor Hannah M. Heller went on to praise Hazell for her willingness to discuss controversial issues such as poverty and child labor in Pakistan.

Researching *The Barefoot Book of Heroines* in over two hundred reference works, Hazell has been able to place each of her subjects—among them monarch Eleanor of Aquitaine, Russian poet Anna Akhmatova, Japanese novelist Murasaki Shikibu, Native American Sacajawea, aviator Amelia Earhart, and Underground Railroad worker Harriet Tubman—in an historical context that allows readers to fully appreciate each woman's contribution to history. Her follow-up work, *The Barefoot Book of Heroes,* follows the same format and includes profiles of Japan's prince Taishi Shotoku, artist Leonardo da Vinci, civil rights organizer Martin Luther King, Jr., and Cherokee leader Sequoya.

Hazell offers some advice to young writers and illustrators. "Keep in mind why you want to do this kind of work," she explained to *SATA*. "Stay close to your vision, and don't be afraid to revise, change, and take leaps of daring if your work isn't expressing what you truly feel."

Biographical and Critical Sources

PERIODICALS

Booklist, July, 1997, Carolyn Phelan, review of *Heroes: Great Men through the Ages,* p. 1814; April 15, 2000, Ilene Cooper, review of *The Barefoot Book of Heroic Children,* p. 1540.
MultiCultural Review, September, 2000, Hannah M. Heller, review of *The Barefoot Book of Heroic Children.*
Publishers Weekly, April 3, 2000, review of *The Barefoot Book of Heroic Children,* p. 82.
Resource Links, February, 1997, Judy Davies, review of *The Barefoot Book of Heroines: Great Women from Many Times and Place.*
School Library Journal, December, 1996, Marilyn Taniguchi, review of *Heroines: Great Women through the Ages,* p. 129; June, 1997, Melissa Hudak, review of *Heroes,* p. 135.
Shambhala Sun, January, 1997, Laurie Fisher Huck, review of *The Barefoot Book of Heroines,* pp. 67-69.

*   *   *

HERMES, Patricia 1936-

Personal

Born February 21, 1936, in Brooklyn, NY; daughter of Fred Joseph (a bank vice president) and Jessie Gould Martin; married Matthew E. Hermes (a research and development director for a chemical company), August 24, 1957 (divorced, 1984); children: Paul, Mark, Timo-

thy, Matthew, Jr., Jennifer. *Education:* St. John's University, B.A., 1957.

Addresses

Home and office—1414 Melville Ave., Fairfield, CT 06430. *Agent*—Dorothy Markinko, McIntosh and Otis, Inc., 310 Madison Ave., New York, NY 10017.

Career

Rollingcrest Junior High School, Takoma Park, MD, teacher of English and social studies, 1957-58; Delcastle Technical High School, Delcastle, DE, teacher of homebound children, 1972-73; writer, 1977—. Teacher of gifted middle-grade children, Norfolk, VA, 1981-82; adult education instructor.

Member

Authors Guild, Authors League of America, Society of Children's Book Writers and Illustrators.

Awards, Honors

Best Book for Young Adults citation, American Library Association, 1985, and Notable Children's Trade Book in the Field of Social Studies citation, National Council for Social Studies/Children's Book Council Joint Committee, both for *A Solitary Secret;* Children's Choice Award, 1987, for *Kevin Corbett Eats Flies;* Crabbery Award and Children's Choice Award, International Reading Association/Children's Book Council, both for *What If They Knew?;* Children's Choice Award for *Friends Are Like That* and *A Place for Jeremy;* Pine Tree Book Award, Iowa Young Reader Medal, Hawaii Nene Award, California Young Reader Medal, Notable Children's Trade Book in the Field of Social Studies citation, National Council for Social Studies/Children's Book Council Joint Committee, all for *You Shouldn't Have to Say Goodbye;* Notable Children's Trade Book in the Field of Social Studies citation, National Council for Social Studies/Children's Book Council Joint Committee, for *Who Will Take Care of Me?;* Children's Choice Award for *Heads, I Win;* Best Book of the Year citation, *School Library Journal,* and Children's Choice Award, both for *Mama, Let's Dance.*

Writings

What If They Knew?, Harcourt (San Diego, CA), 1980.
Nobody's Fault?, Harcourt (San Diego, CA), 1981.
You Shouldn't Have to Say Goodbye, Harcourt (San Diego, CA), 1982.
Who Will Take Care of Me?, Harcourt (San Diego, CA), 1983.
Friends Are Like That, Harcourt (San Diego, CA), 1984.
A Solitary Secret, Harcourt (San Diego, CA), 1985.
Kevin Corbett Eats Flies, illustrations by Carol Newsom, Harcourt (San Diego, CA), 1986.
A Place for Jeremy, Harcourt (San Diego, CA), 1987.
A Time to Listen: Preventing Youth Suicide (nonfiction), Harcourt (San Diego, CA), 1987.

Heads, I Win, illustrations by Carol Newsom, Harcourt (San Diego, CA), 1988.

Be Still My Heart, Putnam's (New York, NY), 1989.

I Hate Being Gifted!, Putnam's (New York, NY), 1990.

(Novelization, with Laurice Elehwany) *My Girl: A Novel,* Pocket Books (New York, NY), 1991.

Mama, Let's Dance, Little, Brown (Boston, MA), 1991.

Take Care of My Girl, Little, Brown (Boston, MA), 1992.

Someone to Count On, Little, Brown (Boston, MA), 1993.

Nothing But Trouble, Trouble, Trouble, Scholastic (New York, NY), 1994.

I'll Pulverize You, William, Pocket Books (New York, NY), 1994.

(With Janet Kovalcik) *My Girl II,* Pocket Books (New York, NY), 1994.

On Winter's Wind, Little, Brown (Boston, MA), 1995.

Everything Stinks, Minstrel Books (New York, NY), 1995.

Thirteen Things Not To Tell a Parent, Pocket Books (New York, NY), 1995.

Boys Are Even Worse Than I Thought, Pocket Books (New York, NY), 1995.

When Snow Lay Soft on the Mountain (picture book), illustrated by Leslie A Baker, Little, Brown (Boston, MA), 1996.

My Secret Valentine, Scholastic (New York, NY), 1996.

Something Scary, illustrated by John Gurney, Scholastic (New York, NY), 1996.

Turkey Trouble, illustrated by John Gurney, Scholastic (New York, NY), 1996.

Christmas Magic, illustrated by John Gurney, Scholastic (New York, NY), 1996.

Hoppy Easter, illustrated by Amy Wummer, Scholastic (New York, NY), 1998.

(Novelization) Robert Rodat and Vince McKewin, *Fly Away Home* (motion picture), Newmarket (New York, NY), 1996.

(Novelization) Tom Benedek, *Zeus and Roxanne* (motion picture), Pocket Books (New York, NY), 1997.

Calling Me Home, Avon (New York, NY), 1998.

Cheat the Moon: A Novel, Little, Brown (Boston, MA), 1998.

Our Strange New Land: Elizabeth's Jamestown Colony Diary, Scholastic (New York, NY), 2000.

In God's Novel, Marshall Cavendish (New York, NY), 2000.

Westward to Home: Joshua's Oregon Trail Diary, Scholastic (New York, NY), 2001.

The Starving Time: Elizabeth's Jamestown Colony Diary, Book Two, Scholastic (New York, NY), 2001.

Sweet By and By, HarperCollins (New York, NY), 2002.

Season of Promise: Elizabeth's Jamestown Colony Diary, Book Three, Scholastic (New York, NY), 2002.

A Perfect Place: Joshua's Oregon Trail Diary, Book Two, Scholastic (New York, NY), 2002.

The Wild Year: Joshua's Oregon Trail Diary, Book Three, Scholastic (New York, NY), 2002.

Contributor to textbooks, including *On Reading and Writing for Kids.* Contributor to magazines, including *Woman's Day, Life and Health, Connecticut, American Baby,* and *Mother's Day,* and newspapers, including the *New York Times. What If They Knew?* has been translated into French, Portuguese, and Japanese;

Patricia Hermes

Friends Are Like That, Japanese; *A Solitary Secret,* Danish; and *Mama, Let's Dance,* Italian.

Sidelights

The author of forty books for middle grade readers and young adults, Patricia Hermes does not shy away from difficult topics. She has written of a young girl who must come to terms with her mother's terminal illness in *You Shouldn't Have to Say Goodbye,* about abandoned children in *Mama, Let's Dance,* and of another young girl in *Cheat the Moon,* who must deal not only with her mother's death but also her father's alcoholic neglect. "As adults, we often try to deceive ourselves that childhood is a safe, pleasant place to be," Hermes once told *SATA.* "It isn't—at least, some of the time. For me, it is important to say this to young people so children know they are not alone." While many of Hermes's characters experience difficult and trying times—life in foster care, uncaring parents, unaccepting classmates— most of the author's young protagonists use these unsettling periods to gain strength and wisdom. And in spite of these difficulties, they manage to have fun, mischief, and a great deal of joy.

Some of Hermes's books begin lighter in tone, such as the companion volumes, *Kevin Corbett Eats Flies* and *Heads, I Win,* or as in the four books from the "Cousins' Club" series. Also, in her books featuring Katie Potts, such as *My Secret Valentine, Something Scary, Turkey Trouble, Christmas Magic,* and *Hoppy Easter,* Hermes uses holidays as a prop for stories about more mundane adolescent problems, such as not being invited to a

Halloween party or wondering if Santa Claus will overlook some small transgressions when handing out presents this year. Additionally, Hermes turns her hand to historical themes in books, including *On Winter's Wind, Calling Me Home, In God's Novel, Westward to Home,* and *The Starving Time.*

Hermes was always interested in books and writing. "I loved to write when I was a kid," she remarked to *SATA.* "I was an avid reader as a kid, just buried in books." Hermes noted that since there were very few books specifically for children and young adults in those days, she spent a lot of time reading classic literature: "I lived with *The Secret Garden.*" Hermes also loved the "Green Gables" books by L. M. Montgomery, *Tom Sawyer* and *Huckleberry Finn,* the Grimm brothers' fairy tales, *A Child's Garden of Verses, The Yearling,* and *Heidi.*

Hermes got a lot of practice reading and writing during the time she came down with rheumatic fever, "which in those days was a big deal. You recuperated by spending months in bed." When not stuck in bed or in the hospital, Hermes—like many of her female characters—was an active tomboy. When she went to college, Hermes majored in speech and English. After graduating, she

Daughter of an alcoholic father, twelve-year-old Gabby longs to travel with her friend to see the ocean but cannot leave her six-year-old brother alone. (Cover illustration by Kamil Vojnar.)

married and taught school for a short time; she also raised a large family. Hermes returned to teaching for several years after her children were older, eventually deciding that it was not what she wanted to do. It was about this time that the author became interested in writing professionally.

"I've always written for myself. I never thought of writing for anybody else," Hermes explained to *SATA.* She eventually took a class at the New School for Social Research in writing nonfiction for adults, a course taught by Russell Freedman, who later won the Newbery Award for his biography of Abraham Lincoln. After finishing a few articles, Hermes "took some things I wrote in the course and sent them out to publishers and to my utter amazement, people started buying them. You get hooked pretty quickly that way." Hermes continued to write nonfiction articles for several years, including many pieces on SIDS (sudden infant death syndrome), which had caused the death of one of her children. One of Hermes's first articles was sold to the *New York Times.*

After that article appeared in the *Times,* Hermes turned to fiction writing for children, completing her first novel, *What If They Knew?,* whose main character has epilepsy and is afraid as a new kid in the school that her secret will be discovered by the others. Though dealing with a serious subject, Hermes's book also employed a light approach in dealing with childhood issues. In 1987, Hermes published a sequel to that debut novel, *A Place for Jeremy.* Both titles were selected as Children's Choice books by the International Reading Association and the Children's Book Council.

With the 1982 *You Shouldn't Have to Say Goodbye,* Hermes presents twelve-year-old Sarah, who is losing her mother to cancer. While confronting this crisis, Sarah moves between fear for her mother and her own daily concerns. In the end, Sarah is left with a journal her mother has written, a book that offers guidance in dealing with life's various trials. "This is moving, but it's not maudlin, although Mom's fortitude and equanimity may be more exemplary than typical," commented a *Bulletin of the Center for Children's Books* contributor. Vicki Hardesty, writing in *Voice of Youth Advocates* found the same novel "an excellent portrayal of a teenager adjusting to the terminal illness of a parent." A book for younger children dealing with death and abandonment is Hermes's *Who Will Take Care of Me?* In this story, Mark and his retarded younger brother Pete live with their grandmother. When she dies, the boys run away to the woods to keep Pete from being sent away to a special school. *School Library Journal* critic Nancy Berkowitz found Mark "sympathetic" and Pete's characterization "honest and unsentimental."

Hermes' first book for young adults, the award-winning *A Solitary Secret,* "is a spellbinding book that drops the reader deep into the soul" of a girl who has endured incest, noted *Voice of Youth Advocates* contributor Marijo Duncan. The unnamed teen, who ages from fourteen to eighteen during the story, tells her story via a journal. Eventually, she shares her secret with a friend's parent. Reverting to books for middle-grade children, Hermes wrote _A Place for Jeremy,_ the sequel to _What If They Knew?_ Jeremy spends part of her fifth-grade year with her grandparents in Brooklyn while her parents are abroad and in the process of adopting a baby. Jeremy calls the unknown child "Stupid Baby," fearing that the infant will steal her parents' affections. A _Publishers Weekly_ contributor remarked that "scenes between Jeremy and her grandfather are heartwarming."

According to the author, _Be Still My Heart,_ another young adult offering, "came about because I saw a girl and a boy in a school hallway, just looking at each other with this adoration in their eyes, and I thought, 'I've got to write about that.'" In the novel, Allison loves David, who loves Leslie, Allison's best friend. David and Allison are brought together when a teacher's husband develops AIDS and becomes a victim of discrimination. The book features an unusual character in the Countess—Allison's grandmother—who advocates the use of condoms. While some reviewers found the story stereotypical and lacking depth, "this book shows through its female characters that looks aren't everything to all boys, and that intelligence, enthusiasm, and conviction are just as appealing," declared _School Library Journal_ contributor Kathryn Havris.

Hermes tackles the plight of the gifted children in _I Hate Being Gifted!_ The story's main character, KT, is proud to be in a class for gifted children, but hates being separated from her two best friends. When another girl threatens to usurp her place in the trio, KT has to learn that intellectual pursuits and a social life are compatible. "KT's narrative voice is authentic and fresh; many readers will recognize themselves and their classmates in this slice of sixth grade life," observed a reviewer for _Publishers Weekly._

Child abandonment is dealt with in _Mama, Let's Dance,_ a book that "tugs at the heart without manipulating its audience," according to _Horn Book_'s Mary M. Burns. The story involves three children—ages sixteen, eleven, and seven—who are left to fend for themselves when their mother abandons them. The children pretend nothing has changed until the youngest becomes seriously ill and the siblings realize that they must reach out to their neighbors for help. Carolyn Noah of _School Library Journal_ found _Mama_ a "tightly woven tale," in which "rhythmic, homey text and genuine characters resonate with authenticity."

An unusual living situation and a missing parent are also the subjects of _Take Care of My Girl._ Eleven-year-old Brady lives in an old house with her grandfather Jake. Years before, Brady's father left to "save the whales" and hasn't been heard from since. Over the course of the story, a school project and Jake's failing health make finding Brady's missing parent a priority. "Hermes writes movingly of a young girl's search for the meaning of family," declared Cindy Darling Codell in _School Library Journal._ And _Booklist_ contributor Janice Del Negro found "the story's weak beginning is overcome

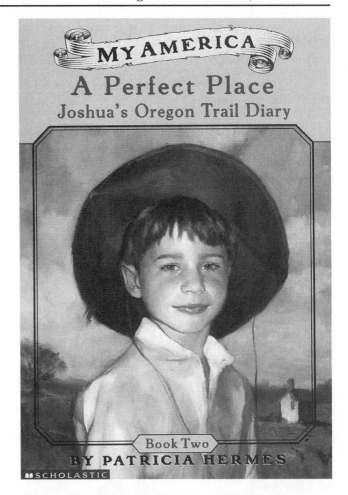

Having traveled to the West along the Oregon Trail, nine-year-old Joshua begins a new life in the Oregon wilderness in this sequel to Westward to Home. _(Cover illustration by Elizabeth B. Parisi.)_

by a slowly accelerating plot, and loose ends ... are tidily if summarily accounted for in a rosy conclusion."

Similarly, in _Someone to Count On_ and in the 1998 _Cheat the Moon,_ young girls are forced to make difficult decisions after the death of a parent. In the former title, Sam and her mother have been traveling around the country since the death of her father, but now they are moving to Colorado to stay on her grandfather's ranch. Just as Sam is settling in, her mother informs her that they are moving on, and Sam is faced with a difficult choice in this "powerful" and "engaging" story with "richly drawn" characters, according to Maeve Visser Knoth in _Horn Book._ In _Cheat the Moon,_ young Gabrielle has to take responsibility for her younger brother Will and herself after her mother dies and her father disappears on alcoholic binges. The beginning writer, Gabrielle, records her feelings in a journal in this "bittersweet tale," as Susan P. Bloom described the novel in _Horn Book._ Debbie Carton, writing in _Booklist,_ called the book a "poignant, compassionate story."

A Time to Listen is Hermes's nonfiction guide intended to help young adults understand issues related to suicide. The book consists of interviews with teens who have tried suicide, parents and friends of victims, and a therapist specializing in the problems confronting young people. "The interviews are probing, but sensitive to the privacy of subjects," commented Libby K. White in *School Library Journal.* "The great myths of teen suicide ... are refuted." *A Time to Listen* includes suggestions for helping depressed friends and overall, it is "a sensible, approachable book for those who need it," concluded Rosemary Moran in *Voice of Youth Advocates.*

Hermes deals more lightheartedly with adolescent issues in two books featuring elementary school friends Kevin Corbett and foster child Bailey Wharton, *Kevin Corbett Eats Flies* and *Heads, I Win.* The title for *Kevin Corbett Eats Flies* "came about because my daughter came home and told me there was a kid in her class eating dead flies off the windowsill," Hermes related in her interview. "As soon as she said that, I said, 'There's the title for my next book.'" In *Kevin Corbett,* the hero regularly gains his classmates' attention by tackling bizarre stunts, like eating flies or the class goldfish. Kevin meets his match, however, in tough but likeable Bailey, who eventually becomes his friend. *Heads, I Win* focuses on Bailey's life both in school and with Ms. Henderson and her four-year-old son. Bailey is afraid that her social worker wants to move her to yet another foster home; to help combat this fear, she decides to run for the class presidency to show everyone how well she is doing in school. Kevin volunteers to be Bailey's campaign manager, "and their analysis of how best to 'buy' individual students makes up much of the humor of the book," wrote Candy Colborn in *School Library Journal,* adding that the "characters are well drawn, and the fifth-grade in-fighting is very realistic."

More of the lighter approach is found in series books from Hermes, including the "Cousins' Club" books and the short novels featuring Katie Potts. The "Cousins' Club" kicks off with *I'll Pulverize You, William,* in which best friends and cousins, Marcie and Meghann, are introduced. The two eleven-year-olds are looking forward to summer until they learn that another, less enjoyable cousin—William—is due to show up. The cousins quickly develop a plan to keep him away from them. Knowing he is allergic to animals, they start a pet-sitting service, but of course things do not go according to plan in this "chipper start" to the series, according to a reviewer for *Publishers Weekly.* A critic for *Kirkus Reviews* also found the book "light and fun." In *Everything Stinks,* Meghann and Marcie are visiting their twin cousins, Jennifer and Amy. Jennifer is of the opinion that everything stinks because she is always treated like a little kid, and she dreams of the time when she will be in charge of everything. When her parents go on vacation, she thinks that time has come, with near disastrous and rather humorous results. Mary Harris Veeder, writing in *Booklist,* felt that Hermes gives some "good descriptions of fifth-grade embarrassments" in the book. Hermes continues the fun in the other titles including *Thirteen Things Not to Tell a Parent* and *Boys Are Even Worse Than I Thought.*

A further change of pace for Hermes is her first picture book, *When Snow Lay Soft on the Mountain,* about young Hallie during a difficult winter on Hairy Bear Mountain when her father is ill and when she badly wants a doll. A contributor for *Kirkus Reviews* called this title a "sweet and sentimental tale." A reviewer for *Publishers Weekly* cautioned against the "treacly ending," but also felt that the book "should satisfy readers in the mood for an old-fashioned moral tale."

Hermes turns to historical times and topics in novels from the new millennium. *On Winter's Wind* is set in Massachusetts in the nineteenth century during the time of slavery. Eleven-year-old Genevieve and her family are having a hard time of it, with the father presumed lost at sea. When she learns that there is a bounty on a slave hidden in her little town, she is sorely tempted to turn the fugitive in, but she is convinced to do otherwise by the Quakers sheltering the young runaway. "Hermes does a fine job of depicting the situation," thought *Booklist*'s Chris Sherman. Knoth, writing in *Horn Book,* also found the tale "poignant."

Hermes remains on the historical track with *Calling Me Home,* set on the Nebraska prairie in the 1850s. Abbie is twelve when her father takes the family from St. Joseph, Missouri, to homestead in Nebraska. She goes from living in a proper house with a piano to a sod house on the prairie; there is no school; no other children are nearby. She enjoys the freedom of the prairie, but also misses the ease of the city, especially when her brother dies during a cholera outbreak. Hermes "takes a fresh path with a feminist angle" on this familiar territory, according to a reviewer for *Publishers Weekly,* who also found the story "solid ... [and] neatly told." Janet Gillen, writing in *School Library Journal,* found that the novel's "strengths lie in Hermes's ability to convey sensitive issues of death and the loss of faith through succinct, well-written scenes."

Closer to contemporary times is the 2002 title, *Sweet By and By,* set during WWII and reminiscent of earlier novels by Hermes dealing with the effects of the death of an adult on a child. Blessing is eleven and has lived with her grandmother in the Tennessee mountains since she was only two. She is secure in the love of her grandmother and is bonded partly by the music they share. Now she must acknowledge the fact that her beloved grandmother is dying and she will have to go on with her life in a new home. A reviewer for *Publishers Weekly* highly commended this "gracefully composed story of love, loss and courage." Other reviewers heaped more praise on the title. *Booklist*'s Kay Weisman felt that the "loving relationship between grandmother and grandchild will touch the heart," and Barbara Auerbach, writing in *School Library Journal,* lauded the "poetic prose" used in this "heartfelt story." Another novel set during World War II is *In God's Novel,* about an eleven-year-old girl in Alabama whose mother suddenly goes "sick crazy," a condition that makes young Missy wonder why God lets bad things happen.

Writing in Scholastic's "My America" series—fictionalized diary accounts of historical times for young readers—Hermes details life in the Jamestown Colony with several books about a young girl called Elizabeth, and also follows the pioneers along the Oregon Trail in the journals of Joshua. *Our Strange New Land* initiates the adventures of Elizabeth, nine, as she records her experiences with Indians, building a new home, and dealing with hunger and death. Shawn Brommer, writing in *School Library Journal,* found the book to be a "quick, easy read." *The Starving Time* furthers Elizabeth's tale, a book in which the "historical details are woven so intricately into the plot that they become an integral part of the story," according to Kristen Oravec in *School Library Journal. Season of Promise* continues the story of Elizabeth, now ten, and the plans of her father to remarry. Hermes writes of the West in *Westward to Home,* the first diary entries of nine-year-old Joshua as he and his family follow the Oregon Trail from St. Joseph, Missouri. John McAndrew, writing in *Childhood Education,* praised the way that Joshua "vividly records his dreams, hopes, frustrations, and fears." Ellen Mandel, writing in *Booklist,* also had praise for the novel, noting that it "will stick in the readers' minds and enrich their studies of the era." Joshua records further adventures in *A Perfect Place,* in which Joshua and his family are settling down to life in Oregon's Willamette Valley. A contributor for *Kirkus Reviews* called this addition to the series "fascinating history," and Sally Bates Goodroe, writing in *School Library Journal,* had similar praise, noting that "details of the life in Oregon Country ... are vividly integrated."

Part of becoming a children's writer, Hermes once told *SATA,* is that there is a childlike part of us "we never lose, if we're lucky. Every good teacher has that. I think that child is a part of me, and she needs to speak—and does—through my books. I don't write for some child out there, I write for the child in me." When asked if she had any advice for young writers, Hermes said, "If I could preach for a minute, I'd say 'If you're going to be a writer, you must be a reader.' It doesn't matter what you read. Forget what those teachers tell you. You don't have to read 'good' literature. Read anything, because eventually, if you become a reader you will someday find good literature. No, there's nothing wrong with trivial reading. Also don't throw away anything you've ever written. I tell kids that if their mothers get in cleaning fits, tell them they can throw away their school books, or their baby brother, but do not throw away anything they've written."

Biographical and Critical Sources

BOOKS

Encyclopedia of Children's Literature, edited by Bernice E. Cullinan and Diane G. Person, Continuum (New York, NY), 2001.
St. James Guide to Young Adult Writers, 2nd edition, edited by Tom Pendergast and Sara Pendergast, St. James Press (Detroit, MI), 1999.

PERIODICALS

Booklist, October 15, 1989, p. 826; November 15, 1992, Janice Del Negro, review of *Take Care of My Girl;* March 15, 1994, p. 128; January 15, 1995, Mary Harris Veeder, review of *Everything Stinks,* p. 928; October 1, 1995, Chris Sherman, review of *On Winter's Wind,* p. 314; June 1, 1998, Debbie Carton, review of *Cheat the Moon,* p. 1766; January 1, 1999, Kay Weisman, review of *Calling Me Home,* p. 876; February 1, 2001, Ellen Mandel, review of *Westward to Home,* p. 1053; October 1, 2002, Kay Weisman, review of *Sweet By and By,* pp. 341-342.
Bulletin of the Center for Children's Books, February, 1983, p. 76; March, 1983, review of *You Shouldn't Have to Say Goodbye,* p. 127; July-August, 1983, p. 211; June, 1985, p. 185; February, 1990, p. 138; December, 1991, p. 91.
Childhood Education, fall, 2001, John McAndrew, review of *Westward to Home,* p. 50.
Horn Book, January-February, 1992, Mary M. Burns, review of *Mama, Let's Dance,* p. 70; January-February, 1994, Maeve Visser Knoth, review of *Someone to Count On,* pp. 69-70; November-December, 1995, Maeve Visser Knoth, review of *On Winter's Wind,* pp. 742-743; September-October, 1998, Susan P. Bloom, review of *Cheat the Moon,* pp. 608-609.
Horn Book Guide, spring, 1994, Maeve Visser Knoth, review of *Someone to Count On,* p. 77; fall, 2001, Erica L. Stahler, review of *Westward to Home,* p. 292.
Kirkus Reviews, December, 15, 1994, review of *I'll Pulverize You, William,* p. 1564; September 15, 1996, review of *When Snow Lay Soft on the Mountain,* p. 1401; November 15, 1998, review of *Calling Me Home,* p. 1669; October 15, 2002, review of *Sweet By and By,* p. 1531, review of *A Perfect Place,* pp. 1530-1531.
Publishers Weekly, April 24, 1987, review of *A Place for Jeremy,* p. 70; November 24, 1989, p. 72; November 23, 1990, review of *I Hate Being Gifted!,* p. 66; October 4, 1991, p. 89; November 2, 1992, p. 72; January 24, 1994, p. 56; November 21, 1994, review of *I'll Pulverize You, William,* pp. 76-77; October 30, 1995, review of *On Winter's Wind,* p. 62; October 21, 1996, review of *When Snow Lay Soft on the Mountain,* p. 82; December 14, 1998, review of *Calling Me Home,* p. 76; May 27, 2002, review of *Our Strange Land,* p. 62; November 11, 2002, review of *Sweet By and By,* p. 64.
School Library Journal, October, 1983, Nancy Berkowitz, review of *Who Will Take Care of Me?,* p. 158; August, 1985, p. 76; March, 1988, Libby K. White, review of *A Time to Listen,* p. 220; August, 1988, Candy Colborn, review of *Heads, I Win,* p. 95; December, 1989, Kathryn Havris, review of *Be Still My Heart,* p. 118; September, 1991, Carolyn Noah, review of *Mama, Let's Dance,* p. 253; December, 1992, Cindy Darling Codell, review of *Take Care of My Girl,* p. 112; May, 1993, p. 23; April, 1994, p. 128; March, 1995, Elaine Lesh Morgan, review of *Everything Stinks,* p. 204; September, 1995, Nancy P. Reeder, review of *On Winter's Wind,* p. 200; January, 1997, Mollie Bynum, review of *When Snow Lay Soft on the*

Mountain, p. 83; June, 1998, Connie Tyrrell Burns, review of *Cheat the Moon,* p. 146; December, 1998, Janet Gillen, review of *Calling Me Home,* p. 1998; August, 2000, Shawn Brommer, review of *Our Strange Land,* p. 156; June, 2001, Kristen Oravec, review of *Westward to Home,* p. 118; October, 2002, Barbara Auerbach, review of *Sweet By and By,* p. 164; November, 2002, Sally Bates Goodroe, review of *A Perfect Place,* p. 124.

Science Books and Films, September-October, 1988, p. 4.

Voice of Youth Advocates, December, 1985, Marijo Duncan, review of *A Solitary Secret,* p. 320; June, 1988, Rosemary Moran, review of *A Time to Listen,* p. 101; October, 1993, Vicki Hardesty, review of *You Shouldn't Have to Say Goodbye,* p. 203; February, 1997, Susan Dunn, review of *Fly Away Home,* pp. 327-328.

Wilson Library Bulletin, February, 1986, p. 47; October, 1989, p. 106.*

*   *   *

HINES, Anna Grossnickle 1946-

Personal

Born July 13, 1946, in Cincinnati, OH; daughter of Earl S. (a mathematical analyst) and Ruth (a personnel service representative; maiden name, Putnam) Grossnickle; married Steve Carlson, August 12, 1965 (divorced, 1973); married Gary Roger Hines (a forest ranger, writer, and musician), June 19, 1976; children: (first marriage) Bethany, Sarah; (second marriage) Lassen. *Education:* Attended San Fernando Valley State College (now California State University, Northridge), 1965-67; Pacific Oaks College, B.A., 1974, M.A., 1979. *Hobbies and other interests:* Needlework, quilting, knitting, gardening, grandparenting.

Addresses

Home—R.R. 4, Box 8057, Milford, PA 18337.

Career

Los Angeles City Children's Centers, Los Angeles, CA, preschool teacher, 1967-68, 1968-70; Columbia Elementary School, Columbia, CA, third grade teacher, 1975-78; full-time writer and illustrator, 1978—.

Member

Society of Children's Book Writers and Illustrators, Children's Literature Council of Pennsylvania.

Awards, Honors

Children's Book of the Year list, Child Study Association of America, 1985, for *All by Myself;* Children's Choice Award, International Reading Association and the Children's Book Council (IRA/CBC), 1987, for *Daddy Makes the Best Spaghetti;* Children's Choice Award, IRA/CBC, 1990, for *Grandma Gets Grumpy;*

Outstanding Science Book for Children, National Science Teachers Association, 1991, for *Remember the Butterflies;* Children's Books of the Year list, Bank Street College, 1991, for *Tell Me Your Best Thing;* Notable Children's Trade Book, National Council for the Social Studies, 1993, for *Flying Firefighters;* Carolyn W. Field Award Honor Book, Pennsylvania Library Association, 1995, for *What Joe Saw.* Other titles by Hines have been selected for the Junior Literary Guild, Book-of-the-Month Club, and other book clubs.

Writings

SELF-ILLUSTRATED, EXCEPT AS NOTED; FOR CHILDREN, EXCEPT AS NOTED

Taste the Raindrops, Greenwillow (New York, NY), 1983.

Come to the Meadow, Clarion (New York, NY), 1984.

Maybe a Band-Aid Will Help, Dutton (New York, NY), 1984.

All by Myself, Clarion (New York, NY), 1985.

Bethany for Real, Greenwillow (New York, NY), 1985.

Cassie Bowen Takes Witch Lessons (juvenile novel), illustrated by Gail Owens, Dutton (New York, NY), 1985.

Daddy Makes the Best Spaghetti, Clarion (New York, NY), 1986.

Don't Worry, I'll Find You, Dutton (New York, NY), 1986.

I'll Tell You What They Say, Greenwillow (New York, NY), 1987.

It's Just Me, Emily, Clarion (New York, NY), 1987.

Keep Your Old Hat, Dutton (New York, NY), 1987.

Grandma Gets Grumpy, Dutton (New York, NY), 1988.

Boys Are Yucko! (sequel to *Cassie Bowen Takes Witch Lessons*), illustrated by Pat Henderson Lincoln, Dutton (New York, NY), 1989.

Sky All Around, Clarion (New York, NY), 1989.

Big Like Me, Greenwillow (New York, NY), 1989.

They Really Like Me, Greenwillow (New York, NY), 1989.

The Secret Keeper, Greenwillow (New York, NY), 1990.

Mean Old Uncle Jack, Clarion (New York, NY), 1990.

The Greatest Picnic in the World, Clarion (New York, NY), 1991.

Remember the Butterflies, Dutton (New York, NY), 1991.

Tell Me Your Best Thing (juvenile novel), illustrated by Karen Ritz, Dutton (New York, NY), 1991.

Jackie's Lunch Box, Greenwillow (New York, NY), 1991.

Moon's Wish, Clarion (New York, NY), 1992.

Rumble Thumble Boom!, Greenwillow (New York, NY), 1992.

Moompa, Toby and Bomp, Clarion (New York, NY), 1993.

Gramma's Walk, Greenwillow (New York, NY), 1993.

Even If I Spill My Milk?, Clarion (New York, NY), 1994.

What Joe Saw, Greenwillow (New York, NY), 1994.

Big Help!, Clarion (New York, NY), 1995.

When the Goblins Came Knocking, Greenwillow (New York, NY), 1995.

When We Married Gary, Greenwillow (New York, NY), 1996.

Miss Emma's Wild Garden, Greenwillow (New York, NY), 1997.

My Own Big Bed, illustrated by Mary Watson, Greenwillow (New York, NY), 1998.

What Can You Do in the Rain?, illustrated by Thea Kliros, Greenwillow (New York, NY), 1998.

What Can You Do in the Wind?, illustrated by Thea Kliros, Greenwillow (New York, NY), 1999.

What Can You Do in the Snow?, illustrated by Thea Kliros, Greenwillow (New York, NY), 1999.

What Can You Do in the Sunshine?, illustrated by Thea Kliros, Greenwillow (New York, NY), 1999.

Not Without Bear, Orchard Books (New York, NY), 2000.

William's Turn, Children's Press (New York, NY), 2001.

Got You!, Children's Press (New York, NY), 2001.

Pieces: A Year in Poems & Quilts, Greenwillow (New York, NY), 2001.

Whose Shoes?, illustrated by LeUyen Pham, Harcourt (San Diego, CA), 2001.

Which Hat Is That? illustrated by LeUyen Pham, Harcourt (San Diego, CA), 2002.

My Grandma Is Coming to Town, illustrated by Melissa Sweet, Candlewick Press (Cambridge, MA), 2003.

ILLUSTRATOR

Gary Hines, *A Ride in the Crummy,* Greenwillow (New York, NY), 1991.

Gary Hines, *Flying Firefighters,* Clarion (New York, NY), 1993.

Gary Hines, *The Day of the High Climber,* Greenwillow (New York, NY), 1994.

Sarah Hines-Stephens, *Bean,* Harcourt (San Diego, CA), 1998.

Sarah Hines-Stephens, *Bean's Games,* Harcourt (San Diego, CA), 1998.

Sarah Hines-Stephens, *Bean's Night,* Harcourt (San Diego, CA), 1998.

Jackie French Koller, *Bouncing on the Bed,* Orchard Books (New York, NY), 1998.

Sarah Hines-Stephens, *Bean Soup,* Harcourt (San Diego, CA), 2000.

Sarah Hines-Stephens, *Soup Too?,* Harcourt (San Diego, CA), 2000.

Sarah Hines-Stephens, *Soup's Oops!,* Harcourt (San Diego, CA), 2000.

Contributor to magazines including *Society of Children's Book Writers Bulletin.*

Adaptations

Daddy Makes the Best Spaghetti and *It's Just Me, Emily* have been adapted for audio cassette.

Sidelights

Author of over forty-five children's titles, many of them award winners, Anna Grossnickle Hines has written and illustrated both picture books and chapter books for primary graders. Additionally, she has illustrated books for her author husband, Gary Hines, and for her daughter, Sarah Hines-Stephens. Hines blends her accomplished art with stories about family and sibling relations, first friendships, and the delights of nature, among other subjects. "My stories come mostly from my experiences and feelings as a child and with my own

Anna Grossnickle Hines

children," Hines once told *SATA*. "The stories are mostly about the discovery, imagination, playfulness, and wonder in young children's everyday lives, so often missed by busy adults." Praised for her understanding of her young audience and depiction of family relationships, as well as for her skill as an artist, Hines is acknowledged as the creator of pleasant, positive, and reassuring works, several of which are noted as especially useful books on their subjects.

Hines resolved at an early age to become a writer of children's books. The oldest of seven children, Hines had plenty of material to work with. Born in Ohio, she moved to California as a child and grew up in Los Angeles, studying art at what was then San Fernando Valley State College. "In early college I was discouraged from pursuing my interest in picture books," Hines told *SATA*. "I was told it was not a worthy interest because a picture book was not truly 'fine art' on the one hand or 'commercial' on the other. To me, the art of the picture book, which can be held in the hands, carried about, taken to bed, is much more personal and intimate than the art which hangs in galleries or museums."

Hines never lost sight of her dream. She married in 1965 and had two daughters, teaching preschool as well. After her first marriage ended in divorce in 1973, Hines finished her college education and married Gary Hines, a forest ranger and a writer/musician. Moving to California's Gold Country in the Sierra Nevada, she taught third grade in a small elementary school. Hines read many books, both to her own children and to the children she taught, and eventually she began to understand what made a good book. Initially, she thought she would simply do illustrations for others, but as she read these books she began to see that she had her own stories to tell. At first she shared these with family and friends, and slowly she began submitting them to publishers. By the time her third child was born, she had collected over a hundred rejection slips. With a new baby in the house, Hines stopped teaching and became busy with household chores. She then decided to make "writing and illustrating a priority," as she reported in *SATA*. "It was a few months after the birth of my third child that I decided I should either pursue my goal of doing children's books more seriously or give it up." She began writing every day, even if only for a matter of minutes. The rest of the family pitched in, helping with chores and child-rearing, and after about twenty months, her renewed efforts paid off. She sold her first picture book, *Taste the Raindrops,* the story of a little child who loves to walk in the rain even though Mother warns against it at first. Hines never looked back.

Hines's second picture book, *Come to the Meadow,* started with an idea for a story about a child playing and discovering things in a meadow. The author developed this concept into the tale of little Mattie, who desperately wants to go to the meadow; everyone in the family is too busy, except for Granny, who finally proposes a picnic there. The word "picnic" is magic for the rest of the family, who suddenly discover that they have the time to spare. A *Publishers Weekly* critic called this early effort a "poetic, unpretentious story," with pictures in "clear green and yellow offset with pristine-white spaces." This theme of the value of extended family, especially including grandparents, comes back in other titles by Hines. *Grandma Gets Grumpy* tells the story of five cousins who spend the night with their grandmother, but quickly learn that she has rules too. "This slice of real life is depicted with such humor and affection that kids are sure to enjoy recognizing themselves and their elders," noted a critic for *Kirkus Reviews,* who added, "The soft, realistic pictures make each character an individual." Writing in *Horn Book,* Ellen Fader commented that Hines uses her "familiar, gentle, colored-pencil illustrations to bring this pleasant story to life," and added that Hines has the "envious ability to focus on the most ordinary situation, mix in a bit of gentle humor, and create, as the result, a charming and intimate glimpse into a preschooler's world." Another grandparent is featured in *Gramma's Walk,* a picture book about young Donnie and Gramma, who is in a wheelchair, and their imagined walk to the seashore. The bond between a boy and his grandfather is also explored in *Moompa, Toby and Bomp,* "a charming tale of simple pleasures," according to Anna DeWind of *School Library Journal.*

Another favorite subject for Hines is child development. In *All by Myself,* she writes about a child taking "a step toward independence," as she described it in *SATA,* by giving up night diapers and going unassisted to the bathroom in the middle of the night. Noting that "*All by Myself* holds a unique position in the growing genre of self-help books for young children," *School Library Journal* reviewer B. P. Goldstone concluded that the book is "a welcome addition to library collections that will help children cope with this problem as well as help to define a growing sense of worth." In *Even If I Spill My Milk?* Hines deals with children's fear of separation. Young Jamie doesn't want his parents to go to a party and leave him with a babysitter, and so tries to delay their departure with a litany of questions. Childhood fear of thunder is dealt with in *Rumble Thumble Boom!,* about a boy and his dog who are afraid of such loud noises. Andrew W. Hunter commented in *School Library Journal* that Hines's "colorful effects enhance the book's use for storytelling with either a group or with a single child." *Booklist*'s Hazel Rochman concluded that "This is one of those read-alouds that will evoke smiles of wry recognition in adults without condescending to kids." The job of introducing a new sibling into the home is explored in *Big Like Me,* as a boy tells his baby sister all the things he will show her when she gets bigger. Denise Wilms noted in *Booklist* that "Hines has an eye for pint-size anatomy," and that the book is an "affectionate and refreshingly positive celebration of a new infant." *Horn Book*'s Fader remarked that the "watercolor and pencil illustrations have a gentle, cozy, and contented feeling which reinforces the mood of this distinctly useful book."

Hines has also explored the world of older children with several juvenile novels. *Cassie Bowen Takes Witch Lessons* tells the story of fourth-grade Cassie, who learns about not only herself, but also about the real meaning of friendship when she is paired with an unpopular girl to do a class assignment. Phyllis Ingram noted in *School Library Journal* that "readers will suffer along with Cassie as she strives to make the right decisions about friendship and loyalty." A reviewer for *Booklist* felt that Hines "carefully constructs a conflict that is true to life, injecting her story with realistic characterizations and dialogue and a solid understanding of the problems of growing up." The sequel, *Boys Are Yucko!,* finds Cassie planning her tenth birthday party, hoping that her divorced father will come, and also dealing with the insistence of her boy-crazy friend Stacy to invite the opposite sex to the event. *Tell Me Your Best Thing* is a story that looks at a young girl's decision to stand up to a class bully. *Publishers Weekly* commented that "the story's quick pace and believable portrayal of third grade angst will appeal to the chapter book set."

Although she has written about a variety of childhood experiences, Hines's major subject would seem to be her own family. The author took inspiration from her own daughter, Sarah, for a trio of books about a young girl and her doll, Abigail. In *Maybe a Band-Aid Will Help,* the doll's leg comes off and the mother is too busy to help Sarah fix it right away. Sarah and Abigail get lost in a shopping mall in *Don't Worry, I'll Find You,* and *Keep Your Old Hat* has Sarah falling out with her friend, Mandy, over who gets to play mother. Her daughter Bethany inspired *Bethany for Real,* which Hines told

When Albert's Grandma comes to visit, he becomes shy but learns to overcome his shyness by playing special games with her. (From My Grandma Is Coming to Town, *illustrated by Melissa Sweet.)*

SATA is "a fun story of the mix-up that results when Bethany pretends to be somebody else." Hines's husband Gary was the model for the father in *Daddy Makes the Best Spaghetti,* a tale of a nurturing dad. "I thought the idea a good one," Hines noted in *SATA,* "and since my husband shares domestic duties in our household, I watched him, waiting for a story to come.... Spaghetti is one of my husband's favorite things to cook, second only to popcorn. His spaghetti is very good, but it got to be a kind of family joke that if he were cooking, it would be spaghetti for dinner ... again." The resulting book, according to Mary M. Burns in *Horn Book,* is "a natural for picture-book programs.... Precise, fine lines combined with clear colors on snowy white backgrounds capture the circumscribed world of the preschooler while celebrating the joys to be found in daily events." A *Kirkus Reviews* critic concluded that "Daddy is bound to

steal the hearts of many young readers." Hines again used personal family experience—her remarriage—for *When We Married Gary.* Young Sarah doesn't remember her father, but Beth does, and when a new man comes into their mother's life, adjustments need to be made. "Hines has done a superb job of tackling a realistic subject—remarriage—without oversimplifying it," noted Lisa Marie Gangemi in *School Library Journal.* Carolyn Phelan, writing in *Booklist,* commented that "Once again, Hines gets the child's perspective and the emotional tone of the story just right."

Hines has also teamed up with her writer husband on several titles, mostly having to do with the outdoors and forestry work. Two of these books are nostalgic reminiscences: in *A Ride in the Crummy,* two boys have an exciting ride in the caboose of a large train, while in its companion volume, *The Day of the High Climber,* two brothers spend the summer at their father's logging camp and marvel at the work of the high climber who must chop top branches off a tree. Donna L. Scanlon, writing in *School Library Journal,* noted that the latter title had a "coziness that is nostalgic but not cloying." Hines has extended this idea of collaborating with family members to working with her daughter Sarah on three board books from 1998, *Bean, Bean's Games,* and *Bean's Night,* and three more in 2000, *Bean Soup, Soup Too?,* and *Soup's Oops!* Bean is a black cat and Soup a white-and-black puppy and the two love to play together.

Hines presents further forays into a child's development in *My Own Big Bed,* the tale of a little girl who has outgrown her crib and is preparing to sleep in a big bed for the first time. This experience is "both exciting and scary" for the narrator, noted a reviewer for *Publishers Weekly.* Now she can get in and out of bed all on her own, but she also has fears about falling out of the bed. Thus, the resourceful young girl props her stuffed animals around the edge of the bed, so that if she does fall out, her landing will be a padded, soft one. "This rite of passage is astutely and economically observed," noted the *Publishers Weekly* critic. Karen Simonetti, reviewing the same title in *Booklist,* found it to be "ideal for bedtime and lapsits." Similarly, Karen James, writing in *School Library Journal,* thought this "warm and reassuring" book would "strike a chord" with youngsters graduating from babyhood, and *Horn Book Guide*'s Patricia Riley praised Hines's tale which "tenderly addresses this childhood transition."

Hines further explores the world of development and activities for young children in a series of board books including *What Can You Do in the Rain?* Jennifer M. Brown, reviewing the titles in *Publishers Weekly,* noted that Hines "invites kids to revel in the weather," suggesting they try waving a flag on a windy day, watch their shadow in the sun, or gaze at the clouds on a rainy day. *Booklist*'s Hazel Rochman also praised the "direct appeal" of the books. In *Miss Emma's Wild Garden,* young Chloe explores her neighbor's garden, which—unlike her father's—is full of wildness and magic. Miss Emma gladly points out all the animals and wild plants to the young girl, who eagerly asks for more. *Booklist*'s Ilene Cooper felt that Hines presented both an "intergenerational story and a mini-nature lesson in one attractive package" with this book.

Pieces: A Year in Poems & Quilts, represents a change of pace for Hines, combining free-verse poems about the seasons with her own quilting as accompanying artwork. "I remember owning a small version of Robert Louis Stevenson's *A Child's Garden of Verses* as a child," Hines remarked on her author Web site in explanation of the inspiration for her book of poems. "I read and enjoyed lots of other poems, too, but it wasn't until my early adulthood that I really fell in love with children's poetry.... Some of my earliest writings were poems, a few of which are in this book. Over the years most of my

efforts have gone into stories, but every now and then I'd write another poem or two, most of them about nature." Then in 1993 she started to go over the poems and discovered that she had almost enough to present a collection about the seasons, and wrote a few more verses to fill in the gaps. However, when it came to the illustrations, Hines wanted to do something special, but could not figure out what that might be. So she set her poems aside for a time and worked on other projects. About this same time, her mother began making quilts, and Hines became interested in the work, as well. She actually began doing quilts as the artwork for her poems as the result of a white lie she told her mother; Hines was working on a quilt as a present for her mother, but needed advice from her on how to proceed. Thus, to cover up the gift, she told her curious mother that the quilt was going to accompany her book of poems. Finally she realized that was in fact how she should illustrate her verses. Working for several years, Hines put together half a dozen quilts to illustrate her poems, and won the enthusiastic support of her editor. Ultimately she delivered thirteen more quilts to her publishers to be scanned for the illustrations and appended a two-page explanation of the quilting process at the end for this 2001 publication.

Reviewers highly praised the resulting blending of verse and artwork. A critic for *Publishers Weekly* called the collection a "deceptively simple, unique collection of poems" and the "series of quilted designs worthy of an exhibition." Likewise, Ilene Cooper commended "this lovely book" which mixes "the intricacies of quilting with the wonders of the changing seasons," in a *Booklist* review. A contributor for *Bulletin of the Center for Children's Books* thought that the "visual appeal and detail of the quilt work will engage young viewers," and a writer for *Kirkus Reviews* also commented that Hines "raises the bar considerably for illustrators working in fabric," and further described the work as a "tour de force."

The 2001 children's book *Whose Shoes?* also started life as a poem. "What little child hasn't tried on big people's shoes?" Hines asked on her author Web site. "I don't remember exactly when I first wrote it, or if there was a particular event that inspired it, but *Whose Shoes?* started out as a poem." Later on, sharing the poem with her writing group, Hines was informed that what she had was really a picture book, and after working on the concept for a time, she came up with the idea of making it a lift-the-flap puzzle-adventure tale. It was decided, also, that Hines would not illustrate the book. Instead she worked with illustrator LeUyen Pham whose "mouse character is so full of energy and charm!" Hines wrote on her Web site. In the story, the little mouse is trying on the shoes of family members on each successive page and readers need to lift the flap to discover whose shoes they are. Anne Parker, reviewing the title in *School Library Journal,* called it "well-written," with rhyming sounds that will "entertain youngsters and have them chiming right along." A critic for *Kirkus Reviews* also praised the "exuberant rhymes" as well as the "clever illustrations." This collaborative effort was so successful that Hines and Pham teamed up for the 2002 *Which Hat Is That?,* employing the same guessing game motif and blend of strong mouse illustrations and rhyming, sing-song text.

Hines's childhood dream of becoming an author and illustrator for children has come true in manifold ways. Writing in *Something about the Author Autobiography Series,* Hines explained her joys and expectations in writing. Acknowledging that in her stories she is the child protagonist and not the adult author, she went on to note that she was "creating the world the way I wanted it to be when I was young. I hope young children, and their parents, will find comfort in my books, maybe even a model of positive family relationships. But mostly I hope they'll enjoy them, and that I'll get to go on creating them for a long, long time."

Biographical and Critical Sources

BOOKS

Hines, Anna Grossnickle, essay in *Something about the Author Autobiography Series,* Gale (Detroit, MI), 1995, pp. 209-228.

PERIODICALS

Booklist, February 1, 1986, review of *Cassie Bowen Takes Witch Lessons,* p. 810; October 1, 1989, Denise Wilms, review of *Big Like Me,* p. 350; September 15, 1992, Hazel Rochman, review of *Rumble Thumble Boom!,* pp. 154-55; March 1, 1996, Carolyn Phelan, review of *When We Married Gary,* p. 1188; March 1, 1997, Ilene Cooper, review of *Miss Emma's Wild Garden,* p. 1172; October 15, 1998, Karen Simonetti, review of *My Own Big Bed,* p. 427; June 1, 1999, Hazel Rochman, review of *What Can You Do in the Rain?,* p. 1842; January 1, 2001, Ilene Cooper, review of *Pieces: A Year in Poems and Quilts,* p. 951.

Bulletin of the Center for Children's Books, December, 1984, p. 67; May, 1985, p. 167; February, 1986, p. 110; September, 1987, p. 9; June, 1988, p. 206; February, 1989, p. 148; February, 1991, p. 142; September, 1995, p. 16; February, 2001, review of *Pieces: A Year in Poems and Quilts,* p. 223.

Horn Book, January-February, 1985, p. 45; July-August, 1985, p. 439; July-August, 1986, p. 440; September-October, 1986, Mary M. Burns, review of *Daddy Makes the Best Spaghetti,* pp. 580-581; July-August, 1987, p. 453; July-August, 1988, Ellen Fader, review of *Grandma Gets Grumpy,* pp. 479-480; May-June, 1989, p. 358; September-October, 1989, Ellen Fader, review of *Big Like Me,* pp. 611-612; November-December, 1994, p. 760; July-August, 1996, p. 450.

Horn Book Guide, spring, 1999, Patricia Riley, review of *My Own Big Bed,* p. 31; fall, 1999, Christie Heppermann, review of *What Can You Do in the Rain?,* p. 234.

Kirkus Reviews, February 15, 1986, review of *Daddy Makes the Best Spaghetti,* p. 303; April 1, 1988, review of *Grandma Gets Grumpy,* p. 539; December 15, 2000, review of *Pieces: A Year in Poems and Quilts;* August 1, 2001, review of *Whose Shoes?,* p. 1124.

New York Times Book Review, September 22, 1985, p. 32; September 7, 1986, p. 26; May 8, 1988, p. 30; September 8, 1996, p. 28.

Publishers Weekly, March 30, 1984, review of *Come to the Meadow,* p. 56; March 21, 1986, p. 86; April 25, 1986, p. 72; August 28, 1987, p. 76; September 25, 1987, p. 107; April 28, 1989, p. 76; July 28, 1989, p. 220; February 23, 1990, p. 219; August 2, 1991, review of *Tell Me Your Best Thing,* pp. 72-73; November 9, 1998, review of *My Own Big Bed,* p. 76; April 12, 1999, Jennifer M. Brown, review of *What Can You Do in the Rain?,* p. 78; January 8, 2001, review of *Pieces: A Year in Poems and Quilts,* p. 67.

School Library Journal, May, 1985, B. P. Goldstone, review of *All by Myself,* p. 76; January, 1986, Phyllis Ingram, review of *Cassie Bowen Takes Witch Lessons,* p. 68; February, 1993, Andrew W. Hunter, review of *Rumble Thumble Boom!,* p. 72; September, 1993, Anna DeWind, review of *Moompa, Toby and Bomp,* p. 208; June, 1994, Donna L. Scanlon, review of *The Day of the High Climber,* p. 101; May, 1996, Lisa Marie Gangemi, review of *When We Married Gary,* p. 92; May, 1997, Marianne Saccardi, review of *Miss Emma's Wild Garden,* p. 100; April, 1999, Karen James, review of *My Own Big Bed,* p. 97; June, 1999, Dawn Amsberry, review of *What Can You Do in the Rain?,* p. 97; March, 2001, Nina Lindsay, review of *Pieces: A Year in Poems and Quilts,* p. 236; August, 2001, Anne Parker, review of *Whose Shoes?,* p. 153.

OTHER

Anna Grossnickle Hines Web Site, http://www.aghines.com/ (March 6, 2002).*

*   *   *

HYDE, Catherine Ryan 1955-

Personal

Born 1955, in Buffalo, NY; daughter of a part-time musician father and a writer mother.

Addresses

Agent—c/o Hardy Agency, 3020 Bridgeway, #204, Sausalito, CA 94965-2839. *E-mail*—ryanhyde@cryanhyde.com.

Career

Novelist and short story writer. Formerly worked as a dog trainer, pastry chef, auto mechanic, shopkeeper, and tour guide at Hearst Castle (California); Cuesta College Writers' Conference, teacher of fiction workshops. Served as member of administrative staff, Santa Barbara Writers' Conference; member of editorial board, *Santa Barbara Review;* member of fiction fellowship panel, Arizona Commission on the Arts, 1998. Pay It Forward Foundation, president and founder.

Awards, Honors

Raymond Carver Short Story Contest honors, 1994, for "Love Is Always Running Away," and 1996, for "Dante"; second-place award, *Bellingham Review* Tobias Wolff Award, 1997, for "Breakage"; numerous Pushcart Prize nominations; citation in *Best American Short Stories 1999,* for "Castration Humor."

Writings

Pay It Forward, Simon & Schuster (New York, NY), 2000.

FOR ADULTS

Funerals for Horses, Russian Hill Press (San Francisco, CA), 1997.
Earthquake Weather (short stories), Russian Hill Press (San Francisco, CA), 1998.
Electric God, Simon & Schuster (New York, NY), 2000.
Walter's Purple Heart, Simon & Schuster (New York, NY), 2002.

Contributor to literary journals, including *Antioch Review, Amherst Review, Sun, Manoa, Puerto del Sol, Virginia Quarterly Review, Ploughshares, New Letters,* and *Michigan Quarterly Review.* Contributor to anthologies, including *Santa Barbara Stories,* John Daniel & Co., 1998; and *California Shorts,* Heyday Books, 1999.

Adaptations

Pay It Forward was adapted as a film starring Kevin Spacey and Helen Hunt, released by Warner Brothers, 2000.

Work in Progress

A collection of short stories, *Subway Dancer and Other Stories;* three novels, *Turtle Park, Chloe Nothing and the Cellar King,* and *Dangerous Dogs;* a partially completed novel, *Love in the Present Tense.*

Sidelights

Catherine Ryan Hyde published her first novel, *Funerals for Horses,* in 1997 with a small publishing house in San Francisco, following this work a year later with a collection of short fiction titled *Earthquake Weather.* Hyde's second novel, *Pay It Forward,* rode the wave of good press generated by her debut work and was a subject of interest in the U.S. film industry before it was even published.

Given an extra-credit assignment by his social studies teacher to think of a plan that would change society, twelve-year-old Trevor McKinney conceives of a "good will chain" in *Pay It Forward.* He will do something good for three people, but rather than have them in his debt, he asks them to "pay it forward" by doing good turns for three other people. One of Trevor's good acts is to try to bring his hard-working single mom, Arlene, together with his social studies teacher, Reuben St. Clair. The two do not seem to have much in common to start.

She is white, pretty, and works two jobs while trying to recover from alcohol addiction; he is black, well-educated, and missing half his face from an explosion in Vietnam. Although the outlook on this romance looks dim at first, like Trevor's other good works, it picks up steam before long. Trevor's extra-credit project soon escalates into a major movement through the work of journalist Chris Chandler, whose articles interweave throughout Hyde's fictional narrative.

Pay It Forward received a great deal of critical attention. Although *Time* contributor R. Z. Sheppard dubbed Trevor's project "an idealistic Ponzi scheme" and found the romantic aspects of the plotline "plodding," *Booklist* reviewer Carolyn Kubisz called the novel a "beautifully written, heartwarming story of one boy's belief in the goodness of humanity." The *Chicago Tribune*'s Scott Eyman praised Hyde's "powerful narrative" as well as her ability to tell the story "with an easy, beneficent wisdom about the ways of the world." A *Publishers Weekly* contributor maintained that "Trevor's ultimate martyrdom, and the extraordinary worldwide success of his project, catapult the drama into the realm of myth, but Hyde's simple prose rarely turns preachy." Ultimately, commented *San Francisco Chronicle* reviewer David Field Sunday, Hyde's "fable speaks to the hunger so many of us feel for something to believe in that can give us hope for a future that looks increasingly bleak."

While Hyde continues to be a meticulous editor of her own prose, and rewrites each of her stories several times before submitting it for publication, she refers to herself as a sporadic writer. "I've been known to write ten pages a day for ten days running before I take a breath," she told a *Publishers Weekly* interviewer, but also admitted to taking breaks of over a month between work. "I'm one of those people who laughingly call themselves inspirational writers," Hyde added, "which basically means someone who has no control over their own creative process."

Biographical and Critical Sources

PERIODICALS

Booklist, December 15, 1999, Carolyn Kubisz, review of *Pay It Forward,* p. 757; November 15, 2000, Carolyn Kubisz, review of *Electric God,* p. 609.
Chicago Tribune, March 3, 2000, Scott Eyman, "Capraesque Fable Fosters Inspirational Feeling."
Library Journal, August, 1997, David A. Berona, review of *Funerals for Horses,* p. 130; April 15, 1998, Charlotte L. Glover, review of *Earthquake Weather,* pp. 117-118; November 1, 2000, Michele Leber, review of *Electric God,* p. 134; April 1, 2002, Michele Leber, review of *Walter's Purple Heart,* p. 138.
New Times, April 30, 1998, Joan McCray Tucker, review of *Earthquake Weather.*
Publishers Weekly, April 28, 1997, review of *Funerals for Horses,* p. 52; February 9, 1998, review of *Earthquake Weather,* p. 75; February 22, 1999, John F. Baker, "On the Map," p. 13; November 1, 1999, review of *Pay It Forward,* p. 72; October 16, 2000, review of *Electric*

God, p. 47; December 4, 2000, "Catherine Ryan Hyde: Understanding All the People," p. 48; February 18, 2002, review of *Walter's Purple Heart,* p. 74.

San Francisco Chronicle, February 6, 2000, David Field Sunday, "One Boy's Attempt to Change the World."

San Jose Mercury News, May 31, 1998, Jill Wolfson, review of *Earthquake Weather.*

San Luis Obispo Telegram-Tribune, April 3, 1998, Michael Ray, review of *Earthquake Weather.*

School Library Journal, July, 2000, Claudia Moore, review of *Pay It Forward,* p. 127; December, 2000, review of *Pay It Forward,* p. 56; September, 2002, Julie Dasso, review of *Walter's Purple Heart,* p. 256.

Time, February 14, 2000, R. Z. Sheppard, review of *Pay It Forward,* p. 86.

OTHER

Book Page, http://www.bookpage.com/ (September 15, 2001), "Meet the Author: Catherine Ryan Hyde."

Catherine Ryan Hyde Web Site, http://www.cryanhyde.com/ (December 11, 2001).

Denver Post, http://www.denverpost.com/ (April 7, 2002), Kelly Milner-Halls, review of *Walter's Purple Heart.*

Pay It Forward Foundation Web Site, http://www.payitforwardfoundation.org/ (January 15, 2002).

Pay It Forward Movement Web Site, http://www.payitforwardmovement.org/ (January 15, 2002).

J–K

JACKSON, Melanie 1956-

Personal

Born October 24, 1956, in Aberdeen, Scotland; daughter of Stanley Bernard (a professor of literature) and Nellie Pearl (a schoolteacher) Chandler; married Barry Mason Jackson (a journalist), June 20, 1981; children: Sarah Nelle. *Education:* University of Toronto, B.A. (with honors), 1978; University of Western Ontario, M.A., 1980. *Religion:* Roman Catholic. *Hobbies and other interests:* Jogging; blues, jazz, and swing music; Tudor history; tennis; old movies.

Addresses

Office—British Columbia School Trustees Association, 4-1580 West Broadway, Vancouver, British Columbia, Canada V6J 5K9. *E-mail*—mjackson@telus.net.

Career

British Columbia School Trustees Association, Vancouver, British Columbia, Canada, staff member, 1980—. Also works as freelance editor, layout compositor, and writer. British Columbia Education Week, past coordinator. Trout Lake Softball League, coordinator.

Member

Children's Writers and Illustrators of British Columbia, Vancouver Children's Literature Roundtable, Kerry's Place Autism Society.

Writings

The Spy in the Alley: A Dinah Galloway Mystery, Orca Book Publishers (Victoria, British Columbia, Canada), 2002.
The Man in the Moonstone, Orca Book Publishers (Victoria, British Columbia, Canada), 2003.

Contributor to magazines and newspapers, including *Vancouver, Western Living,* and *Chatelaine.*

Sidelights

Melanie Jackson told *SATA*: "I have wanted to be a writer since as long as I can remember—a mystery writer, for the most part. I wrote my first mystery story at age seven. I'm not sure why I liked stories so much, except that my parents read to me a lot. When I could print, I wrote down my favorite words (for example, 'princess,'), cut each of them out, and kept them in a red, zip-up coin purse.

"I suppose I want to tell a good yarn, get across that art and creativity are very important parts of life (my heroine is a Judy Garland-like singer, and her singing is always involved in solving mysterious problems), and create on paper the ideas and people who live so vividly in my imagination. Because certain stories and films have made such a strong impression on me, I want to create strong stories of my own. In sum, I guess I believe that imagination, whatever its source, mustn't stay bottled up. You have to use it. To think is to exist, yes, but for some to create is to exist as well.

"As a working mother, I have reserved early morning for my original-draft writing. I write in longhand in an exercise book. Editing and revising I can do at other times of the day, but the early-morning time is the special one.

"Dinah (my heroine) evolved from paler versions of herself in countless unpublished stories. The character came first; her family, friends, and foes, and the plot are almost secondary to her glorious self. Other characters have inspired me. These are Dinah's literary ancestors: curious Alice in *Alice in Wonderland* by Lewis Carroll, *Harriet the Spy* by Louise Fitzhugh, *Anne of Green Gables* by Lucy Maud Montgomery, creative Jo March in *Little Women* by Louisa May Alcott, *Eloise* by Kaye Thompson (herself a singer!), *Ramona* by Beverly Cleary, and also Otis Spofford (an old favorite)."

Jackson commented that her writing reflects "a very positive view! The only thing I wonder about is the sudden shift, when kids reach their mid-teens, to supplying them with too many brooding, solemn, life-is-woeful books. I hope we can retain some humor for them.

"My advice to aspiring writers is read a lot. Write about what you know. Someday you may be writing science fiction best-sellers about Urk from the planet Blorg, but for now, look around you for material."

*   *   *

JANOVER, Caroline (Davis) 1943-

Personal

Born May 4, 1943, in Waterbury, CT; daughter of Leverett Davis (a lobster fisherman and English teacher) and Nina (a child psychologist; maiden name, Chandler) Murray; married Andrew G. Janover, June 22, 1967; children: James, Michael. *Education:* Attended Lake Forest College, 1962-64; Sarah Lawrence College, B.A., 1966; Boston University, M.A., 1969; Fairleigh Dickinson University, M.A., 1980. *Politics:* Democrat. *Religion:* Episcopalian. *Hobbies and other interests:* "Weeding my flower gardens, walking through the woods in comfortable shoes, taking naps while listening to Phish and Mozart, being alone for a whole day, cooking pasta, and attending Nantucket family reunions."

Addresses

Office—Ridge School, 325 West Ridgewood Ave., Ridgewood, NJ 07450. *E-mail*—cjanover@aol.com.

Career

Dalton School, New York, NY, elementary teacher, 1968-77; Ridge School, Ridgewood, NJ, learning disabilities teacher and consultant, 1979—. National speaker on "ways to increase the skills and self-esteem of children with learning differences, specializing in the multiple intelligence of the dyslexic learner."

Member

International Dyslexia Association, Learning Disabilities Association, League of Women Voters.

Awards, Honors

Outstanding Teacher Award from the governor of New Jersey, 1988; Special Educator of the Year Award, Ridgewood School District, 1991; Best Book for the Teen Age citation, New York Public Library, 1995, for *The Worst Speller in Junior High.*

Writings

Josh: A Boy with Dyslexia, Waterfront Books (Burlington, VT), 1988.

Caroline Janover

The Worst Speller in Junior High, Free Spirit Publishing (Minneapolis, MN), 1995.
Zipper, the Kid with ADHD, illustrated by Rick Powell, Woodbine House (Bethesda, MD), 1997.
How Many Days until Tomorrow?, illustrated by Charlotte Fremaux, Woodbine House (Bethesda, MD), 2000.

Contributor to books, including *Their World 1993,* National Center for Learning Disabilities. Contributor to the periodical *Learning Consultant Journal.*

Sidelights

Caroline Janover, a specialist in teaching students with learning disabilities, is the author of several books about children who rise to the challenge of a learning difference. Janover experienced firsthand the problems that learning disabled children face in school. She once commented that "growing up with a learning difference isn't easy. When I was in elementary school, I had an extremely difficult time learning how to read, write, and spell. My second year in the second grade, my teacher made me stand in the wastepaper basket because I wrote my letters backward and lost my place in the reading group. A reading specialist tested me and discovered that I was severely dyslexic. When my teacher heard the news, she looked horrified. 'Is dyslexia contagious?,' she asked."

Upon graduation from college, Janover won a full scholarship to attend graduate school and became a teacher so that she could "work with children who are smart but who need to be taught a different way to learn." After both of her sons were found to have dyslexia as well, Janover began writing novels for them "and for the millions of other creative, intelligent, and talented young people who grow up with learning differences." Although she received over 100 rejection letters the author explained, "I never gave up hope of being published. Having dyslexia has taught me that if you believe in yourself, work hard, and never give up hope, you can one day reach your dream!"

Janover's first book, *Josh: A Boy with Dyslexia,* focuses on a fifth-grader who is teased by his older brother and the kids on the block because he gets lost walking to school and runs the bases backward in kick-ball. Using clever compensating strategies, Josh saves the day in a crisis and wins the respect of his brother and classmates at school. This title was recently made available through a "print-on-demand" service through iuniverse.com.

The Worst Speller in Junior High also deals with learning differences. This novel features thirteen-year-old Katie Kelso, who wants to become a "PK" (popular kid) and write for the school literary magazine despite her poor spelling skills. Katie, who is beginning her first year of junior high, worries about making friends, attracting boys, and doing well in her classes. To add to these concerns, her mother is diagnosed with breast cancer, forcing Katie to babysit for her bothersome younger brothers. In the end, with the help of her parents, teachers, and new boyfriend Brian, Katie succeeds in feeling good about herself both as a student and as a friend. A critic in *Publishers Weekly* found Katie "an engaging heroine" who overcomes her difficulties while "inviting and maintaining the reader's affections." Although Katie's triumph over dyslexia occasionally "overwhelms the story," according to *Booklist* contributor Kay Weisman, "the dialogue rings true, and preteen social issues are well handled."

Janover added: "In 1997 I published *Zipper: The Kid with ADHD,* a book dedicated to my oldest son, Jamie. Written at a third-to-sixth-grade reading level, the story is a funny but realistic tale about a fifth-grader who acts before he thinks. Zipper has millions of thoughts bounding in his brain. He forgets chores and homework assignments, behaves impulsively, and drives his parents and teachers crazy. Underneath it all, Zipper is a smart, well-intentioned young man. Zipper begins to take control of his impulsive behaviors when he is inspired to earn the object of his dreams, a drum set!" A *Booklist* critic commented: "Janover's story will enlighten and reassure children who see themselves or others in the character of Zipper." Another reviewer reported in *Intervention in School and Clinic:* "This book is a great story for teaching understanding and acceptance of individuals with disabilities.... General and special educators alike should consider putting it on the required reading list."

Janover wrote: "In *How Many Days until Tomorrow?* Josh, a twelve-year-old boy with dyslexia, is forced to

Twelve-year-old Josh, who has dyslexia, discovers that he has other talents when he spends the summer with his bookish older brother and gruff grandfather on an island in Maine. (From How Many Days until Tomorrow?, *illustrated by Charlotte Fremaux.)*

spend a summer on a remote island off the coast of Maine. His teasing older brother and grandparents he hardly knows make rugged island living a torture, especially because his grandfather (alias Grumps) rarely says a kind word. At the end of the summer, Josh uses his ingenuity to save his grandfather's life, learning that, in many ways, he is just as smart as his 'gifted' older brother." A *School Library Journal* contributor wrote: "Josh's life is not easy but his complaints and defeats never come across as whining or pathetic. He shows heroism every day as he struggles with his disability.... A fine novel that happens to have a dyslexic hero."

Biographical and Critical Sources

PERIODICALS

Booklist, February 1, 1995, Kay Weisman, review of *The Worst Speller in Junior High,* p. 1005; February, 1998, review of *Zipper: The Kid with ADHD.*
Intervention in School and Clinic, March, 1999, review of *Zipper.*
Kliatt, March, 1995, p. 8.
Publishers Weekly, November 21, 1994, p. 78, review of *The Worst Speller in Junior High.*
School Library Journal, September, 1988, p. 183; February, 1995, p. 98; May, 2001, review of *How Many Days until Tomorrow?*

JOHNSON, Stephen T. 1964-

Personal

Born 1964, in Madison, WI. *Education:* University of Kansas, B.F.A., 1987; attended Universite de Bordeaux and the Conservatoire des Beaux-Arts, Bordeaux, France, 1984-85.

Addresses

Agent—c/o Author Mail, Penguin Putnam, 375 Hudson Street, New York, NY 10014

Career

Illustrator; guest lecturer and instructor. Illustrator of cover art for magazines, including *Forbes* and *Time;* illustrator of CD covers for record companies; creator of artwork for State Ballet of Missouri, Association of Kansas Theatre, and Georgia Department of Industry, Trade, and Tourism. *Exhibitions:* Works were exhibited in a one-man show at the Center for the Arts Gallery, Moorhead State University, Moorhead, MN, 1991; works have also appeared in several group exhibitions, including the Society of Illustrators Museum and the Norman Rockwell Museum, and in public collections, including the National Portrait Gallery.

Awards, Honors

Best of Show Award, Lawrence Art Center, 1987; Philip Isenberg Memorial Award, Pastel Society of America, 1992; David Humphrey's Memorial Award, Allied Artists of America, 1992; Alice Melrose Memorial

In Love as Strong as Ginger, *written by Lenore Look, Katie learns how hard her grandmother is working at a crab cannery. (Illustrated by Stephen T. Johnson.)*

Award, Audubon Artists, 1993; Knickerbocker Artists Award, Salmagundi Club, 1993; H. K. Holbein Award, Pastel Society of America, 1993; Yarka Art Materials Award, Audubon Artists, 1994; Washington Square Outdoor Award, Salmagundi Club, 1995; Caldecott Honor Book, 1995, for *Alphabet City.*

Writings

SELF-ILLUSTRATED

Alphabet City, Viking (New York, NY), 1995.
City by Numbers, Viking (New York, NY), 1998.
My Little Red Toolbox, Harcourt (San Diego, CA), 2000.
My Little Blue Robot, Silver Whistle (San Diego, CA), 2002.
As the City Sleeps, Viking (New York, NY), 2002.

ILLUSTRATOR

Robert D. San Souci, *The Samurai's Daughter: A Japanese Legend,* Dial Books (New York, NY), 1992.
Melissa Hayden, *The Nutcracker Ballet,* Andrews & McMeel (Kansas City, MO), 1992.
Robert D. San Souci, *The Snow Wife,* Dial Books (New York, NY), 1993.
Charles Dickens, *A Christmas Carol,* adapted by Donna Martin, Andrews & McMeel (Kansas City, MO), 1993.
Sheila MacGill-Callahan, *When Solomon Was King,* Dial Books (New York, NY), 1995.
Steven Schnur, *The Tie Man's Miracle: A Chanukah Tale,* Morrow (New York, NY), 1995.
Robert Burleigh, *Hoops,* Silver Whistle (San Diego, CA), 1997.
Lenore Look, *Love as Strong as Ginger,* Atheneum (New York, NY), 1999.
Dori Chaconas, *On a Wintry Morning,* Viking (New York, NY), 2000.
Steve Sanfield, *The Girl Who Wanted a Song,* Harcourt (San Diego, CA), 1996.
Robert Burleigh, *Goal,* Harcourt (San Diego, CA), 2001.
Jane Yolen, *The Hurrying Child,* Silver Whistle (San Diego, CA), 2001.
Diane Siebert, *Tour America,* Sea Star Books (New York, NY), 2003.

Sidelights

Stephen T. Johnson had already illustrated several books before he won the prestigious Caldecott Honor Book citation with his first solo effort, *Alphabet City.* Reviewers have considered *Alphabet City* to be an artistic inspiration for older children as well as a didactic picture book for young children. Indeed, this wordless book "invites young and old alike to take a new look at familiar surroundings, discovering the alphabet without ever looking in a book or reading from a sign," according to Nancy Menaldi-Scanlan in *School Library Journal.* Johnson employs a medley of media, including gouache, watercolor, pastels, and charcoal to create illustrations so realistic critics likened them to photographs. But, "this is hardly an alphabet book for preschoolers," stated *Booklist* contributor Ilene Cooper, who noted that some of Johnson's depictions of letters might puzzle adult eyes, much less the children for whom it is intended. "Nevertheless," Cooper observed, "the artwork is quite amazing."

Johnson used the same idea as the basis for *City by Numbers,* in which ordinary sights around New York City, including the Brooklyn Bridge and Central Park, are shown to exhibit the form of a number from one to twenty-one. "The stunningly realistic paintings in this wonderful book invite readers of all ages to view their world in a new and playful way," asserted David J. Whitin in *Teaching Children Mathematics.* Whether as inspiration for younger children exploring math concepts, or for older children becoming interested in the art of form, readers cannot fail to be affected by Johnson's "deep sense of the rhythm and harmony of city life," wrote GraceAnne A. DeCandido in *Booklist.* Johnson offers a spookier vision of the city in his *As the City Sleeps,* an "eerie ramble" through phantasmagoric city streets at night that a contributor to *Publishers Weekly* found "mesmerizing."

Johnson is also the creator of two books, *My Little Red Toolbox* and *My Little Blue Robot,* whose sturdy cardboard pages release smaller pieces that can interact with other pieces of the book. Thus, *My Little Red Toolbox* features a paper wrench and bolts to tighten, as well as a saw and an erasable drawing board. And in *My Little Blue Robot* little hands can create a robot out of the pieces that can be removed from the book.

Johnson's artwork has also contributed to the success of picture books by other authors. His diminutive, intimate pastel-and-watercolor illustrations grace Lenore Look's book *Love as Strong as Ginger,* a nostalgic vision of her grandmother, whose backbreaking work in a cannery helped establish the family of recent Chinese immigrants. "Sometimes sketchy, the illustrations imply a mood rather than tell a story, and in this way intensify the emotional content of the text," explained a contributor to *Publishers Weekly.* Likewise, in Robert Burleigh's *Hoops,* Johnson's illustrations are considered a valuable contribution to the author's poetic tribute to the feel of playing the game. Indeed, "the drawings create a loose storyline for the staccato text," remarked a contributor to *Publishers Weekly.* For *Booklist* reviewer Carolyn Phelan, "the drawings create context and characters as they express the players' moves and emotions."

Johnson has found a grateful audience in picture book readers who applaud the emotive quality of his artwork. Employing charcoal, gouache, and watercolor to create effects either realistic or impressionistic, focusing in on subjects of various racial composition in rural settings or city streets, Johnson's illustrations are considered to enrich and deepen the stories they accompany or stand alone as artistic inspirations to young people exploring letters, numbers, and shapes.

Biographical and Critical Sources

PERIODICALS

Booklist, January 1, 1996, Ilene Cooper, review of *Alphabet City,* p. 824; November 15, 1997, Carolyn Phelan, review of *Hoops,* p. 558; February 15, 1999, Grace-Anne A. DeCandido, review of *City by Numbers,* p. 1065; October 15, 1999, Hazel Rochman, review of *Love as Strong as Ginger,* p. 443; April 15, 2001, Kelly Milner Halls, review of *Goal,* p. 1562; September 1, 2001, Gillian Engberg, review of *Goal,* p. 101.

Early Childhood Education Journal, summer, 2001, Pauline Devay Zeece, review of *My Little Red Toolbox,* p. 238.

Horn Book Magazine, November, 1998, Lolly Robinson, review of *City by Numbers,* p. 708; May, 1999, review of *Love as Strong as Ginger,* p. 318.

Kirkus Reviews, September 15, 1998, review of *City by Numbers,* p. 1385; October 1, 2002, review of *As the City Sleeps,* p. 1492.

Plays, October, 2001, review of *Goal,* p. 70.

Publishers Weekly, November 11, 1996, review of *The Girl Who Wanted a Song,* p. 74; October 6, 1997, review of *Hoops,* p. 83; May 24, 1999, review of *Love as Strong as Ginger,* p. 79; August 7, 2000, "All in a Day's Work," review of *My Little Red Toolbox,* p. 97; October 23, 2000, review of *On a Wintry Morning,* p. 74; August 12, 2002, "Otherworldly Tips," review of *My Little Blue Robot,* p. 302; October 21, 2002, review of *As the City Sleeps,* p. 73.

School Library Journal, January, 1996, Nancy Menaldi-Scanlon, review of *Alphabet City,* pp. 85-86; July, 1997, John Philbrook, review of *The Girl Who Wanted a Song,* p. 74; November, 1997, Connie C. Rockman, review of *Hoops,* p. 105; February, 1999, Pam Gosner, review of *City by Numbers,* p. 99; July, 1999, Margaret A. Change, review of *Love as Strong as Ginger,* p. 76; November, 2000, Jane Marino, review of *On a Wintry Morning,* p. 112.

Teaching Children Mathematics, March, 2000, David J. Whitin, review of *City by Numbers,* p. 470.*

*   *   *

KERRY, Lois
See DUNCAN, Lois

L

LANDAU, Elaine 1948-

Personal

Born February 15, 1948, in Lakewood, NJ; daughter of James and May (a department store manager; maiden name, Tudor) Garmiza; married Edward William Landau (an electrical engineer), December 16, 1968; children: Michael Brent. *Education:* New York University, B.A., 1970; Pratt Institute, M.L.S., 1975. *Religion:* Jewish. *Hobbies and other interests:* Botany.

Addresses

Home—11810 Southwest 92nd Lane, Miami, FL 33186.

Career

Reporter on community newspaper in New York, NY, 1970-72; Simon & Schuster, New York, NY, editor, 1972-73; Tuckahoe Public Library, Tuckahoe, NY, director, 1975-79; Sparta Public Library, Sparta, NJ, director.

Member

Society of Children's Book Writers and Illustrators, American Library Association.

Awards, Honors

New Jersey Institute of Technology awards, 1977, for both *Death: Everyone's Heritage* and *Hidden Heroines: Women in American History,* 1981, for both *Occult Visions: A Mystical Gaze into the Future* and *The Teen Guide to Dating,* and 1989, for both *Alzheimer's Disease* and *Surrogate Mothers;* NCSS/CBC Notable Children's Trade Book in the Field of Social Studies, 1990, for *We Have AIDS,* 1991, for *We Survived the Holocaust,* 2002, for *Columbus Day: Celebrating a Famous Explorer* and *Heroine of the Titanic: The Real Unsinkable Molly Brown,* and 2003, for *Osama bin Laden: A War against the West;* ALA Quick Picks for Reluctant Young Adult

Elaine Landau

Readers, 1991, for *We Have AIDS;* Science Books and Films (SB&F) Annual Best Children's Science Book List, 1991, for *Neptune,* 1994, for *Rabies,* 1996, for *ESP* and *The Curse of Tutankhamen,* 1997, for *Ocean Mammals* and *Tropical Forest Mammals,* and 1998, for *Joined at Birth; The Lives of Conjoined Twins;* Society of School Librarians, "Best of 1993," for *The White Power Movement;* NSTA/CBC Outstanding Science Trade Books for Children, 1994, for *Rabies; Booklist* Selection of the Best Rain Forest Books of the Decade, 1997, for *Tropical Rain Forests around the World,* and *Tropical Forest Mammals;* SB&F Best Science Books for Junior High and High School Readers, 1998, for *Tourette Syndrome* and *Joined at Birth; The Lives of Conjoined Twins;* Ohio Farm Bureau Award for Children's Literature, 2000, for *Corn;* New York Public Library Books for the Teenage, 2001, for *Heroine of the Titanic: The Real Unsinkable Molly Brown; Voya* 7th Annual Nonfiction Honor List, 2001, for *Heroine of the Titanic: The Real Unsinkable Molly Brown;* Society of School Librarians International Book Award, Honor Book, 2002, for *Osama bin Laden: A War against the West; Booklist* Top 10 Biographies for Youth, 2002, for *Osama bin Laden: A War against the West;* International Reading Association Young Adult's Choice, 2003, for *Slave Narratives: The Journey to Freedom;* Texas Bluebonnet Award Master List, 2003-2004, for *Smokejumpers.*

Writings

(With Jesse Jackson) *Black in America: A Fight for Freedom,* Messner (New York, NY), 1973.

Woman, Woman! Feminism in America, Messner (New York, NY), 1974.

Hidden Heroines: Women in American History, Messner (New York, NY), 1975.

Death: Everyone's Heritage, Messner (New York, NY), 1976.

Yoga for You, Messner (New York, NY), 1977.

Occult Visions: A Mystical Gaze into the Future, illustrated by Carol Gjertsen, Messner (New York, NY), 1979.

The Teen Guide to Dating, Messner (New York, NY), 1980.

The Smart Spending Guide for Teens, Messner (New York, NY), 1982.

Why Are They Starving Themselves?: Understanding Anorexia Nervosa and Bulimia, Messner (New York, NY), 1983.

Child Abuse: An American Epidemic, Messner (New York, NY), 1984, 2nd edition, 1990.

Growing Old in America, Messner (New York, NY), 1985.

Different Drummer: Homosexuality in America, Messner (New York, NY), 1986.

Sexually Transmitted Diseases, Enslow (Berkeley Heights, NJ), 1986.

Alzheimer's Disease, Franklin Watts (New York, NY), 1987.

The Homeless, Messner (New York, NY), 1987.

On the Streets: The Lives of Adolescent Prostitutes, Messner (New York, NY), 1987.

Surrogate Mothers, Franklin Watts (New York, NY), 1988.

Teenagers Talk about School—and Open Their Hearts about Their Closest Concerns, Messner (New York, NY), 1988.

The Sioux, Franklin Watts (New York, NY), 1989.

Black Market Adoption and the Sale of Children, Franklin Watts (New York, NY), 1990.

Cowboys, Franklin Watts (New York, NY), 1990.

Teenage Violence, Messner (New York, NY), 1990.

Tropical Rain Forests around the World, Franklin Watts (New York, NY), 1990.

Nazi War Criminals, Franklin Watts (New York, NY), 1990.

Lyme Disease, Franklin Watts (New York, NY), 1990.

We Have AIDS, Franklin Watts (New York, NY), 1990.

Weight: A Teenage Concern, Lodestar (New York, NY), 1991.

Wildflowers around the World, Franklin Watts (New York, NY), 1991.

We Survived the Holocaust, Franklin Watts (New York, NY), 1991.

Armed America: The Status of Gun Control, Messner (New York, NY), 1991.

Dyslexia, Franklin Watts (New York, NY), 1991.

Mars, Franklin Watts (New York, NY), 1991.

Chemical and Biological Warfare, Lodestar (New York, NY), 1991.

Interesting Invertebrates: A Look at Some Animals without Backbones, Franklin Watts (New York, NY), 1991.

Colin Powell: Four-Star General, Franklin Watts (New York, NY), 1991.

A survivor of the Titanic disaster, Margaret Brown— better known as the "Unsinkable Molly Brown"— championed social and political causes and ran for the U.S. Congress, as Landau portrays in **Heroine of the Titanic.** *(Photo from the Colorado Historical Society.)*

Jupiter, Franklin Watts (New York, NY), 1991.

Robert Fulton, Franklin Watts (New York, NY), 1991.

Saturn, Franklin Watts (New York, NY), 1991.

Neptune, Franklin Watts (New York, NY), 1991.

Endangered Plants, Franklin Watts (New York, NY), 1992.

The Warsaw Ghetto Uprising, New Discovery (New York, NY), 1992.

Terrorism: America's Growing Threat, Lodestar (New York, NY), 1992.

Big Brother Is Watching: Secret Police and Intelligence Services, Walker (New York, NY), 1992.

Teens and the Death Penalty, Enslow (Berkeley Heights, NJ), 1992.

The Cherokees, Franklin Watts (New York, NY), 1992.

State Birds: Including the Commonwealth of Puerto Rico, Franklin Watts (New York, NY), 1992.

State Flowers: Including the Commonwealth of Puerto Rico, Franklin Watts (New York, NY), 1992.

Bill Clinton, Franklin Watts (New York, NY), 1993.

Sexual Harassment, Walker (New York, NY), 1993.

Yeti: Abominable Snowman of the Himalayas, Millbrook Press (Brookfield, CT), 1993.

The White Power Movement: America's Racist Hate Groups, Millbrook Press (Brookfield, CT), 1993.

Sasquatch: Wild Man of the Woods, Millbrook Press (Brookfield, CT), 1993.

The Loch Ness Monster, Millbrook Press (Brookfield, CT), 1993.

Rabies, Lodestar (New York, NY), 1993.

The Right to Die, Franklin Watts (New York, NY), 1993.

Interracial Dating and Marriage, Messner (New York, NY), 1993.

Environmental Groups: The Earth Savers, Enslow (Berkeley Heights, NJ), 1993.

Allergies, Twenty-first Century Books (Brookfield, CT), 1994.

Epilepsy, Twenty-first Century Books (Brookfield, CT), 1994.

Deafness, Twenty-first Century Books (Brookfield, CT), 1994.

Teenage Drinking, Enslow (Berkeley Heights, NJ), 1994.

The Chilulas, Franklin Watts (New York, NY), 1994.

Blindness, Twenty-first Century Books (Brookfield, CT), 1994.

The Beauty Trap, New Discovery (New York, NY), 1994.

Sibling Rivalry: Brothers and Sisters at Odds, Millbrook Press (Brookfield, CT), 1994.

Diabetes, Twenty-first Century Books (Brookfield, CT), 1994.

The Pomo, Franklin Watts (New York, NY), 1994.

Cancer, Twenty-first Century Books (Brookfield, CT), 1994.

The Hopi, Franklin Watts (New York, NY), 1994.

Breast Cancer, Franklin Watts (New York, NY), 1995.

Your Legal Rights: From Custody Battles to School Searches, the Headline-making Cases that Affect Your Life, Walker (New York, NY), 1995.

Hooked: Talking about Addiction, Millbrook Press (Brookfield, CT), 1995.

Ghosts, Millbrook Press (Brookfield, CT), 1995.

Tuberculosis, Franklin Watts (New York, NY), 1995.

The Abenaki, Franklin Watts (New York, NY), 1996.

Temperate Forest Mammals, Children's Press (New York, NY), 1996.

Tropical Forest Mammals, Children's Press (New York, NY), 1996.

ESP, Millbrook Press (Brookfield, CT), 1996.

UFO's, Millbrook Press (Brookfield, CT), 1996.

Mountain Mammals, Children's Press (New York, NY), 1996.

Stalking, Franklin Watts (New York, NY), 1996.

The Ottawas, Franklin Watts (New York, NY), 1996.

Fortune Telling, Millbrook Press (Brookfield, CT), 1996.

Foretelling the Future, Millbrook Press (Brookfield, CT), 1996.

Grassland Mammals, Children's Press (New York, NY), 1996.

Desert Mammals, Children's Press (New York, NY), 1996.

Ocean Mammals, Children's Press (New York, NY), 1996.

Near-Death Experiences, Millbrook Press (Brookfield, CT), 1996.

The Shawnee, Franklin Watts (New York, NY), 1996.

The Curse of Tutankhamen, Millbrook Press (Brookfield, CT), 1996.

Bill Clinton and His Presidency, Franklin Watts (New York, NY), 1997.

Joined at Birth: The Lives of Conjoined Twins, Franklin Watts (New York, NY), 1997.

Short Stature: From Folklore to Fact, Franklin Watts (New York, NY), 1997.

Standing Tall: Unusually Tall People, Franklin Watts (New York, NY), 1997.

Living with Albinism, Franklin Watts (New York, NY), 1997.

The Sumerians, Millbrook Press (Brookfield, CT), 1997.

Your Pet Cat, Children's Press (New York, NY), 1997.

Your Pet Dog, Children's Press (New York, NY), 1997.

Your Pet Gerbil, Children's Press (New York, NY), 1997.

Your Pet Hamster, Children's Press (New York, NY), 1997.

Your Pet Iguana, Children's Press (New York, NY), 1997.

Your Pet Tropical Fish, Children's Press (New York, NY), 1997.

Minibeasts As Pets, Children's Press (New York, NY), 1997.

Parrots and Parakeets as Pets, Children's Press (New York, NY), 1997.

Wild Children: Growing Up without Human Contact, Franklin Watts (New York, NY), 1998.

Multiple Births, Franklin Watts (New York, NY), 1998.

Tourette Syndrome, Franklin Watts (New York, NY), 1998.

Apatosaurus, Children's Press (New York, NY), 1999.

Pterodactyls, Children's Press (New York, NY), 1999.

Stegosaurus, Children's Press (New York, NY), 1999.

Triceratops, Children's Press (New York, NY), 1999.

Tyrannosaurus Rex, Children's Press (New York, NY), 1999.

Velociraptor, Children's Press (New York, NY), 1999.

Angelfish, Children's Press (New York, NY), 1999.

Electric Fish, Children's Press (New York, NY), 1999.

Jellyfish, Children's Press (New York, NY), 1999.

Piranhas, Children's Press (New York, NY), 1999.

Sea Horses, Children's Press (New York, NY), 1999.

Siamese Fighting Fish, Children's Press (New York, NY), 1999.

Apples, Children's Press (New York, NY), 1999.

Bananas, Children's Press (New York, NY), 1999.

Corn, Children's Press (New York, NY), 1999.

Sugar, Children's Press (New York, NY), 1999.

Tomatoes, Children's Press (New York, NY), 1999.

Wheat, Children's Press (New York, NY), 1999.

Australia and New Zealand, Children's Press (New York, NY), 1999.

India, Children's Press (New York, NY), 1999.

Israel, Children's Press (New York, NY), 1999.

Korea, Children's Press (New York, NY), 1999.

Norway, Children's Press (New York, NY), 1999.

Puerto Rico, Children's Press (New York, NY), 1999.

Parkinson's Disease, Franklin Watts (New York, NY), 1999.

Jupiter, Franklin Watts (New York, NY), 1999.

Mars, Franklin Watts (New York, NY), 1999.

Saturn, Franklin Watts (New York, NY), 1999.

Air Crashes, Franklin Watts (New York, NY), 1999.

Fires, Franklin Watts (New York, NY), 1999.

Space Disasters, Franklin Watts (New York, NY), 1999.

Maritime Disasters, Franklin Watts (New York, NY), 1999.

Canada, Children's Press (New York, NY), 2000.

France, Children's Press (New York, NY), 2000.

Dominican Republic, Children's Press (New York, NY), 2000.

Egypt, Children's Press (New York, NY), 2000.

Peru, Children's Press (New York, NY), 2000.

Land Mines: 100 Million Hidden Killers, Enslow Publishers (Berkeley Heights, NJ), 2000.

Pizza: The Pie That's Not a Dessert, Rourke Press (Vero Beach, FL), 2000.

John F. Kennedy, Jr., Twenty-first Century Books (Brookfield, CT), 2000.

The New Nuclear Reality, Twenty-first Century Books (Brookfield, CT), 2000.

Holocaust Memories: Speaking the Truth in Their Own Words, Franklin Watts (New York, NY), 2001.

Slave Narratives: The Journey to Freedom, Franklin Watts (New York, NY), 2001.

Autism, Franklin Watts (New York, NY), 2001.

Heroine of the Titanic: The Real Unsinkable Molly Brown, Clarion Books (New York, NY), 2001.

Ice Cream: The Cold Creamy Treat, Rourke Press (Vero Beach, FL), 2001.

Chocolate: Savor the Flavor, Rourke Press (Vero Beach, FL), 2001.

Pretzels: One of the World's Oldest Snack Foods, Rourke Press (Vero Beach, FL), 2001.

Chewing Gum: A Sticky Treat, Rourke Press (Vero Beach, FL), 2001.

Hamburgers: Bad News for Cows, Rourke Press (Vero Beach, FL), 2001.

Canals, Children's Press (New York, NY), 2001.

Bridges, Children's Press (New York, NY), 2001.

Tunnels, Children's Press (New York, NY), 2001.

Skyscrapers, Children's Press (New York, NY), 2001.

Independence Day: Birthday of the United States, Enslow Publishers (Berkeley Heights, NJ), 2001.

Columbus Day: Celebrating a Famous Explorer, Enslow Publishers (Berkeley Heights, NJ), 2001.

Thanksgiving Day: A Time to Be Thankful, Enslow Publishers (Berkeley Heights, NJ), 2001.

Spinal Cord Injuries, Enslow Publishers (Berkeley Heights, NJ), 2001.

Presidential Election 2000, Children's Press (New York, NY), 2002.

Prince William: W. O. W., William of Wales, Millbrook Press (Brookfield, CT), 2002.

Smokejumpers, photographs by Ben Klaffke, Millbrook Press (Brookfield, CT), 2002.

Head and Brain Injuries, Enslow Publishers (Berkeley Heights, NJ), 2002.

St. Patrick's Day, Enslow Publishers (Berkeley Heights, NJ), 2002.

Valentine's Day: Candy, Love, and Hearts, Enslow Publishers (Berkeley Heights, NJ), 2002.

Veterans Day: Remembering Our War Heroes, Enslow Publishers (Berkeley Heights, NJ), 2002.

Earth Day: Keeping Our Planet Clean, Enslow Publishers (Berkeley Heights, NJ), 2002.

Mardi Gras: Music, Parades, and Costumes, Enslow Publishers (Berkeley Heights, NJ), 2002.

Osama bin Laden: A War against the West, Twenty-first Century Books (Brookfield, CT), 2002.

Popcorn!, illustrated by Brian Lies, Charlesbridge (Watertown, MA), 2003.

Fearsome Alligators, Enslow Publishers (Berkeley Heights, NJ), 2003.

Scary Sharks, Enslow Publishers (Berkeley Heights, NJ), 2003.

Sinister Snakes, Enslow Publishers (Berkeley Heights, NJ), 2003.

Killer Bees, Enslow Publishers (Berkeley Heights, NJ), 2003.

Creepy Spiders, Enslow Publishers (Berkeley Heights, NJ), 2003.

Landau provides answers to common questions about a tasty treat in **Popcorn!,** *illustrated by Brian Lies.*

Fierce Cats, Enslow Publishers (Berkeley Heights, NJ), 2003.

A Healthy Diet, Franklin Watts (New York, NY), 2003.

Alcohol, Franklin Watts (New York, NY), 2003.

Cigarettes, Franklin Watts (New York, NY), 2003.

Cocaine, Franklin Watts (New York, NY), 2003.

The Civil Rights Movement, Franklin Watts (New York, NY), 2003.

A President's Work: A Look at the Executive Branch, Lerner Books (Minneapolis, MN), 2003.

Friendly Foes: A Look at Political Parties, Lerner Books (Minneapolis, MN), 2003.

Contributor of reviews to *New York Times Book Review.*

Sidelights

A prolific author of nonfiction for younger readers, Elaine Landau has been praised by reviewers for her well-researched and well-written books. In topics ranging from the legendary Loch Ness Monster to the presidency of Bill Clinton and the terrorist Osama bin Laden, and from UFO's and ESP to up-to-the minute advances in Alzheimer's Disease research, Landau presents factual information often highlighted by case studies, interviews, and other information that provides readers with added insight into the topic at hand.

Born in New Jersey in 1948, Landau had written her first book by the time she was nine years old, composing it "in the children's room of my local library," as she once recalled to *SATA.* "I spent a lot of time in that room, reading and growing, while remaining safely hidden from a mother, older sister, and aunt who assured me that to dream of becoming an author was an unrealistic career aspiration." But Landau was not to be discouraged by the advice of her family. "The relative hasn't been born who can dampen the magic of a well-spun story," she declared. "Besides, I was a very determined little girl. So determined that by the time I was fifteen, I had written over two dozen books—the longest of which was a full nine pages!"

When Landau was in her mid-twenties and living in New York City, she published the first of her many books. "Although being a 'real' author is often a very lonely occupation (you can't entertain friends while completing a chapter), it is also my greatest joy," she once explained. "I've always loved the idea of reaching out to share my thoughts and feelings with others, and I still can't think of a better way to do so."

Many of Landau's books have been of particular interest to modern teens facing a far different world than that of previous generations, a fact that makes older nonfiction books irrelevant. Eating disorders are dealt with in detail in *Why Are They Starving Themselves?: Understanding Anorexia Nervosa and Bulimia,* which contains interviews with several women and teens, as well as a list of resources on where to get help for both anorexics and their families. The book received a starred review from *Booklist.* Landau's related work, *Weight: A Teenage Concern,* published in 1991, examines the social pres-

sures on young women to be thin, and the prejudice that overweight teens often face. "Readers will enjoy the testimonials of teens and appreciate the author's non-judgmental tone," according to *Voice of Youth Advocates* reviewer Joyce Hamilton. *The Beauty Trap,* which Landau published in 1994, focuses on the root cause of eating disorders: society's obsession with physical beauty and how that obsession is internalized and acted upon by women. Providing basic information on the consequences of falling into the beauty trap in four chapters, the book also includes a list of organizations that offers readers more information on ways to break the cycle. "Landau's insightful and disturbing examination" of modern culture's obsession with the physical appearance of women and girls "should be required reading for all young girls, their parents, and their teachers," according to Jeanne Triner in *Booklist.*

Other books of interest to teen readers have concerned topics of equal seriousness. *Teenage Drinking,* published in 1994, involves readers in the personal life of teens whose lives are controlled by the out-of-control drinking of either themselves or someone close to them. Praised for her ability to "reveal the impact and danger of alcoholism much more clearly and compellingly than the typical statistics and charts" by *Voice of Youth Advocates* reviewer Joanne Eglash, Landau combines stories of young alcoholics with information and advice to family members and friends. Similarly, in *Hooked: Talking about Addiction,* the author divides her discussion into causes of addiction, its effect, and the steps that must be taken in the recovery process, using three case histories of teens as the focus of the book. Susan Dove Lempke, writing in *Booklist,* felt that Landau's book is a "good jumping-off point for students who want to learn about addictions." *Teenagers Talk about School—and Open Their Hearts about Their Closest Concerns,* which features interviews with a wide variety of students across the United States, encompasses many of the topics covered in more detail in Landau's other books. "Teens will surely recognize themselves and their friends in Landau's bittersweet mosaic of the American teen social environment," according to Libby K. White, reviewing the 1988 work for *School Library Journal.*

Sexuality figures prominently in teen life, and Landau has written several books dealing with various aspects of human sexual relationships, from dating to marriage. *Interracial Dating and Marriage* covers everything from the history of cross-race relationships between men and women to interviews with those involved with partners of a different race. White praised the book in *School Library Journal,* calling Landau's approach "warmly supportive of those who find love outside their own group," adding that "there is no attempt to minimize potential difficulties." Concerns over the medical hazards associated with sexual intercourse are covered in 1986's *Sexually Transmitted Diseases* and *We Have AIDS,* a 1990 work that "will surely help to dispel the notion among teenagers that, 'it can't happen to me,'" according to *Appraisal* reviewer Tippin McDaniel. Landau speaks with nine young adults that have contracted the deadly disease, illustrating the fact that

AIDS does strike across racial, cultural, and economic boundaries. The AIDS epidemic also serves as one of Landau's topics in her *Different Drummer: Homosexuality in America.* Examining homosexuality as it currently exists throughout the American social fabric—from same-sex parenting to homophobia—the author "aims to foster a better understanding of homosexuality rather than to offer direct support to those who are questioning their sexual orientation," in the words of Stephanie Zvirin in *Booklist.*

Landau has also examined social issues such as child abuse, sexual harassment, homelessness, and surrogate parenting. *The Homeless,* published in 1987, features several interviews that illustrate the serious plight of Americans with no permanent place to live. Landau's "writing is sober, the text carefully organized, the topic important," noted Zena Sutherland in *Bulletin of the Center for Children's Books.* In *Surrogate Mothers,* the author discusses the various causes of infertility, and the ethics involved in some of the solutions to this problem. In addition to providing an in-depth examination of the "Baby M" case, Landau also includes several other case studies involving couples who wished to have children but, for various reasons, were unable to either bear children of their own or adopt. "The clarity of the writing and the organization of the material work together to capture and hold the reader's interest," commented Leonard J. Garigliano in *Appraisal.*

Additionally, Landau has turned her attention to medical topics. Her 1987 title *Alzheimer's Disease* is constructed to help young readers understand this devastating illness. Using real life stories as an opener, Landau goes on to describe the progressive effects of the disease, including loss of memory and physical debilitation. Landau takes a similar approach in *Parkinson's Disease* and *Living with Albinism.* In the former title, she explains the basics of this motor disorder, from its subsequent tremors to speech problems as well as the problems doctors have in diagnosing it. Landau "has crafted another well-written, well-organized overview," declared Christine A. Moesch in a *School Library Journal* review of this title.

Also writing in *School Library Journal,* Joyce Adams Burner found Landau's *Living with Albinism* a "positive book, written without sensationalism." Focusing on one eleven-year-old with the condition, Landau again personalizes medical problems and thereby makes them more understandable. *Spinal Cord Injuries* is another title with appeal for young teens, a survey that includes the personal histories of celebrities such as Gloria Estefan and Christopher Reeves. *Booklist*'s Roger Leslie called the book "informative" as well as "accessible."

Noting that "kids are fascinated by those who look different from them," *Booklist*'s Ilene Cooper found that Landau answers such queries "in a straightforward way" in two different books: *Short Stature: From Folklore to Fact,* and *Joined at Birth: The Lives of Conjoined Twins.* The author deals with height in *Short Stature,* a book that lets young readers know that people with dwarfism can lead normal and productive lives. In *Joined at Birth,*

Landau takes a look at several examples of such cases, from Eng and Chang to Angela and Amy Lakesberg, who shared a heart before they were separated, and to Abigail and Brittany Hensel, twins sharing one body from below the waist. Thomas Plaut, reviewing the latter title in *Science Books and Films,* felt the "writing style is comfortable and suited to late elementary school youngsters," and Cooper also praised the text, noting that "as always, Landau's writing is clear and cogent." In *Tourette Syndrome* Landau investigates this neurological condition that gives rise to tics and overly verbal behavior. Again using case histories—from athletes to an actor and a surgeon—to explain the disorder, Landau employs an "unadorned style and easily understandable language," according to Randy Meyer in *Booklist.* Christine A. Moesch, writing in *School Library Journal,* also noted that the "writing is clear and well organized," providing for young readers an "excellent overview of a misunderstood condition." Similarly, Kevin S. Beach, writing in *Voice of Youth Advocates,* found that the "attractive format and accessible reading level make this an effective guide."

Natural history is another specialty for Landau, who has written books about the planets, dinosaurs, and plants and animals. Working in the "True Book" series, she has written about a wide array of fish, including angelfish and piranhas. Writing in *School Library Journal,* Karey Wehner called the books of this series "clearly written, well-organized, and attractively formatted introductions." Carolyn Phelan, reviewing *Jellyfish* and *Siamese Fighting Fish* in *Booklist,* commented on the "distinctive look" of the books, dealing with types of fish that are of "special interest to children." Animals as pets is the subject for another series, dealing with the acquisition, care, and feeding of animals from fish to dogs. Reviewing *Your Pet Tropical Fish* in *Teacher Librarian,* Jessica Higgs remarked that it was a "good title for younger readers."

Landau also turns her attention to flora as well as fauna in *Apples* and *Corn,* "simple introductions to food staples," according to Ilene Cooper in *Booklist.* In 2000 *Corn* was awarded the Ohio Farm Bureau Award for Children's Literature. Corn is again examined in Landau's first picture book, *Popcorn!* Kay Weisman noted of the book in *Booklist,* that Landau "uses a lighthearted approach in this picture book for older children." *School Library Journal*'s Barbara L. McMullin wrote, "Children will love this enjoyable, oversized compilation of historical facts, legends, trivia, and recipes."

History and biography provide further inspiration for Landau. Her *John F. Kennedy, Jr.* is a "poignant tribute," according to William McLoughlin in a *School Library Journal* review. Landau tells of the last days and tragic airplane death of this young man who was the son of the assassinated president, John F. Kennedy. McLaughlin further noted that this biography was an "appealing choice." Peter D. Sieruta, writing in *Horn Book Guide,* found the biography "balanced and well-rounded." *Booklist*'s Cooper also had praise for the profile, noting that Landau does "an excellent job" in detailing the events in the life of this young man who "meant more to his country than just his resumé." In *Heroine of the Titanic: The Real Unsinkable Molly Brown,* Landau provides a "realistic biography of an independent and strong-willed woman," according to Andrew Medlar writing in *School Library Journal.* A socialite and social activist, Margaret Brown organized relief for survivors when the ship she was sailing on, the famous Titanic, sunk in 1912. Landau traces the humble origins of Brown until her marriage with a wealthy silver miner thrust her into the socialite role. However, she remained a tireless crusader for social justice, crusading for miners' rights, and her strong character came to the fore when the Titanic went down and she took charge of her lifeboat, helping to rescue others in the water. "Landau hits just the right tone in this complete portrait," Medlar concluded. Another biography with contemporary appeal is Landau's 2002 *Osama bin Laden: A War against the West.* Cooper, writing in *Booklist,* noted the urgent need for such a book, praising the author's "absorbing" narrative. "Landau, who is known for her solid research, applies her considerable talents here," Cooper further remarked. A contributor for *Kirkus Reviews* wrote that the story of bin Laden's transformation from son of a privileged family to international terrorist is "intrinsically chilling."

History of a more general nature is presented in several volumes from Landau, including *Maritime Disasters, Space Disasters,* and *Slave Narratives.* In the first two titles, the author deals with disasters such as the Titanic, the Lusitania, and the Andrea Doria as examples of accidents at sea, and with the Challenger and several other less high-profile disasters in space. Kathy Broderick praised both *Space Disasters* and *Maritime Disasters* in *Booklist,* calling them "clearly written," and sure to "enhance a school's curriculum." In her *Slave Narratives: The Journey to Freedom,* Landau combines both a general historical outlook with four first-person voices and testimonies of one-time slaves, replaying the daily drudgery and terror of the slave life, as well as the dangers of escape and of finding a new home. Edith Ching, reviewing the title in *School Library Journal,* thought it was a "good introduction to the topic as well as a telling account about slave life in various circumstances."

Landau also deals with current affairs in titles such as *The New Nuclear Reality* and *Land Mines.* Anne G. Brouse found the former title to be a "clearly written, accessible overview" in a *School Library Journal* review, and John Peters, writing in *Booklist,* felt this "systematic look ... will leave readers marveling that the world hasn't already been bombed into radioactive slag." Landau points out nuclear dangers which include rogue states with nuclear weapons, the selling of such weapons by the former Soviet Union, and the danger of such weapons falling into the hands of terrorists. *Land Mines* paints an equally chilling picture of the thousands of mines in the world and the awful toll they take on a civilian population. "Landau offers important and persuasive facts about this problem in an effective resource for students," wrote Lynn Evarts in a *Voice of Youth*

Advocates review. Further social history, of a less urgent sort, is served up in the "Finding Out About Holidays" series, in which Landau profiles such national holidays as Thanksgiving and Columbus Day. Reviewing *Columbus Day: Celebrating a Famous Explorer,* Janie Schomberg noted in *School Library Journal* that "Landau gently challenges the myths and assumptions about Columbus" in a book that "gives readers food for thought about the man, the period, and how the holiday might be interpreted and celebrated in today's world."

Writing nonfiction remains Landau's chosen occupation. "Being a nonfiction writer is like taking an unending voyage in a sea of fascinating facts," Landau explained to *SATA.* "Through extensive research and travel, I've learned about desert camels, dolphin intelligence, UFO's, the Loch Ness Monster, and some very deadly diseases. The best part of the experience is sharing the information with young people across America. Even though I may never meet all my readers, I feel as though I'm talking to them whenever they open one of my books."

Biographical and Critical Sources

PERIODICALS

Appraisal, winter, 1989, Leonard J. Garigliano, review of *Surrogate Mothers,* pp. 44-45; summer, 1990, Tippin McDaniel, review of *We Have AIDS,* pp. 31-32; winter, 1991, p. 35; winter, 1994, pp. 55-56; winter, 1995, pp. 118-119; summer, 1996, p. 54.

Booklist, November 1, 1979, p. 450; March 15, 1986, Stephanie Zvirin, *Different Drummer: Homosexuality in America,* p. 1074; December 15, 1987, p. 710; February 1, 1989, p. 932; May 1, 1993, p. 1586; March 15, 1994, Jeanne Triner, review of *The Beauty Trap,* p. 1340; June 1, 1995, Merri Monks, review of *Tuberculosis,* p. 1744; September 15, 1997, Ilene Cooper, review of *Joined at Birth* and *Short Stature,* p. 228, April Judge, review of *Bill Clinton and His Presidency,* p. 228; December 1, 1997, Carolyn Phelan, "The Rain Forest Collection," pp. 628-629; January 1, 1998, Lauren Peterson, review of *The Sumerians,* p. 805; July, 1998, Randy Meyer, review of *Tourette Syndrome,* pp. 1870-1871; November 15, 1998, Karen Hutt, review of *Multiple Births* and *Living with Albinism,* p. 583; June 1, 1999, Carolyn Phelan, review of *Jellyfish* and *Siamese Fighting Fish,* p. 1818; July, 1999, Roger Leslie, review of *Parkinson's Disease,* p. 1936; October 15, 1999, Ilene Cooper, review of *Apples* and *Corn,* p. 449; February 1, 2000, Kathy Broderick, review of *Space Disasters* and *Maritime Disasters,* p. 1020; July, 2000, John Peters, review of *The New Nuclear Reality,* p. 2017; December 15, 2000, Ilene Cooper, review of *John F. Kennedy, Jr.,* p. 806; August, 2001, Hazel Rochman, review of *Slave Narratives,* p. 2105; September 1, 2001, Hazel Rochman, review of *Holocaust Memories,* p. 94; September 15, 2001, Gillian Engberg, review of *Thanksgiving Day,* p. 234; January 1, 2002, Ilene Cooper, review of *Osama bin Laden,* p. 834; February 1, 2002, Roger Leslie, review of *Spinal Cord Injuries,*

p. 933; June 1, 2002, Susan Dove Lempke, review of *Smokejumpers;* February 1, 2003, Kay Weisman, review of *Popcorn!*

Bulletin of the Center for Children's Books, December, 1976, pp. 59-60; October, 1983, p. 31; June, 1986, pp. 187-188; January, 1988, Zena Sutherland, review of *The Homeless,* pp. 94-95; November, 1988, p. 76; June, 1991, p. 242; September, 1993, p. 15; February, 1994, pp. 191-192.

Horn Book Guide, fall, 1998, Gail Hedges, review of *Tourette Syndrome* and *Living with Albinism,* p. 389; fall, 1999, Gail Hedges, review of *Parkinson's Disease,* p. 353; spring, 2001, Peter D. Sieruta, review of *John F. Kennedy, Jr.,* p. 146.

Kirkus Reviews, November 15, 1975, p. 1292; December 15, 1982, p. 1339; May 1, 1986, p. 722; October 15, 1991, p. 1345; June 15, 1993, review of *Sexual Harassment,* p. 787; December 1, 1993, review of *The Right to Die,* p. 1525; February 1, 2002, review of *Osama bin Laden,* p. 183.

Publishers Weekly, May 7, 2001, review of *Heroine of the Titanic,* p. 248.

School Library Journal, February, 1976, p. 46; March, 1980, p. 134; February, 1981; September, 1983, p. 131; November, 1987, p. 110; January, 1989, Libby K. White, review of *Teenagers Talk about School—and Open Their Hearts about Their Closest Concerns,* p. 100; June, 1990, Nancy E. Curran, review of *Black Market Adoption and the Sale of Children,* p. 142; September, 1993, Libby K. White, review of *Interracial Dating and Marriage,* p. 257; January, 1994, p. 138; March, 1994, p. 243; January, 1996, p. 134; September, 1997, Rosie Peasley, review of *Bill Clinton and His Presidency,* p. 232; March, 1998, Cynthia M. Sturgis, review of *The Sumerians* et al., pp. 234-235; July, 1998, Christine A. Moesch, review of *Tourette Syndrome,* p. 107; August, 1998, Joyce Adams Burner, review of *Living with Albinism,* p. 177; June, 1999, Christine A. Moesch, review of *Parkinson's Disease,* pp. 148, 150; August, 1999, Karey Wehner, review of *Piranhas* and *Siamese Fighting Fish,* p. 147; February, 2000, John Peters, review of *Mars* and *Jupiter,* p. 135, Eldon Younce, review of *Space Disasters* and *Maritime Disasters,* p. 135; September, 2000, Anne G. Brouse, review of *The New Nuclear Reality,* p. 250; February, 2001, Joyce Adams Burner, review of *Hamburgers* and *Chewing Gum,* p. 113; March, 2001, William McLoughlin, review of *John F. Kennedy, Jr.,* p. 271; July, 2001, Andrew Medlar, review of *Heroine of the Titanic,* p. 126; August, 2001, Edith Ching, review of *Slave Narratives,* p. 200; September, 2001, Janie Schomberg, review of *Columbus Day* and *Independence Day,* p. 216; December, 2001, Linda Beck, review of *Autism,* p. 165; January, 2002, Pamela K. Bomboy, review of *Thanksgiving Day,* p. 120; July, 2002, Anne Chapman Callaghan, review of *Smokejumpers;* March, 2003, Pamela K. Bomboy, review of *The 2000 Presidential Election,* p. 220; April, 2003, Barbara L. McMullin, review of *Popcorn!*

Science Books and Films, May, 1998, Thomas Plaut, review of *Joined at Birth,* p. 114.

Teacher Librarian, March, 1999, Jessica Higgs, review of *Your Pet Tropical Fish,* p. 48.

Voice of Youth Advocates, April, 1981, p. 45; December, 1987, pp. 46-47; April, 1989, p. 60; August, 1990, p. 177; June, 1991, Joyce Hamilton, review of *Weight: A Teenage Concern,* p. 126; December, 1991, p. 337; June, 1992, Colleen Macklin, review of *Teens and the Death Penalty;* August, 1993, p. 179; February, 1994, p. 397; December, 1994, Joanne Eglash, review of *Teenage Drinking,* p. 300; February, 1995, p. 360; December, 1998, Kevin S. Beach, review of *Tourette Syndrome,* p. 382; February, 2001, Lynn Evarts, review of *Land Mines,* p. 443.

OTHER

Elaine Landau Web Site, http://www.elainelandau.com (May 11, 2003).

* * *

LAWRINSON, Julia 1969-

Personal

Born September 21, 1969, in Perth, Western Australia; married John Farrell (an angling teacher), May 24, 2003; children: Annie. *Education:* Murdoch University, graduate diploma of education, 1998; Edith Cowan University, B.A. (Hons), 1999, currently completing Ph.D.

Addresses

Agent—c/o Fremantle Arts Centre Press, Box 158, North Fremantle, 6159 Western Australia. *E-mail*—skatingtheedge@hotmail.com

Career

Edith Cowan University, Western Australia, university tutor in literature, drama, and children's literature; teacher of English as a second language, 1993—. State Literature Centre of Western Australia, chair.

Awards, Honors

Western Australia Premier's Award for Young Adult Writing, 2001; Centenary Medal recipient, 2003.

Writings

FOR CHILDREN

Obsession, Fremantle Arts Centre Press (Fremantle, Western Australia), 2001.

Skating the Edge, Fremantle Arts Centre Press (Fremantle, Western Australia), 2002.

Loz and Al, Fremantle Arts Centre Press (Fremantle, Western Australia), 2003.

Work in Progress

Suburban Freak Show.

Julia Lawrinson

Sidelights

Julia Lawrinson told *SATA:* "After being permanently suspended from a State high school in Western Australia at the age of fifteen, I spent the remainder of my teenage years on the fringes of society. By the time I was twenty, I had worked in a country roadhouse, in numerous supermarkets and at a cinema, as well as having spent time in two psychiatric hospitals. These things developed my critical eye and gave me a take on the world that was decidedly left-of-centre. The Australian writer David Malouf once said that if you lived to the age of twenty, you possess enough material to write for sixty years. I believe that if your life is unconventional, you could probably stretch that to a hundred.

"I write mainly for teenagers because the things I write about match the intensity of teenage experience. From a technical point of view, you can't hedge, waffle or fake it in YA lit, because your audience will spot it and call you on it straight away. I love the impassioned responses I get from readers: when someone tells you that you've made them re-examine everything in their lives, it's a precious thing."

In Lawrinson's first young adult novel *Obsession,* fifteen-year-old Charlie has moved to a new school, and is alternately bullied by the older students and dismissive of those who would befriend her. This situation offers little comfort to the daughter of an alcoholic mother with an intolerable new boyfriend. Being a part of the school play is the only bright spot in Charlie's new life, and as rehearsals progress, she becomes entranced by the beauty and talent of fellow drama student Kate. Charlie's feelings for Kate, expressed in the diary that provides the novel's narrative, continue to grow until she realizes that she has fallen in love. Although the reader will recognize Charlie's feelings before Charlie herself does, according to Helen Purdie in *Magpies,* the girl's feelings are "handled sympathetically and touchingly, even with humour."

Purdie also praised the skill with which Lawrinson populates her fictional world. Charlie's new friends Julie and Milka are fully-realized, interesting characters in their own right, the critic noted, and Lawrinson's depiction of the bullies Arron and Macca are "chillingly accurate," Purdie continued. Authenticity and passion are two qualities Lawrinson values highly in young adult literature, according to her statements to *SATA,* and the language she uses in *Obsession* reflects this commitment, according to Purdie, who commented that while the book's slang is occasionally harsh, it is always justified by the context, as are the novel's references to sexuality and illicit drug-use. If Barbara Jo McKee, writing in *Kliatt* dubbed *Obsession* "a touching account of a doomed relationship," Purdie found the book to be a bit more intense than that, calling it "one for the mature young adult who enjoys realism."

Lawrinson's second young adult novel, *Skating the Edge,* partially set in an adolescent psychiatric hospital, was described by Brett D'Arcy of *West Australian* as "an imaginatively conceived and skillfully executed novel by an author who obviously has a big future ahead of her." Caitlin, the teenaged narrator of the story, is asked to piece together answers after her friend's suicide. D'Arcy noted, "Lawringson manages to imbue her prose with a strong sense of warmth and passion and, above all, purpose." *Viewpoint*'s Ruth Starke commented, "One of the strengths of *Skating the Edge* is its affectionate portrayal of friendship," adding that "The story rips along at a great pace with occasional flashes of humour and the end is particularly satisfying."

Biographical and Critical Sources

PERIODICALS

Kliatt, November, 2001, Barbara Jo McKee, review of *Obsessions,* p. 16.
Magpies, July, 2001, Helen Purdie, review of *Obsessions,* p. 41.
Viewpoint, spring, 2002, Ruth Starke, review of *Skating the Edge,* p. 31.
West Australian, August 24, 2002, Brett D'Arcy, review of *Skating the Edge.*

*　　*　　*

LOUISE, Heidi
See ERDRICH, Louise

M

MARKUSEN, Bruce (Stanley Rodriguez) 1965-

Personal

Born January 30, 1965, in Bronxville, NY; son of Stanley and Grace (Rodriguez) Markusen; married Sue Bartow (a pharmacy technician), May 20, 2000. *Ethnicity:* "Puerto Rican." *Education:* Hamilton College, B.A., 1987. *Politics:* Republican. *Religion:* Catholic.

Addresses

Office—National Baseball Hall of Fame, P.O. Box 590, Cooperstown, NY 13326. *Agent*—Robert Wilson, P.O. Box 613, Hastings-on-Hudson, NY. *E-mail*—bmark@telenet.net.

Career

WIBX Radio, Utica, NY, sports director, 1987-95; National Baseball Hall of Fame, Cooperstown, NY, senior researcher, 1995-99, manager of program presentations, 2000—. Author, internet writer, collector of baseball cards, volunteer at Bassett Hospital, Cooperstown, NY. Greater Utica Sports Hall of Fame, committee member, 1993-95.

Member

Society for American Baseball Research (SABR).

Awards, Honors

Seymour Medal, SABR, 1999, for *Baseball's Last Dynasty;* McFarland-SABR Research Award, 2002, for article, "The First All-Black Lineup."

Writings

Baseball's Last Dynasty: Charlie Finley's Oakland A's, Masters Press-Contemporary Books (Indianapolis, IN), 1998, revised and expanded as *A Baseball Dynasty:*

In Roberto Clemente, *Bruce Markusen examines the life and baseball career of "The Great One."*

Charlie Finley's Swingin' A's, St. Johann Press (Haworth, NJ), 2002.
Roberto Clemente: The Great One, Sport Publishing (Champaign, IL), 1998.
The Orlando Cepeda Story, Pinata Books (Houston, TX), 2001.

Author of introduction to Jonah Winter, *Beisbol: Pioneros y Leyendas del Beisbol Latino,* Lee and Low (New

York, NY), 2001. Contributor of articles on baseball history published in various major league team publications as well as *Elysian Fields Quarterly, Baseball Digest, Albany Times Union, Sports Collectors Digest, Freeman's Journal, Vineline: Monthly Newspaper of the Chicago Cubs, Chicago Cubs Quarterly,* and *Oldtyme Baseball News.*

Work in Progress

Fall Classics: The Ten Greatest World Series; Melting Pots and Pittsburgh Lumber, both baseball books, and a young adult gothic horror novel, *Haunted House of the Vampire.*

Sidelights

Baseball fan Bruce Markusen is the author of several books about famous baseball players. His first book, *Baseball's Last Dynasty: Charlie Finley's Oakland A's,* is an award-winning account of a triumphant baseball team that appeared to be the beginning of a new trend in American baseball in the 1970s but turned out to be the last of its kind. In 1968, owner Charlie Finley moved his perpetually losing Athletics baseball team to Oakland, California, and through the addition of such future Baseball Hall of Famers as Reggie Jackson and "Catfish" Hunter, brought in five division crowns and three World Series between 1971 and 1975. Some fans were shocked at the shaggy appearance of the players and their disdain for the traditions of professional baseball, seeing the players' behavior as another symptom of the cultural upheavals of the time. In fact, according to Markusen's account, Finley's team "was built in the old baseball world of the reserve clause and was disbanded with the onset of free agency," as *Booklist* contributor Wes Lukowsky put it, a fact which made the Oakland A's of the early 1970s one of the last teams of its kind.

As a portrait of a baseball team, "Markusen has a colorful cast of characters and a wealth of engaging episodes to work with," observed Jules Tygiel in *Nine.* Finley served as his own general manager effectively, according to the author, but alienated his best players through his excessive frugality. And despite the large personalities sported by the A's star players, "Finley ... dominates this book as he did the team," according to Tygiel. Yet, however well researched Markusen's portraits of individual teams members and managers, *Baseball's Last Dynasty* lacks something in placing the team in its proper historical context, some critics remarked. According to Tygiel, Markusen fails to place the team in the broader context of baseball or national history. "The book lacks ... a historical or biographical thread that would turn this into a compelling narrative rather than five years of baseball statistics and a blizzard of detail," remarked a *Publishers Weekly* critic similarly. But, despite its flaws, "at his best, Markusen reminds us of how good the 1970s Athletics were," concluded Tygiel.

For his second book project, this Cooperstown Baseball Hall of Fame researcher presents a full-scale biography of Roberto Clemente, the first Latin American player to be inducted into the Hall of Fame. In *Roberto Clemente: The Great One,* Markusen takes Clemente from his humble birth in Puerto Rico to a professional baseball career that began in the racially turbulent 1950s and ended abruptly in 1972 with the player's untimely death. A contributor to *Publishers Weekly* noted that, with the rise of Latin American players in the professional baseball leagues in the United States, Markusen has written the story of a "hero to so many modern-day heroes."

Markusen told *SATA:* "As an avid fan of baseball and its history, the genre of horror, and modern-day film and television, I have a wide range of interests that I feel driven to write about and analyze. I am particularly interested in the culture of the 1960s and 1970s, perhaps because those were the years in which I was raised. The culture of that era, particularly how it is reflected in the sport of baseball, serves as a source of inspiration and motivation."

Biographical and Critical Sources

PERIODICALS

Booklist, May 15, 1998, Wes Lukowsky, review of *Baseball's Last Dynasty,* p. 1586.
Library Journal, May 15, 1998, Morey Berger, review of *Baseball's Last Dynasty,* p. 92; December, 1998, William O. Scheeren, review of *Roberto Clemente,* p. 116.
Nine, fall, 2000, Jules Tygiel, review of *Baseball's Last Dynasty,* p. 103.
Publishers Weekly, May 25, 1998, review of *Baseball's Last Dynasty,* p. 77; November 2, 1998, "The Other Great One," p. 68.

*　　　*　　　*

MARSHALL, Bonnie C. 1941-
(Bonnie Carey)

Personal

Born June 9, 1941, in Concord, NH; daughter of Sumner E. and Agnes (McNeil) Marshall; children: Lorrie Jean, Peter Dean Carey. *Education:* Boston University, B.A. (summa cum laude), 1962; Assumption College M.A.T., 1966; University of North Carolina at Chapel Hill, Ph.D., 1983; Certificates from Moscow State University, 1975, Leningrad (USSR) State University, 1985, Herzen Pedagogical Institute, 1989, 1990.

Addresses

Home and office—PO Box 1447, Meredith, NH 03253.

Career

Literary translator; writer; poet; scholar; teacher; folklorist. Hale High School Raleigh, NC, teacher of Russian and English, 1972-80; visiting positions at Duke Univer-

Bonnie C. Marshall

sity, 1980, Wake Forest University, 1982, Randolph-Macon Woman's College, 1982, College of the Holy Cross, 1984-85, University of Montana, 1983-84, 1985-86, University of South Alabama, 1987-88; Davidson College, Davidson, NC, assistant professor of Russian (developed Russian program), 1988-93; ACTR Resident Director, Summer Program for Russian Teachers in St. Petersburg, Russia, 1989-90; School for Global Education, St. Petersburg, Russia, 1994, English instructor; American Academy of Foreign Languages, Moscow, Russia, 1995-96; Johnson C. Smith University, Charlotte, NC, adjunct associate professor of Russian and curriculum coordinator of the Russian program and distance learning, 1992, 2000-2002.

Member

American Association for the Advancement of Slavic Studies, American Women in Slavic Studies, Russian-American Cultural Center (Boston, MA; board of directors, 1998—), Southern Conference on Slavic Studies, Student Award Committee (executive council, 1994-95).

Awards, Honors

Chicago Book Clinic Certificate of Award for *Baba Yaga's Geese and Other Russian Stories*, 1974; *Search Behind the Lines* nominated for Mildred Batchelder Award, 1976; *Grasshopper to the Rescue,* Junior Literary Guild selection, 1979; ACTR variable term research

grant, Gorky Institute of World Literature, Moscow, USSR, 1991; ACTR Research Scholar Program, Moscow Linguistics University, Moscow, Russia, 1993; Phi Beta Kappa.

Writings

AS BONNIE CAREY; EXCEPT AS NOTED

(Adapter and translator) *Baba Yaga's Geese and Other Russian Stories,* illustrated by Guy Fleming, Indiana University Press (Bloomington, IN), 1973.

(Translator) Yevgeny Ryss *Search Behind the Lines,* Morrow (New York, NY), 1974.

(Translator) Anatoli Aleksin *Alik the Detective,* Morrow (New York, NY), 1977.

(Translator) *Grasshopper to the Rescue,* illustrated by Lady McCrady, Morrow (New York, NY), 1979.

(Reteller, as Bonnie C. Marshall) *Tales from the Heart of the Balkans,* Libraries Unlimited (Littleton, CO), 2001.

Translations include the plays *Vassilissa the Beautiful* by Catherine Chernyak, and *The Scarlet Flower* by L. Brausevich and I. Karnaukhova; other translations have appeared in periodicals, including *Jack and Jill, Christian Science Monitor, Fiction, Bee Hive, Daisy,* and *Serb World;* poetry has appeared in *The Long View Journal, Poet Lore, Twigs, Teens Today,* and *Hearthstone;* also the author of numerous academic articles; book reviewer for *World Literature Today.*

Work in Progress

Adaptation and retelling, *The White Swan and Other Stories from Russia.*

Sidelights

Bonnie C. Marshall, formerly working under the name Bonnie Carey, is a Russian language scholar who has blended her research and linguistic skills with translation to publish several books of Russian and Balkan folk tales and myths, including *Baba Yaga's Geese and Other Russian Stories, Grasshopper to the Rescue,* and the 2001 *Tales from the Heart of the Balkans.* Marshall noted for *SATA* that her longtime desire has been to expose "American youth to the folklore and children's literature of Russia and the former Yugoslavia." With the opening of those countries in the 1990s, her work was made easier. "Since it is only within recent years that oral traditions have been recorded for many of the Russian and South Slavic ethnic groups, it is exciting to be involved in pioneering efforts to render new folk tales into English."

Born in 1941, Marshall was raised on a farm in New England, imbibing the folk and fairy tales of her native region in both their oral and written forms. Books were Marshall's connection to a bigger world, and soon she had graduated from folk tales to mysteries, and from there to French literature and on to Russian literature. She was eleven years old when she first tried her hand at poetry. Her high school years were spent in the small New Hampshire town of Penacook, named after a Native

American tribe. During this time she developed an interest in Native American lore and the tales of women such as Hannah Duston, a white woman who was said to not only have eluded her Indian captors, but to have scalped them, as well.

Graduating from high school, Marshall attended Boston University, Assumption College, and the University of North Carolina at Chapel Hill, going deeper into her love of Russian literature with the attainment of degrees in Russian. While earning her doctorate, she studied in the then Soviet Union, at Moscow State University in 1975, and later—once she had attained her Ph.D.—at Leningrad State University in 1985. Since that time, Marshall has often traveled in Russia, researching and teaching. Additionally, she developed several Russian language programs in the United States.

Marshall began publishing children's books in 1973, with a translation and adaptation about the famous Russian folk character, Baba Yaga. With *Baba Yaga's Geese and Other Russian Stories,* Marshall presented the classic Russian witch who flies through the air accompanied by her flock of geese. Marshall added other folk tales, including one about a bear who enjoys playing blind man's bluff, an aged mushroom who instructs a young girl in the virtues of patience, and the tale of two frogs. Her collection includes not only folk tales, but also fables, original stories, and even riddles translated from the Russian, which add an "unusual dimension" to the collection, in the opinion of a contributor for *Booklist.* That same reviewer also praised the "short, lively [selections] abounding with folk wit and wisdom." Martha L. Savage, reviewing the book in *Library Journal,* felt it was an "interesting collection."

Marshall enlarged upon her writing skills with plays for children's theater and by storytelling. A translation of one Russian children's play, *Vassilissa the Beautiful,* was shown throughout the schools of North Carolina in the early 1970s as part of a cultural enrichment project. Marshall, now a grandmother, continues to tell stories in local schools and libraries in her native New Hampshire, where she returned to live after raising her two children.

Book publication has also continued to form a part of Marshall's creative efforts. *Grasshopper to the Rescue* is the translation of a cumulative Georgian story about an ant who falls into a river and is ultimately saved by his friend, the grasshopper. However, first the grasshopper must get acorns for the pig before he will fetch bristles so that the grasshopper can weave a rope to throw to the ant. But before the grasshopper can get the oak tree to give up his acorns, the insect must scare the raven out of the branches of the tree. And this is just the beginning of the grasshopper's travails, but ultimately he does succeed in helping the ant. Denise M. Wilms, reviewing the title for *Booklist,* found the repetition in the story "overextended," but also noted that the "droll pictures keep things moving fast enough to satisfy." Writing in *School Library Journal,* Patricia Dooley had similar concerns, finding the text "too jerky and clause-ridden," but also noting that the "narrative does make its point."

Over twenty years were to pass until Marshall's next children's book publication, *Tales from the Heart of the Balkans,* a "diverse collection," according to Donna L. Scanlon in *School Library Journal.* Marshall provides a brief outline to the history of the Balkans and also information on the oral tradition of the region. Her assortment includes both folk and fairy tales, which could work either for independent reading or for group reading and storytelling. Scanlon felt that readers who got beyond what she found to be an unattractive cover "will be well rewarded."

"For me, life and scholarship have always been inseparable facets of the same coin," Marshall concluded for *SATA.* "My approach to literature, too, has been a combination of the spontaneity of a creative artist and an analytical scholar. My efforts, in general, are always focused on undeveloped areas, because to work in such areas is a true adventure."

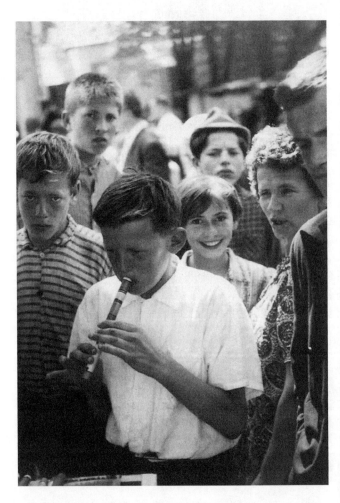

In Tales from the Heart of the Balkans *Marshall translates and retells thirty-three folk stories and provides background on the region's history. (Photo by Joel M. Halpern.)*

Biographical and Critical Sources

PERIODICALS

Booklist, January 1, 1974, review of *Baba Yaga's Geese and Other Russian Stories*, p. 487; March 15, 1979, Denise M. Wilms, review of *Grasshopper to the Rescue*, p. 1156.

Citizen, November 30, 2001, Bea Lewis, "Meredith Author completes new book," p. D1.

Library Journal, November 15, 1973, Martha L. Savage, review of *Baba Yaga's Geese and Other Russian Stories*, p. 3448.

News and Observer (Raleigh, NC), October 22, 1973, Mary Day Mordecai, "Folk Tale Brought to Life for Americans by Raleigh Translator"; November 11, 1973, Ardia Kimzey, "Raleigh Author's 'Folk Book of the Year'".

School Library Journal, April, 1979, Patricia Dooley, review of *Grasshopper to the Rescue*, p. 41; October, 1984, Ann Donovan, review of *Search behind the Lines*, p. 108; February, 2002, Donna L. Scanlon, review of *Tales form the Heart of the Balkans*, p. 124.

Sunday Concord Monitor (Concord, NH), October 10, 1993, p. B3.

* * *

McPHERSON, James M(unro) 1936-

Personal

Born October 11, 1936, in Valley City, ND; son of James Munro (a high school teacher and administrator) and Miriam (an elementary school teacher; maiden name, Osborn) McPherson; married Patricia A. Rasche (an editor), December 28, 1957; children: Joanna. *Education:* Gustavus Adolphus College, B.A. (magna cum laude), 1958; Johns Hopkins University, Ph.D. (with highest distinction), 1963. *Politics:* Democratic. *Religion:* Presbyterian. *Hobbies and other interests:* Tennis, bicycling, sailing, reading mystery and adventure novels, playing with his granddaughter.

Addresses

Home—15 Randall Rd., Princeton, NJ 08540-3609. *Office*—Department of History, Dickinson Hall, Princeton University, Princeton, NJ 08544.

Career

Author, editor, educator, preservationist, and consultant. Princeton University, Princeton, NJ, instructor, 1962-65, assistant professor, 1965-68, associate professor, 1968-72, professor of history, 1972-82, Edwards Professor of American History, 1982-91, George Henry Davis '86 Professor of American History, 1991—. Commonwealth Fund Lecturer, University College, London, England, 1982. Fellow, Behavioral Sciences Center, Stanford University, 1982-83. Consultant on the film *Gettysburg,* Turner Pictures, 1993; on the television documentary *The Civil War* by Ken Burns, Public Broadcasting System, 1999; and on the television documentary *Abraham and Mary Lincoln: A House Divided,* Public Broadcasting System, 2001; also consultant, Social Science program, Educational Research Council, Cleveland, OH. President, Protect Historic America, 1993-94; Society of American Historians, 2000-01; and American Historical Association, 2003—. Member of board of directors, Civil War Trust and Association for the Preservation of Civil War Sites (now the Civil War Preservation Trust), 1991-93; member of Civil War Sites Advisory Committee, a committee created by the U.S. Congress, 1991-93; Member of advisory board, George Tyler Moore College of the Study of the Civil War, Shepherdstown, WV. Member of board of advisors, Lincoln Forum. Member of editorial board of magazine *Civil War History.*

McPherson provided the narration for the video *Abraham Lincoln,* Atlas Video, 1990; is interviewed in the documentary *Smithsonian's Great Battles of the Civil War, Volume One,* Mastervision Studio, 1992, on the videos *The Civil War Legends: Robert E. Lee* and *The Civil War Legends: Abraham Lincoln* (both from Acorn Video), and on the audio cassette *American Heritage's Great Minds of History,* Simon & Schuster, 1999. He also provided the audio commentary on the DVD of the film *Gettysburg,* Turner Home Entertainment, 2000.

Member

Organization of American Historians, Society of American Historians, American Philosophical Society, American Historical Association (president 2003-04), Southern Historical Association, Phi Beta Kappa.

Awards, Honors

Woodrow Wilson National Fellowship, 1958; Danforth fellow, 1958-62; Proctor & Gamble faculty fellowship; Anisfield Wolff Award in Race Relations, Cleveland Foundation, 1965, for *The Struggle for Equality: Abolitionists and the Negro in the Civil War and Reconstruction;* Guggenheim fellow, 1967-58; Huntington fellowship, National Endowment for the Humanities, 1977-78; Huntington Seaver fellow, 1987-88; National Book Award nomination, 1988, National Book Critics Circle nomination, 1988, Pulitzer Prize in history, 1989, Distinguished Book Award, U.S. Military Academy, West Point, 1989, and citation, 100 Best English-Language Books of the 20th Century, Board of the Modern Library, 1999, all for *Battle Cry of Freedom: The Civil War Era;* Lincoln Prize, 1998, for *For Cause and Comrades: Why Men Fought in the Civil War;* Michael Award, New Jersey Literary Hall of Fame, 1989; Gustavus Adolphus College Alumni Award, Gustavus Alumni Association, 1990; R. Stanton Avery fellow, Huntington Library, 1995-96; Theodore and Franklin D. Roosevelt Prize in Naval History, 1998, with wife, Patricia McPherson, for *Lamson of the Gettysburg: The Civil War Letters of Lieutenant Roswell H. Lamson, U.S. Navy;* Jefferson Lecturer in the Humanities, National Endowment for the Humanities, 2000; Richard Nelson Current Award of Achievement, 2002; recipient of honorary degrees from Gustavus Adolphus College,

Gettysburg College, Muhlenberg College, Lehigh University, Bowdoin College, and Monmouth University.

Writings

FOR CHILDREN; NONFICTION

Marching Toward Freedom: The Negro in the Civil War, 1861-1865, Knopf (New York, NY), 1968, published as *Marching Toward Freedom: Blacks in the Civil War,* Facts on File (New York, NY), 1991.

(With Joyce Oldham Appleby and Alan Brinkley) *The American Journey* (textbook; student edition), National Geographic Society/Glencoe/McGraw-Hill (New York, NY), 1998, also published as *The American Journey: Building a Nation,* teacher's wraparound edition, National Geographic Society/Glencoe/McGraw-Hill (New York, NY), 2000.

Fields of Fury: The American Civil War, Atheneum (New York, NY), 2002.

(With Appleby, Brinkley, Albert S. Broussard, and Donald A. Ritchie) *The American Vision* (textbook), National Geographic Society/Glencoe/McGraw-Hill (New York, NY), 2003.

FOR ADULTS; NONFICTION

The Struggle for Equality: Abolitionists and the Negro in the Civil War and Reconstruction, Princeton University Press (Princeton, NJ), 1964, 2nd edition with new preface by the author, 1995.

The Negro's Civil War: How American Negroes Felt and Acted in the War for the Union, Pantheon (New York, NY), 1965, University of Illinois Press (Urbana, IL), 1982, published as *The Negro's Civil War: How American Blacks Felt and Acted During the War for the Union,* Ballantine Books (New York, NY), 1991.

The Abolitionist Legacy: From Reconstruction to the NAACP, Princeton University Press (Princeton, NJ), 1975, 2nd edition, with a new preface by the author, 1995.

Ordeal by Fire: The Civil War and Reconstruction, Knopf (New York, NY), 1982, McGraw-Hill (New York, NY), 2001, published as *The Civil War* (reprint of the second part of *Ordeal by Fire*), Knopf (New York, NY), 1982, McGraw-Hill (New York, NY), 1982, published as two separate volumes, *Ordeal by Fire: The Coming of War* and *Ordeal by Fire: The Civil War,* McGraw-Hill (New York, NY), 1993, 3rd edition, McGraw-Hill (New York, NY), 2001.

Images of the Civil War, paintings by Mort Künstler, Gramercy Books (New York, NY), 1982.

Battle Cry of Freedom: The Civil War Era, Oxford University Press (New York, NY), 1988, published as collector's edition, Easton Press (Norwalk, CT), 2002.

Gettysburg (companion volume to film of the same name), paintings by Mort Künstler, Turner Publishing (Atlanta, GA), 1993, Rutledge Hill Press (Nashville, TN), 1998.

What They Fought For, 1861-1865, Louisiana State University Press (Baton Rouge, LA), 1994.

Drawn with the Sword: Reflections on the American Civil War, Oxford University Press (New York, NY), 1996.

For Cause and Comrades: Why Men Fought in the Civil War, Oxford University Press (New York, NY), 1997.

James M. McPherson

Crossroads of Freedom: Antietam, Oxford University Press (New York, NY), 2002.

Hallowed Ground: A Walk in Gettysburg, Crown (New York, NY), 2003

ESSAYS AND LECTURES

Lincoln and the Strategy of Unconditional Surrender, Gettysburg College (Gettysburg, PA), 1984.

How Lincoln Won the War with Metaphor, Louis A. Warren Lincoln Library and Museum (Fort Wayne, IN), 1985.

Abraham Lincoln and the Second American Revolution, Oxford University Press (New York, NY), 1990, published as collector's edition, Easton Press (Norwalk, CT), 1991.

Why the Confederacy Lost, edited by Gabor S. Boritt, Oxford University Press (New York, NY), 1992.

Is Blood Thicker than Water? Crises of Nationalism in the Modern World, Vintage Canada (Toronto, Ontario, Canada), 1998, Vintage Books (New York, NY), 1999.

(With Douglas J. Wilson) *Accepting the Prize: Two Historians Speak,* Lincoln and Soldiers Institute (Gettysburg, PA), 2000.

"For a Vast Future Also": Lincoln and the Millennium, National Endowment for the Humanities (Washington, DC), 2000.

EDITOR

(With others) *Blacks in America: Bibliographical Essays,* Doubleday (Garden City, NY), 1971.

(With Corner Vann Woodward and J. Morgan Kousser) *Region, Race, and Reconstruction: Essays in Honor of C. Vann Woodward,* Oxford University Press (New York, NY), 1982.

Battle Chronicles of the Civil War, six volumes, Grey Castle Press (Lakeville, CT), Macmillan (New York, NY), 1989.

(Consulting editor) Steve O'Brien and others, editors, *American Political Leaders: From Colonial Times to the Present,* ABC-CLIO (Santa Barbara, CA), 1991.

The Atlas of the Civil War, Macmillan (New York, NY), 1994.

"We Cannot Escape History": Lincoln and the Last Best Hope on Earth, University of Illinois Press (Urbana, IL), 1995.

(With Bruce Catton) *The American Heritage New History of the Civil War,* Viking (New York, NY), 1996, revised edition, with contributing editor Noah Andre Trudeau, MetroBooks (New York, NY), 2001.

(With wife, Patricia R. McPherson) *Lamson of the Gettysburg: The Civil War Letters of Lieutenant Roswell H.*

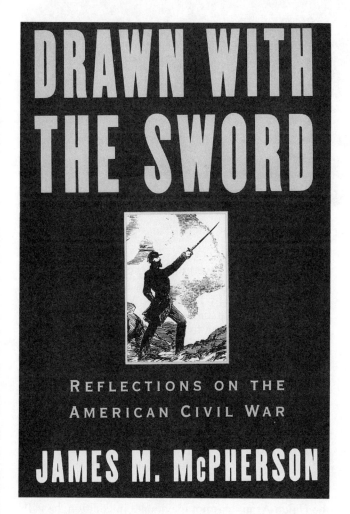

The author's masterfully written series of essays interprets such questions as why the North won the Civil War and who really freed the slaves.

Lamson, U.S. Navy, Oxford University Press (New York, NY), 1997.

(With William J. Cooper) *Writing the Civil War: The Quest to Understand,* University of South Carolina Press (Columbia, SC), 1998.

To the Best of My Ability: The American Presidents, Dorling Kindersley (New York, NY), 2000, revised edition, 2001.

Encyclopedia of Civil War Biographies, Sharpe Reference (Armonk, NY), 2000.

(Editor and contributor, with Alan Brinkley and David Rubel) *Days of Destiny: Crossroads in American History: America's Greatest Historians Examine Thirty-One Uncelebrated Days that Changed the Course of History,* DK Publishing (New York, NY), 2001.

The Civil War Reader, 1862, Simon & Schuster (New York, NY), 2002.

Also author of *How Abolitionists Fought on After the Civil War,* Princeton University (Princeton, NJ), a reprint in book form of an article from the quarterly magazine *University,* 1968-69; *White Liberals and Black Power in Negro Education, 1865-1915,* 1969; *First Black Power Bid in U.S. Education,* Princeton University (Princeton, NJ), from *University,* 1970; and *Who Freed the Slaves? Lincoln and Emancipation,* Lincoln Memorial Association (Redlands, CA), 1993. McPherson's works have been translated into other languages, including French, German, and Spanish. Contributor to books, including *The Anti-Slavery Vanguard: New Essays on Abolitionism,* edited by Martin M. Duberman, Princeton University Press (Princeton, NJ), 1965; *Towards a New Past: Dissenting Essays in American History,* edited by Barton J. Bernstein, Pantheon (New York, NY), 1968; and *How I Met Lincoln: Some Distinguished Enthusiasts Reveal Just How They Fell Under His Spell,* compiled by Harold Holzer, American Heritage (New York, NY), 1999. Contributor of forewords and afterwords to books, including *Brother Against Brother,* edited by Diane Stine Thomas, Silver Burdett Press (Englewood Cliffs, NJ), 1990; *Personal Memoirs of Ulysses S. Grant,* by Ulysses S. Grant, Penguin Books (New York, NY), 1999; and *The Birth of the Grand Old Republican Party: The Republicans' First Generation,* edited by Robert F. Engs and Randall M. Miller, University of Pennsylvania Press (Philadelphia, PA), 2002. Contributor to periodicals, including *American Historical Review, Caribbean Studies, Journal of American History, Journal of Negro History, Mid-America, Phylon,* and others.

Adaptations

Battle Cry of Freedom: The Civil War Era was released on audio tape by Books on Tape, 1989; *Abraham Lincoln: The Second American Revolution* was released on audio tape by Books on Tape, 1992; *Crossroads of Freedom: Antietam* was released as an audio CD by Oxford University Press, 2002.

Sidelights

An American author of nonfiction for children and adults, James M. McPherson generally is considered the

McPherson writes an account of the Civil War for young readers in **Fields of Fury.** *(Illustration from Corbis.)*

preeminent living expert on the American Civil War. The war, which took place from 1861 to 1865, pitted the Union Army from the northern United States against the Confederate Army from the southern United States. More than six hundred thousand soldiers died in the Civil War—more than in any other war involving Americans. A prolific writer, McPherson has written and edited numerous books about the Civil War and its aftermath, the Reconstruction, and of president Abraham Lincoln. McPherson is noted for his coverage of African Americans during the mid-nineteenth century, especially their service as soldiers and their efforts to secure their freedom from slavery, and of the abolitionists who worked to obtain equal rights for the freed slaves. He is also a preservationist, working to protect Civil War battlefields and other important sites as well as resource materials in libraries and other places. Finally, McPherson is credited with helping to initiate a resurgence of interest in the Civil War among the American public. Several of his books have been bestsellers and are

considered to have paved the way for the success of the films *Glory* and *Gettysburg* and the television documentary *The Civil War* by Ken Burns. McPherson wrote the text for a book of paintings by Mort Künstler that was issued as a companion to the motion picture *Gettsyburg* and also provided narration on the DVD of the film; in addition, McPherson served as a consultant in the making of the Ken Burns documentary.

McPherson perhaps is best known for *Battle Cry of Freedom: The Civil War Era,* an informational book for adults that was published in 1988 and won the Pulitzer Prize for history the next year. Often acknowledged as the best single-volume study of the Civil War, *Battle Cry of Freedom* offers readers a reassessment of the war and its outcome. McPherson theorizes that the victory of the Union Army was not inevitable; in addition, he calls the Civil War a turning point in American history, a revolutionary event that brought sweeping changes to society, such as the end of slavery and a new emphasis on industrialization. A professor of history at Princeton University for more than forty years, McPherson directs most of his works to readers at the college level and above; however, several of his books, especially *Battle Cry of Freedom,* have appeal for young people and are used as supplemental reading in high schools. As an author for children, McPherson has written informational books about the Civil War and its soldiers, both black and white; he also is the coauthor of textbooks on the history of America for students in middle school.

Thematically, McPherson emphasizes the moral and ideological aspects of war. He is noted for being empathic in his treatment of the soldiers who fought on both sides of the Civil War and for writing works that stress the human dimension of this event. In several of his books, McPherson draws upon letters and diaries, many of which are unpublished, and he also includes little-known facts about his subjects. As a literary stylist, McPherson characteristically uses a narrative approach rather than the topical or thematic approaches that historians often favor. He is credited for the thoroughness of his research and for writing with authority,

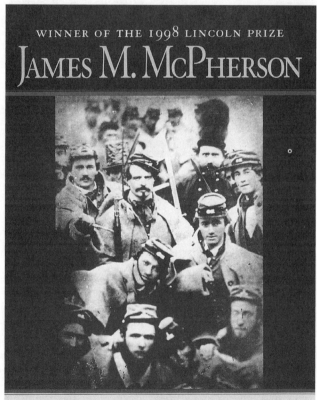

Through the letters and diaries of both Confederate and Union soldiers, McPherson shows why they fought for their ideals of liberty, justice, and patriotism. (Cover photo by Archive Photos.)

balance, eloquence, and clarity. In addition, McPherson has been commended for his ability to satisfy both scholars and general readers with his works, which are praised for providing accurate facts and insightful opinions in an accessible, engaging manner. McPherson occasionally is accused of not offering many new revelations about the Civil War and for not making clear whose side he is on in the controversies surrounding it. However, he usually is viewed as an exceptional historian as well as a writer of integrity and literary skill whose works demonstrate his respect for both his subject and his audience. Writing in *Salon,* Kathleen Whittamore stated, "As anyone who reads James McPherson knows, the broadest topics deliver the gold. This Princeton historian is an expert silversmith with detail, but a true artist when he solders the big questions.... Other writers in the Civil War may be better at emotive drama (Shelby Foote) or crackling narrative (Bruce Catton), but if you want the most astute synthesis possible, McPherson's the man." Calling McPherson "a remarkable and admirable figure," David Walsh of the *World Socialist Web site* projected, "When, in the future, historians consider the ideological landscape of our time, in all its general dreariness and moral and political renegacy, it seems certain that some consideration will be given to James McPherson as a contradictory figure of the period itself. And it will be noted—with approval and appreciation, one trusts—that he contributed to an intellectual ferment with far-reaching consequences." In his assessment of McPherson in *America,* Tom O'Brien concluded that his "whole corpus displays patriotism, not as the last refuge of a scoundrel, but as the civic-mindedness of a first-class mind and first-class person. Would American history suffer if there were even more of him?"

Born in Valley City, North Dakota, McPherson grew up in a small town in Minnesota. He is the son of James Munro McPherson, a high school teacher and administrator, and Miriam Osborn McPherson, an elementary school teacher who went back to get her degree after her children were grown. The author told Joseph Deitch of *Publishers Weekly* that having two teachers as parents "clearly had an influence on me. I see them as role models." Some of McPherson's siblings also became educators: both of his sisters have taught in elementary schools and one of his brothers was a teacher at the university level. McPherson's interest in the Civil War perhaps also has roots in his family background: his great-grandfather and great-great-grandfather both fought in the Union Army, a fact of which McPherson was unaware until he became a historian. McPherson was first inspired to study the past by a history teacher at his high school, a man who had fought in World War II. The author told Joseph Deitch of *Publishers Weekly* that he and his classmates "got a lot of personal reminiscences about the war that aroused my interest in the historical dimensions and in the war itself." After high school, McPherson went to Gustavus Adolphus College in Saint Peter, Minnesota. McPherson once told *SATA,* "I became fascinated with American history while in college, and it was natural that I should combine my interest in teaching and history to become a teacher of history and a writer of books about American history that I hope have been useful in teaching and learning."

While attending Gustavus Adolphus College, McPherson married Patricia A. Rasche; the couple have a daughter, Joanna. With her husband, Patricia McPherson served as the coeditor of a collection of letters by Lieutenant Roswell H. Lamson, one of the most talented naval officers of the Civil War. After graduating from college, James McPherson decided to attend graduate school to acquire his doctorate in history. At the time, the Civil Rights Movement was beginning to take place in the South. McPherson told David Walsh of the *World Socialist Web Site,* "This was in the late '50s, at the time of the Little Rock school desegregation crisis and the Montgomery bus boycott. I was just becoming conscious of what was going on in the world at this time, so I thought, 'This is a strange place, this South.' So I decided that maybe I'd like to find out more about it, study Southern history." McPherson decided to attend graduate school at Johns Hopkins University in Baltimore, Maryland. He told Walsh, "I really went to Hopkins because C. Vann Woodward [a specialist on Southern history and on segregation] was there. And when I got there, ... I was suddenly struck by the parallels between the times in which I was living and what had happened exactly, I mean exactly in some cases, 100 years earlier." In 1982, McPherson coedited *Region, Race, and Reconstruction,* a volume of essays in honor of his mentor C. Vann Woodward. As he noted in a statement that he made to the U.S. House of Representatives regarding the preservation of historical documents, a statement that was reprinted in *National Humanities Alliance (NHA) Testimony,* McPherson also chose to attend John Hopkins for another reason: "its proximity to Washington and to one of the great research libraries of the world, the Library of Congress. Nor was I disappointed in the wealth of sources in that marvelous institution just up the street. I remember with fondness my many trips from Baltimore on the old Pennsylvania Railroad or the B & O or by car-pooling with other graduate students in an ancient Volkswagen Beetle or Chevrolet gas-guzzler. I spent many hundreds of happy hours going over books, pamphlets, and newspapers as well as manuscript collections for my doctoral dissertation...."

As a northerner, McPherson became fascinated by the role that the North had played in trying to change race relations in the South. He studied eighteenth-century abolitionists and wrote about their role during and after the Civil War in trying to obtain equal rights, equal justice, and education for the freed slaves. In an interview with William R. Ferris in *Humanities,* McPherson recalled, "I did my Ph.D. dissertation on people that I called—perhaps with a little bit of exaggeration— the civil rights activists of the 1860s, the abolitionists, both black and white." He told Amy Lifson on the *National Endowment for the Humanities* Web site, "I was struck by all of these parallels between what was a freedom crusade of the 1860s and a freedom crusade of the 1960s. My first entreé into Civil War scholarship focused on that very theme." While attending Johns

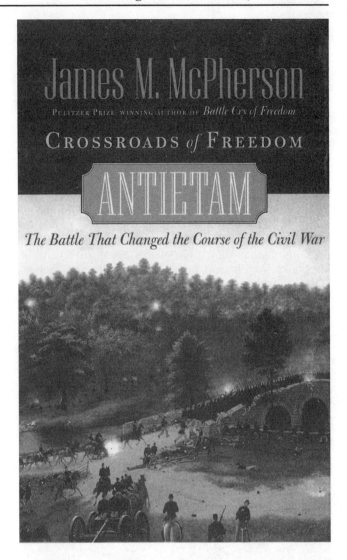

McPherson presents an intriguing version of the pivotal 1862 Civil War battle that took place in Antietam, Maryland. (Cover painting by Captain James Hope.)

Hopkins, McPherson participated in civil rights activities in the Baltimore area. In 1962, he moved to Princeton, New Jersey, to work as an instructor of history at Princeton University. The next year, McPherson received his doctorate from Johns Hopkins. His doctoral dissertation became his first book, *The Struggle for Equality: Abolitionism and the Negro in the Civil War and Reconstruction,* a volume published in 1964. In *NHA Testimony,* McPherson called this work "a study of the continuing activities of abolitionists on behalf of civil rights and education for freed slaves after the abolition of slavery." He added, "The challenges and excitement of discovery in this research really launched my career as a historian."

One year after the publication of *The Struggle for Equality,* McPherson produced *The Negro's Civil War: How American Negroes Felt and Acted in the War for the Union* (later published as *The Negro's Civil War: How American Blacks Felt and Acted During the War for the Union*). With *Marching Toward Freedom: The*

Negro in the Civil War (later published as *Marching Toward Freedom: Blacks in the Civil War*), McPherson adapted material from *The Negro's Civil War* for a young audience. In this work, which was published in 1968, McPherson presents children with a history of how African Americans served in the Civil War, first in supporting roles and then, after they were allowed to enlist, as effective soldiers. The author supplements his story with passages from diaries, letters, speeches, newspapers, and songs as well as prints and photographs from the period. Writing in the *New York Times Book Review* about McPherson's accomplishment in *Marching Toward Freedom,* Mel Watkins commented, "Using numerous quotes from politicians, slaves, and freedmen, he shows that military and political expediency, not idealism, dictated the Union's altered stance." A writer in *Commonweal* dubbed *Marching Toward Freedom* a "well-documented account" and "an impressive study" before noting, "Its brevity is an additional asset." Writing in *Book World,* Paul M. Angle said, "Mr. McPherson brings a fresh approach. Half of the text, perhaps more, consists of quotations from what the historians call first-hand sources.... Skillfully used by the author, these sources give the book an unusual degree of directness (read 'punch') and realism. The story—and the facts—give more credit to the black man than to the white." A critic in *Booklist* concluded, "Numerous excerpts ... add authenticity and conviction to McPherson's telling portrayal of Negro attitudes and experiences, including impressive performances on the battlefield." McPherson told *SATA,* "I enjoyed the experience of writing *Marching Toward Freedom.* My two youngest brothers were then in junior high and high school, and I tried out the book on them as I was writing it in order to see whether it would appeal to a high-school age audience. They liked it, and I hope that other students who have read it have also liked it."

In 1972, McPherson became a full professor of history at Princeton; in 1982, he became the Edwards Professor of American History at the school. In addition to his academic career, McPherson continued to write and edit books on the Civil War and its key players. Asked by C. Vann Woodward and Richard Hofstadter to contribute a volume to the Oxford History of the United States, a multi-volume collection of individual books by historians that was published by Oxford University Press, he began to write about the period 1848 to 1865. In 1988, McPherson produced *Battle Cry of Freedom: The Civil War Era,* the book that established him as perhaps the best historian ever to have written about the War Between the States. In this work, which takes its title from a song adopted by both the North and the South, the author outlines the history of the period by incorporating its most relevant political, social, economic, and military aspects. In addition, he combines scholarship on the subject with his own research and interpretations and tells the story of the Civil War as if he were writing fiction, with plot, conflict, character development, and other literary characteristics.

Battle Cry of Freedom was a best-seller in both hardcover and paperback. In addition, critical commen-

tary on the volume was almost unanimously laudatory. McPherson was praised for his ability to synthesize a wealth of information—material that previous writers had taken from three to eight volumes to decipher—and place it into a single, cohesive, well-written volume. Writing in the *New York Times Book Review,* Hugh Brogan noted, "This is the best one-volume treatment of a subject I have ever come across. It may actually be the best ever published. It is comprehensive and succinct, scholarly without being pedantic, eloquent but unrhetorical. It is compellingly readable. I was swept away, feeling as if I had never heard the saga before. It is most welcome.... A deeply satisfying book." Huston Horn of the *Los Angeles Times Book Review* commented, "Deftly coordinated, gracefully composed, charitably argued, and suspensefully laid out, McPherson's book is just the compass of the tumultuous middle years of the 18th century it was intended to be, and as narrative history, it is surpassing. Bright with details and fresh quotations, sold with carefully-arrived-at conclusions, it must surely be, of the 50,000 books written on the Civil War, the finest compression of that national paroxysm ever fitted between two covers." Martin Flagg of the *Times Educational Supplement* called McPherson's book "a miracle of lucidity, proportion, and ripe judgment. It is also, for a one-volume chronicle, marvelously inclusive, and one cannot imagine a more telling or compelling account of this, the most tragic episode (and enduring trauma) of American history." Writing in *School Library Journal,* Audrey B. Eaglon dubbed *Battle Cry of Freedom* "probably the best one-volume history of the Civil War ever written; it reads like a suspense novel, pulling readers into the story of a nation riven by conflict."

In 1991, McPherson became the George Henry Davis '86 Professor of American History at Princeton. In the same year, the United States Senate appointed McPherson to the Civil War Sites Advisory Commission, which was responsible for determining the major battle sites of the war, evaluating their condition, and recommending proposals for their preservation. As a teacher, he has taken his students on regular tours of Civil War battlefields; for example, they go to Pennsylvania every spring to visit Gettysburg. At the battlefields, McPherson often is asked by his students why the soldiers were willing to fight—and to stay in the war—when they knew that they may not be coming home. These questions prompted *For Cause and Comrades: Why Men Fought in the Civil War,* a title published in 1997. In order to create this work, McPherson studied the diaries and letters of over a thousand enlistees from both the Union and Confederate armies. He concluded that the soldiers were motivated by courage, self-respect, and group cohesion and were sustained by duty, faith, personal honor, patriotism, and ideology, especially the preservation of liberty. Writing about *For Cause and Comrades* in *Kliatt Young Adult Paperback Book Guide,* Raymond L. Puffer commented, "A good scholar can always be depended upon to come up with an interesting new approach to a worked-over subject. In this title, Princeton historian McPherson shows again why he deserves to be called the dean of Civil War scholars."

Puffer concluded by calling *For Cause and Comrades* a "legitimate and readable antidote to the romanticized motives so often cited in other works. This book also packs a visceral punch; it is full of fascinating quotations and first-person recollections, making it an often vivid experience for the reader. This is 'living history' indeed." Calling *For Cause and Comrades* "one of the most comprehensive and valuable analyses of the Civil War ever written," Daniel Baracskay of *Presidential Studies Quarterly* commended the author's "painstaking detail and incredible insight" before concluding that McPherson "has provided a tremendous contribution to the study of the Civil War, and the disciplines of history and political science.... McPherson has set a new standard for research for times to come." Roland Green of *Booklist* observed that, in *For Cause and Comrades,* McPherson "has written more eloquently than almost any Civil War historian since Bruce Catton. The result is an invaluable book, though a saddening one." *For Cause and Comrades* was awarded the Lincoln Prize in 1998.

In 2002, McPherson produced *Fields of Fury: the American Civil War,* a history of the war for children that spans events from the initial Confederate attack at Fort Sumter to the triumph of the Union at Appomattox. McPherson defines major battles; provides eyewitness accounts, many by children; profiles historical luminaries; gives personal anecdotes from the soldiers; and addresses such issues as slavery, the roles of women and African Americans, health care on the battlefield, treatment of prisoners of war, and the effects of Reconstruction. McPherson also includes sidebars of information; a timeline; and many photographs, drawings, and maps. With this volume, the author is credited for doing for a young audience what he did for adults with *Battle Cry of Freedom.* Writing in *School Library Journal,* Starr E. Smith commented, "A distinguished historian has used his formidable talents to produce a concise, accessible, and appealing history in an attractive format.... McPherson summarizes the major facts of the war and relates anecdotes that bring to life the conflict's participants.... A good pick for researchers and browsers alike." Noting that there is always a need for another good overview on the Civil War, a critic in *Kirkus Reviews* declared that *Fields of Fury* "fills that need." The reviewer called the work a "thoughtfully and clearly constructed offering that will appeal to history buffs, young and old, and a must for any Civil War history collection." Carolyn Phelan of *Booklist* stated, "This large-format book provides an attractive and readable introduction to the Civil War.... McPherson writes with authority, offering a broad overview as well as many details and anecdotes that give his account a human dimension." Phelan concluded by calling *Fields of Fury* a "good balance of information and illustration on a topic of perennial interest."

McPherson continues to write and edit books on his specialties, to teach at Princeton, to serve as a consultant and on committees, and to act as a crusader for the preservation of the major battle sites of the Civil War. He has argued publicly against the exploitation of these sites by commercial vendors; in addition, he guides both new students and the general public through battlefields and other locations that are relevant to the war. In his interview with William R. Ferris of *Humanities,* McPherson suggested why he thinks that the Civil War has an enduring fascination: "One reason is the continuing salience of many of the issues over which the war was fought. Even though the War resolved the issues of Union and slavery, it didn't entirely resolve the issues that underlay those two questions. The relationships between the national government and regions, race relations, the role of government in trying to bring about change in race relations—these issues are still important in American society today.... The continuing relevance of these issues, I think, is one reason for the continuing fascination with the Civil War." When asked why writers in academia do not create more books for general readers, McPherson said, "Look at the large membership in the history book club, the interest in the History Channel on television, and the interest in documentaries by Ken Burns and by other historical filmmakers. There is a real hunger out there which is not always reached by academic historians. I think they ought to reach out more than they do, and that is what I try to do." He concluded, "I think it's possible to break new ground or offer new interpretations or to write a narrative work of history in such a way as it can appeal to a general audience, but also have something for a more academic and specialized audience. It has something to do with being convinced that history is a story of change over time, with a beginning, a development, a climax of consequences, and writing that story in such a way as it will retain the interest of a broad audience, but also have something new and interesting in the way of insight or interpretation for the specialist as well. It is not easy to explain. I just try to do it, and sometimes I think I've succeeded."

Biographical and Critical Sources

PERIODICALS

America, September 16, 2002, Tom O'Brien, "A Qualified Victory," p. 23.

Booklist, October 1, 1968, review of *Marching Toward Freedom: The Negro in the Civil War, 1861-1865,* pp. 189-190; February 1, 1997, Roland Green, review of *For Cause and Comrades: Why Men Fought in the Civil War,* p. 924; November 15, 2002, Carolyn Phelan, review of *Fields of Fury: The American Civil War,* p. 586.

Book World, May 5, 1968, Paul M. Angle, "The Battle Against Prejudice," p. 30.

Commonweal, May 24, 1968, review of *Marching Toward Freedom: The Negro in the Civil War, 1861-1865,* p. 302.

Humanities, May-June, 2000, William R. Ferris, "'The War that Never Goes Away:' A Conversation with Civil War Historian James M. McPherson."

Kirkus Reviews, September 1, 2002, review of *Fields of Fury: The American Civil War,* p. 1315.

Kliatt Young Adult Paperback Book Guide, January, 1999, Raymond L. Puffer, review of *For Cause and Comrades: Why Men Fought in the Civil War,* p. 31.

Los Angeles Times Book Review, March 20, 1988, Huston Horn, "The Finest One-Volume Civil War Ever Written," p. 10.

New York Times Book Review, May 5, 1968, Mel Watkins, review of *Marching Toward Freedom: The Negro in the Civil War, 1861-1865,* p. 49; February 14, 1988, Hugh Brogan, review of *Battle Cry of Freedom: The Civil War Era,* p. 1.

Presidential Studies Quarterly, summer, 1997, Daniel Baracskay, review of *For Cause and Comrades: Why Men Fought in the Civil War,* p. 612.

Publishers Weekly, January 18, 1991, Joseph Deitch, "James M. McPherson: The Civil War Historian Continues to Find New Material about That Profoundly Influential Conflict," p. 40.

School Library Journal, March, 1989, Audrey B. Eaglon, "Beautiful Losers," p. 131; October, 2002, Starr E. Smith, review of *Fields of Fury: The American Civil War,* p. 188.

Times Educational Supplement, March 13, 1992, Martin Flagg, review of *Battle Cry of Freedom: The Civil War Era,* p. 28.

OTHER

National Endowment for the Humanities, http://www.neh.fed.us/ (March 22, 2003), Amy Lifson, "Meet James McPherson."

National Humanities Alliance (NHA) Testimony, http://www.nhalliance.org/ (April 18, 1991), "James M. McPherson, 18 April 1991."

Salon, http://www.salon.com/ (March 22, 2003), Katherine Whittamore, review of *Drawn with the Sword.*

World Socialist Web site, http://www.wsws.org/ (May 19, 1999), David Walsh, "Historian James M. McPherson and the Cause of Intellectual Integrity."

N-O

NELSON, Robin Laura 1971-

Personal

Born September 20, 1971, in New Ulm, MN; daughter of David and Tamra (Merritt) Nesheim; married Cory Nelson, 1995; children: Zachary, Maren. *Education:* Hamline University, B.A. (summa cum laude), 1994, Certification in Elementary Education, 1995; College of St. Catherine, St. Paul, MN, Certificate for Pre-K, 1995.

Addresses

Home—Minneapolis, MN. *Agent*—c/o Author Mail, Lerner Publishing Group, 241 First Ave., N., Minneapolis, MN 55401.

Career

Writer, 2002—. St. Mark's Lutheran School, Hacienda Heights, CA, fourth grade teacher, 1995-1997; substitute teacher, 1997-99; Sylvan Learning Center, Bloomington, MN, lead teacher, 1997-2000; Lerner Publishing Group, Minneapolis, MN, curriculum product developer, 2000-2002.

Writings

NONFICTION

A Cloudy Day, Lerner Publications (Minneapolis, MN), 2001.

A Rainy Day, Lerner Publications (Minneapolis, MN), 2001.

A Snowy Day, Lerner Publications (Minneapolis, MN), 2001.

A Sunny Day, Lerner Publications (Minneapolis, MN), 2001.

A Windy Day, Lerner Publications (Minneapolis, MN), 2001.

Where Is My Home?, Lerner Publications (Minneapolis, MN), 2001.

Where Is My Town?, Lerner Publications (Minneapolis, MN), 2001.

Where Is My State?, Lerner Publications (Minneapolis, MN), 2001.

Where Is My Country?, Lerner Publications (Minneapolis, MN), 2001.

Where Is My Continent?, Lerner Publications (Minneapolis, MN), 2001.

A Day, Lerner Publications (Minneapolis, MN), 2001.

Months, Lerner Publications (Minneapolis, MN), 2001.

A Week, Lerner Publications (Minneapolis, MN), 2001.

Hearing, Lerner Publications (Minneapolis, MN), 2001.

Seeing, Lerner Publications (Minneapolis, MN), 2001.

Smelling, Lerner Publications (Minneapolis, MN), 2001.

Tasting, Lerner Publications (Minneapolis, MN), 2001.

Touching, Lerner Publications (Minneapolis, MN), 2001.

Pet Fish, Lerner Publications (Minneapolis, MN), 2002.

Pet Frog, Lerner Publications (Minneapolis, MN), 2002.

Pet Guinea Pig, Lerner Publications (Minneapolis, MN), 2002.

Pet Hamster, Lerner Publications (Minneapolis, MN), 2002.

Pet Hermit Crab, Lerner Publications (Minneapolis, MN), 2002.

Earth Day, Lerner Publications (Minneapolis, MN), 2002.

Independence Day, Lerner Publications (Minneapolis, MN), 2002.

Martin Luther King, Jr. Day, Lerner Publications (Minneapolis, MN), 2002.

Memorial Day, Lerner Publications (Minneapolis, MN), 2002.

Presidents' Day, Lerner Publications (Minneapolis, MN), 2002.

From Flower to Honey, Lerner Publications (Minneapolis, MN), 2002.

Being A Leader, Lerner Publications (Minneapolis, MN), 2002.

Being Fair, Lerner Publications (Minneapolis, MN), 2002.

Being Responsible, Lerner Publications (Minneapolis, MN), 2002.

Following Rules, Lerner Publications (Minneapolis, MN), 2002.

Respecting Others, Lerner Publications (Minneapolis, MN), 2002.

Freezing and Melting, Lerner Publications (Minneapolis, MN), 2003.

The Water Cycle, Lerner Publications (Minneapolis, MN), 2003.

We Use Water, Lerner Publications (Minneapolis, MN), 2003.

What Is Water?, Lerner Publications (Minneapolis, MN), 2003.

Where Is Water?, Lerner Publications (Minneapolis, MN), 2003.

Communication Then and Now, Lerner Publications (Minneapolis, MN), 2003.

Home Then and Now, Lerner Publications (Minneapolis, MN), 2003.

School Then and Now, Lerner Publications (Minneapolis, MN), 2003.

Toys and Games Then and Now, Lerner Publications (Minneapolis, MN), 2003.

Transportation Then and Now, Lerner Publications (Minneapolis, MN), 2003.

Dairy, Lerner Publications (Minneapolis, MN), 2003.

Fats, Oils, and Sweets, Lerner Publications (Minneapolis, MN), 2003.

Fruits, Lerner Publications (Minneapolis, MN), 2003.

Grains, Lerner Publications (Minneapolis, MN), 2003.

Meat and Protein, Lerner Publications (Minneapolis, MN), 2003.

Vegetables, Lerner Publications (Minneapolis, MN), 2003.

From Cocoa Bean to Chocolate, Lerner Publications (Minneapolis, MN), 2003.

From Cotton to T-Shirt, Lerner Publications (Minneapolis, MN), 2003.

From Egg to Chicken, Lerner Publications (Minneapolis, MN), 2003.

From Foal to Horse, Lerner Publications (Minneapolis, MN), 2003.

Beginning readers learn facts about the weather in Robin Laura Nelson's **A Rainy Day.** *(Photo by L. S. Stepanowicz.)*

From Kernel to Corn, Lerner Publications (Minneapolis, MN), 2003.

From Sea to Salt, Lerner Publications (Minneapolis, MN), 2003.

From Sheep to Sweater, Lerner Publications (Minneapolis, MN), 2003.

From Wax to Crayon, Lerner Publications (Minneapolis, MN), 2003.

From Metal to Airplane, Lerner Publications (Minneapolis, MN), 2004.

From Peanut to Peanut Butter, Lerner Publications (Minneapolis, MN), 2004.

Float and Sink, Lerner Publications (Minneapolis, MN), 2004.

Gravity, Lerner Publications (Minneapolis, MN), 2004.

Magnets, Lerner Publications (Minneapolis, MN), 2004.

Push and Pull, Lerner Publications (Minneapolis, MN), 2004.

Ways Things Move, Lerner Publications (Minneapolis, MN), 2004.

Happy, Lerner Publications (Minneapolis, MN), 2004.

Sad, Lerner Publications (Minneapolis, MN), 2004.

Angry, Lerner Publications (Minneapolis, MN), 2004.

Afraid, Lerner Publications (Minneapolis, MN), 2004.

Food, Lerner Publications (Minneapolis, MN), 2004.

Clothing, Lerner Publications (Minneapolis, MN), 2004.

Shelter, Lerner Publications (Minneapolis, MN), 2004.

Jobs, Lerner Publications (Minneapolis, MN), 2004.

Circle, Lerner Publications (Minneapolis, MN), 2004.

Rectangle, Lerner Publications (Minneapolis, MN), 2004.

Square, Lerner Publications (Minneapolis, MN), 2004.

Triangle, Lerner Publications (Minneapolis, MN), 2004.

Sidelights

Author of over seventy titles for Minnesota's Lerner Publications, Robin Laura Nelson has written on science topics including weather, time, water, and the senses; on social science topics such as values, emotions, and holidays; and on a variety of other themes from history to the story of where food comes from. "There is a growing need for nonfiction books in the classroom, particularly at the primary grades," Nelson told *SATA.* "Nonfiction books for emergent readers were scarce. I am happy to be writing books that address this need in our schools. I hope that my books help students develop the nonfiction reading skills that they need to be successful."

Born in New Ulm, Minnesota, in 1971, Nelson trained as an elementary school and pre-kindergarten teacher, then taught in Minnesota schools for five years before going to work for Lerner Publishing Group as a curriculum product developer. After two years of researching, writing, and editing nonfiction books for emergent readers and teaching guides for the K-6 classroom, Nelson decided to branch out as a freelance writer for primary school children.

Nelson's publications began with the 2001 *A Cloudy Day,* the first of five introductory titles on weather. Other books in the series focus on rain, snow, sun and wind. Reviewing *A Snowy Day* and *A Sunny Day* in *School Library Journal,* Holly T. Sneeringer felt that these small beginning readers have "just the right dose of fact and fun." Sneeringer further praised the "simple sentences" as well as the photographic illustrations for making the message clear and effective. Repetition also comes into play in the books, allowing emergent readers to establish a rhythm to their reading.

The "Where Is?" series focuses on "geopolitical concepts," according to Be Astengo writing in *School Library Journal* in a review of *Where Is My Continent?* Again, Nelson mixes simple sentences with descriptive photographs, yet Astengo felt that the writing was so "simplistic" that little information was imparted in the seventeen sentences in the book. However, Astengo also felt the book will "fill a niche" for kindergarten children. The calendar is introduced in Nelson's *A Day, Months,* and *A Week.* Reviewing the first title in *School Library Journal,* Karen Land found that the book combines "fun facts and a simple math activity."

The senses take center stage in another series from Nelson, with titles including *Hearing, Seeing, Smelling, Tasting,* and *Touching.* The one-sentence-per-page format was again in use in these titles, in conjunction with full-color illustrations. Geared for kindergartners, the syntax and information is kept basic. However, Lisa Gangemi Kropp, reviewing *Smelling* in *School Library Journal,* felt that such measures went too far, and that the book contains "little information, and [is] too simplistic."

A further series from Nelson deals with pets, including frogs, hamsters, and even the hermit crab. Reviewing *Pet Frog* in *School Library Journal,* Cathie Bashaw remarked on the fact that "children of various ethnic backgrounds" were caring for the animals. Simple factual sentences on each page combine with a "Fun Facts" section, and in some cases labeled diagrams. Information included in the sixteen-sentence books includes reasons the animal is a good pet, the requirements of feeding and cleaning, and the appropriate living environment for each pet. *Booklist*'s Kathy Broderick, in a review of *Pet Fish,* noted that new readers "may enjoy reading these books on their own."

Nelson has also written about important public holidays in such titles as *Earth Day, Independence Day,* and *Presidents' Day,* noting both why and how such days are celebrated. Civic values and morals are presented in such books as *Being a Leader* and *Being Responsible.* Everything young readers might want to know about water is presented in *Freezing and Melting, The Water Cycle, We Use Water,* and other titles. Children also find out about the production cycle in such books as *From Cocoa Bean to Chocolate,* which traces the sweet stuff from the plant to the chocolate bar. *From Sheep to Sweater* does the same for wool, tracing it from sheep to shearing to wool spinning to knitting into a sweater. Other products from honey to T-shirts are examined in the same series.

"I enjoy writing nonfiction for children," Nelson concluded to *SATA.* "I hope that children learn as much from my books as I do while researching them. I expect to continue writing nonfiction for young readers as well as eventually writing nonfiction for older children. I also look forward to crossing into new territory and a new genre and write fiction for children someday."

Biographical and Critical Sources

PERIODICALS

Booklist, October 15, 2002, Kathy Broderick, review of *Pet Fish,* p. 433.

School Library Journal, January, 2002, Karen Land, review of *A Day,* p. 122; February, 2002, Be Astengo, review of *Where Is My Continent?,* p. 125; April, 2002, Holly T. Sneeringer, review of *A Snowy Day* and *A Sunny Day,* p. 138; August, 2002, Lisa Gangemi Kropp, review of *Smelling,* p. 178; October, 2002, Cathie Bashaw, review of *Pet Frog,* p. 150.

* * *

NICOLSON, Cynthia Pratt 1949-

Personal

Born August 2, 1949, in Winnipeg, Manitoba, Canada; married Donald Nicolson (an architect); children: Sara, Ian, Vanessa. *Education:* University of Winnipeg, B.Sc. *Hobbies and other interests:* Kayaking, snow-shoeing.

Addresses

Home—Box C-5 Bowen Island, British Columbia VON 1GO, Canada. *E-mail*—cpnicolson@yahoo.com

Career

Writer. Elementary school teacher.

Awards, Honors

Shortlisted for Silver Birch, Red Cedar, and Hackmatack awards; science writing award, American Institute of Physics, 2001, for *Exploring Space.*

Writings

FOR CHILDREN

Earthdance: How Volcanoes, Earthquakes, Tidal Waves and Geysers Shake Our Restless Planet, illustrated by Bill Slavin, Kids Can Press (Toronto, Ontario, Canada), 1994.

The Earth, illustrated by Bill Slavin, Kids Can Press (Toronto, Ontario, Canada), 1996.

The Stars, illustrated by Bill Slavin, Kids Can Press (Toronto, Ontario, Canada), 1998.

The Planets, illustrated by Bill Slavin, Kids Can Press (Toronto, Ontario, Canada), 1998.

Comets, Asteroids, and Meteorites, illustrated by Bill Slavin, Kids Can Press (Toronto, Ontario, Canada), 1999.

Exploring Space, illustrated by Bill Slavin, Kids Can Press (Toronto, Ontario, Canada), 2000.

Baa! The Most Interesting Book You'll Ever Read about Genes and Cloning, illustrated by Rose Cowles, Kids Can Press (Toronto, Ontario, Canada), 2001.

Volcano!, Kids Can Press (Toronto, Ontario, Canada), 2001.

Earthquake!, Kids Can Press (Toronto, Ontario, Canada), 2001.

Hurricane!, Kids Can Press (Toronto, Ontario, Canada), 2002.

Tornado!, Kids Can Press (Toronto, Ontario, Canada), 2003.

Contributor to *Owl* magazine.

Sidelights

Cynthia Pratt Nicolson writes science books for children that are filled with information stretching across the breadth of her chosen subjects. For example, in *Baa! The Most Interesting Book You'll Ever Read about Genes and Cloning,* she offers discussions of Mendel, cells, chromosomes, and DNA, provides anecdotes about famous cases where DNA testing has proven crucial, and details simple experiments that students can do themselves in order to bring the science under discussion to life. "Though she doesn't quite get to everything," noted a contributor to *Kirkus reviews,* "she does give readers the big picture." Likewise, *Booklist* reviewer Carolyn Phelan remarked that Nicolson's "explanation of scientific concepts are brief, but surprisingly clear." For *Quill & Quire* reviewer Sheree Haughian, *Baa!* has the benefit of being both enjoyable to read and a practical guide for students and science teachers. Haughian dubbed this book "certainly the first engaging book for children about the topic."

Responses to Nicolson's other science books for children, created in a similar format, have been similarly positive. Her book *Exploring Space,* which received the science writing award from the American Institute of Physics, discusses this vast subject in a series of brief chapters covering the ancients' relationship to the stars, the invention of the telescope, space travel, and developments in the arena of human dwellings in space. As in her other books, "coverage is broad rather than deep," remarked Carolyn Phelan in *Booklist.* Relevant additional information is added in sidebars, and a number of simple science experiments help the author illustrate various points, adding up to "an excellent classroom resource and a good addition to a library collection on astronomy and space exploration," according to Dennis W. Cheek, a contributor to *Science Books and Films.*

Volcano is Nicolson's first book in a series on natural disasters, and applies the format developed for her earlier science titles. *Resource Links* reviewer Shirley Jean Sheppard stated, "Nicolson captures the beauty and the horror of these forces of destruction," but teachers ought to be aware of the book's potential to frighten younger children. Still, *Quill & Quire* reviewer Wendy A. Lewis declared that "*Volcano*'s clever newspaper-

Young readers explore the science of volcanoes through activities, learn how scientists study volcanoes, and read about famous eruptions in Cynthia Pratt Nicolson's Volcano! *(Photo by J. D. Griggs.)*

style design with front-page disaster headlines is perfect for this subject matter." *Earthquake!,* the second book in the series, relies upon this same format "and is equally detailed and succinct," remarked Heather Myers in *Resource Links.* A third book, *Hurricane!* discusses how hurricanes form, how scientists measure them, and their impact on the human environment. Sidebars highlight the worst hurricanes in human history, and provide experiments to help illustrate concepts discussed in the text.

Nicolson told *SATA:* "I can see a volcano from my back deck! My home is on Bowen Island, B.C., and the volcano is Mount Baker in Washington State. Sometimes, as I stare at Mount Baker in the distance, I try to imagine it blasting ash into the sky. There were no mountains, or even big hills, where I grew up in Winnipeg. I was born there on August 2, 1949, a scorching day when the temperature reached 38 degree C (100 degrees F).

"One of the most exciting things that happened to me as a kid was learning to read. By age nine or so, I was a real bookworm who walked to and from school with my nose in a book. Some of my favourites were *The House at Pooh Corner,* the 'Little House' series, and *Anne of Green Gables.* As I read, I often lost track of everything that was going on around me. One day, in grade five, I looked up from a Nancy Drew mystery and found that my whole class was in the middle of a spelling test. It was like suddenly waking up from a wonderful dream!

As I grew older, I got busy with other things—running on the track team, canoeing, traveling—but I always loved reading. Creating a book seemed like a wonderful thing to do, but for some reason I thought only other people could be writers, not me. Instead, I studied science at the University of Winnipeg and became a teacher. In 1980, my husband Don and I moved to Bowen Island with our baby daughter. For the first time, I saw the enormous slugs that live on the West Coast. I knew this would make an interesting topic for kids, so I learned everything I could about these slimy creatures. Then, I got brave and sent my slug article to *Owl* magazine. I still remember the day I went to the mailbox and opened their reply saying they wanted to publish it. Maybe I could be a writer after all! Since 1980, I've written lots of articles for *Owl* and eleven science books for Kids Can Press. I really enjoy learning new things about the natural world and writing about science gives me a chance to do that. Don and I now have three children—Sara, Ian, and Vanessa—who are quite grown up, and a little white dog who knows how to sneeze on command. In the summer, I love kayaking in the ocean around Bowen, and in the winter, we take our snowshoes up to the mountains on the mainland. In addition to writing, I enjoy teaching grade five at the school here on the island. Some of my students remind me of myself as a kid—and they are probably like many of you. There's nothing they like better than getting lost in a really good book."

Biographical and Critical Sources

PERIODICALS

Booklist, December 1, 2000, Carolyn Phelan, review of *Exploring Space,* p. 731; December 1, 2001, Hazel Rochman, review of *Volcano!,* p. 656; January 1, 2002, Carolyn Phelan, review of *Baa! The Most Interesting Book You'll Ever Read about Genes and Cloning,* p. 853.

Horn Book Guide, fall, 2001, Harry Clement Stubbs, review of *Exploring Space,* p. 384.

Kirkus Reviews, August 15, 2001, review of *Baa!,* p. 1219; October 1, 2002, review of *Hurricane!* p. 1476.

Quill & Quire, August, 2001, Wendy A. Lewis, review of *Volcano!,* p. 29; September, 2001, Sheree Haughian, review of *Baa!,* p. 54.

Resource Links, December, 2001, Shirley Jean Sheppard, review of *Volcano!,* p. 28; April, 2002, Heather Myers, review of *Earthquake!,* p. 36.

School Library Journal, May, 2002, Patricia Manning, review of *Earthquake!,* p. 175.

Science Books and Films, May, 2001, Dennis W. Cheek, review of *Exploring Space,* p. 127.

*   *   *

NORTH, Milou
See ERDRICH, Louise

*   *   *

ORR, Wendy 1953-
(Sally George)

Personal

Born November 19, 1953, in Edmonton, Alberta, Canada; citizenship, Canadian and Australian; daughter of Anthony M. (an air force pilot) and Elizabeth Ann (a teacher and homemaker; maiden name, Jenkins) Burridge; married Thomas H. Orr (a farmer), January 11, 1975; children: James Anthony, Susan Elizabeth. *Education:* London School of Occupational Therapy, diploma, 1975; LaTrobe University, B.Sc., 1982. *Hobbies and other interests:* Animals, reading, gardening, people, travel, tai chi.

Addresses

Agent—Debbie Golvan, Golvan Arts Management, P.O. Box 766, Kew, Victoria 3101, Australia. *E-mail*—wendy@wendyorr.com.

Career

Albury Community Health, Albury, Australia, occupational therapist, 1975-80; Language and Development Clinic, Shepparton, Australia, occupational therapist, 1982-91; author, 1988—.

Member

Australian Society of Authors, Australian Children's Book Council, Red Hill Readers.

Awards, Honors

Shared first place award, Ashton Scholastic Picture Book Awards, 1987, for *Amanda's Dinosaur;* shortlist, Book of the Year for Junior Readers, Australian Children's Book Council, 1993, for *Leaving It to You;* winner, Book of the Year for Junior Readers, Australian Children's Book Council, 1995, for *Ark in the Park;* Australian Family Therapy Association, recommendation, 1995, for *Ark in the Park,* and high commendation, 1997, for *Peeling the Onion;* honor book, Children's Book Council of Australia, 1997, included among Best Books for Young Adults, American Library Association, Books for the Teen Age, New York Public Library, both 1998, and "Best of the Best" list, American Library Association, all for *Peeling the Onion;* shortlist, Audio Book of the Year for adults, for *The House at Evelyn's Pond.*

Writings

Amanda's Dinosaur, illustrated by Gillian Campbell, Ashton Scholastic (Australia), 1988.

The Tin Can Puppy (picture book), illustrated by Brian Kogler, HarperCollins Australia/Angus & Robertson (Sydney, New South Wales, Australia), 1990.

Bad Martha, illustrated by Carol McLean Carr, Angus & Robertson (Sydney, New South Wales, Australia), 1991.

Aa-Choo! (picture book), illustrated by Ruth Ohi, Annick Press (Toronto, Ontario, Canada), 1992.

Leaving It to You, Angus & Robertson (Sydney, New South Wales, Australia), 1992.

The Great Yackandandah Billy Cart Race, illustrated by Neil Curtis, HarperCollins Australia (Sydney, New South Wales, Australia), 1993.

Mindblowing! (middle-grade reader), illustrated by Ruth Ohi, Allen & Unwin Australia (St. Leonards, New South Wales, Australia), 1994, published as *A Light in Space,* Annick Press (Toronto, Ontario, Canada), 1994.

Ark in the Park, illustrated by Kerry Millard, HarperCollins Australia/Angus & Robertson (Sydney, New South Wales, Australia), 1994, Henry Holt (New York, NY), 2000.

The Laziest Boy in the World, illustrated by Farbio Nardo, HarperCollins Australia/Angus & Robertson (Sydney, New South Wales, Australia), 1994.

Yasou Nikki, illustrated by Kim Gamble, HarperCollins Australia (Sydney, New South Wales, Australia), 1995.

Dirtbikes, HarperCollins Australia (Sydney, New South Wales, Australia), 1995.

The Bully Biscuit Gang, HarperCollins Australia (Sydney, New South Wales, Australia), 1995.

Jessica Joan, illustrated by Ann James, Reed Books (Australia), 1995.

Grandfather Martin, illustrated by Kate Ellis, Houghton Mifflin (Boston, MA), 1996.

Alroy's Very Nearly Clean Bedroom, illustrated by Bettina Guthridge, Longman & Cheshire, 1996, Sundance Publishing (Littleton, MA), 1997.

Peeling the Onion (young adult), Allen & Unwin Australia (St. Leonards, New South Wales, Australia), 1996, Holiday House (New York, NY), 1997.

Nim's Island, illustrated by Kerry Millard, Knopf (New York, NY), 2001.

Poppy's Path, illustrated by Ritva Voutila, Koala Books (Australia), 2001.

The House at Evelyn's Pond (adult novel), Allen & Unwin Australia (St. Leonards, New South Wales, Australia), 2001.

Spook's Shack, illustrated by Kerry Millard, Allen & Unwin (St. Leonards, New South Wales, Australia), 2003.

"MICKI AND DANIEL" PICTURE BOOK SERIES

Pegasus and Ooloo Mooloo, illustrated by Ruth Ohi, Annick Press (Toronto, Ontario, Canada), 1993.

The Wedding, illustrated by Ruth Ohi, Annick Press (Toronto, Ontario, Canada), 1993.

The Train to the City, illustrated by Ruth Ohi, Annick Press (Toronto, Ontario, Canada), 1993.

Published in Australia as "Micki Moon and Daniel Day" series, illustrated by Mike Spoor, Allen & Unwin Australia (St. Leonards, New South Wales, Australia).

UNDER PSEUDONYM SALLY GEORGE

Bad Dog George, Thomas Nelson Australia (Melbourne, Victoria, Australia), 1994.

Breakfast in Bed, Thomas Nelson Australia (Melbourne, Victoria, Australia), 1994.

George at the Zoo, Thomas Nelson Australia (Melbourne, Victoria, Australia), 1994.

Orr's works have been translated into French, Japanese, Italian, German, Spanish, Basque, Korean, Thai, Dutch, and Danish.

Work in Progress

Three children's books; research for an adult novel.

Sidelights

Australian author Wendy Orr has written books for children and young adults that are noted for their elements of fantasy and humor. Orr was lucky enough to have a father who worked for the Royal Canadian Air Force. She spent her childhood in locations all across Canada, traveling to France, and living for a time in Colorado. Her broad experiences were put to good use later, when she began her career as a writer.

"My parents instilled a love of language early," Orr once commented, "with books at bedtime and my father's stories of our dog's great-great-great-grandfather, in the car. My own first 'book' was written when I was eight. 'Glossy the Horse' was a full four pages long and bore a striking resemblance to *Black Beauty,* which my mother had just read to us. Dramatic poems followed; how

Wendy Orr

delighted my grandmother must have been to receive a 'Poem on Death' for her sixtieth birthday!

"On leaving high school," she added, "I spent a year studying animal care in Kingston, Ontario, went to England for a holiday, and stayed for three years to complete a diploma at the London School of Occupational Therapy. In my final year, 1975, I met and married an Australian farmer holidaying in the United Kingdom and returned to New South Wales with him after graduation.

"The business of growing up, and starting a career and family took over and except for an article on 'Living in Wheelchairs' when I was a student, my writing was limited to patient records and weekly epistles to my parents. At the end of 1982, however, when I had completed a bachelor of applied science and another post-graduate certificate, I decided that it was time to do what I had always wanted. In December 1986 I entered the Ashton Scholastic competition for a picture book manuscript. *Amanda's Dinosaur,* which shared the first place, was published in 1988 and subsequently had rights sold to Canada, New Zealand, and the United States."

Orr's picture-book series "Micki and Daniel" centers on the friendship between two young children and their pets, Pegasus, a miniature horse, and Ooloo Mooloo, a parrot. Although some critics have found these stories somewhat constrained by the author's attempt to be "politically correct," others have considered their adventures amusing and appealing to children. "It is refreshing to see stories of friendship featuring human children instead of the more usual animal quasi-adults," remarked Sarah Ellis in her *Quill & Quire* review of *The Wedding* and *The Train to the City.* In *Pegasus and Ooloo Mooloo,* Micki and Daniel find the animals that accompany them throughout the rest of the series. The four encounter evil circus-owners who want to steal Pegasus, the miniature horse, but Ooloo Mooloo the parrot saves the day when he makes a noise like a police siren and scares the bad guys away. Although some critics mentioned what they considered a lack of focus in the story, noting that the parrot rather than one of the children saves the day, others praised both the setup for the series and the intrinsic interest of the characters. *The Wedding,* the second book in the series, was found to be successful in its rendering of the story of a wedding ceremony in which Micki and Daniel are invited to take part, but their pets are not. Ooloo Mooloo and Pegasus

Following an auto accident that leaves her with a broken neck, karate champion Anna has to rebuild herself physically and mentally. (Cover illustration by Jacqui Henshaw.)

insist on joining in nonetheless, "and it all adds up to a satisfying slapstick climax," according to Ellis.

Orr's science fiction adventure *Mindblowing!,* published outside Australia under the title *A Light in Space,* was widely praised as a fast-paced, compelling story of a boy who meets a being from outer space who, though friendly to him, intends to capture the earth's oxygen for her own planet. "This is top-quality science fiction," a reviewer for *Books in Canada* reported. Critics noted the skillful way in which the author contrasts the viewpoints of the human boy and the alien girl who intends to mine the earth's oxygen for her own planet, despite the deadly effect this would have on the earth's inhabitants. "The plot of this light book is entertaining and fast paced, while the characters are well drawn," remarked J. R. Wytenbroek in *Quill & Quire.* Although Wytenbroek faulted Orr for failing to dramatize the resolution to her story, Anne Connor, reviewing *A Light in Space* for *School Library Journal,* praised Orr's character development and suspenseful plot, dubbing the novel "unusual and fun."

Orr's picture books for preschoolers and first readers include *The Tin Can Puppy,* in which Dylan, who has been told he is too young to take care of the pet he so badly wants, finds a puppy in a tin can in the dump while he is looking for wheels for his cart. Dylan takes the puppy home and hides him, and when his parents discover the puppy, Dylan is allowed to keep him. This is "a slight story," according to Joyce Banks in a review for *School Librarian,* "but told in an amusing, percipient and economical way." Similarly, Orr's *Aa-Choo!,* in which Megan wakes up one morning too sick to go to daycare, presents a common problem critics felt would be appreciated by the preschool audience for whom the book is intended. When no one can take the day off of work to stay home with her, Megan goes to work with her mother, camps out under her mother's desk during an important meeting, and has a few adventures while exploring the office looking for the bathroom. "The delicate dilemma of what to do when a young child is ill and parents have to work is treated gently and humorously," stated Theo Hersh in *Canadian Materials.* Although Phyllis Simon found the story "rather contrived" in her review in *Quill & Quire,* Hersh called *Aa-Choo!* "a book working parents will want to share with their children."

Orr's books for preschoolers and young readers share a humorous approach to the common and uncommon dilemmas faced by her young heroes. Often employing elements of fantasy or science fiction, the author is noted for blending realistic human characters and their animal or alien counterparts in a way that illuminates the hearts and minds of each. While Orr is occasionally faulted for creating slim plots or both showing and telling readers about her characters, her most successful books are ones in which critics find a solid blend of character development, swift pacing, and humorous viewpoint.

"I tend to carry an idea for a story in my head for a year or so before I start writing," Orr explained, "the characters develop further as I redraft and the plot usually changes considerably from my first ideas. Although much of my work verges on fantasy, it has also of course been influenced by my own life. My childhood in a French village gave me the emotional background for *Ark in the Park*—like Sophie, I not only longed for the normalcy of nearby grandparents, but was lucky enough to find some. Similarly, *Yasou Nikki* was loosely based on my own first day of school, when a little girl named Jacqueline took me under her wing, taught me to speak French, and remained a close friend ever after. And *Leaving It to You,* while not drawn on any particular situation, was of course influenced by my first job as a community based occupational therapist in Albury—both by my memories of the people that I met, and of myself, as an idealistic young therapist coming to terms with life.

"In fact, once I'd finished *A Light in Space* I realized that despite being science fiction, it had also been influenced by my own life and concerns at the time of writing. It was actually started the week before [a car accident in 1991 that dramatically curtailed my mobility], and was written in the two years following—I am sure that some of the issues of control versus independence in the story must have been influenced by my own disabilities and fight to regain independence."

Peeling the Onion, a novel for young adults, centers on a similar theme. In this work, seventeen year-old protagonist Anna is tragically disabled in a car accident. While learning to make physical adjustments in order to function independently, Anna must also cope with the reactions of her family and friends, recognizing the inevitable strains that are put upon these relationships. Reviewing *Peeling the Onion* for *Australian Bookseller & Publisher,* Olivia Craze wrote that Orr "mixes the spicy ingredients of authentic characters and relationships with a compelling plot to produce a novel full of power and honesty, touched with humour." Anne Briggs, writing in *Magpies,* reported that in *Peeling the Onion* Orr "displays yet again her precise observation of family relationships and her flair for creating original and richly individual characters of all ages."

Orr told *SATA,* "My husband and I now live in a few acres of bush, or woods, south of Melbourne, Australia. Our daughter is in university, and our son is working in London and engaged to be married.

"Although I still enjoy and am continuing to write for children, a few years ago a story idea appeared that grew into the adult novel *The House at Evelyn's Pond.* As a Canadian migrant to Australia, I was intrigued by the thought that there must be other families who had followed their husbands to different countries, their new country. Although reviewers tend to presume this novel is autobiographical, the intersections of my main character's life with my own are geographical rather than personal. (There is, however, considerable irony as my son, soon after the publication of the novel, met a Norwegian girl while traveling in Asia. They are now engaged to be married, so that one or both of them will

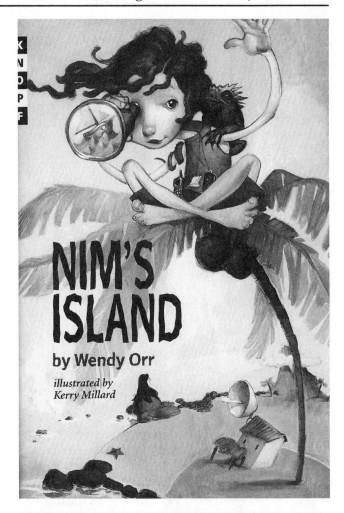

Nim must rely on a sea lion, an iguana, and a new e-mail friend for help while her father is away from their island home. (Cover illustration by Glin Dibley.)

at some time find themselves experiencing the same situation.)

"My intention is to alternate between adult and children's fiction from now on, as I enjoy both the greater depth of reflection possible with adult fiction, and the fun of word play and fantasy with children's writing. Currently I have three children's books in various stages of writing and planning, and am about to start a new adult novel."

Biographical and Critical Sources

PERIODICALS

Australian Bookseller & Publisher, July, 1996, Olivia Craze, review of *Peeling the Onion,* p. 78.
Books in Canada, May, 1993, pp. 30-31; February, 1995, review of *A Light in Space,* p. 50.
Canadian Materials, May, 1992, Theo Hersh, review of *Aa-Choo!,* p. 161.
Magpies, September, 1996, Anne Briggs, review of *Magpies,* p. 38.
Quill & Quire, March, 1992, Phyllis Simon, review of *Aa-Choo!,* p. 66; July, 1993, Sarah Ellis, review of *The*

Wedding and *The Train to the City,* pp. 55-56;
December, 1994, J. R. Wytenbroek, review of *A Light
in Space,* pp. 33-34.
School Librarian, November, 1993, Joyce Banks, review of
The Tin Can Puppy, p. 156.
School Library Journal, February, 1995, Anne Connor,
review of *A Light in Space,* p. 100.*

*   *   *

ORWIN, Joanna 1944-

Personal

Born November 28, 1944, in Nelson, New Zealand;
daughter of Richard Arthur (an ear, nose, and throat
specialist) and Joan Frances (Sladden) Lucas; married
Donald Francis Ginn Orwin, 1968 (deceased, 1989);
children: John, Sally, Kate. *Education:* University of
Canterbury, B.Sc. (Hons), 1968, B.A., 1992. *Hobbies
and other interests:* "Over the years I have sailed small
boats, wind surfed, and snow skied. Now I mainly tramp
(hike) in the New Zealand back country, garden, attend
Masters swimming training, and always spend time
reading, and going to films, and theatre."

Addresses

Home and office—227 Aonhead Rd., Christchurch 8004,
New Zealand. *E-mail*—joanna.orwin@clear.net.nz.

Career

Forest and Range Experiment Station (later Forest
Research Institute, then Landcare Research), plant ecologist and science editor, 1967-75, science editor, 1982-
96, science writing trainer, 1996-98; writer of children's
books, 1980-87, 1998—; freelance writer since 1998.

Member

New Zealand Society of Authors, New Zealand Book
Council, New Zealand Children's Book Foundation,
New Zealand Historic Places Trust.

Awards, Honors

Shortlist, New Zealand Children's Book of the Year,
1985, for *Ihaka and the Prophecy;* New Zealand
Children's Book of the Year, 1986, for *The Guardian of
the Land;* shortlist, New Zealand Children's Book of the
Year, 1988, for *Watcher in the Forest;* Award in
History, Historical Branch, New Zealand Internal Affairs, 1992, for *Four Generations from Maoridom;*
winner, senior fiction category, New Zealand Post
Children's Book Awards, 2002, for *Owl;* Award in
History, New Zealand History Research Trust Fund,
2003, for *Kauri Book.*

Joanna Orwin

Writings

FOR CHILDREN

Ihaka and the Summer Wandering, Oxford University Press
(Auckland, New Zealand), 1982.
Ihaka and the Prophecy, Oxford University Press (Auck-
land, New Zealand), 1984.
The Guardian of the Land, Oxford University Press
(Auckland, New Zealand), 1985.
The Watcher in the Forest, Oxford University Press
(Auckland, New Zealand), 1987.
(With Syd Cormack) *Four Generations from Maoridom:
The Memoirs of a South Island Kaumatua and
Fisherman,* University of Otaga Press (Dunedin, New
Zealand), 1997.
The Tar Dragon (picture book), Ashton Scholastic, 1997.
Owl, Longacre Press, 2001.

Contributor of articles to periodicals, including *Forest
and Bird, Terra Nova, New Zealand Forest Industries,
New Zealand Rod and Rifle,* and *Growing Today.*

Work in Progress

A teenage novel based on parallel historical and modern
stories, "Out of Time," accepted for publication by
Longacre Press; and a commissioned book on New

Zealand Kauri—history, natural history, and cultural content—to be completed by the end of 2003.

Sidelights

Joanna Orwin told *SATA:* "Becoming involved in writing fiction was chance and opportunity—space and time suddenly appeared in my life, and I needed to fill it productively. I was unemployed, home with a young baby, two children at primary school, and have never been good at not having mental occupation. I hadn't ever planned on writing, or not consciously. Books were about reading—I am first and foremost a reader. The writing became compulsive during the 1980s, then life and a return to paid work as a science editor intervened for many years. Finding time to write fiction still has to compete with the demands of earning some sort of living (which I am now managing to do by various sorts of non-fiction writing), time for my adult family, gardening an increasingly unruly quarter acre, and walking in the back country.

"All of my books for children have grown from particular New Zealand landscapes. Landscape and its power to move and influence people has always intrigued and provoked me. Stories that used the power of place to create atmosphere and authenticity had the most impact on me as a child—and still do. As I grew older I became interested in the natural processes that form landscapes, and ended up studying geomorphology (the science of landforms) and botany at university. This led me into a job as a plant ecologist—one of the main attractions was being able to spend time in the mountains. So, when I came to write fiction, it seemed natural to try and recreate an authentic landscape and people it with characters who were strongly influenced by that landscape.

"My latest published book, *Owl,* is my attempt to use Maori myth as the basis of a story, as a metaphor for what is happening to the MacIntyre family. I was trying to use myth in a modern context, but using it the way it's always been used—as an explanation and pattern for human behaviour.

"I think it's important to have stories that grow out of our own experience and reflect our culture, our place in the world. My books will therefore continue to reflect New Zealand landscapes and the New Zealand experience, while inevitably being about the concerns and emotions that are common to young people wherever they are living."

Biographical and Critical Sources

PERIODICALS

Magpies, November, 2001, Raymond Huber, review of *Owl,* p. 8.

P

PERETTI, Frank E. 1951-

Personal

Born January 13, 1951, in Lethbridge, Alberta, Canada; son of Gene E. (a minister) and Joyce E. (a homemaker; maiden name, Schneider) Peretti; married Barbara Jean Ammon (a homemaker), June 24, 1972. *Education:* Attended University of California—Los Angeles, 1976-78. *Politics:* Conservative. *Religion:* Christian. *Hobbies and other interests:* Carpentry, sculpturing, bicycling, hiking, music, aviation.

Addresses

Home—ID. *Agent*—c/o Blanton/Harrell, Inc., 2910 Poston Ave., Nashville, TN 37203.

Career

Licensed minister; associate pastor of community church in Washington state, 1978-84; K-2 Ski Factory, Washington state, production worker (ski maker), 1985-88; writer and public speaker, 1986—. Has worked as a musician and storyteller.

Awards, Honors

Gold Medallion Award, Evangelical Christian Publishers Association, and Readers' and Editors' Choice awards, *Christianity Today,* all for *Piercing the Darkness.*

Writings

"COOPER KIDS ADVENTURES" SERIES

The Door in the Dragon's Throat, Crossway (Westchester, IL), 1986.
Escape from the Island of Aquarius, Crossway (Westchester, IL), 1986.
The Tombs of Anak, Crossway (Westchester, IL), 1987.
Trapped at the Bottom of the Sea, Crossway (Westchester, IL), 1988.

Frank E. Peretti

The Secret of the Desert Stone, Word Publications (Nashville, TN), 1996.
The Deadly Curse of Toco-Rey, Word Publications (Nashville, TN), 1996.
The Legend of Annie Murphy, Word Publications (Nashville, TN), 1997.
Flying Blind, Tommy Nelson (Nashville, TN), 1997.

"VERITAS PROJECT" SERIES

Hangman's Curse, Tommy Nelson (Nashville, TN), 2001.

Nightmare Academy, Tommy Nelson (Nashville, TN), 2002.

OTHER

This Present Darkness (novel), Crossway (Westchester, IL), 1986.

Tilly (novel; based on his radio play), Crossway (Westchester, IL), 1988.

Piercing the Darkness (also see below), Crossway Books (Westchester, IL), 1989.

All Is Well, illustrated by Robert Sauber, Word (Dallas, TX), 1991.

Prophet, Crossway Books (Westchester, IL), 1992.

The Oath, Word Publications (Nashville, TN), 1995.

The Visitation, Word Publications (Nashville, TN), 1999.

This Present Darkness and *Piercing the Darkness,* Crossway Books (Westchester, IL), 2000.

The Wounded Spirit (memoir), Word Publications (Nashville, TN), 2000 published as *No More Bullies: For Those Who Wound or Are Wounded,* Word Publications (Nashville, TN), 2003.

No More Victims, Word Publications (Nashville, TN), 2001.

(Reteller, with Sharon Lamson, Cheryl McKay, and Bill Ross) *Wild & Wacky Totally True Bible Stories: All About Obedience,* Tommy Nelson (Nashville, TN), 2002.

(Reteller, with Bill Ross) *Wild & Wacky Totally True Bible Stories: All About Faith,* Tommy Nelson (Nashville, TN), 2002.

(Reteller, with Bill Ross) *Wild & Wacky Totally True Bible Stories: All About Courage,* Tommy Nelson (Nashville, TN), 2002.

(Reteller, with Bill Ross) *Wild & Wacky Totally True Bible Stories: All About Helping Others,* Tommy Nelson (Nashville, TN), 2002.

Author of the radio drama *Tilly.* The *Wild & Wacky Totally True Bible Stories* series has been produced on videocassette and DVD. Contributor to Christian periodicals.

Sidelights

Frank E. Peretti is a bestselling author of Christian fiction, with over nine million copies of his books sold. "Mr. Peretti's publisher acclaims him the successor to C. S. Lewis; the *Darkness* novels have sold millions. Yet the author's name is virtually unknown outside the Christian community," wrote Jared Lobdell in the *National Review.* Writing in *Christianity Today,* Michael G. Maudlin called Peretti the "great fundamentalist novelist, the father of the blockbuster Christian fiction."

Hailed in *Time* and *Newsweek* as the creator of the crossover Christian thriller, Peretti is the son of a minister and an ordained minister himself, and writes evangelical stories that celebrate the divine power of God and prayer. In his writing, inspired by conservative Christian theology, angels vanquish demons and good always prevails over evil. "The battle against the demonic has always been Peretti's principle theme," wrote Etta Wilson in *BookPage.* With novels such as

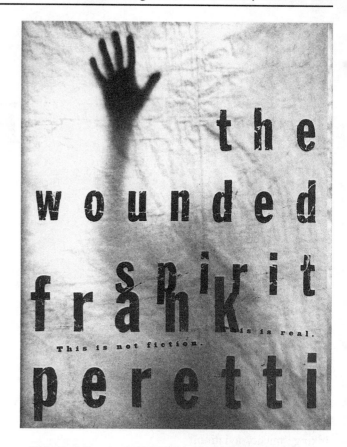

Tormented as a child because of a disfiguring illness, Peretti calls for other wounded spirits and their tormenters to seek healing and forgiveness in his nonfiction account. (Cover photo by Annette Fournet.)

This Present Darkness, Piercing the Darkness, Prophet, The Oath, and *The Visitation,* Peretti almost single-handedly created the genre of Christian thrillers for adult readers. His books for young readers, including the titles in the "Cooper Kids Adventures" series and the "Veritas Project" series, have done the same for middle-grade and young adult readers.

Born in 1951, in Canada, Peretti had, as Jeremy Lott noted in *Christianity Today,* "a hellish childhood." A glandular birth defect known as cystic hygroma led to infected and swollen lymph nodes in his neck as a baby, a condition that caused a baseball-sized lump on his throat. When his father's Pentecostal ministry led the family from Canada to Seattle, Washington, the infant Peretti had the first of seven operations. However, once the cyst was removed, his tongue became affected, swelling and elongating, turning black, and oozing blood. "I was having trouble eating—imagine trying to swallow, even to chew, without the help of your tongue," Peretti told Lott. More operations followed, but the child's tongue—affected by toxins sent by the lymph glands—continued to protrude from his mouth, making speaking another trying event in his life. Even the faith healer Oral Roberts could do nothing for the symptoms the child showed.

When Peretti was at home, people did not stare or torment him for his differences. At school, however, he was embarrassed not only by his long, black tongue, but also by his diminutive size. As he told Jana Riess in *Publishers Weekly,* he looked like a "small, frail freak" as a kid. He began to retreat from public life of any sort, feeling safe only at home with his loving parents and siblings, and tucked away in his room with comic books, trading cards, and an active imagination that created stories starring various movie monsters. As Peretti noted in his memoir, *The Wounded Spirit,* "I think part of me wanted to be one, at least a monster who wins. I wouldn't have minded being Frankenstein. At least monsters could do something about their pain." He began to write monster stories, and he and his brother even built their own monsters, one of them called Xenarthex.

Peretti's condition slowly improved, aided in part by a speech therapist who trained Peretti at age twelve to be able to talk with his tongue inside his mouth. His Christian background also helped him through these difficult years, as he has commented. By the time he was in high school in Seattle, his story-telling skills had attracted a group of neighborhood kids. After graduating, he began playing banjo with a local bluegrass group. Married in 1972, he left the band and started a Christian music ministry, then studied English and film at UCLA for a time before he assisted in pastoring a small Assembly of God church on Vashon Island, Washington, with his father.

Peretti gave up the ministry in 1985, however, working in a ski factory, and began writing short stories and his first adult novel, *This Present Darkness.* Once the novel was finished, Peretti tried unsuccessfully to get his manuscript published with mainstream publishers. Finally Crossway Books, a Christian publishing house in Illinois, bought the book. *This Present Darkness* features protagonist Pastor Hank Busche and his heroic efforts to save a small college town from the Legions of Hell. The demons, in the guise of the Universal Consciousness Society, conspire to purchase the college and then subjugate humankind with the help of a Satanic professor, a New Age minister, a corrupt multinational corporation, and a police chief. Pastor Busche is aided in his efforts by a skeptical reporter who begins to see that this nefarious plot means to subjugate not only the townspeople, but the entire human race. The conspiracy is dramatically defeated when Pastor Busche summons an army of angels to repel the demons.

Published in 1986, this debut novel sold poorly for a year, suffering from poor distribution and a lack of promotion. Then the Christian singer Amy Grant began to praise the book to her audience, and word of mouth picked up. By 1988, the novel was selling 40,000 copies a month and Peretti was deep into a sequel, *Piercing the Darkness.* Peretti had a succession of blockbuster novels thereafter, including *Prophet, The Oath,* and *The Visitation.*

Peretti's first nonfiction book, *The Wounded Spirit,* was inspired by the 1999 shootings at Columbine High School that left thirteen people dead. Peretti explores the causes of youth violence and suggests some possible solutions by relating experiences from his own childhood and young adult years. In the book he details his painful youth and the cystic hygroma which caused him to be branded as an outsider, suffering the jibes and taunts of fellow students. Peretti compares this to the condition of Eric Harris and Dylan Klebold, the perpetrators of the Columbine tragedy, who had been teased and ostracized for their differences. It was a high school gym teacher who finally came to Peretti's aid, merely by being someone with whom a troubled young man could speak about his problems. Peretti urges those who hurt others to be kinder and more aware of the effects of their actions. He also encourages those who are injured by the pettiness and insensitivity of others to speak out about their pain, rather than letting resentments build. Reviewing *The Wounded Spirit* in *Publishers Weekly,* a critic stated: "This book is full of painful stories, but also memorable moments of hope, as Peretti recounts instances when a peer or a teacher stood up for him. This remarkable memoir will inspire readers to undertake similar acts of courageous compassion."

Peretti has also written a number of books specifically for young readers. In 1990, he created the first in a series of exotic adventure stories featuring Christian archaeologist Dr. Jake Cooper and his children, Jay and Lila. The first, *The Door in the Dragon's Throat,* involves a treasure hunt in the Middle East, while the second, *Escape from the Island of Aquarius,* tells of a manhunt for a missionary missing amongst a satanic cult in the South Pacific. In eight books, Peretti takes readers into cave tombs with a mysterious religion, and even into a battle between Soviet and CIA agents. In *The Secret of the Desert Stone,* the children and their father investigate a bizarre two-mile high stone that appears overnight in Togwana. *The Deadly Curse of Toco-Rey* finds the trio in the jungles of Central America fighting the eponymous curse. *The Legend of Annie Murphy* has them dealing with a hundred-year-old ghost. And in *Flying Blind,* the importance of faith is emphasized when Jay must try to land his uncle's Cessna after suffering a head injury that has left him temporarily blind.

In the "Veritas Project" series, inaugurated in 2001 with *Hangman's Curse,* Peretti has developed books targeted at both teens and "tweens." Again using a family as the center of action, the author posits a secret government project, the Veritas Project, which is meant to aid the FBI in breaking drug rings and solving other crimes. *School Library Journal*'s Elaine Fort Weischedel called the series an "evangelical Christian X-Files." Featured in each title are Nate and Sarah Springfield, and their twin children, Elijah and Elisha. In the debut title in the series, *Hangman's Curse,* the family goes undercover in a small town high school to try and solve a baffling crime. A mysterious curse has struck several of the football players, leaving them raving and crazed, tied to their hospital beds. In their delirium, they all mutter the name Abel Frye. Elijah and Elisha befriend many of the kids at school in an attempt to get to the bottom of this Abel Frye mystery. Soon it becomes clear that the deadly madness is connected to a spider breeding in the walls of the school, and Elisha is put into mortal danger.

Weischedel felt that Peretti "develops the plot nicely," and that the religiosity of the Springfield family "does not interrupt the flow of the story, nor does anyone get preachy." Weischedel concluded, "Young teens should enjoy this fast-paced and atmospheric novel." A contributor for *Publishers Weekly* similarly praised *Hangman's Curse*, noting that Peretti's "comfortably paced, compelling performance consistently draws readers along." The same reviewer concluded, "Peretti has an obvious knack ... for emphasizing his beliefs without preaching."

Peretti returns to the "Veritas Project" with the 2002 title, *Nightmare Academy,* in which the project team has a new assignment—to find out what really happened to two runaways. The Springfield twins go undercover again, posing as runaways themselves, ending up in an academy where there is no such thing as absolute truth.

Peretti has also coauthored, with Bill Ross, a series of books about the Bible, "Wild & Wacky Totally True Bible Stories," humorous retellings of stories that deal with themes including courage, helping others, obedience, and faith. A character named Mr. Henry relates the experiences of various biblical figures as they pertain to the topic at hand and how they connect to today's world. The books have also been adapted for videocassette and DVD, with Peretti himself playing the "absent-minded professor-type host," according to Kirsten Martindale in *School Library Journal.* Martindale further noted that the series "embraces biblical philosophy and religious values" and will have viewers "smiling their way through some traditionally serious subjects."

Commenting on the appeal of Peretti's novels, Lobdell wrote, "Whatever their genre may be, it is not 'fantasy.' ... Still, Mr. Peretti deserves his sales, and many readers will get exactly what they want from his books."

Biographical and Critical Sources

BOOKS

Peretti, Frank E., *The Wounded Spirit* (memoir), Word Publications (Nashville, TN), 2000.

PERIODICALS

Booklist, September 1, 1995, John Mort, review of *The Oath,* p. 6; June, 1999, John Mort, review of *The Visitation,* p. 1743.
Bookstore Journal, January, 1988, p. 163.
Christianity Today, April 29, 1996, Michael G. Maudlin, review of *The Oath,* p. 24; August 9, 1999, Susan Wise Bauer, review of *The Visitation,* p. 70; March 4, 2001, Jeremy Lott, review of *The Wounded Spirit,* p. 99.
Dallas Morning News, December 2, 2000, Berta Delgado, "Author Tells All to Help Heal Others," p. 1G.
Harper's, September, 1996, Vince Passaro, review of *The Oath,* pp. 64-70.
Journal of Popular Culture, winter, 1994, Jay R. Howard, "Vilifying the Enemy: The Christian Right and the Novels of Frank Peretti," pp. 193-206.
Library Journal, August, 1989, p. 165; October 15, 1989, p. 50; November 1, 1991, p. 68; September 1, 1995, p. 158.
Nation, February 19, 1996, Donna Minkowitz, review of *The Oath,* pp. 25-28.
National Review, August 20, 1990, Jared Lobdell, review of *This Present Darkness,* pp. 45-47.
People, June 18, 1990, Andrew Abrahams, "Moved by the Spirit of the Lord, Frank Peretti Writes Theological Thrillers That Sell to Heaven," pp. 62-63.
Publishers Weekly, May 15, 1995, p. 15; August 17, 1998, Carol Chapman Stertzer, "Frank Peretti," p. S28; July 31, 2000, Marcia Nelson, "Post-Columbine Reflections," p. 44; October 30, 2000, review of *The Wounded Spirit,* p. 68, Jana Riess, "PW Talks with Frank Peretti," p. 69; May 14, 2001, review of *Hangman's Curse,* p. 40.
School Library Journal, February, 1986, p. 89; May, 1986, p. 96; July, 2001, Elaine Fort Weischedel, review of *Hangman's Curse,* p. 112; Kirsten Martindale, review of *Mr. Henry's Wild & Wacky World* (videocassettes), p. 64.
Seattle Times, September 1, 1999, Sally Macdonald, "'Christian Thrillers' Convert Readers," p. B1; June, 2002.
Time, November 13, 1995, Martha Duffy, review of *The Oath,* p. 105.
Voice Literary Supplement, July, 1990, p. 15.

OTHER

BookPage, http://www.bookpage.com/ (January 6, 2001), Etta Wilson, "Maturity Marks Frank Peretti's *The Visitation.*"
Frank Peretti Home Page, http://thewoundedspirit.com/ (June 11, 2002).
Steeling the Mind of America, http://www.steelingthemind.com/ (January 6, 2001), "Steeling Speaker, Frank Peretti page."*

*   *   *

PLUCKROSE, Henry (Arthur) 1931-

Personal

Born October 23, 1931, in London, England; son of Henry and Ethel Pluckrose; married Helen Fox, May 31, 1955; children: Patrick, Elspeth, Hilary. *Education:* Attended St. Mark and St. John College, 1952-54, and Institute of Education, London, part-time, 1958-60; College of Preceptors, F.C.P., 1976.

Addresses

Home—3 Butts Lane, Danbury, Essex, England. *Office*—Evans Brothers Ltd., Montague House, Russell Sq., London WC1B 5BX, England.

Henry Pluckrose introduces the Czech people, geography, climate, and cities to young readers. (Top right cover photo by Michael Short; bottom photos by Gavin Hellier.)

Career

Teacher of elementary school-aged children in inner London, England, 1954-68; Prior Weston School, London, headteacher, beginning 1968; Evans Brothers Ltd., London, editor for art and craft in education, 1968—. *Military service:* British Army, Royal Army Education Corps, 1950-52.

Writings

Let's Make Pictures, Mills & Boon (London, England), 1965, 2nd edition, 1972, Taplinger (New York, NY), 1967.

Creative Arts and Crafts: A Handbook for Teachers in Primary Schools, Macdonald (London, England), 1966, 2nd edition, 1969, Roy (New York, NY), 1967.

Introducing Crayon Techniques, Watson-Guptill (New York, NY), 1967.

Let's Work Large: A Handbook of Art Techniques for Teachers in Primary Schools, Taplinger (New York, NY), 1967.

Introducing Acrylic Painting, Watson-Guptill (New York, NY), 1968.

(Compiler) *The Art and Craft Book,* Evans Brothers (London, England), 1969.

(Editor, with Frank Peacock) *A Dickens Anthology,* Mills & Boon (London, England), 1970.

Creative Themes, Evans Brothers (London, England), 1969, International Publications Service (Levittown, PA), 1970.

(Editor) *A Book of Crafts,* Regnery (Chicago, IL), 1971.

Art & Craft Today, Evans Brothers (London, England), 1971.

Art, Citation Press (New York, NY), 1972.

(Compiler) *A Craft Collection,* Evans Brothers (London, England), 1973.

Open School, Open Society, Evans Brothers (London, England), 1975.

Seen in Britain, Mills & Boon (London, England), 1977.

A Sourcebook of Picture Making, Evans Brothers (London, England), 1977.

(Editor, with Peter Wilby) *The Condition of English Schools,* Penguin (London, England), 1980.

(Editor, with Peter Wilby) *Education 2000,* Temple Smith (London, England), 1980.

Print Ideas, Evans Brothers (London, England), 1980.

Talk about Growing, illustrated by Chris Fairclough, Watts (London, England), 1980.

Play and Learn Book, Watts (London, England), 1981.

"THINGS" SERIES

Things to See, F. Watts (New York, NY), 1971.

Things to Touch, F. Watts (New York, NY), 1971.

Things to Hear, F. Watts (New York, NY), 1973.

Things That Move, F. Watts (New York, NY), 1973.

Things Big and Small, F. Watts (New York, NY), 1974.

Things Have Shapes, F. Watts (New York, NY), 1974.

Things That Pull, F. Watts (New York, NY), 1974.

Things That Push, F. Watts (New York, NY), 1974.

Things Light and Heavy, F. Watts (New York, NY), 1975.

Things That Cut, F. Watts (New York, NY), 1975.

Things Left and Right, F. Watts (New York, NY), 1975.

Things That Grow, F. Watts (New York, NY), 1975.

Things That Float, F. Watts (New York, NY), 1975.

Things That Hold, F. Watts (New York, NY), 1975.

Things Hard and Soft, F. Watts (New York, NY), 1976.

Things Up and Down, F. Watts (New York, NY), 1976.

Things to Smell, F. Watts (New York, NY), 1977.

Things Hot and Cold, F. Watts (New York, NY), 1977.

"STARTING POINT" SERIES; EDITOR

Let's Use the Locality, Mills & Boon (London, England), 1971.

Let's Paint, Mills & Boon (London, England), 1971.

Let's Print, Mills & Boon (London, England), 1971.

Let's Make a Picture, Mills & Boon (London, England), 1971.

Let's Make a Puppet, Mills & Boon (London, England), 1971.

"ON LOCATION" SERIES

Castles, Mills & Boon (London, England), 1973.

Churches, Mills & Boon (London, England), 1973.

Houses, Mills & Boon (London, England), 1974.

Farms, Mills & Boon (London, England), 1974.

Monasteries, Mills & Boon (London, England), 1975.

"SMALL WORLD" SERIES; EDITOR

Apes, F. Watts (New York, NY), 1979.

Dinosaurs, F. Watts (New York, NY), 1979.

Birds, F. Watts (New York, NY), 1979.

Lions and Tigers, F. Watts (New York, NY), 1979.

Ants, F. Watts (New York, NY), 1980.

Bees and Wasps, F. Watts (New York, NY), 1980.

Reptiles, F. Watts (New York, NY), 1980.

Bears, F. Watts (New York, NY), 1980.

Elephants, F. Watts (New York, NY), 1980.

Horses, F. Watts (New York, NY), 1980.

Birds, F. Watts (New York, NY), 1981.

Whales, F. Watts (New York, NY), 1981.

Eskimos, F. Watts (New York, NY), 1981.

Plains Indians, F. Watts (New York, NY), 1981.

Butterflies and Moths, F. Watts (New York, NY), 1981.

Ancient Greeks, F. Watts (New York, NY), 1981.

Romans, F. Watts (New York, NY), 1982.

Jungles, F. Watts (New York, NY), 1982.

Aborigines, F. Watts (New York, NY), 1982.

Arctic Lands, F. Watts (New York, NY), 1982.

Vikings, F. Watts (New York, NY), 1982.

"THINKABOUT" SERIES

Big and Little, illustrated by Chris Fairclough, F. Watts (New York, NY), 1986.

Floating and Sinking, illustrated by Chris Fairclough, F. Watts (New York, NY), 1986.

Hearing, illustrated by Chris Fairclough, F. Watts (New York, NY), 1986.

Hot and Cold, illustrated by Chris Fairclough, F. Watts (New York, NY), 1986.

Seeing, illustrated by Chris Fairclough, F. Watts (New York, NY), 1986.

Shape, illustrated by Chris Fairclough, F. Watts (New York, NY), 1986.

Smelling, illustrated by Chris Fairclough, F. Watts (New York, NY), 1986.

Tasting, illustrated by Chris Fairclough, F. Watts (New York, NY), 1986.

Touching, illustrated by Chris Fairclough, F. Watts (New York, NY), 1986.

"FRESH START" SERIES

Crayons, illustrated by Chris Fairclough, F. Watts (New York, NY), 1987.

Paints, illustrated by Chris Fairclough, F. Watts (New York, NY), 1987.

Decorated Lettering, illustrated by Chris Fairclough, F. Watts (New York, NY), 1990.

Book Craft, illustrated by Chris Fairclough, F. Watts (New York, NY), 1992.

"KNOWABOUT" SERIES

Knowabout Capacity, illustrated by Chris Fairclough, F. Watts (New York, NY), 1988.

Knowabout Counting, illustrated by Chris Fairclough, F. Watts (New York, NY), 1988.

Knowabout Lengths, illustrated by Chris Fairclough, F. Watts (New York, NY), 1988.

Knowabout Numbers, illustrated by Chris Fairclough, F. Watts (New York, NY), 1988.

Knowabout Pattern, illustrated by Chris Fairclough, F. Watts (New York, NY), 1988.

Knowabout Sorting, illustrated by Chris Fairclough, F. Watts (New York, NY), 1988.

Knowabout Time, illustrated by Chris Fairclough, F. Watts (New York, NY), 1988.

Knowabout Weight, illustrated by Chris Fairclough, F. Watts (New York, NY), 1988.

"LOOK AT" SERIES

Faces, illustrated by Mike Galletly, F. Watts (New York, NY), 1988.

Feet, illustrated by Mike Galletly, F. Watts (New York, NY), 1988.

Teeth, illustrated by Mike Galletly, F. Watts (New York, NY), 1988.

Paws and Claws, illustrated by Simon Roulstone, F. Watts (New York, NY), 1988.

Fur and Feathers, illustrated by Simon Roulstone, F. Watts (New York, NY), 1989.

Fingers and Feelers, F. Watts (New York, NY), 1990.

Homes, Holes, and Hives, F. Watts (New York, NY), 1990.

Tongues and Tasters, F. Watts (New York, NY), 1990.

Whoops, Words, and Whistles, F. Watts (New York, NY), 1990.

"WAYS TO" SERIES

Move It!, illustrated by Chris Fairclough, F. Watts (New York, NY), 1989.

Build It!, F. Watts (New York, NY), 1990.

Change It!, F. Watts (New York, NY), 1990.

Clean It!, illustrated by Chris Fairclough, F. Watts (New York, NY), 1990.

Store It!, illustrated by Chris Fairclough, F. Watts (New York, NY), 1990.

Wear It!, F. Watts (New York, NY), 1990.

Cut It!, F. Watts (New York, NY), 1990.

Join It!, illustrated by Chris Fairclough, F. Watts (New York, NY), 1990.

Pluckrose's book encourages young children to see, touch, and talk about a concept central to mathematics.

"READABOUT" SERIES

Tools, illustrated by Chris Fairclough, F. Watts (New York, NY), 1992.

Machines, illustrated by Chris Fairclough, F. Watts (New York, NY), 1992.

Directions, illustrated by Chris Fairclough, F. Watts (New York, NY), 1992.

Communications, illustrated by Chris Fairclough, F. Watts (New York, NY), 1992.

Energy, illustrated by Chris Fairclough, F. Watts (New York, NY), 1992.

Wheels, illustrated by Chris Fairclough, F. Watts (New York, NY), 1992.

"WALKABOUT" SERIES

Changing Seasons, Children's Press (New York, NY), 1994.

In the Air, Children's Press (New York, NY), 1994.

Minibeasts, Children's Press (New York, NY), 1994.

Seashore, Children's Press (New York, NY), 1994.

Tree, Children's Press (New York, NY), 1994.

Under the Ground, Children's Press (New York, NY), 1994.

Weather, Children's Press (New York, NY), 1994.

"FIND OUT ABOUT" SERIES

Paper, F. Watts (New York, NY), 1994.

Metal, F. Watts (New York, NY), 1994.

Rock and Stone, F. Watts (New York, NY), 1994.

Wood, F. Watts (New York, NY), 1994.

"EXPLORING OUR SENSES" SERIES

Hearing, illustrated by Chris Fairclough, Gareth Stevens (Milwaukee, WI), 1995.

Seeing, illustrated by Chris Fairclough, Gareth Stevens (Milwaukee, WI), 1995.

Smelling, illustrated by Chris Fairclough, Gareth Stevens (Milwaukee, WI), 1995.

Tasting, illustrated by Chris Fairclough, Gareth Stevens (Milwaukee, WI), 1995.

Touching, illustrated by Chris Fairclough, Gareth Stevens (Milwaukee, WI), 1995.

"MATH COUNTS" SERIES

Capacity, Children's Press (Chicago, IL), 1995.

Counting, Children's Press (Chicago, IL), 1995.

Length, Children's Press (New York, NY), 1995.

Numbers, Children's Press (New York, NY), 1995.

Pattern, Children's Press (New York, NY), 1995.

Shape, Children's Press (New York, NY), 1995.

Size, Children's Press (New York, NY), 1995.

Sorting, Children's Press (New York, NY), 1995.

Time, Children's Press (New York, NY), 1995.

Weight, Children's Press (New York, NY), 1995.

"NEW LOOK" SERIES

Inside and Outside, illustrated by Stephen Shoot, Children's Press (Chicago, IL), 1995.

Holes, illustrated by Stephen Shoot, Children's Press (Chicago, IL), 1995.

Beginnings and Endings, illustrated by Stephen Shoot, Children's Press (Chicago, IL), 1996.

Walls, illustrated by Stephen Shoot, Children's Press (Chicago, IL), 1996.

"SENSES" SERIES

Eating and Tasting, Raintree Steck-Vaughn (Austin, TX), 1998.

Listening and Hearing, Raintree Steck-Vaughn (Austin, TX), 1998.

Looking and Seeing, Raintree Steck-Vaughn (Austin, TX), 1998.

Sniffing and Smelling, Raintree Steck-Vaughn (Austin, TX), 1998.

Touching and Feeling, Raintree Steck-Vaughn (Austin, TX), 1998.

"PICTURE A COUNTRY" SERIES

France, F. Watts (New York, NY), 1998.

Egypt, F. Watts (New York, NY), 1998.

Germany, F. Watts (New York, NY), 1998.

India, F. Watts (New York, NY), 1998.

Italy, F. Watts (New York, NY), 1998.

Jamaica, F. Watts (New York, NY), 1998.

Japan, F. Watts (New York, NY), 1998.

Spain, F. Watts (New York, NY), 1998.

Australia, F. Watts (New York, NY), 1999.

China, F. Watts (New York, NY), 1999.

Czech Republic, F. Watts (New York, NY), 1999.

Russia, F. Watts (New York, NY), 1999.

"MACHINES AT WORK" SERIES

In the Supermarket, F. Watts (New York, NY), 1998.

Building A Road, illustrated by Teri Gower, F. Watts (New York, NY), 1998.

On a Building Site, F. Watts (New York, NY), 1998.

On the Farm, illustrated by Teri Gower, F. Watts (New York, NY), 1998.

On the Move, illustrated by Teri Gower, F. Watts (New York, NY), 1998.

Under the Ground, F. Watts (New York, NY), 1999.

"LET'S EXPLORE" SERIES

What Shape Is It?, F. Watts (London, England), 1999, published as *Discovering Shapes,* Gareth Stevens (Milwaukee, WI), 2001.

What Size Is It?, F. Watts (London, England), 1999, published as *Measuring Size,* Gareth Stevens (Milwaukee, WI), 2001.

How Many Are There?, F. Watts (London, England), 1999, published as *Numbers and Counting,* Gareth Stevens (Milwaukee, WI), 2001.

Air, Gareth Stevens (Milwaukee, WI), 2001.

Day and Night, Gareth Stevens (Milwaukee, WI), 2001.

Earth, Gareth Stevens (Milwaukee, WI), 2001.

Fire, Gareth Stevens (Milwaukee, WI), 2001.

My Day, Gareth Stevens (Milwaukee, WI), 2001.

Seasons, Gareth Stevens (Milwaukee, WI), 2001.

Sorting and Sets, Gareth Stevens (Milwaukee, WI), 2001.

Time, Gareth Stevens (Milwaukee, WI), 2001.

Water, Gareth Stevens (Milwaukee, WI), 2001.

Pluckrose describes farm machines at work in **On the Farm.** *(Photo by JCB Landpower Ltd.)*

Sidelights

Author of over two hundred nonfiction titles for young and very young readers, Henry Pluckrose has "always been an exception" to the dry-as-toast approach to educational books, according to a reviewer for *Books for Keeps.* The British writer's success comes, as this same critic noted, from Pluckrose's ability "to enter into a partnership with his reader, gently tapping that reader's experience to allow more things to be learnt than his books 'teach'." Pluckrose has written for a dozen series both in his native England and in the United States. Among these are the popular "Thinkabout," "Know-about," "Readabout," "Walkabout," and "Look At" series; his subjects range from basic concept books, to titles dealing with math, science, art, history, and geography. In the "Small World" series, which he edited, Pluckrose tackles topics from the Plains Indians of North America to ants and apes.

Born in London, England, in 1931, Pluckrose grew up in the difficult generation that experienced both the De-pression and the Second World War as children. After serving in the British Army from 1950 to 1952, Pluckrose went to college and became an educator, teaching elementary school children in inner London from the early 1950s to 1968. His work in education, as well as his experiences as a father of three, convinced him there were not enough titles for young children on a wide range of basic skills and concepts.

Interest in the use of arts and crafts in education led to some of Pluckrose's earliest titles. In 1965 he published *Let's Make Pictures,* an easy-to-follow guide for bud-ding young artists. Writing both for the student and the instructor, he assembled many titles around the art theme; one of the most popular was *The Art and Craft Book,* a collection of writings by a variety of contribu-tors on topics from puppet-making to designing class-room space. A contributor for the *Times Literary Supplement* found the range of contributions to the guide "impressivley wide," and commended Pluckrose for producing a book "which is useful and interesting." *A Craft Collection* from 1973 similarly presents a variety of projects in media from clay to fabrics, employing a "deliberately experimental approach," according to a reviewer for the *Times Literary Supplement,* while also supplying sufficient instructions for each project. *Print Ideas* further expands on the use of arts and crafts in the classroom in a "thoroughy practical introduction to printing," according to a contributor for the *Junior Bookshelf.* Experimentation again is the key word in this art how-to. C. Lynham, writing in *School Librarian* praised the author for a book that "goes further and says more than many of its predecessors."

From such stand-alone titles, Pluckrose moved to series work, and some of the first work was again in the arts, for the "Starting Point" books. Basic concept books, however, soon became his focus. His "Things" series explores topics from sight to hearing to touch and comparison of qualities, all designed to teach very young children about the five senses. Reviewing his *Things Light and Heavy,* a reviewer for *Growing Point* noted the use of photographs with a brief text as well as simple activities, and dubbed the whole a "practical arrangement of contrasting objects." Reviewing *Things That Float* in *Growing Point,* a contributor praised the use of questions with each picture which "encourage observation, reason and memory." A reviewer for *Junior Bookshelf* praised the "excellent" use of black-and-white photography in the same title, while another reviewer for *Junior Bookshelf* lauded *Things That Push,* noting that Pluckrose demonstrates that he "understands the mind of a young child, and knows how to get the information across with the minimum strain."

More basic concepts are served up in the "Thinkabout" series, with photographic illustrations by Chris Fairclough, with whom Pluckrose often collaborates. Geared for ages two to seven, these books, similarly to the "Things" series, examine concepts such as big and little, hot and cold, the five senses, and the nature of floating versus sinking. Designed as part picture book and part springboard for discussion between young child and parent or teacher, the books focus on everyday elements of life that small children and their adults can too often take for granted. Again the author blends brief text with "handsome photography," as a reviewer noted in a *Booklist* review of *Big and Little* and several other titles in the series. Writing about several books in the series in *Appraisal: Science Books for Young People,* a reviewer noted that "preschoolers may find these [titles] appealing," but also complained of the "homogeniety of the families and communities portrayed." Denise M. Wilms, in a *Booklist* review of *Hearing* and the other four books in the series on the senses, remarked that Pluckrose puts together "striking full-color photographs with simple texts that invite readers to think about their personal environment." Wilms concluded that the titles provide "handsome, effective lessons." Reviewing *Hearing* and other titles on the senses in *British Books News,* Elizabeth J. King felt that "anyone with small children will find [the books] invaluable as a starting point for talk and exploration." Sr. Edna Demanche echoed this sentiment in a *Science Books and Films* review of *Seeing* and other titles in the series: "Any parent or primary teacher who wants a top-flight teaching aid will find it in this set of books." Demanche further praised the "vivid, full-page photographs [that] seem to leap off the page," as well as Pluckrose's "scant, direct text [that] points the direction for discussion with very young children."

With his "Knowabout" and "Math Counts" series, Pluckrose assumes a similar approach to mathematical concepts such as numbers, counting, lengths, pattern, and measurement. The "Knowabout" books again combine the photography of Fairclough with brief, succinct text from Pluckrose in works geared at children three to six. Phillis Wilson, writing in *Booklist,* found that *Counting* and other titles in the series are "no shelf-sitters." Wilson further noted that "skilful connections are evident as Pluckrose's text, in tandem with the photos, generate dialogue." Pluckrose employs simple objects from the home, nature, and shop for more abstract titles such as *Capacity* and *Weight.* Reviewing *Pattern* and other titles in the series, *Booklist*'s Wilson praised the books as "examples of quality bookmaking," and remarked that they would also be useful for English-as-a-second language instruction. A critic for *Kirkus Reviews* in a review of *Length* and other titles called the entire series "useful" and "high-quality," while Roger Sutton, reviewing *Counting* in *Bulletin of the Center for Children's Books,* praised the use of "familiar objects," such as fingers or stairs, and the "very simple question" placed on each page. Renee Steinberg, writing in *School Library Journal,* found that *Counting* and other series titles combine "vibrantly colored photographs of familiar objects ... with informative text and related questions to encourage active shared participation." Much of the same ground is covered in "Math Counts," a series of ten books from Children's Press also dealing with capacity, counting, shape, sorting, and measurement. "This series will fill a void in most school and public libraries for good books on these ten topics," wrote a reviewer for *Appraisal.* Writing in *Science Books and Films,* Victor Mastrovincenzo and Christopher Mastrovincenzo lauded the "colorful and striking photography" in *Counting* and other titles in the "Math Counts" series, finding that such images allow very young children "to easily visualize and understand some elementary topics of mathematics." The same reviewers also noted that the books in the series "stimulate children's thinking and encourage them to experiment with and experience mathematics all around them."

Similar generalized concept books are found in series such as "Readabout" and "Find Out About," both of which adopt the same format as "Thinkabout" and "Knowabout" in presenting an introduction to topics such as materials (rock and stone, metal, wood, paper), and machines. Reviewing *Paper* and other titles in the "Find Out About" series, a contributor for *Books for Keeps* commended the books for taking a "strong, unequivocal line about the environment, stressing the need for conservation and the recycling of waste." In a *Books for Keeps* review of titles in the "Readabout" series, a critic noted that Pluckrose's brief text is "effective, making useful points that can be applied beyond the pages of the book." Fundamental concepts of physics are presented in *Energy* and *Wheels,* books designed to "stimulate interest, observation, and thought rather than to inform," wrote Kevin Steinberger in *Magpies.* Steinberger went on to conclude that these "attractive books will be very useful in the infant classroom in many ways." Stuart Hannabuss, writing in *School Librarian,* also had praise for the series. In a review of *Directions* and *Machines,* he commented that both Pluckrose and Fairclough "are well known and deservedly successful in this field," and that "discussion and independent research activities spring out on every page."

A plethora of subjects are offered in the "Small World" series, edited by Pluckrose in collaboration with a variety of photographers. These picture book introductions generally are geared for a primary school audience, have more text than Pluckrose's more basic concept books, and are less focused thematically, Reviewing *Arctic Lands* and *Vikings* in *Booklist,* Ilene Cooper praised Pluckrose for bringing "rather involved subjects" to primary grade readers with his "simple yet meaningful texts." In a *Booklist* review of several animal books in the series, including *Apes,* Barbara Elleman felt that the mixture of brief text and illustrations "give young readers a satisfactory introduction to . . . different animal groups," and Peter Dance, writing in the *Times Literary Supplement,* lauded the "clear, simple texts" in *Ants* and other animal books in the series. Reviewing *Butterflies and Moths* in *School Librarian,* C. M. Ball felt that the brief information "is interesting and likely to encourage questions and further reading." *Romans* and *Ancient Greeks,* two further titles in the "Small World" series also were commended by David N. Pauli, writing in *School Library Journal.* Pauli wrote that teachers "couldn't do better than to introduce these two books" to children learning about past cultures. Barbara Hawkins in *School Library Journal* also commented on the "succinctly covered" information and "well-executed color illustrations, including many cutaway diagrams," which grace series books such as *Reptiles.* However, some reviewers voiced dissatisfaction with similar aspects of the books. Barbara B. Murphy, writing in *School Library Journal* on *Bears* and other series titles, felt the texts "occasionally become confusing due to oversimplification." Joan C. Heidelberg, writing in *Science Books and Films,* remarked that *Dinosaurs* "offers little new information from what has been published in earlier children's books." Cooper, writing in *Booklist,* pointed to "a few confusing statements" in *Romans* and *Ancient Greeks,* and Donna J. Neylon in *School Library Journal* forgave what she considered "only . . . fair quality" writing in *Vikings* because there are so few books dealing with the topic for primary grade students. Harsher criticism came from Marion Glastonbury, reviewing *Aborigines* in the *Times Educational Supplement.* Glastonbury thought that Pluckrose's title "does much to perpetuate" such "educationally unhelpful" concepts as a belief that people from other countries or races are necessarily more superstitious or aggressive or, as the same reviewer put it, "freaks."

Pluckrose returns to more focused thematic approaches in several other series, each dealing with scientific and practical topics. His "Look At" series examines parts of the human body and parts of other animals' bodies, as well. Wilms, writing in *Booklist,* found that his *Fur and Feathers* would help in "sharpening children's observations skills and comprehension of analogous physiological structures." In a *Booklist* review of *Faces* and other titles in the series dealing with parts of the human body, Wilms wrote that the "beautifully photographed books encourage youngsters to look and learn about parts of their body that they no doubt take for granted." Reviewing *Faces* in *Appraisal,* Louise Ritsema commented that an effort is made to "involve the child in observation and experimentation, with the use of stimulating questions relating to the illustrations." Anne Rowe, in a *School Librarian* review of *Paws and Claws,* commended the books in the series as an "exciting new approach to the natural world." A contributor for *Books*

On the Move *provides photos and descriptions of machines that help people travel.*

for Keeps, in a review of *Feet* and other titles in the series, felt they provide an "excellent introduction to . . . parts of the body." And in a review of *Tongues and Tasters, School Librarian*'s Lynda Jones concluded, "This is the sort of material that teachers in primary education have been wanting for years."

Pluckrose tackles the senses in two separate series, "Exploring Our Senses" for Gareth Stevens Publishing, and "Senses" for Raintree. Reviewing the latter series, a contributor for *Horn Book Guide* remarked that the books combine simple text with color photos to "encourage articulate and thoughtful observation" rather than to provide anatomical descriptions. "Exploring Our Senses" also takes the picture book approach to the subject, encouraging young readers to begin thinking about the senses. Kenneth Skau, writing in *Appraisal,* felt the books in "Exploring Our Senses" were most appropriate for pre-school children, "because they are relatively simplistic." Pluckrose's "Machines at Work" series employs the familiar blend of color photography and simple text to introduce machines at home, on the farm, at building sites, and airports. *Booklist*'s Hazel Rochman felt that *On the Farm* and *On the Move* "will appeal to those preschoolers who are fascinated by machines." P. Jenkins, writing in *Books for Your Children,* found the entire set of six books a "really jolly series." A more hands-on approach is taken with the "Ways To" series, describing basic functions such as cleaning, joining, cutting, and wearing. Targeted at preschoolers to second graders, the books combine basic information with color photographs, along with questions to stimulate involvement and suggested activities. A reviewer for *Books for Keeps* thought that the books in the series "provide an approach to their subjects which children could valuably extend to other areas." Focusing on specific action verbs, the books employ "excellent color photographs," according to Pamela K. Bomboy in *School Library Journal,* and "will be useful as trade-book supplements in science classes." Reviewing *Cut It!* and *Join It!* in *Bulletin of the Center for Children's Books,* Roger Sutton praised the books' design as having the "eyecatching appeal of an upscale housewares catalog." Sutton also lauded the fact that concepts are "logically introduced and developed."

In addition to language arts, Pluckrose deals with actual arts in the "Fresh Start" series. In titles such as *Crayons, Paints,* and *Book Craft,* Pluckrose offers a wealth of craft projects for eager young artists. With *Book Craft,* he presents projects from simple folded paper books to ones with sewn sections. Derek Lomas, writing in *School Librarian,* felt that "techniques are explained simply" and that there are "plenty of clear, coloured photographs to supplement the text." A contributor for *Junior Bookshelf* found *Paints* and *Crayons* to be "instructive and useful," and a critic for *Kirkus Reviews* called the same titles "two inspiring introductions to the versatility of easily obtained art materials" as well as a "fine resource for teachers and parents." Wilms in *Booklist* also felt that both those activity books "present a nice batch of ideas for working."

Pluckrose takes to the road in the "Picture a Country" series for Watts. Geared for kindergarten through third grade, each of the thirty-page books in the series devotes two pages to the basic geography of the country, along with cultural information such as schooling, home life, work, and typical food. Additionally, color photographs are accompanied by captions. A reviewer for *Horn Book Guide* felt that four books in the series "proffer overgeneralized facts," while another contributor for the same publication, in a review for *India* and *Japan,* complained that the books provide "very little in the way of concrete information." Another critic for *Horn Book Guide* called the entries on *Germany* and *Italy* a "bland, overgeneralized introduction." Elizabeth Talbot, writing in *School Library Journal,* found what she termed "egregious errors" in titles on *China, Czech Republic,* and *Russia.* However, other critics found more to like in the series. *School Librarian*'s Janet Fisher called *Australia* and *China* "useful additions to the library," and Ann W. Moore, in a *School Library Journal* review of *Egypt* and *France,* felt the books "are attractive and could spawn much discussion."

In his over two hundred titles, Pluckrose has proved himself to be not only a versatile writer, but also a tireless promoter of basic concept books for the very young. His books about art, math, and basic science concepts have introduced a generation of readers to principles and ideas they will later more fully explore in school, while works on geography and history ply readers with questions and make them more aware of the world around them.

Biographical and Critical Sources

PERIODICALS

Appraisal: Science Books for Young People, fall, 1986, review of "Thinkabout" series, pp. 117-118; autumn, 1989, Louise Ritsema, review of *Faces,* pp. 74-75; spring-summer, 1995, Kenneth Skau, review of "Exploring Our Senses" series, p. 65; winter-spring, 1996, review of "Math Counts" series, pp. 79-80.

Booklist, December 1, 1979, Barbara Elleman, review of *Apes,* p. 552; July 1, 1981, review of *Bees and Wasps,* p. 1393; July, 1982, Ilene Cooper, review of *Ancient Greeks* and *Romans,* p. 1439; January 15, 1983, Ilene Cooper, review of *Arctic Lands* and *Vikings,* p. 673; May 1, 1986, Denise M. Wilms, review of *Hearing,* p. 1316; November 1, 1987, review of *Big and Little,* p. 484; April 15, 1988, Denise M. Wilms, review of *Paints* and *Crayons,* p. 1437; May 1, 1988, Phillis Wilson, review of *Counting,* p. 1528; November 1, 1988, Phillis Wilson, review of *Pattern,* p. 486; October 1, 1989, Denise Wilms, review of *Paws and Claws,* p. 354; February 1, 1989, Denise M. Wilms, review of *Faces,* p. 941; December 1, 1998, Hazel Rochman, review of *On the Farm* and *On the Move,* p. 682.

Books for Keeps, March, 1988, review of "Look At" series, p. 24; September, 1990, review of "Ways To" series, p. 18; January, 1992, review of "Readabout" series, p. 14; May, 1993, review of "Walkabout" series, p. 22; September, 1994, review of *Paper,* p. 14.

Books for Your Children, autumn, 1990, P. Jenkins, review of "Machines at Work" series, p. 21.

British Book News, March, 1986, Elizabeth J. King, review of *Hearing,* p. 27.

Bulletin of the Center for Children's Books, June, 1988, Roger Sutton, review of *Counting,* p. 214; February, 1990, Roger Sutton, review of *Cut It!* and *Join It!,* p. 145.

Growing Point, April, 1975, review of *Things Light and Heavy,* p. 2594; March, 1976, review of *Things That Float* and *Things That Hold,* p. 2814.

Horn Book Guide, fall, 1998, review of "Senses" series, p. 390, review of *Italy* and *Germany,* pp. 424-425, review of *Japan* and *India,* p. 425; fall, 1999, review of "Picture a Country" series, p. 391.

Junior Bookshelf, April, 1975, review of *Things That Push,* p. 111; April, 1976, review of *Things That Float,* pp. 94-95; October, 1980, review of *Print Ideas,* pp. 255-256; February, 1988, review of *Crayons* and *Paints,* p. 35.

Kirkus Reviews, March 1, 1988, review of *Crayons* and *Paints,* p. 368; October 1, 1988, review of "Knowabout" series, pp. 1474-1475.

Magpies, November, 1992, Kevin Steinberger, review of *Energy* and *Wheels,* p. 35.

School Librarian, December, 1980, C. Lynham, review of *Print Ideas,* p. 405; June, 1981, C. M. Ball, review of *Butterflies and Moths,* p. 147; November, 1989, Anne

Rowe, review of *Paws and Claws,* p. 156; February, 1991, Lynda Jones, review of *Tongues and Tasters,* p. 26; August, 1992, Stuart Hannabuss, review of *Directions* and *Machines,* p. 109, Derek Lomas, review of *Book Craft,* p. 109; winter, 1999, Janet Fisher, review of *Australia* and *China,* p. 204.

School Library Journal, February, 1980, Barbara B. Murphy, review of *Bears,* p. 49; September, 1981, Barbara Hawkins, review of *Reptiles,* pp. 112-113; October, 1982, David N. Pauli, review of *Ancient Greeks* and *Romans,* p. 144; March, 1983, Donna J. Neylon, review of *Vikings,* p. 166; November, 1983, review of *Arctic Lands,* p. 39; October, 1986, Denise L. Moll, review of "Thinkabout" series, p. 166; October, 1988, Renee Steinberg, review of *Counting,* p. 136; April, 1989, Denise L. Moll, review of *Length,*

pp. 97-98; June, 1990, Pamela K. Bomboy, review of "Ways To" series, p. 115; February, 1999, Ann W. Moore, review of *Egypt* and *France,* p. 101; January, 2000, Elizabeth Talbot, review of *China, Czech Republic,* and *Russia,* pp. 125-126.

Science Books and Films, November, 1980, Joan C. Heidelberg, review of *Dinosaurs,* p. 92; November, 1986, Sr. Edna Demanche, review of *Hearing,* pp. 106-107; January, 1996, Victor Mastrovincenzo and Christopher Mastrovincenzo, review of *Counting,* p. 15.

Times Educational Supplement, November 5, 1982, Marion Glastonbury, review of *Aborigines,* p. 22.

Times Literary Supplement, April, 15, 1970, review of *The Art and Craft Book,* p. 4271; March 27, 1981, Peter Dance, review of *Ants,* p. 347.*

R

REYNOLDS, Marilynn 1940-

Personal

Born June 1, 1940, in Sudbury, Ontario, Canada; married Norman Reynolds (an executive), May 5, 1962; children: Natalie, Maureen. *Education:* University of Alberta, B.A., 1961; Grant MacEwan College, Diploma in Fine Art, 1986. *Hobbies and other interests:* Music, art.

Addresses

Home—13516-81 Ave. NW, Edmonton, Alberta, Canada T5R 3N5.

Career

Writer. *Edmonton Journal,* Edmonton, Alberta, Canada, reporter, 1961-64, book reviewer, 1968-72; *Western Living Magazine,* Edmonton, writer and Edmonton editor, 1980s.

Member

Society of Children's Book Writers and Illustrators, Canadian Society of Children's Authors, Illustrators, and Performers, Writers Guild of Alberta, Children's Literature Roundtable, Young Alberta Book Society.

Awards, Honors

IODE Provincial Creative Writing Scholarship, 1957; Canadian Children's Book Centre Choice, 1993, short-listed, Tiny Torgi award, CNIB, shortlisted, Henry Kreisel Award, all for *Belle's Journey;* Canadian Children's Book Centre Choice, and Pick of the Lists, American Booksellers Association, 1997, for *The New Land;* Canadian Children's Book Centre Choice, and Pick of the Lists, American Booksellers Association, nominee, Children's Book of the Year, Canadian Library Association, shortlisted, Storyteller Award, Western Writers of America, shortlisted, R. Ross Annett Award,

An old horse brings a girl through a blizzard in Marilynn Reynolds's heroic survival story **Belle's Journey,** *illustrated by Stephen McCallum.*

nominee, Amelia Frances Howard-Gibbon Award, honorable mention, ALCUIN Award for book design, all 1999, and all for *The Prairie Fire;* winner, Amelia Frances Howard-Gibbon Award for illustration, Our Choice, Canadian Children's Book Centre, Storytelling World Award, 2001, all for *The Magnificent Piano Recital;* Our Choice, Canadian Children's Book Centre, 2001, for *A Present for Mrs. Kazinski;* shortlist, Blue Spruce Award, Ontario Library Association, for *The*

Young Percy works with his family to overcome the prairie fire heading for his home in Reynolds's **The Prairie Fire,** *illustrated by Don Kilby.*

Name of the Child; The Name of the Child was listed in *Resource Links* "Year's Best, 2002."

Writings

Belle's Journey, illustrated by Stephen McCallum, Orca Book Publishers (Custer, WA), 1993.

A Dog for a Friend, illustrated by Stephen McCallum, Orca Book Publishers (Custer, WA), 1994.

The New Land: A First Year on The Prairie, illustrated by Stephen McCallum, Orca Book Publishers (Custer, WA), 1997.

The Prairie Fire, illustrated by Don Kilby, Orca Book Publishers (Custer, WA), 1999.

The Magnificent Piano Recital, illustrated by Laura Fernandez and Rick Jacobson, Orca Book Publishers (Custer, WA), 2001.

A Present for Mrs. Kazinski, illustrated by Lynn Smith-Ary, Orca Book Publishers (Custer, WA), 2001.

The Name of the Child, illustrated by Don Kilby, Orca Book Publishers (Custer, WA), 2002.

Belle's Journey has been translated into German and Japanese; *A Present for Mrs. Kazinski* has been translated into Korean; Reynolds's work has been included in anthologies including *I Remember When* and *Personal Histories,* by David Booth.

Sidelights

"Marilynn Reynolds has a gift for translating her memories into stories set in an earlier era of Canadian history," wrote Valerie Nielsen in *Canadian Materials.* The Canadian author pens picture books often set on the prairies of her native country in the early decades of the twentieth century, capturing sights and sounds of a bygone age through the stories her mother and grandmother once told her. Reynolds tells of a perilous journey home in *Belle's Journey,* of pioneer life in *The New Land,* of a near tragedy in *The Prairie Fire.* Moving away from the country, she presents the power of music in *The Magnificent Piano Recital* and the bond of intergenerational love in *A Present for Mrs. Kazinski,* while in *The Name of the Child* a young boy learns to overcome his fears to save a baby. Reynolds's award-winning titles are aimed at young readers from four to eight years old; three of her titles have been illustrated by Stephen McCallum, noted for his "cinematic approach to illustrations which are gentle and warm," according to Karen Jollimore in *Resource Links.*

Born in Sudbury, Ontario, in 1940, Reynolds demonstrated an early love for and talent in writing, winning the IODE Provincial Creative Writing Scholarship to the Banff School of Fine Arts while still a high school student. She earned her bachelor's degree in English from the University of Alberta, and went on to write for adults for many years, as a reporter on the *Edmonton Journal,* then as a book reviewer, and finally as editor of *Western Living* magazine. It was only in 1993 that she finally turned her hand to writing picture books.

Reynolds once told *SATA* that her first children's book, *Belle's Journey,* is based on the experiences of her mother and grandmother. Reynolds began to write about these experiences in a book she presented to her mother for her 72nd birthday. "There were five children's stories in the book, all loosely based on tales my grandmother and mother had told me about their lives on the Canadian prairies during the 1920s. One of the stories in my book was about a little girl and her old school pony who are lost in a blizzard. That story has been published separately as the picture book *Belle's Journey.*"

Reynolds further explained to *SATA:* "Although *Belle's Journey* is a work of fiction it has its origins in two near-tragedies. The first occurred when my grandmother and mother were traveling the eight miles home from the nearest town in a wagon pulled by my mother's school pony. A terrible blizzard blew in and they were lost for hours. When the wagon suddenly stopped my grandmother realized that the wind had stopped blowing and the horse had seen something she recognized—the windmill in their own farmyard. The horse managed to bring them home and when my grandfather went out into the fields the next morning he saw the tracks of the wagon wheels in a giant circle in the snow. The horse had been pulling them around and around in one spot for hours!"

Yet that was only half of what found its way into the pages of *Belle's Journey.* "The second story that inspired *Belle's Journey* was told by my mother, who said that during the 1920s she was riding the same pony home from a concert at the school and the weather was so cold that she had frostbite in her legs. The horse was in very bad shape, covered with frost, with her eyes frozen wide open." When Reynolds decided to use such tales as the inspiration for a book, she needed to telescope events somewhat. "When I came to write my story I combined both real-life events," she commented to *SATA.* "Because there is so much prejudice against older people in our society I decided to make the horse a very old one who manages to use her strength, courage, and experi-

ence to save the child's life. *Belle's Journey* is dedicated to my mother, the little girl who rode her pony eight miles to a piano lesson and eight miles home."

Gernot Wieland, writing in *Canadian Literature,* called *Belle's Journey* an "archetypal Canadian" story, the "journey from an inhospitable wilderness to the coziness and warmth of a home." Similarly, a reviewer for *Resource Links* called the book a "tale of prairie perseverance." Young Molly takes piano lessons eight miles away from her home, and the old workhorse, Belle, takes her there and back. Too old to pull a plough any longer, the horse may be sold by Molly's father and replaced with a younger pony that Molly can enter in the fair, but until that time Belle is consigned the lazy occupation of serving as taxi for the young piano player. Then one winter day child and horse are caught in a blizzard on their way back from the piano teacher's. Belle plods on through the snow, Molly shivering on the horse's back. Finally the two arrive back home, and there is no more talk of selling the loyal old horse.

Wieland commented on the two journeys in the book: one Molly's safe return from the teacher's, and the other Belle's "journey into the hearts of Molly and Father." Wieland also found a metaphor in the horse's "stubborn defiance against the fierceness of the winter storm," which transforms itself into a "symbol of those early prairie settlers who struggled against the onslaught of the elements to eke out a living in a dangerous and threatening environment." A reviewer for the *Alberta Report* found the picture book to be "highly evocative of prairie life," while Carole Carpenter, writing in *Canadian Children's Literature,* felt the story demonstrates the "steadfast devotion of animal to the child entrusted to its care," and praised Reynolds's "easy but profoundly moving telling." Carpenter concluded, "Many children surely will claim this story, embracing it as their own because it speaks to them in a manner they know and recognize as traditional through its evident humanity."

Belle's Journey won the debut author a clutch of awards and let her know she was on the right track with her picture book inspiration. Her second book, *A Dog for a Friend,* was also one of the stories in the book Reynolds wrote for her mother on her seventy-second birthday. It, too, was inspired by family stories about life in the west during the 1920s. "My mother told me how much she longed for a dog when she was small, and how her father finally went to town and brought one home in the pocket of his jacket," Reynolds told *SATA.* "And my grandmother often regaled me with her story about bringing a runt pig into the house to save its life—and having the wealthy young Englishman who employed her take the runt into his own bed to stop it from crying."

Reynolds once again combined a pair of stories from her grandmother's and mother's youth to come up with one resonant tale. "I loved these stories when I was small, and in my book, I used the real-life events to create a story about a little girl who wants a dog but who ends up adopting a pig instead. In my book, the kind-hearted mother takes the pig to bed!" In *A Dog for a Friend*, Jesse is a lonely little girl living on the Canadian prairie during the 1920s. She longs for a dog, but her luck instead brings her a pig, and the runt of the litter at that. Reluctant at first to consider the pig an actual pet, she soon is won over by her Harold the pig, and when a real puppy finally comes her way, the animal seems "anticlimactic," according to Annette Goldsmith in *Books in Canada*. Goldsmith also commended Reynolds for her "modest but thoroughly engaging picture-books about country life."

Reynolds stuck with prairie tales for her third title, *The New Land: A First Year on the Prairie*, a chronicle of one family's journey from Europe to farmstead in Canada in the early years of the twentieth century. Reynolds, who spent many summers with her grandparents in Saskatchewan, once again resurrected memories of stories she was told as a child to paint this "complete and vivid picture of the early life and experiences of the pioneers," as Karen Jollimore noted in *Resource Links*. The book deals with the first year on the prairie of this immigrant family, and the difficulties they face. After traveling by sea, rail, and wagon, they arrive at their land and have to dig a well, construct a sod house and barn, and then make it through the bitterly cold first winter. Spring brings planting and prairie flowers; they put in wheat, a kitchen garden, and apple trees.

Shirley Wilton, reviewing the title in *School Library Journal*, commended this "quiet story" for being "simple and direct." Gwyneth Evans, found universal themes in the tale. Writing in *Quill and Quire*, she commented on how the story seems "deliberately general rather than specific in references, suggesting the experience of tens of thousands of families." Evans further noted that *The New Land* is an "attractive book that conveys a simple and practical account." However, partly because of its lack of specificity, Evans ultimately found this to be a "useful book, but not one to grip the heart." On the other hand, Jollimore praised Reynolds's book for portraying "the pioneer experience in such a way that the reader feels like a part of the family," and *Booklist*'s Carolyn Phelan felt the book "will be useful for school units on immigration to the American and Canadian prairies."

Another prairie tale is presented in *The Prairie Fire*, in which young Percy shows his usefulness when a fire breaks out near the family homestead. Percy is too young to help his father plough, and instead is relegated to taking care of the workhorse, Maude. But when he sees a black cloud on the horizon, he recognizes it as a prairie fire, and warns his parents. Then he must overcome his own fear to help save the farm. "Marilynn Reynolds has a gift for bringing stories of earlier times on the prairies to life," wrote Nielsen in a *Canadian Materials* review of *The Prairie Fire*. Nielsen further observed that *The Prairie Fire* is "both a fascinating picture book for primary grade children and a valuable information resource for older readers who are studying the prairies." More critical praise came from a contributor for *Kirkus Reviews* who called it an "exciting story

... realistically told," and from Elizabeth Bush in *Bulletin of the Center for Children's Books*, who remarked that Reynolds's narrative "is direct and tense, and she effectively conveys to young listeners that an act of the greatest bravery may be a simple, clearheaded response in the face of necessity." *Quill and Quire*'s Evans also lauded the effort, noting that Reynolds "is able to draw the reader into the drama of everyday life, and her story is well matched by the sensitive and detailed realism of [Don] Kilby's coloured pencil illustrations."

Reynolds moves away from prairie settings for *The Magnificent Piano Recital*, a tale of "the power of music and the admiration that gifted musicians inspire," according to Lauren Peterson in *Booklist*. Recently arrived in town, Arabella is new in her school and does not hit it off with her teacher, Mrs. Bat. Her mother is a piano teacher, and Arabella practices hard all winter; then in the spring Arabella's mother holds a recital at which the young girl shines. Suddenly she gains popularity and even Mrs. Bat likes her. Peterson found the picture book to be a "thought-provoking story that children may want to talk about," but Jane Marino, writing in *School Library Journal*, found the work to be "ultimately unsuccessful." Marino complained of "stiff prose" and "cardboard characters," yet a reviewer for *Quill and Quire* found the book "a gentle story filled with feminine touches." The same reviewer also commended the "pleasingly rhythmic prose," and the "carefully balanced" characters and scenes.

In *A Present for Mrs. Kazinski* Reynolds deals with contemporary matters in an intergenerational tale dealing with a young boy and an octogenarian. Frank and his mom live on the first floor and Mrs. Kazinski on the top in the same building. Frank loves the old woman and wants to do something special for her eightieth birthday. Consulting other residents of the building, he finally strikes on the idea of giving her a kitten, even though he has grown to love the stray animal. The old woman is touched by the gift, but also sees that the young boy has grown close to the animal, so asks him to help her take care of the pet. Kate McLean, reviewing the title in *School Library Journal*, felt it would "find an appreciative audience at many libraries." A contributor for *Kirkus Reviews* also found much to like in the picture book, calling it a "charming evocation of a classic sentiment."

Reynolds returns to historical, country settings with her 2002 title, *The Name of the Child*. Lloyd is shipped out of the city in 1918, one step ahead of the deadly Spanish Flu epidemic, to stay with his aunt and uncle and their newborn baby. But after a fitful night at the farm, kept awake by coyotes, he discovers that both his aunt and uncle have come down with the flu, and he must take care of the baby, somehow getting it to distant neighbors who have a milk cow to feed it. Such a trip forces easily-frightened Lloyd to drive a wagon down a muddy and deserted road on a rainy night, overcoming some of his own worst fears in the process. "Reynolds writes well," commented *Booklist*'s Carolyn Phelan, "creating a convincing historical context as well as a vivid story." More praise came from Joanne de Groot in *Resource Links* who felt that this "charming story works on a number of different levels." And though a critic for *Kirkus Reviews* found the illustrations too "static and gloomy," the same writer commended the "gripping" story, "set in a period and place not often seen in American picture books."

Biographical and Critical Sources

PERIODICALS

Alberta Report, December 23, 1996, review of *Belle's Journey,* pp. 38-39.

Booklist, October 15, 1997, Carolyn Phelan, review of *The New Land,* pp. 415-416; January 1, 2000, John Peters, review of *The Prairie Fire,* p. 937; March 1, 2001, Lauren Peterson, review of *The Magnificent Piano Recital,* p. 1288; October 15, 2001, Shelle Rosenfeld, review of *A Present for Mrs. Kazinski,* pp. 401-402; January 1, 2002, Carolyn Phelan, review of *The Name of the Child,* p. 900.

Books in Canada, September, 1998, Annette Goldsmith, review of *A Dog for a Friend,* p. 34.

Bulletin of the Center for Children's Books, November, 1999, Elizabeth Bush, review of *The Prairie Fire,* p. 104.

Canadian Children's Literature, fall, 1996, Carole Carpenter, review of *Belle's Journey,* pp. 132-136.

Canadian Literature, spring, 1996, Gernot Wieland, review of *Belle's Journey,* pp. 195-196.

Canadian Materials, December 10, 1999, Valerie Nielsen, review of *The Prairie Fire;* February 16, 2001, Valerie Nielsen, review of *The Magnificent Piano Recital.*

Kirkus Reviews, November 1, 1999, review of *The Prairie Fire,* p. 1747; October 1, 2002, review of *The Name of the Child,* p. 1478.

Maclean's, November 22, 1999, "Pages of Wonder," p. 98.

Quill and Quire, Gwyneth Evans, April, 1997, review of *New Land,* p. 36; May, 1999, Gwyneth Evans, review of *The Prairie Fire,* p. 36; October, 2000, review of *The Magnificent Piano Recital,* pp. 44-45.

Reading Teacher, December, 1998, review of *The New Land,* p. 387.

Resource Links, June, 1997, Karen Jollimore, review of *New Land,* p. 208; August, 1997, review of *Belle's Journey,* p. 253; December, 2002, Joanne de Groot, review of *Name of the Child,* pp. 13-14.

School Library Journal, July, 1997, Shirley Wilton, review of *The New Land,* pp. 73-74; January, 2000, Susan Knell, review of *The Prairie Fire,* p. 110l; April, 2001, Jane Marino, review of *The Magnificent Piano Recital,* p. 121; October, 2001, Kate McLean, review of *A Present for Mrs. Kazinski,* p. 130.

Teacher Librarian, April, 2000, review of *Prairie Fire,* p. 20.

OTHER

CANSCAIP, http://www.canscaip.org/ (March 8, 2003), "Members: Marilynn Reynolds."

Children's Literature, http://www.childrenslit.com/ (March 8, 2003), "Meet Authors and Illustrators: Marilynn Reynolds."

YABS, http://www.yabs.ab.ca/ (March 8, 2003), "Marilynn Reynolds."

*   *   *

RHYNES, Martha E. 1939-

Personal

Born December 5, 1939, in Dallas, TX; daughter of Raymond Jerome (an oil pipeline superintendent) and Juanita (a schoolteacher; maiden name, Wallace) Eubank; married Willard E. Rhynes (a veterinarian and rancher); children: six. *Ethnicity:* "White." *Education:* Attended Texas Women's University and Oklahoma State University; East Central University, B.A. (with honors), 1975, M.A., 1980; graduate study at University of Oklahoma, 1985, Drake University, 1989, and Tulsa Junior College, 1992. *Religion:* United Methodist. *Hobbies and other interests:* Square dancing, duplicate bridge.

Addresses

Home—Route 1, Box 192, Stonewall, OK 74871. *Office*—605 Ann, Ada, OK 74820. *E-mail*—emmy ryan@tds.net.

Martha E. Rhynes

Career

Stonewall School, Stonewall, OK, middle and high school English teacher, 1976-94; East Central University, Ada, OK, adjunct professor of composition, 1994-98. Public speaker; judge of essay contests.

Member

National Council of Teachers of English, Oklahoma Council of Teachers of English, Oklahoma Writing project, Oklahoma Writer's Federation Inc., Society of Children's Book Writers and Illustrators, Ada Library Friends (member of board of directors), Ada Writer's Club, Douglas Bible Club, Owls Book Club.

Awards, Honors

Fellow of National Endowment for the Humanities, 1989; lifetime achievement award, Oklahoma Council of Teachers of English.

Writings

The Secret of the Pack Rat's Nest (young adult novel), 1stBooks Library (Bloomington, IN), 2002.
I, Too, Sing America: The Story of Langston Hughes (young adult biography), Morgan Reynolds (Greensboro, NC), 2002.
Gwendolyn Brooks: Poet from Chicago (young adult biography), Morgan Reynolds (Greensboro, NC), 2003.

Contributor to periodicals, e-zines, and literary encyclopedias, including *Living with Teens, Institute of Children's Literature, Inscriptions, Critical Survey of Short Fiction, Cyclopedia of Literary Places,* and *Cyclopedia of World Authors.*

Work in Progress

Wrinkled Sox, a historical novel set in the 1940s; *How to Write Scary Stories,* for young adults; *Reading and Writing with the Five Senses,* for young adults; *Ralph Ellison: A Biography.*

Sidelights

Martha E. Rhynes told *SATA:* "In my teens I, a city girl from Houston, married a large-animal veterinarian and rancher from Oklahoma. I was a stay-at-home wife and mother of six (four boys and two girls) until my youngest children (twins) started school. At that time I returned to college and eventually graduated from East Central University in Oklahoma.

"I began a second career by teaching literature and composition to students in grades seven through twelve at Stonewall, a rural school located near my ranch home. Later I served as an adjunct professor of freshman composition at East Central University. Encouraging teens to enjoy reading and writing was a challenge, but I loved it.

"After twenty years in the classroom, I retired to care for my elderly parents. From my home office I began a third career, writing articles for 'e-zines,' journals, encyclopedias, book reviews, and author profiles. Morgan Reynolds published *I, Too, Sing America: The Story of Langston Hughes* in 2002. I chose to research and write about Hughes because my students liked his jazzy rhythms and dream themes.

"My husband and I live on our family-operated commercial ranch, where we raise black baldy cattle. Two sons and their families live nearby. When I am not writing at the computer, I enjoy square dancing, playing duplicate bridge, and reading."

Biographical and Critical Sources

PERIODICALS

Booklist, February 15, 2002, Gillian Engberg, review of *I, Too, Sing America: The Story of Langston Hughes,* p. 1033
School Library Journal, May, 2002, Carol Jones Collins, review of *I, Too, Sing America: The Story of Langston Hughes,* p. 176; April, 2003, Sunny Shore, review of *Gwendolyn Brooks: Poet from Chicago,* p. 190.

*   *   *

ROUNDS, Glen (Harold) 1906-2002

OBITUARY NOTICE—See index for *SATA* sketch: Born April 4, 1906, near Wall, SD; died September 27, 2002, in Pinehurst, NC. Author and illustrator. Rounds was the author and illustrator of over fifty books for children and young adults, often drawing on his early life growing up in Montana in the early twentieth century. During his early career, he worked various jobs ranging from cowboy and railroad hand to baker, carnival medicine man, and textile designer. His interest in art led him to attend the Kansas City Art Institute from 1926 to 1927 and the Art Student's League in New York City in 1930 and 1931. Rounds began approaching publishers with his work in the mid-1930s, and his tenacity eventually paid off with his first collection of original tall tales about Paul Bunyan, *Ol' Paul, the Mighty Logger* (1936). This was followed by dozens of other fiction and nonfiction works that were often about frontier life, including the "Whitey" series about a young cowboy, the tall-tale series featuring his character Mr. Yowder, and nature books such as *Wild Orphan* (1961) and *The Beaver: How He Works* (1976). After contracting severe arthritis in his right arm in 1989, Rounds learned to draw with his left hand and continued to write and illustrate books, including his most recent works, *Sod Houses on the Great Plains* (1995) and *Beaver* (1999). In addition to his own books, Rounds also illustrated the works of other authors such as Vance Randolph, Wilson Gage, Jane Yolen, and Eric A. Kimmel.

OBITUARIES AND OTHER SOURCES:

BOOKS

St. James Guide to Children's Writers, fifth edition, St. James (Detroit, MI), 1999.

Writers Directory, 17th edition, St. James (Detroit, MI), 2002.

PERIODICALS

Los Angeles Times, September 30, 2002, p. B9.

New York Times, September 28, 2002, p. B15.

Washington Post, September 30, 2002, p. B4.

S

SANDERS, Nancy I. 1960-

Personal

Born May 17, 1960, in Everett, PA; daughter of Richard J. (a dairy farmer) and Phyllis (a homemaker; maiden name, Harden) Hershberger; married Jeffrey L. Sanders (an elementary school teacher), May 23, 1982; children: Daniel M., Benjamin L. *Ethnicity:* "Caucasian." *Religion:* Christian (interdenominational).

Addresses

Home—6361 Prescott Court, Chino, CA 91710.

Career

Freelance writer, 1985—. TCC Manuscript Critique Service, editor, 1992-2000.

Member

Society of Children's Book Writers and Illustrators.

Writings

FOR CHILDREN

Favorite Bible Heroes: Activities for Ages 4 and 5, Rainbow Publishers, 1993.

Bible Crafts on a Shoestring Budget for Grades 3 and 4, Rainbow Publishers, 1993.

Amazing Bible Puzzles: Old Testament, Concordia (St. Louis, MO), 1993.

Amazing Bible Puzzles: New Testament, Concordia (St. Louis, MO), 1993.

Jumbo Bible Bulletin Boards: More Bible Stories for Preschool and Primary, Christian Education Publishers, 1994.

Jumbo Bible Bulletin Boards: Fall and Winter, Preschool and Primary, Christian Education Publishers, 1994.

Jonah: Six Fun Surprises, illustrated by Bill Stroble, Tyndale House (Wheaton, IL), 1994.

Nancy I. Sanders

Moses: Six Fun Surprises, illustrated by Bill Stroble, Tyndale House (Wheaton, IL), 1994.

My Book about Ben and Me, Concordia (St. Louis, MO), 1994.

My Book about Sara and Me, Concordia (St. Louis, MO), 1994.

Cents-ible Bible Crafts, Concordia (St. Louis, MO), 1994.

The Fall into Sin, Concordia (St. Louis, MO), 1995.

Jesus Walks on the Water, Concordia (St. Louis, MO), 1995.

WA-A-AY COOL Bible Puzzles, Concordia (St. Louis, MO), 1996.

Red Hot Bible Puzzles, Concordia (St. Louis, MO), 1996.

Marshal Matt and the Gummy Worm Mystery, Concordia (St. Louis, MO), 1996.

Marshal Matt and the Case of the Secret Code, Concordia (St. Louis, MO), 1996.

Young readers learn about a famous biblical figure in Sanders's **Noah.** *(Illustrated by Eira Reeves.)*

Marshal Matt and the Topsy-Turvy Trail Mystery, Concordia (St. Louis, MO), 1996.

Marshal Matt and the Puzzling Prints Mystery, Concordia (St. Louis, MO), 1996.

Marshal Matt and the Slippery Snacks Mystery, illustrated by Larry Nolte, Concordia (St. Louis, MO), 1996.

Marshal Matt and the Case of the Freezing Fingers, Concordia (St. Louis, MO), 1997.

Old Testament Days: An Activity Guide, Chicago Review Press (Chicago, IL), 1999.

(With Nanette Williams) *Unforgettable Edible Bible Crafts,* illustrated by Becky Radtke, Concordia (St. Louis, MO), 1999.

A Kid's Guide to African American History, Chicago Review Press (Chicago, IL), 2000.

15 American History Mini Books, Scholastic (New York, NY), 2000.

Fresh and Fun: November, Scholastic (New York, NY), 2001.

The Pet I'll Get, Reader's Digest Children's Publishers (New York, NY), 2001.

My Many Hats, Reader's Digest Children's Publishers (New York, NY), 2001.

Noah, illustrated by Eira Reeves, John Hunt Publishers (New Alresford, Hampshire, England), 2001.

Solomon, John Hunt Publishers (New Alresford, Hampshire, England), 2001.

Zacchaeus, John Hunt Publishers (New Alresford, Hampshire, England), 2001.

Mary and Martha, John Hunt Publishers (New Alresford, Hampshire, England), 2001.

Can't Catch Me, Reader's Digest Children's Publishers (New York, NY), 2001.

Off to the Fair, Reader's Digest Children's Publishers (New York, NY), 2001.

25 Read & Write Mini-Books that Teach Word Families, Scholastic (New York, NY), 2001.

Munch and Learn Math Storymats, Scholastic (New York, NY), 2002.

Easy-to-Read Nursery Rhyme Plays, Scholastic (New York, NY), 2002.

Easter, Children's Press (Danbury, CT), 2002.

Earth Day, Children's Press (Danbury, CT), 2002.

Independence Day, Children's Press (Danbury, CT), 2002.

Passover, Children's Press (Danbury, CT), 2002.

Grammar Manipulatives, Scholastic (New York, NY), 2003.

25 Read & Write Mini-Books that Teach Phonix, Scholastic (New York, NY), 2003.

FOR CHILDREN; WITH SUSAN TITUS OSBORN

Moon Rocks and Dinosaur Bones, illustrated by Julie Durrell, Concordia (St. Louis, MO), 1999.

Lost and Found, illustrated by Julie Durrell, Concordia (St. Louis, MO), 1999.

Hidden Treasure, illustrated by Julie Durrell, Concordia (St. Louis, MO), 1999.

Comet Campout, illustrated by Julie Durrell, Concordia (St. Louis, MO), 1999.

Cooks, Cakes, and Chocolate Shakes, Concordia (St. Louis, MO), 2000.

The Super-Duper Seed Surprise, illustrated by Rhonda Krum, Concordia (St. Louis, MO), 2000.

FOR CHILDREN; WITH SHERYL CRAWFORD

25 Science Plays for Emergent Readers, Scholastic (New York, NY), 2000.

15 Irresistible Mini-Plays for Teaching Math, Scholastic (New York, NY), 2000.

15 Easy-to-Read Mini-Book Plays, Scholastic (New York, NY), 2001.

15 Easy & Irresistible Mini-Books, Scholastic (New York, NY), 2002.

15 Easy-to-Read Holiday & Seasonal Mini-Book Plays, Scholastic (New York, NY), 2002.

15 Easy-to-Read Neighborhood & Community Mini-Book Plays, Scholastic (New York, NY), 2002.

15 Easy-to-Read Nursery Rhyme Mini-Book Plays, Teaching Resources (New York, NY), 2003.

Author of twenty-five "read and write mini-books" that teach word families, Scholastic (New York, NY), 2001; fifteen "easy-to-read mini-book plays" (with Sheryl Crawford), Scholastic (New York, NY), 2001. Contributor to magazines, including *R-A-D-A-R* and *Clubhouse Jr.*

OTHER

To Follow Yahweh's Plan (for adults), Writer's Press (Seattle, WA), 2001.

Contributor to *The Complete Handbook for Christian Writing and Speaking,* Promise Publishers, 1994. Contributor to periodicals, including *Better Homes and Gardens, Today's Christian Woman, Virtue, Helping Hand, Pockets, Discoveries, Power and Light, On the Line, My Friend, R-A-D-A-R, Clubhouse Jr.,* and *Society of Children's Book Writers and Illustrators Bulletin.* Contributing editor, *Christian Communicator,* 1992-2000; assistant editor, *Trails 'n' Treasures,* 1998-99.

Sidelights

"'Relationship' is the key word in my writing career," Nancy I. Sanders once told *SATA,* "My main love is for the picture book because of the relationship this type of book builds between the reader and the child. I want to write picture books that unite the adult with the child as they experience the books together—fostering communication, encouraging time together, and developing a common bond of love for the story and thus for life.

"I write for both the mainstream and the Christian market. One of the reasons I write for the Christian market is because I believe that a relationship with Jesus is integral to all other relationships in life. I write curriculum and teacher resource materials to help create a positive relationship between the teacher and student. I write books for beginner readers to provide positive models for relationships with peers. I write books in

general to help nurture the relationship of the readers with their own identities to increase their self-esteem.

"One of the highlights of my career thus far was when a woman approached me at a writer's conference. She said that *Jonah* is her granddaughter's favorite book. 'Every evening we have to snuggle together and read this book from beginning to end before I tuck her into bed.'

"My desire is for the words I write to be bridges connecting people to build positive relationships in life."

*   *   *

SCHEEDER, Louis 1946-

Personal

Born December 26, 1946, in New York, NY. *Education:* Georgetown University, B.A., 1968; New York University, M.A., 1995.

Addresses

Home—7 Stuyvesant Oval, No. 9D, New York, NY 10009. *Agent*—Jack Tantleff, Abrams Artists, 275 Seventh Ave., New York, NY 10001. *E-mail*—ls36@nyu.edu.

Career

New York University, New York, NY, master teacher and director of classical studio at Tisch School of the Arts. Theatrical director; consultant in theatrical advertising and other theater topics.

Awards, Honors

Mayor's Arts Award, achievement in the arts, Washington, DC, 1982; award for academic excellence in performance studies, 1995.

Writings

(With Shane Ann Younts) *All the Words on Stage,* Smith & Kraus (Lyme, NH), 2002.

Contributor to encyclopedias and reference directories. Contributor of articles and reviews to periodicals, including *Mid-Atlantic Almanak* and *Chronicle of Higher Education.*

Biographical and Critical Sources

PERIODICALS

Choice, September, 2002, W. Baker, review of *All the Words on Stage,* p. 67.

SCHWARZ, (Silvia Tessa) Viviane 1977-

Personal

Born April 7, 1977, in Hannover, Germany; daughter of Wolfgang (a professor of medicine) and Ursula (a teacher and writer) Schwarz; companion of Joel Stewart (an illustrator). *Education:* Attended University of Bonn; Falmouth College of Arts, B.A. (with first class honors), 2002, M.A., 2003. *Hobbies and other interests:* Toymaking, bookbinding, running a small press.

Addresses

Agent—c/o Author Mail, Candlewick Press, 2067 Massachusetts Ave., 3rd Floor, Cambridge, MA 02140. *E-mail*—viv@moonsheep.co.uk.

Career

Writer and illustrator. Moonsheep Studio, Falmouth, Cornwall, England, cofounder.

Viviane Schwarz

Awards, Honors

Parent's Choice selection, Silver Honor Award, 2002, for *The Adventures of a Nose.*

Writings

The Adventures of a Nose (picture book), illustrated by Joel Stewart, Candlewick Press (Cambridge, MA), 2002.

Contributor of illustrations to *Der Bunte Hund.* Schwarz's book has been translated into seven languages.

Work in Progress

Picture books; a novel; research for a master's degree in "authorial illustration."

Sidelights

Viviane Schwarz told *SATA*: "I began writing before I could read. The main reason for learning to read was to try and find out what I was writing all the time. These days I am writing stories because I want to read them.

"I see myself not quite as a writer or illustrator, but rather as a cartographer of places that don't exist, and a collector of all sorts of things. Still, I believe that stories should be more than just collected bits and bobs; I want them to be going somewhere, whether limping, ticking like clockwork, crawling, or rushing. So, I'm someone who herds a collection of all sorts of things through a place that never existed while scribbling down a map of it all.

"I am writing in my second language. This should be a problem, but it doesn't seem to be. It is actually a relief to get out of a language that I know too well—like moving out of my parents' house, out into the world, stumbling through it, being a bit rubbish, but free.

"My first book was a picture book, now translated into seven languages or so (including German—not by me, oddly), featuring a nose with legs, which seems a good start in many ways. The next years should show if my English skills get me through writing a whole novel. I think they will.

"Eventually, I am planning an epic work on pigeons— some time in the far future, I feel. Right now I am doing a master's degree in authorial illustration, which takes up most of my time. My main influences are Tove Jansson, Bruno Schulz, Edward Gorey, and Mervyn Peake.

"In my spare time, I like to sew sheep, restore parasols, make pinhole cameras, and generally fiddle about with silly things. The only thing I am sure about in this world is that it runs on silliness, which isn't always funny."

Biographical and Critical Sources

PERIODICALS

Publishers Weekly, February 25, 2002, review of *The Adventures of a Nose,* p. 66.

School Library Journal, May, 2002, Sally R. Dow, review of *The Adventures of a Nose,* p. 126.

OTHER

Moonsheep Studios, http://www.moonsheep.co.uk/ (May 23, 2003).

*   *   *

SCOLTOCK, Jack 1942-
(A. Zebra)

Personal

Born August 19, 1942, in Derry, Northern Ireland; son of James Frederick (an engineer) and Kathleen (a homemaker; maiden name, McGuinness) Scoltock; married Ursula Bridge Bradley (a hairdresser), December 2, 1967; children: Jason, Justine. *Religion:* "Lapsed Catholic." *Hobbies and other interests:* Scuba diving.

Addresses

Home—27 Caw Park, Waterside, Derry, Northern Ireland BT471LZ. *Office*—Marine Sports, 119 Spencer Rd., Derry, Northern Ireland BT471AE.

Career

Worked as a bricklayer in Derry, Northern Ireland and England, 1959-67; Molins Engineering, Maydown, Campsie, Derry, engineering inspector, 1971-85; Marine Sports (a scuba-diving equipment business), Derry, Northern Ireland, owner, 1985—. Writer.

Awards, Honors

Best Fiction Award for short story, Downtown Radio (Newtownards, Northern Ireland), 1990, for "County Champion Three Times."

Writings

FOR CHILDREN

Quest of the Royal Twins, illustrated by Jeannette Dunne, Wolfhound Press (Dublin, Ireland), 1988.

(Under pseudonym A. Zebra) *A Rumble in the Jungle,* illustrated by Cathy Dineen, Wolfhound Press (Dublin, Ireland), 1989.

Badger, Beano and the Magic Mushroom, illustrated by Jeannette Dunne, Wolfhound Press (Dublin, Ireland), 1990.

Jeremy's Adventure, illustrated by Aileen Caffrey, Wolfhound Press (Dublin, Ireland), 1991.

Justine's Secret Challenge, Wolfhound Press (Dublin, Ireland), 1992.

Seek the Enchanted Antlers, Wolfhound Press (Dublin, Ireland), 1992.

Fairy Girl, Wolfhound Press (Dublin, Ireland), 1992.

The Magic Harp, Wolfhound Press (Dublin, Ireland), 1994.

The Magic Sword, illustrated by Aileen Caffrey, Wolfhound Press (Dublin, Ireland), 1995.

The Sand Clocker: Spanish Armada Stowaway, Wolfhound Press (Dublin, Ireland), 1996.

Midnight Mission, Wolfhound Press (Dublin, Ireland), 1997.

A Sense of Survival, Wolfhound Press (Dublin, Ireland), 1997.

Also author of *The Magic of Fungie,* Wolfhound Press (Dublin, Ireland), and of the e-book, *Commaric,* a young adult fantasy-horror novel available at www. diskuspublishers.com; author of play, *Hope in the Derry Workhouse,* and other plays written for special needs performers. Contributor of short stories to anthologies, including *Devenish Island,* Western Library Board, 1986, and *Borderlines,* Holiday Projects West, 1988. Also contributor to periodicals, including *Tater, Fingerpost, Treasure Hunting, Writer's Companion, Derry*

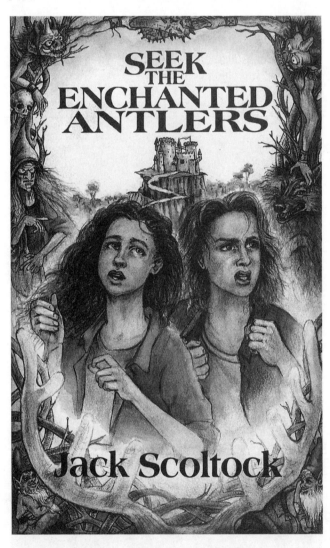

In a secret world inside Errigal mountain, Sinead and Johnny face fierce creatures and threatening powers in this fantasy adventure. (Cover illustration by Aileen Caffrey.)

Journal, Belfast Telegraph, Northern Woman, and *Sentinel.*

Adaptations

The short story, "County Champion Three Times," was performed by local actors on Downtown Radio in Derry, Northern Ireland, 1990.

Work in Progress

At work on the sixth Badger, Beano book.

Sidelights

Jack Scoltock once told *SATA:* "I was born in Derry and grew up in the 'Waterside' part of the city. I had a happy childhood, though when I was very young, my father and mother divorced. I was always an avid reader of comic books, which I still collect and read, though I can't get American or Canadian comics now (too expensive). I firmly believe that reading comics was what developed my imagination. Being the eldest of a family of three I used to pretend I could see things in the light bulb, and I would make up stories for my brother and sister in our bedroom at night. They still remember this. The local cinema, 'The Midland,' was also a great developer of my imagination. Like many other children in Waterside I spent many happy hours there.

"I joined the Brooke Park Library when I was old enough and my favourite novels were Mark Twain's *Huckleberry Finn, Tom Sawyer,* and, particularly, *A Connecticut Yankee in King Arthur's Court.* These were books I read often. *A Connecticut Yankee,* a story in which the hero is transported to another time, really caught my imagination and some of my children's novels have this theme of being transported to other worlds and times. My favourite modern writer is Terry Brooks.

"I started scribbling when I had an accident to my ankle, which ended my bricklaying career. In 1971 I was one of the thirteen Derry divers who found the Spanish Armada wreck of 'La Trinidad Valencera' off the coast of Donegal, Ireland, twenty-five miles away. As an active diver with the Derry Sub-Aqua Club my imagination developed even further.

"In Derry most of us were poor, but we were happy. The traumatic experience of the troubles changed all that. Over twenty years ago when the bombing and killing of both Protestant and Catholic sections of the community where I live began, I started to write as a way of relaxation. My writing really began to develop then. Two of my short stories about this situation followed, one an allegory called *A Rumble in the Jungle,* about the animals in the jungle seeking their animal rights (civil rights) and one animal, one say (one man, one vote). My publisher advised me to use the pseudonym A. Zebra because of the touchy subject matter. It was published in 1989. Though life here in Derry is much more peaceful,

I am still writing and hope to be able to write for a long time to come.

"In 1988, my first novel, *Quest of the Royal Twins,* was published. I do produce quite an amount of writing during the winter. My shop does more trade in the summer, so I am lucky enough to have more time for my writing in the slacker winter months.

"My novel *Jeremy's Adventure* is about animal experimentation, which I abhor. I believe that the young should be educated about this so they can be aware that the makeup and shampoo their parents are using are animal experimentation-free. Children don't like to be preached to, but through writing they can be educated in an enjoyable way about animal experimentation.

"I hope to be writing until I die. My hobby is writing, and this plus the feedback I receive from children give me a lot of enjoyment. I have never been particularly concerned about criticism from adults. It is the children's opinions I value most."

*   *   *

SHERRARD, Valerie (Anne) 1957-

Personal

Born May 16, 1957, in Moosejaw, Saskatchewan, Canada; daughter of Robert Allan (an air force mechanic) and Pauline May (a homemaker; maiden name, Hill) Russell; married Brent Ronald Sherrard (a carpenter), June 26, 1999; children: Anthony Philip Vucenovic, Rebecca Leah Bullock (deceased), Pamela Sarah Bullock. *Ethnicity:* "Anglo-Saxon." *Education:* Attended high school. *Politics:* "Vote person, not party." *Religion:* Christian.

Addresses

Home—P.O. Box 575, Miramichi, New Brunswick, Canada E1N 3A8. *E-mail*—valerie@nbnet.nb.ca.

Career

Glenelg Youth Alliance (group home for adolescents), Miramichi, New Brunswick, Canada, executive director, 1984—. Foster parent to more than seventy teenagers, between 1986 and 1999.

Member

Writers' Union of Canada, New Brunswick Foster Families Association (past president).

Writings

Out of the Ashes (young adult novel), Dundurn Press (Toronto, Ontario, Canada), 2002.

Work in Progress

Two young adult novels featuring Shelby Belgarden, the heroine of *Out of the Ashes; Kate,* a young adult novel; *Sarah's Legacy,* a juvenile novel.

Sidelights

Valerie Sherrard told *SATA:* "Back in February of 1991 I had an unusual experience. I'd been working on a novel, but it wasn't me, and it was going nowhere (as generally happens when we attempt to write something that doesn't come naturally). Each session began with a warmup exercise, in the hope that things would start to flow. One morning, I realized I had just typed the words 'Chapter Two.' Going back, I saw that my warmup (normally a paragraph or two about anything at all) had become a full chapter. When I read it, it seemed worth saving. From that day, I woke early every morning and wrote. Chapter after chapter poured out until, at the end of a month, I found myself with a completed two-hundred-page manuscript.

"This experience taught me something, although it was a number of years before I fully understood the lesson. In order to produce anything remotely worthy of print, I had to step aside and allow a story to grow and develop on its own. Every attempt to wrestle control from the characters has resulted in flat, lifeless words on paper. Once I saw that, for me, this was how it worked, I found it relatively easy to let a story have its own voice.

"I am still an early morning writer, finding that the words flow easiest at that time. I rarely write more than a chapter (1,200-1,600 words) a day, although I did once write fourteen chapters over a ten-day period. When a story wants to 'rest'—I let it. Sometimes this will be for a few days, other times it may be months. It doesn't matter. When it is ready, it will continue to tell itself.

"I would not say that I have been particularly influenced by any specific writers, although I have great respect for many. I am especially fond of those who are able to infuse a book with life and to keep the voice and rhythm steady.

"I write for young people because they are dear to my heart, because I like and respect them. It is my hope that any influence my work may have on teens will be to help them look more deeply inside themselves, and more carefully at the world around them."

Biographical and Critical Sources

PERIODICALS

Daily Gleaner: Weekend Books, June 1, 2002, Ingrid Mueller, review of *Out of the Ashes,* p. B7.
Quill & Quire, August, 2002, Wendy A. Lewis, review of *Out of the Ashes,* p. 32.

SILL, Cathryn 1953-

Personal

Born February 8, 1953, in Asheville, NC; daughter of Jack Howard (an accountant) and Mary (a homemaker; maiden name, Jarvis) Powell; married John Sill (an author and illustrator), March 16, 1975. *Education:* Western Carolina University, B.S.Ed., 1975. *Religion:* Christian.

Addresses

Home—105 Wilkie St., Franklin, NC 28734.

Career

Macon County Board of Education, Franklin, NC, elementary schoolteacher, 1976—; children's writer, 1988—.

Writings

FOR CHILDREN

(With husband, John Sill, and Ben Sill) *A Field Guide to Little Known and Seldom Seen Birds of North America,* illustrated by John Sill, Peachtree (Atlanta, GA), 1988.
(With Ben Sill and John Sill) *Another Field Guide to Little Known and Seldom Seen Birds of North America,* illustrated by John Sill, Peachtree (Atlanta, GA), 1990.
About Birds: A Guide for Children, illustrated by John Sill, Peachtree (Atlanta, GA), 1991.
(With Ben Sill and John Sill) *Beyond Birdwatching* illustrated by John Sill, Peachtree (Atlanta, GA), 1993.
About Mammals: A Guide for Children, illustrated by John Sill, Peachtree (Atlanta, GA), 1997.
About Reptiles: A Guide for Children, illustrated by John Sill, Peachtree (Atlanta, GA), 1999.
About Amphibians: A Guide for Children, illustrated by John Sill, Peachtree (Atlanta, GA), 2000.
About Insects: A Guide for Children, illustrated by John Sill, Peachtree (Atlanta, GA), 2000.
About Fish: A Guide for Children, illustrated by John Sill, Peachtree (Atlanta, GA), 2002.
About Arachnids, illustrated by John Sill, Peachtree (Atlanta, GA), 2003.

Sidelights

Cathryn Sill started out writing about birds, but soon expanded her subject matter to include amphibians, mammals, insects, and other creatures in a format that has been universally praised as effective and enjoyable for very young children as well as early readers of science books. *About Birds: A Guide for Children* is an early example of the format that Sill and her husband, illustrator John Sill, created so successfully. It spotlights John Sill's realistic watercolor illustrations, and pairs them with brief statements about birds in general or specific species. Each full-page illustration appears in small form in the volume Afterword, along with more detailed information about the bird or concept being showcased. The result is "a wonderful visual introduc-

Cathryn Sill defines and describes the life of amphibians in her easy-to-read guide **About Amphibians,** *illustrated by John Sill.*

tion for small children," remarked Kathleen T. Horning in *Booklist. School Library Journal* contributor Ellen Fader also offered praise for Sill's efforts, observing that "Little else on this subject exists at such a young level," making this "a priority purchase" for many librarians.

Cathryn Sill once told *SATA:* "I enjoy natural history and particularly birds. I am also very fond of teaching. I wanted a simple, informative book about birds to use in my kindergarten classroom. The illustrations needed to be accurate as well as beautiful. Since my husband, John, is an artist and illustrator, we enjoyed working together on *About Birds.*"

About Birds was shortly followed by *About Mammals: A Guide for Children,* using the format which reviewers had deemed so useful for working with young children. Here, Sill successfully discusses "how varied animals can be in regard to what they eat, where they live, and how they may act, move, or look," according to

Katherine E. Gillen in *Science Books and Films.* "This is ideal for storytimes," remarked Susan Oliver in *School Library Journal.* Next came *About Reptiles: A Guide for Children,* another successful entry in this series, this time offering basic information about varieties, life cycle, habitat, and food preferences for these creatures.

Likewise, *About Insects: A Guide for Children* uses simple, declarative sentences to convey information about the variety of insects in the world, from silverfish to the mayfly. A contributor to *Appraisal: Science Books for Young People,* remarked that this book "is clearly targeted to the very youngest of children and would be best read to a group of inquisitive, budding naturalists." Similarly, *Booklist* reviewer Gillian Engberg dubbed this book "excellent classroom or pleasure reading for science and nature fans." Sill's next book, *About Amphibians: A Guide for Children,* covers the life cycle and habitat of a variety of amphibians. *School Library Journal* reviewer Patricia Manning compared this book favorably to Sill's earlier books, noting that despite a few minor errors of fact, "this book is inviting, informative, and eye-catching." For a contributor to *Kirkus Reviews,* "the text captures the essential characteristics of amphibians with admirable brevity." In *About Fish: A Guide for Children,* Sill briefly discusses fish movement, gills, and means of self-protection in a work that *Booklist* reviewer Carolyn Phelan described as "simple enough for a preschool teacher to read aloud in class, and easy enough for new readers to read for themselves."

Biographical and Critical Sources

PERIODICALS

Appraisal: Science Books for Young People, review of *About Insects,* p. 98.
Booklist, December 15, 1991, Kathleen T. Horning, review of *About Birds,* p. 772; June 1, 1999, Carolyn Phelan, review of *About Reptiles,* p. 1835; February 1, 2000, Gillian Engberg, review of *About Insects,* p. 1026; May 15, 2001, Carolyn Phelan, review of *About Amphibians,* p. 1754; March 1, 2002, Carolyn Phelan, review of *About Fish,* p. 1138; March 1, 2003, Carolyn Phelan, review of *About Arachnids,* p. 1201.
Horn Book Guide, fall, 1999, review of *About Reptiles,* p. 345.
Kirkus Reviews, February 1, 2001, review of *About Amphibians,* p. 189; January 15, 2003, review of *About Arachnids,* p. 147.
School Library Journal, February, 1992, Ellen Fader, review of *About Birds,* p. 84; June, 1997, Susan Oliver, review of *About Mammals,* p. 113; July, 1999, Karey Wehner, review of *About Reptiles,* p. 90; July, 2000, Karey Wehner, review of *About Insects,* p. 98; June, 2001, Patricia Manning, review of *About Amphibians,* p. 141.
Science Books and Films, October, 1997, Katherine E. Gillen, review of *About Mammals,* p. 210.*

* * *

SIMMONS, Andra 1939-

Personal

Born December 9, 1939, in Covina, CA; daughter of Charles J., Jr. (a rancher and developer) and Ruth (a homemaker; maiden name, Goodrich) Hurst; married John A. Simmons (a designer), October 15, 1967; children: Robert A. *Education:* Attended Oregon State University, 1958-60; University of California—Santa Barbara, degree, 1962.

Addresses

Home and office—Hurst Ranch Educational Center, 1015 South Citrus St., West Covina, CA 91791. *Agent*—Kendra Marcus, Book Stop Literary Agency, 67 Meadow Lane, Orinda, CA 94563.

Career

Hurst Ranch Educational Center, West Covina, CA, director. Also worked as an elementary school teacher.

Writings

Ten Little Angels, illustrated by Jone Hallmark, Harcourt Brace and Co. (San Diego, CA), 2001.

Sidelights

Andra Simmons told *SATA* how she became a writer: "It was simply a process developed over time with a love of words and rhymes and a passion for reading. Ah, and perhaps, most important of all, following my Dad's motto, 'If you can dream it, you can do it,' and, after years of persistence, I did."

* * *

SMITH, Derek 1943-

Personal

Born July 30, 1943, in Long Whatton, England; children: Becky Rees. *Hobbies and other interests:* Films, reading, walking.

Addresses

Home and office—82B Earlham Grove, Forest Gate, London, England E7 9AR. *E-mail*—ds@earlham.freeserve.co.uk.

Career

Gardener, writer, book publisher.

Member

Newham Writers Workshop, Amnesty International.

Awards, Honors

Named in the Pick of the Year 1996 list by the Federation for Children's Book Groups, and shortlisted, Children's Book Award, 1997, for *Frances Fairweather Demon Striker!;* David Thomas prize, best self-published children's book of 1999, for *The Good Wolf;* 100 Best Books for 2001, The Book Trust, for *Lucy-Anne's Changing Ways.*

Writings

FOR CHILDREN

Hard Cash, Faber & Faber (London, England), 1991.
The Magical World of Lucy-Anne, illustrated by Tony Kenyon, Walker (London, England), 1995.
Frances Fairweather Demon Striker!, Faber & Faber (London, England), 1996.
The Good Wolf, illustrated by Abi Bown, Earlham Books (London, England), 1999.

Derek Smith

Lucy-Anne's Changing Ways, illustrated by Abi Bown, Earlham Books (London, England), 2000.
Half a Bike, Faber & Faber (London, England), 2001.

OTHER

The Strikers of Hanbury Street & Other East End Tales, AP Ltd., 2002.

Sidelights

Derek Smith's early readers and young adult novels are noted for their humor, pacing, and subtle depths. Smith introduced the world to Lucy-Anne in *The Magical World of Lucy-Anne,* a series of short stories for beginning readers that reviewers found delightful. In this book, and its follow-up, *Lucy-Anne's Changing Ways,* Lucy-Anne's imagination turns the events of an ordinary day—riding the bus with her father, taking in the laundry from the line in the yard, and so forth—into extraordinary adventures. In addition, Lucy-Anne's imagination comes in handy when her Dad's beans stop growing, or when the snowman's frozen neck needs a rub. "The conversations she has in all six adventures show great imagination on the author's part," remarked a contributor to the *Junior Bookshelf.* Smith's character "will be loved by children for many years to come," concluded a reviewer for the *Book Trust.* For a slightly older crowd, Smith wrote *The Good Wolf,* a sort of twisted fairy tale about a wolf who can't bear to be a carnivore, and helps save Little Red Riding Hood and the Three Pigs from his own bloodthirsty relatives. Although David Churchill writing in *School Librarian* remarked that a vegetarian willing to put his own

siblings to death in defense of his principles "sounds a bit bleak," "the story-telling, with its dilemmas, tension, action and humour . . . is so good" that Smith pulls it off.

Smith's young adult novels are more firmly grounded in realism than his early-reader fare. Reviewers were more than usually affected by the dilemma that faces ten-year-old Frances in *Frances Fairweather Demon Striker!,* a girl whose love of football drives her to disguise herself as a boy in order to play. When Frances's teacher and father forbid her to participate on the girl's football team because of her poor schoolwork, Frances becomes Frank, an ace footballer for the boys' team and all is well, until the day the boys' team faces off against the girls'. Some reviewers predicted that many young readers would be initially attracted to the football element, but would find themselves with a much more intriguing story on their hands, one that might make them question what it means to be a boy or girl. "The puzzles of identity thrown up by Frances/Frank's dilemma are an intriguing addition to a satisfying story," concluded Peter Andrews in *School Librarian.*

Also for the young adult crowd is *Hard Cash,* a novel in which a couple of poor urban would-be orphans find a load of obviously stolen cash and decide to spend it. Reviewers noted that the option of turning in the money for a reward hardly occurs to these children, whose primary role models are their drunken or criminal parents. When Shorty and Warby realize that they can't spend their loot in the local shops, they enlist the help of their friends and siblings, and then Shorty's ne'er-do-well father is on to them and the action of the plot begins to snowball. *School Librarian* reviewer Marcus Crouch called *Hard Cash* "an immoral story with a last-minute moral ending," and added that "Derek Smith handles the first-person narrative brilliantly." Just as reviewers were pleasantly surprised to uncover another level to Smith's novel *Frances Fairweather Demon Striker!,* so they found that the humor, fast-pacing, and action-packed plot of *Hard Cash* are just the beginning of this story. "There are some sound, hard lessons in this cautionary tale," remarked a contributor to *Junior Bookshelf,* continuing: "There is also much understanding, much exploration of complicated relationships, much destruction of illusions." Similarly, Roy in Smith's young adult novel *Half a Bike* is a kid whose lack of family resources, in terms of emotional as well as financial support, leads him to behave in ways with serious consequences.

Derek Smith told *SATA:* "I have lived most of my life in the East End of London. I have for many years been involved in community projects in the area—as writer-in-residence for Soapbox Theatre in Newham in London, as one of the founders of Page One bookshop in Stratford (London), and as a co-op development worker in the London Borough of Tower Hamlets. I have had plays performed on radio, television and the stage in the UK as well as my published work for children.

"I didn't begin writing for children until I was forty-eight. I had up to that time been writing mostly plays. I began with them as I thought they would be easier (with no description) but quickly found they had their own difficulties.

"My first novel was a total mess. I had been writing plays and had no understanding of things like viewpoint. Well, I hadn't needed to until then. So I went on a writing course at the City Lit Institute in London. It helped a lot, and I now run a course for grown ups, Writing for Children, at City University, also in London.

"I don't completely plan my children's novels. When I start writing the story, I know about the main characters, the place, and how the story starts. I often know the ending—but I am very vague about the chunk in the middle. I find if I plan too much then I get bored with the story and don't want to write it. As I am writing the early chapters I keep a notebook in which I am thinking ahead. I liken it to a walk in a thick fog. When I am writing chapter one, I can see vaguely to chapter three. When I get to chapter three I can see just about to chapter five, and so on. Though it does help a lot to know where I am trying to end up.

"I live in the London Borough of Newham and I go regularly to Newham Writers Workshop. This meets once a week at a local community arts centre, and ends up round the pub. They are a group of writers, from beginners to published writers, who live in the area. I find the meetings really enjoyable as writing can be a lonely business and it's good to meet other people who understand your problems and share your successes and commiserate on your rejections.

"I now survive on my writing, but not in the purest sense. Writing itself makes me about a quarter of my income. I make a little in my teaching at City University, but most comes from story-writing workshops I run in schools. I do about seventy a year in the London area."

Biographical and Critical Sources

PERIODICALS

Books for Keeps, September, 1996, review of *Frances Fairweather Demon Striker!* p. 13.
Book Trust, summer, 2002, review of *Lucy-Anne's Changing Ways.*
Guardian, June 20, 1991, Beverly Pangram, review of *Hard Cash.*
Junior Bookshelf, August, 1991, review of *Hard Cash,* p. 181; April, 1996, review of *The Magical World of Lucy-Anne,* p. 71, August, 1996, review of *Frances Fairweather Demon Striker!* p. 160.
Liverpool Echo, June 25, 1996, review of *Frances Fairweather Demon Striker!*
Lollipops, January, 1997, review of *The Magical World of Lucy-Anne.*
New Englander, August 13, 1996, Janet Croft.
Observer, April 8, 1991, Naomi Lewis, review of *Hard Cash,* p. 50.
School Librarian, November, 1991, Marcus Crouch, review of *Hard Cash,* p. 154; May, 1996, Angela Lepper, review of *The Magical World of Lucy-Anne,* p. 65;

August, 1996, Peter Andrews, review of *Frances Fairweather Demon Striker!* p. 109; March, 2000, David Churchill, review of *The Good Wolf.*
Sunday Times, June 16, 1991, Susan Marling, review of *Hard Cash.*
Yorkshire Evening Post, December 8, 1994, Richard Beaumont, review of *Hard Cash.*

*   *   *

STAFFORD, Liliana 1950-

Personal

Born March 18, 1950, in Sussex, England; married Edward Stafford (a teacher), September 25, 1971; children: Helen, Robert, Hermine, Sophia, Brian, Julia. *Education:* Attended College Nedlands for two years. *Politics:* Labour.

Addresses

Home—17 Pilgrim Way, Hamilton Hill, Perth 6163 Western Australia. *E-mail*—ziliensk@iinet.net.au

Career

Writer. Owner of a small horse riding business, 1980-90.

Awards, Honors

Notable Book, Children's Book Council, 2001, for *Amelia Elicott's Garden.*

Writings

FOR CHILDREN

Just Dragon, illustrated by Margaret Power, Cygnet Books (Nedlands, Western Australia), 2000.
The Snow Bear, illustrated by Lambert Davis, Scholastic (New York, NY), 2000.
Amelia Elicott's Garden (picture book), illustrated by Stephen Michael King, Margaret Hamilton Books (Hunters Hill, New South Wales, Australia), 2000.
Chiko Book One: Through the Starting Flags (juvenile novel), illustrated by Alena Kennedy, Cygnet Young Fiction (Crawley, Western Australia), 2001.
Chiko Book Two: A Race Is Run (juvenile novel), illustrated by Irene Young, Cygnet Young Fiction (Crawley, Western Australia), 2001.
Digger (novel), University of Western Australia Press, 2002.
Grandpa's Gate (picture book), University of Western Australia Press, 2002.
The Stone Elephant, Benchmark Press (West Palm Beach, FL), 2002.

Amelia Elicott's Garden has been published in Taiwan, Korea, and America, as well as in Australia.

Liliana Stafford

Work in Progress

Stone Elephant, a picture book; *Shar,* a novel; *Into the Island,* a novel set in Ireland.

Sidelights

Liliana Stafford has lived in Australia most of her adult life. Her young adult novels, *Chiko, Book One: Through the Starting Flags* and *Chiko, Book Two: A Race Is Run,* about a young girl and her show pony, "capture completely the joyous essence of riding in the Australian bush," according to a reviewer in the *Roleystone Courier Journal.* In the first book, young Penny graduates from her comfortable old pony Mustard to Chiko, with whom Penny learns to race and jump in preparation for an important show. In the second book, the relationship between horse and girl must change as Penny soon grows too tall to ride little Chiko. "This is a thrilling bedtime story that will make kids want to leap into their beds, snuggle under their quilts and read another chapter," remarked Leonie Allen in the *Brisbane Courier Mail.*

The Snow Bear, received significant critical attention in the United States. Set in a village in northern Canada, *The Snow Bear* tells the story of the friendship that grows between Bruun, a little boy, and a polar bear who

wanders into town and is feeding at the town dump. The bear is confined to bear jail until the time when he is judged to be so hungry that he will want to go back to the wilderness area to feed herself. But Bruun secretly feeds the bear, and then, when she won't leave town after being released, leads her out onto the ice, only to be trapped by a winter storm. Throughout that winter, the bear cares for Bruun, teaches him how to survive, and brings him back to town in the spring. Bruun grows up and finds the bear again in her last year of life, and is finally able to return the favor. A contributor to *Kirkus Reviews,* felt that the story exhibited both "narrative gaps and credibility issues," but Connie Forst, writing in *Resource Links,* proclaimed *The Snow Bear* "a book that will definitely tug on some emotions while providing a great read."

Liliana Stafford told *SATA:* "Writing for me is now a way of life. I work intermittently throughout the day, taking time out for a walk around the lake with our dog Mitzy, a swim at the beach or a browse through the markets and book shops of Freemantle.

"I began writing in 1988 and was writing for nearly twelve years before I was published. Finally three of my picture books came out in the same year. I didn't plan it that way, it just happened.

"*The Snow Bear* was written in the summer with the temperature around 36 degrees Celsius. I had been thinking for months about the interaction between humans and the natural world and had written some notes under the heading 'Shelter.' One night I was sitting up late after the children had gone to bed when into my head came a picture of a polar bear that had been caught in a storm. At the same time the words 'The Snow Bear' were there and I knew I had a new picture book.

"I researched polar bears in our local library and read about the bear jail in Churchill, Minnesota, and two weeks later I had my story. A Canadian friend asked me how I could write about polar bears in Canada when I had never been there. I don't have an answer except I worked for ten years with horses and children and understood something of how they relate. The rest is called research.

"When I first started writing I worked in a series of notebooks then on an old computer that took one chapter per disk. Now I have a new laptop computer but I still scribble in notebooks sometimes.

"The most important thing about writing that I am still learning is trusting the story to emerge. Walking helps, and scribbling in a notebook, but sometimes it is just a matter of timing. Some stories take years, others days or weeks. They control the pace. I can only be ready and willing to put in the work.

"Currently I am working on a junior novel set on the west coast of Ireland in the Gaelic-speaking area. We visited this area two years ago and I came home with a very thick notebook full of jottings and pieces of a novel. Writing it has allowed me to explore questions of emigration and Irish mythology that have long held my attention. When all the disparate pieces of a story start coming together in a coherent whole is when I become excited. At these times I wouldn't swap writing for anything else in the world."

Biographical and Critical Sources

PERIODICALS

Brisbane Courier Mail, September 18, 2001, Leonie Allen, review of *Chiko Book One* and *Chiko Book Two*.
Childhood Education, summer, 2002, Amy S. Easter, review of *The Snow Bear*, p. 240.
Kirkus Reviews, September 15, 2001, review of *The Snow Bear*, p. 1369.
Resource Links, December, 2001, Connie Forst, review of *The Snow Bear*, p. 11.
Roleystone Courier Journal, June, 2001, "Local Character—Book Hero."
School Library Journal, January, 2001, Meghan R. Malone, review of *Just Dragon*, p. 108; December, 2001, Lisa Dennis, review of *The Snow Bear*, p. 112.*

*   *   *

STEPHENS, Rebecca 1961-

Personal

Born March 10, 1961, in Sevenoaks, Kent, England; daughter of Stanley John Cecil (an advertising executive) and Janet Elizabeth (a medical secretary; maiden name, Haine; present surname, Hogg) Stephens; married Jovan Masic (a trading executive); children: Anna Jane Dubravka. *Ethnicity:* "British, Caucasian." *Education:* University of London, B.Sc. (with honors), 1983. *Religion:* Christian. *Hobbies and other interests:* Trekking, photography.

Addresses

Home and office—28 Crookham Rd., London SW6 4EQ, England. *E-mail*—rebecca.stephens@virgin.net.

Career

Financial Times, London, England, deputy editor, 1985-93; freelance writer. Mountaineer, beginning 1989, including ascent of Mount Everest, 1993, and Seven Summits, 1994; leader of treks in the Himalayas. Broadcaster, including appearances on the series *Tomorrow's World*, presented by the British Broadcasting Corp.; lecturer for schools and businesses. Sir Edmund Hillary Himalayan Trust, member of board of trustees.

Member

Royal Geographical Society (fellow), Alpine Club.

Awards, Honors

Member, Order of the British Empire.

Writings

On Top of the World, Macmillan (New York, NY), 1994.
Everest (juvenile), Dorling Kindersley Publishing (New York, NY), 2001.

Contributor to British newspapers.

Work in Progress

A book on the Seven Summits, "the highest mountain on each of the seven continents."

Biographical and Critical Sources

PERIODICALS

Financial Times, March 13, 1993, Rebecca Stephens, "Everest: The Ultimate High," p. WFT2; June 10, 1993, Rebecca Stephens, "Rebecca's Story: How I Climbed Everest," p. WFT1.
Times (London, England), May 12, 1993, Walter Ellis, "Heights of Ambition," p. 12; May 18, 1993, Alice Thomson, "Day of the Spiderwoman," p. 14.

*   *   *

STEWART, Gail B. 1949-

Personal

Born August 12, 1949, in Chicago, IL; daughter of Arthur R. (a reporter) and Barbara (a homemaker; maiden name, Colberg) Stewart; married Carl Frantzén (a writer), March, 1979; children: Ted, Elliot, Flynn. *Education:* Gustavus Adolphus College, B.A., 1971; attended University of Minnesota, 1977-79; University of St. Thomas, M.A., 1975. *Hobbies and other interests:* Reading and crossword puzzles.

Addresses

Agent—c/o Lucent Books, P. O. Box 289001, San Diego, CA 92198. *E-mail*—gstewart@mninter.net.

Career

Writer. English teacher, 1971-82; University of Minnesota, teaching assistant, 1977-79.

Awards, Honors

Voices of Youth Award, 1997, for *Gay and Lesbian Youth;* New York Readers Award, 1992.

Writings

JUVENILE NONFICTION

China, Crestwood House (Mankato, MN), 1988.
Stunt People, Crestwood House (Mankato, MN), 1988.

Gail B. Stewart gives a history of gangs in America and includes four first-person accounts of gang life. (Cover photos by Natasha Frost.)

Smoke Jumpers and Forest Firefighters, Crestwood House (Mankato, MN), 1988.

Coal Miners, Crestwood House (Mankato, MN), 1988.

Offshore Oil Rig Workers, Crestwood House (Mankato, MN), 1988.

The Facts About Teen Suicide, Crestwood House (Mankato, MN), 1988.

Motorcycle Racing, Crestwood House (New York, NY), 1988.

1900s, Crestwood House (New York, NY), 1989.

1910s, Crestwood House (New York, NY), 1989.

1920s, Crestwood House (New York, NY), 1989.

1930s, Crestwood House (New York, NY), 1989.

Peer Pressure, Crestwood House (New York, NY), 1989.

Chicago, Rourke Enterprises (Vero Beach, FL), 1989.

Death, Crestwood House (New York, NY), 1989.

Child Abuse, Crestwood House (New York, NY), 1989.

Adoption, Crestwood House (New York, NY), 1989.

In Space, Rourke Enterprises (Vero Beach, FL), 1989.

New York, Rourke Enterprises (Vero Beach, FL), 1989.

In the Deserts, Rourke Enterprises (Vero Beach, FL), 1989.

On the Water, Rourke Enterprises (Vero Beach, FL), 1989.

In the Future, Rourke Enterprises (Vero Beach, FL), 1989.

In the Mountains, Rourke Enterprises (Vero Beach, FL), 1989.

In the Polar Regions, Rourke Enterprises (Vero Beach, FL), 1989.

Houston, Rourke Enterprises (Vero Beach, FL), 1989.

Los Angeles, Rourke Enterprises (Vero Beach, FL), 1989.

Discrimination, Crestwood House (New York, NY), 1989.

Lumbermen, illustrated by Mark E. Ahlstrom, Rourke Enterprises (Vero Beach, FL), 1990.

South Africa, Crestwood House (New York, NY), 1990.

The Soviet Union, Crestwood House (New York, NY), 1990.

Acid Rain, Lucent Books (San Diego, CA), 1990.

Rivermen, illustrated by Joe Nordstrom, Rourke Enterprises (Vero Beach, FL), 1990.

Scouts, illustrated by Tom Casmer, Rourke Enterprises (Vero Beach, FL), 1990.

Panama, Crestwood House (New York, NY), 1990.

Northern Ireland, Crestwood House (New York, NY), 1990.

Poland, Crestwood House (New York, NY), 1990.

Trappers and Traders, illustrated by Tom Casmer, Rourke Enterprises (Vero Beach, FL), 1990.

Drought, Crestwood House (New York, NY), 1990.

Texans, illustrated by Joe Nordstrom, Rourke Enterprises (Vero Beach, FL), 1990.

Drug Trafficking, Lucent Books (San Diego, CA), 1990.

Germany, Crestwood House (New York, NY), 1990.

Lebanon, Crestwood House (New York, NY), 1990.

Colombia, Crestwood House (New York, NY), 1991.

El Salvador, Crestwood House (New York, NY), 1991.

The Philippines, Crestwood House (New York, NY), 1991.

Cuba, Crestwood House (New York, NY), 1991.

Romania, Crestwood House (New York, NY), 1991.

The Revolutionary War, Lucent Books (San Diego, CA), 1991.

Antarctica, Crestwood House (New York, NY), 1991.

Ethiopia, Crestwood House (New York, NY), 1991.

Iraq, Crestwood House (New York, NY), 1991.

World War I, Lucent Books (San Diego, CA), 1991.

(With Jane Duden) *1980s,* Crestwood House (New York, NY), 1991.

Microscope: Bringing the Unseen World into Focus, Lucent Books (San Diego, CA), 1992.

Benjamin Franklin, Lucent Books (San Diego, CA), 1992.

What Happened to Judge Crater?, illustrated by Marcy Ramsey, Crestwood House (New York, NY), 1992.

Where Lies Butch Cassidy?, illustrated by Yoshi Miyaki, Crestwood House (New York, NY), 1992.

Why Buy Quantrill's Bones?, illustrated by James Watling, Crestwood House (New York, NY), 1992.

Liberia, Crestwood House (New York, NY), 1992.

India, Crestwood House (New York, NY), 1992.

Egypt, Crestwood House (New York, NY), 1992.

The Baltic States, Crestwood House (New York, NY), 1992.

The New Deal, New Discovery Books (New York, NY), 1993.

Alexander the Great, Lucent Books (San Diego, CA), 1994.

Hitler's Reich, Lucent Books (San Diego, CA), 1994.

Cowboys in the Old West, Lucent Books (San Diego, CA), 1995.

The Quarter Horse, photography by William Muñoz, Capstone Press (Minneapolis, MN), 1995.

The Appaloosa Horse, photography by William Muñoz, Capstone Press (Minneapolis, MN), 1995.

The Thoroughbred Horse: Born to Run, illustrated by Ron Colbroth, Capstone Press (Minneapolis, MN), 1995.

Horseback Riding, Capstone Press (Minneapolis, MN), 1995.

Life in the Eskimo Village, Lucent Books (San Diego, CA), 1995.

Life in the Warsaw Ghetto, Lucent Books (San Diego, CA), 1995.

The Arabian Horse, photography by William Muñoz, Capstone Press (Minneapolis, MN), 1995.

Life During the French Revolution, Lucent Books (San Diego, CA), 1995.

Mustangs and Wild Horses, photography by William Muñoz, Capstone Press (Minneapolis, MN), 1996.

The Shetland Pony, photography by William Muñoz, Capstone Press (Minneapolis, MN), 1996.

The Palomino Horse, photography by William Muñoz, Capstone Press (Minneapolis, MN), 1996.

The Pinto Horse, photography by William Muñoz, Capstone Press (Minneapolis, MN), 1996.

The Elderly, Lucent Books (San Diego, CA), 1996.

People with AIDS, Lucent Books (San Diego, CA), 1996.

The Homeless, Lucent Books (San Diego, CA), 1996.

Teen Mothers, Lucent Books (San Diego, CA), 1996.

Teens in Prison, photography by Natasha Frost, Lucent Books (San Diego, CA), 1997.

Battered Women, photography by Natasha Frost, Lucent Books (San Diego, CA), 1997.

Gangs, photography by Natasha Frost, Lucent Books (San Diego, CA), 1997.

Illegal Immigrants, photography by Natasha Frost, Lucent Books (San Diego, CA), 1997.

Teen Runaways, photography by Natasha Frost, Lucent Books (San Diego, CA), 1997.

Gay and Lesbian Youth, photography by Natasha Frost, Lucent Books (San Diego, CA), 1997.

The Death Penalty, Greenhaven Press (San Diego, CA), 1998.

Drugs and Sports, Greenhaven Press (San Diego, CA), 1998.

Life During the Spanish Inquisition, Lucent Books (San Diego, CA), 1998.

Militias, Lucent Books (San Diego, CA), 1998.

Mothers on Welfare, photography by Theodore E. Roseen, Lucent Books (San Diego, CA), 1998.

Teens and Depression, photography by Theodore E. Roseen, Lucent Books (San Diego, CA), 1998.

Teen Fathers, photography by Theodore E. Roseen, Lucent Books (San Diego, CA), 1998.

Diabetes, Lucent Books (San Diego, CA), 1999.

F. Scott Fitzgerald, Lucent Books (San Diego, CA), 1999.

Homeless Teens, photography by husband, Carl Frantzén, Lucent Books (San Diego, CA), 1999.

1970s, Lucent Books (San Diego, CA), 1999.

Teen Dropouts, photography by Carl Frantzén, Lucent Books (San Diego, CA), 1999.

Soccer, Lucent Books (San Diego, CA), 2000.

Teen Addicts, photography by Carl Frantzén, Lucent Books (San Diego, CA), 2000.

Teen Alcoholics, Lucent Books (San Diego, CA), 2000.

Teen Parenting, Lucent Books (San Diego, CA), 2000.

Teens and Divorce, Lucent Books (San Diego, CA), 2000.

Teens with Eating Disorders, Lucent Books (San Diego, CA), 2000.

Weapons of War, Lucent Books (San Diego, CA), 2000.

America Under Attack: September 11, 2001, Lucent Books (San Diego, CA), 2001.

Phobias, Lucent Books (San Diego, CA), 2001.

Suez Canal, Lucent Books (San Diego, CA), 2001.

Teens with Disabilities, photography by Carl Frantzén, Lucent Books (San Diego, CA), 2001.

Teens and Violence, Lucent Books (San Diego, CA), 2002.

Divorce, Kidhaven Press (San Diego, CA), 2002.

Drugs, Kidhaven Press (San Diego, CA), 2002.

Guns and Violence, Kidhaven Press (San Diego, CA), 2002.

Teens With Cancer, Lucent Books (San Diego, CA), 2002.

Terrorism, Lucent Books (San Diego, CA), 2002.

Tuberculosis, Lucent Books (San Diego, CA), 2002.

Great Women Comedians, Lucent Books (San Diego, CA), 2003.

Life in Elizabethan London, Lucent Books (San Diego, CA), 2003.

Life of a Soldier in Washington's Army, Lucent Books (San Diego, CA), 2003.

Microscopes, Kidhaven Press (San Diego, CA), 2003.

Child Abuse, Kidhaven Press (San Diego, CA), 2003.

People with Mental Illness, photography by Carl Frantzén, Lucent Books (San Diego, CA), 2003.

Racism, Kidhaven Press (San Diego, CA), 2003.

Sleep Disorders, Lucent Books (San Diego, CA), 2003.

***Stewart gives a history of soccer and describes memorable moments and personalities in* Soccer.** *(Photo by Ezra O. Shaw)*

Four teens discuss their alcoholism and the ways they have dealt with their addiction. (Cover photos by Carl Franzen.)

Smoking, Kidhaven Press (San Diego, CA), 2003.
Defending the Borders, Lucent Books (San Diego, CA), 2004.
Lyme Disease, Lucent Books (San Diego, CA), 2004.
Saddam Hussein, Blackbirch Press (San Diego, CA), 2004.
Teens in Mexico, Lucent Books (San Diego, CA), 2004.

Sidelights

Gail B. Stewart is a versatile, prolific writer who has produced more than one hundred volumes of nonfiction for young readers. She began her writing career in 1988, when she issued seven books. The next year she published nineteen additional titles, and in the ensuing years she has often produced as many as ten or more works. Her writings include histories, biographies, books on nations, and even geographical accounts. She has also produced books on animals, jobs, and mysteries, such as the whereabouts of outlaw Butch Cassidy's corpse.

Stewart has published several books on various issues of particular concern to teenagers. *Teens with Disabilities* won praise from *School Library Journal* reviewer Kim Harris, who noted the book's "well-done, informal approach." *Teens with Eating Disorders,* meanwhile,

was considered "flawed" by *Booklist* reviewer Catherine Andronik, who nonetheless concluded that "selections from it should be required reading for teens facing the new stress of college life," and *Teen Alcoholics* was acknowledged by *Booklist* reviewer Mary Romano Marks as a "realistic portrait of seemingly typical teens faced with an all too common problem." Still another book, *Teen Dropouts,* received praise from *Booklist* reviewer Roger Leslie, who declared that Stewart "opens eyes and creates a connection between ... teens and readers of any age, and from any life experience." Stewart explored related issues in *Teens and Depression,* which Mary Romano Marks acknowledged in *Booklist* for "in-depth accounts," and *Teen Fathers,* which Roger Leslie, another *Booklist* critic, noted for its "complex, exasperating, and poignant ... first-person accounts."

Stewart's other books on teen issues include *Gangs,* wherein—as Susan Dove Lempke wrote in *Booklist*—"teens are allowed to speak frankly ... about their lives and the world they see around them," and *Teens in Prison,* which includes what Lempke described in *Booklist* as "eye-opening" revelations. Lempke also wrote in *Booklist* that two other books, *Gay and Lesbian Youth* and *Teen Runaways* serve to "vividly illustrate the difficulties many young people face."

In addition to writing about teen issues, Stewart has published books on subjects ranging from sports to history. *Drugs and Sports,* for example, was described by *Booklist* reviewer Jean Franklin as an "informative examination," and *Soccer* was noted in *School Library Journal* as an examination of "the origins and philosophy of this sport." Stewart's history writings, meanwhile, include *Life During the Spanish Inquisition,* which *Booklist* critic Mary Romano Marks found "candid and objective," and *Life During the French Revolution,* which Frances Bradburn, also writing in *Booklist,* noted for its "unerring ability to capture the fascinating scenario." Another history volume, *Life in the Warsaw Ghetto,* includes what *Booklist* reviewer Hazel Rochman described as "astonishing stories of heroism and endurance," while the lighter *Cowboys in the Old West* constitutes what April Judge affirmed in *Booklist* as a "comprehensive, well-researched title."

Among Stewart's other writings are books on various issues and developments in society. Such books include *Militias,* which Marks acknowledged, in *Booklist,* for its "smooth, engaging style." Another *Booklist* reviewer, Merri Monks noted that Stewart's *People with AIDS* and *The Elderly* both aim to "reveal the problems—and the strengths—of individuals ... considered outsiders."

Stewart told *SATA,* "I began writing professionally by accident. I was copyediting a book on motorcycle racing when it was evident that the author was incapable of making the changes necessary for the book to go to print. It later was evident that the author had plagiarized large sections of his book. Because the book's due date was written in stone, so to speak, it had to be finished, and fast! I knew I could write, and I took it on. I had fun with it, and never did a minute of editing after that!

Now, more than one hundred books later, I marvel at the accidental way it all began."

Biographical and Critical Sources

PERIODICALS

Booklist, March 15, 1995, Hazel Rochman, review of *Life in the Warsaw Ghetto,* p. 1329; May 1, 1995, April Judge, review of *Cowboys in the Old West,* p. 1559; June 1, 1995, Frances Bradburn, review of *Life During the French Revolution,* p. 1748; March 1, 1996, Merri Monks, reviews of *People with AIDS* and *The Elderly,* p. 1174; March 1, 1997, Susan Dove Lempke, reviews of *Teen Runaways* and *Gay and Lesbian Youth,* p. 1155; May 15, 1997, Susan Dove Lempke, reviews of *Gangs* and *Teens in Prison,* p. 1572; January 1, 1998, Mary Romano Marks, reviews of *Life During the Spanish Inquisition,* p. 788, and *Militias,* pp. 788-789; April 15, 1998, Roger Leslie, review of *Teen Fathers,* p. 1434; May 15, 1998, Mary Romano Marks, review of *Teens and Depression,* p. 1616; August, 1998, Jean Franklin, review of *Drugs and Sports,* pp. 1989-1990; April 15, 1999, Roger Leslie, review of *Teen Dropouts,* p. 1523; March 15, 2000, Mary Romano Marks, review of *Teen Alcoholics,* p. 1368; February 1, 2001, Catherine Andronik, review of *Teens with Eating Disorders,* p. 1045; June 1, 2002, Carolyn Phelan, review of *Terrorism,* p. 1720.

School Library Journal, March 2001, Kim Harris, review of *Teens with Disabilities,* p. 279; June, 2001, Christolon Blair, review of *Soccer,* p. 181; October, 2001, Marilyn Fairbanks, review of *Phobias,* p. 192; December, 2001, Mary R. Hofmann, review of *Teens with Cancer,* p. 171; August, 2002, Tim Wadham, review of *Great Women Comedians,* p. 218; September, 2002, Louise L. Sherman, review of *Terrorism,* p. 253; September, 2002, Wendy Lukehart, review of *America Under Attack: September 11, 2001,* p. 251; March, 2003, Christine A. Moesch, review of *Leukemia,* p. 244; April, 2003, Eldon Younce, reviews of *Weapons of War,* and *Life of a Soldier in Washington's Army,* p. 188.

*   *   *

SULLIVAN, Kathryn A. 1954-

Personal

Born January 22, 1954, in Elmhurst, IL; daughter of Joseph (a government employee) and Rose Marie (a homemaker; maiden name, Wright) Sullivan. *Education:* Northern Illinois University, B.A., 1975, M.A., 1977; Nova University, D.Sc., 1991. *Hobbies and other interests:* Reading.

Addresses

Home—670 Winona St., Winona, MN 55987. *Office*—Library, Winona State University, Winona, MN 55987. *E-mail*—kathy@kathrynsullivan.webhostpals.com.

Career

West Chicago Public Library, West Chicago, IL, periodicals librarian, 1977-78; Winona State University, Winona, MN, periodicals librarian, 1978-99, distance learning librarian, 1999—.

Member

American Library Association, Minnesota Library Association, Electronically Published Internet Connection (EPIC), EGuild.

Awards, Honors

Eppie Award, fantasy category, EPIC, 2002, for *The Crystal Throne.*

Writings

The Crystal Throne (fantasy novel), RFI West, 2000.

Contributor of short stories to little magazines and Internet periodicals.

Work in Progress

Agents and Adepts, for RFI West; *Talking to Trees,* a young adult fantasy; another fantasy "set in the same universe as *The Crystal Throne* but several centuries earlier."

Sidelights

Kathryn A. Sullivan told *SATA:* "I came up with the original idea of *The Crystal Throne* when I was fourteen. I wrote other novels as well, but this was the book I was most pleased with, and I continued to polish it and develop that universe further until the book was finally published. The reason for its success, I think, is that I tried not to lose the fourteen-year-old's enthusiasm. *The Crystal Throne* is about two twelve-year-olds pulled into a magical world and asked to break a curse. The girl is a fantasy reader (as I was) but the boy doesn't believe in magic. They have to work together as a team in order to succeed."

Biographical and Critical Sources

PERIODICALS

Shadow Keep Zine, April 15, 2001, Bob Yosco, review of *The Crystal Throne.*

OTHER

Write Lifestyle, http://www.geocities.com/theritelifestyle/ (February, 2001), Brenda Gayle, review of *The Crystal Throne.*

T–U

TIPENE, Tim 1972-

Personal

Surname is pronounced "Tee-pene;" born June 12, 1972, in Henderson, New Zealand; son of Willie and Annette (Sherman) Tipene. *Education:* Carrington Polytechnic (now Unitec), earned certificate in community skills and therapy and graduate certificate in child and adolescent mental health; Waitemata Health, certificate in Maori family therapy, 2001. *Religion:* "Spiritual."

Addresses

Home—59 Duffy Rd., Waitakere, Auckland, New Zealand. *Office*—Warrior Kids, P.O. Box 95-008, Swanson, New Zealand. *E-mail*—warriorkids@xtra.co.nz.

Career

Mount Tabor Trust, Kaukapakapa, Auckland, New Zealand, residential support person, 1992-94; Families for NonViolence Trust (founded originally as Kura Toa Trust), Auckland, New Zealand, founder and principal, 1994—. Creator and presenter of Warrior Kids (life-skills program), 1994—; martial arts instructor, including classes in self defense for women; teacher of anger management lessons for men; Mensline, telephone counselor.

Awards, Honors

Selection as notable book, New Zealand Children's Book Foundation, 1999, for *The Wooden Fish;* selection as White Ravens Book, Bologna Children's Book Fair, and nomination for the Esther Glen Medal, New Zealand Lianza Children's Book Awards, both 2002, both for *Taming the Taniwha.*

Writings

The Wooden Fish (picture book), Reed Publishing, 1999.

Taming the Taniwha (picture book), illustrated by Henry Campbell, Huia Publishers (Wellington, New Zealand), 2001.

(With Catherine Hannken) *Taming Taniwha* (resource manual), Kura Toa Trust, 2001.

The Warrior Kids Manuals, Families For Nonviolence (Auckland, New Zealand), 2002.

Contributor to periodicals, including *Learning Media School Journal, Certified Male, New Zealand Martial Arts,* and *Education Today.*

Adaptations

The story of *Taming the Taniwha* was recorded and performed in a musical adaptation by Heartstrings.

Work in Progress

Stories for children and young adults.

Biographical and Critical Sources

OTHER

New Zealand Book Council, http://www.bookcouncil.org.nz/writers/ (January 16, 2003).

Warrior Kids, http://www.warriorkids.org/ (May 12, 2003).

*   *   *

UNZNER, Christa 1958-
(Christa Unzner-Fischer)

Personal

Born March 4, 1958, in Schoneiche, East Germany (now Germany); daughter of Heinz (a graphic artist) and Thea (a graphic artist; maiden name, Fammermann) Unzner; married Peter Fischer Sternaux (a graphic artist), September 18, 1982 (divorced, 1991). *Education:* Attended Berlin School of Advertising and Design, 1976-79. *Hobbies and other interests:* Literature, music, traveling.

Addresses

Home—Woehlertstrasse 14, 10115 Berlin, Germany.

Career

Dewag Werbung (advertising agency), Berlin, Germany, graphic artist for three years; freelance illustrator at Kinderbuchverlag, Altberliner Verlag, Verlag Neues Leben, all in Berlin, Germany, and Editions Nathan and Monchaltdorf, both in Paris, France, 1982—; Nord-Sued Verlag, Gossau, Switzerland, illustrator, 1991—. *Exhibitions:* Beginning in 1982, has had personal exhibitions and group exhibitions in Germany, France, Poland, and Czechoslovakia.

Awards, Honors

Wettbewerb Award for children's illustrations; Schonste Buchere Award.

Writings

(And illustrator, under name Christa Unzner-Fischer) *Im Spielzeugland,* Der Kinderbuchverlag (Berlin, West Germany), 1985.

ILLUSTRATOR

Wolfram Hänel, *Jasmine and Rex,* translated by Rosemary Lanning, North-South (New York, NY), 1995.

Dorothea Lachner, *Smoky's Special Easter Present,* translated by Marianne Martens, North-South (New York, NY), 1996.

Dorothea Lachner, *Meredith, the Witch Who Wasn't,* translated by J. Alison James, North-South (New York, NY), 1997.

Anne Liersch, *A House Is Not a Home,* translated by J. Alison James, North-South (New York, NY), 1999.

Ursel Scheffler, *The Man with the Black Glove,* translated by Rosemary Lanning, North-South (New York, NY), 1999.

Dorothea Lachner, *Meredith's Mixed Up Magic,* translated by J. Alison James, North-South (New York, NY), 2000.

Anne Liersch, *Nell and Fluffy,* translated by J. Alison James, North-South (New York, NY), 2001.

Mischa Damjan, *The Clown Said No,* translated by Anthea Bell, North-South (New York, NY), 2001.

Wolfram Hänel, *Weekend with Grandmother,* North-South (New York, NY), 2002.

Udo Weigelt, *Miranda's Ghosts,* translated by Marisa Miller, North-South (New York, NY), 2002.

Dorothea Lachner, *Meredith and Her Magical Book of Spells,* translated by J. Alison James, North-South (New York, NY), 2003.

ILLUSTRATOR; UNDER NAME CHRISTA UNZNER-FISCHER

Jurij Brezan, *Die Reise nach Krakau,* Verlag Neues Leben (Berlin, West Germany), 1982.

Karl Mundstock, *Ali und die Bande vom Lauseplatz,* Der Kinderbuchverlag (Berlin, West Germany), 1982.

Erna Linde and Guenter Linde, *Liebe geht durch den Magen,* Verlag Neues Leben (Berlin, West Germany), 1982.

Das Malvenhaus (anthology), Der Kinderbuchverlag (Berlin, West Germany), 1983.

Von Witzbolden, Spassvoegeln und Schelmen (anthology), Verlag Neues Leben (Berlin, West Germany), 1983.

Uta Mauersberger, *Die Geschichte vom Plumpser,* Der Kinderbuchverlag (Berlin, West Germany), 1984.

Arthur Schnitzler, *Therese,* Verlag Neues Leben (Berlin, West Germany), 1985.

Elisabeth Hering, *Kostbarkeiten aus dem deutschen Marchenschatz,* Altberliner Verlag, 1985.

Gunter Preuss, *Feen sterben nicht,* Der Kinderbuchverlag (Berlin, West Germany), 1985.

Der Fuchs und die Weintrauben (fable), Altberliner Verlag, 1985.

Hanna Kuenzel, *Vom Joerg, der Zahnweh hatte,* Der Kinderbuchverlag (Berlin, West Germany), 1986.

Mein Vater, meine Mutter (anthology), Verlag Neues Leben (Berlin, West Germany), 1986.

Dunkel wars, der Mond schien helle (nursery rhymes), Altberliner Verlag, 1987.

Gerhard Dahne, *Kostbarkeiten aus dem deutschen Sagenschatz,* Altberliner Verlag, 1987.

Heinrich Hoffmann von Fallersleben, *Kitzlein, Spitzlein und Fritzlein,* Der Kinderbuchverlag (Berlin, West Germany), 1987.

Daumengross und starker Hans (fairy tale), Der Kinderbuchverlag (Berlin, West Germany), 1988.

Uta Mauersberger, *Kleine Hexe Annabell,* Der Kinderbuchverlag (Berlin, West Germany), 1988.

Liebeszauber (anthology), Verlag Tribune, 1988.

Reinhard Griebner, *Himmelhochjauchzend Zutodebetruebt,* Der Kinderbuchverlag (Berlin, West Germany), 1989.

Heinz Kahlau, *Die Hasin Paula,* Verlag Junge Welt, 1989.

Der Mond ist aufgegangen (lullaby), Altberliner Verlag, 1989.

Ruth Zechlin, *Eine Kuh, die sass im Schwalbennest* (lullaby), Verlag Edition Peters Leipzig, 1989.

Leo Lenvers, *Jean-le-Niais,* Edition Fernard Nathan (Paris, France), 1990.

Genevieve Laurencin, *Un gros ballon tout petit,* Edition Fernand Nathan (Paris, France), 1991.

Barbara Haupt, *Mein Bruder Joscha,* Hoch Verlag (Stuttgart, Germany), 1991.

Gebrueder Grimm, *Blanche-Neige,* Edition Fernand Nathan, 1992.

Anneliese Probst, *Sagen und Maerchen aus dem Harz,* Altberliner Verlag, 1992.

Anneliese Probst, *Sagen und Maerchen aus Thueringen,* Altberliner Verlag, 1992.

Joachiem Walter, *Kuddelmuddelkunterbunt und Ausserueberordentlich,* Der Kinderbuchverlag, 1992.

Ingrid Ostheeren, *Der echte Nikolaus bin ich,* Nord-Sued Verlag (Gossau, Switzerland), 1993.

Wolfram Hänel, *Waldemar und die weite Welt,* Nord-Sued Verlag (Gossau, Switzerland), 1993.

Andreas Greve, *Kluger kleiner Balthasar,* Nord-Sued Verlag (Gossau, Switzerland), 1994.

ILLUSTRATOR; UNDER NAME CHRISTA UNZNER-FISCHER; IN ENGLISH TRANSLATION

Gerda Marie Scheidl, *Loretta and the Little Fairy,* translated by J. Alison James, North-South (New York, NY), 1992, originally published as *Loretta und die kleine Fee,* Nord-Sued Verlag (Gossau, Switzerland).

Hermann Moers, *Annie's Dancing Day,* translated by Rosemary Lanning, North-South (New York, NY), 1992.

Ingrid Ostheeren, *Martin and the Pumpkin Ghost,* translated by J. Alison James, North-South (New York, NY), 1994.

Wolfram Hänel, *The Extraordinary Adventures of an Ordinary Hat,* translated by Alison James, North-South (New York, NY), 1994.

Work in Progress

Illustrator for *Ich bin der kleine Koenig* by Anthonie Schneider for North-South Books.

Sidelights

Christa Unzner is a prolific German illustrator of children's picture books, noted for the expressive features of her characters' faces and her detailed backgrounds. Since 1992, Unzner, who previously published under the name Unzner-Fischer, has illustrated books written by a variety of authors and put forth by North-South Books. Wolfram Hänel's *Jasmine and Rex* is a chapter-book variation on the Romeo and Juliet story with animals playing all the roles. Unzner contributes "expressive pen-and-ink and watercolor illustrations," remarked Linda Wicher in *School Library Journal.* Also by Hänel is *Weekend with Grandmother,* the story of a boy's quiet adventures with his grandmother. "Unzner's watercolor-over-ink sketches adorn every page and bring warmth and dimension to the story," observed a contributor to *Kirkus Reviews.*

With Dorothea Lachner, Unzner has produced several gently scary books about Meredith, a very unusual witch. In *Meredith, the Witch Who Wasn't,* crafty Meredith likes to make things with her hands, but that doesn't earn her any points with the other witches. To earn their approval, she must learn to cast spells; but despite practicing, her spells never amount to much and she is relieved of her status as witch. Then, one day, an elderly witch visits Meredith's tree house, and seeing how well she has managed to make everything herself, returns Meredith's powers to her. *School Library Journal* reviewer Lisa Smith praised Lachner's "upbeat story" and Unzner's "illustrations that are full of humorous details." Meredith returns in *Meredith's Mixed Up Magic,* in which the hapless witch accidentally conjures up an uninvited guest, and when the two square off, flinging spells at each other, the result is humorous mayhem. As in the earlier book, "the art is full of amusing details and captures the action fully," according to *School Library Journal* reviewer Jeanne Clancy Watkins. Another charmingly frightening picture book is Udo Weigelt's *Miranda's Ghosts,* in which a young girl returning home from a Halloween party

decides to give some of the creatures who come out at night in her bedroom a taste of their own medicine. "Unzner's ghosts leer, their eyes pop, and long, fiendishly distorted noses protrude from amorphous expressions," remarked a reviewer for *Publishers Weekly.*

A more earnest entry in the picture-book category is Anne Liersch's *A House Is Not a Home,* in which a group of animal friends decide to build a home for the impending winter when Badger steps in and takes charge, alienating everyone with his know-it-all attitude. The other animals decide to go off and build the kind of home they want to live in and leave Badger to himself but welcome him back once he realizes the error of his ways. *Booklist* contributor Mart Segal preferred Unzner's paintings of the forest in different seasons to her rendition of the animal characters in the foreground, some of whom have "a slightly angry or mean look," which may alarm some children.

Unzner has also contributed the illustrations to Dorothea Lachner's *Smoky's Special Easter Present* the story of a pet rabbit who goes into the city to find an Easter present for the girl who owns him, and to Mischa Damjan's *The Clown Said No,* which is the story of a group of circus performers who leave the circus and create their own show.

"I grew up painting and drawing. I think I even had paper and pencil in my hand before I started walking," Christa Unzner once told *SATA:* "And when my parents didn't give in to my little-girl dreams of becoming a ballet dancer, I stuck with drawing.

"I grew up in Schoeneiche near Berlin (East Berlin) in a house with a large, beautiful garden. My parents, both graphic artists, gave my brother and me a very creative atmosphere and raised us up to think independently, which wasn't exactly easy, living behind the iron curtain. After school I did an apprenticeship as a window decorator and then studied at the School of Advertising and Design in Berlin. I studied there for one year under my father, who has had a very important influence on my life. He was my toughest critic and my strongest supporter. He died in 1993.

"After my studies, I worked for three years in an advertising agency. Advertising didn't really interest me—I always wanted to illustrate picture books. So I started applying to various publishing companies, and since 1982 I have been working as a freelance illustrator. I worked for the Kinderbuchverlag in Berlin, the Altberliner Verlag, and the Verlag Neues Leben.

"I got married and lived with my husband and a black cat in Berlin. Since 1986, I have made many trips to France—to both the south of France and to Paris, which always gives me a fresh point of view and inspires my work. After the Berlin Wall came down, France also gave me a new beginning. I started working for Editions Nathan in Paris and also applied to various German companies. Today I work exclusively for Nord-Sued

Verlag in Switzerland, and since 1991 I've illustrated fifteen books for them.

"In the beginning of my career in East Germany, I was very insecure and was constantly looking to find my own personal style. Later, my work changed dramatically—perhaps because of personal changes in my life, but perhaps also because of political changes. I no longer work with the pressure of having to be successful, but now I work because of the pleasure I get out of being able to support myself by making beautiful books for children. Perhaps because of this my illustrations have become more lively. My drawings have become much freer and more open. I usually make oversized picture books to illustrate texts that I am offered. I would like to eventually try to write and illustrate something of my own creation but have not got around to trying this yet.

"In 1991 my husband and I divorced. I still live in Berlin, but my work is no longer the most important thing for me in my life. Now my work is closely linked with my personal goals and dreams. Most of the time, I'm at my desk, but just as before, I love to travel—usually with my boyfriend to Italy where his parents live and also to the south of France. I feel at home there, because my uncle lives there, and we are very close. Music and nature are great sources of relaxation and inspiration for me. Before I used to surround myself with people, but these days I avoid this and concentrate on contacts and friends that are of substance."

Biographical and Critical Sources

PERIODICALS

American Bookseller, March, 1993.
Booklist, September 1, 1997, Julie Corsaro, review of *Meredith, the Witch Who Wasn't,* p. 133, November 1, 1999, Mart Segal, review of *A House Is Not a Home,* p. 539.
Kid's Home Library, September, 1992.
Kirkus Reviews, March 15, 2002, review of *Weekend with Grandmother,* p. 412.
Publishers Weekly, June 6, 1994; September 23, 2002, review of *Miranda's Ghosts,* p. 72.
School Library Journal, July, 1995, Jeanne Clancy Watkins, review of *You Shall Be King!,* p. 68; January, 1996, Linda Wicher, review of *Jasmine and Rex,* p. 84; September, 1996, Joy Fleishhacker, review of *Smoky's Special Easter Present,* p. 182; November, 1997, Lisa Smith, review of *Meredith, the Witch Who Wasn't,* p. 91; November, 1999, Christine A. Moesch, review of *A House Is Not a Home,* December, 1999, Lisa Smith, review of *The Man with the Black Glove,* p. 112; January, 2001, Jeanne Clancy Watkins, review of *Meredith's Mixed Up Magic,* p. 102; April, 2001, Lisa Dennis, review of *Nell and Fluffy,* p. 117; July, 2002, Amy Lilien-Harper, review of *The Clown Said No,* p. 87; February, 2003, Kathleen Kelly MacMillan, review of *Miranda's Ghosts,* p. 124.*

*   *   *

UNZNER-FISCHER, Christa
See UNZNER, Christa

V

VANDE VELDE, Vivian 1951-

Personal

Born June 18, 1951, in New York, NY; daughter of Pasquale (a linotype operator) and Marcelle (Giglio) Brucato; married Jim Vande Velde (a computer analyst), April 20, 1974; children: Elizabeth. *Education:* Attended State University of New York at Brockport, 1969-70, and Rochester Business Institute, 1970-71. *Religion:* Catholic. *Hobbies and other interests:* Reading, needlecrafts, "quiet family things."

Career

Writer.

Member

Society of Children's Book Writers and Illustrators, Rochester Area Children's Writers and Illustrators.

Awards, Honors

Child Study Association Book of the Year, 1986, Bro-Dart Foundation Elementary School Library Collection, International Reading Association (IRA) List, National Council of Teachers of English Notable Trade Books in the Language Arts, and the New York Public Library Children's Books 100 Titles for Reading and Sharing, all for *A Hidden Magic;* Author of the Month Award, *Highlights for Children,* 1988; "Pick of the Lists" citation, American Booksellers Association (ABA), "Best Book for Young Adults" and "Quick Pick for Reluctant Young Adult Readers" citations, American Library Association (ALA), "Popular Paperback for Young Adults" citation, Young Adult Library Services Association, Blue Ribbon Book award, Bulletin of the Center for Children's Books, and Nevada Young Readers award, 1998, all for *Companions of the Night;* "Quick Pick" and "Recommended Books for the Reluctant Young Adult Reader" citations, ALA, Junior Library Guild Selection, New York Public Library Books for the Teen Age, and Texas Lone Star reading list citation, Texas Library Association, all for *Dragon's Bait;* Junior Guild Selection for *A Well-Timed Enchantment;* "Best Book for Young Adults" and "Quick Pick for Reluctant Young Adult Readers" citations, ALA, "Young Adult's Choice" citation, IRA, and winner of "Tellable" stories, 1996, all for *Tales from the Brothers Grimm and the Sisters Weird;* "Quick Pick" citation, ALA, for *Curses, Inc.;* "Quick Pick for Reluctant Young Adult Readers" citation, ALA, 1999, for *Ghost of a Hanged Man;* Edgar Allan Poe Award for best young adult mystery, 2000, for *Never Trust a Dead Man;* Anne Spencer Lindgergh Prize in Children's Literature, 2001/2002, and New York Public Library Books for the Teen Age, 2003, both for *Heir Apparent;* Black-Eyed Susan Award (Maryland), 2002, for *There's a Dead Person Following My Sister Around;* and Volunteer State Book Award (Tennessee), 2002, for *Smart Dog.*

Writings

Once Upon a Test: Three Light Tales of Love, illustrated by Diane Dawson Hearn, A. Whitman (Morton Grove, IL), 1984.

A Hidden Magic, illustrated by Trina Schart Hyman, Crown (New York, NY), 1985.

A Well-Timed Enchantment, Crown (New York, NY), 1990.

User Unfriendly, Harcourt (San Diego, CA), 1991.

Dragon's Bait, Harcourt (San Diego, CA), 1992.

Tales from the Brothers Grimm and the Sisters Weird, Harcourt (San Diego, CA), 1995.

Companions of the Night, Harcourt (San Diego, CA), 1995.

Curses, Inc., Harcourt (San Diego, CA), 1997.

The Conjurer Princess, HarperPrism (New York, NY), 1997.

The Changeling Prince, HarperPrism (New York, NY), 1998.

Ghost of a Hanged Man, Marshall Cavendish (Tarrytown, NY), 1998.

A Coming Evil, Houghton Mifflin (Boston, MA), 1998.

Smart Dog, Harcourt Brace (San Diego, CA), 1998.

Spellbound, Science Fiction Book Club (New York, NY), 1998.

Never Trust a Dead Man, Harcourt Brace (San Diego, CA), 1999.

There's a Dead Person Following My Sister Around, Harcourt Brace (San Diego, CA), 1999.

Magic Can Be Murder, Harcourt Brace (San Diego, CA), 2000.

Troll Teacher, illustrated by Mary Jane Auch, Holiday House (New York, NY), 2000.

The Rumpelstiltskin Problem, Houghton Mifflin (Boston, MA), 2000.

Alison, Who Went Away, Houghton Mifflin (Boston, MA), 2001.

Being Dead: Stories, Harcourt Brace (San Diego, CA), 2001.

Heir Apparent, Harcourt Brace (San Diego, CA), 2002.

Wizard at Work, Harcourt Brace (San Diego, CA), 2003.

Witch's Wishes, Holiday House (New York, NY), 2003.

Contributor of short stories to *Cricket, Disney Adventures, Electric Company, Highlights for Children, Kid City, School, Storyworks,* and *Young American.* Contributor to anthologies, including *A Wizard's Dozen, A Nightmare's Dozen, Girls to the Rescue,* and several Bruce Coville anthologies.

Sidelights

Vivian Vande Velde is the author of two dozen books for young readers that blend fantasy with mystery elements, or that turn fairy tales on their heads with fresh new perspectives and with humorous touches. Vande Velde once commented that she has been "making up stories" since she was a child just to please herself. She recalled, "most of my stories were a mish-mash; I might take part of the Cinderella story here, part of the legend of Ivanhoe there, throw in a dash of Superman." Now that Vande Velde makes her career as a writer, and her stories are entertaining others as well, she still has fun with the characters and plots of well-known tales. Offbeat, fantastic, and even sarcastic, Vande Velde's books contain intriguing, suspenseful situations and provocative messages that eschew traditional themes and story-types. Christy Tyson of *Voice of Youth Advocates* noted that Vande Velde's early books *Dragon's Bait* and *User Unfriendly* "have been very popular." Vande Velde has gone on to write about vampires in *Companions of the Night,* to take a new look at fairy tales in *Tales from the Brothers Grimm and the Sisters Weird* and *The Rumpelstiltskin Problem,* to tell of a sixteen-year-old who turns to magic to help find her kidnapped sister in *The Conjurer Princess,* to play with the conventions of the Western in *Ghost of a Hanged Man,* to create magical mysteries in *Never Trust a Dead Man* and *Magic Can Be Murder,* and even to tackle a realistic novel in *Alison, Who Went Away.* But whatever genre the inventive Vande Velde is writing in, one thing remains the same: the high entertainment value of her books.

Born in New York City in 1951, Vande Velde grew up in New York state, enjoying reading and story-making.

Vivian Vande Velde

Such skills, however, did not lead to a successful time in school, where she was a self-confessed average student, even in English classes. Graduating from high school, she moved on to college for a year, but quit when she had exhausted all the literature course offerings she was interested in. Thereafter she attended a business school and trained as a secretary. Married in 1974, Vande Velde soon was a stay-at-home mom with a daughter, and this is when she began thinking of making a career in writing, enrolling in a writing course. Feedback from that class finally directed her to fantasy writing.

One of Vande Velde's early books exemplifies her talent for transforming old tales into new ones. According to Karen P. Smith of *School Library Journal, A Hidden Magic* is a "delightful parody of the classic fairy tale genre." Vande Velde's princess, instead of being beautiful, is plain. Her handsome prince is far from noble—he's spoiled and vain. Moreover, the princess in the story does not have to be saved by a prince—she saves him. At the close of the story, the princess refuses to marry the prince. Readers may be surprised by the man she prefers. "[Vande] Velde's approach remains fresh and definitely amusing," remarked Smith.

It was another five years before Vande Velde published her next book, *A Well-Timed Enchantment,* about a teenage girl sent back in time by T-shirt-wearing elves after she has accidentally messed up history by dropping her digital watch into a wishing well. Her next novel, *User Unfriendly,* in the words of Diane G. Yates of *Voice of Youth Advocates,* contains an "interesting premise . . . nicely developed with some lively fights and mildly scary situations." The story takes place in cyberspace and a teenager's basement. After Arvin's friend pirates an interactive computer game, he assures Arvin and five other high school pals that it's fine to use. But Arvin, his friends, and even his mother have no idea that playing the game without anyone monitoring their play will be truly dangerous. As they begin to play the game, they discover that there are glitches and holes in the program. They find themselves playing the roles of medieval characters and fighting for survival, with no hope of quitting the game before they finish their quest. To make matters worse, Arvin's mother begins to display terrifying symptoms of an unknown illness. Arvin has to win the game by facing orcs and wolves and rescuing a princess who has been kidnapped. According to a *Kirkus Reviews* critic, the "adventures" in this book "are vivid and diverting." A reviewer commented in *Publishers Weekly* that some readers "will not be able to put this swashbuckler down."

Selwyn has to join forces with the man he is accused of murdering, brought back from the dead in the form of a bat, to find the real killer. (Cover illustration by Tristan Elwell.)

Alys, the protagonist in *Dragon's Bait,* feels ready to die after she has been accused and condemned for witchcraft. Her punishment is to be devoured by a dragon, and she is tied up on a hill to await her fate. There is no one who can save Alys (her father died when he heard the sentence placed upon her), and she thinks her life is over. But instead of eating her, the dragon decides to help her. Moreover, the dragon, Selendrile, is only a part-time dragon. He can assume human form, and by doing so, he helps Alys get back at those who falsely accused her. As a *Publishers Weekly* reviewer asserted, this novel with a "gently feminist slant" is also a "gripping adventure" which "probes the issues associated with revenge." A *Kirkus Reviews* critic noted that the novel's subtexts include the notion that "revenge is not nearly as sweet as advertised," and that readers won't find easy answers in this book: "lessons—if any—are a little hard to follow."

While, according to Kim Carter of *Voice of Youth Advocates,* the dragon is the "only truly unusual element" in *Dragon's Bait,* the fantastic element in *Companions of the Night* is a handsome, college student vampire. Kerry, just sixteen and with a driver's permit instead of license, drives out alone late at night to the laundromat to recover her little brother's toy bear. Yet Kerry finds something else: Ethan, a young man thought to be a vampire, about to be killed by a mob. When Kerry saves him, she is accused of being a vampire herself; when she returns home, she finds that her father and brother have been kidnapped by the vampire hunters. Eventually, Kerry learns that Ethan really is a vampire, but she asks him to help her find her family anyway. Despite the fact that she doesn't quite know whether to fear him or trust him, Kerry finds herself attracted to Ethan. As Deborah Stevenson wrote in *Bulletin of the Center for Children's Books,* the novel is "an intellectual adventure more than a sensual one, its challenges more cerebral than hormonal.... It's a freshly written thriller, an offbeat love story, an engaging twist on the vampire novel, and an exciting tale of moral complexity." "*Companions of the Night* should attract a loyal following of its own," concluded Marilyn Makowski of *School Library Journal.*

Tales from the Brothers Grimm and the Sisters Weird consists of thirteen familiar folktales, revised in "both amusing and touching versions" as Ann A. Flowers of *Horn Book* explained. In one story, Rumpelstiltskin is a young, handsome elf. In another, Hansel and Gretel are murderers. The wolf in the story of Little Red Riding Hood is Granny's friend, the princess in the story of the Princess and the Pea requests more mattresses on her own, and the beauty in the Beauty and the Beast story is not pleased with the Beast's human appearance. "[Vande] Velde challenges readers' notions of good, bad, and ugly," observed Luann Toth in *School Library Journal.* A *Kirkus Reviews* critic remarked that the work is "Terrific fun." Vande Velde returned to fairy tales with her year 2000 *The Rumpelstiltskin Problem,* a book that presents six variations on that tale. Susan L. Rogers, writing in *School Library Journal,* found this offering to be an "interesting experiment." A reviewer for *Publish-*

ers *Weekly* had stronger praise, writing that "Vande Velde's takes on this fairy tale are always humorous and often heartwarming."

In her later fantasy novels, Vande Velde has taken her penchant for unusual situations and combined it with in-depth examinations of moral issues. *The Conjurer Princess,* for instance, begins as a standard adventure when sixteen-year-old Lylene determines to rescue her older sister from the man who kidnapped her and murdered her fiancé on their wedding day. Lylene first turns to magic to aid her on her quest, promising to work for a wizard as payment for magical training. When magic proves less helpful than she had hoped, Lylene enlists the aid of two soldiers who turn out to be violent mercenaries. Many people have been hurt by the time Lylene finds her sister, only to realize that perhaps her rescue attempt was ill-advised in the first place. As Diane G. Yates remarked in *Voice of Youth Advocates,* "Vande Velde packs a lot into an enjoyable, short, quickly read narrative," including a portrayal of Lylene's growing maturity.

The 1998 novel *The Changeling Prince* likewise illuminates issues of fate and responsibility. Weiland has lived an uneasy existence since the sinister sorceress Daria transformed him from a wolf cub into a human child. He is only one of a group of similarly changed people who live their lives in fear of when Daria might suddenly become angry and return them to their animal forms. When Daria decides to leave her fortress and move into a town, Weiland has a new adjustment to make. He learns to live among the townspeople and eventually makes a friend, the thief Shile. As Daria's power becomes more evil, Weiland finally must make a stand. *Voice of Youth Advocates* contributor Nancy Eaton found the protagonist compelling, writing that "Weiland's detailed agonies of indecision evoke compassion in the reader: everything could go either way; there are no right choices." The result, the critic concluded, is a work that "raises thoughtful questions about individual responsibility."

In *Ghost of a Hanged Man,* the author combines an element of the supernatural with yet another genre, the Western. The infamous criminal Jake Barnette is sentenced to hang in the summer of 1877, and no one really takes it seriously when he swears in court he will revenge himself against those responsible for his punishment. The next spring, however, floods spill through the town, forcing several coffins—including Barnette's—to emerge from the inundated cemetery. When the foreman of Barnette's jury and the judge who presided at the trial suddenly die, the young son of the town sheriff knows he must take action before his family is destroyed. "This unsettling novel has many appealing elements," Carrie Schadle noted in *School Library Journal* including the sinister ghost, Old West setting, and the scared yet brave protagonists. Janice M. Del Negro likewise found the "colorful characters" and "easy immediacy" of the dialogue appealing, and concluded in *Bulletin of the Center for Children's Books* that "Vande Velde has a knack for creepy understatement that effectively delivers

unexpected chills, and the climax . . . brings the book to its shuddery, satisfying conclusion."

A murder mystery also figures in 1999's *Never Trust a Dead Man,* albeit one with a more lighthearted approach. Seventeen-year-old Selwyn has been wrongly convicted of murder by his medieval village, and has been sentenced to be entombed alive in the burial cave of his supposed victim, Farold. Selwyn has almost resigned himself to his fate when the imperious witch Elswyth enters the cave while looking for spell components. She makes Selwyn a bargain: she will release him from the cave and give him one week to find the real killers in exchange for years of his service. Elswyth complicates the deal by resurrecting the spirit of the annoying Farold as a bat and disguising Selwyn as a beautiful girl. As this unlikely duo of sleuths searches for the answer, many mishaps and humorous truths follow in their wake, making for an entertaining adventure. "Favoring the comic over the macabre," Kitty Flynn wrote in *Horn Book,* "Vande Velde offers a funny and imaginative murder mystery that intrigues as much as it entertains." A *Kirkus Reviews* critic similarly hailed the novel, writing that "the sympathetic hero, original humor, sharp dialogue, and surprising plot twists make this read universally appealing and difficult to put down."

Vande Velde's first picture book, *Troll Teacher,* had its start with a seed of truth and then with the author asking herself 'But what if?' "During the summer between second grade and third," Vande Velde once explained, "my daughter was talking with a friend who was trying to make her nervous about her upcoming teacher. 'Oooh, I've heard about her,' the friend said (though she lived in a town an hour and a half away). 'Isn't she the one who gives three hours of homework every night? And when girls have long hair, she likes to pull on their hair and make them cry.' I started thinking: What if there really was a teacher that was this bad? Or worse? Or—worst of all—what if there was a teacher who wasn't even human?" From that premise Vande Velde wrote *Troll Teacher* as a short story, and it became a picture book after her friend, writer-illustrator M. J. Auch, created her own illustrations for the story and sent it to her publisher. The result proved to be a successful collaborative effort. Reviewing the picture book in *Booklist,* Marta Segal noted, "As in her young adult novels, Vande Velde vividly captures a young person's feelings about being the only one in the world who really understands what's going on."

With *Magic Can Be Murder,* Vande Velde "throws murder, witchcraft, and romance into the brew," according to Laura Glaser in *School Library Journal.* Nola and her witch mother live in something of a medieval netherworld, traveling from town to town to work. Nola manages to use her powers to good effect, solving a murder, saving herself and her mother, and even finding true love in a book that is, according to Glaser, "most likely to cast a spell on Vande Velde's fans." *Booklist*'s Helen Rosenberg praised this "lighthearted mystery," concluding that kids "who like mystery and fantasy fans ... will like this."

Mysteries of a more serious nature are presented in *Alison, Who Went Away.* Fourteen-year-old Susan, or Sibyl as she has taken to calling herself, "lives in the shadow of her older sister, Alison," as *Booklist's* Frances Bradburn pointed out. Missing, Alison is something of an enigma to her sister and readers alike. While Susan thinks her rebellious sister has merely run away, the reader begins to believe otherwise, for we learn that Susan's is a "family in denial," as Betty S. Evans noted in *School Library Journal.* Things come to a climax in a student play in which Susan acts. Vande Velde's first venture into realistic fiction, *Alison, Who Went Away* is a "high-school story laced with a dose of sadness and mystery," according to Bradburn.

Being Dead is a collection of seven "deliciously creepy tales," according to Miranda Doyle in *School Library Journal.* Doyle went on to note that most of the tales "deal with everyday teens in seemingly ordinary situations." Once lulled by the commonplace, the reader will be all the more shocked when things turn decidedly "gruesome," as Doyle further mentioned. A critic for *Kirkus Reviews* concluded that Vande Velde "again chills, charms, moves and startles with her customary effectiveness." Similarly, GraceAnne A. DeCandido, writing in *Booklist,* praised Vande Velde's "sure hand," and went on to prophesy that "these spirits are destined to find their audience." And *Horn Book's* Anita L. Burkam, noted that humor is the furthest thing from Vande Velde's mind in these stories. "Long known for stories that leaven supernatural elements with comedy," Burkam wrote, "Vande Velde here forgoes the humor to present a set of ghost stories for readers who enjoy being really scared."

In her 2002 novel, *Heir Apparent,* Vande Velde tells a "plausible, suspenseful" story, according to a contributor for *Kirkus Reviews,* of a girl in the near future who becomes trapped in a total immersion virtual reality game. Giannine becomes stranded in a game of kings and intrigue called "Heir Apparent" after some anti-fantasy protestors purposely damaged the equipment; now if she does not become successor to the medieval throne within three days, her brain could suffer permanent damage. The critic for *Kirkus Reviews* added that the book is "riveting reading for experienced gamers and tyros alike." A reviewer for *Publishers Weekly* also had praise for the title, noting that "hilarious characters ... plus fantastical elements ... will spur readers on toward the satisfying conclusion." Similarly, Lana Miles, writing in *School Library Journal,* commented that "all of the elements of a good fantasy are present in this adventure." Miles further lauded the book as a "unique combination of futuristic and medieval themes."

As fantastic as Vande Velde's stories are, readers may not be surprised to learn that her "stories aren't usually based on things that really happened." Yet facing dragons that turn into humans and vampires in a small New York town seems to do wonders for building

character. Vande Velde once commented that her stories, based "on real feelings," force her characters to meet unexpected challenges. "Often the people in my stories are uncomfortable with the way they look, or they feel clumsy, or they find themselves having to take charge in a situation for which they are totally unprepared." She continued, "Most of my characters are quite surprised to find—by the story's end—that they can cope after all." A contributor for *The Oxford Companion to Fairy Tales* summed up Vande Velde's achievement in much of her fiction: "Though shocking, the tales are told in a light comic vein aimed at exposing social contradictions in such a manner that young adults can easily grasp the targets of criticism."

Biographical and Critical Sources

BOOKS

The Oxford Companion to Fairy Tales, edited by Jack Zipes, Oxford University Press (New York, NY), 2000, p. 534.

Reginald, Robert, *Science Fiction and Fantasy Literature, 1975-1991,* Gale (Detroit, MI), 1992.

PERIODICALS

Booklist, April 1, 1995, p. 1389; September 1, 1998, p. 121; November 15, 1998, Chris Sherman, review of *Ghost of a Hanged Man,* p. 591; April 1, 1999, Holly Koelling, review of *Never Trust a Dead Man,* p. 1402; September 1, 1999, Candace Smith, review of *There's a Dead Person Following My Sister Around,* p. 124; November 15, 2000, Marta Segal, review of *Troll Teacher,* p. 650; December 15, 2000, Helen Rosenberg, review of *Magic Can Be Murder,* p. 809; April 1, 2001, Frances Bradburn, review of *Alison, Who Went Away,* p. 1459; September 1, 2001, GraceAnne A. DeCandido, review of *Being Dead,* p. 97; February 1, 2003, Gillian Engberg, review of *Heir Apparent,* p. 982; April 15, 2003, GraceAnne A. DeCandido, review of *Wizard at Work,* p. 1466.

Bulletin of the Center for Children's Books, July-August, 1995, Deborah Stevenson, review of *Companions of the Night,* pp. 373-374; October, 1998, Deborah Stevenson, review of *Ghost of a Hanged Man,* p. 75; October, 1999, Janice M. Del Negro, review of *There's a Dead Person Following My Sister Around,* p. 72; February, 2001, Janice M. Del Negro, review of *The Rumpelstiltskin Problem,* p. 239; September, 2001, Janice M. Del Negro, review of *Being Dead,* p. 29.

Horn Book, March-April, 1996, Ann A. Flowers, review of *Tales from the Brothers Grimm and the Sisters Weird,* pp. 201-202; May-June, 1998, Kitty Flynn, review of *Never Trust a Dead Man,* pp. 339-340; November-December, 1998, Kitty Flynn, review of *Ghost of a Hanged Man,* p. 742; November-December, 2001, Anita L. Burkam, review of *Being Dead,* p. 758.

Kirkus Reviews, August 1, 1991, review of *User Unfriendly,* p. 1017; August 1, 1992, review of *Dragon's Bait,* p. 994; August 1, 1995, review of *Tales from the Brothers Grimm and the Sisters Weird,* p. 1118; October 15, 1998, review of *A Coming Evil,* p. 1539; March 15, 1999, review of *Never Trust a Dead Man;*

August 1, 2001, review of *Being Dead,* p. 1133; March 1, 2003, review of *Wizard at Work,* p. 401.

Magazine of Fantasy and Science Fiction, June, 1996, p. 27; August, 1999, Michelle West, review of *Never Trust a Dead Man,* p. 45; March, 2002, Michelle West, review of *Being Dead,* pp. 34-39.

New York Times Book Review, March 9, 2003, review of *Heir Apparent,* p. 24.

Publishers Weekly, August 23, 1991, review of *User Unfriendly,* pp. 63-64; July 27, 1992, review of *Dragon's Bait,* p. 63; August 10, 1998, review of *Smart Dog,* p. 389; November 9, 1998, review of *Ghost of a Hanged Man,* p. 77; August 30, 1999, review of *There's a Dead Person Following My Sister Around,* p. 85; October 2, 2000, review of *Magic Can Be Murder,* p. 82, review of *The Rumpelstiltskin Problem,* p. 82; February 5, 2001, review of *Alison, Who Went Away,* p. 89; September 16, 2002, review of *Heir Apparent,* p. 69.

School Library Journal, December, 1985, Karen P. Smith, review of *A Hidden Magic,* pp. 95-96; September, 1992, p. 261; May, 1995, Marilyn Makowski, review of *Companions of the Night,* pp. 123-124; January, 1996, Luann Toth, review of *Tales from the Brothers Grimm and the Sisters Weird,* p. 126; October, 1998, Carrie Schadle, review of *Ghost of a Hanged Man,* p. 147; November, 1998, p. 131; May, 1999, Laura Glaser, review of *Never Trust a Dead Man,* p. 131; September, 1999, Timothy Capehart, review of *There's a Dead Person Following My Sister Around,* pp. 229-230; October, 2000, Gay Lynn Van Vleck, review of *Troll Teacher,* p. 140; November, 2000, Laura Glaser, review of *Magic Can Be Murder,* p. 164, Susan L. Rogers, review of *The Rumpelstiltskin Problem,* p. 177; April, 2001, Betty S. Evans, review of *Alison, Who Went Away,* p. 151; September, 2001, Miranda Doyle, review of *Being Dead,* p. 234; October, 2002, Lana Miles, review of *Heir Apparent,* p. 174.

Science Fiction Chronicle, October, 1995, p. 50.

Voice of Youth Advocates, December, 1991, Diane G. Yates, review of *User Unfriendly,* p. 327; April, 1993, Kim Carter, review of *Dragon's Bait,* p. 48; October, 1995, Christy Tyson, review of *Companions of the Night,* pp. 238-239; February, 1998, Diane G. Yates, review of *The Conjurer Princess,* pp. 396-397 June, 1998, Nancy Eaton, review of *The Changeling Prince,* pp. 134, 136; February, 1998, review of *The Conjurer Princess,* p. 396.

OTHER

Vivian Vande Velde-All Books, http://www.non.com/ (March 14, 2003).

*   *   *

Van LEEUWEN, Jean 1937-

Personal

Surname pronounced "Van *Loo*-en"; born December 26, 1937, in Glen Ridge, NJ; daughter of Cornelius (a clergyman) and Dorothy (a teacher; maiden name, Charlton) Van Leeuwen; married Bruce David Gavril (a

digital computer systems designer), July 7, 1968; children: David Andrew, Elizabeth Eva. *Education:* Syracuse University, B.A., 1959. *Hobbies and other interests:* Gardening, reading, antiques, music.

Addresses

Home—7 Colony Row, Chappaqua, NY 10514.

Career

Began career working for *TV Guide;* Random House, Inc., New York, NY, began as assistant editor, became associate editor of juvenile books, 1963-68; Viking Press, Inc., New York, NY, associate editor of juvenile books, 1968-70; Dial Press, New York, NY, senior editor of juvenile books, 1970-73; currently full-time writer.

Awards, Honors

New Jersey Institute of Technology award, 1972, for *I Was a 98-Pound Duckling;* Art Books for Children award, 1974, for adaptation of Hans Christian Andersen's *The Emperor's New Clothes;* New Jersey Institute of Technology award, 1975 and 1976, for *Too Hot for Ice Cream;* Ethical Culture School award, 1975, William Allen White award, 1978, and South Carolina Children's Book award, 1979, all for *The Great Christmas Kidnapping Caper; Seems Like This Road Goes on Forever* was named one of the best books of 1979, American Library Association (ALA), Young Adult Services Division; Massachusetts Honor Book Award, 1981, for *The Great Cheese Conspiracy;* Pick of the Lists selection, American Booksellers Association, and Parents' Choice Remarkable Books for Literature selection, both for *The Great Rescue Operation;* International Reading Association Teachers' Choice selection, Pick of the Lists selection, American Booksellers Association, and Best in Kids' Entertainment selection, *Parents'* magazine, all for *Going West.*

More Tales of Oliver Pig, Amanda Pig and Her Big Brother Oliver, Tales of Amanda Pig, and *More Tales of Amanda Pig* all won the *Booklist* Children's Editors' Choice award; *More Tales of Oliver Pig, Amanda Pig and Her Big Brother Oliver,* and *More Tales of Amanda Pig* were noted on the American Booksellers Association Pick of the Lists; *Amanda Pig and Her Big Brother Oliver, Benjy and the Power of Zingies,* and *Benjy in Business* were all listed as Child Study Association Children's Books of the Year; *Oliver, Amanda, and Grandmother Pig* and *Going West* were listed in New York Public Library: 100 Titles for Reading and Sharing; *Oliver, Amanda, and Grandmother Pig* and *Tales of Amanda Pig* received the Library of Congress Books of the Year award; *More Tales of Oliver Pig, Amanda Pig and Her Big Brother Oliver,* and *Tales of Amanda Pig* have all been named ALA Notable Books.

Writings

(Editor) *A Time of Growing,* Random House (New York, NY), 1967.

Timothy's Flower, illustrated by Moneta Barnett, Random House (New York, NY), 1967.

One Day in Summer, illustrated by Richard Fish, Random House (New York, NY), 1969.

The Great Cheese Conspiracy, Random House (New York, NY), 1969.

(Adaptor) Hans Christian Andersen, *The Emperor's New Clothes,* illustrated by Jack Delano and Irene Delano, Random House (New York, NY), 1971.

I Was a 98-Pound Duckling, Dial (New York, NY), 1972.

Too Hot for Ice Cream, illustrated by Martha Alexander, Dial (New York, NY), 1974.

The Great Christmas Kidnapping Caper, illustrated by Steven Kellogg, Dial (New York, NY), 1975.

Seems Like This Road Goes on Forever, Dial (New York, NY), 1979.

The Great Rescue Operation, illustrated by Margot Apple, Dial (New York, NY), 1982.

Benjy and the Power of Zingies, illustrated by Margot Apple, Dial (New York, NY), 1982.

Benjy in Business, illustrated by Margot Apple, Dial (New York, NY), 1983.

Benjy the Football Hero, illustrated by Gail Owens, Dial (New York, NY), 1985.

Dear Mom, You're Ruining My Life, Dial (New York, NY), 1989.

Going West, illustrated by Thomas B. Allen, Dial (New York, NY), 1991.

The Great Summer Camp Catastrophe, illustrated by Diane deGroat, Dial (New York, NY), 1992.

Emma Bean, illustrated by Juan Wijngaard, Dial (New York, NY), 1993.

Two Girls in Sister Dresses, illustrated by Linda Benson, Dial (New York, NY), 1994.

Bound for Oregon, Dial (New York, NY), 1994.

Across the Wide Dark Sea, illustrated by Thomas B. Allen, Dial (New York, NY), 1995.

Blue Sky, Butterfly, Dial (New York, NY), 1996.

A Fourth of July on the Plains, illustrated by Henri Sorensen, Dial (New York, NY), 1997.

Touch the Sky Summer, illustrated by Dan Andreasen, Dial (New York, NY), 1997.

Nothing Here But Trees, illustrated by Phil Boatwright, Dial (New York, NY), 1998.

Growing Ideas (biography), photographs by David Gavril, Richard C. Owen (Katonah, NY), 1998.

The Tickle Stories, illustrated by Mary Whyte, Dial (New York, NY), 1998.

The Strange Adventures of Blue Dog, illustrated by Marco Ventura, Dial (New York, NY), 1999.

Sorry, illustrated by Brad Sneed, Phyllis Fogelman Books (New York, NY), 2001.

"Wait for Me!" Said Maggie McGee, illustrated by Jacqueline Rogers, Phyllis Fogelman Books (New York, NY), 2001.

Lucy Was There..., Phyllis Fogelman Books (New York, NY), 2002.

The Amazing Air Balloon, illustrated by Marco Ventura, Phyllis Fogelman Books (New York, NY), 2003.

The Great Googlestein Museum Mystery, illustrated by R. W. Alley, Phyllis Fogelman Books (New York, NY), 2003.

When the White Man Came to Our Shores, illustrated by James Bernardin, Phyllis Fogelman Books (New York, NY), 2004.

"OLIVER AND AMANDA PIG" SERIES

Tales of Oliver Pig, illustrated by Arnold Lobel, Dial (New York, NY), 1979.

More Tales of Oliver Pig, illustrated by Arnold Lobel, Dial (New York, NY), 1981.

Amanda Pig and Her Big Brother Oliver, illustrated by Ann Schweninger, Dial (New York, NY), 1982.

Tales of Amanda Pig, illustrated by Ann Schweninger, Dial (New York, NY), 1983.

More Tales of Amanda Pig, illustrated by Ann Schweninger, Dial (New York, NY), 1985.

Oliver, Amanda, and Grandmother Pig, illustrated by Ann Schweninger, Dial (New York, NY), 1987.

Oliver and Amanda's Christmas, illustrated by Ann Schweninger, Dial (New York, NY), 1989.

Oliver Pig at School, illustrated by Ann Schweninger, Dial (New York, NY), 1990.

Amanda Pig on Her Own, illustrated by Ann Schweninger, Dial (New York, NY), 1991.

Oliver and Amanda's Halloween, illustrated by Ann Schweninger, Dial (New York, NY), 1992.

Oliver and Amanda and the Big Snow, illustrated by Ann Schweninger, Dial (New York, NY), 1995.

Amanda Pig, School Girl, Dial (New York, NY), 1997.

Amanda Pig and Her Best Friend Lollipop, illustrated by Ann Schweninger, Penguin Putnam (New York, NY), 1998.

Oliver and Albert, Friends Forever, illustrated by Ann Schweninger, Phyllis Fogelman Books (New York, NY), 2000.

Amanda Pig and the Awful, Scary Monster, illustrated by Ann Schweninger, Phyllis Fogelman Books (New York, NY), 2003.

"PIONEER DAUGHTERS" SERIES

Hannah of Fairfield, illustrated by Donna Diamond, Dial (New York, NY), 1999.

Hannah's Helping Hands, illustrated by Donna Diamond, Phyllis Fogelman Books (New York, NY), 1999.

Hannah's Winter of Hope, illustrated by Donna Diamond, Phyllis Fogelman Books (New York, NY), 2000.

Sidelights

Jean Van Leeuwen is the award-winning author of over fifty books for young readers. Equally adept and entertaining in picture books as she is in chapter books and novels for middle graders and young adults, Van Leeuwen has charmed young readers for over three decades. Her stories about the jovial pig siblings, Oliver and Amanda, number in the double digits and have drawn praise from fans and critics alike. Other books that have survived over time include *The Great Cheese Conspiracy,* featuring a trio of meddlesome mice, and its several sequels. But Van Leeuwen does not entertain only with animal protagonists. Characters in the "Benjy" stories, and in *I Was a 98-Pound Duckling, Too Hot for Ice Cream, Dear Mom, You're Ruining My Life,* and *Blue Sky, Butterfly* are only too real and deal with contemporary issues in both humorous and heart-wrenching ways. This prolific and versatile writer has also mined a historical vein in her fiction, with books such as *Going West* and *Bound for Oregon,* both set during pioneering days in America. And with the "Pioneer Daughters" series of novels, Van Leeuwen takes audiences back to the Revolutionary War in a trio of novels that explores life in the eighteenth-century through the adventures of young Hannah.

Van Leeuwen had a long and close relationship with the printed word before she became a writer, and loved to read as a child. She was working as a children's book editor when she rediscovered her childhood ambition to write and in 1967 joyfully saw the publication of her first book, *Timothy's Flower. Timothy's Flower* was warmly received by critics. A reviewer for the *Bulletin of the Center for Children's Books* credited the "simple, unpretentious style" of the prose for the book's success-ful rendering of how a flower improves the life of a poor boy. Van Leeuwen's early works also include *A Time of Growing,* an anthology of fictional reminiscences of adolescence by established authors, which she edited, and the picture book *One Day in Summer,* described by a *Bulletin of the Center for Children's Books* critic as a "quiet" story with possibly limited appeal due to the "static quality" of the plot.

During this time Van Leeuwen married Bruce Gavril, a computer systems designer who became her technical consultant. Her husband was also the inspiration for the character Raymond in *The Great Cheese Conspiracy* and its sequels. Van Leeuwen describes Raymond as the one "with brains": "a thinker, problem solver, and saver of seemingly useless objects—just like Bruce." *The Great Cheese Conspiracy* features three mice—Raymond, Marvin, the brave but foolhardy leader of the gang, and Fats, whose laziness and passion for food often land him and his friends in trouble—in a story about the trio's efforts to rob a cheese store. Van Leeuwen's mouse books have typically received praise from critics. For example, one *Bulletin of the Center for Children's Books* reviewer, writing about *The Great Rescue Operation,* noted that Marvin, Raymond, and Fats "are distinct—if exaggerated—personalities, the style is colorful and breezy, the plot—deliberately unrestrained—is nicely structured and paced."

In the first sequel to *The Great Cheese Conspiracy, The Great Christmas Kidnapping Caper,* the three mice move into a dollhouse in Macy's department store, where they are befriended by Mr. Dunderhoff, who annually plays Santa Claus. When Mr. Dunderhoff is abducted by the store's greedy competitor, the mice use all their ingenuity to rescue him. A critic described the result as "zestful and surprising" in *Publishers Weekly;* a *Bulletin of the Center for Children's Books* reviewer commented that the "story has a happy blend of humor in dialogue, Christmas setting, local color, and silly situations." The trio are put to the test again in *The*

Great Rescue Operation, in which Marvin and Raymond wake up one day to find that Fats has disappeared along with the doll carriage in which he likes to nap. The friends' attempts to rescue Fats from what they fear is a horrible fate at the hands of a scientist lead to "slapstick humor and nonstop action," according to Caroline S. Parr in the *School Library Journal.* Doris Orgel similarly described the story in her *New York Times Book Review* article as a "funny, lively and appealing book." The three mice again leave Macy's in *The Great Summer Camp Catastrophe,* in which they are inadvertently packed off with a box of cookies to summer camp in Vermont. "What will grab readers," observed Jacqueline Rose in the *School Library Journal,* "is the action-packed plot, with its series of near disasters." And in *The Great Googlestein Museum Mystery,* the trio of mice once again depart their home at Macy's department store and spend a fine time at the Guggenheim Museum.

In the early years of her marriage to Gavril, Van Leeuwen published her first young adult novel, *I Was a 98-Pound Duckling,* a comical account of a girl's thirteenth summer, when she and her best friend are consumed with thoughts of boys and dates and following the beauty regimen outlined in a teen magazine. Although several reviewers noted the lack of originality in the story's plot, a *Bulletin of the Center for Children's Books* contributor remarked: "Kathy tells her story ... with such wry humor and candor that it gives a fresh vitality to a familiar pattern." In a *Publishers Weekly* review, a contributor declared: "This is a witty and charming book."

In the early 1970s Van Leeuwen left publishing to care for her two small children but was determined to continue to write. Her first effort, *Too Hot for Ice Cream,* dubbed by a *Publishers Weekly* critic as "a curiously charming book," tells the story of the everyday adventures of two sisters who spend a hot day in a city park when their father cannot take them to the beach. A more far-reaching consequence of Van Leeuwen's decision to stay home to raise her children is the series of first-reader books filled with stories about Oliver and Amanda Pig, based on her experiences with her own children.

Tales of Oliver Pig, and the subsequent books in this series, fifteen strong and growing, have been warmly received for their gentle humor and loving portrayal of the everyday trials and joys of living with small children. Mary Gordon described the relationship between Amanda and Oliver Pig, which is at the center of each of the books in this series, in the *New York Times Book Review:* "The younger Pigs are occasionally perfectly dreadful to each other. But remember, they are siblings, and one of the great values of these books is their ability to dramatize the ridiculous and trivial and sickeningly frequent fights that siblings engage in every day of their lives, and yet suggest the siblings' essential fondness for each other, their dependency, their mutual good will."

More Tales of Oliver Pig, the first sequel to Van Leeuwen's successful *Tales of Oliver Pig,* features stories about Oliver's first efforts at gardening, how he adjusts to being cared for by his grandmother, and his attempts to stall at bed-time. A *Bulletin of the Center for Children's Books* critic singled out the "gentle humor in the simple, fluent writing style" for praise in its review of this work. In response to her daughter's request, Van Leeuwen's next work in this series shifted the focus away from Oliver toward his younger sister, Amanda. The stories in *Amanda Pig and Her Big Brother Oliver* highlight Amanda's frustrations at being unable to do some of the things her big brother can do and her parents' sympathetic responses. "Never cloying, the humor is genuine, the incidents right on the younger-sibling mark," remarked a *School Library Journal* reviewer.

Critics noted that Amanda is more than an envious younger sister in *Tales of Amanda Pig,* the next work in this series. The stories in this volume find her refusing to eat a fried egg, scaring the clock-monster in the front hall with the help of her father, and switching roles with her sleepy mother at bed-time. Though a reviewer in *School Library Journal* found "the domestic drama . . . a bit dull this time out," a contributor to *Kirkus Reviews* praised "the same irreproachable, unforced child psychology, and if anything more sly by-play" in this installment. Amanda "maintains her pluck, imagination and vulnerability," according to a *School Library Journal* critic, in *More Tales of Amanda Pig,* in which she plays house with her brother, becomes jealous of visiting cousins, and gives her father her favorite toy for his birthday. *Horn Book* reviewer Karen Jameyson found the story to be as "comfortable as an easy chair, as warm and filling as a cup of cocoa."

In *Oliver, Amanda, and Grandmother Pig,* the Pig family enjoys a week-long visit by Grandmother Pig, who cannot do everything younger adults can do but can tell stories and give good hugs. This was followed by *Oliver and Amanda's Christmas,* in which the two young pigs learn to keep Christmas secrets, bake cookies, and select the perfect Christmas tree. Reviewers compared this work favorably with earlier books in the series; Betsy Hearne, writing in *Bulletin of the Center for Children's Books,* described it to be "as comfortable as tradition."

Oliver and Amanda are starting to grow up in the next two works in this series. In *Oliver Pig at School,* Oliver experiences his first day of kindergarten, befriending a scary classmate and making and eating a necklace in art class. Martha V. Parravano praised "the author's understanding of childhood experiences" in her review in *Horn Book.* In *Amanda Pig on Her Own,* Amanda learns to enjoy the adventures she can have when her big brother is away at school. Reviewing the work in *Bulletin of the Center for Children's Books,* Ruth Ann Smith particularly enjoyed Van Leeuwen's ability to "combine gentle humor with ingenuous dialogue."

Van Leeuwen has continued her easy-reader series with seasonal tales such as *Oliver and Amanda's Halloween* and *Oliver and Amanda and the Big Snow.* In the former title, the little pigs make a jack-o'-lantern and help prepare doughnuts as they get ready for Halloween. Brother and sister have to learn to compromise over the pumpkin's expression in "this warmhearted installment," as a critic described the book in *Publishers Weekly.* In *Oliver and Amanda and the Big Snow,* the porcine siblings go out to play after a snow storm and Amanda proves herself adept at snow games. "The warm interactions among family members continue to make these gentle stories a delight for early readers," wrote Hanna B. Zeiger in a *Horn Book* review. *Booklist's* Carolyn Phelan also noted the "gentle humor" in this tale. Susan Dove Lempke, reviewing the same title in *Bulletin of the Center for Children's Books,* noted that though the series had, at the time, been going strong for sixteen years, the "family adventures are as fresh and funny as ever." Lempke concluded that "young readers will wish they could bundle up and join Oliver and Amanda outside." And Gale W. Sherman minced no words in her *School Library Journal* review: "An outstanding selection for beginning-to-read collections."

Oliver got his first day in school and so does Amanda in *Amanda Pig, School Girl,* and it is every bit as fantastic as she always hoped it would be. Amanda even meets a new friend whom she dubs Lollipop. *Horn Book's* Martha V. Parravano praised this title for its "thorough understanding of the emotions and situations of childhood," while *School Library Journal's* Virginia Opocensky felt that fans of the series "will applaud this addition to the tales of Oliver and Amanda." Friendship is celebrated in two further titles in the series, *Amanda Pig and Her Best Friend Lollipop* and *Oliver and Albert, Friends Forever.* In the former title, Amanda continues her progress out into a wider world than family. She and her new friend have good times together at each other's houses and also have their first sleepover. "Amanda is as engaging a character as ever," noted *Horn Book's* Parravano, and *Booklist's* Carolyn Phelan noted that this "pleasant entry" in the series is written with "simplicity and affection." Oliver makes friends with the new boy in school in *Oliver and Albert, Friends Forever,* playing kickball and collecting bugs. Albert is not an easy friend at first, bookish and ignorant of the rules of the easiest games, but Oliver finds he is willing to learn and takes him under his wing. Leslie S. Hilverding, reviewing the title in *School Library Journal,* felt that the tale provides a "sweet and simple beginning chapter book about friendship." Shelle Rosenfeld, writing in *Booklist,* also noted the theme of friendship, writing that this tale "illustrates the importance of appreciating and respecting differences." Rosenfeld concluded that *Oliver and Albert, Friends Forever* is an "entertaining story."

Van Leeuwen has also written several chapter books for slightly older readers, featuring Benjy, a third-grade boy critics have described as a lovable academic and athletic underachiever. A reviewer commented in *Horn Book,* "Like Henry Huggins, Ellen Tebbits, and Ramona, Benjy is an engaging personality—one not quickly forgotten." In *Benjy and the Power of Zingies,* Benjy decides his only chance against the school bully who picks on him is to build up his body by eating Zingies breakfast cereal. A *Bulletin of the Center for Children's Books* critic praised the book's "light-hearted" and "often funny" treatment of life in the third grade. This was followed by *Benjy in Business,* in which Benjy attempts to earn enough money to buy a special baseball mitt he hopes will improve his game. "Benjy displays a sturdy tenacity that makes his extended effort credible and enjoyable," commented Carolyn Noah in the *School Library Journal.* Ilene Cooper remarked in *Booklist* that some of the action in the third work in this series, *Benjy the Football Hero,* may be lost on readers not familiar with the rules of the game at the book's center, but the critic added "this has the same good humor and engaging characters of the other Benjy books." About the series as a whole, Robert E. Unsworth remarked in *School Library Journal* that "Van Leeuwen has a fine ability to see the humor in the tribulations of nine year olds and she writes about them with understanding."

Although she is best known for her picture books and simple stories for first readers, Van Leeuwen has said that she has always enjoyed writing for older children and adolescents. One of her first attempts for this age group, *Seems Like This Road Goes on Forever,* draws on the author's understanding of the kinds of expectations and pressures put on children of members of the clergy. Mary Alice, the daughter of an overly strict minister, retraces with the help of a psychologist the steps that brought her to a hospital bed with a broken leg, unable to communicate or think clearly about her recent past. Although a reviewer in *Bulletin of the Center for Children's Books* found this a "slow-paced" if "convincing account of an emotional breakdown," a *New York Times Book Review* contributor concluded that it "is finely written, though cheerless—which it must be, I suppose, in order to be told properly." In a more lighthearted vein, *Dear Mom, You're Ruining My Life* is a novel for upper elementary school grades inspired by Van Leeuwen's daughter, Elizabeth. "As a sixth grader," the author wrote in her *SAAS* essay, "she was acutely embarrassed by everything about her family: our rusty old car, her father who actually insisted on *talking* to her friends, and especially me." A critic in *Kirkus Reviews* called the resulting portrait of life in the sixth grade "a genuinely funny look at a roller-coaster year."

Writing for middle graders, Van Leeuwen tells the story of an eleven-year-old trying to cope with her parents' separation in her 1996 novel, *Blue Sky, Butterfly.* Young Twig feels isolated from both her mom and her older brother after her father leaves, and they all try and cope with the changed circumstances in their lives. Finally, through the intervention of a grandmother and the healing influences of a garden, she is able to deal with her life. Reviewing the novel in *Horn Book Guide,* Patricia Riley called attention to Van Leeuwen's "well-drawn, interesting characters," and *Booklist*'s Susan Dove Lempke noted that Van Leeuwen "evokes the desolate period immediately following parental breakup" with "aching sharpness."

Returning to the picture book format, Van Leeuwen continues to provide warm, wholesome stories for young readers, dealing with family relations and friendship, among other themes. *Touch the Sky Summer* is narrated by Luke and tells of a special vacation taken with his family by the lake. "Children who have visited lakeside cabins will enjoy the vicarious experience, related in a natural-sounding text," wrote Phelan in a *Booklist* review. *School Library Journal*'s Opocensky also praised this story of a "happy family and an idyllic setting," calling it a "warm, wonderful read." A grandfather puts his three grandchildren to bed with tall tales from his childhood on the farm in *The Tickle Stories,* a book "perfect for bedtime stalling," commented Linda Perkins in a *Booklist* review. In *The Strange Adventures of Blue Dog,* a small wooden toy dog comes to life for a time and lives some very dog-like adventures.

Family relations are the subject of two further picture book titles from 2001. In *Sorry,* two brothers who cannot apologize to each other over a bowl of oatmeal manage to turn this into a feud that lasts generations. Finally, through the intercession of two great-grandchildren, the chasm between families is bridged with the word "sorry" when these children are on the verge of fighting over an apple. "Familiar themes of feuding families and the power of a simple apology dominate this story," wrote Susan L. Rogers in a *School Library Journal* review. Rogers went on to note that this "folkloric comic satire with overtones of universal truths should appeal to a wide range of readers and listeners." Further positive remarks came from a *Publishers Weekly* reviewer who commented that "regret permeates this unforgiving story of a needless feud, rendered in poignant detail." And combining these two sentiments, *Booklist*'s Shelle Rosenfeld concluded, "Humorous yet poignant, the story shows how a single word can make all the difference."

Family dynamics of a less serious sort are at the center of *"Wait for Me!" Said Maggie McGee,* in which the youngest of eight children is left out of the games of her older siblings. Too young to ride a tricycle or even get to the cookie jar, Maggie longs for the day when she can go to school. Once she does, she manages to help her older brother remember his lines in the school play and as a result becomes one of the gang. "Maggie McGee is a spunky, appealing role model for the youngest among us," remarked Rosalyn Pierini in a *School Library Journal* review. And *Booklist*'s Gillian Engberg had more laudatory words for the book, noting that with "gentle, poignant humor, Van Leeuwen tells a charming, straightforward story most younger siblings can relate to."

Van Leeuwen credits her advancing age with her increased interest in the past. In her *SAAS* essay she states: "In my writing . . . I find that I am starting to look backward. I have always been fascinated by history, not the history of big events and dates that I was taught in school, but of people and how they lived. I have written recently about my own childhood. I have ideas of writing about my family history, and perhaps, if I can find the right way to do it, about our country's history."

Van Leeuwen's reminiscence of her childhood, *Two Girls in Sister Dresses,* evokes the author's feelings about her younger sister. The book was highly praised for its realistic yet sensitive portrayal of the relationship between sisters. Phelan noted in her review in *Booklist* that *Two Girls in Sister Dresses* is written with Van Leeuwen's "accustomed simplicity and finesse." Also memorable for its nostalgic atmosphere is *Emma Bean,* which details the life of a homemade stuffed rabbit, a gift to Molly at birth from her grandmother. Critics noted similarities between *Emma Bean* and the children's classic, *The Velveteen Rabbit,* but Annie Ayres argued in her *Booklist* review that Van Leeuwen's "warmly sentimental book" is for those children not yet ready for the "more sophisticated and emotionally weighty themes" of the latter title.

Van Leeuwen has also produced historical books for young readers: *Going West,* a fictional journal of seven-year-old Hannah as she and her family travel west by wagon in the days of the pioneers, and *Bound for Oregon,* based on the real-life journey of Mary Ellen Todd and her family on the Oregon trail in the 1850s. Although more serious than many of the works for which she is best known, these books have been praised for the author's signature emphasis on a warm and supportive family atmosphere. A *Publishers Weekly* critic called *Going West* a "haunting evocation of times past," and further remarked, "Into a gentle text brimming with family warmth and love, Van Leeuwen ... packs a wealth of emotional moments." In *Bound for Oregon,* Van Leeuwen presents another pioneer tale, narrated by nine-year-old Mary Ellen. A description primarily of life on the trail, the "concrete details ... will draw readers," noted *Booklist*'s Phelan, who also felt that the book was a "fine introduction" to such a life. A reviewer for *Publishers Weekly* thought that the "contrast between the tenderness of Mary Ellen's perceptions and the hardships of the frontier is deeply moving," while *Horn Book*'s Ellen Fader praised the "especially vivid and well-rounded" characters and dubbed the book "inspiring reading."

More novel-length historical fiction is served up in the trilogy of books about Hannah Perley and her family during the Revolutionary War in Fairfield, Connecticut. In the initial volume, *Hannah of Fairfield,* the nine-year-old protagonist faces the approach of war, and Hannah's older brother Ben is eager to join General Washington's army. But the focus in this first novel is more on the domestic side of life than on the battlefield, and Hannah rails against having to do "girl's" work all the time when she would rather be working with the animals. *Booklist*'s Hazel Rochman felt that this "simply written docu-novel will give middle-grade readers a strong sense of what it was like to be a young girl then." Similarly, a critic for *Kirkus Reviews* wrote that Hannah's story "will entertain and inspire anyone who is interested in the past." In *Hannah's Helping Hands,* the young girl and her family try to keep a sense of normalcy as the war goes on all around them. Details of farming life are interspersed in the narrative as are bits of war history, supplied by brother Ben. Hannah is instrumental in saving her

family's farm animals when the British attack, though their home and many others are burned to the ground. "Van Leeuwen has provided a refreshing approach to the period that is accessible to reluctant readers," noted Cheryl Cufari in a *School Library Journal* review of this second novel in the series. And with *Hannah's Winter of Hope,* the family is living in the father's clock shop until their home can be rebuilt. The long cold winter of 1799-80 comes to life in this novel, with Ben captured by the English. However, toward the end of the winter he is finally released and returns home. "Van Leeuwen is brilliant at showing the effects of war through the prism of one family's life," wrote Connie Fletcher in a *Booklist* review of the final novel in the trilogy.

History for a younger audience also finds its way into Van Leeuwen's picture books. *Across the Wide Dark Sea* tells of life on the *Mayflower* as it makes its way across the Atlantic to the New World. Storms and suffering make the nine-week trip harrowing, and upon arrival there is a harsh winter and Indians to contend with. *Booklist*'s Phelan praised Van Leeuwen for "telling a particular story that reflects the broader immigrant experience." *A Fourth of July on the Plains* is another of Van Leeuwen's historical tales based on real accounts, this one from a diary account of a celebration on the Oregon Trail in 1852. Jesse is too young to go hunting with the men and the women do not need his help sewing a flag for the Fourth of July, so he and other young boys scrape together whistles and bells and make a parade for the adults as a surprise. Rochman, writing in *Booklist,* observed that this story "combines a child's voice and viewpoint with handsome paintings that capture the pioneer experience." A reviewer for *Publishers Weekly* voiced similar opinions, noting that Van Leeuwen's tale provides "a likeably informal child's view of pioneer life, as well as an enthusiastic appreciation for the rituals, both solemn and boisterous, of the Fourth." *Nothing Here But Trees* once again gives insight to the pioneer experience through the eyes of a young narrator. The setting is Ohio in the early nineteenth century and a boy and his brother help Pa clear the land, build fences, plant corn, and harvest their crop. "This is close to Laura Ingalls Wilder country," commented *Booklist*'s Rochman, and a contributor for *Kirkus Reviews* called the picture book "engaging, entertaining, unsentimental."

That same three-word description could be used to describe much of Van Leeuwen's work for young readers. Reviewers have consistently praised the warm yet realistic celebrations of family life found in her books, emphasizing her gentle humor and insightful portrayal of common childhood experiences. For example, in a review of *Oliver, Amanda, and Grandmother Pig,* Karen Jameyson concluded in *Horn Book:* "With perceptiveness and gentle humor Jean Van Leeuwen shapes even the most mundane subjects into pleasing, warm tales." Such warm tales are Van Leeuwen's staple product; they are what readers have come to expect when they pick up one of her numerous titles.

Biographical and Critical Sources

PERIODICALS

Booklist, September 1, 1985, Ilene Cooper, review of *Benjy the Football Hero,* p. 72; July, 1993, Annie Ayres, review of *Emma Bean,* p. 1977; May 1, 1992, p. 1603; April 1, 1994, Carolyn Phelan, review of *Two Girls in Sister Dresses,* p. 1453; October 1, 1994, Carolyn Phelan, review of *Bound for Oregon,* p. 329; September 15, 1995, Carolyn Phelan, review of *Across the Wide Sea,* p. 161; January 1, 1996, Carolyn Phelan, review of *Oliver and Amanda and the Big Snow,* p. 850; June 1, 1996, Susan Dove Lempke, review of *Blue Sky, Butterfly,* p. 1724; May 15, 1997, Hazel Rochman, review of *A Fourth of July on the Plains,* p. 1582; June 1, 1997, Carolyn Phelan, review of *Touch the Sky Summer,* p. 1723; May 1, 1998, Linda Perkins, review of *The Tickle Stories,* p. 1524; July, 1998, Carolyn Phelan, review of *Amanda Pig and Her Best Friend Lollipop,* p. 1892; September 1, 1998, Hazel Rochman, review of *Nothing Here But Trees,* p. 129; March 1, 1999, Hazel Rochman, review of *Hannah of Fairfield,* p. 1215; August, 2000, Connie Fletcher, review of *Hannah's Winter of Hope,* p. 2142; December 1, 2000, Shelle Rosenfeld, review of *Oliver and Albert, Friends Forever,* p. 727; May 15, 2001, Gillian Engberg, review of *"Wait for Me!" Said Maggie McGee,* p. 1761; June 1, 2001, Shelle Rosenfeld, review of *Sorry,* p. 1896.

Bulletin of the Center for Children's Books, February, 1968, p. 103; June, 1968, review of *Timothy's Flower,* p. 166; July, 1969, review of *One Day in Summer,* p. 184; September, 1973, review of *I Was a 98-Pound Duckling,* p. 19; February, 1975, p. 100; November, 1975, review of *The Great Christmas Kidnapping Caper;* October, 1979, review of *Seems Like This Road Goes on Forever;* July, 1981, review of *More Tales of Oliver Pig,* p. 221; July-August, 1982; review of *The Great Rescue Operation;* March, 1983, review of *Benjy and the Power of Zingies;* January, 1986, p. 98; May, 1989, pp. 238-239; October, 1989, Betsy Hearne, review of *Oliver and Amanda's Christmas,* p. 47; September, 1990, p. 18; March, 1991, Ruth Ann Smith, review of *Amanda Pig on Her Own,* pp. 180-181; November, 1994, p. 107; December, 1995, Susan Dove Lempke, review of *Oliver and Amanda and the Big Snow,* p. 143.

Horn Book, February, 1975; December, 1979, p. 660; August, 1981, p. 419; June, 1982, p. 294; December, 1982, pp. 646-647; April, 1983, review of *Benjy and the Power of Zingies,* pp. 168-169; December, 1983, p. 713; February, 1984, pp. 48-49; March-April, 1986, Karen Jameyson, review of *More Tales of Amanda Pig,* pp. 199-200; September, 1987, Karen Jameyson, review of *Oliver, Amanda, and Grandmother Pig,* pp. 606-607; November, 1989, p. 754; September-October, 1990, Martha V. Parravano, review of *Oliver Pig at School,* p. 599; March-April, 1992, p. 199; July-August, 1994, pp. 447-448; March-April, 1995, Ellen Fader, review of *Bound for Oregon,* p. 197; September-October, 1995, Hanna B. Zeiger, review of *Oliver and Amanda and the Big Snow,* p. 628; May-

June, 1997, Martha V. Parravano, review of *Amanda Pig, Schoolgirl,* p. 329; July-August, 1998, Martha V. Parravano, review of *Amanda Pig and Her Best Friend Lollipop,* pp. 499-500; September-October, 2000, p. 584.

Horn Book Guide, spring, 1995, p. 85; fall, 1996, Patricia Riley, review of *Blue Sky, Butterfly,* p. 298; fall, 1996, p. 283; fall, 1998, p. 309; spring, 1999, p. 60; fall, 1999, p. 270.

Kirkus Reviews, October 1, 1967, p. 1202; April 15, 1969, p. 436; October 1, 1972, p. 1155; September 1, 1982, p. 997; December 1, 1982, p. 1293; September 1, 1983, review of *Tales of Amanda Pig;* May 15, 1989, review of *Dear Mom, You're Ruining My Life,* p. 772; June 1, 1992, p. 724; August 1, 1993, p. 1008; April 15, 1996, pp. 608-609; April 15, 1998, p. 588; September 1, 1998, review of *Nothing Here But Trees,* p. 1294; January 1, 1999, review of *Hannah of Fairfield,* p. 73; May 1, 1999, p. 729.

New York Times Book Review, November 5, 1967; November 30, 1975, p. 26; June 24, 1979; November 11, 1979, review of *Seems Like This Road Goes on Forever;* May 3, 1981; April 25, 1982, Doris Orgel, "Mice in Macy's"; November 13, 1983; May 19, 1985; November 10, 1985, Mary Gordon, "Pig Tales"; January 10, 1988, p. 36.

Publishers Weekly, December 4, 1967, p. 44; September 25, 1972, review of *I Was a 98-Pound Duckling;* October 7, 1974, review of *Too Hot for Ice Cream,* p. 63; September 8, 1975, review of *The Great Christmas Kidnapping Caper;* August 14, 1987, p. 107; December 13, 1991, review of *Going West,* p. 55; September 2, 1992, review of *Oliver and Amanda's Halloween,* p. 59; August 2, 1993, p. 79; April 25, 1994, p. 78; September 5, 1994, review of *Bound for Oregon,* p. 112; May 19, 1997, review of *A Fourth of July on the Plains,* pp. 75-76; June 7, 1999, p. 82; July 27, 1999, p. 93; May 21, 2001, review of *Sorry,* p. 107.

School Library Journal, October, 1975, p. 78; May, 1979, p. 76; December, 1979, p. 93; May, 1981, p. 80; August, 1982, Caroline S. Parr, review of *The Great Rescue Operation,* p. 123; December, 1982, review of *Amanda Pig and Her Big Brother Oliver,* p. 75; January, 1983, p. 80; December, 1983, Carolyn Noah, review of *Benjy in Business,* p. 70; December, 1983, review of *Tales of Amanda Pig,* p. 80; May, 1985, Robert E. Unsworth, review of *Benjy the Football Hero,* p. 111; December, 1985, review of *More Tales of Amanda Pig,* p. 110; March, 1988, p. 177; June, 1989, pp. 109-110; October, 1989, p. 45; May, 1991, p. 85; March, 1992, p. 225; April, 1992, Jacqueline Rose, review of *The Great Summer Camp Catastrophe,* p. 126; June, 1994; October, 1994, p. 128; September, 1995, pp. 187-188; December, 1995, Gale W. Sherman, review of *Oliver and Amanda and the Big Snow,* p. 92; June, 1996, p. 126; May, 1997, p. 116; July, 1997, Virginia Opocensky, review of *Touch the Sky Summer* and *Amanda Pig, School Girl,* p. 77; July, 1998, p. 84; November, 1998, p. 99; May, 1999, pp. 99-100; July, 1999, p. 82; November, 1999, Cheryl Cufari, review of *Hannah's Helping Hands,* pp. 131-132; July, 2000, p. 89; November, 2000,

Leslie S. Hilverding, review of *Oliver and Albert, Friends Forever,* p. 136; May, 2001, Susan L. Rogers, review of *Sorry,* p. 138; July, 2001, Rosalyn Pierini, review of *"Wait for Me!" Said Maggie McGee,* p. 90.
Time, December 3, 1979, p. 100.
Times Educational Supplement, June 8, 1984.

Wilson Library Bulletin, April, 1995, p. 112

OTHER

Meet Jean Van Leeuwen, http://www.eduplace.com/ (February 24, 2002).
Official Jean Van Leeuwen Web site, http://www.jeanvanleeuwen.com/ (May 6, 2003).

Autobiography Feature

Jean Van Leeuwen

I had a book-filled childhood. It was not that my family was a particularly literary one. I was just irresistibly attracted to books. Any time, anywhere, I was likely to be found with a book in my hand. I read riding in the car, even though it made me dizzy. I read when the family went visiting, even though my mother said it was rude. I read late at night under the covers, by flashlight, when I was supposed to be asleep. And I would read almost anything, just as long as it had a story. What I liked best of all was to stretch out on my bed with a book, so far lost inside some other world that when I heard my mother's voice, summoning me to dinner, I would look around and blink, wondering where I was.

The books I remember from my childhood were not, for the most part, fine literature. When I was very young, I had a Mother Goose book and a few picture books, my favorite one being about a very long dog named Pretzel. And for awhile, later on, my aunt Ruthie gave me fine editions of children's classics for my birthday, books like *Black Beauty, Little Women,* and *Hans Brinker; or, the Silver Skates.* This was a wonderful gift to give a child. I loved owning these books, touching them, placing them on my bookshelf, although they were almost too beautiful to read.

But most of what I recall reading were series books, like the Bobbsey Twins and Nancy Drew and the Hardy Boys. I had a series, handed down from my aunt, called the "Honey Bunch" books, about the most sickeningly sweet little girl who ever lived. And a series, which must have come from my grandfather, about children on a farm. This one was for when I was truly desperate, as the writing was terribly old-fashioned. It wasn't the stories themselves, I suspect, that appealed to me as much as the luxury of all those volumes lined up on the shelf, all those other lives waiting to be looked into.

My family was made up primarily of preachers and teachers. My father was a minister, and so was his brother. My mother was a teacher, and so were her two sisters. Her mother had been a teacher once, too. And her father, my maternal grandfather, had been a minister, rather a famous

Jean Van Leeuwen

one, I gather. His name was John Edward Charlton. Not only was he a minister, but a writer as well. He was the author of six books, three of them collections of the stories he told to children during his church services. He also wrote poetry and magazine articles. If writing ability is handed down in the genes, perhaps mine came from him.

John Charlton was born in Leeds, England, the son of a coffee and tea merchant. When he was nine years old, he came to the United States with his family. He grew up outside of Boston and began preaching at the age of seventeen, while he was still a student. I have newspaper articles from the time which refer to my grandfather as "the boy preacher." Upon graduating from Boston University (from which he eventually earned four academic degrees), he became pastor of the Methodist Episcopal Church of Newton Highlands, Massachusetts. That same year, 1905, he married Mabelle Perley, a young schoolteacher from Ipswich. And in 1909, my mother, Dorothy Elizabeth Charlton, was born.

All of my mother's maternal ancestors came from New England. In fact, *The Perley Family History,* a fat red book which always impressed me as a child, traces them back to the seventeenth century. All of my father's ancestors came from Holland, Michigan, and—some generations back—from Holland itself. But my parents met in New Jersey.

My grandfather's ministry took him from churches in the Massachusetts towns of Worcester, Salem, and Fall River eventually to the Morrow Memorial Church, a large congregation in Maplewood, New Jersey. There he stayed for nineteen years. During this time, my mother graduated from high school and from Wheaton College in Massachusetts, then returned to New Jersey to become an elementary-school teacher. And in 1933, in what must have seemed a replay of her parents' courtship, the young teacher met a young preacher.

My father, Cornelius Van Leeuwen, came from a background so Dutch that he and three of his cousins had the same name. All of them were named after their grandfather. His mother was Cornelia and his father Martin. Martin Van Leeuwen was the oldest of fourteen children. Most of this hardworking, conservative, religious clan lived in the community of Holland, Michigan.

My father grew up in Holland, and attended Hope College there. But when he decided to become a minister, he enrolled at New Brunswick Theological Seminary in New Jersey, a more liberal school than the one in his hometown. During his senior year, he was sent out to preach at a small Dutch Reformed church in nearby Middlebush. In May 1934, this church invited him to become its regular pastor. And in June of that year, he and my mother were married, by her father, at the Morrow Memorial Church in Maplewood.

One request which my father had made of my mother when they were married was not to have any babies on weekends, the busiest time for a minister. I arrived bright and early on the morning of December 26, 1937, not only a Sunday morning but right in the middle of the Christmas season as well. By this time my parents had moved to Rutherford, New Jersey, a suburb of New York City, where my father was minister of the Rutherford Congregational Church. This small town, neither rich nor poor, only a mile square and surrounded by other suburban towns, was the setting for my childhood.

Looking back, I remember my early years as a secure, carefree time. I had a little sister, Barbara, who was two years younger (born on a Saturday). And a baby brother, named John Charlton but called Jack, who was six years younger (born on a Sunday). We lived in a pleasant house on a pleasant, tree-lined street, with a swing set in the

"My maternal grandfather, Reverend John Charlton, with his family. My mother is on her mother's lap," about 1913

backyard and kids to play with across the street. In due course, I went to school, and learned to read from a teacher named Miss Bean. Then, when I was eight, we moved to a larger house a few streets away. It is this house, and this block, which I remember best. It was my world.

The block I lived on was one of small old houses set close together, tall shade trees, and neat grassy backyards that seem tiny now but were vast to me back then. It was a short block, bounded on one end by the hill we walked down to go to school and sledded down when it snowed, and on the other by the railroad tracks. The railroad tracks were a natural barrier, one I was forbidden by my parents to cross on pain of death by locomotive. And though I yearned to rebel, to explore the inviting woods and factory yards beyond as some of my more adventurous friends did, I never quite dared. So almost everything that happened to me happened on my block.

The block was heavily populated with children, most of them boys. Although I was naturally somewhat shy and a bookworm, I was also a tomboy. I rode bikes with the boys, played cowboys, climbed trees, and played endless games of baseball in the street. With my best friend, Freddy, who lived across the street, I built secret forts in our backyard. I can remember long lazy summer days of playing ball against the front steps or looking for four-leaf clovers in the backyard, listening all the while for the bell of the ice-cream truck, which always arrived in time to cool us off. And summer evenings after supper, when all the kids on the block played hide-and-seek around the tele-phone pole until the streetlights came on.

During the summer we always went away for a month, in the early years to my grandparents' summer house in Gloucester, Massachusetts, and later to Lake George, in the Adirondack Mountains of New York. I loved both places, the seashore and the mountains. My grandparents' house was perched on a rocky cliff overlooking the ocean, and although I was only five or six when we went there, I still can remember how it felt to climb down those rocks to the sandy beach below, to smell the seaweed and the salty air, to lie in bed at night listening to waves lapping endlessly at the shore. And I have equally vivid memories of the blue skies, crisp mountain air, and clear waters of Lake George. Here, as our family first rented a cottage and later built one of our own, I learned to swim and play tennis, handle boats, and for the first time really see the world of nature. Both of these places are a part of me, and both have been frequent settings for my writing.

Not everything in my childhood was completely idyllic. For years I had a terrible longing for a dog. This need of mine was like a constant nagging toothache. I read dog books, collected china dogs, and paid daily visits to the neighbors' Irish setter, fantasizing that he was mine. Eventually, when I was about twelve, we got a dog, and I was delighted. But I remember all those evening stars that I wished on fruitlessly, and the disappointment on Christmas

The author's paternal grandparents, Martin and Corne-lia Van Leeuwen, on their wedding day, about 1905

mornings when once again no puppy waited for me under the tree.

My shyness was sometimes a problem. I was afraid to talk to grown-ups, and my mother recalls that when she sent me on an errand, I would go only if Barbara went with me and did the talking. Having a little sister who not only had an outgoing personality, but was also pretty and annoyingly good all the time was a trial to me. She played quietly with her dolls with other girls, and was always clean and neat. I ran wild with the boys, had skinned knees and rumpled clothes, and always felt a little bit bad.

But probably the biggest pressure in my early life came from being a minister's child. I have an image in my mind of myself at about four, dressed in ruffles and patent-leather shoes, trying to sit still on a hard wooden church pew, while my mother drew pictures and fed me Lifesavers in an attempt to keep me quiet through the service. Our lives were dominated by the church. Its schedule was ours, its activities, its people. We children spent hours there, it seemed, on Sunday mornings, from Sunday school until everyone went home at last after the service and we wandered through the pews picking up discarded bulletins. We participated in everything: Sunday school, Youth Fellowship, family suppers, Christmas pageants, choir. And we had to be "good" children: well behaved, attentive, quiet, polite. If we weren't, what would people think of the minister's family?

It was these expectations that I found difficult to deal with. I didn't like playing a part, smiling when I wanted to frown, shaking hands in the church vestibule when I wanted to be outside playing baseball, singing in the choir because it was expected, not because I liked to sing. I hated conformity, and was filled with scorn at the very idea of allowing my life to be ruled by "What will people think?" Yet I lacked the courage for open rebellion. So I adopted a protective camouflage. On the outside, I was well behaved, attentive, quiet, and polite, sitting with my family in church on a Sunday morning. But inside, my mind drifted, escaped into fantasy, ran free. As a teenager, I finally did stage a tiny rebellion, occasionally staying home from church. But even then I did it the cowardly way, inventing mysterious stomachaches which arrived early Sunday mornings and conveniently departed by afternoon.

During all of these years I read constantly, going to the library and coming home with stacks of books, as many as I could carry. I would develop passions for certain kinds of stories—dog stories, horse stories, mysteries, historical fiction—and proceed to read everything in that category on the shelves. By the time I was in sixth grade, I felt as if I had read just about every book in the small basement children's room of the Rutherford Public Library. It was then that I had an inspiration. I'd read so many books, why couldn't I write one of my own? It seemed simple enough to me.

At that time I was in my horse-story period. I had just finished *Black Beauty,* and decided I would write a book about a girl and her horse. I got a clean new notebook, sharpened my pencils, and fearlessly plunged right in. For a little while, the project went well. I wrote about three chapters. But then I found myself faltering, slowing down. And finally the book ground to a complete stop. Looking back, I can see that I knew nothing about constructing a story, and less than nothing about horses. My total experience consisted of clinging tightly to the saddle while an elderly pony walked around a track. So, very early, I learned the important lesson of writing about things you know. And I also learned that writing was hard work. Discouraged, I put away that first effort, and with it, for some time to come, my writing ambitions.

At about this same time, our class was assigned to do reports on careers. Each of us was to choose a career that we thought might interest us, and write a report about it. All of the girls were talking about which career to choose. The choices for women at that time, at least as we perceived them, were limited. As I recall, every single girl in my class planned to be either a nurse, a teacher, or a secretary. Once again, a small spark of rebellion flared inside me. I didn't want to be like everyone else. I didn't want to follow in my mother's footsteps and become a teacher. So I went off to the library to find myself a career. After exploring a number of reference books, I finally came up with one: book editor. I don't recall why I selected it, perhaps because it seemed remarkable to me to be paid for the pleasure of reading books, but it turned out to be a prophetic choice.

I n the summer of 1952, just before I entered high school, my father was invited to attend a conference in California. My parents decided that this would be an ideal opportunity for a family cross-country trip. I recall visiting numerous national parks, crossing the desert, dipping my feet in the Pacific Ocean for the first time, making snowballs in July in the California mountains, touring a Hollywood studio. But what I remember most about the trip was a sense of widening horizons. The country was so vast and it was filled with so many people. What were their lives like? I had always been curious, peering into the lighted windows of other people's houses as we drove home from my grandmother's house in the dark. Now I gazed out of the car window for three straight weeks, absorbing the changing landscape, observing all sorts of people, speculating about how they lived. When we stopped, I eavesdropped on their conversations, looking for clues.

I'm not sure if this is the exact moment it started, but I think it is when I became a confirmed Observer of the Passing Scene. To this day, wherever I am, I continue, rather like a spy sent from another planet, to observe the human race. I do it on trains and buses, in restaurants, grocery stores, while driving car pools for my children—any place where I come in contact with people. And I have come to feel that this detective-like curiosity is a necessary quality for a writer.

Back home that fall, I entered high school. My preoccupation was more with figuring out how to be popular than any intellectual pursuit. Still, from time to time, I continued to do some writing. I went through a period of trying to imitate the short stories in women's magazines. Before I began each one, I would carefully cut out pictures of my main characters and paste them into a notebook. It's not clear to me why I did this, but in retrospect it seems rather a good idea. Without being aware of it, I was getting to know my characters, I remember particularly a story I wrote about a Seeing Eye dog (again, a subject about which I knew almost nothing), which was

praised by my English teacher. I did well in all of my writing assignments. But no one ever encouraged me to take it seriously, to think of actually becoming a writer.

Something happened in my junior year, though, that did make me think about it. We were reading Ernest Hemingway's *For Whom the Bell Tolls* in English, and we were assigned a book report. I handed mine in, and was surprised when the teacher asked to see me after school. Closing the door, she looked at me very seriously and asked if I had copied my report from some other source. Alarmed, I answered that I hadn't. She didn't seem quite sure whether to believe me or not, and after a moment mumbled something about the writing being too good to have been done by a high-school student. I felt humiliated and highly offended at being accused of cheating, and I went home angry. But later, looking over the paper, I saw that in a sense my English teacher had been right. I had loved the book and Hemingway's writing. When it came time to do my book report, without realizing it or knowing I could, I had imitated his style. And much later, I saw that in her bungling way my teacher had paid me a compliment. I wasn't ready yet to imagine that I could become a writer, but just maybe I had a little bit of talent.

*

I went off to college in 1955 without any clear idea of my future. I had chosen Syracuse University, a university large enough to offer degrees in many different fields. At

"My mother, Dorothy Charlton Van Leeuwen, holding me at age twelve weeks."

first I thought I would major in English. But that seemed to lead to a teaching career, and I still didn't think I wanted to continue in the family teaching tradition. Then I took some psychology courses, and liked them so much that I decided psychology would be my major. But to become a psychologist meant going to graduate school, and I was eager to leave the academic world and enter the real world. So, in my junior year, I switched from the School of Liberal Arts to the School of Journalism, where I declared a major in magazine. I still had vague thoughts about writing, but didn't know what kind of writing or how I could make a living at it. If I couldn't be a writer, I would at least be associated with words. I fixed on a new ambition: to become editor in chief of one of the top women's magazines in New York.

Upon graduating from college in 1959, I went off with three friends for a summer tour of Europe. This was something I had dreamed of for a long time. The trip was everything I had hoped it would be. We stayed in youth hostels in Germany, college dormitories in Paris, and lived for a week with a farm family in southern France. It was another widening of my horizons. And it was also a last interlude of freedom before all of us tied ourselves down to full-time jobs. I enjoyed every minute of it, and returned refreshed and eager to take on the challenge of moving to New York City and finding an exciting job in publishing.

I had imagined myself taking the magazine world by storm. In reality it didn't work out quite that way. Day after day, I commuted from my parents' house in New Jersey into the city. There I walked the streets, carrying a newspaper opened to the classified section, with all possible jobs circled in red. With my journalism school degree, I was determined not to start as a secretary, yet secretarial jobs seemed to be the only ones available. I went to employment agencies, but they had nowhere to send me. I followed up the meager leads offered by college friends. Finally I found my way to a women's magazine which didn't have a job available, but would let me try a free-lance writing assignment, which might later lead to a job.

This, I thought, was my Big Chance. The assignment was a travel article, and I remember working so hard on it, rewriting over and over again, trying to get the chatty style just right, determined to impress the editor so she would have to give me a job. The results were a huge anticlimax. I heard nothing from the magazine for weeks, and when I finally got up enough courage to call, the editor didn't seem to remember who I was. She had no comments to give me on the article, and they had changed their minds about the job possibility. I was back to pavement pounding and ad circling.

Eventually, after about two months of this, my luck changed. I was hired as an assistant editor at *TV Guide* magazine. It wasn't exactly the glamorous job I had envisioned. It wasn't with a women's magazine, the salary was pitifully low, and it entailed very little writing. Most of the job consisted of talking on the telephone with publicity people at the local TV stations, verifying their program schedule, then writing the two-or three-line blurbs describing the programs that went into the listings. "So-and-so's guests tonight are . . . " Still it was a start. I had a real job on a real magazine in New York City.

Now I could move into the city. As soon as I received my first paycheck, I rented an apartment with two other

The author (right) with her brother Jack and sister Barbara at Niagara Falls, 1952

girls in Manhattan. One of the girls was my best friend from high school, and this was something the two of us had planned for years. The apartment we found was in an old brownstone building on a busy, noisy street. The one bedroom was crowded. The kitchen was so tiny that the stove and refrigerator were one unit, and when you washed the dishes, you had to stack them in the bedroom. But we didn't care. We had a fireplace and a view of a backyard with an actual tree growing in it. And most important, we were living in New York City.

It was an exciting time for all of us, on our own for the first time, just embarking on our careers. None of the three of us had any money, so we furnished our apartment with odds and ends begged from our families. We tramped around to thrift shops, finding bargain tables and lamps, painting and fixing them up, sewing curtains for the windows. Because we couldn't afford pictures for the walls, we invited a cartoonist friend to decorate one entire wall with a giant cartoon. Through our jobs and college acquaintances, we were meeting other young single people. We went to parties, and developed a circle of friends. We were beginning to feel at home in New York.

After a year or so, however, I found myself growing restless with my job at *TV Guide*. It was too easy, too much of a routine. I longed for more of a challenge. Trying to find a way to do more writing, I proposed articles to the editor. But this was just the local edition; most of the articles were written at the national headquarters in Pennsylvania. Occasionally I did get to write longer blurbs, when one of the local stations had a special program. But they only amounted to a paragraph or two. And once I wrote a real article about a children's show. But even that was just two pages long. It was becoming clear to me that this was as much as I could aspire to at the magazine.

So again I began looking for a job. And once again, the magazine world did not seem eager to embrace me. After several months of frustration, I finally decided to try book publishing. I answered an ad placed by a company called Abelard-Schuman for someone to do library promotion work. I wasn't familiar with the company's books, and didn't even know what library promotion was, but somehow I got the job.

My new job was quite a change from *TV Guide.* I discovered that library promotion work involved sending out books for review, producing catalogs, updating mailing lists, attending meetings and conventions. Because books are published twice a year, rather than once a week, the pace was slower. And instead of television people, I was dealing with librarians and book reviewers. Although I was now doing even less writing than I had before, I enjoyed the job more. Because suddenly I was intimately involved with something I had always loved: books.

Abelard-Schuman was a small, family-owned company, where everyone seemed to do a little bit of everything. This was a good opportunity for me, as I soon realized that I was more interested in the editorial side of publishing than the sales and promotion side. I volunteered my services to Frances Schwartz, the children's book editor, to write copy for book jackets. After awhile I began to stay late, reading manuscripts and writing reports on them. As I became more and more involved, I felt a growing sense of excitement. Here was something I truly liked doing. As the months went by, a new ambition began to take shape in my head. I would become a children's book editor.

I confided this ambition to another editor, Peggy Jackson. She took me under her wing, teaching me all she knew about copyediting and artwork and production. And when there was an opening in the editorial department, I approached Frances Schwartz about it. Would she make me an assistant editor? I was overjoyed when she said yes.

This began a most satisfying ten years as a children's book editor. I read avidly, catching up with all the fine books that had been published since I was a child. I learned about print orders, permissions, copyrights, color separations: all the nitty-gritty of book publishing. I experienced the exhilaration of discovering a good manuscript hidden in the stacks of unsolicited manuscripts that it was my job to read. And the pleasure of working with an author through months of revision, helping to shape and polish a story to make it the best it could be. And the thrill of holding in my hand the first copy of the first book I had edited.

In 1963 I moved to Random House as an assistant editor in the children's book department. At that time the Random House offices were in the Archdiocese Building on Madison Avenue behind St. Patrick's Cathedral. It was a wonderful old building, perfect for a publisher, with high ceilings, marble staircases, and even little garret rooms on the top floor, one of which for a time served as my office. Bennett Cerf was in charge of everything, in a grand office on the first floor.

One day, after I had been there only a few weeks, I was summoned to his office. I went with a fair amount of fear and trembling, convinced that I had unknowingly made some horrendous mistake and was about to be fired. Sitting behind his impressive wood-paneled desk, with rich draperies behind and plush carpeting underfoot, he smiled at me. He looked exactly as he did on television, on the game show "What's My Line?"

"I have a letter here," he said, and proceeded to read it to me. It was from, of all people, my mother. It told how

Jean with her father at her high-school graduation, 1955

much she enjoyed watching him on television and how pleased she was that I was now working for him. I was greatly relieved, and also greatly embarrassed. And Bennett Cerf was most cordial, bidding me welcome and promising to write to my mother that he was pleased to have me, too.

I stayed at Random House for five years. At first, I was assistant editor to Janet Finnie, who was in charge of the nonfiction "Allabout" series. Most of the books I worked on were science books, illustrated with photographs, so I became something of an expert in photo research. From Janet I learned valuable lessons about integrity, checking and rechecking accuracy before committing words to the printed page. I also learned about tenacity, pursing a lead for just the right photograph beyond the point where it seemed to come to a dead end. And I lost a good bit of my shyness in the process of telephoning world-renowned experts in all kinds of fields. Eventually I progressed from assistant editor to associate editor, in charge of a nature series called "Gateway Books."

Random House was a fun place to work. You never knew what famous person you would meet in the lobby or glimpse out the window, from the Kennedys to the Pope. And, with the offices of Alfred A. Knopf and Pantheon in the same building, there was a group of young editors with whom to be friendly. For a time I shared an office with Jane Yolen, who was going through the exciting experience of having her first book published. Other assistant editors were Jane Feder, Polly Berends, and Alice Bach, all of whom later went on to write for children. It was a stimulating place and time.

Whether it was due to this environment or to my daily exposure to manuscripts, both good and bad, I once again began to have the urge to write. This time I felt determined to succeed. But I knew I needed guidance. So I signed up for an evening course at Hunter College, taught by picture-book author William Lipkind. He encouraged me and, after the course ended, invited me to join a writers' workshop. Later I participated in another workshop, organized by Jane Yolen. These small, supportive groups were an ideal place to try out ideas, receive constructive criticism, and gain confidence as a writer.

Finally I completed a picture book which I thought was ready to submit to a publisher. It was called *Timothy's Flower,* and was based on a small boy whom I had observed in my New York City neighborhood. I wanted to submit it to Random House, but at the last minute developed cold feet. What if it was terrible? All of the editors and all my friends would know about it.

I was rescued from this dilemma by my friend and fellow editor Alice Bach, who simply told the editor in chief, Walter Retan, that I had written a manuscript. He asked to see it, I gave it to him, and—miracle of miracles—he liked it. The process of editing and finding an artist began. And at last, in 1967, I experienced the biggest thrill of my career, holding in my hand the first copy of my first published book. Nothing else, I think, has ever quite matched the excitement of seeing my name actually spelled out on the cover of a book for the first time.

Two more big changes in my life took place the following year, and they happened almost simultaneously. In May, I accepted a new job as associate editor at Viking Press. There, under editor in chief Velma Varner, I would be able to work on fiction for older readers, which was turning out to be my favorite kind of children's literature. And in July, I was married. Bruce Gavril, my new husband, was a mechanical engineer by training, now working in computer science at IBM's T. J. Watson Research Laboratory. Though our fields were very different, both of us were doing creative work, so he understood and supported my writing. I immediately enlisted him as my technical consultant, a role which he has continued to play admirably through the years.

He also was the inspiration for one of the characters in a new book I was writing. In my years of living in the city, I had always been impressed by its bustle, so many people busily doing so many things. I had the idea of writing about a gang of mice, operating in this world but unnoticed by it, having big adventures. The setting for the story was an old movie theater. The leader of the gang was Marvin, tough and daring, but none too smart. He needed an assistant with brains, and this was Raymond, a thinker, problem solver, and saver of seemingly useless objects—just like Bruce. The trio was rounded out by Fats, a genial bumbler with a passion for cheese. The plot of the story revolved around the gang's attempt to rob a nearby cheese shop. *The Great Cheese Conspiracy,* my first book for older readers, was published by Random House in 1969.

The early years of our marriage were busy and productive. I was working full time and enjoying it, and also fitting in time for writing. I embarked on a book of another type, a growing-up story based on my own adolescence, entitled *I Was a 98-Pound Duckling.* And, in 1970, I became senior editor at Dial Press, working for

"Bruce and I with my parents on our wedding day," July 7, 1968

Phyllis Fogelman. Soon she became my editor as well, as I also moved to Dial as an author. This rewarding association with a perceptive editor, so important to a writer, has continued to this day.

It was not long, however, before Bruce and I were facing new challenges. First, Bruce left IBM to strike out on his own, hoping to develop, patent, and sell an invention in the computer field. This adventure, which was planned to last a year, went on for seven. And then, in 1972, our first child, David, was born. I returned to work, while Bruce took care of David. Although it was difficult for him to accomplish complicated technical work while feeding and diapering a baby, he enjoyed the hours spent getting to know his son. And we were glad that his unusual career circumstances had provided this opportunity for family closeness.

Then, a year later, our second child arrived. Born on Halloween, two months premature, Elizabeth weighed only three and a half pounds. And she was sick with hyaline membrane disease, an unfinished condition of the lungs. The days after her birth were filled with anxiety. But she was a strong baby and, day by day, she improved. When Elizabeth was four weeks old, we were able to take her home from the hospital.

Faced with caring for a tiny infant, still weighing under five pounds, and a bouncy toddler, it seemed time for me to leave publishing and become a full-time mother. We were living then in a two-bedroom apartment, the same one in which Bruce had lived before we were married. The second bedroom was Bruce's office, where he worked on his invention. That left only the living room for the babies. We had two cribs, a playpen, and a changing table lined up in there, and a little later, a tricycle and a motorcycle under the dining-room table. It was crowded, and we couldn't afford to move or even go anywhere. The biggest treat for Bruce and me was going out to a movie once a week. Still, we were together, a family of four, and it was a happy time.

Having two young children so close together kept me very much a full-time mother. But I wanted to be at least a part-time writer, too. I tried working at night, but once the children were in bed I found myself also falling asleep. The only real time available was their nap time. And, since one of the babies napped in the living room and the other in the bedroom, the only space available was our tiny kitchen. To make matters worse, David didn't really like to take naps, and often he would sit in his crib, singing and talking to his stuffed animals. I would be sitting at my portable typewriter in the kitchen, trying to think deep thoughts to the tune of the ABC song from "Sesame Street." Desperation being the mother of invention, I finally hit on a solution to the problem. I ran the dishwasher. Whether it was empty or full, I ran the dishwasher at nap time every day. And sometimes I ran it twice.

Although I wanted to write longer stories for older children, I realized that nap times weren't long enough to do it. I had only an hour or two a day, at most, to work. So I decided to try a picture book. But what would it be about? I seized on the subject closest to me: my children. I had been struck by some of the amusing things they said and did, and began taking notes. These notes eventually grew into a series of short stories about a small boy named Oliver and his baby sister, Amanda.

When I had accumulated five of them, I was ready to send them off to my editor, Phyllis Fogelman, for her reaction. Before I did, however, I had a change of heart about the characters. I had always loved animal stories, and my children did, too. So I decided to change Oliver and Amanda from people to animals. For several days I agonized over what kind of animals they should be. I was very fond of rabbits, but the comfortable chubbiness of pigs appealed to me, too. And while many picture books, most notably *Peter Rabbit,* had featured rabbit characters, very few had been written about pigs. So I decided finally on pigs.

The author and her husband in Vermont on their eighth wedding anniversary, 1976

It happened that Dial Press was about to launch a series of "Easy-to-Read" books for beginning readers, and *Tales of Oliver Pig* was selected as one of the first in the series. I had to revise the manuscript, making everything shorter—words, sentences, entire stories. This was quite a challenge, since I had become accustomed to writing for older children. But I found I enjoyed it. And, thanks to David and Elizabeth, I also found myself full of ideas for new Oliver and Amanda stories. I completed a second book, *More Tales of Oliver Pig,* and made notes for still more books to come.

At this point change entered our lives again. Bruce decided to return to his old job at IBM. The outlook for selling his invention was too uncertain, especially given his new role as a father. The T. J. Watson research facility was located in Yorktown Heights, New York, about thirty-five miles north of New York City. At last we could move from our cramped apartment to a house, where the children would have their own bedrooms and a yard to play in. We found a house in Chappaqua, New York, and moved into it early in the summer of 1977.

At first, the move from city to country was a bit bewildering to our children. David was afraid to set foot in the grass lest he be attacked by bees. And Elizabeth was so unaccustomed to the spaciousness of a house that every time I left her side, she would call out, "Mommy, where are you?" But soon they adjusted and couldn't remember ever having had a previous life.

That fall David entered kindergarten, and Elizabeth attended nursery school, so I was beginning to have more time to write. Again, I was able to undertake longer books. I completed a young-adult novel, *Seems Like This Road Goes On Forever.* Then I went back to more stories about the pig family. Elizabeth had noticed that there were two books about Oliver, but none about Amanda, and thought it was high time for me to write a book starring her. After that, I began another mouse book for older readers. A pattern was beginning to emerge in my work, of mixing picture books with longer novels, animal stories with people stories, humorous books and those with more serious themes. I found the mix refreshing and energizing, and I have continued working in this way through the years.

Our new suburban life brought me close to nature once again. Deer wandered through our yard at night, and raccoons and skunks paid us unexpected visits. A squirrel even dropped down the chimney for a visit, which we didn't find quite as amusing. I planted a garden and hung a bird feeder. The children made friends with other children in the neighborhood, and soon there were bikes in the driveway, forts being constructed under the pine trees, baseball games in the front yard. As they both entered elementary school, they became engaged in even more activities: soccer, Scouts, swimming, piano lessons, ballet.

All of this provided wonderful material for new books. David was the kind of child who always seemed to have one all-consuming interest in his life, from dinosaurs as a four year old through Indians, nature, sports, cartooning, and most recently as a teenager, photography. His enthusiasms were contagious, and he had a knack for doing interesting offbeat things, like opening a nature museum in his room or walking into the office of a local newspaper as a sixth grader and convincing the editor to publish his cartoons. Creative, determined, marching to his own drummer, David has kept us on our toes as parents. And he made a great book character. He was the inspiration for Benjy in *Benjy and the Power of Zingies,* and its two sequels.

Elizabeth is a much different personality: sunny, sensitive to people, and committed to doing her best in anything she undertakes. She, too, has given me story ideas. As a sixth grader she was acutely embarrassed by everything about her family: our rusty old car, her father who actually insisted on *talking* to her friends, and especially me, who did everything imaginable wrong, from having subnormal fashion sense to trying too hard in the parent-child volleyball game at school. This led to the writing of *Dear Mom: You're Ruining My Life.* And I am currently collecting material for a sequel.

Writing is by nature a solitary occupation, one of its few real disadvantages, to my way of thinking. Over the years I have missed the camaraderie of an office, the stimulation of daily contact with other people committed to children's books. And I have also missed editing, which I had found extremely satisfying. A way to bring at least a measure of this back into my life was presented to me soon after we moved to Chappaqua. A writers' workshop for children's books was already in existence in town, led by Ann Tobias, a former Harper editor. Ann planned to return to publishing full-time, and offered the leadership of the group to me. I was delighted at the idea. For the past ten years I have found my involvement with this workshop to be continuously rewarding. I've had the opportunity to discover new talent and attempt to nurture it. I have exercised my editing skills, encouraging writers to revise and revise again. And in a number of cases I have had the great pleasure of seeing manuscripts accepted and careers launched. In my own small way, I feel I am helping to pass the torch to a new writing generation.

*

I am often asked to speak at schools, and I enjoy doing it. For one thing, it allows me not to write for a day and not feel too guilty about it. And it also releases me from my self-imposed solitary confinement to mingle for awhile in the real world. It's fun to meet the actual readers of my books. I always have the feeling of having completed a cycle, seeing at last the thing I created in the hands of those for whom it was created.

One of the questions which I am invariably asked on these occasions is "Where do you get your ideas?" I have thought a lot about this question, because it seems to me it is a bigger one than it appears at first. The girl in the pink sweatshirt in the back row is not just asking what made you think of writing about pigs or mice or sixth graders. There is a puzzlement in the question which goes deeper. What she is really asking, I believe, is "How do you *do* it? How do you keep all those balls in the air? How do you create something out of nothing?"

Creativity is a mysterious process which, after more than twenty years of writing, I still only dimly understand. But it does seem to proceed in an orderly fashion. For me, each book begins with a thunderbolt from the sky. I will be walking along, minding my own business, when suddenly

an idea strikes me. And I know, with a sense of complete conviction, that this is a book.

Once, I was waiting for a light to change on a street corner in New York City, and I glimpsed a teenage boy driving a car that I instinctively felt didn't belong to him. That was it. Some chord was struck, some sense of recognition that seems almost mystical to me. The teenage boy eventually became a teenage girl, the city became the country, but the car remained. And the book became *Seems Like This Road Goes On Forever.*

On another occasion I was having milk and cookies at the kitchen table with my first-grade son after school. David was telling me how he had taken the quarter I'd given him for ice cream and given it to a very large friend, in exchange for punching the nose of the neighborhood bully who'd been tormenting him. Again, I knew instantly that here was a book. And some time later, it was: *Benjy and the Power of Zingies.*

After this initial magical moment, the hard work begins. Invariably, I am in the middle of some other project, so I make a few notes, put them in a folder, and, consciously at least, forget about the idea for a time. However, the subconscious apparently never rests. Though I am not aware of it, the idea continues to simmer inside my head. Every now and then, while I'm out walking or showering or making dinner or doing the laundry, another thought comes to me. It may be about plot or character, or perhaps just a snatch of dialogue. I jot it down and add it to the folder. In this way, usually very slowly, the story begins to accumulate, to take shape and form. And finally, somewhat like a baby chick patiently pecking its way out of the egg, a whole book emerges.

This whole book exists only in my head, however, and on the few scraps of paper in a file folder. It still has to be written. Usually I make an outline then, to organize my thoughts. And then, months or even years after the first idea, I begin to write. Sometimes the writing brings surprises, subsidiary characters who demand to take center stage, or plot turns that don't work and have to be revised. Sometimes major elements of the story need to be rethought. But by and large, this stage is the easy part for me, the fun part. The hard work has already been done.

It used to be that I didn't fully trust this process. I would try to force it or rush it along. But I've learned over the years to be patient. Just as you can't speed up the chick pecking out of the egg, you can't hatch a book until it is ready. And I've also learned to listen to my subconscious. I give it the opportunity to speak to me, on long solitary walks or sometimes long sleepless hours in the middle of the night, and I trust what it has to say.

In December of 1987 I had my fiftieth birthday. As this momentous occasion approached, I found myself growing more and more depressed. I had enjoyed my forties. They had been satisfying, productive, growing years. I didn't want to leave them behind. Becoming fifty seemed to symbolize being over the hill, sliding down to old age. To combat my depression, I organized a birthday celebration, a joint party with three old friends from my single days in New York who were also about to experience this very significant birthday. At some point during the preparations for the party, my feelings underwent a change.

Jean with her husband Bruce, daughter Elizabeth, and son David, Chappaqua, New York, 1986

I realized that reaching fifty was, in fact, cause for celebration. And that the only way to deal with it was to look forward rather than back, to make the years ahead just as productive as the ones behind. Suddenly I was eager for that birthday party.

Now my children are poised on the edge of the nest. One is learning to drive the car. The other has her first job. Soon they will be flying off into their own lives. More change undoubtedly awaits us: a quieter house certainly, perhaps a career change for Bruce, possibly another move. I find that I am unperturbed by this. Wherever we may go, I know that everything I value—and my writing most of all—will go along with me.

Through the years, I have become more and more attached to the simple things, those that endure. I love old houses, flower gardens, stone walls, the spreading arms of aged trees. The smell of bread baking, the sound of Mozart on the radio, the sight of birds fluttering at the feeder outside my kitchen window. Rocky, hilly landscapes that seem unchanged for centuries. Sometimes I think my New England blood is pulling me back to my roots. I am a modest collector of antiques, and I relish the feel of wood that has been polished by many hands. I love sitting at a farm table that served generations of families before ours, sleeping under a patchwork quilt stitched by my great-grandmother, holding a teddy bear loved by a long-ago child.

In my writing, too, I find that I am starting to look backward. I have always been fascinated by history, not the history of big events and dates that I was taught in school, but of people and how they lived. I have written recently about my own childhood. I have ideas of writing about my family history, and perhaps, if I can find the right way to do it, about our country's history.

I receive quite a lot of letters from children. Most of them are complimentary; others contain complaints or suggestions for new books. As an avenue of direct contact with my audience, I treasure them all. One which I received some years ago but have never forgotten came from a ten-year-old girl. She had just finished reading *I Was a 98-Pound Duckling,* and wrote in some detail about what she liked about the book. And then she concluded her letter by

saying: "I am only ten years old. But when I get to be thirteen, I will know what to do."

At the moment I read that, I knew why I was writing books for children.

POSTSCRIPT

Jean Van Leeuwen provided the following update to *SATA* in 2003:

Much has happened in my writing life during the fifteen years that have passed. Perhaps most important has been my acting on a long-time impulse to write about the past. This expansion of my creative field of vision began, as so many literary adventures do, with a trip to my local library.

There, one day in 1990, I happened to come across an adult book about women settlers in Kansas. The book contained actual diaries and letters written by these women more than a hundred and fifty years ago. I picked it up and took it home to read, just for fun. As I read, however, I found myself growing more and more excited. One woman's experience in particular captured my imagination. She wrote that she was so lonely living out there on the plains, far from any neighbors, that she would lie down in the fields with the sheep, just to have some company. Something about that one short statement set off a little light bulb in my head. And I decided to write a book for children about a pioneer family who pack everything they have into a wagon and move west.

I immediately plunged into the research. For the first time since college days, I hung out in the library, taking notes, finding references in books to other sources, tracking down first-person accounts in university libraries and historical societies, talking to librarians there about other possible sources. I found that I loved it! It was like being a detective, one of my early childhood ambitions. It wasn't too long before I had enough material to write a picture book, which I called *Going West*. When the book came out, I was especially pleased to discover that the artist, Thomas Allen, had chosen to illustrate the episode in the story where the mother lies down in the fields with the sheep, just to have some company.

While I was gathering all of this background information for *Going West,* I came across something else which fascinated me: tales of pioneers who traveled farther west on the Oregon Trail. Once again, I was hooked. What fun it would be to write a longer story, this one based on the diaries that many travelers kept as they rode west. And how exciting if I could find a diary written by a child. Perhaps it could even be published just as written. I put my new detective skills to work locating this kind of material, and soon my desk was stacked high with copies of old diaries. Some were written by men, some by women. But sadly, I couldn't find a single one that had been written by a child.

I was close to giving up on my idea when, by chance, I stumbled upon a little book called *On to Oregon*. Originally published in an Idaho newspaper in the early nineteen hundreds, it was told from the point of view of a nine-year-old girl, Mary Ellen Todd. She had traveled with her family from their home in Arkansas out to Oregon in 1852. This wasn't a diary but a reminiscence, written down years later. And it wasn't even written by Mary Ellen herself, but by

David and Elizabeth, 1996

her daughter, who had heard over and over again her mother's tales of the Oregon Trail during her childhood. Still, this was an exciting discovery. Mary Ellen's journey had been filled with adventure and hardship, and it was described in detail that made me almost feel I was traveling alongside her. The only problem was the writing style, which was so old-fashioned that I felt it would put off today's readers. So I decided to retell her story, keeping all of the true events but adding background details, dialogue, and descriptive action to make it more immediate and appealing.

In order to feel confident enough to write about the Oregon Trail, I had to do a lot more research. While I couldn't travel the entire route of the Oregon Trail, I could go to Oregon. There I spent many hours at the Oregon Historical Society. I went to museums where I could look at and sometimes touch a genuine old wagon, a water bucket, a sunbonnet, a cooking pot. I visited places along the trail where I could see the remnants of wagon wheel ruts, as well as the too-steep mountains which the family had to climb and then descend in a wagon pulled by half-dead oxen. With some difficulty, I managed to locate the beautiful valley where the Todd family first settled when they arrived in Oregon after six months of hard traveling.

Only after seeing all of these artifacts did I feel ready to tell Mary Ellen's story.

This book, retitled *Bound for Oregon,* was published in 1994. An interesting postscript to the story came when, a couple of years later, I received a letter from a descendent of the Todd family. He and I began corresponding, and he told me much about what happened to the family after their arrival in Oregon. Mary Ellen's father established a pottery business, as he had in Arkansas. The family moved from their first cabin to another. My new friend discovered the location where this cabin had stood, and visited the site. And one day I received a mysterious package with an Oregon postmark. Opening it, I found some broken fragments of pottery—pottery which Mary Ellen's father had made! My friend had located the site of his kiln and, digging into the surrounding earth, uncovered these bits of the past. I was amazed, and thrilled to have such a wonderful souvenir of this book. I keep those little pieces of pottery on my desk to this day for inspiration.

Since *Bound for Oregon,* I have continued to write books of historical fiction. In the picture-book format, I have written about the Mayflower journey in *Across the Wide Dark Sea.* I told of a holiday celebration on the Oregon Trail in *A Fourth of July on the Plains.* I wrote about settling the Ohio wilderness in *Nothing Here But Trees*. And, most recently, I recounted the story of the first person to go up in a hot-air balloon in America (a thirteen-year-old boy) in *The Amazing Air Balloon*. I continue to be fascinated by the stories of pioneers, whose dogged determination, faith, and courage tamed the vast wilderness that was once America. I tell their stories in the first person, trying to present them in as immediate a way as I can so that modern-day readers can share the feelings of these long-ago children.

I have also written a trilogy of books for slightly older readers about the American Revolution. This project began with the realization that a good deal of the history of those tumultuous times took place right in my own neighborhood of Westchester County, New York, and nearby Connecticut. George Washington had headquarters in White Plains, a town not far from mine. Battles were fought there. And towns along the Connecticut coast had been attacked by the British after they captured New York City. Once again, I went to the library and began to read.

My reading soon led me to the historical society in Fairfield, Connecticut. This old town also happened to be the home of my Aunt Ruthie, the same aunt who had long ago given me gifts of classic children's books. Sitting in the library of the historical society, I read first-person accounts of the burning of the town by the British in 1779. And right away, I knew I had a story to tell.

It seemed fitting that this project should involve my now-elderly aunt. She had always been such an enthusiastic supporter of my writing, distributing my books to all her friends. Now I could visit her at the same time I spent hours poring over books, magazines, newspaper clippings, maps, and files of old papers at the Fairfield Historical Society. As with *Bound for Oregon*, I didn't feel satisfied just reading about the time period. I needed to know first-hand about all the activities that a Colonial-period family would engage in, like spinning, dyeing and weaving wool, cooking, candle-making, sheep-shearing, using herbal medicine, caring for farm animals. Soon I was attending demonstrations of Colonial crafts. I tried my hand at spinning and dyeing and candle-making. I visited a restored house which had stood in Fairfield since before the Revolution. I took a tour of a demonstration farm along with a group of nursery-school children, gathering eggs and holding a baby lamb in my arms. And I asked a lot of questions. The research for the first book, *Hannah of Fairfield*, took longer than the actual writing. Fortunately, the second and third volumes, *Hannah's Helping Hands* and *Hannah's Winter of Hope,* went a little faster.

I have not been concentrating solely on historical fiction, however. As I always did in the past, I continue to mix up the kinds of books I write. Over the years, I have steadily added to my "Oliver and Amanda Pig" series. Although my children are no longer the direct inspiration they once were, I find that some little everyday event—a child's remark overheard in the supermarket, a snowstorm, a glimpse of children selling lemonade on a street corner—will trigger memories of my family's past which slowly grow into stories. After each of these books is written, I am convinced that I'll never have an idea for another. But, thankfully, they keep on coming.

On a recent visit to an elementary school, I talked to a group of second-graders about my "Oliver and Amanda

Pig" books. A couple of weeks later, I received in the mail some of the children's own writing efforts. Their topic was their favorite toy. One boy wrote about a treasured Batman cape. As I read his composition, my mind flashed back to my own son's Batman cape, which I had made from a fragment of blue cloth and which he'd worn seemingly constantly during his super-hero period when he was four or five. It had been part of his Halloween costume two years in a row. I had nearly forgotten about it, but now, suddenly, it loomed large. My mind was flooded with memories of David saving the world in that cape. And, thanks to this unexpected memory jog, I knew right away that I would write an Oliver Pig book about it.

Along with the "Oliver and Amanda Pig" books, I have also published picture books like *Emma Bean, The Tickle Stories*, and *Sorry,* as well as contemporary novels such as *Blue Sky, Butterfly* and *Lucy Was There* . . . . I enjoy the change from a serious story to a humorous one, from a picture book to a novel, from animals to human characters, from the past to the present. After digging through all the research material necessary to write about Connecticut in the eighteenth century or Oregon in the nineteenth, it is quite a relief to come back to the twenty-first century. And, after writing a picture book or a contemporary novel, I can't wait to once again journey into the past.

Two of my most recent books demonstrate this point perfectly. Back in 1969, I published my first book for older readers, *The Great Cheese Conspiracy*. Since then, three more books have come out about my mouse heroes, Marvin, Raymond, and Fats. I had great fun writing these comic fantasies, as it was a chance to let my imagination run wild and think of crazy adventures for the New York City mice, like riding on a kite over Central Park or marching in a parade down Fifth Avenue. Every time I wrote one, I would get letters from readers suggesting creative ideas for their further adventures. For some time, I had been thinking of and making notes for a new story, this one to take place in an art museum. But it took a batch of letters from some schoolchildren in Oklahoma to apply the

Jean and Bruce, 2003

spark of inspiration that got me started on the book. Even for a book like this, I had to do research—kind of odd research, I have to admit. I hung around the Guggenheim Museum trying to view it through the eyes of a mouse. I studied the pigeons in Central Park in preparation for a little mouse vs. pigeon skirmish I had in mind. I learned all about Rollerblades, though this time I wasn't brave enough to try them myself. And I came up with another comic tale, *The Great Googlestein Museum Mystery*, in which one member of the mouse gang becomes an acclaimed artist.

Right after finishing this book, I embarked on another historical novel. This one, like *Going West*, came out of my reading about the settlement of the west. In this case, the location was the dense forests of Ohio. And like that first book, it was just the briefest mention of a true incident which inspired me. Two boys are left alone in a half-built cabin while their father goes back east to bring out the rest of the family. The father does not return. The boys have to find ways to survive on their own for many months. That was all the information I had. But once again, this little glimpse into the pioneer past captured my imagination. This time, however, I knew I had a bigger challenge to take on. Since I had little knowledge either of survival skills or of early-nineteenth-century Ohio, I would have to do double research. This research, which has gone on for the past year, has taken me on an intriguing journey, along winding trails that led through the library and the internet and historical societies and on to nature centers and camping stores and into the woods. As with any detective work, detours along the way sometimes brought me to abrupt dead ends and other times to exciting discoveries. It has been quite a trip. And it was a thrill to learn from the survival expert who read the completed manuscript that I'd gotten most—though not all—things right.

True to form, I am resting now from my strenuous research labors. I have been working on a new story about Amanda Pig. And just recently I had a new idea for a short, contemporary novel. It is gestating at the moment, my scribbled notes for it accumulating in a file folder. Hopefully, some day soon the voice of the main character will begin speaking inside my head, the first sentence of this new story will announce itself, and the writing will begin. This is the way my writing life goes and, I hope, will continue to go.

Since my husband retired a few years ago and our children have moved on to their own lives, it has been fairly quiet at our house. My Aunt Ruthie passed away three years ago, followed soon after by my mother, her sister. I miss them both, along with their connection to my past. I continue to enjoy running a writers' workshop and speaking at schools about my work. I also volunteer at the elementary school which my children attended, helping first-graders with their own writing. Besides being fun and rewarding, this helps me keep in touch with what is going on inside the heads of six-year-olds these days.

And one more thing. My son David, former Oliver Pig and long-time cartoonist, has written and illustrated his first children's book, *Hector and the Noisy Neighbor,* due to be published in 2004. This makes me very proud.

W

WALLACE, Ian 1950-

Personal

Born March 31, 1950, in Niagara Falls, Ontario, Canada; son of Robert Amiens and Kathleen (Watts) Wallace; married Debra Wiedman. *Education:* Graduated from Ontario College of Art, 1973; graduate studies, 1973-74. *Hobbies and other interests:* Walking, movies, travel, dining out.

Addresses

Home—184 Major St., Toronto, Ontario, Canada M5S 2L3.

Career

Writer and illustrator of children's books. Staff writer and illustrator for Kids Can Press, 1974-76; Art Gallery of Ontario, Toronto, information officer, 1976-80. Artist. *Exhibitions:* "Chin Chiang and the Dragon's Dance," Art Gallery of Ontario, 1986; "Once upon a Time," Vancouver Art Gallery, 1988; "Canada at Bologna," Bologna Children's Book Fair, 1990.

Member

Writers Union of Canada, Canadian Children's Book Centre, Canadian Society of Children's Authors, Illustrators and Performers (CANSCAIP).

Awards, Honors

Runner-up for City of Toronto Book Awards, 1976, "Our Choice" Selection, Children's Book Centre, 1977-81, Canada Council grants, 1980, 1981, 1983, 1986, 1987, Imperial Order of Daughters of the Empire (IODE) Book Award, 1984, Amelia Frances Howard-Gibbon Illustrator's Award, 1984, International Board on Books for Young People Honor List citation, 1986, all for *Chin Chiang and the Dragon's Dance;* Ontario Arts Council grants, 1985, 1988; American Library

Ian Wallace

Association Notable Book citation, 1987, and White Raven Award, International Youth Library, 1987, both for *Very Last First Time;* Mr. Christie Award and Elizabeth Mrazik Cleaver Award, both for *The Name of the Tree;* nominee from Canada for Hans Christian Anderson medal (illustration), 1994; Gibbon Medal short list, 1994, for *Hansel & Gretel;* IODE Book Award, 1997, for *A Winter's Tale;* and Smithsonian Notable Book, 1999, and IBBY Honour Book, 2000, both for *Boy of the Deeps.*

Writings

JUVENILE

Julie News (self-illustrated), Kids Can Press (Toronto, Ontario, Canada), 1974.

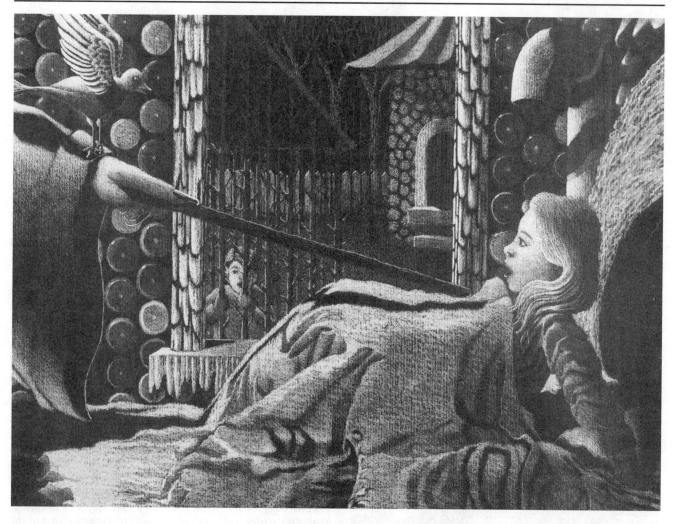

Wallace sets his self-illustrated retelling of **Hansel** *and* **Gretel** *on the Atlantic coast of North America.*

(With Angela Wood) *The Sandwich,* Kids Can Press (Toronto, Ontario, Canada), 1975, revised edition, 1985.

The Christmas Tree House (self-illustrated), Kids Can Press (Toronto, Ontario, Canada), 1976.

Chin Chiang and the Dragon's Dance (self-illustrated), Atheneum (New York, NY), 1984.

The Sparrow's Song (self-illustrated), Viking (New York, NY), 1986.

Morgan the Magnificent (self-illustrated), Macmillan (New York, NY), 1987.

Mr. Kneebone's New Digs (self-illustrated), Groundwood (Toronto, Ontario, Canada), 1991.

(Reteller) Brothers Grimm, *Hansel and Gretel* (self-illustrated), Groundwood (Toronto, Ontario, Canada), 1994.

A Winter's Tale (self-illustrated), Groundwood (Toronto, Ontario, Canada), 1997.

Boy of the Deeps (self-illustrated), DK Ink (New York, NY), 1999.

Duncan's Way (self-illustrated), DK Ink (New York, NY), 2000.

The True Story of Trapper Jack's Left Big Toe (self-illustrated), Groundwood (Toronto, Ontario, Canada), 2002.

The Naked Lady (self-illustrated), Roaring Brook Press (Brookfield, CT), 2002.

ILLUSTRATOR

Jan Andrews, *Very Last First Time,* Atheneum (New York, NY), 1985, Groundwood Books (Toronto, Ontario, Canada), 2003, published as *Eva's Ice Adventure,* Methuen (London, England), 1986.

Tim Wynne-Jones, *Architect of the Moon,* Groundwood Books (Toronto, Ontario, Canada), 1988, published as *Builder of the Moon,* Macmillan (New York, NY), 1989.

Celia Barker Lottridge, *The Name of the Tree: A Bantu Folktale,* Macmillan (New York, NY), 1990.

Teddy Jam, *The Year of the Fire,* Macmillan (New York, NY), 1993.

Bud Davidge, *The Mummer's Song,* Orchard Books (New York, NY), 1994.

W. D. Valgardson, *Sarah and the People of Sand River,* Groundwood (Toronto, Ontario, Canada), 1996.

Contributor to periodicals, including *Canadian Books for Young People.*

Sidelights

Canadian author/illustrator Ian Wallace has produced a number of award-winning self-illustrated picture books, including *Chin Chiang and the Dragon's Dance, Morgan the Magnificent, A Winter's Tale, Boy of the Deeps,* and *Duncan's Way.* One of Wallace's major themes is "the initiation process by which a child moves to understanding of self and the larger world," according to a contributor for *St. James Guide to Children's Writers.* Dealing with subjects such as young boys and girls from a variety of social and ethnic backgrounds who are on the cusp of growing up, as well as with the aged poor in his own books, Wallace also is a talented illustrator of the works of other writers such as Tim Wynne-Jones. In a profile of the author/writer in *Language Arts,* Jon C. Stott noted, "As admirers of Ian Wallace's books know, they're not only beautiful and engaging, they're very carefully planned and structured. Reading one of them is a total experience."

Born on the Canadian side of Niagara Falls in 1950, Wallace spent peaceful Sunday afternoons on family road trips, seeing how many trees of a certain species or how many cows he could count. "My first exposure to the world of art came not through pictures hung on gallery and museum walls," Wallace once told *SATA,* "but through the picture books my brothers and I carted out of our local library." The stories he encountered in

On her first winter camping trip with her father and brother, Abigail comes up with a way to save a fawn tangled in fishing line in Wallace's self-illustrated work A Winter's Tale.

these books transported him out of provincial Ontario to exotic and not so exotic locales around the world. One of his favorite books from those years is *Wind in the Willows* by Kenneth Grahame, and the image of Toad flying along in his orange bi-plane. "Just as important," Wallace continued to *SATA,* "[these books] made us keenly aware of the fact that a painter was not merely somebody who, like our father, picked up a brush or roller and stroked or rolled it over the walls of our house whenever the rooms had grown tired around the edges. But rather, an artist was someone who made dreams real." By age thirteen, Wallace had decided that he wanted to be one such person himself. From a simple declaration, the impulse to become an artist continued to grow through Wallace's teenage years, in part nourished by his parents, and he spent hours alone with pencil and paper learning how to sketch.

After attending the Ontario College of Art, Wallace worked as a staff writer and illustrator for a Canadian children's book publisher. Ultimately such work led him to trying his hand at his own titles; *The Sandwich* and *The Christmas Tree House* are two early examples of his picture book work. In the former title, young Vincenzo despairs about being teased for eating a mortadella and provolone sandwich, but is reassured by his father that it is okay to be different. Nick and his friend Gloria discover a tree house in *The Christmas Tree House,* and they think it is the work of Don Valley Rose, who everyone figures is an evil old witch. However, when Nick makes friends with the old eccentric, he learns that she is actually a kind person. Reviewing the artwork in that book, Stott commented that the "greypencil illustrations suggest the wintry settings and create a luminous quality which reflects the warmth of new friendship the children experience."

Chin Chiang and the Dragon's Dance, Wallace's next title, was six years in the works. "I cannot stress enough the value of time," Wallace told *SATA.* "Time to allow the right words to come forth, time to allow the drawings to formulate in the head before they appear on the paper, and time to allow both to be as polished as a piece of rare jade." *Chin Chiang* is the story of a young boy who wants to participate in the Chinese New Year celebrations for the Year of the Dragon, yet his stage fright gets in the way. The boy is getting ready for his first dragon dance, but his shyness sends him fleeing the street and his grandfather for the rooftop of the local library. Here he meets an old lady named Pu Yee who assists him in learning the steps to the dance without him even knowing it. He is then able to return and take part in the dance and his place in his own cultural heritage, his fears of failure left behind.

Wallace's years of work paid off; critics were full of praise and the picture book won numerous awards. Writing in the *Globe and Mail,* Sandra Martin lauded the "astonishing panoply of 16 watercolor paintings" which are "subtle yet brilliantly colored." Martin was so impressed with the "authenticity and meticulous care" of the artwork that she remarked the illustrations "speak eloquently of centuries of Chinese heritage transplanted onto the Canadian West coast." Mingshoi Cai, writing in *Children's Literature in Education,* felt that same title "captures the spirit of young people who try to carry on the cultural tradition," while Lee Galda, writing in the *Reading Teacher,* praised the manner in which the book "explodes with a cacophony of sound and a crescendo-ing intensity of brilliant colours, resplendent with exquisite details of Westcoast Chinese culture."

The Sparrow's Song, Wallace's next self-illustrated title, is set in the Niagara Falls region where the artist grew up, but is transposed to the early years of the 20th century. Young Charles kills a sparrow and his sister Katie takes care of the baby sparrow left motherless by this cruel act. Together they both learn important lessons: she of forgiveness, and he of repentance, as they work together gathering food for the fledgling and teach it to fly. Carole Gerson, reviewing the book in *Canadian Children's Literature,* noted that "text and illustrations interact magically" in this picture book. The contributor for *St. James Guide to Children's Writers* also praised Wallace's "free flowing depictions of water, rocks, and trees [that] symbolize the ever-changing panorama of nature." Several reviewers also commented on the background of the gorge and Niagara falls in the illustrations which acts like a spiritual power for the young children.

The circus is the inspiration for *Morgan the Magnificent,* the tale of another little child, like Chin, frozen by stage fright. Morgan lives alone with her single father and dreams of being a circus performer, using the beams in the barn for her tightrope-walking stage. One day she sneaks off to the circus and into the tent of the star aerialist, Anastasia. There she puts on the woman's costume and climbs up to the highwire only to be petrified once she realizes what she has done and where she is. Ultimately saved by Anastasia and cajoled into performing her own act, Morgan is wiser at the end of her adventure, for she understands both her strengths and limitations. Wallace employs various viewpoints in his illustrations in order to bring the viewer into the action of the story, both from the perspective of the highwire itself looking down, and from the spectator on the ground looking up. Catherine Sheldrick Ross, reviewing *Morgan the Magnificent* in *Canadian Literature,* called attention to the "spare and dramatic" text, and to the fact that Wallace's golden-hued pictures "do not so much illustrate the text as extend and enrich it." Ulrike Walker, writing in *Canadian Children's Literature,* similarly found that the title is an "excellent, meticulous-ly designed picture book." Walker also commented on the happy ending, brought about with the help of Anastasia: "The secure 'reality' of the father's farm world is happily mingled with Morgan's own dream world," Walker wrote.

During much of the late 1980s, Wallace concentrated on illustrating the books of others, including *Architect of the Moon* by Wynne-Jones, the Bantu tale, *The Name of the Tree,* Teddy Jam's *The Year of the Fire,* and Bud Davidge's *The Mummer's Song.* Reviewing *The Name of the Tree* in *Reading Teacher,* Galda praised Wallace's

New to the Yukon, Josh sets out to get a look at Trapper Jack's tenth toe, allegedly kept in an empty tobacco tin at the Sourdough Saloon. (From The True Story of Trapper Jack's Left Big Toe, *written and illustrated by Wallace.)*

artwork, which works "beautifully to convey the mood of intense heat." According to Denia Lewis Hester in a *School Library Journal* review of that same title, "Wallace masterfully utilizes muted pinks, grays, and greens that bring to life the cracked, dry land that threatens the animals' very existence."

With the 1991 *Mr. Kneebone's New Digs,* Wallace returns to a theme initially worked in *The Christmas Tree,* namely the situation of the elderly poor in an urban environment. April Moth lives in a miserable one-room flat with her dog, Mr. Kneebone. She grows so disgusted with the rat-infested place that she sets off to find better lodgings, and ends up in a cave in the park, at least safe from the big buildings of the city. She at last has found a bit of independence in the city, but it is a fragile independence. Lynn Wytenbroek, writing in *Canadian Literature,* praised Wallace's "wonderful pastel pictures ... [which] help make the book come alive." Annette Goldsmith, writing in *Quill and Quire,* also commented on the "quite lovely" illustrations, but was less im-pressed with the book as a whole, calling it a "disap-pointment" for long-time fans. Theo Hersh, however, found more to like in the book in a *Canadian Materials* review, describing the artwork as "among Wallace's best," and further remarking that the "complex, unset-tling book" was both "unusual" and "wonderful."

Adapting the work of the Brother's Grimm, Wallace provides his own take on a classic fairy tale in *Hansel and Gretel*, a work that "may well be his most ambitious book," according to Raymond E. Jones and Jon C. Stott in *Canadian Children's Books: A Critical Guide to Authors and Illustrators*. The same authors pointed out that with so many retellings of this classic tale, "the creator of a new version faces the challenge of providing pictures that both enhance the traditional meanings of the story and communicate new ones. Wallace succeeds admirably on both counts." Wallace's retelling remains true to the original tale in spirit, but does modernize and localize parts of it, making the father a poor Atlantic Coast fisherman. Jones and Stott found the illustrations for this book "the darkest of any in Wallace's books." Reviewing *Hansel and Gretel* in *Booklist*, Hazel Rochman found the retelling "sinister but not gruesome." *School Library Journal*'s Judith Constantinides called the book a "brooding, surrealistic version of the classic

fairy tale" and a "distinguished book to savor." Similarly, Patty Lawlor, reviewing the same title in *Quill and Quire*, concluded that "Wallace offers readers the opportunity to experience *Hansel and Gretel* in an intriguing and provocative picture-book format."

More uplifting material is presented in *A Winter's Tale* in which nine-year-old Abigail takes her first winter camping trip with her father and in the process helps to save a trapped fawn. *Booklist*'s Linda Perkins found that "the story is a successful vehicle for Wallace's exquisite art," while Audrey Laski, writing in *School Librarian*, called it an "enchanting picture story." Deborah Stevenson, reviewing the work in *Bulletin of the Center for Children's Books*, thought the tale was "appealing," and a "rare outdoor rite-of-passage story about a girl." A young boy has his own rite of passage in *Boy of the Deeps*, in which young James goes to his first day of work in the Nova Scotian coal mines at the turn of the

In Wallace's self-illustrated **The Naked Lady**, *Tom Sims is introduced to the wonderful world of art when he befriends a sculptor who moves in next door.*

20th century. This momentous day is made even more dramatic with a cave-in, which traps the boy and his father far beneath the earth. A reviewer for *Publishers Weekly* felt that Wallace's "taut yet descriptive narrative appeals to the senses," while *Booklist*'s Rochman noted that the illustrations in shades of "black, brown, and blue are lit with the flickering glow of miners' lamps in the dark." *Quill and Quire*'s Hadley Dyer remarked that "Wallace is one of the few children's book illustrators unafraid to let sombre colours dominate," and went on to conclude that the book would appeal to anyone who appreciates that "rare combination of fine writing and illustration."

Another adolescent boy is featured in *Duncan's Way,* which recounts the way in which a boy helps his out-of-work father. Duncan's family have long been fishermen in Newfoundland, but now the cod are not plentiful and after eighteen months of unemployment, something needs to be done. Duncan suddenly hits on the idea of using the family boat as a floating delivery van for a bakery. Linda Ludke, reviewing the work in *School Library Journal,* praised both the artwork, which "capture[s] the beauty of the landscape," and the text, which "eloquently conveys Duncan's anxiety." A contributor for *Publishers Weekly* also commended this simple tale: "Wallace creates some memorable portraits within this larger picture of a vanishing way of life."

Another rite of passage is served up in *The True Story of Trapper Jack's Left Big Toe,* set in the Yukon Territory. Josh and Gabe hear that a local trapper's amputated toe resides in a tobacco tin in the town's saloon, and conspire to get a look at it. First, however, they run into the trapper himself, who explains how his toe came to be frostbitten and subsequently amputated, and then he takes the youths to the saloon himself so they can get a look at it. A contributor for *Kirkus Reviews* called this a "great" and "well-paced" story. *Horn Book*'s Betty Carter likewise praised the "fast-moving plot and ample dialogue." Linda Berezowsk, writing in *Resource Links,* found that Wallace's illustrations "complement the script and provide a strong visual setting for the story," and Lauren Peterson of *Booklist* also praised the artwork, noting that Wallace "adds to the fun [of this tall tale] with nicely rendered, superrealistic illustrations." And a contributor for *Publishers Weekly* called the book a "wry and absorbing initiation story."

In the 2002 publication, *The Naked Lady,* Wallace tells the semi-autobiographical story of his own beginnings as an artist. Young Tom takes a welcoming pie to the new neighbor, Pieter, and is shocked to see a statue of a naked lady in the man's yard. When the widowed sculptor informs Tom the statue is nude rather than naked, a friendship and mentorship begins between the lonely older man and the inquisitive farm boy, reflecting Wallace's own first teacher-student relationship as an artist. Reviewers responded warmly to this tribute. A contributor for *Publishers Weekly* applauded the "clean lines and uncluttered composition" of the artwork which in turn "reflect[s] the directness and economy of the prose." The same reviewer called the book a "heartfelt

tribute to the important role of mentors in any artist's life." Carolyn Janssen, reviewing the book in *School Library Journal,* likewise found the story to be "inspiring" as well as "appealing and enriching." And a contributor for *Kirkus Reviews* dubbed the tale "haunting" and "beautifully written and illustrated."

In an article for *Five Owls,* Wallace described his illustration process, and the importance of patience. "I always wait for the moment of revelation when I can smell the characters' blood in the media I am using, when I can see the tracks their history has left on the paper's tooth, and when I can watch them climb out of the dark and into the light of my studio. When that moment comes, I can finally say, 'So *that's* what that character or that situation is all about!'"

Jones and Stott concluded that Wallace is "one of Canada's major picture-book artists," and that his books "present a significant and strong vision of life. They emphasize not only the individual's successful quest for self-worth, but also the importance of individuals understanding themselves in relation to family, friends, community, tradition, and the powerful world of nature of which they are a part." Writing in *St. James Guide to Children's Writers,* Wallace explained his mission as a children's book author and illustrator. "In my work as an author I do not sit down to write stories, nor do I consciously choose stories to illustrate because they will be distinguished as being multi-cultural or Canadian or whatever flag one chooses to wave over them. I write or illustrate stories because first and foremost they are stories that will intrigue, inspire, and touch young readers. The characters who inhabit these tales are people who have earned my sympathy and are ones with whom I can empathize on a personal level. They are universal characters with universal emotions and universal experiences that make us human. They are characters who struggle, who test limits, and who endure. But most importantly they are characters who through the story go through some kind of change. At the end of a good story, a reader comes away with the confidence that the protagonist will never be the same and will treasure the memory. It is my hope that the reader of my books will never be the same either."

Biographical and Critical Sources

BOOKS

Children's Literature Review, Volume 37, Gale (Detroit, MI), 1996.

Continuum Encyclopedia of Children's Literature, edited by Bernice E. Cullinan and Diane G. Person, Continuum International (New York, NY), 2001.

Jones, Raymond E., and Jon C. Scott, *Canadian Children's Books: A Critical Guide to Authors and Illustrators,* Oxford University Press (Toronto, Ontario, Canada), 2000, pp. 459-565.

St. James Guide to Children's Writers, edited by Sara Pendergast and Tom Pendergast, St. James Press (Detroit, MI), 1999.

Writers on Writing, Overlea House (Toronto, Ontario, Canada), 1989.

PERIODICALS

Booklist, June 1, 1996, Hazel Rochman, review of *Hansel and Gretel,* p. 1729; November 1, 1996, Carolyn Phelan, review of *Sarah and the People of Sand River,* p. 496; October 15, 1997, Linda Perkins, review of *A Winter's Tale,* p. 417; March 15, 1999, Hazel Rochman, review of *Boy of the Deeps,* p. 1336; February 15, 2000, Susan Dove Lempke, review of *Duncan's Way,* p. 1122; June 1, 2002, Lauren Peterson, review of *The True Story of Trapper Jack's Left Big Toe,* p. 1744.

Bulletin of the Center for Children's Books, January, 1998, Deborah Stevenson, review of *A Winter's Tale,* p. 180.

Canadian Children's Literature, no. 57-58, 1990, Carole Gerson, review of *The Sparrow's Song,* pp. 135-136; no. 60, 1990, Ulrike Walker, review of *Morgan the Magnificent,* pp. 113-114.

Canadian Literature, autumn, 1989, Catherine Sheldrick Ross, review of *Morgan the Magnificent,* pp. 246-247; autumn, 1992, Lynn Wytenbroek, review of *Mr. Kneebone's New Digs,* p. 162.

Canadian Materials, May, 1991, Joan McGrath, "Making Friends," pp. 153-156; March, 1992, Theo Hersh, review of *Mr. Kneebone's New Digs,* p. 85.

Children's Literature in Education, September, 1994, Mingshoi Cai, review of *Chin Chiang and the Dragon's Dance,* p. 169.

Emergency Librarian, September, 1990, review of *Chin Chiang and the Dragon's Dance,* p. 51.

Five Owls, May-June, 1999, Ian Wallace, "Waiting for the Raven," pp. 102-103.

Globe and Mail (Toronto, Ontario, Canada), August 4, 1984, Sandra Martin, review of *Chin Chiang and the Dragon's Dance;* November 1, 1986.

Horn Book, May-June, 2002, Betty Carter, review of *The True Story of Trapper Jack's Left Big Toe,* p. 323.

Horn Book Guide, spring, 2001, Carolyn Shute, review of *Duncan's Way,* p. 52.

Kirkus Reviews, March 15, 1999, review of *Boy of the Deeps,* pp. 458-459; April 1, 2002, review of *The True Story of Trapper Jack's Left Big Toe,* p. 501; October 1, 2002, review of *The Naked Lady,* p. 1483.

Language Arts, April, 1989, Jon C. Stott, "Profile: Ian Wallace," pp. 443-449.

Maclean's, December 9, 2002, review of *The Naked Lady,* p. 77.

Publishers Weekly, September 23, 1996, review of *Sarah and the People of Sand River,* p. 76; April 26, 1999, review of *Boy of the Deeps,* p. 83; March 6, 2000, review of *Duncan's Way,* p. 110; March 18, 2002, review of *The True Story of Trapper Jack's Left Big Toe,* p. 104; November 11, 2002, review of *The Naked Lady,* p. 63.

Quill and Quire, November, 1991, Annette Goldsmith, review of *The Name of the Tree,* p. 26; October, 1994, Patty Lawlor, review of *Hansel and Gretel,* pp. 40-41; March, 1999, Hadley Dyer, review of *Boy of the Deeps,* p. 67.

Reading Teacher, February, 1991, Lee Galda, review of *The Name of the Tree,* p. 411; April, 1992, Lee Galda, review of *Chin Chiang and the Dragon's Dance,* p. 635.

Resource Links, April, 2001, review of *Duncan's Way,* p. 49; June, 2002, Linda Berezowsk, review of *The True Story of Trapper Jack's Left Big Toe,* pp. 8-10.

School Librarian, spring, 1998, Audrey Laski, review of *A Winter's Tale,* p. 37.

School Library Journal, March, 1990, Denia Lewis Hester, review of *The Name of the Tree,* p. 209; June, 1990, p. 80; May, 1996, Judith Constantinides, review of *Hansel and Gretel,* p. 104; December, 1996, Sally R. Dow, review of *Sarah and the People of Sand River,* p. 108; December, 1997, Patricia Manning, review of *A Winter's Tale,* p. 102; July, 1999, Kathleen Whalin, review of *Boy of the Deeps,* p. 82; March, 2000, Linda Ludke, review of *Duncan's Way,* p. 219; April, 2002, Beth Tegart, review of *The True Story of Trapper Jack's Left Big Toe,* p. 159; November, 2002, Carolyn Janssen, review of *The Naked Lady,* p. 139.

OTHER

Meet the Author/Illustrator: Ian Wallace (videotape), Meade Education Services, 1990.

* * *

WALLACE, Nancy Elizabeth 1948-

Personal

Born May 16, 1948, in Bronx, NY; daughter of John and Alexine Wallace; married Peter E. Banks (a high school teacher). *Education:* University of Connecticut, B.A., M.A. *Hobbies and other interests:* Sailing, camping, theater, museums, gardening, bike riding.

Addresses

Agent—Sterling Lord Literistic, 65 Bleecker St., New York, NY 10012.

Career

Author. Yale-New Haven Hospital, New Haven, CT, director of Volunteer Services, coordinator of Child Life Program, preschool teacher, day care teacher, consultant, 1972-92. Volunteer of ABC—A Better Chance and Read to Grow, a Connecticut literacy program.

Member

Society of Children's Book Writers and Illustrators.

Awards, Honors

Honors award, National Parenting Publications, featured selection, Children's Book of the Month Club, both 1995, both for *Snow;* Featured selection, Children's Book of the Month Club, 1999, Gold award, Oppenheim Toy Portfolio, 2000, both for *Rabbit's Bedtime;* Featured selection, Junior Library Guild, 2000, for *Tell-a-Bunny;* Best Book of the Year citation, Bank Street College of Education, 2000, for *Apples, Apples, Apples;* Best Book of the Year citation, Bank Street College of Education, 2001, for *Count Down to Clean Clean Up!;* Foreword

Press award, 2001 for *A Taste of Honey;* original art and writing materials included in archives of the Northeast Children's Literature Collection, the Dodd Center, University of Connecticut.

Writings

SELF-ILLUSTRATED PICTURE BOOKS

Snow, Golden Books (New York, NY), 1995.

Rabbit's Bedtime, Houghton Mifflin (Boston, MA), 1999, Spanish translation by Annie Garcia Kaplan published as *Hora de dormir del conejo/Rabbit's Bedtime* (bilingual edition), Houghton Mifflin (Boston, MA), 2000.

Tell-a-Bunny, Winslow Press (Delray Beach, FL), 2000.

Apples, Apples, Apples, Winslow Press (Delray Beach, FL), 2000.

Paperwhite, Houghton Mifflin (Boston, MA), 2000.

A Taste of Honey, Winslow Press (Delray Beach, FL), 2001.

Count Down to Clean Up!, Houghton Mifflin (Boston, MA), 2001.

Pumpkin Day!, Marshall Cavendish (Tarrytown, NY), 2002.

Recycle Every Day!, Marshall Cavendish (Tarrytown, NY), 2003.

Baby Day!, Houghton Mifflin (Boston, MA), 2003.

The Sun, the Moon and the Stars, Houghton Mifflin (Boston, MA), 2003.

Leaves, Leaves, Leaves, Marshall Cavendish (Tarrytown, NY), 2003.

Work in Progress

Seeds, Seeds, Seeds, Marshall Cavendish (Tarrytown, NY), 2004.

Sidelights

Nancy Elizabeth Wallace told *SATA:* "I keep a quote by Joseph Campbell on my desk, 'If you follow your bliss, you put yourself on a kind of track that has been there the whole while, waiting for you, and the life that you ought to be living is the one you are living.'

"I had worked for years at Yale-New Haven Hospital (YNHH) on Pediatrics as a child-life specialist (therapeutic play) and coordinator of the program. We used play, art, music, creative writing, medical play, and puppetry to help infants, toddlers, preschool and school-age children, and adolescents to cope with the stress of being in the hospital. These experiences gave children an important sense of normalcy, choice, and control, and the opportunity to express their thoughts, fears, fantasies, and misconceptions. In this acute care setting, we worked with pediatric patients with burns, cardiac problems, spinal column injuries, cancer, and cystic fibrosis. I prepared children for surgery, medical tests, even to have limbs amputated; and provided play for children up to within hours of their death. I burned out.

"Next came Volunteer Services, administering the YNHH program with over one thousand volunteers,

Nancy Elizabeth Wallace

many in highly sophisticated patient support and educator roles. While I was director, we initiated a creative arts program; it won an American Hospital Association Award. Musicians visited patients' bedsides in the intensive care units, art docents brought prints to patients and gave mini lectures, comedians brought laughter to the AIDS floor. The power of the arts was clear to me. But it was one of those eighty-hour-a-week positions, with no boundaries; there was always more, more, more that could be done. There was little time or energy for my family and friends. I needed to find a better life balance.

"So, I registered for two adult education courses; a three-session Scherenschnitte class (a traditional form of paper cutting) and for what I thought was a ten-session children's book writing course. The emphasis would be on illustration; the other students were all artists! I thought, 'Okay, well, I'll try cutting paper for my illustrations.' After submitting an assignment, the instructor told me, 'You've found your medium.'

"I sent my work out and received rejections. Then one project was picked out of the 'slush pile' and at the first meeting with the editor, *Snow* was accepted on the spot. *Snow* was published in 1995. Because I was now a published author I was hired by LEARN to be an author-in-residence to work with inner-city and suburban school children, helping them to write and illustrate their own books.

"Because I was a children's book author and had worked at Yale-New Haven Hospital, in 1998 when a committee with a vision of creating a 'Books for Babies' literacy program was forming, I was invited to join them and to write 'the book'! *Rabbit's Bedtime,* illustrated with cut paper, is about balance and taking time to do the important little BIG things in life. It was sent to Houghton Mifflin. It was accepted within hours! It was published in nine months! In under a year, an extraordinary group of business people, bankers, the medical community, philanthropists, librarians, the New Haven Foundation, and dedicated citizens had worked together to initiate Read to Grow, a continuum of programs to address literacy in our community. I am honored and extremely grateful to be a part of Read to Grow. My book, *Rabbit's Bedtime,* or the bilingual version, *Hora de dormir del conejo,* is given to every newborn at three Connecticut Hospitals; and Read to Grow keeps growing! My new book, *Baby Day!* and the bilingual version *Dí del Bebé,* will also become part of Books for Babies/ Read to Grow. A fourth hospital is being added in Hartford."

Wallace's first picture book, *Snow,* was warmly received by critics who praised both the nostalgic, fun-loving story and Wallace's colorful cut-paper illustrations. In this story, a grandfather rabbit recalls the fun he and his brother had long ago, when the first snow of the winter finally arrived. "The strength of this gentle book is the way it captures the quiet magic and cozy charm of a cold, snowy day with loved ones," contended Roni Schotter in the *New York Times Book Review.* Likewise, Patricia Pearl Dole, writing in *School Library Journal,* noted that the style of Wallace's illustrations, characterized by bright colors, spare shapes, and an auspicious use of white space, "gives a feeling of primitive exuberance to the pictures." Susan Dove Lempke, writing in *Booklist,* also focused her review on Wallace's artwork, noting that the illustrations for *Snow* "are striking and evocative of both the serenity and the playfulness of children in the snow."

Critics noted a similarity between Wallace's next book, *Rabbit's Bedtime,* and the classic children's book *Goodnight Moon.* Here a young rabbit prepares for bed,

Wallace employs cut-paper illustrations in her self-illustrated work Apples, Apples, Apples.

recalling the events of the day in a sweet and simple rhyme. "Each activity is impressively captured in Wallace's distinct cut-paper artwork," remarked a contributor to *Kirkus Reviews*. Although Sue Sherif, writing in *School Library Journal*, felt that the overall effect of the book was almost too sweet, "the clean design and the book's small, square format make it a likely success," she predicted. Wallace's *Tell-a-Bunny* depicts the silly results when Sunny asks her friends to spread the word about a surprise party she wants to throw. With each phone call, the facts about the party get more and more mixed up until Sunny's friends arrive at her house at six in the morning (instead of six at night), ready for fun. "Whether or not kids are familiar with 'telephone,' they'll recognize the humorous confusion that miscommunication can bring," observed Steven Engelfried in *School Library Journal*.

In *Apples, Apples, Apples,* Wallace adds a recipe for applesauce, instructions for making prints from apples, famous apple sayings, and an apple song to a story about a bunny family that goes to an apple orchard. Additional information about growing apples and the history of the fruit are planted on signs throughout the orchard, for older readers. "Bold shapes and monochromatic backgrounds keep the pictures clean and uncluttered," remarked Joy Fleishhacker in *School Library Journal*. Although some reviewers noted that Wallace treads familiar ground in composing a story about a trip to an apple orchard, "what sets this book apart is its wonderful paper-cut artwork," noted Ilene Cooper in *Booklist*. Wallace's artwork and the innate attractions of the natural world work their magic in *Paperwhite* as well, according to reviewers. Here a young friend and an old friend plant a narcissus bulb in the dead of winter and await its bloom as the first sign of spring. While they wait, they make cookies and knit scarves, string beads, and play the piano. The result "is a lovely paean to the simple acts shared by friends," remarked Wendy Lukehart in *School Library Journal*. As in her other stories, Wallace's illustrations add further dimensions to her text; here they show the passing days through subtle changes in the light as little Lucy Rabbit arrives each day at 4:30. *Paperwhite* celebrates "both the wonders of nature and the pleasures of a loving intergenerational friendship," concluded a contributor to *Publishers Weekly*.

Like *Apples, Apples, Apples* and *Paperwhite*, the story of *A Taste of Honey* is engineered to both instruct preschoolers and entertain them. Here, little Lily Bear asks question after question of her Poppy Bear, who explains to her the process of where honey comes from, starting with the jar on the shelf and leading inevitably back to bees. Sidebars offer additional information, but the main text and the colorful cut-paper illustrations are geared toward a preschool audience. The result is "a picture book well designed to explain and entertain," concluded Carolyn Phelan in *Booklist*.

With *Count Down to Clean Up!*, Wallace collects a group of ten of her signature bunnies, giving each a characteristic color and a clue to their interests. As the group travels down the street, one by one the bunnies disappear into the shops along the way, gathering supplies for a fix-up project at the local park. "Children will delight in figuring out who went where and who got what," predicted GraceAnne A. DeCandido in *Booklist*. Wallace's brightly colored paper illustrations make use of found paper; thus, "she has cleverly combined the medium with a message of caring for the local community and its resources," remarked Roxanne Burg in *School Library Journal*.

Pumpkin Day!, like *Apples, Apples, Apples*, celebrates a commonplace autumn activity for young children. And like *Rabbit's Bedtime*, it depicts with warmth a family enjoying being together. Here, Wallace's rabbit family spends a day in a pumpkin field, where they learn about the different kinds of pumpkins and how they are grown. Pumpkins are later carved into jack-o-lanterns, the seeds baked, and pumpkin muffins consumed. The pumpkin fields contain further pumpkin facts on signposts and the book contains a recipe for making the muffins at home. Again, a portion of the success of the book was attributed to Wallace's illustrations. "The origami-and-paper collages placed against pure backgrounds are the best Wallace has done to date, and that's saying something," enthused Ilene Cooper in a *Booklist* review.

Biographical and Critical Sources

PERIODICALS

Booklist, November 15, 1995, Susan Dove Lempke, review of *Snow*, p. 565; May 15, 2000, Helen Rosenberg, review of *Tell-a-Bunny*, p. 1750; October 15, 2000, Ilene Cooper, review of *Apples, Apples, Apples*, p. 448; November 15, 2000, Shelley Townsend-Hudson, review of *Paperwhite*, p. 651; January 1, 2001, Isabel Schon, review of *Hora de dormir del conejo/ Rabbit's Bedtime*, p. 973; February 15, 2001, Carolyn Phelan, review of *A Taste of Honey*, p. 1142; September 15, 2001, GraceAnne A. DeCandido, review of *Count Down to Clean Up!*, p. 233; August, 2002, Ilene Cooper, review of *Pumpkin Day!*, p. 1963.

Horn Book Guide, July-December, 2000, Elena Abos Alvarez-Bviza, review of *Paperwhite*, p. 25.

Kirkus Reviews, September 15, 1995, review of *Snow*, p. 1360; September 1, 1999, review of *Rabbit's Bedtime*, p. 1423; August 1, 2001, review of *Count Down to Clean Up!*, p. 1134; August 1, 2002, review of *Pumpkin Day!*, p. 1146.

New York Times Book Review, November 12, 1995, Roni Schotter, review of *Snow*, p. 42.

Publishers Weekly, November 6, 1995, review of *Snow*, p. 93; June 26, 2000, review of *Apples, Apples, Apples*, p. 74; September 4, 2000, review of *Paperwhite*, p. 107; March 19, 2001, review of *A Taste of Honey*, p. 99.

School Library Journal, December, 1995, Patricia Pearl Dole, review of *Snow*, p. 93; November, 1999, Sue Sherif, review of *Rabbit's Bedtime*, p. 132; May, 2000, Steven Engelfried, review of *Tell-a-Bunny*, p. 156; September, 2000, Joy Fleishhacker, review of *Apples*,

Apples, Apples, p. 211; October, 2000, Wendy Lukehart, review of *Paperwhite,* p. 141; June, 2001, Janet M. Bair, review of *A Taste of Honey,* p. 141; October, 2001, Roxanne Burg, review of *Count Down to Clean Up!,* p. 133; November, 2002, Melinda Piehler, review of *Pumpkin Day!,* p. 140.

Teaching Children Mathematics, January, 2002, David Whitin, review of *Paperwhite,* p. 299.

Y–Z

YACCARINO, Dan 1965-

Personal

Born May 20, 1965, in Monclair, NJ. *Education:* Graduated from the Parsons School of Design, New York, NY, 1987.

Addresses

Home—New York, NY. *Agent*—c/o Author Mail, HarperCollins/Joanna Cotler Books, 1350 6th Avenue, New York, NY 10019.

Career

Freelance artist, writer, and producer. Images created for advertising campaigns, including Cotton Inc., AT&T, Gardenburger, Sony, and Nikkei. *Exhibitions:* Has exhibited sculptures and large-scale paintings in galleries in New York, Tokyo, Los Angeles, and Rome.

Awards, Honors

ADDE Award, How Magazine Society of Illustrators of Los Angeles; AIGA Award, The Association of Educational Publishers; Parent's Choice Award; ALA Notable and Parent Guide Award; has received awards from the Society of Illustrators, Communication Arts, and American Illustration; invited to read his books at 2002 Easter festivities at the White House.

Writings

SELF-ILLUSTRATED BOOKS FOR CHILDREN; EXCEPT AS NOTED

Big Brother Mike, Hyperion (New York, NY), 1993.
If I Had a Robot, Viking (New York, NY), 1996.
An Octopus Followed Me Home, Viking (New York, NY), 1997.
Good Night, Mr. Night, Harcourt (San Diego, CA), 1997.
Zoom! Zoom! Zoom! I'm Off to the Moon, Scholastic, Inc. (New York, NY), 1997.

Dan Yaccarino

Deep in the Jungle, Atheneum (New York, NY), 2000.
Oswald, Atheneum (New York, NY), 2001.
Unlovable, Holt (New York, NY), 2001.
So Big!, HarperFestival (New York, NY), 2001.
The Lima Bean Monster, illustrated by Adam McCauley, Walker & Company (New York, NY), 2001.
Where the Four Winds Blow, Joanna Cotler Books (New York, NY), 2003.

Also author, with Lisa Desimini, David Ricceri, and Sara Schwartz, of *All Year Round: A Book to Benefit Children in Need,* for Scholastic, and illustrator for *Discover 2000: The New York State 2000 Summer Reading Program,* by Lisa von Drasek.

On the first day of school, galactic space exchange student Johnny has a hard time coping on planet Meep, while his counterpart Blorp Glorp takes things in stride on Earth. (*From* First Day on a Strange New Planet, *written and illustrated by Yaccarino.*)

"BLAST OFF BOY AND BLORP" SERIES; SELF-ILLUSTRATED

First Day on a Strange New Planet, Hyperion (New York, NY), 2000.

New Pet, Hyperion (New York, NY), 2001.

The Big Science Fair, Hyperion (New York, NY), 2002.

ILLUSTRATOR

Catherine Friend, *The Sawfin Stickleback: A Very Fishy Story,* Hyperion (New York, NY), 1994.

Eve Merriam, *Bam! Bam! Bam!,* Holt (New York, NY), 1995.

M. C. Helldorfer, *Carnival,* Viking (New York, NY), 1996.

W. Nikola-Lisa, *One Hole in the Road,* Holt (New York, NY), 1996.

Kevin Henkes, *Circle Dogs,* Greenwillow Press (New York, NY), 1998.

Five Little Pumpkins, HarperFestival (New York, NY), 1998.

Laura Godwin, *Little White Dog,* Hyperion (New York, NY), 1998.

Andrea Zimmerman and David Clemesha, *Trashy Town,* HarperCollins (New York, NY), 1999.

Rebecca Kai Dotlich, *Away We Go!,* HarperFestival (New York, NY), 2000.

Naomi Shihab Nye, *Come with Me: Poems for a Journey,* Greenwillow Books (New York, NY), 2000.

Laurie Myers, *Surviving Brick Johnson,* Clarion Books (New York), 2000.

Robert Burleigh, *I Love Going through This Book,* HarperCollins (New York, NY), 2001.

Abigail Tabby, *Baby Face,* HarperFestival (New York, NY), 2001.

Jack Prelutsky, *Halloween Countdown,* HarperFestival (New York, NY), 2002.

I Met a Bear, HarperFestival (New York, NY), 2002.

Margaret Wise Brown, *The Good Little Bad Little Pig,* Hyperion (New York, NY), 2002.

Dan Yaccarino's Mother Goose, Little Golden Books (New York, NY), 2003.

ILLUSTRATOR, PLAY-AND-LEARN KIT

Paul Kepple and Ann Keech, *Move It!,* Running Press (Philadelphia, PA), 1998.

Paul Kepple and Ann Keech, *Bugs,* Running Press (Philadelphia, PA), 1999.

Also animator for television commercials. Yaccarino's illustrations have been featured on maps, Jack in the Box, picture frames, growth charts, sewing cards, stationary, playing cards, travel games, bed linens, and other products. Yaccarino has contributed illustrations to magazines, including *Rolling Stone, Playboy, New York,* and *Fast Company.*

Adaptations

Yaccarino has adapted several of his books for animation; *Oswald* was adapted for an animated television series, Nickelodeon network, 2001. Several of Yaccarino's characters have been made into plush toys.

Work in Progress

Writing and illustrating children's books; television and feature film projects.

Sidelights

Dan Yaccarino is a children's book writer and illustrator who first broke into print with his self-illustrated *Big Brother Mike,* a "visually offbeat take on sibling rivalry," according to a reviewer for *Publishers Weekly.* Since that time, Yaccarino has authored many more titles of his own as well as illustrated numerous books by other authors, including the works of Jack Prelutsky and Margaret Wise Brown. Best known for *Oswald,* which has become a popular and critically acclaimed series on the Nickelodeon network, Yaccarino has also penned a trio of books about Blast Off Boy and Blorp, a pair of "unlikely intergalactic exchange students," according to a contributor for *Kirkus Reviews.* Other books from the versatile and prolific author/artist include *Deep in the Jungle, Good Night, Mr. Night, The Lima Bean Monster,* and the juvenile fantasy novel from 2003, *Where the Four Winds Blow.* Writing in *Bulletin of the Center for Children's Books,* Deborah Stevenson applauded the "retro air" to much of Yaccarino's work. "There's no glamorized, adult-appealing nostalgia here," Stevenson further commented. "Rather there's a robustness reminiscent of the energetic illustrative work of the colorful 1950s and even at times ... of Diego Rivera's glistening monumental figures." Employing bold, bright colors and sturdy figures, Yaccarino's illustrations have a "refreshening unfussiness," according to Stevenson.

Yaccarino has parlayed a career in editorial illustration and advertising with children's illustration. With his first solo title, *Big Brother Mike,* he tells a story of typical older brother and younger brother relationships, including the usual ups and downs. While older brother Mike can come to the aid of the younger narrator against bullies or to help him bury his pet hamster, he can also be irritating when battling for the television remote control. A reviewer for *Publishers Weekly* called this a "spunky first book." *Booklist*'s Lisa Napoli recognized Yaccarino's "ability to use color, form and composition to show feelings" in this debut title, and a critic for *Kirkus Reviews* also had praise for his "vibrantly expressive illustrations, with emotion-indicative colors."

In his second solo effort, *If I Had a Robot,* Yaccarino tells of young Phil, who dreams of having a robot so that the machine could finish up his vegetables for him or go to school and do his homework for him. Once again, reviewers focused on Yaccarino's "visually emphatic" illustrations, as John Peters characterized them in *School Library Journal. Booklist*'s Susan Dove Lempke also commented on the "retro-style artwork ... [which] carries through the time-honored concept" of childish wish-fulfillment. A contributor for *Publishers Weekly* likewise felt that the book's "main appeal comes from the quirky sci-fi illustrations." Yaccarino returns to a similar premise in *The Lima Bean Monster,* in which

Sammy unwittingly unleashes a monster when trying to get rid of unwanted food stuffs. In this case, lima beans need to be emptied from the plate, and Sammy does so by slipping them into his sock and then burying them in a vacant lot. When a Lima Bean Monster results from this and starts to eat all the adults in the neighborhood, Sammy and the other kids protect them by gathering around the monster and eating him up. Sally R. Dow, writing in *School Library Journal,* found this a "fast-paced story ... [with] surefire appeal for youngsters who won't touch their vegetables."

Working on a bedtime premise, Yaccarino presents a bowler-hatted Mr. Night, who puts the world to bed and also helps children fall asleep in the picture book *Good Night, Mr. Night.* "Simple forms and Matisse-like colors match the innocence of the story, told in a series of simple lines," wrote a critic for *Kirkus Reviews.* Writing in *Bulletin of the Center for Children's Books,* Janice M. DelNegro commented on Yaccarino's "Rousseauian landscape," concluding that the book is a "storytime natural," and that young readers would "appreciate Yaccarino's controlled text and flamingly colorful illustrations." Similarly, a reviewer for *Publishers Weekly* called the book a "calming bedtime tale" and further remarked that the "quiet narration and undulating illustrations have an almost hypnotic quality." Lauren Peterson, writing in *Booklist,* felt *Good Night, Mr. Night* was a "gentle bedtime tale that stirs the imagination." Peterson also went on to praise Yaccarino's "rich, vibrant" double-page spreads, which "complement the text beautifully."

Moon exploration is the focus of *Zoom! Zoom! Zoom! I'm Off to the Moon,* about a boy astronaut who takes an

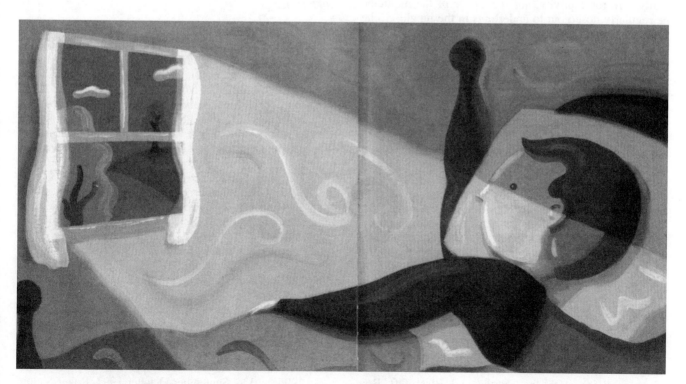

Mr. Night walks the earth, putting the world to bed in Yaccarino's self-illustrated **Good Night, Mr. Night.**

adventurous trip to the moon done in rhyming narrative. The text itself climbs diagonally up the page, reducing in size as the boy's spaceship takes off and gains altitude. A contributor for *Publishers Weekly* called this an "effervescent" picture book that readers could use as a "launch pad for their own imaginations," and "Horn Book'"s Roger Sutton felt the book is "a perfect space story for the toddler realm" and a "lilting bedtime story." Sutton also commented on Yaccarino's signature "rounded retro shapes" in the illustrations, reminiscent of 1950s toys. Shelley Townsend-Hudson, reviewing the same title in *Booklist,* felt that Yaccarino's "fanciful illustrations pull children into this exuberant picture book and make the launch a special event." More rhyming text is presented in *An Octopus Followed Me Home,* in which a child whines to be allowed to keep the stray octopus that has followed her home. But her father reminds her of all the other animals that have followed her home, including the crocodile under the bed and the giraffe with its neck up the chimney. No more, says dad, but then the last page shows an even more monstrous critter following the girl home. *Booklist*'s Hazel Rochman felt that the verses and "bright illustrations give an uproarious spin" to the usual tale of a kid pleading to keep a stray. A reviewer for *Publishers Weekly* wrote that Yaccarino "specializes in simple text and whimsically distorted shapes," and *Newsweek*'s Malcolm Jones, Jr., dubbed the tale a "beguilingly simple can-I-keep-it story."

A reviewer for *Publishers Weekly* called Yaccarino's year 2000 title, *Deep in the Jungle* "perhaps his best book yet," and a "tongue-in-cheek look at an arrogant king of beasts." Tricked one day into leaving the jungle for the confines of a zoo, the lion decides he does not really care for captivity, nor for a taste of the medicine he regularly dosed out to underlings in the jungle. So he eats his tamer, and returns home where he helps the other jungle animals against another trickster trying to get them into the zoo. The same reviewer concluded that Yaccarino "humorously twists the savage-versus-civilized formula." *Booklist*'s Connie Fletcher felt that Yaccarino's "bright and cartoony" illustrations help take the "bite out of the tale."

Yaccarino has also penned three titles in a series about an earthling student, Johnny Smith, and an alien boy from the planet Meep, Blorp Gorp, who trade places. Smith, dubbed Blast Off Boy, is chosen from millions of applicants to represent Earth on Meep; at the same time Blorp, all green except for his black eyes, tries to adjust to his new life at Blast Off Boy's former elementary school. *First Day on a Strange Planet* chronicles the outset of this strange arrangement. While Blast Off Boy becomes the center of attention on Meep, Blorp is put in detention. A reviewer for *Publishers Weekly* felt that Yaccarino "puts a fresh and funny spin on ordinary events like lunchtime and gym class" in this "auspicious debut" to the series. Stevenson, reviewing the same title in *Bulletin of the Center for Children's Books,* found the book "an enjoyable armchair excursion into space." Blorp is living with the Smiths and Blast Off Boy resides with Blorp's family on Meep in the second title

of the series, *New Pet.* A critic for *Kirkus Reviews* thought that while this second book "won't send any young readers into orbit, it will appeal to those who adore aliens of any variety." John Peters, writing in *Booklist,* had higher praise for the book, commending Yaccarino's "daffy spin on familiar themes," and noting that the author/illustrator once again "deftly intertwin[es] his two story lines." The dual story line continues in *The Big Science Fair,* and both students are preparing for fairs on each planet: Blorp with real exuberance and Blast Off Boy with more of a sense of dread, faced with "all the brainy aliens [who] are planning their macaroni models of hydrogen molecules," as a contributor for *Kirkus Reviews* noted. The same critic concluded that the series is a "welcome addition to the library of those just blasting off out of easy readers." Marlene Gawron, writing in *School Library Journal,* thought that Yaccarino's name should be added to the list of those authors "who have nailed the schoolroom scene."

Another popular offering from Yaccarino is the 2001 *Oswald,* illustrated with computer-generated images. In this cumulative story, Oswald and his dog, Weenie, move to a new city and though the eight-armed wonder is worried that they will remain friendless, the canine is not so worried. Attempting to catch a runaway piano, they in fact begin to meet a cast of odd new locals, including trees that can walk and hat-wearing eggs. Gillian Engberg, writing in *Booklist,* felt that youngsters three to seven would enjoy the "zany, random comedy."

Biographical and Critical Sources

PERIODICALS

Booklist, March 15, 1993, Lisa Napoli, review of *Big Brother Mike,* p. 1363; July, 1996, Susan Dove Lempke, review of *If I Had a Robot,* p. 1831; August, 1997, Hazel Rochman, review of *An Octopus Followed Me Home,* p. 1908; November 1, 1997, Lauren Peterson, review of *Good Night, Mr. Night,* p. 485; November 15, 1997, Shelley Townsend-Hudson, review of *Zoom! Zoom! Zoom! I'm Off to the Moon,* p. 568; December 15, 1998, Carolyn Phelan, review of *Five Little Pumpkins,* p. 754; March 1, 2000, Connie Fletcher, review of *Deep in the Jungle,* p. 1253; July, 2001, Gillian Engberg, review of *Oswald,* p. 2022; September 1, 2001, John Peters, review of *The Lima Bean Monster,* p. 118; December 1, 2001, John Peters, review of *New Pet,* p. 645.

Bulletin of the Center for Children's Books, September, 1996, p. 38; September 1, 1998, Deborah Stevenson, "Rising Star: Dan Yaccarino"; January, 1998, Janice M. DelNegro, review of *Good Night, Mr. Night,* p. 182; December, 2000, Deborah Stevenson, review of *First Day on a Strange New Planet,* p. 167; June, 2001, Deborah Stevenson, review of *Oswald,* pp. 392-393.

Horn Book, July-August, 1995, pp. 452-453; May-June, 1996, p. 324; September-October 1997, Roger Sutton, review of *Zoom! Zoom! Zoom! I'm Off to the Moon,*

p. 567; March-April, 2000, review of *Deep in the Jungle,* p. 191.

Horn Book Guide, fall, 1993, p. 280; spring, 1997, p. 54; spring, 1999, Marilyn Bousqin, review of *Five Little Pumpkins,* p. 20; spring, 2001, Anita L. Burkam, review of *First Day on a Strange New Planet,* p. 68.

Kirkus Reviews, March 1, 1993, review of *Big Brother Mike,* p. 308; July 15, 1997, p. 1119; August 15, 1997, review of *Good Night, Mr. Night,* p. 1315; December 15, 2000, review of *So Big!,* p. 1768; September 1, 2001, review of *New Pet,* p. 1304; November 1, 2001, review of *Unlovable,* p. 1556; October 1, 2002, review of *The Big Science Fair,* p. 1484.

Newsweek, December 1, 1997, Malcolm Jones, Jr., review of *An Octopus Followed Me Home,* p. 78.

New York Times Book Review, March 16, 1997, p. 26; May 11, 1997, p. 24; July 21, 1997, p. 200.

Publishers Weekly, March 15, 1993, review of *Big Brother Mike,* p. 85; October 3, 1994, p. 68; January 30, 1995, p. 99; December 18, 1995, p. 53; June 24, 1996, review of *If I Had a Robot,* p. 58; August 12, 1996, pp. 82-83; July 21, 1997, review of *Good Night, Mr. Night,* and *Zoom! Zoom! Zoom! I'm Off to the Moon,* p. 200; October 20, 1997, review of *An Octopus Followed Me Home,* pp. 74-75; January 3, 2000, review of *Deep in the Jungle,* p. 75; October 30, 2000, review of *First Day on a Strange New Planet,* p. 75; July 30, 2001, review of *The Lima Bean Monster,*

p. 84; December 17, 2001, review of *Unlovable,* pp. 89-90.

School Library Journal, August, 1993, p. 155; December, 1994, p. 74; July, 1995, p. 73; September, 1996, John Peters, review of *If I Had a Robot,* p. 195; March, 1996, p. 189; September, 1996, p. 195; October, 1996, p. 103; October, 1997, p. 114; December, 1997, Susan M. Moore, review of *Zoom! Zoom! Zoom! I'm Off to the Moon,* p. 103; January, 1998, p. 95; February, 1999, Blair Christolon, review of *Five Little Pumpkins,* pp. 83-84; February, 2000, Joy Fleishhacker, review of *Deep in the Jungle,* p. 106; July, 2001, Linda M. Kenton, review of *Oswald,* p. 91; September, 2001, Sally R. Dow, review of *The Lima Bean Monster,* p. 209; December, 2001, Gay Lynn Van Vleck, review of *New Pet,* p. 116; January, 2002, Karen Land, review of *Unlovable,* p. 114; December, 2002, Marlene Gawron, review of *The Big Science Fair,* p. 114.

Time, December 9, 1996, pp. 78-79.

OTHER

Dan Yaccarino Homepage, http://www.danyaccarino.com/ (March 9, 2003).

*   *   *

ZEBRA, A.
See SCOLTOCK, Jack

Cumulative Indexes

Illustrations Index

(In the following index, the number of the *volume* in which an illustrator's work appears is given *before* the colon, and the *page number* on which it appears is given *after* the colon. For example, a drawing by Adams, Adrienne appears in Volume 2 on page 6, another drawing by her appears in Volume 3 on page 80, another drawing in Volume 8 on page 1, and so on and so on....)

YABC

Index references to *YABC* refer to listings appearing in the two-volume *Yesterday's Authors of Books for Children,* also published by The Gale Group. *YABC* covers prominent authors and illustrators who died prior to 1960.

A

Aas, Ulf 5: 174
Abbé, S. van See van Abbé, S.
Abel, Raymond 6: 122; 7: 195; 12: 3; 21: 86; 25: 119
Abelliera, Aldo 71: 120
Abolafia, Yossi 60: 2; 93: 163
Abrahams, Hilary 26: 205; 29: 24-25; 53: 61
Abrams, Kathie 36: 170
Abrams, Lester 49: 26
Accorsi, William 11: 198
Acs, Laszlo 14: 156; 42: 22
Adams, Adrienne 2: 6; 3: 80; 8: 1; 15: 107; 16: 180; 20: 65; 22: 134-135; 33: 75; 36: 103, 112; 39: 74; 86: 54; 90: 2, 3
Adams, Connie J. 129: 68
Adams, John Wolcott 17: 162
Adams, Lynn 96: 44
Adams, Norman 55: 82
Adams, Pam 112: 1, 2
Adams, Sarah 98: 126
Adamson, George 30: 23, 24; 69: 64
Addams, Charles 55: 5
Ade, Rene 76: 198
Adinolfi, JoAnn 115: 42
Adkins, Alta 22: 250
Adkins, Jan 8: 3; 69: 4
Adler, Peggy 22: 6; 29: 31
Adler, Ruth 29: 29
Adragna, Robert 47: 145
Agard, Nadema 18: 1
Agee, Jon 116: 8, 9, 10
Agre, Patricia 47: 195
Ahl, Anna Maria 32: 24
Ahlberg, Allan 68: 6-7, 9
Ahlberg, Janet 68: 6-7, 9
Aicher-Scholl, Inge 63: 127
Aichinger, Helga 4: 5, 45
Aitken, Amy 31: 34
Akaba, Suekichi 46: 23; 53: 127
Akasaka, Miyoshi YABC 2: 261
Akino, Fuku 6: 144
Alain 40: 41
Alajalov 2: 226
Alborough, Jez 86: 1, 2, 3
Albrecht, Jan 37: 176
Albright, Donn 1: 91
Alcala, Alfredo 91: 128
Alcorn, John 3: 159; 7: 165; 31: 22; 44: 127; 46: 23, 170
Alcorn, Stephen 110: 4; 125: 106; 128: 172
Alcott, May 100: 3
Alda, Arlene 44: 24
Alden, Albert 11: 103
Aldridge, Andy 27: 131
Aldridge, George 105: 125
Alex, Ben 45: 25, 26
Alexander, Ellen 91: 3
Alexander, Lloyd 49: 34

Alexander, Martha 3: 206; 11: 103; 13: 109; 25: 100; 36: 131; 70: 6, 7; 136: 3, 4, 5
Alexander, Paul 85: 57; 90: 9
Alexeieff, Alexander 14: 6; 26: 199
Alfano, Wayne 80: 69
Aliki See Brandenberg, Aliki
Allamand, Pascale 12: 9
Allan, Judith 38: 166
Alland, Alexandra 16: 255
Allen, Gertrude 9: 6
Allen, Graham 31: 145
Allen, Jonathan B. 131: 3, 4
Allen, Pamela 50: 25, 26-27, 28; 81: 9, 10; 123: 4-5
Allen, Rowena 47: 75
Allen, Thomas B. 81: 101; 82: 248; 89: 37; 104: 9
Allen, Tom 85: 176
Allender, David 73: 223
Alley, R. W. 80: 183; 95: 187
Allison, Linda 43: 27
Allon, Jeffrey 119: 174
Allport, Mike 71: 55
Almquist, Don 11: 8; 12: 128; 17: 46; 22: 110
Aloise, Frank 5: 38; 10: 133; 30: 92
Althea See Braithwaite, Althea
Altschuler, Franz 11: 185; 23: 141; 40: 48; 45: 29; 57: 181
Alvin, John 117: 5
Ambrus, Victor G. 1: 6-7, 194; 3: 69; 5: 15; 6: 44; 7: 36; 8: 210; 12: 227; 14: 213; 15: 213; 22: 209; 24: 36; 28: 179; 30: 178; 32: 44, 46; 38: 143; 41: 25, 26, 27, 28, 29, 30, 31, 32; 42: 87; 44: 190; 55: 172; 62: 30, 144, 145, 148; 86: 99, 100, 101; 87: 66, 137; 89: 162; 134: 160
Ames, Lee J. 3: 12; 9: 130; 10: 69; 17: 214; 22: 124
Amon, Aline 9: 9
Amoss, Berthe 5: 5
Amundsen, Dick 7: 77
Amundsen, Richard E. 5: 10; 24: 122
Ancona, George 12: 11; 55: 144
Andersen, Bethanne 116: 167
Anderson, Alasdair 18: 122
Anderson, Bob 139: 16
Anderson, Brad 33: 28
Anderson, C. W. 11: 10
Anderson, Carl 7: 4
Anderson, Catherine Corley 72: 2
Anderson, Cecil 127: 152
Anderson, David Lee 118: 176
Anderson, Doug 40: 111
Anderson, Erica 23: 65
Anderson, Laurie 12: 153, 155
Anderson, Lena 99: 26
Anderson, Scoular 138: 13
Anderson, Susan 90: 12
Anderson, Wayne 23: 119; 41: 239; 56: 7; 62: 26
Andreasen, Daniel 86: 157; 87: 104; 103: 201, 202
Andrew, Ian 111: 37; 116: 12
Andrew, John 22: 4

Andrews, Benny 14: 251; 31: 24; 57: 6, 7
Anelay, Henry 57: 173
Angel, Marie 47: 22
Angelo, Valenti 14: 8; 18: 100; 20: 232; 32: 70
Anglund, Joan Walsh 2: 7, 250-251; 37: 198, 199, 200
Anholt, Catherine 74: 8; 131: 7; 141: 5
Anholt, Laurence 141: 4
Anno, Mitsumasa 5: 7; 38: 25, 26-27, 28, 29, 30, 31, 32; 77: 3, 4
Antal, Andrew 1: 124; 30: 145
Apostolou, Christy Hale See Hale, Christy
Apple, Margot 33: 25; 35: 206; 46: 81; 53: 8; 61: 109; 64: 21, 22, 24, 25, 27; 71: 176; 77: 53; 82: 245; 92: 39; 94: 180; 96: 107
Appleyard, Dev 2: 192
Aragonés, Sergio 48: 23, 24, 25, 26, 27
Araneus 40: 29
Arbo, Cris 103: 4
Archambault, Matthew 85: 173; 138: 19, 20
Archer, Janet 16: 69
Ardizzone, Edward 1: 11, 12; 2: 105; 3: 258; 4: 78; 7: 79; 10: 100; 15: 232; 20: 69, 178; 23: 223; 24: 125; 28: 25, 26, 27, 28, 29, 30, 31, 33, 34, 35, 36, 37; 31: 192, 193; 34: 215, 217; 60: 173; 64: 145; 87: 176; YABC 2: 25
Arenella, Roy 14: 9
Argent, Kerry 103: 56; 138: 17
Armer, Austin 13: 3
Armer, Laura Adams 13: 3
Armer, Sidney 13: 3
Armitage, David 47: 23; 99: 5
Armitage, Eileen 4: 16
Armstrong, George 10: 6; 21: 72
Armstrong, Shelagh 102: 114
Arno, Enrico 1: 217; 2: 22, 210; 4: 9; 5: 43; 6: 52; 29: 217, 219; 33: 152; 35: 99; 43: 31, 32, 33; 45: 212, 213, 214; 72: 72; 74: 166; 100: 169
Arnold, Emily 76: 7, 9, 10
Arnold, Katya 115: 11
Arnold, Tedd 116: 14; 133: 152
Arnosky, Jim 22: 20; 70: 9, 10, 11; 118: 3, 5
Arnsteen, Katy Keck 105: 97; 116: 145
Arrowood, Clinton 12: 193; 19: 11; 65: 210
Artell, Mike 89: 8
Arting, Fred J. 41: 63
Artzybasheff, Boris 13: 143; 14: 15; 40: 152, 155
Aruego, Ariane 6: 4
Aruego, Jose 4: 140; 6: 4; 7: 64; 33: 195; 35: 208; 68: 16, 17; 75: 46; 93: 91, 92; 94: 197; 109: 65, 67; 125: 2, 3, 4, 5; 127: 188
Asare, Meshack 86: 9; 139: 19
Ascensios, Natalie 105: 139
Asch, Frank 5: 9; 66: 2, 4, 6, 7, 9, 10; 102: 18, 19, 21
Ashby, Gail 11: 135
Ashby, Gwynneth 44: 26
Ashley, C. W. 19: 197
Ashmead, Hal 8: 70

Aska, Warabe *56:* 10
Assel, Steven *44:* 153; *77:* 22, 97
Astrop, John *32:* 56
Atene, Ann *12:* 18
Atherton, Lisa *38:* 198
Atkinson, Allen *60:* 5
Atkinson, J. Priestman *17:* 275
Atkinson, Janet *86:* 147; *103:* 138
Atkinson, Mike *127:* 74
Atkinson, Wayne *40:* 46
Attebery, Charles *38:* 170
Atwood, Ann *7:* 9
Aubrey, Meg Kelleher *77:* 159
Augarde, Steve *25:* 22
Austerman, Miriam *23:* 107
Austin, Margot *11:* 16
Austin, Robert *3:* 44
Austin, Virginia *81:* 205; *127:* 221
Auth, Tony *51:* 5
Avedon, Richard *57:* 140
Averill, Esther *1:* 17; *28:* 39, 40, 41
Axeman, Lois *2:* 32; *11:* 84; *13:* 165; *22:* 8; *23:* 49; *61:* 116; *101:* 124
Ayer, Jacqueline *13:* 7
Ayer, Margaret *15:* 12; *50:* 120
Ayers, Alan *91:* 58; *107:* 169
Ayliffe, Alex *95:* 164
Ayto, Russell *111:* 5; *112:* 54
Azarian, Mary *112:* 9, 10; *114:* 129; *117:* 171; *137:* 163

B

B. T. B. *See* Blackwell, Basil T.
Babbitt, Bradford *33:* 158
Babbitt, Natalie *6:* 6; *8:* 220; *68:* 20; *70:* 242, 243
Baca, Maria *104:* 5
Bacchus, Andy *94:* 87
Bacha, Andy *109:* 169
Bachem, Paul *48:* 180; *67:* 65
Back, Adam *63:* 125
Back, George *31:* 161
Backhouse, Colin *78:* 142
Bacon, Bruce *4:* 74
Bacon, Paul *7:* 155; *8:* 121; *31:* 55; *50:* 42; *56:* 175; *62:* 82, 84
Bacon, Peggy *2:* 11, 228; *46:* 44
Bailey, Peter *58:* 174; *87:* 221
Baker, Alan *22:* 22; *61:* 134; *93:* 11, 12
Baker, Charlotte *2:* 12
Baker, Garin *89:* 65
Baker, Jeannie *23:* 4; *88:* 18, 19, 20
Baker, Jim *22:* 24
Baker, Joe *82:* 188; *111:* 55; *124:* 70
Baker, Leslie *112:* 214; *132:* 103, 246
Baldridge, Cyrus LeRoy *19:* 69; *44:* 50
Balet, Jan *11:* 22
Balian, Lorna *9:* 16; *91:* 16
Balit, Christina *102:* 24
Ballantyne, R. M. *24:* 34
Ballis, George *14:* 199
Baltzer, Hans *40:* 30
Banbery, Fred *58:* 15
Banfill, A. Scott *98:* 7; *112:* 59
Bang, Molly Garrett *24:* 37, 38; *69:* 8, 9, 10; *111:* 7, 9, 10, 11; *140:* 11
Banik, Yvette Santiago *21:* 136
Banner, Angela *See* Maddison, Angela Mary
Bannerman, Helen *19:* 13, 14
Bannon, Laura *6:* 10; *23:* 8
Bantock, Nick *74:* 229; *95:* 6
Baptist, Michael *37:* 208
Baracca, Sal *135:* 206
Barasch, Lynne *126:* 16
Barbarin, Lucien C., Jr. *89:* 88
Barbour, Karen *96:* 5; *74:* 209
Bare, Arnold Edwin *16:* 31

Bare, Colleen Stanley *32:* 33
Bargery, Geoffrey *14:* 258
Barker, Carol *31:* 27
Barker, Cicely Mary *49:* 50, 51
Barkley, James *4:* 13; *6:* 11; *13:* 112
Barks, Carl *37:* 27, 28, 29, 30-31, 32, 33, 34
Barling, Joy *62:* 148
Barling, Tom *9:* 23
Barlow, Gillian *62:* 20
Barlow, Perry *35:* 28
Barlowe, Dot *30:* 223
Barlowe, Wayne *37:* 72; *84:* 43; *105:* 5
Barnard, Bryn *88:* 53; *13:* 55
Barner, Bob *29:* 37; *128:* 33; *136:* 19, 20
Barnes, Hiram P. *20:* 28
Barnes, Tim *137:* 28
Barnes-Murphy, Rowan *88:* 22
Barnett, Ivan *70:* 14
Barnett, Moneta *16:* 89; *19:* 142; *31:* 102; *33:* 30, 31, 32; *41:* 153; *61:* 94, 97
Barney, Maginel Wright *39:* 32, 33, 34; *YABC 2:* 306
Barnum, Jay Hyde *11:* 224; *20:* 5; *37:* 189, 190
Baron, Alan *80:* 3; *89:* 123
Barr, George *60:* 74; *69:* 64
Barragan, Paula S. *134:* 116
Barrall, Tim *115:* 152
Barrauds *33:* 114
Barrer-Russell, Gertrude *9:* 65; *27:* 31
Barret, Robert *85:* 134
Barrett, Angela *40:* 136, 137; *62:* 74; *75:* 10; *76:* 142
Barrett, Jennifer *58:* 149
Barrett, John E. *43:* 119
Barrett, Moneta *74:* 10
Barrett, Peter *55:* 169; *86:* 111
Barrett, Robert *62:* 145; *77:* 146; *82:* 35
Barrett, Ron *14:* 24; *26:* 35
Barron, John N. *3:* 261; *5:* 101; *14:* 220
Barrow, Ann *136:* 27
Barrows, Walter *14:* 268
Barry, Ethelred B. *37:* 79; *YABC 1:* 229
Barry, James *14:* 25
Barry, Katharina *2:* 159; *4:* 22
Barry, Robert E. *6:* 12
Barry, Scott *32:* 35
Bartenbach, Jean *40:* 31
Barth, Ernest Kurt *2:* 172; *3:* 160; *8:* 26; *10:* 31
Bartlett, Alison *101:* 88
Barton, Byron *8:* 207; *9:* 18; *23:* 66; *80:* 181; *90:* 18, 19, 20, 21; *126:* 29, 30
Barton, Harriett *30:* 71
Barton, Jill *129:* 108; *135:* 120
Bartram, Robert *10:* 42
Bartsch, Jochen *8:* 105; *39:* 38
Bascove, Barbara *45:* 73
Base, Graeme *101:* 15, 16, 17, 18
Bash, Barbara *132:* 9
Baskin, Leonard *30:* 42, 43, 46, 47; *49:* 125, 126, 128, 129, 133
Bass, Saul *49:* 192
Bassett, Jeni *40:* 99; *64:* 30
Basso, Bill *99:* 139
Batchelor, Joy *29:* 41, 47, 48
Bate, Norman *5:* 16
Bates, Leo *24:* 35
Batet, Carmen *39:* 134
Batherman, Muriel *31:* 79; *45:* 185
Battaglia, Aurelius *50:* 44
Batten, John D. *25:* 161, 162
Battles, Asa *32:* 94, 95
Bauernschmidt, Marjorie *15:* 15
Baum, Allyn *20:* 10
Baum, Willi *4:* 24-25; *7:* 173
Bauman, Leslie *61:* 121
Baumann, Jill *34:* 170
Baumhauer, Hans *11:* 218; *15:* 163, 165, 167
Baxter, Glen *57:* 100

Baxter, Leon *59:* 102
Baxter, Robert *87:* 129
Bayley, Dorothy *37:* 195
Bayley, Nicola *40:* 104; *41:* 34, 35; *69:* 15; *129:* 33, 34, 35
Baynes, Pauline *2:* 244; *3:* 149; *13:* 133, 135, 137-141; *19:* 18, 19, 20; *32:* 208, 213, 214; *36:* 105, 108; *59:* 12, 13, 14, 16, 17, 18, 20; *100:* 158, 159, 243; *133:* 3, 4
Beame, Rona *12:* 40
Bear's Heart *73:* 215
Beard, Dan *22:* 31, 32
Beard, J. H. *YABC 1:* 158
Bearden, Romare *9:* 7; *22:* 35
Beardsley, Aubrey *17:* 14; *23:* 181; *59:* 130, 131
Bearman, Jane *29:* 38
Beaton, Cecil *24:* 208
Beaton, Clare *125:* 28
Beaucé, J. A. *18:* 103
Beaujard, Sophie *81:* 54
Beck, Charles *11:* 169; *51:* 173
Beck, Ian *138:* 27
Beck, Ruth *13:* 11
Becker, Harriet *12:* 211
Beckett, Sheilah *25:* 5; *33:* 37, 38
Beckhoff, Harry *1:* 78; *5:* 163
Beckman, Kaj *45:* 38, 39, 40, 41
Beckman, Per *45:* 42, 43
Beddows, Eric *72:* 70
Bedford, F. D. *20:* 118, 122; *33:* 170; *41:* 220, 221, 230, 233
Bee, Joyce *19:* 62
Beeby, Betty *25:* 36
Beech, Carol *9:* 149
Beek *25:* 51, 55, 59
Beekman, Doug *125:* 146, 148
Beerbohm, Max *24:* 208
Beeson, Bob *108:* 57
Begin, Maryjane *82:* 13
Behr, Joyce *15:* 15; *21:* 132; *23:* 161
Behrens, Hans *5:* 97
Beier, Ellen *135:* 170; *139:* 47
Beinicke, Steve *69:* 18
Beisner, Monika *46:* 128, 131; *112:* 127
Belden, Charles J. *12:* 182
Belina, Renate *39:* 132
Bell, Corydon *3:* 20
Bell, Graham *54:* 48
Bell, Thomas P. *76:* 182
Bellamy, Glen *127:* 15
Beltran, Alberto *43:* 37
Bemelmans, Ludwig *15:* 19, 21; *100:* 27
Ben-Ami, Doron *75:* 96; *84:* 107; *108:* 132; *110:* 63
Benda, Wladyslaw T. *15:* 256; *30:* 76, 77; *44:* 182
Bender, Robert *77:* 162; *79:* 13
Bendick, Jeanne *2:* 24; *68:* 27, 28
Benioff, Carol *121:* 42
Benner, Cheryl *80:* 11
Bennett, Charles H. *64:* 6
Bennett, F. I. *YABC 1:* 134
Bennett, Jill *26:* 61; *41:* 38, 39; *45:* 54
Bennett, Rainey *15:* 26; *23:* 53
Bennett, Richard *15:* 45; *21:* 11, 12, 13; *25:* 175
Bennett, Susan *5:* 55
Benoit, Elise *77:* 74
Benson, Linda *60:* 130; *62:* 91; *75:* 101; *79:* 156; *134:* 129
Benson, Patrick *68:* 162
Bentley, Carolyn *46:* 153
Bentley, Roy *30:* 162
Benton, Thomas Hart *2:* 99
Berelson, Howard *5:* 20; *16:* 58; *31:* 50
Berenstain, Jan *12:* 47; *64:* 33, 34, 36, 37, 38, 40, 42, 44; *135:* 25, 28, 31, 35
Berenstain, Stan *12:* 47; *64:* 33, 34, 36, 37, 38, 40, 42, 44; *135:* 25, 28, 31, 35
Berenzy, Alix *65:* 13; *73:* 6; *78:* 115

Berg, Joan *1:* 115; *3:* 156; *6:* 26, 58
Berg, Ron *36:* 48, 49; *48:* 37, 38; *67:* 72
Bergen, David *115:* 44
Berger, Barbara *77:* 14
Berger, William M. *14:* 143; *YABC 1:* 204
Bergherr, Mary *74:* 170
Bergin, Mark *114:* 8, 9
Bergstreser, Douglas *69:* 76
Bergum, Constance R. *121:* 14, 15
Bering, Claus *13:* 14
Berkeley, Jon *139:* 218
Berkowitz, Jeanette *3:* 249
Berman, Paul *66:* 14
Bernadette *See* Watts, Bernadette
Bernardin, James *112:* 24
Bernath, Stefen *32:* 76
Bernhard, Durga *80:* 13
Bernstein, Michel J. *51:* 71
Bernstein, Ted *38:* 183; *50:* 131
Bernstein, Zena *23:* 46
Berridge, Celia *86:* 63
Berrill, Jacquelyn *12:* 50
Berry, Erick *See* Best, Allena
Berry, William D. *14:* 29; *19:* 48
Berry, William A. *6:* 219
Berson, Harold *2:* 17, 18; *4:* 28, 29, 220;
    9: 10; *12:* 19; *17:* 45; *18:* 193; *22:* 85;
    34: 172; *44:* 120; *46:* 42; *80:* 240
Berton, Patsy *99:* 16
Bertschmann, Harry *16:* 1
Besco, Don *70:* 99
Beskow, Elsa *20:* 13, 14, 15
Bess, Clayton *63:* 94
Best, Allena *2:* 26; *34:* 76
Betera, Carol *74:* 68
Bethell, Thomas N. *61:* 169
Bethers, Ray *6:* 22
Bettina *See* Ehrlich, Bettina
Betts, Ethel Franklin *17:* 161, 164, 165;
    YABC 2: 47
Betz, Rudolf *59:* 161
Bewick, Thomas *16:* 40-41, 43-45, 47; *54:*
    150; *YABC 1:* 107
Beyer, Paul J. III *74:* 24
Bezencon, Jacqueline *48:* 40
Biamonte, Daniel *40:* 90
Bianchi, John *91:* 19
Bianco, Pamela *15:* 31; *28:* 44, 45, 46
Bible, Charles *13:* 15
Bice, Clare *22:* 40
Bierman, Don *57:* 184
Biggers, John *2:* 123
Bileck, Marvin *3:* 102; *40:* 36, 37
Bilibin, Ivan *61:* 8, 9, 12, 13, 14, 15, 151,
    152, 154, 162
Billington, Patrick *98:* 71
Bimen, Levent *5:* 179
Binch, Caroline *81:* 18; *140:* 15, 16
Bing, Christopher *126:* 34
Binger, Bill *121:* 46
Binks, Robert *25:* 150
Binzen, Bill *24:* 47
Birch, Reginald *15:* 150; *19:* 33, 34, 35,
    36; *37:* 196, 197; *44:* 182; *46:* 176;
    YABC 1: 84; *2:* 34, 39
Birchall, Mark *123:* 188
Bird, Esther Brock *1:* 36; *25:* 66
Birkett, Rachel *78:* 206
Birling, Paul *109:* 30
Birmingham, Christian *132:* 243
Birmingham, Lloyd P. *12:* 51; *83:* 13
Biro, Val *1:* 26; *41:* 42; *60:* 178; *67:* 23,
    24; *84:* 242, 243
Bischoff, Ilse *44:* 51
Bishop, Gavin *97:* 17, 18
Bishop, Kathleen Wong *115:* 67
Bishop, Rich *56:* 43
Bite, I. *60:* 14
Bittinger, Ned *93:* 117

Bjorklund, Lorence *3:* 188, 252; *7:* 100; *9:*
    113; *10:* 66; *19:* 178; *33:* 122, 123; *35:*
    36, 37, 38, 39, 41, 42, 43; *36:* 185; *38:*
    93; *47:* 106; *66:* 194; *YABC 1:* 242
Bjorkman, Steve *91:* 199
Blackburn, Loren H. *63:* 10
Blackford, John *137:* 105
Blackwell, Basil T. *YABC 1:* 68, 69
Blackwood, Gary L. *118:* 17
Blades, Ann *16:* 52; *37:* 213; *50:* 41; *69:*
    21; *99:* 215
Blair, Jay *45:* 46; *46:* 155
Blaisdell, Elinore *1:* 121; *3:* 134; *35:* 63
Blake, Quentin *3:* 170; *10:* 48; *13:* 38; *21:*
    180; *26:* 60; *28:* 228; *30:* 29, 31; *40:*
    108; *45:* 219; *46:* 165, 168; *48:* 196; *52:*
    10, 11, 12, 13, 14, 15, 16, 17; *73:* 41,
    43; *78:* 84, 86; *80:* 250, 251; *84:* 210,
    211, 212; *87:* 177; *96:* 24, 26, 28;
    *124:*79; *125:* 32, 34
Blake, Robert J. *37:* 90; *53:* 67; *54:* 23
Blake, William *30:* 54, 56, 57, 58, 59, 60
Blanchard, N. Taylor *82:* 140
Blass, Jacqueline *8:* 215
Blazek, Scott R. *91:* 71
Bleck, Cathie *118:* 116
Blegvad, Erik *2:* 59; *3:* 98; *5:* 117; *7:* 131;
    11: 149; *14:* 34, 35; *18:* 237; *32:* 219;
    60: 106; *66:* 16, 17, 18, 19; *70:* 233; *76:*
    18; *82:* 106; *87:* 45; *100:* 188; *129:* 125;
    132: 17, 18, 19, 20; *YABC 1:* 201
Blessen, Karen *93:* 126
Bliss, Corinne Demas *37:* 38
Bloch, Lucienne *10:* 12
Blondon, Herve *129:* 48
Bloom, Lloyd *35:* 180; *36:* 149; *47:* 99;
    62: 117; *68:* 231; *72:* 136; *75:* 185; *83:*
    99; *108:* 19
Blossom, Dave *34:* 29
Blumenschein, E. L. *YABC 1:* 113, 115
Blumer, Patt *29:* 214
Blundell, Kim *29:* 36
Bluthenthal, Diana Cain *93:* 32; *104:* 106
Blythe, Benjamin *128:* 7
Blythe, Gary *112:* 52
Boardman, Gwenn *12:* 60
Bober, Richard *125:* 145; *132:* 40
Bobri *30:* 138; *47:* 27
Bock, Vera *1:* 187; *21:* 41
Bock, William Sauts *8:* 7; *14:* 37; *16:* 120;
    21: 141; *36:* 177; *62:* 203
Bodecker, N(iels) M(ogens) *8:* 13; *14:* 2;
    17: 55-57; *73:* 22, 23, 24
Boehm, Linda *40:* 31
Bogacki, Tomek *138:* 31, 32
Bogdan, Florentina *107:* 43
Bohdal, Susi *22:* 44; *101:* 20
Bohlen, Nina *58:* 13
Boies, Alex *96:* 53
Bolam, Emily *101:* 216
Bolian, Polly *3:* 270; *4:* 30; *13:* 77; *29:*
    197
Bolle, Frank *87:* 100
Bollen, Roger *79:* 186; *83:* 16
Bolling, Vickey *114:* 44
Bollinger, Peter *101:* 7; *128:* 198
Bolognese, Don *2:* 147, 231; *4:* 176; *7:*
    146; *17:* 43; *23:* 192; *24:* 50; *34:* 108;
    36: 133; *71:* 24, 25; *103:* 131; *129:* 39,
    40
Bolton, A. T. *57:* 158
Bond, Arnold *18:* 116
Bond, Barbara Higgins *21:* 102
Bond, Bruce *52:* 97
Bond, Felicia *38:* 197; *49:* 55, 56; *89:* 170;
    90: 171; *126:* 37
Bonn, Pat *43:* 40
Bonners, Susan *41:* 40; *85:* 36; *94:* 99, 100
Bonsall, Crosby *23:* 6
Boon, Debbie *103:* 6
Boon, Emilie *86:* 23, 24
Boore, Sara *60:* 73

Booth, Franklin *YABC 2:* 76
Booth, Graham *32:* 193; *37:* 41, 42
Borda, Juliette *102:* 188
Bordier, Georgette *16:* 54
Boren, Tinka *27:* 128
Borges, Jose Francisco *119:* 62
Borja, Robert *22:* 48
Born, Adolf *49:* 63
Bornstein, Ruth *14:* 44; *88:* 45, 46; *107:* 30
Borten, Helen *3:* 54; *5:* 24
Bosin, Blackbear *69:* 104
Bossom, Naomi *35:* 48
Bostock, Mike *83:* 221; *114:* 14
Boston, Peter *19:* 42
Bosustow, Stephen *34:* 202
Boszko, Ron *75:* 47
Bottner, Barbara *14:* 46
Boucher, Joelle *41:* 138
Boulat, Pierre *44:* 40
Boulet, Susan Seddon *50:* 47
Bouma, Paddy *118:* 25; *128:* 16
Bour, Daniele *66:* 145
Bourke-White, Margaret *15:* 286-287; *57:*
    102
Boutet de Monvel, M. *30:* 61, 62, 63, 65
Bowen, Betsy *105:* 222
Bowen, Richard *42:* 134
Bowen, Ruth *31:* 188
Bower, Ron *29:* 33
Bowers, David *95:* 38; *115:* 20; *127:* 169,
    170
Bowman, Leslie *85:* 203; *105:* 108; *116:*
    76; *128:* 234
Bowser, Carolyn Ewing *22:* 253
Boyd, Patti *45:* 31
Boyle, Eleanor Vere *28:* 50, 51
Boynton, Sandra *57:* 13, 14, 15; *107:* 36,
    37
Bozzo, Frank *4:* 154
Brabbs, Derry *55:* 170
Brace, Eric *132:* 193, 194
Brackers de Hugo, Pierre *115:* 21
Bradford, Ron *7:* 157
Bradley, David P. *69:* 105
Bradley, Richard D. *26:* 182
Bradley, William *5:* 164
Brady, Irene *4:* 31; *42:* 37; *68:* 191
Bragg, Michael *32:* 78; *46:* 31
Bragg, Ruth Gembicki *77:* 18
Brainerd, John W. *65:* 19
Braithwaite, Althea *23:* 12-13; *119:* 16
Bralds, Braldt *90:* 28; *91:* 151
Bram, Elizabeth *30:* 67
Bramley, Peter *4:* 3
Brandenberg, Aliki *2:* 36-37; *24:* 222; *35:*
    49, 50, 51, 52, 53, 54, 56, 57; *75:* 15,
    17; *92:* 205; *113:* 18, 19, 20
Brandenburg, Alexa *75:* 19
Brandenburg, Jim *47:* 58
Brandi, Lillian *31:* 158
Brandon, Brumsic, Jr. *9:* 25
Bransom, Paul *17:* 121; *43:* 44
Braren, Loretta Trezzo *87:* 193
Braun, Wendy *80:* 17, 18
Brautigam, Don *115:* 175, 176
Brazell, Derek *75:* 105; *79:* 9
Breathed, Berkeley *86:* 27, 28, 29
Brennan, Steve *83:* 230; *101:* 184
Brenner, Fred *22:* 85; *36:* 34; *42:* 34
Brett, Bernard *22:* 54
Brett, Harold M. *26:* 98, 99, 100
Brett, Jan *30:* 135; *42:* 39; *71:* 31, 32; *130:*
    23, 24, 25, 26, 27
Brewer, Paul *106:* 115
Brewer, Sally King *33:* 44
Brewster, Patience *40:* 68; *45:* 22, 183; *51:*
    20; *66:* 144; *89:* 4; *97:* 30, 31
Brick, John *10:* 15
Brickman, Robin *131:* 88
Bridge, David R. *45:* 28
Bridgman, L. J. *37:* 77
Bridwell, Norman *4:* 37; *138:* 36, 37, 40

Brierley, Louise *91:* 22; *96:* 165
Briggs, Raymond *10:* 168; *23:* 20, 21; *66:* 29, 31, 32; *131:* 28, 29
Brigham, Grace A. *37:* 148
Bright, Robert *24:* 55
Brighton, Catherine *107:* 39
Brinckloe, Julie *13:* 18; *24:* 79, 115; *29:* 35; *63:* 140; *81:* 131
Brion *47:* 116
Brisley, Joyce L. *22:* 57
Brisson, James F. *110:* 60
Brittingham, Geoffrey *88:* 37
Brix-Henker, Silke *81:* 194
Brock, Charles E. *15:* 97; *19:* 247, 249; *23:* 224, 225; *36:* 88; *42:* 41, 42, 43, 44, 45; *100:* 189; *YABC 1:* 194, 196, 203
Brock, Emma *7:* 21
Brock, Henry Matthew *15:* 81; *16:* 141; *19:* 71; *34:* 115; *40:* 164; *42:* 47, 48, 49; *49:* 66
Brocksopp, Arthur *57:* 157
Broda, Ron *136:* 180
Brodkin, Gwen *34:* 135
Brodovitch, Alexi *52:* 22
Bromhall, Winifred *5:* 11; *26:* 38
Brooke, L. Leslie *16:* 181-183, 186; *17:* 15-17; *18:* 194
Brooker, Christopher *15:* 251
Brooker, Krysten *111:* 94; *140:* 28
Brooks, Maya Itzna *92:* 153
Brooks, Ron *94:* 15
Broomfield, Maurice *40:* 141
Brotman, Adolph E. *5:* 21
Brown, Buck *45:* 48
Brown, Christopher *62:* 124, 125, 127, 128
Brown, Craig McFarland *73:* 28; *84:* 65
Brown, Dan *61:* 167; *115:* 183, 184; *116:* 28, 29
Brown, David *7:* 47; *48:* 52
Brown, Denise *11:* 213
Brown, Ford Madox *48:* 74
Brown, Judith Gwyn *1:* 45; *7:* 5; *8:* 167; *9:* 182, 190; *20:* 16, 17, 18; *23:* 142; *29:* 117; *33:* 97; *36:* 23, 26; *43:* 184; *48:* 201, 223; *49:* 69; *86:* 227; *110:* 188
Brown, Kathryn *98:* 26
Brown, Laurie Krasny *99:* 30
Brown, Marc (Tolon) *10:* 17, 197; *14:* 263; *51:* 18; *53:* 11, 12, 13, 15, 16-17; *75:* 58; *80:* 24, 25, 26; *82:* 261; *99:* 29
Brown, Marcia *7:* 30; *25:* 203; *47:* 31, 32, 33, 34, 35, 36-37, 38, 39, 40, 42, 43, 44; *YABC 1:* 27
Brown, Margery W. *5:* 32-33; *10:* 3
Brown, Martin *101:* 43
Brown, Mary Barrett *97:* 74
Brown, Palmer *36:* 40
Brown, Paul *25:* 26; *26:* 107
Brown, Richard *61:* 18; *67:* 30
Brown, Rick *78:* 71
Brown, Robert S. *85:* 33
Brown, Ruth *55:* 165; *86:* 112, 113; *105:* 16, 17, 18
Brown, Trevor *99:* 160; *139:* 247
Browne, Anthony *45:* 50, 51, 52; *61:* 21, 22, 23, 24, 25; *105:* 21, 22, 23, 25
Browne, Dik *8:* 212; *67:* 32, 33, 35, 37, 39
Browne, Gordon *16:* 97; *64:* 114, 116, 117, 119, 121
Browne, Hablot K. *15:* 65, 80; *21:* 14, 15, 16, 17, 18, 19, 20; *24:* 25
Browning, Coleen *4:* 132
Browning, Mary Eleanor *24:* 84
Bruce, Robert *23:* 23
Brude, Dick *48:* 215
Brule, Al *3:* 135
Bruna, Dick *43:* 48, 49, 50; *76:* 27, 28
Brundage, Frances *19:* 244
Brunhoff, Jean de *24:* 57, 58
Brunhoff, Laurent de *24:* 60; *71:* 35, 36, 37
Brunkus, Denise *84:* 50; *123:* 117
Brunson, Bob *43:* 135

Bryan, Ashley F. *31:* 44; *72:* 27, 28, 29; *107:* 92; *116:* 192; *132:* 24
Bryant, Michael *93:* 74
Brychta, Alex *21:* 21
Bryer, Diana *107:* 121
Bryson, Bernarda *3:* 88, 146; *39:* 26; *44:* 185; *131:* 40
Buba, Joy *12:* 83; *30:* 226; *44:* 56
Buchanan, Lilian *13:* 16
Bucholtz-Ross, Linda *44:* 137
Buchs, Thomas *40:* 38
Buck, Margaret Waring *3:* 30
Buehner, Mark *104:* 12, 15; *105:* 160; *119:* 98
Buehr, Walter *3:* 31
Buff, Conrad *19:* 52, 53, 54
Buff, Mary *19:* 52, 53
Bull, Charles Livingston *18:* 207; *88:* 175, 176
Bullen, Anne *3:* 166, 167
Bullock, Kathleen *77:* 24
Bumgarner-Kirby, Claudia *77:* 194
Burbank, Addison *37:* 43
Burchard, Peter *3:* 197; *5:* 35; *6:* 158, 218
Burckhardt, Marc *94:* 48; *110:* 89
Burger, Carl *3:* 33; *45:* 160, 162
Burgeson, Marjorie *19:* 31
Burgess, Anne *76:* 252
Burgess, Gelett *32:* 39, 42
Burke, Phillip *95:* 117
Burkert, Nancy Ekholm *18:* 186; *22:* 140; *24:* 62, 63, 64, 65; *26:* 53; *29:* 60, 61; *46:* 171; *YABC 1:* 46
Burleson, Joe *104:* 35
Burn, Doris *6:* 172
Burn, Jeffrey *89:* 125
Burnard, Damon *115:* 23
Burnett, Virgil *44:* 42
Burningham, John *9:* 68; *16:* 60-61; *59:* 28, 29, 30, 31, 32, 33, 35; *111:* 18, 19, 21
Burns, Howard M. *12:* 173
Burns, Jim *47:* 70; *86:* 32; *91:* 197; *123:* 16
Burns, M. F. *26:* 69
Burns, Raymond *9:* 29
Burns, Robert *24:* 106
Burr, Dan *65:* 28; *108:* 134
Burr, Dane *12:* 2
Burra, Edward *YABC 2:* 68
Burrell, Galen *56:* 76
Burri, René *41:* 143; *54:* 166
Burridge, Marge Opitz *14:* 42
Burris, Burmah *4:* 81
Burroughs, John Coleman *41:* 64
Burroughs, Studley O. *41:* 65
Burton, Marilee Robin *46:* 33
Burton, Virginia Lee *2:* 43; *44:* 49, 51; *100:* 46, 47; *YABC 1:* 24
Busoni, Rafaello *1:* 186; *3:* 224; *6:* 126; *14:* 5; *16:* 62-63
Butchkes, Sidney *50:* 58
Butler, Geoff *94:* 20
Butler, Ralph *116:* 212
Butterfield, Ned *1:* 153; *27:* 128; *79:* 63
Butterworth, Nick *106:* 43, 44
Buxton, John *123:* 12
Buzelli, Christopher *105:* 149
Buzonas, Gail *29:* 88
Buzzell, Russ W. *12:* 177
Byard, Carole *39:* 44; *57:* 18, 19, 20; *60:* 60; *61:* 93, 96; *69:* 210; *78:* 246; *79:* 227
Byars, Betsy *46:* 35
Byfield, Barbara Ninde *8:* 18
Byfield, Graham *32:* 29
Byrd, Robert *13:* 218; *33:* 46
Byrd, Samuel *123:* 104

C

Cabat, Erni *74:* 38
Cabban, Vanessa *138:* 73
Cabrera, Jane *103:* 24
Caddy, Alice *6:* 41
Cady, Harrison *17:* 21, 23; *19:* 57, 58
Caffrey, Aileen *72:* 223; *141:* 154
Caldecott, Randolph *16:* 98, 103; *17:* 32-33, 36, 38-39; *26:* 90; *100:* 49, 50; *YABC 2:* 172
Calder, Alexander *18:* 168
Calderon, W. Frank *25:* 160
Caldwell, Ben *105:* 75
Caldwell, Clyde *98:* 100; *116:* 39
Caldwell, Doreen *23:* 77; *71:* 41
Caldwell, John *46:* 225
Call, Greg *126:* 135
Callahan, Kevin *22:* 42
Callahan, Philip S. *25:* 77
Callan, Jamie *59:* 37
Calvin, James *61:* 92
Camburn-Bracalente, Carol A. *118:* 22
Cameron, Julia Margaret *19:* 203
Cameron, Scott *99:* 18
Camm, Martin *140:* 208, 209, 210
Campbell, Ann *11:* 43; *123:* 182
Campbell, Bill *89:* 39
Campbell, Ken *126:* 143
Campbell, Robert *55:* 120
Campbell, Rod *51:* 27; *98:* 34
Campbell, Walter M. *YABC 2:* 158
Camps, Luis *28:* 120-121; *66:* 35
Cann, Helen *124:* 50; *141:* 78
Cannon, Janell *78:* 25; *128:* 40
Canright, David *36:* 162
Canty, Thomas *85:* 161; *92:* 47; *113:* 192; *134:* 60
Caporale, Wende *70:* 42
Capp, Al *61:* 28, 30, 31, 40, 41, 43, 44
Caras, Peter *36:* 64
Caraway, Caren *57:* 22
Caraway, James *3:* 200-201
Carbe, Nino *29:* 183
Cares, Linda *67:* 176
Carigiet, Alois *24:* 67
Carle, Eric *4:* 42; *11:* 121; *12:* 29; *65:* 32, 33, 34, 36; *73:* 63, 65
Carlson, Nancy L. *41:* 116; *56:* 25; *90:* 45
Carmi, Giora *79:* 35
Carpenter, Nancy *76:* 128; *86:* 173; *89:* 171; *131:* 186; *134:* 8; *138:* 215
Carr, Archie *37:* 225
Carrick, Donald *5:* 194; *39:* 97; *49:* 70; *53:* 156; *63:* 15, 16, 17, 18, 19, 21; *80:* 131; *86:* 151; *118:* 24
Carrick, Malcolm *28:* 59, 60
Carrick, Paul *118:* 26
Carrick, Valery *21:* 47
Carrier, Lark *71:* 43
Carroll, Jim *88:* 211; *140:* 177
Carroll, Lewis *See* Dodgson, Charles L.
Carroll, Michael *72:* 5
Carroll, Pamela *84:* 68; *128:* 214
Carroll, Ruth *7:* 41; *10:* 68
Carter, Abby *81:* 32; *97:* 121; *102:* 61
Carter, Barbara *47:* 167, 169
Carter, David A. *114:* 24, 25
Carter, Don *124:* 54
Carter, Harry *22:* 179
Carter, Helene *15:* 38; *22:* 202, 203; *YABC 2:* 220-221
Cartlidge, Michelle *49:* 65; *96:* 50, 51
Cartwright, Reg *63:* 61, 62; *78:* 26
Carty, Leo *4:* 196; *7:* 163; *58:* 131
Cary *4:* 133; *9:* 32; *20:* 2; *21:* 143
Cary, Page *12:* 41
Casale, Paul *71:* 63; *109:* 122; *136:* 28
Case, Sandra E. *16:* 2
Caseley, Judith *87:* 36

Casilla, Robert *78:* 7
Casino, Steve *85:* 193
Cassel, Lili *See* Wronker, Lili Cassel
Cassel-Wronker, Lili *See* Wronker, Lili Cassel
Cassels, Jean *8:* 50
Cassen, Melody *140:* 51
Cassity, Don *104:* 24
Cassler, Carl *75:* 137, 138; *82:* 162
Casson, Hugh *65:* 38, 40, 42, 43
Castellon, Federico *48:* 45, 46, 47, 48
Castle, Jane *4:* 80
Castro, Antonio *84:* 71
Catalano, Dominic *94:* 79
Catalanotto, Peter *63:* 170; *70:* 23; *71:* 182; *72:* 96; *74:* 114; *76:* 194, 195; *77:* 7; *79:* 157; *80:* 28, 67; *83:* 157; *85:* 27; *108:* 11; *113:* 30, 31, 33, 34, 36; *114:* 27, 28, 29; *117:* 53; *124:* 168
Catania, Tom *68:* 82
Cather, Carolyn *3:* 83; *15:* 203; *34:* 216
Catrow, David *117:* 179
Cauley, Lorinda Bryan *44:* 135; *46:* 49
Cayard, Bruce *38:* 67
Cazet, Denys *52:* 27; *99:* 39, 40
Cecil, Randy *127:* 132, 133
Cellini, Joseph *2:* 73; *3:* 35; *16:* 116; *47:* 103
Cepeda, Joe *90:* 62; *109:* 91; *134:* 172
Chabrian, Debbi *45:* 55
Chabrian, Deborah *51:* 182; *53:* 124; *63:* 107; *75:* 84; *79:* 85; *82:* 247; *89:* 93; *101:* 197
Chagnon, Mary *37:* 158
Chalmers, Mary *3:* 145; *13:* 148; *33:* 125; *66:* 214
Chamberlain, Christopher *45:* 57
Chamberlain, Margaret *46:* 51; *106:* 89
Chamberlain, Nigel *78:* 140
Chambers, C. E. *17:* 230
Chambers, Dave *12:* 151
Chambers, Jill *134:* 110
Chambers, Mary *4:* 188
Chambliss, Maxie *42:* 186; *56:* 159; *93:* 163, 164; *103:* 178
Champlin, Dale *136:* 124
Chan, Harvey *96:* 236; *99:* 153
Chandler, David P. *28:* 62
Chaney, Howard *139:* 27
Chang, Warren *101:* 209
Chapel, Jody *68:* 20
Chapman, C. H. *13:* 83, 85, 87
Chapman, Frederick T. *6:* 27; *44:* 28
Chapman, Gaynor *32:* 52, 53
Chappell, Warren *3:* 172; *21:* 56; *27:* 125
Charles, Donald *30:* 154, 155
Charlip, Remy *4:* 48; *34:* 138; *68:* 53, 54; *119:*29, 30
Charlot, Jean *1:* 137, 138; *8:* 23; *14:* 31; *48:* 151; *56:* 21
Charlot, Martin *64:* 72
Charlton, Michael *34:* 50; *37:* 39
Charmatz, Bill *7:* 45
Chartier, Normand *9:* 36; *52:* 49; *66:* 40; *74:* 220
Chase, Lynwood M. *14:* 4
Chast, Roz *97:* 39, 40
Chastain, Madye Lee *4:* 50
Chatterton, Martin *68:* 102
Chau, Tungwai *140:* 35
Chauncy, Francis *24:* 158
Chee, Cheng-Khee *79:* 42; *81:* 224
Chen, Chih-sien *90:* 226
Chen, Tony *6:* 45; *19:* 131; *29:* 126; *34:* 160
Cheney, T. A. *11:* 47
Cheng, Judith *36:* 45; *51:* 16
Chermayeff, Ivan *47:* 53
Cherry, David *93:* 40
Cherry, Lynne *34:* 52; *65:* 184; *87:* 111; *99:* 46, 47
Chesak, Lina *135:* 118

Chess, Victoria *12:* 6; *33:* 42, 48, 49; *40:* 194; *41:* 145; *69:* 80; *72:* 100; *92:* 33, 34; *104:* 167
Chessare, Michele *41:* 50; *56:* 48; *69:* 145
Chesterton, G. K. *27:* 43, 44, 45, 47
Chestnutt, David *47:* 217
Chesworth, Michael *75:* 24, 152; *88:* 136; *94:* 25; *98:* 155
Chetham, Celia *134:* 34
Chetwin, Grace *86:* 40
Chevalier, Christa *35:* 66
Chew, Ruth *7:* 46; *132:* 147
Chewning, Randy *92:* 206
Chichester Clark, Emma *72:* 121; *77:* 212; *78:* 209; *87:* 143; *117:* 37, 39, 40
Chifflart *47:* 113, 127
Child, Lauren *119:* 32
Chin, Alex *28:* 54
Cho, Shinta *8:* 126
Chodos, Margaret *52:* 102, 103, 107
Chollick, Jay *25:* 175
Choma, Christina *99:* 169
Chorao, Kay *7:* 200-201; *8:* 25; *11:* 234; *33:* 187; *35:* 239; *69:* 35; *70:* 235; *123:* 174
Chowdhury, Subrata *62:* 130
Christelow, Eileen *38:* 44; *83:* 198, 199; *90:* 57, 58
Christensen, Bonnie *93:* 100
Christensen, Gardell Dano *1:* 57
Christensen, James C. *140:* 226
Christiana, David *90:* 64; *135:* 13
Christiansen, Per *40:* 24
Christie, Gregory *116:* 107; *127:* 20, 21
Christy, Howard Chandler *17:* 163-165, 168-169; *19:* 186, 187; *21:* 22, 23, 24, 25
Chronister, Robert *23:* 138; *63:* 27; *69:* 167
Church, Frederick *YABC 1:* 155
Chute, Marchette *1:* 59
Chwast, Jacqueline *1:* 63; *2:* 275; *6:* 46-47; *11:* 125; *12:* 202; *14:* 235
Chwast, Seymour *3:* 128-129; *18:* 43; *27:* 152; *92:* 79; *96:* 56, 57, 58
Cieslawksi, Steve *101:* 142; *127:* 116
Cirlin, Edgard *2:* 168
Clairin, Georges *53:* 109
Clapp, John *105:* 66; *109:* 58; *126:* 7; *129:* 148; *130:* 165
Clark, Brenda *119:* 85
Clark, David *77:* 164; *134:* 144, 145
Clark, Emma Chichester *See* Chichester Clark, Emma
Clark, Victoria *35:* 159
Clarke, Gus *72:* 226; *134:* 31
Clarke, Harry *23:* 172, 173
Clarke, Peter *75:* 102
Claverie, Jean *38:* 46; *88:* 29
Clayton, Robert *9:* 181
Cleaver, Elizabeth *8:* 204; *23:* 36
Cleland, T. M. *26:* 92
Clemens, Peter *61:* 125
Clement, Charles *20:* 38
Clement, Rod *97:* 42
Clement, Stephen *88:* 3
Clementson, John *84:* 213
Clevin, Jörgen *7:* 50
Clifford, Judy *34:* 163; *45:* 198
Clokey, Art *59:* 44
Clouse, James *84:* 15
Clouse, Nancy L. *78:* 31; *114:* 90
Coalson, Glo *9:* 72, 85; *25:* 155; *26:* 42; *35:* 212; *53:* 31; *56:* 154; *94:* 37, 38, 193
Cober, Alan E. *17:* 158; *32:* 77; *49:* 127
Cober-Gentry, Leslie *92:* 111
Cocca-Leffler, Maryann *80:* 46; *136:* 60; *139:* 193
Cochran, Bobbye *11:* 52
CoConis, Ted *4:* 41; *46:* 41; *51:* 104
Cocozza, Chris *87:* 18; *110:* 173; *111:* 149
Coerr, Eleanor *1:* 64; *67:* 52
Coes, Peter *35:* 172

Cogancherry, Helen *52:* 143; *69:* 131; *77:* 93; *78:* 220; *109:* 204; *110:* 129
Coggins, Jack *2:* 69
Cohen, Alix *7:* 53
Cohen, Sheldon *105:* 33, 34
Cohen, Vincent O. *19:* 243
Cohen, Vivien *11:* 112
Coker, Paul *51:* 172
Colbert, Anthony *15:* 41; *20:* 193
Colby, C. B. *3:* 47
Cole, Babette *58:* 172; *96:* 63, 64
Cole, Brock *68:* 223; *72:* 36, 37, 38, 192; *127:* 23; *136:* 64, 65
Cole, Gwen *87:* 185
Cole, Herbert *28:* 104
Cole, Michael *59:* 46
Cole, Olivia H. H. *1:* 134; *3:* 223; *9:* 111; *38:* 104
Colin, Paul *102:* 59; *123:* 118; *126:* 152
Collicott, Sharleen *98:* 39
Collier, Bryan *126:* 54
Collier, David *13:* 127
Collier, John *27:* 179
Collier, Steven *50:* 52
Collins, Heather *66:* 84; *67:* 68; *81:* 40; *98:* 192, 193; *129:* 95, 96, 98
Collins, Ross *140:* 23, 24
Colon, Raul *108:* 112; *113:* 5; *117:* 167; *134:* 112
Colonna, Bernard *21:* 50; *28:* 103; *34:* 140; *43:* 180; *78:* 150
Comport, Sally Wern *117:* 169
Conde, J. M. *100:* 120
Condon, Grattan *54:* 85
Cone, Ferne Geller *39:* 49
Cone, J. Morton *39:* 49
Conklin, Paul *43:* 62
Connolly, Howard *67:* 88
Connolly, Jerome P. *4:* 128; *28:* 52
Connolly, Peter *47:* 60
Conoly, Walle *110:* 224
Conover, Chris *31:* 52; *40:* 184; *41:* 51; *44:* 79
Contreras, Gerry *72:* 9
Converse, James *38:* 70
Conway *62:* 62
Conway, Michael *69:* 12; *81:* 3; *92:* 108
Cook, G. R. *29:* 165
Cook, Joel *108:* 160
Cookburn, W. V. *29:* 204
Cooke, Donald E. *2:* 77
Cooke, Tom *52:* 118
Coomaraswamy, A. K. *50:* 100
Coombs, Charles *43:* 65
Coombs, Deborah *139:* 175
Coombs, Patricia *2:* 82; *3:* 52; *22:* 119; *51:* 32, 33, 34, 35, 36-37, 38, 39, 40, 42, 43
Cooney, Barbara *6:* 16-17, 50; *12:* 42; *13:* 92; *15:* 145; *16:* 74, 111; *18:* 189; *23:* 38, 89, 93; *32:* 138; *38:* 105; *59:* 48, 49, 51, 52, 53; *74:* 222; *81:* 100; *91:* 25; *96:* 71, 72, 74; *100:* 149; *YABC 2:* 10
Cooper, Floyd *79:* 95; *81:* 45; *84:* 82; *85:* 74; *91:* 118; *96:* 77, 78; *103:* 149
Cooper, Heather *50:* 39
Cooper, Helen *102:* 42, 43, 44
Cooper, Mario *24:* 107
Cooper, Marjorie *7:* 112
Cope, Jane *61:* 201; *108* 52
Copelman, Evelyn *8:* 61; *18:* 25
Copley, Heather *30:* 86; *45:* 57
Corbett, Grahame *30:* 114; *43:* 67
Corbino, John *19:* 248
Corcos, Lucille *2:* 223; *10:* 27; *34:* 66
Corey, Robert *9:* 34
Corlass, Heather *10:* 7
Cornell, James *27:* 60
Cornell, Jeff *11:* 58
Cornell, Laura *94:* 179; *95:* 25
Corrigan, Barbara *8:* 37
Corwin, Judith Hoffman *10:* 28
Cory, Fanny Y. *20:* 113; *48:* 29

Cosgrove, Margaret *3:* 100; *47:* 63; *82:* 133
Costabel, Eva Deutsch *45:* 66, 67
Costanza, John *58:* 7, 8, 9
Costello, Chris *86:* 78
Costello, David F. *23:* 55
Cote, Nancy *126:* 139
Couch, Greg *94:* 124; *110:* 13
Councell, Ruth Tietjen *79:* 29
Courtney, Cathy *58:* 69, 144; *59:* 15; *61:* 20, 87
Courtney, R. *35:* 110
Counihan, Claire *133:* 106
Cousineau, Normand *89:* 180; *112:* 76
Couture, Christin *41:* 209
Covarrubias, Miguel *35:* 118, 119, 123, 124, 125
Coville, Katherine *32:* 57; *36:* 167; *92:* 38
Covington, Neverne *113:* 87
Cowell, Cressida *140:* 39
Cowell, Lucinda *77:* 54
Cox *43:* 93
Cox, Charles *8:* 20
Cox, David *56:* 37; *90:* 63; *119:* 38
Cox, Palmer *24:* 76, 77
Cox, Steve *140:* 96
Coxe, Molly *69:* 44
Crabb, Gordon *70:* 39
Crabtree, Judith *98:* 42
Craft, Kinuko *22:* 182; *36:* 220; *53:* 122, 123, 148, 149; *74:* 12; *81:* 129; *86:* 31; *89:* 139; *127:* 27, 28, 29; *132:* 142; *139:* 38
Craig, David *136:* 198
Craig, Helen *49:* 76; *62:* 70, 71, 72; *69:* 141; *94:* 42, 43, 44; *112:* 53; *135:* 101, 102
Crane, Alan H. *1:* 217
Crane, H. M. *13:* 111
Crane, Jack *43:* 183
Crane, Walter *18:* 46-49, 53, 54, 56-57, 59-61; *22:* 128; *24:* 210, 217; *100:* 70, 71
Cravath, Lynne W. *98:* 45
Crawford, Denise *137:* 213
Crawford, Will *43:* 77
Credle, Ellis *1:* 69
Crespi, Francesca *87:* 90
Cressy, Michael *124:* 55
Crews, Donald *32:* 59, 60; *76:* 42, 43, 44
Crews, Nina *97:* 49
Crichlow, Ernest *74:* 88; *83:* 203
Crofut, Bob *80:* 87; *81:* 47
Crofut, Susan *23:* 61
Croll, Carolyn *80:* 137; *102:* 52
Cross, Peter *56:* 78; *63:* 60, 65
Crowe, Elizabeth *88:* 144
Crowell, Pers *3:* 125
Cruikshank, George *15:* 76, 83; *22:* 74, 75, 76, 77, 78, 79, 80, 81, 82, 84, 137; *24:* 22, 23
Crump, Fred H. *11:* 62
Cruz, Ray *6:* 55; *70:* 234; *123:* 173
Csatari, Joe *44:* 82; *55:* 152; *63:* 25, 28; *102:* 58
Cuffari, Richard *4:* 75; *5:* 98; *6:* 56; *7:* 13, 84, 153; *8:* 148, 155; *9:* 89; *11:* 19; *12:* 55, 96, 114; *15:* 51, 202; *18:* 5; *20:* 139; *21:* 197; *22:* 14, 192; *23:* 15, 106; *25:* 97; *27:* 133; *28:* 196; *29:* 54; *30:* 85; *31:* 35; *36:* 101; *38:* 171; *42:* 97; *44:* 92, 192; *45:* 212, 213; *46:* 36, 198; *50:* 164; *54:* 80, 136, 137, 145; *56:* 17; *60:* 63; *66:* 49, 50; *70:* 41; *71:* 132; *77:* 157; *78:* 58, 149; *79:* 120; *85:* 2, 152
Cugat, Xavier *19:* 120
Cumings, Art *35:* 160
Cummings, Chris *29:* 167
Cummings, Pat *42:* 61; *61:* 99; *69:* 205; *71:* 57, 58; *78:* 24, 25; *93:* 75; *107:* 49, 50
Cummings, Richard *24:* 119
Cunette, Lou *20:* 93; *22:* 125
Cunningham, Aline *25:* 180

Cunningham, David *11:* 13
Cunningham, Imogene *16:* 122, 127
Cupples, Pat *107:* 12; *126:* 109
Curlee, Lynn *98:* 48; *141:* 39
Curry, John Steuart *2:* 5; *19:* 84; *34:* 36
Curry, Tom *127:* 131
Curtis, Bruce *23:* 96; *30:* 88; *36:* 22
Cusack, Margaret *58:* 49, 50, 51
Cushman, Doug *65:* 57; *101:* 39, 40; *133:* 179
Cyrus, Kurt *132:* 39
Czechowski, Alicia *95:* 21
Czernecki, Stefan *117:* 173

D

Dabcovich, Lydia *25:* 105; *40:* 114; *99:* 75, 76
Dacey, Bob *82:* 175
d'Achille, Gino *127:* 175, 176
Dailey, Don *78:* 197
Dain, Martin J. *35:* 75
Dale, Penny *127:* 224
Dale, Rae *72:* 197
Daley, Joann *50:* 22
Dalton, Anne *40:* 62; *63:* 119
Daly, Deborah M. *74:* 213
Daly, Jim *103:* 60
Daly, Jude *138:* 118, 119
Daly, Nicholas *37:* 53; *76:* 48, 49
Daly, Niki *107:* 15; *114:* 38, 39, 40
Daly, Paul *97:* 205
Dalziel, Brothers *33:* 113
D'Amato, Alex *9:* 48; *20:* 25
D'Amato, Janet *9:* 48; *20:* 25; *26:* 118
Daniel, Alan *23:* 59; *29:* 110; *76:* 50, 53, 55, 56; *115:* 74; *134:* 70
Daniel, Lea *76:* 53, 55
Daniel, Lewis C. *20:* 216
Daniels, Beau *73:* 4
Daniels, Steve *22:* 16
Daniels, Stewart *56:* 12
Dann, Bonnie *31:* 83
Dann, Penny *82:* 128
Danska, Herbert *24:* 219
Danyell, Alice *20:* 27
Darley, F.O.C. *16:* 145; *19:* 79, 86, 88, 185; *21:* 28, 36; *35:* 76, 77, 78, 79, 80-81; *YABC 2:* 175
Darling, Lois *3:* 59; *23:* 30, 31
Darling, Louis *1:* 40-41; *2:* 63; *3:* 59; *23:* 30, 31; *43:* 54, 57, 59; *121:* 53
Darrow, David R. *84:* 101
Darrow, Whitney, Jr. *13:* 25; *38:* 220, 221
Darwin, Beatrice *43:* 54
Darwin, Len *24:* 82
Dastolfo, Frank *33:* 179
Dauber, Liz *1:* 22; *3:* 266; *30:* 49
Daugherty, James *3:* 66; *8:* 178; *13:* 27-28, 161; *18:* 101; *19:* 72; *29:* 108; *32:* 156; *42:* 84; *YABC 1:* 256; *2:* 174
d'Aulaire, Edgar Parin *5:* 51; *66:* 53
d'Aulaire, Ingri Parin *5:* 51; *66:* 53
Davalos, Felipe *99:* 197
Davenier, Christine *125:* 88; *127:* 32; *128:* 152
David, Jonathan *19:* 37
Davidson, Kevin *28:* 154
Davidson, Raymond *32:* 61
Davie, Helen K. *77:* 48, 49
Davis, Allen *20:* 11; *22:* 45; *27:* 222; *29:* 157; *41:* 99; *47:* 99; *50:* 84; *52:* 105
Davis, Bette J. *15:* 53; *23:* 95
Davis, Dimitris *45:* 95
Davis, Jim *32:* 63, 64
Davis, Lambert *110:* 23, 24
Davis, Marguerite *31:* 38; *34:* 69, 70; *100:* 34; *YABC 1:* 126, 230

Davis, Nelle *69:* 191
Davis, Paul *78:* 214
Davis, Yvonne LeBrun *94:* 144
Davisson, Virginia H. *44:* 178
DaVolls, Andy *85:* 53
Dawson, Diane *24:* 127; *42:* 126; *52:* 130; *68:* 104
Day, Alexandra *67:* 59; *97:* 54
Day, Rob *94:* 110; *127:* 24
Dean, Bob *19:* 211
de Angeli, Marguerite *1:* 77; *27:* 62, 65, 66, 67, 69, 70, 72; *100:* 75, 76; *YABC 1:* 166
DeArmond, Dale *70:* 47
Deas, Michael *27:* 219, 221; *30:* 156; *67:* 134; *72:* 24; *75:* 155; *84:* 206; *88:* 124
de Bosschère, Jean *19:* 252; *21:* 4
De Bruyn, M(onica) G. *13:* 30-31
De Cuir, John F. *1:* 28-29
Deeter, Catherine *74:* 110; *103:* 150; *137:* 50
Degen, Bruce *40:* 227, 229; *57:* 28, 29; *56:* 156; *75:* 229; *76:* 19; *81:* 36, 37; *92:* 26; *93:* 199; *97:* 56, 58, 59; *124:* 40
De Grazia *14:* 59; *39:* 56, 57
DeGrazio, George *88:* 40
de Groat, Diane *9:* 39; *18:* 7; *23:* 123; *28:* 200-201; *31:* 58, 59; *34:* 151; *41:* 152; *43:* 88; *46:* 40, 200; *49:* 163; *50:* 89; *52:* 30, 34; *54:* 43; *63:* 5; *70:* 136; *71:* 99; *73:* 117, 156; *77:* 34; *85:* 48; *86:* 201; *87:* 142; *90:* 72, 73, 143; *95:* 182; *111:* 123; *118:* 160; *126:* 8; *130:* 130; *138:* 93, 94
de Groot, Lee *6:* 21
Deines, Brian *110:* 139
DeJohn, Marie *89:* 78
Dekhteryov, B. *61:* 158
de Kiefte, Kees *94:* 107
Delacre, Lulu *36:* 66
Delaney, A. *21:* 78
Delaney, Molly *80:* 43
Delaney, Ned *28:* 68; *56:* 80; *102:* 11
DeLapine, Jim *79:* 21
De La Roche Saint Andre, Anne *75:* 37
de Larrea, Victoria *6:* 119, 204; *29:* 103; *72:* 203; *87:* 199
Delessert, Étienne *7:* 140; *46:* 61, 62, 63, 65, 67, 68; *130:* 38, 39, 40, 41, 42; *YABC 2:* 209
Delulio, John *15:* 54
DeLuna, Tony *88:* 95
Demarest, Chris L. *45:* 68-69, 70; *73:* 172, 173, 176; *78:* 106; *82:* 48, 49; *89:* 212; *92:* 86; *128:* 57, 58
De Mejo, Oscar *40:* 67
Demi *11:* 135; *15:* 245; *66:* 129, 130; *89:* 216; *102:* 66, 67, 68
Denetsosie, Hoke *13:* 126; *82:* 34
Dennis, Morgan *18:* 68-69; *64:* 89
Dennis, Wesley *2:* 87; *3:* 111; *11:* 132; *18:* 71-74; *22:* 9; *24:* 196, 200; *46:* 178; *69:* 94, 96; *129:* 62
Denslow, W. W. *16:* 84-87; *18:* 19-20, 24; *29:* 211; *100:* 21
Denton, Kady MacDonald *110:* 82; *130:* 70
Denton, Terry *72:* 163
DePalma, Mary Newell *132:* 114; *139:* 75
de Paola, Tomie *8:* 95; *9:* 93; *11:* 69; *25:* 103; *28:* 157; *29:* 80; *39:* 52-53; *40:* 226; *46:* 187; *59:* 61, 62, 63, 64, 65, 66, 67, 68, 69, 71, 72, 74; *62:* 19; *108:* 63, 67, 68, 70
Deraney, Michael J. *77:* 35; *78:* 148
deRosa, Dee *70:* 48; *71:* 210; *91:* 78
Dervaux, Isabelle *111:* 117
De Saulles, Tony *119:* 39
Deshaprabhu, Meera Dayal *86:* 192
Desimini, Lisa *86:* 68; *94:* 47; *96:* 7; *104:* 107; *125:* 194; *131:* 180
de St. Menin, Charles *70:* 17

Detmold, Edward J. *22:* 104, 105, 106, 107; *35:* 120; *64:* 5; *YABC 2:* 203
Detrich, Susan *20:* 133
Deutermann, Diana *77:* 175
DeVelasco, Joseph E. *21:* 51
de Veyrac, Robert *YABC 2:* 19
DeVille, Edward A. *4:* 235
de Visser, John *55:* 119
Devito, Bert *12:* 164
Devlin, Harry *11:* 74; *74:* 63, 65; *136:* 77, 78
Dewan, Ted *108:* 73
Dewar, Nick *133:* 122
Dewey, Ariane *7:* 64; *33:* 195; *35:* 208; *68:* 16, 17; *75:* 46; *93:* 91; *94:* 197; *109:* 65, 66, 67; *125:* 2, 3, 4, 5; *127:* 188
Dewey, Jennifer (Owings) *58:* 54; *64:* 214; *65:* 207; *88:* 169; *103:* 45
Dewey, Kenneth *39:* 62; *51:* 23; *56:* 163
de Zanger, Arie *30:* 40
Diamond, Donna *21:* 200; *23:* 63; *26:* 142; *35:* 83, 84, 85, 86-87, 88, 89; *38:* 78; *40:* 147; *44:* 152; *50:* 144; *53:* 126; *69:* 46, 47, 48, 201; *71:* 133; *123:* 19
Dias, Ron *71:* 67
Diaz, David *80:* 213; *96:* 83, 84; *108:* 228; *110:* 29
Dibley, Glin *138:* 83; *141:* 128
DiCesare, Joe *70:* 38; *71:* 63, 106; *79:* 214; *93:* 147; *116:* 217
Dick, John Henry *8:* 181
Dickens, Frank *34:* 131
Dickey, Robert L. *15:* 279
Dickson, Mora *84:* 21
Dietz, James *128:* 223
di Fate, Vincent *37:* 70; *90:* 11; *93:* 60; *109:* 219, 220
Di Fiori, Lawrence *10:* 51; *12:* 190; *27:* 97; *40:* 219; *93:* 57; *130:* 45
Digby, Desmond *97:* 180
Di Grazia, Thomas *32:* 66; *35:* 241
Dillard, Annie *10:* 32
Dillard, Sarah *136:* 186
Dillon, Corinne B. *1:* 139
Dillon, Diane *4:* 104, 167; *6:* 23; *13:* 29; *15:* 99; *26:* 148; *27:* 136, 201; *51:* 29, 48, 51, 52, 53, 54, 55, 56-57, 58, 59, 60, 61, 62; *54:* 155; *56:* 69; *58:* 127, 128; *61:* 95; *62:* 27; *64:* 46; *68:* 3; *69:* 209; *74:* 89; *79:* 92; *86:* 89; *92:* 28, 177; *93:* 7, 210; *94:* 239, 240; *97:* 167; *106:* 58, 59, 61, 64; *107:* 3; *139:* 246
Dillon, Leo *4:* 104, 167; *6:* 23; *13:* 29; *15:* 99; *26:* 148; *27:* 136, 201; *51:* 29, 48, 51, 52, 53, 54, 55, 56-57, 58, 59, 60, 61, 62; *54:* 155; *56:* 69; *58:* 127, 128; *61:* 95; *62:* 27; *64:* 46; *68:* 3; *69:* 209; *74:* 89; *79:* 92; *86:* 89; *92:* 28, 177; *93:* 7, 210; *94:* 239, 240; *97:* 167; *106:* 58, 59, 61, 64; *107:* 3; *139:* 246
Dillon, Sharon Saseen *59:* 179, 188
DiMaccio, Gerald *121:* 80
DiMaggio, Joe *36:* 22
Dinan, Carol *25:* 169; *59:* 75
Dines, Glen *7:* 66-67
Dinesen, Thomas *44:* 37
Dinnerstein, Harvey *42:* 63, 64, 65, 66, 67, 68; *50:* 146
Dinsdale, Mary *10:* 65; *11:* 171
Dinyer, Eric *86:* 148; *109:* 163; *110:* 239; *124:*11
DiSalvo-Ryan, DyAnne *59:* 77; *62:* 185; *117:* 46
Disney, Walt *28:* 71, 72, 73, 76, 77, 78, 79, 80, 81, 87, 88, 89, 90, 91, 94
DiTerlizzi, Tony *105:* 7
Divito, Anna *83:* 159
Dixon, Don *74:* 17; *109:* 196
Dixon, Larry *127:* 125
Dixon, Maynard *20:* 165
Doares, Robert G. *20:* 39
Dobias, Frank *22:* 162

Dobrin, Arnold *4:* 68
Dobson, Steven Gaston *102:* 103
Dockray, Tracy *139:* 77
Docktor, Irv *43:* 70
Dodd, Ed *4:* 69
Dodd, Julie *74:* 73
Dodd, Lynley *35:* 92; *86:* 71; *132:* 45, 46, 47
Dodge, Bill *96:* 36; *118:* 7, 8, 9; *133:* 135
Dodgson, Charles L. *20:* 148; *33:* 146; *YABC 2:* 98
Dodson, Bert *9:* 138; *14:* 195; *42:* 55; *54:* 8; *60:* 49; *101:* 125
Dodson, Liz Brenner *105:* 117; *111:* 15
Dohanos, Stevan *16:* 10
Dolce, J. Ellen *74:* 147; *75:* 41
Dolch, Marguerite P. *50:* 64
Dolesch, Susanne *34:* 49
Dollar, Diane *57:* 32
Dolobowsky, Mena *81:* 54
Dolson, Hildegarde *5:* 57
Domanska, Janina *6:* 66-67; *YABC 1:* 166
Domi *134:* 113
Dominguez, El *53:* 94
Domjan, Joseph *25:* 93
Domm, Jeffrey C. *84:* 69; *135:* 70
Donahey, William *68:* 209
Donahue, Dorothy *76:* 170
Donahue, Vic *2:* 93; *3:* 190; *9:* 44
Donald, Elizabeth *4:* 18
Donato *85:* 59
Doney, Todd L. W. *87:* 12; *93:* 112; *98:* 135; *101:* 57; *104:* 40; *118:* 163; *135:* 162, 163
Donna, Natalie *9:* 52
Donohue, Dorothy *95:* 2; *132:* 30
Dooling, Michael *82:* 19; *105:* 55; *106:* 224; *125:* 135
Doran, Ben-Ami *128:* 189
Doré, Gustave *18:* 169, 172, 175; *19:* 93, 94, 95, 96, 97, 98, 99, 100, 101, 102, 103, 104, 105; *23:* 188; *25:* 197, 199
Doremus, Robert *6:* 62; *13:* 90; *30:* 95, 96, 97; *38:* 97
Dorfman, Ronald *11:* 128
Doriau *86:* 59; *91:* 152
Dorros, Arthur *78:* 42, 43; *91:* 28
dos Santos, Joyce Audy *57:* 187, 189
Doty, Roy *28:* 98; *31:* 32; *32:* 224; *46:* 157; *82:* 71
Doucet, Bob *132:* 238
Dougherty, Charles *16:* 204; *18:* 74
Doughty, Thomas *118:* 31; *140:* 60
Douglas, Aaron *31:* 103
Douglas, Carole Nelson *73:* 48
Douglas, Goray L. *13:* 151
Dowd, Jason *132:* 51, 52
Dowd, Vic *3:* 244; *10:* 97
Dowden, Anne Ophelia *7:* 70-71; *13:* 120
Dowdy, Mrs. Regera *29:* 100
Downing, Julie *60:* 140; *81:* 50; *86:* 200; *99:* 129
Doyle, Janet *56:* 31
Doyle, Richard *21:* 31, 32, 33; *23:* 231; *24:* 177; *31:* 87
Draper, Angie *43:* 84
Drath, Bill *26:* 34
Drawson, Blair *17:* 53; *126:* 65
Drescher, Henrik *105:* 60, 62, 63
Drescher, Joan *30:* 100, 101; *35:* 245; *52:* 168; *137:* 52
Drew, Patricia *15:* 100
Drummond, V. H. *6:* 70
Drury, Christian Potter *105:* 97
Dubanevich, Arlene *56:* 44
Ducak, Danilo *99:* 130; *108:* 214
Duchesne, Janet *6:* 162; *79:* 8
Duda, Jana *102:* 155
Dudash, Michael *32:* 122; *77:* 134; *82:* 149
Duer, Douglas *34:* 177
Duffy, Daniel Mark *76:* 37; *101:* 196; *108:* 147, 148

Duffy, Joseph *38:* 203
Duffy, Pat *28:* 153
Dugin, Andrej *77:* 60
Dugina, Olga *77:* 60
Duke, Chris *8:* 195; *139:* 164
Duke, Kate *87:* 186; *90:* 78, 79, 80, 81
Dulac, Edmund *19:* 108, 109, 110, 111, 112, 113, 114, 115, 117; *23:* 187; *25:* 152; *YABC 1:* 37; *2:* 147
Dulac, Jean *13:* 64
Dumas, Philippe *52:* 36, 37, 38, 39, 40-41, 42, 43, 45; *119:*40, 41, 42
Dunaway, Nancy *108:* 161
Dunbar, James *76:* 63
Duncan, Beverly *72:* 92
Duncan, John *116:* 94
Dunn, H. T. *62:* 196
Dunn, Harvey *34:* 78, 79, 80, 81
Dunn, Iris *5:* 175
Dunn, Phoebe *5:* 175
Dunne, Jeanette *72:* 57, 173, 222
Dunn-Ramsey, Marcy *117:* 131
Dunnington, Tom *3:* 36; *18:* 281; *25:* 61; *31:* 159; *35:* 168; *48:* 195; *79:* 144; *82:* 230
Dunrea, Olivier *59:* 81; *118:* 53, 54; *124:* 43
Duntze, Dorothee *88:* 28
Dupasquier, Philippe *86:* 75; *104:* 76
DuQuette, Keith *90:* 83
Durrell, Julie *82:* 62; *94:* 62
Dutz *6:* 59
Duvoisin, Roger *2:* 95; *6:* 76-77; *7:* 197; *28:* 125; *30:* 101, 102, 103, 104, 105, 107; *47:* 205; *84:* 254
Dyer, Dale *141:* 71
Dyer, Jane *75:* 219; *129:* 28
Dypold, Pat *15:* 37

E

E. V. B. *See* Boyle, Eleanor Vere (Gordon)
Eachus, Jennifer *29:* 74; *82:* 201
Eadie, Bob *63:* 36
Eagle, Bruce *95:* 119
Eagle, Ellen *82:* 121; *89:* 3
Eagle, Jeremy *141:* 71
Eagle, Michael *11:* 86; *20:* 9; *23:* 18; *27:* 122; *28:* 57; *34:* 201; *44:* 189; *73:* 9; *78:* 235; *85:* 43
Earle, Edwin *56:* 27
Earle, Olive L. *7:* 75
Earle, Vana *27:* 99
Early, Lori *132:* 2
Early, Margaret *72:* 59
East, Stella *131:* 223
Eastman, P. D. *33:* 57
Easton, Reginald *29:* 181
Eaton, Tom *4:* 62; *6:* 64; *22:* 99; *24:* 124
Ebel, Alex *11:* 89
Ebert, Len *9:* 191; *44:* 47
Echevarria, Abe *37:* 69
Eckersley, Maureen *48:* 62
Eckert, Horst *72:* 62
Ede, Janina *33:* 59
Edens, Cooper *49:* 81, 82, 83, 84, 85; *112:* 58
Edens, John *109:* 115
Edgar, Sarah E. *41:* 97
Edliq, Emily S. *131:* 107
Edrien *11:* 53
Edwards, Freya *45:* 102
Edwards, George Wharton *31:* 155
Edwards, Gunvor *2:* 71; *25:* 47; *32:* 71; *54:* 106
Edwards, Jeanne *29:* 257
Edwards, Linda Strauss *21:* 134; *39:* 123; *49:* 88-89

Egge, David *102:* 71
Eggenhofer, Nicholas *2:* 81
Eggleton, Bob *74:* 40; *81:* 190, 191; *105:* 6; *121:* 183
Egielski, Richard *11:* 90; *16:* 208; *33:* 236; *38:* 35; *49:* 91, 92, 93, 95, 212, 213, 214, 216; *79:* 122; *106:* 67, 68, 69; *134:* 135
Ehlert, Lois *35:* 97; *69:* 51; *112:* 7; *113:* 208; *128:* 63, 64, 65
Ehrlich, Bettina *1:* 83
Eichenberg, Fritz *1:* 79; *9:* 54; *19:* 248; *23:* 170; *24:* 200; *26:* 208; *50:* 67, 68, 69, 70, 71, 72, 73, 74, 75, 77, 79, 80, 81; *60:* 165; *100:* 137; *YABC 1:* 104-105; *2:* 213
Einsel, Naiad *10:* 35; *29:* 136
Einsel, Walter *10:* 37
Einzig, Susan *3:* 77; *43:* 78; *67:* 155; *129:* 154
Eitzen, Allan *9:* 56; *12:* 212; *14:* 226; *21:* 194; *38:* 162; *76:* 218
Eldridge, H. *54:* 109
Eldridge, Harold *43:* 83
Elgaard, Greta *19:* 241
Elgin, Kathleen *9:* 188; *39:* 69
Ellacott, S. E. *19:* 118
Elliott, Mark *93:* 69; *105:* 108; *107:* 123; *140:* 53
Elliott, Sarah M. *14:* 58
Ellis, Dianne *130:* 208
Ellis, Jan Davey *88:* 50; *115:* 80
Ellis, Richard *130:* 47, 48
Ellison, Pauline *55:* 21
Elmer, Richard *78:* 5
Elmore, Larry *90:* 8
Elwell, Tristan *110:* 39; *121:* 182; *127:* 46; *137:* 144; *141:* 173
Elzbieta *88:* 80, 81
Emberley, Ed *8:* 53; *70:* 53, 54
Emberley, Michael *34:* 83; *80:* 72; *119:* 47, 48
Emerling, Dorothy *104:* 27
Emery, Leslie *49:* 187
Emmett, Bruce *49:* 147; *80:* 175; *101:* 206
Emry-Perrott, Jennifer *61:* 57
Engel, Diana *70:* 57
Engle, Mort *38:* 64
Englebert, Victor *8:* 54
English, Mark *101:* 207
Enos, Randall *20:* 183
Enright, Maginel Wright *19:* 240, 243; *39:* 31, 35, 36
Enrique, Romeo *34:* 135
Epstein, Stephen *50:* 142, 148
Erdrich, Louise *141:* 62
Erhard, Walter *1:* 152
Erickson, Phoebe *11:* 83; *59:* 85
Erikson, Mel *31:* 69
Eriksson, Eva *63:* 88, 90, 92, 93
Ering, Timothy Basil *131:* 100
Ernst, Lisa Campbell *47:* 147; *95:* 47
Esco, Jo *61:* 103
Escourido, Joseph *4:* 81
Escriva, Vivi *119:* 51
Esté, Kirk *33:* 111
Estep, David *73:* 57
Estes, Eleanor *91:* 66
Estoril, Jean *32:* 27
Estrada, Pau *74:* 76
Estrada, Ric *5:* 52, 146; *13:* 174
Etchemendy, Teje *38:* 68
Etheredges, the *73:* 12
Ets, Marie Hall *2:* 102
Eulalie *YABC 2:* 315
Evans, Greg *73:* 54, 55, 56
Evans, Katherine *5:* 64
Ewart, Claire *76:* 69
Ewing, Carolyn *66:* 143; *79:* 52
Ewing, Juliana Horatia *16:* 92
Eyolfson, Norman *98:* 154

F

Fabian, Limbert *136:* 114
Facklam, Paul *132:* 62
Falconer, Ian *125:* 66
Falconer, Pearl *34:* 23
Falkenstern, Lisa *70:* 34; *76:* 133; *78:* 171; *127:* 16
Falls, C. B. *1:* 19; *38:* 71, 72, 73, 74
Falter, John *40:* 169, 170
Falwell, Cathryn *118:* 77; *137:* 185
Fancher, Lou *138:* 219; *141:* 64
Fanelli, Sara *89:* 63; *126:* 69
Farmer, Andrew *49:* 102
Farmer, Peter *24:* 108; *38:* 75
Farnsworth, Bill *93:* 189; *116:* 147; *124:* 8; *135:* 52
Farquharson, Alexander *46:* 75
Farrell, David *40:* 135
Farris, David *74:* 42
Fasolino, Teresa *118:* 145
Fatigati, Evelyn *24:* 112
Faul-Jansen, Regina *22:* 117
Faulkner, Jack *6:* 169
Fava, Rita *2:* 29
Fax, Elton C. *1:* 101; *4:* 2; *12:* 77; *25:* 107
Fay *43:* 93
Federspiel, Marian *33:* 51
Fedorov, Nickolai Ivanovich *110:* 102
Feelings, Tom *5:* 22; *8:* 56; *12:* 153; *16:* 105; *30:* 196; *49:* 37; *61:* 101; *69:* 56, 57; *93:* 74; *105:* 88
Fehr, Terrence *21:* 87
Feiffer, Jules *3:* 91; *8:* 58; *61:* 66, 67, 70, 74, 76, 77, 78; *111:* 47, 48, 49, 50; *132:* 122
Feigeles, Neil *41:* 242
Feldman, Elyse *86:* 7
Feller, Gene *33:* 130
Fellows, Muriel H. *10:* 42
Felstead, Cathie *116:* 85
Felts, Shirley *33:* 71; *48:* 59
Fennelli, Maureen *38:* 181
Fenton, Carroll Lane *5:* 66; *21:* 39
Fenton, Mildred Adams *5:* 66; *21:* 39
Ferguson, Walter W. *34:* 86
Fernandes, Eugenie *77:* 67
Fernandes, Stanislaw *70:* 28
Fernandez, Fernando *77:* 57
Fernandez, Laura *77:* 153; *101:* 117; *131:* 222
Fetz, Ingrid *11:* 67; *12:* 52; *16:* 205; *17:* 59; *29:* 105; *30:* 108, 109; *32:* 149; *43:* 142; *56:* 29; *60:* 34; *85:* 48; *87:* 146
Fiammenghi, Gioia *9:* 66; *11:* 44; *12:* 206; *13:* 57, 59; *52:* 126, 129; *66:* 64; *85:* 83; *91:* 161
Fiedler, Joseph Daniel *96:* 42; *113:* 173; *129:* 164
Field, Rachel *15:* 113
Fielding, David *70:* 124
Fine, Peter K. *43:* 210
Finger, Helen *42:* 81
Fink, Sam *18:* 119
Finlay, Winifred *23:* 72
Finney, Pat *79:* 215
Fiore, Peter *99:* 196; *125:* 139
Fiorentino, Al *3:* 240
Firmin, Charlotte *29:* 75; *48:* 70
Firmin, Peter *58:* 63, 64, 65, 67, 68, 70, 71
Firth, Barbara *81:* 208; *127:* 218
Fischel, Lillian *40:* 204
Fischer, Hans *25:* 202
Fischer-Nagel, Andreas *56:* 50
Fischer-Nagel, Heiderose *56:* 50
Fisher, Chris *79:* 62
Fisher, Cynthia *117:* 45; *137:* 118

Fisher, Leonard Everett *3:* 6; *4:* 72, 86; *6:* 197; *9:* 59; *16:* 151, 153; *23:* 44; *27:* 134; *29:* 26; *34:* 87, 89, 90, 91, 93, 94, 95, 96; *40:* 206; *50:* 150; *60:* 158; *73:* 68, 70, 71, 72, 73; *YABC 2:* 169
Fisher, Lois *20:* 62; *21:* 7
Fisk, Nicholas *25:* 112
Fitschen, Marilyn *2:* 20-21; *20:* 48
Fitzgerald, F. A. *15:* 116; *25:* 86-87
Fitzhugh, Louise *1:* 94; *9:* 163; *45:* 75, 78
Fitzhugh, Susie *11:* 117
Fitzpatrick, Jim *109:* 130
Fitzpatrick, Marie-Louise *125:* 69, 70
Fitzsimmons, Arthur *14:* 128
Fix, Philippe *26:* 102
Flack, Marjorie *21:* 67; *100:* 93; *YABC 2:* 122
Flagg, James Montgomery *17:* 227
Flavin, Teresa *132:* 115
Flax, Zeona *2:* 245
Fleishman, Seymour *14:* 232; *24:* 87
Fleming, Denise *71:* 179; *81:* 58; *126:* 71, 72, 73
Fleming, Guy *18:* 41
Flesher, Vivienne *85:* 55
Fletcher, Claire *80:* 106
Flint, Russ *74:* 80
Floate, Helen *111:* 163
Floethe, Richard *3:* 131; *4:* 90
Floherty, John J., Jr. *5:* 68
Flora, James *1:* 96; *30:* 111, 112
Florian, Douglas *19:* 122; *83:* 64, 65; *125:* 71, 72, 74, 76; *128:* 130
Flory, Jane *22:* 111
Flower, Renee *125:* 109
Floyd, Gareth *1:* 74; *17:* 245; *48:* 63; *62:* 35, 36, 37, 39, 40, 41; *74:* 245; *79:* 56
Fluchère, Henri A. *40:* 79
Flynn, Barbara *7:* 31; *9:* 70
Fogarty, Thomas *15:* 89
Folger, Joseph *9:* 100
Folkard, Charles *22:* 132; *29:* 128, 257-258
Foott, Jeff *42:* 202
Forberg, Ati *12:* 71, 205; *14:* 1; *22:* 113; *26:* 22; *48:* 64, 65
Ford, George *24:* 120; *31:* 70, 177; *58:* 126; *81:* 103; *107:* 91; *136:* 100
Ford, H. J. *16:* 185-186
Ford, Pamela Baldwin *27:* 104
Foreman, Michael *2:* 110-111; *67:* 99; *73:* 78, 79, 80, 81, 82; *93:* 146; *135:* 55, 56, 57
Forrester, Victoria *40:* 83
Forsey, Chris *140:* 210
Fortnum, Peggy *6:* 29; *20:* 179; *24:* 211; *26:* 76, 77, 78; *39:* 78; *58:* 19, 21, 23, 27; *YABC 1:* 148
Foster, Brad W. *34:* 99
Foster, Genevieve *2:* 112
Foster, Gerald *7:* 78
Foster, Laura Louise *6:* 79
Foster, Marian Curtis *23:* 74; *40:* 42
Foster, Sally *58:* 73, 74
Foucher, Adèle *47:* 118
Fowler, Mel *36:* 127
Fowler, Richard *87:* 219
Fox, Charles Phillip *12:* 84
Fox, Jim *6:* 187
Fox-Davies, Sarah *76:* 150
Fracé, Charles *15:* 118
Frailey, Joy *72:* 108
Frame, Paul *2:* 45, 145; *9:* 153; *10:* 124; *21:* 71; *23:* 62; *24:* 123; *27:* 106; *31:* 48; *32:* 159; *34:* 195; *38:* 136; *42:* 55; *44:* 139; *60:* 39, 40, 41, 42, 43, 44, 46; *73:* 183
Frampton, David *85:* 72; *102:* 33; *139:* 182
Francois, André *25:* 117
Francoise *See* Seignobosc, Francoise
Frank, Lola Edick *2:* 199
Frank, Mary *4:* 54; *34:* 100
Franké, Phil *45:* 91

Frankel, Alona *66:* 70
Frankel, Julie *40:* 84, 85, 202
Frankenberg, Robert *22:* 116; *30:* 50; *38:* 92, 94, 95; *68:* 111
Frankfeldt, Gwen *84:* 223; *110:* 92
Franklin, John *24:* 22
Franson, Leanne R. *111:* 57, 58
Frascino, Edward *9:* 133; *29:* 229; *33:* 190; *48:* 80, 81, 82, 83, 84-85, 86
Frasconi, Antonio *6:* 80; *27:* 208; *53:* 41, 43, 45, 47, 48; *145:* 73: 226; *131:* 68
Fraser, Betty *2:* 212; *6:* 185; *8:* 103; *31:* 72, 73; *43:* 136; *111:* 76
Fraser, Eric *38:* 78; *41:* 149, 151
Fraser, F. A. *22:* 234
Fraser, Mary Ann *137:* 63
Frasier, Debra *69:* 60; *112:* 67
Frazee, Marla *72:* 98; *105:* 79, 80
Frazetta, Frank *41:* 72; *58:* 77, 78, 79, 80, 81, 82, 83
Freas, John *25:* 207
Fredrickson, Mark *103:* 33
Freeland, Michael J. *118:* 115
Freeman, Don *2:* 15; *13:* 249; *17:* 62-63, 65, 67-68; *18:* 243; *20:* 195; *23:* 213, 217; *32:* 155; *55:* 129
Freeman, Irving *67:* 150
Freeman, Pietri *140:* 223
Fregosi, Claudia *24:* 117
Fremaux, Charlotte Murray *138:* 29; *141:* 95
French, Fiona *6:* 82-83; *75:* 61; *109:* 170; *132:* 79, 80, 81, 82
Frendak, Rodney *126:* 97, 98
Freynet, Gilbert *72:* 221
Friedman, Judith *43:* 197; *131:* 221
Friedman, Marvin *19:* 59; *42:* 86
Frinta, Dagmar *36:* 42
Frith, Michael K. *15:* 138; *18:* 120
Fritz, Ronald *46:* 73; *82:* 124
Fromm, Lilo *29:* 85; *40:* 197
Frost, A. B. *17:* 6-7; *19:* 123, 124, 125, 126, 127, 128, 129, 130; *100:* 119; *YABC 1:* 156-157, 160; *2:* 107
Frost, Kristi *118:* 113
Fry, Guy *2:* 224
Fry, Rosalie *3:* 72; *YABC 2:* 180-181
Fry, Rosalind *21:* 153, 168
Fryer, Elmer *34:* 115
Fuchs, Bernie *110:* 10
Fuchs, Erich *6:* 84
Fuchshuber, Annegert *43:* 96
Fufuka, Mahiri *32:* 146
Fujikawa, Gyo *39:* 75, 76; *76:* 72, 73, 74
Fulford, Deborah *23:* 159
Fuller, Margaret *25:* 189
Fulweiler, John *93:* 99
Funai, Mamoru *38:* 105
Funk, Tom *7:* 17, 99
Furchgott, Terry *29:* 86
Furness, William Henry, Jr. *94:* 18
Furukawa, Mel *25:* 42

G

Gaadt, David *78:* 212; *121:* 166
Gaadt, George *71:* 9
Gaber, Susan *99:* 33; *115:* 57, 58
Gaberell, J. *19:* 236
Gabler, Mirko *99:* 71
Gackenbach, Dick *19:* 168; *41:* 81; *48:* 89, 90, 91, 92, 93, 94; *54:* 105; *79:* 75, 76, 77
Gad, Victor *87:* 161
Gaetano, Nicholas *23:* 209
Gaffney-Kessell, Walter *94:* 219
Gag, Flavia *17:* 49, 52

Gág, Wanda *100:* 101, 102; *YABC 1:* 135, 137-138, 141, 143
Gagnon, Cécile *11:* 77; *58:* 87
Gal, Laszlo *14:* 127; *52:* 54, 55, 56; *65:* 142; *68:* 150; *81:* 185; *96:* 104, 105
Galazinski, Tom *55:* 13
Galdone, Paul *1:* 156, 181, 206; *2:* 40, 241; *3:* 42, 144; *4:* 141; *10:* 109, 158; *11:* 21; *12:* 118, 210; *14:* 12; *16:* 36-37; *17:* 70-74; *18:* 111, 230; *19:* 183; *21:* 154; *22:* 150, 245; *33:* 126; *39:* 136, 137; *42:* 57; *51:* 169; *55:* 110; *66:* 80, 82, 139; *72:* 73; *100:* 84
Gale, Cathy *140:* 22
Gallagher, S. Saelig *105:* 154
Gallagher, Sears *20:* 112
Galloway, Ewing *51:* 154
Galouchko, Annouchka Gravel *95:* 55
Galster, Robert *1:* 66
Galsworthy, Gay John *35:* 232
Galvez, Daniel *125:* 182
Gamble, Kim *112:* 64, 65; *124:* 77
Gammell, Stephen *7:* 48; *13:* 149; *29:* 82; *33:* 209; *41:* 88; *50:* 185, 186-187; *53:* 51, 52-53, 54, 55, 56, 57, 58; *54:* 24, 25; *56:* 147, 148, 150; *57:* 27, 66; *81:* 62, 63; *87:* 88; *89:* 10; *106:* 223; *126:* 2; *128:* 71, 73, 74, 77
Gamper, Ruth *84:* 198
Gampert, John *58:* 94
Ganly, Helen *56:* 56
Gannett, Ruth Chrisman *3:* 74; *18:* 254; *33:* 77, 78
Gantschev, Ivan *45:* 32
Garafano, Marie *73:* 33
Garbot, Dave *131:* 106
Garbutt, Bernard *23:* 68
Garcia *37:* 71
Garcia, Manuel *74:* 145
Gardner, Earle *45:* 167
Gardner, Joan *40:* 87
Gardner, Joel *40:* 87, 92
Gardner, John *40:* 87
Gardner, Lucy *40:* 87
Gardner, Richard See Cummings, Richard
Gargiulo, Frank *84:* 158
Garland, Michael *36:* 29; *38:* 83; *44:* 168; *48:* 78, 221, 222; *49:* 161; *60:* 139; *71:* 6, 11; *72:* 229; *74:* 142; *89:* 187; *93:* 183; *104:* 110; *131:* 55; *139:* 209
Garland, Peggy *60:* 139
Garland, Sarah *62:* 45; *135:* 67, 68
Garn, Aimee *75:* 47
Garner, Joan *128:* 170
Garneray, Ambroise Louis *59:* 140
Garnett, Eve *3:* 75
Garnett, Gary *39:* 184
Garns, Allen *80:* 125; *84:* 39
Garraty, Gail *4:* 142; *52:* 106
Garrett, Agnes *46:* 110; *47:* 157
Garrett, Edmund H. *20:* 29
Garrett, Tom *107:* 194
Garrick, Jacqueline *67:* 42, 43; *77:* 94
Garrison, Barbara *19:* 133; *104:* 146; *109:* 87
Garro, Mark *108:* 131; *128:* 210
Garvey, Robert *98:* 222
Garza, Carmen Lomas *80:* 211
Gates, Frieda *26:* 80
Gaughan, Jack *26:* 79; *43:* 185
Gaver, Becky *20:* 61
Gawing, Toby *72:* 52
Gay, Marie-Louise *68:* 76-77, 78; *102:* 136; *126:* 76, 78, 81, 83; *127:* 55, 56
Gay, Zhenya *19:* 135, 136
Gaydos, Tim *62:* 201
Gazsi, Ed *80:* 48
Gazzo, Gabriel *73:* 85
Geary, Clifford N. *1:* 122; *9:* 104; *51:* 74
Gee, Frank *33:* 26

Geer, Charles *1:* 91; *3:* 179; *4:* 201; *6:* 168; *7:* 96; *9:* 58; *10:* 72; *12:* 127; *39:* 156, 157, 158, 159, 160; *42:* 88, 89, 90, 91; *55:* 111, 116
Gehm, Charlie *36:* 65; *57:* 117; *62:* 60, 138
Geisel, Theodor Seuss *1:* 104-105, 106; *28:* 108, 109, 110, 111, 112, 113; *75:* 67, 68, 69, 70, 71; *89:* 127, 128; *100:* 106, 107, 108
Geisert, Arthur *92:* 67, 68; *133:* 72, 73, 74
Geldart, William *15:* 121; *21:* 202
Genia *4:* 84
Gentry, Cyrille R. *12:* 66
Genzo, John Paul *136:* 74
George, Jean *2:* 113
George, Lindsay Barrett *95:* 57
Geraghty, Paul *130:* 60, 61
Gérard, Jean Ignace *45:* 80
Gérard, Rolf *27:* 147, 150
Gerber, Mark *61:* 105
Gerber, Mary Jane *112:* 124
Gerber, Stephanie *71:* 195
Gergely, Tibor *54:* 15, 16
Geritz, Franz *17:* 135
Gerlach, Geff *42:* 58
Gerrard, Roy *47:* 78; *90:* 96, 97, 98, 99
Gershinowitz, George *36:* 27
Gerstein, Mordicai *31:* 117; *47:* 80, 81, 82, 83, 84, 85, 86; *51:* 173; *69:* 134; *107:* 122
Gervase *12:* 27
Getz, Arthur *32:* 148
Gewirtz, Bina *61:* 81
Giancola, Donato *95:* 146
Gibbons, Gail *23:* 78; *72:* 77, 78, 79; *82:* 182; *104:* 65
Gibbs, Tony *40:* 95
Gibran, Kahlil *32:* 116
Gider, Iskender *81:* 193
Giesen, Rosemary *34:* 192-193
Giffard, Hannah *83:* 70
Giguère, George *20:* 111
Gilbert, John *19:* 184; *54:* 115; *YABC 2:* 287
Gilbert, W. S. *36:* 83, 85, 96
Gilbert, Yvonne *116:* 70; *128:* 84
Gilchrist, Jan Spivey *72:* 82, 83, 84-85, 87; *77:* 90; *105:* 89, 91; *130:* 63, 64
Giles, Will *41:* 218
Gili, Phillida *70:* 73
Gill, Margery *4:* 57; *7:* 7; *22:* 122; *25:* 166; *26:* 146, 147
Gillen, Denver *28:* 216
Gillette, Henry J. *23:* 237
Gilliam, Stan *39:* 64, 81
Gillies, Chuck *62:* 31
Gilliland, Jillian *87:* 58
Gilman, Alec *98:* 105
Gilman, Esther *15:* 124
Gilman, Phoebe *104:* 70, 71
Ginsberg, Sari *111:* 184
Ginsburg, Max *62:* 59; *68:* 194
Giovanopoulos, Paul *7:* 104; *60:* 36
Giovine, Sergio *79:* 12; *93:* 118; *139:* 118
Githens, Elizabeth M. *5:* 47
Gladden, Scott *99:* 108; *103:* 160
Gladstone, Gary *12:* 89; *13:* 190
Gladstone, Lise *15:* 273
Glanzman, Louis S. *2:* 177; *3:* 182; *36:* 97, 98; *38:* 120, 122; *52:* 141, 144; *71:* 191; *91:* 54, 56
Glaser, Milton *3:* 5; *5:* 156; *11:* 107; *30:* 26; *36:* 112; *54:* 141
Glass, Andrew *36:* 38; *44:* 133; *48:* 205; *65:* 3; *68:* 43, 45; *90:* 104, 105
Glass, Marvin *9:* 174
Glasser, Judy *41:* 156; *56:* 140; *69:* 79; *72:* 101
Glattauer, Ned *5:* 84; *13:* 224; *14:* 26
Glauber, Uta *17:* 76
Gleeson, J. M. *YABC 2:* 207
Glegg, Creina *36:* 100

Glienke, Amelie *63:* 150
Gliewe, Unada *3:* 78-79; *21:* 73; *30:* 220
Gliori, Debi *72:* 91; *138:* 82
Glovach, Linda *7:* 105
Gobbato, Imero *3:* 180-181; *6:* 213; *7:* 58; *9:* 150; *18:* 39; *21:* 167; *39:* 82, 83; *41:* 137, 251; *59:* 177
Goble, Paul *25:* 121; *26:* 86; *33:* 65; *69:* 68-69; *131:* 79, 80
Goble, Warwick *46:* 78, 79
Godal, Eric *36:* 93
Godfrey, Michael *17:* 279
Goembel, Ponder *42:* 124
Goffe, Toni *61:* 83, 84, 85; *89:* 11; *90:* 124
Goffstein, M. B. *8:* 71; *70:* 75, 76, 77
Golbin, Andrée *15:* 125
Goldfeder, Cheryl *11:* 191
Goldsborough, June *5:* 154-155; *8:* 92, *14:* 226; *19:* 139; *54:* 165
Goldsmith, Robert *110:* 77
Goldstein, Leslie *5:* 8; *6:* 60; *10:* 106
Goldstein, Nathan *1:* 175; *2:* 79; *11:* 41, 232; *16:* 55
Goldstrom, Robert *98:* 36
Golembe, Carla *79:* 80, 81; *136:* 91
Golin, Carlo *74:* 112
Gómez, Elizabeth *127:* 70; *133:* 76
Gomi, Taro *64:* 102; *103:* 74, 76
Gon, Adriano *101:* 112
Gonzalez, Maya Christina *104:* 3; *136:* 92
Goodall, John S. *4:* 92-93; *10:* 132; *66:* 92, 93; *YABC 1:* 198
Goode, Diane *15:* 126; *50:* 183; *52:* 114-115; *76:* 195; *84:* 94; *99:* 141; *114:* 76, 77, 78
Goodelman, Aaron *40:* 203
Goodenow, Earle *40:* 97
Goodfellow, Peter *62:* 95; *94:* 202
Goodman, Joan Elizabeth *50:* 86
Goodman, Vivian *82:* 251
Goodnow, Patti *117:* 33
Goodwin, Harold *13:* 74
Goodwin, Philip R. *18:* 206
Goor, Nancy *39:* 85, 86
Goor, Ron *39:* 85, 86
Gorbachev, Valeri *89:* 96; *112:* 97
Gordon, Gwen *12:* 151
Gordon, Margaret *4:* 147; *5:* 48-49; *9:* 79
Gordon, Mike *101:* 62, 63, 64
Gordon, Russell *136:* 204; *137:* 214
Gordon, Walter *138:* 9
Gore, Leonid *89:* 51; *94:* 74; *136:* 8
Gorecka-Egan, Erica *18:* 35
Gorey, Edward *1:* 60-61; *13:* 169; *18:* 192; *20:* 201; *29:* 90, 91, 92-93, 94, 95, 96, 97, 98, 99, 100; *30:* 129; *32:* 90; *34:* 200; *45:* 48; *68:* 24, 25; *69:* 79; *70:* 80, 82, 83, 84; *85:* 136; *127:* 62
Gorsline, Douglas *1:* 98; *6:* 13; *11:* 113; *13:* 104; *15:* 14; *28:* 117, 118; *YABC 1:* 15
Gorton, Julia *108:* 94
Gosfield, Josh *118:* 165, 166
Gosner, Kenneth *5:* 135
Gotlieb, Jules *6:* 127
Goto, Scott *115:* 86; *136:* 69
Gottlieb, Dale *67:* 162; *107:* 16
Goudey, Ray *97:* 86
Gough, Alan *91:* 57
Gough, Philip *23:* 47; *45:* 90
Gould, Chester *49:* 112, 113, 114, 116, 117, 118
Govern, Elaine R. *26:* 94
Gower, Teri *102:* 184
Gowing, Toby *60:* 25; *63:* 33; *78:* 70, 252; *83:* 228; *86:* 187; *93:* 145; *108:* 133; *110:* 217
Grabianski *20:* 144
Grabianski, Janusz *39:* 92, 93, 94, 95
Graboff, Abner *35:* 103, 104
Graef, Renee *61:* 188; *72:* 207

Graham, A. B. *11:* 61
Graham, Bob *101:* 66, 67, 68
Graham, L. *7:* 108
Graham, Margaret Bloy *11:* 120; *18:* 305, 307
Graham, Mark *88:* 208
Grahame-Johnstone, Janet *13:* 61
Grahame-Johnstone, Anne *13:* 61
Grainger, Sam *42:* 95
Gramatky, Hardie *1:* 107; *30:* 116, 119, 120, 122, 123
Granahan, Julie *84:* 84
GrandPre, Mary *84:* 131; *109:* 199; *118:* 76
Grandville, J. J. *45:* 81, 82, 83, 84, 85, 86, 87, 88; *47:* 125; *64:* 10
Granger, Paul *39:* 153
Grant, (Alice) Leigh *10:* 52; *15:* 131; *20:* 20; *26:* 119; *48:* 202
Grant, Gordon *17:* 230, 234; *25:* 123, 124, 125, 126; *52:* 69; *YABC 1:* 164
Grant, Renee *77:* 40
Grant, Shirley *109:* 45
Graves, Elizabeth *45:* 101
Gray, Harold *33:* 87, 88
Gray, Les *82:* 76; *83:* 232
Gray, Reginald *6:* 69
Greder, Armin *76:* 235
Green, Ann Canevari *62:* 48
Green, Eileen *6:* 97
Green, Elizabeth Shippen *139:* 109
Green, Jonathan *86:* 135; *105:* 109
Green, Ken *111:* 68
Green, Michael *32:* 216
Green, Robina *87:* 138
Greene, Jeffrey *117:* 93
Greenaway, Kate *17:* 275; *24:* 180; *26:* 107; *41:* 222, 232; *100:* 115, 116; *YABC 1:* 88-89; *2:* 131, 133, 136, 138-139, 141
Greenberg, Melanie Hope *72:* 93; *80:* 125; *101:* 174; *133:* 180
Greenwald, Sheila *1:* 34; *3:* 99; *8:* 72
Greger, Carol *76:* 86
Gregorian, Joyce Ballou *30:* 125
Gregory, Fran *130:* 4; *140:* 93
Gregory, Frank M. *29:* 107
Greiffenhagen, Maurice *16:* 137; *27:* 57; *YABC 2:* 288
Greiner, Robert *6:* 86
Gretter, J. Clemens *31:* 134
Gretz, Susanna *7:* 114
Gretzer, John *1:* 54; *3:* 26; *4:* 162; *7:* 125; *16:* 247; *18:* 117; *28:* 66; *30:* 85, 211; *33:* 235; *56:* 16
Grey Owl *24:* 41
Gri *25:* 90
Grieder, Walter *9:* 84
Griesbach/Martucci *59:* 3
Grifalconi, Ann *2:* 126; *3:* 248; *11:* 18; *13:* 182; *46:* 38; *50:* 145; *66:* 99, 100, 101, 104, 106; *69:* 38; *70:* 64; *87:* 128; *90:* 53; *93:* 49; *128:* 48; *133:* 79, 81
Griffin, Gillett Good *26:* 96
Griffin, James *30:* 166
Griffin, John Howard *59:* 186
Griffin, Rachel *131:* 23
Griffith, Gershom *94:* 214
Griffiths, Dave *29:* 76
Grimsdell, Jeremy *83:* 75
Grimwood, Brian *82:* 89
Gringhuis, Dirk *6:* 98; *9:* 196
Gripe, Harald *2:* 127; *74:* 98
Grisha *3:* 71
Grohmann, Susan *84:* 97
Gropper, William *27:* 93; *37:* 193
Gros *60:* 199
Grose, Helen Mason *YABC 1:* 260; *2:* 150
Grossman, Nancy *24:* 130; *29:* 101
Grossman, Robert *11:* 124; *46:* 39
Groth, John *15:* 79; *21:* 53, 54; *83:* 230
Gruelle, Johnny *35:* 107
Gschwind, William *11:* 72
Guay, Rebecca *110:* 95, 96; *135:* 240

Guback, Georgia *88:* 102
Guerguerion, Claudine *105:* 73
Guevara, Susan *97:* 87
Guggenheim, Hans *2:* 10; *3:* 37; *8:* 136
Guilbeau, Honoré *22:* 69
Guillette, Joseph *137:* 37
Guisewite, Cathy *57:* 52, 53, 54, 56, 57
Gukova, Julia *95:* 104
Gundersheimer, Karen *35:* 240; *82:* 100
Gunderson, Nick *57:* 120
Gurney, James *76:* 97; *86:* 32
Gurney, John *75:* 39, 82; *110:* 175
Gusman, Annie *38:* 62
Gustafson, Scott *34:* 111; *43:* 40
Gustavson, Adam *104:* 10
Guthridge, Bettina *108:* 79
Guthrie, R. Dale *64:* 143
Guthrie, Robin *20:* 122
Gutierrez, Alan *136:* 31, 32
Gutierrez, Rudy *97:* 162
Gutmann, Bessie Pease *73:* 93, 94
Gwynne, Fred *41:* 94, 95
Gyberg, Bo-Erik *38:* 131

H

Haas, Irene *17:* 77; *87:* 46; *96:* 117
Hack, Konrad *51:* 127
Hader, Berta H. *16:* 126
Hader, Elmer S. *16:* 126
Haeffele, Deborah *76:* 99
Haemer, Alan *62:* 109
Hafner, Marylin *22:* 196, 216; *24:* 44; *30:* 51; *35:* 95; *51:* 25, 160, 164; *86:* 16; *105:* 196; *121:* 93, 94
Hagerty, Sean *62:* 181
Hague, Michael *32:* 128; *48:* 98, 99, 100-101, 103, 105, 106-107, 108, 109, 110; *49:* 121; *51:* 105; *64:* 14, 15; *79:* 134; *80:* 91, 92; *83:* 135; *100:* 241; *102:* 29; *129:* 101, 103, 104
Hair, Jonathan *115:* 135
Halas, John *29:* 41, 47, 48
Haldane, Roger *13:* 76; *14:* 202
Hale, Christy *79:* 124; *84:* 200; *114:* 201; *128:* 2, 3
Hale, Irina *26:* 97
Hale, James Graham *88:* 207
Hale, Kathleen *17:* 79; *66:* 114, 116, 118
Haley, Gail E. *43:* 102, 103, 104, 105; *78:* 65, 67; *136:* 106, 107
Hall, Amanda *96:* 110
Hall, Chuck *30:* 189
Hall, Douglas *15:* 184; *43:* 106, 107; *86:* 100; *87:* 82; *129:* 72
Hall, H. Tom *1:* 227; *30:* 210
Hall, Melanie *116:* 48, 49
Hall, Sydney P. *31:* 89
Hall, Vicki *20:* 24
Hallinan, P. K. *39:* 98
Hallman, Tom *98:* 166
Hally, Greg *101:* 200
Halperin, Wendy Anderson *96:* 151; *125:* 96, 97, 98, 99; *139:* 22; *140:* 84
Halpern, Joan *10:* 25
Halsey, Megan *96:* 172; *114:* 185
Halstead, Virginia *125:* 105
Halverson, Janet *49:* 38, 42, 44
Hallensleben, Georg *134:* 5, 6
Hamanaka, Sheila *71:* 100
Hamann, Brad *78:* 151
Hamann, Sigune *104:* 115
Hamberger, John *6:* 8; *8:* 32; *14:* 79; *34:* 136; *88:* 78
Hamil, Tom *14:* 80; *43:* 163
Hamilton, Bill and Associates *26:* 215
Hamilton, Helen S. *2:* 238
Hamilton, J. *19:* 83, 85, 87

Hamilton, Laurie *116:* 210
Hamilton, Todd Cameron *84:* 15
Hamlin, Janet *97:* 136; *124:* 90; *137:* 157
Hamlin, Louise *71:* 135
Hammond, Chris *21:* 37
Hammond, Elizabeth *5:* 36, 203
Hampshire, Michael *5:* 187; *7:* 110-111; *48:* 150; *51:* 129
Hampson, Denman *10:* 155; *15:* 130
Hampton, Blake *41:* 244
Handford, Martin *64:* 105, 106-07, 109
Handforth, Thomas *42:* 100, 101, 102, 103, 104, 105, 107
Handville, Robert *1:* 89; *38:* 76; *45:* 108, 109
Hane, Roger *17:* 239; *44:* 54
Haney, Elizabeth Mathieu *34:* 84
Hanke, Ted *71:* 10
Hanley, Catherine *8:* 161
Hann, Jacquie *19:* 144
Hanna, Cheryl *91:* 133
Hanna, Wayne A. *67:* 145
Hannon, Mark *38:* 37
Hanson, Joan *8:* 76; *11:* 139
Hanson, Peter E. *52:* 47; *54:* 99, 100; *73:* 21; *84:* 79; *116:* 144
Hansson, Gunilla *64:* 111, 112
Hardcastle, Nick *121:* 82
Hardy, David A. *9:* 96; *119:* 74
Hardy, Paul *YABC 2:* 245
Harlan, Jerry *2:* 96
Harlin, Greg *89:* 194; *103:* 82; *118:* 161; *121:* 167
Harness, Cheryl *106:* 80; *131:* 87
Harnischfeger *18:* 121
Harper, Arthur *YABC 2:* 121
Harper, Betty *126:* 90
Harper, Piers *79:* 27; *105:* 102
Harrington, Glenn *82:* 18; *94:* 66, 68
Harrington, Jack *83:* 162
Harrington, Richard *5:* 81
Harris, Jim *127:* 130
Harris, John *83:* 25
Harris, Nick *86:* 177
Harris, Susan Yard *42:* 121
Harrison, Florence *20:* 150, 152
Harrison, Harry *4:* 103
Harrison, Jack *28:* 149
Harrison, Mark *105:* 157
Harrison, Ted *56:* 73
Harsh, Fred *72:* 107
Harston, Jerry *105:* 143
Hart, Lewis *98:* 115
Hart, William *13:* 72
Hartelius, Margaret *10:* 24
Hartshorn, Ruth *5:* 115; *11:* 129
Harvey, Bob *48:* 219
Harvey, Gerry *7:* 180
Harvey, Lisa *97:* 21
Harvey, Paul *88:* 74
Harvey, Roland *71:* 88; *123:* 63
Hassall, Joan *43:* 108, 109
Hassell, Hilton *YABC 1:* 187
Hasselriis, Else *18:* 87; *YABC 1:* 96
Hastings, Glenn *89:* 183
Hastings, Ian *62:* 67
Hauman, Doris *2:* 184; *29:* 58, 59; *32:* 85, 86, 87
Hauman, George *2:* 184; *29:* 58, 59; *32:* 85, 86, 87
Hausherr, Rosmarie *15:* 29
Hawkes, Kevin *78:* 72; *104:* 198; *105:* 197; *112:* 109; *126:* 87
Hawkins, Jacqui *112:* 86
Hawkinson, John *4:* 109; *7:* 83; *21:* 64
Hawkinson, Lucy *21:* 64
Hawthorne, Mike *140:* 228
Haxton, Elaine *28:* 131
Haydock, Robert *4:* 95
Hayes, Geoffrey *26:* 111; *44:* 133; *91:* 85
Haynes, Max *72:* 107
Hays, Michael *73:* 207; *83:* 93; *139:* 197

Haywood, Carolyn *1:* 112; *29:* 104
Heale, Jonathan *104:* 117
Healy, Daty *12:* 143
Healy, Deborah *58:* 181, 182; *101:* 111
Heap, Sue *102:* 207
Hearn, Diane Dawson *79:* 99; *113:* 13
Hearon, Dorothy *34:* 69
Heaslip, William *57:* 24, 25
Hechtkopf, H. *11:* 110
Hedderwick, Mairi *30:* 127; *32:* 47; *36:* 104; *77:* 86
Hefter, Richard *28:* 170; *31:* 81, 82; *33:* 183
Hehenberger, Shelly *126:* 91
Heigh, James *22:* 98
Heighway, Richard *25:* 160; *64:* 4
Heine, Helme *67:* 86; *135:* 91, 92
Heinly, John *45:* 113
Hellard, Susan *81:* 21
Hellebrand, Nancy *26:* 57
Heller, Linda *46:* 86
Heller, Ruth M. *66:* 125; *77:* 30, 32
Hellmuth, Jim *38:* 164
Helms, Georgeann *33:* 62
Helweg, Hans *41:* 118; *50:* 93; *58:* 22, 26
Henba, Bobbie *90:* 195
Henderson, Dave *73:* 76; *75:* 191, 192, 193, 194; *82:* 4
Henderson, Douglas *103:* 68
Henderson, Kathy *55:* 32
Henderson, Keith *35:* 122
Henderson, Meryl *127:* 58, 60
Hendry, Linda *80:* 104; *83:* 83
Henkes, Kevin *43:* 111; *108:* 106, 107, 108
Henneberger, Robert *1:* 42; *2:* 237; *25:* 83
Henriquez, Celeste *103:* 137
Henriquez, Elsa *82:* 260
Henriquez, Emile F. *89:* 88
Henry, Everett *29:* 191
Henry, Matthew *117:* 58
Henry, Paul *93:* 121
Henry, Thomas *5:* 102
Hensel *27:* 119
Henshaw, Jacqui *141:* 127
Henstra, Friso *8:* 80; *36:* 70; *40:* 222; *41:* 250; *73:* 100, 101
Henterly, Jamichael *93:* 4
Heo, Yumi *89:* 85, 86; *94:* 89, 90
Hepple, Norman *28:* 198
Herbert, Helen *57:* 70
Herbert, Wally *23:* 101
Herbster, Mary Lee *9:* 33
Hergé *See* Rémi, Georges
Hermansen, Pal *133:* 113
Hermanson, Dennis *10:* 55
Hermes, Gertrude *54:* 161
Herr, Margo *57:* 191
Herr, Susan *83:* 163
Herriman, George *140:* 74, 75, 76, 77, 78
Herriman, Lisa *87:* 190
Herring, Michael *121:* 76
Herrington, Roger *3:* 161
Hescox, Richard *85:* 86; *90:* 30; *139:* 35
Heslop, Mike *38:* 60; *40:* 130
Hess, Lydia J. *85:* 17
Hess, Mark *111:* 146; *113:* 207
Hess, Paul *134:* 47
Hess, Richard *42:* 31
Hester, Ronnie *37:* 85
Heuser, Olga J. *121:* 116
Heustis, Louise L. *20:* 28
Hewitson, Jennifer *74:* 119; *124:* 167
Hewitt, Kathryn *80:* 126
Hewitt, Margaret *84:* 112
Heyduck-Huth, Hilde *8:* 82
Heyer, Carol *74:* 122; *130:* 72, 73
Heyer, Hermann *20:* 114, 115
Heyer, Marilee *102:* 108
Heyman, Ken *8:* 33; *34:* 113
Heywood, Karen *48:* 114
Hickling, P. B. *40:* 165

Hickman, Steve *85:* 58; *136:* 33
Hierstein, Judy *56:* 40
Higginbottom, J. Winslow *8:* 170; *29:* 105, 106
Higgins, Chester *101:* 79
Higham, David *50:* 104
Hildebrandt, Greg *8:* 191; *55:* 35, 36, 38, 39, 40, 42, 46
Hildebrandt, Tim *8:* 191; *55:* 44, 45, 46
Hilder, Rowland *19:* 207
Hill, Eric *66:* 127, 128; *133:* 91
Hill, Gregory *35:* 190
Hill, Pat *49:* 120
Hillenbrand, Will *84:* 115; *92:* 76, 80; *93:* 131; *104:* 168; *128:* 137
Hillier, Matthew *45:* 205
Hillman, Priscilla *48:* 115
Hills, Tad *113:* 4; *137:* 147
Himler, Ronald *6:* 114; *7:* 162; *8:* 17, 84, 125; *14:* 76; *19:* 145; *26:* 160; *31:* 43; *38:* 116; *41:* 44, 79; *43:* 52; *45:* 120; *46:* 43; *54:* 44, 83; *58:* 180; *59:* 38; *68:* 146; *69:* 231; *70:* 98; *71:* 177, 178; *77:* 219; *79:* 212; *83:* 62; *89:* 5; *91:* 160; *92:* 91, 92, 93; *94:* 93; *95:* 69, 174, 194; *99:* 99, 112; *113:* 92; *118:* 114; *137:* 73, 74, 77, 167
Himmelman, John C. *47:* 109; *65:* 87; *94:* 96, 97
Hinds, Bill *37:* 127, 130
Hines, Anna Grossnickle *51:* 90; *74:* 124; *95:* 78, 79, 80, 81
Hines, Bob *135:* 149, 150
Hiroko *99:* 61
Hiroshige *25:* 71
Hirsh, Marilyn *7:* 126
Hiscock, Bruce *137:* 80, 81
Hissey, Jane *103:* 90; *130:* 81
Hitch, Jeff *99:* 206; *128:* 86
Hitz, Demi *11:* 135; *15:* 245; *66:* 129, 130
Hnizdovsky, Jacques *32:* 96; *76:* 187
Ho, Kwoncjan *15:* 132
Hoban, Lillian *1:* 114; *22:* 157; *26:* 72; *29:* 53; *40:* 105, 107, 195; *41:* 80; *69:* 107, 108; *71:* 98; *77:* 168; *106:* 50; *113:* 86; *136:* 118
Hoban, Tana *22:* 159; *104:* 82, 83, 85
Hoberman, Norman *5:* 82
Hobson, Sally *77:* 185
Hockerman, Dennis *39:* 22; *56:* 23
Hodgell, P. C. *42:* 114
Hodges, C. Walter *2:* 139; *11:* 15; *12:* 25; *23:* 34; *25:* 96; *38:* 165; *44:* 197; *45:* 95; *100:* 57; *YABC 2:* 62-63
Hodges, David *9:* 98
Hodgetts, Victoria *43:* 132
Hofbauer, Imre *2:* 162
Hoff, Syd *9:* 107; *10:* 128; *33:* 94; *72:* 115, 116, 117, 118; *138:* 114, 115
Hoffman, Rosekrans *15:* 133; *50:* 219; *63:* 97
Hoffman, Sanford *38:* 208; *76:* 174; *88:* 160, 161
Hoffmann, Felix *9:* 109
Hoffnung, Gerard *66:* 76, 77
Hofsinde, Robert *21:* 70
Hogan, Inez *2:* 141
Hogarth, Burne *41:* 58; *63:* 46, 48, 49, 50, 52, 53, 54, 55, 56
Hogarth, Paul *41:* 102, 103, 104; *YABC 1:* 16
Hogarth, William *42:* 33
Hogenbyl, Jan *1:* 35
Hogner, Nils *4:* 122; *25:* 144
Hogrogian, Nonny *3:* 221; *4:* 106-107; *5:* 166; *7:* 129; *15:* 2; *16:* 176; *20:* 154; *22:* 146; *25:* 217; *27:* 206; *74:* 127, 128, 129, 149, 152; *127:* 99; *YABC 2:* 84, 94
Hokanson, Lars *93:* 111
Hokusai *25:* 71
Hol, Colby *126:* 96
Holberg, Richard *2:* 51

Holbrook, Kathy *107:* 114
Holdcroft, Tina *38:* 109
Holden, Caroline *55:* 159
Holder, Heidi *36:* 99; *64:* 9
Holiday, Henry *YABC 2:* 107
Holl, F. *36:* 91
Holland, Brad *45:* 59, 159
Holland, Gay W. *128:* 105
Holland, Janice *18:* 118
Holland, Marion *6:* 116
Holldobler, Turid *26:* 120
Holling, Holling C. *15:* 136-137
Hollinger, Deanne *12:* 116
Holm, Sharon Lane *114:* 84; *115:* 52
Holmes, B. *3:* 82
Holmes, Bea *7:* 74; *24:* 156; *31:* 93
Holmes, Dave *54:* 22
Holmes, Lesley *135:* 96
Holmgren, George Ellen *45:* 112
Holt, Norma *44:* 106
Holtan, Gene *32:* 192
Holz, Loretta *17:* 81
Hom, Nancy *79:* 195
Homar, Lorenzo *6:* 2
Homer, Winslow *128:* 8; *YABC 2:* 87
Honey, Elizabeth *112:* 95, 96; *137:* 93, 94
Honeywood, Varnette P. *110:* 68, 70
Hong, Lily Toy *76:* 104
Honigman, Marian *3:* 2
Honoré, Paul *42:* 77, 79, 81, 82
Hood, Alun *69:* 145, 218; *72:* 41; *80:* 226; *87:* 4; *95:* 139
Hood, Susan *12:* 43
Hook, Christian *104:* 103
Hook, Frances *26:* 188; *27:* 127
Hook, Jeff *14:* 137; *103:* 105
Hook, Richard *26:* 188
Hooks *63:* 30
Hoover, Carol A. *21:* 77
Hoover, Russell *12:* 95; *17:* 2; *34:* 156
Hope, James *141:* 116
Hopkins, Chris *99:* 127
Hoppin, Augustus *34:* 66
Horder, Margaret *2:* 108; *73:* 75
Horen, Michael *45:* 121
Horne, Daniel *73:* 106; *91:* 153; *109:* 127; *110:* 232
Horne, Richard *111:* 80
Horse, Harry *128:* 195
Horvat, Laurel *12:* 201
Horvath, Ferdinand Kusati *24:* 176
Horvath, Maria *57:* 171
Horwitz, Richard *57:* 174
Hotchkiss, De Wolfe *20:* 49
Hough, Charlotte *9:* 112; *13:* 98; *17:* 83; *24:* 195
Houlihan, Ray *11:* 214
Housman, Laurence *25:* 146, 147
Houston, James *13:* 107; *74:* 132, 134, 135
Hovland, Gary *88:* 172
How, W. E. *20:* 47
Howard, Alan *16:* 80; *34:* 58; *45:* 114
Howard, J. N. *15:* 234
Howard, John *33:* 179
Howard, Kim *116:* 71
Howard, Rob *40:* 161
Howe, John *115:* 47
Howe, John F. *79:* 101; *80:* 150
Howe, Phillip *79:* 117
Howe, Stephen *1:* 232
Howell, Karen *119:* 123
Howell, Pat *15:* 139
Howell, Troy *23:* 24; *31:* 61; *36:* 158; *37:* 184; *41:* 76, 235; *48:* 112; *56:* 13; *57:* 3; *59:* 174; *63:* 5; *74:* 46; *89:* 188; *90:* 231; *95:* 97; *98:* 130; *99:* 189
Howes, Charles *22:* 17
Hranilovich, Barbara *127:* 51
Hu, Ying-Hwa *116:* 107
Huang, Benrei *137:* 55
Huang, Zhong-Yang *117:* 30, 32
Hubbard, Woodleigh Marx *98:* 67; *115:* 79

Hubley, Faith *48:* 120-121, 125, 130, 131, 132, 134
Hubley, John *48:* 125, 130, 131, 132, 134
Hudnut, Robin *14:* 62
Huerta, Catherine *76:* 178; *77:* 44, 45; *90:* 182
Huffaker, Sandy *10:* 56
Huffman, Joan *13:* 33
Huffman, Tom *13:* 180; *17:* 212; *21:* 116; *24:* 132; *33:* 154; *38:* 59; *42:* 147
Hughes, Arthur *20:* 148, 149, 150; *33:* 114, 148, 149
Hughes, Darren *95:* 44
Hughes, David *36:* 197
Hughes, Shirley *1:* 20, 21; *7:* 3; *12:* 217; *16:* 163; *29:* 154; *63:* 118; *70:* 102, 103, 104; *73:* 169; *88:* 70; *110:* 118, 119
Hugo, Victor *47:* 112
Hull, Cathy *78:* 29
Hull, Richard *95:* 120; *123:* 175
Hulsmann, Eva *16:* 166
Hummel, Berta *43:* 137, 138, 139
Hummel, Lisl *29:* 109; *YABC 2:* 333-334
Humphrey, Henry *16:* 167
Humphreys, Graham *25:* 168
Humphries, Tudor *76:* 66; *80:* 4; *124:* 4, 5
Hunt, James *2:* 143
Hunt, Jonathan *84:* 120
Hunt, Paul *119:* 104; *129:* 135; *139:* 160
Hunt, Robert *110:* 206, 235
Hunter, Anne *133:* 190
Hurd, Clement *2:* 148, 149; *64:* 127, 128, 129, 131, 133, 134, 135, 136; *100:* 37, 38
Hurd, Peter *24:* 30, 31,; *YABC 2:* 56
Hurd, Thacher *46:* 88-89; *94:* 114, 115, 116; *123:* 81-82, 84
Hürlimann, Ruth *32:* 99
Hussar, Michael *114:* 113; *117:* 159
Hustler, Tom *6:* 105
Hutchins, Laurence *55:* 22
Hutchins, Pat *15:* 142; *70:* 106-107, 108
Hutchinson, Sascha *95:* 211
Hutchinson, William M. *6:* 3, 138; *46:* 70
Hutchison, Paula *23:* 10
Hutton, Clarke *YABC 2:* 335
Hutton, Kathryn *35:* 155; *89:* 91
Hutton, Warwick *20:* 91
Huyette, Marcia *29:* 188
Hyatt, John *54:* 7
Hyde, Maureen *82:* 17; *121:* 145, 146
Hyman, David *117:* 64
Hyman, Trina Schart *1:* 204; *2:* 194; *5:* 153; *6:* 106; *7:* 138, 145; *8:* 22; *10:* 196; *13:* 96; *14:* 114; *15:* 204; *16:* 234; *20:* 82; *22:* 133; *24:* 151; *25:* 79, 82; *26:* 82; *29:* 83; *31:* 37, 39; *34:* 104; *38:* 84, 100, 128; *41:* 49; *43:* 146; *46:* 91, 92, 93, 95, 96, 97, 98, 99, 100, 101, 102, 103, 104-105, 108, 109, 111, 197; *48:* 60, 61; *52:* 32; *60:* 168; *66:* 38; *67:* 214; *72:* 74; *75:* 92; *79:* 57; *82:* 95, 238; *89:* 46; *95:* 91, 92, 93; *100:* 33, 199; *132:* 12

Ichikawa, Satomi *29:* 152; *41:* 52; *47:* 133, 134, 135, 136; *78:* 93, 94; *80:* 81
Ide, Jacqueline *YABC 1:* 39
Ilsley, Velma *3:* 1; *7:* 55; *12:* 109; *37:* 62; *38:* 184
Inga *1:* 142
Ingman, Bruce *134:* 50
Ingpen, Robert *109:* 103, 104; *132:* 138; *137:* 177
Ingraham, Erick *21:* 177; *84:* 256; *103:* 66
Inkpen, Mick *99:* 104, 105; *106:* 44
Innocenti, Roberto *21:* 123; *96:* 122

Inoue, Yosuke *24:* 118
Iofin, Michael *97:* 157
Iosa, Ann *63:* 189
Ipcar, Dahlov *1:* 124-125; *49:* 137, 138, 139, 140-141, 142, 143, 144, 145
Irvin, Fred *13:* 166; *15:* 143-144; *27:* 175
Irving, Jay *45:* 72
Irving, Laurence *27:* 50
Isaac, Joanne *21:* 76
Isadora, Rachel *43:* 159, 160; *54:* 31; *79:* 106-107, 108; *121:* 100, 102
Ishmael, Woodi *24:* 111; *31:* 99
Ives, Ruth *15:* 257

J

Jabar, Cynthia *101:* 201
Jackness, Andrew *94:* 237
Jackson, Julian *91:* 104, 106
Jackson, Michael *43:* 42
Jackson, Shelley *79:* 71; *99:* 109
Jacob, Murv *89:* 30
Jacobi, Kathy *62:* 118
Jacobs, Barbara *9:* 136
Jacobs, Lou, Jr. *9:* 136; *15:* 128
Jacobson, Rick *131:* 222
Jacobus, Tim *79:* 140; *109:* 126; *129:* 180
Jacques, Robin *1:* 70; *2:* 1; *8:* 46; *9:* 20; *15:* 187; *19:* 253; *32:* 102, 103, 104; *43:* 184; *73:* 135; *YABC 1:* 42
Jaffee, Al *66:* 131, 132
Jagr, Miloslav *13:* 197
Jahn-Clough, Lisa *88:* 114
Jahnke, Robert *84:* 24
Jainschigg, Nicholas *80:* 64; *91:* 138; *95:* 63; *99:* 25; *108:* 50
Jakesavic, Nenad *85:* 102
Jakobsen, Kathy *116:* 83
Jakubowski, Charles *14:* 192
Jambor, Louis *YABC 1:* 11
James, Ann *73:* 50; *82:* 113
James, Brian *140:* 91
James, Derek *35:* 187; *44:* 91; *61:* 133; *74:* 2; *80:* 57; *86:* 88; *130:* 30
James, Gilbert *YABC 1:* 43
James, Harold *2:* 151; *3:* 62; *8:* 79; *29:* 113; *51:* 195; *74:* 90
James, Kennon *126:* 211
James, Robin *50:* 106; *53:* 32, 34, 35
James, Will *19:* 150, 152, 153, 155, 163
Janosch *See* Eckert, Horst
Janovitch, Marilyn *68:* 168
Janovitz, Marilyn *87:* 187; *130:* 198
Jansons, Inese *48:* 117
Jansson, Tove *3:* 90; *41:* 106, 108, 109, 110, 111, 113, 114
Jaques, Faith *7:* 11, 132-33; *21:* 83, 84; *69:* 114, 116; *73:* 170
Jaques, Frances Lee *29:* 224
Jauss, Anne Marie *1:* 139; *3:* 34; *10:* 57, 119; *11:* 205; *23:* 194
Jeffers, Susan *17:* 86-87; *25:* 164-165; *26:* 112; *50:* 132, 134-135; *70:* 111, 112-113; *137:* 107, 108, 109, 110, 111
Jefferson, Louise E. *4:* 160
Jenkin-Pearce, Susie *78:* 16
Jenkins, Debra Reid *85:* 202; *114:* 89
Jenkins, Jean *98:* 79, 102
Jenkins, Patrick *72:* 126
Jenkins, Steve *124:* 177
Jenks, Aleta *73:* 117; *124:* 225
Jenkyns, Chris *51:* 97
Jensen, Bruce *95:* 39
Jensinius, Kirsten *56:* 58
Jeram, Anita *89:* 135; *102:* 122, 123; *129:* 112
Jernigan, E. Wesley *85:* 92
Jerome, Karen A. *72:* 194

Jeruchim, Simon 6: 173; 15: 250
Jeschke, Susan 20: 89; 39: 161; 41: 84; 42: 120
Jessel, Camilla 29: 115
Jiang, Cheng An 109: 108
Jiang, Wei 109: 108
Jimenez, Maria 77: 158; 93: 127
Jobling, Curtis 138: 74
Jocelyn, Marthe 118: 83; 137: 219
Joerns, Consuelo 38: 36; 44: 94
John, Diana 12: 209
John, Helen 1: 215; 28: 204
Johns, Elizabeth 127: 33
Johns, Jasper 61: 172
Johns, Jeanne 24: 114
Johnson, Bruce 9: 47
Johnson, Cathy 92: 136
Johnson, Crockett *See* Leisk, David
Johnson, D. William 23: 104
Johnson, Gillian 119: 175
Johnson, Harper 1: 27; 2: 33; 18: 302; 19: 61; 31: 181; 44: 46, 50, 95
Johnson, Ingrid 37: 118
Johnson, James Ralph 1: 23, 127
Johnson, James David 12: 195
Johnson, Jane 48: 136
Johnson, Joel Peter 98: 18; 128: 111
Johnson, John E. 34: 133
Johnson, Kevin 72: 44
Johnson, Kevin Eugene 109: 215
Johnson, Larry 47: 56; 123: 107
Johnson, Margaret S. 35: 131
Johnson, Meredith Merrell 71: 181; 83: 158; 89: 103; 104: 88
Johnson, Milton 1: 67; 2: 71; 26: 45; 31: 107; 60: 112; 68: 96
Johnson, Pamela 16: 174; 52: 145; 62: 140; 73: 116; 85: 64
Johnson, Paul Brett 83: 95; 132: 119
Johnson, Stephen 80: 15; 131: 35; 141: 96
Johnson, Steve 138: 219; 141: 64
Johnson, William R. 38: 91
Johnson-Petrov, Arden 115: 206
Johnston, David McCall 50: 131, 133
Johnston, Lynne 118: 85, 87, 89
Johnstone, Anne 8: 120; 36: 89
Johnstone, Janet Grahame 8: 120; 36: 89
Jonas, Ann 50: 107, 108, 109; 135: 113
Jones, Bob 71: 5; 77: 199
Jones, Carol 5: 131; 72: 185, 186
Jones, Chuck 53: 70, 71
Jones, Davy 89: 176
Jones, Elizabeth Orton 18: 124, 126, 128-129
Jones, Harold 14: 88; 52: 50
Jones, Holly 127: 3
Jones, Jeff 41: 64
Jones, Laurian 25: 24, 27
Jones, Margaret 74: 57
Jones, Randy 131: 104
Jones, Richard 127: 222
Jones, Robert 25: 67
Jones, Wilfred 35: 115; YABC 1: 163
Jordan, Charles 89: 58
Jordan, Martin George 84: 127
Jordan, Richard 84: 36
Jorgenson, Andrea 91: 111
Joseph, James 53: 88
Joudrey, Ken 64: 145; 78: 6
Joyce, William 72: 131, 132, 133, 134; 73: 227
Joyner, Jerry 34: 138
Jucker, Sita 5: 93
Judkis, Jim 37: 38
Juhasz, Victor 31: 67
Jullian, Philippe 24: 206; 25: 203
Jung, Tom 91: 217
Junge, Walter 67: 150
Jupo, Frank 7: 148-149
Justice, Martin 34: 72

K

Kabatova-Taborska, Zdenka 107: 153
Kahl, David 74: 95; 97: 35; 109: 174; 110: 213
Kahl, M. P. 37: 83
Kahl, Virginia 48: 138
Kahn, Katherine Janus 90: 135
Kakimoo, Kozo 11: 148
Kalett, Jim 48: 159, 160, 161
Kalin, Victor 39: 186
Kalman, Maira 96: 131, 132; 137: 115
Kalmenoff, Matthew 22: 191
Kalow, Gisela 32: 105
Kamen, Gloria 1: 41; 9: 119; 10: 178; 35: 157; 78: 236; 98: 82
Kaminsky, Jef 102: 153
Kandell, Alice 35: 133
Kane, Henry B. 14: 90; 18: 219-220
Kane, Robert 18: 131
Kanfer, Larry 66: 141
Kappes, Alfred 28: 104
Karalus, Bob 41: 157
Karas, G. Brian 80: 60; 99: 179; 115: 41; 118: 50; 136: 168
Karasz, Ilonka 128: 163
Karlin, Eugene 10: 63; 20: 131
Karlin, Nurit 63: 78; 103: 110
Karpinski, Tony 134: 160
Kasamatsu, Shiro 139: 155
Kasparavicius, Kestutis 139: 210
Kassian, Olena 64: 94
Kastner, Jill 79: 135; 117: 84, 85
Kasuya, Masahiro 41: 206-207; 51: 100
Katona, Robert 21: 85; 24: 126
Kauffer, E. McKnight 33: 103; 35: 127; 63: 67
Kaufman, Angelika 15: 156
Kaufman, Joe 33: 119
Kaufman, John 13: 158
Kaufman, Stuart 62: 64; 68: 226; 137: 44
Kaufmann, John 1: 174; 4: 159; 8: 43, 1; 10: 102; 18: 133-134; 22: 251
Kaye, Graham 1: 9; 67: 7, 8
Kaye, M. M. 62: 95
Kazalovski, Nata 40: 205
Keane, Bil 4: 135
Kearney, David 72: 47; 121: 83
Keating, Pamel T. 77: 37
Keats, Ezra Jack 3: 18, 105, 257; 14: 101, 102; 33: 129; 57: 79, 80, 82, 83, 84, 87
Keegan, Marcia 9: 122; 32: 93
Keeler, Patricia A. 81: 56
Keely, Jack 119: 95
Keely, John 26: 104; 48: 214
Keen, Eliot 25: 213
Keeping, Charles 9: 124, 185; 15: 28, 134; 18: 115; 44: 194, 196; 47: 25; 52: 3; 54: 156; 69: 123, 124; 74: 56
Keith, Eros 4: 98; 5: 138; 31: 29; 43: 220; 52: 91, 92, 93, 94; 56: 64, 66; 60: 37; 79: 93
Keleinikov, Andrei 65: 101, 102
Kelen, Emery 13: 115
Keller, A. J. 62: 198
Keller, Arthur I. 26: 106
Keller, Dick 36: 123, 125
Keller, Holly 45: 79; 76: 118, 119, 120, 121; 108: 137, 138, 140
Keller, Katie 79: 222; 93: 108
Keller, Ronald 45: 208
Kelley, True 41: 114, 115; 42: 137; 75: 35; 92: 104, 105; 124: 62; 130: 100, 101
Kellogg, Steven 8: 96; 11: 207; 14: 130; 20: 58; 29: 140-141; 30: 35; 41: 141; 57: 89, 90, 92, 93, 94, 96; 59: 182; 73: 141; 77: 129; 130: 105, 106; YABC 1: 65, 73
Kelly, Geoff 97: 196; 112: 25
Kelly, Kathleen M. 71: 109

Kelly, Laura 89: 217
Kelly, Walt 18: 136-141, 144-146, 148-149
Kemble, E. W. 34: 75; 44: 178; YABC 2: 54, 59
Kemp-Welsh, Lucy 24: 197; 100: 214
Kendrick, Dennis 79: 213
Kennaway, Adrienne 60: 55, 56
Kennedy, Paul Edward 6: 190; 8: 132; 33: 120
Kennedy, Richard 3: 93; 12: 179; 44: 193; 100: 15; YABC 1: 57
Kent, Jack 24: 136; 37: 37; 40: 81; 84: 89; 86: 150; 88: 77
Kent, Rockwell 5: 166; 6: 129; 20: 225, 226, 227, 229; 59: 144
Kenyon, Tony 81: 201; 127: 74
Kepes, Juliet 13: 119
Kerins, Anthony 76: 84
Kerr, Judity 24: 137
Kerr, Phyllis Forbes 72: 141
Kessler, Leonard 1: 108; 7: 139; 14: 107, 227; 22: 101; 44: 96; 67: 79; 82: 123
Kesteven, Peter 35: 189
Ketcham, Hank 28: 140, 141, 142
Kettelkamp, Larry 2: 164
Key, Alexander 8: 99
Khalsa, Dayal Kaur 62: 99
Kiakshuk 8: 59
Kidd, Chip 94: 23
Kidd, Tom 64: 199; 81: 189
Kiddell-Monroe, Joan 19: 201; 55: 59, 60; 87: 174; 121: 112
Kidder, Harvey 9: 105; 80: 41
Kidwell, Carl 43: 145
Kieffer, Christa 41: 89
Kiesler, Kate 110: 105; 136: 142
Kiff, Ken 40: 45
Kilbride, Robert 37: 100
Kilby, Don 141: 144
Kim, Glenn 99: 82
Kimball, Anton 78: 114; 119: 105
Kimball, Yeffe 23: 116; 37: 88
Kincade, Orin 34: 116
Kindersley, Barnabas 96: 110
Kindred, Wendy 7: 151
King, Colin 53: 3
King, Robin 10: 164-165
King, Stephen Michael 141: 31
King, Tara Calahan 139: 172
King, Tony 39: 121
Kingman, Dong 16: 287; 44: 100, 102, 104
Kingsley, Charles YABC 2: 182
Kingston, Maxine Hong 53: 92
Kipling, John Lockwood YABC 2: 198
Kipling, Rudyard YABC 2: 196
Kipniss, Robert 29: 59
Kirchherr, Astrid 55: 23
Kirchhoff, Art 28: 136
Kirk, David 117: 88, 89
Kirk, Ruth 5: 96
Kirk, Tim 32: 209, 211; 72: 89; 83: 49
Kirmse, Marguerite 15: 283; 18: 153
Kirsch, Vincent X. 124: 207
Kirschner, Ruth 22: 154
Kish, Ely 73: 119; 79: 2
Kitamura, Satoshi 62: 102; 98: 91; 101: 147; 138: 2
Kitchel, JoAnn E. 133: 32
Kitchen, Herbert Thomas 70: 126
Kittelsen, Theodor 62: 14
Kiuchi, Tatsuro 114: 71
Klapholz, Mel 13: 35
Klein, Bill 89: 105
Klein, Robert 55: 77
Klein, Suzanna 63: 104
Kleinman, Zalman 28: 143
Kliban, B. 35: 137, 138
Kline, Michael 127: 66
Knabel, Lonnie 73: 103; 75: 187, 228
Kneen, Maggie 140: 139
Knight, Ann 34: 143
Knight, Christopher 13: 125

Knight, Hilary *1:* 233; *3:* 21; *15:* 92, 158-159; *16:* 258-260; *18:* 235; *19:* 169; *35:* 242; *46:* 167; *52:* 116; *69:* 126, 127; *132:* 129; *YABC 1:* 168-169, 172
Knorr, Peter *126:* 92, 93
Knotts, Howard *20:* 4; *25:* 170; *36:* 163
Knutson, Barbara *112:* 134
Knutson, Kimberley *115:* 90
Kobayashi, Ann *39:* 58
Kocsis, J. C. *See* Paul, James
Koehn, Ilse *34:* 198; *79:* 123
Koelsch, Michael *99:* 182; *107:* 164; *109:* 239; *138:* 142
Koering, Ursula *85:* 46
Koering, Ursula *3:* 28; *4:* 14; *44:* 5; *64:* 140, 141
Koerner, Henry *See* Koerner, W.H.D.
Koerner, W.H.D. *14:* 216; *21:* 88, 89, 90, 91; *23:* 211
Koffler, Camilla *36:* 113
Koide, Yasuko *50:* 114
Kolado, Karen *102:* 228
Komoda, Kiyo *9:* 128; *13:* 214
Konashevich, Vladimir *61:* 160
Konashevicha, V. *YABC 1:* 26
Konigsburg, E. L. *4:* 138; *48:* 141, 142, 144, 145; *94:* 129, 130; *126:* 129, 130, 131
Kooiker, Leonie *48:* 148
Koonook, Simon *65:* 157
Koontz, Robin Michal *136:* 155
Koopmans, Loek *101:* 121
Kopper, Lisa *72:* 152, 153; *105:* 135, 136
Korach, Mimi *1:* 128-129; *2:* 52; *4:* 39; *5:* 159; *9:* 129; *10:* 21; *24:* 69
Koren, Edward *5:* 100; *65:* 65, 67
Koscielniak, Bruce *99:* 122
Koshkin, Alexander *92:* 180
Kossin, Sandy *10:* 71; *23:* 105
Kostin, Andrej *26:* 204
Kotzky, Brian *68:* 184
Kovacevic, Zivojin *13:* 247
Kovalski, Maryann *58:* 120; *84:* 88; *97:* 124, 125, 126
Krahn, Fernando *2:* 257; *34:* 206; *49:* 152
Kramer, Anthony *33:* 81
Kramer, David *96:* 162; *109:* 132
Kramer, Frank *6:* 121
Krantz, Kathy *35:* 83
Kratter, Paul *139:* 65
Kraus, Robert *13:* 217; *65:* 113; *93:* 93, 94
Kredel, Fritz *6:* 35; *17:* 93-96; *22:* 147; *24:* 175; *29:* 130; *35:* 77; *YABC 2:* 166, 300
Krementz, Jill *17:* 98; *49:* 41
Krenina, Katya *117:* 106; *125:* 133
Kresin, Robert *23:* 19
Krieger, Salem *54:* 164
Kriegler, Lyn *73:* 29
Krommes, Beth *128:* 141
Krone, Mike *101:* 71
Kronheimer, Ann *135:* 119
Kruck, Gerald *88:* 181
Krupinski, Loretta *67:* 104; *102:* 131
Krupp, Robin Rector *53:* 96, 98
Krush, Beth *1:* 51, 85; *2:* 233; *4:* 115; *9:* 61; *10:* 191; *11:* 196; *18:* 164-165; *32:* 72; *37:* 203; *43:* 57; *60:* 102, 103, 107, 108, 109
Krush, Joe *2:* 233; *4:* 115; *9:* 61; *10:* 191; *11:* 196; *18:* 164-165; *32:* 72, 91; *37:* 203; *43:* 57; *60:* 102, 103, 107, 108, 109
Krych, Duane *91:* 43
Krykorka, Vladyana *96:* 147
Kubinyi, Laszlo *4:* 116; *6:* 113; *16:* 118; *17:* 100; *28:* 227; *30:* 172; *49:* 24, 28; *54:* 23
Kubricht, Mary *73:* 118
Kucharik, Elena *139:* 31
Kuchera, Kathleen *84:* 5
Kuhn, Bob *17:* 91; *35:* 235
Kukalis, Romas *90:* 27; *139:* 37
Kuklin, Susan *63:* 82, 83, 84

Kunhardt, Dorothy *53:* 101
Kunhardt, Edith *67:* 105, 106
Künstler, Mort *10:* 73; *32:* 143
Kurchevsky, V. *34:* 61
Kurczok, Belinda *121:* 118
Kurelek, William *8:* 107
Kuriloff, Ron *13:* 19
Kuskin, Karla *2:* 170; *68:* 115, 116; *111:* 116
Kutzer, Ernst *19:* 249
Kuzma, Steve *57:* 8; *62:* 93
Kuznetsova, Berta *74:* 45
Kvasnosky, Laura McGee *93:* 103

L

LaBlanc, André *24:* 146
Laboccetta, Mario *27:* 120
Labrosse, Darcia *58:* 88; *108:* 77
LaCava, Vince *95:* 118
Laceky, Adam *32:* 121
Lacis, Astra *85:* 117
La Croix *YABC 2:* 4
Ladwig, Tim *98:* 212; *117:* 76
La Farge, Margaret *47:* 141
LaFave, Kim *64:* 177; *72:* 39; *97:* 146; *99:* 172; *106:* 123
Lagarrigue, Jerome *136:* 102
Laimgruber, Monika *11:* 153
Laite, Gordon *1:* 130-131; *8:* 209; *31:* 113; *40:* 63; *46:* 117
LaMarche, Jim *46:* 204; *61:* 56; *94:* 69; *114:* 22; *129:* 163
Lamb, Jim *10:* 117
Lambase, Barbara *101:* 185
Lambert, J. K. *38:* 129; *39:* 24
Lambert, Sally Anne *133:* 191
Lambert, Saul *23:* 112; *33:* 107; *54:* 136
Lambert, Stephen *109:* 33
Lambo, Don *6:* 156; *35:* 115; *36:* 146
Lamut, Sonja *57:* 193
Lamut, Sonya *85:* 102
Landa, Peter *11:* 95; *13:* 177; *53:* 119
Landau, Jacob *38:* 111
Landis, Joan *104:* 23
Landon, Lucinda *79:* 31
Landshoff, Ursula *13:* 124
Lane, Daniel *112:* 60
Lane, John R. *8:* 145
Lane, John *15:* 176-177; *30:* 146
Lang, G. D. *48:* 56
Lang, Gary *73:* 75
Lang, Jerry *18:* 295
Lange, Dorothea *50:* 141
Langner, Nola *8:* 110; *42:* 36
Lanino, Deborah *105:* 148
Lantz, Paul *1:* 82, 102; *27:* 88; *34:* 102; *45:* 123
Larkin, Bob *84:* 225
Laroche, Giles *126:* 140
Larrecq, John *44:* 108; *68:* 56
Larsen, Suzanne *1:* 13
Larson, Gary *57:* 121, 122, 123, 124, 125, 126, 127
Larsson, Carl *35:* 144, 145, 146, 147, 148-149, 150, 152, 153, 154
Larsson, Karl *19:* 177
Lartitegui, Ana G. *105:* 167
La Rue, Michael D. *13:* 215
Lasker, Joe *7:* 186-187; *14:* 55; *38:* 115; *39:* 47; *83:* 113, 114, 115
Latham, Barbara *16:* 188-189; *43:* 71
Lathrop, Dorothy *14:* 117, 118-119; *15:* 109; *16:* 78-79, 81; *32:* 201, 203; *33:* 112; *YABC 2:* 301
Lattimore, Eleanor Frances *7:* 156
Lauden, Claire *16:* 173
Lauden, George, Jr. *16:* 173

Laune, Paul *2:* 235; *34:* 31
Lauré, Jason *49:* 53; *50:* 122
Lauter, Richard *63:* 29; *67:* 111; *77:* 198
Lavallee, Barbara *74:* 157; *92:* 154; *96:* 126
Lave, Fitz Hugh *59:* 139
Lavis, Stephen *43:* 143; *87:* 137, 164, 165
Lawrence, John *25:* 131; *30:* 141; *44:* 198, 200
Lawrence, Stephen *20:* 195
Lawson, Carol *6:* 38; *42:* 93, 131
Lawson, George *17:* 280
Lawson, Robert *5:* 26; *6:* 94; *13:* 39; *16:* 11; *20:* 100, 102, 103; *54:* 3; *66:* 12; *100:* 144, 145; *YABC 2:* 222, 224-225, 227-235, 237-241
Layfield, Kathie *60:* 194
Lazare, Jerry *44:* 109; *74:* 28
Lazarevich, Mila *17:* 118
Lazarus, Claire *103:* 30
Lazarus, Keo Felker *21:* 94
Lazzaro, Victor *11:* 126
Lea, Tom *43:* 72, 74
Leacroft, Richard *6:* 140
Leaf, Munro *20:* 99
Leake, Donald *70:* 41
Leander, Patricia *23:* 27
Lear, Edward *18:* 183-185
Lebenson, Richard *6:* 209; *7:* 76; *23:* 145; *44:* 191; *87:* 153
Le Cain, Errol *6:* 141; *9:* 3; *22:* 142; *25:* 198; *28:* 173; *68:* 128, 129; *86:* 49
Lechon, Daniel *113:* 211
Leder, Dora *129:* 172
Leduc, Bernard *102:* 36
Lee, Alan *62:* 25, 28
Lee, Bryce *99:* 60; *101:* 195
Lee, Dom *83:* 118, 120; *93:* 123; *121:* 121, 126
Lee, Doris *13:* 246; *32:* 183; *44:* 111
Lee, Hector Viveros *115:* 96
Lee, Jared *93:* 200
Lee, Jody *81:* 121; *82:* 225; *91:* 155; *100:* 182
Lee, Jody A. *127:* 124, 126, 127 *See also* Lee, Jody
Lee, Manning de V. *2:* 200; *17:* 12; *27:* 87; *37:* 102, 103, 104; *YABC 2:* 304
Lee, Marie G. *138:* 157
Lee, Paul *97:* 100; *105:* 72, 209; *109:* 177; *128:* 113
Lee, Robert J. *3:* 97; *67:* 124
Lee, Victor *96:* 228; *105:* 182; *140:* 196
Leech, Dorothy *98:* 76
Leech, John *15:* 59
Leedy, Loreen *84:* 142; *128:* 144, 145, 146
Leeman, Michael *44:* 157
Leeming, Catherine *87:* 39
Lees, Harry *6:* 112
LeFever, Bill *88:* 220, 221
Legènisel *47:* 111
Legrand, Edy *18:* 89, 93
Lehman, Barbara *73:* 123
Lehrman, Rosalie *2:* 180
Leichman, Seymour *5:* 107
Leighton, Clare *25:* 130; *33:* 168; *37:* 105, 106, 108, 109
Leisk, David *1:* 140-141; *11:* 54; *30:* 137, 142, 143, 144
Leister, Brian *89:* 45; *106:* 37; *114:* 67
Leloir, Maurice *18:* 77, 80, 83, 99
Lemieux, Michèle *100:* 148; *139:* 153
Lemke, Horst *14:* 98; *38:* 117, 118, 119
Lemke, R. W. *42:* 162
Lemon, David Gwynne *9:* 1
LeMoult, Adolph *82:* 116
Lenn, Michael *136:* 89
Lennon, John *114:* 100
Lennox, Elsie *95:* 163
Lenski, Lois *1:* 144; *26:* 135, 137, 139, 141; *100:* 153, 154
Lent, Blair *1:* 116-117; *2:* 174; *3:* 206-207; *7:* 168-169; *34:* 62; *68:* 217; *133:* 101

Leonard, Richard *91:* 128
Leone, Leonard *49:* 190
Lerner, Carol *86:* 140, 141, 142
Lerner, Judith *116:* 138
Lerner, Sharon *11:* 157; *22:* 56
Leroux-Hugon, Hélène *132:* 139
Leslie, Cecil *19:* 244
Lessac, Frane *80:* 182, 207; *96:* 182
Lester, Alison *50:* 124; *90:* 147, 148; *129:* 130
Le Tord, Bijou *49:* 156; *95:* 112
Levai, Blaise *39:* 130
Levin, Ted *12:* 148
Levine, David *43:* 147, 149, 150, 151, 152; *64:* 11
Levine, Joe *71:* 88
Levine, Marge *81:* 127
Levit, Herschel *24:* 223
Levstek, Ljuba *131:* 192; *134:* 216
Levy, Jessica Ann *19:* 225; *39:* 191
Levy, Lina *117:* 126
Lewin, Betsy *32:* 114; *48:* 177; *90:* 151; *91:* 125; *92:* 85; *115:* 105
Lewin, Ted *4:* 77; *8:* 168; *20:* 110; *21:* 99, 100; *27:* 110; *28:* 96, 97; *31:* 49; *45:* 55; *48:* 223; *60:* 20, 119, 120; *62:* 139; *66:* 108; *71:* 12; *72:* 21; *74:* 226; *76:* 139, 140; *77:* 82; *79:* 87; *85:* 49, 177; *86:* 55; *88:* 182; *93:* 28, 29; *94:* 34, 182, 194; *99:* 156; *104:* 8; *115:* 123; *118:* 74; *119:* 114, 116; *131:* 54
Lewis, Allen *15:* 112
Lewis, E. B. *88:* 143; *93:* 109; *119:* 79; *124:* 113; *128:* 49
Lewis, Jan *81:* 22
Lewis, Kim *136:* 165
Lewis, Richard W. *52:* 25
Lewis, Robin Baird *98:* 193
Leydon, Rita Flodén *21:* 101
Lieblich, Irene *22:* 173; *27:* 209, 214
Lieder, Rick *108:* 197
Lies, Brian *92:* 40; *141:* 101
Liese, Charles *4:* 222
Life, Kay *79:* 49
Lifton, Robert Jay *66:* 154
Lightburn, Ron *86:* 153; *91:* 122
Lightfoot, Norman R. *45:* 47
Lignell, Lois *37:* 114
Lill, Debra *121:* 70
Lilly, Charles *8:* 73; *20:* 127; *48:* 53; *72:* 9, 16; *77:* 98; *102:* 94
Lilly, Ken *37:* 224
Lim, John *43:* 153
Limona, Mercedes *51:* 183
Lincoln, Patricia Henderson *27:* 27; *78:* 127
Lindahn, Ron *84:* 17
Lindahn, Val *84:* 17
Lindberg, Howard *10:* 123; *16:* 190
Lindberg, Jeffrey *64:* 77; *77:* 71; *79:* 54; *80:* 149
Linden, Seymour *18:* 200-201; *43:* 140
Linder, Richard *27:* 119
Lindman, Maj *43:* 154
Lindsay, Norman *67:* 114
Lindsay, Vachel *40:* 118
Line, Les *27:* 143
Linell *See* Smith, Linell
Lionni, Leo *8:* 115; *72:* 159, 160, 161
Lipinsky, Lino *2:* 156; *22:* 175
Lippincott, Gary A. *70:* 35; *119:* 118
Lippman, Peter *8:* 31; *31:* 119, 120, 160
Lisi, Victoria *89:* 145
Lisker, Sonia O. *16:* 274; *31:* 31; *44:* 113, 114
Lisowski, Gabriel *47:* 144; *49:* 157
Lissim, Simon *17:* 138
Little, Ed *89:* 145
Little, Harold *16:* 72
Little, Mary E. *28:* 146
Litty, Julie *111:* 63
Livesly, Lorna *19:* 216
Livingston, Susan *95:* 22

Llerena, Carlos Antonio *19:* 181
Lloyd, Errol *11:* 39; *22:* 178
Lloyd, Megan *77:* 118; *80:* 113; *97:* 75; *117:*94, 95
Lo, Koon-chiu *7:* 134
Loates, Glen *63:* 76
Lobel, Anita *6:* 87; *9:* 141; *18:* 248; *55:* 85, 86, 87, 88, 93, 104; *60:* 67; *78:* 263; *82:* 110; *96:* 157, 159; *101:* 84; *132:* 35
Lobel, Arnold *1:* 188-189; *5:* 12; *6:* 147; *7:* 167, 209; *18:* 190-191; *25:* 39, 43; *27:* 40; *29:* 174; *52:* 127; *55:* 89, 91, 94, 95, 97, 98, 99, 100, 101, 102, 103, 105, 106; *60:* 18, 31; *66:* 181, 183; *75:* 57; *82:* 246; *136:* 146
Locker, Thomas *109:* 134
Lodge, Bernard *107:* 125, 126
Lodge, Jo *112:* 119
Loefgren, Ulf *3:* 108
Loescher, Ann *20:* 108
Loescher, Gil *20:* 108
Loew, David *93:* 184
Lofting, Hugh *15:* 182-183; *100:* 161, 162
Lofts, Pamela *60:* 188
Loh, George *38:* 88
Lomberg, Jon *58:* 160
Lonette, Reisie *11:* 211; *12:* 168; *13:* 56; *36:* 122; *43:* 155
Long, Loren *99:* 176
Long, Miles *115:* 174
Long, Sally *42:* 184
Long, Sylvia *74:* 168; *132:* 63
Longoni, Eduardo *73:* 85
Longtemps, Ken *17:* 123; *29:* 221; *69:* 82
Looser, Heinz *YABC 2:* 208
Lopshire, Robert *6:* 149; *21:* 117; *34:* 166; *73:* 13
Lord, John Vernon *21:* 104; *23:* 25; *51:* 22
Lorenz, Albert *40:* 146; *115:* 127
Loretta, Sister Mary *33:* 73
Lorraine, Walter H. *3:* 110; *4:* 123; *16:* 192; *103:* 119
Loss, Joan *11:* 163
Louderback, Walt *YABC 1:* 164
Lousada, Sandra *40:* 138
Low, Joseph *14:* 124, 125; *18:* 68; *19:* 194; *31:* 166; *80:* 239
Low, William *62:* 175; *80:* 147; *112:* 194
Lowenheim, Alfred *13:* 65-66
Lowenstein, Sallie *116:* 90, 91
Lowitz, Anson *17:* 124; *18:* 215
Lowrey, Jo *8:* 133
Lubell, Winifred *1:* 207; *3:* 15; *6:* 151
Lubin, Leonard B. *19:* 224; *36:* 79, 80; *45:* 128, 129, 131, 132, 133, 134, 135, 136, 137, 139, 140, 141; *70:* 95; *YABC 2:* 96
Lucht, Irmgard *82:* 145
Ludwig, Helen *33:* 144, 145
Lufkin, Raymond *38:* 138; *44:* 48
Luhrs, Henry *7:* 123; *11:* 120
Lujan, Tonita *82:* 33
Lupo, Dom *4:* 204
Lustig, Loretta *30:* 186; *46:* 134, 135, 136, 137
Luzak, Dennis *52:* 121; *99:* 142
Lydbury, Jane *82:* 98
Lydecker, Laura *21:* 113; *42:* 53
Lynch, Charles *16:* 33
Lynch, Marietta *29:* 137; *30:* 171
Lynch, P. J. *126:* 228; *129:* 110; *132:* 247
Lyon, Carol *102:* 26
Lyon, Elinor *6:* 154
Lyon, Fred *14:* 16
Lyons, Oren *8:* 193
Lyster, Michael *26:* 41

M

Maas, Dorothy *6:* 175
Maas, Julie *47:* 61
Macaulay, David *46:* 139, 140-141, 142, 143, 144-145, 147, 149, 150; *72:* 167, 168, 169; *137:* 129, 130, 131, 132
MacCarthy, Patricia *69:* 141
Macdonald, Alister *21:* 55
Macdonald, Roberta *19:* 237; *52:* 164
MacDonald, Norman *13:* 99
MacDonald, Suse *54:* 41; *109* 138; *130:* 156
Mace, Varian *49:* 159
Macguire, Robert Reid *18:* 67
Machetanz, Fredrick *34:* 147, 148
MacInnes, Ian *35:* 59
MacIntyre, Elisabeth *17:* 127, 128
Mack, Stan *17:* 129; *96:* 33
Mackay, Donald *17:* 60
MacKaye, Arvia *32:* 119
Mackenzie, Stuart *73:* 213
MacKenzie, Garry *33:* 159
Mackie, Clare *87:* 134
Mackinlay, Miguel *27:* 22
MacKinstry, Elizabeth *15:* 110; *42:* 139, 140, 141, 142, 143, 144, 145
MacLeod, Lee *91:* 167
Maclise, Daniel *YABC 2:* 257
Madden, Don *3:* 112-113; *4:* 33, 108, 155; *7:* 193; *78:* 12; *YABC 2:* 211
Maddison, Angela Mary *10:* 83
Maestro, Giulio *8:* 124; *12:* 17; *13:* 108; *25:* 182; *54:* 147; *59:* 114, 115, 116, 117, 118, 121, 123, 124, 125, 126, 127; *68:* 37, 38; *106:* 129, 130, 131, 136, 137, 138
Maffia, Daniel *60:* 200
Maggio, Viqui *58:* 136, 181; *74:* 150; *75:* 90; *85:* 159; *90:* 158; *109:* 184
Magnus, Erica *77:* 123
Magnuson, Diana *28:* 102; *34:* 190; *41:* 175
Magovern, Peg *103:* 123
Maguire, Sheila *41:* 100
Magurn, Susan *91:* 30
Mahony, Will *37:* 120
Mahony, Will *85:* 116
Mahood, Kenneth *24:* 141
Maik, Henri *9:* 102
Maione, Heather Harms *106:* 5
Maisto, Carol *29:* 87
Maitland, Antony *1:* 100, 176; *8:* 41; *17:* 246; *24:* 46; *25:* 177, 178; *32:* 74; *60:* 65, 195; *67:* 156; *87:* 131; *101:* 110
Mak, Kam *72:* 25; *75:* 43; *87:* 186; *97:* 24; *102:* 154
Makie, Pam *37:* 117
Maktima, Joe *116:* 191
Maland, Nick *99:* 77
Male, Alan *132:* 64
Malone, James Hiram *84:* 161
Malone, Nola Langner *82:* 239
Malsberg, Edward *51:* 175
Malvern, Corinne *2:* 13; *34:* 148, 149
Mancusi, Stephen *63:* 198, 199
Mandelbaum, Ira *31:* 115
Manders, John *138:* 152, 155
Manet, Edouard *23:* 170
Mangurian, David *14:* 133
Manham, Allan *42:* 109; *77:* 180; *80:* 227
Manley, Matt *103:* 167; *117:* 98
Manniche, Lise *31:* 121
Manning, Jane *96:* 203
Manning, Jo *63:* 154
Manning, Samuel F. *5:* 75
Mantel, Richard *57:* 73; *63:* 106; *82:* 255
Maraja *15:* 86; *YABC 1:* 28; *2:* 115

Marcellino, Fred *20:* 125; *34:* 222; *53:* 125; *58:* 205; *61:* 64, 121, 122; *68:* 154, 156-157, 158, 159; *72:* 25; *86:* 184; *98:* 181; *118:* 129, 130, 131
Marchesi, Stephen *34:* 140; *46:* 72; *50:* 147; *66:* 239; *70:* 33; *73:* 18, 114, 163; *77:* 47, 76, 147; *78:* 79; *80:* 30; *81:* 6; *89:* 66; *93:* 21, 130; *94:* 94; *97:* 66; *98:* 96; *114:* 115, 116
Marchiori, Carlos *14:* 60
Marciano, John Bemelmans *118:* 133
Marcus, Barry David *139:* 248
Margules, Gabriele *21:* 120
Mariana *See* Foster, Marian Curtis
Mariano, Michael *52:* 108
Marino, Dorothy *6:* 37; *14:* 135
Mario, Heide Stetson *101:* 202
Maris, Ron *71:* 123
Maritz, Nicolaas *85:* 123
Mark, Mona *65:* 105; *68:* 205; *116:* 213
Markham, R. L. *17:* 240
Marks, Alan *104:* 104; *109:* 182
Marks, Cara *54:* 9
Marokvia, Artur *31:* 122
Marquez, Susan *108:* 121
Marrella, Maria Pia *62:* 116
Marriott, Pat *30:* 30; *34:* 39; *35:* 164, 165, 166; *44:* 170; *48:* 186, 187, 188, 189, 191, 192, 193; *91:* 92
Mars, W. T. *1:* 161; *3:* 115; *4:* 208, 225; *5:* 92, 105, 186; *8:* 214; *9:* 12; *13:* 121; *27:* 151; *31:* 180; *38:* 102; *48:* 66; *62:* 164, 165; *64:* 62; *68:* 229; *79:* 55
Marschall, Ken *85:* 29
Marsh, Christine *3:* 164
Marsh, James *73:* 137
Marsh, Reginald *17:* 5; *19:* 89; *22:* 90, 96
Marshall, Anthony D. *18:* 216
Marshall, James *6:* 160; *40:* 221; *42:* 24, 25, 29; *51:* 111, 112, 113, 114, 115, 116, 117, 118, 119, 120, 121; *64:* 13; *75:* 126, 127, 128, 129; *102:* 10, 12
Marshall, Janet *97:* 154
Marstall, Bob *55:* 145; *84:* 153, 170; *104:* 145
Martchenko, Michael *50:* 129, 153, 155, 156, 157; *83:* 144, 145
Marten, Ruth *129:* 52
Martin, Charles E. *70:* 144
Martin, David Stone *24:* 232; *62:* 4
Martin, Fletcher *18:* 213; *23:* 151
Martin, René *7:* 144; *42:* 148, 149, 150
Martin, Richard E. *51:* 157; *131:* 203
Martin, Ron *32:* 81
Martin, Stefan *8:* 68; *32:* 124, 126; *56:* 33
Martinez, Ed *58:* 192; *72:* 231; *77:* 33; *80:* 214
Martinez, John *6:* 113; *118:* 13; *139:* 143
Marton, Jirina *95:* 127, 128
Martorell, Antonio *84:* 6; *97:* 161
Martucci, Griesbach *52:* 106
Marvin, Frederic *83:* 86
Marx, Robert F. *24:* 143
Masefield, Judith *19:* 208, 209
Masheris, Robert *78:* 51
Mason, George F. *14:* 139
Mason, Robert *84:* 96
Massey, Barbara *68:* 142
Massie, Diane Redfield *16:* 194
Massie, Kim *31:* 43
Mataya, David *121:* 66
Mathers, Petra *119:* 135
Mathewuse, James *51:* 143
Mathieu, Joseph *14:* 33; *39:* 206; *43:* 167; *56:* 180; *79:* 126; *94:* 147
Matsubara, Naoko *12:* 121
Matsuda, Shizu *13:* 167
Matte, L'Enc *22:* 183
Mattelson, Marvin *36:* 50, 51
Matthews, F. Leslie *4:* 216
Mattingly, David *71:* 76, 77; *82:* 64; *91:* 216, 217; *109:* 25

Matulay, Laszlo *5:* 18; *43:* 168
Matus, Greta *12:* 142
Mauldin, Bill *27:* 23
Mauterer, Erin Marie *119:* 5
Mawicke, Tran *9:* 137; *15:* 191; *47:* 100
Mawson, Matt *74:* 115
Max, Peter *45:* 146, 147, 148-149, 150
Maxie, Betty *40:* 135
Maxwell, John Alan *1:* 148
Mayan, Earl *7:* 193
Mayer, Danuta *117:* 103
Mayer, Marianna *32:* 132
Mayer, Mercer *11:* 192; *16:* 195-196; *20:* 55, 57; *32:* 129, 130, 132, 133, 134; *41:* 144, 248, 252; *58:* 186; *73:* 140, 142, 143; *137:* 137, 138
Mayhew, James *85:* 121; *138:* 187
Mayhew, Richard *3:* 106
Mayo, Gretchen Will *38:* 81; *84:* 166
Mays, Victor *5:* 127; *8:* 45, 153; *14:* 245; *23:* 50; *34:* 155; *40:* 79; *45:* 158; *54:* 91; *66:* 240
Mazal, Chanan *49:* 104
Maze, Deborah *71:* 83
Mazellan, Ron *75:* 97, 98
Mazetti, Alan *112:* 72
Mazille, Capucine *96:* 168
Mazza, Adriana Saviozzi *19:* 215
Mazzella, Mary Jo *82:* 165
Mazzetti, Alan *45:* 210
McAfee, Steve *135:* 146
McAlinden, Paul *112:* 128
McBride, Angus *28:* 49; *103:* 40
McBride, Will *30:* 110
McCaffery, Janet *38:* 145
McCallum, Graham *78:* 78
McCallum, Stephen *141:* 143
McCann, Gerald *3:* 50; *4:* 94; *7:* 54; *41:* 121
McCay, Winsor *41:* 124, 126, 128-129, 130-131; *134:* 77, 79
McClary, Nelson *1:* 111
McClintock, Barbara *57:* 135; *95:* 130
McClintock, Theodore *14:* 141
McCloskey, Robert *1:* 184-185; *2:* 186-187; *17:* 209; *39:* 139, 140, 141, 142, 143, 146, 147, 148; *85:* 150, 151; *100:* 172, 173, 174
McClung, Robert *2:* 189; *68:* 166, 167
McClure, Gillian *31:* 132
McConnel, Jerry *31:* 75, 187
McConnell, Mary *102:* 49
McCord, Kathleen Garry *78:* 236
McCormack, John *66:* 193
McCormick, A. D. *35:* 119
McCormick, Dell J. *19:* 216
McCrady, Lady *16:* 198; *39:* 127
McCrea, James *3:* 122; *33:* 216
McCrea, Ruth *3:* 122; *27:* 102; *33:* 216
McCue, Lisa *65:* 148, 149; *77:* 54; *80:* 132
McCully, Emily Arnold *2:* 89; *4:* 120-121, 146, 197; *5:* 2, 129; *7:* 191; *11:* 122; *15:* 210; *33:* 23; *35:* 244; *37:* 122; *39:* 88; *40:* 103; *50:* 30, 31, 32, 33, 34, 35, 36-37; *52:* 89, 90; *57:* 6; *62:* 3; *70:* 195; *86:* 82; *96:* 192; *97:* 93; *110:* 143, 144; *117:* 47
McCurdy, Michael *13:* 153; *24:* 85; *81:* 160; *82:* 157, 158; *86:* 125; *97:* 92; *117:* 178; *132:* 6
McCusker, Paul *99:* 19
McDaniel, Jerry *132:* 135
McDermott, Beverly Brodsky *11:* 180
McDermott, Gerald *16:* 201; *74:* 174-175
McDermott, Mike *96:* 187
McDonald, Jill *13:* 155; *26:* 128
McDonald, Ralph J. *5:* 123, 195
McDonough, Don *10:* 163
McElmurry, Jill *137:* 148
McElrath-Eslick, Lori *129:* 145
McEntee, Dorothy *37:* 124
McEwan, Keith *88:* 116

McFall, Christie *12:* 144
McGaw, Laurie *109:* 243
McGee, Barbara *6:* 165
McGinley-Nally, Sharon *131:* 19
McGinnis, Robert *110:* 113
McGovern, Tara *98:* 171
McGraw, Sheila *83:* 146
McGregor, Malcolm *23:* 27
McHale, John *138:* 190
McHugh, Tom *23:* 64
McIntosh, Jon *42:* 56
McKay, Donald *2:* 118; *32:* 157; *45:* 151, 152
McKeating, Eileen *44:* 58
McKee, David *10:* 48; *21:* 9; *70:* 154, 155; *107:* 139, 140, 141; *134:* 218
McKee, Diana *109:* 185
McKie, Roy *7:* 44
McKillip, Kathy *30:* 153
McKinney, Ena *26:* 39
McKinnon, James *136:* 75
McLachlan, Edward *5:* 89
McLaren, Chesley *133:* 53
McLaren, Kirsty *123:* 99; *124:* 226
Mclean, Andrew *113:* 117, 118, 120, 121
McLean, Meg *94:* 196
McLean, Sammis *32:* 197
McLean, Wilson *90:* 29; *113:* 195
McLoughlin, John C. *47:* 149
McLoughlin, Wayne *102:* 230; *134:* 178
McMahon, Robert *36:* 155; *69:* 169
McManus, Shawn *85:* 71
McMillan, Bruce *22:* 184
McMullan, James *40:* 33; *67:* 172; *87:* 142; *99:* 63, 64
McNaught, Harry *12:* 80; *32:* 136
McNaughton, Colin *39:* 149; *40:* 108; *92:* 144, 145, 146; *134:* 104, 106
McNicholas, Maureen *38:* 148
McPhail, David *14:* 105; *23:* 135; *37:* 217, 218, 220, 221; *47:* 151, 152, 153, 154, 155, 156, 158-159, 160, 162-163, 164; *71:* 211; *81:* 139, 140, 142; *86:* 123; *132:* 150; *140:* 129, 131, 132
McPhee, Richard B. *41:* 133
McPheeters, Neal *78:* 132; *86:* 90; *99:* 162; *111:* 141
McQuade, Jacqueline *124:* 223
McQueen, Lucinda *28:* 149; *41:* 249; *46:* 206; *53:* 103
McVay, Tracy *11:* 68
McVicker, Charles *39:* 150
Mead, Ben Carlton *43:* 75
Meade, Holly *90:* 102; *94:* 101
Mecray, John *33:* 62
Meddaugh, Susan *20:* 42; *29:* 143; *41:* 241; *77:* 50; *84:* 173, 174, 175, 176-77, 178; *125:* 160, 161, 162
Meehan, Dennis B. *56:* 144
Meents, Len W. *73:* 147, 150
Meers, Tony *99:* 113
Meisel, Paul *98:* 137; *124:* 18
Melendez, Francisco *72:* 180
Melo, John *16:* 285; *58:* 203
Meloni, Maria Teresa *98:* 62
Meltzer, Ericka *See* O'Rourke, Ericka
Menasco, Milton *43:* 85
Mendelson, Steven T. *86:* 154
Mendelssohn, Felix *19:* 170
Mendola, Christopher *88:* 223
Meng, Heinz *13:* 158
Merian, Maria Sibylla *140:* 88
Mero, Lee *34:* 68
Merrill, Frank T. *16:* 147; *19:* 71; *YABC 1:* 226, 229, 273
Merriman, Rachel *98:* 108; *114:* 122
Meryman, Hope *27:* 41
Meryweather, Jack *10:* 179
Messick, Dale *64:* 150, 151, 152
Meth, Harold *24:* 203
Meyer, Herbert *19:* 189
Meyer, Renate *6:* 170

Meyers, Bob *11:* 136
Meynell, Louis *37:* 76
Micale, Albert *2:* 65; *22:* 185
Miccuci, Charles *82:* 163
Middleton-Sandford, Betty *2:* 125
Mieke, Anne *45:* 74
Mighell, Patricia *43:* 134
Miglio, Paige *101:* 203
Mikolaycak, Charles *9:* 144; *12:* 101; *13:* 212; *21:* 121; *22:* 168; *30:* 187; *34:* 103, 150; *37:* 183; *43:* 179; *44:* 90; *46:* 115, 118-119; *49:* 25; *78:* 121, 122, 205, 207; *81:* 4
Milelli, Pascal *129:* 66; *135:* 153
Miles, Elizabeth *117:* 77
Miles, Jennifer *17:* 278
Milhous, Katherine *15:* 193; *17:* 51
Millais, John E. *22:* 230, 231
Millar, H. R. *YABC 1:* 194-195, 203
Millard, C. E. *28:* 186
Millard, Kerry *105:* 124
Miller, Don *15:* 195; *16:* 71; *20:* 106; *31:* 178
Miller, Edna *29:* 148
Miller, Edward *115:* 64
Miller, Frank J. *25:* 94
Miller, Grambs *18:* 38; *23:* 16
Miller, Ian *99:* 128
Miller, Jane *15:* 196
Miller, Marcia *13:* 233
Miller, Marilyn *1:* 87; *31:* 69; *33:* 157
Miller, Mitchell *28:* 183; *34:* 207
Miller, Shane *5:* 140
Miller, Virginia *81:* 206
Mills, Elaine *72:* 181
Mills, Judith Christine *130:* 168, 169
Mills, Lauren *92:* 170
Mills, Yaroslava Surmach *35:* 169, 170; *46:* 114
Millsap, Darrel *51:* 102
Milone, Karen *89:* 169
Miner, Julia *98:* 69
Minor, Wendell *39:* 188; *52:* 87; *56:* 171; *58:* 116; *62:* 56; *66:* 109; *74:* 93; *78:* 129; *94:* 67; *117:* 12, 13; *124:* 84, 86; *136:* 121
Mirocha, Paul *81:* 133
Mitchell, Judith *109:* 117
Mitchell, Mark *91:* 208
Mitgutsch, Ali *76:* 161
Mitsuhashi, Yoko *45:* 153
Miyake, Yoshi *38:* 141
Mizumura, Kazue *10:* 143; *18:* 223; *36:* 159
Mochi, Ugo *8:* 122; *38:* 150
Mock, Paul *55:* 83; *123:* 32
Modarressi, Mitra *90:* 236; *126:* 168
Modell, Frank *39:* 152
Mogenson, Jan *74:* 183
Mohn, Susan *89:* 224
Mohr, Mark *133:* 201
Mohr, Nicholasa *8:* 139; *113:* 127
Molan, Christine *60:* 177; *84:* 183
Moldon, Peter L. *49:* 168
Molk, Laurel *92:* 150
Momaday, N. Scott *48:* 159
Mombourquette, Paul *112:* 91; *126:* 142
Montiel, David *69:* 106; *84:* 145
Montresor, Beni *2:* 91; *3:* 138; *38:* 152, 153, 154, 155, 156-157, 158, 159, 160; *68:* 63
Montserrat, Pep *128:* 135
Moon, Carl *25:* 183, 184, 185
Moon, Eliza *14:* 40
Moon, Ivan *22:* 39; *38:* 140
Moore, Adrienne *67:* 147
Moore, Agnes Kay Randall *43:* 187
Moore, Cyd *117:* 107, 108
Moore, Gustav *127:* 181, 182
Moore, Jackie *128:* 79
Moore, Janet *63:* 153
Moore, Mary *29:* 160

Moore, Yvette *101:* 11, 12
Mora, Raul Mina *20:* 41
Moraes, Odilon *102:* 144
Moran, Rosslyn *111:* 26
Moran, Tom *60:* 100
Mordvinoff, Nicolas *15:* 179
Morgan, Jacqui *58:* 57
Morgan, Mary *114:* 133, 134, 135; *123:* 11
Morgan, Tom *42:* 157
Morice, Dave *93:* 142
Morin, Paul *73:* 132; *79:* 130; *88:* 140; *137:* 143
Morozumi, Atsuko *110:* 155
Morrill, Leslie *18:* 218; *29:* 177; *33:* 84; *38:* 147; *42:* 127; *44:* 93; *48:* 164, 165, 167, 168, 169, 170, 171; *49:* 162; *63:* 136, 180; *70:* 72; *71:* 70, 91, 92; *72:* 228; *80:* 163, 164, 165; *90:* 121; *121:* 88
Morrill, Rowena A. *84:* 16; *98:* 163
Morris *47:* 91
Morris, Frank *55:* 133; *60:* 28; *76:* 2
Morris, Harry O. *119:* 138
Morris, Jackie *128:* 194
Morris, Oradel Nolen *128:* 180
Morris, Tony *62:* 146; *70:* 97
Morrison, Bill *42:* 116; *66:* 170; *69:* 40
Morrison, Gordon *87:* 150; *113:* 93; *128:* 181, 182
Morrow, Gray *2:* 64; *5:* 200; *10:* 103, 114; *14:* 175
Morton, Lee Jack *32:* 140
Morton, Marian *3:* 185
Mosberg, Hilary *117:* 195; *118:* 164
Moser, Barry *56:* 68, 117, 118, 119, 120, 121, 122, 123, 124; *59:* 141; *60:* 160; *79:* 91, 147, 149, 151, 152; *82:* 81; *90:* 118; *91:* 35; *95:* 210; *97:* 91, 93; *102:* 152; *126:* 4; *128:* 175; *133:* 141; *138:* 167, 171, 174
Moser, Cara *90:* 118; *138:* 167
Moses, Grandma *18:* 228
Moskof, Martin Stephen *27:* 152
Mosley, Francis *57:* 144
Moss, Donald *11:* 184
Moss, Geoffrey *32:* 198
Moss, Marissa *71:* 130; *104:* 127
Most, Bernard *48:* 173; *91:* 142, 143; *134:* 120
Mowry, Carmen *50:* 62
Moxley, Sheila *96:* 174
Moyers, William *21:* 65
Moyler, Alan *36:* 142
Mozley, Charles *9:* 87; *20:* 176, 192, 193; *22:* 228; *25:* 205; *33:* 150; *43:* 170, 171, 172, 173, 174; *YABC 2:* 89
Mueller, Hans Alexander *26:* 64; *27:* 52, 53
Mugnaini, Joseph *11:* 35; *27:* 52, 53; *35:* 62
Mujica, Rick *72:* 67; *88:* 95; *111:* 53
Muller, Robin *86:* 161
Muller, Steven *32:* 167
Müller, Jörg *35:* 215; *67:* 138, 139
Mullins, Edward S. *10:* 101
Mullins, Patricia *51:* 68
Multer, Scott *80:* 108
Munari, Bruno *15:* 200
Munch, Edvard *140:* 143
Munowitz, Ken *14:* 148; *72:* 178, 179
Munro, Roxie *58:* 134; *136:* 177; *137:* 218
Munsinger, Lynn *33:* 161; *46:* 126; *71:* 92; *82:* 80; *89:* 218; *92:* 125; *94:* 157, 158, 159, 160; *98:* 196; *103:* 198
Munson, Russell *13:* 9
Muñoz, William *42:* 160
Murdocca, Sal *73:* 212; *98:* 132; *111:* 168
Murphy, Bill *5:* 138; *130:* 170
Murphy, Jill *37:* 142; *70:* 166
Murphy, Kelly *130:* 212
Murr, Karl *20:* 62
Murray, Ossie *43:* 176
Mussino, Attilio *29:* 131; *100:* 164
Mutchler, Dwight *1:* 25

Myers, Bernice *9:* 147; *36:* 75; *81:* 146, 147, 148
Myers, Duane O. *99:* 145
Myers, Lou *11:* 2

N

Nachreiner, Tom *29:* 182
Nacht, Merle *65:* 49
Nadler, Ellis *88:* 91
Najaka, Marlies *62:* 101
Nakai, Michael *30:* 217; *54:* 29
Nakatani, Chiyoko *12:* 124
Narahashi, Keiko *77:* 188; *82:* 213; *115:* 142, 143, 144
Nascimbene, Yan *133:* 128
Nash, Lesa *87:* 135
Nash, Linell *46:* 175
Nash, Scott *130:* 36
Naso, John *33:* 183
Nason, Thomas W. *14:* 68
Nasser, Muriel *48:* 74
Nast, Thomas *21:* 29; *28:* 23; *51:* 132, 133, 134, 135, 136, 137, 138, 139, 141
Nasta, Vincent *78:* 185
Natale, Vincent *76:* 3; *78:* 125; *112:* 47
Natchev, Alexi *96:* 177
Nathan, Charlott *125:* 151
Natti, Susanna *20:* 146; *32:* 141, 142; *35:* 178; *37:* 143; *71:* 49; *93:* 98; *125:* 166, 168; *126:* 228
Navarra, Celeste Scala *8:* 142
Naylor, Penelope *10:* 104
Nazz, James *72:* 8
Nebel, M. *45:* 154
Neebe, William *7:* 93
Needler, Jerry *12:* 93
Neel, Alice *31:* 23
Neely, Beth *119:* 184
Neely, Keith R. *46:* 124
Neff, Leland *78:* 74
Negri, Rocco *3:* 213; *5:* 67; *6:* 91, 108; *12:* 159
Neidigh, Sherry *128:* 53
Neill, John R. *18:* 8, 10-11, 21, 30; *100:* 22
Neilsen, Terese *116:* 74
Nelson, Craig *62:* 151; 153
Nelson, Gail White *68:* 140
Nelson, Jennifer *129:* 152
Nelson, S. D. *131:* 34
Ness, Evaline *1:* 164-165; *2:* 39; *3:* 8; *10:* 147; *12:* 53; *26:* 150, 151, 152, 153; *49:* 30, 31, 32; *56:* 30; *60:* 113
Neville, Vera *2:* 182
Nevwirth, Allan *79:* 168
Newberry, Clare Turlay *1:* 170
Newbold, Greg *108:* 125
Newfeld, Frank *14:* 121; *26:* 154
Newman, Ann *43:* 90
Newsom, Carol *40:* 159; *44:* 60; *47:* 189; *65:* 29; *70:* 192; *80:* 36; *85:* 137, 138; *92:* 167
Newsom, Tom *49:* 149; *71:* 13, 62; *75:* 156; *91:* 113
Newton, Jill *83:* 105
Ng, Michael *29:* 171
Nicholson, William *15:* 33-34; *16:* 48
Nickens, Bessie *104:* 153
Nicklaus, Carol *45:* 194; *62:* 132, 133
Nickless, Will *16:* 139
Nicolas *17:* 130, 132-133; *YABC 2:* 215
Niebrugge, Jane *6:* 118
Nielsen, Cliff *95:* 207, 208; *105:* 58; *114:* 112; *124:* 12; *125:* 91, 92; *132:* 224; *135:* 187; *136:* 40; *137:* 168
Nielsen, Jon *6:* 100; *24:* 202

Nielsen, Kay *15:* 7; *16:* 211-213, 215, 217; *22:* 143; *YABC 1:* 32-33
Niland, Deborah *25:* 191; *27:* 156; *135:* 50
Niland, Kilmeny *25:* 191; *75:* 143
Nino, Alex *59:* 145
Ninon *1:* 5; *38:* 101, 103, 108
Nissen, Rie *44:* 35
Nivola, Claire A. *78:* 126; *140:* 147
Nixon, K. *14:* 152
Noble, Louise *61:* 170
Noble, Marty *97:* 168; *125:* 171
Noble, Trinka Hakes *39:* 162; *84:* 157
Noguchi, Yoshie *30:* 99
Nolan, Dennis *42:* 163; *67:* 163; *78:* 189; *82:* 225; *83:* 26; *92:* 169, 170; *103:* 166; *111:* 35; *112:* 213; *127:* 171
Noll, Sally *82:* 171
Nolte, Larry *121:* 63, 65
Nones, Eric Jon *61:* 111; *76:* 38; *77:* 177
Noonan, Daniel *100:* 224
Noonan, Julia *4:* 163; *7:* 207; *25:* 151; *91:* 29; *95:* 149
Norcia, Ernie *108:* 155; *140:* 47
Nordenskjold, Birgitta *2:* 208
Norman, Elaine *77:* 72, 176; *94:* 35; *136:* 63
Norman, Mary *36:* 138, 147
Norman, Michael *12:* 117; *27:* 168
Northway, Jennifer *85:* 96
Novak, Matt *104:* 132, 133
Novelli, Luca *61:* 137
Nugent, Cynthia *106:* 189
Numeroff, Laura Joffe *28:* 161; *30:* 177
Nussbaumer, Paul *16:* 219; *39:* 117
Nutt, Ken *72:* 69; *97:* 170
Nyce, Helene *19:* 219
Nygren, Tord *30:* 148; *127:* 164

O

Oakley, Graham *8:* 112; *30:* 164, 165; *84:* 188, 189, 190, 191, 192
Oakley, Thornton *YABC 2:* 189
Oberheide, Heide *118:* 37
Obligado, Lilian *2:* 28, 66-67; *6:* 30; *14:* 179; *15:* 103; *25:* 84; *61:* 138, 139, 140, 141, 143
Obrant, Susan *11:* 186
O'Brien, Anne Sibley *53:* 116, 117
O'Brien, John *41:* 253; *72:* 12; *89:* 59, 60; *98:* 16
O'Brien, Teresa *87:* 89
O'Brien, Tim *93:* 25; *136:* 94
O'Clair, Dennis *127:* 25
Odell, Carole *35:* 47
Odom, Mel *99:* 164
O'Donohue, Thomas *40:* 89
Oechsli, Kelly *5:* 144-145; *7:* 115; *8:* 83, 183; *13:* 117; *20:* 94; *81:* 199
Offen, Hilda *42:* 207
Ogden, Bill *42:* 59; *47:* 55
Ogg, Oscar *33:* 34
Ohi, Ruth *90:* 175, 177; *131:* 63; *135:* 106
Ohlsson, Ib *4:* 152; *7:* 57; *10:* 20; *11:* 90; *19:* 217; *41:* 246; *82:* 106; *92:* 213
Ohtomo, Yasuo *37:* 146; *39:* 212, 213
O'Keefe, Jennifer *136:* 184
O'Kelley, Mattie Lou *36:* 150
Oliver, Jenni *23:* 121; *35:* 112
Oller, Erika *128:* 186; *134:* 126
Olschewski, Alfred *7:* 172
Olsen, Ib Spang *6:* 178-179; *81:* 164
Olson, Alan *77:* 229
Olugebefola, Ademola *15:* 205
O'Malley, Kevin *94:* 180; *106:* 8; *113:* 108; *136:* 70
O'Neil, Dan IV *7:* 176

O'Neill, Catharine *72:* 113; *84:* 78; *134:* 153
O'Neill, Jean *22:* 146
O'Neill, Michael J. *54:* 172
O'Neill, Rose *48:* 30, 31
O'Neill, Steve *21:* 118
Ono, Chiyo *7:* 97
Orbaan, Albert *2:* 31; *5:* 65, 171; *9:* 8; *14:* 241; *20:* 109
Orbach, Ruth *21:* 112
Orfe, Joan *20:* 81
Org, Ed *119:* 93
Ormai, Stella *72:* 129
Ormerod, Jan *55:* 124; *70:* 170, 171; *90:* 39; *132:* 172, 173, 174
Ormsby, Virginia H. *11:* 187
O'Rourke, Ericka *108:* 216; *117:* 194; *111:* 142; *119:* 194; *137:* 152
O'Rourke, Ericka Meltzer *See* O'Rourke, Ericka
Orozco, José Clemente *9:* 177
Orr, Forrest W. *23:* 9
Orr, N. *19:* 70
Ortiz, Vilma *88:* 158
Osborn, Robert *65:* 49
Osborne, Billie Jean *35:* 209
Osmond, Edward *10:* 111
O'Sullivan, Tom *3:* 176; *4:* 55; *78:* 195
Otani, June *124:* 42
Otto, Svend *22:* 130, 141; *67:* 188, 189
Oudry, J. B. *18:* 167
Oughton, Taylor *5:* 23; *104:* 136
Övereng, Johannes *44:* 36
Overlie, George *11:* 156
Owens, Carl *2:* 35; *23:* 521
Owens, Gail *10:* 170; *12:* 157; *19:* 16; *22:* 70; *25:* 81; *28:* 203, 205; *32:* 221, 222; *36:* 132; *46:* 40; *47:* 57; *54:* 66, 67, 68, 69, 70, 71, 72, 73; *71:* 100; *73:* 64; *77:* 157; *80:* 32; *82:* 3; *99:* 226
Owens, Mary Beth *113:* 202, 203
Owens, Nubia *84:* 74
Oxenbury, Helen *3:* 150-151; *24:* 81; *68:* 174, 175, 176; *81:* 209; *84:* 213, 245; *129:* 56
Oz, Robin *88:* 167

P

Padgett, Jim *12:* 165
Page, Homer *14:* 145
Paget, Sidney *24:* 90, 91, 93, 95, 97
Paget, Walter *64:* 122
Pak *12:* 76
Pak, Yu Cha *86:* 174
Paladino, Lance *134:* 30
Palazzo, Tony *3:* 152-153
Palecek, Josef *56:* 136; *89:* 158
Palen, Debbie *135:* 88
Palencar, John Jude *84:* 12, 45; *85:* 87; *92:* 187; *99:* 128; *110:* 204
Palin, Nicki *81:* 201; *89:* 161
Palladini, David *4:* 113; *40:* 176, 177, 178-179, 181, 224-225; *50:* 138; *78:* 186
Pallarito, Don *43:* 36
Palmer, Heidi *15:* 207; *29:* 102
Palmer, Jan *42:* 153; *82:* 161
Palmer, Juliette *6:* 89; *15:* 208
Palmer, Kate Salley *104:* 143
Palmer, Lemuel *17:* 25, 29
Palmisciano, Diane *110:* 62
Palmquist, Eric *38:* 133
Panesis, Nicholas *3:* 127
Panton, Doug *52:* 99
Paparone, Pamela *129:* 174
Papas, William *11:* 223; *50:* 160
Papin, Joseph *26:* 113
Papish, Robin Lloyd *10:* 80

Paradis, Susan *40:* 216
Paraquin, Charles H. *18:* 166
Paris, Peter *31:* 127
Parisi, Elizabeth B. *141:* 82
Park, Nick *113:* 143
Park, Seho *39:* 110
Park, W. B. *22:* 189
Parker, Ant *82:* 87, 88; *104:* 121
Parker, Lewis *2:* 179
Parker, Nancy Winslow *10:* 113; *22:* 164; *28:* 47, 144; *52:* 7; *69:* 153; *91:* 171, 174; *132:* 175
Parker, Robert *4:* 161; *5:* 74; *9:* 136; *29:* 39
Parker, Robert Andrew *11:* 81; *29:* 186; *39:* 165; *40:* 25; *41:* 78; *42:* 123; *43:* 144; *48:* 182; *54:* 140; *74:* 141; *91:* 24; *111:* 115
Parkin, Trevor *140:* 151
Parkins, David *114:* 123
Parkinson, Kathy *71:* 143
Parkinson, Keith *70:* 66
Parks, Gordon, Jr. *33:* 228
Parnall, Peter *5:* 137; *16:* 221; *24:* 70; *40:* 78; *51:* 130; *69:* 17, 155; *136:* 22, 23, 24
Parnall, Virginia *40:* 78
Parr, Todd *134:* 139, 140
Parrish, Anne *27:* 159, 160
Parrish, Dillwyn *27:* 159
Parrish, Maxfield *14:* 160, 161, 164, 165; *16:* 109; *18:* 12-13; *YABC 1:* 149, 152, 267; *2:* 146, 149
Parry, David *26:* 156
Parry, Marian *13:* 176; *19:* 179
Partch, Virgil *45:* 163, 165
Pascal, David *14:* 174
Pasquier, J. A. *16:* 91
Pasternak, Robert *119:* 53
Paterson, Diane *13:* 116; *39:* 163; *59:* 164, 165, 166, 167; *72:* 51, 53; *129:* 175
Paterson, Helen *16:* 93
Patkau, Karen *112:* 123
Paton, Jane *15:* 271; *35:* 176
Patrick, John *139:* 190
Patrick, Pamela *90:* 160; *93:* 211; *105:* 12
Patterson, Geoffrey *54:* 75
Patterson, Robert *25:* 118
Patz, Nancy *111:* 40
Paul, James *4:* 130; *23:* 161
Paul, Korky *102:* 85
Paull, Grace *24:* 157; *87:* 127
Paulsen, Ruth Wright *79:* 160, 164
Pavlov, Elena *80:* 49
Payne, Adam S. *135:* 166
Payne, Joan Balfour *1:* 118
Payson, Dale *7:* 34; *9:* 151; *20:* 140; *37:* 22
Payzant, Charles *21:* 147
Peacock, Ralph *64:* 118
Peake, Mervyn *22:* 136, 149; *23:* 162, 163, 164; *YABC 2:* 307
Pearson, Larry *38:* 225
Pearson, Tracey Campbell *64:* 163, 164, 167, 168, 169; *118:*51
Peat, Fern B. *16:* 115
Peck, Anne Merriman *18:* 241; *24:* 155
Peck, Beth *66:* 242; *79:* 166; *80:* 136; *91:* 34; *95:* 9; *101:* 77
Pedersen, Judy *66:* 217; *121:* 36
Pedersen, Vilhelm *YABC 1:* 40
Pederson, Sharleen *12:* 92
Peek, Merle *39:* 168
Peet, Bill *2:* 203; *41:* 159, 160, 161, 162, 163; *78:* 158, 159, 160, 161
Peguero, Adrian *116:* 133
Peguero, Gerard *116:* 133
Pels, Winslow Pinney *55:* 126
Peltier, Leslie C. *13:* 178
Pendle, Alexy *7:* 159; *13:* 34; *29:* 161; *33:* 215; *86:* 62
Pendola, Joanne *76:* 203; *81:* 125; *105:* 181

Pene du Bois, William *4:* 70; *10:* 122; *26:* 61; *27:* 145, 211; *35:* 243; *41:* 216; *68:* 180, 181; *73:* 45
Penfound, David *102:* 185
Pennington, Eunice *27:* 162
Peppé, Mark *28:* 142
Peppé, Rodney *4:* 164-165; *74:* 187, 188, 189
Pepper, Hubert *64:* 143
Percy, Graham *63:* 2
Perkins, David *60:* 68
Perkins, Lucy Fitch *72:* 199
Perl, Susan *2:* 98; *4:* 231; *5:* 44-45, 118; *6:* 199; *8:* 137; *12:* 88; *22:* 193; *34:* 54-55; *52:* 128; *YABC 1:* 176
Perrone, Donna *78:* 166
Perry, Patricia *29:* 137; *30:* 171
Perry, Roger *27:* 163
Perske, Martha *46:* 83; *51:* 108, 147
Pesek, Ludek *15:* 237
Peters, David *72:* 205
Petersham, Maud *17:* 108, 147-153
Petersham, Miska *17:* 108, 147-153
Peterson, Eric *109:* 125
Peterson, Nisse *99:* 27
Peterson, R. F. *7:* 101
Peterson, Russell *7:* 130
Petie, Haris *2:* 3; *10:* 41, 118; *11:* 227; *12:* 70
Petrides, Heidrun *19:* 223
Petruccio, Steven James *67:* 159; *127:* 5
Pettingill, Ondre *64:* 181; *70:* 64
Peyo *40:* 56, 57
Peyton, K. M. *15:* 212
Pfeifer, Herman *15:* 262
Pfister, Marcus *83:* 165, 166, 167
Pfloog, Jan *124:* 60
Phillips, Craig *70:* 151
Phillips, Douglas *1:* 19
Phillips, F. D. *6:* 202
Phillips, Louise *133:* 67
Phillips, Thomas *30:* 55
Philpot, Glyn *54:* 46
Phiz *See* Browne, Hablot K.
Piatti, Celestino *16:* 223
Pica, Steve *115:* 181
Picarella, Joseph *13:* 147
Picart, Gabriel *121:* 165
Pickard, Charles *12:* 38; *18:* 203; *36:* 152
Picken, George A. *23:* 150
Pickens, David *22:* 156
Pienkowski, Jan *6:* 183; *30:* 32; *58:* 140, 141, 142, 143, 146, 147; *73:* 3; *87:* 156, 157; *131:* 189
Pilkey, Dav *68:* 186; *115:* 164, 166
Pimlott, John *10:* 205
Pincus, Harriet *4:* 186; *8:* 179; *22:* 148; *27:* 164, 165; *66:* 202
Pini, Wendy *89:* 166
Pinkett, Neil *60:* 8
Pinkney, Brian *81:* 184, 185; *94:* 107; *113:* 146, 147; *117:* 121, 166; *132:* 145
Pinkney, Jerry *8:* 218; *10:* 40; *15:* 276; *20:* 66; *24:* 121; *33:* 109; *36:* 222; *38:* 200; *41:* 165, 166, 167, 168, 169, 170, 171, 173, 174; *44:* 198; *48:* 51; *53:* 20; *56:* 61, 68; *58:* 184; *60:* 59; *61:* 91; *71:* 146, 148, 149; *72:* 17; *73:* 149; *74:* 159, 192; *75:* 45; *80:* 206; *81:* 44; *85:* 144; *95:* 50; *107:* 158, 159, 160; *108:* 164; *112:* 114, 115; *133:* 58
Pinkwater, Daniel Manus *46:* 180, 181, 182, 185, 188, 189, 190; *76:* 178, 179, 180
Pinkwater, Manus *8:* 156; *46:* 180 *See also* Pinkwater, Daniel Manus
Pinkwater, Jill *114:* 160, 161
Pinto, Ralph *10:* 131; *45:* 93
Piñón, Mark *74:* 22
Pistolesi *73:* 211
Pittman, Helena Clare *71:* 151
Pitz, Henry C. *4:* 168; *19:* 165; *35:* 128; *42:* 80; *YABC 2:* 95, 176

Pitzenberger, Lawrence J. *26:* 94
Player, Stephen *82:* 190
Plecas, Jennifer *84:* 201; *106:* 124
Plowden, David *52:* 135, 136
Plummer, William *32:* 31
Podwal, Mark *56:* 170, 173; *101:* 154, 155, 157
Pogány, Willy *15:* 46, 49; *19:* 222, 256; *25:* 214; *44:* 142, 143, 144, 145, 146, 147, 148
Pohrt, Tom *67:* 116; *104:* 80
Poirson, V. A. *26:* 89
Polacco, Patricia *74:* 195, 196-197, 198; *123:* 121-123
Polgreen, John *21:* 44
Politi, Leo *1:* 178; *4:* 53; *21:* 48; *47:* 173, 174, 176, 178, 179, 180, 181
Pollema-Cahill, Phyllis *123:* 126
Pollen, Samson *64:* 80
Polonsky, Arthur *34:* 168
Polseno, Jo *1:* 53; *3:* 117; *5:* 114; *17:* 154; *20:* 87; *32:* 49; *41:* 245
Pomaska, Anna *117:* 148
Ponter, James *5:* 204
Poole, Colin *111:* 27
Poortvliet, Rien *6:* 212; *65:* 165, 166-67
Popp, Wendy *72:* 122
Poppel, Hans *71:* 154, 155
Porfirio, Guy *76:* 134
Portal, Colette *6:* 186; *11:* 203
Porter, George *7:* 181
Porter, Janice Lee *136:* 175
Porter, John *113:* 47
Porter, Pat Grant *84:* 112; *125:* 101
Porter, Walter *124:* 175
Postma, Lidia *79:* 17
Potter, Beatrix *100:* 194, 195; *132:* 179, 180, 181, 182; *YABC 1:* 208-210, 212, 213
Potter, Giselle *117:* 123
Potter, Katherine *104:* 147
Potter, Miriam Clark *3:* 162
Poulin, Stephane *98:* 140, 141
Powell, Ivan *67:* 219
Power, Margaret *105:* 122
Powers, Richard M. *1:* 230; *3:* 218; *7:* 194; *26:* 186
Powledge, Fred *37:* 154
Powzyk, Joyce *74:* 214
Poydar, Nancy *96:* 149
Pracher, Richard *91:* 166
Prachatická, Markéta *126:* 126
Prater, John *103:* 142, 143, 144
Pratt, Charles *23:* 29
Pratt, George *116:* 208
Prebenna, David *73:* 174
Preiss-Glasser, Robin *123:* 176
Press, Jenny *116:* 95
Pretro, Korinna *91:* 126
Price, Christine *2:* 247; *3:* 163, 253; *8:* 166
Price, Cynthia *118:* 156
Price, Edward *33:* 34
Price, Garrett *1:* 76; *2:* 42
Price, Hattie Longstreet *17:* 13
Price, Norman *YABC 1:* 129
Price, Willard *48:* 184
Priceman, Marjorie *81:* 171; *136:* 169
Primavera, Elise *26:* 95; *58:* 151; *73:* 37; *80:* 79; *86:* 156; *105:* 161
Primrose, Jean *36:* 109
Prince, Alison *86:* 188, 189
Prince, Leonora E. *7:* 170
Pritchett, Shelley *116:* 148
Prittie, Edwin J. *YABC 1:* 120
Prosmitsky, Jenya *132:* 33
Provensen, Alice *37:* 204, 215, 222; *70:* 176, 177, 178, 180, *71:* 213
Provensen, Martin *37:* 204, 215, 222; *70:* 176, 177, 178, 180; *71:* 213
Pucci, Albert John *44:* 154
Pudlo *8:* 59
Pulver, Harry, Jr. *129:* 159

Punchatz, Don *99:* 57
Purdy, Susan *8:* 162
Pursell, Weimer *55:* 18
Purtscher, Alfons *97:* 6
Puskas, James *5:* 141
Pyk, Jan *7:* 26; *38:* 123
Pyle, Chuck *99:* 149
Pyle, Howard *16:* 225-228, 230-232, 235; *24:* 27; *34:* 124, 125, 127, 128; *59:* 132; *100:* 198

Q

Quackenbush, Robert *4:* 190; *6:* 166; *7:* 175, 178; *9:* 86; *11:* 65, 221; *41:* 154; *43:* 157; *70:* 185, 186; *71:* 137; *85:* 47; *92:* 148; *133:* 154, 164, 169
Quennell, Marjorie (Courtney) *29:* 163, 164
Quidor, John *19:* 82
Quirk, John *62:* 170
Quirk, Thomas *12:* 81

R

Rackham, Arthur *15:* 32, 78, 214-227; *17:* 105, 115; *18:* 233; *19:* 254; *20:* 151; *22:* 129, 131, 132, 133; *23:* 175; *24:* 161, 181; *26:* 91; *32:* 118; *64:* 18; *100:* 9, 16, 203, 204; *YABC 1:* 25, 45, 55, 147; *2:* 103, 142, 173, 210
Racz, Michael *56:* 134
Radcliffe, Andrew *82:* 215
Rader, Laura *101:* 219
Rafilson, Sidney *11:* 172
Raglin, Tim *125:* 24
Raible, Alton *1:* 202-203; *28:* 193; *35:* 181; *110:* 207
Raine, Patricia *82:* 74; *88:* 154
Ramhorst, John *117:* 11
Ramsey, James *16:* 41
Ramsey, Marcy Dunn *82:* 11
Ramus, Michael *51:* 171
Rand, Paul *6:* 188
Rand, Ted *67:* 9, 10, 121, 123; *74:* 190; *84:* 170; *103:* 170; *112:* 6; *114:* 73; *139:* 168
Randazzo, Tony *81:* 98
Randell, William *55:* 54
Rane, Walter *93:* 144
Ransome, Arthur *22:* 201
Ransome, James E. *74:* 137; *75:* 80; *84:* 181; *94:* 108; *117:* 115; *123:* 128-130
Rantz, Don *119:* 184
Rao, Anthony *28:* 126
Raphael, Elaine *23:* 192; *71:* 24, 25
Rappaport, Eva *6:* 190
Raschka, Christopher *80:* 187, 189, 190; *97:* 211; *115:*210; *117:* 151, 152, 153, 154
Raskin, Ellen *2:* 208-209; *4:* 142; *13:* 183; *22:* 68; *29:* 139; *36:* 134; *38:* 173, 174, 175, 176, 177, 178, 179, 180, 181; *60:* 163; *86:* 81
Rathmann, Peggy *93:* 32; *94:* 168
Ratkus, Tony *77:* 133
Ratzkin, Lawrence *40:* 143
Rau, Margaret *9:* 157
Raverat, Gwen *YABC 1:* 152
Ravid, Joyce *61:* 73
Ravielli, Anthony *1:* 198; *3:* 168; *11:* 143
Ravilious, Robin *77:* 169
Rawlins, Donna *72:* 198; *73:* 15, 129
Rawlins, Janet *76:* 79
Rawlinson, Debbie *75:* 132
Ray, Deborah Kogan *8:* 164; *29:* 238; *50:* 112, 113; *62:* 119; *78:* 191

Ray, Jane *96:* 166; *97:* 104
Ray, Ralph *2:* 239; *5:* 73
Rayevsky, Robert *64:* 17; *70:* 173; *80:* 204; *117:* 79
Raymond, Larry *31:* 108; *97:* 109
Rayner, Mary *22:* 207; *47:* 140; *72:* 191; *87:* 171, 172
Raynes, John *71:* 19
Raynor, Dorka *28:* 168
Raynor, Paul *24:* 73
Rayyan, Omar *110:* 222; *112:* 17; *125:* 131
Razzi, James *10:* 127
Read, Alexander D. *20:* 45
Reader, Dennis *71:* 157
Reasoner, Charles *53:* 33, 36, 37
Reczuch, Karen *115:* 132
Reed, Joseph *116:* 139
Reed, Lynn Rowe *115:* 173
Reed, Tom *34:* 171
Reeder, Colin *74:* 202; *77:* 113
Rees, Mary *134:* 219
Reese, Bob *60:* 135
Reeves, Eira B. *130:* 173, 174; *141:* 151
Regan, Dana *117:* 116
Regan, Laura *103:* 198
Reid, Barbara *82:* 178; *92:* 17; *93:* 169, 170
Reid, Stephen *19:* 213; *22:* 89
Reim, Melanie *104:* 151
Reinert, Kirk *89:* 138
Reinertson, Barbara *44:* 150; *62:* 103
Reiniger, Lotte *40:* 185
Reisberg, Mira *119:* 2
Reiser, Lynn *81:* 175; *138:* 184
Reiss, John J. *23:* 193
Relf, Douglas *3:* 63
Relyea, C. M. *16:* 29; *31:* 153
Rémi, Georges *13:* 184
Remington, Frederic *19:* 188; *41:* 178, 179, 180, 181, 183, 184, 185, 186, 187, 188; *62:* 197
Remkiewicz, Frank *67:* 102; *77:* 171; *80:* 130; *113:* 107
Rendon, Maria *116:* 141; 192; *134:* 152
Renfro, Ed *79:* 176
Renlie, Frank *11:* 200
Reschofsky, Jean *7:* 118
Rethi *60:* 181
Réthi, Lili *2:* 153; *36:* 156
Reusswig, William *3:* 267
Rey, H. A. *1:* 182; *26:* 163, 164, 166, 167, 169; *69:* 172, 173, 174, 175; *86:* 195, 196, 197; *100:* 211; *YABC 2:* 17
Reynolds, Doris *5:* 71; *31:* 77
Rhead, Louis *31:* 91; *100:* 228
Rhodes, Andrew *38:* 204; *50:* 163; *54:* 76; *61:* 123, 124; *87:* 200
Ribbons, Ian *3:* 10; *37:* 161; *40:* 76
Ricci, Regolo *93:* 22
Rice, Elizabeth *2:* 53, 214
Rice, Eve *34:* 174, 175; *91:* 172
Rice, James *22:* 210; *93:* 173
Richards, George *40:* 116, 119, 121; *44:* 179
Richards, Henry *YABC 1:* 228, 231
Richardson, Ernest *2:* 144
Richardson, Frederick *18:* 27, 31
Richardson, John *110:* 88
Richman, Hilda *26:* 132
Richmond, George *24:* 179
Riddell, Chris *114:* 170, 195
Riddle, Tohby *74:* 204
Riding, Peter *63:* 195
Rieniets, Judy King *14:* 28
Riger, Bob *2:* 166
Riggio, Anita *73:* 191; *85:* 63; *137:* 184
Riley, Jon *74:* 70
Riley, Kenneth *22:* 230
Ringgold, Faith *71:* 162; *114:* 173, 174, 176
Ringi, Kjell *12:* 171
Rios, Tere *See* Versace, Marie
Ripper, Charles L. *3:* 175

Ripplinger, Henry *117:* 31
Ritchie, William *74:* 183
Ritz, Karen *41:* 117; *72:* 239; *87:* 125; *102:* 7; *106:* 6
Rivkin, Jay *15:* 230
Rivoche, Paul *45:* 125
Roach, Marilynne *9:* 158
Robbin, Jodi *44:* 156, 159
Robbins, Frank *42:* 167
Robbins, Ruth *52:* 102
Roberts, Cliff *4:* 126
Roberts, Doreen *4:* 230; *28:* 105
Roberts, Jim *22:* 166; *23:* 69; *31:* 110
Roberts, Tony *109:* 195, 214
Roberts, W. *22:* 2, 3
Robins, Arthur *137:* 172
Robinson, Aminah Brenda Lynn *86:* 205; *103:* 55
Robinson, Charles [1870-1937] *17:* 157, 171, 172, 173, 175, 176; *24:* 207; *25:* 204; *YABC 2:* 308, 309, 310, 331
Robinson, Charles *3:* 53; *5:* 14; *6:* 193; *7:* 150; *7:* 183; *8:* 38; *9:* 81; *13:* 188; *14:* 248-249; *23:* 149; *26:* 115; *27:* 48; *28:* 191; *32:* 28; *35:* 210; *36:* 37; *48:* 96; *52:* 33; *53:* 157; *56:* 15; *62:* 142; *77:* 41; *111:* 148
Robinson, Jerry *3:* 262
Robinson, Joan G. *7:* 184
Robinson, Lolly *90:* 227
Robinson, T. H. *17:* 179, 181-183; *29:* 254
Robinson, W. Heath *17:* 185, 187, 189, 191, 193, 195, 197, 199, 202; *23:* 167; *25:* 194; *29:* 150; *YABC 1:* 44; *2:* 183
Roche, Christine *41:* 98
Roche, Denis *99:* 184
Roche, P. K. *57:* 151, 152
Rocker, Fermin *7:* 34; *13:* 21; *31:* 40; *40:* 190, 191
Rocklen, Margot *101:* 181
Rockwell, Anne *5:* 147; *33:* 171, 173; *71:* 166, 167, 168; *114:* 183, 184
Rockwell, Gail *7:* 186
Rockwell, Harlow *33:* 171, 173, 175
Rockwell, Lizzy *114:* 182
Rockwell, Norman *23:* 39, 196, 197, 199, 200, 203, 204, 207; *41:* 140, 143; *123:* 47; *YABC 2:* 60
Rockwood, Richard *119:* 75
Rodegast, Roland *43:* 100
Rodgers, Frank *69:* 177
Rodriguez, Joel *16:* 65
Roeckelein, Katrina *134:* 223
Roennfeldt, Robert *66:* 243
Roever, J. M. *4:* 119; *26:* 170
Roffey, Maureen *33:* 142, 176, 177
Rogasky, Barbara *46:* 90
Rogers, Carol *2:* 262; *6:* 164; *26:* 129
Rogers, Forest *87:* 160; *101:* 76
Rogers, Frances *10:* 130
Rogers, Gregory *104:* 76; *126:* 57
Rogers, Jacqueline *78:* 249; *80:* 34; *86:* 54; *103:* 70; *115:* 72; *129:* 173; *131:* 57, 225
Rogers, Walter S. *31:* 135, 138; *67:* 65, 168; *100:* 81
Rogers, William A. *15:* 151, 153-154; *33:* 35
Rogoff, Barbara *95:* 20
Rohmann, Eric *103:* 152
Rojankovsky, Feodor *6:* 134, 136; *10:* 183; *21:* 128, 129, 130; *25:* 110; *28:* 42; *68:* 120
Rolfsen, Alf *62:* 15
Romain, Trevor *134:* 157
Roman, Barbara J. *103:* 171
Romas *114:* 111
Romano, Robert *64:* 68
Root, Barry *80:* 212; *90:* 196
Root, Kimberly Bulcken *86:* 72; *98:* 21; *108:* 111; *127:* 114
Roper, Bob *65:* 153
Roraback, Robin *111:* 156

Rorer, Abigail *43:* 222; *85:* 155
Rosales, Melodye *80:* 35
Rosamilia, Patricia *36:* 120
Rose, Carl *5:* 62
Rose, David S. *29:* 109; *70:* 120
Rose, Gerald *68:* 200, 201; *86:* 48
Rose, Ted *93:* 178
Rosenbaum, Jonathan *50:* 46
Rosenberg, Amye *74:* 207, 208
Rosenberry, Vera *87:* 22, 26
Rosenblum, Richard *11:* 202; *18:* 18
Rosier, Lydia *16:* 236; *20:* 104; *21:* 109; *22:* 125; *30:* 151, 158; *42:* 128; *45:* 214; *77:* 227, 228
Rosing, Jens *85:* 142
Ross *See* Thomson, Ross
Ross, Christine *83:* 172-173
Ross, Clare Romano *3:* 123; *21:* 45; *48:* 199
Ross, Dave *32:* 152; *57:* 108
Ross, Herbert *37:* 78
Ross, John *3:* 123; *21:* 45
Ross, Johnny *32:* 190
Ross, Larry *47:* 168; *60:* 62
Ross, Ruth *109:* 233
Ross, Tony *17:* 204; *56:* 132; *65:* 176, 177, 179; *90:* 123; *123:* 186-187, 190; *130:* 188, 190, 191, 192; *132:* 242
Rossetti, Dante Gabriel *20:* 151, 153
Roth, Arnold *4:* 238; *21:* 133
Roth, Marci *135:* 223
Roth, Rob *105:* 98
Roth, Roger *61:* 128
Roth, Stephanie *136:* 171, 172
Roth, Susan L. *80:* 38; *93:* 78; *134:* 165, 166
Rothman, Michael *139:* 62
Rotondo, Pat *32:* 158
Roughsey, Dick *35:* 186
Rouille, M. *11:* 96
Rounds, Glen *8:* 173; *9:* 171; *12:* 56; *32:* 194; *40:* 230; *51:* 161, 162, 166; *56:* 149; *70:* 198, 199; *YABC 1:* 1-3; *112:* 163
Roundtree, Katherine *114:* 88
Rowan, Evadne *52:* 51
Rowe, Eric *111:* 161
Rowe, Gavin *27:* 144; *72:* 47; *88:* 201
Rowe, John *132:* 70, 71
Rowell, Kenneth *40:* 72
Rowen, Amy *52:* 143
Rowena *116:* 101
Rowland, Jada *83:* 73
Rowles, Daphne *58:* 24
Roy, Jeroo *27:* 229; *36:* 110
Royo *118:* 32
Rubel, Nicole *18:* 255; *20:* 59; *81:* 66, 67; *95:* 169, 170; *119:* 60; *135:* 177, 179, 180
Rubel, Reina *33:* 217
Rud, Borghild *6:* 15
Ruddell, Gary *110:* 238; *116:* 207
Rudolph, Norman Guthrie *17:* 13
Rue, Leonard Lee III *37:* 164
Ruelle, Karen Gray *126:* 193
Ruff, Donna *50:* 173; *72:* 203; *78:* 49; *80:* 120, 121; *93:* 162
Ruffins, Reynold *10:* 134-135; *41:* 191, 192-193, 194-195, 196; *125:* 187, 188, 189
Ruhlin, Roger *34:* 44
Ruiz, Art *95:* 154; *110:* 91
Runnerstroem, Bengt Arne *75:* 161
Ruse, Margaret *24:* 155
Rush, Ken *98:* 74
Rush, Peter *42:* 75
Russell, E. B. *18:* 177, 182
Russell, Jim *53:* 134
Russell, P. Craig *80:* 196
Russo, Marisabina *84:* 51; *106:* 164
Russo, Susan *30:* 182; *36:* 144
Russon, Mary *87:* 145
Ruth, Rod *9:* 161

Rutherford, Alexa *110:* 108
Rutherford, Jenny *78:* 5
Rutherford, Meg *25:* 174; *34:* 178, 179; *69:* 73; *72:* 31
Rutland, Jonathan *31:* 126
Ryan, Will *86:* 134
Ryden, Hope *8:* 176
Rylant, Cynthia *112:* 170, 172
Rymer, Alta M. *34:* 181
Rystedt, Rex *49:* 80

S

Saaf, Chuck *49:* 179
Saaf, Donald *101:* 220; *124:* 180
Sabaka, Donna R. *21:* 172
Sabin, Robert *45:* 35; *60:* 30; *99:* 161
Sacker, Amy *16:* 100
Saelig, S. M. *129:* 73
Saffioti, Lino *36:* 176; *48:* 60
Saflund, Birgitta *94:* 2
Sagsoorian, Paul *12:* 183; *22:* 154; *33:* 106; *87:* 152
Sahlberg, Myron *57:* 165
Saint Exupéry, Antoine de *20:* 157
Saldutti, Denise *39:* 186; *57:* 178
Sale, Morton *YABC 2:* 31
Salter, George *72:* 128, 130
Saltzberg, Barney *135:* 184, 185
Saltzman, David *86:* 209
Salwowski, Mark *71:* 54
Salzman, Yuri *86:* 12
Sambourne, Linley *YABC 2:* 181
Sampson, Katherine *9:* 197
Samson, Anne S. *2:* 216
San Souci, Daniel *40:* 200; *96:* 199, 200; *113:* 171
Sancha, Sheila *38:* 185
Sand, George X. *45:* 182
Sandberg, Lasse *15:* 239, 241
Sanders, Beryl *39:* 173
Sanderson, Ruth *21:* 126; *24:* 53; *28:* 63; *33:* 67; *41:* 48, 198, 199, 200, 201, 202, 203; *43:* 79; *46:* 36, 44; *47:* 102; *49:* 58; *62:* 121, 122; *85:* 3; *109:* 207, 208, 209, 210
Sandia *119:* 74
Sandin, Joan *4:* 36; *6:* 194; *7:* 177; *12:* 145, 185; *20:* 43; *21:* 74; *26:* 144; *27:* 142; *28:* 224, 225; *38:* 86; *41:* 46; *42:* 35; *59:* 6; *80:* 136; *94:* 188; *140:* 116
Sandland, Reg *39:* 215
Sandoz, Edouard *26:* 45, 47
Sanford, John *66:* 96, 97
Sankey, Tom *72:* 103
Santore, Charles *54:* 139
Santoro, Christopher *74:* 215
Santos, Jesse J. *99:* 24
Sapieha, Christine *1:* 180
Saport, Linda *123:* 137-138
Sara *See* De La Roche Saint Andre, Anne
Sarg, Tony *YABC 2:* 236
Sargent, Claudia *64:* 181
Sargent, Robert *2:* 217
Saris *1:* 33
Sarony *YABC 2:* 170
Sasek, Miroslav *16:* 239-242
Sassman, David *9:* 79
Sätty *29:* 203, 205
Sauber, Robert *40:* 183; *76:* 256; *78:* 154; *87:* 92
Saunders, Dave *85:* 163, 164, 165
Savadier, Elivia *84:* 50
Savage, Naomi *56:* 172
Savage, Steele *10:* 203; *20:* 77; *35:* 28
Savio *76:* 4
Savitt, Sam *8:* 66, 182; *15:* 278; *20:* 96; *24:* 192; *28:* 98

Sawyer, Kem Knapp *84:* 228, 229
Say, Allen *28:* 178; *69:* 182, 183, 232; *110:* 194, 195, 196
Sayles, Elizabeth *82:* 93; *105:* 155; *109:* 116
Scabrini, Janet *13:* 191; *44:* 128
Scanlan, Peter *83:* 27
Scanlon, Paul *83:* 87
Scannell, Reece *105:* 105
Scarry, Huck *35:* 204-205
Scarry, Richard *2:* 220-221; *18:* 20; *35:* 193, 194-195, 196, 197, 198, 199, 200-201, 202; *75:* 165, 167, 168
Schachner, Judith Byron *88:* 180; *92:* 163; *93:* 102
Schaeffer, Mead *18:* 81, 94; *21:* 137, 138, 139; *47:* 128
Schaffer, Amanda *90:* 206
Schanzer, Rosalyn *138:* 192, 193
Scharl, Josef *20:* 132; *22:* 128
Scheel, Lita *11:* 230
Scheib, Ida *29:* 28
Schermer, Judith *30:* 184
Schick, Eleanor *82:* 210, 211
Schick, Joel *16:* 160; *17:* 167; *22:* 12; *27:* 176; *31:* 147, 148; *36:* 23; *38:* 64; *45:* 116, 117; *52:* 5, 85; *104:* 159
Schields, Gretchen *75:* 171, 203
Schindelman, Joseph *1:* 74; *4:* 101; *12:* 49; *26:* 51; *40:* 146; *56:* 158; *73:* 40
Schindler, Edith *7:* 22
Schindler, S. D. *38:* 107; *46:* 196; *74:* 162; *75:* 172, 173; *99:* 133; *112:* 177; *118:* 185, 186; *121:* 71; *136:* 159
Schlesinger, Bret *7:* 77
Schmid, Eleanore *12:* 188; *126:* 196, 197
Schmiderer, Dorothy *19:* 224
Schmidt, Bill *73:* 34; *76:* 220, 222, 224
Schmidt, Elizabeth *15:* 242
Schmidt, George Paul *132:* 122
Schmidt, Karen Lee *54:* 12; *71:* 174; *92:* 56; *94:* 190, 191; *127:* 103
Schmidt, Lynette *76:* 205
Schneider, Rex *29:* 64; *44:* 171
Schoberle, Cecile *80:* 200; *92:* 134
Schoenherr, Ian *32:* 83
Schoenherr, John *1:* 146-147, 173; *3:* 39, 139; *17:* 75; *29:* 72; *32:* 83; *37:* 168, 169, 170; *43:* 164, 165; *45:* 160, 162; *51:* 127; *66:* 196, 197, 198; *68:* 83; *72:* 240; *75:* 225; *88:* 176
Scholder, Fritz *69:* 103
Schomburg, Alex *13:* 23
Schongut, Emanuel *4:* 102; *15:* 186; *47:* 218, 219; *52:* 147, 148, 149, 150
Schoonover, Frank *17:* 107; *19:* 81, 190, 233; *22:* 88, 129; *24:* 189; *31:* 88; *41:* 69; *YABC 2:* 282, 316
Schottland, Miriam *22:* 172
Schramm, Ulrik *2:* 16; *14:* 112
Schreiber, Elizabeth Anne *13:* 193
Schreiber, Ralph W. *13:* 193
Schreiter, Rick *14:* 97; *23:* 171; *41:* 247; *49:* 131
Schroeder, Binette *56:* 128, 129
Schroeder, E. Peter *12:* 112
Schroeder, Ted *11:* 160; *15:* 189; *30:* 91; *34:* 43
Schrotter, Gustav *22:* 212; *30:* 225
Schubert, Dieter *101:* 167, 168
Schubert-Gabrys, Ingrid *101:* 167, 168
Schucker, James *31:* 163
Schuett, Stacey *72:* 137
Schulke, Debra *57:* 167
Schulke, Flip *57:* 167
Schulz, Charles M. *10:* 137-142; *118:* 192, 193, 194, 196, 199
Schutzer, Dena *109:* 32
Schwark, Mary Beth *51:* 155; *72:* 175
Schwartz, Amy *47:* 191; *82:* 100; *83:* 178, 179, 180, 181; *129:* 107; *131:* 197, 198
Schwartz, Carol *124:* 41; *130:* 199

Schwartz, Charles *8:* 184
Schwartz, Daniel *46:* 37
Schwartz, Joanie *124:* 170
Schwartzberg, Joan *3:* 208
Schweitzer, Iris *2:* 137; *6:* 207
Schweninger, Ann *29:* 172; *82:* 246
Schwinger, Laurence *84:* 44; *91:* 61
Scofield, Penrod *61:* 107; *62:* 160
Scott, Anita Walker *7:* 38
Scott, Art *39:* 41
Scott, Frances Gruse *38:* 43
Scott, Julian *34:* 126
Scott, Roszel *33:* 238
Scott, Sally *87:* 27
Scott, Trudy *27:* 172
Scribner, Joanne *14:* 236; *29:* 78; *33:* 185; *34:* 208; *78:* 75
Scrofani, Joseph *31:* 65; *74:* 225
Seaman, Mary Lott *34:* 64
Searle, Ronald *24:* 98; *42:* 172, 173, 174, 176, 177, 179; *66:* 73, 74; *70:* 205, 206, 207
Searle, Townley *36:* 85
Sebree, Charles *18:* 65
Sedacca, Joseph M. *11:* 25; *22:* 36
Seder, Jason *108:* 102
Seeley, Laura L. *97:* 105
Segar, E. C. *61:* 179, 181
Ségur, Adrienne *27:* 121
Seibold, J. Otto *83:* 188, 190, 191
Seignobosc, Françoise *21:* 145, 146
Sejima, Yoshimasa *8:* 187
Selig, Sylvie *13:* 199
Seltzer, Isadore *6:* 18; *133:* 59
Seltzer, Meyer *17:* 214
Selznick, Brian *79:* 192; *104:* 25; *117:* 175; *126:* 156; *134:* 171
Sempé, Jean-Jacques *47:* 92; *YABC 2:* 109
Sendak, Maurice *1:* 135; *190:* 3; *204:* 7; *142;* *15:* 199; *17:* 210; *27:* 181, 182, 183, 185, 186, 187, 189, 190-191, 192, 193, 194, 195, 197, 198, 199, 203; *28:* 181; *32:* 108; *33:* 148, 149; *35:* 238; *44:* 180, 181; *45:* 97, 99; *46:* 174; *73:* 225; *91:* 10, 11 *YABC 1:* 167; *113:* 163, 165, 167, 168; *118:* 153; *127:* 161
Sengler, Johanna *18:* 256
Senn, Steve *60:* 145
Seredy, Kate *1:* 192; *14:* 20-21; *17:* 210
Sergeant, John *6:* 74
Servello, Joe *10:* 144; *24:* 139; *40:* 91; *70:* 130, 131
Seton, Ernest Thompson *18:* 260-269, 271
Seuss, Dr. *See* Geisel, Theodor
Severin, John Powers *7:* 62
Sewall, Marcia *15:* 8; *22:* 170; *37:* 171, 172, 173; *39:* 73; *45:* 209; *62:* 117; *69:* 185, 186; *71:* 212; *90:* 232; *96:* 127; *102:* 101; *107:* 129; *119:* 176, 177, 178, 180
Seward, James *70:* 35
Seward, Prudence *16:* 243
Sewell, Helen *3:* 186; *15:* 308; *33:* 102; *38:* 189, 190, 191, 192
Seymour, Stephen *54:* 21
Shachat, Andrew *82:* 179
Shahn, Ben *39:* 178; *46:* 193
Shalansky, Len *38:* 167
Shanks, Anne Zane *10:* 149
Shannon, David *57:* 137; *107:* 184; *112:* 216; *135:* 12
Sharp, Paul *52:* 60
Sharp, William *6:* 131; *19:* 241; *20:* 112; *25:* 141
Sharratt, Nick *102:* 207, 208; *104:* 163
Shaw, Barclay *74:* 14, 16; *118:* 138
Shaw, Charles *21:* 135; *38:* 187; *47:* 124; *126:* 219
Shaw, Charles G. *13:* 200
Shea, Edmund *56:* 19
Shearer, Ted *43:* 193, 194, 195, 196

Shecter, Ben *16:* 244; *25:* 109; *33:* 188, 191; *41:* 77
Shed, Greg *74:* 94; *84:* 204; *129:* 149
Shefcik, James *48:* 221, 222; *60:* 141
Shefelman, Karl *58:* 168
Shefts, Joelle *48:* 210
Shein, Bob *139:* 189
Shekerjian, Haig *16:* 245
Shekerjian, Regina *16:* 245; *25:* 73
Shemie, Bonnie *96:* 207
Shenton, Edward *45:* 187, 188, 189; *YABC 1:* 218-219, 221
Shepard, Ernest H. *3:* 193; *4:* 74; *16:* 101; *17:* 109; *25:* 148; *33:* 152, 199, 200, 201, 202, 203, 204, 205, 206, 207; *46:* 194; *98:* 114; *100:* 111, 178, 179, 217, 219, 220, 221; *YABC 1:* 148, 153, 174, 176, 180-181
Shepard, Mary *4:* 210; *22:* 205; *30:* 132, 133; *54:* 150, 152, 153, 157, 158; *59:* 108, 109, 111; *100:* 246
Shepperson, Rob *96:* 153
Sherman, Theresa *27:* 167
Sherwan, Earl *3:* 196
Shields, Charles *10:* 150; *36:* 63
Shields, Leonard *13:* 83, 85, 87
Shiffman, Lena *139:* 167
Shigley, Neil K. *66:* 219
Shillabeer, Mary *35:* 74
Shilston, Arthur *49:* 61; *62:* 58
Shimin, Symeon *1:* 93; *2:* 128-129; *3:* 202; *7:* 85; *11:* 177; *12:* 139; *13:* 202-203; *27:* 138; *28:* 65; *35:* 129; *36:* 130; *48:* 151; *49:* 59; *56:* 63, 65, 153
Shine, Andrea *104:* 165; *128:* 34
Shinn, Everett *16:* 148; *18:* 229; *21:* 149, 150, 151; *24:* 218
Shinn, Florence Scovel *63:* 133, 135
Shore, Robert *27:* 54; *39:* 192, 193; *YABC 2:* 200
Shortall, Leonard *4:* 144; *8:* 196; *10:* 166; *19:* 227, 228-229, 230; *25:* 78; *28:* 66, 167; *33:* 127; *52:* 125; *73:* 12, 212
Shortt, T. M. *27:* 36
Shpitalnik, Vladimir *83:* 194
Shtainments, Leon *32:* 161
Shulevitz, Uri *3:* 198-199; *17:* 85; *22:* 204; *27:* 212; *28:* 184; *50:* 190, 191, 192, 193, 194-195, 196, 197, 198, 199, 201; *106:* 181, 182, 183
Shupe, Bobbi *139:* 80, 81
Shute, A. B. *67:* 196
Shute, Linda *46:* 59; *74:* 118
Siberell, Anne *29:* 193
Sibley, Don *1:* 39; *12:* 196; *31:* 47
Sibthorp, Fletcher *94:* 111, 112
Sidjakov, Nicolas *18:* 274
Siebel, Fritz *3:* 120; *17:* 145
Siegel, Hal *74:* 246
Siegl, Helen *12:* 166; *23:* 216; *34:* 185, 186
Sill, John *140:* 194; *141:* 157
Sills, Joyce *5:* 199
Silva, Simon *108:* 122
Silver, Maggie *85:* 210
Silveria, Gordon *96:* 44
Silverstein, Alvin *8:* 189
Silverstein, Shel *33:* 211; *92:* 209, 210
Silverstein, Virginia *8:* 189
Silvey, Joe *135:* 203
Simard, Remy *95:* 156
Simmons, Elly *110:* 2; *127:* 69; *134:* 181
Simon, Eric M. *7:* 82
Simon, Hilda *28:* 189
Simon, Howard *2:* 175; *5:* 132; *19:* 199; *32:* 163, 164, 165
Simont, Marc *2:* 119; *4:* 213; *9:* 168; *13:* 238, 240; *14:* 262; *16:* 179; *18:* 221; *26:* 210; *33:* 189, 194; *44:* 132; *58:* 122; *68:* 117; *73:* 204, 205, 206; *74:* 221; *126:* 199, 200; *133:* 195
Sims, Agnes *54:* 152

Sims, Blanche *44:* 116; *57:* 129; *75:* 179, 180; *77:* 92; *104:* 192
Singer, Edith G. *2:* 30
Singer, Gloria *34:* 56; *36:* 43
Singer, Julia *28:* 190
Siomades, Lorianne *134:* 45
Siracusa, Catherine *68:* 135; *82:* 218
Sis, Peter *67:* 179, 181, 183, 184, 185; *96:* 96, 98; *106:* 193, 194, 195
Sivard, Robert *26:* 124
Sivertson, Liz *116:* 84
Skardinski, Stanley *23:* 144; *32:* 84; *66:* 122; *84:* 108
Slackman, Charles B. *12:* 201
Slade, Paul *61:* 170
Slark, Albert *99:* 212
Slater, Rod *25:* 167
Sloan, Joseph *16:* 68
Sloane, Eric *21:* 3; *52:* 153, 154, 155, 156, 157, 158, 160
Slobodkin, Louis *1:* 200; *3:* 232; *5:* 168; *13:* 251; *15:* 13, 88; *26:* 173, 174, 175, 176, 178, 179; *60:* 180
Slobodkina, Esphyr *1:* 201
Small, David *50:* 204-205; *79:* 44; *95:* 189, 190, 191; *126:* 203, 204; *136:* 119
Small, W. *33:* 113
Smalley, Janet *1:* 154
Smedley, William T. *34:* 129
Smee, David *14:* 78; *62:* 30
Smith, A. G., Jr. *35:* 182
Smith, Alvin *1:* 31, 229; *13:* 187; *27:* 216; *28:* 226; *48:* 149; *49:* 60
Smith, Anne Warren *41:* 212
Smith, Barry *75:* 183
Smith, Carl *36:* 41
Smith, Craig *97:* 197
Smith, Doris Susan *41:* 139
Smith, E. Boyd *19:* 70; *22:* 89; *26:* 63; *YABC 1:* 4-5, 240, 248-249
Smith, Edward J. *4:* 224
Smith, Eunice Young *5:* 170
Smith, Gary *113:* 216
Smith, George *102:* 169
Smith, Howard *19:* 196
Smith, J. Gerard *95:* 42
Smith, Jacqueline Bardner *27:* 108; *39:* 197
Smith, Jay J. *61:* 119
Smith, Jeff *93:* 191
Smith, Jessie Willcox *15:* 91; *16:* 95; *18:* 231; *19:* 57, 242; *21:* 29, 156, 157, 158, 159, 160, 161; *34:* 65; *100:* 223; *YABC 1:* 6; *2:* 180, 185, 191, 311, 325
Smith, Jos. A. *52:* 131; *72:* 120; *74:* 151; *84:* 147, 148; *85:* 146; *87:* 96; *94:* 219; *96:* 97; *104:* 33; *108:* 126, 127, 128; *111:* 140; *136:* 145
Smith, Kenneth R. *47:* 182
Smith, Kevin Warren *89:* 112
Smith, L. H. *35:* 174
Smith, Lane *76:* 211, 213; *88:* 115; *105:* 202, 203, 204, 205; *131:* 207
Smith, Lee *29:* 32
Smith, Linell Nash *2:* 195
Smith, Maggie Kaufman *13:* 205; *35:* 191; *110:* 158
Smith, Mavis *101:* 219
Smith, Moishe *33:* 155
Smith, Philip *44:* 134; *46:* 203
Smith, Ralph Crosby *2:* 267; *49:* 203
Smith, Robert D. *5:* 63
Smith, Sally J. *84:* 55
Smith, Susan Carlton *12:* 208
Smith, Terry *12:* 106; *33:* 158
Smith, Virginia *3:* 157; *33:* 72
Smith, William A. *1:* 36; *10:* 154; *25:* 65
Smith-Moore, J. J. *98:* 147
Smolinski, Dick *84:* 217
Smoljan, Joe *112:* 201
Smollin, Mike *39:* 203
Smyth, Iain *105:* 207
Smyth, M. Jane *12:* 15

Smythe, Theresa *141:* 37
Sneed, Brad *125:* 25
Snyder, Andrew A. *30:* 212
Snyder, Jerome *13:* 207; *30:* 173
Snyder, Joel *28:* 163
Soentpiet, Chris K. *97:* 208; *110:* 33
Sofia *1:* 62; *5:* 90; *32:* 166; *86:* 43
Sofilas, Mark *93:* 157
Sokol, Bill *37:* 178; *49:* 23
Sokolov, Kirill *34:* 188
Solbert, Ronni *1:* 159; *2:* 232; *5:* 121; *6:* 34; *17:* 249
Solonevich, George *15:* 246; *17:* 47
Soma, Liana *81:* 118
Soman, David *90:* 122; *102:* 126; *140:* 120
Sommer, Robert *12:* 211
Sorel, Edward *4:* 61; *36:* 82; *65:* 191, 193; *126:* 214
Sorensen, Henrik *62:* 16
Sorensen, Svend Otto *22:* 130, 141; *67:* 188, 189
Sotomayor, Antonio *11:* 215
Souhami, Jessica *112:* 128
Souza, Diana *71:* 139
Sovak, Jan *115:* 190
Soyer, Moses *20:* 177
Spaenkuch, August *16:* 28
Spain, Valerie *105:* 76
Spain, Sunday Sahara *133:* 204
Spanfeller, James *1:* 72, 149; *2:* 183; *19:* 230, 231, 232; *22:* 66; *36:* 160, 161; *40:* 75; *52:* 166; *76:* 37
Sparks, Mary Walker *15:* 247
Speidel, Sandra *78:* 233; *94:* 178; *134:* 180
Speirs, John *67:* 178
Spence, Geraldine *21:* 163; *47:* 196
Spence, Jim *38:* 89; *50:* 102
Spencer, Laurie *113:* 12
Spencer, Mark *57:* 170
Sperling, Andrea *133:* 182
Spiegel, Doris *29:* 111
Spiegelman, Art *109:* 227
Spier, Jo *10:* 30
Spier, Peter *3:* 155; *4:* 200; *7:* 61; *11:* 78; *38:* 106; *54:* 120, 121, 122-123, 124-125, 126, 127, 128-129, 130, 131, 132-133, 134
Spilka, Arnold *5:* 120; *6:* 204; *8:* 131
Spirin, Gennady *95:* 196, 197; *113:* 172; *128:* 9; *129:* 49; *134:* 210
Spivak, I. Howard *8:* 10; *13:* 172
Spohn, David *72:* 233
Spohn, Kate *87:* 195
Spollen, Christopher J. *12:* 214
Spooner, Malcolm *40:* 142
Spowart, Robin *82:* 228; *92:* 149; *133:* 131
Sprattler, Rob *12:* 176
Spring, Bob *5:* 60
Spring, Ira *5:* 60
Springer, Harriet *31:* 92
Spudvilas, Anne *110:* 74
Spurll, Barbara *78:* 199; *88:* 141, 142; *99:* 215
Spurrier, Steven *28:* 198
Spuvilas, Anne *85:* 114
Spy *See* Ward, Leslie
Squires, Stuart *127:* 74
St. John, J. Allen *41:* 62
Stabin, Victor *101:* 131
Stadler, John *62:* 33
Staffan, Alvin E. *11:* 56; *12:* 187
Stahl, Ben *5:* 181; *12:* 91; *49:* 122; *71:* 128; *87:* 206; *112:* 107
Stair, Gobin *35:* 214
Stallwood, Karen *73:* 126
Stamaty, Mark Alan *12:* 215
Stammen, JoEllen McAllister *113:* 14
Stampnick, Ken *51:* 142
Stanley, Diane *3:* 45; *37:* 180; *80:* 217, 219
Starcke, Helmut *86:* 217
Starr, Branka *73:* 25
Stasiak, Krystyna *49:* 181; *64:* 194

Staub, Leslie *103:* 54
Staunton, Ted *112:* 192
Stead, L. *55:* 51, 56
Steadman, Broeck *97:* 185, 186; *99:* 56; *121:* 48
Steadman, Ralph *32:* 180; *123:* 143, 145
Steckler, June *90:* 178
Steichen, Edward *30:* 79
Steig, William *18:* 275-276; *70:* 215, 216, 217, 218; *111:* 173, 174, 175, 176, 177
Stein, Harve *1:* 109
Steinberg, Saul *47:* 193
Steinel, William *23:* 146
Steiner, Charlotte *45:* 196
Steiner, Joan *110:* 219
Steirnagel, Michael *80:* 56
Stemp, Eric *60:* 184
Stephens, Alice Barber *66:* 208, 209
Stephens, Charles H. *YABC 2:* 279
Stephens, Pat *126:* 110; *128:* 101
Stephens, William M. *21:* 165
Steptoe, John *8:* 197; *57:* 9; *63:* 158, 159, 160, 161, 163, 164, 165, 166, 167; *96:* 4; *105:* 87
Stern, Simon *15:* 249-250; *17:* 58; *34:* 192-193
Sterret, Jane *53:* 27
Stevens, David *62:* 44
Stevens, Janet *40:* 126; *57:* 10, 11; *80:* 112; *90:* 221, 222; *109:* 156; *130:* 34
Stevens, Mary *11:* 193; *13:* 129; *43:* 95
Stevenson, Harvey *66:* 143; *80:* 201, 221
Stevenson, James *42:* 182, 183; *51:* 163; *66:* 184; *71:* 185, 187, 188; *78:* 262; *87:* 97; *113:* 182, 183, 184, 185
Stevenson, Sucie *92:* 27; *104:* 194, 195; *112:* 168
Stewart, April Blair *75:* 210
Stewart, Arvis *33:* 98; *36:* 69; *60:* 118; *75:* 91; *127:* 4
Stewart, Charles *2:* 205
Stiles, Fran *26:* 85; *78:* 56; *82:* 150
Stillman, Susan *44:* 130; *76:* 83
Stimpson, Tom *49:* 171
Stinemetz, Morgan *40:* 151
Stinson, Paul *110:* 86
Stirnweis, Shannon *10:* 164
Stites, Joe *86:* 96
Stobbs, William *1:* 48, 49; *3:* 68; *6:* 20; *17:* 117, 217; *24:* 150; *29:* 250; *60:* 179; *87:* 204, 205, 206
Stock, Catherine *37:* 55; *65:* 198; *72:* 7; *99:* 225; *114:* 197, 198, 199; *126:* 3
Stockman, Jack *113:* 24
Stoeke, Janet Morgan *90:* 225; *136:* 196
Stoerrle, Tom *55:* 147
Stolp, Jaap *49:* 98
Stolp, Todd *89:* 195
Stone, David L. *87:* 154
Stone, David *9:* 173
Stone, David K. *4:* 38; *6:* 124; *9:* 180; *43:* 182; *60:* 70
Stone, Helen V. *6:* 209
Stone, Helen *44:* 121, 122, 126
Stone, Kazuko G. *134:* 43
Stone, Phoebe *86:* 212; *134:* 213
Stoud, Virginia A. *89:* 31
Stover, Jill *82:* 234
Stratton, Helen *33:* 151
Stratton-Porter, Gene *15:* 254, 259, 263-264, 268-269
Streano, Vince *20:* 173
Street, Janet Travell *84:* 235
Streeter, Clive *121:* 2
Stringer, Lauren *129:* 187
Strodl, Daniel *47:* 95
Strogart, Alexander *63:* 139
Stromoski, Rick *111:* 179; *124:* 161, 190
Strong, Joseph D., Jr. *YABC 2:* 330
Ströyer, Poul *13:* 221
Strugnell, Ann *27:* 38
Struzan, Drew *117:* 6

Stubbs, William *73:* 196
Stubis, Talivaldis *5:* 182, 183; *10:* 45; *11:* 9; *18:* 304; *20:* 127
Stubley, Trevor *14:* 43; *22:* 219; *23:* 37; *28:* 61; *87:* 26
Stuck, Marion *104:* 44
Stuecklen, Karl W. *8:* 34, 65; *23:* 103
Stull, Betty *11:* 46
Stutzman, Mark *119:* 99
Stutzmann, Laura *73:* 185
Suba, Susanne *4:* 202-203; *14:* 261; *23:* 134; *29:* 222; *32:* 30
Sueling, Barbara *98:* 185
Sueling, Gwenn *98:* 186
Sugarman, Tracy *3:* 76; *8:* 199; *37:* 181, 182
Sugita, Yutaka *36:* 180-181
Suh, John *80:* 157
Sullivan, Dorothy *89:* 113
Sullivan, Edmund J. *31:* 86
Sullivan, James F. *19:* 280; *20:* 192
Sully, Tom *104:* 199, 200
Sumichrast, Jözef *14:* 253; *29:* 168, 213
Sumiko *46:* 57
Summers, Leo *1:* 177; *2:* 273; *13:* 22
Summers, Mark *118:* 144
Sutton, Judith *94:* 164
Svarez, Juan *56:* 113
Svolinsky, Karel *17:* 104
Swain, Su Zan Noguchi *21:* 170
Swan, Susan *22:* 220-221; *37:* 66; *60:* 146
Swann, Susan *86:* 55
Swanson, Karl *79:* 65; *89:* 186
Swayne, Sam *53:* 143, 145
Swayne, Zoa *53:* 143, 145
Sweat, Lynn *25:* 206; *57:* 176; *73:* 184
Sweet, Darrell K. *60:* 9; *69:* 86; *74:* 15; *75:* 215; *76:* 130, 131; *81:* 96, 122; *82:* 253; *83:* 11; *84:* 14; *85:* 37; *89:* 140; *90:* 6; *91:* 137, 139; *95:* 160, 161; *126:* 25
Sweet, Darryl *1:* 163; *4:* 136
Sweet, Melissa *71:* 94; *72:* 172; *111:* 82; *139:* 53, 58; *141:* 88
Sweet, Ozzie *31:* 149, 151, 152
Sweetland, Robert *12:* 194
Swiatkowska, Gabi *132:* 43
Swope, Martha *43:* 160; *56:* 86, 87, 89
Sylvester, Natalie G. *22:* 222
Szafran, Gene *24:* 144
Szasz, Susanne *13:* 55, 226; *14:* 48
Szekeres, Cyndy *2:* 218; *5:* 185; *8:* 85; *11:* 166; *14:* 19; *16:* 57, 159; *26:* 49, 214; *34:* 205; *60:* 150, 151, 152, 153, 154; *73:* 224; *74:* 218; *131:* 213, 215
Szpura, Beata *81:* 68; *119:* 65

T

Taback, Simms *40:* 207; *52:* 120; *57:* 34; *80:* 241; *104:* 202, 203
Taber, Patricia *75:* 124
Tabor, Nancy Maria Grande *89:* 210
Taddei, Richard *112:* 13, 14
Tadiello, Ed *133:* 200
Tafuri, Nancy *39:* 210; *75:* 199, 200; *92:* 75; *130:* 215, 216, 217
Tailfeathers, Gerald *86:* 85
Tait, Douglas *12:* 220; *74:* 105, 106
Takabayashi, Mari *113:* 112; *130:* 22
Takahashi, Hideko *136:* 160
Takakjian, Portia *15:* 274
Takashima, Shizuye *13:* 228
Talarczyk, June *4:* 173
Talbott, Hudson *84:* 240
Tallarico, Tony *116:* 197
Tallon, Robert *2:* 228; *43:* 200, 201, 202, 203, 204, 205, 206, 207, 209
Tamas, Szecskó *29:* 135

Tamburine, Jean *12:* 222
Tandy, H. R. *13:* 69
Tandy, Russell H. *65:* 9; *100:* 30, 131
Tang, Charles *81:* 202; *90:* 192
Tang, Susan *80:* 174; *108:* 158
Tang, You-shan *63:* 100
Tankersley, Paul *69:* 206; *133:* 219
Tannenbaum, Robert *48:* 181
Tanner, Jane *87:* 13; *97:* 37
Tanner, Tim *72:* 192; *84:* 35
Tanobe, Miyuki *23:* 221
Tarabay, Sharif *110:* 149; *113:* 123
Tarkington, Booth *17:* 224-225
Tarlow, Phyllis *61:* 198
Tauss, Herbert *95:* 179
Tauss, Marc *117:* 160; *126:* 155
Taylor, Ann *41:* 226
Taylor, Dahl *129:* 157
Taylor, Geoff *93:* 156
Taylor, Isaac *41:* 228
Teague, Mark *83:* 6; *139:* 241
Teale, Edwin Way *7:* 196
Teason, James *1:* 14
Teeple, Lyn *33:* 147
Tee-Van, Helen Damrosch *10:* 176; *11:* 182
Teicher, Dick *50:* 211
Teichman, Mary *77:* 220; *124:* 208; *127:* 22
Temertey, Ludmilla *96:* 232; *104:* 43, 45; *109:* 244
Tempest, Margaret *3:* 237, 238; *88:* 200
Temple, Frances *85:* 185, 186, 187
Temple, Herbert *45:* 201
Templeton, Owen *11:* 77
Tenggren, Gustaf *18:* 277-279; *19:* 15; *28:* 86; *YABC 2:* 145
Tennent, Julie *81:* 105
Tenney, Gordon *24:* 204
Tenniel, John *74:* 234, 235; *100:* 89; *YABC 2:* 99
Tepper, Matt *116:* 80
Terkel, Ari *103:* 162
Terry, Will *131:* 73
Teskey, Donald *71:* 51
Thacher, Mary M. *30:* 72
Thackeray, William Makepeace *23:* 224, 228
Thamer, Katie *42:* 187
Thelwell, Norman *14:* 201
Theobalds, Prue *40:* 23
Theurer, Marilyn Churchill *39:* 195
Thiesing, Lisa *89:* 134; *95:* 202
Thiewes, Sam *133:* 114
Thistlethwaite, Miles *12:* 224
Thollander, Earl *11:* 47; *18:* 112; *22:* 224
Thomas, Allan *22:* 13
Thomas, Art *48:* 217
Thomas, Eric *28:* 49
Thomas, Harold *20:* 98
Thomas, Jacqui *125:* 95
Thomas, Mark *42:* 136
Thomas, Martin *14:* 255
Thompson, Arthur *34:* 107
Thompson, Carol *85:* 189; *95:* 75; *102:* 86
Thompson, Colin *95:* 204
Thompson, Ellen *51:* 88, 151; *60:* 33; *67:* 42; *77:* 148; *78:* 75, 219; *79:* 122, 170; *84:* 219; *85:* 97; *87:* 37; *88:* 192, 194; *89:* 80; *93:* 37; *98:* 59; *132:* 14
Thompson, George W. *22:* 18; *28:* 150; *33:* 135
Thompson, John *58:* 201; *102:* 226; *124:* 154; *128:* 228; *129:* 157
Thompson, Julie *44:* 158
Thompson, Katherine *132:* 146
Thompson, K. Dyble *84:* 6
Thompson, Sharon *74:* 113
Thomson, Arline K. *3:* 264
Thomson, Hugh *26:* 88
Thomson, Ross *36:* 179
Thorkelson, Gregg *95:* 183, 184; *98:* 58
Thornberg, Dan *104:* 125
Thorne, Diana *25:* 212
Thornhill, Jan *77:* 213

Thorpe, Peter *58:* 109
Thorvall, Kerstin *13:* 235
Threadgall, Colin *77:* 215
Thurber, James *13:* 239, 242-245, 248-249
Thurman, Mark *63:* 173
Tibbles, Jean-Paul *115:* 200
Tibbles, Paul *45:* 23
Tibo, Gilles *67:* 207; *107:* 199, 201
Tichenor, Tom *14:* 207
Tichnor, Richard *90:* 218
Tiegreen, Alan *36:* 143; *43:* 55, 56, 58; *77:* 200; *94:* 216, 217; *121:* 54, 59
Tierney, Tom *113:* 198, 200, 201
Tilley, Debbie *102:* 134; *133:* 226; *137:* 101
Tilney, F. C. *22:* 231
Timbs, Gloria *36:* 90
Timmins, Harry *2:* 171
Tinkelman, Murray *12:* 225; *35:* 44
Titherington, Jeanne *39:* 90; *58:* 138; *75:* 79; *135:* 161
Tolbert, Jeff *128:* 69
Tolford, Joshua *1:* 221
Tolkien, J. R. R. *2:* 243; *32:* 215
Tolmie, Ken *15:* 292
Tomei, Lorna *47:* 168, 171
Tomes, Jacqueline *2:* 117; *12:* 139
Tomes, Margot *1:* 224; *2:* 120-121; *16:* 207; *18:* 250; *20:* 7; *25:* 62; *27:* 78, 79; *29:* 81, 199; *33:* 82; *36:* 186, 187, 188, 189, 190; *46:* 129; *56:* 71; *58:* 183; *70:* 228; *75:* 73, 75; *80:* 80; *83:* 97; *90:* 205
Toner, Raymond John *10:* 179
Tong, Gary *66:* 215
Tongier, Stephen *82:* 32
Toothill, Harry *6:* 54; *7:* 49; *25:* 219; *42:* 192
Toothill, Ilse *6:* 54
Topolski, Feliks *44:* 48
Torbert, Floyd James *22:* 226
Torgersen, Don *55:* 157
Tormey, Bertram M. *75:* 3, 4
Torrey, Helen *87:* 41
Torrey, Marjorie *34:* 105
Toschik, Larry *6:* 102
Totten, Bob *13:* 93
Toy, Julie *128:* 112
Trachok, Cathy *131:* 16
Tracy, Libba *82:* 24
Trail, Lee *55:* 157
Trang, Winson *89:* 151
Trapani, Iza *116:* 202
Travers, Bob *49:* 100; *63:* 145
Treatner, Meryl *95:* 180
Tremain, Ruthven *17:* 238
Tresilian, Stuart *25:* 53; *40:* 212
Trez, Alain *17:* 236
Trezzo, Loretta *86:* 45
Trier, Walter *14:* 96
Trimby, Elisa *47:* 199
Trinkle, Sally *53:* 27
Tripp, F. J. *24:* 167
Tripp, Wallace *2:* 48; *7:* 28; *8:* 94; *10:* 54, 76; *11:* 92; *31:* 170, 171; *34:* 203; *42:* 57; *60:* 157; *73:* 182
Trivas, Irene *53:* 4; *54:* 168; *82:* 46, 101
Trnka, Jiri *22:* 151; *43:* 212, 213, 214, 215; *YABC 1:* 30-31
Troughton, Joanna *37:* 186; *48:* 72
Troyer, Johannes *3:* 16; *7:* 18
Trudeau, G. B. *35:* 220, 221, 222; *48:* 119, 123, 126, 127, 128-129, 133
Truesdell, Sue *55:* 142; *108:* 219, 220
Tryon, Leslie *84:* 7; *139:* 214
Tseng, Jean *72:* 195; *94:* 102; *119:* 126
Tseng, Mou-sien *72:* 195; *94:* 102; *119:* 126
Tsinajinie, Andy *2:* 62
Tsugami, Kyuzo *18:* 198-199
Tuckwell, Jennifer *17:* 205
Tudor, Bethany *7:* 103

Tudor, Tasha *18:* 227; *20:* 185, 186, 187; *36:* 111; *69:* 196, 198; *100:* 44; *YABC 2:* 46, 314
Tuerk, Hanne *71:* 201
Tulloch, Maurice *24:* 79
Tunis, Edwin *1:* 218-219; *28:* 209, 210, 211, 212
Tunnicliffe, C. F. *62:* 176; 177; 178, 179; 181
Turkle, Brinton *1:* 211, 213; *2:* 249; *3:* 226; *11:* 3; *16:* 209; *20:* 22; *50:* 23; *67:* 50; *68:* 65; *79:* 205, 206, 207; *128:* 47; *YABC 1:* 79
Turner, Gwenda *59:* 195
Turska, Krystyna *12:* 103; *31:* 173, 174-175; *56:* 32, 34; *100:* 66
Tusa, Tricia *72:* 242; *111:* 180, 181
Tusan, Stan *6:* 58; *22:* 236-237
Tworkov, Jack *47:* 207
Tyers, Jenny *89:* 220
Tylden-Wright, Jenny *114:* 119
Tyrol, Adelaide Murphy *103:* 27
Tyrrell, Frances *107:* 204
Tzimoulis, Paul *12:* 104

U

Uchida, Yoshiko *1:* 220
Uderzo *47:* 88
Ueno, Noriko *59:* 155
Ulm, Robert *17:* 238
Ulrich, George *73:* 15; *75:* 136, 139; *99:* 150
Ulriksen, Mark *101:* 58
Unada *84:* 67 *See* Gliewe, Unada
Underhill, Liz *53:* 159
Underwood, Clarence *40:* 166
Unger, Jim *67:* 208
Ungerer, Tomi *5:* 188; *9:* 40; *18:* 188; *29:* 175; *33:* 221, 222-223, 225; *71:* 48; *106:* 209, 210, 211, 212
Unwin, Nora S. *3:* 65, 234-235; *4:* 237; *44:* 173, 174; *YABC 1:* 59; *2:* 301
Urbanovic, Jackie *86:* 86
Uris, Jill *49:* 188, 197
Ursell, Martin *50:* 51
Utpatel, Frank *18:* 114
Utz, Lois *5:* 190

V

Vagin, Vladimir *66:* 10
Vaillancourt, Francois *107:* 199
Vainio, Pirkko *123:* 157-158
Vallejo, Boris *62:* 130; *72:* 212; *91:* 38; *93:* 61
Van Abbé, S. *16:* 142; *18:* 282; *31:* 90; *YABC 2:* 157, 161
Van Allsburg, Chris *37:* 205, 206; *53:* 161, 162, 163, 165, 166, 167, 168, 169, 170-171; *105:* 215, 216, 217, 218
Vance, James *65:* 28
Van Der Linde, Henry *99:* 17
van der Meer, Ron *98:* 204, 205
van der Meer, Atie *98:* 204, 205
Vandivert, William *21:* 175
Van Dongen, H. R. *81:* 97
Van Everen, Jay *13:* 160; *YABC 1:* 121
Van Horn, William *43:* 218
van Lawick, Hugo *62:* 76, 79
Van Loon, Hendrik Willem *18:* 285, 289, 291
Van Munching, Paul *83:* 85
Van Rynbach, Iris *102:* 192
Van Sciver, Ruth *37:* 162

VanSeveren, Joe *63:* 182
Van Stockum, Hilda *5:* 193
Van Wely, Babs *16:* 50; *79:* 16
Van Wright, Cornelius *72:* 18; *102:* 208; *116:* 107
Van Zyle, Jon *103:* 125
Vardzigulyants, Ruben *90:* 54
Varga, Judy *29:* 196
Vargo, Kurt *79:* 224
Varley, Susan *61:* 199; *63:* 176, 177; *101:* 148; *134:* 220
Vasconcellos, Daniel *80:* 42
Vasiliu, Mircea *2:* 166, 253; *9:* 166; *13:* 58; *68:* 42
Vaughn, Frank *34:* 157
Vavra, Robert *8:* 206
Vawter, Will *17:* 163
Vayas, Diana *71:* 61
Vazquez, Carlos *125:* 184
Veeder, Larry *18:* 4
Velasquez, Eric *45:* 217; *61:* 45; *63:* 110, 111; *88:* 162; *90:* 34, 144; *94:* 213; *107:* 147; *132:* 192; *138:* 213
Velasquez, Jose A. *63:* 73
Velez, Walter *71:* 75; *91:* 154; *121:* 181
Velthuijs, Max *110:* 228, 229
Vendrell, Carme Solé *42:* 205
Venezia, Mike *54:* 17
Venti, Anthony Bacon *124:* 103; *126:* 26
Venturo, Piero *61:* 194, 195
Ver Beck, Frank *18:* 16-17
Verkaaik, Ben *110:* 209
Verling, John *71:* 27
Verney, John *14:* 225; *75:* 8
Verrier, Suzanne *5:* 20; *23:* 212
Versace, Marie *2:* 255
Verstraete, Randy *108:* 193
Vestal, H. B. *9:* 134; *11:* 101; *27:* 25; *34:* 158
Vicatan *59:* 146
Vickrey, Robert *45:* 59, 64
Victor, Joan Berg *30:* 193
Viereck, Ellen *3:* 242; *14:* 229
Vigna, Judith *15:* 293; *102:* 194, 195, 196, 197
Vilato, Gaspar E. *5:* 41
Villiard, Paul *51:* 178
Vimnèra, A. *23:* 154
Vincent, Eric *34:* 98
Vincent, Félix *41:* 237
Vincent, Gabrielle *121:* 175
Vip *45:* 164
Viskupic, Gary *83:* 48
Vitale, Stefano *109:* 71, 107; *114:* 219, 220; *123:* 106; *138:* 232
Vivas, Julie *51:* 67, 69; *96:* 225
Voake, Charlotte *114:* 221, 222
Vo-Dinh, Mai *16:* 272; *60:* 191
Vogel, Ilse-Margret *14:* 230
Voigt, Erna *35:* 228
Vojnar, Kamil *95:* 31; *114:* 4; *115:* 62; *121:* 90; *124:* 72; *130:* 31; *141:* 81
Vojtech, Anna *42:* 190; *108:* 222, 223
von Roehl, Angela *126:* 191
von Schmidt, Eric *8:* 62; *50:* 209, 210
von Schmidt, Harold *30:* 80
Vosburgh, Leonard *1:* 161; *7:* 32; *15:* 295, 296; *23:* 110; *30:* 214; *43:* 181
Voss, Tom *127:* 104
Voter, Thomas W. *19:* 3, 9
Vroman, Tom *10:* 29
Vulliamy, Clara *72:* 65

W

Waber, Bernard *47:* 209, 210, 211, 212, 213, 214; *95:* 215, 216, 217
Wack, Jeff *95:* 140; *110:* 90

Wagner, John *8:* 200; *52:* 104
Wagner, Ken *2:* 59
Waide, Jan *29:* 225; *36:* 139
Wainwright, Jerry *14:* 85
Wakeen, Sandra *47:* 97
Waldherr, Kris *81:* 186
Waldman, Bruce *15:* 297; *43:* 178
Waldman, Neil *35:* 141; *50:* 163; *51:* 180;
   54: 78; *77:* 112; *79:* 162; *82:* 174; *84:* 5,
   56, 106; *94:* 232, 233, 234; *96:* 41; *111:*
   139; *113:* 9; *118:* 30
Waldrep, Richard *111:* 147
Walker, Charles *1:* 46; *4:* 59; *5:* 177; *11:*
   115; *19:* 45; *34:* 74; *62:* 168; *72:* 218
Walker, Dugald Stewart *15:* 47; *32:* 202;
   33: 112
Walker, Gil *8:* 49; *23:* 132; *34:* 42
Walker, Jeff *55:* 154; *123:* 116
Walker, Jim *10:* 94
Walker, Mort *8:* 213
Walker, Norman *41:* 37; *45:* 58
Walker, Stephen *12:* 229; *21:* 174
Wallace, Beverly Dobrin *19:* 259
Wallace, Cly *87:* 93
Wallace, Ian *53:* 176, 177; *56:* 165, 166;
   58: 4; *98:* 4; *101:* 191; *112:* 124; *141:*
   197, 198, 199, 200
Wallace, John *105:* 228
Wallace, Nancy Elizabeth *141:* 204
Wallenta, Adam *123:* 180
Waller, S. E. *24:* 36
Wallner, Alexandra *15:* 120
Wallner, John C. *9:* 77; *10:* 188; *11:* 28;
   14: 209; *31:* 56, 118; *37:* 64; *51:* 186,
   187, 188-189, 190-191, 192-193, 194, 195;
   52: 96; *53:* 23, 26; *71:* 99; *73:* 158; *89:*
   215; *141:* 9
Wallower, Lucille *11:* 226
Walotsky, Ron *93:* 87
Walsh, Ellen Stoll *99:* 209
Walters, Audrey *18:* 294
Walther, Tom *31:* 179
Walton, Garry *69:* 149
Walton, Tony *11:* 164; *24:* 209
Waltrip, Lela *9:* 195
Waltrip, Mildred *3:* 209; *37:* 211
Waltrip, Rufus *9:* 195
Wan *12:* 76
Wappers, G. *121:* 40
Ward, Fred *52:* 19
Ward, Helen *72:* 244
Ward, John *42:* 191; *96:* 54; *97:* 110; *123:*
   105; *124:* 71
Ward, Keith *2:* 107; *132:* 69
Ward, Leslie *34:* 126; *36:* 87
Ward, Lynd *1:* 99, 132, 133, 150; *2:* 108,
   158, 196, 259; *18:* 86; *27:* 56; *29:* 79,
   187, 253, 255; *36:* 199, 200, 201, 202,
   203, 204, 205, 206, 207, 209; *43:* 34; *56:*
   28; *60:* 116; *100:* 65
Ward, Peter *37:* 116
Warhola, James *92:* 5; *115:* 85, 87; *118:*
   174, 175, 177
Warner, Peter *14:* 87
Warnick, Elsa *113:* 223
Warren, Betsy *2:* 101
Warren, Jim *85:* 81
Warren, Marion Cray *14:* 215
Warshaw, Jerry *30:* 197, 198; *42:* 165
Wasden, Kevin *102:* 162
Washington, Nevin *20:* 123
Washington, Phyllis *20:* 123
Wasserman, Amy L. *92:* 110
Waterman, Stan *11:* 76
Watkins-Pitchford, D. J. *6:* 215, 217
Watling, James *67:* 210; *78:* 112; *101:* 81;
   *117:*189, 190; *127:* 119, 120
Watson, Aldren A. *2:* 267; *5:* 94; *13:* 71;
   19: 253; *32:* 220; *42:* 193, 194, 195, 196,
   197, 198, 199, 200, 201; *YABC 2:* 202
Watson, G. *83:* 162

Watson, Gary *19:* 147; *36:* 68; *41:* 122; *47:*
   139
Watson, J. D. *22:* 86
Watson, Karen *11:* 26
Watson, Mary *117:* 193
Watson, Richard Jesse *62:* 188, 189
Watson, Wendy *5:* 197; *13:* 101; *33:* 116;
   46: 163; *64:* 12; *74:* 242, 243; *91:* 21
Watt, Mélanie *136:* 206
Watterson, Bill *66:* 223, 225, 226
Watts, Bernadette *4:* 227; *103:* 182, 183
Watts, James *59:* 197; *74:* 145; *86:* 124
Watts, John *37:* 149
Watts, Stan *116:* 205
Weatherby, Mark Alan *77:* 141
Webb, Jennifer *110:* 79
Webb, Sophie *135:* 214
Webber, Helen *3:* 141
Webber, Irma E. *14:* 238
Weber, Erik *56:* 19, 20
Weber, Florence *40:* 153
Weber, Jill *127:* 227, 228
Weber, Roland *61:* 204
Weber, William J. *14:* 239
Webster, Jean *17:* 241
Wegman, William *78:* 243
Wegner, Fritz *14:* 250; *20:* 189; *44:* 165;
   86: 62
Weidenear, Reynold H. *21:* 122
Weihs, Erika *4:* 21; *15:* 299; *72:* 201; *107:*
   207, 208
Weil, Lisl *7:* 203; *10:* 58; *21:* 95; *22:* 188,
   217; *33:* 193
Weiman, Jon *50:* 162, 165; *52:* 103; *54:*
   78, 79, 81; *78:* 80; *82:* 107; *93:* 82; *97:*
   69; *105:* 179
Weiner, Sandra *14:* 240
Weiner, Scott *55:* 27
Weinhaus, Karen Ann *53:* 90; *71:* 50; *86:*
   124
Weisgard, Leonard *1:* 65; *2:* 191, 197, 204,
   264-265; *5:* 108; *21:* 42; *30:* 200, 201,
   203, 204; *41:* 47; *44:* 125; *53:* 25; *85:*
   196, 198, 200, 201; *100:* 139, 207; *YABC*
   2: 13
Weiss, Ellen *44:* 202
Weiss, Emil *1:* 168; *7:* 60
Weiss, Harvey *1:* 145, 223; *27:* 224, 227;
   68: 214; *76:* 245, 246, 247
Weiss, Nicki *33:* 229
Weissman, Bari *49:* 72; *90:* 125; *139:* 142
Welch, Sheila Kelly *130:* 221
Welkes, Allen *68:* 218
Wellington, Monica *99:* 223
Welliver, Norma *76:* 94
Wellner, Fred *127:* 53
Wells, Frances *1:* 183
Wells, H. G. *20:* 194, 200
Wells, Haru *53:* 120, 121
Wells, Rosemary *6:* 49; *18:* 297; *60:* 32;
   66: 203; *69:* 215, 216; *114:* 227; *118:*
   149, 150
Wells, Rufus III *56:* 111, 113
Wells, Susan *22:* 43
Wendelin, Rudolph *23:* 234
Wengenroth, Stow *37:* 47
Werenskiold, Erik *15:* 6; *62:* 17
Werner, Honi *24:* 110; *33:* 41; *88:* 122
Werth, Kurt *7:* 122; *14:* 157; *20:* 214; *39:*
   128
West, Harry A. *124:* 38
Westcott, Nadine Bernard *68:* 46; *84:* 49;
   86: 133; *106:* 199; *111:* 78; *113:* 111;
   130: 224; *139:* 54
Westerberg, Christine *29:* 226
Westerduin, Anne *105:* 229
Weston, Martha *29:* 116; *30:* 213; *33:* 85,
   100; *53:* 181, 182, 183, 184; *77:* 95; *80:*
   152; *119:* 196, 197, 198, 199; *127:* 189;
   133: 196
Wetherbee, Margaret *5:* 3
Wexler, Jerome *49:* 73

Whalley, Peter *50:* 49
Wheatley, Arabelle *11:* 231; *16:* 276
Wheeler, Cindy *49:* 205
Wheeler, Dora *44:* 179
Wheelright, Rowland *15:* 81; *YABC 2:* 286
Whelan, Michael *56:* 108; *70:* 27, 29, 67,
   68, 148; *74:* 18; *84:* 14; *91:* 195, 196;
   95: 147; *98:* 150, 151; *106:* 157; *113:*
   218, 220; *116:* 99, 100
Whelan, Patrick *135:* 145
Whistler, Rex *16:* 75; *30:* 207, 208
White, Craig *110:* 130; *119:* 193; *130:* 33
White, David Omar *5:* 56; *18:* 6
White, Joan *83:* 225
White, Martin *51:* 197; *85:* 127
Whitear *32:* 26
Whitehead, Beck *86:* 171
Whithorne, H. S. *7:* 49
Whitney, George Gillett *3:* 24
Whitney, Jean *99:* 53
Whitson, Paul *102:* 161
Whittam, Geoffrey *30:* 191
Whyte, Mary *96:* 127
Wiberg, Harald *38:* 127; *93:* 215
Wick, Walter *77:* 128
Wickstrom, Sylvie *106:* 87
Widener, Terry *105:* 230; *106:* 7
Wiese, Kurt *3:* 255; *4:* 206; *14:* 17; *17:*
   18-19; *19:* 47; *24:* 152; *25:* 212; *32:* 184;
   36: 211, 213, 214, 215, 216, 217, 218;
   45: 161; *100:* 92
Wiesner, David *33:* 47; *51:* 106; *57:* 67;
   58: 55; *64:* 78, 79, 81; *69:* 233; *72:* 247,
   248-49, 251, 252-53, 254; *83:* 134; *104:*
   31; *117:* 197, 199, 200, 202; *139:* 223,
   224
Wiesner, William *4:* 100; *5:* 200, 201; *14:*
   262
Wiggins, George *6:* 133
Wijngaard, Juan *111:* 36; *114:* 124
Wikkelsoe, Otto *45:* 25, 26
Wikland, Ilon *5:* 113; *8:* 150; *38:* 124, 125,
   130; *127:* 162
Wikler, Madeline *114:* 233
Wilbur, C. Keith, M.D. *27:* 228
Wilburn, Kathy *53:* 102; *68:* 234
Wilcox, Cathy *105:* 123
Wilcox, J. A. J. *34:* 122
Wilcox, R. Turner *36:* 219
Wild, Jocelyn *46:* 220-221, 222; *80:* 117
Wilde, George *7:* 139
Wildsmith, Brian *16:* 281-282; *18:* 170-171;
   66: 25; *69:* 224-225, 227; *77:* 103; *83:*
   218; *124:* 214, 217, 219
Wildsmith, Mike *140:* 229
Wilhelm, Hans *58:* 189, 191; *73:* 157; *77:*
   127; *135:* 229, 230, 233, 234
Wilkin, Eloise *36:* 173; *49:* 208, 209, 210
Wilkinson, Barry *50:* 213
Wilkinson, Gerald *3:* 40
Wilkon, Jozef *31:* 183, 184; *71:* 206, 207,
   209; *133:* 222
Wilks, Mike *34:* 24; *44:* 203
Willey, Bee *103:* 129; *139:* 159
Willhoite, Michael A. *71:* 214
Williams, Berkeley, Jr. *64:* 75
Williams, Ferelith Eccles *22:* 238
Williams, Garth *1:* 197; *2:* 49, 270; *4:* 205;
   15: 198, 302-304, 307; *16:* 34; *18:* 283,
   298-301; *29:* 177, 178, 179, 232-233,
   241-245, 248; *40:* 106; *66:* 229, 230, 231,
   233, 234; *71:* 192; *73:* 218, 219, 220;
   78: 261; *100:* 251, 252, 255; *136:* 117;
   YABC 2: 15-16, 19
Williams, J. Scott *48:* 28
Williams, Jennifer *102:* 201
Williams, Jenny *60:* 202; *81:* 21; *88:* 71
Williams, Kit *44:* 206-207, 208, 209, 211,
   212
Williams, Marcia *97:* 214
Williams, Maureen *12:* 238
Williams, Patrick *14:* 218

Williams, Richard *44:* 93; *72:* 229; *74:* 133; *78:* 155, 237; *91:* 178; *110:* 212; *136:* 201, 202, 203
Williams, Sam *124:* 222
Williams, Sophy *135:* 236
Williams, Vera B. *53:* 186, 187, 188, 189; *102:* 201, 202, 203
Williamson, Mel *60:* 9
Willingham, Fred *104:* 206
Willmore, J. T. *54:* 113, 114
Wilson, Charles Banks *17:* 92; *43:* 73
Wilson, Connie *113:* 179
Wilson, Dagmar *10:* 47
Wilson, Dawn *67:* 161; *81:* 120; *113:* 158
Wilson, Edward A. *6:* 24; *16:* 149; *20:* 220-221; *22:* 87; *26:* 67; *38:* 212, 214, 215, 216, 217
Wilson, Forrest *27:* 231
Wilson, Gahan *35:* 234; *41:* 136
Wilson, George *76:* 87
Wilson, Helen Miranda *140:* 61
Wilson, Jack *17:* 139
Wilson, Janet *77:* 154; *96:* 114; *99:* 219, 220; *106:* 122; *130:* 210
Wilson, John *22:* 240
Wilson, Maurice *46:* 224
Wilson, Patten *35:* 61
Wilson, Peggy *15:* 4; *84:* 20
Wilson, Rowland B. *30:* 170
Wilson, Sarah *50:* 215
Wilson, Tom *33:* 232
Wilson, W. N. *22:* 26
Wilton, Nicholas *103:* 52
Wilwerding, Walter J. *9:* 202
Wimmer, Mike *63:* 6; *70:* 121; *75:* 186; *76:* 21, 22, 23; *91:* 114; *97:* 45, 68; *98:* 28; *107:* 130
Winborn, Marsha *78:* 34; *99:* 70
Winchester, Linda *13:* 231
Wind, Betty *28:* 158
Windham, Kathryn Tucker *14:* 260
Winfield, Alison *115:* 78
Winfield, Wayne *72:* 23
Wing, Gary *64:* 147
Wing, Ron *50:* 85
Wingerter, Linda S. *132:* 199
Winick, Judd *124:* 227, 228, 229
Winslow, Will *21:* 124
Winsten, Melanie Willa *41:* 41
Winter, Milo *15:* 97; *19:* 221; *21:* 181, 203, 204, 205; *64:* 19; *YABC 2:* 144
Winter, Paula *48:* 227
Winters, Greg *70:* 117
Winters, Nina *62:* 194
Wise, Louis *13:* 68
Wiseman, Ann *31:* 187
Wiseman, B. *4:* 233
Wishnefsky, Phillip *3:* 14
Wiskur, Darrell *5:* 72; *10:* 50; *18:* 246
Wisniewski, David *95:* 220, 221
Wisniewski, Robert *95:* 10; *119:* 192
Witt, Dick *80:* 244
Wittman, Sally *30:* 219
Wittner, Dale *99:* 43
Woehr, Lois *12:* 5
Wohlberg, Meg *12:* 100; *14:* 197; *41:* 255
Wohnoutka, Mike *137:* 68
Woldin, Beth Weiner *34:* 211
Wolf, Elizabeth *133:* 151
Wolf, J. *16:* 91
Wolf, Janet *78:* 254
Wolf, Linda *33:* 163
Wolfe, Corey *72:* 213
Wolff, Ashley *50:* 217; *81:* 216

Wondriska, William *6:* 220
Wong, Janet S. *98:* 225
Wonsetler, John C. *5:* 168
Wood, Audrey *50:* 221, 222, 223; *81:* 219, 221
Wood, Don *50:* 220, 225, 226, 228-229; *81:* 218, 220; *139:* 239, 240
Wood, Grant *19:* 198
Wood, Heather *133:* 108
Wood, Ivor *58:* 17
Wood, Muriel *36:* 119; *77:* 167
Wood, Myron *6:* 220
Wood, Owen *18:* 187; *64:* 202, 204-05, 206, 208, 210
Wood, Ruth *8:* 11
Woodbridge, Curtis *133:* 138
Wooding, Sharon L. *66:* 237
Woodruff, Liza *132:* 239
Woods, John, Jr. *109:* 142
Woodson, Jack *10:* 201
Woodson, Jacqueline *94:* 242
Woodward, Alice *26:* 89; *36:* 81
Wool, David *26:* 27
Woolley, Janet *112:* 75
Woolman, Steven *106:* 47
Wooten, Vernon *23:* 70; *51:* 170
Worboys, Evelyn *1:* 166-167
Word, Reagan *103:* 204
Worth, Jo *34:* 143
Worth, Wendy *4:* 133
Wosmek, Frances *29:* 251
Wrenn, Charles L. *38:* 96; *YABC 1:* 20, 21
Wright, Barbara Mullarney *98:* 161
Wright, Dare *21:* 206
Wright-Frierson, Virginia *58:* 194; *110:* 246
Wright, George *YABC 1:* 268
Wright, Joseph *30:* 160
Wronker, Lili Cassel *3:* 247; *10:* 204; *21:* 10
Wyant, Alexander Helwig *110:* 19
Wyatt, David *97:* 9; *101:* 44; *114:* 194; *140:* 20
Wyatt, Stanley *46:* 210
Wyeth, Andrew *13:* 40; *YABC 1:* 133-134
Wyeth, Jamie *41:* 257
Wyeth, N. C. *13:* 41; *17:* 252-259, 264-268; *18:* 181; *19:* 80, 191, 200; *21:* 57, 183; *22:* 91; *23:* 152; *24:* 28, 99; *35:* 61; *41:* 65; *100:* 206; *YABC 1:* 133, 223; *2:* 53, 75, 171, 187, 317
Wyman, Cherie R. *91:* 42

X

Xuan, YongSheng *119:* 202, 207, 208; *140:* 36

Y

Yaccarino, Dan *141:* 208, 209
Yakovetic, Joe *59:* 202; *75:* 85
Yalowitz, Paul *93:* 33
Yamaguchi, Marianne *85:* 118
Yang, Jay *1:* 8; *12:* 239
Yap, Weda *6:* 176
Yaroslava *See* Mills, Yaroslava Surmach
Yashima, Taro *14:* 84

Yates, John *74:* 249, 250
Yee, Wong Herbert *115:* 216, 217
Yeo, Brad *135:* 121
Ylla *See* Koffler, Camilla
Yohn, F. C. *23:* 128; *YABC 1:* 269
Yorke, David *80:* 178
Yoshida, Toshi *77:* 231
Youll, Paul *91:* 218
Youll, Stephen *92:* 227; *118:* 136, 137
Young, Ed *7:* 205; *10:* 206; *40:* 124; *63:* 142; *74:* 250, 251, 252, 253; *75:* 227; *81:* 159; *83:* 98; *94:* 154; *115:* 160; *137:* 162; *YABC 2:* 242
Young, Mary O'Keefe *77:* 95; *80:* 247; *134:* 214; *140:* 213
Young, Noela *8:* 221; *89:* 231; *97:* 195
Yun, Cheng Mung *60:* 143

Z

Zacharow, Christopher *88:* 98
Zacks, Lewis *10:* 161
Zadig *50:* 58
Zaffo, George *42:* 208
Zagwyn, Deborah Turney *138:* 227
Zaid, Barry *50:* 127; *51:* 201
Zaidenberg, Arthur *34:* 218, 219, 220
Zalben, Jane Breskin *7:* 211; *79:* 230, 231, 233
Zallinger, Jean *4:* 192; *8:* 8, 129; *14:* 273; *68:* 36; *80:* 254; *115:* 219, 220, 222
Zallinger, Rudolph F. *3:* 245
Zebot, George *83:* 214
Zeck, Gerry *40:* 232
Zeiring, Bob *42:* 130
Zeldich, Arieh *49:* 124; *62:* 120
Zeldis, Malcah *86:* 239; *94:* 198
Zelinsky, Paul O. *14:* 269; *43:* 56; *49:* 218, 219, 220, 221, 222-223; *53:* 111; *68:* 195; *102:* 219, 220, 221, 222
Zelvin, Diana *72:* 190; *76:* 101; *93:* 207
Zemach, Margot *3:* 270; *8:* 201; *21:* 210-211; *27:* 204, 205, 210; *28:* 185; *49:* 22, 183, 224; *53:* 151; *56:* 146; *70:* 245, 246; *92:* 74
Zemsky, Jessica *10:* 62
Zepelinsky, Paul *35:* 93
Zerbetz, Evon *127:* 34
Zhang, Ange *101:* 190
Ziegler, Jack *84:* 134
Zimdars, Berta *129:* 155
Zimic, Tricia *72:* 95
Zimmer, Dirk *38:* 195; *49:* 71; *56:* 151; *65:* 214; *84:* 159; *89:* 26
Zimmermann, H. Werner *101:* 223; *112:* 197
Zimnik, Reiner *36:* 224
Zinkeisen, Anna *13:* 106
Zinn, David *97:* 97
Zoellick, Scott *33:* 231
Zonia, Dhimitri *20:* 234-235
Zudeck, Darryl *58:* 129; *63:* 98; *80:* 52
Zug, Mark *88:* 131
Zuma *99:* 36
Zvorykin, Boris *61:* 155
Zweifel, Francis *14:* 274; *28:* 187
Zwerger, Lisbeth *54:* 176, 178; *66:* 246, 247, 248; *130:* 230, 231, 232, 233
Zwinger, Herman H. *46:* 227
Zwolak, Paul *67:* 69, 71, 73, 74

Author Index

The following index gives the number of the volume in which an author's biographical sketch, Autobiography Feature, Brief Entry, or Obituary appears.

This index includes references to all entries in the following series, which are also published by The Gale Group.

YABC—*Yesterday's Authors of Books for Children: Facts and Pictures about Authors and Illustrators of Books for Young People from Early Times to 1960*

CLR—*Children's Literature Review: Excerpts from Reviews, Criticism, and Commentary on Books for Children*

SAAS—*Something about the Author Autobiography Series*

A

Aardema, Verna 1911-2000 ....*107*
  Obituary *119*
  Earlier sketches in SATA *4, 68*
  See also CLR *17*
  See also SAAS *8*
  See Vugteveen, Verna Aardema
Aaron, Chester 1923- *74*
  Earlier sketch in SATA *9*
  See also SAAS *12*
Aaseng, Nate
  See Aaseng, Nathan
Aaseng, Nathan 1953- *88*
  Brief entry *38*
  Earlier sketch in SATA *51*
  See also CLR *54*
  See also SAAS *12*
Abbas, Jailan 1952- *91*
Abbott, Alice
  See Borland, Kathryn Kilby
  and Speicher, Helen Ross S(mith)
Abbott, Jacob 1803-1879 ....*22*
Abbott, Manager Henry
  See Stratemeyer, Edward L.
Abbott, R(obert) Tucker 1919-1995 ....*61*
  Obituary *87*
Abbott, Sarah
  See Zolotow, Charlotte (Gertrude) S(hapiro)
Abdelsayed, Cindy 1962- *123*
Abdul, Raoul 1929- *12*
Abel, Raymond 1911- *12*
Abell, Kathleen 1938- *9*
Abelove, Joan *110*
Abels, Harriette S(heffer) 1926- *50*
Abercrombie, Barbara (Mattes) 1939- *16*
Abernethy, Robert G(ordon) 1927- *5*
Abisch, Roslyn Kroop 1927- *9*
Abisch, Roz
  See Abisch, Roslyn Kroop
Abodaher, David J. (Naiph) 1919- *17*
Abolafia, Yossi 1944- *60*
  Brief entry *46*
Abrahall, Clare Hoskyns
  See Hoskyns-Abrahall, Clare (Constance Drury)
Abrahams, Hilary (Ruth) 1938- *29*
Abrahams, Robert David 1905-1998 ....*4*
Abrams, Joy 1941- *16*
Abrams, Lawrence F. *58*
  Brief entry *47*
Abrashkin, Raymond 1911-1960 ....*50*
Achebe, (Albert) Chinua(lumogu) 1930- *40*
  Brief entry *38*
  Earlier sketch in SATA *38*
  See also CLR *20*
Ackerman, Diane 1948- *102*
Ackerman, Eugene (Francis) 1888-1974 ....*10*
Ackerman, Karen 1951- *126*

Ackerman, Susan Yoder 1945- *92*
Ackison, Wendy Wassink 1956- *103*
Ackley, Peggy Jo 1955- *58*
Acorn, John (Harrison) 1958- *79*
Acs, Laszlo (Bela) 1931- *42*
  Brief entry *32*
Acuff, Selma Boyd 1924- *45*
Ada, Alma Flor 1938- *84*
  Earlier sketch in SATA *43*
  See also CLR *62*
Adair, Gilbert 1944- *98*
Adair, Ian 1942- *53*
Adair, Margaret Weeks (?)-1971 ....*10*
Adam, Cornel
  See Lengyel, Cornel Adam
Adam, Mark
  See Alexander, Marc
Adam, Robert 1948- *93*
Adams, Adrienne 1906- *90*
  Earlier sketch in SATA *8*
  See also CLR *73*
Adams, Andy 1859-1935
  See YABC *1*
Adams, Barbara Johnston 1943- *60*
Adams, Bruin
  See Ellis, Edward S(ylvester)
Adams, Captain Bruin
  See Ellis, Edward S(ylvester)
Adams, Captain J. F. C.
  See Ellis, Edward S(ylvester)
Adams, Dale
  See Quinn, Elisabeth
Adams, Daniel
  See Nicole, Christopher (Robin)
Adams, Debra
  See Speregen, Devra Newberger
Adams, Douglas (Noel) 1952-2001 ....*116*
  Obituary *128*
Adams, Edith
  See Shine, Deborah
Adams, Florence 1932- *61*
Adams, Harriet S(tratemeyer) 1892(?)-1982 ....*1*
  Obituary *29*
Adams, Hazard 1926- *6*
Adams, John Anthony 1944- *67*
Adams, Laurie 1941- *33*
Adams, Lowell
  See Joseph, James (Herz)
Adams, Nicholas
  See Smith, Sherwood
Adams, Nicholas
  See Doyle, Debra
  and Macdonald, James D.
Adams, Nicholas
  See Pine, Nicholas
Adams, Pam 1919- *112*
Adams, Richard (George) 1920- *69*
  Earlier sketch in SATA *7*
  See also CLR *20*
Adams, Ruth Joyce *14*
Adams, Tricia
  See Kite, Pat
Adams, William Taylor 1822-1897 ....*28*

Adam Smith, Janet (Buchanan) 1905-1999 ....*63*
Adamson, Gareth 1925-1982(?) *46*
  Obituary *30*
Adamson, George Worsley 1913- *30*
Adamson, Graham
  See Groom, Arthur William
Adamson, Joy(-Friederike Victoria) 1910-1980 ....*11*
  Obituary *22*
Adamson, Wendy Writson 1942- *22*
Addona, Angelo F. 1925- *14*
Addy, Sharon Hart 1943- *108*
Addy, Ted
  See Winterbotham, R(ussell) R(obert)
Adelberg, Doris
  See Orgel, Doris
Adelson, Leone 1908- *11*
Adkins, Jan 1944- *69*
  Earlier sketch in SATA *8*
  See also CLR *77*
  See also SAAS *19*
Adler, C(arole) S(chwerdtfeger) 1932- *126*
  Earlier sketches in SATA *26, 63, 102*
  See also CLR *78*
  See also SAAS *15*
Adler, David A. 1947- *106*
  Earlier sketches in SATA *14, 70*
Adler, Irene
  See Penzler, Otto
  and Storr, Catherine (Cole)
Adler, Irving 1913- *29*
  Earlier sketch in SATA *1*
  See also CLR *27*
  See also SAAS *15*
Adler, Larry 1939- *36*
Adler, Peggy *22*
Adler, Ruth 1915-1968 ....*1*
Adlerman, Daniel 1963- *96*
Adlerman, Kimberly M. 1964- *96*
Adoff, Arnold 1935- *96*
  Earlier sketches in SATA *5, 57*
  See also CLR *7*
  See also SAAS *15*
Adorjan, Carol (Madden) 1934- *71*
  Earlier sketch in SATA *10*
Adrian, Frances
  See Polland, Madeleine A(ngela Cahill)
Adrian, Mary
  See Jorgensen, Mary Venn
Adshead, Gladys L(ucy) 1896-1985 ....*3*
Aesop 620(?)B.C.-560(?)B.C. *64*
  See also CLR *14*
Aesop, Abraham
  See Newbery, John
Affabee, Eric
  See Stine, R(obert) L(awrence)
Agapida, Fray Antonio
  See Irving, Washington
Agard, John *138*
Agard, Nadema 1948- *18*
Agarwal, Deepa 1947- *141*
Agee, Jon 1960- *116*

Agell, Charlotte 1959- 99
Agent Orange
    See Moseley, James W(illett)
Aghill, Gordon
    See Garrett, (Gordon) Randall (Phillip)
    and Silverberg, Robert
Agle, Nan Hayden 1905- *3*
    See also SAAS *10*
Agnew, Edith J(osephine) 1897-1988 ......*11*
Ahern, Margaret McCrohan 1921- *10*
Ahl, Anna Maria 1926- *32*
Ahlberg, Allan 1938- *120*
    Brief entry *35*
    Earlier sketch in SATA *68*
    See also CLR *18*
Ahlberg, Janet 1944-1994 ....*120*
    Brief entry *32*
    Obituary *83*
    Earlier sketch in SATA *68*
    See also CLR *18*
Aichinger, Helga 1937- *4*
Aiken, Clarissa (M.) Lorenz
    1899-1992 ....*12*
    Obituary *109*
Aiken, Conrad (Potter) 1889-1973 ....*30*
    Earlier sketch in SATA *3*
Aiken, Joan (Delano) 1924- *73*
    Autobiography Feature *109*
    Earlier sketches in SATA *2, 30*
    See also CLR *19*
    See also SAAS *1*
Ainsley, Alix
    See Steiner, Barbara A(nnette)
Ainsworth, Catherine Harris 1910- *56*
Ainsworth, Norma *9*
Ainsworth, Ruth (Gallard) 1908- *73*
    Earlier sketch in SATA *7*
Ainsworth, William Harrison
    1805-1882 ....*24*
Aistrop, Jack 1916- *14*
Aitken, Amy 1952- *54*
    Brief entry *40*
Aitken, Dorothy 1916- *10*
Aitmatov, Chingiz (Torekulovich)
    1928- *56*
    See Aytmatov, Chingiz
Akaba, Suekichi 1910- *46*
Akers, Floyd
    See Baum, L(yman) Frank
Aks, Patricia 1926-1994 ....*68*
Alagoa, Ebiegberi Joe 1933- *108*
Alain
    See Brustlein, Daniel
Alan, Robert
    See Silverstein, Robert Alan
Alarcon, Francisco X(avier) 1954- *104*
Albert, Burton 1936- *22*
Albert, Richard E. 1909-1999 ....*82*
Albert, Susan Wittig 1940- *107*
Alberts, Frances Jacobs 1907-1989 ....*14*
Albertson, Susan
    See Wojciechowski, Susan
Albion, Lee Smith *29*
Alborough, Jez 1959- *86*
Albrecht, Lillie (Vanderveer H.)
    1894-1985 ....*12*
Albyn, Carole Lisa 1955- *83*
Alcock, Gudrun 1908- *56*
    Brief entry *33*
Alcock, Vivien 1924- *76*
    Brief entry *38*
    Earlier sketch in SATA *45*
    See also CLR *26*
Alcorn, John 1935- *31*
    Brief entry *30*
Alcorn, Stephen 1958- *110*
Alcott, Louisa May 1832-1888 ....*100*
    See also YABC *1*
    See also CLR *38*
Alda, Arlene 1933- *106*
    Brief entry *36*
    Earlier sketch in SATA *44*

Alden, Isabella (Macdonald)
    1841-1930 ....*115*
    See also YABC *2*
Alden, Sue
    See Francis, Dorothy Brenner
Alderman, Clifford Lindsey
    1902-1988 ....*3*
Alderson, Sue Ann 1940- *59*
    Brief entry *48*
Alding, Peter
    See Jeffries, Roderic (Graeme)
Aldis, Dorothy (Keeley) 1896-1966 ....*2*
Aldiss, Brian W(ilson) 1925- *34*
Aldon, Adair
    See Meigs, Cornelia Lynde
Aldous, Allan (Charles) 1911- *27*
Aldrich, Ann
    See Meaker, Marijane (Agnes)
Aldrich, Bess Streeter 1881-1954
    See CLR *70*
Aldrich, Thomas (Bailey)
    1836-1907 ....*114*
    Earlier sketch in SATA *17*
Aldridge, (Harold Edward) James
    1918- *87*
Aldridge, Josephine Haskell *14*
Alegria, Ricardo E(nrique) 1921- *6*
Aleksin, Anatolii Georgievich 1924- *36*
Alenov, Lydia 1948- *61*
Alex, Ben (a pseudonym) 1946- *45*
Alex, Marlee (a pseudonym) 1948- *45*
Alexander, Anna B(arbara Cooke) 1913- ...*1*
Alexander, Anne
    See Alexander, Anna B(arbara Cooke)
Alexander, Ellen 1938- *91*
Alexander, Frances (Laura) 1888-1979 ......*4*
Alexander, Jocelyn Anne Arundel
    1930- *22*
Alexander, Linda 1935- *2*
Alexander, Lloyd (Chudley) 1924- *135*
    Earlier sketches in SATA *3, 49, 81, 129*
    See also CLR *48*
    See also SAAS *19*
Alexander, Marc 1929- *117*
Alexander, Martha 1920- *136*
    Earlier sketches in SATA *11, 70*
Alexander, Rae Pace
    See Alexander, Raymond Pace
Alexander, Raymond Pace
    1898-1974 ....*22*
Alexander, Rod
    See Pellowski, Michael (Joseph)
Alexander, Sally Hobart 1943- *84*
Alexander, Sue 1933- *136*
    Earlier sketches in SATA *12, 89*
    See also SAAS *15*
Alexeieff, Alexandre A. 1901-1979 ....*14*
Alger, Horatio, Jr.
    See Stratemeyer, Edward L.
Alger, Horatio, Jr. 1832-1899 ....*16*
    See also CLR *87*
Alger, Leclaire (Gowans) 1898-1969 ......*15*
Aliki
    See CLR *71*
    See Brandenberg, Aliki (Liacouras)
Alkema, Chester Jay 1932- *12*
Al-Khalili, Jim 1962- *124*
Alkiviades, Alkis 1953- *105*
Allamand, Pascale 1942- *12*
Allan, Mabel Esther 1915-1998 ....*75*
    Earlier sketches in SATA *5, 32*
    See also CLR *43*
    See also SAAS *11*
Allan, Nicholas 1956- *123*
    Earlier sketch in SATA *79*
Allan-Meyer, Kathleen 1918- *51*
    Brief entry *46*
Allard, Harry
    See Allard, Harry G(rover), Jr.
Allard, Harry G(rover), Jr. 1928- *102*
    Earlier sketch in SATA *42*
    See also CLR *85*

Allee, Marjorie Hill 1890-1945 ....*17*
Allen, Adam
    See Epstein, Beryl (M. Williams)
    and Epstein, Samuel
Allen, Alex B.
    See Heide, Florence Parry
Allen, Allyn
    See Eberle, Irmengarde
Allen, Bob 1961- *76*
Allen, Gertrude E(lizabeth) 1888-1984 ......*9*
Allen, Grace
    See Hogarth, Grace (Weston Allen)
Allen, Jeffrey (Yale) 1948- *42*
Allen, John
    See Perry, Ritchie (John Allen)
Allen, Jonathan B(urgess) 1957- *131*
    See Allen, Jonathan Dean
Allen, Jonathan Dean
    See Allen, Jonathan B(urgess)
Allen, Judy (Christina) 1941- *124*
    Earlier sketch in SATA *80*
Allen, Kenneth S. 1913-1981 ....*56*
Allen, Leroy 1912- *11*
Allen, Linda 1925- *33*
Allen, Marjorie 1931- *22*
Allen, Maury 1932- *26*
Allen, Merritt Parmelee 1892-1954 ....*22*
Allen, Nancy Kelly 1949- *127*
Allen, Nina (Stroemgren) 1935- *22*
Allen, Pamela (Kay) 1934- *123*
    Earlier sketches in SATA *50, 81*
    See also CLR *44*
Allen, Rodney F. 1938-1999 ....*27*
Allen, Roger MacBride 1957- *105*
Allen, Ruth
    See Peterson, Esther (Allen)
Allen, Samuel W(ashington) 1917- *9*
Allen, T. D.
    See Allen, Terril Diener
Allen, Terril Diener 1908- *35*
Allen, Terry D.
    See Allen, Terril Diener
Allen, Thomas B(enton) 1929- *140*
    Earlier sketch in SATA *45*
Allen, Tom
    See Allen, Thomas B(enton)
Allerton, Mary
    See Govan, (Mary) Christine Noble
Alleyn, Ellen
    See Rossetti, Christina (Georgina)
Allington, Richard L(loyd) 1947- *39*
    Brief entry *35*
Allison, Amy 1956- *138*
Allison, Bob *14*
Allison, Diane Worfolk *78*
Allison, Linda 1948- *43*
Allman, Barbara 1950- *137*
Allmendinger, David F(rederick), Jr.
    1938- *35*
Allred, Gordon T(hatcher) 1930- *10*
Allsop, Kenneth 1920-1973 ....*17*
Almedingen, E. M. *3*
    See Almedingen, Martha Edith von
Almon, Russell
    See Clevenger, William R(ussell)
    and Downing, David A(lmon)
Almond, David 1951- *114*
    See also CLR *85*
Almquist, Don 1929- *11*
Alphin, Elaine Marie 1955- *139*
    Earlier sketches in SATA *80, 130*
Alsop, Mary O'Hara 1885-1980 ....*34*
    Obituary *24*
    Earlier sketch in SATA *2*
Alter, Anna 1974- *135*
Alter, Judith (MacBain) 1938- *101*
    Earlier sketch in SATA *52*
Alter, Judy
    See Alter, Judith (MacBain)
Alter, Robert Edmond 1925-1965 ....*9*
Althea
    See Braithwaite, Althea

Altman, Linda Jacobs 1943- 21
Altman, Suzanne
  See Orgel, Doris
  and Schecter, Ellen
Altschuler, Franz 1923- 45
Altsheler, Joseph A(lexander) 1862-1919
  See YABC 1
Alvarez, John
  See del Rey, Lester
Alvarez, Joseph A. 1930- 18
Alvarez, Julia 1950- 129
Alyer, Philip A.
  See Stratemeyer, Edward L.
Amann, Janet 1951- 79
Amato, Carol A. 1942- 92
Amato, Mary 1961- 140
Ambrose, Stephen E(dward)
  1936-2002 138
  Earlier sketch in SATA 40
Ambrus, Gyozo Laszlo 1935- 41
  See Ambrus, Victor G.
Ambrus, Victor G. 1
  See also SAAS 4
  See Ambrus, Gyozo Laszlo
Amerman, Lockhart 1911-1969 3
Ames, Evelyn 1908-1990 13
  Obituary 64
Ames, Gerald 1906-1993 11
  Obituary 74
Ames, Lee J(udah) 1921- 3
Ames, Mildred 1919-1994 85
  Earlier sketches in SATA 22, 81
Ammon, Richard 1942- 124
Amon, Aline 1928- 9
Amoss, Berthe 1925- 112
  Earlier sketch in SATA 5
Anastasio, Dina 1941- 94
  Brief entry 30
  Earlier sketch in SATA 37
Anckarsvard, Karin Inez Maria
  1915-1969 6
Ancona, George 1929- 85
  Earlier sketch in SATA 12
  See also SAAS 18
Anders, Isabel 1946- 101
Andersdatter, Karla M(argaret) 1938- 34
Andersen, Hans Christian
  1805-1875 100
  See also YABC 1
  See also CLR 6
Andersen, Ted
  See Boyd, Waldo T.
Andersen, Yvonne 1932- 27
Anderson, Bernice G(oudy)
  1894-1997 33
Anderson, Bob 1944- 139
  Earlier sketch in SATA 136
Anderson, Brad(ley Jay) 1924- 33
  Brief entry 31
Anderson, C. C.
  See Anderson, Catherine Corley
Anderson, C(larence) W(illiam)
  1891-1971 11
Anderson, Catherine C.
  See Anderson, Catherine Corley
Anderson, Catherine Corley 1909- 72
Anderson, Clifford
  See Gardner, Richard (M.)
Anderson, Daryl Shon 1963- 93
Anderson, Dave
  See Anderson, David Poole
Anderson, David Poole 1929- 60
  See Anderson, Dave
Anderson, Eloise Adell 1927- 9
Anderson, George
  See Groom, Arthur William
Anderson, Grace Fox 1932- 43
Anderson, J(ohn) R(ichard) L(ane)
  1911-1981 15
  Obituary 27
Anderson, Joy 1928- 1

Anderson, Kevin J(ames) 1962- 117
  Earlier sketch in SATA 74
Anderson, Kirsty 1978- 108
Anderson, Laurie Halse 1961- 132
  Earlier sketch in SATA 95
Anderson, LaVere Francis Shoenfelt
  1907-1998 27
Anderson, Leone Castell 1923- 53
  Brief entry 49
Anderson, Lisa G. 1963- 108
Anderson, Lonzo 2
  See Anderson, John L(onzo)
Anderson, Lucia (Lewis) 1922- 10
Anderson, M. T(obin) 1968- 97
Anderson, Madelyn Klein 28
Anderson, Margaret J(ean) 1931- 27
  See also SAAS 8
Anderson, Mary 1939- 82
  Earlier sketch in SATA 7
  See also SAAS 23
Anderson, Mona 1910- 40
Anderson, Mrs. Melvin
  See Anderson, Catherine Corley
Anderson, Norman Dean 1928- 22
Anderson, Peggy Perry 1953- 84
Anderson, Poul (William) 1926-2001 90
  Autobiography Feature 106
  Brief entry 39
  See also CLR 58
Anderson, Rachel 1943- 86
  Earlier sketch in SATA 34
  See also SAAS 18
Anderson, Richard
  See Anderson, J(ohn) R(ichard) L(ane)
Anderson, (Tom) Scoular 138
Anderson, Susan 1952- 90
Anderson, W. B.
  See Schultz, James Willard
Anderson, Wayne 1946- 56
Andre, Evelyn M(arie) 1924- 27
Andreassen, Karl
  See Boyd, Waldo T.
Andrew, Ian (Peter) 1962- 116
Andrew, Prudence (Hastings) 1924- 87
Andrews, Benny 1930- 31
Andrews, Eleanor Lattimore
  See Lattimore, Eleanor Frances
Andrews, Elton V.
  See Pohl, Frederik
Andrews, F(rank) Emerson
  1902-1978 22
Andrews, J(ames) S(ydney) 1934- 4
Andrews, Jan 1942- 98
  Brief entry 49
  Earlier sketch in SATA 58
Andrews, Julie 1935- 7
  See also CLR 85
Andrews, Roy Chapman 1884-1960 19
Andrews, Tamra 1959- 129
Andrews, Wendy
  See Sharmat, Marjorie Weinman
Andrews, William G(eorge) 1930- 74
Andrezel, Pierre
  See Blixen, Karen (Christentze Dinesen)
Andriani, Renee
  See Williams-Andriani, Renee
Andrist, Ralph K. 1914- 45
Andryszewski, Tricia 1956- 88
Angel, Marie 1923- 47
Angeles, Peter A. 1931- 40
Angeletti, Roberta 1964- 124
Angeli, Marguerite (Lofft) de
  See de Angeli, Marguerite (Lofft)
Angell, Madeline 1919- 18
Angelo, Valenti 1897- 14
Angelou, Maya 1928- 136
  Earlier sketch in SATA 49
  See also CLR 53
Angier, Bradford -1997 12
Anglund, Joan Walsh 1926- 2
  See also CLR 1

Ango, Fan D.
  See Longyear, Barry B(rookes)
Angrist, Stanley W(olff) 1933- 4
Anholt, Catherine 1958- 131
  Earlier sketch in SATA 74
Anholt, Laurence 1959- 141
  Earlier sketch in SATA 74
Anita
  See Daniel, Anita
Anmar, Frank
  See Nolan, William F(rancis)
Annett, Cora
  See Scott, Cora Annett (Pipitone)
Annie-Jo
  See Blanchard, Patricia
Annixter, Jane
  See Sturtzel, Jane Levington
Annixter, Paul
  See Sturtzel, Howard A(llison)
Anno, Mitsumasa 1926- 77
  Earlier sketches in SATA 5, 38
  See also CLR 14
Anrooy, Francine Van
  See Van Anrooy, Francine
Ansary, Mir Tamim 1948- 140
Anstey, Caroline 1958- 81
Antell, Will D. 1935- 31
Anthony, Barbara 1932- 29
Anthony, C. L.
  See Smith, Dorothy Gladys
Anthony, Edward 1895-1971 21
Anthony, John
  See Beckett, Ronald Brymer
  and Ciardi, John (Anthony)
  and Sabini, John Anthony
Anthony, Joseph 1964- 103
Anthony, Patricia 1947- 109
Anthony, Piers 1934- 84
  Autobiography Feature 129
  See also SAAS 22
Anthony, Susan C(arol) 1953- 87
Anticaglia, Elizabeth 1939- 12
Antle, Nancy 1955- 102
Anton, Michael J(ames) 1940- 12
Antonacci, Robert J(oseph) 1916- 45
  Brief entry 37
Anvil, Christopher
  See Crosby, Harry C., Jr.
Aoki, Hisako 1942- 45
Apfel, Necia H(alpern) 1930- 51
  Brief entry 41
Aphrodite, J.
  See Livingston, Carole
Apikuni
  See Schultz, James Willard
Apostolou, Christine Hale 1955- 128
  Earlier sketch in SATA 82
Appel, Allen (R.) 1945- 115
Appel, Benjamin 1907-1977 39
  Obituary 21
Appel, Martin E(liot) 1948- 45
Appel, Marty
  See Appel, Martin E(liot)
Appelbaum, Diana Muir Karter
  1953- 132
Appelt, Kathi 1954- 129
  Earlier sketch in SATA 83
Apperley, Dawn 1969- 135
Appiah, Peggy 1921- 84
  Earlier sketch in SATA 15
  See also SAAS 19
Apple, Margot 64
  Brief entry 42
Applebaum, Stan 1922- 45
Applegate, K. A.
  See Applegate, Katherine (Alice)
Applegate, Katherine (Alice) 1956- 109
  See Applegate, K. A.

Appleton, Victor 67
    Earlier sketch in SATA *1*
    See Doyle, Debra
    and Macdonald, James D.
    and Rotsler, (Charles) William
    and Stratemeyer, Edward L.
    and Vardeman, Robert E(dward)
Appleton, Victor II 67
    Earlier sketch in SATA *1*
Apsler, Alfred 1907-1982 ....*10*
Aragones, Sergio 1937- *48*
    Brief entry *39*
Araujo, Frank P. 1937- *86*
Arbo, Cris 1950- *103*
Arbuthnot, May Hill 1884-1969 ....*2*
Archambault, John *112*
    Earlier sketch in SATA *67*
Archbold, Rick 1950- *97*
Archer, Jules 1915- *85*
    Earlier sketch in SATA *4*
    See also SAAS *5*
Archer, Marion Fuller 1917- *11*
Archibald, Joe
    See Archibald, Joseph S(topford)
Archibald, Joseph S(topford) 1898-1986 ....*3*
    Obituary *47*
Ardai, Charles 1969- *85*
Arden, Barbi
    See Stoutenburg, Adrien (Pearl)
Arden, William
    See Lynds, Dennis
Ardizzone, Edward (Jeffrey Irving)
    1900-1979 ....*28*
    Obituary *21*
    Earlier sketch in SATA *1*
    See also CLR *3*
Ardley, Neil (Richard) 1937- *121*
    Earlier sketch in SATA *43*
Arehart-Treichel, Joan 1942- *22*
Arenella, Roy 1939- *14*
Argent, Kerry 1960- *138*
Arkin, Alan (Wolf) 1934- *59*
    Brief entry *32*
Arlen, Leslie
    See Nicole, Christopher (Robin)
Arley, Robert
    See Jackson, Mike
Armer, Alberta (Roller) 1904-1986 ....*9*
Armer, Laura Adams 1874-1963 ....*13*
Armistead, John 1941- *130*
Armitage, David 1943- *99*
    Brief entry *38*
Armitage, Frank
    See Carpenter, John (Howard)
Armitage, Ronda (Jacqueline) 1943- *99*
    Brief entry *38*
    Earlier sketch in SATA *47*
Armour, Richard (Willard)
    1906-1989 ....*14*
    Obituary *61*
Arms-Doucet, Sharon 1951- *125*
Armstrong, George D. 1927- *10*
Armstrong, Gerry (Breen) 1929- *10*
Armstrong, Jeannette (C.) 1948- *102*
Armstrong, Jennifer 1961- *111*
    Autobiography Feature *120*
    Earlier sketch in SATA *77*
    See also CLR *66*
    See also SAAS *24*
Armstrong, Louise *43*
    Brief entry *33*
Armstrong, Martin Donisthorpe
    1882-1974 ....*115*
Armstrong, Richard 1903-1986 ....*11*
Armstrong, William H(oward)
    1914-1999 ....*4*
    Obituary *111*
    See also CLR *1*
    See also SAAS *7*
Arndt, Ursula (Martha H.) *56*
    Brief entry *39*
Arneson, D(on) J(on) 1935- *37*

Arnett, Caroline
    See Cole, Lois Dwight
Arnett, Jack
    See Goulart, Ron(ald Joseph)
Arnette, Robert
    See Silverberg, Robert
Arno, Enrico 1913-1981 ....*43*
    Obituary *28*
Arnold, Caroline 1944- *131*
    Brief entry *34*
    Earlier sketches in SATA *36, 85*
    See also CLR *61*
    See also SAAS *23*
Arnold, Elliott 1912-1980 ....*5*
    Obituary *22*
Arnold, Emily 1939- *76*
    Earlier sketch in SATA *50*
    See McCully, Emily Arnold
Arnold, Katya 1947- *115*
    Earlier sketch in SATA *82*
Arnold, Marsha Diane 1948- *93*
Arnold, Nick 1961- *113*
Arnold, Oren 1900-1980 ....*4*
Arnold, Susan (Riser) 1951- *58*
Arnold, Tedd 1949- *116*
    Earlier sketch in SATA *69*
Arnoldy, Julie
    See Bischoff, Julia Bristol
Arnosky, James Edward 1946- *22*
    See also CLR *15*
    See Arnosky, Jim
Arnosky, Jim *118*
    Earlier sketch in SATA *70*
    See Arnosky, James Edward
Arnott, Kathleen 1914- *20*
Arnov, Boris, Jr. 1926- *12*
Arnow, Harriette (Louisa) Simpson
    1908-1986 ....*42*
    Obituary *47*
Arnsteen, Katy Keck 1934- *68*
Arnstein, Helene S(olomon) 1915- *12*
Arntson, Herbert E(dward)
    1911-1982 ....*12*
Aroner, Miriam *82*
Aronson, Marc *126*
Aronson, Virginia 1954- *122*
Arora, Shirley (Lease) 1930- *2*
Arriey, Richmond
    See Delany, Samuel R(ay), Jr.
Arrington, Stephen L(ee) 1948- *97*
Arrowood, (McKendrick Lee) Clinton
    1939- *19*
Artell, Mike 1948- *134*
    Earlier sketches in SATA *89, 134*
Arthur, Robert (Andrew) 1909-1969
    See Arthur, Robert, (Jr.)
Arthur, Robert, (Jr.) 1909-1969 ....*118*
    See Arthur, Robert (Andrew)
Arthur, Ruth M(abel) 1905-1979 ....*26*
    Earlier sketch in SATA *7*
Artis, Vicki Kimmel 1945- *12*
Artzybasheff, Boris (Miklailovich)
    1899-1965 ....*14*
Aruego, Ariane
    See Dewey, Ariane
Aruego, Jose (Espiritu) 1932- *125*
    Earlier sketches in SATA *6, 68*
    See also CLR *5*
Arundel, Honor (Morfydd) 1919-1973 ......*4*
    Obituary *24*
    See also CLR *35*
Arundel, Jocelyn
    See Alexander, Jocelyn Anne Arundel
Arvey, Michael 1948- *79*
Asare, Meshack (Yaw) 1945- *139*
    Earlier sketch in SATA *86*
Asaro, Catherine (Ann) 1955- *101*
Asay, Donna Day 1945- *127*
Asbjornsen, Peter Christen
    1812-1885 ....*15*
Asch, Frank 1946- *102*
    Earlier sketches in SATA *5, 66*

Ash, Jutta 1942- *38*
Ashabranner, Brent (Kenneth)
    1921- *130*
    Earlier sketches in SATA *1, 67*
    See also CLR *28*
    See also SAAS *14*
Ashbless, William
    See Powers, Tim(othy Thomas)
Ashby, Gwynneth 1922- *44*
Ashby, Yvonne 1955- *121*
Ashe, Arthur (Robert, Jr.)
    1943-1993 ....*65*
    Obituary *87*
Ashe, Geoffrey (Thomas) 1923- *17*
    Autobiography Feature *125*
Ashe, Mary Ann
    See Lewis, Mary (Christianna)
Asher, Sandra Fenichel 1942- *118*
    See Asher, Sandy
Asher, Sandy *71*
    Brief entry *34*
    Earlier sketch in SATA *36*
    See also SAAS *13*
    See Asher, Sandra Fenichel
Asheron, Sara
    See Moore, Lilian
Ashey, Bella
    See Breinburg, Petronella
Ashford, Daisy
    See Ashford, Margaret Mary
Ashford, Jeffrey
    See Jeffries, Roderic (Graeme)
Ashford, Margaret Mary 1881-1972 ....*10*
Ashley, Bernard 1935- *79*
    Brief entry *39*
    Earlier sketch in SATA *47*
    See also CLR *4*
Ashley, Elizabeth
    See Salmon, Annie Elizabeth
Ashley, Ray
    See Abrashkin, Raymond
Ashton, Lorayne
    See Gottfried, Theodore Mark
Ashton, Warren T.
    See Adams, William Taylor
Asimov, Isaac 1920-1992 ....*74*
    Earlier sketches in SATA *1, 26*
    See also CLR *79*
Asinof, Eliot 1919- *6*
Aska, Warabe *56*
    See Masuda, Takeshi
Asprin, Robert L(ynn) 1946- *92*
Asquith, Cynthia Mary Evelyn (Charteris)
    1887-1960 ....*107*
Astley, Juliet
    See Lofts, Norah (Robinson)
Aston, James
    See White, T(erence) H(anbury)
Ata, Te 1895-1995 ....*119*
Atene, Ann
    See Atene, (Rita) Anna
Atene, (Rita) Anna 1922- *12*
Atheling, William, Jr.
    See Blish, James (Benjamin)
Atkins, Jeannine 1953- *113*
Atkinson, Allen G. 1953(?)-1987 ....*60*
    Brief entry *46*
    Obituary *55*
Atkinson, M. E.
    See Frankau, Mary Evelyn Atkinson
Atkinson, Margaret Fleming *14*
Attema, Martha 1949- *94*
Atticus
    See Davies, Hunter
    and Fleming, Ian (Lancaster)
    and Pawle, Gerald Strachan
    and Wilson, (Thomas) Woodrow
Atwater, Florence (Hasseltine Carroll)
    1896-1979 ....*66*
    Earlier sketch in SATA *16*
    See also CLR *19*

Atwater, Montgomery Meigs
  1904-1976 ....*15*
Atwater, Richard (Tupper)
  1892-1948 ....*66*
  Brief entry *27*
  Earlier sketch in SATA *54*
  See also CLR *19*
Atwater-Rhodes, Amelia 1984- *124*
Atwell, Debby 1953- *87*
Atwood, Ann (Margaret) 1913-1992 ....*7*
Atwood, Margaret (Eleanor) 1939- *50*
Aubrey, Meg Kelleher 1963- *83*
Aubry, Claude B. 1914-1984 ....*29*
  Obituary *40*
Auch, Mary Jane *138*
Auclair, Joan 1960- *68*
Auel, Jean M(arie) 1936- *91*
Auer, Martin 1951- *77*
Augarde, Steve 1950- *25*
Augelli, John P(at) 1921- *46*
Augustine, Mildred
  See Benson, Mildred (Augustine Wirt)
Ault, Phil
  See Ault, Phillip H(alliday)
Ault, Phillip H(alliday) 1914- *23*
Ault, Rosalie Sain 1942- *38*
Ault, Roz
  See Ault, Rosalie Sain
Aung, (Maung) Htin 1909- *21*
Aunt Weedy
  See Alcott, Louisa May
Austen, Carrie
  See Bennett, Cherie
Austin, Carrie
  See Seuling, Barbara
Austin, Elizabeth S. 1907-1977 ....*5*
Austin, Harry
  See McInerny, Ralph (Matthew)
Austin, Margot 1909(?)-1990 ....*11*
  Obituary *66*
Austin, Oliver L(uther), Jr. 1903-1988 ......*7*
  Obituary *59*
Austin, Patricia 1950- *137*
Austin, R. G.
  See Gelman, Rita Golden
  and Lamb, Nancy
Austin, Virginia *80*
Auteur, Hillary
  See Gottfried, Theodore Mark
Auth, Tony
  See Auth, William Anthony, Jr.
Auth, William Anthony, Jr. 1942- *51*
Autry, Gloria Diener
  See Allen, Terril Diener
Auvil, Peggy A(ppleby) 1954- *122*
Averill, Esther (Holden) 1902-1992 ....*28*
  Obituary *72*
  Earlier sketch in SATA *1*
Avery, Al
  See Montgomery, Rutherford George
Avery, Gillian (Elise) 1926- *137*
  Earlier sketches in SATA *7, 75*
  See also SAAS *6*
Avery, Kay 1908- *5*
Avery, Lorraine
  See Older, Effin
  and Older, Jules
Avery, Lynn
  See Cole, Lois Dwight
Avi *108*
  Earlier sketch in SATA *71*
  See also CLR *68*
  See Wortis, Avi
Avishai, Susan 1949- *82*
Awdry, Christopher Vere 1940- *67*
Awdry, Wilbert Vere 1911-1997 ....*94*
  See also CLR *23*
Axelrod, Amy *131*
Axton, David
  See Koontz, Dean R(ay)
Ayars, James S(terling) 1898-1986 ....*4*

Aye, A. E.
  See Edwards, Hazel (Eileen)
Aye, A. K.
  See Edwards, Hazel (Eileen)
Ayer, Eleanor H. 1947-1998 ....*121*
  Earlier sketch in SATA *78*
Ayer, Jacqueline 1930- *13*
Ayer, Margaret (?)-1981 ....*15*
Aylesworth, Jim 1943- *139*
  Earlier sketches in SATA *38, 89*
Aylesworth, Thomas G(ibbons)
  1927-1995 ....*88*
  Earlier sketch in SATA *4*
  See also CLR *6*
  See also SAAS *17*
Aylward, Marcus
  See Alexander, Marc
Aymar, Brandt 1911- *22*
Ayme, Marcel (Andre) 1902-1967 ....*91*
  See also CLR *25*
Ayres, Becky
  See Hickox, Rebecca (Ayres)
Ayres, Pam 1947- *90*
Aytmatov, Chingiz
  See Aitmatov, Chingiz (Torekulovich)
Ayto, Russell 1960- *111*
Azaid
  See Zaidenberg, Arthur
Azar, Penny 1952- *121*
Azarian, Mary 1940- *112*

B

Baastad, Babbis Friis
  See Friis-Baastad, Babbis Ellinor
Bab
  See Gilbert, W(illiam) S(chwenck)
Babbis, Eleanor
  See Friis-Baastad, Babbis Ellinor
Babbitt, Lucy Cullyford 1960- *85*
Babbitt, Natalie (Zane Moore)
  1932- *106*
  Earlier sketches in SATA *6, 68*
  See also CLR *53*
  See also SAAS *5*
Babcock, Chris 1963- *83*
Babcock, Dennis Arthur 1948- *22*
Baber, Carolyn Stonnell 1936- *96*
Baca, Maria 1951- *104*
Bach, Alice (Hendricks) 1942- *93*
  Brief entry *27*
  Earlier sketch in SATA *30*
Bach, Mary 1960- *125*
Bach, Richard (David) 1936- *13*
Bache, Ellyn 1942- *124*
Bachman, Fred 1949- *12*
Bachman, Richard
  See King, Stephen (Edwin)
Bachrach, Deborah *80*
Bacmeister, Rhoda W(arner)
  1893-1991 ....*11*
Bacon, Betty
  See Bacon, Elizabeth
Bacon, Elizabeth 1914-2001 ....*3*
  Obituary *131*
Bacon, Joan Chase
  See Bowden, Joan Chase
Bacon, Josephine Dodge (Daskam)
  1876-1961 ....*48*
Bacon, Margaret Frances
  Obituary *50*
  See Bacon, Peggy
Bacon, Margaret Hope 1921- *6*
Bacon, Martha Sherman 1917-1981 ....*18*
  Obituary *27*
  See also CLR *3*
Bacon, Melvin (L.) 1950- *93*
Bacon, Peggy 1895-1987 ....*2*
  See Bacon, Margaret Frances

Bacon, R(onald) L(eonard) 1924- *84*
  Earlier sketch in SATA *26*
Baden, Robert 1936- *70*
Baden-Powell, Robert (Stephenson Smyth)
  1857-1941 ....*16*
Badt, Karin L(uisa) 1963- *91*
Baehr, Kingsley M. 1937- *89*
Baehr, Patricia (Goehner) 1952- *65*
Baer, Jill
  See Gilbert, (Agnes) Joan (Sewell)
Baer, Judy 1951- *71*
Baerg, Harry J(ohn) 1909-1996 ....*12*
Baeten, Lieve 1954- *83*
Bagert, Brod 1947- *80*
Baggette, Susan K. 1942- *126*
Bagnold, Enid 1889-1981 ....*25*
  Earlier sketch in SATA *1*
Bahlke, Valerie Worth 1933-1994 ....*81*
  See Worth, Valerie
Bahous, Sally 1939- *86*
Bahr, Mary M(adelyn) 1946- *95*
Bahr, Robert 1940- *38*
Bahti, Tom 1926-1972 ....*57*
  Brief entry *31*
Bailey, Alice Cooper 1890-1978 ....*12*
Bailey, Anne 1958- *71*
Bailey, Bernadine (Freeman)
  1901-1995 ....*14*
Bailey, Carolyn Sherwin 1875-1961 ....*14*
Bailey, Debbie 1954- *123*
Bailey, Donna (Veronica Anne)
  1938- *68*
Bailey, Jane H(orton) 1916- *12*
Bailey, John (Robert) 1940- *52*
Bailey, Linda 1948- *107*
Bailey, Maralyn Collins (Harrison)
  1941- *12*
Bailey, Matilda
  See Radford, Ruby L(orraine)
Bailey, Maurice Charles 1932- *12*
Bailey, Pearl (Mae) 1918-1990 ....*81*
Bailey, Ralph Edgar 1893-1982 ....*11*
Baillie, Allan (Stuart) 1943- *87*
  See also CLR *49*
  See also SAAS *21*
Baines, John (David) 1943- *71*
Bains, Larry
  See Sabin, Louis
Baird, Alison 1963- *138*
Baird, Bil *30*
  Obituary *52*
  See Baird, William Britton
Baird, Thomas (P.) 1923-1990 ....*45*
  Brief entry *39*
  Obituary *64*
Baird, William Britton 1904-1987 ....*30*
  See Baird, Bil
Baity, Elizabeth Chesley 1907-1989 ....*1*
Baiul, Oksana 1977- *108*
Bakeless, John (Edwin) 1894-1978 ....*9*
Bakeless, Katherine Little 1895-1992 ....*9*
Baker, Alan 1951- *93*
  Earlier sketch in SATA *22*
Baker, Augusta 1911-1998 ....*3*
Baker, Betty Lou 1928-1987 ....*73*
  Obituary *54*
  Earlier sketch in SATA *5*
Baker, Carin Greenberg 1959- *79*
Baker, Charlotte 1910- *2*
Baker, (Mary) Elizabeth (Gillette) 1923- ...*7*
Baker, Gayle Cunningham 1950- *39*
Baker, James W. 1924- *65*
  Earlier sketch in SATA *22*
Baker, James W. 1926- *122*
Baker, Janice E(dla) 1941- *22*
Baker, Jeannie 1950- *88*
  Earlier sketch in SATA *23*
  See also CLR *28*
Baker, Jeffrey J(ohn) W(heeler) 1931- *5*
Baker, Jim
  See Baker, James W.
Baker, Ken 1962- *133*

Baker, Laura Nelson 1911- 3
Baker, Margaret 1890-1965 4
Baker, Margaret J(oyce) 1918- *12*
  See also SAAS 8
Baker, Mary Gladys Steel
  1892-1974 ....*12*
Baker, (Robert) Michael (Graham)
  1938- 4
Baker, Nina (Brown) 1888-1957 ....*15*
Baker, Pamela J. 1947- 66
Baker, Rachel 1904-1978 2
  Obituary 26
Baker, Samm Sinclair 1909-1997 ....*12*
  Obituary 96
Baker, Susan (Catherine) 1942-1991 29
Balaam
  See Lamb, G(eoffrey) F(rederick)
Balan, Bruce 1959- *113*
Balcavage, Dynise 1965- *137*
Balch, Glenn 1902-1989 3
  Obituary 83
  See also SAAS 11
Balderose, Nancy Ward 1952- *93*
Baldry, Cherith 1947- 72
Balducci, Carolyn (Feleppa) 1946- 5
Baldwin, Alex
  See Butterworth, W(illiam) E(dmund III)
Baldwin, Anne Norris 1938- 5
Baldwin, Clara 11
Baldwin, Gordo
  See Baldwin, Gordon C.
Baldwin, Gordon C. 1908-1983 ....*12*
  See Baldwin, Gordo
  and Gordon, Lew
Baldwin, James 1841-1925 24
Baldwin, James (Arthur) 1924-1987 9
  Obituary 54
Baldwin, Louis 1919- *110*
Baldwin, Margaret
  See Weis, Margaret (Edith)
Baldwin, Stan(ley C.) 1929- 62
  Brief entry 28
Bales, Carol Ann 1940- 57
  Brief entry 29
Balet, Jan (Bernard) 1913- 11
Balgassi, Haemi 1971- *131*
Balian, Lorna 1929- 91
  Earlier sketch in SATA 9
Balit, Christina 1961- *102*
Ball, Duncan 1941- 73
Ball, Zachary
  See Janas, Frankie-Lee
  and Masters, Kelly R(ay)
Ballantine, Lesley Frost
  See Frost, Lesley
Ballantyne, R(obert) M(ichael)
  1825-1894 24
Ballard, J(ames) G(raham) 1930- *93*
Ballard, John 1945- *110*
Ballard, Lowell C(lyne) 1904-1986 ....*12*
  Obituary 49
Ballard, (Charles) Martin 1929- 1
Ballard, Mignon F(ranklin) 1934- *64*
  Brief entry 49
Ballard, Robert D(uane) 1942- 85
  See also CLR 60
Ballard, Robin 1965- *126*
Ballouhey, Pierre 1944- 90
Balogh, Penelope 1916-1975 1
  Obituary 34
Balow, Tom 1931- *12*
Baltazzi, Evan S(erge) 1921- 90
Baltimore, J.
  See Catherall, Arthur
Baltzer, Hans (Adolf) 1900- 40
Bambara, Toni Cade 1939-1995 ....*112*
Bamfylde, Walter
  See Bevan, Tom
Bamman, Henry A. 1918- *12*
Banat, D. R.
  See Bradbury, Ray (Douglas)
Bancroft, Griffing 1907-1999 6

Bancroft, Laura
  See Baum, L(yman) Frank
Bandel, Betty 1912- 47
Baner, Skulda Vanadis 1897-1964 ....*10*
Banfill, A. Scott 1956- 98
Bang, Betsy 1912- 48
  Brief entry 37
Bang, Garrett
  See Bang, Molly Garrett
Bang, Molly Garrett 1943- *111*
  Earlier sketches in SATA 24, 69
  See also CLR 8
Bang-Campbell, Monika *140*
Banjo, The
  See Paterson, A(ndrew) B(arton)
Banke, Cecile de
  See de Banke, Cecile
Banks, Kate 1960- *134*
Banks, Lynne Reid
  See CLR 86
  See Reid Banks, Lynne
Banks, Michael A. 1951- *101*
Banks, Sara (Jeanne Gordon Harrell) 26
  See Harrell, Sara (Jeanne) Gordon
Bannatyne-Cugnet, (Elizabeth) Jo(-Anne)
  1951- *101*
Banner, Angela
  See CLR 24
  See Maddison, Angela Mary
Bannerman, Helen (Brodie Cowan Watson)
  1862(?)-1946 ....*19*
  See also CLR 21
Banning, Evelyn I. 1903-1993 36
Bannon, Laura (?)-1963 6
Bantock, Nick 1950(?)- 95
Barasch, Lynne 1939- *126*
  Earlier sketch in SATA 74
Barbalet, Margaret 1949- 77
Barbary, James
  See Beeching, Jack
Barbash, Shepard 1957- 84
Barbe, Walter Burke 1926- 45
Barber, Antonia
  See Anthony, Barbara
Barber, Lynda
  See Graham-Barber, Lynda
Barber, Lynda Graham
  See Graham-Barber, Lynda
Barber, Richard (William) 1941- 35
Barbera, Joe
  See Barbera, Joseph Roland
Barbera, Joseph Roland 1911- 51
Barberis, Juan C(arlos) 1920- 61
Barbour, Karen 1956- *121*
  Earlier sketch in SATA 63
Barbour, Ralph Henry 1870-1944 16
Barclay, Bill
  See Moorcock, Michael (John)
Barclay, Isabel
  See Dobell, I(sabel) M(arian) B(arclay)
Barclay, William Ewert
  See Moorcock, Michael (John)
Bare, Arnold Edwin 1920- 16
Bare, Colleen Stanley 32
Bargar, Gary W. 1947-1985 63
Barish, Matthew 1907-2000 ....*12*
Barkan, Joanne *127*
  Earlier sketch in SATA 77
Barker, Albert W. 1900- 8
Barker, Carol (Minturn) 1938- 31
Barker, Cicely Mary 1895-1973 49
  Brief entry 39
  See also CLR 88
Barker, Melvern 1907-1989 11
Barker, S(quire) Omar 1894-1985 ....*10*
Barker, Will 1913-1983 8
Barkin, Carol 1944- 52
  Earlier sketch in SATA 42
Barklem, Jill 1951- 96
  See also CLR 31
Barkley, James Edward 1941- 6
Barks, Carl 1901-2000 37

Barley, Janet Crane 1934- 95
Barnaby, Ralph S(tanton) 1893-1986 9
Barnard, A. M.
  See Alcott, Louisa May
Barnard, Bryn 1956- *115*
Barne, Kitty
  See Barne, Marion Catherine
Barne, Marion Catherine 1883-1957 97
  See Barne, Kitty
Barner, Bob 1947- *136*
  Earlier sketch in SATA 29
Barnes, (Frank) Eric Wollencott
  1907-1962 22
Barnes, Joyce Annette 1958- 85
Barnes, Laura T. 1958- *119*
Barnes, Loutricia
  See Barnes-Svarney, Patricia L(ou)
Barnes, Michael 1934- 55
Barnes-Murphy, Frances 1951- 88
Barnes-Murphy, Rowan 1952- 88
Barnes-Svarney, Patricia L(ou) 1953- *67*
Barnet, Nancy 1954- 84
Barnett, Ivan 1947- 70
Barnett, Lincoln (Kinnear)
  1909-1979 36
Barnett, Moneta 1922-1976 33
Barnett, Naomi 1927- 40
Barney, Maginel Wright
  1881(?)-1966 39
  Brief entry 32
Barnhart, Clarence L(ewis)
  1900-1993 48
  Obituary 78
Barnouw, Victor 1915-1989 43
  Brief entry 28
Barnstone, Willis 1927- 20
Barnum, Jay Hyde 1888(?)-1962 20
Barnum, P. T., Jr.
  See Stratemeyer, Edward L.
Barnum, Richard 67
  Earlier sketch in SATA 1
Barnum, Theodore
  See Stratemeyer, Edward L.
Baron, Kathy 1954- 90
Baron, Virginia Olsen 1931- 46
  Brief entry 28
Barr, Donald 1921- 20
Barr, George 1907-1992 2
Barr, Jene 1922-1985 16
  Obituary 42
  See Cohen, Jene Barr
Barr, Nevada 1952(?)- *126*
  Earlier sketch in SATA 115
Barrer, Gertrude
  See Barrer-Russell, Gertrude
Barrer-Russell, Gertrude 1921- 27
Barrett, Angela (Jane) 1955- 75
Barrett, Ethel 87
  Brief entry 44
Barrett, Joyce Durham 1943- 138
Barrett, Judi
  See Barrett, Judith
Barrett, Judith 1941- 26
Barrett, Robert T(heodore) 1949- 92
Barrett, Ron 1937- 14
Barrett, Susan (Mary) 1938- 113
Barrett, Tracy 1955- *115*
  Earlier sketch in SATA 84
Barrie, J(ames) M(atthew)
  1860-1937 100
  See also YABC 1
  See also CLR 16
Barrington, Michael
  See Moorcock, Michael (John)
Barris, George 1925- 47
Barrol, Grady
  See Bograd, Larry
Barron, Rex 1951- 84
Barron, T(homas) A(rchibald)
  1952- *126*
  Earlier sketch in SATA 83
  See also CLR 86

Barron, Tom
  See Barron, T(homas) A(rchibald)
Barrow, Lloyd H. 1942- *73*
Barry, Dana (Marie Malloy) 1949- *139*
Barry, James P(otvin) 1918- *14*
Barry, Katharina Watjen 1936- *4*
Barry, Robert (Everett) 1931- *6*
Barry, Scott 1952- *32*
Barry, Sheila Anne *91*
Bartenbach, Jean 1918- *40*
Barth, Edna 1914-1980 ....*7*
  Obituary *24*
Barthelme, Donald 1931-1989 ....*7*
  Obituary *62*
Bartholomew, Barbara 1941- *86*
  Brief entry *42*
Bartholomew, Jean
  See Beatty, Patricia (Robbins)
Bartlett, Philip A. *1*
Bartlett, Robert Merrill 1899-1995 ....*12*
Bartoletti, Susan Campbell 1958- *135*
  Earlier sketches in SATA *88, 129*
Barton, Byron 1930- *126*
  Earlier sketches in SATA *9, 90*
Barton, Jill(ian) 1940- *75*
Barton, May Hollis *67*
  Earlier sketch in SATA *1*
Barton, Pat *59*
  See Arrowsmith, Pat
Barton, Pat 1928- *59*
Bartos-Hoeppner, Barbara 1923- *5*
Bartsch, Jochen 1906- *39*
Baruch, Dorothy W(alter) 1899-1962 ....*21*
Barunga, Albert 1912(?)-1977 ....*120*
Bas, Rutger
  See Rutgers van der Loeff-Basenau,
  An(na) Maria Margaretha
Base, Graeme (Rowland) 1958- *101*
  Earlier sketch in SATA *67*
  See also CLR *22*
Bash, Barbara 1948- *132*
Bashevis, Isaac
  See Singer, Isaac Bashevis
Baskin, Leonard 1922-2000 ....*120*
  Brief entry *27*
  Earlier sketch in SATA *30*
Baskin, Nora Raleigh 1961- *129*
Bason, Lillian 1913- *20*
Bassett, Jeni 1959- *64*
  Brief entry *43*
Bassett, John Keith
  See Keating, Lawrence A.
Bassett, Lisa 1958- *61*
Bassil, Andrea 1948- *96*
Bastyra, Judy *108*
Bat-Ami, Miriam 1950- *122*
  Earlier sketch in SATA *82*
Bate, Lucy 1939- *18*
Bate, Norman (Arthur) 1916- *5*
Bateman, Teresa 1957- *112*
Bates, Barbara S(nedeker) 1919- *12*
Bates, Betty *19*
  See Bates, Elizabeth
Bates, Katharine Lee 1859-1929 ....*113*
  See Lincoln, James
Batey, Tom 1946- *52*
  Brief entry *41*
Batherman, Muriel
  See Sheldon, Muriel
Batson, Larry 1930- *35*
Batt, Tanya Robyn 1970- *131*
Battaglia, Aurelius 1910- *50*
  Brief entry *33*
Batten, H(arry) Mortimer 1888-1958 ....*25*
Batten, Mary 1937- *102*
  Earlier sketch in SATA *5*
Batterberry, Ariane Ruskin 1935- *13*
Batterberry, Michael Carver 1932- *32*
Battle-Lavert, Gwendolyn 1951- *85*
  See Lavert, Gwendolyn Battle
Battles, (Roxy) Edith 1921- *7*
Baudouy, Michel-Aime 1909- *7*

Bauer, Caroline Feller 1935- *98*
  Brief entry *46*
  Earlier sketch in SATA *52*
  See also SAAS *24*
Bauer, Fred 1934- *36*
Bauer, Helen 1900-1988 ....*2*
Bauer, Joan 1951- *117*
Bauer, Marion Dane 1938- *113*
  Earlier sketches in SATA *20, 69*
  See also SAAS *9*
Bauer, Steven 1948- *125*
Bauerschmidt, Marjorie 1926- *15*
Baughman, Dorothy 1940- *61*
Baum, Allyn Z(elton) 1924-1997 ....*98*
  Earlier sketch in SATA *20*
Baum, L. Frank
  See Thompson, Ruth Plumly
Baum, L(yman) Frank 1856-1919 ....*100*
  Earlier sketch in SATA *18*
  See also CLR *15*
Baum, Louis 1948- *64*
  Brief entry *52*
Baum, Louis F.
  See Baum, L(yman) Frank
Baum, Willi 1931- *4*
Baumann, Amy (Brown) Beeching
  1922- *10*
Baumann, Hans 1914- *2*
  See also CLR *35*
Baumann, Kurt 1935- *21*
Baumgartner, Barbara 1939- *86*
Baurys, Flo(rence) 1938- *122*
Bawden, Nina (Mary Mabey) 1925- *72*
  Earlier sketch in SATA *4*
  See also CLR *51*
  See also SAAS *16*
  See Kark, Nina Mary
Bay, Jeanette Graham 1928- *88*
Bayer, Harold
  See Gregg, Andrew K.
Bayley, Nicola 1949- *129*
  Earlier sketches in SATA *41, 69*
Baylor, Byrd 1924- *136*
  Earlier sketches in SATA *16, 69*
  See also CLR *3*
Baynes, Pauline (Diana) 1922- *133*
  Earlier sketches in SATA *19, 59*
BB
  See Watkins-Pitchford, Denys James
Beach, Charles
  See Reid, (Thomas) Mayne
Beach, Charles Amory *1*
Beach, Edward L(atimer) 1918-2002 ....*12*
  Obituary *140*
Beach, Lisa 1957- *111*
Beach, Lynn
  See Lance, Kathryn
Beach, Stewart T(aft) 1899-1979 ....*23*
Beachcroft, Nina 1931- *18*
Beagle, Peter S(oyer) 1939- *130*
  Earlier sketch in SATA *60*
Beaglehole, Helen 1946- *117*
Beale, Fleur *107*
Bealer, Alex W(inkler III) 1921-1980 ......*8*
  Obituary *22*
Beales, Valerie 1915- *74*
Beals, Carleton 1893-1979 ....*12*
Beame, Rona 1934- *12*
Beamer, (George) Charles (Jr.)
  1942- *43*
Bean, Normal
  See Burroughs, Edgar Rice
Beaney, Jan
  See Udall, Jan Beaney
Beaney, Jane
  See Udall, Jan Beaney
Bear, Greg(ory Dale) 1951- *105*
  Earlier sketch in SATA *65*
Bearanger, Marie
  See Messier, Claire
Beard, Charles A(ustin) 1874-1948 ....*18*
Beard, Dan(iel Carter) 1850-1941 ....*22*

Beard, Darleen Bailey 1961- *96*
Bearden, Romare (Howard)
  1914(?)-1988 ....*22*
  Obituary *56*
Beardmore, Cedric
  See Beardmore, George
Beardmore, George 1908-1979 ....*20*
Bearman, Jane (Ruth) 1917- *29*
Beaton, Clare 1947- *125*
Beatty, Elizabeth
  See Holloway, Teresa (Bragunier)
Beatty, Hetty Burlingame 1907-1971 ....*5*
Beatty, Jerome, Jr. 1918- *5*
Beatty, John (Louis) 1922-1975 ....*6*
  Obituary *25*
Beatty, Patricia (Robbins) 1922-1991 .....*73*
  Obituary *68*
  Earlier sketches in SATA *1, 30*
  See also SAAS *4*
Bechard, Margaret 1953- *85*
Bechtel, Louise Seaman 1894-1985 ....*4*
  Obituary *43*
Beck, Barbara L. 1927- *12*
Beck, Ian (Archibald) 1947- *138*
Becker, Beril 1901-1999 ....*11*
Becker, Deborah Zimmett 1955- *138*
  Earlier sketch in SATA *134*
Becker, John (Leonard) 1901- *12*
Becker, Joyce 1936- *39*
Becker, May Lamberton 1873-1958 ....*33*
Becker, Neesa 1951- *123*
Beckett, Sheilah 1913- *33*
Beckman, Delores 1914- *51*
Beckman, Gunnel 1910- *6*
  See also CLR *25*
  See also SAAS *9*
Beckman, Kaj
  See Beckman, Karin
Beckman, Karin 1913- *45*
Beckman, Per (Frithiof) 1913- *45*
Bedard, Michael 1949- *93*
  See also CLR *35*
Beddows, Eric
  See Nutt, Ken
Bedford, A. N.
  See Watson, Jane Werner
Bedford, Annie North
  See Watson, Jane Werner
Bedoukian, Kerop 1907-1981 ....*53*
Bee, Jay
  See Brainerd, John W(hiting)
Beebe, B(urdetta) F(aye) *1*
  See Johnson, B(urdetta) F(aye)
Beebe, (Charles) William 1877-1962 ....*19*
Beeby, Betty 1923- *25*
Beech, Webb
  See Butterworth, W(illiam) E(dmund III)
Beechcroft, William
  See Hallstead, William F(inn III)
Beeching, Jack 1922- *14*
Beeler, Janet
  See Shaw, Janet
Beeler, Nelson F(rederick)
  1910-1978 ....*13*
Beere, Peter 1951- *97*
Beers, Dorothy Sands 1917- *9*
Beers, Lorna 1897-1989 ....*14*
Beers, V(ictor) Gilbert 1928- *130*
  Earlier sketch in SATA *9*
Beeton, Max
  See Redding, Robert Hull
Begay, Shonto 1954- *137*
Begaye, Lisa Shook
  See Beach, Lisa
Begin, Maryjane 1963- *82*
Begin-Callanan, Maryjane
  See Begin, Maryjane
Begley, Kathleen A(nne) 1948- *21*
Behan, Leslie
  See Gottfried, Theodore Mark
Behn, Harry 1898-1973 ....*2*
  Obituary *34*

Behnke, Frances L. 8
Behr, Joyce 1929- *15*
Behrens, June York 1925- *19*
Behrman, Carol H(elen) 1925- *14*
Beifuss, John, (Jr.) 1959- *92*
Beil, Karen Magnuson 1950- *124*
Beiler, Edna 1923- *61*
Beinicke, Steve 1956- *69*
Beirne, Barbara 1933- *71*
Beiser, Arthur 1931- *22*
Beiser, Germaine 1931- *11*
Beistle, Shirley
    See Climo, Shirley
Belair, Richard L. 1934- *45*
Belaney, Archibald Stansfeld
    1888-1938 ....*24*
    See Grey Owl
Belbin, David 1958- *106*
Belden, Wilanne Schneider 1925- *56*
Belfrage, Sally 1936-1994 ....*65*
    Obituary *79*
Belknap, B. H.
    See Ellis, Edward S(ylvester)
Belknap, Boynton
    See Ellis, Edward S(ylvester)
Belknap, Boynton M.D.
    See Ellis, Edward S(ylvester)
Bell, Anthea 1936- *88*
Bell, Clare (Louise) 1952- *99*
Bell, Corydon Whitten 1894-1980 ....*3*
Bell, David Owen 1949- *99*
Bell, Emerson
    See Stratemeyer, Edward L.
Bell, Emily Mary
    See Cason, Mabel Earp
Bell, Frank
    See Benson, Mildred (Augustine Wirt)
Bell, Gertrude (Wood) 1911-1987 ....*12*
Bell, Gina *7*
    See Balzano, Jeanne (Koppel)
Bell, Jadrien
    See Golden, Christie
Bell, Janet
    See Clymer, Eleanor
Bell, Janet Cheatham 1937- *127*
Bell, Krista (Anne Blakeney) 1950- *126*
Bell, Margaret E(lizabeth) 1898-1990 ....*2*
Bell, Mary Reeves 1946- *88*
Bell, Norman (Edward) 1899- *11*
Bell, Raymond Martin 1907-1999 ....*13*
Bell, Thelma Harrington 1896-1985 ....*3*
Bell, William 1945- *90*
Bellairs, John (Anthony) 1938-1991 ....*68*
    Obituary *66*
    Earlier sketch in SATA *2*
    See also CLR *37*
Beller, Susan Provost 1949- *128*
    Earlier sketch in SATA *84*
Bellingham, Brenda 1931- *99*
    Brief entry *51*
Bello, Rosario de
    See De Bello, Rosario
Belloc, (Joseph) Hilaire (Pierre Sebastien
    Rene Swanton) 1870-1953 ....*112*
    See also YABC *1*
Belloc, Joseph Peter Rene Hilaire
    See Belloc, (Joseph) Hilaire (Pierre
    Sebastien Rene Swanton)
Belloc, Joseph Pierre Hilaire
    See Belloc, (Joseph) Hilaire (Pierre
    Sebastien Rene Swanton)
Belloli, Andrea P. A. 1947- *86*
Bellville, Cheryl Walsh 1944- *54*
    Brief entry *49*
Bell-Zano, Gina *7*
    See Balzano, Jeanne (Koppel)
Belpre, Pura 1899-1982 ....*16*
    Obituary *30*
Belting, Natalia Maree 1915-1997 ....*6*
Belton, John Raynor 1931- *22*
Belton, Sandra (Yvonne) 1939- *134*
    Earlier sketch in SATA *85*

Beltran, Alberto 1923- *43*
Beltran-Hernandez, Irene 1945- *74*
Belvedere, Lee
    See Grayland, Valerie (Merle Spanner)
Bemelmans, Ludwig 1898-1962 ....*100*
    Earlier sketch in SATA *15*
    See also CLR *6*
Benander, Carl D. 1941- *74*
Benary, Margot
    See Benary-Isbert, Margot
Benary-Isbert, Margot 1889-1979 ....*2*
    Obituary *21*
    See also CLR *12*
Benasutti, Marion 1908-1992 ....*6*
Benchley, Nathaniel (Goddard)
    1915-1981 ....*25*
    Obituary *28*
    Earlier sketch in SATA *3*
Benchley, Peter (Bradford) 1940- *89*
    Earlier sketch in SATA *3*
Bender, Edna 1941- *92*
Bender, Esther 1942- *88*
Bender, Lucy Ellen 1942- *22*
Bender, Robert 1962- *79*
Bendick, Jeanne 1919- *135*
    Earlier sketches in SATA *2, 68*
    See also CLR *5*
    See also SAAS *4*
Bendick, Robert L(ouis) 1917- *11*
Benedict, Andrew
    See Arthur, Robert, (Jr.)
Benedict, Dorothy Potter 1889-1979 ....*11*
    Obituary *23*
Benedict, Lois Trimble 1902-1967 ....*12*
Benedict, Rex 1920-1995 ....*8*
Benedict, Stewart H(urd) 1924- *26*
Beneduce, Ann K(eay) *128*
Benet, Laura 1884-1979 ....*3*
    Obituary *23*
Benet, Stephen Vincent 1898-1943
    See YABC *1*
Benet, Sula 1906-1982 ....*21*
    Obituary *33*
Ben-Ezer, Ehud 1936- *122*
Benezra, Barbara (Beardsley) 1921- *10*
Benham, Leslie 1922- *48*
Benham, Lois (Dakin) 1924- *48*
Benham, Mary Lile 1914- *55*
Benjamin, Nora
    See Kubie, Nora Gottheil Benjamin
Benjamin, Saragail Katzman 1953- *86*
Benner, Cheryl 1962- *80*
Benner, Judith Ann 1942- *94*
Bennett, Alice
    See Ziner, Florence
Bennett, Cherie 1960- *97*
Bennett, Dorothea
    See Young, Dorothea Bennett
Bennett, James (W.) 1942- *93*
Bennett, Jay 1912- *87*
    Brief entry *27*
    Earlier sketch in SATA *41*
    See also SAAS *4*
Bennett, Jill (Crawford) 1934- *41*
Bennett, John 1865-1956
    See YABC *1*
Bennett, Penelope (Agnes) 1938- *94*
Bennett, Rachel
    See Hill, Margaret (Ohler)
Bennett, Rainey 1907-1998 ....*15*
    Obituary *111*
Bennett, Richard 1899- *21*
Bennett, Russell H(oradley) 1896- *25*
Bennett, William (John) 1943- *102*
Benning, Elizabeth
    See Rice, Bebe Faas
Benson, Elizabeth P(olk) 1924- *65*
Benson, Kathleen 1947- *111*
    Earlier sketch in SATA *62*
Benson, Linda M(aria) 1959- *84*

Benson, Mildred (Augustine Wirt)
    1905-2002 ....*100*
    Obituary *135*
    Earlier sketch in SATA *65*
    See Keene, Carolyn
Benson, Mildred Wirt
    See Benson, Mildred (Augustine Wirt)
Benson, Millie
    See Benson, Mildred (Augustine Wirt)
Benson, Sally 1900-1972 ....*35*
    Obituary *27*
    Earlier sketch in SATA *1*
Bentley, Judith (McBride) 1945- *89*
    Earlier sketch in SATA *40*
Bentley, Nancy (L.) 1946- *78*
Bentley, Phyllis Eleanor 1894-1977 ....*6*
    Obituary *25*
Bentley, Roy 1947- *46*
Bentley, William (George) 1916- *84*
ben Uzair, Salem
    See Horne, Richard Henry
Bercaw, Edna Coe 1961- *124*
Berck, Judith 1960- *75*
Berelson, Howard 1940- *5*
Berends, Polly Berrien 1939- *50*
    Brief entry *38*
Berenstain, Jan(ice) 1923- *135*
    Earlier sketches in SATA *12, 64, 129*
    See also CLR *19*
    See also SAAS *20*
Berenstain, Michael 1951- *45*
Berenstain, Stan(ley) 1923- *135*
    Earlier sketches in SATA *12, 64, 129*
    See also CLR *19*
    See also SAAS *20*
Berenzy, Alix 1957- *65*
Beresford, Elisabeth 1926- *141*
    Earlier sketches in SATA *25, 86*
    See also SAAS *20*
Berg, Dave
    See Berg, David
Berg, David 1920-2002 ....*27*
    Obituary *137*
Berg, Elizabeth 1948- *104*
Berg, Jean Horton 1913- *6*
Berg, Joan
    See Victor, Joan Berg
Berg, Ron 1952- *48*
Bergaust, Erik 1925-1978 ....*20*
Bergel, Colin J. 1963- *137*
Bergen, Joyce 1949- *95*
Berger, Barbara (Helen) 1945- *77*
Berger, Gilda 1935- *88*
    Brief entry *42*
Berger, Josef 1903-1971 ....*36*
Berger, Melvin H. 1927- *88*
    Autobiography Feature *124*
    Earlier sketch in SATA *5*
    See also CLR *32*
    See also SAAS *2*
Berger, Phil 1942-2001 ....*62*
Berger, Samantha (Allison) 1969- *140*
Berger, Terry 1933- *8*
Bergey, Alyce (Mae) 1934- *45*
Bergin, Mark 1961- *114*
Bergman, Donna 1934- *73*
Bergman, Tamar 1939- *95*
Bergum, Constance R. 1952- *121*
Berkey, Barry Robert 1935- *24*
Berkowitz, Freda Pastor 1908-1994 ....*12*
Berkus, Clara Widess 1909- *78*
Berlan, Kathryn Hook 1946- *78*
Berlfein, Judy Reiss 1958- *79*
Berliner, Don 1930- *33*
Berliner, Franz 1930- *13*
Berlitz, Charles (L. Frambach)
    1914- *32*
Berman, Linda 1948- *38*
Berman, Paul (Lawrence) 1949- *66*
Berna, Paul 1910-1994 ....*15*
    Obituary *78*
    See also CLR *19*

Bernadette
    See Watts, (Anna) Bernadette
Bernard, Bruce 1928-2000 78
    Obituary 124
Bernard, George I. 1949- 39
Bernard, Jacqueline (de Sieyes)
    1921-1983 8
    Obituary 45
Bernard, Patricia 1942- 106
Bernardin, James (B.) 1966- 112
Bernards, Neal 1963- 71
Bernays, Anne
    See Kaplan, Anne Bernays
Bernhard, Durga T. 1961- 80
Bernhard, Emery 1950- 80
Bernstein, Daryl (Evan) 1976- 81
Bernstein, Joanne E(ckstein) 1943- 15
Bernstein, Margery 1933- 114
Bernstein, Theodore M(enline)
    1904-1979 12
    Obituary 27
Berrien, Edith Heal
    See Heal, Edith
Berrill, Jacquelyn (Batsel) 1905- 12
Berrington, John
    See Brownjohn, Alan
Berry, B. J.
    See Berry, Barbara J.
Berry, Barbara J. 1937- 7
Berry, Erick
    See Best, (Evangel) Allena Champlin
Berry, James 1925- 110
    Earlier sketch in SATA 67
    See also CLR 22
Berry, Joy
    See Berry, Joy Wilt
Berry, Joy Wilt 1944- 58
    Brief entry 46
Berry, William D(avid) 1926- 14
Berson, Harold 1926- 4
Bertin, Charles-Francois
    See Berlitz, Charles (L. Frambach)
Bertolet, Paul
    See McLaughlin, Frank
Berton, Pierre (Francis Demarigny)
    1920- 99
Bertrand, Cecile 1953- 76
Bertrand, Diane Gonzales 1956- 106
Bertrand, Lynne 1963- 81
Beskow, Elsa (Maartman) 1874-1953 20
    See also CLR 17
Bess, Clayton
    See CLR 39
    See Locke, Robert
Best, (Evangel) Allena Champlin
    1892-1974 2
    Obituary 25
Best, Cari 1951- 107
Best, (Oswald) Herbert 1894-1980 2
Bestall, A(lfred) E(dmeades)
    1892-1986 97
    Obituary 48
Betancourt, Jeanne 1941- 96
    Brief entry 43
    Earlier sketch in SATA 55
Beth, Mary
    See Miller, Mary Beth
Bethancourt, T. Ernesto 11
    See also CLR 3
    See Paisley, Tom
Bethel, Dell 1929- 52
Bethell, Jean (Frankenberry) 1922- 8
Bethers, Ray 1902-1973 6
Bethke, Bruce Raymond 1955- 114
Bethlen, T. D.
    See Silverberg, Robert
Bethune, J. G.
    See Ellis, Edward S(ylvester)
Bethune, J. H.
    See Ellis, Edward S(ylvester)
Betteridge, Anne
    See Potter, Margaret (Newman)

Bettina
    See Ehrlich, Bettina Bauer
Bettmann, Otto Ludwig 1903-1998 46
Betts, James
    See Haynes, Betsy
Betz, Eva Kelly 1897-1968 10
Bevan, Tom 1868-1930(?)
    See YABC 2
Bewick, Thomas 1753-1828 16
Beyer, Audrey White 1916- 9
Beyer, Paul J. III 1950- 74
Beynon, John
    See Harris, John (Wyndham Parkes Lucas)
    Beynon
Bezencon, Jacqueline (Buxcel) 1924- 48
Bial, Morrison David 1917- 62
Bial, Raymond 1948- 116
    Earlier sketch in SATA 76
Biala
    See Brustlein, Janice Tworkov
Biale, Rachel 1952- 99
Bialk, Elisa
    See Krautter, Elisa (Bialk)
Bianchi, John 1947- 91
Bianchi, Robert S(teven) 1943- 92
Bianco, Margery
    See Bianco, Margery Williams
Bianco, Margery Williams
    1881-1944 15
    See also CLR 19
Bianco, Pamela 1906- 28
Bibby, Violet 1908- 24
Bible, Charles 1937- 13
Bibo, Bobette
    See Gugliotta, Bobette
Bice, Clare 1909-1976 22
Bickerstaff, Isaac
    See Swift, Jonathan
Biegel, Paul 1925- 79
    Earlier sketch in SATA 16
    See also CLR 27
    See also SAAS 18
Biemiller, Carl L(udwig), Jr.)
    1912-1979 40
    Obituary 21
Bienenfeld, Florence L(ucille) 1929- 39
Bierhorst, John (William) 1936- 91
    Earlier sketch in SATA 6
    See also SAAS 10
Biggar, Joan R(awlins) 1936- 120
Biggle, Lloyd, Jr. 1923- 65
Bilal, Abdel W(ahab) 1970- 92
Bilbrough, Norman 1941- 111
Bileck, Marvin 1920- 40
Bilibin, Ivan (Iakolevich) 1876-1942 61
Bill, Alfred Hoyt 1879-1964 44
Billam, Rosemary 1952- 61
Billings, Charlene W(interer) 1941- 41
Billingsley, Franny 1954- 132
Billington, Elizabeth T(hain) 50
    Brief entry 43
Billout, Guy (Rene) 1941- 10
    See also CLR 33
Bilson, Geoffrey 1938-1987 99
Binch, Caroline (Lesley) 1947- 140
    Earlier sketch in SATA 81
Bing, Christopher (H.) 126
Bingham, Sam(uel A.) 1944- 96
Bingley, Margaret (Jane Kirby)
    1947- 72
Binkley, Anne
    See Rand, Ann (Binkley)
Binzen, Bill 24
    See Binzen, William
Birch, David (W.) 1913- 89
Birch, Reginald B(athurst)
    1856-1943 19
Birchman, David 1949- 72
Birchmore, Daniel A. 1951- 92
Bird, Carmel 1940- 124
Bird, E(lzy) J(ay) 1911- 58

Birdseye, Tom 1951- 98
    Earlier sketch in SATA 66
Birenbaum, Barbara 1941- 65
Birmingham, Lloyd P(aul) 1924- 83
    Earlier sketch in SATA 12
Birney, Betty G. 1947- 98
Biro, B.
    See Biro, B(alint) S(tephen)
Biro, B(alint) S(tephen) 1921- 67
    See Biro, Val
Biro, Val 1
    See also CLR 28
    See also SAAS 13
    See Biro, B(alint) S(tephen)
Bischoff, Julia Bristol 1909-1970 12
Bishop, Bonnie 1943- 37
Bishop, Claire Huchet 1899(?)-1993 14
    Obituary 74
    See also CLR 80
Bishop, Courtney
    See Ruemmler, John D(avid)
Bishop, Curtis (Kent) 1912-1967 6
Bishop, Gavin 1946- 97
Bishop, Kathleen Wong 1954- 120
Bishop, Kathy
    See Bishop, Kathleen Wong
Bishop, Nic 1955- 107
Bisset, Donald 1910-1995 86
    Earlier sketch in SATA 7
Bisson, Terry (Ballantine) 1942- 99
Bitter, Gary G(len) 1940- 22
Bixby, William (Courtney) 1920-1986 6
    Obituary 47
Bjoerk, Christina 1938- 99
    Earlier sketch in SATA 67
    See also CLR 22
Bjork, Christina
    See Bjoerk, Christina
Bjorklund, Lorence F. 1913-1978 35
    Brief entry 32
Black, Algernon David 1900-1993 12
    Obituary 76
Black, Irma Simonton 1906-1972 2
    Obituary 25
Black, Mansell
    See Trevor, Elleston
Black, MaryAnn
    See Easley, MaryAnn
Black, Susan Adams 1953- 40
Blackall, Bernie 1956- 126
Blackburn, Claire
    See Altman, Linda Jacobs
Blackburn, John(ny) Brewton 1952- 15
Blackburn, Joyce Knight 1920- 29
Blackett, Veronica Heath 1927- 12
Blackie, Jean Cutler 1943- 79
Blacklin, Malcolm
    See Chambers, Aidan
Blacklock, Dyan 1951- 112
Blackman, Malorie 1962- 128
    Earlier sketch in SATA 83
Blackton, Peter
    See Wilson, Lionel
Blackwood, Alan 1932- 70
Blackwood, Gary L. 1945- 118
    Earlier sketch in SATA 72
Blade, Alexander
    See Garrett, (Gordon) Randall (Phillip)
    and Hamilton, Edmond
    and Silverberg, Robert
Blades, Ann (Sager) 1947- 69
    Earlier sketch in SATA 16
    See also CLR 15
Bladow, Suzanne Wilson 1937- 14
Blaine, John
    See Goodwin, Harold L(eland)
Blaine, Marge
    See Blaine, Margery Kay
Blaine, Margery Kay 1937- 11
Blair, Alison
    See Lerangis, Peter
Blair, Anne Denton 1914- 46

Blair, David Nelson 1954- *80*
Blair, Eric (Arthur) 1903-1950 ....*29*
  See Orwell, George
Blair, Jay 1953- *45*
Blair, Lucile
  See Yeakley, Marjory Hall
Blair, Margaret Whitman 1951- *124*
Blair, Pauline Hunter *131*
  Earlier sketch in SATA *3*
  See Clarke, Pauline
Blair, Ruth Van Ness 1912-1999 ....*12*
Blair, Shannon
  See Kaye, Marilyn
Blair, Walter 1900-1992 ....*12*
  Obituary *72*
Blaisdell, Bob
  See Blaisdell, Robert
Blaisdell, Robert 1959- *105*
Blake, Jon 1954- *78*
Blake, Olive
  See Supraner, Robyn
Blake, Quentin (Saxby) 1932- *125*
  Earlier sketches in SATA *9, 52, 96*
  See also CLR *31*
Blake, Robert 1949- *42*
Blake, Walker E.
  See Butterworth, W(illiam) E(dmund III)
Blake, William 1757-1827 ....*30*
  See also CLR *52*
Blakely, Gloria 1950- *139*
Blakely, Roger K. 1922- *82*
Blakeney, Jay D.
  See Chester, Deborah
Blakey, Nancy 1955- *94*
Blanc, Esther S. 1913-1997 ....*66*
Blanchard, Patricia *125*
Blanchet, M(uriel) Wylie
  1891-1961 ....*106*
Blanco, Richard L(idio) 1926- *63*
Bland, E.
  See Nesbit, E(dith)
Bland, Edith Nesbit
  See Nesbit, E(dith)
Bland, Fabian
  See Nesbit, E(dith)
Blank, Clarissa Mabel 1915-1965 ....*62*
Blassingame, Wyatt Rainey
  1909-1985 ....*34*
  Obituary *41*
  Earlier sketch in SATA *1*
Blatchford, Claire H. 1944- *94*
Blauer, Ettagale 1940- *49*
Bledsoe, Glen L(eonard) 1951- *108*
Bledsoe, Karen E(lizabeth) 1962- *108*
Bledsoe, Lucy Jane 1957- *97*
Bleeker, Sonia *2*
  Obituary *26*
  See Zim, Sonia Bleeker
Blegen, Daniel M. 1950- *92*
Blegvad, Erik 1923- *132*
  Earlier sketches in SATA *14, 66*
Blegvad, Lenore 1926- *66*
  Earlier sketch in SATA *14*
Blish, James (Benjamin) 1921-1975 ....*66*
Blishen, Edward (William)
  1920-1996 ....*66*
  Obituary *93*
  Earlier sketch in SATA *8*
Bliss, Corinne Demas 1947- *37*
  See Demas, Corinne
Bliss, Reginald
  See Wells, H(erbert) G(eorge)
Bliss, Ronald G(ene) 1942- *12*
Bliven, Bruce, Jr. 1916-2002 ....*2*
Blixen, Karen (Christentze Dinesen)
  1885-1962 ....*44*
  See Dinesen, Isak
Blizzard, Gladys S. (?)-1992 ....*79*
Blobaum, Cindy 1966- *123*
Bloch, Lucienne 1909-1999 ....*10*
Bloch, Marie Halun 1910-1998 ....*6*
  See also SAAS *9*

Bloch, Robert (Albert) 1917-1994 ....*12*
  Obituary *82*
Blochman, Lawrence G(oldtree)
  1900-1975 ....*22*
Block, Francesca Lia 1962- *116*
  Earlier sketch in SATA *80*
  See also CLR *33*
  See also SAAS *21*
Block, Irvin 1917- *12*
Blomgren, Jennifer (Alice) 1954- *136*
Blood, Charles Lewis 1929- *28*
Bloom, Freddy 1914-2000 ....*37*
  Obituary *121*
Bloom, Lloyd 1947- *108*
  Brief entry *43*
Bloomfield, Michaela 1966- *70*
Bloor, Edward (William) 1950- *98*
Blos, Joan W(insor) 1928- *109*
  Brief entry *27*
  Earlier sketches in SATA *33, 69*
  See also CLR *18*
  See also SAAS *11*
Blough, Glenn O(rlando) 1907-1995 ....*1*
Blue, Rose 1931- *93*
  Autobiography Feature *117*
  Earlier sketches in SATA *5, 91*
  See also SAAS *24*
Blue, Zachary
  See Stine, R(obert) L(awrence)
Bluggage, Oranthy
  See Alcott, Louisa May
Blumberg, Leda 1956- *59*
Blumberg, Rhoda 1917- *123*
  Earlier sketches in SATA *35, 70*
  See also CLR *21*
Blume, Judy (Sussman) 1938- *79*
  Earlier sketches in SATA *2, 31*
  See also CLR *69*
Blumenthal, Shirley 1943- *46*
Blutig, Eduard
  See Gorey, Edward (St. John)
Bly, Janet (Chester) 1945- *43*
Bly, Stephen A(rthur) 1944- *116*
  Earlier sketch in SATA *43*
Blyler, Allison Lee 1966- *74*
Blyton, Carey 1932-2002 ....*9*
  Obituary *138*
Blyton, Enid (Mary) 1897-1968 ....*25*
  See also CLR *31*
Boardman, Fon Wyman, Jr.
  1911-2000 ....*6*
Boardman, Gwenn R. *12*
  See Petersen, Gwenn Boardman
Boase, Wendy 1944-1999 ....*28*
  Obituary *110*
Boatner, Mark Mayo III 1921- *29*
Bobbe, Dorothie de Bear 1905-1975 ....*1*
  Obituary *25*
Bober, Natalie S. 1930- *134*
  Earlier sketch in SATA *87*
  See also SAAS *23*
Bobette, Bibo
  See Gugliotta, Bobette
Bobritsky, Vladimir *47*
  Brief entry *32*
  See Bobri, Vladimir V.
Bochak, Grayce 1956- *76*
Bock, Hal
  See Bock, Harold I.
Bock, Harold I. 1939- *10*
Bock, William Sauts Netamux'we
  1939- *14*
Bode, Janet 1943-1999 ....*96*
  Obituary *118*
  Earlier sketch in SATA *60*
Bodecker, N(iels) M(ogens)
  1922-1988 ....*73*
  Obituary *54*
  Earlier sketch in SATA *8*
Boden, Hilda
  See Bodenham, Hilda Morris
Bodenham, Hilda Morris 1901- *13*

Bodett, Tom *70*
  See Bodett, Thomas Edward
Bodie, Idella F(allaw) 1925- *89*
  Earlier sketch in SATA *12*
Bodker, Cecil 1927- *133*
  Earlier sketch in SATA *14*
  See also CLR *23*
Bodker, Cecil 1927-
  See Bodker, Cecil
Bodsworth, (Charles) Fred(erick)
  1918- *27*
Boeckman, Charles 1920- *12*
Boelts, Maribeth 1964- *78*
Boerst, William J. 1939- *121*
Boesch, Mark J(oseph) 1917- *12*
Boesen, Victor 1908- *16*
Bogacki, Tomek *138*
Bogaerts, Gert 1965- *80*
Bogan, Paulette 1960- *129*
Bogart, Jo Ellen 1945- *92*
  See also CLR *59*
Boggs, Ralph Steele 1901-1994 ....*7*
Bograd, Larry 1953- *89*
  Earlier sketch in SATA *33*
  See also SAAS *21*
Bohdal, Susi 1951- *101*
  Earlier sketch in SATA *22*
Bohlen, Nina 1931- *58*
Bohlmeijer, Arno 1956- *94*
Bohner, Charles (Henry) 1927- *62*
Bohnhoff, Maya Kaathryn 1954- *88*
Boissard, Janine 1932- *59*
Boland, Janice *98*
Bolden, Tonya (Wilyce) 1959- *138*
  Earlier sketch in SATA *79*
Boles, Paul Darcy 1916-1984 ....*9*
  Obituary *38*
Bolian, Polly 1925- *4*
Bollen, Roger 1941(?)- *83*
  Brief entry *29*
Bolliger, Max 1929- *7*
Bolognese, Don(ald Alan) 1934- *129*
  Earlier sketches in SATA *24, 71*
Bolotin, Norman (Phillip) 1951- *93*
Bolton, Carole 1926- *6*
Bolton, Elizabeth
  See St. John, Nicole
Bolton, Evelyn
  See Bunting, (Anne) Eve(lyn)
Bonar, Veronica
  See Bailey, Donna (Veronica Anne)
Bond, B. J.
  See Heneghan, James
Bond, Bruce 1939- *61*
Bond, Felicia 1954- *126*
  Earlier sketch in SATA *49*
Bond, Gladys Baker 1912- *14*
Bond, Higgins 1951- *83*
Bond, J. Harvey
  See Winterbotham, R(ussell) R(obert)
Bond, (Thomas) Michael 1926- *58*
  Earlier sketch in SATA *6*
  See also CLR *1*
  See also SAAS *3*
Bond, Nancy (Barbara) 1945- *82*
  Earlier sketch in SATA *22*
  See also CLR *11*
  See also SAAS *13*
Bond, Rebecca 1972- *130*
Bond, Ruskin 1934- *87*
  Earlier sketch in SATA *14*
Bondie, J. D.
  See Cunningham, Chet
Bone, Ian 1956- *117*
Bonehill, Captain Ralph
  See Stratemeyer, Edward L.
Bonham, Barbara Thomas 1926- *7*
Bonham, Frank 1914-1989 ....*49*
  Obituary *62*
  Earlier sketch in SATA *1*
  See also SAAS *3*
Boniface, William 1963- *102*

Bonn, Pat
  See Bonn, Patricia Carolyn
Bonn, Patricia Carolyn 1948- *43*
Bonner, Mary Graham 1890-1974 ....*19*
Bonner, Mike 1951- *121*
Bonners, Susan 1947- *85*
  Brief entry *48*
Bonsall, Crosby Barbara (Newell)
  1921-1995 ....*23*
  Obituary *84*
Bonsall, Joseph S. 1948- *119*
Bonsignore, Joan 1959- *140*
Bontemps, Arna(ud Wendell)
  1902-1973 ....*44*
  Obituary *24*
  Earlier sketch in SATA *2*
  See also CLR *6*
Bonzon, Paul-Jacques 1908-1978 ....*22*
Boock, Paula 1964- *134*
Booher, Dianna Daniels 1948- *33*
Book, Rick 1949- *119*
Bookman, Charlotte
  See Zolotow, Charlotte (Gertrude)
  S(hapiro)
Boon, Debbie 1960- *103*
Boon, Emilie (Laetitia) 1958- *86*
Boone, Charles Eugene
  See Boone, Pat
Boone, Pat 1934- *7*
Boorman, Linda (Kay) 1940- *46*
Boorstin, Daniel J(oseph) 1914- *52*
Booth, Ernest Sheldon 1915-1984 ....*43*
Booth, Graham (Charles) 1935- *37*
Borden, Louise (Walker) 1949- *141*
  Earlier sketches in SATA *68, 104*
Bordier, Georgette 1924- *16*
Borgman, James (Mark) 1954- *122*
Borgman, Jim
  See Borgman, James (Mark)
Boring, Mel 1939- *35*
Borja, Corinne 1929- *22*
Borja, Robert 1923- *22*
Borland, Hal *5*
  Obituary *24*
  See Borland, Harold Glen
Borland, Kathryn Kilby 1916- *16*
Borlenghi, Patricia 1951- *79*
Born, Adolf 1930- *49*
Bornstein-Lercher, Ruth 1927- *88*
  Earlier sketch in SATA *14*
Borski, Lucia Merecka *18*
Borten, Helen Jacobson 1930- *5*
Borton, Elizabeth
  See Trevino, Elizabeth B(orton) de
Borton, Lady 1942- *98*
Borton de Trevino, Elizabeth
  See Trevino, Elizabeth B(orton) de
Bortstein, Larry 1942- *16*
Bortz, Alfred B(enjamin) 1944- *139*
  Earlier sketch in SATA *74*
Bortz, Fred
  See Bortz, Alfred B(enjamin)
Bosco, Jack
  See Holliday, Joseph
Boshell, Gordon 1908- *15*
Boshinski, Blanche 1922- *10*
Bosman, Paul 1929- *107*
Bosse, Malcolm (Joseph, Jr.)
  1926-2002 ....*136*
  Earlier sketch in SATA *35*
Bosserman, (Charles) Phillip 1931- *84*
Bossom, Naomi 1933- *35*
Bostock, Mike 1962- *114*
Boston, L(ucy) M(aria Wood)
  1892-1990 ....*19*
  Obituary *64*
  See also CLR *3*
Bostrom, Kathleen (Susan) Long
  1954- *139*
  Earlier sketch in SATA *137*
Bosworth, J. Allan 1925- *19*
Bothwell, Jean (?)-1977 ....*2*

Botkin, B(enjamin) A(lbert)
  1901-1975 ....*40*
Botsford, Ward 1927- *66*
Botting, Douglas (Scott) 1934- *43*
Bottner, Barbara 1943- *93*
  Autobiography Feature *121*
  Earlier sketch in SATA *14*
  See also SAAS *26*
Bottone, Frank G., Jr. 1969- *141*
Bouchard, David 1952- *117*
Boucher, (Clarence) Carter 1954- *129*
Boughton, Richard 1954- *75*
Boulet, Susan Seddon 1941- *50*
Boulle, Pierre (Francois Marie-Louis)
  1912-1994 ....*22*
  Obituary *78*
Boulton, Jane 1921- *91*
Bouma, Paddy 1947- *128*
Bour, Daniele 1939- *62*
Bourdon, David 1934-1998 ....*46*
Bourne, Lesley
  See Marshall, Evelyn
Bourne, Miriam Anne 1931-1989 ....*16*
  Obituary *63*
Boutet de Monvel, (Louis) M(aurice)
  1850(?)-1913 ....*30*
  See also CLR *32*
Bova, Ben(jamin William) 1932- *133*
  Earlier sketches in SATA *6, 68*
  See also CLR *3*
Bovaird, Anne E(lizabeth) 1960- *90*
Bowden, Joan Chase 1925- *51*
  Brief entry *38*
Bowen, Alexandria Russell *97*
Bowen, Andy Russell
  See Bowen, Alexandria Russell
Bowen, Betty Morgan
  See West, Betty
Bowen, Catherine (Shober) Drinker
  1897-1973 ....*7*
Bowen, David
  See Bowen, Joshua David
Bowen, Fred 1953- *136*
Bowen, Joshua David 1930- *22*
Bowen, Rhys
  See Quin-Harkin, Janet
Bowen, Robert Sydney 1900-1977 ....*52*
  Obituary *21*
Bowermaster, Jon 1954- *135*
  Earlier sketch in SATA *77*
Bowers, Terrell L. 1945- *101*
Bowers, Terry
  See Bowers, Terrell L.
Bowie, C. W.
  See Wirths, Claudine (Turner) G(ibson)
Bowie, Jim
  See Norwood, Victor G(eorge) C(harles)
  and Stratemeyer, Edward L.
Bowkett, Stephen 1953- *67*
Bowler, Jan Brett
  See Brett, Jan (Churchill)
Bowman, Crystal 1951- *105*
Bowman, James Cloyd 1880-1961 ....*23*
Bowman, John S(tewart) 1931- *16*
Bowman, Kathleen (Gill) 1942- *52*
  Brief entry *40*
Boyce, George A(rthur) 1898- *19*
Boyd, Candy Dawson 1946- *72*
  See also CLR *50*
Boyd, Pauline
  See Schock, Pauline
Boyd, Selma
  See Acuff, Selma Boyd
Boyd, Waldo T. 1918- *18*
Boyer, Robert E(rnst) 1929- *22*
Boyes, Vivien (Elizabeth) 1952- *106*
Boyle, Ann (Peters) 1916- *10*
Boyle, Eleanor Vere (Gordon)
  1825-1916 ....*28*
Boyle, Robert H. 1928- *65*
Boylston, Helen Dore 1895-1984 ....*23*
  Obituary *39*

Boynton, Sandra (Keith) 1953- *107*
  Brief entry *38*
  Earlier sketch in SATA *57*
Boz
  See Dickens, Charles (John Huffam)
Bracken, Charles
  See Pellowski, Michael (Joseph)
Brackers de Hugo, Pierre 1960- *115*
Brackett, Dolli Tingle 1911(?)-1993 ......*137*
Brackett, Virginia (Roberts Meredith)
  1950- *121*
Bradbury, Bianca (Ryley) 1908-1982 ......*56*
  Earlier sketch in SATA *3*
Bradbury, Edward P.
  See Moorcock, Michael (John)
Bradbury, Ray (Douglas) 1920- *123*
  Earlier sketches in SATA *11, 64*
Bradfield, Carl 1942- *91*
Bradford, Ann (Liddell) 1917- *56*
  Brief entry *38*
Bradford, Barbara Taylor 1933- *66*
Bradford, Karleen 1936- *96*
  Earlier sketch in SATA *48*
Bradford, Lois J(ean) 1936- *36*
Bradford, Richard (Roark)
  1932-2002 ....*59*
  Obituary *135*
Bradley, Duane
  See Sanborn, Duane
Bradley, Marion Zimmer
  1930-1999 ....*139*
  Obituary *116*
  Earlier sketch in SATA *90*
  See Chapman, Lee
  and Dexter, John
  and Gardner, Miriam
  and Ives, Morgan
  and Rivers, Elfrida
Bradley, Virginia 1912- *23*
Bradley, Will
  See Strickland, (William) Brad(ley)
Bradman, Tony 1954- *81*
Bradshaw, Gillian (Joan) 1949- *118*
Bradshaw, Gillian (Marucha) 1956- *127*
Bradstreet, T. J.
  See Thesman, Jean
Brady, Esther Wood 1905-1987 ....*31*
  Obituary *53*
Brady, Irene 1943- *4*
Brady, Kimberley S(mith) 1953- *101*
Brady, Lillian 1902- *28*
Bragdon, Elspeth MacDuffie 1897-1980 ....*6*
Bragdon, Lillian Jacot *24*
Bragg, Mabel Caroline 1870-1945 ....*24*
Bragg, Michael 1948- *46*
Bragg, Ruth Gembicki 1943- *77*
Brahm, Sumishta 1954- *58*
Brailsford, Frances
  See Wosmek, Frances
Brainerd, John W(hiting) 1918- *65*
Braithwaite, Althea 1940- *23*
  Autobiography Feature *119*
  See also SAAS *24*
Bram, Elizabeth 1948- *30*
Brancato, Robin F(idler) 1936- *97*
  See also CLR *32*
  See also SAAS *9*
Branch, Muriel Miller 1943- *94*
Brand, Christianna
  See Lewis, Mary (Christianna)
Brand, Rebecca
  See Charnas, Suzy McKee
Brandel, Marc 1919- *71*
Brandenberg, Alexa (Demetria)
  1966- *97*
Brandenberg, Aliki (Liacouras)
  1929- *113*
  Earlier sketches in SATA *2, 35, 75*
  See Aliki
Brandenberg, Franz 1932- *75*
  Earlier sketches in SATA *8, 35*
Brandenburg, Jim 1945- *87*

Brandhorst, Carl T(heodore)
1898-1988 ....*23*
Brandis, Marianne 1938- *96*
Earlier sketch in SATA *59*
Brandon, Brumsic, Jr. 1927- *9*
Brandon, Curt
See Bishop, Curtis (Kent)
Brandreth, Gyles 1948- *28*
Brandt, Catharine 1905-1997 ....*40*
Brandt, Keith
See Sabin, Louis
Brandt, Sue R(eading) 1916- *59*
Branfield, John (Charles) 1931- *11*
Branford, Henrietta 1946-1999 ....*106*
Branley, Franklyn M(ansfield)
1915-2002 ....*136*
Earlier sketches in SATA *4, 68*
See also CLR *13*
See also SAAS *16*
Branscum, Robbie (Tilley)
1937-1997 ....*72*
Obituary *96*
Earlier sketch in SATA *23*
See also SAAS *17*
Bransom, (John) Paul 1885-1979 ....*43*
Bratton, Helen 1899-1986 ....*4*
Bratun, Katy 1950- *83*
Braude, Michael 1936- *23*
Braun, Lilian Jackson 1916(?)- *109*
Brautigan, Richard (Gary) 1935-1984 ......*56*
Braymer, Marjorie Elizabeth
1911-1988 ....*6*
Breathed, (Guy) Berke(ley) 1957- *86*
Brecht, Edith 1895-1975 ....*6*
Obituary *25*
Breck, Vivian
See Breckenfeld, Vivian Gurney
Breckenfeld, Vivian Gurney
1895-1992 ....*1*
Breda, Tjalmar
See DeJong, David C(ornel)
Bredeson, Carmen 1944- *98*
Breinburg, Petronella 1927- *11*
See also CLR *31*
Breisky, William J(ohn) 1928- *22*
Brennan, Gale (Patrick) 1927- *64*
Brief entry *53*
Brennan, Herbie
See Brennan, J(ames) H(erbert)
Brennan, J(ames) H(erbert) 1940- *140*
Brennan, Jan
See Brennan, J(ames) H(erbert)
Brennan, Joseph Lomas 1903-2000 ....*6*
Brennan, Linda Crotta 1952- *130*
Brenner, Anita 1905-1974 ....*56*
Brenner, Barbara (Johnes) 1925- *124*
Earlier sketches in SATA *4, 42, 76*
See also SAAS *14*
Brenner, Fred 1920- *36*
Brief entry *34*
Brent, Stuart *14*
Breslin, Theresa *70*
Breslow, Maurice (A.) 1935- *72*
Breslow, Susan 1951- *69*
Brett, Bernard 1925- *22*
Brett, Grace N(eff) 1900-1975 ....*23*
Brett, Jan (Churchill) 1949- *130*
Earlier sketches in SATA *42, 71*
See also CLR *27*
Brewer, James D. 1951- *108*
Brewer, Sally King 1947- *33*
Brewster, Benjamin
See Folsom, Franklin (Brewster)
Brewster, Hugh 1950- *95*
Brewster, Patience 1952- *97*
Brewton, John E(dmund) 1898-1982 ....*5*
Brian, Janeen (Paulette) 1948- *141*
Brick, John 1922-1973 ....*10*
Bride, Nadja
See Nobisso, Josephine

Bridgers, Sue Ellen 1942- *90*
Autobiography Feature *109*
Earlier sketch in SATA *22*
See also CLR *18*
See also SAAS *1*
Bridges, Laurie
See Bruck, Lorraine
Bridges, Ruby (Nell) 1954- *131*
Bridges, William (Andrew) 1901-1984 ......*5*
Bridwell, Norman (Ray) 1928- *138*
Earlier sketches in SATA *4, 68*
Brier, Howard M(axwell) 1903-1969 ....*8*
Brierley, (Louise) 1958- *59*
Briggs, Katharine Mary 1898-1980 ....*101*
Obituary *25*
Briggs, Peter 1921-1975 ....*39*
Obituary *31*
Briggs, Raymond (Redvers) 1934- *131*
Earlier sketches in SATA *23, 66*
See also CLR *10*
Bright, Robert (Douglas Sr.)
1902-1988 ....*63*
Obituary *60*
Earlier sketch in SATA *24*
Bright, Sarah
See Shine, Deborah
Brightfield, Richard 1927- *65*
Brief entry *53*
Brightfield, Rick
See Brightfield, Richard
Brighton, Catherine 1943- *107*
Earlier sketch in SATA *65*
Brill, Marlene Targ 1945- *124*
Earlier sketch in SATA *77*
Brimberg, Stanlee 1947- *9*
Brimner, Larry Dane 1949- *79*
Autobiography Feature *112*
Brin, David 1950- *65*
Brin, Ruth Firestone 1921- *22*
Brinckloe, Julie (Lorraine) 1950- *13*
Brindel, June (Rachuy) 1919- *7*
Brindle, Max
See Fleischman, (Albert) Sid(ney)
Brindze, Ruth 1903-1984 ....*23*
Brink, Carol Ryrie 1895-1981 ....*100*
Obituary *27*
Earlier sketches in SATA *1, 31*
See also CLR *30*
Brinsmead, H. F.
See Brinsmead, H(esba) F(ay)
Brinsmead, H. F(ay)
See Aalben, Patrick
and Brinsmead, H(esba) F(ay)
Brinsmead, H(esba) F(ay) 1922- *78*
Earlier sketch in SATA *18*
See also CLR *47*
See also SAAS *5*
Briquebec, John
See Rowland-Entwistle, (Arthur) Theodore
(Henry)
Brisbane, Henry R.
See Ellis, Edward S(ylvester)
Brisco, P. A.
See Matthews, Patricia (Anne)
Brisco, Patty
See Matthews, Patricia (Anne)
and Matthews, Clayton (Hartley)
Briscoe, Jill (Pauline) 1935- *56*
Brief entry *47*
Brisley, Joyce Lankester 1896-1978 ....*22*
Obituary *84*
Brisson, Pat 1951- *128*
Autobiography Feature *133*
Earlier sketch in SATA *67*
Britt, Dell 1934- *1*
Brittain, Bill
See SAAS *7*
See Brittain, William (E.)
Brittain, C. Dale 1948- *82*
Brittain, William (E.) 1930- *76*
Earlier sketch in SATA *36*
See Brittain, Bill

Brittingham, Geoffrey (Hugh) 1959- *76*
Britton, Kate *49*
See Stegeman, Janet Allais
Britton, Louisa
See McGuire, Leslie (Sarah)
Britton, Rick 1952- *82*
Bro, Marguerite (Harmon)
1894-1977 ....*19*
Obituary *27*
Broadhead, Helen Cross 1913- *25*
Brochmann, Elizabeth 1938- *41*
Brock, Betty 1923- *4*
Brock, C(harles) E(dmund)
1870-1938 ....*42*
Brief entry *32*
Brock, Delia
See Ephron, Delia
Brock, Emma L(illian) 1886-1974 ....*8*
Brock, H(enry) M(atthew)
1875-1960 ....*42*
Brockett, Eleanor Hall 1913-1967 ....*10*
Brockman, C(hristian) Frank
1902-1985 ....*26*
Broderick, Dorothy M. 1929- *5*
Brodeur, Ruth Wallace
See Wallace-Brodeur, Ruth
Brodie, Sally
See Cavin, Ruth (Brodie)
Brodsky, Beverly
See McDermott, Beverly Brodsky
Brody, Wendy
See Staub, Wendy Corsi
Broeger, Achim 1944- *31*
Broekel, Rainer Lothar 1923- *38*
Broekel, Ray
See Broekel, Rainer Lothar
Broekstra, Lorette 1964- *124*
Broger, Achim
See Broeger, Achim
Brokamp, Marilyn 1920- *10*
Broman, Fred
See Moseley, James W(illett)
Bromhall, Winifred *26*
Brommer, Gerald F(rederick) 1927- *28*
Brondfield, Jerome 1913- *22*
Brondfield, Jerry
See Brondfield, Jerome
Bronner, Stephen Eric 1949- *101*
Bronowski, Jacob 1908-1974 ....*55*
Bronson, Lynn
See Lampman, Evelyn Sibley
Brook, Judith (Penelope) 1926- *59*
Brief entry *51*
Brook, Judy
See Brook, Judith (Penelope)
Brooke, L(eonard) Leslie 1862-1940 ....*17*
See also CLR *20*
Brooke, William J. 1946- *139*
Brooke-Haven, P.
See Wodehouse, P(elham) G(renville)
Brookins, Dana 1931- *28*
Brooks, Anita *5*
See Abramovitz, Anita (Zeltner Brooks)
Brooks, Bill 1939- *59*
Brooks, Bruce 1950- *112*
Brief entry *53*
Earlier sketch in SATA *72*
See also CLR *25*
Brooks, Caryl 1924- *84*
Brooks, Charlotte K(endrick)
1918-1998 ....*24*
Obituary *112*
Brooks, George
See Baum, L(yman) Frank
Brooks, Gwendolyn (Elizabeth)
1917-2000 ....*6*
Obituary *123*
See also CLR *27*
Brooks, Jerome 1931- *23*
Brooks, Lester 1924- *7*

Brooks, Martha 1944- *121*
  Autobiography Feature *134*
  Earlier sketch in SATA *68*
Brooks, Maurice (Graham) 1900- *45*
Brooks, Polly Schoyer 1912- *12*
Brooks, Ron(ald George) 1948- *94*
  Brief entry *33*
Brooks, Terry 1944- *60*
Brooks, Walter R(ollin) 1886-1958 ....*17*
Brooks-Hill, Helen (Mason)
  1908-1994 ....*59*
Broome, Errol 1937- *105*
Brophy, Nannette 1963- *73*
Brosnan, James Patrick 1929- *14*
Brosnan, Jim
  See Brosnan, James Patrick
Brostoff, Anita 1931- *132*
Brothers Hildebrandt, The
  See Hildebrandt, Greg
  and Hildebrandt, Tim(othy)
Broun, Emily
  See Sterne, Emma Gelders
Brouwer, S. W.
  See Brouwer, Sigmund (W.)
Brouwer, Sigmund (W.) 1959- *109*
Brow, Thea 1934- *60*
Brower, Millicent *8*
Brower, Pauline 1929- *22*
Browin, Frances Williams 1898-1986 ....*5*
Brown, Alexis
  See Baumann, Amy (Brown) Beeching
Brown, Anne Ensign 1937- *61*
Brown, Beverly Swerdlow *97*
Brown, Bill
  See Brown, William L(ouis)
Brown, Billye Walker
  See Cutchen, Billye Walker
Brown, Bob
  See Brown, Robert Joseph
Brown, Buck 1936- *45*
Brown, Cassie 1919-1986 ....*55*
Brown, Conrad 1922- *31*
Brown, Craig McFarland 1947- *73*
Brown, David
  See Brown, David A(lan)
  and Myller, Rolf
Brown, Dee (Alexander) 1908-2002 ......*110*
  Obituary *141*
  Earlier sketch in SATA *5*
Brown, Drew T. III 1955- *83*
Brown, Drollene P. 1939- *53*
Brown, Eleanor Frances 1908-1987 ....*3*
Brown, Elizabeth M(yers) 1915- *43*
Brown, Fern G. 1918- *34*
Brown, (Robert) Fletch 1923- *42*
Brown, Fornan 1901-1996 ....*71*
  Obituary *88*
Brown, George Earl 1883-1964 ....*11*
Brown, George Mackay 1921-1996 ....*35*
Brown, Irene Bennett 1932- *3*
Brown, Irving
  See Adams, William Taylor
Brown, Ivor (John Carnegie) 1891-1974 ...*5*
  Obituary *26*
Brown, Jane Clark 1930- *81*
Brown, Janet Mitsui *87*
Brown, Joe David 1915-1976 ....*44*
Brown, Joseph E(dward) 1929- *59*
  Brief entry *51*
Brown, Judith Gwyn 1933- *20*
Brown, Kathryn 1955- *98*
Brown, Ken (James) *129*
Brown, Kevin 1960- *101*
Brown, Laurene Krasny 1945- *99*
  Earlier sketch in SATA *54*
Brown, Laurie Krasny
  See Brown, Laurene Krasny
Brown, Lloyd Arnold 1907-1966 ....*36*
Brown, Mahlon A.
  See Ellis, Edward S(ylvester)

Brown, Marc (Tolon) 1946- *80*
  Earlier sketches in SATA *10, 53*
  See also CLR 29
Brown, Marcia (Joan) 1918- *47*
  Earlier sketch in SATA *7*
  See also CLR 12
Brown, Margaret Wise 1910-1952 ....*100*
  See also YABC 2
  See also CLR 10
Brown, Margery (Wheeler) *78*
  Earlier sketch in SATA *5*
Brown, Marion Marsh 1908-2001 ....*6*
Brown, Myra Berry 1918- *6*
Brown, Palmer 1919- *36*
Brown, Pamela (Beatrice) 1924-1989 ....*5*
  Obituary *61*
Brown, Reeve Lindbergh
  See Lindbergh, Reeve
Brown, Richard E. 1946- *61*
Brown, Robert Joseph 1907-1989 ....*14*
Brown, Roderick (Langmere) Haig-
  See Haig-Brown, Roderick (Langmere)
Brown, Rosalie *9*
  See Moore, Rosalie (Gertrude)
Brown, Roswell
  See Webb, Jean Francis (III)
Brown, Roy (Frederick) 1921-1982 ....*51*
  Obituary *39*
Brown, Ruth 1941- *105*
Brown, Scott 1971- *134*
Brown, Sue Ellen 1954- *81*
Brown, Tricia 1954- *114*
Brown, Vinson 1912-1991 ....*19*
Brown, Walter R(eed) 1929- *19*
Brown, Will
  See Ainsworth, William Harrison
Brown, William L(ouis) 1910-1964 ....*5*
Browne, Anthony (Edward Tudor)
  1946- *105*
  Brief entry *44*
  Earlier sketches in SATA *45, 61*
  See also CLR 19
Browne, Dik *38*
  See Browne, Richard Arthur Allen
Browne, Hablot Knight 1815-1882 ....*21*
Browne, Matthew
  See Rands, William Brighty
Browne, Richard Arthur Allen
  1917-1989 ....*67*
  Brief entry *38*
  See Browne, Dik
Browne, Vee F(rances) 1956- *90*
Browning, Robert 1812-1889
  See YABC 1
Brownjohn, Alan 1931- *6*
Brownlee, Walter 1930- *62*
Brownlow, Kevin 1938- *65*
Brownridge, William R(oy) 1932- *94*
Bruce, (William) Harry 1934- *77*
Bruce, Mary 1927- *1*
Bruchac, Joseph III 1942- *131*
  Earlier sketches in SATA *42, 89*
  See also CLR 46
Bruck, Lorraine 1921- *55*
  Brief entry *46*
  See Bridges, Laurie
Bruemmer, Fred 1929- *47*
Bruna, Dick 1927- *76*
  Brief entry *30*
  Earlier sketch in SATA *43*
  See also CLR 7
Brunhoff, Jean de 1899-1937 ....*24*
  See also CLR 4
Brunhoff, Laurent de 1925- *71*
  Earlier sketch in SATA *24*
  See also CLR 4
Brunskill, Elizabeth Ann Flatt 1966- *88*
Brush, Karen A(lexandra) 1960- *85*
Brussel-Smith, Bernard 1914- *58*
Brust, Steven K. (Zoltan) 1955- *121*
  Earlier sketch in SATA *86*
Brustlein, Daniel 1904- *40*

Brustlein, Janice Tworkov -2000 ....*40*
  Obituary *126*
Brutschy, Jennifer 1960- *84*
Bryan, Ashley F. 1923- *132*
  Earlier sketches in SATA *31, 72*
  See also CLR 66
Bryant, Bernice (Morgan) 1908-1976 ......*11*
Bryant, Jennifer F(isher) 1960- *94*
Brychta, Alex 1956- *21*
Brynie, Faith H(ickman) 1946- *113*
Bryson, Bernarda 1905- *9*
Buba, Joy Flinsch 1904- *44*
Buchan, Bryan 1945- *36*
Buchan, John 1875-1940
  See YABC 2
Buchanan, Debby 1952- *82*
Buchanan, Deborah Leevonne
  See Buchanan, Debby
Buchanan, Paul 1959- *116*
Buchanan, Sue 1937- *138*
Buchanan, Sue 1939- *139*
Buchheimer, Naomi Barnett
  See Barnett, Naomi
Buchignani, Walter 1965- *84*
Buchwald, Art(hur) 1925- *10*
Buchwald, Emilie 1935- *7*
Buck, Gisela 1941- *101*
Buck, Lewis 1925- *18*
Buck, Margaret Waring 1905-1997 ....*3*
Buck, Pearl S(ydenstricker)
  1892-1973 ....*25*
  Earlier sketch in SATA *1*
Buck, Siegfried 1941- *101*
Buckeridge, Anthony (Malcolm)
  1912- *85*
  Earlier sketch in SATA *6*
Buckholtz, Eileen (Garber) 1949- *54*
  Brief entry *47*
Buckler, Ernest 1908-1984 ....*47*
Buckless, Andrea K. 1968- *117*
Buckley, Helen E(lizabeth) 1918- *90*
  Earlier sketch in SATA *2*
Buckley, James, Jr. 1963- *114*
Buckmaster, Henrietta *6*
  See Stephens, Henrietta Henkle
Budd, Lillian (Peterson) 1897-1989 ....*7*
Buehler, Stephanie Jona 1956- *83*
Buehner, Caralyn M. 1963- *104*
Buehner, Mark 1959- *104*
Buehr, Walter Franklin 1897-1971 ....*3*
Buell, Janet 1952- *106*
Buergel, Paul-Hermann H. 1949- *83*
Buettner, Dan 1960- *95*
Buff, Conrad 1886-1975 ....*19*
Buff, Mary (E. Marsh) 1890-1970 ....*19*
Buffett, Jimmy 1946- *110*
  Earlier sketch in SATA *76*
Buffie, Margaret 1945- *107*
  Earlier sketch in SATA *71*
  See also CLR 39
Bugni, Alice 1951- *122*
Bujold, Lois McMaster 1949- *136*
Bulfinch, Thomas 1796-1867 ....*35*
Bull, Angela (Mary) 1936- *45*
Bull, Emma 1954- *99*
  Autobiography Feature *103*
Bull, Norman John 1916- *41*
Bull, Schuyler M. 1974- *138*
Bulla, Clyde Robert 1914- *139*
  Earlier sketches in SATA *2, 41, 91*
  See also SAAS 6
Bullock, Kathleen (Mary) 1946- *77*
Bullock, Robert (D.) 1947- *92*
Bulpin, (Barbara) Vicki *92*
Bumstead, Kathleen Mary 1918-1987 ......*53*
Bundles, A'Lelia Perry 1952- *76*
Bunin, Catherine 1967- *30*
Bunin, Sherry 1925- *30*
Bunkers, Suzanne L. 1950- *136*
Bunting, A. E.
  See Bunting, (Anne) Eve(lyn)

Bunting, Eve
  See Bunting, (Anne) Eve(lyn)
Bunting, (Anne) Eve(lyn) 1928- *110*
  Earlier sketches in SATA *18, 64*
  See also CLR *82*
  See Bunting, Eve
Bunting, Glenn (Davison) 1957- *22*
Burack, Sylvia K. 1916- *35*
Burbank, Addison (Buswell)
  1895-1961 ....*37*
Burch, Joann J(ohansen) *75*
Burch, Robert J(oseph) 1925- *74*
  Earlier sketch in SATA *1*
  See also CLR *63*
Burchard, Peter Duncan 1921- *74*
  Earlier sketch in SATA *5*
  See also SAAS *13*
Burchard, S. H.
  See Burchard, Sue
Burchard, Sue 1937- *22*
Burchardt, Nellie 1921- *7*
Burdett, Lois *117*
Burdick, Eugene (Leonard)
  1918-1965 ....*22*
Burford, Eleanor
  See Hibbert, Eleanor Alice Burford
Burgan, Michael 1960- *118*
Burger, Carl 1888-1967 ....*9*
Burgess, Ann Marie
  See Gerson, Noel Bertram
Burgess, Barbara Hood 1926- *69*
Burgess, Em
  See Burgess, Mary Wyche
Burgess, (Frank) Gelett 1866-1951 ....*32*
  Brief entry *30*
Burgess, Mary Wyche 1916- *18*
Burgess, Melvin 1954- *96*
Burgess, Michael
  See Gerson, Noel Bertram
Burgess, Robert F(orrest) 1927- *4*
Burgess, Thornton Waldo 1874-1965 ......*17*
Burgess, Trevor
  See Trevor, Elleston
Burgwyn, Mebane Holoman
  1914-1992 ....*7*
Burke, David 1927- *46*
Burke, Dianne O'Quinn 1940- *89*
Burke, Janine 1952- *139*
Burke, Patrick 1958- *114*
Burke, Ralph
  See Garrett, (Gordon) Randall (Phillip)
  and Silverberg, Robert
Burkert, Nancy Ekholm 1933- *24*
  See also SAAS *14*
Burke-Weiner, Kimberly 1962- *95*
Burks, Brian 1955- *95*
Burland, Brian (Berkeley) 1931- *34*
Burland, C. A.
  See Burland, Cottie (Arthur)
Burland, Cottie (Arthur) 1905-1983 ....*5*
Burleigh, Robert 1936- *98*
  Earlier sketch in SATA *55*
Burlingame, (William) Roger 1889-1967 ...*2*
Burman, Ben Lucien 1896-1984 ....*6*
  Obituary *40*
Burn, Doris 1923- *1*
Burnard, Damon 1963- *115*
Burnett, Constance Buel 1893-1975 ....*36*
Burnett, Frances (Eliza) Hodgson
  1849-1924 ....*100*
  See also YABC *2*
  See also CLR *24*
Burnford, Sheila (Philip Cochrane Every)
  1918-1984 ....*3*
  Obituary *38*
  See also CLR *2*
Burnham, Sophy 1936- *65*
Burningham, John (Mackintosh)
  1936- *111*
  Earlier sketches in SATA *16, 59*
  See also CLR *9*

Burns, Diane L. 1950- *81*
  See also SAAS *24*
Burns, Eloise Wilkin
  See Wilkin, Eloise
Burns, Florence M. 1905-1988 ....*61*
Burns, Khephra 1950- *92*
Burns, Marilyn 1941- *96*
  Brief entry *33*
Burns, Olive Ann 1924-1990 ....*65*
Burns, Paul C. *5*
Burns, Ray
  See Burns, Raymond (Howard)
Burns, Raymond (Howard) 1924- *9*
Burns, Theresa 1961- *84*
Burns, William A. 1909-1999 ....*5*
Burr, Dan 1951- *65*
Burr, Lonnie 1943- *47*
Burrell, Roy E(ric) C(harles) 1923- *72*
Burroughs, Edgar Rice 1875-1950 ....*41*
Burroughs, Jean Mitchell 1908- *28*
Burroughs, Polly 1925- *2*
Burroway, Janet (Gay) 1936- *23*
Burstein, Chaya M(alamud) 1923- *64*
Burstein, Fred 1950- *83*
Burstein, John 1949- *54*
  Brief entry *40*
Bursztynski, Sue 1953- *114*
Burt, Jesse Clifton 1921-1976 ....*46*
  Obituary *20*
Burt, Olive Woolley 1894-1981 ....*4*
Burton, Gennett 1945- *95*
Burton, Hester (Wood-Hill) 1913- *74*
  Earlier sketch in SATA *7*
  See also CLR *1*
  See also SAAS *8*
Burton, Leslie
  See McGuire, Leslie (Sarah)
Burton, Marilee Robin 1950- *82*
  Earlier sketch in SATA *46*
Burton, Maurice 1898-1992 ....*23*
Burton, Robert (Wellesley) 1941- *22*
Burton, Virginia Lee 1909-1968 ....*100*
  Earlier sketch in SATA *2*
  See also CLR *11*
Burton, William H(enry) 1890-1964 ....*11*
Busby, Cylin 1970- *118*
Buscaglia, (Felice) Leo(nardo)
  1924-1998 ....*65*
  See Buscaglia, Leo F.
Buscaglia, Leo F.
  See Buscaglia, (Felice) Leo(nardo)
Busch, Phyllis S. 1909- *30*
Bush, Anne Kelleher 1959- *97*
Bush, Catherine 1961- *128*
Bushnell, Jack 1952- *86*
Busoni, Rafaello 1900-1962 ....*16*
Busselle, Rebecca 1941- *80*
Butcher, Kristin 1951- *140*
Butenko, Bohdan 1931- *90*
Butler, Beverly Kathleen 1932- *7*
Butler, Bill
  See Butler, William (Arthur) Vivian
  and Butler, Ernest Alton
  and Butler, William Huxford
Butler, Charles (Cadman) 1963- *121*
Butler, Dorothy 1925- *73*
Butler, Geoff 1945- *94*
Butler, M. Christina 1934- *72*
Butler, Octavia E(stelle) 1947- *84*
  See also CLR *65*
Butler, Vivian
  See Butler, William (Arthur) Vivian
Butler, William
  See Butler, William (Arthur) Vivian
Butler, William (Arthur) Vivian
  1927-1987 ....*79*
  See Marric, J. J.
Butters, Dorothy Gilman *5*
  See Gilman, Dorothy
Butterworth, Emma Macalik 1928- *43*
Butterworth, Nick 1946- *106*

Butterworth, Oliver 1915-1990 ....*1*
  Obituary *66*
Butterworth, W(illiam) E(dmund III)
  1929- *5*
  See Griffin, W. E. B.
Butts, Ellen R(ubinstein) 1942- *93*
Buxton, Ralph
  See Silverstein, Alvin
  and Silverstein, Virginia B(arbara
  Opshelor)
Buzzeo, Toni 1951- *135*
Byalick, Marcia 1947- *141*
  Earlier sketch in SATA *97*
Byard, Carole (Marie) 1941- *57*
Byars, Betsy (Cromer) 1928- *80*
  Autobiography Feature *108*
  Earlier sketches in SATA *4, 46*
  See also CLR *72*
  See also SAAS *1*
Byfield, Barbara Ninde 1930- *8*
Byman, Jeremy 1944- *129*
Bynum, Janie *133*
Byrd, Elizabeth 1912-1989 ....*34*
Byrd, Robert (John) 1942- *112*
  Earlier sketch in SATA *33*

                    C

C. 3. 3.
  See Wilde, Oscar (Fingal O'Flahertie
  Wills)
Cabaniss, J(ames) Allen 1911-1997 ....*5*
Cabat, Erni 1914- *74*
Cable, Mary 1920- *9*
Cabot, Meg(gin) 1967- *127*
  See also CLR *85*
Cabot, Patricia
  See Cabot, Meg(gin)
Cabral, O. M.
  See Cabral, Olga
Cabral, Olga 1909- *46*
Cabrera, Jane 1968- *103*
Cabrera, Marcela 1966- *90*
Cade, Toni
  See Bambara, Toni Cade
Cadmus and Harmonia
  See Buchan, John
Cadnum, Michael 1949- *121*
  Earlier sketch in SATA *87*
  See also CLR *78*
Caduto, Michael J. 1955- *103*
Cadwallader, Sharon 1936- *7*
Cady, (Walter) Harrison
  1877(?)-1970 ....*19*
Caffey, Donna (J.) 1954- *110*
Cagle, Malcolm W(infield) 1918- *32*
Cahn, Rhoda 1922- *37*
Cahn, William 1912-1976 ....*37*
Cain, Arthur H(omer) 1913- *3*
Caine, Geoffrey
  See Walker, Robert W(ayne)
Caines, Jeannette (Franklin) 1938- *78*
  Brief entry *43*
  See also CLR *24*
Cairns, Trevor 1922- *14*
Calabro, Marian 1954- *79*
Caldecott, Moyra 1927- *22*
Caldecott, Randolph (J.) 1846-1886 ......*100*
  Earlier sketch in SATA *17*
  See also CLR *14*
Calder, Charlotte 1952- *125*
Calder, David 1932-1997 ....*105*
Calder, Lyn
  See Calmenson, Stephanie
Calder, Marie D(onais) 1948- *96*
Calderone-Stewart, Lisa
  See Calderone-Stewart, Lisa-Marie
Calderone-Stewart, Lisa-Marie
  1958- *123*
Caldwell, Doreen (Mary) 1942- *71*

Caldwell, John C(ope) 1913- 7
Calhoun, B. B. 1961- 98
Calhoun, Chad
    See Cunningham, Chet
    and Goulart, Ron(ald Joseph)
Calhoun, Dia 1959- 129
Calhoun, Mary 2
    See also CLR 42
    See Wilkins, Mary Huiskamp
Calhoun, T. B.
    See Bisson, Terry (Ballantine)
Calif, Ruth 1922- 67
Calkins, Franklin
    See Stratemeyer, Edward L.
Call, Hughie Florence 1890-1969 1
Callahan, Dorothy M(onahan) 1934- 39
    Brief entry 35
Callahan, Philip Serna 1923- 25
Callan, Jamie 1954- 59
Callaway, Bernice (Anne) 1923- 48
Callaway, Kathy 1943- 36
Callen, Larry
    See Callen, Lawrence Willard, Jr.
Callen, Lawrence Willard, Jr. 1927- 19
Calley, Karin 1965- 92
Calmenson, Stephanie 1952- 139
    Brief entry 37
    Earlier sketches in SATA 51, 84
Calvert, Elinor H.
    See Lasell, Elinor H.
Calvert, John
    See Leaf, (Wilbur) Munro
Calvert, Patricia 1931- 132
    Earlier sketches in SATA 45, 69
    See also SAAS 17
Camburn, Carol A.
    See Camburn-Bracalente, Carol A.
Camburn-Bracalente, Carol A.
    1962- 118
Cameron, Ann 1943- 129
    Earlier sketches in SATA 27, 89
    See also SAAS 20
Cameron, Edna M. 1905-1999 3
Cameron, Eleanor (Frances)
    1912-1996 25
    Obituary 93
    Earlier sketch in SATA 1
    See also CLR 72
    See also SAAS 10
Cameron, Elizabeth
    See Nowell, Elizabeth Cameron
Cameron, Elizabeth Jane 1910-1976 32
    Obituary 30
Cameron, Ian
    See Payne, Donald Gordon
Cameron, M(alcolm) G(ordon) Graham
    See Graham-Cameron, M(alcolm) G(ordon)
Cameron, M. Graham
    See Graham-Cameron, M(alcolm) G(ordon)
Cameron, Mike Graham
    See Graham-Cameron, M(alcolm) G(ordon)
Cameron, Polly 1928- 2
Cameron, Scott 1962- 84
Camp, Lindsay 1957- 133
Camp, Walter (Chauncey) 1859-1925
    See YABC 1
Campbell, (Elizabeth) Andrea 1963- 50
Campbell, Ann R. 1925- 11
Campbell, Bill 1960- 89
Campbell, Bruce
    See Epstein, Samuel
Campbell, Camilla 1905-1992 26
Campbell, Carole R. 1939- 125
Campbell, Hope 1925- 20
Campbell, Hugh 1930- 90
Campbell, Jane
    See Edwards, Jane Campbell
Campbell, Julie
    See Tatham, Julie Campbell
Campbell, Patricia J(ean) 1930- 45
Campbell, Patty
    See Campbell, Patricia J(ean)

Campbell, Peter A. 1948- 99
Campbell, R. W.
    See Campbell, Rosemae Wells
Campbell, Robin
    See Strachan, Ian
Campbell, Rod 1945- 98
    Brief entry 44
    Earlier sketch in SATA 51
Campbell, Rosemae Wells 1909- 1
Campion, Nardi Reeder 1917- 22
Campling, Elizabeth 1948- 53
Camps, Luis 1928- 66
Canales, Viola 1957- 141
Canfield, Dorothea F.
    See Fisher, Dorothy (Frances) Canfield
Canfield, Dorothea Frances
    See Fisher, Dorothy (Frances) Canfield
Canfield, Dorothy
    See Fisher, Dorothy (Frances) Canfield
Canfield, Jane White 1897-1984 32
    Obituary 38
Canfield, Muriel 1935- 94
Cann, Helen 1969- 124
Cann, Kate 1954- 103
Cannan, Joanna 82
    See Pullein-Thompson, Joanna Maxwell
Cannon, A(nn) E(dwards) 93
Cannon, Bettie (Waddell) 1922- 59
Cannon, Curt
    See Hunter, Evan
Cannon, Eileen E(mily) 1948- 119
Cannon, Frank
    See Mayhar, Ardath
Cannon, Janell 1957- 128
    Earlier sketch in SATA 78
Cannon, Marian G. 1923- 85
Cannon, Taffy
    See Cannon, Eileen E(mily)
Canusi, Jose
    See Barker, S(quire) Omar
Canyon, Christopher 1966- 104
Capek, Michael 1947- 96
Capes, Bernard (Edward Joseph)
    1854-1918 116
Caplin, Alfred Gerald 1909-1979 61
    Obituary 21
    See Capp, Al
Caponigro, John Paul 1965- 84
Capote, Truman 1924-1984 91
Capp, Al 61
    See Caplin, Alfred Gerald
Cappel, Constance 1936- 22
Cappetta, Cynthia 1949- 125
Capps, Benjamin (Franklin) 1922- 9
Captain Kangaroo
    See Keeshan, Robert J.
Captain Wheeler
    See Ellis, Edward S(ylvester)
Captain Young of Yale
    See Stratemeyer, Edward L.
Capucilli, Alyssa Satin 1957- 115
Capucine
    See Mazille, Capucine
Caraher, Kim(berley Elizabeth)
    1961- 105
Caraker, Mary 1929- 74
Caras, Roger A(ndrew) 1928-2001 12
    Obituary 127
Caravantes, Peggy 1935- 140
Caraway, Caren 1939- 57
Carbone, Elisa
    See Carbone, Elisa Lynn
Carbone, Elisa Lynn 1954- 137
    Earlier sketch in SATA 81
Carbonnier, Jeanne 1894-1974 3
    Obituary 34
Card, Orson Scott 1951- 127
    Earlier sketch in SATA 83
Carew, Jan (Rynveld) 1925- 51
    Brief entry 40
Carey, Bonnie 1941-
    See Marshall, Bonnie C.

Carey, Ernestine Gilbreth 1908- 2
Carey, Lisa 110
Carey, M. V.
    See Carey, Mary V(irginia)
Carey, Mary V(irginia) 1925-1994 44
    Brief entry 39
Carey, Peter 1943- 94
Carey, Valerie Scho 1949- 60
Carigiet, Alois 1902-1985 24
    Obituary 47
    See also CLR 38
Carini, Edward 1923- 9
Carkeet, David 1946- 75
Carle, Eric 1929- 120
    Earlier sketches in SATA 4, 65
    See also CLR 72
    See also SAAS 6
Carleton, Captain L. C.
    See Ellis, Edward S(ylvester)
Carleton, Captain Latham C.
    See Ellis, Edward S(ylvester)
Carleton, Latham C.
    See Ellis, Edward S(ylvester)
Carling, Amelia Lau 1949- 119
Carlisle, Clark
    See Holding, James (Clark Carlisle, Jr.)
Carlisle, Olga Andreyev 1930- 35
Carlsen, G(eorge) Robert 1917- 30
Carlsen, Ruth C(hristoffer) 1918- 2
Carlson, Bernice Wells 1910- 8
Carlson, Dale (Bick) 1935- 1
Carlson, Daniel (Bick) 1960- 27
Carlson, Laurie (Winn) 1952- 101
Carlson, Melody 1956- 113
Carlson, Nancy L(ee) 1953- 90
    Brief entry 45
    Earlier sketch in SATA 56
Carlson, Natalie Savage 1906-1997 68
    Earlier sketch in SATA 2
    See also SAAS 4
Carlson, Susan Johnston 1953- 88
Carlson, Vada F. 1897- 16
Carlstrom, Nancy White 1948- 92
    Brief entry 48
    Earlier sketch in SATA 53
Carlton, Keith
    See Robertson, Keith (Carlton)
Carlyon, Richard 55
Carmer, Carl (Lamson) 1893-1976 37
    Obituary 30
Carmer, Elizabeth Black 1904- 24
Carmi, Giora 1944- 79
Carmichael, Carrie 40
    See Carmichael, Harriet
Carol, Bill J.
    See Knott, William C(ecil, Jr.)
Caron, Romi
    See Caron-Kyselkova', Romana
Caron-Kyselkova', Romana 1967- 94
Caroselli, Remus F(rancis) 1916- 36
Carpelan, Bo (Gustaf Bertelsson) 1926- 8
Carpenter, (John) Allan 1917- 81
    Earlier sketch in SATA 3
Carpenter, Angelica Shirley 1945- 71
Carpenter, Frances 1890-1972 3
    Obituary 27
Carpenter, John (Howard) 1948- 58
Carpenter, Johnny
    See Carpenter, John (Howard)
Carpenter, Patricia (Healy Evans)
    1920- 11
Carr, Glyn
    See Styles, (Frank) Showell
Carr, Harriett H(elen) 1899-1977 3
Carr, Jan 1953- 132
    Earlier sketch in SATA 89
Carr, M. J.
    See Carr, Jan
Carr, Mary Jane 1899-1988 2
    Obituary 55
Carr, Philippa
    See Hibbert, Eleanor Alice Burford

Carr, Roger Vaughan 1937- *95*
Carrel, Annette Felder 1929- *90*
Carrick, Carol (Hatfield) 1935- *118*
  Earlier sketches in SATA *7, 63*
  See also SAAS *18*
Carrick, Donald (F.) 1929-1989 ....*63*
  Earlier sketch in SATA *7*
Carrick, Malcolm 1945- *28*
Carrier, Lark 1947- *71*
  Brief entry *50*
Carrier, Roch 1937- *105*
Carrighar, Sally 1898-1985 ....*24*
Carrington, G. A.
  See Cunningham, Chet
Carrington, Marsha Gray 1954- *111*
Carris, Joan Davenport 1938- *44*
  Brief entry *42*
Carroll, Curt
  See Bishop, Curtis (Kent)
Carroll, Elizabeth
  See Barkin, Carol
  and James, Elizabeth
Carroll, Jenny
  See Cabot, Meg(gin)
Carroll, (Archer) Latrobe 1894-1996 ....*7*
Carroll, Laura
  See Parr, Lucy
Carroll, Lewis
  See CLR *18*
  See Dodgson, Charles L(utwidge)
Carroll, Raymond 1924- *86*
  Brief entry *47*
Carruth, Hayden 1921- *47*
Carryl, Charles E(dward)
  1841-1920 ....*114*
Carse, Robert 1902-1971 ....*5*
Carson, J(ohn) Franklin 1920-1981 ....*1*
  Obituary *107*
Carson, Rachel
  See Carson, Rachel Louise
Carson, Rachel Louise 1907-1964 ....*23*
  See Carson, Rachel
Carson, Rosalind
  See Chittenden, Margaret
Carson, S. M.
  See Gorsline, (Sally) Marie
Carter, Alden R(ichardson) 1947- *137*
  Earlier sketch in SATA *67*
  See also CLR *22*
  See also SAAS *18*
Carter, Andy 1948- *134*
Carter, Angela (Olive) 1940-1992 ....*66*
  Obituary *70*
Carter, Anne Laurel 1953- *135*
Carter, Asa Earl
  See Carter, Forrest
Carter, Avis Murton
  See Allen, Kenneth S.
Carter, Bruce
  See Hough, Richard (Alexander)
Carter, Carol S(hadis) 1948- *124*
Carter, David A. 1957- *114*
Carter, Don 1958- *124*
Carter, Dorothy Sharp 1921- *8*
Carter, Forrest 1927(?)-1979 ....*32*
Carter, Helene 1887-1960 ....*15*
Carter, (William) Hodding 1907-1972 ......*2*
  Obituary *27*
Carter, James Earl, Jr. 1924- *79*
Carter, Jimmy
  See Carter, James Earl, Jr.
Carter, Katharine J(ones) 1905-1984 ....*2*
Carter, Lin(wood Vrooman)
  1930-1988 ....*91*
Carter, Mike 1936- *138*

Carter, Nick
  See Avallone, Michael (Angelo, Jr.)
  and Ballard, (Willis) Todhunter
  and Crider, (Allen) Bill(y)
  and Cassiday, Bruce (Bingham)
  and Dey, Frederic (Merrill) Van
  Rensselaer
  and Garside, (Clifford) Jack
  and Hayes, Ralph E(ugene)
  and Henderson, M(arilyn) R(uth)
  and Lynds, Dennis
  and Lynds, Gayle (Hallenbeck)
  and Randisi, Robert J(oseph)
  and Rasof, Henry
  and Stratemeyer, Edward L.
  and Smith, Martin Cruz
  and Swain, Dwight V(reeland)
  and Vardeman, Robert E(dward)
  and Wallmann, Jeffrey M(iner)
  and White, Lionel
Carter, Peter 1929- *57*
Carter, Phyllis Ann
  See Eberle, Irmengarde
Carter, Samuel (Thomson) III
  1904-1988 ....*37*
  Obituary *60*
Carter, William E. 1926-1983 ....*1*
  Obituary *35*
Cartlidge, Michelle 1950- *96*
  Brief entry *37*
  Earlier sketch in SATA *49*
Cartner, William Carruthers 1910- *11*
Cartwright, Ann 1940- *78*
Cartwright, Reg(inald Ainsley) 1938- *64*
Cartwright, Sally 1923- *9*
Carusone, Al 1949- *89*
Carver, John
  See Gardner, Richard (M.)
Carwell, L'Ann
  See McKissack, Patricia (L'Ann) C(arwell)
Cary
  See Cary, Louis F(avreau)
Cary, Louis F(avreau) 1915- *9*
Caryl, Jean
  See Kaplan, Jean Caryl Korn
Casanova, Mary 1957- *136*
  Earlier sketch in SATA *94*
Cascone, A.G.
  See Cascone, Annette
  and Cascone, Gina
Cascone, Annette 1960- *103*
Cascone, Gina 1955- *103*
Case, Marshal T(aylor) 1941- *9*
Case, Michael
  See Howard, Robert West
Caseley, Judith 1951- *87*
  Brief entry *53*
Casewit, Curtis W(erner) 1922- *4*
Casey, Barbara 1944- *79*
Casey, Brigid 1950- *9*
Casey, Tina 1959- *141*
Casilla, Robert 1959- *75*
Cason, Mabel Earp 1892-1965 ....*10*
Cass, Joan E(velyn) *1*
Cass-Beggs, Barbara 1904- *62*
Cassedy, Sylvia 1930-1989 ....*77*
  Obituary *61*
  Earlier sketch in SATA *27*
  See also CLR *26*
Cassel, Lili
  See Wronker, Lili Cassel
Casson, Hugh Maxwell 1910-1999 ....*65*
  Obituary *115*
Cassutt, Michael (Joseph) 1954- *78*
Castaldo, Nancy Fusco 1962- *93*
Castaneda, Omar S. 1954- *71*
Castell, Megan
  See Williams, Jeanne
Castellanos, Jane Mollie Robinson
  1913- *9*
Castellon, Federico 1914-1971 ....*48*
Castillo, Edmund L. 1924- *1*

Castle, Lee
  See Ogan, George F.
  and Ogan, Margaret E. (Nettles)
Castle, Paul
  See Howard, Vernon (Linwood)
Castle, Robert
  See Hamilton, Edmond
Caswell, Brian 1954- *97*
Caswell, Helen (Rayburn) 1923- *12*
Catalano, Dominic 1956- *76*
Catalano, Grace (A.) 1961- *99*
Catalanotto, Peter 1959- *114*
  Autobiography Feature *113*
  Earlier sketch in SATA *70*
  See also CLR *68*
  See also SAAS *25*
Cate, Dick
  See Cate, Richard Edward Nelson
Cate, Richard Edward Nelson 1932- *28*
Cather, Willa (Sibert) 1873-1947 ....*30*
Catherall, Arthur 1906-1980 ....*74*
  Earlier sketch in SATA *3*
  See Ruthin, Margaret
Cathon, Laura E(lizabeth) 1908-1991 ......*27*
Catlett, Elizabeth 1919(?)- *82*
Catlin, Wynelle 1930- *13*
Cato, Heather *105*
Cato, Sheila *114*
Cattell, James 1954- *123*
Catton, (Charles) Bruce 1899-1978 ....*2*
  Obituary *24*
Catz, Max
  See Glaser, Milton
Caudell, Marian 1930- *52*
Caudill, Rebecca 1899-1985 ....*1*
  Obituary *44*
Cauley, Lorinda Bryan 1951- *46*
  Brief entry *43*
Cauman, Samuel 1910-1971 ....*48*
Causley, Charles (Stanley) 1917- *66*
  Earlier sketch in SATA *3*
  See also CLR *30*
Cavallaro, Ann (Abelson) 1918- *62*
Cavallo, Diana 1931- *7*
Cavanagh, Helen (Carol) 1939- *98*
  Brief entry *37*
  Earlier sketch in SATA *48*
Cavanah, Frances 1899-1982 ....*31*
  Earlier sketch in SATA *1*
Cavanna, Betty *30*
  Earlier sketch in SATA *1*
  See also SAAS *4*
  See Harrison, Elizabeth (Allen) Cavanna
Cave, Kathryn 1948- *123*
  Earlier sketch in SATA *76*
Cavendish, Peter
  See Horler, Sydney
Cavin, Ruth (Brodie) 1918- *38*
Cavoukian, Raffi 1948- *68*
Cawley, Winifred 1915- *13*
Caxton, Pisistratus
  See Lytton, Edward G(eorge) E(arle)
  L(ytton) Bulwer-Lytton Baron
Cazeau, Charles J(ay) 1931- *65*
Cazet, Denys 1938- *99*
  Brief entry *41*
  Earlier sketch in SATA *52*
Cazzola, Gus 1934- *73*
Cebulash, Mel 1937- *91*
  Earlier sketch in SATA *10*
Ceder, Georgiana Dorcas -1985 ....*10*
Celenza, Anna Harwell *133*
Celestino, Martha Laing 1951- *39*
Cerf, Bennett (Alfred) 1898-1971 ....*7*
Cerf, Christopher (Bennett) 1941- *2*
Cerullo, Mary M. 1949- *86*
Cervon, Jacqueline
  See Moussard, Jacqueline
Cetin, Frank Stanley 1921- *2*
Chadwick, Lester *67*
  Earlier sketch in SATA *1*
Chaffee, Allen *3*

Chaffin, Lillie D(orton) 1925- 4
Chaikin, Miriam 1928- 102
    Earlier sketch in SATA 24
Challand, Helen J(ean) 1921- 64
Challans, Mary 1905-1983 23
    Obituary 36
    See Renault, Mary
Chalmers, Mary (Eileen) 1927- 6
    See also SAAS 14
Chamberlain, Margaret 1954- 46
Chamberlin, Kate 1945- 105
Chambers, Aidan 1934- 108
    Earlier sketches in SATA 1, 69
    See also SAAS 12
Chambers, Catherine E.
    See St. John, Nicole
Chambers, John W. 1933- 57
    Brief entry 46
Chambers, Kate
    See St. John, Nicole
Chambers, Margaret Ada Eastwood
    1911- 2
Chambers, Peggy
    See Chambers, Margaret Ada Eastwood
Chambers, Robert W(illiam)
    1865-1933 107
Chan, Gillian 1954- 102
Chance, James T.
    See Carpenter, John (Howard)
Chance, John T.
    See Carpenter, John (Howard)
Chance, Stephen
    See Turner, Philip (William)
Chandler, Caroline A(ugusta)
    1906-1979 22
    Obituary 24
Chandler, David P(orter) 1933- 28
Chandler, Edna Walker 1908-1982 11
    Obituary 31
Chandler, Jennifer
    See Westwood, Jennifer
Chandler, Karen 1959- 122
Chandler, Linda S(mith) 1929- 39
Chandler, Robert 1953- 40
Chandler, Ruth Forbes 1894-1978 2
    Obituary 26
Chandonnet, Ann F. 1943- 92
Chaney, Jill 1932- 87
Chang, Chih-Wei 1966- 111
Chang, Cindy 1968- 90
Chang, Margaret (Scrogin) 1941- 71
Chang, Raymond 1939- 71
Chanin, Michael 1952- 84
Channel, A. R.
    See Catherall, Arthur
Chapian, Marie 1938- 29
Chapin, Tom 1945- 83
Chapman, Allen 67
    Earlier sketch in SATA 1
Chapman, Cheryl O(rth) 1948- 80
Chapman, (Constance) Elizabeth (Mann)
    1919- 10
Chapman, Gaynor 1935- 32
Chapman, Gillian 1955- 120
Chapman, Jane 1970- 122
Chapman, Jean 104
    Earlier sketch in SATA 34
    See also CLR 65
Chapman, Lee
    See Bradley, Marion Zimmer
Chapman, Lynne F(erguson) 1963- 94
Chapman, Vera (Ivy May)
    1898-1996 33
Chapman, Walker
    See Silverberg, Robert
Chappell, Audrey 1954- 72
Chappell, Warren 1904-1991 68
    Obituary 67
    Earlier sketch in SATA 6
    See also SAAS 10
Charbonneau, Eileen 1951- 118
    Earlier sketch in SATA 84

Charbonnet, Gabrielle 1961- 81
Chardiet, Bernice (Kroll) 1927(?)- 27
Charles, Donald
    See Meighan, Donald Charles
Charles, Louis
    See Stratemeyer, Edward L.
Charles, Nicholas J.
    See Kuskin, Karla (Seidman)
Charlip, Remy 1929- 119
    Earlier sketches in SATA 4, 68
    See also CLR 8
Charlot, Jean 1898-1979 8
    Obituary 31
Charlot, Martin (Day) 1944- 64
Charlton, Michael (Alan) 1923- 34
Charmatz, Bill 1925- 7
Charnas, Suzy McKee 1939- 110
    Earlier sketch in SATA 61
Charosh, Mannis 1906- 5
Chartier, Normand L. 1945- 66
Chase, Alice
    See McHargue, Georgess
Chase, Alyssa 1965- 92
Chase, Andra 1942- 91
Chase, Emily
    See Aks, Patricia
    and Garwood, Julie
    and Sachs, Judith
    and White, Carol
Chase, Mary (Coyle) 1907-1981 17
    Obituary 29
Chase, Mary Ellen 1887-1973 10
Chase, Richard 1904-1988 64
    Obituary 56
Chase, Samantha
    See Glick, Ruth (Burtnick)
Chast, Roz 1954- 97
Chastain, Madye Lee 1908-1989 4
Chataway, Carol 1955- 140
Chatterjee, Debjani 1952- 83
Chauncy, Nan(cen Beryl Masterman)
    1900-1970 6
    See also CLR 6
Chaundler, Christine 1887-1972 1
    Obituary 25
Chee, Cheng-Khee 1934- 79
Cheese, Chloe 1952- 118
Chekhonte, Antosha
    See Chekhov, Anton (Pavlovich)
Chekhov, Anton (Pavlovich)
    1860-1904 90
Chen, Anthony 1929- 6
Chen, Ju-Hong 1941- 78
Chen, Sara
    See Odgers, Sally Farrell
Chen, Tony
    See Chen, Anthony
Chen, Yuan-tsung 1932- 65
Chenault, Nell
    See Smith, Linell Nash
Chenery, Janet (Dai) 1923- 25
Cheney, Cora 1916-1999 3
    Obituary 110
Cheney, Glenn (Alan) 1951- 99
Cheney, Ted
    See Cheney, Theodore Albert
Cheney, Theodore A. Rees
    See Cheney, Theodore Albert
Cheney, Theodore Albert 1928- 11
Cheng, Andrea 1957- 128
Cheng, Christopher 1959- 106
Cheng, Judith 1955- 36
Cheng, Shan
    See Jiang, Cheng An
Cheripko, Jan 1951- 83
Chermayeff, Ivan 1932- 47
Chernoff, Dorothy A.
    See Ernst, (Lyman) John
Chernoff, Goldie Taub 1909- 10
Cherry, Lynne 1952- 99
    Earlier sketch in SATA 34

Cherryh, C. J. 93
    See Cherry, Carolyn Janice
Cherryholmes, Anne
    See Price, Olive
Chesler, Bernice 1932-2002 59
Chess, Victoria (Dickerson) 1939- 92
    Earlier sketch in SATA 33
Chester, Deborah 1957- 85
Chester, Kate
    See Guccione, Leslie Davis
Chesterton, G(ilbert) K(eith)
    1874-1936 27
Chetin, Helen 1922- 6
Chetwin, Grace 86
    Brief entry 50
Chevalier, Christa 1937- 35
Chevalier, Tracy 1964- 128
Chew, Ruth 1920- 7
Chichester Clark, Emma 1955- 117
    See Clark, Emma Chichester
Chidsey, Donald Barr 1902-1981 3
    Obituary 27
Chiefari, Janet D. 1942- 58
Chien-min, Lin
    See Rumford, James
Child, L. Maria
    See Child, Lydia Maria
Child, Lauren 1965- 119
Child, Lincoln B. 1957- 113
Child, Lydia Maria 1802-1880 67
Child, Mrs.
    See Child, Lydia Maria
Child, Philip 1898-1978 47
Children's Shepherd, The
    See Westphal, Arnold Carl
Childress, Alice 1920-1994 81
    Earlier sketches in SATA 7, 48
    See also CLR 14
Childs, H(alla) Fay (Cochrane)
    1890-1971 1
    Obituary 25
Chilton, Charles (Frederick William)
    1917- 102
Chimaera
    See Farjeon, Eleanor
Chin, Richard (M.) 1946- 52
Chinery, Michael 1938- 26
Chin-Lee, Cynthia D. 1958- 102
Chipperfield, Joseph Eugene
    1912-1980(?) 87
    Earlier sketch in SATA 2
Chislett, Gail (Elaine) 1948- 58
Chittenden, Elizabeth F. 1903-1999 9
Chittenden, Margaret 1935- 28
Chittum, Ida 1918- 7
Chmielarz, Sharon Lee 1940- 72
Choate, Judith (Newkirk) 1940- 30
Chocolate, Debbi 1954- 96
Chocolate, Deborah M. Newton
    See Chocolate, Debbi
Choi, Sook Nyul 1937- 73
    Autobiography Feature 126
    See also CLR 53
Choldenko, Gennifer 1957- 135
Chorao, (Ann Mc)Kay (Sproat)
    1936- 69
    Earlier sketch in SATA 8
Chown, Marcus 1959- 137
Choyce, Lesley 1951- 94
Chrisman, Arthur Bowie 1889-1953 124
    See also YABC 1
Christelow, Eileen 1943- 90
    Autobiography Feature 120
    Brief entry 35
    Earlier sketch in SATA 38
Christensen, Bonnie 1951- 110
Christensen, Gardell Dano 1907-1991 1
Christensen, Laurie
    See Steding, Laurie
Christesen, Barbara 1940- 40
Christgau, Alice Erickson 1902-1977 13
Christian, Mary Blount 1933- 9

Christie, Agatha (Mary Clarissa)
1890-1976 36
Christie, Gregory
See Christie, R. Gregory
Christie, Philippa 129
Earlier sketches in SATA *1, 67*
See also CLR *9*
See Pearce, Philippa
Christie, R. Gregory 1971- 127
Christopher, John
See CLR *2*
See Youd, (Christopher) Samuel
Christopher, Louise
See Hale, Arlene
Christopher, Matt(hew Frederick)
1917-1997 80
Obituary 99
Earlier sketches in SATA *2, 47*
See also CLR *33*
See also SAAS *9*
Christopher, Milbourne 1914(?)-1984 46
Christy, Howard Chandler
1873-1952 21
Chrystie, Frances N(icholson)
1904-1986 60
Chu, Daniel 1933- 11
Chukovsky, Kornei (Ivanovich)
1882-1969 34
Earlier sketch in SATA *5*
Church, Richard 1893-1972 3
Churchill, E(lmer) Richard 1937- 11
Churchill, Elizabeth
See Hough, Richard (Alexander)
Chute, B(eatrice) J(oy) 1913-1987 2
Obituary 53
Chute, Marchette (Gaylord)
1909-1994 1
Chwast, Jacqueline 1932- 6
Chwast, Seymour 1931- 96
Earlier sketch in SATA *18*
Ciardi, John (Anthony) 1916-1986 65
Obituary 46
Earlier sketch in SATA *1*
See also CLR *19*
See also SAAS *26*
Ciment, James D. 1958- 140
Citra, Becky 1954- 137
Clair, Andree 19
Clampett, Robert 44
See Clampett, Bob
Clapp, John 1968- 109
Clapp, Patricia 1912- 74
Earlier sketch in SATA *4*
See also SAAS *4*
Clare, Ellen
See Sinclair, Olga
Clare, Helen
See Clarke, Pauline
Claremont, Chris(topher Simon)
1950- 87
Clark, Ann Nolan 1896-1995 82
Obituary 87
Earlier sketch in SATA *4*
See also CLR *16*
See also SAAS *16*
Clark, Champ 1923- 47
Clark, Christopher (Anthony) Stuart
See Stuart-Clark, Christopher (Anthony)
Clark, Clara Gillow 1951- 84
Clark, David
See Hardcastle, Michael
Clark, David Allen
See Ernst, (Lyman) John
Clark, Emma Chichester 69
See Chichester Clark, Emma
Clark, Frank J(ames) 1922- 18
Clark, Garel
See Garelick, May
Clark, Halsey
See Deming, Richard
Clark, Joan
See Benson, Mildred (Augustine Wirt)

Clark, Joan 1934- 96
Earlier sketch in SATA *59*
Clark, Leonard 1905-1981 30
Obituary 29
Clark, M. R.
See Clark, Mavis Thorpe
Clark, Margaret (D.) 1943- 126
Clark, Margaret Goff 1913- 82
Earlier sketch in SATA *8*
Clark, Mary Higgins 1929- 46
Clark, Mavis Thorpe 1909-1999 74
Earlier sketch in SATA *8*
See also CLR *30*
See also SAAS *5*
Clark, Merle
See Gessner, Lynne
Clark, Patricia Denise 1921- 117
See Lorrimer, Claire
Clark, Patricia Finrow 1929- 11
Clark, Ronald William 1916-1987 2
Obituary 52
Clark, Van D(eusen) 1909-1974 2
Clark, Virginia
See Gray, Patricia (Clark)
Clark, Walter Van Tilburg 1909-1971 8
Clarke, Arthur C(harles) 1917- 115
Earlier sketches in SATA *13, 70*
Clarke, Clorinda 1917- 7
Clarke, Gus 1948- 134
Clarke, J.
See Clarke, Judith
Clarke, James Hall
See Rowland-Entwistle, (Arthur) Theodore
(Henry)
Clarke, Joan B. 1921- 42
Brief entry 27
Clarke, John
See Laklan, Carli
and Sontup, Dan(iel)
Clarke, Judith 1943- 110
Earlier sketch in SATA *75*
See also CLR *61*
Clarke, Julia 1950- 138
Clarke, Kenneth 1957- 107
Clarke, Lea
See Rowland-Entwistle, (Arthur) Theodore
(Henry)
Clarke, Mary Stetson 1911-1994 5
Clarke, Michael
See Newlon, (Frank) Clarke
Clarke, Pauline 1921- 131
See also CLR *28*
See Blair, Pauline Hunter
and Clare, Helen
Clarke-Rich, Elizabeth L. 1934- 103
Clarkson, E(dith) Margaret 1915- 37
Clarkson, Ewan 1929- 9
Claverie, Jean 1946- 38
Clay, Patrice 1947- 47
Claypool, Jane 103
See Miner, Jane Claypool
Clayton, Elaine 1961- 94
Clayton, Lawrence (Otto, Jr.) 1945- 75
Clayton, Sandra 1951- 110
Cleary, Beverly (Atlee Bunn)
1916- 121
Earlier sketches in SATA *2, 43, 79*
See also CLR *72*
See also SAAS *20*
Cleary, Brian P. 1959- 132
Earlier sketch in SATA *93*
Cleaver, Bill 22
Obituary 27
See also CLR *6*
See Cleaver, William J(oseph)
Cleaver, Carole 1934- 6
Cleaver, Elizabeth (Ann Mrazik)
1939-1985 23
Obituary 43
See also CLR *13*
Cleaver, Hylton Reginald 1891-1961 49

Cleaver, Vera (Allen) 1919-1993 76
Earlier sketch in SATA *22*
See also CLR *6*
Cleishbotham, Jebediah
See Scott, Sir Walter
Cleland, Mabel
See Widdemer, Mabel Cleland
Clem, Margaret H(ollingsworth)
1923- 90
Clemens, Samuel Langhorne
1835-1910 100
See also YABC *2*
See Twain, Mark
Clemens, Virginia Phelps 1941- 35
Clement, Rod 97
Clements, Andrew 1949- 104
Clements, Bruce 1931- 94
Earlier sketch in SATA *27*
Clemons, Elizabeth
See Nowell, Elizabeth Cameron
Clerk, N. W.
See Lewis, C(live) S(taples)
Cleveland-Peck, Patricia 80
Cleven, Cathrine
See Cleven, Kathryn Seward
Cleven, Kathryn Seward 2
Clevenger, William R(ussell) 1954- 84
Clevin, Joergen 1920- 7
Clevin, Jorgen
See Clevin, Joergen
Clewes, Dorothy (Mary) 1907-2003 86
Obituary 138
Earlier sketch in SATA *1*
Clifford, David
See Rosenberg, Eth(el) Clifford
Clifford, Eth 92
See also SAAS *22*
See Rosenberg, Eth(el) Clifford
Clifford, Harold B(urton) 1893-1988 10
Clifford, Margaret Cort 1929- 1
Clifford, Martin
See Hamilton, Charles (Harold St. John)
Clifford, Mary Louise Beneway
1926- 23
Clifford, Peggy
See Clifford, Margaret Cort
Clifford, Rachel Mark
See Lewis, Brenda Ralph
Clifton, (Thelma) Lucille 1936- 128
Earlier sketches in SATA *20, 69*
See also CLR *5*
Climo, Shirley 1928- 77
Autobiography Feature 110
Brief entry 35
Earlier sketch in SATA *39*
See also CLR *69*
Clinton, Cathryn
See Hoellwarth, Cathryn Clinton
Clinton, Dirk
See Silverberg, Robert
Clinton, Jon
See Prince, J(ack) H(arvey)
Clish, (Lee) Marian 1946- 43
Clive, Clifford
See Hamilton, Charles (Harold St. John)
Clokey, Art 1921- 59
Cloudsley-Thompson, J(ohn) L(eonard)
1921- 19
Clouse, Nancy L. 1938- 78
Clutha, Janet Paterson Frame 1924- 119
See Frame, Janet
Clymer, Eleanor 1906-2001 85
Obituary 126
Earlier sketch in SATA *9*
See also SAAS *17*
Clyne, Patricia (Edwards) 31
Coalson, Glo 1946- 94
Earlier sketch in SATA *26*
Coates, Anna 1958- 73
Coates, Belle 1896-1986 2
Coates, Ruth Allison 1915- 11
Coats, Alice M(argaret) 1905-1976 11

Coatsworth, Elizabeth (Jane)
　1893-1986 ....*100*
　Obituary *49*
　Earlier sketches in SATA *2, 56*
　See also CLR *2*
Cobalt, Martin
　See Mayne, William (James Carter)
Cobb, Mary 1931- *88*
Cobb, Vicki 1938- *136*
　Earlier sketches in SATA *8, 69, 131*
　See also CLR *2*
　See also SAAS *6*
Cobbett, Richard
　See Pluckrose, Henry (Arthur)
Cober, Alan E(dwin) 1935-1998 ....*7*
　Obituary *101*
Cobham, Sir Alan
　See Hamilton, Charles (Harold St. John)
Cocagnac, Augustin Maurice(-Jean)
　1924- *7*
Cocca-Leffler, Maryann 1958- *136*
　Earlier sketch in SATA *80*
Cochran, Bobbye A. 1949- *11*
Cockett, Mary *3*
Cody, C. S.
　See Waller, Leslie
Cody, Jess
　See Cunningham, Chet
Coe, Anne (E.) 1949- *95*
Coe, Douglas
　See Epstein, Beryl (M. Williams)
　and Epstein, Samuel
Coen, Rena Neumann 1925- *20*
Coerr, Eleanor (Beatrice) 1922- *67*
　Earlier sketch in SATA *1*
Cofer, Judith Ortiz 1952- *110*
　See Ortiz Cofer, Judith
Coffey, Brian
　See Koontz, Dean R(ay)
Coffin, Geoffrey
　See Mason, F(rancis) van Wyck
Coffin, M. T.
　See Stanley, George Edward
Coffman, Ramon Peyton 1896-1989 ....*4*
Cogan, Karen 1954- *125*
Coggins, Jack (Banham) 1914- *2*
Cohen, Barbara 1932-1992 ....*77*
　Obituary *74*
　Earlier sketch in SATA *10*
　See also SAAS *7*
Cohen, Daniel (E.) 1936- *70*
　Earlier sketch in SATA *8*
　See also CLR *43*
　See also SAAS *4*
Cohen, Jene Barr
　See Barr, Jene
Cohen, Joan Lebold 1932- *4*
Cohen, Judith Love 1933- *78*
Cohen, Miriam 1926- *106*
　Earlier sketch in SATA *29*
　See also SAAS *11*
Cohen, Nora *75*
Cohen, Paul S. 1945- *58*
Cohen, Peter Zachary 1931- *4*
Cohen, Robert Carl 1930- *8*
Cohen, Sholom 1951- *94*
Cohn, Angelo 1914- *19*
Coit, Margaret Louise 1919- *2*
Colbert, Anthony 1934- *15*
Colbert, Nancy A. 1936- *139*
Colby, C(arroll) B(urleigh)
　1904-1977 ....*35*
　Earlier sketch in SATA *3*
Colby, Jean Poindexter 1909-1993 ....*23*
Cole, Annette
　See Steiner, Barbara A(nnette)
Cole, Babette 1949- *96*
　Earlier sketch in SATA *61*
Cole, Betsy 1940- *83*
Cole, Brock 1938- *136*
　Earlier sketch in SATA *72*
　See also CLR *18*

Cole, Davis
　See Elting, Mary
Cole, Hannah 1954- *74*
Cole, Jack -1974
　See Stewart, John (William)
Cole, Jackson
　See Germano, Peter B.
　and Schisgall, Oscar
Cole, Jennifer
　See Zach, Cheryl (Byrd)
Cole, Joanna 1944- *120*
　Brief entry *37*
　Earlier sketches in SATA *49, 81*
　See also CLR *40*
Cole, Lois Dwight 1903-1979 ....*10*
　Obituary *26*
Cole, Michael 1947- *59*
Cole, Sheila R(otenberg) 1939- *95*
　Earlier sketch in SATA *24*
Cole, William (Rossa) 1919-2000 ....*71*
　Earlier sketch in SATA *9*
　See also SAAS *9*
Coleman, Andrew
　See Pine, Nicholas
Coleman, Clare
　See Bell, Clare (Louise)
Coleman, Mary Ann 1928- *83*
Coleman, Michael (Lee) 1946- *108*
　Autobiography Feature *133*
Coleman, William L(eRoy) 1938- *49*
　Brief entry *34*
Coles, Robert (Martin) 1929- *23*
Colin, Ann
　See Ure, Jean
Collard, Sneed B. III 1959- *139*
　Earlier sketches in SATA *84, 136*
Collicott, Sharleen 1937- *98*
Collier, Bryan *126*
Collier, Christopher 1930- *70*
　Earlier sketch in SATA *16*
Collier, Ethel 1903-1999 ....*22*
Collier, James Lincoln 1928- *70*
　Earlier sketch in SATA *8*
　See also CLR *3*
　See also SAAS *21*
Collier, Jane
　See Collier, Zena
Collier, Steven 1942- *61*
Collier, Zena 1926- *23*
　See Collier, Jane
Collings, Gillian 1939- *102*
Collington, Peter 1948- *99*
　Earlier sketch in SATA *59*
Collins, Ace 1953- *82*
Collins, Andrew J.
　See Collins, Ace
Collins, David R(aymond) 1940- *121*
　Earlier sketch in SATA *7*
Collins, Heather 1946- *81*
Collins, Hunt
　See Hunter, Evan
Collins, Michael
　See Lynds, Dennis
Collins, Michael 1930- *58*
Collins, Pat(ricia) Lowery 1932- *31*
Collins, Paul 1936- *126*
Collinson, A. S.
　See Collinson, Alan S.
Collinson, Alan S. 1934- *80*
Collinson, Roger (Alfred) 1936- *133*
Collodi, Carlo
　See CLR *5*
　See Lorenzini, Carlo
Colloms, Brenda 1919- *40*
Colman, Hila *53*
　Earlier sketch in SATA *1*
　See also SAAS *14*
Colman, Penny (Morgan) 1944- *114*
　Earlier sketch in SATA *77*
Colman, Warren (David) 1944- *67*
Colombo, John Robert 1936- *50*
Colonius, Lillian 1911-1992 ....*3*

Colorado, Antonio J.
　See Colorado (Capella), Antonio J(ulio)
Colorado (Capella), Antonio J(ulio)
　1903-1994 ....*23*
　Obituary *79*
Colt, Martin
　See Epstein, Beryl (M. Williams)
　and Epstein, Samuel
Colum, Padraic 1881-1972 ....*15*
　See also CLR *36*
Columbus, Chris(topher) 1959- *97*
Columella
　See Moore, Clement Clarke
Colver, Anne 1908- *7*
Colvin, James
　See Moorcock, Michael (John)
Colwell, Eileen (Hilda) 1904-2002 ....*2*
Coman, Carolyn *127*
Combs, Lisa M.
　See McCourt, Lisa
Combs, Robert
　See Murray, John
Comfort, Jane Levington
　See Sturtzel, Jane Levington
Comfort, Mildred Houghton
　1886-1976 ....*3*
Comins, Ethel M(ae) *11*
Comins, Jeremy 1933- *28*
Commager, Henry Steele 1902-1998 ....*23*
　Obituary *102*
Compere, Mickie
　See Davidson, Margaret
Compestine, Ying Chang 1963- *140*
Compton, Patricia A. 1936- *75*
Comte, The Great
　See Hawkesworth, Eric
Comus
　See Ballantyne, R(obert) M(ichael)
Comyns, Nance
　See Comyns-Toohey, Nantz
Comyns-Toohey, Nantz 1956- *86*
Conan Doyle, Arthur
　See Doyle, Sir Arthur Conan
Condit, Martha Olson 1913- *28*
Condon, Judith *83*
Condy, Roy 1942- *96*
Cone, Ferne Geller 1921- *39*
Cone, Molly (Lamken) 1918- *115*
　Earlier sketches in SATA *1, 28*
　See also SAAS *11*
Cone, Patrick 1954- *89*
Coney, Michael G(reatrex) 1932- *61*
Coney, Michael Greatrex
　See Coney, Michael G(reatrex)
Coney, Mike
　See Coney, Michael G(reatrex)
Conford, Ellen 1942- *110*
　Earlier sketches in SATA *6, 68*
　See also CLR *71*
Conger, Lesley
　See Suttles, Shirley (Smith)
Conklin, Gladys Plemon 1903- *2*
Conklin, Paul *43*
　Brief entry *33*
Conkling, Hilda 1910- *23*
Conley-Weaver, Robyn 1963- *125*
Conlon-McKenna, Marita 1956- *71*
Conly, Jane Leslie 1948- *112*
　Earlier sketch in SATA *80*
Conly, Robert Leslie 1918(?)-1973 ....*23*
　See O'Brien, Robert C.
Connolly, Jerome P(atrick) 1931- *8*
Connolly, Pat 1943- *74*
Connolly, Peter 1935- *105*
　Earlier sketch in SATA *47*
Conover, Chris 1950- *31*
Conquest, Owen
　See Hamilton, Charles (Harold St. John)
Conrad, Joseph 1857-1924 ....*27*

Conrad, Pam 1947-1996 ....*133*
    Brief entry *49*
    Obituary *90*
    Earlier sketches in SATA *52, 80*
    See also CLR *18*
    See also SAAS *19*
Conroy, Jack *19*
    See Conroy, John Wesley
Conroy, Robert
    See Goldston, Robert (Conroy)
Constant, Alberta Wilson 1908-1981 ......*22*
    Obituary *28*
Conway, Diana C(ohen) 1943- *91*
Conway, Gordon
    See Hamilton, Charles (Harold St. John)
Cook, Bernadine 1924- *11*
Cook, Fred J(ames) 1911- *2*
Cook, Glen (Charles) 1944- *108*
Cook, Hugh (Walter Gilbert) 1956- *85*
Cook, Jean Thor 1930- *94*
Cook, Joel 1934- *79*
Cook, Joseph Jay 1924- *8*
Cook, Lyn
    See Waddell, Evelyn Margaret
Cook, Roy
    See Silverberg, Robert
Cooke, Ann
    See Cole, Joanna
Cooke, Arthur
    See Lowndes, Robert A(ugustine) W(ard)
Cooke, Barbara
    See Alexander, Anna B(arbara Cooke)
Cooke, David Coxe 1917- *2*
Cooke, Donald Ewin 1916-1985 ....*2*
    Obituary *45*
Cooke, Frank E. 1920- *87*
Cooke, Jean (Isobel Esther) 1929- *74*
Cooke, John Estes
    See Baum, L(yman) Frank
Cooke, Trish 1962- *129*
Cookson, Catherine (McMullen)
    1906-1998 ....*9*
    Obituary *116*
Coolidge, Olivia E(nsor) 1908- *26*
    Earlier sketch in SATA *1*
Cooling, Wendy *111*
Coombs, Charles I(ra) 1914-1994 ....*43*
    Earlier sketch in SATA *3*
    See also SAAS *15*
Coombs, Chick
    See Coombs, Charles I(ra)
Coombs, Patricia 1926- *51*
    Earlier sketch in SATA *3*
    See also SAAS *22*
Cooney, Barbara 1917-2000 ....*96*
    Obituary *123*
    Earlier sketches in SATA *6, 59*
    See also CLR *23*
Cooney, Caroline B. 1947- *130*
    Brief entry *41*
    Earlier sketches in SATA *48, 80, 113*
Cooney, Nancy Evans 1932- *42*
Coontz, Otto 1946- *33*
Cooper, Ann (Catharine) 1939- *104*
Cooper, Elisha 1971- *99*
Cooper, Elizabeth Keyser -1992 ....*47*
Cooper, Floyd *96*
    See also CLR *60*
Cooper, Gordon 1932- *23*
Cooper, Helen 1932- *102*
Cooper, Henry S(potswood) F(enimore), Jr.
    1933- *65*
Cooper, Ilene *97*
    Earlier sketch in SATA *66*
Cooper, James Fenimore 1789-1851 ....*19*
Cooper, John R. *1*
Cooper, Kay 1941- *11*
Cooper, Lee Pelham 1926- *5*
Cooper, Lester (Irving) 1919-1985 ....*32*
    Obituary *43*
Cooper, Lettice (Ulpha) 1897-1994 ....*35*
    Obituary *82*

Cooper, M. E.
    See Lerangis, Peter
Cooper, Melrose
    See Kroll, Virginia L(ouise)
Cooper, Michael L. 1950- *117*
    Earlier sketch in SATA *79*
Cooper, Patrick 1949- *134*
Cooper, Susan (Mary) 1935- *104*
    Earlier sketches in SATA *4, 64*
    See also CLR *67*
    See also SAAS *6*
Cope, Jane U(rsula) 1949- *108*
Copeland, Helen 1920- *4*
Copeland, Paul W. *23*
Coplans, Peta 1951- *84*
Copley (Diana) Heather Pickering
    1918- *45*
Coppard, A(lfred) E(dgar) 1878-1957
    See YABC *1*
Coralie
    See Anderson, Catherine Corley
Corbett, Grahame *43*
    Brief entry *36*
Corbett, Scott 1913- *42*
    Earlier sketch in SATA *2*
    See also CLR *1*
    See also SAAS *2*
Corbett, W(illiam) J(esse) 1938- *102*
    Brief entry *44*
    Earlier sketch in SATA *50*
    See also CLR *19*
Corbin, Sabra Lee
    See Malvern, Gladys
Corbin, William
    See McGraw, William Corbin
Corby, Dan
    See Catherall, Arthur
Corcoran, Barbara (Asenath) 1911- *125*
    Earlier sketches in SATA *3, 77*
    See also CLR *50*
    See also SAAS *20*
Corcos, Lucille 1908-1973 ....*10*
Cordell, Alexander
    See Graber, Alexander
Cordell, Alexander
    See Graber, (George) Alexander
Corella, Joseph
    See Odgers, Sally Farrell
Coren, Alan 1938- *32*
Corey, Dorothy *23*
Corey, Shana 1974- *133*
Corfe, Thomas Howell 1928- *27*
Corfe, Tom
    See Corfe, Thomas Howell
Corfield, Robin Bell 1952- *74*
Corlett, William 1938- *46*
    Brief entry *39*
Cormack, M(argaret) Grant 1913- *11*
Cormack, Maribelle B. 1902-1984 ....*39*
Cormier, Robert (Edmund)
    1925-2000 ....*83*
    Obituary *122*
    Earlier sketches in SATA *10, 45*
    See also CLR *55*
Cornelius, Carol 1942- *40*
Cornell, J.
    See Cornell, Jeffrey
Cornell, James (Clayton, Jr.) 1938- *27*
Cornell, Jean Gay 1920- *23*
Cornell, Jeffrey 1945- *11*
Cornish, Sam(uel James) 1935- *23*
Cornwall, Nellie
    See Sloggett, Nellie
Correy, Lee
    See Stine, G(eorge) Harry
Corrick, James A. 1945- *76*
Corrigan, (Helen) Adeline 1909- *23*
Corrigan, Barbara 1922- *8*
Corrin, Sara 1918- *86*
    Brief entry *48*
Corrin, Stephen *86*
    Brief entry *48*

Cort, M. C.
    See Clifford, Margaret Cort
Cort, Margaret
    See Clifford, Margaret Cort
Corwin, Judith H(offman) 1946- *10*
Cory, Rowena
    See Lindquist, Rowena Cory
Cosby, Bill
    See Cosby, William Henry, Jr.
Cosby, William Henry, Jr. 1937- *110*
    Earlier sketch in SATA *66*
    See Cosby, Bill
Cosgrove, Margaret (Leota) 1926- *47*
Cosgrove, Stephen E(dward) 1945- *53*
    Brief entry *40*
Coskey, Evelyn 1932- *7*
Cosner, Shaaron 1940- *43*
Cossi, Olga 1921- *102*
    Earlier sketch in SATA *67*
Costabel, Eva Deutsch 1924- *45*
Costabel-Deutsch, Eva
    See Costabel, Eva Deutsch
Costello, David F(rancis) 1904-1990 ....*23*
Cott, Jonathan 1942- *23*
Cottam, Clarence 1899-1974 ....*25*
Cottle, Joan 1960- *135*
Cottler, Joseph 1899-1996 ....*22*
Cottonwood, Joe 1947- *92*
Cottrell, Leonard 1913-1974 ....*24*
Cottringer, Anne 1952- *97*
Counsel, June 1926- *70*
Countryman, The
    See Whitlock, Ralph
Courlander, Harold 1908-1996 ....*6*
    Obituary *88*
Coursen, Valerie 1965(?)- *102*
Courtney, Dayle
    See Goldsmith, Howard
Cousins, Linda 1946- *90*
Cousins, Margaret 1905-1996 ....*2*
    Obituary *92*
Cousteau, Jacques-Yves 1910-1997 ....*98*
    Earlier sketch in SATA *38*
Couture, Christin 1951- *73*
Coville, Bruce 1950- *118*
    Earlier sketches in SATA *32, 77*
Covington, Dennis *109*
Covington, Linda
    See Windsor, Linda
Cowan, Catherine *121*
Cowell, Cressida 1966- *140*
Cowen, Eve
    See Werner, Herma
Cowen, Ida 1898-1993 ....*64*
Cowie, Leonard W(allace) 1919- *4*
Cowles, Kathleen
    See Krull, Kathleen
Cowley, (Cassia) Joy 1936- *90*
    Autobiography Feature *118*
    Earlier sketch in SATA *4*
    See also CLR *55*
    See also SAAS *26*
Cowley, Marjorie 1925- *111*
Cox, (Christopher) Barry 1931- *62*
Cox, Clinton 1934- *108*
    Earlier sketch in SATA *74*
Cox, David (Dundas) 1933- *56*
Cox, Donald William 1921- *23*
Cox, Jack
    See Cox, John Roberts
Cox, John Roberts 1915-1981 ....*9*
Cox, Judy 1954- *117*
Cox, Palmer 1840-1924 ....*24*
    See also CLR *24*
Cox, Vic 1942- *88*
Cox, Victoria
    See Garretson, Victoria Diane
Cox, Wally *25*
    See Cox, Wallace (Maynard)

Cox, William R(obert) 1901-1988 ....*46*
    Brief entry *31*
    Obituary *57*
    See Ward, Jonas
Coxe, Molly 1959- *101*
    Earlier sketch in SATA *69*
Coxon, Michele 1950- *76*
Coy, Harold 1902-1986 ....*3*
Coy, John 1958- *120*
Craats, Rennay 1973- *131*
Crabtree, Judith 1928- *98*
    Earlier sketch in SATA *63*
Cracker, Edward E.B.
    See Odgers, Sally Farrell
Craft, K. Y.
    See Craft, Kinuko Y(amabe)
Craft, Kinuko
    See Craft, Kinuko Y(amabe)
Craft, Kinuko Y(amabe) 1940- *127*
    Earlier sketch in SATA *65*
Craft, Ruth 1935- *87*
    Brief entry *31*
Craig, A. A.
    See Anderson, Poul (William)
Craig, Alisa
    See MacLeod, Charlotte (Matilda)
Craig, Helen 1934- *94*
    Earlier sketches in SATA *46, 49*
Craig, John Eland
    See Chipperfield, Joseph Eugene
Craig, John Ernest 1921- *23*
Craig, Kit
    See Reed, Kit
Craig, M. F.
    See Craig, Mary (Francis) Shura
Craig, M. Jean *17*
Craig, M. S.
    See Craig, Mary (Francis) Shura
Craig, Margaret (Maze) 1911-1964 ....*9*
Craig, Mary
    See Craig, Mary (Francis) Shura
Craig, Mary Shura
    See Craig, Mary (Francis) Shura
Craig, Mary (Francis) Shura
    1923-1991 ....*86*
    Obituary *65*
    Earlier sketch in SATA *6*
    See also SAAS *7*
Craig, Ruth 1922- *95*
Craik, Mrs.
    See Craik, Dinah Maria (Mulock)
Craik, Dinah Maria (Mulock)
    1826-1887 ....*34*
    See Craik, Mrs.
    and Mulock, Dinah Maria
Crane, Barbara (Joyce) 1934- *31*
Crane, Caroline 1930- *11*
Crane, M. A.
    See Wartski, Maureen (Ann Crane)
Crane, Stephen (Townley) 1871-1900
    See YABC *2*
Crane, Walter 1845-1915 ....*100*
    Earlier sketch in SATA *18*
    See also CLR *56*
Crane, William D(wight) 1892-1976 ....*1*
Cranfield, Ingrid 1945- *74*
Cranshaw, Stanley
    See Fisher, Dorothy (Frances) Canfield
Crary, Elizabeth (Ann) 1942- *99*
    Brief entry *43*
Crary, Margaret (Coleman) 1906-1986 .....*9*
Cravath, Lynne W. 1951- *98*
Craven, Thomas 1889-1969 ....*22*
Crawford, Charles P. 1945- *28*
Crawford, Deborah 1922- *6*
Crawford, John E(dmund) 1904-1971 ......*3*
Crawford, Mel 1925- *44*
    Brief entry *33*
Crawford, Phyllis 1899- *3*
Cray, Roberta
    See Emerson, Ru
Crayder, Dorothy *7*

Crayder, Teresa
    See Colman, Hila
Crayon, Geoffrey
    See Irving, Washington
Craz, Albert G. 1926- *24*
Crebbin, June 1938- *80*
Crecy, Jeanne
    See Williams, Jeanne
Credle, Ellis 1902-1998 ....*1*
Creech, Sharon 1945- *139*
    Earlier sketch in SATA *94*
    See also CLR *42*
Creeden, Sharon 1938- *91*
Creighton, Jill 1949- *96*
Crenson, Victoria 1952- *88*
Cresp, Gael 1954- *119*
Crespo, George 1962- *82*
Cresswell, Helen 1934- *79*
    Earlier sketches in SATA *1, 48*
    See also CLR *18*
    See also SAAS *20*
Cressy, Michael 1955- *124*
Cressy, Mike
    See Cressy, Michael
Cretan, Gladys (Yessayan) 1921- *2*
Cretzmeyer, Stacy (Megan) 1959- *124*
Crew, Gary 1947- *110*
    Earlier sketch in SATA *75*
    See also CLR *42*
Crew, Helen (Cecilia) Coale 1866-1941
    See YABC *2*
Crew, Linda (Jean) 1951- *137*
    Earlier sketch in SATA *71*
Crews, Donald 1938- *76*
    Brief entry *30*
    Earlier sketch in SATA *32*
    See also CLR *7*
Crews, Nina 1963- *97*
Crichton, (John) Michael 1942- *88*
    Earlier sketch in SATA *9*
Crider, (Allen) Bill(y) 1941- *99*
Crilley, Mark 1966- *120*
Crisman, Ruth 1914- *73*
Crisp, Marta Marie 1947- *128*
Crisp, Marty
    See Crisp, Marta Marie
Crispin, A(nn) C(arol) 1950- *86*
Cristall, Barbara *79*
Crofford, Emily (Ardell) 1927- *61*
Crofut, William E. III 1934- *23*
Croll, Carolyn 1945-1994 ....*102*
    Brief entry *52*
    Earlier sketch in SATA *56*
Croman, Dorothy Young
    See Rosenberg, Dorothy
Cromie, Alice Hamilton 1914- *24*
Cromie, William J(oseph) 1930- *4*
Crompton, Anne Eliot 1930- *73*
    Earlier sketch in SATA *23*
Crompton, Richmal
    See Lamburn, Richmal Crompton
Cronbach, Abraham 1882-1965 ....*11*
Crone, Ruth 1919- *4*
Cronin, A(rchibald) J(oseph)
    1896-1981 ....*47*
    Obituary *25*
Cronin, Doreen (A.) 1911- *125*
Crook, Beverly Courtney *38*
    Brief entry *35*
Crook, Connie Brummel
    See Crook, Constance
Crook, Constance *98*
Crosby, Alexander L. 1906-1980 ....*2*
    Obituary *23*
Crosby, Harry C., Jr. *102*
Crosher, G. R. *14*
Cross, Gilbert B. 1939- *60*
    Brief entry *51*
Cross, Gillian (Clare) 1945- *110*
    Earlier sketches in SATA *38, 71*
    See also CLR *28*

Cross, Helen Reeder
    See Broadhead, Helen Cross
Cross, Peter 1951- *95*
Cross, Verda 1914- *75*
Cross, Wilbur Lucius III 1918- *2*
Crossland, Caroline 1964- *83*
Crossley-Holland, Kevin (John William)
    1941- *120*
    Earlier sketches in SATA *5, 74*
    See also CLR *84*
    See also SAAS *20*
Crouch, Marcus 1913-1996 ....*4*
Crout, George C(lement) 1917- *11*
Crow, Donna Fletcher 1941- *40*
Crowe, Andrew *111*
Crowe, John
    See Lynds, Dennis
Crowe, (Bettina) Peter Lum 1911- *6*
Crowell, Grace Noll 1877-1969 ....*34*
Crowell, Pers 1910-1990 ....*2*
Crowell, Robert Leland 1909-2001 ....*63*
Crowfield, Christopher
    See Stowe, Harriet (Elizabeth) Beecher
Crowley, Arthur McBlair 1945- *38*
Crowley, John 1942- *140*
    Earlier sketch in SATA *65*
Crownfield, Gertrude 1867-1945
    See YABC *1*
Crowther, James Gerald 1899-1983 ....*14*
Cruikshank, George 1792-1878 ....*22*
    See also CLR *63*
Crum, Shutta *134*
Crummel, Susan Stevens 1949- *130*
Crump, Fred H., Jr. 1931- *76*
    Earlier sketch in SATA *11*
Crump, J(ames) Irving 1887-1979 ....*57*
    Obituary *21*
Crump, William D(rake) 1949- *138*
Crunden, Reginald
    See Cleaver, Hylton Reginald
Crunk, T.
    See Crunk, Tony
Crunk, Tony 1956- *130*
Crutcher, Chris(topher C.) 1946- *99*
    Earlier sketch in SATA *52*
    See also CLR *28*
Cruz, Ray(mond) 1933- *6*
Cruz Martinez, Alejandro (?)-1987 ....*74*
Cuetara, Mittie 1957- *106*
Cuffari, Richard 1925-1978 ....*66*
    Obituary *25*
    Earlier sketch in SATA *6*
Cullen, Countee 1903-1946 ....*18*
Culliford, Pierre 1928-1992 ....*40*
    Obituary *74*
Cullinan, Bernice E(llinger) 1926- *135*
Culp, Louanna McNary 1901-1965 ....*2*
Culper, Felix
    See McCaughrean, Geraldine
Cumbaa, Stephen 1947- *72*
Cumming, Primrose Amy 1915- *24*
Cumming, Robert 1945- *65*
Cummings, Betty Sue 1918- *15*
    See also SAAS *9*
Cummings, Parke 1902-1987 ....*2*
    Obituary *53*
Cummings, Pat (Marie) 1950- *107*
    Earlier sketches in SATA *42, 71*
    See also CLR *48*
    See also SAAS *13*
Cummings, Phil 1957- *123*
    Earlier sketch in SATA *74*
Cummings, Priscilla 1951- *129*
Cummings, Richard
    See Gardner, Richard (M.)
Cummins, Maria Susanna 1827-1866
    See YABC *1*
Cuneo, Mary Louise -2001 ....*85*
Cunliffe, John Arthur 1933- *86*
    Earlier sketch in SATA *11*

Cunliffe, Marcus (Falkner)
  1922-1990 37
  Obituary 66
Cunningham, Bob
  See May, Julian
Cunningham, Captain Frank
  See Glick, Carl (Cannon)
Cunningham, Cathy
  See Cunningham, Chet
Cunningham, Chet 1928- 23
  See Calhoun, Chad
  and Cody, Jess
  and Dalton, Kit
  and Fletcher, Dirk
Cunningham, Dale S(peers) 1932- *11*
Cunningham, Dru *91*
Cunningham, E. V.
  See Fast, Howard (Melvin)
Cunningham, Julia (Woolfolk)
  1916- *132*
  Earlier sketches in SATA *1, 26*
  See also SAAS *2*
Cunningham, Lawrence J. 1943- *125*
Cunningham, Virginia
  See Holmgren, Virginia C(unningham)
Curiae, Amicus
  See Fuller, Edmund (Maybank)
Curie, Eve 1904- *1*
Curlee, Lynn 1947- *141*
  Earlier sketch in SATA *98*
Curley, Daniel 1918-1988 23
  Obituary *61*
Curley, Marianne 1959- *131*
Currie, Robin 1948- *120*
Currie, Stephen 1960- *132*
  Earlier sketch in SATA *82*
Curry, Ann (Gabrielle) 1934- 72
Curry, Jane L(ouise) 1932- 90
  Autobiography Feature *138*
  Earlier sketches in SATA *1, 52*
  See also CLR *31*
  See also SAAS *6*
Curry, Peggy Simson 1911-1987 8
  Obituary 50
Curtis, Bruce (Richard) 1944- 30
Curtis, Chara M(ahar) 1950- 78
Curtis, Christopher Paul 1954(?)- *140*
  Earlier sketch in SATA *93*
  See also CLR *68*
Curtis, Gavin 1965- *107*
Curtis, Jamie Lee 1958- 95
  See also CLR *88*
Curtis, Patricia 1921- *101*
  Earlier sketch in SATA *23*
Curtis, Peter
  See Lofts, Norah (Robinson)
Curtis, Philip (Delacourt) 1920- 62
Curtis, Richard (Alan) 1937- 29
Curtis, Richard Hale
  See Deming, Richard
  and Levinson, Leonard
  and Rothweiler, Paul Roger
Curtis, Wade
  See Pournelle, Jerry (Eugene)
Curtiss, A(rlene) B. 1934- 90
Cusack, Margaret 1945- 58
Cushman, Doug 1953- *101*
  Earlier sketch in SATA *65*
Cushman, Jerome 2
Cushman, Karen 1941- 89
  See also CLR *55*
Cusick, Richie Tankersley 1952- *140*
  Earlier sketch in SATA *67*
Cutchen, Billye Walker 1930- 15
Cutchins, Judy 1947- 59
Cutler, Daniel S(olomon) 1951- 78
Cutler, (May) Ebbitt 1923- 9
Cutler, Ivor 1923- 24
Cutler, Jane 1936- *118*
  Earlier sketch in SATA *75*
Cutler, Samuel
  See Folsom, Franklin (Brewster)

Cutlip, Kimbra L(eigh-Ann) 1964- *128*
Cutrate, Joe
  See Spiegelman, Art
Cutt, W(illiam) Towrie 1898-1981 16
  Obituary 85
Cuyler, Margery S(tuyvesant) 1948- 99
  Earlier sketch in SATA *39*
Cuyler, Stephen
  See Bates, Barbara S(nedeker)
Cyrus, Kurt 1954- *132*

D

Dabcovich, Lydia 99
  Brief entry 47
  Earlier sketch in SATA *58*
Dace, Dolores B(oelens) 1929- 89
Dadey, Debbie 1959- *136*
  Earlier sketch in SATA *73*
Dahl, Borghild (Margarethe)
  1890-1984 7
  Obituary 37
Dahl, Roald 1916-1990 73
  Obituary 65
  Earlier sketches in SATA *1, 26*
  See also CLR *41*
Dahlstedt, Marden (Stewart)
  1921-1983 8
  Obituary *110*
Dain, Martin J. 1924-2000 35
Dakos, Kalli 1950- *115*
  Earlier sketch in SATA *80*
Dale, DeArmond 1914- 70
Dale, Gary
  See Reece, Colleen L.
Dale, George E.
  See Asimov, Isaac
Dale, Jack
  See Holliday, Joseph
Dale, Kim 1957- *123*
Dale, Margaret J(essy) Miller 1911- 39
Dale, Norman
  See Denny, Norman (George)
Dale, Penny 1954- 70
Dalgliesh, Alice 1893-1979 17
  Obituary 21
  See also CLR *62*
Dalkey, Kara (Mia) 1953- *132*
Dallas, Ruth
  See Mumford, Ruth
Dalmas, John
  See Jones, John R(obert)
Dalton, Annie 1948- *140*
  Earlier sketch in SATA *40*
Dalton, Kit
  See Cunningham, Chet
Dalton, Pamela
  See Johnson, Pamela
Dalton, Sean
  See Chester, Deborah
Dalton, Sheila *108*
Daly, Jim
  See Stratemeyer, Edward L.
Daly, Kathleen N(orah) *124*
  Brief entry 37
Daly, Maureen 1921- *129*
  Earlier sketch in SATA *2*
  See also SAAS *1*
Daly, Nicholas 1946- *114*
  Earlier sketches in SATA *37, 76*
  See also CLR *41*
  See Daly, Niki
Daly, Niki
  See SAAS *21*
  See Daly, Nicholas
D'Amato, Alex 1919- 20
D'Amato, Janet (Potter) 1925- 9
Damerow, Gail (Jane) 1944- 83
Damrell, Liz 1956- 77

Damrosch, Helen
  See Tee-Van, Helen Damrosch
Dana, Barbara 1940- 22
Dana, Richard Henry, Jr. 1815-1882 26
Danachair, Caoimhin O
  See Danaher, Kevin
Danaher, Kevin 1913- 22
Danakas, John 1963- 94
D'Andrea, Kate
  See Steiner, Barbara A(nnette)
Dangerfield, Balfour
  See McCloskey, (John) Robert
Daniel, Alan 1939- 76
  Brief entry 53
Daniel, Anita 1893(?)-1978 23
  Obituary 24
Daniel, Anne
  See Steiner, Barbara A(nnette)
Daniel, Becky 1947- 56
Daniel, Colin
  See Windsor, Patricia
Daniel, Hawthorne 1890- 8
Daniel, (Donna) Lee 1944- 76
Daniel, Rebecca
  See Daniel, Becky
Daniels, Guy 1919-1989 ....*11*
  Obituary 62
Daniels, Lucy
  See Oldfield, Jenny
Daniels, Max
  See Gellis, Roberta (Leah Jacobs)
Daniels, Olga
  See Sinclair, Olga
Daniels, Patricia 1955- 93
Daniels, Zoe
  See Laux, Constance
Dank, Gloria Rand 1955- 56
  Brief entry 46
Dank, Leonard D(ewey) 1929- 44
Dank, Milton 1920- 31
Dann, Max 1955- 62
Dantz, William R.
  See Philbrick, (W.) Rodman
Danziger, Paula 1944- *102*
  Brief entry 30
  Earlier sketches in SATA *36, 63*
  See also CLR *20*
Darby, Gene Kegley
  See Darby, Jean (Kegley)
Darby, J. N.
  See Govan, (Mary) Christine Noble
Darby, Jean (Kegley) 1921- 68
Darby, Patricia (Paulsen) 14
Darby, Ray(mond) 1912-1982 7
d'Arcy, Willard
  See Cox, William R(obert)
Dare, Geena
  See McNicoll, Sylvia (Marilyn)
Darian, Shea 1959- 97
Daringer, Helen Fern 1892-1986 1
Darke, Marjorie 1929- 87
  Earlier sketch in SATA *16*
Darley, F(elix) O(ctavius) C(arr)
  1822-1888 35
Darling, David J. 1953- 60
  Brief entry 44
Darling, Kathy
  See Darling, Mary Kathleen
Darling, Lois (MacIntyre) 1917-1989 3
  Obituary 64
Darling, Louis, (Jr.) 1916-1970 3
  Obituary 23
Darling, Mary Kathleen 1943- *124*
  Earlier sketches in SATA *9, 79*
Darling, Sandra
  See Day, Alexandra
Darroll, Sally
  See Odgers, Sally Farrell
Darrow, Whitney, (Jr.) 1909-1999 13
  Obituary *115*
Darwin, Len
  See Darwin, Leonard

Darwin, Leonard 1916- 24
Dasent, Sir George Webbe
   1817-1896 62
   Brief entry 29
Daskam, Josephine Dodge
   See Bacon, Josephine Dodge (Daskam)
D'ath, Justin 1953- 106
Dauer, Rosamond 1934- 23
Daugherty, Charles Michael 1914- 16
Daugherty, James (Henry)
   1889-1974 13
   See also CLR 78
Daugherty, Richard D(eo) 1922- 35
d'Aulaire, Edgar Parin 1898-1986 66
   Obituary 47
   Earlier sketch in SATA 5
   See also CLR 21
d'Aulaire, Ingri (Mortenson Parin)
   1904-1980 66
   Obituary 24
   Earlier sketch in SATA 5
   See also CLR 21
Dave, Dave
   See Berg, David
Daveluy, Paule Cloutier 1919- 11
Davenier, Christine 1961- 127
Daves, Michael 1938- 40
David, A. R.
   See David, A(nn) Rosalie
David, A(nn) Rosalie 1946- 103
David, Jonathan
   See Ames, Lee J(udah)
David, Lawrence 1963- 111
David, Rosalie
   See David, A(nn) Rosalie
Davidson, Alice Joyce 1932- 54
   Brief entry 45
Davidson, Basil 1914- 13
Davidson, (Marie) Diane 1924- 91
Davidson, Hugh
   See Hamilton, Edmond
Davidson, Jessica 1915-1986 5
Davidson, Judith 1953- 40
Davidson, Lionel 1922- 87
Davidson, Margaret 1936- 5
Davidson, Marion
   See Garis, Howard R(oger)
Davidson, Mary R. 1885-1973 9
Davidson, Mary S. 1940- 61
Davidson, Mickie
   See Davidson, Margaret
Davidson, Nicole
   See Jensen, Kathryn
Davidson, R.
   See Davidson, Raymond
Davidson, Raymond 1926- 32
Davidson, Rosalie 1921- 23
Davie, Helen K(ay) 1952- 77
Davies, Andrew (Wynford) 1936- 27
Davies, Bettilu D(onna) 1942- 33
Davies, Hunter 1936- 55
   Brief entry 45
Davies, Joan 1934- 50
   Brief entry 47
Davies, Nicola 1958- 99
Davies, Peter J(oseph) 1937- 52
Davies, Sumiko 1942- 46
Davis, Bette J. 1923- 15
Davis, Burke 1913- 4
Davis, Christopher 1928- 6
Davis, D(elbert) Dwight 1908-1965 33
Davis, Daniel S(heldon) 1936- 12
Davis, David R. 1948- 106
Davis, Donald (D) 1944- 93
Davis, Gibbs 1953- 102
   Brief entry 41
   Earlier sketch in SATA 46
Davis, Grania 1943- 88
   Brief entry 50
Davis, H(arold) L(enoir) 1896-1960 114
Davis, Hubert J(ackson) 1904-1997 31

Davis, James Robert 1945- 32
   See Davis, Jim
Davis, Jenny 1953- 74
Davis, Jim
   See Davis, James Robert
Davis, Julia 1900(?)-1993 6
   Obituary 75
Davis, Karen (Elizabeth) 1944- 109
Davis, Leslie
   See Guccione, Leslie Davis
Davis, Louise Littleton 1921- 25
Davis, Maggie S. 1943- 57
Davis, Marguerite 1889- 34
Davis, Mary L(ee) 1935- 9
Davis, Mary Octavia 1901-1976 6
Davis, Nelle 1958- 73
Davis, Ossie 1917- 81
   See also CLR 56
Davis, Paxton 1925-1994 16
Davis, Robert 1881-1949
   See YABC 1
Davis, Robin W(orks) 1962- 87
Davis, Russell Gerard 1922- 3
Davis, Tim(othy N.) 1957- 94
Davis, Verne Theodore 1889-1973 6
Davis, Yvonne 1927- 115
Davol, Marguerite W. 1928- 82
DaVolls, Andy (P.) 1967- 85
DaVolls, Linda 1966- 85
Davys, Sarah
   See Manning, Rosemary (Joy)
Dawes, Claiborne 1935- 111
Dawson, Elmer A. 67
   Earlier sketch in SATA 1
Dawson, Imogen (Zoe) 1948-
   See Dawson, Imogen (Zoe)
Dawson, Imogen (Zoe) 1948- 126
   Earlier sketch in SATA 90
Dawson, Mary 1919- 11
Day, A(rthur) Grove 1904-1994 59
Day, Alexandra 97
   Earlier sketch in SATA 67
   See also CLR 22
   See also SAAS 19
Day, Beth (Feagles) 1924- 33
Day, Donna
   See Asay, Donna Day
Day, Edward C. 1932- 72
Day, Jon 1936(?)- 79
Day, Nancy 1953- 140
Day, Nancy Raines 1951- 93
Day, Shirley 1962- 94
Day, Thomas 1748-1789
   See YABC 1
Day, Trevor 1955- 124
Dazey, Agnes J(ohnston) 2
Dazey, Frank M. 2
Deacon, Alexis 1978- 139
Deacon, Eileen
   See Geipel, Eileen
Deacon, Richard
   See McCormick, (George) Donald (King)
Dean, Anabel 1915- 12
Dean, Karen Strickler 1923- 49
de Angeli, Marguerite (Lofft)
   1889-1987 100
   Obituary 51
   Earlier sketches in SATA 1, 27
   See also CLR 1
Deans, Sis Boulos 1955- 136
   Earlier sketch in SATA 78
DeArmand, Frances Ullmann
   1904(?)-1984 10
   Obituary 38
DeArmond, Dale Burlison
   See Dale, DeArmond
   and DeArmond, Dale
Deary, Terry 1946- 101
   Brief entry 41
   Earlier sketch in SATA 51
Deaver, Julie Reece 1953- 68
de Banke, Cecile 1889-1965 11

De Bello, Rosario 1923- 89
de Bono, Edward 1933- 66
de Brissac, Malcolm
   See Dickinson, Peter (Malcolm)
de Brunhoff, Jean
   See Brunhoff, Jean de
De Brunhoff, Laurent
   See Brunhoff, Laurent de
de Bruyn, Monica (Jean) G(rembowicz)
   1952- 13
DeBry, Roger K. 1942- 91
de Camp, Catherine Crook
   1907-2000 83
   Earlier sketch in SATA 12
de Camp, L(yon) Sprague
   1907-2000 83
   Earlier sketch in SATA 9
DeCandido, Keith R. A. 112
Dechausay, Sonia E. 94
Decker, Duane 1910-1964 5
DeClements, Barthe (Faith) 1920- 131
   Earlier sketches in SATA 35, 71
   See also CLR 23
de Conte, Sieur Louis
   See Clemens, Samuel Langhorne
Dedman, Stephen 108
Dee, Catherine 1964- 138
Dee, Ruby 77
   See Wallace, Ruby Ann
Deedy, John 1923- 24
Deegan, Paul Joseph 1937- 48
   Brief entry 38
Deem, James M(organ) 1950- 134
   Earlier sketch in SATA 75
Deeter, Catherine 1947- 137
DeFelice, Cynthia (C.) 1951- 121
   Earlier sketch in SATA 79
Defoe, Daniel 1660(?)-1731 22
   See also CLR 61
DeFord, Deborah H. 123
deFrance, Anthony
   See DiFranco, Anthony (Mario)
Degen, Bruce 1945- 97
   Brief entry 47
   Earlier sketch in SATA 57
DeGering, Etta (Belle) Fowler
   1898-1996 7
De Goldi, Kate
   See De Goldi, Kathleen Domenica
De Goldi, Kathleen Domenica
   1959- 123
De Grazia, Ted 39
   See De Grazia, Ettore
de Groat, Diane 1947- 90
   Earlier sketch in SATA 31
deGros, J. H.
   See Villiard, Paul
de Grummond, Lena Young 62
   Earlier sketch in SATA 6
de Hamel, Joan Littledale 1924- 86
De Haven, Tom 1949- 72
de Hugo, Pierre
   See Brackers de Hugo, Pierre
Deiss, Joseph Jay 1915- 12
de Jenkins, Lyll Becerra 1925-1997 102
DeJong, David C(ornel) 1905-1967 10
de Jong, Dola 7
   See de Jong, Dorothea Rosalie
DeJong, Meindert 1906-1991 2
   Obituary 68
   See also CLR 73
DeJonge, Joanne E. 1943- 56
Deka, Connie
   See Laux, Constance
de Kay, Ormonde (Jr.) 1923-1998 7
   Obituary 106
de Kiriline, Louise
   See Lawrence, Louise de Kiriline
Dekker, Carl
   See Laffin, John (Alfred Charles)
   and Lynds, Dennis

deKruif, Paul (Henry) 1890-1971 ....*50*
  Earlier sketch in SATA 5
Delacre, Lulu 1957- *36*
DeLaCroix, Alice 1940- *75*
De Lage, Ida 1918- *11*
de la Mare, Walter (John)
  1873-1956 ....*16*
  See also CLR 23
Delaney, Harry 1932- *3*
Delaney, Michael 1955- *96*
Delaney, Ned *28*
  See Delaney, Thomas Nicholas III
Delano, Hugh 1933- *20*
Delany, Samuel R(ay), Jr. 1942- *92*
De la Ramee, Marie Louise (Ouida)
  1839-1908 ....*20*
  See Ouida
de la Roche, Mazo 1879-1961 ....*64*
De La Roche Saint Andre, Anne
  1950- *75*
Delaune, (Jewel) Lynn (de Grummond) ......
  7
DeLaurentis, Louise Budde 1920- *12*
Delderfield, Eric R(aymond)
  1909-1995 ....*14*
Delderfield, Ronald Frederick
  1912-1972 ....*20*
DeLeeuw, Adele (Louise) 1899-1988 ......*30*
  Obituary *56*
  Earlier sketch in SATA 1
De Leon, Nephtali 1945- *97*
Delessert, Etienne 1941- *130*
  Brief entry *27*
  Earlier sketch in SATA 46
  See also CLR 81
Delgado, James P. 1958- *122*
de Lint, Charles (Henri Diederick Hofsmit)
  1951- *115*
Delmar, Roy
  See Wexler, Jerome (LeRoy)
Deloria, Vine (Victor), Jr. 1933- *21*
del Rey, Lester 1915-1993 ....*22*
  Obituary *76*
Delrio, Martin
  See Macdonald, James D.
Delton, Judy 1931-2001 ....*77*
  Obituary *130*
  Earlier sketch in SATA 14
  See also SAAS 9
Delulio, John 1938- *15*
Delving, Michael
  See Williams, Jay
Demarest, Chris(topher) L(ynn)
  1951- *128*
  Brief entry *44*
  Earlier sketches in SATA 45, 82
Demarest, Doug
  See Barker, Will
Demas, Corinne 1947- *131*
  See Bliss, Corinne Demas
Demas, Vida 1927- *9*
De Mejo, Oscar 1911-1992 ....*40*
de Messieres, Nicole 1930- *39*
Demi
  See Hitz, Demi
Demijohn, Thom
  See Disch, Thomas M(ichael)
  and Sladek, John
Deming, Richard 1915-1983 ....*24*
  See Queen, Ellery
Demuth, Patricia Brennan 1948- *84*
  Brief entry *51*
Dengler, Marianna (Herron) 1935- *103*
Dengler, Sandy 1939- *54*
  Brief entry *40*
Denim, Sue
  See Pilkey, Dav(id Murray, Jr.)
Denmark, Harrison
  See Zelazny, Roger (Joseph)
Dennard, Deborah 1953- *136*
  Earlier sketch in SATA 78

Denney, Diana 1910-2000 ....*25*
  Obituary *120*
Dennis, Morgan 1891(?)-1960 ....*18*
Dennis, Wesley 1903-1966 ....*18*
Denny, Norman (George) 1901-1982 ......*43*
Denslow, Sharon Phillips 1947- *68*
Denslow, W(illiam) W(allace)
  1856-1915 ....*16*
  See also CLR 15
Denton, Kady MacDonald *110*
  Earlier sketch in SATA 66
  See also CLR 71
Denver, Walt
  See Redding, Robert Hull
  and Sherman, Jory (Tecumseh)
Denzel, Justin F(rancis) 1917-1999 ....*46*
  Brief entry *38*
Denzer, Ann Wiseman
  See Wiseman, Ann (Sayre)
DePalma, Mary Newell 1961- *139*
dePaola, Thomas Anthony 1934- *108*
  Earlier sketches in SATA 11, 59
  See dePaola, Tomie
dePaola, Tomie
  See CLR 81
  See also SAAS 15
  See dePaola, Thomas Anthony
dePaola, Paul 1949- *74*
DePauw, Linda Grant 1940- *24*
DeRan, David 1946- *76*
Derby, Sally 1934- *132*
  Earlier sketch in SATA 89
de Regniers, Beatrice Schenk (Freedman)
  1914-2000 ....*68*
  Obituary *123*
  Earlier sketch in SATA 2
  See also SAAS 6
Dereske, Jo 1947- *72*
Derleth, August (William) 1909-1971 ....*5*
Derman, Martha (Winn) *74*
Derman, Sarah Audrey 1915- *11*
DeRoberts, Lyndon
  See Silverstein, Robert Alan
de Roo, Anne Louise 1931-1997 ....*84*
  Earlier sketch in SATA 25
  See also CLR 63
deRosa, Dee *70*
Derrick, Lionel
  See Cunningham, Chet
Derrickson, Jim 1959- *141*
Derry Down Derry
  See Lear, Edward
Dervaux, Isabelle 1961- *106*
Derwent, Lavinia *14*
Desai, Anita 1937- *126*
  Earlier sketch in SATA 63
De Saulles, Tony 1958- *119*
Desbarats, Peter 1933- *39*
de Selincourt, Aubrey 1894-1962 ....*14*
Deshpande, Chris 1950- *69*
Desimini, Lisa 1964- *86*
Desjarlais, John (J.) 1953- *71*
Desmoinaux, Christel 1967- *103*
Desmond, Adrian J(ohn) 1947- *51*
Desmond, Alice Curtis 1897-1990 ....*8*
DeSpain, Pleasant 1943- *87*
Desputeaux, Helene 1959- *95*
Dessen, Sarah 1970- *120*
Detine, Padre
  See Olsen, Ib Spang
de Trevino, Elizabeth B.
  See Trevino, Elizabeth B(orton) de
de Trevino, Elizabeth Borton
  See Trevino, Elizabeth B(orton) de
Detwiler, Susan Dill 1956- *58*
Deuker, Carl 1950- *82*
Deutsch, Babette 1895-1982 ....*1*
  Obituary *33*
Deutsch, Eva Costabel
  See Costabel, Eva Deutsch
Deutsch, Helen 1906-1992 ....*76*
Devaney, John 1926-1994 ....*12*

de Varona, Frank J. 1943- *83*
Devereux, Frederick L(eonard), Jr.
  1914-1993 ....*9*
Devi, Nila
  See Woody, Regina Jones
deVinck, Christopher 1951- *85*
DeVito, Cara 1956- *80*
Devlin, Harry 1918- *136*
  Earlier sketches in SATA 11, 74
Devlin, (Dorothy) Wende 1918- *74*
  Earlier sketch in SATA 11
Devon, Paddie 1953- *92*
Devons, Sonia 1974- *72*
Devorah-Leah *111*
de Vos, Gail 1949- *122*
DeVries, Douglas 1933- *122*
De Waard, E(lliott) John 1935- *7*
Dewan, Ted 1961- *108*
Dewdney, Selwyn (Hanington)
  1909-1979 ....*64*
DeWeese, Gene
  See DeWeese, Thomas Eugene
DeWeese, Jean
  See DeWeese, Thomas Eugene
DeWeese, Thomas Eugene 1934- *46*
  Brief entry *45*
Dewey, Ariane 1937- *109*
  Earlier sketch in SATA 7
Dewey, Jennifer (Owings) 1941- *103*
  Brief entry *48*
  Earlier sketch in SATA 58
Dewey, Kenneth Francis 1940- *39*
deWit, Dorothy (May Knowles)
  1916-1980 ....*39*
  Obituary *28*
Dexter, Alison 1966- *125*
Dexter, John
  See Bradley, Marion Zimmer
Deyneka, Anita 1943- *24*
Deyrup, Astrith Johnson 1923- *24*
Dhondy, Farrukh 1944- *65*
  See also CLR 41
Diamond, Arthur 1957- *76*
Diamond, Donna 1950- *69*
  Brief entry *30*
  Earlier sketch in SATA 35
Diamond, Petra
  See Sachs, Judith
Diamond, Rebecca
  See Sachs, Judith
Dias, Earl Joseph 1916- *41*
Dias, Ron 1937- *71*
Diaz, David 1959(?)- *96*
  See also CLR 65
DiCamillo, Kate 1964- *121*
Di Certo, J(oseph) J(ohn) 1933- *60*
DiCianni, Ron 1952- *107*
Dick, Trella Lamson 1889-1974 ....*9*
Dickens, Charles (John Huffam)
  1812-1870 ....*15*
Dickens, Frank
  See Huline-Dickens, Frank William
Dickens, Monica (Enid) 1915-1992 ....*4*
  Obituary *74*
Dickinson, Emily (Elizabeth)
  1830-1886 ....*29*
Dickinson, Mary 1949- *48*
  Brief entry *41*
Dickinson, Peter (Malcolm) 1927- *95*
  Earlier sketches in SATA 5, 62
  See also CLR 29
Dickinson, Susan 1931- *8*
Dickinson, Terence 1943- *102*
Dickinson, W(illiam) Croft
  1897-1963 ....*13*
Dickson, Gordon R(upert) 1923-2001 ......*77*
Dickson, Naida 1916- *8*
Diehn, Gwen 1943- *80*
Dieterich, Michele M. 1962- *78*
Dietz, David H(enry) 1897-1984 ....*10*
  Obituary *41*

Dietz, Lew 1907-1997 ....*11*
  Obituary *95*
Di Fiori, Larry
  See Di Fiori, Lawrence
Di Fiori, Lawrence 1934- *130*
DiFranco, Anthony (Mario) 1945- *42*
Digby, Anne 1935- *72*
Digges, Jeremiah
  See Berger, Josef
D'Ignazio, Fred(erick) 1949- *39*
  Brief entry *35*
Di Grazia, Thomas (?)-1983 ....*32*
Dikty, Julian May
  See May, Julian
Dillard, Annie 1945- *140*
  Earlier sketch in SATA *10*
Dillard, Kristine 1964- *113*
Dillard, Polly Hargis 1916- *24*
Diller, Harriett 1953- *78*
Dillon, Barbara 1927- *44*
  Brief entry *39*
Dillon, Diane (Claire) 1933- *106*
  Earlier sketches in SATA *15, 51*
  See also CLR *44*
Dillon, Eilis 1920-1994 ....*74*
  Autobiography Feature *105*
  Obituary *83*
  Earlier sketch in SATA *2*
  See also CLR *26*
Dillon, Jana (a pseudonym) 1952- *117*
Dillon, Leo 1933- *106*
  Earlier sketches in SATA *15, 51*
  See also CLR *44*
Dillon, Sharon Saseen
  See Saseen, Sharon (Dillon)
Dils, Tracey E. 1958- *83*
Dilson, Jesse 1914- *24*
Dinan, Carolyn *59*
  Brief entry *47*
Dines, (Harry) Glen 1925-1996 ....*7*
Dinesen, Isak
  See Blixen, Karen (Christentze Dinesen)
Dinessi, Alex
  See Schembri, Jim
Dinneen, Betty 1929- *61*
Dinnerstein, Harvey 1928- *42*
Dinsdale, Tim(othy Kay) 1924-1987 ....*11*
Dirk
  See Gringhuis, Richard H.
Dirks, Wilhelmina 1916- *59*
Dirks, Willy
  See Dirks, Wilhelmina
DiSalvo-Ryan, DyAnne 1954- *59*
Disch, Thomas M(ichael) 1940- *92*
  See also CLR *18*
  See also SAAS *15*
  See Disch, Tom
Disch, Tom
  See Disch, Thomas M(ichael)
Disher, Garry 1949- *125*
  Earlier sketch in SATA *81*
Disney, Walt(er Elias) 1901-1966 ....*28*
  Brief entry *27*
Di Valentin, Maria (Amelia) Messuri
  1911-1985 ....*7*
Dixon, Ann R. 1954- *127*
  Earlier sketch in SATA *77*
Dixon, Dougal 1947- *127*
  Earlier sketch in SATA *45*
Dixon, Franklin W. *100*
  Earlier sketches in SATA *1, 67*
  See also CLR *61*
  See McFarlane, Leslie (Charles)
  and Stratemeyer, Edward L.
Dixon, Jeanne 1936- *31*
Dixon, Paige
  See Corcoran, Barbara (Asenath)
Dixon, Peter L(ee) 1931- *6*
Dixon, Rachel 1952- *74*
Djoleto, (Solomon Alexander) Amu
  1929- *80*

Doak, Annie
  See Dillard, Annie
Doane, Pelagie 1906-1966 ....*7*
Dobell, I(sabel) M(arian) B(arclay)
  1909-1998 ....*11*
Dobie, J(ames) Frank 1888-1964 ....*43*
Dobler, Lavinia G. 1910- *6*
Dobrin, Arnold 1928- *4*
Dobson, Jill 1969- *140*
Dobson, Julia 1941- *48*
Dobson, Mary 1954- *117*
Dockery, Wallene T. 1941- *27*
Dockray, Tracy 1962- *139*
Dockrey, Karen 1955- *103*
Doctor, Bernard
  See Doctor, Bernard Aquina
Doctor, Bernard Aquina 1950- *81*
Doctor X
  See Nourse, Alan E(dward)
Dodd, Ed(ward Benton) 1902-1991 ....*4*
  Obituary *68*
Dodd, Lynley (Stuart) 1941- *132*
  Earlier sketches in SATA *35, 86*
  See also CLR *62*
Dodd, Quentin 1972- *137*
Dodds, Bill 1952- *78*
Dodds, Dayle Ann 1952- *75*
Dodge, Bertha S(anford) 1902-1995 ....*8*
Dodge, Fremont
  See Grimes, Lee
Dodge, Gil
  See Hano, Arnold
Dodge, Mary (Elizabeth) Mapes
  1831(?)-1905 ....*100*
  Earlier sketch in SATA *21*
  See also CLR *62*
Dodgson, Charles L(utwidge)
  1832-1898 ....*100*
  See also YABC *2*
  See also CLR *2*
  See Carroll, Lewis
Dodson, Kenneth MacKenzie
  1907-1999 ....*11*
Dodson, Susan 1941- *50*
  Brief entry *40*
Dogyear, Drew
  See Gorey, Edward (St. John)
Doherty, Berlie 1943- *111*
  Earlier sketch in SATA *72*
  See also CLR *21*
  See also SAAS *16*
Doherty, Charles Hugh 1913- *6*
Doherty, Craig A. 1951- *83*
Doherty, Katherine M(ann) 1951- *83*
Dokey, Cameron 1956- *97*
Dolan, Edward F(rancis), Jr. 1924- *94*
  Brief entry *31*
  Earlier sketch in SATA *45*
Dolan, Ellen M(eara) 1929-1998 ....*88*
Dolan, Sean J. 1958- *74*
Dolce, J. Ellen 1948- *75*
Dolch, Edward William 1889-1961 ....*50*
Dolch, Marguerite Pierce 1891-1978 ....*50*
Dollar, Diane (Hills) 1933- *57*
Dolson, Hildegarde *5*
  See Lockridge, Hildegarde (Dolson)
Domanska, Janina 1913(?)-1995 ....*68*
  Obituary *84*
  Earlier sketch in SATA *6*
  See also CLR *40*
  See also SAAS *18*
Dominguez, Angel 1953- *76*
Domino, John
  See Averill, Esther (Holden)
Domjan, Joseph (Spiri) 1907-1992 ....*25*
Domm, Jeffrey C. 1958- *84*
Donalds, Gordon
  See Shirreffs, Gordon D(onald)
Donaldson, Bryna
  See Stevens, Bryna
Donaldson, Gordon 1913-1993 ....*64*
  Obituary *76*

Donaldson, Joan 1953- *78*
Donaldson, Julia 1948- *132*
  Earlier sketch in SATA *82*
Donaldson, Stephen R(eeder) 1947- *121*
Doner, Kim 1955- *91*
Doney, Todd L. W. 1959- *104*
Donkin, Nance (Clare) 1915- *95*
Donna, Natalie 1934-1979 ....*9*
Donoghue, Emma 1969- *101*
Donoughue, Carol 1935- *139*
Donovan, John 1928-1992 ....*72*
  Brief entry *29*
  See also CLR *3*
Donovan, Mary Lee 1961- *86*
Donze, Mary Terese 1911- *89*
Doob, Leonard W(illiam) 1909-2000 ....*8*
Dooley, Norah 1953- *74*
Dooling, Michael 1958- *105*
Dor, Ana
  See Ceder, Georgiana Dorcas
Dore, (Louis Christophe Paul) Gustave
  1832-1883 ....*19*
Doremus, Robert 1913- *30*
Doren, Marion (Walker) 1928- *57*
Dorenkamp, Michelle 1957- *89*
Dorflinger, Carolyn 1953- *91*
Dorian, Edith M(cEwen) 1900-1983 ....*5*
Dorian, Harry
  See Hamilton, Charles (Harold St. John)
Dorian, Marguerite *7*
Dorin, Patrick C(arberry) 1939- *59*
  Brief entry *52*
Dorman, Michael 1932- *7*
Dorman, N. B. 1927- *39*
Dorris, Michael (Anthony)
  1945-1997 ....*75*
  Obituary *94*
  See also CLR *58*
Dorris, Michael A.
  See Dorris, Michael (Anthony)
Dorritt, Susan
  See Schlein, Miriam
Dorros, Arthur (M.) 1950- *122*
  Earlier sketch in SATA *78*
  See also CLR *42*
  See also SAAS *20*
Dorson, Richard M(ercer) 1916-1981 ......*30*
Doss, Helen (Grigsby) 1918- *20*
Doss, Margot Patterson *6*
dos Santos, Joyce Audy 1949- *57*
  Brief entry *42*
  See Zarins, Joyce Audy
Dothers, Anne
  See Chess, Victoria (Dickerson)
Dottig
  See Grider, Dorothy
Dotts, Maryann J. 1933- *35*
Doty, Jean Slaughter 1929- *28*
Doty, Roy 1922- *28*
Doubtfire, Dianne (Abrams) 1918- *29*
Dougherty, Charles 1922- *18*
Douglas, Blaise 1960- *101*
Douglas, Carole Nelson 1944- *73*
Douglas, Garry
  See Kilworth, Garry (D.)
Douglas, James McM.
  See Butterworth, W(illiam) E(dmund III)
Douglas, Kathryn
  See Ewing, Kathryn
Douglas, Leonard
  See Bradbury, Ray (Douglas)
Douglas, Marjory Stoneman
  1890-1998 ....*10*
Douglas, Michael
  See Crichton, (John) Michael
Douglas, Michael
  See Bright, Robert (Douglas Sr.)
Douglass, Barbara 1930- *40*
Douglass, Frederick 1817(?)-1895 ....*29*
Douty, Esther M(orris) 1909-1978 ....*8*
  Obituary *23*
Dow, Emily R. 1904-1987 ....*10*

Dow, Vicki
  See McVey, Vicki
Dowd, John David 1945- *78*
Dowdell, Dorothy (Florence) Karns
  1910- *12*
Dowden, Anne Ophelia 1907- *7*
  See also SAAS *10*
Dowdey, Landon Gerald 1923- *11*
Dowdy, Mrs. Regera
  See Gorey, Edward (St. John)
Dowling, Terry 1947- *101*
Downer, Marion 1892(?)-1971 ....*25*
Downey, Fairfax D(avis) 1893-1990 ....*3*
  Obituary *66*
Downie, John 1931- *87*
Downie, Mary Alice (Dawe) 1934- *87*
  Earlier sketch in SATA *13*
Downing, David A(lmon) 1958- *84*
Downing, Julie 1956- *81*
Downing, Paula E. 1951- *80*
Downing, Warwick 1931- *138*
Downing, Wick
  See Downing, Warwick
Doyle, A. Conan
  See Doyle, Sir Arthur Conan
Doyle, Sir Arthur Conan 1859-1930 ....*24*
  See Conan Doyle, Arthur
Doyle, Brian 1935- *104*
  Earlier sketch in SATA *67*
  See also CLR *22*
  See also SAAS *16*
Doyle, Charlotte (Lackner) 1937- *94*
Doyle, Conan
  See Doyle, Sir Arthur Conan
Doyle, Debra 1952- *105*
Doyle, John
  See Graves, Robert (von Ranke)
Doyle, Malachy 1954- *120*
  See also CLR *83*
Doyle, Richard 1824-1883 ....*21*
Doyle, Sir A. Conan
  See Doyle, Sir Arthur Conan
Dr. A
  See Asimov, Isaac
  and Silverstein, Alvin
  and Silverstein, Virginia B(arbara
  Opshelor)
Dr. Alphabet
  See Morice, Dave
Dr. Fred
  See Bortz, Alfred B(enjamin)
Dr. Seuss
  See CLR *53*
  See Geisel, Theodor Seuss
  and LeSieg, Theo.
  and Seuss, Dr.
  and Stone, Rosetta
Dr. Zed
  See Penrose, Gordon
Drabble, Margaret 1939- *48*
Drackett, Phil(ip Arthur) 1922- *53*
Draco, F.
  See Davis, Julia
Dracup, Angela 1943- *74*
Dragisic, Patricia *116*
Dragonwagon, Crescent 1952- *133*
  Earlier sketches in SATA *11, 41, 75*
  See also SAAS *14*
Drake, David (Allen) 1945- *85*
Drake, Frank
  See Hamilton, Charles (Harold St. John)
Drake, Jane 1954- *82*
Drakeford, Dale B(enjamin) 1952- *113*
Draper, Hastings
  See Jeffries, Roderic (Graeme)
Draper, Sharon M(ills) 1957- *98*
  See also CLR *57*
Drapier, M. B.
  See Swift, Jonathan
Drawson, Blair 1943- *126*
  Earlier sketch in SATA *17*

Dresang, Eliza (Carolyn Timberlake)
  1941- *19*
Drescher, Henrik 1955- *105*
  Earlier sketch in SATA *67*
  See also CLR *20*
Drescher, Joan E(lizabeth) 1939- *137*
  Earlier sketch in SATA *30*
Drew, Patricia (Mary) 1938- *15*
Drewery, Mary 1918- *6*
Drewry, Henry N(athaniel) 1924- *138*
Drial, J. E.
  See Laird, Jean E(louise)
Drimmer, Frederick 1916-2000 ....*60*
  Obituary *124*
Driskill, J. Lawrence 1920- *90*
Driskill, Larry
  See Driskill, J. Lawrence
Driving Hawk, Virginia
  See Sneve, Virginia Driving Hawk
Drucker, Malka 1945- *111*
  Brief entry *29*
  Earlier sketch in SATA *39*
Drucker, Olga Levy 1927- *79*
Drummond, V(iolet) H(ilda)
  1911-2000 ....*6*
Drummond, Walter
  See Silverberg, Robert
Drury, Clare Marie
  See Hoskyns-Abrahall, Clare (Constance
  Drury)
Drury, Roger W(olcott) 1914- *15*
Dryden, Pamela
  See St. John, Nicole
D.T., Hughes
  See Hughes, Dean
Duane, Diane (Elizabeth) 1952- *95*
  Brief entry *46*
  Earlier sketch in SATA *58*
Dubanevich, Arlene 1950- *56*
Dubelaar, Thea 1947- *60*
du Blane, Daphne
  See Groom, Arthur William
Du Bois, Shirley Graham
  1907(?)-1977 ....*24*
  See Graham, Shirley
Du Bois, W(illiam) E(dward) B(urghardt)
  1868-1963 ....*42*
du Bois, William Pene
  See Pene du Bois, William (Sherman)
Duboise, Novella 1911-1999 ....*88*
Dubosarsky, Ursula 1961- *107*
DuBose, LaRocque (Russ) 1926- *2*
Dubrovin, Vivian 1931- *139*
  Earlier sketch in SATA *65*
Ducey, Jean Sparks 1915- *93*
Du Chaillu, Paul (Belloni)
  1835(?)-1903 ....*26*
Ducharme, Dede Fox
  See Ducharme, Lilian Fox
Ducharme, Lilian Fox 1950- *122*
Ducornet, Erica 1943- *7*
Ducornet, Rikki
  See Ducornet, Erica
Duden, Jane 1947- *136*
Duder, Tessa 1940- *117*
  Earlier sketch in SATA *80*
  See also CLR *43*
  See also SAAS *23*
Dudley, Helen
  See Hope Simpson, Jacynth
Dudley, Nancy
  See Cole, Lois Dwight
Dudley, Robert
  See Baldwin, James
Dudley, Ruth H(ubbell) 1905-2001 ....*11*
Dudley-Smith, T.
  See Trevor, Elleston
Due, Linnea A. 1948- *64*
Dueck, Adele 1955- *97*
Dueland, Joy V(ivian) *27*
Duerr, Gisela 1968- *89*
Duey, Kathleen 1950- *132*

Dufault, Joseph Ernest Nephtali
  See James, Will(iam Roderick)
Duff, Maggie
  See Duff, Margaret K.
Duff, Margaret K. *37*
Duffey, Betsy (Byars) 1953- *131*
  Earlier sketch in SATA *80*
Duffy, Carol Ann 1955- *95*
Dugan, Jack
  See Butterworth, W(illiam) E(dmund III)
Dugan, Michael (Gray) 1947- *15*
Duggan, Alfred Leo 1903-1964 ....*25*
Duggan, Maurice (Noel) 1922-1974 ....*40*
  Obituary *30*
Duggleby, John 1952- *94*
Dugin, Andrej 1955- *77*
Dugina, Olga 1964- *77*
du Jardin, Rosamond Neal 1902-1963 ....*2*
Duke, Kate 1956- *90*
  See also CLR *51*
Duke, Will
  See Gault, William Campbell
Dulac, Edmund 1882-1953 ....*19*
Dumas, Alexandre (pere) 1802-1870 ....*18*
Dumas, Jacqueline 1946- *55*
Dumas, Philippe 1940- *119*
  Earlier sketch in SATA *52*
du Maurier, Daphne 1907-1989 ....*27*
  Obituary *60*
Dumbleton, Mike 1948- *124*
  Earlier sketch in SATA *73*
Dunbar, Joyce 1944- *112*
  Earlier sketch in SATA *76*
Dunbar, Paul Laurence 1872-1906 ....*34*
Dunbar, Robert E(verett) 1926- *32*
Duncan, Alexandra
  See Moore, Ishbel (Lindsay)
Duncan, Alice Faye 1967- *95*
Duncan, Gregory
  See McClintock, Marshall
Duncan, Jane
  See Cameron, Elizabeth Jane
Duncan, Julia K. *1*
  See Benson, Mildred (Augustine Wirt)
Duncan, Lois 1934- *141*
  Earlier sketches in SATA *1, 36, 75, 133*
  See also CLR *29*
  See also SAAS *2*
Duncan, Norman 1871-1916
  See YABC *1*
Duncan, Terence
  See Nolan, William F(rancis)
Duncombe, Frances (Riker)
  1900-1994 ....*25*
  Obituary *82*
Dunlap, Julie 1958- *84*
Dunleavy, Deborah 1951- *133*
Dunlop, Agnes M. R. (?)-1982 ....*87*
  See Kyle, Elisabeth
Dunlop, Eileen (Rhona) 1938- *76*
  Earlier sketch in SATA *24*
  See also SAAS *12*
Dunn, Anne M. 1940- *107*
Dunn, Harvey T(homas) 1884-1952 ....*34*
Dunn, Herb
  See Gutman, Dan
Dunn, John M. (III) 1949- *93*
Dunn, Judy
  See Spangenberg, Judith Dunn
Dunn, Mary Lois 1930- *6*
Dunnahoo, Terry Janson 1927- *7*
Dunne, Jeanette 1952- *72*
Dunne, Kathleen 1933- *126*
Dunne, Marie
  See Clark, Ann Nolan
Dunne, Mary Collins 1914- *11*
Dunne, Mary Jo
  See Dunne, Mary Collins
Dunnett, Margaret (Rosalind)
  1909-1977 ....*42*

Dunrea, Olivier (Jean-Paul Dominique)
  1953- *118*
  Brief entry *46*
  Earlier sketch in SATA *59*
Dunton, Dorothy 1912- *92*
Dupasquier, Philippe 1955- *86*
Dupuy, T(revor) N(evitt) 1916-1995 ......*4*
  Obituary *86*
DuQuette, Keith 1960- *90*
Durant, Alan 1958- *121*
Durant, John 1902- *27*
Durell, Ann 1930- *66*
Durrant, Lynda 1954- *96*
Durrell, Gerald (Malcolm) 1925-1995 ......*8*
  Obituary *84*
Durrell, Julie 1955- *94*
Durrett, Deanne 1940- *92*
Du Soe, Robert C. 1892-1958
  See YABC *2*
Dussling, Jennifer 1970- *96*
DuTemple, Lesley A. 1952- *113*
Dutz
  See Davis, Mary Octavia
Duval, Katherine
  See James, Elizabeth
Duvall, Evelyn Millis 1906- *9*
Duvall, Jill D(onovan) 1932- *102*
Duvoisin, Roger (Antoine)
  1904-1980 ....*30*
  Obituary *23*
  Earlier sketch in SATA *2*
  See also CLR *23*
Dwiggins, Don(ald J.) 1913-1988 ....*4*
  Obituary *60*
Dwight, Allan
  See Cole, Lois Dwight
Dwyer, Deanna
  See Koontz, Dean R(ay)
Dwyer, K. R.
  See Koontz, Dean R(ay)
Dyck, Peter J. 1914- *75*
Dyer, James (Frederick) 1934- *37*
Dyess, John (Foster) 1939- *76*
Dygard, Thomas J. 1931-1996 ....*97*
  Obituary *92*
  Earlier sketch in SATA *24*
  See also SAAS *15*
Dyke, John 1935- *35*

E

E. V. L.
  See Lucas, E(dward) V(errall)
Eagar, Frances (Elisabeth Stuart)
  1940-1978 ....*11*
  Obituary *55*
Eager, Edward (McMaken)
  1911-1964 ....*17*
  See also CLR *43*
Eager, George B. 1921- *56*
Eagle, Ellen 1953- *61*
Eagle, Kin
  See Adlerman, Daniel
  and Adlerman, Kimberly M.
Eagle, Mike 1942- *11*
Earle, Olive L(ydia) 1888-1982 ....*7*
Earle, William
  See Johns, W(illiam) E(arle)
Earls, Nick 1963- *95*
Early, Jack
  See Scoppettone, Sandra
Early, Jon
  See Johns, W(illiam) E(arle)
Early, Margaret 1951- *72*
Earnshaw, Brian 1929- *17*
Earnshaw, Micky
  See Earnshaw, Spencer Wright
Earnshaw, Spencer Wright 1939- *88*
Easley, MaryAnn *94*

Eastman, Charles A(lexander) 1858-1939
  See YABC *1*
Eastman, P(hilip) D(ey) 1909-1986 ....*33*
  Obituary *46*
Easton, Kelly 1960- *141*
Eastwick, Ivy (Ethel) O(live) *3*
Eaton, Anne T(haxter) 1881-1971 ....*32*
Eaton, George L.
  See Verral, Charles Spain
Eaton, Janet
  See Givens, Janet E(aton)
Eaton, Jeanette 1886-1968 ....*24*
Eaton, Tom 1940- *22*
Ebel, Alex 1927- *11*
Eber, Dorothy (Margaret) Harley
  1930- *27*
Eberle, Irmengarde 1898-1979 ....*2*
  Obituary *23*
Eble, Diane 1956- *74*
Eboch, Chris *113*
Eckblad, Edith Berven 1923- *23*
Eckert, Allan W. 1931- *91*
  Brief entry *27*
  Earlier sketch in SATA *29*
  See also SAAS *21*
Eckert, Horst 1931- *72*
  Earlier sketch in SATA *8*
  See Janosch
Ecklar, Julia (Marie) 1964- *112*
Eddings, David (Carroll) 1931- *91*
Ede, Janina 1937- *33*
Edell, Celeste *12*
Edelman, Lily (Judith) 1915-1981 ....*22*
Edelson, Edward 1932- *51*
Edens, Cooper 1945- *112*
  Earlier sketch in SATA *49*
Edens, (Bishop) David 1926- *39*
Edey, Maitland A(rmstrong)
  1910-1992 ....*25*
  Obituary *71*
Edgeworth, Maria 1768-1849 ....*21*
Edgy, Wardore
  See Gorey, Edward (St. John)
Edison, Theodore
  See Stratemeyer, Edward L.
Edler, Tim(othy) 1948- *56*
Edmiston, Jim 1948- *80*
Edmonds, I(vy) G(ordon) 1917- *8*
Edmonds, Walter D(umaux)
  1903-1998 ....*27*
  Obituary *99*
  Earlier sketch in SATA *1*
  See also SAAS *4*
Edmund, Sean
  See Pringle, Laurence P(atrick)
Edsall, Marian (Stickney) 1920- *8*
Edwards, Al
  See Nourse, Alan E(dward)
Edwards, Anne 1927- *35*
Edwards, Audrey 1947- *52*
  Brief entry *31*
Edwards, Becky (Jane) 1966- *125*
Edwards, Bertram
  See Edwards, Herbert Charles
Edwards, Bronwen Elizabeth
  See Rose, Wendy
Edwards, Cecile Pepin 1916- *25*
Edwards, Dorothy 1914-1982 ....*88*
  Obituary *31*
  Earlier sketch in SATA *4*
Edwards, F. E.
  See Nolan, William F(rancis)
Edwards, Frank B. 1952- *93*
Edwards, Gunvor *32*
Edwards, Harvey 1929- *5*
Edwards, Hazel (Eileen) 1945- *135*
Edwards, Herbert Charles 1912- *12*
Edwards, Jane Campbell 1932- *10*
Edwards, Julia
  See Stratemeyer, Edward L.
Edwards, Julie
  See Andrews, Julie

Edwards, Linda Strauss 1948- *49*
  Brief entry *42*
Edwards, Michelle 1955- *70*
Edwards, Monica le Doux Newton
  1912-1998 ....*12*
Edwards, Olwen
  See Gater, Dilys
Edwards, Page (Lawrence, Jr.)
  1941-1999 ....*59*
Edwards, R. T.
  See Goulart, Ron(ald Joseph)
Edwards, Sally (Cary) 1929- *7*
Edwards, Samuel
  See Gerson, Noel Bertram
Egan, E(dward) W(elstead) 1922- *35*
Egan, Lorraine Hopping 1960- *134*
  Earlier sketch in SATA *91*
Egan, Tim 1957- *89*
Egermeier, Elsie E(milie) 1890-1986 ......*65*
Eggenberger, David 1918- *6*
Eggleston, Edward 1837-1902 ....*27*
Egielski, Richard 1952- *106*
  Earlier sketches in SATA *11, 49*
Egypt, Ophelia Settle 1903-1984 ....*16*
  Obituary *38*
Ehlert, Lois (Jane) 1934- *128*
  Earlier sketches in SATA *35, 69*
  See also CLR *28*
Ehling, Katalin Olah 1941- *93*
Ehrenfreund, Norbert 1921- *86*
Ehrlich, Amy 1942- *132*
  Earlier sketches in SATA *25, 65, 96*
Ehrlich, Bettina Bauer 1903-1985 ....*1*
Eichenberg, Fritz 1901-1990 ....*50*
  Earlier sketch in SATA *9*
Eichler, Margrit 1942- *35*
Eichner, James A. 1927- *4*
Eidson, Thomas 1944- *112*
Eifert, Virginia (Louise) S(nider)
  1911-1966 ....*2*
Eige, (Elizabeth) Lillian 1915- *65*
Eiken, J. Melia 1967- *125*
Einsel, Naiad *10*
Einsel, Walter 1926- *10*
Einzig, Susan 1922- *43*
Eiseman, Alberta 1925- *15*
Eisenberg, Azriel (Louis) 1903-1985 ......*12*
Eisenberg, Lisa 1949- *57*
  Brief entry *50*
Eisenberg, Phyllis Rose 1924- *41*
Eisner, Vivienne
  See Margolis, Vivienne
Eisner, Will(iam Erwin) 1917- *31*
Eitzen, Allan 1928- *9*
Eitzen, Ruth (Carper) 1924- *9*
Ekwensi, C. O. D.
  See Ekwensi, Cyprian (Odiatu Duaka)
Ekwensi, Cyprian (Odiatu Duaka)
  1921- *66*
Elam, Richard M(ace, Jr.) 1920- *9*
Elborn, Andrew
  See Clements, Andrew
  and Clements, Andrew
Eldon, Kathy 1946- *107*
Elfman, Blossom 1925- *8*
Elgin, Kathleen 1923- *39*
Elia
  See Lamb, Charles
Eliot, A. D.
  See Jewett, (Theodora) Sarah Orne
Eliot, Alice
  See Jewett, (Theodora) Sarah Orne
Eliot, Anne
  See Cole, Lois Dwight
Eliot, Dan
  See Silverberg, Robert
Elish, Dan 1960- *129*
  Earlier sketch in SATA *68*
Elisha, Ron 1951- *104*
Elkin, Benjamin 1911-1995 ....*3*
Elkins, Dov Peretz 1937- *5*
Ellacott, S(amuel) E(rnest) 1911- *19*

Ellen, Jaye
  See Nixon, Joan Lowery
Eller, Scott
  See Holinger, William (Jacques)
  and Shepard, Jim
Ellestad, Myrvin H. 1921- *120*
Elliot, David 1952- *122*
Elliot, Don
  See Silverberg, Robert
Elliott, Bruce
  See Field, Edward
Elliott, Don
  See Silverberg, Robert
Elliott, Elizabeth Shippen Green
  See Green, Elizabeth Shippen
Elliott, Janice 1931-1995 ....*119*
Elliott, Joey
  See Houk, Randy
Elliott, Louise *111*
Elliott, Odette 1939- *75*
Elliott, Sarah M(cCarn) 1930- *14*
Elliott, William
  See Bradbury, Ray (Douglas)
Ellis, (Mary) Amabel (Nassau Strachey)
  Williams
  See Williams-Ellis, (Mary) Amabel
  (Nassau Strachey)
Ellis, Anyon
  See Rowland-Entwistle, (Arthur) Theodore
  (Henry)
Ellis, Deborah 1961- *129*
Ellis, E. S.
  See Ellis, Edward S(ylvester)
Ellis, Edward S(ylvester) 1840-1916
  See YABC *1*
Ellis, Ella Thorp 1928- *127*
  Earlier sketch in SATA *7*
  See also SAAS *9*
Ellis, Harry Bearse 1921- *9*
Ellis, Herbert
  See Wilson, Lionel
Ellis, Mel(vin Richard) 1912-1984 ....*7*
  Obituary *39*
Ellis, Richard 1938- *130*
Ellis, Sarah 1952- *131*
  Earlier sketch in SATA *68*
  See also CLR *42*
Ellison, Emily *114*
Ellison, Lucile Watkins
  1907(?)-1979 ....*50*
  Obituary *22*
Ellison, Virginia H(owell) 1910- *4*
Ellsberg, Edward 1891-1983 ....*7*
Elmer, Robert 1958- *99*
Elmore, (Carolyn) Patricia 1933- *38*
  Brief entry *35*
El-Moslimany, Ann P(axton) 1937- *90*
Elspeth
  See Bragdon, Elspeth MacDuffie
Elting, Mary 1906- *88*
  Earlier sketch in SATA *2*
  See also SAAS *20*
Elwart, Joan Potter 1927- *2*
Elwood, Ann 1931- *55*
  Brief entry *52*
Elwood, Roger 1943- *58*
Elya, Susan M(iddleton) 1955- *106*
Elzbieta *88*
Emberley, Barbara A(nne) 1932- *70*
  Earlier sketch in SATA *8*
  See also CLR *5*
Emberley, Ed(ward Randolph) 1931- *70*
  Earlier sketch in SATA *8*
  See also CLR *81*
Emberley, Michael 1960- *119*
  Earlier sketches in SATA *34, 80*
Embry, Margaret Jacob 1919-1975 ....*5*
Emecheta, (Florence Onye) Buchi
  1944- *66*
Emerson, Alice B. *67*
  Earlier sketch in SATA *1*
  See Benson, Mildred (Augustine Wirt)

Emerson, Kathy Lynn 1947- *63*
Emerson, Ru 1944- *107*
  Earlier sketch in SATA *70*
Emerson, Sally 1952- *111*
Emerson, William K(eith) 1925- *25*
Emert, Phyllis R(aybin) 1947- *93*
Emery, Anne (McGuigan) 1907- *33*
  Earlier sketch in SATA *1*
Emmens, Carol Ann 1944- *39*
Emmett, Jonathan 1965- *138*
Emory, Jerry 1957- *96*
Emrich, Duncan (Black Macdonald)
  1908-1970(?) *11*
Emslie, M. L.
  See Simpson, Myrtle L(illias)
Ende, Michael (Andreas Helmuth)
  1929-1995 ....*130*
  Brief entry *42*
  Obituary *86*
  Earlier sketch in SATA *61*
  See also CLR *14*
Enderle, Judith (Ann) Ross 1941- *89*
  Autobiography Feature *114*
  Earlier sketch in SATA *38*
  See also SAAS *26*
Enell, Trinka (Gochenour) 1951- *79*
Enfield, Carrie
  See Smith, Susan Vernon
Engdahl, Sylvia Louise 1933- *4*
  Autobiography Feature *122*
  See also CLR *2*
  See also SAAS *5*
Engel, Diana 1947- *70*
Engelhart, Margaret S. 1924- *59*
Engelmann, Kim (V.) 1959- *87*
England, George Allan 1877-1936 ....*102*
Engle, Eloise *9*
  See Paananen, Eloise (Katherine)
Englebert, Victor 1933- *8*
English, James W(ilson) 1915- *37*
Engstrom, Elizabeth 1951- *110*
Enright, D(ennis) J(oseph)
  1920-2002 ....*25*
  Obituary *140*
Enright, Elizabeth (Wright) 1909-1968 ......*9*
  See also CLR *4*
Ensor, Robert (T.) 1922- *93*
Entwistle, (Arthur) Theodore (Henry)
  Rowland
  See Rowland-Entwistle, (Arthur) Theodore
  (Henry)
Enys, Sarah L.
  See Sloggett, Nellie
Epanya, Christian A(rthur Kingue)
  1956- *91*
Ephraim, Shelly S(chonebaum)
  1952- *97*
Ephron, Delia 1944- *65*
  Brief entry *50*
Epler, Doris M. 1928- *73*
Epp, Margaret A(gnes) 1913- *20*
Epple, Anne Orth 1927- *20*
Epstein, Anne Merrick 1931- *20*
Epstein, Beryl (M. Williams) 1910- *31*
  Earlier sketch in SATA *1*
  See also CLR *26*
  See also SAAS *17*
Epstein, Perle S(herry) 1938- *27*
Epstein, Rachel S. 1941- *102*
Epstein, Samuel 1909-2000 ....*31*
  Earlier sketch in SATA *1*
  See also CLR *26*
  See also SAAS *17*
Erdman, Loula Grace 1905(?)-1976 ....*1*
Erdoes, Richard 1912- *33*
  Brief entry *28*
Erdrich, Louise 1954- *141*
  Earlier sketch in SATA *94*
Erickson, Betty J(ean) 1923- *97*
Erickson, John R. 1943- *136*
  Earlier sketch in SATA *70*
Erickson, Jon 1948- *141*

Erickson, Phoebe *59*
Erickson, Russell E(verett) 1932- *27*
Erickson, Sabra Rollins 1912-1995 ....*35*
Ericson, Walter
  See Fast, Howard (Melvin)
Erikson, Mel 1937- *31*
Erlanger, Baba
  See Trahey, Jane
Erlbach, Arlene 1948- *115*
  Earlier sketch in SATA *78*
Erlich, Lillian (Feldman) 1910-1983 ....*10*
Ernst, (Lyman) John 1940- *39*
Ernst, Kathryn (Fitzgerald) 1942- *25*
Ernst, Lisa Campbell 1957- *95*
  Brief entry *44*
  Earlier sketch in SATA *55*
Ervin, Janet Halliday 1923- *4*
Erwin, Will
  See Eisner, Will(iam Erwin)
Esbensen, Barbara J(uster)
  1925-1996 ....*97*
  Brief entry *53*
  Earlier sketch in SATA *62*
Eseki, Bruno
  See Mphahlele, Ezekiel
Eshmeyer, R. E. *29*
  See Eschmeyer, R(einhart) E(rnst)
Eskridge, Ann E. 1949- *84*
Espeland, Pamela (Lee) 1951- *128*
  Brief entry *38*
  Earlier sketch in SATA *52*
Espriella, Don Manuel Alvarez
  See Southey, Robert
Espy, Willard R(ichardson)
  1910-1999 ....*38*
  Obituary *113*
Essrig, Harry 1912- *66*
Estep, Irene Compton *5*
Esterl, Arnica 1933- *77*
Estes, Eleanor (Ruth) 1906-1988 ....*91*
  Obituary *56*
  Earlier sketch in SATA *7*
  See also CLR *70*
Estoril, Jean
  See Allan, Mabel Esther
Estrada, Pau 1961- *74*
Etchemendy, Nancy 1952- *38*
Etchison, Birdie L(ee) 1937- *38*
Etchison, Craig 1945- *133*
Etherington, Frank 1945- *58*
Ets, Marie Hall 1893-1984 ....*2*
  See also CLR *33*
Eunson, (John) Dale 1904-2002 ....*5*
  Obituary *132*
Evanoff, Vlad 1916- *59*
Evans, Douglas 1953- *93*
Evans, Eva (Knox) 1905-1998 ....*27*
Evans, Freddi Williams 1957- *134*
Evans, Greg 1947- *73*
Evans, Hubert Reginald 1892-1986 ....*118*
  Obituary *48*
Evans, Katherine (Floyd) 1901-1964 ....*5*
Evans, Larry
  See Evans, Laurence Chubb
Evans, Laurence Chubb 1939- *88*
Evans, Lawrence Watt
  See Watt-Evans, Lawrence
Evans, Mari 1923- *10*
Evans, Mark *19*
Evans, Nancy 1950- *65*
Evans, Patricia Healy
  See Carpenter, Patricia (Healy Evans)
Evans, (Alice) Pearl 1927- *83*
Evans, Shirlee 1931- *58*
Evans, Tabor
  See Cameron, Lou
  and Knott, William C(ecil, Jr.)
  and Wallmann, Jeffrey M(iner)
Evarts, Esther
  See Benson, Sally
Evarts, Hal G. (Jr.) 1915-1989 ....*6*

Everett, Gail
    See Hale, Arlene
Evernden, Margery 1916- 5
Eversole, Robyn Harbert 1971- 74
Evslin, Bernard 1922-1993 83
    Brief entry 28
    Obituary 77
    Earlier sketch in SATA 45
Ewart, Claire 1958- 76
Ewen, David 1907-1985 4
    Obituary 47
Ewing, Juliana (Horatia Gatty)
    1841-1885 16
    See also CLR 78
Ewing, Kathryn 1921- 20
Eyerly, Jeannette (Hyde) 1908- 86
    Earlier sketch in SATA 4
    See also SAAS 10
Eyre, Dorothy
    See McGuire, Leslie (Sarah)
Eyre, Katherine Wigmore 1901-1970 26
Ezzell, Marilyn 1937- 42
    Brief entry 38

F

Fabe, Maxene 1943- 15
Faber, Doris (Greenberg) 1924- 78
    Earlier sketch in SATA 3
Faber, Harold 1919- 5
Fabre, Jean Henri (Casimir)
    1823-1915 22
Facklam, Margery (Metz) 1927- 132
    Earlier sketches in SATA 20, 85
Fadiman, Clifton (Paul) 1904-1999 11
    Obituary 115
Fahs, Sophia Blanche Lyon
    1876-1978 102
Fair, David 1952- 96
Fair, Sylvia 1933- 13
Fairfax-Lucy, Brian (Fulke Cameron-Ramsay)
    1898-1974 6
    Obituary 26
Fairfield, Flora
    See Alcott, Louisa May
Fairman, Joan A(lexandra) 1935- 10
Faithfull, Gail 1936- 8
Falconer, Ian 125
Falconer, James
    See Kirkup, James
Falconer, Lee N.
    See May, Julian
Falkner, Leonard 1900-1977 12
Fall, Andrew
    See Arthur, Robert, (Jr.)
Fall, Thomas
    See Snow, Donald Clifford
Falls, C(harles) B(uckles) 1874-1960 38
    Brief entry 27
Falstein, Louis 1909-1995 37
Fanelli, Sara 1969- 126
    Earlier sketch in SATA 89
Fanning, Leonard M(ulliken) 1888-1967 5
Faralla, Dana 1909- 9
Faralla, Dorothy W.
    See Faralla, Dana
Farb, Peter 1929-1980 12
    Obituary 22
Farber, Norma 1909-1984 75
    Obituary 38
    Earlier sketch in SATA 25
Farish, Terry 1947- 82
Farjeon, (Eve) Annabel 1919- 11
Farjeon, Eleanor 1881-1965 2
    See also CLR 34
Farley, Carol (J.) 1936- 137
    Earlier sketch in SATA 4
Farley, Walter (Lorimer) 1915-1989 132
    Earlier sketches in SATA 2, 43
Farlow, James O(rville, Jr.) 1951- 75

Farmer, Nancy 1941- 117
    Earlier sketch in SATA 79
Farmer, Patti 1948- 79
Farmer, Penelope (Jane) 1939- 105
    Brief entry 39
    Earlier sketch in SATA 40
    See also CLR 8
    See also SAAS 22
Farmer, Peter 1950- 38
Farmer, Philip Jose 1918- 93
Farnham, Burt
    See Clifford, Harold B(urton)
Farnsworth, Bill 1958- 135
    Earlier sketch in SATA 84
Farquhar, Margaret C(utting)
    1905-1988 13
Farquharson, Alexander 1944- 46
Farquharson, Martha
    See Finley, Martha
Farr, Diana (Pullein-Thompson) 82
    See Pullein-Thompson, Diana
Farr, Finis (King) 1904-1982 10
Farrar, Susan Clement 1917- 33
Farrell, Ben
    See Cebulash, Mel
Farrell, Patrick
    See Odgers, Sally Farrell
Farrell, Sally
    See Odgers, Sally Farrell
Farrington, S(elwyn) Kip, Jr.
    1904-1983 20
Farthing, Alison 1936- 45
    Brief entry 36
Farthing-Knight, Catherine 1933- 92
Fassler, Joan (Grace) 1931- 11
Fast, Howard (Melvin) 1914-2003 7
    Autobiography Feature 107
Fasulo, Michael 1963- 83
Fatchen, Max 1920- 84
    Earlier sketch in SATA 20
    See also SAAS 20
Fate, Marilyn
    See Collins, Paul
Father Goose
    See Ghigna, Charles
Fatigati, (Frances) Evelyn 1948- 24
Fatio, Louise 1904-1993 6
Faulhaber, Martha 1926- 7
Faulkner, Anne Irvin 1906- 23
Faulkner, Frank
    See Ellis, Edward S(ylvester)
Faulkner, Nancy
    See Faulkner, Anne Irvin
Faulknor, Cliff(ord Vernon) 1913- 86
Favole, Robert J(ames) 1950- 125
Fax, Elton Clay 1909-1993 25
Faxon, Lavinia
    See Russ, Lavinia (Faxon)
Feagles, Anita M(acRae) 1927- 9
Feagles, Elizabeth
    See Day, Beth (Feagles)
Feague, Mildred H. 1915- 14
Fecher, Constance
    See Heaven, Constance (Christina)
Feder, Chris Welles 1938- 81
Feder, Harriet K. 1928- 73
Feder, Paula (Kurzband) 1935- 26
Feelings, Muriel (Lavita Grey)
    1938- 16
    See also CLR 5
    See also SAAS 8
Feelings, Thomas 1933- 8
    See Feelings, Tom
Feelings, Tom 69
    See also CLR 58
    See also SAAS 19
    See Feelings, Thomas
Fehler, Gene 1940- 74
Fehrenbach, T(heodore) R(eed, Jr.)
    1925- 33
Feiffer, Jules (Ralph) 1929- 111
    Earlier sketches in SATA 8, 61

Feig, Barbara Krane 1937- 34
Feikema, Feike
    See Manfred, Frederick (Feikema)
Feil, Hila 1942- 12
Feilen, John
    See May, Julian
Feinberg, Barbara Jane 1938- 58
    See Feinberg, Barbara Silberdick
Feinberg, Barbara Silberdick 1938- 123
    See Feinberg, Barbara Jane
Feldman, Anne (Rodgers) 1939- 19
Feldman, Elane 79
Felix
    See Vincent, Felix
Fellows, Muriel H. 10
Felsen, Henry Gregor 1916-1995 1
    See also SAAS 2
Feltenstein, Arlene (H.) 1934- 119
Felton, Harold William 1902-1991 1
Felton, Ronald Oliver 1909- 3
Felts, Shirley 1934- 33
Fenderson, Lewis H., Jr. 1907-1983 47
    Obituary 37
Fenner, Carol (Elizabeth) 1929-2002 89
    Obituary 132
    Earlier sketch in SATA 7
    See also SAAS 24
Fenner, Phyllis R(eid) 1899-1982 1
    Obituary 29
Fenten, Barbara D(oris) 1935- 26
Fenten, D(onald) X. 1932- 4
Fenton, Carroll Lane 1900-1969 5
Fenton, Edward 1917-1995 7
    Obituary 89
Fenton, Mildred Adams 1899-1995 21
Fenwick, Patti
    See Grider, Dorothy
Feravolo, Rocco Vincent 1922- 10
Ferber, Edna 1887-1968 7
Fergus, Charles 114
Ferguson, Alane 1957- 85
Ferguson, Bob
    See Ferguson, Robert Bruce
Ferguson, Cecil 1931- 45
Ferguson, Robert Bruce 1927-2001 13
Ferguson, Sarah (Margaret) 1959- 110
    Earlier sketch in SATA 66
Ferguson, Walter (W.) 1930- 34
Fergusson, Erna 1888-1964 5
Fermi, Laura 1907-1977 6
    Obituary 28
Fern, Eugene A. 1919-1987 10
    Obituary 54
Fernandes, Eugenie 1943- 139
    Earlier sketch in SATA 77
Ferrari, Maria 123
Ferrell, Nancy Warren 1932- 70
Ferrier, Lucy
    See Penzler, Otto
Ferris, Helen Josephine 1890-1969 21
Ferris, James Cody 1
    See McFarlane, Leslie (Charles)
Ferris, Jean 1939- 105
    Brief entry 50
    Earlier sketch in SATA 56
Ferris, Jeri Chase 1937- 84
Ferry, Charles 1927- 92
    Earlier sketch in SATA 43
    See also CLR 34
    See also SAAS 20
Fetz, Ingrid 1915- 30
Feydy, Anne Lindbergh
    Brief entry 32
    See Sapieyevski, Anne Lindbergh
Fiammenghi, Gioia 1929- 66
    Earlier sketch in SATA 9
Fiarotta, Noel 15
    See Ficarotta, Noel
Fiarotta, Phyllis 15
    See Ficarotta, Phyllis
Fichter, George S. 1922-1993 7

Fidler, Kathleen (Annie) 1899-1980 87
  Obituary 45
  Earlier sketch in SATA 3
Fiedler, Jean(nette Feldman) 4
Field, Dorothy 1944- 97
Field, Edward 1924- 109
  Earlier sketch in SATA 8
Field, Eugene 1850-1895 16
Field, Gans T.
  See Wellman, Manly Wade
Field, James 1959- 113
Field, Peter
  See Drago, Harry Sinclair
  and Hobson, Laura Z(ametkin)
Field, Rachel (Lyman) 1894-1942 15
  See also CLR 21
Fielding, Kate
  See Oldfield, Jenny
Fienberg, Anna 1956- 112
Fife, Dale (Odile Hollerbach) 1901- 18
Fighter Pilot, A
  See Johnston, H(ugh) A(nthony) S(tephen)
Figler, Jeanie 1949- 123
Figley, Marty Rhodes 1948- 88
Figueroa, Pablo 1938- 9
Fijan, Carol 1918- 12
Filderman, Diane E(lizabeth) 1959- 87
Files, Meg 1946- 107
Fillmore, Parker H(oysted) 1878-1944
  See YABC 1
Filstrup, Chris
  See Filstrup, E(dward) Christian
Filstrup, E(dward) Christian 1942- 43
Finchler, Judy 1943- 93
Finder, Martin
  See Salzmann, Siegmund
Fine, Anne 1947- 111
  Earlier sketches in SATA 29, 72
  See also CLR 25
  See also SAAS 15
Finger, Charles J(oseph)
  1869(?)-1941 42
Fink, William B(ertrand) 1916- 22
Finke, Blythe Foote 1922- 26
Finkel, George (Irvine) 1909-1975 8
Finkelstein, Norman H. 1941- 137
  Earlier sketch in SATA 73
Finlay, Alice Sullivan 1946- 82
Finlay, Winifred Lindsay Crawford
  (McKissack) 1910-1989 23
Finlayson, Ann 1925- 8
Finley, Martha 1828-1909 43
Finley, Mary Peace 1942- 83
Finney, Jack 109
  See Finney, Walter Braden
Finney, Shan 1944- 65
Firer, Ben Zion
  See Firer, Benzion
Firer, Benzion 1914- 64
Fireside, Bryna J. 1932- 73
Firmin, Charlotte 1954- 29
Firmin, Peter 1928- 58
  Earlier sketch in SATA 15
Fischbach, Julius 1894-1988 10
Fischer, John
  See Fluke, Joanne
Fischer, R. J.
  See Fluke, Joanne
Fischer-Nagel, Andreas 1951- 56
Fischer-Nagel, Heiderose 1956- 56
Fischler, Shirley (Walton) 66
Fischler, Stan(ley I.) 66
  Brief entry 36
Fisher, Aileen (Lucia) 1906- 73
  Earlier sketches in SATA 1, 25
  See also CLR 49
Fisher, Barbara 1940- 44
  Brief entry 34
Fisher, Chris 1958- 80
Fisher, Clavin C(argill) 1912- 24

Fisher, Dorothy (Frances) Canfield 1879-
  1958
  See YABC 1
  See also CLR
Fisher, Gary L. 1949- 86
Fisher, John (Oswald Hamilton)
  1909- 15
Fisher, Laura Harrison 1934- 5
Fisher, Leonard Everett 1924- 120
  Autobiography Feature 122
  Earlier sketches in SATA 4, 34, 73
  See also CLR 18
  See also SAAS 1
Fisher, Lois I. 1948- 38
  Brief entry 35
Fisher, Margery (Turner) 1913-1992 20
  Obituary 74
Fisher, Marshall Jon 1963- 113
Fisher, Nikki
  See Strachan, Ian
Fisher, Robert (Tempest) 1943- 47
Fisher, Suzanne
  See Staples, Suzanne Fisher
Fishman, Cathy Goldberg 1951- 106
Fisk, Nicholas 25
  See Higginbottom, David
Fisk, Pauline 1948- 66
Fiske, Tarleton
  See Bloch, Robert (Albert)
Fitch, Clarke
  See Sinclair, Upton (Beall)
Fitch, John IV
  See Cormier, Robert (Edmund)
Fitch, Sheree 1956- 108
Fitschen, Dale 1937- 20
Fitzalan, Roger
  See Trevor, Elleston
Fitzgerald, Captain Hugh
  See Baum, L(yman) Frank
Fitzgerald, Edward Earl 1919-2001 20
Fitzgerald, F(rancis) A(nthony)
  1940- 15
Fitzgerald, John D(ennis)
  1907(?)-1988 20
  Obituary 56
  See also CLR 1
Fitzgerald, Merni Ingrassia 1955- 53
Fitzgibbon, Terry 1948- 121
Fitzhardinge, Joan Margaret 1912- 73
  Earlier sketch in SATA 2
  See Phipson, Joan
Fitzhugh, Louise (Perkins)
  1928-1974 45
  Obituary 24
  Earlier sketch in SATA 1
  See also CLR 72
Fitzhugh, Percy Keese 1876-1950 65
Fitzpatrick, Marie-Louise 1962- 125
FitzRalph, Matthew
  See McInerny, Ralph (Matthew)
Fitz-Randolph, Jane (Currens) 1915- 51
Fitzsimons, Cecilia (A. L.) 1952- 97
Flack, Marjorie 1897-1958 100
  See also YABC 2
  See also CLR 28
Flack, Naomi John White -1999 40
  Brief entry 35
Flannery, Kate
  See De Goldi, Kathleen Domenica
Flatt, Lizann
  See Brunskill, Elizabeth Ann Flatt
Fleagle, Gail S(hatto) 1940- 117
Fleetwood, Jenni 1947- 80
Fleischer, Jane
  See Oppenheim, Joanne
Fleischhauer-Hardt, Helga 1936- 30
Fleischman, Paul 1952- 110
  Brief entry 32
  Earlier sketches in SATA 39, 72
  See also CLR 66
  See also SAAS 20

Fleischman, (Albert) Sid(ney) 1920- 96
  Earlier sketches in SATA 8, 59
  See also CLR 15
Fleischner, Jennifer 1956- 93
Fleisher, Paul 1948- 132
  Earlier sketch in SATA 81
Fleisher, Robbin 1951-1977 52
  Brief entry 49
Fleishman, Seymour 1918- 66
  Brief entry 32
Fleming, A. A.
  See Arthur, Robert, (Jr.)
Fleming, Alice Mulcahey 1928- 9
Fleming, Candace 1962- 94
Fleming, Denise 1950- 126
  Earlier sketch in SATA 81
Fleming, Ian (Lancaster) 1908-1964 9
Fleming, Ronald Lee 1941- 56
Fleming, Stuart
  See Knight, Damon (Francis)
Fleming, Susan 1932- 32
Fleming, Thomas (James) 1927- 8
Fleming, Virginia (Edwards) 1923- 84
Flesch, Y.
  See Flesch, Yolande (Catarina)
Flesch, Yolande (Catarina) 1950- 55
Fletcher, Charlie May Hogue 1897-1977 ...3
Fletcher, Colin 1922- 28
Fletcher, Dirk
  See Cunningham, Chet
Fletcher, George U.
  See Pratt, (Murray) Fletcher
Fletcher, Helen Jill 1910- 13
Fletcher, Ralph 1953- 105
Fletcher, Susan (Clemens) 1951- 110
  Earlier sketch in SATA 70
Fleur, Paul
  See Pohl, Frederik
Flexner, James Thomas 1908- 9
Flint, Helen 1952- 102
Flint, Russ 1944- 74
Flitner, David P(erkins), Jr. 1949- 7
Floethe, Louise Lee 1913- 4
Floethe, Richard 1901-1998 4
Floherty, John Joseph 1882-1964 25
Flood, Bo
  See Flood, Nancy Bo
Flood, Nancy Bo 1945- 130
Flood, Pansie Hart 1964- 140
Flood, William 1942- 129
Flooglebuckle, Al
  See Spiegelman, Art
Flora, James (Royer) 1914-1998 30
  Obituary 103
  Earlier sketch in SATA 1
  See also SAAS 6
Florian, Douglas 1950- 125
  Earlier sketches in SATA 19, 83
Flory, Jane Trescott 1917- 22
Flournoy, Valerie (Rose) 1952- 95
Flowerdew, Phyllis -1994 33
Flowers, Pam 1946- 136
Flowers, Sarah 1952- 98
Floyd, Gareth 1940- 62
  Brief entry 31
Fluchere, Henri 1914- 40
Fluke, Joanne 88
Flynn, Barbara 1928- 9
Flynn, Jackson
  See Bensen, Donald R.
  and Shirreffs, Gordon D(onald)
Flynn, Nicholas
  See Odgers, Sally Farrell
Flynn, Rachel 1953- 109
Fodor, R(onald) V(ictor) 1944- 25
Fogelin, Adrian 1951- 129
Foley, (Anna) Bernice Williams
  1902-1987 28
Foley, June 1944- 44
Foley, (Mary) Louise Munro 1933- 106
  Brief entry 40
  Earlier sketch in SATA 54

Folke, Will
  See Bloch, Robert (Albert)
Folsom, Franklin (Brewster)
  1907-1995 ....*5*
  Obituary *88*
Folsom, Michael (Brewster)
  1938-1990 ....*40*
  Obituary *88*
Fontenot, Mary Alice 1910- *91*
  Earlier sketch in SATA *34*
Foon, Dennis 1951- *119*
Fooner, Michael *22*
Foote, Timothy (Gilson) 1926- *52*
Forberg, Ati *22*
  See Forberg, Beate Gropius
Forbes, Anna 1954- *101*
Forbes, Bryan 1926- *37*
Forbes, Cabot L.
  See Hoyt, Edwin P(almer), Jr.
Forbes, Esther 1891-1967 ....*100*
  Earlier sketch in SATA *2*
  See also CLR *27*
Forbes, Graham B. *1*
Forbes, Kathryn
  See McLean, Kathryn (Anderson)
Forbes, Robert
  See Arthur, Robert, (Jr.)
Ford, Albert Lee
  See Stratemeyer, Edward L.
Ford, Barbara *56*
  Brief entry *34*
Ford, Brian J(ohn) 1939- *49*
Ford, Carolyn (Mott) 1938- *98*
Ford, Elbur
  See Hibbert, Eleanor Alice Burford
Ford, Ellen 1949- *89*
Ford, George (Jr.) *31*
Ford, Hilary
  See Youd, (Christopher) Samuel
Ford, Hildegarde
  See Morrison, Velma Ford
Ford, Jerome W. 1949- *78*
Ford, Jerry
  See Ford, Jerome W.
Ford, Juwanda G(ertrude) 1967- *102*
Ford, Marcia
  See Radford, Ruby L(orraine)
Ford, Peter 1936- *59*
Ford, S. M.
  See Uhlig, Susan
Foreman, Michael 1938- *135*
  Earlier sketches in SATA *2, 73, 129*
  See also CLR *32*
  See also SAAS *21*
Forest, Antonia *29*
Forest, Dial
  See Gault, William Campbell
Forest, Heather 1948- *120*
Forester, C(ecil) S(cott) 1899-1966 ....*13*
Forman, Brenda 1936- *4*
Forman, James
  See Forman, James D(ouglas)
Forman, James D(ouglas) 1932- *70*
  Earlier sketch in SATA *8*
Forrest, Elizabeth
  See Salsitz, Rhondi Vilott
Forrest, Sybil
  See Markun, Patricia Maloney
Forrestal, Elaine 1941- *117*
Forrester, Helen *48*
  See Bhatia, Jamunadevi
Forrester, Marian
  See Schachtel, Roger (Bernard)
Forrester, Sandra 1949- *90*
Forrester, Victoria 1940- *40*
  Brief entry *35*
Forsee, (Frances) Aylesa -1986 ....*1*
Forsey, Chris 1950- *59*
Forshay-Lunsford, Cin 1965- *60*
Forster, E(dward) M(organ)
  1879-1970 ....*57*

Fort, Paul
  See Stockton, Francis Richard
Forte, Maurizio 1961- *110*
Fortey, Richard (Alan) 1946- *109*
Forth, Melissa D(eal) *96*
Fortnum, Peggy *26*
  See Nuttall-Smith, Margaret Emily Noel
Forward, Robert L(ull) 1932-2002 ....*82*
Foster, Alan Dean 1946- *70*
Foster, Brad W. 1955- *34*
Foster, Doris Van Liew 1899-1993 ....*10*
Foster, E(lizabeth) C(onnell) 1902- *9*
Foster, Elizabeth 1902- *12*
Foster, Elizabeth 1905-1963 ....*10*
Foster, F. Blanche 1919- *11*
Foster, G(eorge) Allen 1907-1969 ....*26*
Foster, Genevieve (Stump) 1893-1979 ......*2*
  Obituary *23*
  See also CLR *7*
Foster, Hal
  See Foster, Harold (Rudolf)
Foster, Harold (Rudolf) 1892-1982 ....*31*
  See Foster, Hal
Foster, Jeanne
  See Williams, Jeanne
Foster, John
  See Foster, John L(ouis)
  and Furcolo, Foster
Foster, John (Thomas) 1925- *8*
Foster, John L(ouis) 1941- *102*
Foster, Laura Louise (James) 1918- *6*
Foster, Leila Merrell 1929- *73*
Foster, Lynne 1937- *74*
Foster, Marian Curtis 1909-1978 ....*23*
Foster, Sally *58*
Foulds, E. V.
  See Foulds, Elfrida Vipont
Foulds, Elfrida Vipont 1902-1992 ....*52*
  See Vipont, Elfrida
Fourie, Corlia 1944- *91*
Fourth Brother, The
  See Aung, (Maung) Htin
Fowke, Edith (Margaret) 1913-1996 ......*14*
Fowles, John (Robert) 1926- *22*
Fox, Aileen 1907- *58*
Fox, Charles Philip 1913- *12*
Fox, Eleanor
  See St. John, Wylly Folk
Fox, Freeman
  See Hamilton, Charles (Harold St. John)
Fox, Geoffrey 1941- *73*
Fox, Grace
  See Anderson, Grace Fox
Fox, Larry *30*
Fox, Lorraine 1922-1976 ....*27*
  Earlier sketch in SATA *11*
Fox, Louisa
  See Kroll, Virginia L(ouise)
Fox, Mary Virginia 1919- *88*
  Brief entry *39*
  Earlier sketch in SATA *44*
Fox, Mem *103*
  See also CLR *23*
  See Fox, Merrion Frances
Fox, Merrion Frances 1946- *51*
  See also CLR *80*
  See Fox, Mem
Fox, Michael W(ilson) 1937- *15*
Fox, Paula 1923- *120*
  Earlier sketches in SATA *17, 60*
  See also CLR *44*
Fox, Robert J. 1927- *33*
Fradin, Dennis
  See Fradin, Dennis Brindell
Fradin, Dennis Brindell 1945- *135*
  Earlier sketches in SATA *29, 90*
Fradin, Judith (Bernette) Bloom
  1945- *90*
Frailey, Paige (Menefee) 1965- *82*
Frame, Janet
  See Clutha, Janet Paterson Frame

Frame, Paul 1913-1994 ....*60*
  Brief entry *33*
  Obituary *83*
Frances, Miss
  See Horwich, Frances R(appaport)
Franchere, Ruth *18*
Francis, Charles
  See Holme, Bryan
Francis, Dee
  See Haas, Dorothy F.
Francis, Dorothy Brenner 1926- *127*
  Earlier sketch in SATA *10*
Francis, Pamela (Mary) 1926- *11*
Franck, Eddie
  See Cooke, Frank E.
Franco, Eloise (Bauder) 1910- *62*
Franco, Johan (Henri Gustave)
  1908-1988 ....*62*
Franco, Marjorie *38*
Francois, Andre 1915- *25*
Francoise
  See Seignobosc, Francoise
Frank, Anne(lies Marie) 1929-1945 ....*87*
  Brief entry *42*
Frank, Daniel B. 1956- *55*
Frank, Helene
  See Vautier, Ghislaine
Frank, Josette 1893-1989 ....*10*
  Obituary *63*
Frank, Lucy 1947- *94*
Frank, Mary 1933- *34*
Frank, R., Jr.
  See Ross, Frank (Xavier), Jr.
Frankau, Mary Evelyn Atkinson
  1899-1974 ....*4*
Frankel, Alona 1937- *66*
Frankel, Bernice *9*
Frankel, Edward 1910- *44*
Frankel, Ellen 1951- *78*
Frankel, Julie 1947- *40*
  Brief entry *34*
Frankenberg, Robert 1911- *22*
Franklin, Cheryl J. 1955- *70*
Franklin, Harold 1926- *13*
Franklin, Kristine L. 1958- *124*
  Earlier sketch in SATA *80*
Franklin, Max
  See Deming, Richard
Franklin, Steve
  See Stevens, Franklin
Franson, Leanne R. 1963- *111*
Franzen, Nils-Olof 1916- *10*
Frascino, Edward *48*
  Brief entry *33*
  See also SAAS *9*
Frasconi, Antonio 1919- *131*
  Earlier sketches in SATA *6, 53*
  See also SAAS *11*
Fraser, Betty
  See Fraser, Elizabeth Marr
Fraser, Elizabeth Marr 1928- *31*
Fraser, Eric (George) 1902-1983 ....*38*
Fraser, Mary Ann 1959- *137*
  Earlier sketch in SATA *76*
  See also SAAS *23*
Fraser, Wynnette (McFaddin) 1925- *90*
Frasier, Debra 1953- *112*
  Earlier sketch in SATA *69*
Fraustino, Lisa Rowe 1961- *84*
Frazee, Marla 1958- *105*
Frazetta, Frank 1928- *58*
Frazier, Neta (Osborn) Lohnes
  1890-1990 ....*7*
Frederic, Mike
  See Cox, William R(obert)
Fredericks, Anthony D. 1947- *113*
Freed, Alvyn M. 1913- *22*
Freedman, Benedict 1919- *27*
Freedman, Jeff 1953- *90*
Freedman, Nancy 1920- *27*

Freedman, Russell (Bruce) 1929- *123*
  Earlier sketches in SATA *16, 71*
  See also CLR *71*
Freeman, Barbara C(onstance) 1906- *28*
Freeman, Bill
  See Freeman, William Bradford
Freeman, Don 1908-1978 ....*17*
  See also CLR *30*
Freeman, Ira Maximilian 1905-1987 ....*21*
Freeman, Lucy (Greenbaum) 1916- *24*
Freeman, Mae (Blacker) 1907- *25*
Freeman, Marcia S. 1937- *102*
Freeman, Martha 1956- *101*
Freeman, Nancy 1932- *61*
Freeman, Peter J.
  See Calvert, Patricia
Freeman, Sarah (Caroline) 1940- *66*
Freeman, William Bradford 1938- *58*
  Brief entry *48*
Fregosi, Claudia (Anne Marie)
  1946- *24*
French, Allen 1870-1946
  See YABC *1*
French, Dorothy Kayser 1926- *5*
French, Fiona 1944- *132*
  Earlier sketches in SATA *6, 75*
  See also CLR *37*
  See also SAAS *21*
French, Jackie 1950- *108*
  See French, Jacqueline Anne
French, Jackie 1953- *139*
French, Kathryn
  See Mosesson, Gloria R(ubin)
French, Michael 1944- *49*
  Brief entry *38*
French, Paul
  See Asimov, Isaac
French, Simon 1957- *86*
Frenette, Liza *126*
Freschet, Gina 1960- *139*
Frewer, Glyn (M.) 1931- *11*
Frey, Darcy *98*
Frick, C. H.
  See Irwin, Constance (H.) Frick
Frick, Constance
  See Irwin, Constance (H.) Frick
Fricke, Aaron 1962- *89*
Fridell, Ron 1943- *124*
Friedlander, Joanne K(ohn) 1930- *9*
Friedman, Estelle (Ehrenwald) 1920- *7*
Friedman, Frieda 1905- *43*
Friedman, Ina R(osen) 1926- *136*
  Brief entry *41*
  Earlier sketch in SATA *49*
Friedman, Jerrold David
  See Gerrold, David
Friedman, Judi 1935- *59*
Friedman, Laurie 1964- *138*
Friedman, Marvin 1930- *42*
  Brief entry *33*
Friedmann, Stan 1953- *80*
Friedrich, Otto (Alva) 1929-1995 ....*33*
Friedrich, Priscilla 1927- *39*
Friendlich, Dick
  See Friendlich, Richard J.
Friendlich, Richard J. 1909- *11*
Friermood, Elisabeth Hamilton
  1903-1992 ....*5*
Friesen, Bernice (Sarah Anne)
  1966- *105*
Friesen, Gayle 1960- *109*
Friesner, Esther M. 1951- *71*
Friis-Baastad, Babbis Ellinor 1921-1970 ....*7*
Frimmer, Steven 1928- *31*
Frischmuth, Barbara 1941- *114*
Friskey, Margaret (Richards) 1901-1995 ....*5*
Fritts, Mary Bahr
  See Bahr, Mary M(adelyn)

Fritz, Jean (Guttery) 1915- *119*
  Autobiography Feature *122*
  Earlier sketches in SATA *1, 29, 72*
  See also CLR *14*
  See also SAAS *2*
Froehlich, Margaret W(alden) 1930- *56*
Frois, Jeanne 1953- *73*
Froissart, Jean 1338(?)-1410(?) *28*
Froman, Elizabeth Hull 1920-1975 ....*10*
Froman, Robert (Winslow) 1917- *8*
Fromm, Lilo 1928- *29*
Frommer, Harvey 1937- *41*
Frost, A(rthur) B(urdett) 1851-1928 ....*19*
Frost, Erica
  See Supraner, Robyn
Frost, Lesley 1899-1983 ....*14*
  Obituary *34*
Frost, Robert (Lee) 1874-1963 ....*14*
  See also CLR *67*
Frost, Shelley 1960- *138*
Fry, Annette R(iley) *89*
Fry, Christopher 1907- *66*
Fry, Edward Bernard 1925- *35*
Fry, Rosalie Kingsmill 1911-1992 ....*3*
  See also SAAS *11*
Fry, Virginia Lynn 1952- *95*
Frye, Sally
  See Moore, Elaine
Fuchs, Bernie 1932- *95*
Fuchs, Erich 1916- *6*
Fuchshuber, Annegert 1940- *43*
Fuertes, Gloria 1918-1998 ....*115*
Fuge, Charles 1966- *74*
Fujikawa, Gyo 1908-1998 ....*76*
  Brief entry *30*
  Obituary *110*
  Earlier sketch in SATA *39*
  See also CLR *25*
  See also SAAS *16*
Fujita, Tamao 1905-1999 ....*7*
Fujiwara, Kim 1957- *81*
Fujiwara, Michiko 1946- *15*
Fuller, Catherine Leuthold 1916- *9*
Fuller, Edmund (Maybank) 1914- *21*
Fuller, Iola
  See McCoy, Iola Fuller
Fuller, John G(rant, Jr.) 1913-1990 ....*65*
Fuller, Kathleen
  See Gottfried, Theodore Mark
Fuller, Lois Hamilton 1915- *11*
Fuller, Margaret
  See Ossoli, Sarah Margaret (Fuller)
Fuller, Maud
  See Petersham, Maud (Sylvia Fuller)
Fuller, Roy (Broadbent) 1912-1991 ....*87*
Fuller, Sarah Margaret
  See Ossoli, Sarah Margaret (Fuller)
Fuller, Sarah Margaret
  See Ossoli, Sarah Margaret (Fuller)
Fults, John Lee 1932- *33*
Funk, Thompson 1911- *7*
Funk, Tom
  See Funk, Thompson
Funke, Lewis 1912-1992 ....*11*
Fuqua, Jonathon Scott 1966- *141*
Furbee, Mary R.
  See Furbee, Mary Rodd
Furbee, Mary Rodd 1954- *138*
Furchgott, Terry 1948- *29*
Furlong, Monica (Mavis) 1930-2003 ....*86*
Furman, Gertrude Lerner Kerman
  1909- *21*
Furniss, Tim 1948- *49*
Furukawa, Toshi 1924- *24*
Fusillo, Archimede 1962- *137*
Futcher, Jane P. 1947- *76*
Fyleman, Rose (Amy) 1877-1957 ....*21*
Fyson, J(enny) G(race) 1904- *42*

G

Gaan, Margaret 1914- *65*
Gaber, Susan 1956- *115*
Gaberman, Judie Angell 1937- *78*
  Earlier sketch in SATA *22*
  See also CLR *33*
Gabhart, Ann 1947- *75*
Gabler, Mirko 1951- *77*
Gabriel, Adriana
  See Rojany, Lisa
Gabrys, Ingrid Schubert
  See Schubert-Gabrys, Ingrid
Gackenbach, Dick 1927- *79*
  Brief entry *30*
  Earlier sketch in SATA *48*
Gadd, Jeremy 1949- *116*
Gaddis, Vincent H. 1913-1997 ....*35*
Gadler, Steve J. 1905-1985 ....*36*
Gaeddert, Lou Ann (Bigge) 1931- *103*
  Earlier sketch in SATA *20*
Gaeddert, Louann
  See Gaeddert, Lou Ann (Bigge)
Gaer, Joseph 1897-1969 ....*118*
Gaer, Yossef
  See Gaer, Joseph
Gaetz, Dayle Campbell 1947- *138*
Gaffney, Timothy R. 1951- *69*
Gaffron, Norma (Bondeson) 1931- *97*
Gag, Wanda (Hazel) 1893-1946 ....*100*
  See also YABC *1*
  See also CLR *4*
Gage, Wilson
  See Steele, Mary Q(uintard Govan)
Gagnon, Cecile 1936- *58*
Gaiman, Neil (Richard) 1960- *85*
Gainer, Cindy 1962- *74*
Gaines, Ernest J(ames) 1933- *86*
  See also CLR *62*
Gaither, Gloria 1942- *127*
Gal, Laszlo 1933- *96*
  Brief entry *32*
  Earlier sketch in SATA *52*
  See also CLR *61*
Galbraith, Kathryn O(sebold) 1945- *85*
Galdone, Paul 1907(?)-1986 ....*66*
  Obituary *49*
  Earlier sketch in SATA *17*
  See also CLR *16*
Galinsky, Ellen 1942- *23*
Gallagher, Lurlene Nora
  See McDaniel, Lurlene
Gallant, Roy A(rthur) 1924- *110*
  Earlier sketches in SATA *4, 68*
  See also CLR *30*
Gallardo, Evelyn 1948- *78*
Gallico, Paul (William) 1897-1976 ....*13*
Gallo, Donald R(obert) 1938- *112*
  Autobiography Feature *104*
Galloway, Owateka (S.) 1981- *121*
Galloway, Priscilla 1930- *112*
  Earlier sketch in SATA *66*
Gallup, Joan 1957- *128*
Galouchko, Annouchka Gravel 1960- *95*
Galt, Thomas Franklin, Jr. 1908-1989 ......*5*
Galt, Tom
  See Galt, Thomas Franklin, Jr.
Galvin, Matthew R(eppert) 1950- *93*
Gamble, Kim 1952- *124*
  Earlier sketch in SATA *81*
Gambrell, Jamey *82*
Gamerman, Martha 1941- *15*
Gammell, Stephen 1943- *128*
  Earlier sketches in SATA *53, 81*
  See also CLR *83*
Ganly, Helen (Mary) 1940- *56*
Gannett, Ruth Chrisman (Arens)
  1896-1979 ....*33*
Gannett, Ruth Stiles 1923- *3*
Gannon, Robert Haines 1931- *8*
Gano, Lila 1949- *76*

Gans, Roma 1894-1996 45
  Obituary 93
Gant, Matthew
  See Hano, Arnold
Gantner, Susan (Verble) 1939- 63
Gantos, Jack
  See CLR 85
  See Gantos, John (Bryan), Jr.
Gantos, John (Bryan), Jr. 1951- 119
  Earlier sketches in SATA 20, 81
  See Gantos, Jack
Ganz, Yaffa 1938- 61
  Brief entry 52
Garafano, Marie 1942- 84
Garant, Andre J. 1968- 123
Garbe, Ruth Moore
  See Moore, Ruth (Ellen)
Garcia, Yolanda P(acheco) 1952- 113
Gard, Janice
  See Latham, Jean Lee
Gard, Joyce
  See Reeves, Joyce
Gard, Robert Edward 1910-1992 18
  Obituary 74
Gardam, Jane (Mary) 1928- 130
  Brief entry 28
  Earlier sketches in SATA 39, 76
  See also CLR 12
  See also SAAS 9
Gardella, Tricia 1944- 96
Garden, Nancy 1938- 114
  Earlier sketches in SATA 12, 77
  See also CLR 51
  See also SAAS 8
Gardiner, John Reynolds 1944- 64
Gardner, Craig Shaw 1949- 99
Gardner, Dic
  See Gardner, Richard (M.)
Gardner, Jane Mylum 1946- 83
Gardner, Jeanne LeMonnier 1925- 5
Gardner, John (Champlin), Jr.
  1933-1982 40
  Obituary 31
Gardner, Martin 1914- 16
Gardner, Miriam
  See Bradley, Marion Zimmer
Gardner, Richard (M.) 1931- 24
Gardner, Richard A. 1931- 13
Gardner, Sandra 1940- 70
Gardner, Sheldon 1934- 33
Gardner, Ted
  See Gardner, Theodore Roosevelt II
Gardner, Theodore Roosevelt II
  1934- 84
Garelick, May 1910-1989 19
Garfield, James B. 1881-1984 6
  Obituary 38
Garfield, Leon 1921-1996 76
  Obituary 90
  Earlier sketches in SATA 1, 32
  See also CLR 21
Garis, Howard R(oger) 1873-1962 13
Garland, Mark (A.) 1953- 79
Garland, Sarah 1944- 135
  Earlier sketch in SATA 62
Garland, Sherry 1948- 114
  Earlier sketch in SATA 73
Garner, Alan 1934- 69
  Autobiography Feature 108
  Earlier sketch in SATA 18
  See also CLR 20
Garner, David 1958- 78
Garner, Eleanor Ramrath 1930- 122
Garner, James Finn 1960(?)- 92
Garnet, A. H.
  See Slote, Alfred
Garnett, Eve C. R. 1900-1991 3
  Obituary 70
Garou, Louis P.
  See Bowkett, Stephen
Garraty, John A(rthur) 1920- 23

Garren, Devorah-Leah
  See Devorah-Leah
Garret, Maxwell R. 1917- 39
Garretson, Victoria Diane 1945- 44
Garrett, Helen 1895- 21
Garrett, Richard 1920- 82
Garrigue, Sheila 1931- 21
Garrison, Barbara 1931- 19
Garrison, Frederick
  See Sinclair, Upton (Beall)
Garrison, Webb B(lack) 1919-2000 25
Garrity, Jennifer Johnson 1961- 124
Garrity, Linda K. 1947- 128
Garst, Doris Shannon 1894-1981 1
Garst, Shannon
  See Garst, Doris Shannon
Garth, Will
  See Hamilton, Edmond
  and Kuttner, Henry
Garthwaite, Marion H(ook) 1893-1981 7
Gascoigne, Bamber 1935- 62
Gaskins, Pearl Fuyo 1957- 134
Gasperini, Jim 1952- 54
  Brief entry 49
Gater, Dilys 1944- 41
Gates, Doris 1901-1987 34
  Obituary 54
  Earlier sketch in SATA 1
  See also SAAS 1
Gates, Frieda 1933- 26
Gates, Viola R. 1931- 101
Gathorne-Hardy, Jonathan G. 1933- 124
  Earlier sketch in SATA 26
Gatti, Anne 1952- 103
Gatty, Juliana Horatia
  See Ewing, Juliana (Horatia Gatty)
Gauch, Patricia Lee 1934- 80
  Earlier sketch in SATA 26
  See also CLR 56
  See also SAAS 21
Gaul, Randy 1959- 63
Gault, Clare 1925- 36
Gault, Frank 1926-1982 36
  Brief entry 30
Gault, William Campbell 1910-1995 8
Gauthier, Gail 1953- 118
Gaver, Becky
  See Gaver, Rebecca
Gaver, Rebecca 1952- 20
Gavin, Jamila 1941- 125
  Earlier sketch in SATA 96
Gay, Amelia
  See Hogarth, Grace (Weston Allen)
Gay, Kathlyn 1930- 9
Gay, Marie-Louise 1952- 126
  Earlier sketch in SATA 68
  See also CLR 27
  See also SAAS 21
Gay, Zhenya 1906-1978 19
Gaze, Gillian
  See Barklem, Jill
Gear, Kathleen M. O'Neal
  See Gear, Kathleen O'Neal
Gear, Kathleen O'Neal 1954- 71
Gear, W. Michael 1955- 71
Geason, Susan 1946- 122
Gedalof, Robin
  See McGrath, Robin
Gedge, Pauline (Alice) 1945- 101
Gee, Maurice (Gough) 1931- 101
  Earlier sketch in SATA 46
  See also CLR 56
Geehan, Wayne (E.) 1947- 107
Geer, Charles 1922- 42
  Brief entry 32
Geeslin, Campbell 1925- 107
Gehman, Mary W. 1923- 86
Gehr, Mary 1910(?)-1997 32
  Obituary 99
Geipel, Eileen 1932- 30
Geis, Darlene Stern 1918(?)-1999 7
  Obituary 111

Geisel, Helen 1898-1967 26
Geisel, Theodor Seuss 1904-1991 100
  Obituary 67
  Earlier sketches in SATA 1, 28, 75
  See also CLR 53
  See Dr. Seuss
Geisert, Arthur (Frederick) 1941- 133
  Brief entry 52
  Earlier sketches in SATA 56, 92
  See also CLR 87
  See also SAAS 23
Geisert, Bonnie 1942- 92
Geldart, William 1936- 15
Gelinas, Paul J. 1904-1996 10
Gellis, Roberta (Leah Jacobs)
  1927- 128
Gellman, Marc 112
Gelman, Amy 1961- 72
Gelman, Jan 1963- 58
Gelman, Rita Golden 1937- 131
  Brief entry 51
  Earlier sketch in SATA 84
Gelman, Steve 1934- 3
Gemming, Elizabeth 1932- 11
Gennaro, Joseph F(rancis), Jr. 1924- 53
Gentile, Petrina 1969- 91
Gentle, Mary 1956- 48
Gentleman, David (William) 1930- 7
George, Barbara
  See Katz, Bobbi
George, Emily
  See Katz, Bobbi
George, Gail
  See Katz, Bobbi
George, Jean
  See George, Jean Craighead
George, Jean Craighead 1919- 124
  Earlier sketches in SATA 2, 68
  See also CLR 1, 80
George, John L(othar) 1916- 2
George, Kristine O'Connell 1954- 110
George, Lindsay Barrett 1952- 95
George, S(idney) C(harles) 1898- 11
George, Sally
  See Orr, Wendy
George, Twig C. 1950- 114
Georgiou, Constantine 1927- 7
Georgiou, Theo
  See Odgers, Sally Farrell
Geraghty, Paul 1959- 130
Gerard, Jean Ignace Isidore
  1803-1847 45
Geras, Adele (Daphne) 1944- 129
  Earlier sketches in SATA 23, 87
  See also SAAS 21
Gerber, Merrill Joan 1938- 127
  Earlier sketch in SATA 64
Gerber, Perren 1933- 104
Gerberg, Mort 1931- 64
Gergely, Tibor 1900-1978 54
  Obituary 20
Geringer, Laura 1948- 94
  Earlier sketch in SATA 29
Gerler, William R(obert) 1917-1996 47
Gernstein, Mordicai 36
Gerrard, Jean 1933- 51
Gerrard, Roy 1935-1997 90
  Brief entry 45
  Obituary 99
  Earlier sketch in SATA 47
  See also CLR 23
Gerrold, David 1944- 66
Gershator, Phillis 1942- 90
Gerson, Corinne 1927- 37
Gerson, Mary-Joan 136
  Earlier sketch in SATA 79
Gerson, Noel Bertram 1914-1988 22
  Obituary 60
Gerstein, Mordicai 1935- 81
  Brief entry 36
  Earlier sketch in SATA 47
Gertridge, Allison 1967- 132

Gervais, Bernadette 1959- *80*
Gesner, Clark 1938- *40*
Gessner, Lynne 1919- *16*
Getz, David 1957- *91*
Getzinger, Donna 1968- *128*
Gevirtz, Eliezer 1950- *49*
Gewe, Raddory
  See Gorey, Edward (St. John)
Ghan, Linda (R.) 1947- *77*
Gherman, Beverly 1934- *123*
  Earlier sketch in SATA *68*
Ghigna, Charles 1946- *108*
Giambastiani, Kurt R. A. 1958- *141*
Giannini, Enzo 1946- *68*
Gibbons, Alan 1953- *124*
Gibbons, Faye 1938- *103*
  Earlier sketch in SATA *65*
Gibbons, Gail (Gretchen) 1944- *104*
  Earlier sketches in SATA *23, 72*
  See also CLR *8*
  See also SAAS *12*
Gibbons, Kaye 1960- *117*
Gibbs, Adrea 1960- *126*
Gibbs, Alonzo (Lawrence) 1915-1992 ......*5*
Gibbs, Tony
  See Gibbs, Wolcott, Jr.
Gibbs, Wolcott, Jr. 1935- *40*
Giblin, James Cross 1933- *122*
  Earlier sketches in SATA *33, 75*
  See also CLR *29*
  See also SAAS *12*
Gibson, Andrew (William) 1949- *72*
Gibson, Betty 1911- *75*
Gibson, Jo
  See Fluke, Joanne
Gibson, William 1914- *66*
Gidal, Nachum
  See Gidal, Tim Nachum
Gidal, Sonia (Epstein) 1922- *2*
Gidal, Tim Nachum 1909-1996 ....*2*
Gidalewitsch, Nachum
  See Gidal, Tim Nachum
Giegling, John A(llan) 1935- *17*
Gifaldi, David 1950- *76*
Giff, Patricia Reilly 1935- *121*
  Earlier sketches in SATA *33, 70*
Giffard, Hannah 1962- *83*
Gifford, Griselda 1931- *42*
Gifford, Kerri 1961- *91*
Gilbert, Ann
  See Taylor, Ann
Gilbert, Anne Yvonne 1951- *128*
Gilbert, Barbara Snow 1954- *97*
Gilbert, Frances
  See Collings, Gillian
Gilbert, Harriett 1948- *30*
Gilbert, (Agnes) Joan (Sewell) 1931- *10*
Gilbert, John (Raphael) 1926- *36*
Gilbert, Nan
  See Gilbertson, Mildred Geiger
Gilbert, Roby Goodale 1966- *90*
Gilbert, Ruth Gallard Ainsworth
  See Ainsworth, Ruth (Gallard)
Gilbert, Sara (Dulaney) 1943- *82*
  Earlier sketch in SATA *11*
Gilbert, Suzie 1956- *97*
Gilbert, W(illiam) S(chwenck)
  1836-1911 ....*36*
Gilbertson, Mildred Geiger 1908-1988 ......*2*
Gilbreath, Alice 1921- *12*
Gilbreth, Frank B(unker), Jr. 1911-2001 ....*2*
Gilchrist, Jan Spivey 1949- *130*
  Earlier sketch in SATA *72*
Gilden, Mel 1947- *97*
Gilfond, Henry *2*
Gilge, Jeanette 1924- *22*
Gili, Phillida 1944- *70*
Gill, Derek (Lewis Theodore)
  1919-1997 ....*9*
Gill, Margery Jean 1925- *22*
Gill, Stephen 1932- *63*
Gillett, Mary (Bledsoe) *7*

Gillette, Henry Sampson 1915- *14*
Gillette, J(an) Lynett 1946- *103*
Gillham, Bill
  See Gillham, W(illiam) E(dwin) C(harles)
Gillham, W(illiam) E(dwin) C(harles)
  1936- *42*
Gilliam, Stan 1946- *39*
  Brief entry *35*
Gilliland, Alexis A(rnaldus) 1931- *72*
Gilliland, (Cleburne) Hap 1918- *92*
Gillmor, Don 1954- *127*
Gilman, Esther 1925- *15*
Gilman, Phoebe 1940-2002 ....*104*
  Obituary *141*
  Earlier sketch in SATA *58*
Gilmore, Iris 1900-1982 ....*22*
Gilmore, Kate 1931- *87*
Gilmore, Mary (Jean Cameron)
  1865-1962 ....*49*
Gilmore, Susan 1954- *59*
Gilroy, Beryl (Agatha) 1924- *80*
Gilson, Barbara
  See Gilson, Charles James Louis
Gilson, Charles James Louis 1878-1943
  See YABC *2*
Gilson, Jamie 1933- *91*
  Brief entry *34*
  Earlier sketch in SATA *37*
Ginsburg, Mirra 1909-2000 ....*92*
  Earlier sketch in SATA *6*
  See also CLR *45*
Giovanni, Nikki 1943- *107*
  Earlier sketch in SATA *24*
  See also CLR *73*
Giovanopoulos, Paul (Arthur) 1939- *7*
Gipson, Fred(erick Benjamin) 1908-1973 ...*2*
  Obituary *24*
Girard, Linda (Walvoord) 1942- *41*
Girion, Barbara 1937- *78*
  Earlier sketch in SATA *26*
  See also SAAS *14*
Girzone, Joseph F(rancis) 1930- *76*
Gise, Joanne
  See Mattern, Joanne
Gittings, Jo (Grenville) Manton 1919- *3*
Gittings, Robert (William Victor)
  1911-1992 ....*6*
  Obituary *70*
Givens, Janet E(aton) 1932- *60*
Gladstone, Eve
  See Werner, Herma
Gladstone, Gary 1935- *12*
Gladstone, M(yron) J. 1923- *37*
Glanville, Brian (Lester) 1931- *42*
Glanzman, Louis S. 1922- *36*
Glaser, Dianne E(lizabeth) 1937- *50*
  Brief entry *31*
Glaser, Isabel Joshlin 1929- *94*
Glaser, Milton 1929- *11*
Glaspell, Susan 1882(?)-1948
  See YABC *2*
Glass, Andrew 1949- *90*
  Brief entry *46*
Glasscock, Amnesia
  See Steinbeck, John (Ernst)
Glassman, Bruce 1961- *76*
Glauber, Uta (Heil) 1936- *17*
Glazer, Thomas (Zachariah)
  1914-2003 ....*9*
Glazer, Tom
  See Glazer, Thomas (Zachariah)
Gleasner, Diana (Cottle) 1936- *29*
Gleason, Judith 1929- *24*
Gleason, Katherine (A.) 1960- *104*
Gleeson, Libby 1950- *118*
  Earlier sketch in SATA *82*
Gleiter, Jan 1947- *111*
Gleitzman, Morris 1953- *88*
  See also CLR *88*
Glen, Maggie 1944- *88*
Glendinning, Richard 1917-1988 ....*24*

Glendinning, Sally
  See Glendinning, Sara W(ilson)
Glendinning, Sara W(ilson)
  1913-1993 ....*24*
Glenn, Mel 1943- *93*
  Brief entry *45*
  Earlier sketch in SATA *51*
  See also CLR *51*
Glenn, Patricia Brown 1953- *86*
Glennon, Karen M. 1946- *85*
Gles, Margaret Breitmaier 1940- *22*
Glick, Carl (Cannon) 1890-1971 ....*14*
Glick, Ruth (Burtnick) 1942- *125*
Gliewe, Unada (Grace) 1927- *3*
Glimmerveen, Ulco 1958- *85*
Glines, Carroll V(ane), Jr. 1920- *19*
Gliori, Debi 1959- *138*
  Earlier sketch in SATA *72*
Globe, Leah Ain 1900- *41*
Glovach, Linda 1947- *105*
  Earlier sketch in SATA *7*
Glover, Denis (James Matthews)
  1912-1980 ....*7*
Glubok, Shirley (Astor) *68*
  Earlier sketch in SATA *6*
  See also CLR *1*
  See also SAAS *7*
Glyman, Caroline A. 1967- *103*
Glynne-Jones, William 1907-1977 ....*11*
Gobbato, Imero 1923- *39*
Gobbletree, Richard
  See Quackenbush, Robert M(ead)
Goble, Dorothy *26*
Goble, Paul 1933- *131*
  Earlier sketches in SATA *25, 69*
  See also CLR *21*
Goble, Warwick (?)-1943 ....*46*
Godden, (Margaret) Rumer
  1907-1998 ....*36*
  Obituary *109*
  Earlier sketch in SATA *3*
  See also CLR *20*
  See also SAAS *12*
Gode, Alexander
  See Gode von Aesch, Alexander (Gottfried Friedrich)
Gode von Aesch, Alexander (Gottfried
  Friedrich) 1906-1970 ....*14*
Godfrey, Jane
  See Bowden, Joan Chase
Godfrey, Martyn
  See Godfrey, Martyn N.
  and Godfrey, Martyn N.
Godfrey, Martyn N. 1949-2000 ....*95*
  See also CLR *57*
  See Godfrey, Martyn
Godfrey, William
  See Youd, (Christopher) Samuel
Godin, Celia (Marilyn) 1948- *66*
Goedecke, Christopher (John) 1951- *81*
Goekler, Susan
  See Wooley, Susan Frelick
Goettel, Elinor 1930- *12*
Goetz, Delia 1898-1996 ....*22*
  Obituary *91*
Goffe, Toni 1936- *61*
Goffstein, Brooke
  See Goffstein, M(arilyn) B(rooke)
Goffstein, M(arilyn) B(rooke) 1940- *70*
  Earlier sketch in SATA *8*
  See also CLR *3*
Goforth, Ellen
  See Francis, Dorothy Brenner
Gogol, Sara 1948- *80*
Golann, Cecil Paige 1921-1995 ....*11*
Golbin, Andree 1923- *15*
Gold, Alison Leslie 1945- *104*
Gold, Phyllis *21*
  See Goldberg, Phyllis
Gold, Robert S(tanley) 1924- *63*
Gold, Sharlya *9*
Goldberg, Grace 1956- *78*

Goldberg, Herbert S. 1926- *25*
Goldberg, Jacob 1943- *94*
Goldberg, Jake
  See Goldberg, Jacob
Goldberg, Jan *123*
  See Curran, Jan Goldberg
Goldberg, Stan J. 1939- *26*
Goldberg, Susan 1948- *71*
Goldberg, Whoopi 1955- *119*
Golden, Christie 1963- *116*
Goldentyer, Debra 1960- *84*
Goldfeder, Cheryl
  See Pahz, (Anne) Cheryl Suzanne
Goldfeder, James
  See Pahz, James Alon
Goldfeder, Jim
  See Pahz, James Alon
Goldfrank, Helen Colodny 1912- *6*
Goldin, Augusta 1906-1999 ....*13*
Goldin, Barbara Diamond 1946- *92*
  Autobiography Feature *129*
  See also SAAS 26
Goldin, David 1963- *101*
Goldman, Alex J. 1917- *65*
Goldman, E(leanor) M(aureen)
  1943- *103*
Goldman, Elizabeth 1949- *90*
Goldsborough, June 1923- *19*
Goldsmith, Howard 1943- *108*
  Earlier sketch in SATA 24
Goldsmith, Oliver 1730-1774 ....*26*
Goldsmith, Ruth M. 1919- *62*
Goldstein, Nathan 1927- *47*
Goldstein, Philip 1910-1997 ....*23*
Goldston, Robert (Conroy) 1927- *6*
Goldstone, Lawrence A.
  See Treat, Lawrence
Golembe, Carla 1951- *79*
Golenbock, Peter 1946- *99*
Goll, Reinhold W(eimar) 1897-1993 ....*26*
Gollub, Matthew 1960- *134*
  Earlier sketch in SATA 83
Gomez, Elizabeth *133*
Gomez-Freer, Elizabeth
  See Gomez, Elizabeth
Gomi, Taro 1945- *103*
  Earlier sketch in SATA 64
  See also CLR 57
Gondosch, Linda 1944- *58*
Gonzalez, Catherine Troxell
  1917-2000 ....*87*
Gonzalez, Christina
  See Gonzalez, Maya Christina
Gonzalez, Gloria 1940- *23*
Gonzalez, Maya
  See Gonzalez, Maya Christina
Gonzalez, Maya Christina 1964- *115*
Goobie, Beth 1959- *128*
Good, Alice 1950- *73*
Goodall, Daphne Machin
  See Machin Goodall, Daphne (Edith)
Goodall, Jane 1934- *111*
Goodall, John S(trickland)
  1908-1996 ....*66*
  Obituary *91*
  Earlier sketch in SATA 4
  See also CLR 25
Goodbody, Slim
  See Burstein, John
Goode, Diane (Capuozzo) 1949- *114*
  Earlier sketches in SATA 15, 84
Goode, Stephen Ray 1943- *55*
  Brief entry *40*
Goodenow, Earle 1913- *40*
Goodin, Sallie (Brown) 1953- *74*
Goodman, Alison 1966- *111*
Goodman, Deborah Lerme 1956- *50*
  Brief entry *49*
Goodman, Elaine 1930- *9*
Goodman, Joan Elizabeth 1950- *94*
  Earlier sketch in SATA 50
Goodman, Walter 1927-2002 ....*9*

Goodrich, Samuel Griswold
  1793-1860 ....*23*
Goodwin, Hal
  See Goodwin, Harold L(eland)
Goodwin, Harold L(eland)
  1914-1990 ....*51*
  Obituary *65*
  Earlier sketch in SATA 13
Goodwin, William 1943- *117*
Goor, Nancy (Ruth Miller) 1944- *39*
  Brief entry *34*
Goor, Ron(ald Stephen) 1940- *39*
  Brief entry *34*
Goossen, Agnes
  See Epp, Margaret A(gnes)
Gorbachev, Valeri 1944- *98*
Gordion, Mark
  See Turtledove, Harry (Norman)
Gordon, Ad
  See Hano, Arnold
Gordon, Amy 1949- *115*
Gordon, Bernard Ludwig 1931- *27*
Gordon, Colonel H. R.
  See Ellis, Edward S(ylvester)
Gordon, Donald
  See Payne, Donald Gordon
Gordon, Dorothy 1893-1970 ....*20*
Gordon, Esther S(aranga) 1935- *10*
Gordon, Frederick *1*
Gordon, Gaelyn 1939-1997
  See CLR 75
Gordon, Gary
  See Edmonds, I(vy) G(ordon)
Gordon, Hal
  See Goodwin, Harold L(eland)
Gordon, Jeffie Ross
  See Enderle, Judith (Ann) Ross
  and Gordon, Stephanie Jacob
Gordon, John
  See Gesner, Clark
Gordon, John (William) 1925- *84*
Gordon, Lew
  See Baldwin, Gordon C.
Gordon, Margaret (Anna) 1939- *9*
Gordon, Mike 1948- *101*
Gordon, Selma
  See Lanes, Selma Gordon
Gordon, Sheila 1927- *88*
  See also CLR 27
Gordon, Shirley 1921- *48*
  Brief entry *41*
Gordon, Sol 1923- *11*
Gordon, Stephanie Jacob 1940- *89*
  Autobiography Feature *114*
  Earlier sketch in SATA 64
  See also SAAS 26
Gordon, Stewart
  See Shirreffs, Gordon D(onald)
Gorelick, Molly C. 1920- *9*
Gorey, Edward (St. John) 1925-2000 ......*70*
  Brief entry *27*
  Obituary *118*
  Earlier sketch in SATA 29
  See also CLR 36
Gorham, Charles Orson 1868-1936 ....*36*
Gorham, Michael
  See Folsom, Franklin (Brewster)
Gormley, Beatrice 1942- *127*
  Brief entry *35*
  Earlier sketch in SATA 39
Gorog, Judith (Katharine Allen)
  1938- *75*
  Earlier sketch in SATA 39
Gorsline, Douglas (Warner)
  1913-1985 ....*11*
  Obituary *43*
Gorsline, (Sally) Marie 1928- *28*
Gorsline, S. M.
  See Gorsline, (Sally) Marie
Gorton, Kaitlyn
  See Emerson, Kathy Lynn

Goryan, Sirak
  See Saroyan, William
Goscinny, Rene 1926-1977 ....*47*
  Brief entry *39*
  See also CLR 37
Goss, Clay(ton E.) 1946- *82*
Goss, Gary 1947- *124*
Gottesman, S. D.
  See Kornbluth, C(yril) M.
  and Lowndes, Robert A(ugustine) W(ard)
  and Pohl, Frederik
Gottfried, Ted
  See Gottfried, Theodore Mark
Gottfried, Theodore Mark 1928- *85*
Gottlieb, Gerald 1923- *7*
Gottlieb, William P(aul) 1917- *24*
Goudey, Alice E(dwards) 1898-1993 .....*20*
Goudge, Eileen 1950- *88*
Goudge, Elizabeth (de Beauchamp)
  1900-1984 ....*2*
  Obituary *38*
Gough, Catherine *24*
  See Mulgan, Catherine
Gough, Philip 1908- *45*
Gough, Sue 1940- *106*
Goulart, Ron(ald Joseph) 1933- *138*
  Earlier sketch in SATA 6
  See Calhoun, Chad
Gould, Alberta 1945- *96*
Gould, Chester 1900-1985 ....*49*
  Obituary *43*
Gould, Jean R(osalind) 1909-1993 ....*11*
  Obituary *77*
Gould, Lilian *6*
Gould, Marilyn 1928- *76*
  Earlier sketch in SATA 15
Gould, Steven (Charles) 1955- *95*
Gourley, Catherine 1950- *95*
Gourse, Leslie 1939- *89*
Govan, (Mary) Christine Noble
  1898-1985 ....*9*
Gove, Doris 1944- *72*
Govern, Elaine 1939- *26*
Graaf, Peter
  See Youd, (Christopher) Samuel
Graber, Alexander 1914-1997 ....*98*
  Earlier sketch in SATA 7
Graber, (George) Alexander
  1914-1997 ....*98*
Graber, Richard (Fredrick) 1927- *26*
Grabianski, Janusz 1928-1976 ....*39*
  Obituary *30*
Graboff, Abner 1919-1986 ....*35*
Grace, F(rances Jane) *45*
Grace, Theresa
  See Mattern, Joanne
Gracza, Margaret Young 1928- *56*
Graduate of Oxford, A
  See Ruskin, John
Graeber, Charlotte Towner *106*
  Brief entry *44*
  Earlier sketch in SATA 56
Graeme, Roderic
  See Jeffries, Roderic (Graeme)
Graff, Polly Anne Colver
  See Colver, Anne
Graff, (S.) Stewart 1908- *9*
Graham, Ada 1931- *11*
Graham, Alastair 1945- *74*
Graham, Arthur Kennon
  See Harrison, David L(ee)
Graham, Bob 1942- *101*
  Earlier sketch in SATA 63
  See also CLR 31
Graham, Brenda Knight 1942- *32*
Graham, Charlotte
  See Bowden, Joan Chase
Graham, Eleanor 1896-1984 ....*18*
  Obituary *38*
Graham, Ennis
  See Molesworth, Mary Louisa
Graham, Frank, Jr. 1925- *11*

Graham, Ian 1953- *112*
Graham, John 1926- *11*
Graham, Kennon
    See Harrison, David L(ee)
Graham, Larry
    See Graham, Lawrence (Otis)
Graham, Lawrence (Otis) 1962- *63*
Graham, Lorenz (Bell) 1902-1989 ....*74*
    Obituary *63*
    Earlier sketch in SATA *2*
    See also CLR *10*
    See also SAAS *5*
Graham, Margaret Bloy 1920- *11*
Graham, Robin Lee 1949- *7*
Graham, Shirley 1907-1977
    See Du Bois, Shirley Graham
Graham-Barber, Lynda 1944- *42*
Graham-Cameron, M.
    See Graham-Cameron, M(alcolm) G(ordon)
Graham-Cameron, M(alcolm) G(ordon)
    1931- *53*
    Brief entry *45*
Graham-Cameron, Mike
    See Graham-Cameron, M(alcolm) G(ordon)
Grahame, Kenneth 1859-1932 ....*100*
    See also YABC *1*
    See also CLR *5*
Gramatky, Hardie 1907-1979 ....*30*
    Obituary *23*
    Earlier sketch in SATA *1*
    See also CLR *22*
Grambling, Lois G. 1927- *71*
Grambo, Rebecca L(ynn) 1963- *109*
Grammer, June Amos 1927- *58*
Grand, Samuel 1912-1988 ....*42*
Grandville, J. J.
    See Gerard, Jean Ignace Isidore
Grandville, Jean Ignace Isidore Gerard
    See Gerard, Jean Ignace Isidore
Granfield, Linda 1950- *96*
Grange, Peter
    See Nicole, Christopher (Robin)
Granger, Michele 1949- *88*
Granowsky, Alvin 1936- *101*
Granstaff, Bill 1925- *10*
Granstroem, Brita 1969- *111*
Granstrom, Brita
    See Granstroem, Brita
Grant, Bruce 1893-1977 ....*5*
    Obituary *25*
Grant, Cynthia D. 1950- *77*
    Earlier sketch in SATA *33*
Grant, Eva 1907-1996 ....*7*
Grant, Gordon 1875-1962 ....*25*
Grant, Gwen(doline Ellen) 1940- *47*
Grant, (Alice) Leigh 1947- *10*
Grant, Matthew G.
    See May, Julian
Grant, Maxwell
    See Gibson, Walter B(rown)
    and Lynds, Dennis
Grant, Myrna (Lois) 1934- *21*
Grant, Neil 1938- *14*
Grant, Nicholas
    See Nicole, Christopher (Robin)
Grant, Richard 1948- *80*
Grant, Skeeter
    See Spiegelman, Art
Grater, Michael 1923- *57*
Gravel, Fern
    See Hall, James Norman
Gravelle, Karen 1942- *78*
Graves, Charles Parlin 1911-1972 ....*4*
Graves, Robert (von Ranke)
    1895-1985 ....*45*
Graves, Valerie
    See Bradley, Marion Zimmer
Gray, Betsy
    See Poole, Gray Johnson
Gray, Caroline
    See Nicole, Christopher (Robin)

Gray, Elizabeth Janet
    See Vining, Elizabeth Gray
Gray, Genevieve S(tuck) 1920-1995 ....*4*
Gray, Harold (Lincoln) 1894-1968 ....*33*
    Brief entry *32*
Gray, Jenny
    See Gray, Genevieve S(tuck)
Gray, Judith A(nne) 1949- *93*
Gray, Les 1929- *82*
Gray, Libba Moore 1937- *83*
Gray, Luli 1945- *90*
Gray, Marian
    See Pierce, Edith Gray
Gray, Nicholas Stuart 1922-1981 ....*4*
    Obituary *27*
Gray, Nigel 1941- *104*
    Earlier sketch in SATA *33*
Gray, (Lucy) Noel (Clervaux)
    1898-1983 ....*47*
Gray, Patricia (Clark) *7*
Gray, Patsey
    See Gray, Patricia (Clark)
Grayland, V. Merle
    See Grayland, Valerie (Merle Spanner)
Grayland, Valerie (Merle Spanner) *7*
Grayson, Devin (Kalile) 1970- *119*
Grayson, Paul 1946- *79*
Graystone, Lynn
    See Brennan, Joseph Lomas
Great Comte, The
    See Hawkesworth, Eric
Greaves, Margaret 1914-1995 ....*87*
    Earlier sketch in SATA *7*
Greaves, Nick 1955- *77*
Gree, Alain 1936- *28*
Green, Adam
    See Weisgard, Leonard (Joseph)
Green, Anne Canevari 1943- *62*
Green, Brian
    See Card, Orson Scott
Green, Cliff(ord) 1934- *126*
Green, Connie Jordan 1938- *80*
Green, D.
    See Casewit, Curtis W(erner)
Green, Elizabeth Shippen
    1871-1954 ....*139*
Green, Hannah
    See Greenberg, Joanne (Goldenberg)
Green, Jane 1937- *9*
Green, Mary Moore 1906- *11*
Green, Morton 1937- *8*
Green, Norma B(erger) 1925- *11*
Green, Phyllis 1932- *20*
Green, Roger (Gilbert) Lancelyn
    1918-1987 ....*2*
    Obituary *53*
Green, (James Le)Roy 1948- *89*
Green, Sheila Ellen 1934- *87*
    Earlier sketch in SATA *8*
Green, Timothy 1953- *91*
Greenaway, Kate 1846-1901 ....*100*
    See also YABC *2*
    See also CLR *6*
Greenbank, Anthony Hunt 1933- *39*
Greenberg, Harvey R. 1935- *5*
Greenberg, Jan 1942- *125*
    Earlier sketch in SATA *61*
Greenberg, Joanne (Goldenberg)
    1932- *25*
Greenberg, Melanie Hope 1954- *72*
Greenberg, Polly 1932- *52*
    Brief entry *43*
Greenblat, Rodney Alan 1960- *106*
Greenburg, Dan 1936- *102*
Greene, Bette 1934- *102*
    Earlier sketch in SATA *8*
    See also CLR *2*
    See also SAAS *16*
Greene, Carla 1916- *67*
    Earlier sketch in SATA *1*

Greene, Carol *102*
    Brief entry *44*
    Earlier sketch in SATA *66*
Greene, Constance C(larke) 1924- *72*
    Earlier sketch in SATA *11*
    See also CLR *62*
    See also SAAS *11*
Greene, Ellin 1927- *23*
Greene, Graham (Henry) 1904-1991 ....*20*
Greene, Jacqueline Dembar 1946- *131*
    Earlier sketch in SATA *76*
Greene, Laura Offenhartz 1935- *38*
Greene, Rhonda Gowler 1955- *101*
Greene, Stephanie 1953- *127*
Greene, Wade 1933- *11*
Greene, Yvonne
    See Flesch, Yolande (Catarina)
Greenfeld, Howard (Scheinman)
    1928- *140*
    Earlier sketch in SATA *19*
Greenfeld, Josh(ua Joseph) 1928- *62*
Greenfield, Eloise 1929- *105*
    Earlier sketches in SATA *19, 61*
    See also CLR *38*
    See also SAAS *16*
Greening, Hamilton
    See Hamilton, Charles (Harold St. John)
Greenlaw, M. Jean 1941- *107*
Greenleaf, Barbara Kaye 1942- *6*
Greenleaf, Peter 1910-1997 ....*33*
Greenlee, Sharon 1935- *77*
Greeno, Gayle 1949- *81*
Greenseid, Diane 1948- *93*
Greenspun, Adele Aron 1938- *76*
Greenstein, Elaine 1959- *82*
Greenwald, Sheila
    See Green, Sheila Ellen
Greenwood, Barbara 1940- *129*
    Earlier sketch in SATA *90*
Greenwood, Pamela D. 1944- *115*
Greer, Richard
    See Garrett, (Gordon) Randall (Phillip)
    and Silverberg, Robert
Gregg, Andrew K. 1929- *81*
Gregg, Charles T(hornton) 1927- *65*
Gregg, Walter H(arold) 1919- *20*
Gregor, Arthur 1923- *36*
Gregor, Lee
    See Pohl, Frederik
Gregori, Leon 1919- *15*
Gregorian, Joyce Ballou 1946-1991 ....*30*
    Obituary *83*
Gregorich, Barbara 1943- *66*
Gregorowski, Christopher 1940- *30*
Gregory, Diana (Jean) 1933- *49*
    Brief entry *42*
Gregory, Harry
    See Gottfried, Theodore Mark
Gregory, Jean
    See Ure, Jean
Gregory, Kristiana 1951- *136*
    Earlier sketch in SATA *74*
Gregory, Philippa 1954- *122*
Gregory, Stephen
    See Penzler, Otto
Gregory, Valiska 1940- *82*
Greisman, Joan Ruth 1937- *31*
Grendon, Stephen
    See Derleth, August (William)
Grenville, Pelham
    See Wodehouse, P(elham) G(renville)
Gretz, Susanna 1937- *7*
Gretzer, John *18*
Grewdead, Roy
    See Gorey, Edward (St. John)
Grey, Carol
    See Lowndes, Robert A(ugustine) W(ard)
Grey, Jerry 1926- *11*
Greybeard the Pirate
    See Macintosh, Brownie

Author Index

Grey Owl
  See CLR *32*
  See Belaney, Archibald Stansfeld
Gri
  See Denney, Diana
Grice, Frederick 1910-1983 6
Grider, Dorothy 1915- *31*
Gridley, Marion E(leanor) 1906-1974 ......*35*
  Obituary *26*
Grieco-Tiso, Pina 1954- *108*
Grieder, Walter 1924- *9*
Griego, Tony A. 1955- *77*
Griese, Arnold A(lfred) 1921- *9*
Griessman, Annette 1962- *116*
Grifalconi, Ann 1929- *133*
  Earlier sketches in SATA *2, 66*
  See also CLR *35*
  See also SAAS *16*
Griffin, Adele 1970- *105*
Griffin, Elizabeth May 1985- *89*
Griffin, Gillett Good 1928- *26*
Griffin, Judith Berry *34*
Griffin, Kitty 1951- *137*
Griffin, Peni R(ae Robinson) 1961- *99*
  Earlier sketch in SATA *67*
Griffin, Steven A(rthur) 1953- *89*
Griffin, W. E. B.
  See Butterworth, W(illiam) E(dmund III)
Griffith, Connie 1946- *89*
Griffith, Gershom 1960- *85*
Griffith, Helen V(irginia) 1934- *87*
  Autobiography Feature *107*
  Earlier sketch in SATA *39*
Griffith, Jeannette
  See Eyerly, Jeannette (Hyde)
Griffiths, Helen 1939- *86*
  Earlier sketch in SATA *5*
  See also CLR *75*
  See also SAAS *5*
Grigson, Jane (McIntire) 1928-1990 ....*63*
Grimes, Lee 1920- *68*
Grimes, Nikki 1950- *136*
  Earlier sketch in SATA *93*
  See also CLR *42*
Grimm, Jacob Ludwig Karl
  1785-1863 ....*22*
Grimm, Wilhelm Karl 1786-1859 ....*22*
Grimm, William C(arey) 1907-1992 ....*14*
Grimsdell, Jeremy 1942- *83*
Grimshaw, Nigel (Gilroy) 1925- *23*
Grimsley, Gordon
  See Groom, Arthur William
Gringhuis, Dirk
  See Gringhuis, Richard H.
Gringhuis, Richard H. 1918-1974 6
  Obituary *25*
Grinnell, George Bird 1849-1938 ....*16*
Gripe, Maria (Kristina) 1923- *74*
  Earlier sketch in SATA *2*
  See also CLR *5*
Groch, Judith (Goldstein) 1929- *25*
Grode, Redway
  See Gorey, Edward (St. John)
Groener, Carl
  See Lowndes, Robert A(ugustine) W(ard)
Groening, Matt 1954- *116*
  Earlier sketch in SATA *81*
Grohmann, Susan 1948- *84*
Grohskopf, Bernice 7
Grol, Lini R(icharda) 1913- *9*
Grollman, Earl A. 1925- *22*
Groom, Arthur William 1898-1964 ....*10*
Gross, Alan 1947- *54*
  Brief entry *43*
Gross, Ernie 1913- *67*
Gross, Philip (John) 1952- *84*
Gross, Ruth Belov 1929- *33*
Gross, Sarah Chokla 1906-1976 9
  Obituary *26*
Grosser, Morton 1931- *74*
Grosser, Vicky 1958- *83*

Grossman, Bill 1948- *126*
  Earlier sketch in SATA *72*
Grossman, Nancy 1940- *29*
Grossman, Patricia 1951- *73*
Grossman, Robert 1940- *11*
Grote, JoAnn A. 1951- *113*
Groten, Dallas 1951- *64*
Groth, John (August) 1908-1988 ....*21*
  Obituary *56*
Groth-Fleming, Candace
  See Fleming, Candace
Grove, Vicki *122*
Grover, Wayne 1934- *69*
Groves, Georgina
  See Symons, (Dorothy) Geraldine
Groves, Maketa 1950- *107*
Groves, Seli *77*
Gruber, Terry (deRoy) 1953- *66*
Gruelle, John (Barton) 1880-1938 ....*35*
  Brief entry *32*
  See Gruelle, Johnny
Gruelle, Johnny
  See CLR *34*
  See Gruelle, John (Barton)
Gruenberg, Sidonie Matsner
  1881-1974 ....*2*
  Obituary *27*
Gruhzit-Hoyt, Olga (Margaret)
  1922- *127*
  Earlier sketch in SATA *16*
Grummer, Arnold E(dward) 1923- *49*
Grunewalt, Pine
  See Kunhardt, Edith
Grupper, Jonathan *137*
Gryski, Camilla 1948- *72*
Guarino, Dagmar
  See Guarino, Deborah
Guarino, Deborah 1954- *68*
Guay, Georgette (Marie Jeanne)
  1952- *54*
Guback, Georgia *88*
Guccione, Leslie Davis 1946- *111*
  Earlier sketch in SATA *72*
Guck, Dorothy 1913- *27*
Guerny, Gene
  See Gurney, Gene
Guest, Elissa Haden 1953- *125*
Guest, Jacqueline 1952- *135*
Guevara, Susan *97*
Gugler, Laurel Dee *95*
Gugliotta, Bobette 1918-1994 7
Guianan, Eve 1965- *102*
Guiberson, Brenda Z. 1946- *124*
  Earlier sketch in SATA *71*
Guile, Melanie 1949- *104*
Guillaume, Jeanette G. Flierl 1899-1990 ...8
Guillot, Rene 1900-1969 7
  See also CLR *22*
Guisewite, Cathy (Lee) 1950- *57*
Gulley, Judie 1942- *58*
Gundrey, Elizabeth 1924- *23*
Gunn, James E(dwin) 1923- *35*
Gunn, Robin Jones 1955- *84*
Gunston, Bill
  See Gunston, William Tudor
Gunston, William Tudor 1927- *9*
Gunther, John 1901-1970
Guravich, Dan 1918- *74*
Gurko, Leo 1914- *9*
Gurko, Miriam 1910(?)-1988 ....*9*
  Obituary *58*
Gurney, Gene 1924- *65*
Gurney, James 1958- *120*
  Earlier sketch in SATA *76*
Gurney, John Steven 1962- *75*
Gustafson, Sarah R.
  See Riedman, Sarah R(egal)
Gustafson, Scott 1956- *34*
Guthrie, A(lfred) B(ertram), Jr.
  1901-1991 ....*62*
  Obituary *67*
Guthrie, Anne 1890-1979 ....*28*

Guthrie, Donna W. 1946- *105*
  Earlier sketch in SATA *63*
Gutman, Bill *128*
  Brief entry *43*
  Earlier sketch in SATA *67*
Gutman, Dan 1955- *139*
  Earlier sketches in SATA *77, 136*
Gutmann, Bessie Pease 1876-1960 ....*73*
Guy, Rosa (Cuthbert) 1925- *122*
  Earlier sketches in SATA *14, 62*
  See also CLR *13*
Guymer, (Wilhelmina) Mary 1909- *50*
Gwynne, Fred(erick Hubbard)
  1926-1993 ....*41*
  Brief entry *27*
  Obituary *75*
Gwynne, Oscar A.
  See Ellis, Edward S(ylvester)
Gwynne, Oswald A.
  See Ellis, Edward S(ylvester)

H

Haab, Sherri 1964- *91*
Haar, Jaap ter
  See CLR *15*
  See ter Haar, Jaap
Haas, Carolyn Buhai 1926- *43*
Haas, Dan 1957- *105*
Haas, Dorothy F. *46*
  Brief entry *43*
  See also SAAS *17*
Haas, Irene 1929- *96*
  Earlier sketch in SATA *17*
Haas, James E(dward) 1943- *40*
Haas, (Katherine) Jessie 1959- *98*
  Autobiography Feature *135*
Habenstreit, Barbara 1937- *5*
Haber, Karen 1955- *78*
Haber, Louis 1910-1988 ....*12*
Hackett, John Winthrop 1910-1997 ....*65*
Haddix, Margaret Peterson 1964- *125*
  Earlier sketch in SATA *94*
Hader, Berta (Hoerner) 1891(?)-1976 .....*16*
Hader, Elmer (Stanley) 1889-1973 ....*16*
Hadithi, Mwenye
  See Hobson, Bruce
Hadley, Franklin
  See Winterbotham, R(ussell) R(obert)
Hadley, Lee 1934-1995 ....*89*
  Brief entry *38*
  Obituary *86*
  Earlier sketch in SATA *47*
  See also CLR *40*
  See Irwin, Hadley
Haeffele, Deborah 1954- *76*
Haenel, Wolfram 1956- *89*
  See also CLR *64*
Hafner, Marylin 1925- *121*
  Earlier sketch in SATA *7*
Hager, Betty 1923- *89*
Hager, Tom 1953- *119*
Haggard, H(enry) Rider 1856-1925 ....*16*
Haggerty, James J(oseph) 1920- *5*
Hagon, Priscilla
  See Allan, Mabel Esther
Hague, (Susan) Kathleen 1949- *49*
  Brief entry *45*
Hague, Michael R. 1948- *129*
  Brief entry *32*
  Earlier sketches in SATA *48, 80*
Hahn, Emily 1905-1997 ....*3*
  Obituary *96*
Hahn, Hannelore *8*
Hahn, James (Sage) 1947- *9*
Hahn, (Mona) Lynn 1949- *9*
Hahn, Mary Downing 1937- *138*
  Brief entry *44*
  Earlier sketches in SATA *50, 81*
  See also SAAS *12*

Hahn, Michael T. 1953- 92
Haig-Brown, Roderick (Langmere)
  1908-1976 12
  See also CLR *31*
Haight, Rip
  See Carpenter, John (Howard)
Haight, Sandy 1949- 79
Haij, Vera
  See Jansson, Tove (Marika)
Haines, Gail Kay 1943- 11
Haining, Peter 1940- 14
Hains, Harriet
  See Watson, Carol
Hakim, Joy 1931- 83
Halacy, D(aniel) S(tephen), Jr. 1919- 36
  See Halacy, Dan
Halacy, Dan
  See SAAS *8*
  See Halacy, D(aniel) S(tephen), Jr.
Haldane, Roger John 1945- 13
Hale, Arlene 1924-1982 49
Hale, Bruce 1957- 123
Hale, Christy
  See Apostolou, Christine Hale
Hale, Edward Everett 1822-1909 16
Hale, Glenn
  See Walker, Robert W(ayne)
Hale, Helen
  See Mulcahy, Lucille Burnett
Hale, Irina 1932- 26
Hale, Kathleen 1898-2000 66
  Obituary 121
  Earlier sketch in SATA *17*
Hale, Linda (Howe) 1929- 6
Hale, Lucretia P.
  See Hale, Lucretia Peabody
Hale, Lucretia Peabody 1820-1900 26
Hale, Nancy 1908-1988 31
  Obituary 57
Haley, Gail E(inhart) 1939- 136
  Brief entry 28
  Earlier sketches in SATA *43, 78*
  See also CLR *21*
  See also SAAS *13*
Haley, Neale 52
Hall, Adam
  See Trevor, Elleston
Hall, Adele 1910- 7
Hall, Anna Gertrude 1882-1967 8
Hall, Barbara 1960- 68
Hall, Beverly B. 1918- 95
Hall, Borden
  See Yates, Raymond F(rancis)
Hall, Brian P(atrick) 1935- 31
Hall, Cameron
  See del Rey, Lester
Hall, Caryl
  See Hansen, Caryl (Hall)
Hall, Donald (Andrew, Jr.) 1928- 97
  Earlier sketch in SATA *23*
Hall, Douglas 1931- 43
Hall, Elizabeth 1929- 77
Hall, Elvajean 1910-1984 6
Hall, James Norman 1887-1951 21
Hall, Jesse
  See Boesen, Victor
Hall, Katy
  See McMullan, Kate (Hall)
Hall, Kirsten Marie 1974- 67
Hall, Lynn 1937- 79
  Earlier sketches in SATA *2, 47*
  See also SAAS *4*
Hall, Malcolm 1945- 7
Hall, Marjory
  See Yeakley, Marjory Hall
Hall, Melanie 1949- 116
  Earlier sketch in SATA *78*
Hall, Patricia 136
Hall, Rosalys Haskell 1914- 7
Hall, Willis 1929- 66
Hallard, Peter
  See Catherall, Arthur

Hallas, Richard
  See Knight, Eric (Mowbray)
Hall-Clarke, James
  See Rowland-Entwistle, (Arthur) Theodore
  (Henry)
Haller, Dorcas Woodbury 1946- 46
Hallett, Mark 1947- 83
Halliburton, Richard 1900-1939(?) 81
Halliburton, Warren J. 1924- 19
Halliday, Brett
  See Dresser, Davis
  and Johnson, (Walter) Ryerson
  and Terrall, Robert
Halliday, William R(oss) 1926- 52
Hallin, Emily Watson 6
Hallinan, P(atrick) K(enneth) 1944- 39
  Brief entry 37
Hallman, Ruth 1929- 43
  Brief entry 28
Hallowell, Tommy
  See Hill, Thomas
Hall-Quest, (Edna) Olga W(ilbourne)
  1899-1986 11
  Obituary 47
Halls, Kelly Milner 1957- 131
Hallstead, William F(inn III) 1924- 11
Hallward, Michael 1889-1982 12
Halperin, Wendy Anderson 1952- 125
  Earlier sketch in SATA *80*
Halpin, Marlene 1927- 88
Halsell, Grace (Eleanor) 1923-2000 13
Halter, Jon C(harles) 1941- 22
Halvorson, Marilyn 1948- 123
Hamalian, Leo 1920- 41
Hamberger, John 1934- 14
Hamblin, Dora Jane 1920- 36
Hambly, Barbara 1951- 108
Hamerstrom, Frances 1907-1998 24
Hamil, Thomas Arthur 1928- 14
Hamill, Ethel
  See Webb, Jean Francis (III)
Hamilton, (John) Alan 1943- 66
Hamilton, Alice
  See Cromie, Alice Hamilton
Hamilton, Anita 1919- 92
Hamilton, Buzz
  See Hemming, Roy G.
Hamilton, Carol (Jean Barber) 1935- 94
Hamilton, Charles (Harold St. John)
  1876-1961 13
Hamilton, Charles 1913-1996 65
  Obituary 93
Hamilton, Clive
  See Lewis, C(live) S(taples)
Hamilton, Dorothy (Drumm)
  1906-1983 12
  Obituary 35
Hamilton, Edith 1867-1963 20
Hamilton, Edmond 1904-1977 118
Hamilton, (Muriel) Elizabeth (Mollie)
  1906- 23
Hamilton, Franklin
  See Silverberg, Robert
Hamilton, Gail
  See Corcoran, Barbara (Asenath)
  and Dodge, Mary Abigail
Hamilton, Kersten 1958- 134
Hamilton, Martha 1953- 123
Hamilton, Mary (E.) 1927- 55
Hamilton, Mollie
  See Kaye, M(ary) M(argaret)
Hamilton, Morse 1943-1998 101
  Earlier sketch in SATA *35*
Hamilton, Peter F. 1960- 109
Hamilton, Priscilla
  See Gellis, Roberta (Leah Jacobs)
Hamilton, Ralph
  See Stratemeyer, Edward L.

Hamilton, Virginia (Esther)
  1936-2002 123
  Obituary 132
  Earlier sketches in SATA *4, 56, 79*
  See also CLR *40*
Hamilton-Paterson, James 1941- 82
Hamlet, Ova
  See Lupoff, Richard A(llen)
Hamley, Dennis 1935- 69
  Earlier sketch in SATA *39*
  See also CLR *47*
  See also SAAS *22*
Hamlin, Peter J. 1970- 84
Hamm, Diane Johnston 1949- 78
Hammer, Charles 1934- 58
Hammer, Richard 1928- 6
Hammerman, Gay M(orenus) 1926- 9
Hammond, Ralph
  See Hammond Innes, Ralph
Hammond, Winifred G(raham)
  1899-1992 29
  Obituary 107
Hammond Innes, Ralph 1913-1998 116
Hammontree, Marie (Gertrude)
  1913- 13
Hampshire, Joyce Gregorian
  See Gregorian, Joyce Ballou
Hampshire, Susan 1942- 98
Hampson, (Richard) Denman 1929- 15
Hamre, Leif 1914- 5
Hamsa, Bobbie 1944- 52
  Brief entry 38
Han, Suzanne Crowder 1953- 89
Hancock, Mary A. 1923- 31
Hancock, Sibyl 1940- 9
Hand, Elizabeth 1957- 118
Handford, Martin (John) 1956- 64
  See also CLR *22*
Handforth, Thomas (Schofield)
  1897-1948 42
Handler, Daniel
  See CLR *79*
  See Snicket, Lemony
Handville, Robert (Tompkins) 1924- 45
Hanel, Wolfram
  See Haenel, Wolfram
Haney, Lynn 1941- 23
Hanff, Helene 1916-1997 97
  Earlier sketch in SATA *11*
Hanley, Boniface Francis 1924- 65
Hanlon, Emily 1945- 15
Hann, Jacquie 1951- 19
Hann, Judith 1942- 77
Hanna, Bill
  See Hanna, William (Denby)
Hanna, Cheryl 1951- 84
Hanna, Jack (Bushnell) 1947- 74
Hanna, Nell(ie L.) 1908- 55
Hanna, Paul R(obert) 1902-1988 9
Hanna, William (Denby) 1910-2001 51
  Obituary 126
Hannam, Charles 1925- 50
Hannon, Ezra
  See Hunter, Evan
Hann-Syme, Marguerite 127
Hano, Arnold 1922- 12
Hanover, Terri
  See Huff, Tanya (Sue)
Hansen, Ann Larkin 1958- 96
Hansen, Brooks 1965- 104
Hansen, Caryl (Hall) 1929- 39
Hansen, Ian V. 1929- 113
Hansen, Joyce (Viola) 1942- 101
  Brief entry 39
  Earlier sketch in SATA *46*
  See also CLR *21*
  See also SAAS *15*
Hansen, Mark Victor 112
Hansen, Ron(ald Thomas) 1947- 56
Hanser, Richard (Frederick)
  1909-1981 13
Hanson, Joan 1938- 8

Hansson, Gunilla 1939- *64*
Harald, Eric
　See Boesen, Victor
Hard, Charlotte (Ann) 1969- *98*
Hardcastle, Michael 1933- *47*
　Brief entry *38*
Harding, Lee 1937- *32*
　Brief entry *31*
Hardt, Helga Fleischhauer
　See Fleischhauer-Hardt, Helga
Hardwick, Richard Holmes, Jr.
　1923- *12*
Hardy, Alice Dale *67*
　Earlier sketch in SATA *1*
Hardy, David A(ndrews) 1936- *9*
Hardy, Jon 1958- *53*
Hardy, Stuart
　See Schisgall, Oscar
Hare, Norma Q(uarles) 1924- *46*
　Brief entry *41*
Harford, Henry
　See Hudson, W(illiam) H(enry)
Hargrave, Leonie
　See Disch, Thomas M(ichael)
Hargrove, James 1947- *57*
　Brief entry *50*
Hargrove, Jim
　See Hargrove, James
Hariton, Anca I. 1955- *79*
Hark, Mildred
　See McQueen, Mildred Hark
Harkaway, Hal
　See Stratemeyer, Edward L.
Harkins, Philip 1912-1997 ....*6*
　Obituary *129*
Harlan, Elizabeth 1945- *41*
　Brief entry *35*
Harlan, Glen
　See Cebulash, Mel
Harlan, Judith 1949- *135*
　Earlier sketch in SATA *74*
　See also CLR *81*
Harler, Ann
　See Van Steenwyk, Elizabeth (Ann)
Harley, Bill 1954- *87*
Harmelink, Barbara (Mary) *9*
Harmer, Mabel 1894-1992 ....*45*
Harmon, Margaret 1906- *20*
Harmon, William (Ruth) 1938- *65*
Harnan, Terry 1920- *12*
Harness, Cheryl 1951- *131*
Harnett, Cynthia (Mary) 1893-1981 ....*5*
　Obituary *32*
Harper, Anita 1943- *41*
Harper, Betty 1946- *126*
Harper, Elaine
　See Hallin, Emily Watson
Harper, Ellen
　See Noble, Marty
Harper, Jo 1932- *97*
Harper, Mary Wood
　See Dixon, Jeanne
Harper, Piers 1966- *105*
Harper, Wilhelmina 1884-1973 ....*4*
　Obituary *26*
Harrah, Michael 1940- *41*
Harrar, George E. 1949- *124*
Harrell, Beatrice Orcutt 1943- *93*
Harrell, Janice 1945- *70*
Harries, Joan 1922- *39*
Harrill, Ronald 1950- *90*
Harrington, Denis J(ames) 1932- *88*
Harrington, Lyn *5*
　See Harrington, Evelyn Davis
Harris, Alan 1944- *71*
Harris, Aurand 1915-1996 ....*37*
　Obituary *91*
Harris, Carol Flynn 1933- *135*
Harris, Catherine
　See Ainsworth, Catherine Harris
Harris, Christie 1907-
　See Harris, Christie (Lucy) Irwin

Harris, Christie (Lucy) Irwin
　1907-2002 ....*74*
　Autobiography Feature *116*
　Earlier sketch in SATA *6*
　See also CLR *47*
　See also SAAS *10*
Harris, Christine 1955- *105*
Harris, Colver
　See Colver, Anne
Harris, David (William) 1942- *118*
Harris, Dorothy Joan 1931- *13*
Harris, Geraldine (Rachel) 1951- *54*
Harris, Jacqueline L. 1929- *62*
Harris, Janet 1932-1979 ....*4*
　Obituary *23*
Harris, Jesse
　See Standiford, Natalie
Harris, Joel Chandler 1848-1908 ....*100*
　See also YABC *1*
　See also CLR *49*
Harris, John (Wyndham Parkes Lucas)
　Beynon 1903-1969 ....*118*
　See Wyndham, John
Harris, Johnson
　See Harris, John (Wyndham Parkes Lucas)
　Beynon
Harris, Jonathan 1921-1997 ....*52*
Harris, Larry Vincent 1939- *59*
Harris, Lavinia
　See St. John, Nicole
Harris, Leon A., Jr. 1926-2000 ....*4*
Harris, Lorle K(empe) 1912-2001 ....*22*
Harris, Marilyn
　See Springer, Marilyn Harris
Harris, Mark Jonathan 1941- *84*
　Earlier sketch in SATA *32*
Harris, Mary K(athleen) 1905-1966 ....*119*
Harris, Robie H. 1940- *90*
　Brief entry *53*
Harris, Robin
　See Shine, Deborah
Harris, Rosemary (Jeanne) *82*
　Earlier sketch in SATA *4*
　See also CLR *30*
　See also SAAS *7*
Harris, Sherwood 1932- *25*
Harris, Steven Michael 1957- *55*
Harris, Trudy 1949- *128*
Harris-Filderman, Diane
　See Filderman, Diane E(lizabeth)
Harrison, C(hester) William 1913- *35*
　See Williams, Coe
Harrison, Carol
　See Harrison, Carol Thompson
Harrison, Carol Thompson *113*
Harrison, David L(ee) 1937- *92*
　Earlier sketch in SATA *26*
Harrison, Deloris 1938- *9*
Harrison, Edward Hardy 1926- *56*
Harrison, Harry (Max) 1925- *4*
Harrison, Michael 1939- *106*
Harrison, Molly (Hodgett)
　1909-2002 ....*41*
Harrison, Sarah 1946- *63*
Harrison, Ted
　See Harrison, Edward Hardy
Harsh, Fred (T.) 1925- *72*
Harshaw, Ruth H(etzel) 1890-1968 ....*27*
Harshman, Marc 1950- *109*
　Earlier sketch in SATA *71*
Hart, Bruce 1938- *57*
　Brief entry *39*
Hart, Carole 1943- *57*
　Brief entry *39*
Hart, Carolyn G(impel) 1936- *74*
Hart, Jan Siegel 1940- *79*
Hart, Virginia 1949- *83*
Harte, (Francis) Bret(t) 1836(?)-1902 .....*26*
Harter, Debbie 1963- *107*
Hartley, Ellen (Raphael) 1915-1980 ....*23*
Hartley, Fred Allan III 1953- *41*
Hartley, William B(rown) 1913-1980 ......*23*

Hartling, Peter
　See CLR *29*
　See Hartling, Peter
Hartling, Peter 1933- *66*
　See Hartling, Peter
Hartman, Evert 1937- *38*
　Brief entry *35*
Hartman, Jane E(vangeline) 1928- *47*
Hartman, Louis F(rancis) 1901-1970 ....*22*
Hartman, Victoria 1942- *91*
Hartnett, Sonya 1968- *130*
　Earlier sketch in SATA *93*
Hartshorn, Ruth M. 1928- *11*
Hartwig, Manfred 1950- *81*
Harvey, Brett 1936- *61*
Harvey, Karen D. 1935- *88*
Harvey, Roland 1945- *123*
　Earlier sketch in SATA *71*
Harwick, B. L.
　See Keller, Beverly L(ou)
Harwin, Brian
　See Henderson, LeGrand
Harwood, Pearl Augusta (Bragdon)
　1903-1998 ....*9*
Haseley, Dennis 1950- *105*
　Brief entry *44*
　Earlier sketch in SATA *57*
Hashmi, Kerri 1955- *108*
Haskell, Arnold L(ionel) 1903-1981(?) *6*
Haskins, James
　See Haskins, James S.
Haskins, James S. 1941- *105*
　Autobiography Feature *132*
　Earlier sketches in SATA *9, 69*
　See also CLR *39*
　See Haskins, Jim
Haskins, Jim
　See SAAS *4*
　See Haskins, James S.
Hasler, Joan 1931- *28*
Hass, Robert 1941- *94*
Hassall, Joan 1906-1988 ....*43*
　Obituary *56*
Hassler, Jon (Francis) 1933- *19*
Hastings, Beverly
　See Barkin, Carol
　and James, Elizabeth
Hastings, Graham
　See Jeffries, Roderic (Graeme)
Hastings, Ian 1912- *62*
Hatch, Lynda S. 1950- *90*
Hathorn, Libby *120*
　Earlier sketch in SATA *74*
　See Hathorn, Elizabeth Helen
Haugaard, Erik Christian 1923- *68*
　Earlier sketch in SATA *4*
　See also CLR *11*
　See also SAAS *12*
Haugaard, Kay *117*
Haugen, Tormod 1945- *66*
Hauman, Doris 1898- *32*
Hauman, George 1890-1961 ....*32*
Hauptly, Denis J(ames) 1945- *57*
Hauser, Jill Frankel 1950- *127*
Hauser, Margaret L(ouise) 1909- *10*
Hausherr, Rosmarie 1943- *86*
Hausman, Gerald 1945- *132*
　Earlier sketches in SATA *13, 90*
Hausman, Gerry
　See Hausman, Gerald
Hauth, Katherine B. 1940- *99*
Hautman, Pete(r Murray) 1952- *128*
　Earlier sketch in SATA *82*
Hautzig, Deborah 1956- *106*
　Earlier sketch in SATA *31*
Hautzig, Esther Rudomin 1930- *68*
　Earlier sketch in SATA *4*
　See also CLR *22*
　See also SAAS *15*
Havel, Jennifer
　See Havill, Juanita

Havighurst, Walter (Edwin)
  1901-1994 ....*1*
  Obituary *79*
Haviland, Virginia 1911-1988 ....*6*
  Obituary *54*
Havill, Juanita 1949- *74*
Hawes, Judy 1913- *4*
Hawes, Louise 1943- *60*
Hawke, Rosanne (Joy) 1953- *124*
Hawkes, Kevin 1959- *78*
Hawkes, Nigel 1943- *119*
Hawkesworth, Eric 1921- *13*
Hawkins, Arthur 1903-1985 ....*19*
Hawkins, Colin 1945- *112*
Hawkins, Jacqui *112*
Hawkins, Laura 1951- *74*
Hawkins, (Helena Ann) Quail
  1905-2002 ....*6*
  Obituary *141*
Hawkinson, John (Samuel) 1912-1994 ......*4*
Hawkinson, Lucy (Ozone)
  1924-1971 ....*21*
Hawks, Robert 1961- *85*
Hawley, Mabel C. *67*
  Earlier sketch in SATA *1*
Hawthorne, Captain R. M.
  See Ellis, Edward S(ylvester)
Hawthorne, Nathaniel 1804-1864
  See YABC *2*
Hay, John 1915- *13*
Hay, Timothy
  See Brown, Margaret Wise
Hayashi, Leslie Ann 1954- *115*
Hayashi, Nancy 1939- *80*
Haycock, Kate 1962- *77*
Haycraft, Howard 1905-1991 ....*6*
  Obituary *70*
Haycraft, Molly Costain 1911- *6*
Hayden, Gwendolen Lampshire
  1904- *35*
Hayden, Robert C(arter), Jr. 1937- *47*
  Brief entry *28*
Hayden, Robert E(arl) 1913-1980 ....*19*
  Obituary *26*
Hayden, Torey L(ynn) 1951- *65*
Hayes, Carlton J(oseph) H(untley)
  1882-1964 ....*11*
Hayes, Daniel 1952- *109*
  Earlier sketch in SATA *73*
Hayes, Geoffrey 1947- *91*
  Earlier sketch in SATA *26*
Hayes, Joe 1945- *131*
  Earlier sketch in SATA *88*
Hayes, John F. 1904-1980 ....*11*
Hayes, Sheila 1937- *51*
  Brief entry *50*
Hayes, Will *7*
Hayes, William D(imitt) 1913-1976 ....*8*
Haynes, Betsy 1937- *94*
  Brief entry *37*
  Earlier sketch in SATA *48*
Haynes, David 1955- *97*
Haynes, Linda
  See Swinford, Betty (June Wells)
Haynes, Mary 1938- *65*
Haynes, Max 1956- *72*
Hays, H(offmann) R(eynolds)
  1904-1980 ....*26*
Hays, Thomas Anthony 1957- *84*
Hays, Tony
  See Hays, Thomas Anthony
Hays, Wilma Pitchford 1909- *28*
  Earlier sketch in SATA *1*
  See also CLR *59*
  See also SAAS *3*
Hayward, Linda 1943- *101*
  Brief entry *39*
Haywood, Carolyn 1898-1990 ....*75*
  Obituary *64*
  Earlier sketches in SATA *1, 29*
  See also CLR *22*
Hazell, Rebecca (Eileen) 1947- *141*

Hazen, Barbara Shook 1930- *90*
  Earlier sketch in SATA *27*
Head, Gay
  See Hauser, Margaret L(ouise)
Headstrom, (Birger) Richard
  1902-1985 ....*8*
Heady, Eleanor B(utler) 1917-1979 ....*8*
Heagy, William D. 1964- *76*
Heal, Edith 1903-1995 ....*7*
Heal, Gillian 1934- *89*
Heale, Jay (Jeremy Peter Wingfield)
  1937- *84*
Healey, Brooks
  See Albert, Burton
Healey, Larry 1927- *44*
  Brief entry *42*
Heaps, Willard A(llison) 1908-1987 ....*26*
Hearn, Diane Dawson 1952- *79*
Hearn, Emily
  See Valleau, Emily
Hearn, Sneed
  See Gregg, Andrew K.
Hearne, Betsy Gould 1942- *95*
  Earlier sketch in SATA *38*
Heath, Charles D(ickinson) 1941- *46*
Heath, Veronica
  See Blackett, Veronica Heath
Heaven, Constance (Christina) 1911- *7*
Hebert-Collins, Sheila 1948- *111*
Hecht, Henri Joseph 1922- *9*
Hechtkopf, Henryk 1910- *17*
Heck, Bessie (Mildred) Holland
  1911-1995 ....*26*
Heckert, Connie K(aye Delp) 1948- *82*
Hedderwick, Mairi 1939- *77*
  Earlier sketch in SATA *30*
Hedges, Sid(ney) G(eorge)
  1897-1974 ....*28*
Heerboth, Sharon
  See Leon, Sharon
Heffernan, John 1949- *121*
Heffron, Dorris 1944- *68*
Hefter, Richard 1942- *31*
Hegarty, Reginald Beaton 1906-1973 ......*10*
Hehenberger, Shelly 1968- *126*
Heidbreder, Robert K. 1947- *130*
Heide, Florence Parry 1919- *118*
  Earlier sketches in SATA *32, 69*
  See also CLR *60*
  See also SAAS *6*
Heiderstadt, Dorothy 1907-2001 ....*6*
Heidi Louise
  See Erdrich, Louise
Heidler, David S(tephen) 1955- *132*
Heidler, Jeanne T. 1956- *132*
Heilbroner, Joan Knapp 1922- *63*
Heiligman, Deborah 1958- *90*
Heilman, Joan Rattner *50*
Heimann, Rolf 1940- *120*
Hein, Lucille Eleanor 1915-1994 ....*20*
Heine, Helme 1941- *135*
  Earlier sketch in SATA *67*
  See also CLR *18*
Heinlein, Robert A(nson) 1907-1988 ......*69*
  Obituary *56*
  Earlier sketch in SATA *9*
  See also CLR *75*
Heins, Ethel L(eah) 1918-1997 ....*101*
Heins, Paul 1909- *13*
Heintze, Carl 1922- *26*
Heinz, Brian J(ames) 1946- *95*
Heinz, W(ilfred) C(harles) 1915- *26*
Heinzen, Mildred
  See Masters, Mildred
Heisel, Sharon E(laine) 1941- *125*
  Earlier sketch in SATA *84*
Heitzmann, William Ray 1948- *73*
Heitzmann, Wm. Ray
  See Heitzmann, William Ray
Helberg, Shirley Adelaide Holden
  1919- *138*

Helfman, Elizabeth S(eaver)
  1911-2001 ....*3*
Helfman, Harry Carmozin 1910-1995 ....*3*
Hellberg, Hans-Eric 1927- *38*
Heller, Linda 1944- *46*
  Brief entry *40*
Heller, Mike
  See Hano, Arnold
Heller, Ruth M. 1924- *112*
  Earlier sketch in SATA *66*
Hellman, Hal
  See Hellman, Harold
Hellman, Harold 1927- *4*
Helman, Andrea (Jean) 1946- *107*
  See Helman, Andrea (Jean)
Helmer, Diana Star 1962- *86*
Helmer, Marilyn *112*
Helps, Racey 1913-1971 ....*2*
  Obituary *25*
Helweg, Hans H. 1917- *50*
  Brief entry *33*
Helyar, Jane Penelope Josephine
  1933- *82*
  Autobiography Feature *138*
  See Poole, Josephine
Hemmant, Lynette 1938- *69*
Hemming, Roy G. 1928-1995 ....*11*
  Obituary *86*
Hemphill, Kris (Harrison) 1963- *118*
Hemphill, Martha Locke 1904-1973 ....*37*
Henba, Bobbie 1926- *87*
Henbest, Nigel 1951- *55*
  Brief entry *52*
Henderley, Brooks *1*
Henderson, Gordon 1950- *53*
Henderson, Kathy 1949- *95*
  Brief entry *53*
  Earlier sketch in SATA *55*
Henderson, LeGrand 1901-1965 ....*9*
Henderson, Nancy Wallace 1916- *22*
Henderson, Zenna (Chlarson) 1917-1983 ...*5*
Hendrickson, Walter Brookfield, Jr.
  1936- *9*
Hendry, Diana 1941- *106*
  Earlier sketch in SATA *68*
Hendry, Frances Mary 1941- *110*
Hendry, Linda (Gail) 1961- *83*
Heneghan, James 1930- *97*
  Earlier sketch in SATA *53*
Henkes, Kevin 1960- *108*
  Earlier sketches in SATA *43, 76*
  See also CLR *23*
Henney, Carolee Wells 1928- *102*
Henriod, Lorraine 1925- *26*
Henriquez, Emile F. 1937- *89*
Henry, Ernest 1948- *107*
Henry, Joanne Landers 1927- *6*
Henry, Maeve 1960- *75*
Henry, Marguerite 1902-1997 ....*100*
  Obituary *99*
  See also CLR *4*
  See also SAAS *7*
Henry, Marie H. 1935- *65*
Henry, Marilyn 1939- *117*
Henry, Marion
  See del Rey, Lester
Henry, O.
  See Porter, William Sydney
Henry, Oliver
  See Porter, William Sydney
Henry, T. E.
  See Rowland-Entwistle, (Arthur) Theodore
  (Henry)
Henschel, Elizabeth Georgie *56*
Henson, James Maury 1936-1990 ....*43*
  Obituary *65*
  See Henson, Jim
Henson, Jim -1990
  See Henson, James Maury
Henstra, Friso 1928- *73*
  Earlier sketch in SATA *8*
  See also SAAS *14*

Hentoff, Nat(han Irving) 1925- *133*
  Brief entry *27*
  Earlier sketches in SATA *42, 69*
  See also CLR *52*
Henty, G(eorge) A(lfred) 1832-1902 ....*64*
  See also CLR *76*
Heo, Yumi *94*
Herald, Kathleen
  See Peyton, Kathleen (Wendy)
Herb, Angela M. 1970- *92*
Herbert, Cecil
  See Hamilton, Charles (Harold St. John)
Herbert, Don(ald Jeffrey) 1917- *2*
Herbert, Frank (Patrick) 1920-1986 ......*37*
  Obituary *47*
  Earlier sketch in SATA *9*
Herbert, Helen (Jean) 1947- *57*
Herbert, Janis 1956- *139*
Herbert, Wally
  See Herbert, Walter William
Herbert, Walter William 1934- *23*
Herbst, Judith 1947- *74*
Herda, D. J. 1948- *80*
Herge
  See CLR *6*
  See Remi, Georges
Heritage, Martin
  See Horler, Sydney
Herkimer, L(awrence) R(ussell)
  1925(?)- *42*
Herlihy, Dirlie Anne 1935- *73*
Herman, Charlotte 1937- *99*
  Earlier sketch in SATA *20*
Hermanson, Dennis (Everett) 1947- *10*
Hermes, Jules 1962- *92*
Hermes, Patricia 1936- *141*
  Earlier sketches in SATA *31, 78*
Hernandez, Natalie Nelson 1929- *123*
Herndon, Ernest *91*
Herold, Ann Bixby 1937- *72*
Herrera, Juan Felipe 1948- *127*
Herrick, Steven 1958- *103*
Herriman, George (Joseph)
  1880-1944 ....*140*
Herriot, James 1916-1995 ....*135*
  Earlier sketch in SATA *86*
  See also CLR *80*
  See Wight, James Alfred
Herrmanns, Ralph 1933- *11*
Herrold, Tracey
  See Dils, Tracey E.
Herron, Edward A(lbert) 1912- *4*
Herschler, Mildred Barger *130*
Hersey, John (Richard) 1914-1993 ....*25*
  Obituary *76*
Hershberger, Priscilla (Gorman)
  1951- *81*
Hershey, Kathleen M. 1934- *80*
Hersom, Kathleen 1911- *73*
Hertz, Grete Janus 1915- *23*
Herzig, Alison Cragin 1935- *87*
Herzog, Brad 1968- *131*
Heslewood, Juliet 1951- *82*
Hess, Lilo 1916- *4*
Hess, Paul 1961- *134*
Hesse, Hermann 1877-1962 ....*50*
Hesse, Karen 1952- *103*
  Autobiography Feature *113*
  Earlier sketch in SATA *74*
  See also CLR *54*
  See also SAAS *25*
Hest, Amy 1950- *129*
  Earlier sketches in SATA *55, 82*
Heuer, Kenneth John 1927- *44*
Heuman, William 1912-1971 ....*21*
Hewes, Agnes Danforth 1874-1963 ....*35*
Hewett, Anita 1918-1989 ....*13*
Hewett, Joan 1930- *140*
  Earlier sketch in SATA *81*
Hewett, Richard 1929- *81*
Hewitson, Jennifer 1961- *97*
Hewitt, Margaret 1961- *84*

Hewitt, Sally 1949- *127*
Hext, Harrington
  See Phillpotts, Eden
Hey, Nigel S(tewart) 1936- *20*
Heyduck-Huth, Hilde 1929- *8*
Heyer, Carol 1950- *130*
  Earlier sketch in SATA *74*
Heyer, Marilee 1942- *102*
  Earlier sketch in SATA *64*
Heyerdahl, Thor 1914-2002 ....*52*
  Earlier sketch in SATA *2*
Heyes, (Nancy) Eileen 1956- *80*
Heyliger, William 1884-1955
  See YABC *1*
Heyman, Ken(neth Louis) 1930- *114*
  Earlier sketch in SATA *34*
Heyward, (Edwin) DuBose
  1885-1940 ....*21*
Heywood, Karen 1946- *48*
Hezlep, William (Earl) 1936- *88*
Hibbert, Christopher 1924- *4*
Hibbert, Eleanor Alice Burford
  1906-1993 ....*2*
  Obituary *74*
  See Holt, Victoria
Hickman, Estella (Lee) 1942- *111*
Hickman, Janet 1940- *127*
  Earlier sketch in SATA *12*
Hickman, Martha Whitmore 1925- *26*
Hickman, Pamela M. 1958- *128*
Hickok, Lorena A. 1893-1968 ....*20*
Hickox, Rebecca (Ayres) *116*
Hicks, Clifford B. 1920- *50*
Hicks, Eleanor B.
  See Coerr, Eleanor (Beatrice)
Hicks, Harvey
  See Stratemeyer, Edward L.
Hicks, Peter 1952- *111*
Hicyilmaz, Gay 1947- *77*
Hieatt, Constance B(artlett) 1928- *4*
Hiebert, Ray Eldon 1932- *13*
Higdon, Hal 1931- *4*
Higginbottom, David 1923- *87*
  See Fisk, Nicholas
Higginbottom, J(effrey) Winslow
  1945- *29*
Higgins, Joanna 1945- *125*
Higgins, Simon (Richard) 1958- *105*
Higginsen, Vy *79*
High, Linda Oatman 1958- *94*
High, Philip E(mpson) 1914- *119*
Higham, David (Michael) 1949- *50*
Higham, Jon Atlas
  See Higham, Jonathan Huw
Higham, Jonathan Huw 1960- *59*
Highet, Helen
  See MacInnes, Helen (Clark)
Hightower, Florence Cole 1916-1981 ....*4*
  Obituary *27*
Highwater, Jamake (Mamake)
  1942(?)-2001 ....*69*
  Brief entry *30*
  Earlier sketch in SATA *32*
  See also CLR *17*
Hildebrandt, Greg 1939- *55*
  Brief entry *33*
Hildebrandt, Tim(othy) 1939- *55*
  Brief entry *33*
Hildebrandts, The
  See Hildebrandt, Greg
  and Hildebrandt, Tim(othy)
Hilder, Rowland 1905-1993 ....*36*
  Obituary *77*
Hildick, E. W.
  See SAAS *6*
  See Hildick, (Edmund) Wallace
Hildick, (Edmund) Wallace
  1925-2001 ....*68*
  Earlier sketch in SATA *2*
  See Hildick, E. W.
Hilgartner, Beth 1957- *58*

Hill, Alexis
  See Craig, Mary (Francis) Shura
  and Glick, Ruth (Burtnick)
Hill, Anthony (Robert) 1942- *91*
Hill, David 1942- *103*
Hill, Donna (Marie) 1921- *124*
  Earlier sketch in SATA *24*
Hill, Douglas (Arthur) 1935- *78*
  Earlier sketch in SATA *39*
Hill, Elizabeth Starr 1925- *24*
Hill, Eric 1927- *133*
  Brief entry *53*
  Earlier sketch in SATA *66*
  See also CLR *13*
Hill, Grace Brooks *67*
  Earlier sketch in SATA *1*
Hill, Grace Livingston 1865-1947
  See YABC *2*
Hill, Helen M(orey) 1915- *27*
Hill, John
  See Koontz, Dean R(ay)
Hill, Johnson
  See Kunhardt, Edith
Hill, Judy I. R.
  See Roberts, Judy I.
Hill, Kathleen Louise 1917- *4*
Hill, Kay
  See Hill, Kathleen Louise
Hill, Kirkpatrick 1938- *126*
  Earlier sketch in SATA *72*
Hill, Lee Sullivan 1958- *96*
Hill, Lorna 1902-1991 ....*12*
Hill, Margaret (Ohler) 1915- *36*
Hill, Meg
  See Hill, Margaret (Ohler)
Hill, Meredith
  See Craig, Mary (Francis) Shura
Hill, Monica
  See Watson, Jane Werner
Hill, Pamela Smith 1954- *112*
Hill, Ralph Nading 1917-1987 ....*65*
Hill, Robert W(hite) 1919-1982 ....*12*
  Obituary *31*
Hill, Ruth A.
  See Viguers, Ruth Hill
Hill, Ruth Livingston
  See Munce, Ruth Hill
Hill, Thomas 1960- *82*
Hillcourt, William 1900-1992 ....*27*
Hillenbrand, Will 1960- *84*
Hiller, Ilo (Ann) 1938- *59*
Hillerman, Tony 1925- *6*
Hillert, Margaret 1920- *91*
  Earlier sketch in SATA *8*
Hillman, Elizabeth 1942- *75*
Hillman, John 1952- *120*
Hillman, Martin
  See Hill, Douglas (Arthur)
Hillman, Priscilla 1940- *48*
  Brief entry *39*
Hills, C(harles) A(lbert) R(eis)
  1955- *39*
Hilton, Irene Pothus -1979 ....*7*
Hilton, James 1900-1954 ....*34*
Hilton, Margaret Lynette 1946- *105*
  Earlier sketch in SATA *68*
  See Hilton, Nette
Hilton, Nette
  See CLR *25*
  See also SAAS *21*
  See Hilton, Margaret Lynette
Hilton, Ralph 1907-1982 ....*8*
Hilton, Suzanne 1922- *4*
Hilton-Bruce, Anne
  See Hilton, Margaret Lynette
Himelstein, Shmuel 1940- *83*
Himler, Ann 1946- *8*
Himler, Ronald (Norbert) 1937- *137*
  Earlier sketches in SATA *6, 92*
Himmelman, John C(arl) 1959- *94*
  Earlier sketch in SATA *47*

Hinckley, Helen
   See Jones, Helen Hinckley
Hind, Dolores (Ellen) 1931- *53*
   Brief entry *49*
Hindin, Nathan
   See Bloch, Robert (Albert)
Hindley, Judy 1940- *120*
Hinds, P(atricia) Mignon *98*
Hines, Anna Grossnickle 1946- *141*
   Brief entry *45*
   Earlier sketches in SATA *51, 95*
   See also SAAS *16*
Hines, Gary (Roger) 1944- *136*
   Earlier sketch in SATA *74*
Hinojosa, Maria (de Lourdes) 1961- *88*
Hinton, S(usan) E(loise) 1950- *115*
   Earlier sketches in SATA *19, 58*
   See also CLR *23*
Hinton, Sam 1917- *43*
Hintz, Martin 1945- *128*
   Brief entry *39*
   Earlier sketch in SATA *47*
Hintz, Stephen V. 1975- *129*
Hippopotamus, Eugene H.
   See Kraus, (Herman) Robert
Hirano, Cathy 1957- *68*
Hirsch, Karen 1941- *61*
Hirsch, Odo *111*
Hirsch, Phil 1926- *35*
Hirsch, S. Carl 1913- *2*
   See also SAAS *7*
Hirschfelder, Arlene B. 1943- *138*
   Earlier sketch in SATA *80*
Hirschi, Ron 1948- *95*
   Earlier sketch in SATA *56*
Hirschmann, Linda (Ann) 1941- *40*
Hirsh, Marilyn 1944-1988 ....*7*
   Obituary *58*
Hirshberg, Al(bert Simon)
   1909-1973 ....*38*
Hiscock, Bruce 1940- *137*
   Earlier sketch in SATA *57*
Hiser, Constance 1950- *71*
Hiser, Iona Seibert -1998 ....*4*
Hislop, Julia Rose Catherine 1962- *74*
Hissey, Jane (Elizabeth) 1952- *103*
   Autobiography Feature *130*
   Earlier sketch in SATA *58*
Hitchcock, Alfred (Joseph)
   1899-1980 ....*27*
   Obituary *24*
Hite, Sid 1954- *136*
   Earlier sketch in SATA *75*
Hitte, Kathryn 1919- *16*
Hitz, Demi 1942- *102*
   Earlier sketches in SATA *11, 66*
   See also CLR *58*
   See Demi
Hitzeroth, Deborah L. 1961- *78*
Hnizdovsky, Jacques 1915- *32*
Ho, Minfong 1951- *94*
   Earlier sketch in SATA *15*
   See also CLR *28*
Hoagland, Edward 1932- *51*
Hoare, Robert J(ohn) 1921-1975 ....*38*
Hoban, Lillian 1925-1998 ....*69*
   Obituary *104*
   Earlier sketch in SATA *22*
   See also CLR *67*
Hoban, Russell (Conwell) 1925- *136*
   Earlier sketches in SATA *1, 40, 78*
   See also CLR *69*
Hoban, Tana 1917- *104*
   Earlier sketches in SATA *22, 70*
   See also CLR *76*
   See also SAAS *12*
Hobart, Lois (Elaine) *7*
Hobbie, Holly 1944-
   See CLR *88*
Hobbs, Valerie 1941- *93*

Hobbs, Will(iam Carl) 1947- *110*
   Autobiography Feature *127*
   Earlier sketch in SATA *72*
   See also CLR *59*
Hoberman, Mary Ann 1930- *111*
   Earlier sketches in SATA *5, 72*
   See also CLR *22*
   See also SAAS *18*
Hobson, Bruce 1950- *62*
Hobson, Burton (Harold) 1933- *28*
Hobson, Laura Z(ametkin)
   1900-1986 ....*52*
   See Field, Peter
Hobson, Sally 1967- *84*
Hochschild, Arlie Russell 1940- *11*
Hockaby, Stephen
   See Mitchell, Gladys (Maude Winifred)
Hockenberry, Hope
   See Newell, Hope Hockenberry
Hodge, Deborah 1954- *122*
Hodge, P. W.
   See Hodge, Paul W(illiam)
Hodge, Paul W(illiam) 1934- *12*
Hodgell, P(atricia) C(hristine) 1951- *42*
Hodges, C(yril) Walter 1909- *2*
Hodges, Carl G. 1902-1964 ....*10*
Hodges, Elizabeth Jamison *1*
Hodges, Margaret Moore 1911- *117*
   Earlier sketches in SATA *1, 33, 75*
   See also SAAS *9*
Hodgetts, Blake Christopher 1967- *43*
Hodgson, Harriet 1935- *84*
Hoehne, Marcia 1951- *89*
Hoellwarth, Cathryn Clinton 1957- *136*
Hoestlandt, Jo(celyne) 1948- *94*
Hoexter, Corinne K. 1927- *6*
Hoeye, Michael 1947- *136*
Hoff, Carol 1900-1979 ....*11*
Hoff, Mary (King) 1956- *74*
Hoff, Syd(ney) 1912- *138*
   Earlier sketches in SATA *9, 72*
   See also CLR *83*
   See also SAAS *4*
Hoffman, Edwin D. *49*
Hoffman, Mary (Margaret) 1945- *97*
   Earlier sketch in SATA *59*
   See also SAAS *24*
   See Lassiter, Mary
Hoffman, Phyllis M(iriam) 1944- *4*
Hoffman, Rosekrans 1926- *15*
Hoffmann, E(rnst) T(heodor) A(madeus)
   1776-1822 ....*27*
Hoffmann, Felix 1911-1975 ....*9*
Hoffmann, Heinrich 1809-1894
   See CLR *70*
Hoffmann, Margaret Jones 1910- *48*
Hoffmann, Peggy
   See Hoffmann, Margaret Jones
Hofher, Catherine Baxley 1954- *130*
Hofher, Cathy
   See Hofher, Catherine Baxley
Hofmeyr, Dianne (Louise) *138*
Hofsepian, Sylvia A. 1932- *74*
Hofsinde, Robert 1902-1973 ....*21*
Hogan, Bernice Harris 1929- *12*
Hogan, Inez 1895-1973 ....*2*
Hogan, James P(atrick) 1941- *81*
Hogan, Linda 1947- *132*
Hogarth, Burne 1911-1996 ....*89*
   Earlier sketch in SATA *63*
Hogarth, Grace (Weston Allen)
   1905-1995 ....*91*
Hogarth, Jr.
   See Kent, Rockwell
Hogarth, (Arthur) Paul 1917-2001 ....*41*
Hogg, Garry 1902-1976 ....*2*
Hogg, Gary 1957- *105*
Hogner, Dorothy Childs *4*
Hogner, Nils 1893-1970 ....*25*

Hogrogian, Nonny 1932- *74*
   Autobiography Feature *127*
   Earlier sketch in SATA *7*
   See also CLR *2*
   See also SAAS *1*
Hoh, Diane 1937- *102*
   Brief entry *48*
   Earlier sketch in SATA *52*
Hoke, John (Lindsay) 1925- *7*
Hol, Coby 1943- *126*
Holabird, Katharine 1948- *135*
   Earlier sketch in SATA *62*
Holbeach, Henry
   See Rands, William Brighty
Holberg, Ruth L(angland) 1889-1984 ....*1*
Holbrook, Kathy 1963- *107*
Holbrook, Peter
   See Glick, Carl (Cannon)
Holbrook, Sabra
   See Erickson, Sabra Rollins
Holbrook, Sara *131*
Holbrook, Stewart Hall 1893-1964 ....*2*
Holcomb, Jerry (Leona) Kimble
   1927- *113*
Holcomb, Nan
   See McPhee, Norma H.
Holden, Elizabeth Rhoda
   See Lawrence, Louise
Holding, James (Clark Carlisle, Jr.)
   1907-1997 ....*3*
Holeman, Linda 1949- *136*
   Earlier sketch in SATA *102*
Holinger, William (Jacques) 1944- *90*
Holisher, Desider 1901-1972 ....*6*
Holl, Adelaide Hinkle 1910- *8*
Holl, Kristi D(iane) 1951- *51*
Holland, Gay W. 1941- *128*
Holland, Isabelle (Christian)
   1920-2002 ....*70*
   Autobiography Feature *103*
   Obituary *132*
   Earlier sketch in SATA *8*
   See also CLR *57*
Holland, Janice 1913-1962 ....*18*
Holland, John L(ewis) 1919- *20*
Holland, Joyce
   See Morice, Dave
Holland, Julia 1954- *106*
Holland, Lynda (H.) 1959- *77*
Holland, Lys
   See Gater, Dilys
Holland, Marion 1908-1989 ....*6*
   Obituary *61*
Hollander, John 1929- *13*
Hollander, Nicole 1940(?)- *101*
Hollander, Paul
   See Silverberg, Robert
Hollander, Phyllis 1928- *39*
Hollander, Zander 1923- *63*
Holldobler, Turid 1939- *26*
Holliday, Joe
   See Holliday, Joseph
Holliday, Joseph 1910- *11*
Holling, Holling C(lancy) 1900-1973 ......*15*
   Obituary *26*
   See also CLR *50*
Hollingsworth, Alvin C(arl) 1930- *39*
Hollingsworth, Mary 1947- *91*
Holloway, Teresa (Bragunier) 1906- *26*
Holm, (Else) Anne (Lise) 1922-1998 ....*1*
   See also CLR *75*
   See also SAAS *7*
Holm, Jennifer L. *120*
Holm, Sharon Lane 1955- *114*
   Earlier sketch in SATA *78*
Holman, Felice 1919- *82*
   Earlier sketch in SATA *7*
   See also SAAS *17*
Holme, Bryan 1913-1990 ....*26*
   Obituary *66*
Holmes, Barbara Ware 1945- *127*
   Earlier sketch in SATA *65*

Holmes, John
  See Souster, (Holmes) Raymond
Holmes, Marjorie (Rose) 1910-2002 ....*43*
Holmes, Martha 1961- *72*
Holmes, Mary Z(astrow) 1943- *80*
Holmes, Oliver Wendell 1809-1894 ......*34*
Holmes, Peggy 1898- *60*
Holmes, Raymond
  See Souster, (Holmes) Raymond
Holmes, Rick
  See Hardwick, Richard Holmes, Jr.
Holmgren, Helen Jean 1930- *45*
Holmgren, Sister George Ellen
  See Holmgren, Helen Jean
Holmgren, Virginia C(unningham)
  1909- *26*
Holmquist, Eve 1921- *11*
Holt, Kimberly Willis 1960- *122*
Holt, Margaret 1937- *4*
Holt, Margaret Van Vechten (Saunders)
  1899-1963 ....*32*
Holt, Michael (Paul) 1929- *13*
Holt, Rackham
  See Holt, Margaret Van Vechten
  (Saunders)
Holt, Rochelle L. *41*
  See DuBois, Rochelle (Lynn) Holt
Holt, Stephen
  See Thompson, Harlan (Howard)
Holt, Victoria
  See Hibbert, Eleanor Alice Burford
Holton, Leonard
  See Wibberley, Leonard (Patrick
  O'Connor)
Holtze, Sally Holmes 1952- *64*
Holtzman, Jerome 1926- *57*
Holub, Joan 1956- *99*
Holubitsky, Katherine 1955- *121*
Holyer, Erna Maria 1925- *22*
Holyer, Ernie
  See Holyer, Erna Maria
Holz, Loretta (Marie) 1943- *17*
Homel, David 1952- *97*
Homze, Alma C. 1932- *17*
Honey, Elizabeth 1947- *137*
  Earlier sketch in SATA *112*
Honeycutt, Natalie 1945- *97*
Hong, Lily Toy 1958- *76*
Honig, Donald 1931- *18*
Honness, Elizabeth H. 1904- *2*
Hoobler, Dorothy *109*
  Earlier sketch in SATA *28*
Hoobler, Thomas *109*
  Earlier sketch in SATA *28*
Hood, Joseph F. 1925- *4*
Hood, Robert E. 1926- *21*
Hood, Sarah
  See Killough, (Karen) Lee
Hook, Brendan 1963- *105*
Hook, Frances 1912-1983 ....*27*
Hook, Geoffrey R(aynor) 1928- *103*
Hook, Jeff
  See Hook, Geoffrey R(aynor)
Hook, Martha 1936- *27*
Hooker, Richard
  See Heinz, W(ilfred) C(harles)
Hooker, Ruth 1920-1998 ....*21*
hooks, bell
  See Watkins, Gloria Jean
Hooks, William H(arris) 1921- *94*
  Earlier sketch in SATA *16*
Hoon, Patricia Easterly 1954- *90*
Hooper, Maureen Brett 1927- *76*
Hooper, Meredith (Jean) 1939- *101*
  Earlier sketch in SATA *28*
Hooper, Patricia 1941- *95*
Hoopes, Lyn Littlefield 1953- *49*
  Brief entry *44*
Hoopes, Ned E(dward) 1932- *21*
Hoopes, Roy 1922- *11*
Hoose, Phillip M. 1947- *137*

Hoover, H(elen) M(ary) 1935- *132*
  Brief entry *33*
  Earlier sketches in SATA *44, 83*
  See also SAAS *8*
Hoover, Helen (Drusilla Blackburn)
  1910-1984 ....*12*
  Obituary *39*
Hope, Christopher (David Tully)
  1944- *62*
Hope, Laura Lee *67*
  Earlier sketch in SATA *1*
Hope Simpson, Jacynth 1930- *12*
Hopf, Alice (Martha) L(ightner)
  1904-1988 ....*5*
  Obituary *55*
Hopkins, Ellen L. 1955- *128*
Hopkins, Jackie (Mims) 1952- *92*
Hopkins, Joseph G(erard) E(dward)
  1909- *11*
Hopkins, Lee Bennett 1938- *125*
  Earlier sketches in SATA *3, 68*
  See also CLR *44*
  See also SAAS *4*
Hopkins, Lyman
  See Folsom, Franklin (Brewster)
Hopkins, Marjorie 1911-1999 ....*9*
Hopkins, Mary R(ice) 1956- *97*
Hopkinson, Amanda 1948- *84*
Hopkinson, Deborah 1952- *108*
  Earlier sketch in SATA *76*
Hoppe, Joanne 1932- *42*
Hoppe, Matthias 1952- *76*
Hopper, Nancy J. 1937- *38*
  Brief entry *35*
Hopping, Lorraine Jean
  See Egan, Lorraine Hopping
Horenstein, Henry 1947- *108*
Horgan, Paul (George Vincent
  O'Shaughnessy) 1903-1995 ....*13*
  Obituary *84*
Horlak, E. E.
  See Tepper, Sheri S.
Horler, Sydney 1888-1954 ....*102*
Hornblow, Arthur, Jr. 1893-1976 ....*15*
Hornblow, Leonora (Schinasi) 1920- *18*
Horne, Richard (George Anthony)
  1960- *111*
Horne, Richard Henry 1803-1884 ....*29*
Horner, Althea (Jane) 1926- *36*
Horner, Dave 1934- *12*
Horner, Jack
  See Horner, John R(obert)
Horner, John R(obert) 1946- *106*
Horniman, Joanne 1951- *98*
Hornos, Axel 1907-1994 ....*20*
Hornstein, Reuben Aaron 1912- *64*
Horowitz, Anthony 1955- *137*
Horowitz, Ruth 1957- *136*
Horse, Harry
  See Horne, Richard (George Anthony)
Horton, Madelyn (Stacey) 1962- *77*
Horvath, Betty 1927- *4*
Horvath, Polly 1957- *140*
  Earlier sketch in SATA *85*
Horwich, Frances R(appaport)
  1908-2001 ....*11*
  Obituary *130*
Horwitz, Elinor Lander *45*
  Brief entry *33*
Horwood, William 1944- *85*
Hosford, Dorothy (Grant) 1900-1952 ......*22*
Hosford, Jessie 1892-1990 ....*5*
Hoshi, Shin'ichi 1926- *101*
Hoskyns-Abrahall, Clare (Constance Drury) .
  ....*13*
Hossack, Sylvia 1939- *83*
Hossack, Sylvie Adams
  See Hossack, Sylvia
Hossell, Karen Price
  See Price, Karen
Hostetler, Marian 1932- *91*
Houck, Carter 1924- *22*

Hough, (Helen) Charlotte 1924- *9*
Hough, Judy Taylor 1932- *63*
  Brief entry *51*
  Earlier sketch in SATA *56*
Hough, Richard (Alexander)
  1922-1999 ....*17*
Houghton, Eric 1930- *7*
Houk, Randy 1944- *97*
Houlehen, Robert J. 1918- *18*
Household, Geoffrey (Edward West)
  1900-1988 ....*14*
  Obituary *59*
Housman, Laurence 1865-1959 ....*25*
Houston, Dick 1943- *74*
Houston, Gloria *81*
  Autobiography Feature *138*
Houston, James A(rchibald) 1921- *74*
  Earlier sketch in SATA *13*
  See also CLR *3*
  See also SAAS *17*
Houston, James D. 1933- *78*
Houston, Jeanne (Toyo) Wakatsuki
  1934- *78*
Houston, Juanita C. 1921- *129*
Houton, Kathleen
  See Kilgore, Kathleen
Howard, Alan 1922- *45*
Howard, Alyssa
  See Buckholtz, Eileen (Garber)
  and Glick, Ruth (Burtnick)
  and Titchener, Louise
Howard, Elizabeth Fitzgerald 1927- *119*
  Earlier sketch in SATA *74*
Howard, Ellen 1943- *99*
  Earlier sketch in SATA *67*
Howard, Jane R(uble) 1924- *87*
Howard, Norman Barry 1949- *90*
Howard, P. M.
  See Howard, Pauline Rodriguez
Howard, Paul 1967- *118*
Howard, Pauline Rodriguez 1951- *124*
Howard, Prosper
  See Hamilton, Charles (Harold St. John)
Howard, Robert West 1908-1988 ....*5*
Howard, Todd 1964- *135*
Howard, Tristan
  See Currie, Stephen
Howard, Vernon (Linwood)
  1918-1992 ....*40*
  Obituary *73*
Howard, Warren F.
  See Pohl, Frederik
Howarth, David (Armine) 1912-1991 ....*6*
  Obituary *68*
Howarth, Lesley 1952- *94*
Howe, Deborah 1946-1978 ....*29*
Howe, James 1946- *111*
  Earlier sketches in SATA *29, 71*
  See also CLR *9*
Howe, John F. 1957- *79*
Howe, Norma 1930- *126*
Howell, Pat 1947- *15*
Howell, S.
  See Styles, (Frank) Showell
Howell, Virginia
  See Ellison, Virginia H(owell)
Howes, Barbara 1914-1996 ....*5*
Howie, Diana (Melson) 1945- *122*
Howker, Janni 1957- *72*
  Brief entry *46*
  See also CLR *14*
  See also SAAS *13*
Howland, Ethan 1963- *131*
Hoy, Linda 1946- *65*
Hoy, Nina
  See Roth, Arthur J(oseph)
Hoyle, Geoffrey 1942- *18*
Hoyt, Edwin P(almer), Jr. 1923- *28*
Hoyt, Erich 1950- *140*
  Earlier sketch in SATA *65*
Hoyt, Olga
  See Gruhzit-Hoyt, Olga (Margaret)

Hrdlitschka, Shelley 1956- *111*
Htin Aung, U.
    See Aung, (Maung) Htin
Huang, Benrei 1959- *86*
Hubalek, Linda K. 1954- *111*
Hubbard, Michelle Calabro 1953- *122*
Hubbard, Patricia 1945- *124*
Hubbard, Woodleigh Marx *98*
Hubbell, Patricia 1928- *132*
    Earlier sketch in SATA 8
Hubley, Faith Elliot 1924-2001 ....*48*
    Obituary *133*
Hubley, John 1914-1977 ....*48*
    Obituary *24*
Huck, Charlotte S. 1922- *136*
    Earlier sketch in SATA 82
Hudson, Cheryl Willis 1948- *81*
Hudson, Jan 1954-1990 ....*77*
    See also CLR 40
Hudson, Jeffrey
    See Crichton, (John) Michael
Hudson, (Margaret) Kirsty 1947- *32*
Hudson, Margaret
    See Shuter, Jane Margaret
Hudson, W(illiam) H(enry)
    1841-1922 ....*35*
Hudson, Wade 1946- *74*
Huelsmann, Eva 1928- *16*
Huerlimann, Bettina 1909-1983 ....*39*
    Earlier sketch in SATA 34
    See Hurlimann, Bettina
Huerlimann, Ruth 1939- *32*
    Earlier sketch in SATA 31
    See Hurlimann, Ruth
Huff, Barbara A. 1929- *67*
Huff, T. S.
    See Huff, Tanya (Sue)
Huff, Tanya (Sue) 1957- *85*
Huff, Vivian 1948- *59*
Huffaker, Sandy 1943- *10*
Huffman, Tom *24*
Huggins, Nathan Irvin 1927-1989 ....*63*
Hughes, Carol 1955- *108*
Hughes, Dean 1943- *139*
    Earlier sketches in SATA 33, 77, 136
    See also CLR 76
Hughes, Eden
    See Butterworth, W(illiam) E(dmund III)
Hughes, Edward James
    See Hughes, Ted
Hughes, (James Mercer) Langston
    1902-1967 ....*33*
    Earlier sketch in SATA 4
    See also CLR 17
Hughes, Libby *71*
Hughes, Matilda
    See MacLeod, Charlotte (Matilda)
Hughes, Monica (Ince) 1925- *119*
    Earlier sketches in SATA 15, 70
    See also CLR 60
    See also SAAS 11
Hughes, Richard (Arthur Warren)
    1900-1976 ....*8*
    Obituary *25*
Hughes, Sara
    See Saunders, Susan
Hughes, Shirley 1927- *110*
    Earlier sketches in SATA 16, 70
    See also CLR 15
Hughes, Ted 1930-1998 ....*49*
    Brief entry *27*
    Obituary *107*
    See also CLR 3
    See Hughes, Edward James
Hughes, Thomas 1822-1896 ....*31*
Hughes, Virginia
    See Campbell, Hope
Hughes, Walter (Llewellyn)
    1910-1993 ....*26*
Hughey, Roberta 1942- *61*
Hugo, Pierre Brackers de
    See Brackers de Hugo, Pierre

Hugo, Victor (Marie) 1802-1885 ....*47*
Huline-Dickens, Frank William
    1931- *34*
Hull, Eleanor (Means) 1913- *21*
Hull, Eric Traviss
    See Harnan, Terry
Hull, H. Braxton
    See Jacobs, Helen Hull
Hull, Jesse Redding
    See Hull, Jessie Redding
Hull, Jessie Redding 1932- *51*
Hull, Katharine 1921-1977 ....*23*
Hulme, Joy N. 1922- *112*
    Earlier sketch in SATA 74
Hults, Dorothy Niebrugge 1898-2000 ....*6*
Humble, Richard 1945- *60*
Hume, Lotta Carswell *7*
Hume, Ruth Fox 1922-1980 ....*26*
    Obituary *22*
Hume, Stephen Eaton 1947- *136*
Hummel, Berta 1909-1946 ....*43*
Hummel, Sister Maria Innocentia
    See Hummel, Berta
Humphrey, Henry (III) 1930- *16*
Humphrey, Sandra McLeod 1936- *95*
Humphreys, Martha 1943- *71*
Humphreys, Susan L.
    See Lowell, Susan
Hundal, Nancy 1957- *128*
Huneck, Stephen 1949- *129*
Hungerford, Hesba Fay
    See Brinsmead, H(esba) F(ay)
Hungerford, Pixie
    See Brinsmead, H(esba) F(ay)
Hunkin, Timothy Mark Trelawney
    1950- *53*
Hunt, Angela Elwell 1957- *75*
Hunt, Francesca
    See Holland, Isabelle (Christian)
Hunt, Irene 1907-2001 ....*91*
    Earlier sketch in SATA 2
    See also CLR 1
Hunt, Janie Louise 1963- *102*
Hunt, Jonathan 1966- *84*
Hunt, Joyce 1927- *31*
Hunt, Linda 1940- *39*
Hunt, Lisa B(ehnke) 1967- *84*
Hunt, Mabel Leigh 1892-1971 ....*1*
    Obituary *26*
Hunt, Morton M(agill) 1920- *22*
Hunt, Nigel
    See Greenbank, Anthony Hunt
Hunt, Peter (Leonard) 1945- *76*
Hunter, Anne B. 1966- *118*
Hunter, Bernice Thurman 1922- *85*
    Brief entry *45*
Hunter, Bobbi Dooley 1945- *89*
Hunter, Captain Marcy
    See Ellis, Edward S(ylvester)
Hunter, Chris
    See Fluke, Joanne
Hunter, Clingham M.D.
    See Adams, William Taylor
Hunter, Dawe
    See Downie, Mary Alice (Dawe)
Hunter, Edith Fisher 1919- *31*
Hunter, Evan 1926- *25*
    See McBain, Ed
Hunter, George E.
    See Ellis, Edward S(ylvester)
Hunter, Hilda 1921- *7*
Hunter, Jim 1939- *65*
Hunter, Kristin 1931-
    See Lattany, Kristin (Elaine Eggleston)
    Hunter
Hunter, Leigh
    See Etchison, Birdie L(ee)
Hunter, Lieutenant Ned
    See Ellis, Edward S(ylvester)
Hunter, Mel 1927- *39*

Hunter, Mollie 1922- *139*
    Earlier sketches in SATA 54, 106
    See also CLR 25
    See also SAAS 7
    See McIlwraith, Maureen Mollie Hunter
Hunter, Ned
    See Ellis, Edward S(ylvester)
Hunter, Norman (George Lorimer)
    1899-1995 ....*84*
    Earlier sketch in SATA 26
Hunter, Ryan Ann
    See Greenwood, Pamela D.
    and Macalaster, Elizabeth G.
Hunter, Sara Hoagland 1954- *98*
Huntington, Amy 1956- *138*
Huntington, Harriet E(lizabeth) 1909- *1*
Huntsberry, William E(mery) 1916- *5*
Hurd, Clement (G.) 1908-1988 ....*64*
    Obituary *54*
    Earlier sketch in SATA 2
    See also CLR 49
Hurd, Edith Thacher 1910-1997 ....*64*
    Obituary *95*
    Earlier sketch in SATA 2
    See also CLR 49
    See also SAAS 13
Hurd, (John) Thacher 1949- *94*
    Autobiography Feature *123*
    Brief entry *45*
    Earlier sketch in SATA 46
Hurlimann, Bettina *39*
    Obituary *34*
    See Huerlimann, Bettina
Hurlimann, Ruth *32*
    Brief entry *31*
    See Huerlimann, Ruth
Hurmence, Belinda 1921- *77*
    See also CLR 25
    See also SAAS 20
Hurst, Carol Otis 1933- *130*
Hurt-Newton, Tania 1968- *84*
Hurwitz, Johanna 1937- *113*
    Earlier sketches in SATA 20, 71
    See also SAAS 18
Hurwood, Bernhardt J. 1926-1987 ....*12*
    Obituary *50*
Husain, Shahrukh 1950- *108*
Hutchens, Paul 1902-1977 ....*31*
Hutchins, Carleen Maley 1911- *9*
Hutchins, Hazel J. 1952- *135*
    Brief entry *51*
    Earlier sketch in SATA 81
    See also SAAS 24
Hutchins, Pat 1942- *111*
    Earlier sketches in SATA 15, 70
    See also CLR 20
    See also SAAS 16
Hutchins, Ross Elliott 1906- *4*
Huthmacher, J. Joseph 1929- *5*
Hutto, Nelson (Allen) 1904-1985 ....*20*
Hutton, Kathryn 1915- *89*
Hutton, Warwick 1939-1994 ....*20*
    Obituary *83*
    See also SAAS 17
Huxley, Aldous (Leonard)
    1894-1963 ....*63*
Huxley, Elspeth (Josceline Grant)
    1907-1997 ....*62*
    Obituary *95*
Hyde, Catherine R(yan) 1955- *141*
Hyde, Dayton O(gden) *9*
Hyde, Hawk
    See Hyde, Dayton O(gden)
Hyde, Margaret O(ldroyd) 1917- *139*
    Earlier sketches in SATA 1, 42, 76
    See also CLR 23
    See also SAAS 8
Hyde, Shelley
    See Reed, Kit
Hyde, Wayne Frederick 1922- *7*
Hylander, Clarence J(ohn) 1897-1964 ....*7*
Hyman, Robin P(hilip) 1931- *12*

Hyman, Trina Schart 1939- 95
　Earlier sketches in SATA *7, 46*
　See also CLR *50*
Hymes, Lucia M(anley) 1907-1998 7
Hyndman, Jane Andrews Lee
　1912-1978 46
　Obituary 23
　Earlier sketch in SATA *1*
Hyndman, Robert Utley 1906-1973 18
Hynes, Pat 98

I

Iannone, Jeanne 7
　See Balzano, Jeanne (Koppel)
Ibbitson, John Perrie 1955- 102
Ibbotson, Eva 1925- 103
　Earlier sketch in SATA *13*
Ibbotson, M. C(hristine) 1930- 5
Ichikawa, Satomi 1949- 78
　Brief entry 36
　Earlier sketch in SATA *47*
　See also CLR *62*
Ignoffo, Matthew 1945- 92
Igus, Toyomi 1953- 112
　Earlier sketch in SATA *76*
Ikeda, Daisaku 1928- 77
Ilowite, Sheldon A. 1931- 27
Ilsley, Velma (Elizabeth) 1918- 12
Imai, Miko 1963- 90
Imershein, Betsy 1953- 62
Immel, Mary Blair 1930- 28
Immell, Myra H. 1941- 92
Impey, Rose 1947- 69
Ingelow, Jean 1820-1897 33
Ingermanson, Randall (Scott) 1958- 134
Ingersoll, Norman 1928- 79
Ingham, Colonel Frederic
　See Hale, Edward Everett
Ingman, Bruce 1963- 134
Ingman, Nicholas 1948- 52
Ingold, Jeanette 128
Ingpen, Robert Roger 1936- 109
Ingraham, Leonard W(illiam) 1913- 4
Ingram, Scott 1948- 92
Ingrams, Doreen 1906-1997 97
　Earlier sketch in SATA *20*
Ingrid, Charles
　See Salsitz, Rhondi Vilott
Ingves, Gunilla (Anna Maria Folkesdotter)
　1939- 101
Inkpen, Mick 1952- 99
Innes, Hammond
　See Hammond Innes, Ralph
Innes, Ralph Hammond
　See Hammond Innes, Ralph
Innocenti, Roberto 1940- 96
　See also CLR *56*
Inyart, Gene 6
　See Namovicz, Gene Inyart
Ionesco, Eugene 1912-1994 7
　Obituary 79
Ipcar, Dahlov (Zorach) 1917- 49
　Earlier sketch in SATA *1*
　See also SAAS *8*
Ireland, Karin 101
Ironside, Jetske 1940- 60
Irvin, Fred 1914- 15
Irvine, Georgeanne 1955- 72
Irvine, Joan 1951- 80
Irving, Alexander
　See Hume, Ruth Fox
Irving, Robert
　See Adler, Irving
Irving, Washington 1783-1859
　See YABC *2*

Irwin, Ann(abelle Bowen) 1915-1998 89
　Brief entry 38
　Obituary 106
　Earlier sketch in SATA *44*
　See also CLR *40*
　See Irwin, Hadley
Irwin, Constance (H.) Frick
　1913-1995 6
Irwin, Hadley
　See CLR *40*
　See also SAAS *14*
　See Hadley, Lee
　and Irwin, Ann(abelle Bowen)
Irwin, Keith Gordon 1885-1964 11
Isaac, Joanne 1934- 21
Isaacs, Anne 1949- 90
Isaacs, Jacob
　See Kranzler, George G(ershon)
Isaacson, Philip M(arshal) 1924- 87
Isadora, Rachel 1953(?)- 121
　Brief entry 32
　Earlier sketches in SATA *54, 79*
　See also CLR *7*
Isbell, Rebecca T(emple) 1942- 125
Isham, Charlotte H(ickock) 1912- 21
Ish-Kishor, Judith 1892-1972 11
Ish-Kishor, Sulamith 1896-1977 17
Ishmael, Woodi 1914-1995 31
　Obituary 109
Isle, Sue 1963- 105
Israel, Elaine 1945- 12
Iterson, S(iny) R(ose) Van
　See Van Iterson, S(iny) R(ose)
Ivanko, John D(uane) 1966- 111
Iverson, Diane 1950- 122
Iverson, Eric G.
　See Turtledove, Harry (Norman)
Ivery, Martha M. 1948- 124
Ives, Morgan
　See Bradley, Marion Zimmer
Iwamatsu, Jun Atsushi 1908-1994 81
　Earlier sketch in SATA *14*
　See Yashima, Taro
Iwasaki (Matsumoto), Chihiro 1918-1974
　See CLR *18*

J

Jac, Lee
　See Morton, Lee Jack, Jr.
Jacka, Martin 1943- 72
Jackson, Alison 1953- 108
　Earlier sketch in SATA *73*
Jackson, C(aary) Paul 1902-1991 6
Jackson, Caary
　See Jackson, C(aary) Paul
Jackson, Dave
　See Jackson, J. David
Jackson, Ellen B. 1943- 115
　Earlier sketch in SATA *75*
Jackson, Garnet Nelson 1944- 87
Jackson, Gina
　See Fluke, Joanne
Jackson, Guida M. 1930- 71
Jackson, J. David 1944- 91
Jackson, Jacqueline 1928- 65
Jackson, Jesse 1908-1983 29
　Obituary 48
　Earlier sketch in SATA *2*
　See also CLR *28*
Jackson, Marjorie 1928- 127
Jackson, Melanie 1956- 141
Jackson, Mike 1946- 91
Jackson, Neta J. 1944- 91
Jackson, O. B.
　See Jackson, C(aary) Paul
Jackson, Robert B(lake) 1926- 8
Jackson, Sally
　See Kellogg, Jean (Defrees)
Jackson, Shirley 1919-1965 2

Jackson, Woody 1948- 92
Jacob, Helen Pierce 1927- 21
Jacobs, Flora Gill 1918- 5
Jacobs, Francine 1935- 43
　Brief entry 42
Jacobs, Frank 1929- 30
Jacobs, Helen Hull 1908-1997 12
Jacobs, Joseph 1854-1916 25
Jacobs, Judy 1952- 69
Jacobs, Laurie A. 1956- 89
Jacobs, Leah
　See Gellis, Roberta (Leah Jacobs)
Jacobs, Leland Blair 1907-1992 20
　Obituary 71
Jacobs, Linda
　See Altman, Linda Jacobs
Jacobs, Lou(is), Jr. 1921- 2
Jacobs, Shannon K. 1947- 77
Jacobs, Susan
　See Quinn, Susan
Jacobs, William Jay 1933- 89
　Earlier sketch in SATA *28*
Jacobson, Daniel 1923- 12
Jacobson, Morris K(arl) 1906- 21
Jacopetti, Alexandra 14
　See Hart, Alexandra
Jacques, Brian 1939- 138
　Earlier sketches in SATA *62, 95*
　See also CLR *21*
Jacques, Robin 1920-1995 32
　Brief entry 30
　Obituary 86
　See also SAAS *5*
Jaekel, Susan M. 1948- 89
Jaffee, Al(lan) 1921- 66
　Earlier sketch in SATA *37*
Jagendorf, Moritz (Adolf) 1888-1981 2
　Obituary 24
Jahn, Joseph Michael 1943- 28
Jahn, Michael
　See Jahn, Joseph Michael
Jahn, Mike
　See Jahn, Joseph Michael
Jahn-Clough, Lisa 1967- 88
Jahsmann, Allan Hart 1916- 28
Jakes, John (William) 1932- 62
James, Andrew
　See Kirkup, James
James, Ann 1952- 117
　Earlier sketch in SATA *82*
James, Brian 1976- 140
James, Bronte
　See Nash, Renea Denise
James, Captain Lew
　See Stratemeyer, Edward L.
James, Dynely
　See Mayne, William (James Carter)
James, Edwin
　See Gunn, James E(dwin)
James, Elizabeth 1942- 97
　Earlier sketches in SATA *39, 45, 52*
James, Emily
　See Standiford, Natalie
James, Harry Clebourne 1896-1978 11
James, J. Alison 1962- 83
James, Josephine
　See Sterne, Emma Gelders
James, Mary
　See Meaker, Marijane (Agnes)
James, Philip
　See del Rey, Lester
　and Moorcock, Michael (John)
James, Robin (Irene) 1953- 50
James, Tegan
　See Odgers, Sally Farrell
James, Will(iam Roderick)
　1892-1942 19
Jameson, W. C. 1942- 93
Jamieson, Ian R.
　See Goulart, Ron(ald Joseph)
Jamiolkowski, Raymond M. 1953- 81
Jane, Mary Childs 1909- 6

Janeczko, Paul B(ryan) 1945- 98
  Earlier sketch in SATA 53
  See also CLR 47
  See also SAAS 18
Janes, Edward C. 1908- 25
Janes, J(oseph) Robert 1935- 101
  Brief entry 50
Janeway, Elizabeth (Hall) 1913- 19
Janger, Kathleen N. 1940- 66
Janice
  See Brustlein, Janice Tworkov
Janosch
  See CLR 26
  See Eckert, Horst
Janover, Caroline (Davis) 1943- 141
  Earlier sketch in SATA 89
Jansen, Jared
  See Cebulash, Mel
Janson, Dora Jane (Heineberg)
  1916- 31
Janson, H(orst) W(oldemar)
  1913-1982 9
Jansson, Tove (Marika) 1914-2001 41
  Earlier sketch in SATA 3
  See also CLR 2
Janus, Grete
  See Hertz, Grete Janus
Jaques, Faith 1923-1997 97
  Earlier sketches in SATA 21, 69
Jaquith, Priscilla 1908- 51
Jaramillo, Mari-Luci 1928- 139
Jarman, Julia 1946- 133
Jarman, Rosemary Hawley 1935- 7
Jarrell, Mary Von Schrader 1914- 35
Jarrell, Randall 1914-1965 7
  See also CLR 6
Jarrett, Roxanne
  See Werner, Herma
Jarrow, Gail 1952- 84
Jarvis, E. K.
  See Ellison, Harlan (Jay)
Jaskol, Julie 1958- 127
Jasner, W. K.
  See Watson, Jane Werner
Jassem, Kate
  See Oppenheim, Joanne
Jauss, Anne Marie 1902(?)-1991 10
  Obituary 69
Javernick, Ellen 1938- 89
Jayne, Lieutenant R. H.
  See Ellis, Edward S(ylvester)
Jaynes, Clare
  See Mayer, Jane Rothschild
Jeake, Samuel, Jr.
  See Aiken, Conrad (Potter)
Jean-Bart, Leslie 1954- 121
Jefferds, Vincent H(arris) 1916- 59
  Brief entry 49
Jefferies, (John) Richard 1848-1887 16
Jeffers, Susan 1942- 137
  Earlier sketches in SATA 17, 70, 129
  See also CLR 30
Jefferson, Sarah
  See Farjeon, (Eve) Annabel
Jeffries, Roderic (Graeme) 1926- 4
Jenkin-Pearce, Susie 1943- 80
Jenkins, Debra Reid
  See Reid Jenkins, Debra
Jenkins, Jean 98
Jenkins, Marie M(agdalen) 1909- 7
Jenkins, Patrick 1955- 72
Jenkins, William A(twell) 1922-1998 9
Jenkyns, Chris 1924- 51
Jennings, Coleman A(lonzo) 1933- 64
Jennings, Dana Andrew 1957- 93
Jennings, Elizabeth (Joan) 1926-2001 66
Jennings, Gary (Gayne) 1928-1999 9
  Obituary 117
Jennings, Patrick 1962- 96
Jennings, Paul 1943- 88
  See also CLR 40
Jennings, Richard (W.) 1945- 136

Jennings, Robert
  See Hamilton, Charles (Harold St. John)
Jennings, S. M.
  See Meyer, Jerome Sydney
Jennings, Sharon (Elizabeth) 1954- 95
Jennison, C. S.
  See Starbird, Kaye
Jennison, Keith Warren 1911-1995 14
Jensen, Kathryn 1949- 81
Jensen, Kristine Mary 1961- 78
Jensen, Niels 1927- 25
Jensen, Vickie (Dee) 1946- 81
Jensen, Virginia Allen 1927- 8
Jeram, Anita 1965- 102
  Earlier sketch in SATA 71
Jerman, Jerry 1949- 89
Jernigan, E. Wesley 1940- 85
Jernigan, Gisela (Evelyn) 1948- 85
Jeschke, Susan 1942- 42
  Brief entry 27
Jessel, Camilla (Ruth) 1937- 29
Jessey, Cornelia
  See Sussman, Cornelia Silver
Jewel
  See Kilcher, Jewel
Jewell, Nancy 1940- 109
  Brief entry 41
Jewett, Eleanore Myers 1890-1967 5
Jewett, (Theodora) Sarah Orne
  1849-1909 15
Jezard, Alison 1919- 57
  Brief entry 34
Jiang, Cheng An 1943- 109
Jiang, Ji-li 1954- 101
Jiang, Zheng An
  See Jiang, Cheng An
Jiler, John 1946- 42
  Brief entry 35
Jimenez, Francisco 1943- 108
Jinks, Catherine 1963- 94
Jobb, Jamie 1945- 29
Jobling, Curtis 131
Jocelyn, Ann Henning 1948- 92
Jocelyn, Marthe 1956- 118
Joerns, Consuelo 44
  Brief entry 33
Joey D
  See Macaulay, Teresa (E.)
Johansen, K(rista) V(ictoria) 1968- 129
John, Joyce 59
Johns, Avery
  See Cousins, Margaret
Johns, Elizabeth 1943- 88
Johns, Janetta
  See Quin-Harkin, Janet
Johns, W(illiam) E(arle) 1893-1968 55
Johns, Captain W. E.
  See Johns, W(illiam) E(arle)
Johnson, A.
  See Johnson, Annabell (Jones)
Johnson, A. E.
  See Johnson, Annabell (Jones)
  and Johnson, Edgar (Raymond)
Johnson, Angela 1961- 102
  Earlier sketch in SATA 69
  See also CLR 33
Johnson, Annabel
  See Johnson, Annabell (Jones)
Johnson, Annabell (Jones) 1921- 72
  Earlier sketch in SATA 2
  See Johnson, Annabel
Johnson, Art 1946- 123
Johnson, Benjamin F., of Boone
  See Riley, James Whitcomb
Johnson, Bettye 1858-1919
  See Rogers, Bettye
Johnson, Caryn
  See Goldberg, Whoopi
Johnson, Caryn E.
  See Goldberg, Whoopi
Johnson, Charles R. 1925- 11

Johnson, Charlotte Buel 46
  See von Wodtke, Charlotte Buel Johnson
Johnson, Chuck
  See Johnson, Charles R.
Johnson, Crockett
  See Leisk, David (Johnson)
Johnson, D(ana) William 1945- 23
Johnson, Daniel Shahid 1954- 73
Johnson, Dinah 130
  See Johnson, Dianne
Johnson, Dolores 1949- 69
Johnson, Dorothy M(arie) 1905-1984 6
  Obituary 40
Johnson, E(ugene) Harper 44
Johnson, Edgar (Raymond)
  1912-1990 72
  Earlier sketch in SATA 2
Johnson, Elizabeth 1911-1984 7
  Obituary 39
Johnson, Eric W(arner) 1918-1994 ....
  Obituary 82
  Earlier sketch in SATA 8
Johnson, Evelyne 1922- 20
Johnson, Fred 19(?)-1982 63
Johnson, Gaylord 1884-1972 7
Johnson, Gerald White 1890-1980 19
  Obituary 28
Johnson, Harper
  See Johnson, E(ugene) Harper
Johnson, James Ralph 1922- 1
Johnson, James Weldon 1871-1938 31
  See also CLR 32
Johnson, Jane 1951- 48
Johnson, Joan J. 1942- 59
Johnson, John E(mil) 1929- 34
Johnson, Johnny 1901-1995
  See Johnson, (Walter) Ryerson
Johnson, La Verne B(ravo) 1925- 13
Johnson, Lee Kaiser 1962- 78
Johnson, Lissa H(alls) 1955- 65
Johnson, Lois Smith 1894-1993 6
Johnson, Lois Walfrid 1936- 130
  Earlier sketches in SATA 22, 91
Johnson, Margaret S(weet)
  1893-1964 35
Johnson, Marguerite Annie
  See Angelou, Maya
Johnson, Meredith Merrell 1952- 104
Johnson, Milton 1932- 31
Johnson, Neil 1954- 135
  Earlier sketch in SATA 73
Johnson, Pamela 1949- 71
Johnson, Patricia Polin 1956- 84
Johnson, Paul Brett 1947- 132
  Earlier sketch in SATA 83
Johnson, Rebecca L. 1956- 67
Johnson, Rick L. 1954- 79
Johnson, (Walter) Ryerson
  1901-1995 10
  Obituary 106
  See Halliday, Brett
Johnson, Scott 1952- 119
  Earlier sketch in SATA 76
Johnson, Sherrie 1948- 87
Johnson, Shirley K(ing) 1927- 10
Johnson, Stephen T. 1964- 141
  Earlier sketch in SATA 84
Johnson, Sue Kaiser 1963- 78
Johnson, Sylvia A. 104
  Brief entry 52
Johnson, William R. 38
Johnson, William Weber 1909-1992 7
Johnston, Agnes Christine
  See Dazey, Agnes J(ohnston)
Johnston, Annie Fellows 1863-1931 37
Johnston, Dorothy Grunbock
  1915-1979 54
Johnston, Ginny 1946- 60
Johnston, H(ugh) A(nthony) S(tephen)
  1913-1967 14
Johnston, Janet 1944- 71

Johnston, Johanna 1914(?)-1982 ....*12*
  Obituary *33*
Johnston, Julie 1941- *110*
  Autobiography Feature *128*
  Earlier sketch in SATA *78*
  See also CLR *41*
  See also SAAS *24*
Johnston, Lynn (Beverley) 1947- *118*
Johnston, Norma *29*
  See St. John, Nicole
Johnston, Portia
  See Takakjian, Portia
Johnston, Susan Taylor 1942- *128*
  Earlier sketch in SATA *83*
  See Johnston, Tony
Johnston, Tony *8*
  See Johnston, Susan Taylor
Jonas, Ann 1932- *135*
  Brief entry *42*
  Earlier sketch in SATA *50*
  See also CLR *74*
Jonell, Lynne *109*
Jones, Adrienne 1915-2000 ....*82*
  Earlier sketch in SATA *7*
  See also SAAS *10*
Jones, Annabel
  See Lewis, Mary (Christianna)
Jones, Betty Millsaps 1940- *54*
Jones, Carol 1942- *79*
Jones, Charles M(artin) 1912-2002 ....*53*
  Obituary *133*
  See Jones, Chuck
Jones, Charlotte Foltz 1945- *122*
  Earlier sketch in SATA *77*
Jones, Chuck
  See Jones, Charles M(artin)
Jones, Constance 1961- *112*
Jones, Diana Wynne 1934- *108*
  Earlier sketches in SATA *9, 70*
  See also CLR *23*
  See also SAAS *7*
Jones, Douglas C(lyde) 1924-1998 ....*52*
Jones, Elizabeth Orton 1910- *18*
Jones, Evan 1915-1996 ....*3*
Jones, Geraldine
  See McCaughrean, Geraldine
Jones, Gillingham
  See Hamilton, Charles (Harold St. John)
Jones, Harold 1904-1992 ....*14*
  Obituary *72*
Jones, Helen Hinckley 1903-1991 ....*26*
Jones, Hettie 1934- *42*
  Brief entry *27*
Jones, Hortense P. 1918- *9*
Jones, J(on) Sydney 1948- *101*
Jones, Jennifer (Berry) 1947- *90*
Jones, John R(obert) 1926- *76*
Jones, Marcia Thornton 1958- *115*
  Earlier sketch in SATA *73*
Jones, Martha T(annery) 1931- *130*
Jones, Mary Alice 1898(?)-1980 ....*6*
Jones, McClure *34*
Jones, Patrick 1961- *136*
Jones, Penelope 1938- *31*
Jones, Rebecca C(astaldi) 1947- *99*
  Earlier sketch in SATA *33*
Jones, Robin D(orothy) 1959- *80*
Jones, Sanford W.
  See Thorn, John
Jones, Terence Graham Parry
  1942- *127*
  See Jones, Terry
  and Monty Python
Jones, Terry *67*
  Brief entry *51*
  See Jones, Terence Graham Parry
Jones, Tim(othy) Wynne
  See Wynne-Jones, Tim(othy)
Jones, Veda Boyd 1948- *119*
Jones, Volcano
  See Mitchell, Adrian

Jones, Weyman (B.) 1928- *4*
  See also SAAS *11*
Jones, William Glynne
  See Glynne-Jones, William
Jonk, Clarence 1906-1987 ....*10*
Joos, Francoise 1956- *78*
Joos, Frederic 1953- *78*
Joosse, Barbara M(onnot) 1949- *96*
  Earlier sketch in SATA *52*
Jordan, Alexis Hill
  See Glick, Ruth (Burtnick)
  and Titchener, Louise
Jordan, Anne Devereaux 1943- *80*
Jordan, Don
  See Howard, Vernon (Linwood)
Jordan, Hope Dahle 1905-1995 ....*15*
Jordan, Jael (Michal) 1949- *30*
Jordan, June (Meyer) 1936-2002 ....*136*
  Earlier sketch in SATA *4*
  See also CLR *10*
Jordan, Lee
  See Scholefield, Alan
Jordan, Martin George 1944- *84*
Jordan, Robert
  See Rigney, James Oliver, Jr.
Jordan, Sherryl 1949- *122*
  Earlier sketch in SATA *71*
  See also SAAS *23*
Jordan, Tanis 1946- *84*
Jorgensen, Mary Venn -1995 ....*36*
Jorgenson, Ivar
  See Silverberg, Robert
Joseph, Anne
  See Coates, Anna
Joseph, Anne
  See Coates, Anna
Joseph, James (Herz) 1924- *53*
Joseph, Joan 1939- *34*
Joseph, Joseph M(aron) 1903-1979 ....*22*
Josephs, Rebecca *14*
  See Talbot, Toby
Josh
  See Clemens, Samuel Langhorne
Joslin, Sesyle *2*
  See Hine, Sesyle Joslin
Joyce, Bill
  See Joyce, William
Joyce, J(ames) Avery 1902-1987 ....*11*
  Obituary *50*
Joyce, Peter 1937- *127*
Joyce, William 1957- *118*
  Brief entry *46*
  Earlier sketch in SATA *72*
  See also CLR *26*
Joyner, Jerry 1938- *34*
Jucker, Sita 1921- *5*
Judah, Aaron 1923- *118*
Judd, Cyril
  See Kornbluth, C(yril) M.
  and Merril, Judith
  and Pohl, Frederik
Judd, Denis (O'Nan) 1938- *33*
Judd, Frances K. *1*
  See Benson, Mildred (Augustine Wirt)
Jude, Conny *81*
Judson, Clara Ingram 1879-1960 ....*38*
  Brief entry *27*
Judy, Stephen
  See Tchudi, Stephen N.
Judy, Stephen N.
  See Tchudi, Stephen N.
Jukes, Mavis 1947- *111*
  Brief entry *43*
  Earlier sketch in SATA *72*
  See also SAAS *12*
Julian, Jane
  See Wiseman, David
Jumpp, Hugo
  See MacPeek, Walter G.
Jupo, Frank J. 1904-1981 ....*7*
Jurmain, Suzanne 1945- *72*

Juster, Norton 1929- *132*
  Earlier sketch in SATA *3*
Justus, May 1898-1989 ....*1*
  Obituary *106*
Juvenilia
  See Taylor, Ann

K

Kabdebo, Tamas
  See Kabdebo, Thomas
Kabdebo, Thomas 1934- *10*
Kabibble, Osh
  See Jobb, Jamie
Kadesch, Robert R(udstone) 1922- *31*
Kaempfert, Wade
  See del Rey, Lester
Kaestner, Erich 1899-1974 ....*14*
  See also CLR *4*
  See Kastner, Erich
Kahl, Jonathan (D.) 1959- *77*
Kahl, M(arvin) P(hilip) 1934- *37*
Kahl, Virginia 1919- *48*
  Brief entry *38*
Kahn, Joan 1914-1994 ....*48*
  Obituary *82*
Kahn, Katherine Janus 1942- *90*
Kahn, Peggy
  See Katz, Bobbi
Kahn, Roger 1927- *37*
Kahukiwa, Robyn 1940- *134*
Kains, Josephine
  See Goulart, Ron(ald Joseph)
Kaizuki, Kiyonori 1950- *72*
Kakimoto, Kozo 1915- *11*
Kalashnikoff, Nicholas 1888-1961 ....*16*
Kalb, Jonah 1926- *23*
Kalbacken, Joan 1925- *96*
Kalechofsky, Roberta 1931- *92*
Kaler, James Otis 1848-1912 ....*15*
Kalish, Claire M. 1947- *92*
Kallen, Stuart A(rnold) 1955- *126*
  Earlier sketch in SATA *86*
Kalman, Bobbie 1947- *63*
Kalman, Maira 1949- *137*
  Earlier sketch in SATA *96*
  See also CLR *32*
Kalnay, Francis 1899-1992 ....*7*
Kaloustian, Rosanne 1955- *93*
Kalow, Gisela 1946- *32*
Kamen, Gloria 1923- *98*
  Earlier sketch in SATA *9*
Kamerman, Sylvia E.
  See Burack, Sylvia K.
Kamm, Josephine (Hart) 1905-1989 ....*24*
Kandel, Michael 1941- *93*
Kandell, Alice S. 1938- *35*
Kane, Bob 1916-1998 ....*120*
Kane, Henry Bugbee 1902-1971 ....*14*
Kane, L. A.
  See Mannetti, Lisa
Kane, Robert W. 1910- *18*
Kane, Wilson
  See Bloch, Robert (Albert)
Kanefield, Teri 1960- *135*
Kaner, Etta 1947- *126*
Kanetzke, Howard W(illiam) 1932- *38*
Kanoza, Muriel Canfield
  See Canfield, Muriel
Kanzawa, Toshiko
  See Furukawa, Toshi
Kaplan, Andrew 1960- *78*
Kaplan, Anne Bernays 1930- *32*
Kaplan, Bess 1927- *22*
Kaplan, Boche 1926- *24*
Kaplan, Elizabeth (A.) 1956- *83*
Kaplan, Irma 1900- *10*
Kaplan, Jean Caryl Korn 1926- *10*
Kaplow, Robert 1954- *70*

Karageorge, Michael
  See Anderson, Poul (William)
Karen, Ruth 1922-1987 9
  Obituary 54
Kark, Nina Mary 1925- 132
  Earlier sketch in SATA 4
  See Bawden, Nina (Mary Mabey)
Karl, Herb 1938- 73
Karl, Jean E(dna) 1927-2000 122
  Earlier sketch in SATA 34
  See also SAAS 10
Karlin, Bernie 1927- 68
Karlin, Eugene 1918- 10
Karlin, Nurit 103
  Earlier sketch in SATA 63
Karnes, Frances A. 1937- 110
Karp, Naomi J. 1926- 16
Karpinski, J. Rick
  See Karpinski, John Eric
Karpinski, John Eric 1952- 81
Karpinski, Rick
  See Karpinski, John Eric
Karr, Kathleen 1946- 127
  Earlier sketch in SATA 82
Karr, Phyllis Ann 1944- 119
Karwoski, Gail Langer 1949- 127
Kashiwagi, Isami 1925- 10
Kassem, Lou 1931- 62
  Brief entry 51
Kastel, Warren
  See Silverberg, Robert
Kastner, Erich
  See Kaestner, Erich
Kastner, Jill (Marie) 1964- 117
  Earlier sketch in SATA 70
Kasuya, Masahiro 1937- 51
Kasza, Keiko 1951- 124
Kataphusin
  See Ruskin, John
Katchen, Carole 1944- 9
Kathryn
  See Searle, Kathryn Adrienne
Katona, Robert 1949- 21
Katsarakis, Joan Harries
  See Harries, Joan
Katz, Avner 1939- 103
Katz, Bobbi 1933- 12
Katz, Fred(eric Phillip) 1938- 6
Katz, Jane B(resler) 1934- 33
Katz, Marjorie P.
  See Weiser, Marjorie P(hillis) K(atz)
Katz, Welwyn Wilton 1948- 96
  Autobiography Feature 118
  Earlier sketch in SATA 62
  See also CLR 45
Katz, William 1940- 98
Katz, William Loren 1927- 13
Kaufman, Bel 57
Kaufman, Jeff 1955- 84
Kaufman, Joe 1911-2001 33
Kaufman, Joseph
  See Kaufman, Joe
Kaufman, Mervyn D. 1932- 4
Kaufmann, Angelika 1935- 15
Kaufmann, John 1931- 18
Kaula, Edna Mason 1906-1987 13
Kaur Khalsa, Dayal
  See Khalsa, Dayal Kaur
Kavaler, Lucy 1930- 23
Kavanagh, Jack 1920- 85
Kavanagh, P(atrick) J(oseph Gregory)
  1931- 122
Kavanaugh, Ian
  See Webb, Jean Francis (III)
Kay, Guy Gavriel 1954- 121
Kay, Helen
  See Goldfrank, Helen Colodny
Kay, Jackie
  See Kay, Jacqueline Margaret
Kay, Jacqueline Margaret 1961- 97
  See Kay, Jackie
Kay, Mara 13

Kay, Verla 1946- 120
Kaye, Geraldine (Hughesdon) 1925- 85
  Earlier sketch in SATA 10
Kaye, Judy
  See Baer, Judy
Kaye, M(ary) M(argaret) 1909- 62
Kaye, Marilyn 1949- 110
  Earlier sketch in SATA 56
Kaye, Mollie
  See Kaye, M(ary) M(argaret)
Keach, James P. 1950- 125
Keams, Geri 1951- 117
Keane, Bil 1922- 4
Keaney, Brian 1954- 106
Kearny, Jillian
  See Goulart, Ron(ald Joseph)
Keating, Bern
  See Keating, Leo Bernard
Keating, Lawrence A. 1903-1966 23
Keating, Leo Bernard 1915- 10
Keats, Emma 1899(?)-1979(?) 68
Keats, Ezra Jack 1916-1983 57
  Obituary 34
  Earlier sketch in SATA 14
  See also CLR 35
Keefer, Catherine
  See Ogan, George F.
  and Ogan, Margaret E. (Nettles)
Keefer, Janice Kulyk 132
  See Kulyk Keefer, Janice
Keegan, Marcia 1943- 104
  Earlier sketch in SATA 9
Keehn, Sally M. 1947- 87
Keel, Frank
  See Keeler, Ronald F(ranklin)
Keeler, Ronald F(ranklin) 1913-1983 47
Keely, Jack 1951- 119
Keen, Martin L. 1913- 4
Keenan, Sheila 1953- 95
Keene, Ann T(odd) 1940- 86
Keene, Carolyn 100
  Earlier sketch in SATA 65
  See Benson, Mildred (Augustine Wirt)
  and McFarlane, Leslie (Charles)
  and Stratemeyer, Edward L.
Keens-Douglas, Richardo 1953- 95
Keeping, Charles (William James)
  1924-1988 69
  Obituary 56
  Earlier sketch in SATA 9
  See also CLR 34
Keeshan, Robert J. 1927- 32
Kehret, Peg 1936- 108
  Earlier sketch in SATA 73
Keillor, Garrison 58
  See Keillor, Gary (Edward)
Keir, Christine
  See Popescu, Christine
Keister, Douglas 1948- 88
Keith, Doug 1952- 81
Keith, Eros 1942- 52
Keith, Hal 1934- 36
Keith, Harold (Verne) 1903-1998 74
  Earlier sketch in SATA 2
Keith, Robert
  See Applebaum, Stan
Keleinikov, Andrei 1924- 65
Kelemen, Julie 1959- 78
Kelen, Emery 1896-1978 13
  Obituary 26
Kelleam, Joseph E(veridge)
  1913-1975 31
Kelleher, Annette 1950- 122
Kelleher, Daria Valerian 1955- 79
Kelleher, Victor (Michael Kitchener)
  1939- 129
  Brief entry 52
  Earlier sketch in SATA 75
  See also CLR 36
Keller, Beverly L(ou) 91
  Earlier sketch in SATA 13

Keller, Charles 1942- 82
  Earlier sketch in SATA 8
Keller, Debra 1958- 94
Keller, Dick 1923- 36
Keller, Emily 96
Keller, Gail Faithfull
  See Faithfull, Gail
Keller, Holly 1942- 108
  Brief entry 42
  Earlier sketch in SATA 76
  See also CLR 45
Keller, Irene (Barron) 1927-2002 36
  Obituary 139
Kelley, Leo P(atrick) 1928- 32
  Brief entry 31
Kelley, Patrick (G.) 1963- 129
Kelley, Patte 1947- 93
Kelley, True (Adelaide) 1946- 130
  Brief entry 39
  Earlier sketches in SATA 41, 92
Kellin, Sally Moffet 1932- 9
Kelling, Furn L. 1914- 37
Kellogg, Gene
  See Kellogg, Jean (Defrees)
Kellogg, Jean (Defrees) 1916-1978 10
Kellogg, Steven (Castle) 1941- 130
  Earlier sketches in SATA 8, 57
  See also CLR 6
Kellow, Kathleen
  See Hibbert, Eleanor Alice Burford
Kelly, Clint 1950- 140
Kelly, Eric P(hilbrook) 1884-1960
  See YABC 1
Kelly, Fiona
  See Coleman, Michael (Lee)
  and Oldfield, Jenny
  and Welford, Sue
Kelly, Jeff
  See Kelly, Jeffrey
Kelly, Jeffrey 1946- 65
Kelly, Joanne (W.) 1934- 87
Kelly, Kate 1958- 91
Kelly, Kathleen M. 1964- 71
Kelly, Laurene 1954- 123
Kelly, Martha Rose 1914-1983 37
Kelly, Marty
  See Kelly, Martha Rose
Kelly, Ralph
  See Geis, Darlene Stern
Kelly, Ralph
  See Geis, Darlene Stern
Kelly, Regina Z(immerman)
  1898-1986 5
Kelly, Rosalie (Ruth) 43
Kelly, Walt(er Crawford) 1913-1973 18
Kelsey, Alice Geer 1896-1982 1
Kemp, Gene 1926- 75
  Earlier sketch in SATA 25
  See also CLR 29
Kempner, Mary Jean 1913-1969 10
Kempton, Jean Welch 1914- 10
Kenda, Margaret 1942- 71
Kendall, Carol (Seeger) 1917- 74
  Earlier sketch in SATA 11
  See also SAAS 7
Kendall, Lace
  See Stoutenburg, Adrien (Pearl)
Kendall, Martha E. 87
Kendall, Russ 1957- 83
Kenealy, James P. 1927- 52
  Brief entry 29
Kenealy, Jim
  See Kenealy, James P.
Kennaway, Adrienne 1945- 60
Kennedy, Brendan 1970- 57
Kennedy, Dana Forrest 1917- 74
Kennedy, Dorothy M(intzlaff) 1931- 53
Kennedy, Doug(las) 1963- 122
Kennedy, John Fitzgerald 1917-1963 11

Kennedy, Joseph Charles 1929- *86*
   Autobiography Feature *130*
   Earlier sketch in SATA *14*
   See Kennedy, X. J.
Kennedy, Pamela (J.) 1946- *87*
Kennedy, Paul E(dward) 1929- *113*
   Earlier sketch in SATA *33*
Kennedy, (Jerome) Richard 1932- *22*
Kennedy, Robert 1938- *63*
Kennedy, T(eresa) A. 1953- *42*
   Brief entry *35*
Kennedy, Teresa
   See Kennedy, T(eresa) A.
Kennedy, William 1928- *57*
Kennedy, X. J.
   See CLR 27
   See also SAAS 22
   See Kennedy, Joseph Charles
Kennell, Ruth Epperson 1893-1977 ....*6*
   Obituary *25*
Kennemore, Tim 1957- *133*
Kennett, David 1959- *121*
Kenny, Herbert Andrew 1912-2002 ....*13*
Kenny, Kathryn
   See Bowden, Joan Chase
   and Krull, Kathleen
   and Sanderlin, Owenita (Harrah)
   and Stack, Nicolete Meredith
Kenny, Kevin
   See Krull, Kathleen
Kensinger, George
   See Fichter, George S.
Kent, Alexander
   See Reeman, Douglas Edward
Kent, David
   See Lambert, David (Compton)
Kent, Deborah Ann 1948- *104*
   Brief entry *41*
   Earlier sketch in SATA *47*
Kent, Jack
   See Kent, John Wellington
Kent, John Wellington 1920-1985 ....*24*
   Obituary *45*
Kent, Lisa 1942- *90*
Kent, Mallory
   See Lowndes, Robert A(ugustine) W(ard)
Kent, Margaret 1894- *2*
Kent, Rockwell 1882-1971 ....*6*
Kent, Sherman 1903-1986 ....*20*
   Obituary *47*
Kenward, Jean 1920- *42*
Kenworthy, Leonard S. 1912-1991 ....*6*
Kenyon, Kate
   See Adorjan, Carol (Madden)
   and Ransom, Candice F.
Kenyon, Ley 1913- *6*
Keown, Elizabeth *78*
Kepes, Juliet A(ppleby) 1919-1999 ....*13*
Kerby, Mona 1951- *75*
Kerigan, Florence 1896-1984 ....*12*
Kerley, Barbara 1960- *138*
Kerman, Gertrude
   See Furman, Gertrude Lerner Kerman
Kerns, Thelma 1929- *116*
Kerr, Bob 1951- *120*
Kerr, Jessica 1901-1991 ....*13*
Kerr, (Anne-) Judith 1923-1970 ....*24*
Kerr, M. E.
   See CLR 29
   See also SAAS *1*
   See Meaker, Marijane (Agnes)
Kerr, Phyllis Forbes 1942- *72*
Kerr, Tom 1950- *77*
Kerry, Frances
   See Kerigan, Florence
Kerry, Lois
   See Duncan, Lois
Kershen, (L.) Michael 1982- *82*
Kerven, Rosalind 1954- *83*
Ker Wilson, Barbara 1929- *121*
   Earlier sketches in SATA *20, 70*
   See also SAAS *18*

Keselman, Gabriela 1953- *128*
Kesey, Ken (Elton) 1935-2001 ....*66*
   Obituary *131*
Kesler, Jay 1935- *65*
Kessel, Joyce Karen 1937- *41*
Kessler, Ethel 1922- *44*
   Brief entry *37*
Kessler, Leonard P. 1921- *14*
Kest, Kristin 1967- *118*
Kesteven, G. R.
   See Crosher, G. R.
Ketcham, Hank
   See Ketcham, Henry King
Ketcham, Henry King 1920-2001 ....*28*
   Brief entry *27*
   Obituary *128*
Ketcham, Sallie 1963- *124*
Ketchum, Liza 1946- *132*
   See Murrow, Liza Ketchum
Ketner, Mary Grace 1946- *75*
Kettelkamp, Larry (Dale) 1933- *2*
   See also SAAS *3*
Ketteman, Helen 1945- *115*
   Earlier sketch in SATA *73*
Kettle, Peter
   See Glover, Denis (James Matthews)
Kevles, Bettyann Holtzmann 1938- *23*
Key, Alexander (Hill) 1904-1979 ....*8*
   Obituary *23*
Key, Samuel M.
   See de Lint, Charles (Henri Diederick
   Hofsmit)
Keyes, Daniel 1927- *37*
Keyes, Fenton 1915-1999 ....*34*
Keyes, Greg
   See Keyes, J. Gregory
Keyes, J. Gregory 1963- *116*
Keyser, Marcia 1933- *42*
Keyser, Sarah
   See McGuire, Leslie (Sarah)
Khalsa, Dayal Kaur 1943-1989 ....*62*
   See also CLR 30
   See Kaur Khalsa, Dayal
Khan, Rukhsana 1962- *118*
Khanshendel, Chiron
   See Rose, Wendy
Khemir, Sabiha *87*
Kherdian, David 1931- *74*
   Autobiography Feature *125*
   Earlier sketch in SATA *16*
   See also CLR 24
Kibbe, Pat (Hosley) *60*
Kidd, Ronald 1948- *92*
   Earlier sketch in SATA *42*
Kiddell, John 1922- *3*
Kiddell-Monroe, Joan 1908-1972 ....*55*
Kidwell, Carl 1910- *43*
Kiefer, Irene 1926- *21*
Kierstead, Vera M. 1913- *121*
Kiesel, Stanley 1925- *35*
Kiesler, Kate (A.) 1971- *90*
Kihn, Greg 1952- *110*
Kikukawa, Cecily H(arder) 1919- *44*
   Brief entry *35*
Kilcher, Jewel 1974- *109*
Kile, Joan 1940- *78*
Kilgore, Kathleen 1946- *42*
Kilian, Crawford 1941- *35*
Killdeer, John
   See Mayhar, Ardath
Killien, Christi 1956- *73*
Killilea, Marie (Lyons) 1913-1991 ....*2*
Killingback, Julia 1944- *63*
Killough, (Karen) Lee 1942- *64*
Kilreon, Beth
   See Walker, Barbara (Jeanne) K(erlin)
Kilworth, Garry (D.) 1941- *94*
Kim, Helen 1899-1970 ....*98*
Kimball, Gayle 1943- *90*
Kimball, Violet T(ew) 1932- *126*
Kimball, Yeffe 1914-1978 ....*37*

Kimbrough, Emily 1899-1989 ....*2*
   Obituary *59*
Kimeldorf, Martin (R.) 1948- *121*
Kimenye, Barbara 1940(?)- *121*
Kimmel, Eric A. 1946- *125*
   Earlier sketches in SATA *13, 80*
Kimmel, Margaret Mary 1938- *43*
   Brief entry *33*
Kimmelman, Leslie (Grodinsky)
   1958- *85*
Kincaid, Jamaica 1949-
   See CLR 63
Kincher, Jonni 1949- *79*
Kindl, Patrice 1951- *128*
   Earlier sketch in SATA *82*
Kindred, Wendy (Good) 1937- *7*
Kines, Pat Decker 1937- *12*
King, Adam
   See Hoare, Robert J(ohn)
King, Alison
   See Martini, Teri
King, (Maria) Anna 1964- *72*
King, Billie Jean 1943- *12*
King, Christopher (L.) 1945- *84*
King, (David) Clive 1924- *28*
King, Colin 1943- *76*
King, Cynthia 1925- *7*
King, Daniel (John) 1963- *130*
King, Elizabeth 1953- *83*
King, Frank R. 1904-1999 ....*127*
King, Jane
   See Currie, Stephen
King, Jeanette (Margaret) 1959- *105*
King, Larry L. 1929- *66*
King, Laurie R. 1952- *88*
King, Marian 1900(?)-1986 ....*23*
   Obituary *47*
King, Martin Luther, Jr. 1929-1968 ....*14*
King, Mary Ellen 1958- *93*
King, Paul
   See Drackett, Phil(ip Arthur)
King, Paula
   See Downing, Paula E.
King, Stephen (Edwin) 1947- *55*
   Earlier sketch in SATA *9*
King, Steve
   See King, Stephen (Edwin)
King, Thomas 1943- *96*
King, Tony 1947- *39*
Kingman, Dong (Moy Shu)
   1911-2000 ....*44*
Kingman, Lee *67*
   Earlier sketch in SATA *1*
   See also SAAS *3*
   See Natti, (Mary) Lee
Kingsland, Leslie William 1912- *13*
Kingsley, Charles 1819-1875
   See YABC 2
   See also CLR 77
Kingsley, Emily Perl 1940- *33*
King-Smith, Dick 1922- *135*
   Brief entry *38*
   Earlier sketches in SATA *47, 80*
   See also CLR 40
Kingston, Maxine (Ting Ting) Hong
   1940- *53*
Kinney, C. Cle(land) 1915- *6*
Kinney, Harrison 1921- *13*
Kinney, Jean Stout 1912- *12*
Kinsey, Elizabeth
   See Clymer, Eleanor
Kinsey, Helen 1948- *82*
Kinsey-Warnock, Natalie 1956- *116*
   Earlier sketch in SATA *71*
Kinzel, Dorothy 1950- *57*
Kinzel, Dottie
   See Kinzel, Dorothy
Kipling, (Joseph) Rudyard
   1865-1936 ....*100*
   See also YABC 2
   See also CLR 65

Kippax, Frank
  See Needle, Jan
Kirby, David K(irk) 1944- 78
Kirby, Margaret
  See Bingley, Margaret (Jane Kirby)
Kirby, Margaret
  See Bingley, Margaret (Jane Kirby)
Kirby, Susan E. 1949- 62
Kirk, Daniel 1952- 107
Kirk, David 1955- 117
Kirk, Ruth (Kratz) 1925- 5
Kirkland, Will
  See Hale, Arlene
Kirkpatrick, Katherine (Anne)
  1964- 113
Kirkup, James 1918- 12
Kirkwood, Kathryn
  See Fluke, Joanne
Kirshenbaum, Binnie 79
Kirshner, David S. 1958- 123
Kish, Eleanor M(ary) 1924- 73
Kish, Ely
  See Kish, Eleanor M(ary)
Kishida, Eriko 1929- 12
Kisinger, Grace Gelvin (Maze)
  1913-1965 10
Kissin, Eva H. 1923- 10
Kissinger, Rosemary K.
  See Updyke, Rosemary K.
Kitamura, Satoshi 1956- 98
  Earlier sketch in SATA 62
  See also CLR 60
Kitchen, Bert
  See Kitchen, Herbert Thomas
Kitchen, Herbert Thomas 1940- 70
Kite, Pat 1940- 78
  See Kite, (L.) Patricia
Kite, (L.) Patricia 78
  See Kite, Pat
Kitt, Tamara
  See de Regniers, Beatrice Schenk
  (Freedman)
Kittinger, Jo S(usenbach) 1955- 96
Kituomba
  See Odaga, Asenath (Bole)
Kitzinger, Sheila 1929- 57
Kiwak, Barbara 1966- 103
Kjelgaard, James Arthur 1910-1959 17
  See also CLR 81
  See Kjelgaard, Jim
Kjelgaard, Jim
  See Kjelgaard, James Arthur
Klagsbrun, Francine (Lifton) 36
Klaits, Barrie 1944- 52
Klaperman, Gilbert 1921- 33
Klaperman, Libby Mindlin
  1921-1982 33
  Obituary 31
Klass, David 1960- 88
Klass, Morton 1927-2001 11
Klass, Sheila Solomon 1927- 99
  Autobiography Feature 126
  Earlier sketch in SATA 45
  See also SAAS 26
Klause, Annette Curtis 1953- 79
Klaveness, Jan O'Donnell 1939- 86
Kleberger, Ilse 1921- 5
Kleeberg, Irene (Flitner) Cumming
  1932- 65
Klein, Aaron E. 1930-1998 45
  Brief entry 28
Klein, Bill 1945- 89
Klein, David 1919-2001 59
Klein, Gerda Weissmann 1924- 44
Klein, H(erbert) Arthur 8
Klein, James 1932- 115
Klein, Leonore (Glotzer) 1916- 6
Klein, Mina C(ooper) 1906-1979 8
Klein, Norma 1938-1989 57
  Earlier sketch in SATA 7
  See also CLR 19
  See also SAAS 1

Klein, Rachel S. 1953- 105
Klein, Robin 1936- 80
  Brief entry 45
  Earlier sketch in SATA 55
  See also CLR 21
Klemin, Diana 65
Klemm, Barry 1945- 104
Klemm, Edward G., Jr. 1910-2001 30
Klemm, Roberta K(ohnhorst)
  1884-1975 30
Kleven, Elisa 1958- 76
  See also CLR 85
Klevin, Jill Ross 1935- 39
  Brief entry 38
Kliban, B(ernard) 1935-1990 35
  Obituary 66
Klimowicz, Barbara 1927- 10
Kline, Christina Baker 1964- 101
Kline, James
  See Klein, James
Kline, Jim
  See Kline, Jim
Kline, Suzy 1943- 99
  Brief entry 48
  Earlier sketch in SATA 67
Kliros, Thea 1935- 106
Klise, M. Sarah 1961- 128
Klug, Ron(ald) 1939- 31
Knaak, Richard A(llen) 1961- 86
Knapp, Edward
  See Kunhardt, Edith
Knapp, Ron 1952- 34
Knebel, Fletcher 1911-1993 36
  Obituary 75
Kneeland, Linda Clarke 1947- 94
Knickerbocker, Diedrich
  See Irving, Washington
Knifesmith
  See Cutler, Ivor
Knigge, Robert (R.) 1921(?)-1987 50
Knight, Anne (Katherine) 1946- 34
Knight, Brenda 112
Knight, Christopher G. 1943- 96
Knight, Damon (Francis) 1922-2002 9
  Obituary 139
Knight, David C(arpenter)
  1925-1984 14
  See also CLR 38
Knight, Eric (Mowbray) 1897-1943 18
Knight, Francis Edgar 1905- 14
Knight, Frank
  See Knight, Francis Edgar
Knight, Hilary 1926- 132
  Earlier sketches in SATA 15, 69
Knight, Joan (M.) 82
Knight, Kathryn Lasky
  See Lasky, Kathryn
Knight, Mallory T.
  See Hurwood, Bernhardt J.
Knight, Theodore O. 1946- 77
Knobloch, Dorothea 1951- 88
Knoepfle, John (Ignatius) 1923- 66
Knott, Bill
  See Knott, William C(ecil, Jr.)
Knott, Will C.
  See Knott, William C(ecil, Jr.)
Knott, William C(ecil, Jr.) 1927- 3
  See Evans, Tabor
  and Knott, Bill
  and Mitchum, Hank
  and Sharpe, Jon
Knotts, Howard (Clayton, Jr.) 1922- 25
Knowles, Anne 1933- 37
Knowles, John 1926-2001 89
  Obituary 134
  Earlier sketch in SATA 8
Knox, Calvin M.
  See Silverberg, Robert
Knox, (Mary) Eleanor Jessie
  1909-2000 59
  Earlier sketch in SATA 30

Knox, James
  See Brittain, William (E.)
Knox, Jolyne 1937- 76
Knudsen, James 1950- 42
Knudsen, R. R.
  See SAAS 18
  See Knudson, Rozanne
Knudson, Richard L(ewis) 1930- 34
Knudson, Rozanne 1932- 79
  Earlier sketch in SATA 7
  See Knudson, R. R.
Knutson, Kimberley 115
Knye, Cassandra
  See Disch, Thomas M(ichael)
Koch, Dorothy Clarke 1924- 6
Koch, Kenneth (Jay) 1925-2002 65
Koch, Phyllis (Mae) McCallum
  1911- 10
Kocsis, J. C.
  See Paul, James
Koda-Callan, Elizabeth 1944- 140
  Earlier sketch in SATA 67
Koehler, Phoebe 1955- 85
Koehler-Pentacoff, Elizabeth 1957- 96
Koehn, Ilse
  See Van Zwienen, Ilse Charlotte Koehn
Koenig, Viviane 1950- 80
Koering, Ursula 1921-1976 64
Koerner, W(illiam) H(enry) D(avid)
  1878-1938 21
Koertge, Ron(ald) 1940- 131
  Earlier sketches in SATA 53, 92
Koff, Richard Myram 1926- 62
Koffinke, Carol 1949- 82
Kogan, Deborah 50
  See Kogan Ray, Deborah
Kogawa, Joy Nozomi 1935- 99
Kohl, Herbert 1937- 47
Kohl, MaryAnn F. 1947- 74
Kohn, Bernice 4
  See Hunt, Bernice (Kohn)
Kohn, Rita (T.) 1933- 89
Kohner, Frederick 1905-1986 10
  Obituary 48
Koide, Tan 1938-1986 50
Koike, Kay 1940- 72
Kolba, St. Tamara 22
Kolibalova, Marketa
  See Kolibalova, Marketa
Kolibalova, Marketa 1953- 126
Koller, Jackie French 1948- 109
  Earlier sketch in SATA 72
  See also CLR 68
Kolodny, Nancy J. 1946- 76
Komaiko, Leah 1954- 97
Komisar, Lucy 1942- 9
Komoda, Beverly 1939- 25
Komoda, Kiyo 1937- 9
Komroff, Manuel 1890-1974 2
  Obituary 20
Konigsburg, E(laine) L(obl) 1930- 126
  Earlier sketches in SATA 4, 48, 94
  See also CLR 81
Koningsberger, Hans 5
  See Koning, Hans
Konkle, Janet Everest 1917- 12
Koob, Theodora (J. Foth) 1918- 23
Kooiker, Leonie
  See Kooyker-Romijn, Johanna Maria
Koons, James
  See Pernu, Dennis
Koontz, Dean R(ay) 1945- 92
Koontz, Robin Michal 1954- 136
  Earlier sketch in SATA 70
Kooyker, Leonie
  See Kooyker-Romijn, Johanna Maria
Kooyker-Romijn, Johanna Maria
  1927- 48
  See Kooyker, Leonie
Kooyker-Romyn, Johanna Maria
  See Kooyker-Romijn, Johanna Maria

Kopper, Lisa (Esther) 1950- *105*
   Brief entry *51*
Korach, Mimi 1922- *9*
Koralek, Jenny 1934- *140*
   Earlier sketch in SATA *71*
Korczak, Janusz *65*
   See Goldszmit, Henryk
Koren, Edward 1935- *5*
Korinets, Iurii Iosifovich
   See Korinetz, Yuri (Iosifovich)
Korinetz, Yuri (Iosifovich) 1923- *9*
   See also CLR *4*
Korman, Bernice 1937- *78*
Korman, Gordon (Richard) 1963- *119*
   Brief entry *41*
   Earlier sketches in SATA *49, 81*
   See also CLR *25*
Korman, Justine 1958- *70*
Kornblatt, Marc 1954- *84*
Korte, Gene J. 1950- *74*
Korty, Carol 1937- *15*
Koscielniak, Bruce 1947- *99*
   Earlier sketch in SATA *67*
Koshin, Alexander (A.) 1952- *86*
Koskenmaki, Rosalie
   See Maggio, Rosalie
Koss, Amy Goldman 1954- *115*
Kossin, Sandy (Sanford) 1926- *10*
Kossman, Nina 1959- *84*
Kotzwinkle, William 1938- *70*
   Earlier sketch in SATA *24*
   See also CLR *6*
Kouhi, Elizabeth 1917- *54*
   Brief entry *49*
Kouts, Anne 1945- *8*
Kovacs, Deborah 1954- *132*
   Earlier sketch in SATA *79*
Kovalski, Maryann 1951- *97*
   Earlier sketch in SATA *58*
   See also CLR *34*
   See also SAAS *21*
Kowalski, Kathiann M. 1955- *96*
Krahn, Fernando 1935- *49*
   Brief entry *31*
   See also CLR *3*
Krakauer, Hoong Yee Lee 1955- *86*
Krakauer, Jon 1954- *108*
Kramer, George
   See Heuman, William
Kramer, Nora 1896(?)-1984 ....*26*
   Obituary *39*
Kramer, Remi (Thomas) 1935- *90*
Krantz, Hazel (Newman) *12*
Kranzler, George G(ershon) 1916- *28*
Kranzler, Gershon
   See Kranzler, George G(ershon)
Krasilovsky, Phyllis 1926- *38*
   Earlier sketch in SATA *1*
   See also CLR *83*
   See also SAAS *5*
Krasne, Betty
   See Levine, Betty K(rasne)
Krasno, Rena 1923- *104*
Kraus, Joanna Halpert 1937- *87*
Kraus, (Herman) Robert 1925-2001 ....*93*
   Obituary *130*
   Earlier sketches in SATA *4, 65*
   See also SAAS *11*
Krauss, Ruth (Ida) 1911-1993 ....*30*
   Obituary *75*
   Earlier sketch in SATA *1*
   See also CLR *42*
Krautter, Elisa (Bialk) 1912(?)-1990 ....*1*
   Obituary *65*
Krautwurst, Terry 1946- *79*
Kray, Robert Clement 1930- *82*
Kredel, Fritz 1900-1973 ....*17*
Kreikemeier, Gregory Scott 1965- *85*
Krementz, Jill 1940- *134*
   Earlier sketches in SATA *17, 71*
   See also CLR *5*
   See also SAAS *8*

Kremer, Marcie
   See Sorenson, Margo
Krenina, Katya 1968- *101*
Krensky, Stephen (Alan) 1953- *136*
   Brief entry *41*
   Earlier sketches in SATA *47, 93*
Kresh, Paul 1919-1997 ....*61*
   Obituary *94*
Kress, Nancy 1948- *85*
Kricher, John C. 1944- *113*
Krieger, Melanie *96*
Kripke, Dorothy Karp *30*
Krisher, Trudy (B.) 1946- *86*
Kristof, Jane 1932- *8*
Kroeber, Theodora (Kracaw) 1897-1979 ....*1*
   See Quinn, Theodora K.
Kroeger, Mary Kay 1950- *92*
Krohn, Katherine E(lizabeth) 1961- *125*
   Earlier sketch in SATA *84*
Kroll, Francis Lynde 1904-1973 ....*10*
Kroll, Steven 1941- *125*
   Autobiography Feature *135*
   Earlier sketches in SATA *19, 66*
   See also SAAS *7*
Kroll, Virginia L(ouise) 1948- *114*
   Earlier sketch in SATA *76*
Krommes, Beth 1956- *128*
Kronenwetter, Michael 1943- *62*
Kroniuk, Lisa
   See Berton, Pierre (Francis Demarigny)
Kropp, Paul (Stephan) 1948- *38*
   Brief entry *34*
Kruess, James
   See CLR *9*
   See Kruss, James
Krull, Kathleen 1952- *80*
   Autobiography Feature *106*
   Brief entry *39*
   Earlier sketch in SATA *52*
   See also CLR *44*
Krumgold, Joseph (Quincy)
   1908-1980 ....*48*
   Obituary *23*
   Earlier sketch in SATA *1*
Krupinski, Loretta 1940- *102*
   Earlier sketch in SATA *67*
Krupnick, Karen 1947- *89*
Krupp, E(dwin) C(harles) 1944- *123*
   Earlier sketch in SATA *53*
Krupp, Robin Rector 1946- *53*
Krush, Beth 1918- *18*
Krush, Joe 1918- *18*
   See Krush, Joseph P.
Kruss, James 1926-1997 ....*8*
   See Kruess, James
Krykorka, Vladyana 1945- *96*
Kubie, Eleanor Gottheil
   See Kubie, Nora Gottheil Benjamin
Kubie, Nora Benjamin
   See Kubie, Nora Gottheil Benjamin
Kubie, Nora Gottheil Benjamin
   1899-1988 ....*39*
   Obituary *59*
Kubinyi, Laszlo 1937- *94*
   Earlier sketch in SATA *17*
Kuenstler, Morton 1927- *10*
Kuharski, Janice 1947- *128*
Kuklin, Susan 1941- *95*
   Earlier sketch in SATA *63*
   See also CLR *51*
Kulling, Monica 1952- *89*
Kullman, Harry 1919-1982 ....*35*
Kumin, Maxine (Winokur) 1925- *12*
Kunhardt, Dorothy (Meserve)
   1901-1979 ....*53*
   Obituary *22*
Kunhardt, Edith 1937- *67*
Kunjufu, Jawanza 1953- *73*
Kunstler, Morton
   See Kuenstler, Morton
Kuntz, J(ohn) L. 1947- *91*
Kuntz, Jerry 1956- *133*

Kupferberg, Herbert 1918-2001 ....*19*
Kuratomi, Chizuko 1939- *12*
   See also CLR *32*
Kurczok, Belinda 1978- *121*
Kurelek, William 1927-1977 ....*8*
   Obituary *27*
   See also CLR *2*
Kurian, George 1928- *65*
Kurjian, Judi(th M.) 1944- *127*
Kurland, Gerald 1942- *13*
Kurland, Michael (Joseph) 1938- *118*
   Earlier sketch in SATA *48*
Kuroi, Ken 1947- *120*
Kurokawa, Mitsuhiro 1954- *88*
Kurten, Bjorn (Olof) 1924-1988 ....*64*
Kurtz, Jane 1952- *139*
   Earlier sketch in SATA *91*
Kurtz, Katherine (Irene) 1944- *126*
   Earlier sketch in SATA *76*
Kurz, Rudolf 1952- *95*
Kushner, Donn (J.) 1927- *52*
   See also CLR *55*
Kushner, Ellen (Ruth) 1955- *98*
Kushner, Jill Menkes 1951- *62*
Kushner, Lawrence 1943- *83*
Kuskin, Karla (Seidman) 1932- *111*
   Earlier sketches in SATA *2, 68*
   See also CLR *4*
   See also SAAS *3*
Kuttner, Paul 1922- *18*
Kuzma, Kay 1941- *39*
Kvale, Velma R(uth) 1898-1979 ....*8*
Kvasnosky, Laura McGee 1951- *93*
Kyle, Benjamin
   See Gottfried, Theodore Mark
Kyle, Elisabeth
   See Dunlop, Agnes M. R.
Kyte, Kathy S. 1946- *50*
   Brief entry *44*

L

L., Barry
   See Longyear, Barry B(rookes)
L., Tommy
   See Lorkowski, Thomas V(incent)
Lace, William W. 1942- *126*
Lachner, Dorothea
   See Knobloch, Dorothea
Lackey, Mercedes R(itchie) 1950- *127*
   Earlier sketch in SATA *81*
Lacoe, Addie *78*
Lacome, Julie 1961- *80*
Lacy, Leslie Alexander 1937- *6*
Ladd, Cheryl (Jean) 1951- *113*
Ladd, Louise 1943- *97*
Ladd, Veronica
   See Miner, Jane Claypool
Laden, Nina 1962- *85*
Lader, Lawrence 1919- *6*
LaDoux, Rita C. 1951- *74*
Lady, A
   See Taylor, Ann
Lady of Quality, A
   See Bagnold, Enid
La Farge, Oliver (Hazard Perry)
   1901-1963 ....*19*
La Farge, Phyllis *14*
LaFaye, A(lexandria R. T.) 1970- *105*
Laffin, John (Alfred Charles) 1922- *31*
LaFontaine, Bruce 1948- *114*
La Fontaine, Jean de 1621-1695 ....*18*
Lager, Claude
   See Lapp, Christiane (Germain)
Lager, Marilyn 1939- *52*
Lagercrantz, Rose (Elsa) 1947- *39*
Lagerloef, Selma (Ottiliana Lovisa)
   1858-1940 ....*15*
   See Lagerlof, Selma (Ottiliana Lovisa)

Lagerlof, Selma (Ottiliana Lovisa) *15*
    See also CLR 7
    See Lagerloef, Selma (Ottiliana Lovisa)
Lagerlof, Selma (Ottiliana Lovisa) 1858-1940
Laiken, Deirdre S(usan) 1948- *48*
    Brief entry *40*
Laimgruber, Monika 1946- *11*
Lain, Anna
    See Lamb, Nancy
Laing, Alexander (Kinnan)
    1903-1976 ....*117*
Laing, Martha
    See Celestino, Martha Laing
Laird, Christa 1944- *108*
    Autobiography Feature *120*
    See also SAAS 26
Laird, Elizabeth (Mary Risk) 1943- *114*
    Earlier sketch in SATA 77
    See also CLR 65
Laird, Jean E(louise) 1930- *38*
Laite, Gordon 1925- *31*
Lake, Harriet
    See Taylor, Paula (Wright)
Laklan, Carli 1907-1988 ....*5*
Lalicki, Barbara *61*
Lally, Soinbhe 1945- *119*
Lamb, Beatrice Pitney 1904-1997 ....*21*
Lamb, Charles 1775-1834 ....*17*
Lamb, Elizabeth Searle 1917- *31*
Lamb, G(eoffrey) F(rederick) *10*
Lamb, Harold (Albert) 1892-1962 ....*53*
Lamb, Lynton (Harold) 1907-1977 ....*10*
Lamb, Mary Ann 1764-1847 ....*17*
Lamb, Nancy 1939- *80*
Lamb, Robert (Boyden) 1941- *13*
Lambert, David (Compton) 1932- *84*
    Brief entry *49*
Lambert, Janet 1895(?)-1973 ....*25*
Lambert, Martha L. *113*
Lambert, Saul 1928- *23*
Lamburn, Richmal Crompton 1890-1969 ...*5*
    See Crompton, Richmal
Lamensdorf, Len
    See Lamensdorf, Leonard
Lamensdorf, Leonard 1930- *120*
Laminack, Lester L. 1956- *120*
Lamorisse, Albert (Emmanuel)
    1922-1970 ....*23*
Lampert, Emily 1951- *52*
    Brief entry *49*
Lamplugh, Lois 1921- *17*
Lampman, Evelyn Sibley 1907-1980 ......*87*
    Obituary *23*
    Earlier sketch in SATA 4
Lamprey, Louise 1869-1951
    See YABC 2
Lampton, Chris
    See Lampton, Christopher F.
Lampton, Christopher
    See Lampton, Christopher F.
Lampton, Christopher F. *67*
    Brief entry *47*
Lamstein, Sarah Marwil 1943- *126*
Lancaster, Bruce 1896-1963 ....*9*
Lance, Kathryn 1943- *76*
Land, Barbara (Neblett) 1923- *16*
Land, Jane
    See Borland, Kathryn Kilby
    and Speicher, Helen Ross S(mith)
Land, Myrick (Ebben) 1922-1998 ....*15*
Land, Ross
    See Borland, Kathryn Kilby
    and Speicher, Helen Ross S(mith)
Landau, Elaine 1948- *141*
    Earlier sketches in SATA 10, 94
Landau, Jacob 1917- *38*
Landeck, Beatrice 1904-1978 ....*15*
Landin, Les 1923- *2*
Landis, J(ames) D(avid) 1942- *60*
    Brief entry *52*
Landis, James D.
    See Landis, J(ames) D(avid)

Landis, Jill Marie 1948- *101*
Landon, Lucinda 1950- *56*
    Brief entry *51*
Landon, Margaret (Dorothea Mortenson)
    1903-1993 ....*50*
Landshoff, Ursula 1908-1989 ....*13*
Lane, Carolyn 1926-1993 ....*10*
Lane, Dakota 1959- *105*
Lane, Jerry
    See Martin, Patricia Miles
Lane, John (Richard) 1932- *15*
Lane, Margaret 1907-1994 ....*65*
    Brief entry *38*
    Obituary *79*
Lane, Rose Wilder 1887-1968 ....*29*
    Brief entry *28*
Lanes, Selma Gordon 1929- *3*
Lanfredi, Judy 1964- *83*
Lang, Andrew 1844-1912 ....*16*
Lang, Paul 1948- *83*
Lang, Susan S. 1950- *68*
Lang, T. T.
    See Taylor, Theodore
Langdo, Bryan 1973- *138*
Lange, John
    See Crichton, (John) Michael
Lange, Suzanne 1945- *5*
Langley, Andrew 1949- *104*
Langley, Charles P(itman) III
    1949- *103*
Langley, Jonathan 1952- *122*
Langner, Nola *8*
    See Malone, Nola Langner
Langone, John (Michael) 1929- *46*
    Brief entry *38*
Langreuter, Jutta 1944- *122*
Langsen, Richard C. 1953- *95*
Langstaff, John (Meredith) 1920- *68*
    Earlier sketch in SATA 6
    See also CLR 3
Langstaff, Launcelot
    See Irving, Washington
Langton, Jane (Gillson) 1922- *140*
    Earlier sketches in SATA 3, 68, 129
    See also CLR 33
    See also SAAS 5
Lanier, Sidney 1842-1881 ....*18*
Lanier, Sterling E(dmund) 1927- *109*
Lanino, Deborah 1964- *123*
Lankford, Mary D. 1932- *112*
    Earlier sketch in SATA 77
Lannin, Joanne (A.) 1951- *121*
Lansdale, Joe R(ichard) 1951- *116*
Lansing, Alfred 1921-1975 ....*35*
Lansing, Karen E. 1954- *71*
Lantier-Sampon, Patricia 1952- *92*
Lantz, Fran
    See Lantz, Francess L(in)
Lantz, Francess L(in) 1952- *109*
    Earlier sketch in SATA 63
Lantz, Paul 1908- *45*
Lantz, Walter 1900-1994 ....*37*
    Obituary *79*
Lanza, Barbara 1945- *101*
Lapp, Christiane (Germain) 1948- *74*
Lappin, Peter 1911-1999 ....*32*
Larkin, Amy
    See Burns, Olive Ann
Larkin, Maia
    See Wojciechowska, Maia (Teresa)
Laroche, Giles 1956- *126*
    Earlier sketch in SATA 71
LaRochelle, David 1960- *115*
LaRose, Linda *125*
Larrabee, Lisa 1947- *84*
Larrecq, John M(aurice) 1926-1980 ....*44*
    Obituary *25*
Larrick, Nancy (Gray) 1910- *4*
Larsen, Anita 1942- *78*
Larsen, Egon 1904- *14*
Larsen, Rebecca 1944- *54*

Larson, Eve
    See St. John, Wylly Folk
Larson, Gary 1950- *57*
Larson, Ingrid D(ana) 1965- *92*
Larson, Jean Russell 1930- *121*
Larson, Kirby 1954- *96*
Larson, Norita D(ittberner) 1944- *29*
Larson, William H. 1938- *10*
Larsson, Carl (Olof) 1853-1919 ....*35*
LaSalle, Charles A.
    See Ellis, Edward S(ylvester)
LaSalle, Charles E.
    See Ellis, Edward S(ylvester)
Lasell, Elinor H. 1929- *19*
Lasell, Fen H.
    See Lasell, Elinor H.
Lasenby, Jack 1931- *103*
    Earlier sketch in SATA 65
Laser, Michael 1954- *117*
Lash, Joseph P. 1909-1987 ....*43*
Lasher, Faith B. 1921- *12*
Lasker, David 1950- *38*
Lasker, Joe *83*
    See also SAAS 17
    See Lasker, Joseph Leon
Lasker, Joseph Leon 1919- *9*
    See Lasker, Joe
Laski, Marghanita 1915-1988 ....*55*
Laskin, Pamela L. 1954- *75*
Lasky, Kathryn 1944- *112*
    Earlier sketches in SATA 13, 69
    See also CLR 11
Lasky Knight, Kathryn
    See Lasky, Kathryn
Lass, Bonnie *131*
Lassalle, C. E.
    See Ellis, Edward S(ylvester)
Lassiter, Mary *59*
    See Hoffman, Mary (Margaret)
Latham, Barbara 1896- *16*
Latham, Frank B(rown) 1910-2000 ....*6*
Latham, Jean Lee 1902-1995 ....*68*
    Earlier sketch in SATA 2
    See also CLR 50
Latham, Mavis
    See Clark, Mavis Thorpe
Latham, Philip
    See Richardson, Robert S(hirley)
Lathrop, Dorothy P(ulis) 1891-1980 ....*14*
    Obituary *24*
Lathrop, Francis
    See Leiber, Fritz (Reuter, Jr.)
Latimer, Jim 1943- *80*
Latta, Rich
    See Latta, Richard
Latta, Richard 1946- *113*
Lattany, Kristin
    See Lattany, Kristin (Elaine Eggleston)
    Hunter
Lattany, Kristin (Eggleston) Hunter
    1931- *132*
Lattany, Kristin (Elaine Eggleston) Hunter
    1931- *132*
    Earlier sketch in SATA 12
    See also CLR 3
    See also SAAS 10
Lattimore, Eleanor Frances 1904-1986 ......*7*
    Obituary *48*
Lattin, Ann
    See Cole, Lois Dwight
Lauber, Patricia (Grace) 1924- *138*
    Earlier sketches in SATA 1, 33, 75
    See also CLR 16
Laugesen, Mary E(akin) 1906-1995 ....*5*
Laughbaum, Steve 1945- *12*
Laughlin, Florence Young 1910-2001 ....*3*
Laughlin, Rosemary 1941- *123*
Laure, Ettagale
    See Blauer, Ettagale
Laure, Jason 1940- *50*
    Brief entry *44*
Laurence, Ester Hauser 1935- *7*

Laurie, Rona 1916- 55
Laurin, Anne
　See McLaurin, Anne
Lauritzen, Jonreed 1902-1979 13
Lauscher, Hermann
　See Hesse, Hermann
Lauture, Denize 1946- 86
Laux, Connie
　See Laux, Constance
Laux, Constance 1952- 97
Laux, Dorothy 1920- 49
Lavallee, Barbara 1941- 74
Lavender, David (Sievert) 1910- 97
　Earlier sketch in SATA *64*
Lavert, Gwendolyn Battle 1951- 131
　See Battle-Lavert, Gwendolyn
Laverty, Donald
　See Blish, James (Benjamin)
　and Knight, Damon (Francis)
Lavigne, Louis-Dominique 107
Lavine, David 1928- 31
Lavine, Sigmund Arnold 1908-1986 82
　Earlier sketch in SATA *3*
　See also CLR *35*
Lavond, Paul Dennis
　See Kornbluth, C(yril) M.
　and Lowndes, Robert A(ugustine) W(ard)
　and Pohl, Frederik
Lawhead, Stephen R. 1950- 109
Lawhead, Steve
　See Lawhead, Stephen R.
Lawlor, Laurie 1953- 137
　Earlier sketch in SATA *80*
Lawrence, Ann (Margaret)
　1942-1987 41
　Obituary 54
Lawrence, Iain 1955- 135
Lawrence, J. T.
　See Rowland-Entwistle, (Arthur) Theodore
　(Henry)
Lawrence, Jerome 1915- 65
Lawrence, John 1933- 30
Lawrence, Louise 1943- 119
　Earlier sketches in SATA *38, 78*
Lawrence, Louise de Kiriline
　1894-1992 13
Lawrence, Lynn
　See Garland, Sherry
Lawrence, Margery H. 1889-1969 120
Lawrence, Michael 1943- 132
Lawrence, Mildred Elwood 1907-1997 3
Lawrence, R(onald) D(ouglas) 1921- 55
Lawrinson, Julia 1969- 141
Lawson, Amy
　See Gordon, Amy
Lawson, Carol (Antell) 1946- 42
Lawson, Don(ald Elmer) 1917-1990 9
Lawson, Joan 1906- 55
Lawson, Julie 1947- 126
　Earlier sketch in SATA *79*
Lawson, Marion Tubbs 1896-1994 22
Lawson, Robert 1892-1957 100
　See also YABC *2*
　See also CLR *73*
Laxdal, Vivienne 1962- 112
Laycock, George (Edwin) 1921- 5
Layne, Laura
　See Knott, William C(ecil, Jr.)
Lazare, Gerald John 1927- 44
Lazare, Jerry
　See Lazare, Gerald John
Lazarevich, Mila 1942- 17
Lazarus, Keo Felker 1913-1993 21
　Obituary 129
Lea, Alec 1907- 19
Lea, Joan
　See Neufeld, John (Arthur)
Leach, Maria 1892-1977 39
　Brief entry 28
Leacock, Elspeth 1946- 131
Leacroft, Helen (Mabel Beal) 1919- 6

Leacroft, Richard (Vallance Becher)
　1914- 6
Leaf, (Wilbur) Munro 1905-1976 20
　See also CLR *25*
Leaf, VaDonna Jean 1929- 26
Leah, Devorah
　See Devorah-Leah
Leakey, Richard E(rskine Frere)
　1944- 42
Leander, Ed
　See Richelson, Geraldine
Lear, Edward 1812-1888 100
　Earlier sketch in SATA *18*
　See also CLR *75*
Lears, Laurie 1955- 127
Leasor, (Thomas) James 1923- 54
Leavitt, Jerome E(dward) 1916- 23
LeBar, Mary E(velyn) 1910-1982 35
LeBlanc, Annette M. 1965- 68
LeBlanc, L(ee) 1913- 54
Lebrun, Claude 1929- 66
Le Cain, Errol (John) 1941-1989 68
　Obituary 60
　Earlier sketch in SATA *6*
Lecourt, Nancy (Hoyt) 1951- 73
Ledbetter, Suzann 1953- 119
Leder, Jane Mersky 1945- 61
　Brief entry 51
Lederer, Muriel 1929- 48
Lederer, William J(ulius) 1912- 62
Lee, Amanda
　See Baggett, Nancy
　and Buckholtz, Eileen (Garber)
　and Glick, Ruth (Burtnick)
Lee, Benjamin 1921- 27
Lee, Betsy 1949- 37
Lee, Carol
　See Fletcher, Helen Jill
Lee, Cora
　See Anderson, Catherine Corley
Lee, Dennis (Beynon) 1939- 102
　Earlier sketch in SATA *14*
　See also CLR *3*
Lee, Dom 1959- 83
　Autobiography Feature 121
　See also SAAS *26*
Lee, Doris Emrick 1905-1983 44
　Obituary 35
Lee, Elizabeth Rogers 1940- 90
Lee, (Nelle) Harper 1926- 11
Lee, Hector Viveros 1962- 115
Lee, Howard
　See Goulart, Ron(ald Joseph)
Lee, Howard N.
　See Goulart, Ron(ald Joseph)
Lee, Huy Voun 1969- 129
Lee, J(oseph) Edward 1953- 130
Lee, Jeanne M. 1943- 138
Lee, John R(obert) 1923-1976 27
Lee, Jordan
　See Scholefield, Alan
Lee, Julian
　See Latham, Jean Lee
Lee, Liz
　See Lee, Elizabeth Rogers
Lee, Lucy
　See Talbot, Charlene Joy
Lee, Lyn 1953- 128
Lee, Manning de Villeneuve
　1894-1980 37
　Obituary 22
Lee, Marian
　See Clish, (Lee) Marian
Lee, Marie G. 1964- 130
　Earlier sketch in SATA *81*
Lee, Mary Price 1934- 82
　Earlier sketch in SATA *8*
Lee, Mildred 6
　See also SAAS *12*
　See Scudder, Mildred Lee
Lee, Richard S. 1927- 82
Lee, Robert C. 1931- 20

Lee, Robert E(dwin) 1918-1994 65
　Obituary 82
Lee, Robert J. 1921- 10
Lee, Sally 1943- 67
Lee, Tammie
　See Townsend, Thomas L.
Lee, Tanith 1947- 134
　Earlier sketches in SATA *8, 88*
Leech, Ben
　See Bowkett, Stephen
Leedy, Loreen (Janelle) 1959- 128
　Brief entry 50
　Earlier sketches in SATA *54, 84*
Lee-Hostetler, Jeri 1940- 63
Leekley, Thomas B(riggs) 1910-2001 23
Leeming, Jo Ann
　See Leeming, Joseph
Leeming, Joseph 1897-1968 26
Leemis, Ralph B. 1954- 72
Leeson, Muriel 1920- 54
Leeson, R. A.
　See Leeson, Robert (Arthur)
Leeson, Robert (Arthur) 1928- 76
　Earlier sketch in SATA *42*
Leffland, Ella 1931- 65
Lefler, Irene (Whitney) 1917- 12
Le Gallienne, Eva 1899-1991 9
　Obituary 68
LeGrand
　See Henderson, LeGrand
Le Guin, Ursula K(roeber) 1929- 99
　Earlier sketches in SATA *4, 52*
　See also CLR *28*
Legum, Colin 1919- 10
Lehman, Barbara 1963- 115
Lehman, Bob 91
Lehman, Elaine 91
Lehn, Cornelia 1920- 46
Lehne, Judith Logan 1947- 93
Lehr, Delores 1920- 10
Lehr, Norma 1930- 71
Leiber, Fritz (Reuter, Jr.) 1910-1992 45
　Obituary 73
Leibold, Jay 1957- 57
　Brief entry 52
Leichman, Seymour 1933- 5
Leigh, Nila K. 1981- 81
Leigh, Tom 1947- 46
Leigh-Pemberton, John 1911-1997 35
Leighton, Clare (Veronica Hope)
　1899-1989 37
Leighton, Margaret (Carver)
　1896-1987 1
　Obituary 52
Leiner, Al(an) 1938- 83
Leiner, Katherine 1949- 93
Leipold, L. Edmond 1902-1983 16
Leisk, David (Johnson) 1906-1975 30
　Obituary 26
　Earlier sketch in SATA *1*
Leister, Mary 1917- 29
Leitch, Patricia 1933- 98
　Earlier sketch in SATA *11*
Leitner, Isabella 1924- 86
Leland, Bob 1956- 92
Leland, Robert E.
　See Leland, Bob
Lember, Barbara Hirsch 1941- 92
LeMieux, A(nne) C(onnelly) 1954- 125
　Earlier sketch in SATA *90*
　See LeMieux, Anne
LeMieux, Anne
　See LeMieux, A(nne) C(onnelly)
Lemieux, Michele 1955- 139
Lemke, Horst 1922- 38
Lenanton, Carola Mary Anima Oman
　See Oman, Carola (Mary Anima)
L'Engle, Madeleine (Camp Franklin)
　1918- 128
　Earlier sketches in SATA *1, 27, 75*
　See also CLR *57*
　See also SAAS *15*

Lengyel, Cornel Adam 1915- 27
Lengyel, Emil 1895-1985 3
  Obituary 42
Lennon, John (Ono) 1940-1980 114
LeNoir, Janice 1941- 89
Lens, Sidney 1912-1986 13
  Obituary 48
Lenski, Lois 1893-1974 100
  Earlier sketches in SATA 1, 26
  See also CLR 26
Lent, Blair 133
  Earlier sketch in SATA 2
Lent, Henry Bolles 1901-1973 17
Lent, John 1948- 108
Leodhas, Sorche Nic
  See Alger, Leclaire (Gowans)
Leokum, Arkady 1916(?)- 45
Leon, Sharon 1959- 79
Leonard, Alison 1944- 70
Leonard, Constance (Brink) 1923- 42
  Brief entry 40
Leonard, Jonathan N(orton)
  1903-1975 36
Leonard, Laura 1923- 75
Leong, Gor Yun
  See Ellison, Virginia H(owell)
Lerangis, Peter 1955- 72
Lerner, Aaron Bunsen 1920- 35
Lerner, Carol 1927- 86
  Earlier sketch in SATA 33
  See also CLR 34
  See also SAAS 12
Lerner, Gerda 1920- 65
Lerner, Harriet 1944- 101
Lerner, Marguerite Rush 1924-1987 11
  Obituary 51
Lerner, Sharon (Ruth) 1938-1982 11
  Obituary 29
Leroe, Ellen W(hitney) 1949- 99
  Brief entry 51
  Earlier sketch in SATA 61
Leroux, Gaston 1868-1927 65
Leroux-Hugon, Helene 1955- 132
LeRoy, Gen 52
  Brief entry 36
LeShan, Eda J(oan) 1922-2002 21
  See also CLR 6
LeSieg, Theo.
  See Dr. Seuss
  and Geisel, Theodor Seuss
  and Seuss, Dr.
  and Stone, Rosetta
Lesinski, Jeanne M. 1960- 120
Leslie, Robert Franklin 1911-1990 7
Leslie, Sarah
  See McGuire, Leslie (Sarah)
LeSourd, Catherine
  See Marshall, (Sarah) Catherine (Wood)
Lessac, Frane 1954- 61
Lessem, Don 1951- 97
Lesser, Rika 1953- 53
Lester, Alison 1952- 129
  Earlier sketches in SATA 50, 90
Lester, Helen 1936- 92
  Earlier sketch in SATA 46
Lester, Julius (Bernard) 1939- 112
  Earlier sketches in SATA 12, 74
  See also CLR 41
Lester, Mike 1955- 131
Le Sueur, Meridel 1900-1996 6
Le Tord, Bijou 1945- 95
  Earlier sketch in SATA 49
Letts, Billie 1938- 121
Leuck, Laura 1962- 85
Leutscher, Alfred (George) 1913- 23
Levai, Blaise 1919- 39
Levenkron, Steven 1941- 86
Leverich, Kathleen 1948- 103
LeVert, (William) John 1946- 55
Levin, Betty 1927- 137
  Earlier sketches in SATA 19, 84
  See also SAAS 11

Levin, Ira 1929- 66
Levin, Marcia Obrasky 1918- 13
Levin, Meyer 1905-1981 21
  Obituary 27
Levin, Miriam (Ramsfelder) 1962- 97
Levine, Abby 1943- 54
  Brief entry 52
Levine, Betty K(rasne) 1933- 66
Levine, David 1926- 43
  Brief entry 35
Levine, Edna S(imon) 35
Levine, Evan 1962- 77
  Earlier sketch in SATA 74
Levine, Gail Carson 1947- 98
  See also CLR 85
Levine, I(srael) E. 1923- 12
Levine, Joan Goldman 11
Levine, Joseph 1910- 33
Levine, Marge 1934- 81
Levine, Rhoda 14
Levine, Sarah 1970- 57
Levine, Shar 1953- 131
Levine-Freidus, Gail
  See Provost, Gail Levine
Levinson, Nancy Smiler 1938- 140
  Earlier sketches in SATA 33, 80
Levinson, Riki 99
  Brief entry 49
  Earlier sketch in SATA 52
Levitin, Sonia (Wolff) 1934- 119
  Autobiography Feature 131
  Earlier sketches in SATA 4, 68
  See also CLR 53
  See also SAAS 2
Levitt, Sidney (Mark) 1947- 68
Levon, O. U.
  See Kesey, Ken (Elton)
Levoy, Myron 49
  Brief entry 37
Levy, Barrie 112
Levy, Constance 1931- 140
  Earlier sketch in SATA 73
  See also SAAS 22
Levy, Elizabeth 1942- 107
  Earlier sketches in SATA 31, 69
  See also SAAS 18
Levy, Marilyn 1937- 67
Levy, Nathan 1945- 63
Levy, Robert 1945- 82
Lewees, John
  See Stockton, Francis Richard
Lewin, Betsy 1937- 90
  Autobiography Feature 115
  Earlier sketch in SATA 32
Lewin, Hugh 1939- 72
  Brief entry 40
  See also CLR 9
Lewin, Ted 1935- 119
  Autobiography Feature 115
  Earlier sketches in SATA 21, 76
Lewis, Alice C. 1936- 46
Lewis, Amanda 1955- 80
Lewis, (Joseph) Anthony 1927- 27
Lewis, Anthony 1966- 120
Lewis, Barbara A. 1943- 73
Lewis, Beverly 1949- 80
Lewis, Brenda Ralph 1932- 72
Lewis, Brian 1963- 128
Lewis, C(live) S(taples) 1898-1963 100
  Earlier sketch in SATA 13
  See also CLR 27
Lewis, Claudia (Louise) 1907-2001 5
Lewis, Cynthia Copeland 1960- 111
Lewis, E(arl) B(radley) 1956- 124
  Earlier sketch in SATA 93
Lewis, E. M. 123
  Earlier sketch in SATA 20
Lewis, Elizabeth Foreman
  1892-1958 121
  See also YABC 2
Lewis, Francine
  See Wells, Helen

Lewis, J. Patrick 1942- 104
  Earlier sketch in SATA 69
Lewis, Jack P(earl) 1919- 65
Lewis, Jean 1924- 61
Lewis, Julinda
  See Lewis-Ferguson, Julinda
Lewis, Kim 1951- 136
  Earlier sketch in SATA 84
Lewis, Linda (Joy) 1946- 67
Lewis, Lucia Z.
  See Anderson, Lucia (Lewis)
Lewis, Marjorie 1929- 40
  Brief entry 35
Lewis, Mary (Christianna)
  1907(?)-1988 64
  Obituary 56
  See Brand, Christianna
Lewis, Mervyn
  See Frewer, Glyn (M.)
Lewis, Michael
  See Untermeyer, Louis
Lewis, Naomi 76
Lewis, Paul
  See Gerson, Noel Bertram
Lewis, Richard 1935- 3
Lewis, Rob 1962- 72
Lewis, Roger
  See Zarchy, Harry
Lewis, Shannon
  See Llywelyn, Morgan
Lewis, Shari 1934-1998 35
  Brief entry 30
  Obituary 104
Lewis, Sylvan R.
  See Aronson, Virginia
Lewis, Thomas P(arker) 1936- 27
Lewis-Ferguson, Julinda 1955- 85
Lewiton, Mina 1904-1970 2
Lexau, Joan M. 130
  Earlier sketches in SATA 1, 36
Ley, Willy 1906-1969 2
Leydon, Rita (Floden) 1949- 21
Leyland, Eric (Arthur) 1911- 37
Li, Xiao Jun 1952- 86
Liatsos, Sandra Olson 1942- 103
Libby, Bill
  See Libby, William M.
Libby, William M. 1927-1984 5
  Obituary 39
Liberty, Gene 1924- 3
Liddell, Kenneth 1912-1975 63
Lidz, Jane 120
Lieberman, E(dwin) James 1934- 62
Liebers, Arthur 1913-1984 12
Lieblich, Irene 1923- 22
Liers, Emil E(rnest) 1890-1975 37
Lies, Brian 1963- 131
Liestman, Vicki 1961- 72
Lietz, Gerald S. 1918- 11
Life, Kay (Guinn) 1930- 83
Lifton, Betty Jean 118
  Earlier sketch in SATA 6
Lifton, Robert Jay 1926- 66
Lightburn, Ron 1954- 91
Lightburn, Sandra 1955- 91
Lightner, A. M.
  See Hopf, Alice (Martha) L(ightner)
Lightner, Alice
  See Hopf, Alice (Martha) L(ightner)
Lignell, Lois 1911- 37
Liles, Maurine Walpole 1935- 81
Lilley, Stephen R(ay) 1950- 97
Lillington, Kenneth (James)
  1916-1998 39
Lilly, Ray
  See Curtis, Richard (Alan)
Lim, John 1932- 43
Liman, Ellen (Fogelson) 1936- 22
Limburg, Peter R(ichard) 1929- 13
Lin, Grace 1974- 111
Lincoln, C(harles) Eric 1924-2000 5

Author Index

Lincoln, James
  See Bates, Katharine Lee
Lindbergh, Anne 81
  See Sapieyevski, Anne Lindbergh
Lindbergh, Anne (Spencer) Morrow
  1906-2001 33
  Obituary 125
Lindbergh, Charles A(ugustus, Jr.)
  1902-1974 33
Lindbergh, Reeve 1945- 116
Lindblom, Steven (Winther) 1946- 94
  Brief entry 39
  Earlier sketch in SATA 42
Linde, Gunnel 1924- 5
Lindenbaum, Pija 1955- 77
Lindgren, Astrid (Anna Emilia Ericsson)
  1907-2002 38
  Obituary 128
  Earlier sketch in SATA 2
  See also CLR 39
Lindgren, Barbro 1937- 120
  Brief entry 46
  Earlier sketch in SATA 63
  See also CLR 86
Lindman, Maj (Jan) 1886-1972 43
Lindop, Edmund 1925- 5
Lindquist, Jennie Dorothea
  1899-1977 13
Lindquist, Rowena Cory 1958- 98
Lindquist, Willis 1908-1988 20
Lindsay, Norman Alfred William
  1879-1969 67
  See also CLR 8
Lindsay, (Nicholas) Vachel
  1879-1931 40
Line, David
  See Davidson, Lionel
Line, Les 1935- 27
Linfield, Esther 40
Lingard, Joan (Amelia) 1932- 114
  Autobiography Feature 130
  Earlier sketches in SATA 8, 74
  See also SAAS 5
Link, Martin 1934- 28
Linnea, Sharon 1956- 82
Lionni, Leo(nard) 1910-1999 72
  Obituary 118
  Earlier sketch in SATA 8
  See also CLR 71
Lipinsky de Orlov, Lino S. 1908- 22
Lipkind, William 1904-1974 15
Lipman, David 1931- 21
Lipman, Matthew 1923- 14
Lippincott, Gary A. 1953- 119
  Earlier sketch in SATA 73
Lippincott, Joseph W(harton)
  1887-1976 17
Lippincott, Sarah Lee 1920- 22
Lippman, Peter J. 1936- 31
Lipsyte, Robert (Michael) 1938- 113
  Earlier sketches in SATA 5, 68
  See also CLR 76
Lisandrelli, Elaine Slivinski 1951- 94
Lisker, Sonia O. 1933- 44
Lisle, Holly 1960- 98
Lisle, Janet Taylor 1947- 96
  Brief entry 47
  Earlier sketch in SATA 59
  See also SAAS 14
Lisle, Seward D.
  See Ellis, Edward S(ylvester)
Lisowski, Gabriel 1946- 47
  Brief entry 31
Liss, Howard 1922-1995 4
  Obituary 84
Lisson, Deborah 1941- 110
  Earlier sketch in SATA 71
List, Ilka Katherine 1935- 6
Liston, Robert A. 1927- 5
Litchfield, Ada B(assett) 1916-1999 5
Litchfield, Jo 1973- 116
Litowinsky, Olga (Jean) 1936- 26

Littke, Lael J. 1929- 140
  Earlier sketches in SATA 51, 83
Little, A. Edward
  See Klein, Aaron E.
Little, Douglas 1942- 96
Little, (Flora) Jean 1932- 106
  Earlier sketches in SATA 2, 68
  See also CLR 4
  See also SAAS 17
Little, Lessie Jones 1906-1986 60
  Obituary 50
Little, Mary E. 1912-1999 28
Littlechild, George 1958- 85
Littledale, Freya (Lota) 1929-1992 74
  Earlier sketch in SATA 2
Littlefield, Bill 1948- 83
Littlefield, Holly 1963- 97
Littlesugar, Amy 1953- 122
Littleton, Mark (R.) 1950- 89
Lively, Penelope (Margaret) 1933- 101
  Earlier sketches in SATA 7, 60
  See also CLR 7
Liversidge, (Henry) Douglas 1913- 8
Livesey, Claire (Warner) 1927- 127
Livingston, Carole 1941- 42
Livingston, Myra Cohn 1926-1996 68
  Obituary 92
  Earlier sketch in SATA 5
  See also CLR 7
  See also SAAS 1
Livingston, Richard R(oland) 1922- 8
Livo, Norma J. 1929- 76
Llerena Aguirre, Carlos (Antonio)
  1952- 19
Llewellyn, Claire 1954- 77
Llewellyn, Grace (Katherine) 1964- 110
Llewellyn, Richard
  See Llewellyn Lloyd, Richard Dafydd
  Vivian
Llewellyn, Sam 1948- 95
Llewellyn Lloyd, Richard Dafydd Vivian
  1906-1983 11
  Obituary 37
  See Llewellyn, Richard
Llewelyn, T. Harcourt
  See Hamilton, Charles (Harold St. John)
Lloyd, A(lan) R(ichard) 1927- 97
Lloyd, Alan
  See Lloyd, A(lan) R(ichard)
Lloyd, E. James
  See James, Elizabeth
Lloyd, Errol 1943- 22
Lloyd, Hugh
  See Fitzhugh, Percy Keese
Lloyd, James
  See James, Elizabeth
Lloyd, Megan 1958- 117
  Earlier sketch in SATA 77
Lloyd, (Mary) Norris 1908-1993 10
  Obituary 75
Lloyd Webber, Andrew 1948- 56
  See Webber, Andrew Lloyd
Llywelyn, Morgan 1937- 109
Lobato, Jose Bento Monteiro
  1882-1948 114
Lobel, Anita (Kempler) 1934- 96
  Earlier sketches in SATA 6, 55
Lobel, Arnold (Stark) 1933-1987 55
  Obituary 54
  Earlier sketch in SATA 6
  See also CLR 5
Lobsenz, Amelia 12
Lobsenz, Norman M(itchell) 1919- 6
Lochak, Michele 1936- 39
Lochlons, Colin
  See Jackson, C(aary) Paul
Locke, Clinton W. 1
Locke, Elsie (Violet) 1912-2001 87
Locke, Lucie 1904-1989 10
Locke, Robert 1944- 63
  See Bess, Clayton

Locker, Thomas 1937- 109
  Earlier sketch in SATA 59
  See also CLR 14
Lockridge, Hildegarde (Dolson)
  1908-1981 121
  See Dolson, Hildegarde
Lockwood, Mary
  See Spelman, Mary
Lodge, Bernard 1933- 107
  Earlier sketch in SATA 33
Lodge, Jo 1966- 112
Loeb, Jeffrey 1946- 57
Loeb, Robert H., Jr. 1917- 21
Loefgren, Ulf 1931- 3
Loeper, John J(oseph) 1929- 118
  Earlier sketch in SATA 10
Loescher, Ann Dull 1942- 20
Loescher, Gil(burt Damian) 1945- 20
Loewer, Jean Jenkins
  See Jenkins, Jean
Loewer, Peter 1934- 98
LoFaro, Jerry 1959- 77
Lofo
  See Heimann, Rolf
Lofting, Hugh (John) 1886-1947 100
  Earlier sketch in SATA 15
  See also CLR 19
Lofts, Norah (Robinson) 1904-1983 8
  Obituary 36
Logan, Jake
  See Knott, William C(ecil, Jr.)
  and Krepps, Robert W(ilson)
  and Pearl, Jacques Bain
  and Riefe, Alan
  and Rifkin, Shepard
  and Smith, Martin Cruz
Logan, Mark
  See Nicole, Christopher (Robin)
Logston, Anne 1962- 112
Logue, Christopher 1926- 23
Logue, Mary 1952- 112
Loh, Morag 1935- 73
Lohans, Alison 1949- 101
Loken, Newton Clayton 1919- 26
Lomas, Steve
  See Brennan, Joseph Lomas
Lomask, Milton (Nachman)
  1909-1991 20
LoMonaco, Palmyra 1932- 102
London, Jack 1876-1916 18
  See London, John Griffith
London, Jane
  See Geis, Darlene Stern
London, Jane
  See Geis, Darlene Stern
London, Jonathan (Paul) 1947- 113
  Earlier sketch in SATA 74
Lonergan, (Pauline) Joy (MacLean)
  1909- 10
Lonette, Reisie (Dominee) 1924- 43
Long, Cathryn J. 1946- 89
Long, Earlene (Roberta) 1938- 50
Long, Helen Beecher 1
Long, Judith Elaine 1953- 20
Long, Judy
  See Long, Judith Elaine
Long, Kim 1949- 69
Long, Sylvia 1948- 120
Longbeard, Frederick
  See Longyear, Barry B(rookes)
Longfellow, Henry Wadsworth
  1807-1882 19
Longfellow, Layne (A.) 1937- 102
Longman, Harold S. 1919- 5
Longsworth, Polly 1933- 28
Longtemps, Kenneth 1933- 17
Longway, A. Hugh
  See Lang, Andrew
Longyear, Barry B(rookes) 1942- 117
Loomans, Diane 1955- 90
Loomis, Christine 113
Loomis, Jennifer A. 1942- 101

Author Index

Loomis, Robert D. 5
Lopez, Angelo (Cayas) 1967- *83*
Lopez, Barry (Holstun) 1945- *67*
Lopshire, Robert M(artin) 1927- *6*
Loraine, Connie
 See Reece, Colleen L.
Lorbiecki, Marybeth 1959- *121*
Lord, Athena V. 1932- *39*
Lord, Beman 1924-1991 ....*5*
 Obituary *69*
Lord, Bette Bao 1938- *58*
Lord, (Doreen Mildred) Douglas
 1904- *12*
Lord, John Vernon 1939- *21*
Lord, Nancy
 See Titus, Eve
Lord, Walter 1917-2002 ....*3*
Lorenz, Albert 1941- *115*
Lorenzini, Carlo 1826-1890 ....*100*
 Earlier sketch in SATA 29
 See Collodi, Carlo
Lorimer, Janet 1941- *60*
Loring, Emilie (Baker) 1864(?)-1951 ......*51*
Lorkowski, Thomas V(incent) 1950- *92*
Lorkowski, Tom
 See Lorkowski, Thomas V(incent)
Lorraine, Walter (Henry) 1929- *16*
Lorrimer, Claire
 See Clark, Patricia Denise
Loss, Joan 1933- *11*
Lothrop, Harriet Mulford Stone
 1844-1924 ....*20*
Lottridge, Celia Barker 1936- *112*
LoTurco, Laura 1963- *84*
Lotz, Wolfgang 1912-1981 ....*65*
Louie, Ai-Ling 1949- *40*
 Brief entry *34*
Louis, Pat
 See Francis, Dorothy Brenner
Louisburgh, Sheila Burnford
 See Burnford, Sheila (Philip Cochrane
 Every)
Lourie, Helen
 See Storr, Catherine (Cole)
Lourie, Peter (King) 1952- *82*
Love, (Kathleen) Ann 1947- *79*
Love, D. Anne 1949- *96*
Love, Douglas 1967- *92*
Love, Katherine (Isabel) 1907- *3*
Love, Sandra (Weller) 1940- *26*
Lovejoy, Jack 1937- *116*
Lovelace, Delos Wheeler 1894-1967 ....*7*
Lovelace, Maud Hart 1892-1980 ....*2*
 Obituary *23*
Lovell, Ingraham
 See Bacon, Josephine Dodge (Daskam)
Loverseed, Amanda (Jane) 1965- *75*
Lovett, Margaret (Rose) 1915- *22*
Low, Alice 1926- *76*
 Earlier sketch in SATA 11
Low, Elizabeth Hammond 1898-1991 ....*5*
Low, Joseph 1911- *14*
Lowe, Jay, Jr.
 See Loeper, John J(oseph)
Lowell, Susan 1950- *127*
 Earlier sketch in SATA 81
Lowenstein, Dyno 1914-1996 ....*6*
Lowenstein, Sallie 1949- *116*
Lowery, Linda 1949- *74*
Lowitz, Anson C. 1901(?)-1978 ....*18*
Lowitz, Sadyebeth Heath 1901-1969 ....*17*
Lowndes, Robert A(ugustine) W(ard)
 1916-1998 ....*117*
Lowry, Janette Sebring 1892-1986 ....*43*
Lowry, Lois 1937- *111*
 Autobiography Feature *127*
 Earlier sketches in SATA 23, 70
 See also CLR 72
 See also SAAS 3
Lowry, Peter 1953- *7*
Lozansky, Edward D. 1941- *62*
Lozier, Herbert 1915- *26*

Lubar, David 1954- *133*
Lubell, Cecil 1912-2000 ....*6*
Lubell, Winifred (A. Milius) 1914- *6*
Lubin, Leonard
 See Lubin, Leonard B.
Lubin, Leonard B. 1943-1994 ....*45*
 Brief entry *37*
Luby, Thia 1954- *124*
Lucado, Max (Lee) 1955- *104*
Lucas, Cedric 1962- *101*
Lucas, E(dward) V(errall) 1868-1938 ....*20*
Lucas, Eileen 1956- *113*
 Earlier sketch in SATA 76
Lucas, George 1944- *56*
Lucas, Jerry 1940- *33*
Lucas, Victoria
 See Plath, Sylvia
Lucashenko, Melissa 1967- *104*
Luccarelli, Vincent 1923- *90*
Luce, Celia (Geneva Larsen) 1914- *38*
Luce, Willard (Ray) 1914-1990 ....*38*
Lucht, Irmgard 1937- *82*
Luckett, Dave 1951- *106*
Luckhardt, Mildred Corell 1898-1990 ....*5*
Ludel, Jacqueline 1945- *64*
Ludlum, Mabel Cleland
 See Widdemer, Mabel Cleland
Ludwig, Helen *33*
Ludwig, Lyndell 1923- *63*
Lueders, Edward (George) 1923- *14*
Luenn, Nancy 1954- *79*
 Earlier sketch in SATA 51
Lufkin, Raymond H. 1897- *38*
Lugard, Flora Louisa Shaw
 1852-1929 ....*21*
Luger, Harriett Mandelay 1914- *23*
Luhrmann, Winifred B(ruce) 1934- *11*
Luis, Earlene W. 1929- *11*
Lum, Peter
 See Crowe, (Bettina) Peter Lum
Lund, Doris Herold 1919- *12*
Lung, Chang
 See Rigney, James Oliver, Jr.
Lunge-Larsen, Lise 1955- *138*
Lunn, Carolyn (Kowalczyk) 1960- *67*
Lunn, Janet (Louise Swoboda)
 1928- *110*
 Earlier sketches in SATA 4, 68
 See also CLR 18
 See also SAAS 12
Lunsford, Cin Forshay
 See Forshay-Lunsford, Cin
Lupoff, Dick
 See Lupoff, Richard A(llen)
Lupoff, Richard A(llen) 1935- *60*
Lurie, Alison 1926- *112*
 Earlier sketch in SATA 46
Lurie, Morris 1938- *72*
Lussert, Anneliese 1929- *101*
Lustig, Arnost 1926- *56*
Lustig, Loretta 1944- *46*
Luther, Rebekah (Lyn) S(tiles)
 1960- *90*
Luttmann, Gail
 See Damerow, Gail (Jane)
Luttrell, Guy L. 1938- *22*
Luttrell, Ida (Alleene) 1934- *91*
 Brief entry *35*
 Earlier sketch in SATA 40
Lutz, Norma Jean 1943- *122*
Lutzeier, Elizabeth 1952- *72*
Lutzker, Edythe 1904-1991 ....*5*
Luzadder, Patrick 1954- *89*
Luzzati, Emanuele 1921- *7*
Luzzatto, Paola Caboara 1938- *38*
Lybbert, Tyler 1970- *88*
Lydon, Michael 1942- *11*
Lyfick, Warren
 See Reeves, Lawrence F.
Lyle, Katie Letcher 1938- *8*

Lynch, Chris 1962- *131*
 Earlier sketch in SATA 95
 See also CLR 58
Lynch, Lorenzo 1932- *7*
Lynch, Marietta 1947- *29*
Lynch, P(atrick) J(ames) 1962- *122*
 Earlier sketch in SATA 79
Lynch, Patricia (Nora) 1898-1972 ....*9*
Lynds, Dennis 1924- *47*
 Brief entry *37*
Lyngseth, Joan
 See Davies, Joan
Lynn, Elizabeth A(nne) 1946- *99*
Lynn, Mary
 See Brokamp, Marilyn
Lynn, Patricia
 See Watts, Mabel Pizzey
Lyon, Elinor 1921- *6*
Lyon, George Ella 1949- *119*
 Earlier sketch in SATA 68
Lyon, Lyman R.
 See de Camp, L(yon) Sprague
Lyons, Dorothy M(arawee) 1907-1997 ......*3*
Lyons, Grant 1941- *30*
Lyons, Marcus
 See Blish, James (Benjamin)
Lyons, Mary E(velyn) 1947- *93*
Lystad, Mary (Hanemann) 1928- *11*
Lytle, Elizabeth Stewart 1949- *79*
Lytle, Robert A. 1944- *119*
Lyttle, Richard B(ard) 1927- *23*
Lytton, Edward G(eorge) E(arle) L(ytton)
 Bulwer-Lytton Baron 1803-1873 ....*23*

M

Ma, Wenhai 1954- *84*
Maar, Leonard (Frank, Jr.) 1927- *30*
Maartens, Maretha 1945- *73*
Maas, Selve -1997 ....*14*
Mabie, Grace
 See Mattern, Joanne
Mac
 See MacManus, Seumas
 and Maccari, Ruggero
Macalaster, Elizabeth G. 1951- *115*
MacAodhagain, Eamon
 See Egan, E(dward) W(elstead)
MacArthur-Onslow, Annette Rosemary
 1933- *26*
Macaulay, David (Alexander) 1946- *137*
 Brief entry *27*
 Earlier sketches in SATA 46, 72
 See also CLR 14
Macaulay, Teresa (E.) 1947- *95*
MacBeth, George (Mann) 1932-1992 ....*4*
 Obituary *70*
MacBride, Roger Lea 1929-1995 ....*85*
MacCarter, Don 1944- *91*
MacClintock, Dorcas 1932- *8*
MacDonald, Amy 1951- *136*
 Earlier sketch in SATA 76
MacDonald, Anne Elizabeth Campbell Bard
 -1958
 See MacDonald, Betty
MacDonald, Anson
 See Heinlein, Robert A(nson)
MacDonald, Betty 1908-1958
 See YABC 1
 See MacDonald, Anne Elizabeth Campbell
 Bard
Macdonald, Blackie
 See Emrich, Duncan (Black Macdonald)
Macdonald, Caroline 1948- *86*
 Obituary *111*
 See also CLR 60
Macdonald, Dwight 1906-1982 ....*29*
 Obituary *33*

MacDonald, George 1824-1905 ....*100*
  Earlier sketch in SATA *33*
  See also CLR *67*
MacDonald, Golden
  See Brown, Margaret Wise
Macdonald, James D. 1954- *114*
  Earlier sketch in SATA *81*
  See Appleton, Victor
Macdonald, Marcia
  See Hill, Grace Livingston
MacDonald, Margaret Read 1940- *94*
Macdonald, Marianne 1934- *113*
Macdonald, Mary
  See Gifford, Griselda
MacDonald, Maryann 1947- *72*
Macdonald, Shelagh 1937- *25*
MacDonald, Suse 1940- *109*
  Brief entry *52*
  Earlier sketch in SATA *54*
Macdonald, Zillah K(atherine)
  1885-1979 ....*11*
MacDonnell, Megan
  See Stevens, Serita (Deborah)
MacDougal, John
  See Blish, James (Benjamin)
MacDougal, John
  See Blish, James (Benjamin)
  and Lowndes, Robert A(ugustine) W(ard)
Mace, Elisabeth 1933- *27*
Mace, Varian 1938- *49*
MacEwen, Gwendolyn (Margaret)
  1941-1987 ....*50*
  Obituary *55*
Macfarlan, Allan A. 1892-1982 ....*35*
MacFarlane, Iris 1922- *11*
MacGill-Callahan, Sheila 1926-2000 ....*78*
MacGregor, Ellen 1906-1954 ....*39*
  Brief entry *27*
MacGregor-Hastie, Roy (Alasdhair Niall)
  1929- *3*
Machetanz, Frederick 1908- *34*
Machin Goodall, Daphne (Edith) *37*
Macht, Norman L(ee) 1929- *122*
MacInnes, Helen (Clark) 1907-1985 ......*22*
  Obituary *44*
Macintosh, Brownie 1950- *98*
MacIntyre, Elisabeth 1916- *17*
Mack, Stan(ley) *17*
Mack, Tracy 1968- *128*
Mackall, Dandi D(aley) 1949- *118*
Mackay, Claire 1930- *97*
  Autobiography Feature *124*
  Earlier sketch in SATA *40*
  See also CLR *43*
Mackay, Constance D'Arcy
  (?)-1966 ....*125*
Mackay, Donald (Alexander) 1914- *81*
MacKaye, Percy (Wallace)
  1875-1956 ....*32*
MacKellar, William 1914- *4*
Macken, Walter 1915-1967 ....*36*
MacKenzie, Jill (Kelly) 1947- *75*
Mackey, Ernan
  See McInerny, Ralph (Matthew)
Mackie, Maron
  See McNeely, Jeannette
Mackin, Edward
  See McInerny, Ralph (Matthew)
MacKinnon, Bernie 1957- *69*
MacKinnon Groomer, Vera 1915- *57*
MacKinstry, Elizabeth 1879-1956 ....*42*
MacLachlan, Patricia 1938- *107*
  Brief entry *42*
  Earlier sketch in SATA *62*
  See also CLR *14*
MacLane, Jack
  See Crider, (Allen) Bill(y)
MacLean, Alistair (Stuart)
  1922(?)-1987 ....*23*
  Obituary *50*
Maclean, Art
  See Shirreffs, Gordon D(onald)

MacLeod, Beatrice (Beach) 1910- *10*
MacLeod, Charlotte (Matilda) 1922- *28*
MacLeod, Doug 1959- *60*
MacLeod, Ellen Jane (Anderson)
  1916- *14*
MacManus, James
  See MacManus, Seumas
MacManus, Seumas 1869-1960 ....*25*
MacMaster, Eve (Ruth) B(owers)
  1942- *46*
MacMillan, Annabelle
  See Quick, Annabelle
MacMillan, Dianne M(arie) 1943- *125*
  Earlier sketch in SATA *84*
Macneill, Janet
  See McNeely, Jeannette
MacPeek, Walter G. 1902-1973 ....*4*
  Obituary *25*
MacPhail, Catherine 1946- *130*
MacPherson, Margaret 1908- *9*
  See also SAAS *4*
MacPherson, Winnie 1930- *107*
Macrae, Travis
  See Feagles, Anita M(acRae)
MacRaois, Cormac 1944- *72*
Macumber, Mari
  See Sandoz, Mari(e Susette)
Macy, Sue 1954- *134*
  Earlier sketch in SATA *88*
Madden, Don 1927- *3*
Maddison, Angela Mary 1923- *10*
  See Banner, Angela
Maddock, Reginald (Bertram)
  1912-1994 ....*15*
Madenski, Melissa (Ann) 1949- *77*
Madian, Jon 1941- *9*
Madison, Arnold 1937- *6*
Madison, Winifred *5*
Madsen, Ross Martin 1946- *82*
Madsen, Susan A(rrington) 1954- *90*
Maehlqvist, (Karl) Stefan 1943- *30*
  See Mahlqvist, (Karl) Stefan
Maestro, Betsy (Crippen) 1944- *106*
  Brief entry *30*
  Earlier sketch in SATA *59*
  See also CLR *45*
Maestro, Giulio 1942- *106*
  Earlier sketches in SATA *8, 59*
  See also CLR *45*
Maeterlinck, Maurice 1862-1949 ....*66*
Magee, Doug 1947- *78*
Magee, Wes 1939- *64*
Maggio, Rosalie 1943- *69*
Magid, Ken(neth Marshall) *65*
Magnus, Erica 1946- *77*
Magorian, James 1942- *92*
  Earlier sketch in SATA *32*
Magorian, Michelle 1947- *128*
  Earlier sketch in SATA *67*
Magovern, Peg *103*
Maguire, Anne
  See Nearing, Penny
Maguire, Gregory (Peter) 1954- *129*
  Earlier sketches in SATA *28, 84*
  See also SAAS *22*
Maguire, Jack 1920-2000 ....*74*
Maguire, Jesse
  See Smith, Sherwood
Maguire, Jessie
  See Smith, Sherwood
Maher, Ramona 1934- *13*
Mahlqvist, (Karl) Stefan *30*
  See Maehlqvist, (Karl) Stefan
Mahon, Julia C(unha) 1916- *11*
Mahony, Elizabeth Winthrop 1948- *8*
  See Winthrop, Elizabeth
Mahood, Kenneth 1930- *24*
Mahy, Margaret (May) 1936- *119*
  Earlier sketches in SATA *14, 69*
  See also CLR *78*
Maiden, Cecil (Edward) 1902-1981 ....*52*

Maidoff, Ilka
  See List, Ilka Katherine
Maifair, Linda Lee 1947- *83*
Maik, Henri
  See Hecht, Henri Joseph
Maillu, David G(ian) 1939- *111*
Maine, Trevor
  See Catherall, Arthur
Mains, Randolph P. 1946- *80*
Maiorano, Robert 1946- *43*
Maisner, Heather 1947- *89*
Maison, Della
  See Katz, Bobbi
Maitland, Antony Jasper 1935- *25*
Maitland, Barbara *102*
Major, Kevin (Gerald) 1949- *134*
  Earlier sketches in SATA *32, 82*
  See also CLR *11*
Majure, Janet 1954- *96*
Makie, Pam 1943- *37*
Makowski, Silk
  See Makowski, Silvia Ann
Makowski, Silvia Ann 1940- *101*
Malam, John 1957- *89*
Malcolm, Dan
  See Silverberg, Robert
Malcolmson, Anne
  See von Storch, Anne B.
Malcolmson, David 1899-1978 ....*6*
Maletta, Dr. Arlene
  See Feltenstein, Arlene (H.)
Mali, Jane Lawrence 1937-1995 ....*51*
  Brief entry *44*
  Obituary *86*
Mallett, Jerry J. 1939- *76*
Mallory, Kenneth 1945- *128*
Mallowan, Agatha Christie
  See Christie, Agatha (Mary Clarissa)
Malmberg, Carl 1904-1979 ....*9*
Malmgren, Dallin 1949- *65*
Malo, John W. 1911-2000 ....*4*
Malone, James Hiram 1930- *84*
Maloney, Pat
  See Markun, Patricia Maloney
Malory, Sir Thomas 1410(?)-1471(?) *59*
  Brief entry *33*
Malvern, Corinne 1905-1956 ....*34*
Malvern, Gladys (?)-1962 ....*23*
Mama G.
  See Davis, Grania
Mammano, Julie (Lynn) 1962- *107*
Mamonova, Tatyana 1943- *93*
Manchel, Frank 1935- *10*
Manchester, William (Raymond)
  1922- *65*
Mandel, Brett H. 1969- *108*
Mandel, Peter (Bevan) 1957-1998 ....*87*
Mandel, Sally Elizabeth 1944- *64*
Mandell, Muriel (Hortense Levin)
  1921- *63*
Manes, Stephen 1949- *99*
  Brief entry *40*
  Earlier sketch in SATA *42*
Manfred, Frederick (Feikema)
  1912-1994 ....*30*
  See Feikema, Feike
Mangin, Marie France 1940- *59*
Mangione, Jerre *6*
  Obituary *104*
  See Mangione, Gerlando
Mango, Karin N. 1936- *52*
Mangurian, David 1938- *14*
Mania, Cathy 1950- *102*
Mania, Robert (C.) 1952- *102*
Maniatty, Taramesha 1978- *92*
Maniscalco, Joseph 1926- *10*
Manley, Deborah 1932- *28*
Manley, Seon 1921- *15*
  See also CLR *3*
  See also SAAS *2*

Mann, Josephine
  See Pullein-Thompson, Josephine (Mary
  Wedderburn)
Mann, Kenny 1946- *91*
Mann, Pamela 1946- *91*
Mann, Patrick
  See Waller, Leslie
Mann, Peggy *6*
  See Houlton, Peggy Mann
Mannetti, Lisa 1953- *57*
  Brief entry *51*
Mannheim, Grete (Salomon)
  1909-1986 ....*10*
Manniche, Lise 1943- *31*
Manning, Rosemary (Joy) 1911-1988 ......*10*
  See Davys, Sarah
  and Voyle, Mary
Manning-Sanders, Ruth (Vernon)
  1895(?)-1988 ....*73*
  Obituary *57*
  Earlier sketch in SATA *15*
Manson, Ainslie Kertland 1938- *115*
Manson, Beverlie 1945- *57*
  Brief entry *44*
Manthorpe, Helen 1958- *122*
Mantinband, Gerda (B.) 1917- *74*
Manton, Jo
  See Gittings, Jo (Grenville) Manton
Manuel, Lynn 1948- *99*
Manushkin, Fran(ces) 1942- *93*
  Earlier sketches in SATA *7, 54*
Man Without a Spleen, A
  See Chekhov, Anton (Pavlovich)
Mapes, Mary A.
  See Ellison, Virginia H(owell)
Maple, Marilyn 1931- *80*
Mappin, Strephyn 1956- *109*
Mara, Barney
  See Roth, Arthur J(oseph)
Mara, Jeanette
  See Cebulash, Mel
Marasmus, Seymour
  See Rivoli, Mario
Marbach, Ethel
  See Pochocki, Ethel (Frances)
Marcal, Annette B.
  See Callaway, Bernice (Anne)
Marcelino
  See Agnew, Edith J(osephine)
Marcellino, Fred 1939-2001 ....*118*
  Obituary *127*
  Earlier sketch in SATA *68*
March, Carl
  See Fleischman, (Albert) Sid(ney)
Marchant, Bessie 1862-1941
  See YABC *2*
Marchant, Catherine
  See Cookson, Catherine (McMullen)
Marcher, Marion Walden 1890-1987 ......*10*
Marchesi, Stephen 1951- *114*
Marchesi, Steve
  See Marchesi, Stephen
  and Older, Effin
  and Older, Jules
Marciano, John Bemelmans *118*
Marco, Lou
  See Gottfried, Theodore Mark
Marcus, Leonard S. 1950- *133*
Marcus, Paul 1953- *82*
Marcus, Rebecca B(rian) 1907- *9*
Marcuse, Aida E. 1934- *89*
Margaret, Karla
  See Andersdatter, Karla M(argaret)
Margolis, Jeffrey A. 1948- *108*
Margolis, Richard J(ules) 1929-1991 ......*86*
  Obituary *67*
  Earlier sketch in SATA *4*
Margolis, Vivienne 1922- *46*
Mariana
  See Foster, Marian Curtis
Marie, Geraldine 1949- *61*

Mariner, Scott
  See Pohl, Frederik
Marino, Dorothy Bronson 1912- *14*
Marino, Jan 1936- *114*
Marino, Nick
  See Deming, Richard
Mario, Anna
  See Odgers, Sally Farrell
Marion, Henry
  See del Rey, Lester
Maris, Ron *71*
  Brief entry *45*
Mark, Jan(et Marjorie) 1943- *114*
  Earlier sketches in SATA *22, 69*
  See also CLR *11*
Mark, Joan T. 1937- *122*
Mark, Pauline (Dahlin) 1913- *14*
Mark, Polly
  See Mark, Pauline (Dahlin)
Mark, Ted
  See Gottfried, Theodore Mark
Marker, Sherry 1941- *76*
Markert, Jennifer 1965- *83*
Markert, Jenny
  See Markert, Jennifer
Markham, Lynne 1947- *102*
Markham, Marion M. 1929- *60*
Markins, W. S.
  See Jenkins, Marie M(agdalen)
Markle, Sandra L(ee) 1946- *92*
  Brief entry *41*
  Earlier sketch in SATA *57*
Marko, Katherine D(olores) *28*
Markoosie
  See CLR *23*
  See Markoosie, Patsauq
Marks, Alan 1957- *77*
Marks, Burton 1930- *47*
  Brief entry *43*
Marks, Hannah K.
  See Trivlepiece, Laurel
Marks, J
  See Highwater, Jamake (Mamake)
Marks, J.
  See Highwater, Jamake (Mamake)
Marks, J(ames) M(acdonald) 1921- *13*
Marks, Laurie J. 1957- *68*
Marks, Mickey Klar -1986 ....*12*
Marks, Peter
  See Smith, Robert Kimmel
Marks, Rita 1938- *47*
Marks, Stan(ley) *14*
Marks-Highwater, J
  See Highwater, Jamake (Mamake)
Marks-Highwater, J.
  See Highwater, Jamake (Mamake)
Markun, Patricia Maloney 1924- *15*
Markusen, Bruce (Stanley Rodriguez)
  1965- *141*
Marley, Louise 1952- *120*
Marlin, Hilda
  See Van Stockum, Hilda
Marlow, Max
  See Nicole, Christopher (Robin)
Marlowe, Amy Bell *67*
  Earlier sketch in SATA *1*
Marney, Dean 1952- *90*
Marokvia, Artur 1909- *31*
Marokvia, Mireille (Journet) 1918- *5*
Marol, Jean-Claude 1946- *125*
Marr, John S(tuart) 1940- *48*
Marric, J. J.
  See Butler, William (Arthur) Vivian
  and Creasey, John
Marrin, Albert 1936- *126*
  Brief entry *43*
  Earlier sketches in SATA *53, 90*
  See also CLR *53*
Marriott, Alice Lee 1910-1992 ....*31*
  Obituary *71*
Marriott, Janice 1946- *134*
Marriott, Pat(ricia) 1920- *35*

Marroquin, Patricio
  See Markun, Patricia Maloney
Mars, W. T.
  See Mars, Witold Tadeusz J.
Mars, Witold Tadeusz J. 1912-1985 ....*3*
Marsden, Carolyn 1950- *140*
Marsden, John 1950- *97*
  Earlier sketch in SATA *66*
  See also CLR *34*
  See also SAAS *22*
Marsh, Carole 1946- *127*
Marsh, Dave 1950- *66*
Marsh, J. E.
  See Marshall, Evelyn
Marsh, James 1946- *73*
Marsh, Jean
  See Marshall, Evelyn
Marsh, Joan F. 1923- *83*
Marsh, Valerie 1954- *89*
Marshall, Anthony D(ryden) 1924- *18*
Marshall, Bonnie C. 1941- *141*
  Earlier sketch in SATA *18*
Marshall, Bridget M(ary) 1974- *103*
Marshall, (Sarah) Catherine (Wood)
  1914-1983 ....*2*
  Obituary *34*
Marshall, Douglas
  See McClintock, Marshall
Marshall, Edward
  See Marshall, James (Edward)
Marshall, Evelyn 1897-1991 ....*11*
Marshall, Felicity 1950- *116*
Marshall, Garry 1934- *60*
Marshall, H. H.
  See Jahn, Joseph Michael
Marshall, James (Edward) 1942-1992 ......*75*
  Earlier sketches in SATA *6, 51*
  See also CLR *21*
Marshall, James Vance
  See Payne, Donald Gordon
Marshall, Janet (Perry) 1938- *97*
Marshall, Jeff
  See Laycock, George (Edwin)
Marshall, Kim
  See Marshall, Michael (Kimbrough)
Marshall, Michael (Kimbrough)
  1948- *37*
Marshall, Percy
  See Young, Percy M(arshall)
Marshall, S(amuel) L(yman) A(twood)
  1900-1977 ....*21*
Marsoli, Lisa Ann 1958- *101*
  Brief entry *53*
Marsten, Richard
  See Hunter, Evan
Marston, Hope Irvin 1935- *127*
  Earlier sketch in SATA *31*
Martchenko, Michael 1942- *95*
  Earlier sketch in SATA *50*
Martel, Suzanne 1924- *99*
Martin, Ann M(atthews) 1955- *126*
  Brief entry *41*
  Earlier sketches in SATA *44, 70*
  See also CLR *32*
Martin, Bill
  See Martin, William Ivan
Martin, Bill, Jr. *67*
  Brief entry *40*
  See Martin, William Ivan
Martin, Charles E(lmer) *70*
  Earlier sketch in SATA *69*
  See Mastrangelo, Charles E(lmer)
Martin, Christopher
  See Hoyt, Edwin P(almer), Jr.
Martin, Claire 1933- *76*
Martin, David Stone 1913-1992 ....*39*
Martin, Donald
  See Honig, Donald
Martin, Dorothy 1921- *47*
Martin, Eugene *1*
Martin, Eva M. 1939- *65*

Martin, Frances M(cEntee)
1906-1998 ....*36*
Martin, Francesca 1947- *101*
Martin, Fred 1948- *119*
Martin, Fredric
See Christopher, Matt(hew Frederick)
Martin, George R(aymond) R(ichard)
1948- *118*
Martin, J(ohn) P(ercival)
1880(?)-1966 ....*15*
Martin, Jacqueline Briggs 1945- *98*
Martin, Jane Read 1957- *84*
Martin, Jeremy
See Levin, Marcia Obrasky
Martin, Les
See Schulman, L(ester) M(artin)
Martin, Linda 1961- *82*
Martin, Lynne 1923- *21*
Martin, Marcia
See Levin, Marcia Obrasky
Martin, Marvin 1926- *126*
Martin, Melanie
See Pellowski, Michael (Joseph)
Martin, Nancy
See Salmon, Annie Elizabeth
Martin, Patricia Miles 1899-1986 ....*43*
Obituary *48*
Earlier sketch in SATA *1*
Martin, Peter
See Chaundler, Christine
Martin, Rene 1891-1977 ....*42*
Obituary *20*
Martin, Rupert (Claude) 1905- *31*
Martin, S. R.
See Mappin, Strephyn
Martin, Stefan 1936- *32*
Martin, Vicky
See Storey, Victoria Carolyn
Martin, Webber
See Silverberg, Robert
Martin, Wendy
See Martini, Teri
Martin, William Ivan 1916- *40*
See Martin, Bill, Jr.
Martineau, Harriet 1802-1876
See YABC 2
Martinet, Jeanne 1958- *80*
Martinez, Ed(ward) 1954- *98*
Martinez, Elizabeth Coonrod 1954- *85*
Martinez, Victor *95*
Martini, Teri 1930- *3*
Martini, Therese
See Martini, Teri
Martinson, Janis
See Herbert, Janis
Marton, Jirina 1946- *95*
Martson, Del
See Lupoff, Richard A(llen)
Martyr, Paula (Jane) *57*
See Lawford, Paula Jane
Maruki, Toshi 1912-2000 ....*112*
See also CLR *19*
Marvin, Isabel R(idout) 1924- *84*
Marx, Patricia Windschill 1948- *112*
Marx, Robert F(rank) 1936- *24*
Marx, Trish
See Marx, Patricia Windschill
Marzani, Carl (Aldo) 1912-1994 ....*12*
Marzollo, Jean 1942- *130*
Earlier sketches in SATA *29, 77*
See also SAAS *15*
Masefield, John (Edward) 1878-1967 ......*19*
Masoff, Joy 1951- *118*
Mason, Ernst
See Pohl, Frederik
Mason, F(rancis) van Wyck
1901-1978 ....*3*
Obituary *26*
Mason, Frank W.
See Mason, F(rancis) van Wyck
Mason, George Frederick 1904-2000 ......*14*

Mason, Miriam E(vangeline) 1900-1973 ....*2*
Obituary *26*
Mason, Tally
See Derleth, August (William)
Mason, Van Wyck
See Mason, F(rancis) van Wyck
Mass, William
See Gibson, William
Masselman, George 1897-1971 ....*19*
Massie, Dianne Redfield 1938- *125*
Earlier sketch in SATA *16*
Massie, Elizabeth *108*
Masson, Sophie 1959- *133*
Masters, Anthony (Richard)
1940-2003 ....*112*
Masters, Kelly R(ay) 1897-1987 ....*3*
Masters, Mildred 1932- *42*
Masters, William
See Cousins, Margaret
Masters, Zeke
See Bensen, Donald R.
and Goulart, Ron(ald Joseph)
Matas, Carol 1949- *93*
Autobiography Feature *112*
See also CLR *52*
Matchette, Katharine E. 1941- *38*
Math, Irwin 1940- *42*
Mathabane, Mark 1960- *123*
Mather, Kirtley F(letcher) 1888-1978 ......*65*
Mathers, Petra 1945- *119*
See also CLR *76*
Matheson, Richard (Christian)
1953- *119*
Mathews, Janet 1914-1992 ....*41*
Mathews, Judith *80*
See Goldberger, Judith M.
Mathews, Louise
See Tooke, Louise Mathews
Mathieu, Joe
See Mathieu, Joseph P.
Mathieu, Joseph P. 1949- *94*
Brief entry *36*
Earlier sketch in SATA *43*
Mathis, Sharon Bell 1937- *58*
Earlier sketch in SATA *7*
See also CLR *3*
See also SAAS *3*
Matloff, Gregory 1945- *73*
Matott, Justin 1961- *109*
Matranga, Frances Carfi 1922- *78*
Matson, Emerson N(els) 1926- *12*
Matsui, Tadashi 1926- *8*
Matsuno, Masako *6*
See Kobayashi, Masako Matsuno
Matte, (Encarnacion) L'Enc 1936- *22*
Mattern, Joanne 1963- *122*
Matthews, Andrew 1948- *138*
Matthews, Caitlin 1952- *122*
Matthews, Downs 1925- *71*
Matthews, Ellen
See Bache, Ellyn
Matthews, Ellen 1950- *28*
Matthews, Jacklyn Meek
See Meek, Jacklyn O'Hanlon
Matthews, John (Kentigern) 1948- *116*
Matthews, Liz
See Pellowski, Michael (Joseph)
Matthews, Morgan
See Pellowski, Michael (Joseph)
Matthews, Patricia (Anne) 1927- *28*
Matthews, William Henry III 1919- *45*
Brief entry *28*
Matthiessen, Peter 1927- *27*
Mattingley, Christobel (Rosemary)
1931- *85*
Earlier sketch in SATA *37*
See also CLR *24*
See also SAAS *18*
Matulay, Laszlo 1912- *43*
Matus, Greta 1938- *12*
Maugham, W. S.
See Maugham, W(illiam) Somerset

Maugham, W(illiam) Somerset
1874-1965 ....*54*
Maugham, William Somerset
See Maugham, W(illiam) Somerset
Maurer, Diane Philippoff
See Maurer-Mathison, Diane V(ogel)
Maurer, Diane Vogel
See Maurer-Mathison, Diane V(ogel)
Maurer-Mathison, Diane V(ogel)
1944- *89*
Mauser, Patricia Rhoads 1943- *37*
Maves, Mary Carolyn 1916- *10*
Maves, Paul B(enjamin) 1913- *10*
Mavor, Salley 1955- *125*
Mawicke, Tran 1911- *15*
Max, Peter 1939- *45*
Maxon, Anne
See Best, (Evangel) Allena Champlin
Maxwell, Arthur S. 1896-1970 ....*11*
Maxwell, Edith 1923- *7*
Maxwell, Gavin 1914-1969 ....*65*
May, Charles Paul 1920- *4*
May, Elaine Tyler 1947- *120*
May, J. C.
See May, Julian
May, Julian 1931- *11*
May, Robert Stephen 1929-1996 ....*46*
May, Robin
See May, Robert Stephen
Mayberry, Florence V(irginia) Wilson ....
10
Maybury, Richard J. 1946- *72*
Mayer, Agatha
See Maher, Ramona
Mayer, Ann M(argaret) 1938- *14*
Mayer, Danuta 1958- *117*
Mayer, Jane Rothschild 1903-2001 ....*38*
Mayer, Marianna 1945- *132*
Earlier sketches in SATA *32, 83*
Mayer, Mercer 1943- *137*
Earlier sketches in SATA *16, 32, 73, 129*
See also CLR *11*
Mayerson, Charlotte Leon *36*
Mayerson, Evelyn Wilde 1935- *55*
Mayfield, Katherine 1958- *118*
Mayfield, Sue 1963- *72*
Mayhar, Ardath 1930- *38*
Mayhew, James (John) 1964- *85*
Maynard, Olga 1920- *40*
Mayne, William (James Carter)
1928- *122*
Earlier sketches in SATA *6, 68*
See also CLR *25*
See also SAAS *11*
Maynes, J. O. Rocky, Jr.
See Maynes, J. Oscar, Jr.
Maynes, J. Oscar, Jr. 1929- *38*
Mayo, Gretchen Will 1936- *84*
Mayo, Margaret (Mary) 1935- *96*
Earlier sketch in SATA *38*
Mays, Lucinda L(a Bella) 1924- *49*
Mays, (Lewis) Victor (Jr.) 1927- *5*
Mazer, Anne 1953- *105*
Earlier sketch in SATA *67*
Mazer, Harry 1925- *105*
Earlier sketches in SATA *31, 67*
See also CLR *16*
See also SAAS *11*
Mazer, Norma Fox 1931- *105*
Earlier sketches in SATA *24, 67*
See also CLR *23*
See also SAAS *1*
Mazille, Capucine 1953- *96*
Mazza, Adriana 1928- *19*
Mazzio, Joann 1926- *74*
Mbugua, Kioi Wa 1962- *83*
McAfee, Carol 1955- *81*
McAllister, Amanda
See Dowdell, Dorothy (Florence) Karns
and Hager, Jean
and Meaker, Eloise
McAllister, Margaret 1956- *117*

McArthur, Nancy 96
McBain, Ed
  See Hunter, Evan
McBratney, Sam 1943- 89
  See also CLR *44*
McBrier, Michael
  See Older, Effin
  and Older, Jules
McCafferty, Jim 1954- 84
McCaffery, Janet 1936- 38
McCaffrey, Anne (Inez) 1926- 116
  Earlier sketches in SATA *8, 70*
  See also CLR *49*
  See also SAAS *11*
McCaffrey, Mary
  See Szudek, Agnes S(usan) P(hilomena)
McCain, Becky Ray 1954- 138
McCain, Murray (David, Jr.) 1926-1981 ...7
  Obituary 29
McCall, Edith (Sansom) 1911- 6
McCall, Virginia Nielsen 1909-2000 13
McCall Smith, Alexander 1948- 73
McCallum, Phyllis
  See Koch, Phyllis (Mae) McCallum
McCallum, Stephen 1960- 91
McCampbell, Darlene Z. 1942- 83
McCann, Edson
  See del Rey, Lester
  and Pohl, Frederik
McCann, Gerald 1916- 41
McCann, Helen 1948- 75
McCannon, Dindga 41
McCants, William D. 1961- 82
McCarter, Neely Dixon 1929- 47
McCarthy, Agnes 1933- 4
McCarthy, Colin (John) 1951- 77
McCarthy, Ralph F. 1950- 139
McCarthy-Tucker, Sherri N. 1958- 83
McCarty, Rega Kramer 1904-1986 10
McCaslin, Nellie 1914- 12
McCaughrean, Geraldine 1951- 139
  Earlier sketches in SATA *87, 136*
  See also CLR *38*
McCaughren, Tom 1936- 75
McCauley, Adam 1965- 128
McCay, (Zenas) Winsor 1869-1934 134
  Earlier sketch in SATA *41*
McClafferty, Carla Killough 1958- 137
McCleery, Patsy R. 1925- 133
  Earlier sketch in SATA *88*
McClintock, Barbara 1955- 95
  Earlier sketch in SATA *57*
McClintock, Marshall 1906-1967 3
McClintock, May Garelick
  See Garelick, May
McClintock, Mike
  See McClintock, Marshall
McClintock, Theodore 1902-1971 14
McClinton, Leon 1933- 11
McCloskey, Kevin 1951- 79
McCloskey, (John) Robert
  1914-2003 100
  Earlier sketches in SATA *2, 39*
  See also CLR *7*
McCloy, James F(loyd) 1941- 59
McClung, Robert M(arshall) 1916- 135
  Earlier sketches in SATA *2, 68*
  See also CLR *11*
  See also SAAS *15*
McClure, Gillian Mary 1948- 31
McColley, Kevin 1961- 80
  See also SAAS *23*
McConduit, Denise Walter 1950- 89
McConnell, James Douglas Rutherford
  1915-1988 40
  Obituary 56
McCord, Anne 1942- 41
McCord, David (Thompson Watson)
  1897-1997 18
  Obituary 96
  See also CLR *9*
McCord, Jean 1924- 34

McCormick, Brooks
  See Adams, William Taylor
McCormick, Dell J. 1892-1949 19
McCormick, (George) Donald (King)
  1911-1998 14
McCormick, Edith (Joan) 1934- 30
McCormick, Patricia 1956- 128
McCourt, Lisa 1964- 117
McCourt, Malachy 1931- 126
McCoy, Iola Fuller 3
McCoy, J(oseph) J(erome) 1917- 8
McCoy, Karen Kawamoto 1953- 82
McCoy, Lois (Rich) 1941- 38
McCrady, Lady 1951- 16
McCrea, James (Craig, Jr.) 1920- 3
McCrea, Ruth (Pirman) 1921- 3
McCreigh, James
  See Pohl, Frederik
McCrumb, Sharyn 1948- 109
McCue, Lisa (Emiline) 1959- 65
McCullen, Andrew
  See Arthur, Robert, (Jr.)
McCullers, (Lula) Carson (Smith)
  1917-1967 27
McCulloch, John Tyler
  See Burroughs, Edgar Rice
McCulloch, Sarah
  See Ure, Jean
McCullough, David (Gaub) 1933- 62
McCullough, Frances Monson 1938- 8
McCullough, Sharon Pierce 1943- 131
McCully, Emily Arnold 134
  Earlier sketches in SATA *5, 110*
  See also CLR *46*
  See also SAAS *7*
  See Arnold, Emily
McCune, Dan
  See Haas, Dorothy F.
McCunn, Ruthanne Lum 1946- 63
McCurdy, Michael (Charles) 1942- 82
  Earlier sketch in SATA *13*
McCutcheon, Elsie (Mary Jackson)
  1937- 60
McCutcheon, John 1952- 97
McDaniel, Becky Bring 1953- 61
McDaniel, Lurlene 1944- 71
McDaniels, Pellom III 1968- 121
McDearmon, Kay 20
McDermott, Beverly Brodsky 1941- 11
McDermott, Gerald (Edward) 1941- 74
  Earlier sketch in SATA *16*
  See also CLR *9*
McDermott, Michael 1962- 76
McDevitt, John Charles 94
  See McDevitt, Jack
McDole, Carol
  See Farley, Carol (J.)
McDonald, Collin 1943- 79
McDonald, Gerald D(oan) 1905-1970 3
McDonald, Jamie
  See Heide, Florence Parry
McDonald, Jill (Masefield)
  1927-1982 13
  Obituary 29
McDonald, Joyce 1946- 101
McDonald, Lucile Saunders
  1898-1992 10
McDonald, Mary Ann 1956- 84
McDonald, Megan 1959- 99
  Earlier sketch in SATA *67*
McDonald, Meme 1954- 112
McDonald, Mercedes 1956- 97
McDonell, Chris 1960- 138
McDonnell, Christine 1949- 115
  Earlier sketch in SATA *34*
McDonnell, Flora (Mary) 1963- 90
McDonnell, Lois Eddy 1914- 10
McDonough, Yona Zeldis 1957- 73
McElligott, Matt(hew) 1968- 135
McElmeel, Sharron L. 1942- 128
McElrath, William N. 1932- 65
McElrath-Eslick, Lori 1960- 96

McEntee, Dorothy (Layng) 1902- 37
McFadden, Kevin Christopher
  1961(?)- 68
  See also CLR *29*
  See Pike, Christopher
McFall, Christie 1918- 12
McFarlan, Donald M(aitland) 1915- 59
McFarland, Kenton D(ean) 1920- 11
McFarland, Martha
  See Smith-Ankrom, M. E.
McFarlane, Leslie (Charles)
  1902-1977 31
  See Dixon, Franklin W.
  and Ferris, James Cody
  and Keene, Carolyn
  and Rockwood, Roy
McFarlane, Peter (William) 1940- 95
McFarlane, Sheryl P. 1954- 86
McFarlane, Todd 1961- 117
McGaw, Jessie Brewer 1913- 10
McGee, Barbara 1943- 6
McGiffin, (Lewis) Lee (Shaffer)
  1908-1978 1
McGill, Ormond 1913- 92
McGinley, Jerry 1948- 116
McGinley, Phyllis 1905-1978 44
  Obituary 24
  Earlier sketch in SATA *2*
McGinnis, Lila S(prague) 1924- 44
McGinty, Alice B. 1963- 134
McGivern, Justin 1985- 129
McGivern, Maureen Daly
  See Daly, Maureen
McGough, Elizabeth (Hemmes)
  1934- 33
McGovern, Ann 1930- 132
  Earlier sketches in SATA *8, 69, 70*
  See also CLR *50*
  See also SAAS *17*
McGowen, Thomas E. 1927- 109
  Earlier sketch in SATA *2*
McGowen, Tom
  See McGowen, Thomas E.
McGrady, Mike 1933- 6
McGrath, Barbara Barbieri 1953- 108
McGrath, Robin 1949- 121
McGrath, Thomas (Matthew)
  1916-1990 41
  Obituary 66
McGraw, Eloise Jarvis 1915-2000 67
  Obituary 123
  Earlier sketch in SATA *1*
  See also SAAS *6*
McGraw, William Corbin 1916-1999 3
McGreal, Elizabeth
  See Yates, Elizabeth
McGregor, Barbara 1959- 82
McGregor, Craig 1933- 8
McGregor, Iona 1929- 25
McGuffey, Alexander Hamilton
  1816-1896 60
McGuigan, Mary Ann 1949- 106
McGuire, Edna 1899- 13
McGuire, Leslie (Sarah) 1945- 94
  Brief entry 45
  Earlier sketch in SATA *52*
McGurk, Slater
  See Roth, Arthur J(oseph)
McHargue, Georgess 1941- 77
  Earlier sketch in SATA *4*
  See also CLR *2*
  See also SAAS *5*
McHugh, (Berit) Elisabet 1941- 55
  Brief entry 44
McIlwraith, Maureen Mollie Hunter 2
  See Hunter, Mollie
McInerney, Judith W(hitelock) 1945- 49
  Brief entry 46
McInerny, Ralph (Matthew) 1929- 93
McKaughan, Larry (Scott) 1941- 75
McKay, Donald 1895- 45

McKay, Hilary (Jane) 1959- 92
See also SAAS 23
McKay, Lawrence, Jr. 1948- *114*
McKay, Robert W. 1921- *15*
McKay, Simon
See Nicole, Christopher (Robin)
McKeating, Eileen 1957- *81*
McKee, David (John) 1935- *107*
Earlier sketch in SATA *70*
See also CLR 38
McKee, Tim 1970- *111*
McKeever, Marcia
See Laird, Jean E(louise)
McKelvey, Carole A. 1942- *78*
McKelvy, Charles 1950- *124*
McKendrick, Melveena (Christine)
1941- *55*
McKenna, Colleen O'Shaughnessy
1948- *136*
Earlier sketch in SATA *76*
McKenzie, Ellen Kindt 1928- *80*
McKie, Robin *112*
McKillip, Patricia A(nne) 1948- *126*
Earlier sketches in SATA 30, 80
McKim, Audrey Margaret 1909-1999 ......*47*
McKinley, (Jennifer Carolyn) Robin
1952- *130*
Brief entry *32*
Earlier sketches in SATA 50, 89
See also CLR *81*
McKinney, Barbara Shaw 1951- *116*
McKinney, Nadine 1938- *91*
McKissack, Fredrick L(emuel)
1939- *117*
Brief entry *53*
Earlier sketch in SATA *73*
See also CLR 55
McKissack, Patricia (L'Ann) C(arwell)
1944- *117*
Earlier sketches in SATA 51, 73
See also CLR 55
McKown, Robin (?)-1976 ....*6*
McLaren, Clemence 1938- *105*
McLaughlin, Frank 1934- *73*
McLaurin, Anne 1953- *27*
McLean, Andrew 1946- *113*
McLean, J. Sloan
See Gillette, Virginia M(ary)
and Wunsch, Josephine (McLean)
McLean, Janet 1946- *113*
McLean, Kathryn (Anderson) 1909-1966 ...*9*
McLean, Virginia Overton 1946- *90*
McLean-Carr, Carol 1948- *122*
McLeish, Kenneth 1940-1997 ....*35*
McLenighan, Valjean 1947- *46*
Brief entry *40*
McLennan, Will
See Wisler, G(ary) Clifton
McLeod, Chum 1955- *95*
McLeod, Emilie Warren 1926-1982 ....*23*
Obituary *31*
McLeod, Kirsty
See Hudson, (Margaret) Kirsty
McLeod, Margaret Vail
See Holloway, Teresa (Bragunier)
McLerran, Alice 1933- *137*
Earlier sketch in SATA 68
McLoughlin, John C. 1949- *47*
McManus, Patrick F(rancis) 1933- *46*
McMeekin, Clark
See McMeekin, Isabel McLennan
McMeekin, Isabel McLennan 1895-1973 ...*3*
McMillan, Bruce 1947- *129*
Earlier sketches in SATA 22, 70
See also CLR 47
McMillan, Naomi
See Grimes, Nikki
McMorey, James L.
See Moyer, Terry J.
McMorrow, Annalisa 1969- *104*
McMullan, Jim 1934- *87*

McMullan, Kate
See McMullan, Kate (Hall)
McMullan, Kate (Hall) 1947- *132*
Brief entry *48*
Earlier sketches in SATA 52, 87
McMurtrey, Martin A(loysias) 1921- *21*
McNair, Kate *3*
McNair, Sylvia 1924-2002 ....*74*
McNaught, Harry *32*
McNaughton, Colin 1951- *134*
Earlier sketches in SATA 39, 92
See also CLR 54
McNaughton, Janet 1953- *110*
McNeely, Jeannette 1918- *25*
McNeer, May (Yonge) 1902-1994 ....*81*
Earlier sketch in SATA *1*
McNeese, Tim 1953- *139*
McNeill, Janet *97*
Earlier sketch in SATA *1*
See Alexander, Janet
McNicoll, Sylvia (Marilyn) 1954- *113*
McNulty, Faith 1918- *139*
Earlier sketches in SATA 12, 84
McPhail, David M(ichael) 1940- *140*
Brief entry *32*
Earlier sketches in SATA 47, 81
McPhee, Norma H. 1928- *95*
McPhee, Richard B(yron) 1934- *41*
McPherson, James M(unro) 1936- *141*
Earlier sketch in SATA 16
McQuay, Mike
See Goulart, Ron(ald Joseph)
McQueen, Lucinda 1950- *58*
Brief entry *48*
McQueen, Mildred Hark 1908-1978 ....*12*
McRae, Russell (William) 1934- *63*
McShean, Gordon 1936- *41*
Mc Swigan, Marie 1907-1962 ....*24*
McVey, Vicki 1946- *80*
McVicker, Charles (Taggart) 1930- *39*
McVicker, Chuck
See McVicker, Charles (Taggart)
McWhirter, A(lan) Ross 1925-1975 ....*37*
Obituary *31*
McWhirter, Norris Dewar 1925- *37*
McWilliams, Karen 1943- *65*
Mdurvwa, Hajara E. 1962- *92*
Meacham, Margaret 1952- *95*
Meachum, Virginia 1918- *133*
Earlier sketch in SATA 87
Mead, Alice 1952- *94*
Mead, Russell (M., Jr.) 1935- *10*
Meade, Ellen *5*
See Roddick, Ellen
Meade, Marion 1934- *127*
Earlier sketch in SATA 23
Meader, Stephen W(arren) 1892-1977 ......*1*
Meadmore, Susan
See Sallis, Susan (Diana)
Meadow, Charles T(roub) 1929- *23*
Meadowcroft, Enid LaMonte
See Wright, Enid Meadowcroft (LaMonte)
Meaker, M. J.
See Meaker, Marijane (Agnes)
Meaker, Marijane (Agnes) 1927- *99*
Autobiography Feature *111*
Earlier sketches in SATA 20, 61
See Aldrich, Ann
and James, Mary
and Kerr, M. E.
and Packer, Vin
Means, Florence Crannell 1891-1980 ....*1*
Obituary *25*
See also CLR 56
Mearian, Judy Frank 1936- *49*
Mecca, Judy Truesdell 1955- *127*
Medary, Marjorie 1890-1980 ....*14*
Meddaugh, Susan 1944- *125*
Earlier sketches in SATA 29, 84
Medearis, Angela Shelf 1956- *123*
Earlier sketch in SATA 72
Medearis, Mary 1915- *5*

Medina, Jane 1953- *122*
Medlicott, Mary 1946- *88*
Mee, Charles L., Jr. 1938- *72*
Earlier sketch in SATA 8
Meek, Jacklyn O'Hanlon 1933- *51*
Brief entry *34*
Meeker, Clare Hodgson 1952- *96*
Meeker, Oden 1919(?)-1976 ....*14*
Meeker, Richard
See Brown, Fornan
Meeks, Esther MacBain *1*
Meggs, Libby Phillips 1943- *130*
Mehdevi, Alexander (Sinclair) 1947- *7*
Mehdevi, Anne (Marie) Sinclair
1947- *8*
Meidell, Sherry 1951- *73*
Meier, Minta 1906- *55*
Meighan, Donald Charles 1929- *30*
Meigs, Cornelia Lynde 1884-1973 ....*6*
See also CLR 55
Meilach, Dona Z(weigoron) 1926- *34*
Meilman, Philip W(arren) 1951- *79*
Meinstereifel, Ronald L. 1960- *134*
Melcher, Marguerite Fellows
1879-1969 ....*10*
Melendez, Francisco 1964- *72*
Melin, Grace Hathaway 1892-1973 ....*10*
Mellersh, H(arold) E(dward) L(eslie)
1897- *10*
Melmoth, Sebastian
See Wilde, Oscar (Fingal O'Flahertie
Wills)
Melnikoff, Pamela (Rita) *97*
Meltzer, Milton 1915- *128*
Autobiography Feature *124*
Earlier sketches in SATA 1, 50, 80
See also CLR 13
See also SAAS 1
Melville, Anne
See Potter, Margaret (Newman)
Melville, Herman 1819-1891 ....*59*
Melwood, Mary
See Lewis, E. M.
Melzack, Ronald 1929- *5*
Memling, Carl 1918-1969 ....*6*
Mendel, Jo
See Bond, Gladys Baker
and Gilbertson, Mildred Geiger
Mendelson, Steven T. 1958-1995 ....*86*
Mendez, Raymond A. 1947- *66*
Mendonca, Susan
Brief entry *45*
See Smith, Susan Vernon
Mendoza, George 1934- *41*
Brief entry *39*
See also SAAS 7
Meng, Heinz (Karl) 1924- *13*
Mennen, Ingrid 1954- *85*
Menotti, Gian Carlo 1911- *29*
Menuhin, Sir Yehudi 1916-1999 ....*40*
Obituary *113*
Menville, Douglas 1935- *64*
Menzel, Barbara Jean 1946- *63*
Mercer, Charles (Edward) 1917-1988 ......*16*
Obituary *61*
Meredith, David William
See Miers, Earl Schenck
Meringoff, Laurene Krasny
See Brown, Laurene Krasny
Meriwether, Louise 1923- *52*
Brief entry *31*
Merlin, Arthur
See Blish, James (Benjamin)
Merlin, Christina
See Heaven, Constance (Christina)
Merriam, Eve 1916-1992 ....*73*
Earlier sketches in SATA 3, 40
See also CLR 14
Merrill, Jane 1946- *42*
Merrill, Jean (Fairbanks) 1923- *82*
Earlier sketch in SATA *1*
See also CLR 52

Merriman, Alex
  See Silverberg, Robert
Merriman, Rachel 1971- *98*
Merrit, Elizabeth
  See Goudge, Eileen
Mertz, Barbara (Gross) 1927- *49*
Meschel, Susan V. 1936- *83*
Messenger, Charles (Rynd Milles)
  1942- *59*
Messick, Dale 1906- *64*
  Brief entry *48*
Messier, Claire 1956- *103*
Messieres, Nicole de
  See de Messieres, Nicole
Messmer, Otto 1892(?)-1983 ....*37*
Metcalf, Doris H(unter) *91*
Metcalf, Suzanne
  See Baum, L(yman) Frank
Metos, Thomas H(arry) 1932- *37*
Metter, Bert(ram Milton) 1927- *56*
Metzenthen, David 1958- *106*
Meyer, Barbara 1939- *77*
Meyer, Carolyn (Mae) 1935- *118*
  Earlier sketches in SATA *9, 70*
  See also SAAS *9*
Meyer, Edith Patterson 1895-1993 ....*5*
Meyer, F(ranklyn) E(dward) 1932- *9*
Meyer, Jean Shepherd *11*
Meyer, Jerome Sydney 1895-1975 ....*3*
  Obituary *25*
Meyer, June
  See Jordan, June (Meyer)
Meyer, Louis A(lbert) 1942- *12*
Meyer, Renate 1930- *6*
Meyer, Susan E. 1940- *64*
Meyers, Susan 1942- *108*
  Earlier sketch in SATA *19*
Meynier, Yvonne (Pollet) 1908- *14*
Mezey, Robert 1935- *33*
Micale, Albert 1913- *22*
Michael, James
  See Scagnetti, Jack
Michael, Manfred
  See Winterfeld, Henry
Michaels, Barbara
  See Mertz, Barbara (Gross)
Michaels, Joanne Louise
  See Teitelbaum, Michael
Michaels, Kristin
  See Williams, Jeanne
Michaels, Molly
  See Untermeyer, Louis
Michaels, Neal
  See Teitelbaum, Michael
Michaels, Ski
  See Pellowski, Michael (Joseph)
Michaels, Steve 1955- *71*
Michaels, William M. 1917- *77*
Michel, Anna 1943- *49*
  Brief entry *40*
Michel, Francois 1948- *82*
Micich, Paul *74*
Micklish, Rita 1931- *12*
Micklos, John J., Jr. 1956- *129*
Micucci, Charles (Patrick, Jr.) 1959- ..*82*
Middleton, Haydn 1955- *85*
Miers, Earl Schenck 1910-1972 ....*1*
  Obituary *26*
Migdale, Lawrence 1951- *89*
Mikaelsen, Ben(jamin John) 1952- *107*
  Earlier sketch in SATA *73*
Miklowitz, Gloria D. 1927- *129*
  Earlier sketches in SATA *4, 68*
  See also SAAS *17*
Mikolaycak, Charles 1937-1993 ....*78*
  Obituary *75*
  Earlier sketch in SATA *9*
  See also SAAS *4*
Mild, Warren (Paul) 1922- *41*
Milelli, Pascal 1965- *135*

Miles, Betty 1928- *78*
  Earlier sketch in SATA *8*
  See also SAAS *9*
Miles, Miska
  See Martin, Patricia Miles
Miles, (Mary) Patricia 1930- *29*
Miles, Patricia A.
  See Martin, Patricia Miles
Milgrom, Harry 1912-1978 ....*25*
Milhous, Katherine 1894-1977 ....*15*
Milios, Rita 1949- *79*
Militant
  See Sandburg, Carl (August)
Millais, Raoul 1901- *77*
Millar, Barbara F. 1924- *12*
Millar, Margaret (Ellis Sturm)
  1915-1994 ....*61*
  Obituary *79*
Millbank, Captain H. R.
  See Ellis, Edward S(ylvester)
Millen, C(ynthia) M. 1955- *114*
Miller, Albert G(riffith) 1905-1982 ....*12*
  Obituary *31*
Miller, Alice P(atricia McCarthy) *22*
Miller, Debbie (S.) 1951- *103*
Miller, Deborah Uchill 1944- *61*
Miller, Don 1923- *15*
Miller, Doris R.
  See Mosesson, Gloria R(ubin)
Miller, Eddie
  See Miller, Edward
Miller, Edna Anita 1920- *29*
Miller, Edward 1905-1974 ....*8*
Miller, Elizabeth 1933- *41*
Miller, Ellanita 1957- *87*
Miller, Eugene 1925- *33*
Miller, Frances A. 1937- *52*
  Brief entry *46*
Miller, Helen M(arkley) -1984 ....*5*
Miller, Jane (Judith) 1925-1989 ....*15*
Miller, Jewel 1956- *73*
Miller, John
  See Samachson, Joseph
Miller, Judi *117*
Miller, Louise (Rolfe) 1940- *76*
Miller, M. L. *85*
Miller, Madge 1918- *63*
Miller, Margaret J.
  See Dale, Margaret J(essy) Miller
Miller, Marilyn (Jean) 1925- *33*
Miller, Marvin *65*
Miller, Mary Beth 1942- *9*
Miller, Maryann 1943- *73*
Miller, Natalie 1917-1976 ....*35*
Miller, Robert H. 1944- *91*
Miller, Ruth White
  See White, Ruth (C.)
Miller, Sandy (Peden) *41*
  Brief entry *35*
  See Miller, Sandra (Peden)
Miller, Virginia
  See Austin, Virginia
Miller, William R. 1959- *116*
Milligan, Spike
  See Milligan, Terence Alan
Milligan, Terence Alan 1918-2002 ....*29*
  Obituary *134*
Millington, Ada
  See Deyneka, Anita
Millman, Isaac 1933- *140*
Mills, Adam
  See Stanley, George Edward
Mills, Claudia 1954- *89*
  Brief entry *41*
  Earlier sketch in SATA *44*
Mills, Elaine (Rosemary) 1941- *72*
Mills, Joyce C. 1944- *102*
Mills, Judith Christine 1956- *130*
Mills, Yaroslava Surmach 1925- *35*
Millspaugh, Ben P. 1936- *77*
Millstead, Thomas E. *30*

Milne, A(lan) A(lexander)
  1882-1956 ....*100*
  See also YABC *1*
  See also CLR *26*
Milne, Lorus J. *5*
  See also CLR *22*
  See also SAAS *18*
Milne, Margery *5*
  See also CLR *22*
  See also SAAS *18*
Milne, Terry
  See Milne, Theresa Ann
Milne, Theresa Ann 1964- *84*
Milnes, Irma McDonough 1924- *101*
Milonas, Rolf
  See Myller, Rolf
Milord, Susan 1954- *74*
Milotte, Alfred G(eorge) 1904-1989 .....*11*
  Obituary *62*
Milstein, Linda 1954- *80*
Milton, Ann *134*
Milton, Hilary (Herbert) 1920- *23*
Milton, John R(onald) 1924- *24*
Milton, Joyce 1946- *101*
  Brief entry *41*
  Earlier sketch in SATA *52*
Milverton, Charles A.
  See Penzler, Otto
Minahan, John A. 1956- *92*
Minar, Barbra (Goodyear) 1940- *79*
Minard, Rosemary 1939- *63*
Minarik, Else Holmelund 1920- *127*
  Earlier sketch in SATA *15*
  See also CLR *33*
Miner, Jane Claypool 1933- *38*
  Brief entry *37*
  See Claypool, Jane
Miner, Lewis S. 1909-1971 ....*11*
Mines, Jeanette (Marie) 1948- *61*
Minier, Nelson
  See Stoutenburg, Adrien (Pearl)
Minnitt, Ronda Jacqueline
  See Armitage, David
Minor, Wendell G. 1944- *109*
  Earlier sketch in SATA *78*
Mintonye, Grace *4*
Miranda, Anne 1954- *109*
  Earlier sketch in SATA *71*
Mirsky, Jeannette 1903-1987 ....*8*
  Obituary *51*
Mirsky, Reba Paeff 1902-1966 ....*1*
Mishica, Clare 1960- *91*
Miskovits, Christine 1939- *10*
Miss Frances
  See Horwich, Frances R(appaport)
Miss Read
  See Saint, Dora Jessie
Mister Rogers
  See Rogers, Fred McFeely
Mitchard, Jacquelyn 1953- *98*
Mitchell, Adrian 1932- *104*
Mitchell, Allison
  See Butterworth, W(illiam) E(dmund III)
Mitchell, B(etty) J(o) 1931- *120*
Mitchell, Clyde
  See Ellison, Harlan (Jay)
Mitchell, Cynthia 1922- *29*
Mitchell, (Sibyl) Elyne (Keith)
  1913- *10*
Mitchell, Gladys (Maude Winifred)
  1901-1983 ....*46*
  Obituary *35*
Mitchell, Jay
  See Roberson, Jennifer
Mitchell, Joyce Slayton 1933- *46*
  Brief entry *43*
Mitchell, K. L.
  See Lamb, Elizabeth Searle
Mitchell, Kathy 1948- *59*
Mitchell, Lori 1961- *128*
Mitchell, Margaree King 1953- *84*
Mitchell, Rhonda *89*

Mitchelson, Mitch
  See Mitchelson, Peter Richard
Mitchelson, Peter Richard 1950- *104*
Mitchison, Naomi Margaret (Haldane)
  1897-1999 ....*24*
  Obituary *112*
Mitchnik, Helen 1901-1982 ....*41*
  Brief entry *35*
Mitchum, Hank
  See Knott, William C(ecil, Jr.)
  and Murray, Stuart A. P.
  and Newton, D(wight) B(ennett)
  and Sherman, Jory (Tecumseh)
Mitgutsch, Ali 1935- *76*
Mitsuhashi, Yoko *45*
  Brief entry *33*
Mitton, Jacqueline 1948- *115*
  Earlier sketch in SATA 66
Mitton, Simon 1946- *66*
Mitton, Tony 1951- *104*
Mizner, Elizabeth Howard 1907- *27*
Mizumura, Kazue *18*
Mobley, Joe A. 1945- *91*
Moche, Dinah (Rachel) L(evine)
  1936- *44*
  Brief entry *40*
Mochi, Ugo (A.) 1889-1977 ....*38*
Mochizuki, Ken 1954- *81*
  See also SAAS 22
Modarressi, Mitra 1967- *126*
Modell, Frank B. 1917- *39*
  Brief entry *36*
Modesitt, Jeanne 1953- *92*
Modesitt, L(eland) E(xton), Jr. 1943- ...*91*
Modrell, Dolores 1933- *72*
Moe, Barbara 1937- *20*
Moerbeek, Kees 1955- *98*
Moeri, Louise 1924- *93*
  Earlier sketch in SATA 24
  See also SAAS 10
Moffett, Jami 1952- *84*
Moffett, Martha (Leatherwood) 1934- *8*
Mogensen, Suzanne A(ncher) 1946- *129*
Mohn, Peter B(urnet) 1934- *28*
Mohn, Viola Kohl 1914- *8*
Mohr, Nicholasa 1938- *97*
  Autobiography Feature *113*
  Earlier sketch in SATA 8
  See also CLR 22
  See also SAAS 8
Mok, Esther 1953- *93*
Molan, Christine 1943- *84*
Molarsky, Osmond 1909- *16*
Moldon, Peter L(eonard) 1937- *49*
Mole, John 1941- *103*
  Earlier sketch in SATA 36
  See also CLR 61
Molesworth, Mary Louisa 1839-1921 ......*98*
Molin, Charles
  See Mayne, William (James Carter)
Molina, Silvia 1946- *97*
Molk, Laurel 1957- *92*
Mollel, Tololwa M. 1952- *88*
Molloy, Anne Baker 1907-1999 ....*32*
Molloy, Paul (George) 1924- *5*
Moloney, James 1954- *94*
Momaday, N(avarre) Scott 1934- *48*
  Brief entry *30*
Monagle, Bernie 1957- *121*
Moncure, Jane Belk 1926- *23*
Monjo, F(erdinand) N(icholas III)
  1924-1978 ....*16*
  See also CLR 2
Monk, Isabell 1952- *136*
Monroe, Lyle
  See Heinlein, Robert A(nson)
Monsell, Helen Albee 1895-1971 ....*24*
Monson-Burton, Marianne 1975- *139*
Montenegro, Laura Nyman 1953- *95*
Montero, Gloria 1933- *109*
Montgomerie, Norah (Mary) 1913- *26*

Montgomery, Constance
  See Cappel, Constance
Montgomery, Elizabeth Rider *34*
  Obituary *41*
  Earlier sketch in SATA 3
  See Julesberg, Elizabeth Rider
  Montgomery
Montgomery, L(ucy) M(aud)
  1874-1942 ....*100*
  See also YABC 1
  See also CLR 8
Montgomery, Raymond A. (Jr.)
  1936- *39*
Montgomery, Rutherford George
  1894-1985 ....*3*
Montgomery, Sy 1958- *114*
  Autobiography Feature *132*
Montgomery, Vivian *36*
Montpetit, Charles 1958- *101*
Montresor, Beni 1926-2001 ....*38*
  Earlier sketch in SATA 3
  See also SAAS 4
Monty Python
  See Chapman, Graham
  and Cleese, John (Marwood)
  and Gilliam, Terry (Vance)
  and Idle, Eric
  and Jones, Terence Graham Parry
  and Palin, Michael (Edward)
Moodie, Fiona 1952- *133*
Moody, Minerva
  See Alcott, Louisa May
Moody, Ralph Owen 1898-1982 ....*1*
Moon, Carl 1879(?)-1948 ....*25*
Moon, Grace (Purdie) 1877(?)-1947 ....*25*
Moon, Lily
  See Warnes, Tim(othy)
Moon, Nicola 1952- *96*
Moon, Pat 1946- *113*
Moon, Sheila (Elizabeth) 1910-1991 ....*5*
  Obituary *114*
Mooney, Bel 1946- *95*
Mooney, Bill *122*
  See Mooney, William F.
Moor, Emily
  See Deming, Richard
Moorcock, Michael (John) 1939- *93*
  See Bradbury, Edward P.
Moore, Anne Carroll 1871-1961 ....*13*
Moore, Cheri
  See Ladd, Cheryl (Jean)
Moore, Clement Clarke 1779-1863 ....*18*
Moore, Cyd 1957- *133*
  Earlier sketch in SATA 83
Moore, Elaine 1944- *86*
Moore, Eva 1942- *103*
  Earlier sketch in SATA 20
Moore, Ishbel (Lindsay) 1954- *140*
Moore, Jack (William) 1941- *46*
  Brief entry *32*
Moore, Janet Gaylord 1905-1992 ....*18*
Moore, Jim 1946- *42*
Moore, John Travers 1908- *12*
Moore, Lilian 1909- *137*
  Earlier sketch in SATA 52
  See also CLR 15
Moore, Margaret R(umberger) 1903- *12*
Moore, Marianne (Craig) 1887-1972 ....*20*
Moore, Patrick (Alfred Caldwell)
  1923- *49*
  Brief entry *39*
  See also SAAS 8
Moore, Regina
  See Dunne, Mary Collins
Moore, Ruth (Ellen) 1908-1989 ....*23*
Moore, Ruth Nulton 1923- *38*
Moore, S(arah) E. *23*
Moore, Tara 1950- *61*
Moore, Yvette 1958- *70*
  Earlier sketch in SATA 69
Mooser, Stephen 1941- *75*
  Earlier sketch in SATA 28

Mora, Francisco X(avier) 1952- *90*
Mora, Pat(ricia) 1942- *134*
  Earlier sketch in SATA 92
  See also CLR 58
Moran, Tom 1943- *60*
Moray Williams, Ursula 1911- *73*
  See also SAAS 9
  See Williams, Ursula Moray
Mordvinoff, Nicolas 1911-1973 ....*17*
More, Caroline
  See Cone, Molly (Lamken)
  and Strachan, Margaret Pitcairn
Moreton, Andrew Esq.
  See Defoe, Daniel
Morey, Charles
  See Fletcher, Helen Jill
Morey, Walt(er Nelson) 1907-1992 ....*51*
  Obituary *70*
  Earlier sketch in SATA 3
  See also SAAS 9
Morgan, Alfred P(owell) 1889-1972 ....*33*
Morgan, Alison (Mary) 1930- *85*
  Earlier sketch in SATA 30
Morgan, Anne 1954- *121*
Morgan, Ellen
  See Bumstead, Kathleen Mary
Morgan, Geoffrey 1916- *46*
Morgan, Helen (Gertrude Louise)
  1921-1990 ....*29*
Morgan, Jane
  See Cooper, James Fenimore
  and Franklin, Jane (Morgan)
  and Moren, Sally M(oore)
Morgan, Lee
  See Meade, Marion
Morgan, Lenore H. 1908-1976 ....*8*
Morgan, Mary 1957- *114*
  Earlier sketch in SATA 81
Morgan, Nina 1953- *110*
Morgan, Pierr 1952- *122*
  Earlier sketch in SATA 77
Morgan, Robin (Evonne) 1941- *80*
Morgan, Sarah (Nicola) 1959- *68*
Morgan, Shirley *10*
  See Kiepper, Shirley Morgan
Morgan, Stacy T(owle) 1959- *104*
Morgan, Stevie
  See Davies, Nicola
Morgan, Tom 1942- *42*
Morgan, Wendy
  See Staub, Wendy Corsi
Morgenstern, Susie Hoch 1945- *133*
Mori, Hana 1909-1990(?) *88*
Mori, Kyoko 1957(?)- *122*
  Autobiography Feature *126*
  See also CLR 64
  See also SAAS 26
Moriarty, William J. 1930- *127*
Morice, Dave 1946- *93*
Morin, Isobel V. 1928- *110*
Morley, Wilfred Owen
  See Lowndes, Robert A(ugustine) W(ard)
Morningstar, Mildred (Whaley)
  1912-1997 ....*61*
  Obituary *114*
Morozumi, Atsuko *110*
Morpurgo, Michael 1943- *93*
  See also CLR 51
Morrah, Dave
  See Morrah, David Wardlaw, Jr.
Morrah, David Wardlaw, Jr.
  1914-1991 ....*10*
Morressy, John 1930- *23*
Morrill, Leslie H(olt) 1934- *48*
  Brief entry *33*
  See also SAAS 22
Morris, Chris(topher Crosby) 1946- *66*
Morris, Deborah 1956- *91*
Morris, Desmond (John) 1928- *14*
Morris, Don 1954- *83*
Morris, Gerald (Paul) 1963- *107*
Morris, Gilbert (Leslie) 1929- *104*

Morris, Janet (Ellen) 1946- 66
Morris, Jay
　　See Tatham, Julie Campbell
Morris, (Margaret) Jean 1924- 98
Morris, Jeffrey B(randon) 1941- 92
Morris, Jill 1936- 119
Morris, Juddi 85
Morris, Judy K. 1936- 61
Morris, Oradel Nolen 128
Morris, Robert A(da) 1933- 7
Morris, William 1913-1994 29
Morrison, Bill 1935- 66
　　Brief entry 37
Morrison, Dorothy Nafus 29
Morrison, Gordon 1944- 128
　　Earlier sketch in SATA 87
Morrison, Joan 1922- 65
Morrison, Lillian 1917- 108
　　Earlier sketch in SATA 3
Morrison, Lucile Phillips 1896- 17
Morrison, Martha A. 1948- 77
Morrison, Meighan 1966- 90
Morrison, Richard
　　See Lowndes, Robert A(ugustine) W(ard)
Morrison, Robert
　　See Lowndes, Robert A(ugustine) W(ard)
Morrison, Roberta
　　See Webb, Jean Francis (III)
Morrison, Taylor 1971- 95
Morrison, Toni 1931- 57
Morrison, Velma Ford 1909- 21
Morrison, Wilbur Howard 1915- 64
Morrison, William
　　See Samachson, Joseph
Morriss, James E(dward) 1932- 8
Morrow, Betty
　　See Bacon, Elizabeth
Morse, Carol
　　See Yeakley, Marjory Hall
Morse, Flo 1921- 30
Morse, Tony 1953- 129
Mort, Vivian
　　See Cromie, Alice Hamilton
Mortimer, Anne 1958- 116
Morton, Anthony
　　See Arthur, Robert, (Jr.)
Morton, Jane 1931- 50
Morton, Lee Jack, Jr. 1928- 32
Morton, Miriam 1918(?)-1985 9
　　Obituary 46
Mosatche, Harriet (S.) 1949- 122
Moscow, Alvin 1925- 3
Mosel, Arlene (Tichy) 1921-1996 7
Moseley, James W(illett) 1931- 139
Moseng, Elisabeth 1967- 90
Moser, Barry (A.) 1940- 138
　　Earlier sketches in SATA 56, 79
　　See also CLR 49
　　See also SAAS 15
Moser, Don(ald Bruce) 1932- 31
Moses, Will 1956- 120
Mosesson, Gloria R(ubin) 24
Mosher, Richard 1949- 120
Moskin, Marietta D(unston) 1928- 23
Moskof, Martin Stephen 1930- 27
Mosley, Francis 1957- 57
Moss, Don(ald) 1920- 11
Moss, Elaine (Dora) 1924- 57
　　Brief entry 31
Moss, Jeff(rey) 1942-1998 73
　　Obituary 106
Moss, Marissa 1959- 104
　　Earlier sketch in SATA 71
Moss, Miriam 1955- 140
　　Earlier sketch in SATA 76
Moss, Thylias (Rebecca Brasier)
　　1954- 108
Most, Bernard 1937- 134
　　Brief entry 40
　　Earlier sketches in SATA 48, 91
Mott, Evelyn Clarke 1962- 133
　　Earlier sketch in SATA 75

Motz, Lloyd 1909- 20
Mould, Edwin
　　See Whitlock, Ralph
Mountain, Robert
　　See Montgomery, Raymond A. (Jr.)
Mountfield, David
　　See Grant, Neil
Moussard, Jacqueline 1924- 24
Mowat, Claire (Angel Wheeler)
　　1933- 123
Mowat, Farley (McGill) 1921- 55
　　Earlier sketch in SATA 3
　　See also CLR 20
Mowry, Jess 1960- 109
　　Autobiography Feature 131
　　See also CLR 65
Moxley, Sheila 1966- 96
Moyer, Terry J. 1937- 94
Moyes, Patricia 63
　　See Haszard, Patricia Moyes
Moyler, Alan (Frank Powell) 1926- 36
Mozley, Charles 1915- 43
　　Brief entry 32
Mphahlele, Es'kia
　　See Mphahlele, Ezekiel
Mphahlele, Ezekiel 1919- 119
　　See Mphahlele, Es'kia
Mr. McGillicuddy
　　See Abisch, Roslyn Kroop
Mr. Sniff
　　See Abisch, Roslyn Kroop
Mr. Tivil
　　See Lorkowski, Thomas V(incent)
Mr. Wizard
　　See Herbert, Don(ald Jeffrey)
Mrs. Fairstar
　　See Horne, Richard Henry
Muchmore, Jo Ann 1937- 103
Mude, O.
　　See Gorey, Edward (St. John)
Mudgeon, Apeman
　　See Mitchell, Adrian
Mueller, Jorg 1942- 67
　　See also CLR 43
Mueller, Virginia 1924- 28
Muggs
　　See Watkins, Lois
Muir, Diana
　　See Appelbaum, Diana Muir Karter
Muir, Frank (Herbert) 1920-1998 30
Muir, Helen 1937- 65
Mukerji, Dhan Gopal 1890-1936 40
　　See also CLR 10
Mulcahy, Lucille Burnett 12
Mulford, Philippa G(reene) 1948- 112
　　Earlier sketch in SATA 43
Mulila, Vigad G.
　　See Maillu, David G(ian)
Mullen, Michael 1937- 122
Muller, Billex
　　See Ellis, Edward S(ylvester)
Muller, Jorg
　　See Mueller, Jorg
Muller, (Lester) Robin 1953- 86
Mullin, Caryl Cude 1969- 130
Mullins, Edward S(wift) 1922- 10
Mullins, Hilary 1962- 84
Mulock, Dinah Maria
　　See Craik, Dinah Maria (Mulock)
Mulvihill, William Patrick 1923- 8
Mumford, Ruth 1919- 86
Mumy, Bill 1954- 112
Mun
　　See Leaf, (Wilbur) Munro
Munari, Bruno 1907-1998 15
　　See also CLR 9
Munce, Ruth Hill 1898- 12
Mundy, Simon (Andrew James Hainault)
　　1954- 64
Munowitz, Ken 1935-1977 14
Munoz, William 1949- 92
　　Earlier sketch in SATA 42

Munro, Alice 1931- 29
Munro, Eleanor 1928- 37
Munro, Roxie 1945- 136
　　Earlier sketch in SATA 58
Munsch, Bob
　　See Munsch, Robert (Norman)
Munsch, Robert (Norman) 1945- 120
　　Brief entry 48
　　Earlier sketches in SATA 50, 83
　　See also CLR 19
Munsinger, Lynn 1951- 94
　　Earlier sketch in SATA 33
Munson, Derek 139
Munson, R. W.
　　See Karl, Jean E(dna)
Munson-Benson, Tunie 1946- 15
Munsterberg, Peggy 1921- 102
Munthe, Nelly 1947- 53
Munves, James (Albert) 1922- 30
Munzer, Martha E. 1899-1999 4
Murch, Mel
　　See Manes, Stephen
Murdoch, David H(amilton) 1937- 96
Murphy, Barbara Beasley 1933- 130
　　Earlier sketch in SATA 5
Murphy, Claire Rudolf 1951- 137
　　Earlier sketch in SATA 76
Murphy, E(mmett) Jefferson 1926- 4
Murphy, Jill (Frances) 1949- 70
　　Earlier sketch in SATA 37
　　See also CLR 39
Murphy, Jim 1947- 124
　　Brief entry 32
　　Earlier sketches in SATA 37, 77
　　See also CLR 53
Murphy, Joseph E., Jr. 1930- 65
Murphy, Pat
　　See Murphy, E(mmett) Jefferson
Murphy, Patricia J. 1963- 132
Murphy, Robert (William)
　　1902-1971 10
Murphy, Shirley Rousseau 1928- 126
　　Earlier sketches in SATA 36, 71
　　See also SAAS 18
Murphy, Stuart J. 1942- 115
Murphy, Tim
　　See Murphy, Jim
Murray, John 1923- 39
Murray, Kirsty 1960- 108
Murray, Marguerite 1917- 63
Murray, Marian 5
Murray, Martine 1965- 125
Murray, (Judith) Michele (Freedman)
　　1933-1974 7
Murray, Ossie 1938- 43
Murrow, Liza Ketchum 1946- 78
　　See Ketchum, Liza
Musgrave, Florence 1902-1999 3
Musgrove, Margaret W(ynkoop)
　　1943- 124
　　Earlier sketch in SATA 26
Mussey, Virginia Howell
　　See Ellison, Virginia H(owell)
Mussey, Virginia T.H.
　　See Ellison, Virginia H(owell)
Mutel, Cornelia F. 1947- 74
Mutz
　　See Kuenstler, Morton
My Brother's Brother
　　See Chekhov, Anton (Pavlovich)
Myers, Arthur 1917- 91
　　Earlier sketch in SATA 35
Myers, Arthur 1917- 91
　　Earlier sketch in SATA 35
Myers, Bernice 81
　　Earlier sketch in SATA 9
Myers, Caroline Elizabeth Clark
　　1887-1980 28
Myers, Edward 1950- 96
Myers, Elisabeth P(erkins) 1918- 36
Myers, (Mary) Hortense (Powner)
　　1913-1987 10

Author Index

Myers, Jack 1913- *83*
Myers, Lou(is) 1915- *81*
Myers, R(obert) E(ugene) 1924- *119*
Myers, Walter Dean 1937- *109*
  Brief entry *27*
  Earlier sketches in SATA *41, 71*
  See also CLR *35*
  See also SAAS *2*
Myers, Walter M.
  See Myers, Walter Dean
Myller, Rolf 1926- *27*
Myra, Harold L(awrence) 1939- *46*
  Brief entry *42*
Myrus, Donald (Richard) 1927- *23*
Mysterious Traveler, The
  See Arthur, Robert, (Jr.)

N

Nadel, Laurie 1948- *74*
Naden, Corinne J. 1930- *79*
Nagel, Andreas Fischer
  See Fischer-Nagel, Andreas
Nagel, Heiderose Fischer
  See Fischer-Nagel, Heiderose
Naidoo, Beverley 1943- *135*
  Earlier sketch in SATA *63*
  See also CLR *29*
Nakae, Noriko 1940- *59*
Nakatani, Chiyoko 1930-1981 ....*55*
  Brief entry *40*
  See also CLR *30*
Nally, Susan W. 1947- *90*
Namioka, Lensey 1929- *89*
  Autobiography Feature *116*
  Earlier sketch in SATA *27*
  See also CLR *48*
  See also SAAS *24*
Nanji, Shenaaz 1954- *131*
Nanogak Agnes 1925- *61*
Napier, Mark
  See Laffin, John (Alfred Charles)
Napoli, Donna Jo 1948- *137*
  Earlier sketch in SATA *92*
  See also CLR *51*
  See also SAAS *23*
Narahashi, Keiko 1959- *115*
  Earlier sketch in SATA *79*
Narayan, R(asipuram) K(rishnaswami)
  1906-2001 ....*62*
Nascimbene, Yan 1949- *133*
Nash, Bruce M(itchell) 1947- *34*
Nash, Linell
  See Smith, Linell Nash
Nash, Mary (Hughes) 1925- *41*
Nash, (Frediric) Ogden 1902-1971 ....*46*
  Earlier sketch in SATA *2*
Nash, Renea Denise 1963- *81*
Nast, Elsa Ruth
  See Watson, Jane Werner
Nast, Thomas 1840-1902 ....*51*
  Brief entry *33*
Nastick, Sharon 1954- *41*
Nathan, Amy *104*
Nathan, Dorothy (Goldeen) (?)-1966 ....*15*
Nathan, Robert (Gruntal) 1894-1985 ....*6*
  Obituary *43*
Nathanson, Laura Walther 1941- *57*
Natti, Susanna 1948- *125*
  Earlier sketch in SATA *32*
Naughton, Bill
  See Naughton, William John (Francis)
Naughton, James Franklin 1957- *85*
Naughton, Jim
  See Naughton, James Franklin
Naughton, William John (Francis)
  1910-1992 ....*86*
Navarra, John Gabriel 1927- *8*
Naylor, Penelope 1941- *10*

Naylor, Phyllis 1933-
  See Naylor, Phyllis Reynolds
Naylor, Phyllis Reynolds 1933- *102*
  Earlier sketches in SATA *12, 66*
  See also CLR *17*
  See also SAAS *10*
  See Naylor, Phyllis
Nazarian, Nikki
  See Nichols, Cecilia Fawn
Nazaroff, Alexander I(vanovich)
  1898-1981 ....*4*
Neal, Harry Edward 1906-1993 ....*5*
  Obituary *76*
Neal, Michael
  See Teitelbaum, Michael
Nearing, Penny 1916- *47*
  Brief entry *42*
Nebel, Gustave E. *45*
  Brief entry *33*
Nebel, Mimouca
  See Nebel, Gustave E.
Nee, Kay Bonner *10*
Needham, Kate 1962- *95*
Needle, Jan 1943- *98*
  Earlier sketch in SATA *30*
  See also CLR *43*
  See also SAAS *23*
Needleman, Jacob 1934- *6*
Neel, David 1960- *82*
Neel, Preston 1959- *93*
Negri, Rocco 1932- *12*
Neier, Aryeh 1937- *59*
Neigoff, Anne *13*
Neigoff, Mike 1920- *13*
Neilson, Frances Fullerton (Jones)
  1910-2001 ....*14*
Neimark, Anne E. 1935- *4*
Neimark, Paul G. 1934- *80*
  Brief entry *37*
Neitzel, Shirley 1941- *134*
  Earlier sketch in SATA *77*
Nell
  See Hanna, Nell(ie L.)
Nelson, Catherine Chadwick 1926- *87*
Nelson, Cordner (Bruce) 1918- *54*
  Brief entry *29*
Nelson, Drew 1952- *77*
Nelson, Esther L. 1928- *13*
Nelson, Jim A.
  See Stotter, Mike
Nelson, Julie L. 1970- *117*
Nelson, Mary Carroll 1929- *23*
Nelson, O. Terry 1941- *62*
Nelson, Peter N. 1953- *73*
Nelson, Richard K(ing) 1941- *65*
Nelson, Robin Laura 1971- *141*
Nelson, Roy Paul 1923- *59*
Nelson, Sharlene (P.) 1933- *96*
Nelson, Ted (W.) 1931- *96*
Nelson, Theresa 1948- *79*
Nerlove, Miriam 1959- *53*
  Brief entry *49*
Nesbit, E(dith) 1858-1924 ....*100*
  See also YABC *1*
  See also CLR *70*
  See Bland, Edith Nesbit
Nesbit, Troy
  See Folsom, Franklin (Brewster)
Nespojohn, Katherine V(eronica)
  1912-1975 ....*7*
Ness, Evaline (Michelow) 1911-1986 ......*26*
  Obituary *49*
  Earlier sketch in SATA *1*
  See also CLR *6*
  See also SAAS *1*
Nestor, William P(rodromos) 1947- *49*
Nethery, Mary *93*
Neuberger, Julia 1950- *78*

Neufeld, John (Arthur) 1938- *81*
  Autobiography Feature *131*
  Earlier sketch in SATA *6*
  See also CLR *52*
  See also SAAS *3*
Neuhaus, David 1958- *83*
Neumeyer, Peter F(lorian) 1929- *13*
Neurath, Marie (Reidemeister)
  1898-1986 ....*1*
Neuschwander, Cindy 1953- *107*
Neusner, Jacob 1932- *38*
Neville, Charles
  See Bodsworth, (Charles) Fred(erick)
Neville, Emily Cheney 1919- *1*
  See also SAAS *2*
Neville, Mary
  See Woodrich, Mary Neville
Nevins, Albert (Francis) J(erome)
  1915-1997 ....*20*
Newberger, Devra
  See Speregen, Devra Newberger
Newberry, Clare Turlay 1903-1970 ....*1*
  Obituary *26*
Newbery, John 1713-1767 ....*20*
Newcombe, Jack *45*
  Brief entry *33*
  See Newcombe, Eugene A.
Newcome, Robert 1955- *91*
Newcome, Zita 1959- *88*
Newell, Crosby
  See Bonsall, Crosby Barbara (Newell)
Newell, Edythe W(eatherford)
  1910-1989 ....*11*
Newell, Hope Hockenberry
  1896-1965 ....*24*
Newfeld, Frank 1928- *26*
Newlon, (Frank) Clarke 1905(?)-1982 ......*6*
  Obituary *33*
Newman, Daisy 1904-1994 ....*27*
  Obituary *78*
Newman, Gerald 1939- *46*
  Brief entry *42*
Newman, Jerry 1935- *82*
Newman, Leslea 1955- *134*
  Earlier sketches in SATA *71, 128*
Newman, Margaret
  See Potter, Margaret (Newman)
Newman, Matthew (Harrison) 1955- *56*
Newman, Robert (Howard)
  1909-1988 ....*87*
  Obituary *60*
  Earlier sketch in SATA *4*
Newman, Shirlee P(etkin) *90*
  Earlier sketch in SATA *10*
Newsom, Carol 1948- *92*
  Earlier sketch in SATA *40*
Newsom, Tom 1944- *80*
Newth, Mette 1942- *140*
Newton, David E(dward) 1933- *67*
Newton, James R(obert) 1935- *23*
Newton, Suzanne 1936- *77*
  Earlier sketch in SATA *5*
Ney, John 1923- *43*
  Brief entry *33*
Ng, Franklin *82*
Nichol, B(arrie) P(hillip) 1944-1988 ....*66*
Nicholas, Louise D.
  See Watkins, Dawn L.
Nicholls, Judith (Ann) 1941- *61*
Nichols, Cecilia Fawn 1906-1987 ....*12*
Nichols, Grace 1950- *98*
Nichols, Janet (Louise) 1952- *67*
Nichols, Judy 1947- *124*
Nichols, Leigh
  See Koontz, Dean R(ay)
Nichols, Paul
  See Hawks, Robert
Nichols, Peter
  See Youd, (Christopher) Samuel
Nichols, (Joanna) Ruth 1948- *15*
Nicholson, C. R.
  See Nicole, Christopher (Robin)

Nicholson, Christina
  See Nicole, Christopher (Robin)
Nicholson, Joyce Thorpe 1919- *35*
Nicholson, Lois P. 1949- *88*
Nicholson, Robin
  See Nicole, Christopher (Robin)
Nicholson, William 1872-1949
  See CLR 76
Nickell, Joe 1944- *73*
Nickelsburg, Janet 1893-1983 ....*11*
Nickerson, Elizabeth *14*
  See Nickerson, Betty
Nickl, Barbara (Elisabeth) 1939- *56*
  See Schroeder, Binette
Nicklaus, Carol *62*
  Brief entry *33*
Nickless, Will 1902-1979(?) *66*
Nic Leodhas, Sorche
  See Alger, Leclaire (Gowans)
Nicol, Ann
  See Turnbull, Ann (Christine)
Nicolas
  See Mordvinoff, Nicolas
Nicolay, Helen 1866-1954
  See YABC 1
Nicole, Christopher (Robin) 1930- *5*
Nicoll, Helen 1937- *87*
Nicolson, Cynthia Pratt 1949- *141*
Ni Dhuibhne, Eilis 1954- *91*
Nielsen, Kay (Rasmus) 1886-1957 ....*16*
  See also CLR 16
Nielsen, Laura F(arnsworth) 1960- *93*
Nielsen, Nancy J. 1951- *77*
Nielsen, Virginia
  See McCall, Virginia Nielsen
Nightingale, Sandy 1953- *76*
Nikolajeva, Maria 1952- *127*
Nikola-Lisa, W. 1951- *71*
Niland, Deborah 1951- *27*
Niland, Kilmeny *75*
Nilsen, Anna
  See Bassil, Andrea
Nilsson, Eleanor 1939- *117*
  Earlier sketch in SATA *81*
  See also SAAS 23
Nimmo, Jenny 1942- *87*
  See also CLR 44
Niven, Larry
  See Niven, Laurence Van Cott
Niven, Laurence Van Cott 1938- *95*
  See Niven, Larry
Nivola, Claire A. 1947- *140*
  Earlier sketch in SATA *84*
Nix, Garth 1963- *97*
  See also CLR 68
Nixon, Hershell Howard 1923- *42*
Nixon, Joan Lowery 1927-2003 ....*115*
  Earlier sketches in SATA *8, 44, 78*
  See also CLR 24
  See also SAAS 9
Nixon, K.
  See Nixon, Kathleen Irene (Blundell)
Nixon, Kathleen Irene (Blundell)
  1894-1988(?) *14*
  Obituary *59*
Nobisso, Josephine 1953- *121*
  Earlier sketch in SATA *78*
Noble, Iris (Davis) 1922-1986 ....*5*
  Obituary *49*
Noble, Marty 1947- *125*
  Earlier sketch in SATA *97*
Noble, Trinka Hakes *123*
  Brief entry *37*
Nodelman, Perry 1942- *101*
Nodset, Joan L.
  See Lexau, Joan M.
Noel Hume, Ivor 1927- *65*
Noestlinger, Christine 1936- *64*
  Brief entry *37*
  See also CLR 12
  See Nostlinger, Christine
Noguere, Suzanne 1947- *34*

Nolan, Dennis 1945- *92*
  Brief entry *34*
  Earlier sketch in SATA *42*
Nolan, Han 1956- *109*
Nolan, Jeannette Covert 1897-1974 ....*2*
  Obituary *27*
Nolan, Paul T(homas) 1919- *48*
Nolan, William F(rancis) 1928- *88*
  Brief entry *28*
Nolen, Jerdine 1953- *105*
Noll, Sally 1946- *82*
Noonan, Julia 1946- *95*
  Earlier sketch in SATA *4*
Nordan, Robert 1934- *133*
Nordhoff, Charles Bernard
  1887-1947 ....*23*
Nordlicht, Lillian *29*
Nordstrom, Ursula 1910-1988 ....*3*
  Obituary *57*
Nordtvedt, Matilda 1926- *67*
Norman, Charles 1904-1996 ....*38*
  Obituary *92*
Norman, Howard
  See Norman, Howard A.
Norman, Howard A. 1949- *81*
Norman, James
  See Schmidt, James Norman
Norman, Jay
  See Arthur, Robert, (Jr.)
Norman, Lilith 1927- *120*
  Earlier sketch in SATA *86*
Norman, Mary 1931- *36*
Norman, Steve
  See Pashko, Stanley
Norment, Lisa 1966- *91*
Norris, Gunilla Brodde 1939- *20*
North, Andrew
  See Norton, Andre
North, Anthony
  See Koontz, Dean R(ay)
North, Captain George
  See Stevenson, Robert Louis (Balfour)
North, Captain George
  See Stevenson, Robert Louis (Balfour)
North, Howard
  See Trevor, Elleston
North, Joan 1920- *16*
North, Milou
  See Erdrich, Louise
North, Robert
  See Withers, Carl A.
North, Sara
  See Bonham, Barbara Thomas
  and Hager, Jean
North, Sterling 1906-1974 ....*45*
  Obituary *26*
  Earlier sketch in SATA *1*
Northeast, Brenda V(ictoria) 1948- *106*
Northmore, Elizabeth Florence
  1906-1974 ....*122*
Norton, Alice Mary *43*
  Earlier sketch in SATA *1*
  See Norton, Andre
Norton, Andre 1912- *91*
  See also CLR 50
  See Norton, Alice Mary
Norton, Browning
  See Norton, Frank R. B(rowning)
Norton, Frank R. B(rowning)
  1909-1989 ....*10*
Norton, Mary 1903-1992 ....*60*
  Obituary *72*
  Earlier sketch in SATA *18*
  See also CLR 6
Nosredna, Trebor
  See Anderson, Bob
Nostlinger, Christine
  See Noestlinger, Christine
Nourse, Alan E(dward) 1928-1992 ....*48*
  See also CLR 33

Novak, Matt 1962- *104*
  Brief entry *52*
  Earlier sketch in SATA *60*
Novelli, Luca 1947- *61*
Nowell, Elizabeth Cameron *12*
Nugent, Nicholas 1949- *73*
Numeroff, Laura Joffe 1953- *90*
  Earlier sketch in SATA *28*
  See also CLR 85
Nunes, Lygia Bojunga 1932- *75*
Nunn, Laura (Donna) Silverstein
  1968- *124*
Nurnberg, Maxwell 1897-1984 ....*27*
  Obituary *41*
Nussbaumer, Paul (Edmund) 1934- *16*
Nutt, Ken 1951- *97*
Nuygen, Mathieu 1967- *80*
Nyberg, (Everett Wayne) Morgan
  1944- *87*
Nyce, (Nellie) Helene von Strecker
  1885-1969 ....*19*
Nyce, Vera 1862-1925 ....*19*
Nye, Naomi Shihab 1952- *86*
  See also CLR 59
Nye, Robert 1939- *6*
Nystrom, Carolyn 1940- *130*
  Earlier sketch in SATA *67*

O

Oakes, Elizabeth H. 1964- *132*
Oakes, Vanya 1909-1983 ....*6*
  Obituary *37*
Oakley, Don(ald G.) 1927- *8*
Oakley, Graham 1929- *84*
  Earlier sketch in SATA *30*
  See also CLR 7
Oakley, Helen (McKelvey) 1906- *10*
Oana, Katherine 1929- *53*
  Brief entry *37*
Oates, Eddie H. 1943- *88*
Oates, Stephen B(aery) 1936- *59*
Obed, Ellen Bryan 1944- *74*
Oberle, Joseph 1958- *69*
Oberman, Sheldon 1949- *85*
  Autobiography Feature *114*
  See also CLR 54
  See also SAAS 26
Obligado, Lilian (Isabel) 1931- *61*
  Brief entry *45*
Obrant, Susan 1946- *11*
O'Brian, E. G.
  See Clarke, Arthur C(harles)
O'Brien, Anne Sibley 1952- *80*
  Brief entry *48*
  Earlier sketch in SATA *53*
O'Brien, Robert C.
  See CLR 2
  See Conly, Robert Leslie
O'Brien, Thomas C(lement) 1938- *29*
O'Callaghan, Julie 1954- *113*
O'Callahan, Jay 1938- *88*
O'Carroll, Ryan
  See Markun, Patricia Maloney
Ochiltree, Dianne 1953- *117*
Ockham, Joan Price
  See Price, Joan
O'Connell, Margaret F(orster)
  1935-1977 ....*30*
  Obituary *30*
O'Connell, Peg
  See Ahern, Margaret McCrohan
O'Connell, Rebecca 1968- *130*
O'Connor, Francine M(arie) 1930- *90*
O'Connor, Genevieve A. 1914- *75*
O'Connor, Jane 1947- *103*
  Brief entry *47*
  Earlier sketch in SATA *59*
O'Connor, Karen 1938- *89*
  Earlier sketch in SATA *34*

O'Connor, Patrick
  See Wibberley, Leonard (Patrick
  O'Connor)
O'Conor, Jane 1958- 78
Odaga, Asenath (Bole) 1937- 130
  Earlier sketch in SATA 67
  See also SAAS 19
O Danachair, Caoimhin
  See Danaher, Kevin
O'Daniel, Janet 1921- 24
O'Day, Cathy
  See Crane, Barbara (Joyce)
O'Dell, Scott 1898-1989 134
  Earlier sketches in SATA 12, 60
  See also CLR 16
Odenwald, Robert P(aul) 1899-1965 11
Odgers, Sally
  See Odgers, Sally Farrell
Odgers, Sally Farrell 1957- 139
  Earlier sketch in SATA 72
O'Donnell, Dick
  See Lupoff, Richard A(llen)
  and Thompson, Don(ald Arthur)
Oechsli, Kelly 1918-1999 5
Oesterle, Virginia Rorby
  See Rorby, Ginny
Ofek, Uriel 1926- 36
  See also CLR 28
Offenbacher, Ami 1958- 91
Offit, Sidney 1928- 10
Ofosu-Appiah, L(awrence) H(enry)
  1920- 13
Ogan, George F. 1912-1983 13
Ogan, M. G.
  See Ogan, George F.
  and Ogan, Margaret E. (Nettles)
Ogan, Margaret E. (Nettles)
  1923-1979 13
Ogburn, Charlton (Jr.) 1911-1998 3
  Obituary 109
Ogilvie, Elisabeth May 1917- 40
  Brief entry 29
Ogilvy, Gavin
  See Barrie, J(ames) M(atthew)
O'Green, Jennifer
  See Roberson, Jennifer
O'Green, Jennifer Roberson
  See Roberson, Jennifer
O'Hagan, Caroline 1946- 38
O'Hanlon, Jacklyn
  See Meek, Jacklyn O'Hanlon
O'Hara, Elizabeth
  See Ni Dhuibhne, Eilis
O'Hara, Kenneth
  See Morris, (Margaret) Jean
O'Hara, Mary
  See Alsop, Mary O'Hara
O'Hara (Alsop), Mary
  See Alsop, Mary O'Hara
O'Hare, Jeff(rey A.) 1958- 105
Ohi, Ruth 1964- 95
Ohiyesa
  See Eastman, Charles A(lexander)
Ohlsson, Ib 1935- 7
Ohmi, Ayano 1959- 115
Ohtomo, Yasuo 1946- 37
o huigin, sean 1942- 138
  See also CLR 75
Oiseau
  See Moseley, James W(illett)
Oke, Janette 1935- 97
O'Keefe, Susan Heyboer 133
O'Keeffe, Frank 1938- 99
O'Kelley, Mattie Lou 1908-1997 97
  Earlier sketch in SATA 36
Okimoto, Jean Davies 1942- 103
  Earlier sketch in SATA 34
Okomfo, Amasewa
  See Cousins, Linda
Olaleye, Isaac O. 1941- 96
  See also SAAS 23
Olcott, Frances Jenkins 1872(?)-1963 19

Old Boy
  See Hughes, Thomas
Oldenburg, E(gbert) William
  1936-1974 35
Older, Effin 1942- 114
Older, Jules 1940- 114
Oldfield, Jenny 1949- 140
Oldfield, Margaret J(ean) 1932- 56
Oldfield, Pamela 1931- 86
Oldham, June 70
Oldham, Mary 1944- 65
Olds, Elizabeth 1896-1991 3
  Obituary 66
Olds, Helen Diehl 1895-1981 9
  Obituary 25
Oldstyle, Jonathan
  See Irving, Washington
O'Leary, Brian (Todd) 1940- 6
O'Leary, Patsy B(aker) 1937- 97
Oliphant, B. J.
  See Tepper, Sheri S.
Oliver, Burton
  See Burt, Olive Woolley
Oliver, Chad
  See Oliver, Symmes C(hadwick)
Oliver, John Edward 1933- 21
Oliver, Marilyn Tower 1935- 89
Oliver, Shirley (Louise Dawkins)
  1958- 74
Oliver, Symmes C(hadwick)
  1928-1993 101
  See Oliver, Chad
Oliviero, Jamie 1950- 84
Olmsted, Lorena Ann 1890-1989 13
Olney, Ross R. 1929- 13
Olschewski, Alfred (Erich) 1920- 7
Olsen, Carol 1945- 89
Olsen, Ib Spang 1921- 81
  Earlier sketch in SATA 6
Olsen, Violet (Mae) 1922-1991 58
Olson, Arielle North 1932- 67
Olson, Gene 1922- 32
Olson, Helen Kronberg 48
Olugebefola, Ademole 1941- 15
Oluonye, Mary N(kechi) 1955- 111
Om
  See Gorey, Edward (St. John)
Oman, Carola (Mary Anima)
  1897-1978 35
O'Meara, Walter (Andrew)
  1897-1989 65
Ommanney, F(rancis) D(ownes)
  1903-1980 23
O Mude
  See Gorey, Edward (St. John)
Oneal, Elizabeth 1934- 82
  Earlier sketch in SATA 30
  See Oneal, Zibby
O'Neal, Reagan
  See Rigney, James Oliver, Jr.
Oneal, Zibby
  See CLR 13
  See Oneal, Elizabeth
O'Neill, Amanda 1951- 111
O'Neill, Gerard K(itchen) 1927-1992 65
O'Neill, Judith (Beatrice) 1930- 34
O'Neill, Mary L(e Duc) 1908(?)-1990 2
  Obituary 64
Onslow, Annette Rosemary MacArthur
  See MacArthur-Onslow, Annette Rosemary
Onyefulu, Ifeoma 1959- 115
  Earlier sketch in SATA 81
Opie, Iona (Margaret Balfour)
  1923- 118
  Earlier sketches in SATA 3, 63
  See also SAAS 6
Opie, Peter (Mason) 1918-1982 118
  Obituary 28
  Earlier sketches in SATA 3, 63
Oppel, Kenneth 1967- 99
Oppenheim, Joanne 1934- 136
  Earlier sketches in SATA 5, 82

Oppenheimer, Joan L(etson) 1925- 28
Optic, Oliver
  See Adams, William Taylor
  and Stratemeyer, Edward L.
Oram, Hiawyn 1946- 101
  Earlier sketch in SATA 56
Orbach, Ruth Gary 1941- 21
Orczy, Emma
  See Orczy, Baroness Emmuska
Orczy, Emma Magdalena Rosalia Maria
  Josefa
  See Orczy, Baroness Emmuska
Orczy, Emmuska
  See Orczy, Baroness Emmuska
Orczy, Baroness Emmuska
  1865-1947 40
  See Orczy, Emma
Orde, A. J.
  See Tepper, Sheri S.
O'Reilly, Jackson
  See Rigney, James Oliver, Jr.
Orgel, Doris 1929- 85
  Earlier sketch in SATA 7
  See also CLR 48
  See also SAAS 19
Orleans, Ilo 1897-1962 10
Orlev, Uri 1931- 135
  Earlier sketch in SATA 58
  See also CLR 30
  See also SAAS 19
Ormai, Stella 57
  Brief entry 48
Ormerod, Jan(ette Louise) 1946- 132
  Brief entry 44
  Earlier sketches in SATA 55, 70
  See also CLR 20
Ormondroyd, Edward 1925- 14
Ormsby, Virginia H(aire) 1906-1990 11
Orr, Katherine S(helley) 1950- 72
Orr, Wendy 1953- 141
  Earlier sketch in SATA 90
Orris
  See Ingelow, Jean
Orth, Richard
  See Gardner, Richard (M.)
Ortiz Cofer, Judith
  See Cofer, Judith Ortiz
Orwell, George
  See CLR 68
  See Blair, Eric (Arthur)
Orwin, Joanna 1944- 141
Osborn, Lois D(orothy) 1915- 61
Osborne, Charles 1927- 59
Osborne, Chester G(orham)
  1915-1987 11
Osborne, David
  See Silverberg, Robert
Osborne, George
  See Silverberg, Robert
Osborne, Leone Neal 1914- 2
Osborne, Mary Pope 1949- 98
  Earlier sketches in SATA 41, 55
  See also CLR 88
Osceola
  See Blixen, Karen (Christentze Dinesen)
Osgood, William E(dward) 1926- 37
O'Shaughnessy, Darren 1972- 129
  See Shan, Darren
O'Shaughnessy, Ellen Cassels 1937- 78
O'Shea, (Catherine) Pat(ricia Shiels)
  1931- 87
  See also CLR 18
Osmond, Edward 1900- 10
Ossoli, Sarah Margaret (Fuller)
  1810-1850 25
  See Fuller, Margaret
  and Fuller, Sarah Margaret
Ostendorf, (Arthur) Lloyd, (Jr.)
  1921-2000 65
  Obituary 125
Otfinoski, Steven 1949- 116
  Earlier sketch in SATA 56

Otis, James
  See Kaler, James Otis
O'Toole, Thomas 1941- *71*
O'Trigger, Sir Lucius
  See Horne, Richard Henry
Otten, Charlotte F(ennema) 1926- *98*
Ottley, Matt 1962- *102*
Ottley, Reginald Leslie 1909-1985 ....*26*
  See also CLR *16*
Otto, Svend
  See Soerensen, Svend Otto
Oughton, Jerrie (Preston) 1937- *131*
  Earlier sketch in SATA *76*
Oughton, (William) Taylor 1925- *104*
Ouida
  See De la Ramee, Marie Louise (Ouida)
Ousley, Odille 1896-1976 ....*10*
Outcalt, Todd 1960- *123*
Overmyer, James E. 1946- *88*
Overton, Jenny (Margaret Mary)
  1942- *52*
  Brief entry *36*
Owen, Annie 1949- *75*
Owen, Caroline Dale
  See Snedeker, Caroline Dale (Parke)
Owen, Clifford
  See Hamilton, Charles (Harold St. John)
Owen, Dilys
  See Gater, Dilys
Owen, (Benjamin) Evan 1918-1984 ....*38*
Owen, (John) Gareth
  See Owen, Gareth
Owen, Gareth 1936- *83*
  See also CLR *31*
  See also SAAS *14*
Owens, Bryant 1968- *116*
Owens, Gail 1939- *54*
Owens, Thomas S(heldon) 1960- *86*
Owens, Tom
  See Owens, Thomas S(heldon)
Oxenbury, Helen 1938- *68*
  Earlier sketch in SATA *3*
  See also CLR *70*
Oxendine, Bess Holland 1933- *90*
Oz, Frank (Richard) 1944- *60*
Ozer, Jerome S. 1927- *59*

P

Pace, Lorenzo 1943- *131*
Pace, Mildred Mastin 1907- *46*
  Brief entry *29*
Pachter, Hedwig (?)-1988 ....*63*
Pack, Janet 1952- *77*
Pack, Robert 1929- *118*
Packard, Edward 1931- *90*
  Earlier sketch in SATA *47*
Packer, Kenneth L. 1946- *116*
Packer, Vin
  See Meaker, Marijane (Agnes)
Pad, Peter
  See Stratemeyer, Edward L.
Page, Eileen
  See Heal, Edith
Page, Eleanor
  See Coerr, Eleanor (Beatrice)
Page, Jake
  See Page, James K(eena), Jr.
Page, James K(eena), Jr. 1936- *81*
Page, Lou Williams 1912-1997 ....*38*
Page, Mary
  See Heal, Edith
Pagnucci, Susan 1944- *90*
Pahz, (Anne) Cheryl Suzanne 1949- *11*
Pahz, James Alon 1943- *11*
Paice, Margaret 1920- *10*
Paige, Harry W(orthington) 1922- *41*
  Brief entry *35*
Paige, Richard
  See Koontz, Dean R(ay)

Paige, Robin
  See Albert, Susan Wittig
Paine, Penelope Colville 1946- *87*
Paine, Roberta M. 1925- *13*
Paisley, Tom 1932- *78*
  See Bethancourt, T. Ernesto
Palatini, Margie *134*
Palazzo, Anthony D.
  See Palazzo, Tony
Palazzo, Tony 1905-1970 ....*3*
Palder, Edward L. 1922- *5*
Palecek, Josef 1932- *56*
Palecek, Libuse 1937- *89*
Palin, Michael (Edward) 1943- *67*
  See Monty Python
Palladini, David (Mario) 1946- *40*
  Brief entry *32*
Pallas, Norvin 1918-1983 ....*23*
Pallotta-Chiarolli, Maria 1960- *117*
Palmer, Bernard (Alvin) 1914-1998 ....*26*
Palmer, C(yril) Everard 1930- *14*
Palmer, (Ruth) Candida 1926- *11*
Palmer, Don
  See Benson, Mildred (Augustine Wirt)
Palmer, Hap 1942- *68*
Palmer, Heidi 1948- *15*
Palmer, Helen Marion
  See Geisel, Helen
Palmer, Jessica 1953- *120*
Palmer, Juliette 1930- *15*
Palmer, Kate Salley 1946- *97*
Palmer, Maria
  See Brennan, J(ames) H(erbert)
  and Strachan, Ian
Palmer, Robin 1909-2000 ....*43*
Paltrowitz, Donna (Milman) 1950- *61*
  Brief entry *50*
Paltrowitz, Stuart 1946- *61*
  Brief entry *50*
Panati, Charles 1943- *65*
Panchyk, Richard 1970- *138*
Panetta, George 1915-1969 ....*15*
Panetta, Joseph N. 1953- *96*
Panik, Sharon 1952- *82*
Panowski, Eileen Thompson 1920- *49*
Pansy
  See Alden, Isabella (Macdonald)
Pantell, Dora (Fuchs) *39*
Panter, Carol 1936- *9*
Papas, Bill
  See Papas, William
Papas, William 1927-2000 ....*50*
Papashvily, George 1898-1978 ....*17*
Papashvily, Helen (Waite)
  1906-1996 ....*17*
Pape, D. L.
  See Pape, Donna (Lugg)
Pape, Donna (Lugg) 1930- *82*
  Earlier sketch in SATA *2*
Paperny, Myra (Green) 1932- *51*
  Brief entry *33*
Paradis, Adrian A(lexis) 1912- *67*
  Earlier sketch in SATA *1*
  See also SAAS *8*
Paradis, Marjorie Bartholomew
  1886(?)-1970 ....*17*
Parenteau, Shirley Laurolyn 1935- *47*
  Brief entry *40*
Parish, Margaret (Cecile) 1927-1988 ....*73*
  See Parish, Peggy
Parish, Margaret Holt
  See Holt, Margaret
Parish, Peggy *17*
  Obituary *59*
  See also CLR *22*
  See Parish, Margaret (Cecile)
Park, Barbara 1947- *123*
  Brief entry *35*
  Earlier sketches in SATA *40, 78*
  See also CLR *34*
Park, Bill *22*
  See Park, W(illiam) B(ryan)

Park, Jordan
  See Kornbluth, C(yril) M.
  and Pohl, Frederik
Park, Linda Sue 1960- *127*
  See also CLR *84*
Park, Nick 1958- *113*
Park, (Rosina) Ruth (Lucia) 1923(?)- *93*
  Earlier sketch in SATA *25*
  See also CLR *51*
Park, W(illiam) B(ryan) 1936- *22*
  See Park, Bill
Parke, Marilyn 1928- *82*
Parker, Elinor Milnor 1906- *3*
Parker, Julie F. 1961- *92*
Parker, Kristy 1957- *59*
Parker, Lois M(ay) 1912-1996 ....*30*
Parker, Margot M. 1937- *52*
Parker, Mary Jessie 1948- *71*
Parker, Nancy Winslow 1930- *132*
  Earlier sketches in SATA *10, 69*
  See also SAAS *20*
Parker, Richard 1915-1990 ....*14*
Parker, Robert
  See Boyd, Waldo T.
Parkes, Lucas
  See Harris, John (Wyndham Parkes Lucas)
  Beynon
Parkhill, John
  See Cox, William R(obert)
Parkinson, Ethelyn M(inerva)
  1906-1999 ....*11*
Parkinson, Kathy *71*
  See Parkinson, Kathryn N.
Parks, Deborah A. 1948- *133*
  Earlier sketch in SATA *91*
Parks, Edd Winfield 1906-1968 ....*10*
Parks, Gordon (Alexander Buchanan)
  1912- *108*
  Earlier sketch in SATA *8*
Parks, Rosa (Louise Lee) 1913- *83*
Parks, Van Dyke 1943- *62*
Parley, Peter
  See Goodrich, Samuel Griswold
Parlin, John
  See Graves, Charles Parlin
Parnall, Peter 1936- *69*
  Earlier sketch in SATA *16*
  See also SAAS *11*
Parotti, Phillip (Elliott) 1941- *109*
Parr, Letitia (Evelyn) 1906-1985(?) *37*
Parr, Lucy 1924- *10*
Parr, Todd *134*
Parrish, Anne 1888-1957 ....*27*
Parrish, Mary
  See Cousins, Margaret
Parrish, (Frederick) Maxfield
  1870-1966 ....*14*
Parry, Marian 1924- *13*
Parson Lot
  See Kingsley, Charles
Parsons, Alexandra 1947- *92*
Parsons, Ellen
  See Dragonwagon, Crescent
Parsons, Martin (Leslie) 1951- *116*
Partch, Virgil Franklin II 1916-1984 ......*39*
  Obituary *39*
Parton, Dolly (Rebecca) 1946- *94*
Partridge, Benjamin W(aring), Jr.
  1915- *28*
Partridge, Cora Cheney
  See Cheney, Cora
Partridge, Elizabeth *134*
Partridge, Jenny (Lilian) 1947- *52*
  Brief entry *37*
Pascal, David 1918- *14*
Pascal, Francine 1938- *80*
  Brief entry *37*
  Earlier sketch in SATA *51*
  See also CLR *25*
Paschal, Nancy
  See Trotter, Grace V(iolet)

Pascudniak, Pascal
  See Lupoff, Richard A(llen)
Pashko, Stanley 1913- 29
Passailaigue, Thomas E.
  See Paisley, Tom
Pateman, Robert 1954- 84
Patent, Dorothy Hinshaw 1940- 120
  Earlier sketches in SATA 22, 69
  See also CLR 19
  See also SAAS 13
Paterson, A(ndrew) B(arton)
  1864-1941 97
Paterson, Banjo
  See Paterson, A(ndrew) B(arton)
Paterson, Diane (R. Cole) 1946- 59
  Brief entry 33
Paterson, John (Barstow) 1932- 114
Paterson, Katherine (Womeldorf)
  1932- 133
  Earlier sketches in SATA 13, 53, 92
  See also CLR 50
Patience, John 1949- 90
Patneaude, David 1944- 85
Paton, Alan (Stewart) 1903-1988 11
  Obituary 56
Paton, Jane (Elizabeth) 1934- 35
Paton, Priscilla 1952- 98
Paton Walsh, Gillian 1937- 109
  Earlier sketches in SATA 4, 72
  See also CLR 65
  See also SAAS 3
  See Paton Walsh, Jill
  and Walsh, Jill Paton
Paton Walsh, Jill
  See Paton Walsh, Gillian
Patrick, Susan
  See Clark, Patricia Denise
Patron, Susan 1948- 76
Patschke, Steve 1955- 125
Patten, Brian 1946- 29
Patterson, Charles 1935- 59
Patterson, Geoffrey 1943- 54
  Brief entry 44
Patterson, Lillie G. -1999 88
  Earlier sketch in SATA 14
Patterson, Nancy Ruth 1944- 72
Pattison, Darcy (S.) 1954- 126
  Earlier sketch in SATA 72
Paul, Aileen 1917- 12
Paul, Ann Whitford 1941- 110
  Earlier sketch in SATA 76
Paul, Elizabeth
  See Crow, Donna Fletcher
Paul, James 1936- 23
Paul, Korky 1951-
  See CLR 87
Paul, Robert
  See Roberts, John G(aither)
Paul, Tessa 1944- 103
Pauli, Hertha (Ernestine) 1909-1973 3
  Obituary 26
Paull, Grace A. 1898- 24
Paulsen, Gary 1939- 111
  Earlier sketches in SATA 22, 50, 54, 79
  See also CLR 82
Paulson, Jack
  See Jackson, C(aary) Paul
Pauquet, Gina Ruck
  See Ruck-Pauquet, Gina
Pausacker, Jenny 1948- 72
  See also SAAS 23
Pausewang, Gudrun 1928- 104
Pavel, Frances 1907- 10
Paxton, Tom 70
  See Paxton, Thomas R.
Payne, Alan
  See Jakes, John (William)
Payne, Bernal C., Jr. 1941- 60
Payne, C. D. 1949- 133
Payne, Donald Gordon 1924- 37
Payne, Emmy
  See West, Emily Govan

Payne, Nina 135
Payson, Dale 1943- 9
Payzant, Charles 18
Paz, A.
  See Pahz, James Alon
Paz, Zan
  See Pahz, (Anne) Cheryl Suzanne
Peace, Mary
  See Finley, Mary Peace
Peake, Mervyn 1911-1968 23
Peale, Norman Vincent 1898-1993 20
  Obituary 78
Pearce, Margaret 104
Peare, Catherine Owens 1911- 9
Pearson, Gayle 1947- 119
  Earlier sketch in SATA 53
Pearson, Kit 1947- 77
  Autobiography Feature 117
  See also CLR 26
Pearson, Mary E. 1955- 134
Pearson, Susan 1946- 91
  Brief entry 27
  Earlier sketch in SATA 39
Pearson, Tracey Campbell 1956- 64
Pease, (Clarence) Howard 1894-1974 2
  Obituary 25
Peavy, Linda 1943- 54
Peck, Anne Merriman 1884-1976 18
Peck, Beth 1957- 79
Peck, Marshall III 1951- 92
Peck, Richard (Wayne) 1934- 97
  Autobiography Feature 110
  Earlier sketches in SATA 18, 55
  See also CLR 15
  See also SAAS 2
Peck, Robert Newton 1928- 111
  Autobiography Feature 108
  Earlier sketches in SATA 21, 62
  See also CLR 45
  See also SAAS 1
Peck, Sylvia 1953- 133
Pederson, Sharleen
  See Collicott, Sharleen
Peebles, Anne
  See Galloway, Priscilla
Peek, Merle 1938- 39
Peel, John 1954- 79
Peel, Norman Lemon
  See Hirsch, Phil
Peeples, Edwin A(ugustus, Jr.)
  1915-1994 6
Peers, Judi(th May West) 1956- 119
Peet, Bill
  See CLR 12
  See Peet, William Bartlett
Peet, Creighton B. 1899-1977 30
Peet, William Bartlett 1915-2002 78
  Obituary 137
  Earlier sketches in SATA 2, 41
  See Peet, Bill
Peguero, Leone 116
Pelaez, Jill 1924- 12
Pelham, David 1938- 70
Pellowski, Anne 1933- 20
Pellowski, Michael (Joseph) 1949- 88
  Brief entry 48
Pellowski, Michael Morgan
  See Pellowski, Michael (Joseph)
Pelta, Kathy 1928- 18
Peltier, Leslie C(opus) 1900-1980 13
Pemberton, John Leigh
  See Leigh-Pemberton, John
Pembury, Bill
  See Groom, Arthur William
Pemsteen, Hans
  See Manes, Stephen
Pendennis, Arthur Esquir
  See Thackeray, William Makepeace
Pender, Lydia Podger 1907- 61
Pendery, Rosemary (Schmitz) 7
Pendle, Alexy 1943- 29

Pendleton, Don
  See Cunningham, Chet
  and Garside, (Clifford) Jack
  and Jagninski, Tom
  and Krauzer, Steven M(ark)
  and Obstfeld, Raymond
Pene du Bois, William (Sherman)
  1916-1993 68
  Obituary 74
  Earlier sketch in SATA 4
  See also CLR 1
Penn, Ruth Bonn
  See Rosenberg, Eth(el) Clifford
Pennage, E. M.
  See Finkel, George (Irvine)
Penner, Fred (Ralph Cornelius)
  1946- 67
Penney, Grace Jackson 1904-2000 35
Penney, Ian 1960- 76
Penney, Sue 1957- 102
Pennington, Eunice 1923- 27
Pennington, Lillian Boyer 1904- 45
Penrose, Gordon 1925- 66
Penson, Mary E. 1917- 78
Penzler, Otto 1942- 38
Pepe, Phil(ip) 1935- 20
Peppe, Rodney (Darrell) 1934- 74
  Earlier sketch in SATA 4
  See also SAAS 10
Percy, Charles Henry
  See Smith, Dorothy Gladys
Percy, Rachel 1930- 63
Perdrizet, Marie-Pierre 1952- 79
Perenyi, Constance (Marie) 1954- 93
Perera, Hilda 1926- 105
Perera, Thomas Biddle 1938- 13
Peretti, Frank E. 1951- 141
  Earlier sketch in SATA 80
Perkins, Al(bert Rogers) 1904-1975 30
Perkins, Lucy Fitch 1865-1937 72
Perkins, Lynne Rae 131
Perkins, (Richard) Marlin 1905-1986 21
  Obituary 48
Perkins, Mitali 1963- 88
Perks, Anne-Marie 1955- 122
Perl, Lila 72
  Earlier sketch in SATA 6
Perl, Susan 1922-1983 22
  Obituary 34
Perlmutter, O(scar) William
  1920-1975 8
Pernu, Dennis 1970- 87
Perrault, Charles 1628-1703 25
  See also CLR 79
Perret, Gene (Richard) 1937- 76
Perrine, Mary 1913- 2
Perrins, Lesley 1953- 56
Perrow, Angeli 1954- 121
Perry, Barbara Fisher
  See Fisher, Barbara
Perry, Patricia 1949- 30
Perry, Phyllis J. 1933- 101
  Earlier sketch in SATA 60
Perry, Ritchie (John Allen) 1942- 105
Perry, Roger 1933- 27
Perry, Steve(n Carl) 1947- 76
Pershall, Mary K. 1951- 70
Pershing, Marie
  See Schultz, Pearle Henriksen
Perske, Robert 1927- 57
Persun, Morgan Reed
  See Watkins, Dawn L.
Peter
  See Stratemeyer, Edward L.
Peters, Alexander
  See Hollander, Zander
Peters, Andrew Fusek 1965- 107
Peters, Caroline
  See Betz, Eva Kelly
Peters, David 1954- 72
Peters, Elizabeth
  See Mertz, Barbara (Gross)

Peters, Emma
See Price, Karen
Peters, Gabriel
See Matott, Justin
Peters, Julie Anne 1952- *128*
Earlier sketch in SATA *82*
Peters, Linda
See Catherall, Arthur
Peters, Lisa Westberg 1951- *115*
Earlier sketch in SATA *74*
Peters, Patricia 1953- *84*
Peters, Russell M. 1929- *78*
Peters, S. H.
See Porter, William Sydney
and Proffitt, Nicholas (Charles)
Petersen, David 1946- *109*
Earlier sketch in SATA *62*
Petersen, Gwenn Boardman 1924- *61*
See Boardman, Gwenn R.
Petersen, P(eter) J(ames) 1941- *118*
Brief entry *43*
Earlier sketches in SATA *48, 83*
Petersen, Palle 1943- *85*
Petersham, Maud (Sylvia Fuller)
1890-1971 ....*17*
See also CLR *24*
Petersham, Miska 1888-1960 ....*17*
See also CLR *24*
Peterson, Cris 1952- *84*
Peterson, Dawn 1934- *86*
Peterson, Esther (Allen) 1934- *35*
Peterson, Hans 1922- *8*
Peterson, Harold L(eslie) 1922-1978 ....*8*
Peterson, Helen Stone 1910- *8*
Peterson, Jean Sunde 1941- *108*
Peterson, Jeanne Whitehouse
See Whitehouse, Jeanne
Peterson, Kathleen B. 1951- *119*
Peterson, Lorraine 1940- *56*
Brief entry *44*
Petie, Haris *10*
See Petty, Roberta
Petrides, Heidrun 1944- *19*
Petrie, Catherine 1947- *52*
Brief entry *41*
Petroski, Catherine (Ann Groom)
1939- *48*
Petrovich, Michael B(oro) 1922- *40*
Petrovskaya, Kyra
See Wayne, Kyra Petrovskaya
Petruccio, Steven James 1961- *67*
Petry, Ann (Lane) 1908-1997 ....*5*
Obituary *94*
See also CLR *12*
Pettit, Jayne 1932- *108*
Pevsner, Stella *131*
Earlier sketches in SATA *8, 77*
See also SAAS *14*
Peyo
See Culliford, Pierre
Peyton, K. M.
See CLR *3*
See also SAAS *17*
See Peyton, Kathleen (Wendy)
Peyton, Kathleen (Wendy) 1929- *62*
Earlier sketch in SATA *15*
See Peyton, K. M.
Pfanner, (Anne) Louise 1955- *68*
Pfeffer, Susan Beth 1948- *83*
Earlier sketch in SATA *4*
See also CLR *11*
See also SAAS *17*
Pfeffer, Wendy 1929- *78*
Pfeiffer, Janet (B.) 1949- *96*
Pfister, Marcus *83*
See also CLR *42*
Pflieger, Pat 1955- *84*
Phelan, Mary Kay 1914- *3*
Phelan, Terry Wolfe 1941- *56*
Phelps, Ethel Johnston 1914- *35*
Philbrick, Rodman
See Philbrick, (W.) Rodman

Philbrick, (W.) Rodman 1951- *122*
Philbrick, W. R.
See Philbrick, (W.) Rodman
Philbrook, Clem(ent E.) 1917- *24*
Phillips, Aileen Paul
See Paul, Aileen
Phillips, Betty Lou
See Phillips, Elizabeth Louise
Phillips, Bob 1940- *95*
Phillips, Elizabeth Louise *58*
Earlier sketch in SATA *48*
Phillips, Irv(ing W.) 1905-2000 ....*11*
Obituary *125*
Phillips, Jack
See Sandburg, Carl (August)
Phillips, Leon
See Gerson, Noel Bertram
Phillips, Loretta (Hosey) 1893-1987 ....*10*
Phillips, Louis 1942- *102*
Earlier sketch in SATA *8*
Phillips, Mary Geisler 1881-1964 ....*10*
Phillips, Michael
See Nolan, William F(rancis)
Phillips, (Woodward) Prentice
1894-1981 ....*10*
Phillpotts, Eden 1862-1960 ....*24*
Phin
See Thayer, Ernest Lawrence
Phipson, Joan
See CLR *5*
See also SAAS *3*
See Fitzhardinge, Joan Margaret
Phiz
See Browne, Hablot Knight
Phleger, Fred B. 1909-1993 ....*34*
Phleger, Marjorie Temple
1908(?)-1986 ....*1*
Obituary *47*
Piatti, Celestino 1922- *16*
Picard, Barbara Leonie 1917- *89*
Earlier sketch in SATA *2*
See also SAAS *10*
Pickard, Charles 1932- *36*
Pickering, James Sayre 1897-1969 ....*36*
Obituary *28*
Pickering, Robert B. 1950- *93*
Pienkowski, Jan (Michal) 1936- *131*
Earlier sketches in SATA *6, 58*
See also CLR *6*
Pierce, Edith Gray 1893-1977 ....*45*
Pierce, Katherine
See St. John, Wylly Folk
Pierce, Meredith Ann 1958- *127*
Brief entry *48*
Earlier sketch in SATA *67*
See also CLR *20*
Pierce, Ruth (Ireland) 1936- *5*
Pierce, Sharon
See McCullough, Sharon Pierce
Pierce, Tamora 1954- *96*
Brief entry *49*
Earlier sketch in SATA *51*
Pierik, Robert 1921- *13*
Piers, Robert
See Anthony, Piers
Pig, Edward
See Gorey, Edward (St. John)
Pike, Bob
See Pike, Robert W(ilson)
Pike, Christopher
See McFadden, Kevin Christopher
Pike, Deborah 1951- *89*
Pike, E(dgar) Royston 1896-1980 ....*22*
Obituary *56*
Pike, R. William 1956- *92*
Pike, Robert W(ilson) 1931- *102*
Pilarski, Laura 1926- *13*
Pilgrim, Anne
See Allan, Mabel Esther
Pilkey, Dav(id Murray, Jr.) 1966- *115*
Earlier sketch in SATA *68*
See also CLR *48*

Pilkington, Francis Meredyth 1907- *4*
Pilkington, Roger (Windle) 1915- *10*
Pincus, Harriet 1938- *27*
Pinczes, Elinor J(ane) 1940- *81*
Pine, Nicholas 1951- *91*
Pine, Tillie S(chloss) 1896-1999 ....*13*
Pini, Richard (Alan) 1950- *89*
Pini, Wendy 1951- *89*
Pinkney, Andrea Davis 1963- *113*
Pinkney, (Jerry) Brian 1961- *74*
See also CLR *54*
Pinkney, Gloria Jean 1941- *85*
Pinkney, J. Brian
See Pinkney, (Jerry) Brian
Pinkney, Jerry 1939- *107*
Brief entry *32*
Earlier sketches in SATA *41, 71*
See also CLR *43*
See also SAAS *12*
Pinkney, John *97*
Pinkney, Sandra L. *128*
Pinkwater, Daniel
See Pinkwater, Daniel Manus
Pinkwater, Daniel Manus 1941- *114*
Earlier sketches in SATA *8, 46, 76*
See also CLR *4*
See also SAAS *3*
Pinkwater, Manus
See Pinkwater, Daniel Manus
Pinner, Joma
See Werner, Herma
Pioneer
See Yates, Raymond F(rancis)
Piowaty, Kim Kennelly 1957- *49*
Piper, Roger
See Fisher, John (Oswald Hamilton)
Pirner, Connie White 1955- *72*
Piro, Richard 1934- *7*
Pirot, Alison Lohans
See Lohans, Alison
Pirsig, Robert M(aynard) 1928- *39*
Pita
See Rendon, Maria
Pitcher, Caroline (Nell) 1948- *128*
Pitre, Felix 1949- *84*
Pitrone, Jean Maddern 1920- *4*
Pittman, Helena Clare 1945- *71*
Pitz, Henry C(larence) 1895-1976 ....*4*
Obituary *24*
Pizer, Vernon 1918- *21*
Place, Marian T(empleton) 1910- *3*
Place, Robin (Mary) 1926- *71*
Plaidy, Jean
See Hibbert, Eleanor Alice Burford
Plain, Belva 1919- *62*
Plath, Sylvia 1932-1963 ....*96*
Platt, Kin 1911- *86*
Earlier sketch in SATA *21*
See also SAAS *17*
Platt, Randall (Beth) 1948- *95*
Platt, Richard 1953- *120*
Playfellow, Robin
See Ellis, Edward S(ylvester)
Playsted, James
See Wood, James Playsted
Plecas, Jennifer 1966- *84*
Plimpton, George (Ames) 1927- *10*
Plomer, William Charles Franklin
1903-1973 ....*24*
Plotz, Helen Ratnoff 1913-2000 ....*38*
Plourde, Lynn 1955- *122*
Plowden, David 1932- *52*
Plowden, Martha Ward 1948- *98*
Plowhead, Ruth Gipson 1877-1967 ....*43*
Plowman, Stephanie 1922- *6*
Pluckrose, Henry (Arthur) 1931- *141*
Earlier sketch in SATA *13*
Plum, J.
See Wodehouse, P(elham) G(renville)
Plum, Jennifer
See Kurland, Michael (Joseph)

Plumme, Don E.
  See Katz, Bobbi
Plummer, Margaret 1911- 2
Pochocki, Ethel (Frances) 1925- 76
Podendorf, Illa (E.) 1903(?)-1983 18
  Obituary 35
Podwal, Mark 1945- 101
Poe, Edgar Allan 1809-1849 23
Poe, Ty (Christopher) 1975- 94
Pogany, William Andrew 1882-1955 44
  See Pogany, Willy
Pogany, Willy
  Brief entry 30
  See Pogany, William Andrew
Pohl, Frederik 1919- 24
Pohlmann, Lillian (Grenfell)
  1902-1997 11
Pohrt, Tom 67
Pointon, Robert
  See Rooke, Daphne (Marie)
Points, Larry (Gene) 1945- 133
Pokeberry, P. J.
  See Mitchell, B(etty) J(o)
POLA
  See Watson, Pauline
Polacco, Patricia Ann 1944- 123
  Earlier sketch in SATA 74
  See also CLR 40
Polatnick, Florence T. 1923- 5
Polder, Markus
  See Kruss, James
Polese, Carolyn 1947- 58
Polese, James 1914- 87
Polette, Nancy (Jane) 1930- 42
Polhamus, Jean Burt 1928- 21
Policoff, Stephen Phillip 1948- 77
Polikoff, Barbara G(arland) 1929- 77
Polisar, Barry Louis 1954- 134
  Earlier sketch in SATA 77
Politi, Leo 1908-1996 47
  Obituary 88
  Earlier sketch in SATA 1
  See also CLR 29
Polking, Kirk 1925- 5
Pollack, Jill S. 1963- 88
Polland, Barbara K(ay) 1939- 44
Polland, Madeleine A(ngela Cahill)
  1918- 68
  Earlier sketch in SATA 6
  See also SAAS 8
Pollema-Cahill, Phyllis 1958- 123
Pollock, Bruce 1945- 46
Pollock, Mary
  See Blyton, Enid (Mary)
Pollock, Penny 1935- 137
  Brief entry 42
  Earlier sketch in SATA 44
Pollowitz, Melinda Kilborn 1944- 26
Polner, Murray 1928- 64
Polonsky, Arthur 1925- 34
Polseno, Jo 17
Pomaska, Anna 1946- 117
Pomerantz, Charlotte 1930- 80
  Earlier sketch in SATA 20
Pomeroy, Pete
  See Roth, Arthur J(oseph)
Pond, Alonzo W(illiam) 1894-1986 5
Pontiflet, Ted 1932- 32
Poole, Gray Johnson 1906- 1
Poole, Josephine 5
  See also SAAS 2
  See Helyar, Jane Penelope Josephine
Poole, (Jane Penelope) Josephine
  See Helyar, Jane Penelope Josephine
Poole, Lynn 1910-1969 1
Poole, Peggy 1925- 39
Poortvliet, Rien 1932- 65
  Brief entry 37
Pope, Elizabeth Marie 1917- 38
  Brief entry 36
Popescu, Christine 1930- 82
  See Pullein-Thompson, Christine

Poploff, Michelle 1956- 67
Popp, K. Wendy 91
Poppel, Hans 1942- 71
Portal, Colette 1936- 6
Porte, Barbara Ann 1943- 93
  Brief entry 45
  Earlier sketch in SATA 57
Porter, A(nthony) P(eyton) 1945- 68
Porter, Connie (Rose) 1959(?)- 129
  Earlier sketch in SATA 81
Porter, Donald Clayton
  See Gerson, Noel Bertram
Porter, Gene(va Grace) Stratton
  See Stratton-Porter, Gene(va Grace)
Porter, Janice Lee 1953- 108
  Earlier sketch in SATA 68
Porter, Katherine Anne 1890-1980 39
  Obituary 23
Porter, Kathryn
  See Swinford, Betty (June Wells)
Porter, Sheena 1935- 24
  See also SAAS 10
Porter, Sue 1951- 76
Porter, William Sydney 1862-1910
  See YABC 2
  See Henry, O.
Posell, Elsa Z(eigerman) -1995 3
Posten, Margaret L(ois) 1915- 10
Potok, Chaim 1929-2002 106
  Obituary 134
  Earlier sketch in SATA 33
Potok, Herbert Harold -2002
  See Potok, Chaim
Potok, Herman Harold
  See Potok, Chaim
Potter, (Helen) Beatrix 1866-1943 132
  Earlier sketch in SATA 100
  See also YABC 1
  See also CLR 73
Potter, Margaret (Newman)
  1926-1998 21
  Obituary 104
  See Betteridge, Anne
Potter, Marian 1915- 9
Potter, Miriam Clark 1886-1965 3
Poulin, Stephane 1961- 98
  See also CLR 28
Poulton, Kimberly 1957(?)- 136
Pournelle, Jerry (Eugene) 1933- 91
  Earlier sketch in SATA 26
Povelite, Kay 1955- 102
Powell, A. M.
  See Morgan, Alfred P(owell)
Powell, E. Sandy 1947- 72
Powell, Pamela 1960- 78
Powell, Patricia Hruby 1966- 136
Powell, Randy 1956- 118
Powell, Richard Stillman
  See Barbour, Ralph Henry
Powell, Robert (Stephenson Smyth) Baden
  See Baden-Powell, Robert (Stephenson
  Smyth)
Powell, Stephanie 1953- 93
Power, Margaret (M.) 1945- 125
  Earlier sketch in SATA 75
Powers, Anne
  See Schwartz, Anne Powers
Powers, Bill 1931- 52
  Brief entry 31
Powers, Margaret
  See Heal, Edith
Powers, Tim(othy Thomas) 1952- 107
Powledge, Fred 1935- 37
Poynter, Margaret 1927- 27
Prachaticka, Marketa
  See Kolibalova, Marketa
Prachatika, Marketa
  See Kolibalova, Marketa
Prager, Arthur 44
Prager, Ellen J. 1962- 136

Pratchett, Terry 1948- 139
  Earlier sketch in SATA 82
  See also CLR 64
Prater, John 1947- 103
  Earlier sketch in SATA 72
Pratt, (Murray) Fletcher 1897-1956 102
Pratt, Kristin Joy 1976- 87
Pratt, Pierre 1962- 95
Preiss, Byron (Cary) 47
  Brief entry 42
Preller, James 1961- 88
Prelutsky, Jack 1940- 118
  Earlier sketches in SATA 22, 66
  See also CLR 13
Prentice, Amy
  See Kaler, James Otis
Prescott, Casey
  See Morris, Chris(topher Crosby)
Presnall, Judith (Ann) Janda 1943- 96
Preston, Douglas 1956- 113
Preston, Edna Mitchell 40
Preston, Lillian Elvira 1918- 47
Preussler, Otfried 1923- 24
Price, Beverley Joan 1931- 98
Price, Christine (Hilda) 1928-1980 3
  Obituary 23
Price, Jennifer
  See Hoover, Helen (Drusilla Blackburn)
Price, Joan 1931- 124
Price, Jonathan (Reeve) 1941- 46
Price, Karen 1957- 125
Price, Lucie Locke
  See Locke, Lucie
Price, Olive 1903-1991 8
Price, Susan 1955- 128
  Earlier sketches in SATA 25, 85
Price, Willard 1887-1983 48
  Brief entry 38
Price-Groff, Claire 127
Priceman, Marjorie 120
  Earlier sketch in SATA 81
Prichard, Katharine Susannah
  1883-1969 66
Prideaux, Tom 1908-1993 37
  Obituary 76
Priestley, Alice 1962- 95
Priestley, Lee (Shore) 1904-1999 27
Priestly, Doug(las Michael) 1954- 122
Prieto, Mariana Beeching 1912-1999 8
Primavera, Elise 1954- 109
  Brief entry 48
  Earlier sketch in SATA 58
Prime, Derek (James) 1931- 34
Prince, Alison (Mary) 1931- 86
  Earlier sketch in SATA 28
Prince, J(ack) H(arvey) 1908- 17
Prince, Maggie 102
Pringle, Eric 138
Pringle, Laurence P(atrick) 1935- 104
  Earlier sketches in SATA 4, 68
  See also CLR 57
  See also SAAS 6
Prior, Natalie Jane 1963- 106
Pritchett, Elaine H(illyer) 1920- 36
Pritts, Kim Derek 1953- 83
Prochazkova, Iva 1953- 68
Proctor, Everitt
  See Montgomery, Rutherford George
Proeysen, Alf 1914-1970
  See CLR 24
  See Proysen, Alf
Professor Scribbler
  See Hollingsworth, Mary
Prose, Francine 1947- 101
Provensen, Alice 1918- 70
  Earlier sketch in SATA 9
  See also CLR 11
Provensen, Martin (Elias) 1916-1987 70
  Obituary 51
  Earlier sketch in SATA 9
  See also CLR 11
Provenzo, Eugene (F., Jr.) 1949- 78

Provost, Gail Levine 1944- 65
Provost, Gary (Richard) 1944-1995 66
Proysen, Alf 67
  See Proeysen, Alf
Pryor, Bonnie H. 1942- 69
Pryor, Boori (Monty) 1950- *112*
Pryor, Helen Brenton 1897-1972 4
Pucci, Albert John 1920- 44
Pudney, John (Sleigh) 1909-1977 24
Pugh, Ellen (Tiffany) 1920- 7
Pullein-Thompson, Christine 3
  See Popescu, Christine
Pullein-Thompson, Diana 3
  See Farr, Diana (Pullein-Thompson)
Pullein-Thompson, Josephine (Mary
  Wedderburn) 82
  Earlier sketch in SATA *3*
Pullman, Philip (Nicholas) 1946- *103*
  Earlier sketch in SATA *65*
  See also CLR *84*
  See also SAAS *17*
Pulver, Harry, Jr. 1960- *129*
Pulver, Robin 1945- *133*
  Earlier sketch in SATA *76*
Puner, Helen W(alker) 1915-1989 37
  Obituary 63
Purdy, Carol 1943- *120*
  Earlier sketch in SATA *66*
Purdy, Susan G(old) 1939- 8
Purnell, Idella 1901-1982 ....*120*
Purscell, Phyllis 1934- 7
Purtill, Richard L. 1931- 53
Pushker, Gloria (Teles) 1927- 75
Pushkin, Aleksandr Sergeevich
  See Pushkin, Alexander (Sergeyevich)
Pushkin, Alexander (Sergeyevich)
  1799-1837 61
  See Pushkin, Aleksandr Sergeevich
Putnam, Alice 1916- 61
Putnam, Arthur Lee
  See Alger, Horatio, Jr.
Putnam, Peter B(rock) 1920-1998 30
  Obituary *106*
Pyle, Howard 1853-1911 ....*100*
  Earlier sketch in SATA *16*
  See also CLR *22*
Pyle, Katharine 1863-1938 66
Pyne, Mable Mandeville 1903-1969 9
Pyrnelle, Louise-Clarke 1850-1907 ....*114*

Q

Quackenbush, Robert M(ead) 1929- 70
  Autobiography Feature *133*
  Earlier sketch in SATA *7*
  See also SAAS *7*
Qualey, Marsha 1953- *124*
  Earlier sketch in SATA *79*
Quammen, David 1948- 7
Quarles, Benjamin (Arthur)
  1904-1996 ....*12*
Quatermass, Martin
  See Carpenter, John (Howard)
Quattlebaum, Mary 1958- *134*
  Earlier sketch in SATA *88*
Quay, Emma *119*
Queen, Ellery
  See Deming, Richard
  and Dannay, Frederic
  and Davidson, Avram (James)
  and Fairman, Paul W.
  and Flora, Fletcher
  and Hoch, Edward D(entinger)
  and Kane, Henry
  and Lee, Manfred B(ennington)
  and Marlowe, Stephen
  and Powell, (Oval) Talmage
  and Sheldon, Walter J(ames)
  and Sturgeon, Theodore (Hamilton)
  and Tracy, Don(ald Fiske)
  and Vance, John Holbrook

Queen, Ellery, Jr.
  See Dannay, Frederic
  and Holding, James (Clark Carlisle, Jr.)
  and Lee, Manfred B(ennington)
Quennell, Marjorie Courtney
  1884-1972 29
Quentin, Brad
  See Bisson, Terry (Ballantine)
Quest, (Edna) Olga W(ilbourne) Hall
  See Hall-Quest, (Edna) Olga W(ilbourne)
Quick, Annabelle 1922-1986 2
Quill, Monica
  See McInerny, Ralph (Matthew)
Quin-Harkin, Janet 1941- *119*
  Earlier sketches in SATA *18, 90*
  See Bowen, Rhys
Quinlan, Susan E(lizabeth) 1954- 88
Quinn, Elisabeth 1881-1962 22
Quinn, Pat 1947- *130*
Quinn, Patrick 1950- 73
Quinn, Rob 1972- *138*
Quinn, Theodora K. *1*
  See Kroeber, Theodora (Kracaw)
Quinn, Vernon
  See Quinn, Elisabeth
Quirk, Anne (E.) 1956- 99
Quixley, Jim 1931- 56
Quyth, Gabriel
  See Jennings, Gary (Gayne)

R

Ra, Carol F. 1939- 76
Raab, Evelyn 1951- *129*
Rabe, Berniece (Louise) 1928- 77
  Earlier sketch in SATA *7*
  See also SAAS *10*
Rabe, Olive H(anson) (?)-1968 13
Rabin, Staton 1958- 84
Rabinowich, Ellen 1946- 29
Rabinowitz, Sandy 1954- 52
  Brief entry 39
Rachlin, Carol K(ing) 1919- 64
Rachlin, Harvey (Brant) 1951- 47
Rachlin, Nahid 64
Rackham, Arthur 1867-1939 ....*100*
  Earlier sketch in SATA *15*
  See also CLR *57*
Radencich, Marguerite C. 1952-1998 79
Radford, Ruby L(orraine) 1891-1971 6
Radin, Ruth Yaffe 1938- *107*
  Brief entry 52
  Earlier sketch in SATA *56*
Radlauer, David 1952- 28
Radlauer, Edward 1921- 15
Radlauer, Ruth Shaw 1926- 98
  Earlier sketch in SATA *15*
Radley, Gail 1951- *112*
  Earlier sketch in SATA *25*
Rae, Gwynedd 1892-1977 37
Raebeck, Lois 1921- 5
Rael, Elsa Okon 1927-
  See CLR *84*
Raffi
  See Cavoukian, Raffi
Raftery, Gerald (Bransfield)
  1905-1986 11
Ragan-Reid, Gale 1956- 90
Rahaman, Vashanti 1953- 98
Rahn, Joan Elma 1929- 27
Raible, Alton (Robert) 1918- 35
Raiff, Stan 1930- 11
Raines, Shirley C(arol) 1945- *128*
Rainey, W. B.
  See Blassingame, Wyatt Rainey
Ralston, Jan
  See Dunlop, Agnes M. R.
Ramal, Walter
  See de la Mare, Walter (John)

Ramanujan, A(ttipat) K(rishnaswami)
  1929-1993 86
Ramstad, Ralph L. 1919- *115*
Rana, Indi
  See Rana, Indira Higham
Rana, Indira Higham 1944- 82
Ranadive, Gail 1944- 10
Rand, Ann (Binkley) 30
Rand, Gloria 1925- *101*
Rand, Paul 1914-1996 6
Randall, Carrie
  See Ransom, Candice F.
Randall, Florence Engel 1917-1997 5
Randall, Janet
  See Young, Janet Randall
  and Young, Robert W(illiam)
Randall, Robert
  See Garrett, (Gordon) Randall (Phillip)
  and Silverberg, Robert
Randall, Ruth (Elaine) Painter
  1892-1971 3
Randell, Beverley
  See Price, Beverley Joan
Randle, Kristen (Downey) 1952- 92
  Autobiography Feature *119*
  See also SAAS *24*
Randolph, Boynton M.D.
  See Ellis, Edward S(ylvester)
Randolph, Geoffrey
  See Ellis, Edward S(ylvester)
Randolph, J. H.
  See Ellis, Edward S(ylvester)
Randolph, Lieutenant J. H.
  See Ellis, Edward S(ylvester)
Rands, William Brighty 1823-1882 17
Raney, Ken 1953- 74
Rankin, Joan 1940- 88
Ranney, Agnes V. 1916-1985 6
Ransom, Candice F. 1952- *135*
  Brief entry 49
  Earlier sketches in SATA *52, 89*
Ransome, Arthur (Michell)
  1884-1967 22
  See also CLR *8*
Ransome, James E. 1961- *123*
  Earlier sketch in SATA *76*
  See also CLR *86*
Rant, Tol E.
  See Longyear, Barry B(rookes)
Raphael, Elaine 23
  See Bolognese, Elaine (Raphael Chionchio)
Rappaport, Eva 1924- 6
Rappoport, Ken 1935- 89
Rarick, Carrie 1911-2002 41
Raschka, Chris
  See Raschka, Christopher
Raschka, Christopher 1959- *117*
  Earlier sketch in SATA *80*
Raskin, Edith Lefkowitz 1908-1987 9
Raskin, Ellen 1928-1984 ....*139*
  Earlier sketches in SATA *2, 38, 136*
  See also CLR *12*
Raskin, Joseph 1897-1982 ....*12*
  Obituary 29
Rathjen, Carl Henry 1909-1984 11
Rathmann, Peggy
  See CLR *77*
Rathmann, Peggy (Margaret Crosby)
  1953- 94
  See Rathmann, Peggy
Ratliff, Thomas M. 1948- *118*
Rattigan, Jama Kim 1951- 99
Ratto, Linda Lee 1952- 79
Rattray, Simon
  See Trevor, Elleston
Ratz de Tagyos, Paul 1958- 76
Rau, Dana Meachen 1971- 94
Rau, Margaret 1913- 9
  See also CLR *8*
Raucher, Herman 1928- 8

Ravielli, Anthony 1916-1997 3
  Obituary 95
Ravilious, Robin 1944- 77
Rawding, F(rederick) W(illiam)
  1930- 55
Rawlings, Marjorie Kinnan
  1896-1953 100
  See also YABC *1*
  See also CLR *63*
Rawls, (Woodrow) Wilson
  1913-1984 22
  See also CLR *81*
Rawlyk, George Alexander 1935- 64
Rawn, Melanie (Robin) 1954- 98
Ray, Carl 1943-1978 63
Ray, Deborah 8
  See Kogan Ray, Deborah
Ray, Delia 1963- 70
Ray, Irene
  See Sutton, Margaret Beebe
Ray, Jane 1960- 72
Ray, JoAnne 1935- 9
Ray, Mary (Eva Pedder) 1932- 127
  Earlier sketch in SATA 2
Ray, Mary Lyn 1946- 90
Rayevsky, Robert 1955- 81
Raymond, Robert
  See Alter, Robert Edmond
Rayner, Mary 1933- 87
  Earlier sketch in SATA 22
  See also CLR *41*
Rayner, William 1929- 55
  Brief entry 36
Raynor, Dorka 28
Rayson, Steven 1932- 30
Razzell, Arthur (George) 1925- 11
Razzell, Mary (Catherine) 1930- 102
Razzi, James 1931- 10
Read, Elfreida 1920- 2
Read, Piers Paul 1941- 21
Reade, Deborah 1949- 69
Reader, Dennis 1929- 71
Readman, Jo 1958- 89
Ready, Kirk L(ewis) 1943- 39
Reaney, James 1926- 43
Reaver, Chap 1935-1993 69
  Obituary 77
Reaver, Herbert R.
  See Reaver, Chap
Reaves, J. Michael
  See Reaves, (James) Michael
Reaves, (James) Michael 1950- 99
Redding, Robert Hull 1919- 2
Redekopp, Elsa 61
Redway, Ralph
  See Hamilton, Charles (Harold St. John)
Redway, Ridley
  See Hamilton, Charles (Harold St. John)
Reece, Colleen L. 1935- 116
Reece, Gabrielle 1970- 108
Reed, Betty Jane 1921- 4
Reed, E.
  See Evans, Mari
Reed, Gwendolyn E(lizabeth) 1932- 21
Reed, Kit 1932- 116
  Earlier sketch in SATA 34
Reed, Neil 1961- 99
Reed, Talbot Baines 1852-1893
  See CLR *76*
Reed, Thomas (James) 1947- 34
Reed, William Maxwell 1871-1962 15
Reeder, Carolyn 1937- 97
  Earlier sketch in SATA 66
  See also CLR *69*
Reeder, Colin (Dawson) 1938- 74
Reeder, Colonel Red
  See Reeder, Russell P(otter), Jr.
Reeder, Russell P(otter), Jr.
  1902-1998 4
  Obituary 101
Reeder, Stephanie Owen 1951- 102
Reed-Jones, Carol 1955- 112

Reef, Catherine 1951- 128
  Earlier sketch in SATA 73
Reeman, Douglas Edward 1924- 63
  Brief entry 28
Rees, Celia 1949- 124
Rees, David (Bartlett) 1936-1993 69
  Obituary 76
  Earlier sketch in SATA 36
  See also SAAS 5
Rees, Ennis (Samuel, Jr.) 1925- 3
Rees, (George) Leslie (Clarence)
  1905-2000 105
  Obituary 135
Reese, Bob
  See Reese, Robert A.
Reese, Della 1931(?)- 114
Reese, Lyn 64
  See Reese, Carolyn Johnson
Reese, Robert A. 1938- 60
  Brief entry 53
Reese, (John) Terence 1913-1996 59
Reeve, Joel
  See Cox, William R(obert)
Reeve, Kirk 1934- 117
Reeves, Faye Couch 1953- 76
Reeves, James 15
  See Reeves, John Morris
Reeves, Jeni 1947- 111
Reeves, John Morris 1909-1978 87
  See Reeves, James
Reeves, Joyce 1911- 17
Reeves, Lawrence F. 1926- 29
Reeves, Ruth Ellen
  See Ranney, Agnes V.
Regan, Dian Curtis 1950- 133
  Earlier sketch in SATA 75
Regehr, Lydia 1903-1991 37
Reger, James P. 1952- 106
Reggiani, Renee 1925- 18
Rehm, Karl M. 1935- 72
Reich, Ali
  See Katz, Bobbi
Reich, Susanna 1954- 113
Reichert, Mickey Zucker
  See Reichert, Miriam Zucker
Reichert, Miriam Zucker 1962- 85
Reid, Alastair 1926- 46
Reid, Barbara 1922- 21
Reid, Barbara (Jane) 1957- 93
  See also CLR *64*
Reid, Desmond
  See Moorcock, Michael (John)
  and McNeilly, Wilfred (Glassford)
Reid, Eugenie Chazal 1924- 12
Reid, John Calvin 21
Reid, (Thomas) Mayne 1818-1883 24
Reid, Meta Mayne 1905-1991 58
  Brief entry 36
Reid Banks, Lynne 1929- 111
  Earlier sketches in SATA 22, 75
  See also CLR *24*
  See Banks, Lynne Reid
Reider, Katja 1960- 126
Reid Jenkins, Debra 1955- 87
Reiff, Stephanie Ann 1948- 47
  Brief entry 28
Reig, June 1933- 30
Reigot, Betty Polisar 1924- 55
  Brief entry 41
Reim, Melanie (K.) 1956- 104
Reinach, Jacquelyn (Krasne)
  1930-2000 28
Reiner, William B(uck) 1910-1976 46
  Obituary 30
Reinfeld, Fred 1910-1964 3
Reiniger, Lotte 1899-1981 40
  Obituary 33
Reinsma, Carol 1949- 91
Reinstedt, Randall A. 1935- 101
Reinstedt, Randy
  See Reinstedt, Randall A.
Reisberg, Mira 1955- 82

Reiser, Lynn (Whisnant) 1944- 138
  Earlier sketch in SATA 81
Reisgies, Teresa (Maria) 1966- 74
Reiss, Johanna (de Leeuw) 1929(?)- 18
  See also CLR *19*
Reiss, John J. 23
Reiss, Kathryn 1957- 76
Reit, Seymour Victory 1918-2001 21
  Obituary 133
Reit, Sy
  See Reit, Seymour Victory
Relf, Patricia 1954- 134
  Earlier sketch in SATA 71
Remi, Georges 1907-1983 13
  Obituary 32
  See Herge
Remington, Frederic 1861-1909 41
Remkiewicz, Frank 1939- 77
Remy, Georges
  See Remi, Georges
Renaud, Bernadette 1945- 66
Renault, Mary
  See Challans, Mary
Rendell, Joan 28
Rendina, Laura (Jones) Cooper
  1902- 10
Rendon, Marcie R. 1952- 97
Rendon, Maria 1965- 116
Renee, Janina 1956- 140
Renfro, Ed 1924- 79
Renick, Marion (Lewis) 1905-1983 1
Renken, Aleda 1907- 27
Renlie, Frank H. 1936- 11
Rennert, Richard Scott 1956- 67
Reno, Dawn E. 1953- 130
Rensie, Willis
  See Eisner, Will(iam Erwin)
Renton, Cam
  See Armstrong, Richard
Renvoize, Jean 5
Resciniti, Angelo G. 1952- 75
Resnick, Michael D(iamond) 1942- 106
  Earlier sketch in SATA 38
Resnick, Mike
  See Resnick, Michael D(iamond)
Resnick, Seymour 1920- 23
Retla, Robert
  See Alter, Robert Edmond
Reuter, Bjarne (B.) 1950- 68
Reuter, Carol (Joan) 1931- 2
Revena
  See Wright, Betty Ren
Revsbech, Vicki
  See Liestman, Vicki
Rey, H(ans) A(ugusto) 1898-1977 100
  Earlier sketches in SATA 1, 26, 69
  See also CLR *5*
Rey, Margret (Elisabeth) 1906-1996 86
  Obituary 93
  Earlier sketch in SATA 26
  See also CLR *5*
Reyher, Becky
  See Reyher, Rebecca Hourwich
Reyher, Rebecca Hourwich
  1897-1987 18
  Obituary 50
Reynolds, C. Buck 1957- 107
Reynolds, John
  See Whitlock, Ralph
Reynolds, Madge
  See Whitlock, Ralph
Reynolds, Malvina 1900-1978 44
  Obituary 24
Reynolds, Marilyn (M.) 1935- 121
  See also SAAS 23
Reynolds, Marilynn 1940- 141
  Earlier sketch in SATA 80
Reynolds, Pamela 1923- 34
Reynolds, Peter H. 1961- 128

Rhine, Richard
  See Silverstein, Alvin
  and Silverstein, Virginia B(arbara
  Opshelor)
Rhoades, Diane 1952- *90*
Rhodes, Bennie (Loran) 1927- *35*
Rhodes, Donna McKee 1962- *87*
Rhodes, Frank Harold Trevor 1926- *37*
Rhue, Morton
  See Strasser, Todd
Rhyne, Nancy 1926- *66*
Rhynes, Martha E. 1939- *141*
Ribbons, Ian 1924- *37*
  Brief entry *30*
  See also SAAS *3*
Ricciuti, Edward R(aphael) 1938- *10*
Rice, Alice (Caldwell) Hegan
  1870-1942 ....*63*
Rice, Bebe Faas 1932- *89*
Rice, Dale R(ichard) 1948- *42*
Rice, Dick
  See Rice, R. Hugh
Rice, Earle, Jr. 1928- *92*
Rice, Edward 1918-2001 ....*47*
  Brief entry *42*
Rice, Elizabeth 1913- *2*
Rice, Eve (Hart) 1951- *91*
  Earlier sketch in SATA *34*
Rice, Inez 1907- *13*
Rice, James 1934- *93*
  Earlier sketch in SATA *22*
Rice, John F. 1958- *82*
Rice, R. Hugh 1929- *115*
Rice, Richard H.
  See Rice, R. Hugh
Rich, Barbara
  See Graves, Robert (von Ranke)
Rich, Elaine Sommers 1926- *6*
Rich, Josephine Bouchard 1912- *10*
Rich, Louise Dickinson 1903-1991 ....*54*
  Obituary *67*
Richard, Adrienne 1921- *5*
  See also SAAS *9*
Richard, James Robert
  See Bowen, Robert Sydney
Richards, Frank
  See Hamilton, Charles (Harold St. John)
Richards, Hilda
  See Hamilton, Charles (Harold St. John)
Richards, Jackie 1925- *102*
Richards, Jean 1940- *135*
Richards, Kay
  See Baker, Susan (Catherine)
Richards, Laura E(lizabeth Howe) 1850-1943
  See YABC *1*
  See also CLR *54*
Richards, Norman 1932- *48*
Richards, R(onald) C(harles) W(illiam)
  1923- *59*
  Brief entry *43*
Richardson, Andrew (William)
  1986- *120*
Richardson, Carol 1932- *58*
Richardson, Grace Lee
  See Dickson, Naida
Richardson, Jean (Mary) *59*
Richardson, Judith Benet 1941- *77*
Richardson, Robert S(hirley) 1902-1981 ....*8*
Richardson, Sandy 1949- *116*
Richardson, Willis 1889-1977 ....*60*
Richelson, Geraldine 1922- *29*
Richemont, Enid 1940- *82*
Richler, Mordecai 1931-2001 ....*98*
  Brief entry *27*
  Earlier sketch in SATA *44*
  See also CLR *17*
Rich-McCoy, Lois
  See McCoy, Lois (Rich)
Richmond, Robin 1951- *75*
Richoux, Pat(ricia) 1927- *7*
Richter, Alice 1941- *30*
Richter, Conrad (Michael) 1890-1968 ....*3*

Richter, Hans Peter 1925-1993 ....*6*
  See also CLR *21*
  See also SAAS *11*
Rickard, Graham 1949- *71*
Riddell, Chris(topher Barry) 1962- *114*
Riddell, Edwina 1955- *82*
Ridden, Brian (John) 1934- *123*
Riddle, Tohby 1965- *74*
Riddles, Libby 1956- *140*
Ridge, Antonia (Florence) (?)-1981 ....*7*
  Obituary *27*
Ridge, Martin 1923- *43*
Ridley, Philip *88*
Ridlon, Marci *22*
  See Balterman, Marcia Ridlon
Riedman, Sarah R(egal) 1902-1995 ....*1*
Riesenberg, Felix, Jr. 1913-1962 ....*23*
Rieu, E(mile) V(ictor) 1887-1972 ....*46*
  Obituary *26*
Rigg, Sharon
  See Creech, Sharon
Riggio, Anita 1952- *73*
Riggs, Stephanie 1964- *138*
Rigney, James Oliver, Jr. 1948- *95*
  See Jordan, Robert
Rikhoff, Jean 1928- *9*
Rikki
  See Ducornet, Erica
Riley, James A. 1939- *97*
Riley, James Whitcomb 1849-1916 ....*17*
Riley, Jocelyn (Carol) 1949- *60*
  Brief entry *50*
Riley, Linda Capus 1950- *85*
Riley, Martin 1948- *81*
Rinaldi, Ann 1934- *117*
  Brief entry *50*
  Earlier sketches in SATA *51, 78*
  See also CLR *46*
Rinard, Judith E(llen) 1947- *140*
  Earlier sketch in SATA *44*
Rinder, Lenore 1949- *92*
Ring, Elizabeth 1920- *79*
Ringdahl, Mark
  See Longyear, Barry B(rookes)
Ringgold, Faith 1930- *114*
  Earlier sketch in SATA *71*
  See also CLR *30*
Ringi, Kjell (Arne Soerensen) 1939- *12*
Rinkoff, Barbara Jean (Rich) 1923-1975 ...*4*
  Obituary *27*
Rinn, Miriam 1946- *127*
Riordan, James 1936- *95*
Rios, Tere
  See Versace, Marie Teresa Rios
Ripken, Cal(vin Edward), Jr. 1960- *114*
Ripley, Catherine 1957- *82*
Ripley, Elizabeth Blake 1906-1969 ....*5*
Ripper, Charles L(ewis) 1929- *3*
Ripper, Chuck
  See Ripper, Charles L(ewis)
Riq
  See Atwater, Richard (Tupper)
Rish, David 1955- *110*
Riskind, Mary 1944- *60*
Rissinger, Matt 1956- *93*
Rissman, Art
  See Sussman, Susan
Rissman, Susan
  See Sussman, Susan
Ritchie, Barbara Gibbons *14*
Ritter, Felix
  See Kruss, James
Ritter, John H. 1951- *137*
  Earlier sketch in SATA *129*
Ritter, Lawrence S(tanley) 1922- *58*
Ritthaler, Shelly 1955- *91*
Ritz, Karen 1957- *80*
Rivera, Geraldo (Miguel) 1943- *54*
  Brief entry *28*
Rivers, Elfrida
  See Bradley, Marion Zimmer
Rivers, Karen 1970- *131*

Riverside, John
  See Heinlein, Robert A(nson)
Rivkin, Ann 1920- *41*
Rivoli, Mario 1943- *10*
Roach, Marilynne K(athleen) 1946- *9*
Roach, Portia
  See Takakjian, Portia
Robb, Laura 1937- *95*
Robbins, Frank 1917- *42*
  Brief entry *32*
Robbins, Ken 1925-1982 ....*94*
  Brief entry *53*
Robbins, Raleigh
  See Hamilton, Charles (Harold St. John)
Robbins, Ruth 1917(?)- *14*
Robbins, Tony
  See Pashko, Stanley
Robbins, Wayne
  See Cox, William R(obert)
Robel, S. L.
  See Fraustino, Lisa Rowe
Roberson, Jennifer 1953- *72*
Roberson, John R(oyster) 1930- *53*
Robert, Adrian
  See St. John, Nicole
Roberts, Bethany *133*
Roberts, Bruce (Stuart) 1930- *47*
  Brief entry *39*
Roberts, Charles G(eorge) D(ouglas)
  1860-1943 ....*88*
  Brief entry *29*
  See also CLR *33*
Roberts, David
  See Cox, John Roberts
Roberts, Elizabeth 1944- *80*
Roberts, Elizabeth Madox 1886-1941 ......*33*
  Brief entry *27*
Roberts, Jim
  See Bates, Barbara S(nedeker)
Roberts, John G(aither) 1913- *27*
Roberts, Judy I. 1957- *93*
Roberts, M. L.
  See Mattern, Joanne
Roberts, Nancy Correll 1924- *52*
  Brief entry *28*
Roberts, Terence
  See Sanderson, Ivan T(erence)
Roberts, Willo Davis 1928- *133*
  Earlier sketches in SATA *21, 70*
  See also SAAS *8*
Robertson, Barbara (Anne) 1931- *12*
Robertson, Don 1929-1999 ....*8*
  Obituary *113*
Robertson, Dorothy Lewis 1912- *12*
Robertson, Ellis
  See Ellison, Harlan (Jay)
  and Silverberg, Robert
Robertson, Janet (E.) 1935- *68*
Robertson, Jennifer Sinclair
  1942-1998 ....*12*
Robertson, Jenny
  See Robertson, Jennifer Sinclair
Robertson, Keith (Carlton)
  1914-1991 ....*85*
  Obituary *69*
  Earlier sketch in SATA *1*
  See also SAAS *15*
Robertson, Stephen
  See Walker, Robert W(ayne)
Robertus, Polly M. 1948- *73*
Robeson, Kenneth
  See Johnson, (Walter) Ryerson
Robeson, Kenneth
  See Dent, Lester
  and Goulart, Ron(ald Joseph)
Robinet, Harriette Gillem 1931- *104*
  Earlier sketch in SATA *27*
  See also CLR *64*
Robins, Deri 1958- *117*
Robins, Patricia
  See Clark, Patricia Denise

Robins, Rollo, Jr.
  See Ellis, Edward S(ylvester)
Robins, Seelin
  See Ellis, Edward S(ylvester)
Robinson, Adjai 1932- 8
Robinson, Aminah Brenda Lynn
  1940- 77
Robinson, Barbara (Webb) 1927- 84
  Earlier sketch in SATA 8
Robinson, C(harles) A(lexander), Jr.
  1900-1965 36
Robinson, Charles 1870-1937 17
Robinson, Charles 1931- 6
Robinson, Dorothy W. 1929- 54
Robinson, Eve
  See Tanselle, Eve
Robinson, Glen(dal P.) 1953- 92
Robinson, Jan M. 1933- 6
Robinson, Jean O. 1934- 7
Robinson, Joan (Mary) G(ale Thomas)
  1910-1988 7
Robinson, Kim Stanley 1952- 109
Robinson, Lee 1948- 110
Robinson, Lloyd
  See Silverberg, Robert
Robinson, Lynda S(uzanne) 1951- 107
Robinson, Marileta 1942- 32
Robinson, Maudie Millian Oller
  1914- 11
Robinson, Nancy K(onheim)
  1942-1994 91
  Brief entry 31
  Obituary 79
  Earlier sketch in SATA 32
Robinson, Ray(mond Kenneth) 1920- 23
Robinson, Shari
  See McGuire, Leslie (Sarah)
Robinson, Spider 1948- 118
Robinson, Sue
  See Robinson, Susan Maria
Robinson, Susan Maria 1955- 105
Robinson, Suzanne
  See Robinson, Lynda S(uzanne)
Robinson, T(homas) H(eath)
  1869-1950 17
Robinson, (Wanda) Veronica 1926- 30
Robinson, W(illiam) Heath
  1872-1944 17
Robison, Bonnie 1924- 12
Robison, Nancy L(ouise) 1934- 32
Robles, Harold E. 1948- 87
Robottom, John 1934- 7
Robson, Eric 1939- 82
Roche, A. K.
  See Abisch, Roslyn Kroop
  and Kaplan, Boche
Roche, Denis (Mary) 1967- 99
Roche, P(atricia) K. 1935- 57
  Brief entry 34
Roche, Terry
  See Poole, Peggy
Rochman, Hazel 1938- 105
Rock, Maxine 1940- 108
Rocker, Fermin 1907- 40
Rocklin, Joanne 1946- 134
  Earlier sketch in SATA 86
Rockwell, Anne F(oote) 1934- 114
  Earlier sketches in SATA 33, 71
  See also SAAS 19
Rockwell, Bart
  See Pellowski, Michael (Joseph)
Rockwell, Harlow 1910-1988 33
  Obituary 56
Rockwell, Norman (Percevel)
  1894-1978 23
Rockwell, Thomas 1933- 70
  Earlier sketch in SATA 7
  See also CLR 6
Rockwood, Joyce 1947- 39

Rockwood, Roy 67
  Earlier sketch in SATA 1
  See McFarlane, Leslie (Charles)
  and Stratemeyer, Edward L.
Rodari, Gianni 1920-1980
  See CLR 24
Rodd, Kathleen Tennant 57
  Obituary 55
  See Rodd, Kylie Tennant
Rodda, Emily 1948(?)- 97
  See also CLR 32
Roddenberry, Eugene Wesley
  1921-1991 45
  Obituary 69
  See Roddenberry, Gene
Roddenberry, Gene
  Obituary 69
  See Roddenberry, Eugene Wesley
Roddy, Lee 1921- 57
Rodenas, Paula 73
Rodgers, Frank 1944- 69
Rodgers, Mary 1931- 130
  Earlier sketch in SATA 8
  See also CLR 20
Rodman, Emerson
  See Ellis, Edward S(ylvester)
Rodman, Eric
  See Silverberg, Robert
Rodman, Maia
  See Wojciechowska, Maia (Teresa)
Rodman, (Cary) Selden 1909-2002 9
Rodowsky, Colby F. 1932- 120
  Earlier sketches in SATA 21, 77
  See also SAAS 22
Rodriguez, Alejo 1941- 83
Rodriguez, Luis J. 1954- 125
Roeder, Virginia Marsh 1926- 98
Roehrig, Catharine H. 1949- 67
Roennfeldt, Robert 1953- 78
Roessel-Waugh, C. C.
  See Waugh, Carol-Lynn Rossel
  and Waugh, Charles G(ordon)
Roets, Lois F. 1937- 91
Roever, J(oan) M(arilyn) 1935- 26
Rofes, Eric Edward 1954- 52
Roffey, Maureen 1936- 33
Rogak, Lisa Angowski 1962- 80
Rogasky, Barbara 1933- 86
Rogers, (Thomas) Alan (Stinchcombe)
  1937- 81
  Earlier sketch in SATA 2
Rogers, Bettye 1858-1919 103
Rogers, Cindy 1950- 89
Rogers, Emma 1951- 74
Rogers, Frances 1888-1974 10
Rogers, Fred McFeely 1928-2003 33
  Obituary 138
Rogers, Jean 1919- 55
  Brief entry 47
Rogers, Matilda 1894-1976 5
  Obituary 34
Rogers, Pamela 1927- 9
Rogers, Paul 1950- 98
  Earlier sketch in SATA 54
Rogers, Robert
  See Hamilton, Charles (Harold St. John)
Rogers, W(illiam) G(arland)
  1896-1978 23
Rohan, Michael Scott 1951- 98
  See Scot, Michael
Rohan, Mike Scott
  See Rohan, Michael Scott
Rohmer, Harriet 1938- 56
Rohrer, Doug 1962- 89
Rojan
  See Rojankovsky, Feodor (Stepanovich)
Rojankovsky, Feodor (Stepanovich)
  1891-1970 21
Rojany, Lisa 94
Rokeby-Thomas, Anna E(lma) 1911- 15
Roland, Albert 1925-2002 11

Roland, Mary
  See Lewis, Mary (Christianna)
Rolerson, Darrell A(llen) 1946- 8
Roll, Winifred 1909-1998 6
Rollins, Charlemae Hill 1897-1979 3
  Obituary 26
Rollock, Barbara T(herese) 1924- 64
Romack, Janice Reed
  See LeNoir, Janice
Romain, Trevor 134
Romanenko, Vitaliy 1962- 101
Romano, Louis G. 1921- 35
Romano, Melora A. 1966- 118
Romijn, Johanna Maria Kooyker
  See Kooyker-Romijn, Johanna Maria
Romyn, Johanna Maria Kooyker
  See Kooyker-Romijn, Johanna Maria
Rongen, Bjoern 1906- 10
Rongen, Bjorn
  See Rongen, Bjoern
Ronson, Mark
  See Alexander, Marc
Rood, Ronald (N.) 1920- 12
Rooke, Daphne (Marie) 1914- 12
Roop, Connie
  See Roop, Constance (Betzer)
Roop, Constance (Betzer) 1951- 116
  Brief entry 49
  Earlier sketch in SATA 54
Roop, Peter (G.) 1951- 116
  Brief entry 49
  Earlier sketch in SATA 54
Roos, Stephen 1945- 128
  Brief entry 41
  Earlier sketches in SATA 47, 77
Roose-Evans, James 1927- 65
Roosevelt, (Anna) Eleanor
  1884-1962 50
Root, Betty 84
Root, Phyllis 1949- 94
  Brief entry 48
  Earlier sketch in SATA 55
Roper, Laura (Newbold) Wood
  1911- 34
Roper, Robert 1946- 78
Roraback, Robin (Ellan) 1964- 111
Rorby, Ginny 1944- 94
Rorer, Abigail 1949- 85
Roscoe, D(onald) T(homas) 1934- 42
Rose, Anne 8
Rose, Deborah Lee 1955- 124
  Earlier sketch in SATA 71
Rose, Elizabeth (Jane Pretty) 1933- 68
  Brief entry 28
Rose, Florella
  See Carlson, Vada F.
Rose, Gerald (Hembdon Seymour)
  1935- 68
  Brief entry 30
Rose, Malcolm 1953- 107
Rose, Nancy A.
  See Sweetland, Nancy A(nn)
Rose, Ted 1940- 93
Rose, Wendy 1948- 12
Rosen, Lillian (Diamond) 1928- 63
Rosen, Michael (Wayne) 1946- 137
  Brief entry 40
  Earlier sketches in SATA 48, 84
  See also CLR 45
Rosen, Michael J(oel) 1954- 86
Rosen, Sidney 1916- 1
Rosen, Winifred 1943- 8
Rosenbaum, Maurice 1907- 6
Rosenberg, Amye 1950- 74
Rosenberg, Dorothy 1906- 40
Rosenberg, Eth(el) Clifford 1915-1953 3
  See Clifford, Eth
Rosenberg, Jane 1949- 58
Rosenberg, Liz 1958- 129
  Earlier sketch in SATA 75

Rosenberg, Maxine B(erta) 1939- *93*
    Brief entry *47*
    Earlier sketch in SATA *55*
Rosenberg, Nancy (Sherman) 1931- *4*
Rosenberg, Sharon 1942- *8*
Rosenberry, Vera 1948- *83*
Rosenblatt, Arthur
    See Rosenblatt, Arthur S.
Rosenblatt, Arthur S. 1938- *68*
    Brief entry *45*
Rosenblatt, Lily 1956- *90*
Rosenbloom, Joseph 1928- *21*
Rosenblum, Richard 1928- *11*
Rosenburg, John M. 1918- *6*
Rosenfeld, Dina 1962- *99*
Rosenthal, Harold 1914-1999 ....*35*
Rosenthal, M(acha) L(ouis)
    1917-1996 ....*59*
Rosenthal, Mark A(lan) 1946- *64*
Rosman, Steven M(ichael) 1956- *81*
Ross, Alan
    See Warwick, Alan R(oss)
Ross, Christine 1950- *83*
Ross, Clare *111*
    Earlier sketch in SATA *48*
    See Romano, Clare
Ross, Dana Fuller
    See Cockrell, Amanda
    and Gerson, Noel Bertram
Ross, Dave *32*
    See Ross, David
Ross, David 1896-1975 ....*49*
    Obituary *20*
Ross, David 1949- *133*
    See Ross, Dave
Ross, Diana
    See Denney, Diana
Ross, Edward S(hearman) 1915- *85*
Ross, Eileen 1950- *115*
Ross, Frank (Xavier), Jr. 1914- *28*
Ross, Jane 1961- *79*
Ross, John 1921- *45*
Ross, Judy 1942- *54*
Ross, Katharine (Reynolds) 1948- *89*
Ross, Kent 1956- *91*
Ross, Lillian Hammer 1925- *72*
Ross, Michael Elsohn 1952- *127*
    Earlier sketch in SATA *80*
Ross, Pat(ricia Kienzle) 1943- *53*
    Brief entry *48*
Ross, Ramon R(oyal) 1930- *62*
Ross, Stewart 1947- *134*
    Earlier sketch in SATA *92*
    See also SAAS *23*
Ross, Tom 1958- *84*
Ross, Tony 1938- *130*
    Earlier sketches in SATA *17, 65*
Ross, Wilda 1915- *51*
    Brief entry *39*
Rossel, Seymour 1945- *28*
Rossel-Waugh, C. C.
    See Waugh, Carol-Lynn Rossel
Rossetti, Christina (Georgina)
    1830-1894 ....*20*
Rossi, Joyce 1943- *116*
Rossotti, Hazel Swaine 1930- *95*
Rostkowski, Margaret I. 1945- *59*
Roth, Arnold 1929- *21*
Roth, Arthur J(oseph) 1925-1993 ....*43*
    Brief entry *28*
    Obituary *75*
    See also SAAS *11*
Roth, David 1940- *36*
Roth, Hano Renee 1931-
    See Roth-Hano, Renee
Roth, Susan L. *134*
Rothberg, Abraham 1922- *59*
Roth-Hano, Renee 1931- *85*
Rothkopf, Carol Z. 1929- *4*
Rothman, Joel 1938- *7*
Rotner, Shelley 1951- *76*
Rottman, S(usan) L(ynn) 1970- *106*

Roueche, Berton 1911-1994 ....*28*
Roughsey, Dick 1921(?)-1985 ....*35*
    See also CLR *41*
Roughsey, Goobalathaldin
    See Roughsey, Dick
Rounds, Glen (Harold) 1906-2002 ....*112*
    Obituary *141*
    Earlier sketches in SATA *8, 70*
Rourke, Constance Mayfield 1885-1941
    See YABC *1*
Rowan, Deirdre
    See Williams, Jeanne
Rowe, Jennifer
    See Rodda, Emily
Rowh, Mark 1952- *90*
Rowland, Florence Wightman
    1900-1997 ....*8*
    Obituary *108*
Rowland-Entwistle, (Arthur) Theodore
    (Henry) 1925- *94*
    Earlier sketch in SATA *31*
Rowling, J(oanne) K(athleen) 1965- *109*
    See also CLR *80*
Rowsome, Frank (Howard), Jr.
    1914-1983 ....*36*
Roy, Gabrielle 1909-1983 ....*104*
Roy, Jacqueline 1954- *74*
Roy, Liam
    See Scarry, Patricia (Murphy)
Roy, Ron(ald) 1940- *110*
    Brief entry *35*
    Earlier sketch in SATA *40*
Roybal, Laura (Husby) 1956- *85*
Royds, Caroline 1953- *55*
Royston, Angela 1945- *120*
Rozakis, Laurie E. 1952- *84*
Rubel, Nicole 1953- *135*
    Earlier sketches in SATA *18, 95*
Rubin, Eva Johanna 1925- *38*
Rubin, Susan Goldman 1939- *132*
    Earlier sketch in SATA *84*
Rubinetti, Donald 1947- *92*
Rubinstein, Gillian 1942-
    See Rubinstein, Gillian (Margaret)
Rubinstein, Gillian (Margaret)
    1942- *105*
    Autobiography Feature *116*
    Earlier sketch in SATA *68*
    See also CLR *35*
    See also SAAS *25*
Rubinstein, Robert E(dward) 1943- *49*
Rublowsky, John M(artin) 1928- *62*
Ruby, Lois (F.) 1942- *95*
    Autobiography Feature *105*
    Brief entry *34*
    Earlier sketch in SATA *35*
Ruchlis, Hy(man) 1913-1992 ....*3*
    Obituary *72*
Rucker, Mike 1940- *91*
Ruckman, Ivy 1931- *93*
    Earlier sketch in SATA *37*
Ruck-Pauquet, Gina 1931- *40*
    Brief entry *37*
Rudley, Stephen 1946- *30*
Rudolph, Marguerita 1908- *21*
Rudomin, Esther
    See Hautzig, Esther Rudomin
Rue, Leonard Lee III 1926- *37*
Ruedi, Norma Paul
    See Ainsworth, Norma
Ruelle, Karen Gray 1957- *126*
    Earlier sketch in SATA *84*
Ruemmler, John D(avid) 1948- *78*
Ruffell, Ann 1941- *30*
Ruffins, Reynold 1930- *125*
    Earlier sketch in SATA *41*
Rugoff, Milton 1913- *30*
Ruhen, Olaf 1911-1989 ....*17*
Rumbaut, Hendle 1949- *84*
Rumford, James 1948- *116*
Rumsey, Marian (Barritt) 1928- *16*

Rumstuckle, Cornelius
    See Brennan, J(ames) H(erbert)
Runnerstroem, Bengt Arne 1944- *75*
Runyan, John
    See Palmer, Bernard (Alvin)
Runyon, Catherine 1947- *62*
Ruoff, A. LaVonne Brown 1930- *76*
Rusch, Kris
    See Rusch, Kristine Kathryn
Rusch, Kristine Kathryn 1960- *113*
Rush, Alison 1951- *41*
Rush, Peter 1937- *32*
Rushford, Patricia H(elen) 1943- *134*
Rushmore, Helen 1898-1994 ....*3*
Rushmore, Robert (William)
    1926-1986 ....*8*
    Obituary *49*
Ruskin, Ariane
    See Batterberry, Ariane Ruskin
Ruskin, John 1819-1900 ....*24*
Russ, Lavinia (Faxon) 1904-1992 ....*74*
Russell, Charlotte
    See Rathjen, Carl Henry
Russell, Ching Yeung 1946- *107*
Russell, Franklin (Alexander) 1926- *11*
Russell, Gertrude Barrer
    See Barrer-Russell, Gertrude
Russell, Helen Ross 1915- *8*
Russell, James 1933- *53*
Russell, Jim
    See Russell, James
Russell, Joan Plummer 1930- *139*
Russell, P. Craig 1951- *80*
Russell, Patrick
    See Sammis, John
Russell, Paul (Gary) 1942- *57*
Russell, Sarah
    See Laski, Marghanita
Russell, Sharman Apt 1954- *123*
Russell, Solveig Paulson 1904-1985 ....*3*
Russo, Marisabina 1950- *106*
Russo, Monica J. 1950- *83*
Russo, Susan 1947- *30*
Rutgers van der Loeff, An
    See Rutgers van der Loeff-Basenau,
    An(na) Maria Margaretha
Rutgers van der Loeff-Basenau, An(na)
    Maria Margaretha 1910- *22*
Ruth, Rod 1912-1987 ....*9*
Rutherford, Douglas
    See McConnell, James Douglas Rutherford
Rutherford, Meg 1932- *34*
Ruthin, Margaret *4*
    See Catherall, Arthur
Rutz, Viola Larkin 1932- *12*
Ruurs, Margriet 1952- *97*
Ryan, Betsy
    See Ryan, Elizabeth (Anne)
Ryan, Cheli Duran *20*
Ryan, Elizabeth (Anne) 1943- *30*
Ryan, Jeanette Mines
    See Mines, Jeanette (Marie)
Ryan, John (Gerald Christopher)
    1921- *22*
Ryan, Margaret 1950- *78*
Ryan, Mary E(lizabeth) 1953- *61*
Ryan, Pam(ela) Munoz *134*
Ryan, Patrick 1957- *138*
Ryan, Peter (Charles) 1939- *15*
Ryan-Lush, Geraldine 1949- *89*
Rybakov, Anatoli (Naumovich)
    1911-1998 ....*79*
    Obituary *108*
Rybolt, Thomas R(oy) 1954- *62*
Rydberg, Ernest E(mil) 1901-1993 ....*21*
Rydberg, Lou(isa Hampton) 1908- *27*
Rydell, Katy 1942- *91*
Rydell, Wendell
    See Rydell, Wendy
Rydell, Wendy *4*
Ryden, Hope *91*
    Earlier sketch in SATA *8*

Ryder, Joanne (Rose) 1946- *122*
  Brief entry *34*
  Earlier sketch in SATA *65*
  See also CLR *37*
Ryder, Pamela
  See Lamb, Nancy
Rye, Anthony
  See Youd, (Christopher) Samuel
Rylant, Cynthia 1954- *112*
  Brief entry *44*
  Earlier sketches in SATA *50, 76*
  See also CLR *86*
  See also SAAS *13*
Rymer, Alta May 1925- *34*

S

S. L. C.
  See Clemens, Samuel Langhorne
S., Svend Otto
  See Soerensen, Svend Otto
Saaf, Donald W(illiam) 1961- *124*
Saal, Jocelyn
  See Sachs, Judith
Sabbeth, Carol (Landstrom) 1957- *125*
Saberhagen, Fred(erick Thomas)
  1930- *89*
  Earlier sketch in SATA *37*
Sabin, Edwin L(egrand) 1870-1952
  See YABC *2*
Sabin, Francene *27*
Sabin, Lou
  See Sabin, Louis
Sabin, Louis 1930- *27*
Sabre, Dirk
  See Laffin, John (Alfred Charles)
Sabuda, Robert (James) 1965- *120*
  Earlier sketch in SATA *81*
Sachar, Louis 1954- *104*
  Brief entry *50*
  Earlier sketch in SATA *63*
  See also CLR *79*
Sachs, Elizabeth-Ann 1946- *48*
Sachs, Judith 1947- *52*
  Brief entry *51*
Sachs, Marilyn (Stickle) 1927- *68*
  Autobiography Feature *110*
  Earlier sketch in SATA *3*
  See also CLR *2*
  See also SAAS *2*
Sackett, S(amuel) J(ohn) 1928- *12*
Sackson, Sid 1920- *16*
Saddler, Allen
  See Richards, R(onald) C(harles) W(illiam)
Saddler, K. Allen
  See Richards, R(onald) C(harles) W(illiam)
Sadie, Stanley (John) 1930- *14*
Sadiq, Nazneen 1944- *101*
Sadler, Catherine Edwards 1952- *60*
  Brief entry *45*
Sadler, Marilyn (June) 1950- *79*
Sadler, Mark
  See Lynds, Dennis
Sagan, Carl (Edward) 1934-1996 ....*58*
  Obituary *94*
Sage, Juniper
  See Brown, Margaret Wise
  and Hurd, Edith Thacher
Sagsoorian, Paul 1923- *12*
Saidman, Anne 1952- *75*
Saint, Dora Jessie 1913- *10*
St. Antoine, Sara L. 1966- *84*
Saint-Exupery, Antoine (Jean Baptiste Marie
  Roger) de 1900-1944 ....*20*
  See also CLR *10*
St. George, Judith 1931- *99*
  Earlier sketch in SATA *13*
  See also CLR *57*
  See also SAAS *12*

St. James, Blakely
  See Gottfried, Theodore Mark
  and Platt, Charles
Saint James, Synthia 1949- *84*
St. John, Nicole *89*
  See also CLR *46*
  See also SAAS *7*
  See Johnston, Norma
St. John, Philip
  See del Rey, Lester
St. John, Wylly Folk 1908-1985 ....*10*
  Obituary *45*
St. Max, E. S.
  See Ellis, Edward S(ylvester)
St. Meyer, Ned
  See Stratemeyer, Edward L.
St. Mox, E. A.
  See Ellis, Edward S(ylvester)
St. Myer, Ned
  See Stratemeyer, Edward L.
St. Tamara
  See Kolba, St. Tamara
Saito, Michiko
  See Fujiwara, Michiko
Sakers, Don 1958- *72*
Sakharnov, S.
  See Sakharnov, Svyatoslav (Vladimirovich)
Sakharnov, Svyatoslav (Vladimirovich)
  1923- *65*
Sakurai, Gail 1952- *87*
Salassi, Otto R(ussell) 1939-1993 ....*38*
  Obituary *77*
Salat, Cristina *82*
Saldutti, Denise 1953- *39*
Salem, Kay 1952- *92*
Salinger, J(erome) D(avid) 1919- *67*
  See also CLR *18*
Salisbury, Graham 1944- *108*
  Earlier sketch in SATA *76*
Salisbury, Joyce E(llen) 1944- *138*
Salkey, (Felix) Andrew (Alexander)
  1928-1995 ....*118*
  Earlier sketch in SATA *35*
Sallis, Susan (Diana) 1929- *55*
Salmon, Annie Elizabeth 1899- *13*
Salsi, Lynn 1947- *130*
Salsitz, R. A. V.
  See Salsitz, Rhondi Vilott
Salsitz, Rhondi Vilott *115*
Salten, Felix
  See Salzmann, Siegmund
Salter, Cedric
  See Knight, Francis Edgar
Saltman, Judith 1947- *64*
Saltzberg, Barney 1955- *135*
Saltzman, David (Charles Laertes)
  1967-1990 ....*86*
Salvadori, Mario (George)
  1907-1997 ....*97*
  Earlier sketch in SATA *40*
Salwood, F. K.
  See Kilworth, Garry (D.)
Salzer, L. E.
  See Wilson, Lionel
Salzman, Marian 1959- *77*
Salzmann, Siegmund 1869-1945 ....*25*
  See Salten, Felix
Samachson, Dorothy (Mirkin)
  1914-1997 ....*3*
Samachson, Joseph 1906-1980 ....*3*
  Obituary *52*
Sammis, John 1942- *4*
Sampson, Emma (Keats) Speed
  1868-1947 ....
Sampson, Fay (Elizabeth) 1935- *42*
  Brief entry *40*
Sampson, Michael 1952- *95*
Samson, Anne S(tringer) 1933- *2*
Samson, Joan 1937-1976 ....*13*
Samson, Suzanne M. 1959- *91*
Samuels, Charles 1902-1982 ....*12*
Samuels, Cynthia K(alish) 1946- *79*

Samuels, Gertrude *17*
Sanborn, Duane 1914-1996 ....*38*
Sancha, Sheila 1924- *38*
Sanchez, Sonia 1934- *136*
  Earlier sketch in SATA *22*
  See also CLR *18*
Sanchez-Silva, Jose Maria 1911- *132*
  Earlier sketch in SATA *16*
  See also CLR *12*
Sand, George X. *45*
Sandak, Cass R(obert) 1950-2001 ....*51*
  Brief entry *37*
Sandberg, (Karin) Inger 1930- *15*
Sandberg, Karl C. 1931- *35*
Sandberg, Lasse (E. M.) 1924- *15*
Sandburg, Carl (August) 1878-1967 ....*8*
  See also CLR *67*
Sandburg, Charles
  See Sandburg, Carl (August)
Sandburg, Charles A.
  See Sandburg, Carl (August)
Sandburg, Helga 1918- *3*
  See also SAAS *10*
Sanderlin, George 1915- *4*
Sanderlin, Owenita (Harrah) 1916- *11*
Sanders, Nancy I. 1960- *141*
  Earlier sketch in SATA *90*
Sanders, Scott Russell 1945- *109*
  Earlier sketch in SATA *56*
Sanders, Winston P.
  See Anderson, Poul (William)
Sanderson, Irma 1912- *66*
Sanderson, Ivan T(erence) 1911-1973 ....*6*
Sanderson, Margaret Love
  See Keats, Emma
  and Sampson, Emma (Keats) Speed
Sanderson, Ruth (L.) 1951- *109*
  Earlier sketch in SATA *41*
Sandin, Joan 1942- *94*
  Earlier sketch in SATA *12*
Sandison, Janet
  See Cameron, Elizabeth Jane
Sandoz, Mari(e Susette) 1900-1966 ....*5*
Sanford, Agnes (White) 1897-1976 ....*61*
Sanford, Doris 1937- *69*
Sanger, Marjory Bartlett 1920- *8*
Sankey, Alice (Ann-Susan) 1910- *27*
San Souci, Daniel *96*
San Souci, Robert D. 1946- *117*
  Earlier sketches in SATA *40, 81*
  See also CLR *43*
Santiago, Esmeralda 1948- *129*
Santos, Helen
  See Griffiths, Helen
Santrey, Louis
  See Sabin, Louis
Santucci, Barbara 1948- *130*
Sapieyevski, Anne Lindbergh
  1940-1993 ....*78*
  Earlier sketch in SATA *35*
  See Feydy, Anne Lindbergh
  and Lindbergh, Anne
Saport, Linda 1954- *123*
Sarac, Roger
  See Caras, Roger A(ndrew)
Sarah, Duchess of York
  See Ferguson, Sarah (Margaret)
Sarasin, Jennifer
  See Sachs, Judith
Sarg, Anthony Frederick
  See Sarg, Tony
Sarg, Tony 1882-1942
  See YABC *1*
Sargent, Pamela 1948- *78*
  Earlier sketch in SATA *29*
Sargent, Robert 1933- *2*
Sargent, Sarah 1937- *44*
  Brief entry *41*
Sargent, Shirley 1927- *11*
Sarnoff, Jane 1937- *10*
Saroyan, William 1908-1981 ....*23*
  Obituary *24*

Sarton, (Eleanor) May 1912-1995 ....*36*
    Obituary *86*
Saseen, Sharon (Dillon) 1949- *59*
Sasek, Miroslav 1916-1980 ....*16*
    Obituary *23*
    See also CLR *4*
Sasso, Sandy Eisenberg 1947- *116*
    Earlier sketch in SATA *86*
Sathre, Vivian 1952- *133*
    Earlier sketch in SATA *79*
Satterfield, Charles
    See del Rey, Lester
    and Pohl, Frederik
Sattgast, L. J.
    See Sattgast, Linda J.
Sattgast, Linda J. 1953- *91*
Sattler, Helen Roney 1921-1992 ....*74*
    Earlier sketch in SATA *4*
    See also CLR *24*
Sauer, Julia Lina 1891-1983 ....*32*
    Obituary *36*
Saul, Carol P. 1947- *117*
    Earlier sketch in SATA *78*
Saul, John (W. III) 1942- *98*
Saul, (Ellen) Wendy 1946- *42*
Saulnier, Karen Luczak 1940- *80*
Saunders, Caleb
    See Heinlein, Robert A(nson)
Saunders, Dave 1939- *85*
Saunders, Julie 1939- *85*
Saunders, (William) Keith
    1910-1994 ....*12*
Saunders, Rubie (Agnes) 1929- *21*
Saunders, Susan 1945- *96*
    Brief entry *41*
    Earlier sketch in SATA *46*
Sauvain, Philip Arthur 1933- *111*
Savadier, Elivia 1950- *79*
Savage, Alan
    See Nicole, Christopher (Robin)
Savage, Blake
    See Goodwin, Harold L(eland)
Savage, Deborah 1955- *76*
Savage, Jeff 1961- *97*
Savageau, Cheryl 1950- *96*
Savery, Constance (Winifred) 1897-1999 ...*1*
Saville, (Leonard) Malcolm
    1901-1982 ....*23*
    Obituary *31*
Saviozzi, Adriana
    See Mazza, Adriana
Savitt, Sam 1917(?)-2000 ....*8*
    Obituary *126*
Savitz, Harriet May 1933- *72*
    Earlier sketch in SATA *5*
    See also SAAS *26*
Sawicki, Mary 1950- *90*
Sawyer, (Frederick) Don(ald) 1947- *72*
Sawyer, Kem Knapp 1953- *84*
Sawyer, Robert J(ames) 1960- *81*
Sawyer, Ruth 1880-1970 ....*17*
    See also CLR *36*
Saxby, H. M.
    See Saxby, (Henry) Maurice
Saxby, (Henry) Maurice 1924- *71*
Saxon, Andrew
    See Arthur, Robert, (Jr.)
Saxon, Antonia
    See Sachs, Judith
Say, Allen 1937- *110*
    Earlier sketches in SATA *28, 69*
    See also CLR *22*
Sayers, Frances Clarke 1897-1989 ....*3*
    Obituary *62*
Sayles, Elizabeth 1956- *108*
Saylor-Marchant, Linda 1963- *82*
Sayre, April Pulley 1966- *131*
    Earlier sketch in SATA *88*
Sazer, Nina 1949- *13*
Scabrini, Janet 1953- *13*
Scagell, Robin 1946- *107*
Scagnetti, Jack 1924- *7*

Scamell, Ragnhild 1940- *77*
Scanlon, Marion Stephany *11*
Scannell, Vernon 1922- *59*
Scarborough, Elizabeth (Ann) 1947- *98*
Scarf, Maggi
    See Scarf, Maggie
Scarf, Maggie 1932- *5*
Scariano, Margaret M. 1924- *86*
Scarlett, Susan
    See Streatfeild, (Mary) Noel
Scarry, Huck
    See Scarry, Richard McClure, Jr.
Scarry, Patricia (Murphy) 1924- *2*
Scarry, Patsy
    See Scarry, Patricia (Murphy)
Scarry, Richard (McClure)
    1919-1994 ....*75*
    Obituary *90*
    Earlier sketches in SATA *2, 35*
    See also CLR *41*
Scarry, Richard McClure, Jr. 1953- *35*
Schachner, Judith Byron 1951- *88*
Schachtel, Roger (Bernard) 1949- *38*
Schaedler, Sally *116*
Schaefer, Jack (Warner) 1907-1991 ....*66*
    Obituary *65*
    Earlier sketch in SATA *3*
Schaefer, Lola M. 1950- *91*
Schaeffer, Mead 1898- *21*
Schaeffer, Susan Fromberg 1941- *22*
Schaer, Brigitte 1958- *112*
Schaller, George B(eals) 1933- *30*
Schanzer, Rosalyn (Good) 1942- *138*
    Earlier sketch in SATA *77*
Schatell, Brian *66*
    Brief entry *47*
Schechter, Betty (Goodstein) 1921- *5*
Schecter, Ellen 1944- *85*
Scheeder, Louis 1946- *141*
Scheer, Julian (Weisel) 1926-2001 ....*8*
Scheffer, Victor B(lanchard) 1906- *6*
Scheffler, Ursel 1938- *81*
Scheffrin-Falk, Gladys 1928- *76*
Scheidl, Gerda Marie 1913- *85*
Scheier, Michael 1943- *40*
    Brief entry *36*
Schell, Mildred 1922- *41*
Schell, Orville (Hickok) 1940- *10*
Scheller, Melanie 1953- *77*
Schellie, Don 1932- *29*
Schembri, Jim 1962- *124*
Schemm, Mildred Walker 1905-1998 ....*21*
    Obituary *103*
Schenker, Dona 1947- *133*
    Earlier sketch in SATA *68*
Scher, Paula 1948- *47*
Scherf, Margaret 1908-1979 ....*10*
Schermer, Judith (Denise) 1941- *30*
Schertle, Alice 1941- *90*
    Earlier sketch in SATA *36*
Schick, Alice 1946- *27*
Schick, Eleanor 1942- *82*
    Earlier sketch in SATA *9*
Schick, Joel 1945- *31*
    Brief entry *30*
Schields, Gretchen 1948- *75*
Schiff, Ken(neth Roy) 1942- *7*
Schiller, Andrew 1919- *21*
Schiller, Barbara (Heyman) 1928- *21*
Schiller, Pamela (Byrne) *127*
Schindel, John 1955- *115*
    Earlier sketch in SATA *77*
Schindelman, Joseph 1923- *67*
    Brief entry *32*
Schindler, S(teven) D. 1952- *118*
    Brief entry *50*
    Earlier sketch in SATA *75*
Schinto, Jeanne 1951- *93*
Schisgall, Oscar 1901-1984 ....*12*
    Obituary *38*
    See Cole, Jackson

Schlee, Ann 1934- *44*
    Brief entry *36*
Schleichert, Elizabeth 1945- *77*
Schlein, Miriam 1926- *130*
    Earlier sketches in SATA *2, 87*
    See also CLR *41*
Schlesinger, Arthur M(eier), Jr.
    1917- *61*
Schlessinger, Laura 1947(?)- *110*
Schloat, G. Warren, Jr. 1914-2000 ....*4*
Schmid, Eleonore 1939- *126*
    Earlier sketches in SATA *12, 84*
Schmiderer, Dorothy 1940- *19*
Schmidt, Annie M. G. 1911-1995 ....*67*
    Obituary *91*
    See also CLR *22*
Schmidt, Diane 1953- *70*
Schmidt, Elizabeth 1915- *15*
Schmidt, Gary D. 1957- *135*
    Earlier sketch in SATA *93*
Schmidt, James Norman 1912-1983 ....*21*
Schmidt, Karen Lee 1953- *94*
Schmidt, Lynette 1952- *76*
Schneider, Antonie 1954- *89*
Schneider, Christine M. 1972(?)- *120*
Schneider, Elisa
    See Kleven, Elisa
Schneider, Herman 1905- *7*
Schneider, Laurie
    See Adams, Laurie
Schneider, Nina 1913- *2*
Schneider, Rex 1937- *44*
Schnirel, James R. 1931- *14*
Schnitter, Jane T. 1958- *88*
Schnitzlein, Danny *134*
Schnur, Steven 1952- *95*
Schoberle, Cecile 1949- *80*
Schock, Pauline 1928- *45*
Schoen, Barbara (Taylor) 1924-1993 ....*13*
Schoenherr, John (Carl) 1935- *66*
    Earlier sketch in SATA *37*
    See also SAAS *13*
Schofield, Sandy
    See Rusch, Kristine Kathryn
Scholastica, Sister Mary
    See Jenkins, Marie M(agdalen)
Scholefield, A. T.
    See Scholefield, Alan
Scholefield, Alan 1931- *66*
Scholefield, Edmund O.
    See Butterworth, W(illiam) E(dmund III)
Scholey, Arthur 1932- *28*
Schone, Virginia *22*
Schongut, Emanuel 1936- *52*
    Brief entry *36*
Schoonover, Frank (Earle)
    1877-1972 ....*24*
Schoor, Gene 1921- *3*
Schories, Pat 1952- *116*
Schotter, Roni *105*
Schraff, Anne E(laine) 1939- *92*
    Earlier sketch in SATA *27*
Schram, Peninnah 1934- *119*
Schrecengost, Maity
    See Schrecengost, S. Maitland
Schrecengost, S. Maitland 1938- *118*
Schrecker, Judie 1954- *90*
Schreiber, Elizabeth Anne (Ferguson)
    1947- *13*
Schreiber, Ralph W(alter) 1942- *13*
Schreiner, Samuel A(gnew), Jr.
    1921- *70*
Schroeder, Alan 1961- *98*
    Earlier sketch in SATA *66*
Schroeder, Binette *56*
    See Nickl, Barbara (Elisabeth)
Schubert, Dieter 1947- *101*
    Earlier sketch in SATA *62*
Schubert-Gabrys, Ingrid 1953- *101*
    Earlier sketch in SATA *62*
Schuerger, Michele R. *110*
Schuett, Stacey 1960- *75*

Schulke, Flip Phelps Graeme 1930- *57*
Schulman, Arlene 1961- *105*
Schulman, Janet 1933- *137*
    Earlier sketch in SATA *22*
Schulman, L(ester) M(artin) 1934- *13*
Schulte, Elaine L(ouise) 1934- *36*
Schultz, Betty K(epka) 1932- *125*
Schultz, Gwendolyn *21*
Schultz, James Willard 1859-1947
    See YABC *1*
Schultz, Pearle Henriksen 1918- *21*
Schulz, Charles M(onroe) 1922-2000 ......*10*
    Obituary *118*
Schumaker, Ward 1943- *96*
Schuman, Michael
    See Schuman, Michael A.
Schuman, Michael A. 1953- *134*
    Earlier sketch in SATA *85*
Schur, Maxine
    See Schur, Maxine Rose
Schur, Maxine Rose 1948- *98*
    Autobiography Feature *135*
    Brief entry *49*
    Earlier sketch in SATA *53*
Schurfranz, Vivian 1925- *13*
Schutzer, A. I. 1922- *13*
Schuyler, Pamela R. 1948- *30*
Schwager, Tina 1964- *110*
Schwandt, Stephen (William) 1947- *61*
Schwark, Mary Beth 1954- *51*
Schwartz, Alvin 1927-1992 ....*56*
    Obituary *71*
    Earlier sketch in SATA *4*
    See also CLR *3*
Schwartz, Amy 1954- *131*
    Brief entry *41*
    Earlier sketches in SATA *47, 83*
    See also CLR *25*
    See also SAAS *18*
Schwartz, Anne Powers 1913-1987 ....*10*
Schwartz, Carol 1954- *77*
Schwartz, Charles W(alsh) 1914- *8*
Schwartz, David M(artin) 1951- *110*
    Earlier sketch in SATA *59*
Schwartz, Elizabeth Reeder 1912- *8*
Schwartz, Ellen 1949- *117*
Schwartz, Jerome L.
    See Lawrence, Jerome
Schwartz, Joel L. 1940- *54*
    Brief entry *51*
Schwartz, Joyce R. 1950- *93*
Schwartz, Julius 1907- *45*
Schwartz, Perry 1942- *75*
Schwartz, Sheila (Ruth) 1929- *27*
Schwartz, Stephen (Lawrence) 1948- *19*
Schwartz, Virginia Frances 1950- *131*
Schwarz, (Silvia Tessa) Viviane
    1977- *141*
Schweitzer, Byrd Baylor
    See Baylor, Byrd
Schweitzer, Iris *59*
    Brief entry *36*
Schweninger, Ann 1951- *98*
    Earlier sketch in SATA *29*
Schwerin, Doris H(alpern) 1922- *64*
Scieszka, Jon 1954- *105*
    Earlier sketch in SATA *68*
    See also CLR *27*
Scillian, Devin *128*
Scioscia, Mary (Hershey) 1926- *63*
Scofield, Penrod 1933- *62*
    Obituary *78*
Scoggin, Margaret C(lara) 1905-1968 ......*47*
    Brief entry *28*
Scoltock, Jack 1942- *141*
    Earlier sketch in SATA *72*
Scoppettone, Sandra 1936- *92*
    Earlier sketch in SATA *9*
    See Early, Jack
Scot, Michael
    See Rohan, Michael Scott

Scotland, Jay
    See Jakes, John (William)
Scott, Alastair
    See Allen, Kenneth S.
Scott, Ann Herbert 1926- *140*
    Brief entry *29*
    Earlier sketches in SATA *56, 94*
Scott, Bill
    See Scott, William N(eville)
Scott, Cora Annett (Pipitone) 1931- *11*
Scott, Dan
    See Barker, S(quire) Omar
Scott, Elaine 1940- *90*
    Earlier sketch in SATA *36*
Scott, Jack Denton 1915-1995 ....*83*
    Earlier sketch in SATA *31*
    See also CLR *20*
    See also SAAS *14*
Scott, Jane (Harrington) 1931- *55*
Scott, John 1912-1976 ....*14*
Scott, John Anthony 1916- *23*
Scott, John M(artin) 1913- *12*
Scott, Mary
    See Mattern, Joanne
Scott, Melissa 1960- *109*
Scott, Richard
    See Rennert, Richard Scott
Scott, Roney
    See Gault, William Campbell
Scott, Sally 1909-1978 ....*43*
Scott, Sally (Elisabeth) 1948- *44*
Scott, W. N.
    See Scott, William N(eville)
Scott, Sir Walter 1771-1832
    See YABC *2*
Scott, Warwick
    See Trevor, Elleston
Scott, William N(eville) 1923- *87*
Scotti, Anna
    See Coates, Anna
Scotti, Anna
    See Coates, Anna
Scribner, Charles, Jr. 1921-1995 ....*13*
    Obituary *87*
Scribner, Joanne L. 1949- *33*
Scribner, Kimball 1917- *63*
Scrimger, Richard 1957- *119*
Scroder, Walter K. 1928- *82*
Scruggs, Sandy 1961- *89*
Scull, Marie-Louise 1943-1993 ....*77*
Scuro, Vincent 1951- *21*
Seabrooke, Brenda 1941- *88*
    Earlier sketch in SATA *30*
Seaman, Augusta Huiell 1879-1950 ....*31*
Seamands, Ruth 1916- *9*
Searcy, Margaret Zehmer 1926- *54*
    Brief entry *39*
Searight, Mary W(illiams) 1918- *17*
Searle, Kathryn Adrienne 1942- *10*
Searle, Ronald (William Fordham)
    1920- *70*
    Earlier sketch in SATA *42*
Sears, Stephen W. 1932- *4*
Sebastian, Lee
    See Silverberg, Robert
Sebestyen, Igen
    See Sebestyen, Ouida
Sebestyen, Ouida 1924- *140*
    Earlier sketch in SATA *39*
    See also CLR *17*
    See also SAAS *10*
Sebrey, Mary Ann 1951- *62*
Sechrist, Elizabeth Hough 1903-1991 ....*2*
Sedges, John
    See Buck, Pearl S(ydenstricker)
Seed, Cecile Eugenie 1930- *86*
    See Seed, Jenny
Seed, Jenny *8*
    See also CLR *76*
    See Seed, Cecile Eugenie
Seeger, Pete(r R.) 1919- *139*
    Earlier sketch in SATA *13*

Seeley, Laura L. 1958- *71*
Seever, R.
    See Reeves, Lawrence F.
Sefozo, Mary 1925- *82*
Sefton, Catherine
    See Waddell, Martin
Segal, Joyce 1940- *35*
Segal, Lore (Groszmann) 1928- *66*
    Earlier sketch in SATA *4*
    See also SAAS *11*
Segar, E(lzie) C(risler) 1894-1938 ....*61*
Seguin, Marilyn W(eymouth) 1951- *91*
Seguin-Fontes, Marthe 1924- *109*
Seibold, J. Otto 1960- *83*
    See also SAAS *22*
Seidel, Ross *95*
Seidelman, James Edward 1926- *6*
Seiden, Art(hur) *107*
    Brief entry *42*
Seidler, Ann (G.) 1925- *131*
Seidler, Tor 1952- *98*
    Brief entry *46*
    Earlier sketch in SATA *52*
Seidman, Laurence Ivan 1925- *15*
Seigel, Kalman 1917-1998 ....*12*
    Obituary *103*
Seignobosc, Francoise 1897-1961 ....*21*
Seitz, Jacqueline 1931- *50*
Seixas, Judith S. 1922- *17*
Sejima, Yoshimasa 1913- *8*
Selberg, Ingrid (Maria) 1950- *68*
Selden, George
    See CLR *8*
    See Thompson, George Selden
Selden, Neil R(oy) 1931- *61*
Self, Margaret Cabell 1902-1996 ....*24*
Selig, Sylvie 1942- *13*
Sellers, Naomi
    See Flack, Naomi John White
Selman, LaRue W. 1927- *55*
Selsam, Millicent E(llis) 1912-1996 ....*29*
    Obituary *92*
    Earlier sketch in SATA *1*
    See also CLR *1*
Seltzer, Meyer 1932- *17*
Seltzer, Richard (Warren, Jr.) 1946- *41*
Selway, Martina 1940- *74*
Selznick, Brian 1966- *117*
    Earlier sketch in SATA *79*
Semel, Nava 1954- *107*
Semloh
    See Holmes, Peggy
Sendak, Jack 1924(?)-1995 ....*28*
Sendak, Maurice (Bernard) 1928- *113*
    Earlier sketches in SATA *1, 27*
    See also CLR *74*
Sender, Ruth M(insky) 1926- *62*
Sengler, Johanna 1924- *18*
Senisi, Ellen B(abinec) 1951- *116*
Senn, J(oyce) A(nn) 1941- *115*
Senn, Steve 1950- *60*
    Brief entry *48*
Serage, Nancy 1924- *10*
Seredy, Kate 1899-1975 ....*1*
    Obituary *24*
    See also CLR *10*
Seroff, Victor I(lyitch) 1902-1979 ....*12*
    Obituary *26*
Serraillier, Ian (Lucien) 1912-1994 ....*73*
    Obituary *83*
    Earlier sketch in SATA *1*
    See also CLR *2*
    See also SAAS *3*
Servello, Joe 1932- *10*
Service, Pamela F. 1945- *64*
Service, Robert
    See Service, Robert W(illiam)
Service, Robert W(illiam)
    1874(?)-1958 ....*20*
    See Service, Robert
Serwadda, W(illiam) Moses 1931- *27*

Serwer-Bernstein, Blanche L(uria)
  1910-1997 ....*10*
Sescoe, Vincent E. 1938- *123*
Seth, Mary
  See Lexau, Joan M.
Seton, Anya 1904(?)-1990 ....*3*
  Obituary *66*
Seton, Ernest (Evan) Thompson
  1860-1946 ....*18*
  See also CLR *59*
Seton-Thompson, Ernest
  See Seton, Ernest (Evan) Thompson
Seuling, Barbara 1937- *98*
  Earlier sketch in SATA *10*
  See also SAAS *24*
Seuss, Dr.
  See Dr. Seuss
  and Geisel, Theodor Seuss
  and LeSieg, Theo.
  and Stone, Rosetta
Severn, Bill
  See Severn, William Irving
Severn, David
  See Unwin, David S(torr)
Severn, William Irving 1914- *1*
Sewall, Marcia 1935- *119*
  Earlier sketches in SATA *37, 69*
Seward, Prudence 1926- *16*
Sewell, Anna 1820-1878 ....*100*
  Earlier sketch in SATA *24*
  See also CLR *17*
Sewell, Helen (Moore) 1896-1957 ....*38*
Sexton, Anne (Harvey) 1928-1974 ....*10*
Seymour, Alta Halverson *10*
Seymour, Jane 1951- *139*
Seymour, Tres 1966- *82*
Shachtman, Tom 1942- *49*
Shackleton, C. C.
  See Aldiss, Brian W(ilson)
Shader, Rachel
  See Sofer, Barbara
Shafer, Robert E(ugene) 1925- *9*
Shaffer, Terea 1968- *79*
Shahan, Sherry 1949- *134*
  Earlier sketch in SATA *92*
Shahn, Bernarda Bryson
  See Bryson, Bernarda
Shaik, Fatima *114*
Shan, Darren
  See O'Shaughnessy, Darren
Shane, Harold Gray 1914-1993 ....*36*
  Obituary *76*
Shanks, Ann Zane (Kushner) *10*
Shannon, David 1959- *107*
  See also CLR *87*
Shannon, George (William Bones)
  1952- *94*
  Earlier sketch in SATA *35*
Shannon, Jacqueline *63*
Shannon, Margaret
  See Silverwood, Margaret Shannon
Shannon, Monica 1905(?)-1965 ....*28*
Shannon, Terry *21*
  See Mercer, Jessie
Shapiro, Irwin 1911-1981 ....*32*
Shapiro, Milton J. 1926- *32*
Shapp, Martha Glauber 1910- *3*
Sharfman, Amalie *14*
Sharma, Partap 1939- *15*
Sharma, Rashmi
  See Singh, Rashmi Sharma
Sharman, Alison
  See Leonard, Alison
Sharmat, Marjorie Weinman 1928- *133*
  Earlier sketches in SATA *4, 33, 74*
Sharmat, Mitchell 1927- *127*
  Earlier sketch in SATA *33*
Sharp, Luke
  See Alkiviades, Alkis

Sharp, Margery 1905-1991 ....*29*
  Obituary *67*
  Earlier sketch in SATA *1*
  See also CLR *27*
Sharpe, Jon
  See Knott, William C(ecil, Jr.)
Sharpe, Mitchell R(aymond) 1924- *12*
Sharpe, Susan 1946- *71*
Sharratt, Nick 1962- *104*
Shasha, Mark 1961- *80*
Shattuck, Roger (Whitney) 1923- *64*
Shaw, Arnold 1909-1989 ....*4*
  Obituary *63*
Shaw, Carolyn V. 1934- *91*
Shaw, Charles (Green) 1892-1974 ....*13*
Shaw, Evelyn S. 1927- *28*
Shaw, Flora Louisa
  See Lugard, Flora Louisa Shaw
Shaw, Janet 1937- *61*
Shaw, Janet Beeler
  See Shaw, Janet
Shaw, Margret 1940- *68*
Shaw, Nancy 1946- *71*
Shaw, Ray *7*
Shaw, Richard 1923- *12*
Shawn, Frank S.
  See Goulart, Ron(ald Joseph)
Shay, Art
  See Shay, Arthur
Shay, Arthur 1922- *4*
Shay, Lacey
  See Shebar, Sharon Sigmond
Shea, George 1940- *54*
  Brief entry *42*
Shea, Pegi Deitz 1960- *137*
  Earlier sketch in SATA *77*
Shearer, John 1947- *43*
  Brief entry *27*
  See also CLR *34*
Shearer, Ted 1919- *43*
Shebar, Sharon Sigmond 1945- *36*
Shecter, Ben 1935- *16*
Shedd, Warner 1934- *87*
Sheedy, Alexandra Elizabeth 1962- *39*
  Earlier sketch in SATA *19*
Sheehan, Ethna 1908-2000 ....*9*
Sheehan, Patty 1945- *77*
Sheehan, Sean 1951- *86*
Shefelman, Janice Jordan 1930- *129*
  Earlier sketch in SATA *58*
Shefelman, Tom (Whitehead) 1927- *58*
Sheffer, H. R.
  See Abels, Harriette S(heffer)
Sheffield, Charles 1935-2002 ....*109*
Sheffield, Janet N. 1926- *26*
Sheikh, Nazneen
  See Sadiq, Nazneen
Shekerjian, Regina Tor *16*
Shelby, Anne 1948- *85*
  Autobiography Feature *121*
  See also SAAS *26*
Sheldon, Ann
  See Antle, Nancy
Sheldon, Ann *67*
  Earlier sketch in SATA *1*
Sheldon, Aure 1917-1976 ....*12*
Sheldon, John
  See Bloch, Robert (Albert)
Sheldon, Muriel 1926- *45*
  Brief entry *39*
Shelley, Frances
  See Wees, Frances Shelley
Shelley, Mary Wollstonecraft (Godwin)
  1797-1851 ....*29*
Shelton, William Roy 1919-1995 ....*5*
  Obituary *129*
Shemie, Bonnie (Jean Brenner)
  1949- *96*
Shemin, Margaretha (Hoeneveld)
  1928- *4*
Shenton, Edward 1895-1977 ....*45*

Shepard, Aaron 1950- *113*
  Earlier sketch in SATA *75*
Shepard, Ernest Howard 1879-1976 ......*100*
  Obituary *24*
  Earlier sketches in SATA *3, 33*
  See also CLR *27*
Shepard, Jim 1956- *90*
Shepard, Mary
  See Knox, (Mary) Eleanor Jessie
Shephard, Esther 1891-1975 ....*5*
  Obituary *26*
Shepherd, Donna Walsh
  See Walsh Shepherd, Donna
Shepherd, Elizabeth *4*
Sherburne, Zoa (Lillian Morin)
  1912-1995 ....*3*
  See also SAAS *18*
Sherlock, Patti *71*
Sherman, D(enis) R(onald) 1934- *48*
  Brief entry *29*
Sherman, Diane (Finn) 1928- *12*
Sherman, Elizabeth
  See Friskey, Margaret (Richards)
Sherman, Harold (Morrow)
  1898-1987 ....*37*
  Obituary *137*
Sherman, Josepha *75*
Sherman, Michael
  See Lowndes, Robert A(ugustine) W(ard)
Sherman, Nancy
  See Rosenberg, Nancy (Sherman)
Sherman, Peter Michael
  See Lowndes, Robert A(ugustine) W(ard)
Sherrard, Valerie (Anne) 1957- *141*
Sherrod, Jane
  See Singer, Jane Sherrod
Sherry, Clifford J. 1943- *84*
Sherry, (Dulcie) Sylvia 1932- *122*
  Earlier sketch in SATA *8*
Sherwan, Earl 1917- *3*
Sherwood, Jonathan
  See London, Jonathan (Paul)
Shetterly, Will(iam Howard) 1955- *78*
  Autobiography Feature *106*
Shiefman, Vicky 1942- *22*
Shields, Brenda Desmond (Armstrong)
  1914- *37*
Shields, Charles 1944- *10*
Shiels, Barbara
  See Adams, Barbara Johnston
Shiffman, Lena 1957- *101*
Shiina, Makoto 1944- *83*
Shimin, Symeon 1902-1984 ....*13*
Shine, Andrea 1955- *104*
Shine, Deborah 1932- *71*
Shinn, Everett 1876-1953 ....*21*
Shinn, Sharon 1957- *110*
Shippen, Katherine B(inney)
  1892-1980 ....*1*
  Obituary *23*
  See also CLR *36*
Shipton, Eric Earle 1907-1977 ....*10*
Shirer, William L(awrence)
  1904-1993 ....*45*
  Obituary *78*
Shirley, Gayle C(orbett) 1955- *96*
Shirley, Jean 1919- *70*
Shirreffs, Gordon D(onald)
  1914-1996 ....*11*
  See Donalds, Gordon
  and Flynn, Jackson
  and Gordon, Stewart
Shirts, Morris A(lpine) 1922- *63*
Shlichta, Joe 1968- *84*
Shmurak, Carole B. 1944- *118*
Shore, June Lewis *30*
Shore, Nancy 1960- *124*
Shore, Robert 1924- *39*
Short, Michael 1937- *65*
Short, Roger
  See Arkin, Alan (Wolf)
Shortall, Leonard W. *19*

Shortt, Tim(othy Donald) 1961- *96*
Shotwell, Louisa Rossiter 1902-1993 ....*3*
Shoup, Barbara 1947- *86*
    See also SAAS 24
Showalter, Jean B(reckinridge) *12*
Showell, Ellen Harvey 1934- *33*
Showers, Paul C. 1910-1999 ....*92*
    Obituary *114*
    Earlier sketch in SATA *21*
    See also CLR 6
    See also SAAS 7
Shpakow, Tanya 1959(?)- *94*
Shpitalnik, Vladimir 1964- *83*
Shreve, Susan Richards 1939- *95*
    Brief entry *41*
    Earlier sketch in SATA *46*
Shriver, Jean Adair 1932- *75*
Shriver, Maria (Owings) 1955- *134*
Shrode, Mary
    See Hollingsworth, Mary
Shtainmets, Leon *32*
Shub, Elizabeth *5*
Shuken, Julia 1948- *84*
Shulevitz, Uri 1935- *106*
    Earlier sketches in SATA *3, 50*
    See also CLR 61
Shulman, Alix Kates 1932- *7*
Shulman, Irving 1913-1995 ....*13*
Shulman, Neil B(arnett) 1945- *89*
Shumsky, Zena
    See Collier, Zena
Shura, Mary Francis
    See Craig, Mary (Francis) Shura
Shusterman, Neal 1962- *140*
    Earlier sketches in SATA *85, 121*
Shuter, Jane Margaret 1955- *90*
Shuttlesworth, Dorothy Edwards *3*
Shwartz, Susan (Martha) 1949- *94*
Shyer, Christopher 1961- *98*
Shyer, Marlene Fanta *13*
Siberell, Anne *29*
Sibley, Don 1922- *12*
Siburt, Ruth 1951- *121*
Siculan, Daniel 1922- *12*
Sidgwick, Ethel 1877-1970 ....*116*
Sidjakov, Nicolas 1924- *18*
Sidney, Frank
    See Warwick, Alan R(oss)
Sidney, Margaret
    See Lothrop, Harriet Mulford Stone
Siegal, Aranka 1930- *88*
    Brief entry *37*
Siegel, Beatrice *36*
Siegel, Helen
    See Siegl, Helen
Siegel, Robert (Harold) 1939- *39*
Siegelson, Kim L. 1962- *114*
Siegl, Helen 1924- *34*
Sierra, Judy 1945- *104*
Silas
    See McCay, (Zenas) Winsor
Silcock, Sara Lesley 1947- *12*
Sill, Cathryn 1953- *141*
    Earlier sketch in SATA *74*
Sill, John 1947- *140*
    Earlier sketch in SATA *74*
Sillitoe, Alan 1928- *61*
Sills, Leslie (Elka) 1948- *129*
Silly, E. S.
    See Kraus, (Herman) Robert
Silsbe, Brenda 1953- *73*
Silva, Joseph
    See Goulart, Ron(ald Joseph)
Silver, Ruth
    See Chew, Ruth
Silverberg, Robert 1935- *91*
    Autobiography Feature *104*
    Earlier sketch in SATA *13*
    See also CLR 59
Silverman, Erica 1955- *112*
    Earlier sketch in SATA *78*
Silverman, Janis L. 1946- *127*

Silverman, Mel(vin Frank) 1931-1966 ......*9*
Silverman, Robin L(andew) 1954- *96*
Silverstein, Alvin 1933- *124*
    Earlier sketches in SATA *8, 69*
    See also CLR 25
Silverstein, Herma 1945- *106*
Silverstein, Robert Alan 1959- *124*
    Earlier sketch in SATA *77*
Silverstein, Shel(don Allan)
    1932-1999 ....*92*
    Brief entry *27*
    Obituary *116*
    Earlier sketch in SATA *33*
    See also CLR 5
Silverstein, Virginia B(arbara Opshelor)
    1937- *124*
    Earlier sketches in SATA *8, 69*
    See also CLR 25
Silverthorne, Elizabeth 1930- *35*
Silverwood, Margaret Shannon
    1966- *137*
    Earlier sketch in SATA *83*
Silvey, Diane F. 1946- *135*
Sim, Dorrith M. 1931- *96*
Simmie, Lois (Ann) 1932- *106*
Simmonds, Posy 1945- *130*
    See also CLR 23
Simmons, Andra 1939- *141*
Simmons, Elly 1955- *134*
Simms, Laura 1947- *117*
Simner, Janni Lee *113*
Simon, Charlie May
    See Fletcher, Charlie May Hogue
Simon, Francesca 1955- *111*
Simon, Gabriel 1972- *118*
Simon, Hilda Rita 1921- *28*
    See also CLR 39
Simon, Howard 1903-1979 ....*32*
    Obituary *21*
Simon, Joe
    See Simon, Joseph H.
Simon, Joseph H. 1913- *7*
Simon, Martin P(aul William)
    1903-1969 ....*12*
Simon, Mina Lewiton
    See Lewiton, Mina
Simon, Norma (Feldstein) 1927- *129*
    Earlier sketches in SATA *3, 68*
Simon, Seymour 1931- *138*
    Earlier sketches in SATA *4, 73*
    See also CLR 63
Simon, Shirley (Schwartz) 1921- *11*
Simon, Solomon 1895-1970 ....*40*
Simonetta, Linda 1948- *14*
Simonetta, Sam 1936- *14*
Simons, Barbara B(rooks) 1934- *41*
Simont, Marc 1915- *126*
    Earlier sketches in SATA *9, 73*
Simpson, Colin 1908-1983 ....*14*
Simpson, Harriette
    See Arnow, Harriette (Louisa) Simpson
Simpson, Jacynth Hope
    See Hope Simpson, Jacynth
Simpson, Margaret 1943- *128*
Simpson, Myrtle L(illias) 1931- *14*
Sims, Blanche (L.) *75*
Simundsson, Elva 1950- *63*
Sinclair, Clover
    See Gater, Dilys
Sinclair, Emil
    See Hesse, Hermann
Sinclair, Jeff 1958- *77*
Sinclair, Olga 1923- *121*
Sinclair, Rose
    See Smith, Susan Vernon
Sinclair, Upton (Beall) 1878-1968 ....*9*
Singer, A. L.
    See Lerangis, Peter
Singer, Arthur 1917-1990 ....*64*
Singer, Isaac
    See Singer, Isaac Bashevis

Singer, Isaac Bashevis 1904-1991 ....*27*
    Obituary *68*
    Earlier sketch in SATA *3*
    See also CLR 1
Singer, Jane Sherrod 1917-1985 ....*4*
    Obituary *42*
Singer, Julia 1917- *28*
Singer, Kurt D(eutsch) 1911- *38*
Singer, Marilyn 1948- *125*
    Brief entry *38*
    Earlier sketches in SATA *48, 80*
    See also CLR 48
    See also SAAS 13
Singer, Muff 1942- *104*
Singer, Susan (Mahler) 1941- *9*
Singh, Rashmi Sharma 1952- *90*
Singleton, Linda Joy 1957- *88*
Sinykin, Sheri Cooper 1950- *133*
    Earlier sketch in SATA *72*
Sipiera, Paul P., (Jr.) 1948- *89*
Siracusa, Catherine (Jane) 1947- *82*
Sirett, Dawn (Karen) 1966- *88*
Sirof, Harriet 1930- *94*
    Earlier sketch in SATA *37*
Sirois, Allen L. 1950- *76*
Sirvaitis (Chernyaev), Karen (Ann)
    1961- *79*
Sis, Peter 1949- *106*
    Earlier sketch in SATA *67*
    See also CLR 45
    See Sis, Peter
Sisson, Rosemary Anne 1923- *11*
Sister Mary Terese
    See Donze, Mary Terese
Sita, Lisa 1962- *87*
Sitomer, Harry 1903-1985 ....*31*
Sitomer, Mindel 1903-1987 ....*31*
Sive, Helen R(obinson) 1951- *30*
Sivulich, Sandra (Jeanne) Stroner 1941- *9*
Skarmeta, Antonio 1940- *57*
Skelly, James R(ichard) 1927- *17*
Skinner, Constance Lindsay 1877-1939
    See YABC 1
Skinner, Cornelia Otis 1901-1979 ....*2*
Skipper, G. C. 1939- *46*
    Brief entry *38*
Skofield, James *95*
    Brief entry *44*
Skold, Betty Westrom 1923- *41*
Skorpen, Liesel Moak 1935- *3*
Skott, Maria
    See Nikolajeva, Maria
Skrypuch, Marsha Forchuk 1954- *134*
Skurzynski, Gloria (Joan) 1930- *122*
    Earlier sketches in SATA *8, 74*
    See also SAAS 9
Skutch, Robert 1925- *89*
Skye, Maggie
    See Werner, Herma
Slackman, Charles B. 1934- *12*
Slade, Arthur G(regory) 1967- *106*
Slade, Richard 1910-1971 ....*9*
Slangerup, Erik Jon 1969- *130*
Slate, Joseph (Frank) 1928- *122*
    Earlier sketch in SATA *38*
Slater, Ray
    See Lansdale, Joe R(ichard)
Slaughter, Hope 1940- *84*
Slaughter, Jean
    See Doty, Jean Slaughter
Slavin, Bill 1959- *76*
Sleator, William (Warner III) 1945- *118*
    Earlier sketches in SATA *3, 68*
    See also CLR 29
Sleigh, Barbara 1906-1982 ....*86*
    Obituary *30*
    Earlier sketch in SATA *3*
Slepian, Jan(ice B.) 1921- *85*
    Brief entry *45*
    Earlier sketch in SATA *51*
    See also SAAS 8
Slicer, Margaret O. 1920- *4*

Slier, Debby
  See Shine, Deborah
Sloan, Carolyn 1937- *116*
  Earlier sketch in SATA *58*
Sloan, Glenna (Davis) 1930- *120*
Sloane, Eric 1910(?)-1985 ....*52*
  Obituary *42*
Sloane, Todd 1955- *88*
Sloat, Teri 1948- *106*
Slobodkin, Florence Gersh 1905-1994 ......*5*
  Obituary *107*
Slobodkin, Louis 1903-1975 ....*26*
  Earlier sketch in SATA *1*
Slobodkina, Esphyr 1908-2002 ....*1*
  Obituary *135*
  See also SAAS *8*
Sloggett, Nellie 1851-1923 ....*44*
Sloss, Lesley Lord 1965- *72*
Slote, Alfred 1926- *72*
  Earlier sketch in SATA *8*
  See also CLR *4*
  See also SAAS *21*
Slote, Elizabeth 1956- *80*
Small, David 1945- *126*
  Brief entry *46*
  Earlier sketches in SATA *50, 95*
  See also CLR *53*
Small, Ernest
  See Lent, Blair
Small, Terry 1942- *75*
Smalls-Hector, Irene 1950- *73*
Smaridge, Norah (Antoinette) 1903-1994 ...*6*
Smee, Nicola 1948- *76*
Smiley, Virginia Kester 1923- *2*
Smith, Anne Warren 1938- *41*
  Brief entry *34*
Smith, Barry (Edward Jervis) 1943- *75*
Smith, Beatrice S(chillinger) *12*
Smith, Betsy Covington 1937- *55*
  Earlier sketch in SATA *43*
Smith, Betty (Wehner) 1904-1972 ....*6*
Smith, Bradford 1909-1964 ....*5*
Smith, Brenda 1946- *82*
Smith, C. Pritchard
  See Hoyt, Edwin P(almer), Jr.
Smith, Caesar
  See Trevor, Elleston
Smith, Craig 1955- *117*
  Earlier sketch in SATA *81*
Smith, Datus C(lifford), Jr.
  1907-1999 ....*13*
  Obituary *116*
Smith, Debra 1955- *89*
Smith, Derek 1943- *141*
Smith, Dick King
  See King-Smith, Dick
Smith, Dodie
  See Smith, Dorothy Gladys
Smith, Doris Buchanan 1934-2002 ....*75*
  Obituary *140*
  Earlier sketch in SATA *28*
  See also SAAS *10*
Smith, Dorothy Gladys 1896-1990 ....*82*
  Obituary *65*
  See Smith, Dodie
Smith, Dorothy Stafford 1905- *6*
Smith, E(lmer) Boyd 1860-1943
  See YABC *1*
Smith, E(dric) Brooks 1917- *40*
Smith, Emma 1923- *52*
  Brief entry *36*
Smith, (Katherine) Eunice (Young)
  1902-1993 ....*5*
Smith, Frances C(hristine) 1904-1986 ....*3*
Smith, Gary R. 1932- *14*
Smith, Geof 1969- *102*
Smith, George Harmon 1920- *5*
Smith, Howard E(verett), Jr. 1927- *12*
Smith, Hugh L(etcher) 1921-1968 ....*5*
Smith, Imogene Henderson 1922- *12*
Smith, Jacqueline B. 1937- *39*

Smith, Janet (Buchanan) Adam
  See Adam Smith, Janet (Buchanan)
Smith, Janice Lee 1949- *54*
Smith, Jean
  See Smith, Frances C(hristine)
Smith, Jean Pajot 1945- *10*
Smith, Jeff(rey Alan) 1958- *93*
Smith, Jeff Allen
  See Smith, Jeff(rey Alan)
Smith, Jenny 1963- *90*
Smith, Jessie
  See Kunhardt, Edith
Smith, Jessie Willcox 1863-1935 ....*21*
  See also CLR *59*
Smith, Joan (Mary) 1933- *54*
  Brief entry *46*
Smith, Johnston
  See Crane, Stephen (Townley)
Smith, Jos(eph) A. 1936- *120*
  Earlier sketch in SATA *73*
Smith, Judie R. 1936- *80*
Smith, Lafayette
  See Higdon, Hal
Smith, Lane 1959- *131*
  Earlier sketch in SATA *76*
  See also CLR *47*
Smith, Lee
  See Albion, Lee Smith
Smith, Lendon H(oward) 1921- *64*
Smith, Linell Nash 1932- *2*
Smith, Lucia B. 1943- *30*
Smith, Marion Hagens 1913- *12*
Smith, Marion Jaques 1899-1987 ....*13*
Smith, Mary Ellen *10*
Smith, Marya 1945- *78*
Smith, Mike
  See Smith, Mary Ellen
Smith, Nancy Covert 1935- *12*
Smith, Norman F. 1920- *70*
  Earlier sketch in SATA *5*
Smith, Patricia Clark 1943- *96*
Smith, Pauline C.
  See Arthur, Robert, (Jr.)
Smith, Pauline C(oggeshall)
  1908-1994 ....*27*
Smith, Philip Warren 1936- *46*
Smith, Rebecca 1946- *123*
Smith, Robert Kimmel 1930- *77*
  Earlier sketch in SATA *12*
Smith, Robert Paul 1915-1977 ....*52*
  Obituary *30*
Smith, Roland 1951- *115*
Smith, Ruth Leslie 1902- *2*
Smith, Sandra Lee 1945- *75*
Smith, Sarah Stafford
  See Smith, Dorothy Stafford
Smith, Sharon 1947- *82*
Smith, Sherwood 1951- *140*
  Earlier sketch in SATA *82*
Smith, Shirley Raines
  See Raines, Shirley C(arol)
Smith, Susan Carlton 1923- *12*
Smith, Susan Mathias 1950- *43*
  Brief entry *35*
Smith, Susan Vernon 1950- *48*
  See Mendonca, Susan
Smith, Ursula 1934- *54*
Smith, Vian (Crocker) 1920-1969 ....*11*
Smith, Wanda VanHoy 1926- *65*
Smith, Ward
  See Goldsmith, Howard
Smith, William A. 1918- *10*
Smith, William Jay 1918- *68*
  Earlier sketch in SATA *2*
  See also SAAS *22*
Smith, Winsome 1935- *45*
Smith, Z. Z.
  See Westheimer, David
Smith-Ankrom, M. E. 1942- *130*
Smith-Griswold, Wendy 1955- *88*
Smith-Rex, Susan J. 1950- *94*

Smithsen, Richard
  See Pellowski, Michael (Joseph)
Smits, Teo
  See Smits, Theodore R(ichard)
Smits, Theodore R(ichard)
  1905-1996 ....*45*
  Brief entry *28*
Smolinski, Dick 1932- *86*
Smothers, Ethel Footman 1944- *76*
Smucker, Barbara (Claassen) 1915- *130*
  Earlier sketches in SATA *29, 76*
  See also CLR *10*
  See also SAAS *11*
Smyth, Iain 1959- *105*
Snedeker, Caroline Dale (Parke) 1871-1956
  See YABC *2*
Snell, Nigel (Edward Creagh) 1936- *57*
  Brief entry *40*
Snellgrove, L(aurence) E(rnest)
  1928- *53*
Snelling, Dennis (Wayne) 1958- *84*
Sneve, Virginia Driving Hawk 1933- *95*
  Earlier sketch in SATA *8*
  See also CLR *2*
Snicket, Lemony 1970- *126*
  See Handler, Daniel
Snodgrass, Mary Ellen 1944- *75*
Snodgrass, Quentin Curtius
  See Clemens, Samuel Langhorne
Snodgrass, Thomas Jefferson
  See Clemens, Samuel Langhorne
Snook, Barbara (Lillian) 1913-1976 ....*34*
Snow, Donald Clifford 1917-1979 ....*16*
Snow, Dorothea J(ohnston) 1909- *9*
Snow, Richard F(olger) 1947- *52*
  Brief entry *37*
Snyder, Anne 1922-2001 ....*4*
  Obituary *125*
Snyder, Bernadette McCarver 1930- *97*
Snyder, Carol 1941- *35*
Snyder, Gerald S(eymour) 1933- *48*
  Brief entry *34*
Snyder, Midori 1954- *106*
Snyder, Paul A. 1946- *125*
Snyder, Zilpha Keatley 1927- *110*
  Autobiography Feature *112*
  Earlier sketches in SATA *1, 28, 75*
  See also CLR *31*
  See also SAAS *2*
Snyderman, Reuven K. 1922- *5*
Soble, Jennie
  See Cavin, Ruth (Brodie)
Sobol, Donald J. 1924- *132*
  Earlier sketches in SATA *1, 31, 73*
  See also CLR *4*
Sobol, Harriet Langsam 1936- *47*
  Brief entry *34*
Sobol, Rose 1931- *76*
Sobott-Mogwe, Gaele 1956- *97*
Soderlind, Arthur E(dwin) 1920- *14*
Soentpiet, Chris K. 1970- *97*
Soerensen, Svend Otto 1916- *67*
Sofer, Barbara 1949- *109*
Sofer, Rachel
  See Sofer, Barbara
Softly, Barbara Frewin 1924- *12*
Sohl, Frederic J(ohn) 1916- *10*
Sokol, Bill
  See Sokol, William
Sokol, William 1923- *37*
Sokolov, Kirill 1930- *34*
Solbert, Romaine G. 1925- *2*
Solbert, Ronni
  See Solbert, Romaine G.
Solheim, James *133*
Solomon, Joan 1930- *51*
  Brief entry *40*
Solomons, Ikey Esquir
  See Thackeray, William Makepeace
Solonevich, George 1915- *15*
Solot, Mary Lynn 1939- *12*
Somerlott, Robert 1928-2001 ....*62*

Somervill, Barbara A(nn) 1948- *140*
Sommer, Angela
    See Sommer-Bodenburg, Angela
Sommer, Carl 1930- *126*
Sommer, Elyse 1929- *7*
Sommer, Robert 1929- *12*
Sommer-Bodenburg, Angela 1948- *63*
Sommer-Bodenburg, Angela 1948- *113*
Sommerdorf, Norma (Jean) 1926- *131*
Sommerfelt, Aimee 1892-1975 ....*5*
Sones, Sonya *131*
Sonneborn, Ruth (Cantor) 1899-1974 ....*4*
    Obituary *27*
Sonnenmark, Laura A. 1958- *73*
Sopko, Eugen 1949- *58*
Sorel, Edward 1929- *126*
    Brief entry *37*
    Earlier sketch in SATA *65*
Sorensen, Henri 1950- *115*
    Earlier sketch in SATA *77*
Sorensen, Svend Otto
    See Soerensen, Svend Otto
Sorensen, Virginia 1912-1991 ....*2*
    Obituary *72*
    See also SAAS *15*
Sorenson, Jane 1926- *63*
Sorenson, Margo 1946- *96*
Sorley Walker, Kathrine *41*
Sorrentino, Joseph N. 1937- *6*
Sortor, June Elizabeth 1939- *12*
Sortor, Toni
    See Sortor, June Elizabeth
Soskin, V. H.
    See Ellison, Virginia H(owell)
Soto, Gary 1952- *120*
    Earlier sketch in SATA *80*
    See also CLR *38*
Sotomayor, Antonio 1902-1985 ....*11*
Souci, Robert D. San
    See San Souci, Robert D.
Soudley, Henry
    See Wood, James Playsted
Soule, Gardner (Bosworth) 1913- *14*
Soule, Jean Conder 1919- *10*
Souster, (Holmes) Raymond 1921- *63*
South, Sheri Cobb 1959- *82*
Southall, Ivan (Francis) 1921- *68*
    Autobiography Feature *134*
    Earlier sketch in SATA *3*
    See also CLR *2*
    See also SAAS *3*
Southey, Robert 1774-1843 ....*54*
Southgate, Vera *54*
Sovak, Jan 1953- *115*
Sowden, Celeste
    See Walters, Celeste
Sowter, Nita *69*
Spagnoli, Cathy 1950- *134*
    Earlier sketch in SATA *79*
Spain, Sahara Sunday 1991- *133*
Spalding, Andrea 1944- *101*
Spanfeller, James J(ohn) 1930- *19*
    See Spanfeller, Jim
Spanfeller, Jim
    See SAAS *8*
    See Spanfeller, James J(ohn)
Spangenberg, Judith Dunn 1942- *5*
Spanyol, Jessica 1965- *137*
Spar, Jerome 1918- *10*
Sparks, Barbara 1942- *78*
Sparks, Beatrice Mathews 1918- *44*
    Brief entry *28*
Sparks, Mary W. 1920- *15*
Spaulding, Douglas
    See Bradbury, Ray (Douglas)
Spaulding, Leonard
    See Bradbury, Ray (Douglas)
Spaulding, Norma *107*
Speare, Elizabeth George 1908-1994 ....*62*
    Obituary *83*
    Earlier sketch in SATA *5*
    See also CLR *8*

Spearing, Judith (Mary Harlow)
    1922- *9*
Speck, Nancy 1959- *104*
Specking, Inez 1890-1960(?) *11*
Speed, Nell
    See Keats, Emma
    and Sampson, Emma (Keats) Speed
Speed, Nell (Ewing) 1878-1913 ....*68*
Speer, Bonnie Stahlman 1929- *113*
Speer-Lyon, Tammie L. 1965- *89*
Speicher, Helen Ross S(mith) 1915- *8*
Speir, Nancy 1958- *81*
Spellman, John W(illard) 1934- *14*
Spellman, Roger G.
    See Cox, William R(obert)
Spelman, Cornelia 1946- *96*
Spelman, Mary 1934- *28*
Spence, Cynthia
    See Eble, Diane
Spence, Eleanor (Rachel) 1928- *21*
    See also CLR *26*
Spence, Geraldine 1931- *47*
Spencer, Ann 1918- *10*
Spencer, Cornelia
    See Yaukey, Grace S(ydenstricker)
Spencer, Donald D(ean) 1931- *41*
Spencer, Elizabeth 1921- *14*
Spencer, Leonard G.
    See Garrett, (Gordon) Randall (Phillip)
    and Silverberg, Robert
Spencer, William 1922- *9*
Spencer, Zane A(nn) 1935- *35*
Speregen, Devra Newberger 1964- *84*
Sperling, Dan(iel Lee) 1949- *65*
Sperry, Armstrong W. 1897-1976 ....*1*
    Obituary *27*
Sperry, Raymond
    See Garis, Howard R(oger)
Sperry, Raymond, Jr. *1*
Spetter, Jung-Hee 1969- *134*
Spicer, Dorothy Gladys -1975 ....*32*
Spiegelman, Art 1948- *109*
Spiegelman, Judith M. *5*
Spielberg, Steven 1947- *32*
Spier, Peter (Edward) 1927- *54*
    Earlier sketch in SATA *4*
    See also CLR *5*
Spilhaus, Athelstan (Frederick)
    1911-1998 ....*13*
    Obituary *102*
Spilka, Arnold 1917- *6*
Spillane, Frank Morrison 1918- *66*
    See Spillane, Mickey
Spillane, Mickey
    See Spillane, Frank Morrison
Spinelli, Eileen 1942- *101*
    Earlier sketch in SATA *38*
Spinelli, Jerry 1941- *110*
    Earlier sketches in SATA *39, 71*
    See also CLR *82*
Spink, Reginald (William)
    1905-1994 ....*11*
Spinka, Penina Keen 1945- *72*
Spinner, Stephanie 1943- *132*
    Earlier sketches in SATA *38, 91*
Spinossimus
    See White, William, Jr.
Spires, Elizabeth 1952- *111*
    Earlier sketch in SATA *71*
Spirin, Gennadii
    See Spirin, Gennady
Spirin, Gennadij
    See Spirin, Gennady
Spirin, Gennady 1948- *134*
    Earlier sketch in SATA *95*
    See also CLR *88*
Spivak, Dawnine *101*
Spohn, David 1948- *72*
Spohn, Kate 1962- *87*
Spollen, Christopher 1952- *12*
Spooner, Michael (Tim) 1954- *92*
Spowart, Robin 1947- *82*

Sprague, Gretchen (Burnham) 1926- *27*
Sprigge, Elizabeth (Miriam Squire)
    1900-1974 ....*10*
Spring, (Robert) Howard 1889-1965 ....*28*
Springer, Margaret 1941- *78*
Springer, Marilyn Harris 1931- *47*
Springer, Nancy 1948- *110*
    Earlier sketch in SATA *65*
Springstubb, Tricia 1950- *78*
    Brief entry *40*
    Earlier sketch in SATA *46*
Spudvilas, Anne 1951- *94*
Spurll, Barbara 1952- *78*
Spykman, E(lizabeth) C(hoate)
    1896-1965 ....*10*
    See also CLR *35*
Spyri, Johanna (Heusser)
    1827-1901 ....*100*
    Earlier sketch in SATA *19*
    See also CLR *13*
Squires, Phil
    See Barker, S(quire) Omar
Srba, Lynne *98*
Sreenivasan, Jyotsna 1964- *101*
S-Ringi, Kjell
    See Ringi, Kjell (Arne Soerensen)
Stacey, Cherylyn 1945- *96*
Stacy, Donald
    See Pohl, Frederik
Stadtler, Bea 1921- *17*
Stafford, Liliana 1950- *141*
Stafford, Paul 1966- *116*
Stahl, Ben(jamin) 1910-1987 ....*5*
    Obituary *54*
Stahl, Hilda 1938-1993 ....*48*
    Obituary *77*
Stair, Gobin (John) 1912- *35*
Stalder, Valerie *27*
Stamaty, Mark Alan 1947- *12*
Stambler, Irwin 1924- *5*
Standiford, Natalie 1961- *81*
Stanek, Lou Willett 1931- *63*
Stang, Judit 1921-1977 ....*29*
Stang, Judy
    See Stang, Judit
Stangl, (Mary) Jean 1928- *67*
Stanhope, Eric
    See Hamilton, Charles (Harold St. John)
Stankevich, Boris 1928- *2*
Stanley, Diane 1943- *115*
    Brief entry *32*
    Earlier sketches in SATA *37, 80*
    See also CLR *46*
    See also SAAS *15*
Stanley, George Edward 1942- *111*
    Earlier sketch in SATA *53*
Stanley, Jerry 1941- *127*
    Earlier sketch in SATA *79*
Stanley, Robert
    See Hamilton, Charles (Harold St. John)
Stanli, Sue
    See Meilach, Dona Z(weigoron)
Stanstead, John
    See Groom, Arthur William
Stanton, Schuyler
    See Baum, L(yman) Frank
Staples, Suzanne Fisher 1945- *105*
    Earlier sketch in SATA *70*
    See also CLR *60*
Stapleton, Marjorie (Winifred) 1932- *28*
Stapp, Arthur D(onald) 1906-1972 ....*4*
Starbird, Kaye 1916- *6*
    See also CLR *60*
Stark, Evan 1942- *78*
Stark, James
    See Goldston, Robert (Conroy)
Stark, Ulf 1944- *124*
Starke, Ruth (Elaine) 1946- *129*
Starkey, Marion L(ena) 1901-1991 ....*13*
Starr, Ward
    See Manes, Stephen

Starret, William
    See McClintock, Marshall
Starr Taylor, Bridget 1959- *99*
Stasiak, Krystyna *49*
Staub, Frank (Jacob) 1949- *116*
Staub, Wendy Corsi 1964- *114*
Staunton, Schuyler
    See Baum, L(yman) Frank
Staunton, Ted 1956- *112*
Steadman, Ralph (Idris) 1936- *123*
    Earlier sketch in SATA *32*
Stearman, Kaye 1951- *118*
Stearns, Monroe (Mather) 1913-1987 ......*5*
    Obituary *55*
Steckler, Arthur 1921-1985 ....*65*
Steding, Laurie 1953- *119*
Steel, Danielle (Fernande) 1947- *66*
Steele, Addison II
    See Lupoff, Richard A(llen)
Steele, Alexander 1958- *116*
Steele, Mary 1930- *94*
Steele, Mary Q(uintard Govan)
    1922-1992 ....*51*
    Obituary *72*
    Earlier sketch in SATA *3*
Steele, (Henry) Max(well) 1922- *10*
Steele, Philip 1948- *140*
    Earlier sketch in SATA *81*
Steele, William O(wen) 1917-1979 ....*51*
    Obituary *27*
    Earlier sketch in SATA *1*
Steelhammer, Ilona 1952- *98*
Steelsmith, Shari 1962- *72*
Stefanik, Alfred T. 1939- *55*
Steffanson, Con
    See Cassiday, Bruce (Bingham)
    and Goulart, Ron(ald Joseph)
Steffens, Bradley 1955- *77*
Stegeman, Janet Allais 1923- *53*
    Brief entry *49*
    See Britton, Kate
Steig, William (H.) 1907- *111*
    Earlier sketches in SATA *18, 70*
    See also CLR *15*
Stein, M(eyer) L(ewis) 1920- *6*
Stein, Mini *2*
Stein, R(ichard) Conrad 1937- *82*
    Earlier sketch in SATA *31*
Stein, Wendy 1951- *77*
Steinbeck, John (Ernst) 1902-1968 ....*9*
Steinberg, Alfred 1917-1995 ....*9*
Steinberg, Fannie 1899-1990 ....*43*
Steinberg, Fred J. 1933- *4*
Steinberg, Phillip Orso 1921- *34*
Steinberg, Rafael (Mark) 1927- *45*
Steinberg, Saul 1914-1999 ....*67*
Steiner, Barbara A(nnette) 1934- *83*
    Earlier sketch in SATA *13*
    See also SAAS *13*
Steiner, Charlotte 1900-1981 ....*45*
Steiner, George 1929- *62*
Steiner, Joan *110*
Steiner, Jorg
    See Steiner, Jorg
Steiner, Jorg 1930- *35*
Steiner, K. Leslie
    See Delany, Samuel R(ay), Jr.
Steiner, Stan(ley) 1925-1987 ....*14*
    Obituary *50*
Steins, Richard 1942- *79*
Stem, Jacqueline 1931- *110*
Steneman, Shep 1945- *132*
Stephanie, Gordon
    See Gordon, Stephanie Jacob
Stephens, Alice Barber 1858-1932 ....*66*
Stephens, Casey
    See Wagner, Sharon B.
Stephens, Mary Jo 1935- *8*
Stephens, Rebecca 1961- *141*
Stephens, Reed
    See Donaldson, Stephen R(eeder)
Stephens, William M(cLain) 1925- *21*

Stephensen, A. M.
    See Manes, Stephen
Stepp, Ann 1935- *29*
Stepto, Michele 1946- *61*
Steptoe, John (Lewis) 1950-1989 ....*63*
    Earlier sketch in SATA *8*
    See also CLR *12*
Sterling, Brett
    See Bradbury, Ray (Douglas)
    and Hamilton, Edmond
    and Samachson, Joseph
Sterling, Dorothy 1913- *83*
    Autobiography Feature *127*
    Earlier sketch in SATA *1*
    See also CLR *1*
    See also SAAS *2*
Sterling, Philip 1907-1989 ....*8*
    Obituary *63*
Sterling, Shirley (Anne) 1948- *101*
Stern, Ellen Norman 1927- *26*
Stern, Judith M. 1951- *75*
Stern, Madeleine B(ettina) 1912- *14*
Stern, Philip Van Doren 1900-1984 ....*13*
    Obituary *39*
Stern, Simon 1943- *15*
Sterne, Emma Gelders 1894- *6*
Steurt, Marjorie Rankin 1888-1978 ....*10*
Stevens, Bryna 1924- *65*
Stevens, Carla M(cBride) 1928- *13*
Stevens, Chambers 1968- *128*
Stevens, Diane 1939- *94*
Stevens, Franklin 1933- *6*
Stevens, Greg
    See Cook, Glen (Charles)
Stevens, Gwendolyn 1944- *33*
Stevens, Jan Romero 1953- *95*
Stevens, Janet 1953- *90*
Stevens, Kathleen 1936- *49*
Stevens, Leonard A. 1920- *67*
Stevens, Lucile Vernon 1899-1994 ....*59*
Stevens, Patricia Bunning 1931- *27*
Stevens, Peter
    See Geis, Darlene Stern
Stevens, Peter
    See Geis, Darlene Stern
Stevens, Serita (Deborah) 1949- *70*
Stevens, Shira
    See Stevens, Serita (Deborah)
Stevenson, Anna (M.) 1905- *12*
Stevenson, Augusta 1869(?)-1976 ....*2*
    Obituary *26*
Stevenson, Burton Egbert 1872-1962 ......*25*
Stevenson, Drew 1947- *60*
Stevenson, Harvey 1960- *80*
Stevenson, James 1929- *113*
    Brief entry *34*
    Earlier sketches in SATA *42, 71*
    See also CLR *17*
Stevenson, Janet 1913- *8*
Stevenson, Robert Louis (Balfour)
    1850-1894 ....*100*
    See also YABC *2*
    See also CLR *11*
Stevenson, Sucie 1956- *104*
Stewart, A(gnes) C(harlotte) *15*
Stewart, Chantal 1945- *121*
Stewart, Charles
    See Zurhorst, Charles (Stewart, Jr.)
Stewart, Elisabeth J(ane) 1927- *93*
Stewart, Elizabeth Laing 1907- *6*
Stewart, Gail B. 1949- *141*
Stewart, George Rippey 1895-1980 ....*3*
    Obituary *23*
Stewart, Jennifer J(enkins) 1960- *128*
Stewart, John (William) 1920- *14*
    See Cole, Jack
Stewart, Mary (Florence Elinor)
    1916- *12*
Stewart, Mary Rainbow
    See Stewart, Mary (Florence Elinor)
Stewart, Melissa 1968- *111*
Stewart, Paul 1955- *114*

Stewart, Robert Neil 1891-1972 ....*7*
Stewart, Scott
    See Zaffo, George J.
Stewart, W(alter) P. 1924- *53*
Stewart, Whitney 1959- *92*
Stewig, John Warren 1937- *110*
    Earlier sketch in SATA *26*
Stickler, Soma Han 1942- *128*
Stidworthy, John 1943- *63*
Stiles, Martha Bennett *108*
    Earlier sketch in SATA *6*
Still, James 1906-2001 ....*29*
    Obituary *127*
Stille, Darlene R(uth) 1942- *126*
Stillerman, Marci *104*
Stillerman, Robbie 1947- *12*
Stilley, Frank 1918- *29*
Stimpson, Gerald
    See Mitchell, Adrian
Stine, G(eorge) Harry 1928-1997 ....*136*
    Earlier sketch in SATA *10*
Stine, Jovial Bob
    See Stine, R(obert) L(awrence)
Stine, R(obert) L(awrence) 1943- *129*
    Earlier sketches in SATA *31, 76*
    See also CLR *37*
Stinetorf, Louise (Allender)
    1900-1992 ....*10*
Stinson, Kathy 1952- *98*
Stirling, Arthur
    See Sinclair, Upton (Beall)
Stirling, Ian 1941- *77*
Stirling, Nora B(romley) 1900-1997 ....*3*
Stirnweis, Shannon 1931- *10*
Stobbs, William 1914-2000 ....*17*
    Obituary *120*
Stock, Carolmarie 1951- *75*
Stock, Catherine 1952- *114*
    Earlier sketch in SATA *65*
Stockdale, Susan 1954- *98*
Stockham, Peter (Alan) 1928- *57*
Stockton, Francis Richard 1834-1902 ......*44*
    See Stockton, Frank R.
Stockton, Frank R.
    Brief entry *32*
    See Stockton, Francis Richard
Stoddard, Edward G. 1923- *10*
Stoddard, Hope 1900-1987 ....*6*
Stoddard, Sandol 1927- *98*
    See Warburg, Sandol Stoddard
Stoehr, Shelley 1969- *107*
Stoeke, Janet Morgan 1957- *136*
    Earlier sketch in SATA *90*
Stoiko, Michael 1919- *14*
Stoker, Abraham 1847-1912 ....*29*
    See Stoker, Bram
Stoker, Bram
    See Stoker, Abraham
Stokes, Cedric
    See Beardmore, George
Stokes, Jack (Tilden) 1923- *13*
Stokes, Olivia Pearl 1916- *32*
Stolz, Mary (Slattery) 1920- *133*
    Earlier sketches in SATA *10, 71*
    See also SAAS *3*
Stone, Alan *1*
    See Svenson, Andrew E(dward)
Stone, David K(arl) 1922- *9*
Stone, Eugenia 1879-1971 ....*7*
Stone, Gene
    See Stone, Eugenia
Stone, Helen V(irginia) *6*
Stone, Idella Purnell
    See Purnell, Idella
Stone, Ikey
    See Purnell, Idella
Stone, Irving 1903-1989 ....*3*
    Obituary *64*
Stone, Jon 1931-1997 ....*39*
    Obituary *95*
Stone, Josephine Rector
    See Dixon, Jeanne

Stone, Lesley
 See Trevor, Elleston
Stone, Peter 1930-2003 65
Stone, Phoebe 134
Stone, Raymond 1
Stone, Rosetta
 See Dr. Seuss
 and Geisel, Theodor Seuss
 and LeSieg, Theo.
 and Seuss, Dr.
Stonehouse, Bernard 1926- 140
 Earlier sketches in SATA *13, 80*
Stones, (Cyril) Anthony 1934- 72
Stong, Phil(ip Duffield) 1899-1957 32
Stoops, Erik D. 1966- 78
Stoppelmoore, Cheryl Jean
 See Ladd, Cheryl (Jean)
Stops, Sue 1936- 86
Storad, Conrad J. 1957- 119
Storey, Margaret 1926- 9
Storey, Victoria Carolyn 1945- 16
Storme, Peter
 See Stern, Philip Van Doren
Storr, Catherine (Cole) 1913-2001 87
 Obituary 122
 Earlier sketch in SATA *9*
Story, Josephine
 See Loring, Emilie (Baker)
Stott, Dorothy (M.) 1958- 99
 Earlier sketch in SATA *67*
Stott, Dot
 See Stott, Dorothy (M.)
Stotter, Mike 1957- 108
Stout, William 1949- 132
Stoutenburg, Adrien (Pearl)
 1916-1982 3
Stoutland, Allison 1963- 130
Stover, Allan C(arl) 1938- 14
Stover, Jill (Griffin) 1958- 82
Stover, Marjorie Filley 1914- 9
Stowe, Harriet (Elizabeth) Beecher 1811-
 1896
 See YABC *1*
Stowe, Leland 1899-1994 60
 Obituary 78
Stowe, Rosetta
 See Ogan, George F.
 and Ogan, Margaret E. (Nettles)
Strachan, Ian 1938- 85
Strachan, Margaret Pitcairn
 1908-1998 14
Strahinich, H. C.
 See Strahinich, Helen C.
Strahinich, Helen C. 1949- 78
Strait, Treva Adams 1909- 35
Strand, Mark 1934- 41
Stranger, Joyce
 See SAAS *24*
 See Wilson, Joyce M(uriel Judson)
Strangis, Joel 1948- 124
Strannigan, Shawn (Alyne) 1956- 93
Strasser, Todd 1950- 107
 Earlier sketches in SATA *41, 45, 71*
 See also CLR *11*
Stratemeyer, Edward L. 1862-1930 100
 Earlier sketches in SATA *1, 67*
 See Appleton, Victor
 and Bowie, Jim
 and Dixon, Franklin W.
 and Keene, Carolyn
Stratford, Philip 1927- 47
Stratton, J. M.
 See Whitlock, Ralph
Stratton, Thomas
 See Coulson, Robert S(tratton)
 and DeWeese, Thomas Eugene
Stratton-Porter, Gene(va Grace)
 1863-1924 15
 See also CLR *87*
 See Porter, Gene(va Grace) Stratton
Strauss, Gwen 1963- 77
Strauss, Joyce 1936- 53

Strauss, Linda Leopold 1942- *127*
Strauss, Susan (Elizabeth) 1954- 75
Strayer, E. Ward
 See Stratemeyer, Edward L.
Streano, Vince(nt Catello) 1945- 20
Streatfeild, (Mary) Noel
 1897(?)-1986 20
 Obituary 48
 See also CLR *83*
Street, Janet Travell 1959- 84
Street, Julia Montgomery 1898-1993 11
Streissguth, Thomas 1958- 116
Strelkoff, Tatiana 1957- 89
Stren, Patti 1949- 88
 Brief entry 41
 See also CLR *5*
Strete, Craig Kee 1950- 96
 Earlier sketch in SATA *44*
Stretton, Barbara (Humphrey) 1936- 43
 Brief entry 35
Strickland, (William) Brad(ley)
 1947- 137
 Earlier sketch in SATA *83*
Strickland, Craig (A.) 1956- 102
Strickland, Dorothy S(alley) 1933- 89
Strickland, Michael R. 1965- 83
Striegel, Jana 1955- 140
Striegel-Wilson, Jana
 See Striegel, Jana
Striker, Lee
 See Clark, Margaret (D.)
Striker, Susan 1942- 63
Stringer, Lauren 1957- 129
Stroeyer, Poul 1923- 13
Stromoski, Rick 1958- 111
Strong, Charles
 See Epstein, Beryl (M. Williams)
 and Epstein, Samuel
Strong, David
 See McGuire, Leslie (Sarah)
Strong, J. J.
 See Strong, Jeremy
Strong, Jeremy 1949- *105*
 Earlier sketch in SATA *36*
Strong, Pat
 See Hough, Richard (Alexander)
Strong, Stacie 1965- 74
Stroud, Bettye 1939- 96
Stroud, Jonathan 1970- 102
Stroyer, Poul
 See Stroeyer, Poul
Strug, Kerri 1977- 108
Stryker, Daniel
 See Morris, Chris(topher Crosby)
 and Stump, Jane Barr
Stuart, David
 See Hoyt, Edwin P(almer), Jr.
Stuart, Derek
 See Foster, John L(ouis)
Stuart, Forbes 1924- 13
Stuart, Ian
 See MacLean, Alistair (Stuart)
Stuart, Jesse (Hilton) 1906-1984 2
 Obituary 36
Stuart, Ruth McEnery 1849(?)-1917 ......*116*
Stuart, Sheila
 See Baker, Mary Gladys Steel
Stuart-Clark, Christopher (Anthony)
 1940- 32
Stubis, Talivaldis 1926- 5
Stubley, Trevor (Hugh) 1932- 22
Stucky, Naomi R. 1922- 72
Stucley, Elizabeth
 See Northmore, Elizabeth Florence
Stultifer, Morton
 See Curtis, Richard (Alan)
Sture-Vasa, Mary
 See Alsop, Mary O'Hara
Sturtevant, Katherine 1950- 130
Sturton, Hugh
 See Johnston, H(ugh) A(nthony) S(tephen)
Sturtzel, Howard A(llison) 1894-1985 1

Sturtzel, Jane Levington 1903-1996 1
Stutson, Caroline 1940- 104
Stuve-Bodeen, Stephanie 1965- 114
Stux, Erica 1929- 140
Styles, (Frank) Showell 1908- 10
Stynes, Barbara White 133
Suba, Susanne 4
Subond, Valerie
 See Grayland, Valerie (Merle Spanner)
Sudbery, Rodie 1943- 42
Sufrin, Mark 1925- 76
Sugarman, Joan G. 1917- 64
Sugarman, Tracy 1921- 37
Sugita, Yutaka 1930- 36
Suhl, Yuri (Menachem) 1908-1986 8
 Obituary 50
 See also CLR *2*
 See also SAAS *1*
Suhr, Joanne 129
Suid, Murray 1942- 27
Sullivan, George (Edward) 1927- 89
 Earlier sketch in SATA *4*
Sullivan, Kathryn A. 1954- 141
Sullivan, Mary Ann 1954- 63
Sullivan, Mary W(ilson) 1907- 13
Sullivan, Pat
 See Messmer, Otto
Sullivan, Paul 1939- 106
Sullivan, Silky
 See Makowski, Silvia Ann
Sullivan, Sue
 See Sullivan, Susan E.
Sullivan, Susan E. 1962- 123
Sullivan, Thomas Joseph, Jr. 1947- 16
Sullivan, Tom
 See Sullivan, Thomas Joseph, Jr.
Sully, Tom 1959- 104
Sumichrast, Jozef 1948- 29
Sumiko
 See Davies, Sumiko
Summerforest, Ivy B.
 See Kirkup, James
Summers, James L(evingston)
 1910-1973 57
 Brief entry 28
Summertree, Katonah
 See Windsor, Patricia
Sun, Chyng Feng 1959- 90
Sunderlin, Sylvia (S.) 1911-1997 28
 Obituary 99
Sung, Betty Lee 26
Supraner, Robyn 1930- 101
 Earlier sketch in SATA *20*
Supree, Burt(on) 1941-1992 73
Surface, Mary Hall 1958- 126
Surge, Frank 1931- 13
Susac, Andrew 1929- 5
Susi, Geraldine Lee 1942- 98
Sussman, Cornelia Silver 1914-1999 59
Sussman, Irving 1908-1996 59
Sussman, Susan 1942- 48
Sutcliff, Rosemary 1920-1992 78
 Obituary 73
 Earlier sketches in SATA *6, 44*
 See also CLR *37*
Sutcliffe, Jane 1957- 138
Sutherland, Colleen 1944- 79
Sutherland, Efua (Theodora Morgue)
 1924-1996 25
Sutherland, Margaret 1941- 15
Sutherland, Zena Bailey 1915-2002 37
 Obituary 137
Suttles, Shirley (Smith) 1922- 21
Sutton, Ann (Livesay) 1923- 31
Sutton, Eve(lyn Mary) 1906-1992 26
Sutton, Felix 1910(?)-1973 31
Sutton, Jane 1950- 52
 Brief entry 43
Sutton, Larry M(atthew) 1931- 29
Sutton, Margaret Beebe 1903-2001 1
 Obituary 131
Sutton, Myron Daniel 1925- 31

Sutton, Roger 1956- *93*
Suzanne, Jamie
  See Hawes, Louise
  and Singleton, Linda Joy
  and Zach, Cheryl (Byrd)
Suzuki, David T(akayoshi) 1936- *138*
Svendsen, Mark (Nestor) 1962- *120*
Svenson, Andrew E(dward)
  1910-1975 ....*2*
  Obituary *26*
  See Stone, Alan
Swain, Gwenyth 1961- *134*
  Earlier sketch in SATA *84*
Swain, Ruth (Freeman) 1951- *119*
Swain, Su Zan (Noguchi) 1916- *21*
Swamp, Jake 1941- *98*
Swan, Susan 1944- *108*
  Earlier sketch in SATA *22*
Swann, Brian (Stanley Frank)
  1940- *116*
Swann, Ruth Rice 1920- *84*
Swanson, Helen M(cKendry) 1919- *94*
Swanson, June 1931- *76*
Swarthout, Glendon (Fred)
  1918-1992 ....*26*
Swarthout, Kathryn 1919- *7*
Swayne, Sam(uel F.) 1907- *53*
Swayne, Zoa (Lourana) 1905- *53*
Sweat, Lynn 1934- *57*
Swede, George 1940- *67*
Sweeney, James B(artholomew)
  1910-1999 ....*21*
Sweeney, Joyce (Kay) 1955- *108*
  Earlier sketches in SATA *65, 68*
Sweeney, Karen O'Connor
  See O'Connor, Karen
Sweet, Sarah C.
  See Jewett, (Theodora) Sarah Orne
Sweetland, Nancy A(nn) 1934- *48*
Swenson, Allan A(rmstrong) 1933- *21*
Swenson, May 1919-1989 ....*15*
Swentzell, Rina 1939- *79*
Swift, Bryan
  See Knott, William C(ecil, Jr.)
Swift, David
  See Kaufmann, John
Swift, Jonathan 1667-1745 ....*19*
  See also CLR *53*
Swift, Merlin
  See Leeming, Joseph
Swiger, Elinor Porter 1927- *8*
Swinburne, Laurence (Joseph) 1924- *9*
Swindells, Robert (Edward) 1939- *80*
  Brief entry *34*
  Earlier sketch in SATA *50*
  See also SAAS *14*
Swinford, Betty (June Wells) 1927- *58*
Swinford, Bob
  See Swinford, Betty (June Wells)
Swithen, John
  See King, Stephen (Edwin)
Switzer, Ellen 1923- *48*
Sybesma, Jetske
  See Ironside, Jetske
Sydney, Frank
  See Warwick, Alan R(oss)
Sylvester, Natalie G(abry) 1922- *22*
Syme, (Neville) Ronald 1913-1992 ....*87*
  Earlier sketch in SATA *2*
Symes, R. F. *77*
Symons, (Dorothy) Geraldine 1909- *33*
Symons, Stuart
  See Stanley, George Edward
Symynkywicz, Jeffrey B(ruce) 1954- *87*
Synge, (Phyllis) Ursula 1930- *9*
Sypher, Lucy Johnston 1907- *7*
Szasz, Suzanne (Shorr) 1915-1997 ....*13*
  Obituary *99*
Szekeres, Cyndy 1933- *131*
  Earlier sketches in SATA *5, 60*
  See also SAAS *13*
Szekessy, Tanja *98*

Szpura, Beata 1961- *93*
Szudek, Agnes S(usan) P(hilomena) *57*
  Brief entry *49*
Szulc, Tad 1926-2001 ....*26*
Szydlow, Jarl
  See Szydlowski, Mary Vigliante
Szydlowski, Mary Vigliante 1946- *94*
Szymanski, Lois 1957- *91*

T

Taback, Simms 1932- *104*
  Brief entry *36*
  Earlier sketch in SATA *40*
Tabor, Nancy Maria Grande 1949- *89*
Tabrah, Ruth Milander 1921- *14*
Tackach, James 1953- *123*
Tafuri, Nancy (E.) 1946- *130*
  Earlier sketches in SATA *39, 75*
  See also CLR *74*
  See also SAAS *14*
Tagg, Christine Elizabeth 1962- *138*
Taha, Karen T(erry) 1942- *71*
Tait, Douglas 1944- *12*
Takabayashi, Mari 1960- *115*
Takakjian, Portia 1930- *15*
Takashima, Shizuye 1928- *13*
Takayama, Sandi 1962- *106*
Talbert, Marc 1953- *99*
  Earlier sketch in SATA *68*
Talbot, Charlene Joy 1928- *10*
Talbot, Toby 1928- *14*
  See Josephs, Rebecca
Talbott, Hudson 1949- *131*
  Earlier sketch in SATA *84*
Talifero, Gerald 1950- *75*
Talker, T.
  See Rands, William Brighty
Tallarico, Tony 1933- *116*
Tallcott, Emogene *10*
Tallis, Robyn
  See Doyle, Debra
  and Macdonald, James D.
  and Smith, Sherwood
  and Tallis, Robyn
  and Zambreno, Mary Frances
Tallon, Robert 1939- *43*
  Brief entry *28*
Talmadge, Marian *14*
Tamar, Erika 1934- *101*
  Earlier sketch in SATA *62*
Tamarin, Alfred H. 1913-1980 ....*13*
Tamburine, Jean 1930- *12*
Tames, Richard (Lawrence) 1946- *102*
  Earlier sketch in SATA *67*
Tamminga, Frederick W(illiam)
  1934- *66*
Tan, Amy (Ruth) 1952- *75*
Tanaka, Beatrice 1932- *76*
Tanaka, Shelley *136*
Tang, Charles 1948- *81*
Tang, You-Shan 1946- *53*
Tania B.
  See Blixen, Karen (Christentze Dinesen)
Tannen, Mary 1943- *37*
Tannenbaum, Beulah Goldstein 1916- *3*
Tannenbaum, D(onald) Leb 1948- *42*
Tanner, Jane 1946- *74*
Tanner, Louise S(tickney) 1922-2000 ....*9*
Tanobe, Miyuki 1937- *23*
Tanselle, Eve 1933- *125*
Tapio, Pat Decker
  See Kines, Pat Decker
Tapp, Kathy Kennedy 1949- *88*
  Brief entry *50*
Tarbescu, Edith 1939- *107*
Tarkington, (Newton) Booth
  1869-1946 ....*17*
Tarr, Judith 1955- *64*

Tarry, Ellen 1906- *16*
  See also CLR *26*
  See also SAAS *16*
Tarshis, Jerome 1936- *9*
Tarsky, Sue 1946- *41*
Tashjian, Janet 1956- *102*
Tashjian, Virginia A. 1921- *3*
Tasker, James 1908- *9*
Tate, Eleanora E(laine) 1948- *94*
  Earlier sketch in SATA *38*
  See also CLR *37*
Tate, Ellalice
  See Hibbert, Eleanor Alice Burford
Tate, Joan 1922- *86*
  Earlier sketch in SATA *9*
  See also SAAS *20*
Tate, Mary Anne
  See Hale, Arlene
Tate, Nikki *134*
Tate, Richard
  See Masters, Anthony (Richard)
Tate, Suzanne 1930- *91*
Tatham, Campbell
  See Elting, Mary
Tatham, Julie
  See Tatham, Julie Campbell
Tatham, Julie Campbell 1908-1999 ....*80*
Taves, Isabella 1915- *27*
Taylor, Alastair 1959- *130*
Taylor, Andrew (John Robert) 1951- *70*
Taylor, Ann 1782-1866 ....*41*
  Brief entry *35*
Taylor, Audilee Boyd 1931- *59*
Taylor, Barbara J. 1927- *10*
Taylor, Ben
  See Strachan, Ian
Taylor, Carl 1937- *14*
Taylor, Cheryl Munro 1957- *96*
Taylor, Cora (Lorraine) 1936- *103*
  Earlier sketch in SATA *64*
  See also CLR *63*
Taylor, Dave 1948- *78*
Taylor, David
  See Taylor, Dave
Taylor, David 1900-1965 ....*10*
Taylor, Elizabeth 1932-1975 ....*13*
Taylor, Florance Walton *9*
Taylor, Florence M(arian Tompkins)
  1892-1983 ....*9*
Taylor, Gage 1942-2000 ....*87*
Taylor, Herb(ert Norman, Jr.)
  1942-1987 ....*22*
  Obituary *54*
Taylor, J. David
  See Taylor, Dave
Taylor, Jane 1783-1824 ....*41*
  Brief entry *35*
Taylor, Jerry D(uncan) 1938- *47*
Taylor, John Robert
  See Taylor, Andrew (John Robert)
Taylor, Judy
  See Hough, Judy Taylor
Taylor, Kenneth N(athaniel) 1917- *26*
Taylor, L(ester) B(arbour), Jr. 1932- *27*
Taylor, Lois Dwight Cole
  See Cole, Lois Dwight
Taylor, Louise Todd 1939- *47*
Taylor, Margaret 1950- *106*
Taylor, Mark 1927- *32*
  Brief entry *28*
Taylor, Mildred D(elois) 1943- *135*
  See also CLR *59*
  See also SAAS *5*
Taylor, Paula (Wright) 1942- *48*
  Brief entry *33*
Taylor, Robert Lewis 1912-1998 ....*10*
Taylor, Sydney (Brenner)
  1904(?)-1978 ....*28*
  Obituary *26*
  Earlier sketch in SATA *1*

Taylor, Theodore 1921- *128*
    Earlier sketches in SATA *5, 54, 83*
    See also CLR *30*
    See also SAAS *4*
Taylor, William 1938- *113*
    Earlier sketch in SATA *78*
    See also CLR *63*
Tazewell, Charles 1900-1972 ....*74*
Tchana, Katrin Hyman 1963- *125*
Tchekhov, Anton
    See Chekhov, Anton (Pavlovich)
Tchen, Richard *120*
Tchudi, Stephen N. 1942- *55*
Teague, Bob
    See Teague, Robert
Teague, Mark (Christopher) 1963- *99*
    Earlier sketch in SATA *68*
Teague, Robert 1929- *32*
    Brief entry *31*
Teal, Val(entine M.) 1902-1997 ....*10*
    Obituary *114*
Teale, Edwin Way 1899-1980 ....*7*
    Obituary *25*
Teasdale, Sara 1884-1933 ....*32*
Tebbel, John (William) 1912- *26*
Teensma, Lynne Bertrand
    See Bertrand, Lynne
Tee-Van, Helen Damrosch
    1893-1976 ....*10*
    Obituary *27*
Tegner, Bruce 1928- *62*
Teitelbaum, Michael 1953- *116*
    Earlier sketch in SATA *59*
Tejima
    See Tejima, Keizaburo
Tejima, Keizaburo 1931- *139*
    See also CLR *20*
Telander, Todd (G.) 1967- *88*
Teleki, Geza 1943- *45*
Telemaque, Eleanor Wong 1934- *43*
Telescope, Tom
    See Newbery, John
Temkin, Sara Anne Schlossberg
    1913-1996 ....*26*
Temko, Florence *13*
Templar, Maurice
    See Groom, Arthur William
Temple, Charles 1947- *79*
Temple, Frances (Nolting)
    1945-1995 ....*85*
Temple, Herbert 1919- *45*
Temple, Paul
    See McConnell, James Douglas Rutherford
Temple, William F(rederick)
    1914-1989 ....*107*
Tenggren, Gustaf 1896-1970 ....*18*
    Obituary *26*
Tennant, Kylie *6*
    See Rodd, Kylie Tennant
Tennant, Veronica 1947- *36*
Tenneshaw, S. M.
    See Beaumont, Charles
    and Garrett, (Gordon) Randall (Phillip)
    and Silverberg, Robert
Tenniel, John 1820-1914 ....*74*
    Brief entry *27*
    See also CLR *18*
Tepper, Sheri S. 1929- *113*
Terada, Alice M. 1928- *90*
Terban, Marvin 1940- *54*
    Brief entry *45*
ter Haar, Jaap 1922- *6*
    See Haar, Jaap ter
Terhune, Albert Payson 1872-1942 ....*15*
Terkel, Susan N(eiburg) 1948- *103*
    Earlier sketch in SATA *59*
Terlouw, Jan (Cornelis) 1931- *30*
Terris, Susan 1937- *77*
    Earlier sketch in SATA *3*
Terry, Luther L(eonidas) 1911-1985 ....*11*
    Obituary *42*

Terry, Margaret
    See Dunnahoo, Terry Janson
Terry, Walter 1913-1982 ....*14*
Terzian, James P. 1915- *14*
Tessendorf, K(enneth) C(harles)
    1925- *75*
Tessler, Stephanie Gordon
    See Gordon, Stephanie Jacob
Tester, Sylvia Root 1939- *64*
    Brief entry *37*
Tether, (Cynthia) Graham 1950- *46*
    Brief entry *36*
Thacher, Mary McGrath 1933- *9*
Thackeray, William Makepeace
    1811-1863 ....*23*
Thaler, Michael C. 1936- *93*
    Brief entry *47*
    Earlier sketch in SATA *56*
Thaler, Mike
    See Thaler, Michael C.
Thaler, Shmuel 1958- *126*
    Earlier sketch in SATA *72*
Thamer, Katie 1955- *42*
Thane, Elswyth 1900-1984(?) *32*
Tharp, Louise (Marshall) Hall
    1898-1992 ....*3*
    Obituary *129*
Thayer, Ernest Lawrence 1863-1940 ....*60*
Thayer, Jane
    See Woolley, Catherine
Thayer, Marjorie -1992 ....*74*
    Brief entry *37*
Thayer, Peter
    See Wyler, Rose
Thelwell, Norman 1923- *14*
Themerson, Stefan 1910-1988 ....*65*
Theroux, Paul (Edward) 1941- *109*
    Earlier sketch in SATA *44*
Thesman, Jean *124*
    Earlier sketch in SATA *74*
Thieda, Shirley Ann 1943- *13*
Thiele, Colin (Milton) 1920- *125*
    Earlier sketches in SATA *14, 72*
    See also CLR *27*
    See also SAAS *2*
Thiesing, Lisa 1958- *95*
Thiry, Joan (Marie) 1926- *45*
Thistlethwaite, Miles 1945- *12*
Thollander, Earl 1922- *22*
Thomas, Abigail 1941- *112*
Thomas, Andrea
    See Hill, Margaret (Ohler)
Thomas, Art(hur Lawrence) 1952- *48*
    Brief entry *38*
Thomas, Carroll
    See Ratliff, Thomas M.
    and Shmurak, Carole B.
Thomas, Dylan (Marlais) 1914-1953 ....*60*
Thomas, Egbert S.
    See Ellis, Edward S(ylvester)
Thomas, Estelle Webb 1899-1982 ....*26*
Thomas, Frances 1943- *92*
Thomas, H. C.
    See Keating, Lawrence A.
Thomas, Ianthe 1951- *139*
    Brief entry *42*
    See also CLR *8*
Thomas, Jane Resh 1936- *90*
    Earlier sketch in SATA *38*
Thomas, Jerry D. 1959- *91*
Thomas, Joan Gale
    See Robinson, Joan (Mary) G(ale Thomas)
Thomas, Joyce Carol 1938- *137*
    Earlier sketches in SATA *40, 78, 123*
    See also CLR *19*
    See also SAAS *7*
Thomas, Lowell Jackson, Jr. 1923- *15*
Thomas, Meredith 1963- *119*
Thomas, Michael
    See Wilks, Michael Thomas
Thomas, Patricia J. 1934- *51*
Thomas, Rob 1965- *97*

Thomas, Vernon (Arthur) 1934- *56*
Thomas, Victoria
    See DeWeese, Thomas Eugene
    and Kugi, Constance Todd
Thomasma, Kenneth R. 1930- *90*
Thomassie, Tynia 1959- *92*
Thompson, Brenda 1935- *34*
Thompson, Carol 1951- *85*
Thompson, China
    See Lewis, Mary (Christianna)
Thompson, Colin (Edward) 1942- *95*
Thompson, David H(ugh) 1941- *17*
Thompson, Eileen
    See Panowski, Eileen Thompson
Thompson, George Selden
    1929-1989 ....*73*
    Obituary *63*
    Earlier sketch in SATA *4*
    See Selden, George
Thompson, Harlan (Howard)
    1894-1987 ....*10*
    Obituary *53*
    See Holt, Stephen
Thompson, Hilary 1943- *56*
    Brief entry *49*
Thompson, Julian F(rancis) 1927- *99*
    Brief entry *40*
    Earlier sketch in SATA *55*
    See also CLR *24*
    See also SAAS *13*
Thompson, K(athryn Carolyn) Dyble
    1952- *82*
Thompson, Kay 1912(?)-1998 ....*16*
    See also CLR *22*
Thompson, Lauren (Stevens) 1962- *132*
Thompson, Ruth Plumly 1891-1976 ....*66*
Thompson, Sharon (Elaine) 1952- *119*
Thompson, Stith 1885-1976 ....*57*
    Obituary *20*
Thompson, Vivian L(aubach) 1911- *3*
Thomson, David (Robert Alexander)
    1914-1988 ....*40*
    Obituary *55*
Thomson, Pat 1939- *122*
    Earlier sketch in SATA *77*
Thomson, Peggy 1922- *31*
Thon, Melanie Rae 1957- *132*
Thorn, John 1947- *59*
Thorndyke, Helen Louise *67*
    Earlier sketch in SATA *1*
    See Benson, Mildred (Augustine Wirt)
Thorne, Ian
    See May, Julian
Thorne, Jean Wright
    See May, Julian
Thornhill, Jan 1955- *77*
Thornton, Hall
    See Silverberg, Robert
Thornton, W. B.
    See Burgess, Thornton Waldo
Thornton, Yvonne S(hirley) 1947- *96*
Thorpe, E(ustace) G(eorge) 1916- *21*
Thorpe, J. K.
    See Nathanson, Laura Walther
Thorvall, Kerstin 1925- *13*
Thorvall-Falk, Kerstin
    See Thorvall, Kerstin
Thrasher, Crystal (Faye) 1921- *27*
Threadgall, Colin 1941- *77*
Thum, Gladys 1920- *26*
Thum, Marcella *28*
    Earlier sketch in SATA *3*
Thundercloud, Katherine
    See Witt, Shirley Hill
Thurber, James (Grover) 1894-1961 ....*13*
Thurman, Judith 1946- *33*
Thurman, Mark (Gordon Ian) 1948- *63*
Thwaite, Ann (Barbara Harrop)
    1932- *14*
Tibbetts, Peggy *127*
Tibbles, Jean-Paul 1958- *115*

Tibo, Gilles 1951- *107*
    Earlier sketch in SATA *67*
Tiburzi, Bonnie 1948- *65*
Ticheburn, Cheviot
    See Ainsworth, William Harrison
Tichenor, Tom 1923-1992 ....*14*
Tichnor, Richard 1959- *90*
Tichy, William 1924- *31*
Tickle, Jack
    See Chapman, Jane
Tiegreen, Alan F. 1935- *94*
    Brief entry *36*
Tierney, Frank M. 1930- *54*
Tierney, Tom 1928- *113*
Tiffault, Benette W. 1955- *77*
Tiller, Ruth L. 1949- *83*
Tilly, Nancy 1935- *62*
Tilton, Madonna Elaine 1929- *41*
Tilton, Rafael
    See Tilton, Madonna Elaine
Timberlake, Carolyn
    See Dresang, Eliza (Carolyn Timberlake)
Timmins, William F(rederick) *10*
Tiner, John Hudson 1944- *32*
Tingle, Dolli (?)-
    See Brackett, Dolli Tingle
Tingum, Janice 1958- *91*
Tinkelman, Murray 1933- *12*
Tinkle, (Julien) Lon 1906-1980 ....*36*
Tinling, Marion (Rose) 1904- *140*
Tipene, Tim 1972- *141*
Tippett, James S(terling) 1885-1958 ....*66*
Titler, Dale M(ilton) 1926- *35*
    Brief entry *28*
Titmarsh, Michael Angelo
    See Thackeray, William Makepeace
Titus, Eve 1922- *2*
Tjong Khing, The 1933- *76*
Tobias, Katherine
    See Gottfried, Theodore Mark
Tobias, Tobi 1938- *82*
    Earlier sketch in SATA *5*
    See also CLR *4*
Todd, Anne Ophelia
    See Dowden, Anne Ophelia
Todd, Barbara K(eith) 1917- *10*
Todd, H(erbert) E(atton) 1908-1988 ....*84*
    Earlier sketch in SATA *11*
Todd, Loreto 1942- *30*
Todd, Pamela 1950- *124*
Todd, Peter
    See Hamilton, Charles (Harold St. John)
Tofel, Richard J. 1957- *140*
Tolan, Stephanie S. 1942- *78*
    Earlier sketch in SATA *38*
Toland, John (Willard) 1912- *38*
Tolkien, J(ohn) R(onald) R(euel)
    1892-1973 ....*100*
    Obituary *24*
    Earlier sketches in SATA *2, 32*
    See also CLR *56*
Toll, Nelly S. 1935- *78*
Tolland, W. R.
    See Heitzmann, William Ray
Tolles, Martha 1921- *76*
    Earlier sketch in SATA *8*
Tolliver, Ruby C(hangos) 1922- *110*
    Brief entry *41*
    Earlier sketch in SATA *55*
Tolmie, Kenneth Donald 1941- *15*
Tolstoi, Lev
    See Tolstoy, Leo (Nikolaevich)
Tolstoy, Leo (Nikolaevich)
    1828-1910 ....*26*
    See Tolstoi, Lev
Tolstoy, Count Leo
    See Tolstoy, Leo (Nikolaevich)
Tomalin, Ruth *29*
Tomes, Margot (Ladd) 1917-1991 ....*70*
    Brief entry *27*
    Obituary *69*
    Earlier sketch in SATA *36*

Tomey, Ingrid 1943- *77*
Tomfool
    See Farjeon, Eleanor
Tomkins, Jasper
    See Batey, Tom
Tomline, F. Latour
    See Gilbert, W(illiam) S(chwenck)
Tomlinson, Jill 1931-1976 ....*3*
    Obituary *24*
Tomlinson, Theresa 1946- *103*
    See also CLR *60*
Tompert, Ann 1918- *139*
    Earlier sketches in SATA *14, 89, 136*
Toner, Raymond John 1908-1986 ....*10*
Tong, Gary S. 1942- *66*
Took, Belladonna
    See Chapman, Vera (Ivy May)
Tooke, Louise Mathews 1950- *38*
Toonder, Martin
    See Groom, Arthur William
Toothaker, Roy Eugene 1928- *18*
Tooze, Ruth (Anderson) 1892-1972 ....*4*
Topek, Susan Remick 1955- *78*
Topping, Audrey R(onning) 1928- *14*
Tor, Regina
    See Shekerjian, Regina Tor
Torbert, Floyd James 1922- *22*
Torgersen, Don Arthur 1934- *55*
    Brief entry *41*
Torley, Luke
    See Blish, James (Benjamin)
Torres, Daniel 1958- *102*
Torres, John A(lbert) 1965- *94*
Torres, Laura 1967- *87*
Torrie, Malcolm
    See Mitchell, Gladys (Maude Winifred)
Toten, Teresa 1955- *99*
Totham, Mary
    See Breinburg, Petronella
Touponce, William F. 1948- *114*
Tournier, Michel (Edouard) 1924- *23*
Towle, Wendy 1963- *79*
Towne, Mary
    See Spelman, Mary
Townsend, Brad W. 1962- *91*
Townsend, John Rowe 1922- *68*
    Autobiography Feature *132*
    Earlier sketch in SATA *4*
    See also CLR *2*
    See also SAAS *2*
Townsend, Sue *93*
    Brief entry *48*
    Earlier sketch in SATA *55*
    See Townsend, Susan Lilian
Townsend, Thomas L. 1944- *59*
Townsend, Tom
    See Townsend, Thomas L.
Townson, Hazel *134*
Toye, William Eldred 1926- *8*
Traherne, Michael
    See Watkins-Pitchford, Denys James
Trahey, Jane 1923-2000 ....*36*
    Obituary *120*
Trapani, Iza 1954- *116*
    Earlier sketch in SATA *80*
Trapp, Maria Augusta von *16*
    See von Trapp, Maria Augusta
Travers, P(amela) L(yndon)
    1899-1996 ....*100*
    Obituary *90*
    Earlier sketches in SATA *4, 54*
    See also CLR *2*
    See also SAAS *2*
Travis, Lucille *133*
    Earlier sketch in SATA *88*
Treadgold, Mary 1910- *49*
Trease, (Robert) Geoffrey 1909-1998 ......*60*
    Obituary *101*
    Earlier sketch in SATA *2*
    See also CLR *42*
    See also SAAS *6*
Treat, Lawrence 1903-1998 ....*59*

Tredez, Alain 1926- *17*
Tredez, Denise 1930- *50*
Treece, Henry 1912-1966 ....*2*
    See also CLR *2*
Tregarthen, Enys
    See Sloggett, Nellie
Tregaskis, Richard 1916-1973 ....*3*
    Obituary *26*
Treherne, Katie Thamer 1955- *76*
Trell, Max 1900-1996 ....*14*
    Obituary *108*
Tremain, Ruthven 1922- *17*
Trembath, Don 1963- *96*
Tremens, Del
    See MacDonald, Amy
Trent, Robbie 1894-1988 ....*26*
Trent, Timothy
    See Malmberg, Carl
Treseder, Terry Walton 1956- *68*
Tresilian, (Cecil) Stuart 1891-(?) *40*
Tressell, Alvin 1916-2000 ....*7*
    See also CLR *30*
Trevino, Elizabeth B(orton) de
    1904- *29*
    Earlier sketch in SATA *1*
    See also SAAS *5*
Trevor, Elleston 1920-1995 ....*28*
    See Hall, Adam
Trevor, Frances
    See Teasdale, Sara
Trevor, Glen
    See Hilton, James
Trevor, (Lucy) Meriol 1919-2000 ....*113*
    Obituary *122*
    Earlier sketch in SATA *10*
Trez, Alain
    See Tredez, Alain
Trez, Denise
    See Tredez, Denise
Trezise, Percy (James) 1923-
    See CLR *41*
Triggs, Tony D. 1946- *70*
Trimble, Marshall I(ra) 1939- *93*
Trimby, Elisa 1948- *47*
    Brief entry *40*
Tripp, Eleanor B(aldwin) 1936- *4*
Tripp, Janet 1942- *108*
Tripp, John
    See Moore, John Travers
Tripp, Nathaniel 1944- *101*
Tripp, Paul 1916-2002 ....*8*
    Obituary *139*
Tripp, Valerie 1951- *78*
Tripp, Wallace (Whitney) 1940- *31*
Trivelpiece, Laurel 1926- *56*
    Brief entry *46*
Trivett, Daphne Harwood 1940- *22*
Trivizas, Eugene 1946- *84*
Trnka, Jiri 1912-1969 ....*43*
    Brief entry *32*
Trollope, Anthony 1815-1882 ....*22*
Trost, Lucille W(ood) 1938- *12*
Trott, Betty 1933- *91*
Trotter, Grace V(iolet) 1900-1991 ....*10*
Trottier, Maxine 1950- *131*
Troughton, Joanna (Margaret) 1947- *37*
Trout, Kilgore
    See Farmer, Philip Jose
Trout, Richard E. *123*
Trudeau, G(arretson) B(eekman)
    1948- *35*
    See Trudeau, Garry B.
Trudeau, Garry B.
    See Trudeau, G(arretson) B(eekman)
Trueman, Terry 1947- *132*
Truesdell, Judy
    See Mecca, Judy Truesdell
Truesdell, Sue
    See Truesdell, Susan G.
Truesdell, Susan G. *108*
    Brief entry *45*
Truss, Jan 1925- *35*

Tryon, Leslie *139*
Tubb, Jonathan N. 1951- *78*
Tubby, I. M.
    See Kraus, (Herman) Robert
Tucker, Caroline
    See Nolan, Jeannette Covert
Tudor, Tasha 1915- *69*
    Earlier sketch in SATA *20*
    See also CLR *13*
Tuerk, Hanne 1951- *71*
Tulloch, Richard (George) 1949- *76*
Tully, John (Kimberley) 1923- *14*
Tumanov, Vladimir A. 1961- *138*
Tung, Angela 1972- *109*
Tunis, Edwin (Burdett) 1897-1973 ....*28*
    Obituary *24*
    Earlier sketch in SATA *1*
    See also CLR *2*
Tunis, John R(oberts) 1889-1975 ....*37*
    Brief entry *30*
Tunnell, Michael O'(Grady) 1950- *103*
Tunnicliffe, C(harles) F(rederick)
    1901-1979 ....*62*
Turk, Hanne
    See Tuerk, Hanne
Turk, Ruth 1917- *82*
Turkle, Brinton 1915- *79*
    Earlier sketch in SATA *2*
Turlington, Bayly 1919-1977 ....*5*
    Obituary *52*
Turnbull, Agnes Sligh 1888-1982 ....*14*
Turnbull, Ann (Christine) 1943- *18*
Turner, Alice K. 1940- *10*
Turner, Ann W(arren) 1945- *113*
    Earlier sketches in SATA *14, 77*
Turner, Bonnie 1932- *75*
Turner, Elizabeth 1774-1846
    See YABC *2*
Turner, Glennette Tilley 1933- *71*
Turner, Josie
    See Crawford, Phyllis
Turner, Megan Whalen 1965- *94*
Turner, Philip (William) 1925- *83*
    Earlier sketch in SATA *11*
    See also SAAS *6*
Turner, Robyn 1947- *77*
Turngren, Ellen (?)-1964 ....*3*
Turska, Krystyna (Zofia) 1933- *31*
    Brief entry *27*
Turteltaub, H. N.
    See Turtledove, Harry (Norman)
Turtledove, Harry (Norman) 1949- *116*
Tusa, Tricia 1960- *111*
    Earlier sketch in SATA *72*
Tusiani, Joseph 1924- *45*
Twain, Mark
    See CLR *66*
    See Clemens, Samuel Langhorne
Tweit, Susan J(oan) 1956- *94*
Tweton, D. Jerome 1933- *48*
Twinem, Neecy 1958- *92*
Tworkov, Jack 1900-1982 ....*47*
    Obituary *31*
Tyers, Jenny 1969- *89*
Tyers, Kathy 1952- *82*
Tyler, Anne 1941- *90*
    Earlier sketch in SATA *7*
Tyler, Linda
    See Tyler, Linda W(agner)
Tyler, Linda W(agner) 1952- *65*
Tyler, Vicki 1952- *64*
Tyne, Joel
    See Schembri, Jim
Tyrrell, Frances 1959- *107*

U

Ubell, Earl 1926- *4*

Uchida, Yoshiko 1921-1992 ....*53*
    Obituary *72*
    Earlier sketch in SATA *1*
    See also CLR *56*
    See also SAAS *1*
Udall, Jan Beaney 1938- *10*
Uden, (Bernard Gilbert) Grant 1910- *26*
Uderzo, Albert 1927-
    See CLR *37*
Udry, Janice May 1928- *4*
Ueno, Noriko
    See Nakae, Noriko
Uhlig, Susan 1955- *129*
Ulam, S(tanislaw) M(arcin)
    1909-1984 ....*51*
Ullman, James Ramsey 1907-1971 ....*7*
Ulm, Robert 1934-1977 ....*17*
Ulmer, Louise 1943- *53*
Ulyatt, Kenneth 1920- *14*
Unada
    See Gliewe, Unada (Grace)
Uncle Gus
    See Rey, H(ans) A(ugusto)
Uncle Ray
    See Coffman, Ramon Peyton
Uncle Shelby
    See Silverstein, Shel(don Allan)
Underhill, Alice Mertie (Waterman)
    1900-1971 ....*10*
Underhill, Liz 1948- *53*
    Brief entry *49*
Unger, Harlow G. 1931- *75*
Unger, Jim 1937- *67*
Ungerer, (Jean) Thomas 1931- *106*
    Earlier sketches in SATA *5, 33*
    See Ungerer, Tomi
Ungerer, Tomi 1931-
    See CLR *77*
    See Ungerer, (Jean) Thomas
Unkelbach, Kurt 1913- *4*
Unnerstad, Edith (Totterman) 1900-1982 ...*3*
    See also CLR *36*
Unobagha, Uzo *139*
    Earlier sketch in SATA *136*
Unrau, Ruth 1922- *9*
Unstead, R(obert) J(ohn) 1915-1988 ....*12*
    Obituary *56*
Unsworth, Walt(er) 1928- *4*
Untermeyer, Bryna Ivens 1909-1985 ......*61*
Untermeyer, Louis 1885-1977 ....*37*
    Obituary *26*
    Earlier sketch in SATA *2*
Unwin, David S(torr) 1918- *14*
Unwin, Nora S(picer) 1907-1982 ....*3*
    Obituary *49*
Unzner, Christa 1958- *141*
    Earlier sketch in SATA *80*
Unzner-Fischer, Christa
    See Unzner, Christa
Updyke, Rosemary K. 1924- *103*
Upitis, Alvis *109*
Ure, Jean 1943- *129*
    Earlier sketches in SATA *48, 78*
    See also CLR *34*
    See also SAAS *14*
Uris, Leon (Marcus) 1924-2003 ....*49*
Ury, Allen B. 1954- *98*
Uschan, Michael V. 1948- *129*
Usher, Margo Scegge
    See McHargue, Georgess
Uston, Ken(neth Senzo) 1935-1987 ....*65*
Uttley, Alice Jane (Taylor)
    1884-1976 ....*88*
    Obituary *26*
    Earlier sketch in SATA *3*
    See Uttley, Alison
Uttley, Alison
    See Uttley, Alice Jane (Taylor)
Utz, Lois (Marie) 1932-1986 ....*5*
    Obituary *50*

V

Vaeth, J(oseph) Gordon 1921- *17*
Vail, Rachel 1966- *94*
Vainio, Pirkko 1957- *123*
    Earlier sketch in SATA *76*
Valen, Nanine 1950- *21*
Valencak, Hannelore *42*
    See Mayer, Hannelore Valencak
Valens, Amy 1946- *70*
Valens, E(vans) G(ladstone), Jr.
    1920-1992 ....*1*
Valentine, Johnny *72*
Valgardson, W(illiam) D(empsey)
    1939- *101*
Valleau, Emily 1925- *51*
Van Abbe, Salaman 1883-1955 ....*18*
Van Allsburg, Chris 1949- *105*
    Earlier sketches in SATA *37, 53*
    See also CLR *13*
Van Anrooy, Francine 1924- *2*
Van Anrooy, Frans
    See Van Anrooy, Francine
Vance, Eleanor Graham 1908-1985 ....*11*
Vance, Gerald
    See Garrett, (Gordon) Randall (Phillip)
    and Silverberg, Robert
Vance, Marguerite 1889-1965 ....*29*
VanCleave, Janice 1942- *116*
    Autobiography Feature *123*
    Earlier sketch in SATA *75*
Vandenburg, Mary Lou 1943- *17*
Vander Boom, Mae M. *14*
Vander-Els, Betty 1936- *63*
van der Linde, Laurel 1952- *78*
van der Meer, Ron 1945- *98*
Van der Veer, Judy 1912-1982 ....*4*
    Obituary *33*
Vanderwerff, Corrine 1939- *117*
Vande Velde, Vivian 1951- *141*
    Earlier sketches in SATA *62, 95*
Vandivert, Rita (Andre) 1905-1986 ....*21*
Van Draanen, Wendelin *122*
Van Duyn, Janet 1910- *18*
Van Dyne, Edith
    See Baum, L(yman) Frank
    and Sampson, Emma (Keats) Speed
    and van Zantwijk, Rudolf (Alexander
    Marinus)
van Frankenhuyzen, Gijsbert 1951- *132*
Van Hook, Beverly H. 1941- *99*
Van Horn, William 1939- *43*
Van Iterson, S(iny) R(ose) *26*
Van Kampen, Vlasta 1943- *54*
Van Laan, Nancy 1939- *105*
van Lawick-Goodall, Jane
    See Goodall, Jane
Van Leeuwen, Jean 1937- *141*
    Earlier sketches in SATA *6, 82, 132*
    See also SAAS *8*
van Lhin, Erik
    See del Rey, Lester
Van Loon, Hendrik Willem
    1882-1944 ....*18*
Van Orden, M(erton) D(ick) 1921- *4*
Van Rensselaer, Alexander (Taylor Mason)
    1892-1962 ....*14*
Van Riper, Guernsey, Jr. 1909-1995 ....*3*
Van Rynbach, Iris 1952- *102*
Vansant, Rhonda Joy Edwards 1950- *92*
Van Steenwyk, Elizabeth (Ann)
    1928- *89*
    Earlier sketch in SATA *34*
Van Stockum, Hilda 1908- *5*
Van Tuyl, Barbara 1940- *11*
van Vogt, A(lfred) E(lton)
    1912-2000 ....*14*
    Obituary *124*
Van Woerkom, Dorothy (O'Brien)
    1924-1996 ....*21*

Van Wormer, Joe
  See Van Wormer, Joseph Edward
Van Wormer, Joseph Edward
  1913-1998 ....*35*
Van Zwienen, Ilse Charlotte Koehn
  1929-1991 ....*34*
  Brief entry *28*
  Obituary *67*
Van Zyle, Jon 1942- *84*
Varga, Judy
  See Stang, Judit
Varley, Dimitry V. 1906-1984 ....*10*
Varley, Susan 1961- *134*
  Earlier sketch in SATA *63*
Vasileva, Tatiana
  See Wassiljewa, Tatjana
Vasiliev, Valery 1949- *80*
Vasilieva, Tatiana
  See Wassiljewa, Tatjana
Vasiliu, Mircea 1920- *2*
Vass, George 1927- *57*
  Brief entry *31*
Vaughan, Carter A.
  See Gerson, Noel Bertram
Vaughan, Harold Cecil 1923- *14*
Vaughan, Marcia (K.) 1951- *95*
  Earlier sketch in SATA *60*
Vaughan, Richard 1947- *87*
Vaughan, Sam(uel) 1928- *14*
Vaughn, Ruth 1935- *14*
Vautier, Ghislaine 1932- *53*
Vavra, Robert James 1935- *8*
Vecsey, George Spencer 1939- *9*
Vedral, Joyce L(auretta) 1943- *65*
Veglahn, Nancy (Crary) 1937- *5*
Velasquez, Gloria (Louise) 1949- *113*
  See Velasquez-Trevino, Gloria (Louise)
Velthuijs, Max 1923- *110*
  Earlier sketch in SATA *53*
Venable, Alan (Hudson) 1944- *8*
Ventura, Piero (Luigi) 1937- *61*
  Brief entry *43*
  See also CLR *16*
Vequin, Capini
  See Quinn, Elisabeth
Verba, Joan Marie 1953- *78*
Verboven, Agnes 1951- *103*
verDorn, Bethea (Stewart) 1952- *76*
Verissimo, Erico (Lopes)
  1905-1975 ....*113*
Verne, Jules (Gabriel) 1828-1905 ....*21*
  See also CLR *88*
Verney, John 1913-1993 ....*14*
  Obituary *75*
Vernon, (Elda) Louise A(nderson)
  1914- *14*
Vernon, Rosemary
  See Smith, Susan Vernon
Vernor, D.
  See Casewit, Curtis W(erner)
Verr, Harry Coe
  See Kunhardt, Edith
Verral, Charles Spain 1904-1990 ....*11*
  Obituary *65*
Versace, Marie Teresa Rios 1917- *2*
Vertreace, Martha M(odena) 1945- *78*
Vesey, A(manda) 1939- *62*
Vesey, Mark (David) 1958- *123*
Vesey, Paul
  See Allen, Samuel W(ashington)
Vestly, Anne-Cath(arina) 1920- *14*
Vevers, (Henry) Gwynne 1916-1988 ....*45*
  Obituary *57*
Viator, Vacuus
  See Hughes, Thomas
Vicar, Henry
  See Felsen, Henry Gregor
Vick, Helen Hughes 1950- *88*
Vicker, Angus
  See Felsen, Henry Gregor
Vickers, Sheena 1960- *94*

Vickery, Kate
  See Kennedy, T(eresa) A.
Victor, Edward 1914- *3*
Victor, Joan Berg 1942- *30*
Vidrine, Beverly Barras 1938- *103*
Viereck, Ellen K. 1928- *14*
Viereck, Phillip 1925- *3*
Viertel, Janet 1915- *10*
Vigliante, Mary
  See Szydlowski, Mary Vigliante
Vigna, Judith 1936- *102*
  Earlier sketch in SATA *15*
Viguers, Ruth Hill 1903-1971 ....*6*
Villiard, Paul 1910-1974 ....*51*
  Obituary *20*
Villiers, Alan (John) 1903-1982 ....*10*
Vilott, Rhondi
  See Salsitz, Rhondi Vilott
Vincent, Eric Douglas 1953- *40*
Vincent, Felix 1946- *41*
Vincent, Gabrielle 1928-2000 ....*121*
  Earlier sketch in SATA *61*
  See also CLR *13*
Vincent, Mary Keith
  See St. John, Wylly Folk
Vincent, William R.
  See Heitzmann, William Ray
Vinegar, Tom
  See Gregg, Andrew K.
Vinest, Shaw
  See Longyear, Barry B(rookes)
Vinge, Joan (Carol) D(ennison)
  1948- *113*
  Earlier sketch in SATA *36*
Vining, Elizabeth Gray 1902-1999 ....*6*
  Obituary *117*
  See Gray, Elizabeth Janet
Vinson, Kathryn 1911-1995 ....*21*
Vinton, Iris 1906(?)-1988 ....*24*
  Obituary *55*
Viola, Herman J(oseph) 1938- *126*
Viorst, Judith 1931- *123*
  Earlier sketches in SATA *7, 70*
  See also CLR *3*
Vip
  See Partch, Virgil Franklin II
Vipont, Charles
  See Foulds, Elfrida Vipont
Vipont, Elfrida
  See Foulds, Elfrida Vipont
Viscott, David S(teven) 1938-1996 ....*65*
Visser, W(illem) F(rederik) H(endrik)
  1900-1968 ....*10*
Vitale, Stefano 1958- *114*
Vivas, Julie 1947- *96*
Vivelo, Jacqueline J. 1943- *63*
Vizzini, Ned 1981- *125*
Vlahos, Olivia 1924- *31*
Vlasic, Bob
  See Hirsch, Phil
Voake, Charlotte *114*
Vo-Dinh, Mai 1933- *16*
Vogel, Carole Garbuny 1951- *105*
  Earlier sketch in SATA *70*
Vogel, Ilse-Margret 1918- *14*
Vogel, John H., Jr. 1950- *18*
Vogt, Esther Loewen 1915-1999 ....*14*
Vogt, Gregory L. *94*
Vogt, Marie Bollinger 1921- *45*
Voight, Virginia Frances 1909-1989 ....*8*
Voigt, Cynthia 1942- *116*
  Brief entry *33*
  Earlier sketches in SATA *48, 79*
  See also CLR *48*
Voigt, Erna 1925- *35*
Voigt-Rother, Erna
  See Voigt, Erna
Vojtech, Anna 1946- *108*
  Earlier sketch in SATA *42*
Vollstadt, Elizabeth Weiss 1942- *121*
Von Ahnen, Katherine 1922- *93*
Vondra, Josef (Gert) 1941- *121*

Von Gunden, Kenneth 1946- *113*
Von Hagen, Victor Wolfgang
  1908-1985 ....*29*
von Klopp, Vahrah
  See Malvern, Gladys
von Schmidt, Eric 1931- *50*
  Brief entry *36*
von Storch, Anne B. 1910- *1*
Vos, Ida 1931- *121*
  Earlier sketch in SATA *69*
  See also CLR *85*
Vosburgh, Leonard (W.) 1912- *15*
Voyle, Mary
  See Manning, Rosemary (Joy)
Vulture, Elizabeth T.
  See Gilbert, Suzie
Vuong, Lynette Dyer 1938- *110*
  Earlier sketch in SATA *60*

W

Waas, Uli
  See Waas-Pommer, Ulrike
Waas-Pommer, Ulrike 1949- *85*
Waber, Bernard 1924- *95*
  Brief entry *40*
  Earlier sketch in SATA *47*
  See also CLR *55*
Wachtel, Shirley Russak 1951- *88*
Wachter, Oralee (Roberts) 1935- *61*
  Brief entry *51*
Waddell, Evelyn Margaret 1918- *10*
Waddell, Martin 1941- *127*
  Autobiography Feature *129*
  Earlier sketches in SATA *43, 81*
  See also CLR *31*
  See also SAAS *15*
Waddy, Lawrence (Heber) 1914- *91*
Wade, Mary Dodson 1930- *79*
Wade, Theodore E., Jr. 1936- *37*
Wademan, Peter John 1946- *122*
Wademan, Spike
  See Wademan, Peter John
Wadsworth, Ginger 1945- *103*
Wagenheim, Kal 1935- *21*
Wagner, Sharon B. 1936- *4*
Wagoner, David (Russell) 1926- *14*
Wahl, Jan (Boyer) 1933- *132*
  Earlier sketches in SATA *2, 34, 73*
  See also SAAS *3*
Waide, Jan 1952- *29*
Wainscott, John Milton 1910-1981 ....*53*
Wainwright, Richard M. 1935- *91*
Wait, Lea 1946- *137*
Waite, Michael P(hillip) 1960- *101*
Waite, P(eter) B(usby) 1922- *64*
Waitley, Douglas 1927- *30*
Wakefield, Jean L.
  See Laird, Jean E(louise)
Wakin, Daniel (Joseph) 1961- *84*
Wakin, Edward 1927- *37*
Walden, Amelia Elizabeth *3*
Waldherr, Kris 1963- *76*
Waldman, Bruce 1949- *15*
Waldman, Neil 1947- *94*
  Earlier sketch in SATA *51*
Waldron, Ann Wood 1924- *16*
Walgren, Judy 1963- *118*
Walker, Addison
  See Walker, (Addison) Mort
Walker, Alice (Malsenior) 1944- *31*
Walker, Barbara (Jeanne) K(erlin)
  1921- *80*
  Earlier sketch in SATA *4*
Walker, Barbara M(uhs) 1928- *57*
Walker, (James) Braz(elton)
  1934-1983 ....*45*
Walker, David G(ordon) 1926- *60*
Walker, David Harry 1911-1992 ....*8*
  Obituary *71*

Walker, Diana 1925- *9*
Walker, Dianne Marie Catherine
    1950- *82*
    See Walker, Kate
Walker, Dick
    See Pellowski, Michael (Joseph)
Walker, Frank 1931-2000 ....*36*
Walker, Holly Beth
    See Bond, Gladys Baker
Walker, Kate
    See Walker, Dianne Marie Catherine
Walker, Kathrine Sorley
    See Sorley Walker, Kathrine
Walker, Lou Ann 1952- *66*
    Brief entry *53*
Walker, Mary Alexander 1927- *61*
Walker, Mildred
    See Schemm, Mildred Walker
Walker, (Addison) Mort 1923- *8*
Walker, Pamela 1948- *24*
Walker, Robert W(ayne) 1948- *66*
Walker, Sally M(acart) 1954- *135*
Walker, Stephen J. 1951- *12*
Walker-Blondell, Becky 1951- *89*
Wallace, Barbara Brooks 1922- *136*
    Earlier sketches in SATA *4, 78*
    See also SAAS *17*
Wallace, Beverly Dobrin 1921- *19*
Wallace, Bill *101*
    Brief entry *47*
    See Wallace, William Keith
    and Wallace, William N.
Wallace, Daisy
    See Cuyler, Margery S(tuyvesant)
Wallace, Ian 1950- *141*
    Earlier sketches in SATA *53, 56*
    See also CLR *37*
Wallace, John 1966- *105*
Wallace, John A(dam) 1915- *3*
Wallace, Karen 1951- *139*
    Earlier sketch in SATA *83*
Wallace, Nancy Elizabeth 1948- *141*
Wallace, Nigel
    See Hamilton, Charles (Harold St. John)
Wallace, Rich 1957- *117*
Wallace, Robert 1932-1999 ....*47*
    Brief entry *37*
Wallace, William Keith 1947- *53*
    See Wallace, Bill
Wallace-Brodeur, Ruth 1941- *88*
    Brief entry *41*
    Earlier sketch in SATA *51*
Wallenta, Adam 1974- *123*
Waller, Leslie 1923- *20*
Walley, Byron
    See Card, Orson Scott
Wallis, Diz 1949- *77*
Wallis, G. McDonald
    See Campbell, Hope
Wallner, Alexandra 1946- *98*
    Brief entry *41*
    Earlier sketch in SATA *51*
Wallner, John C. 1945- *133*
    Earlier sketches in SATA *10, 51*
Wallower, Lucille *11*
Walsh, Ann 1942- *62*
Walsh, Ellen Stoll 1942- *99*
    Earlier sketch in SATA *49*
Walsh, George Johnston 1889-1981 ....*53*
Walsh, Gillian Paton
    See Paton Walsh, Gillian
Walsh, Jill Paton
    See CLR *65*
    See Paton Walsh, Gillian
Walsh, Mary Caswell 1949- *118*
Walsh, V. L.
    See Walsh, Vivian
Walsh, Vivian 1960- *120*
Walsh Shepherd, Donna 1948- *78*
Walter, Frances V. 1923- *71*

Walter, Mildred Pitts 1922- *133*
    Brief entry *45*
    Earlier sketch in SATA *69*
    See also CLR *61*
    See also SAAS *12*
Walter, Villiam Christian
    See Andersen, Hans Christian
Walter, Virginia *134*
    See Walter, Virginia A.
Walters, Audrey 1929- *18*
Walters, Celeste 1938- *126*
Walters, Eric (Robert) 1957- *99*
Walters, Hugh
    See Hughes, Walter (Llewellyn)
Walther, Thomas A. 1950- *31*
Walther, Tom
    See Walther, Thomas A.
Waltner, Elma 1912-1987 ....*40*
Waltner, Willard H. 1909- *40*
Walton, Darwin McBeth 1926- *119*
Walton, Fiona L. M. 1959- *89*
Walton, Richard J. 1928- *4*
Walton, Rick 1957- *101*
Waltrip, Lela (Kingston) 1904-1995 ....*9*
Waltrip, Mildred 1911- *37*
Waltrip, Rufus (Charles) 1898-1988 ....*9*
Walworth, Nancy Zinsser 1917- *14*
Wangerin, Walter, Jr. 1944- *98*
    Brief entry *37*
    Earlier sketch in SATA *45*
Waniek, Marilyn Nelson 1946- *60*
    See Nelson, Marilyn
Wannamaker, Bruce
    See Moncure, Jane Belk
Warbler, J. M.
    See Cocagnac, Augustin Maurice(-Jean)
Warburg, Sandol Stoddard *14*
    See Stoddard, Sandol
Ward, E. D.
    See Gorey, Edward (St. John)
    and Lucas, E(dward) V(errall)
Ward, Ed
    See Stratemeyer, Edward L.
Ward, Helen 1962- *72*
Ward, John (Stanton) 1917- *42*
Ward, Jonas
    See Ard, William (Thomas)
    and Cox, William R(obert)
    and Garfield, Brian (Wynne)
Ward, Lynd (Kendall) 1905-1985 ....*36*
    Obituary *42*
    Earlier sketch in SATA *2*
Ward, Martha (Eads) *5*
Ward, Melanie
    See Curtis, Richard (Alan)
    and Lynch, Marilyn
Ward, Tom
    See Stratemeyer, Edward L.
Wardell, Dean
    See Prince, J(ack) H(arvey)
Wardlaw, Lee 1955- *115*
    Earlier sketch in SATA *79*
Ware, Cheryl 1963- *101*
Ware, Chris 1967- *140*
Ware, Leon (Vernon) 1909-1976 ....*4*
Warner, Frank A. *67*
    Earlier sketch in SATA *1*
Warner, Gertrude Chandler 1890-1979 ......*9*
    Obituary *73*
Warner, J(ohn) F. 1929- *75*
Warner, Lucille Schulberg *30*
Warner, Matt
    See Fichter, George S.
Warner, Oliver (Martin Wilson)
    1903-1976 ....*29*
Warner, Sally 1946- *131*
Warner, Sunny (B.) 1931- *108*
Warnes, Tim(othy) 1971- *116*
Warnick, Elsa 1942- *113*
Warren, Andrea 1946- *98*
Warren, Betsy
    See Warren, Elizabeth Avery

Warren, Billy
    See Warren, William Stephen
Warren, Cathy 1951- *62*
    Brief entry *46*
Warren, Elizabeth
    See Supraner, Robyn
Warren, Elizabeth Avery 1916- *46*
    Brief entry *38*
Warren, Jackie M. 1953- *135*
Warren, Joshua P(aul) 1976- *107*
Warren, Joyce W(illiams) 1935- *18*
Warren, Mary Phraner 1929- *10*
Warren, Robert Penn 1905-1989 ....*46*
    Obituary *63*
Warren, Scott S. 1957- *79*
Warren, William Stephen 1882-1968 ....*9*
Warrick, Patricia Scott 1925- *35*
Warsh
    See Warshaw, Jerry
Warshaw, Jerry 1929- *30*
Warshaw, Mary 1931- *89*
Warshofsky, Fred 1931- *24*
Warshofsky, Isaac
    See Singer, Isaac Bashevis
Wartski, Maureen (Ann Crane)
    1940- *50*
    Brief entry *37*
Warwick, Alan R(oss) 1900-1973 ....*42*
Wa-Sha-Quon-Asin
    See Belaney, Archibald Stansfeld
Wa-sha-quon-asin
    See Belaney, Archibald Stansfeld
Washburn, (Henry) Bradford (Jr.)
    1910- *38*
Washburn, Jan(ice) 1926- *63*
Washburn, Carolyn Kott 1944- *86*
Washburne, Heluiz Chandler
    1892-1970 ....*10*
    Obituary *26*
Washington, Booker T(aliaferro)
    1856-1915 ....*28*
Washington, Donna L. 1967- *98*
Wasserstein, Wendy 1950- *94*
Wassiljewa, Tatjana 1928- *106*
Watanabe, Shigeo 1928- *131*
    Brief entry *32*
    Earlier sketch in SATA *39*
    See also CLR *8*
Waters, John F(rederick) 1930- *4*
Waters, Tony 1958- *75*
Waterton, Betty (Marie) 1923- *99*
    Brief entry *34*
    Earlier sketch in SATA *37*
Watkins, Dawn L. *126*
Watkins, Gloria Jean 1952(?)- *115*
    See hooks, bell
Watkins, Lois 1930- *88*
Watkins, Peter 1934- *66*
Watkins, Yoko Kawashima 1933- *93*
Watkins-Pitchford, Denys James
    1905-1990 ....*87*
    Obituary *66*
    Earlier sketch in SATA *6*
    See also SAAS *4*
Watling, James 1933- *117*
    Earlier sketch in SATA *67*
Watson, Aldren A(uld) 1917- *42*
    Brief entry *36*
Watson, Amy Zakrzewski 1965- *76*
Watson, B. S.
    See Teitelbaum, Michael
Watson, Carol 1949- *78*
Watson, Clyde 1947- *68*
    Earlier sketch in SATA *5*
    See also CLR *3*
Watson, James 1936- *106*
    Earlier sketch in SATA *10*
Watson, Jane Werner 1915- *54*
    Earlier sketch in SATA *3*
Watson, John H.
    See Farmer, Philip Jose
Watson, Mary 1953- *117*

Watson, N. Cameron 1955- *81*
Watson, Nancy Dingman *32*
Watson, Pauline 1925- *14*
Watson, Richard F.
  See Silverberg, Robert
Watson, Richard Jesse 1951- *62*
Watson, Sally (Lou) 1924- *3*
Watson, Wendy (McLeod) 1942- *74*
  Earlier sketch in SATA *5*
Watson Taylor, Elizabeth 1915- *41*
Watt, Melanie 1975- *136*
Watt, Thomas 1935- *4*
Watterson, Bill 1958- *66*
Watt-Evans, Lawrence 1954- *121*
  See Evans, Lawrence Watt
Watts, (Anna) Bernadette 1942- *103*
  Earlier sketch in SATA *4*
Watts, Ephraim
  See Horne, Richard Henry
Watts, Franklin (Mowry) 1904-1978 ....*46*
  Obituary *21*
Watts, Irene N(aemi) 1931- *111*
  Earlier sketch in SATA *56*
Watts, Isaac 1674-1748 ....*52*
Watts, James K(ennedy) M(offitt)
  1955- *59*
Watts, Julia 1969- *103*
Watts, Mabel Pizzey 1906-1994 ....*11*
Watts, Nigel 1957- *121*
Waugh, C. C. Roessel
  See Waugh, Carol-Lynn Rossel
  and Waugh, Charles G(ordon)
Waugh, Carol-Lynn Rossel 1947- *41*
Waugh, Dorothy -1996 ....*11*
Waugh, Virginia
  See Sorensen, Virginia
Wax, Wendy A. 1963- *73*
Wayland, April Halprin 1954- *78*
  See also SAAS *26*
Wayne, (Anne) Jenifer 1917-1982 ....*32*
Wayne, Kyra Petrovskaya 1918- *8*
Wayne, Richard
  See Decker, Duane
Waystaff, Simon
  See Swift, Jonathan
Weales, Gerald (Clifford) 1925- *11*
Weary, Ogdred
  See Gorey, Edward (St. John)
Weatherford, Carole Boston 1956- *138*
Weatherly, Myra (S.) 1926- *130*
Weaver, Harriett E. 1908-1993 ....*65*
Weaver, John L. 1949- *42*
Weaver, Robyn
  See Conley-Weaver, Robyn
Weaver, Robyn M.
  See Conley-Weaver, Robyn
Weaver, Ward
  See Mason, F(rancis) van Wyck
Weaver, Will(iam Weller) 1950- *109*
  Earlier sketch in SATA *88*
Weaver-Gelzer, Charlotte 1950- *79*
Webb, Christopher
  See Wibberley, Leonard (Patrick
  O'Connor)
Webb, Jacquelyn
  See Pearce, Margaret
  and Pearce, Margaret
Webb, Jean Francis (III) 1910-1991 ....*35*
Webb, Kaye 1914- *60*
Webb, Lois Sinaiko 1922- *82*
Webb, Margot 1934- *67*
Webb, Sharon 1936- *41*
Webb, Sophie 1958- *135*
Webber, Andrew Lloyd
  See Lloyd Webber, Andrew
Webber, Irma E(leanor Schmidt)
  1904-1995 ....*14*
Weber, Alfons 1921- *8*
Weber, Bruce 1942- *120*
  Earlier sketch in SATA *73*
Weber, Debora 1955- *58*
Weber, Jill 1950- *127*

Weber, Judith E(ichler) 1938- *64*
Weber, Ken(neth J.) 1940- *90*
Weber, Lenora Mattingly 1895-1971 ....*2*
  Obituary *26*
Weber, Michael 1945- *87*
Weber, William J(ohn) 1927- *14*
Webster, Alice Jane Chandler
  1876-1916 ....*17*
Webster, David 1930- *11*
Webster, Frank V. *67*
  Earlier sketch in SATA *1*
Webster, Gary
  See Garrison, Webb B(lack)
Webster, James 1925-1981 ....*17*
  Obituary *27*
Webster, Jean
  See Webster, Alice Jane Chandler
Wechter, Nell (Carolyn) Wise
  1913-1989 ....*127*
  Earlier sketch in SATA *60*
Weck, Thomas L. 1942- *62*
Wedd, Kate
  See Gregory, Philippa
Weddle, Ethel Harshbarger
  1897-1996 ....*11*
Weems, David B(urnola) 1922- *80*
Wees, Frances Shelley 1902-1982 ....*58*
Weevers, Peter 1944- *59*
Wegen, Ronald 1946-1985 ....*99*
Wegman, William (George) 1943- *135*
  Earlier sketches in SATA *78, 129*
Wegner, Fritz 1924- *20*
Weidhorn, Manfred 1931- *60*
Weidt, Maryann N. 1944- *85*
Weihs, Erika 1917- *107*
  Earlier sketch in SATA *15*
Weik, Mary Hays 1898(?)-1979 ....*3*
  Obituary *23*
Weil, Ann Yezner 1908-1969 ....*9*
Weil, Lisl 1910- *7*
Weilerstein, Sadie Rose 1894-1993 ....*3*
  Obituary *75*
Wein, Elizabeth E(ve) 1964- *82*
Weinberg, Larry
  See Weinberg, Lawrence (E.)
Weinberg, Lawrence (E.) *92*
  Brief entry *48*
Weinberger, Tanya 1939- *84*
Weiner, Sandra 1922- *14*
Weingarten, Violet (Brown)
  1915-1976 ....*3*
  Obituary *27*
Weingartner, Charles 1922- *5*
Weinstein, Nina 1951- *73*
Weir, Bob 1947- *76*
Weir, Diana (R.) Loiewski 1958- *111*
Weir, Joan S(herman) 1928- *99*
Weir, LaVada *2*
Weir, Rosemary (Green) 1905-1994 ....*21*
Weir, Wendy 1949- *76*
Weis, Margaret (Edith) 1948- *92*
  Earlier sketch in SATA *38*
Weisberger, Bernard A(llen) 1922- *21*
Weiser, Marjorie P(hillis) K(atz)
  1934- *33*
Weisgard, Leonard (Joseph)
  1916-2000 ....*85*
  Obituary *122*
  Earlier sketches in SATA *2, 30*
  See also SAAS *19*
Weiss, Adelle 1920- *18*
Weiss, Ann E(dwards) 1943- *69*
  Earlier sketch in SATA *30*
  See also SAAS *13*
Weiss, Edna
  See Barth, Edna
Weiss, Ellen 1953- *44*
Weiss, Harvey 1922- *76*
  Earlier sketches in SATA *1, 27*
  See also CLR *4*
  See also SAAS *19*
Weiss, Jaqueline Shachter 1926- *65*

Weiss, Malcolm E. 1928- *3*
Weiss, Miriam
  See Schlein, Miriam
Weiss, Mitch 1951- *123*
Weiss, Nicki 1954- *86*
  Earlier sketch in SATA *33*
Weiss, Renee Karol 1923- *5*
Weitzman, David L. 1936- *122*
Wekesser, Carol A. 1963- *76*
Welber, Robert *26*
Welch, Amanda (Jane) 1945- *75*
Welch, Jean-Louise
  See Kempton, Jean Welch
Welch, Pauline
  See Bodenham, Hilda Morris
Welch, Ronald
  See Felton, Ronald Oliver
Welch, Sheila Kelly 1945- *130*
Welch, Willy 1952- *93*
Welford, Sue 1942- *75*
Weller, George (Anthony)
  1907-2002 ....*31*
  Obituary *140*
Welling, Peter J. 1947- *135*
Wellington, Monica 1957- *99*
  Earlier sketch in SATA *67*
Wellman, Alice 1900-1984 ....*51*
  Brief entry *36*
Wellman, Manly Wade 1903-1986 ....*6*
  Obituary *47*
Wellman, Paul I(selin) 1898-1966 ....*3*
Wellman, Sam(uel) 1939- *122*
Wells, H(erbert) G(eorge) 1866-1946 ......*20*
  See also CLR *64*
Wells, Helen
  See Campbell, Hope
Wells, Helen 1910-1986 ....*49*
  Earlier sketch in SATA *2*
Wells, J. Wellington
  See de Camp, L(yon) Sprague
Wells, June
  See Swinford, Betty (June Wells)
Wells, Robert
  See Welsch, Roger L(ee)
Wells, Rosemary 1943- *114*
  Earlier sketches in SATA *18, 69*
  See also CLR *69*
  See also SAAS *1*
Wells, Susan (Mary) 1951- *78*
Wels, Byron G(erald) 1924-1993 ....*9*
Welsbacher, Anne 1955- *89*
Welsch, Roger L(ee) 1936- *82*
Welsh, David
  See Hills, C(harles) A(lbert) R(eis)
Weltner, Linda R(iverly) 1938- *38*
Welton, Jude 1955- *79*
Welty, S. F.
  See Welty, Susan F.
Welty, Susan F. 1905- *9*
Wendelin, Rudolph 1910-2000 ....*23*
Wentworth, Robert
  See Hamilton, Edmond
Werlin, Nancy 1961- *119*
  Earlier sketch in SATA *87*
Werner, Elsa Jane
  See Watson, Jane Werner
Werner, Herma 1926- *47*
  Brief entry *41*
Werner, Jane
  See Watson, Jane Werner
Werner, K.
  See Casewit, Curtis W(erner)
Wersba, Barbara 1932- *58*
  Autobiography Feature *103*
  Earlier sketch in SATA *1*
  See also CLR *78*
  See also SAAS *2*
Werstein, Irving 1914(?)-1971 ....*14*
Werth, Kurt 1896-1983 ....*20*
Wesley, Alison
  See Barnes, Michael
Wesley, Mary (Aline) 1912-2002 ....*66*

Wesley, Valerie Wilson 1947- *106*
West, Andrew
  See Arthur, Robert, (Jr.)
West, Anna 1938- *40*
West, Barbara
  See Price, Olive
West, Betty 1921- *11*
West, Bruce 1951- *63*
West, C. P.
  See Wodehouse, P(elham) G(renville)
West, Dorothy
  See Benson, Mildred (Augustine Wirt)
West, Emily Govan 1919- *38*
West, Emmy
  See West, Emily Govan
West, James
  See Withers, Carl A.
West, Jerry
  See Svenson, Andrew E(dward)
West, John
  See Arthur, Robert, (Jr.)
West, Owen
  See Koontz, Dean R(ay)
Westall, Robert (Atkinson)
  1929-1993 ....*69*
  Obituary *75*
  Earlier sketch in SATA 23
  See also CLR 13
  See also SAAS 2
Westaway, Jane 1948- *121*
Westcott, Nadine Bernard 1949- *130*
Westerberg, Christine 1950- *29*
Westerduin, Anne 1945- *105*
Westervelt, Virginia Veeder 1914- *10*
Westheimer, David 1917- *14*
Westmacott, Mary
  See Christie, Agatha (Mary Clarissa)
Westman, Barbara *70*
Westman, Paul (Wendell) 1956- *39*
Westmoreland, William C(hilds)
  1914- *63*
Weston, Allen
  See Hogarth, Grace (Weston Allen)
  and Norton, Andre
Weston, Carol 1956- *135*
Weston, John (Harrison) 1932- *21*
Weston, Martha 1947- *119*
  Earlier sketch in SATA 53
Westphal, Arnold Carl 1897- *57*
Westrup, Hugh *102*
Westwood, Jennifer 1940- *10*
Wexler, Jerome (LeRoy) 1923- *14*
Weyland, Jack 1940- *81*
Weyn, Suzanne 1955- *101*
  Earlier sketch in SATA 63
Wezyk, Joanna 1966- *82*
Whaley, Joyce Irene 1923- *61*
Whalin, W. Terry 1953- *93*
Whalin, W. Terry 1953- *93*
Wharf, Michael
  See Weller, George (Anthony)
Wharmby, Margot *63*
Wheatley, Arabelle 1921- *16*
Wheeler, Cindy 1955- *49*
  Brief entry *40*
Wheeler, Deborah (Jean Ross) 1947- *83*
Wheeler, Janet D. *1*
Wheeler, Jill C. 1964- *136*
  Earlier sketch in SATA 86
Wheeler, Jody 1952- *84*
Wheeler, Opal 1898- *23*
Whelan, Elizabeth M(urphy) 1943- *14*
Whelan, Gloria (Ann) 1923- *128*
  Earlier sketch in SATA 85
Whipple, A(ddison) B(eecher) C(olvin)
  1918- *64*
Whipple, Cal
  See Whipple, A(ddison) B(eecher) C(olvin)
Whistler, Reginald John 1905-1944 ....*30*
Whistler, Rex
  See Whistler, Reginald John
Whitcher, Susan (Godsil) 1952- *96*

Whitcomb, Jon 1906-1988 ....*10*
  Obituary *56*
White, Anne Terry 1896-1980 ....*2*
White, Carolyn 1948- *130*
White, Dale
  See Place, Marian T(empleton)
White, Dori 1919- *10*
White, E(lwyn) B(rooks) 1899-1985 ......*100*
  Obituary *44*
  Earlier sketches in SATA 2, 29
  See also CLR 21
White, Eliza Orne 1856-1947
  See YABC 2
White, Florence M(eiman) 1910- *14*
White, Laurence B(arton), Jr. 1935- *10*
White, Martin 1943- *51*
White, Nancy 1942- *126*
White, Ramy Allison *67*
  Earlier sketch in SATA 1
White, Robb 1909-1990 ....*83*
  Earlier sketch in SATA 1
  See also CLR 3
  See also SAAS 1
White, Ruth (C.) 1942- *117*
  Earlier sketch in SATA 39
White, T(erence) H(anbury)
  1906-1964 ....*12*
White, Tekla N. 1934- *115*
White, Timothy (Thomas Anthony)
  1952-2002 ....*60*
White, William, Jr. 1934- *16*
Whitehead, Don(ald) F. 1908-1981 ....*4*
Whitehouse, Arch
  See Whitehouse, Arthur George Joseph
Whitehouse, Arthur George Joseph
  1895-1979 ....*14*
  Obituary *23*
Whitehouse, Elizabeth S(cott)
  1893-1968 ....*35*
Whitehouse, Jeanne 1939- *29*
Whitelaw, Nancy 1933- *76*
Whitinger, R. D.
  See Place, Marian T(empleton)
Whitley, Mary Ann
  See Sebrey, Mary Ann
Whitley, Peggy 1938- *140*
Whitlock, Ralph 1914-1995 ....*35*
Whitman, Alice
  See Marker, Sherry
Whitman, Sylvia (Choate) 1961- *135*
  Earlier sketch in SATA 85
Whitman, Walt(er) 1819-1892 ....*20*
Whitmore, Arvella 1922- *125*
Whitney, Alex(andra) 1922- *14*
Whitney, David C(harles) 1921- *48*
  Brief entry *29*
Whitney, Phyllis A(yame) 1903- *30*
  Earlier sketch in SATA 1
  See also CLR 59
Whitney, Sharon 1937- *63*
Whitney, Thomas P(orter) 1917- *25*
Whittington, Mary K(athrine) 1941- *75*
Whitworth, John 1945- *123*
Whybrow, Ian *132*
Whyte, Mal(colm Kenneth, Jr.)
  1933- *62*
Whyte, Mary 1953- *94*
Wiater, Stanley 1953- *84*
Wibbelsman, Charles J(oseph) 1945- *59*
Wibberley, Leonard (Patrick O'Connor)
  1915-1983 ....*45*
  Obituary *36*
  Earlier sketch in SATA 2
  See also CLR 3
  See Holton, Leonard
Wiberg, Harald (Albin) 1908- *93*
  Brief entry *40*
Wickens, Elaine *86*
Widdemer, Mabel Cleland 1902-1964 ....*5*
Widener, Terry 1950- *105*
Widerberg, Siv 1931- *10*
Wieler, Diana (Jean) 1961- *109*

Wiener, Lori 1956- *84*
Wier, Ester (Alberti) 1910-2000 ....*3*
Wiese, Kurt 1887-1974 ....*36*
  Obituary *24*
  Earlier sketch in SATA 3
  See also CLR 86
Wiesel, Elie(zer) 1928- *56*
Wiesner, David 1956- *139*
  Earlier sketches in SATA 72, 117
  See also CLR 84
Wiesner, Portia
  See Takakjian, Portia
Wiesner, William 1899-1984 ....*5*
Wiggers, Raymond 1952- *82*
Wiggin, Eric E(llsworth) 1939- *88*
Wiggin (Riggs), Kate Douglas (Smith) 1856-
  1923
  See YABC 1
  See also CLR 52
Wiggins, VeraLee (Chesnut)
  1928-1995 ....*89*
Wight, James Alfred 1916-1995 ....*55*
  Brief entry *44*
  See Herriot, James
Wignell, Edel 1936- *69*
Wijnberg, Ellen *85*
Wikland, Ilon 1930- *93*
  Brief entry *32*
Wikler, Madeline 1943- *114*
Wilber, Donald N(ewton) 1907-1997 ......*35*
Wilbur, C. Keith 1923- *27*
Wilbur, Frances 1921- *107*
Wilbur, Richard (Purdy) 1921- *108*
  Earlier sketch in SATA 9
Wilburn, Kathy 1948- *68*
Wilcox, Charlotte 1948- *72*
Wilcox, R(uth) Turner 1888-1970 ....*36*
Wilcox, Roger
  See Collins, Paul
Wild, Jocelyn 1941- *46*
Wild, Robin (Evans) 1936- *46*
Wild, Robyn 1947- *117*
Wilde, D. Gunther
  See Hurwood, Bernhardt J.
Wilde, Oscar (Fingal O'Flahertie Wills)
  1854(?)-1900 ....*24*
Wilder, Laura (Elizabeth) Ingalls
  1867-1957 ....*100*
  Earlier sketches in SATA 15, 29
  See also CLR 2
Wildsmith, Brian 1930- *124*
  Earlier sketches in SATA 16, 69
  See also CLR 52
  See also SAAS 5
Wilhelm, Hans 1945- *135*
  Earlier sketch in SATA 58
  See also CLR 46
  See also SAAS 21
Wilkie, Katharine E(lliott)
  1904-1980 ....*31*
Wilkin, Eloise 1904-1987 ....*49*
  Obituary *54*
Wilkins, Frances 1923- *14*
Wilkins, Marilyn (Ruth) 1926- *30*
Wilkins, Marne
  See Wilkins, Marilyn (Ruth)
Wilkins, Mary Huiskamp 1926- *139*
  Earlier sketch in SATA 84
  See Calhoun, Mary
Wilkins, Mary Huiskamp Calhoun
  See Wilkins, Mary Huiskamp
Wilkinson, (Thomas) Barry 1923- *50*
  Brief entry *32*
Wilkinson, Beth 1925- *80*
Wilkinson, Brenda 1946- *91*
  Earlier sketch in SATA 14
  See also CLR 20
Wilkinson, (John) Burke 1913-2000 ....*4*
Wilkinson, Sylvia 1940- *56*
  Brief entry *39*
Wilkon, Jozef 1930- *133*
  Earlier sketches in SATA 31, 71

Wilks, Michael Thomas 1947- *44*
Wilks, Mike
  See Wilks, Michael Thomas
Will
  See Lipkind, William
Willard, Barbara (Mary) 1909-1994 ....*74*
  Earlier sketch in SATA *17*
  See also CLR *2*
  See also SAAS *5*
Willard, Mildred Wilds 1911-1978 ....*14*
Willard, Nancy 1936- *127*
  Brief entry *30*
  Earlier sketches in SATA *37, 71*
  See also CLR *5*
Willcox, Isobel 1907-1996 ....*42*
Willett, Edward (C.) 1959- *115*
Willey, Margaret 1950- *86*
Willey, Robert
  See Ley, Willy
Willhoite, Michael A. 1946- *71*
Williams, Barbara 1925- *107*
  Earlier sketch in SATA *11*
  See also CLR *48*
  See also SAAS *16*
Williams, Barbara 1937- *62*
Williams, Beryl
  See Epstein, Beryl (M. Williams)
Williams, Brian (Peter) 1943- *54*
Williams, Carol Lynch 1959- *110*
Williams, Charles
  See Collier, James Lincoln
Williams, Clyde C. 1881-1974 ....*8*
  Obituary *27*
Williams, Coe
  See Harrison, C(hester) William
Williams, Cynthia G. 1958- *123*
Williams, Donna Reilly 1945- *83*
Williams, (Marcia) Dorothy 1945- *97*
  Earlier sketch in SATA *71*
Williams, Eric (Ernest) 1911-1983 ....*14*
  Obituary *38*
Williams, Ferelith Eccles *22*
  See Eccles Williams, Ferelith
Williams, Frances B.
  See Browin, Frances Williams
Williams, Garth (Montgomery)
  1912-1996 ....*66*
  Obituary *90*
  Earlier sketch in SATA *18*
  See also CLR *57*
  See also SAAS *7*
Williams, Guy R(ichard) 1920- *11*
Williams, Hawley
  See Heyliger, William
Williams, Helen 1948- *77*
Williams, J. R.
  See Williams, Jeanne
Williams, J. Walker
  See Wodehouse, P(elham) G(renville)
Williams, Jay 1914-1978 ....*41*
  Obituary *24*
  Earlier sketch in SATA *3*
  See also CLR *8*
Williams, Jeanne 1930- *5*
  See Foster, Jeanne
  and Michaels, Kristin
Williams, Jenny 1939- *60*
Williams, Karen Lynn 1952- *99*
  Earlier sketch in SATA *66*
Williams, Kit 1946(?)- *44*
  See also CLR *4*
Williams, Leslie 1941- *42*
Williams, Linda 1948- *59*
Williams, Lynn
  See Hale, Arlene
Williams, Margery
  See Bianco, Margery Williams
Williams, Mark
  See Arthur, Robert, (Jr.)
Williams, Mark London 1959- *140*
Williams, Maureen 1951- *12*

Williams, Michael
  See St. John, Wylly Folk
Williams, Patrick J.
  See Butterworth, W(illiam) E(dmund III)
Williams, Pete
  See Faulknor, Cliff(ord Vernon)
Williams, S. P.
  See Hart, Virginia
Williams, Sam *124*
Williams, Selma R(uth) 1925- *14*
Williams, Sherley Anne 1944-1999 ....*78*
  Obituary *116*
Williams, Sheron 1955- *77*
Williams, Shirley
  See Williams, Sherley Anne
Williams, Slim
  See Williams, Clyde C.
Williams, Sophy 1965- *135*
Williams, Suzanne (Bullock) 1953- *71*
Williams, Ursula Moray *3*
  See Moray Williams, Ursula
Williams, Vera B(aker) 1927- *102*
  Brief entry *33*
  Earlier sketch in SATA *53*
  See also CLR *9*
Williams-Andriani, Renee 1963- *98*
Williams-Ellis, (Mary) Amabel (Nassau
  Strachey) 1894-1984 ....*29*
  Obituary *41*
Williams-Garcia, Rita 1957- *98*
  See also CLR *36*
Williamson, Gwyneth 1965- *109*
Williamson, Henry (William)
  1895-1977 ....*37*
  Obituary *30*
Williamson, Joanne S(mall) 1926- *122*
  Earlier sketch in SATA *3*
Willis, Charles
  See Clarke, Arthur C(harles)
Willis, Connie 1945- *110*
  See also CLR *66*
Willis, Jeanne (Mary) 1959- *123*
  Earlier sketch in SATA *61*
Willis, Meredith Sue 1946- *101*
Willis, Nancy Carol 1952- *139*
  Earlier sketch in SATA *93*
Willis, Paul J. 1955- *113*
Willms, Russ *95*
Willoughby, Lee Davis
  See Avallone, Michael (Angelo, Jr.)
  and Brandner, Gary (Phil)
  and Deming, Richard
  and DeAndrea, William L(ouis)
  and Streib, Dan(iel Thomas)
  and Toombs, John
  and Webb, Jean Francis (III)
Willson, Robina Beckles *27*
  See Beckles Willson, Robina (Elizabeth)
Wilma, Dana
  See Faralla, Dana
Wilson, April *80*
Wilson, Barbara Ker
  See Ker Wilson, Barbara
Wilson, Beth P(ierre) *8*
Wilson, Budge 1927- *55*
  See Wilson, Marjorie
Wilson, Carletta 1951- *81*
Wilson, Carter 1941- *6*
Wilson, Charles Morrow 1905-1977 ....*30*
Wilson, Darryl B(abe) 1939- *90*
Wilson, Dirk
  See Pohl, Frederik
Wilson, Dorothy Clarke 1904- *16*
Wilson, Edward A(rthur) 1886-1970 ......*38*
Wilson, Ellen (Janet Cameron) (?)-1976 ....*9*
  Obituary *26*
Wilson, Eric (H.) 1940- *34*
  Brief entry *32*
Wilson, Erica *51*
Wilson, Forrest 1918- *27*
Wilson, Gahan 1930- *35*
  Brief entry *27*

Wilson, Gina 1943- *85*
  Brief entry *34*
  Earlier sketch in SATA *36*
Wilson, (Leslie) Granville 1912- *14*
Wilson, Hazel (Hutchins) 1898-1992 ....*3*
  Obituary *73*
Wilson, J(erry) M. 1964- *121*
Wilson, Jacqueline 1945- *102*
  Brief entry *52*
  Earlier sketch in SATA *61*
Wilson, John 1922- *22*
Wilson, Johnniece Marshall 1944- *75*
Wilson, Joyce M(uriel Judson) *84*
  Earlier sketch in SATA *21*
  See Stranger, Joyce
Wilson, Linda Miller 1936- *116*
Wilson, Lionel 1924- *33*
  Brief entry *31*
Wilson, Marjorie
  Brief entry *51*
  See Wilson, Budge
Wilson, Maurice (Charles John)
  1914- *46*
Wilson, Nancy Hope 1947- *138*
  Earlier sketch in SATA *81*
Wilson, Nick
  See Ellis, Edward S(ylvester)
Wilson, Ron(ald William) 1941- *38*
Wilson, Sarah 1934- *50*
Wilson, Tom 1931- *33*
  Brief entry *30*
Wilson, Walt(er N.) 1939- *14*
Wilson-Max, Ken 1965- *93*
Wilton, Elizabeth 1937- *14*
Wilwerding, Walter Joseph 1891-1966 ......*9*
Wimmer, Mike 1961- *70*
Winborn, Marsha (Lynn) 1947- *75*
Winch, John 1944- *117*
Winchester, James H(ugh)
  1917-1985 ....*30*
  Obituary *45*
Winchester, Stanley
  See Youd, (Christopher) Samuel
Winders, Gertrude Hecker -1987 ....*3*
Windham, Basil
  See Wodehouse, P(elham) G(renville)
Windham, Kathryn T(ucker) 1918- *14*
Windrow, Martin
  See Windrow, Martin Clive
Windrow, Martin C.
  See Windrow, Martin Clive
Windrow, Martin Clive 1944- *68*
Windsor, Claire
  See Hamerstrom, Frances
Windsor, Linda 1950- *124*
Windsor, Patricia 1938- *78*
  Earlier sketch in SATA *30*
  See also SAAS *19*
Wineman-Marcus, Irene 1952- *81*
Winer, Yvonne 1934- *120*
Winfield, Arthur M.
  See Stratemeyer, Edward L.
Winfield, Edna
  See Stratemeyer, Edward L.
Winfield, Julia
  See Armstrong, Jennifer
Wing, Natasha (Lazutin) 1960- *82*
Winick, Judd 1970- *124*
Winks, Robin William 1930- *61*
Winn, Alison
  See Wharmby, Margot
Winn, Chris 1952- *42*
Winn, Janet Bruce 1928- *43*
Winn, Marie 1936(?)- *38*
Winnick, Karen B(eth) B(inkoff)
  1946- *51*
Winslow, Barbara 1947- *91*
Winston, Clara 1921-1983 ....*54*
  Obituary *39*
Winston, Richard 1917-1979 ....*54*
Winter, Janet 1926- *126*
Winter, Milo (Kendall) 1888-1956 ....*21*

Winter, Paula Cecelia 1929- *48*
Winter, R. R.
    See Winterbotham, R(ussell) R(obert)
Winterbotham, R(ussell) R(obert)
    1904-1971 ....*10*
Winterbotham, Russ
    See Winterbotham, R(ussell) R(obert)
Winterfeld, Henry 1901-1990 ....*55*
Winters, J. C.
    See Cross, Gilbert B.
Winters, Jon
    See Cross, Gilbert B.
Winters, Kay 1936- *103*
Winters, Nina 1944- *62*
Winters, Paul A. 1965- *106*
Winterton, Gayle
    See Adams, William Taylor
Winthrop, Elizabeth *76*
    Autobiography Feature *116*
    See Mahony, Elizabeth Winthrop
Winton, Ian (Kenneth) 1960- *76*
Winton, Tim 1960- *98*
Wirt, Ann
    See Benson, Mildred (Augustine Wirt)
Wirt, Mildred A.
    See Benson, Mildred (Augustine Wirt)
Wirtenberg, Patricia Z(arrella) 1932- *10*
Wirth, Beverly 1938- *63*
Wirths, Claudine (Turner) G(ibson)
    1926-2000 ....*104*
    Earlier sketch in SATA *64*
Wise, William 1923- *4*
Wise, Winifred E. *2*
Wiseman, Ann (Sayre) 1926- *31*
Wiseman, B(ernard) 1922-1995 ....*4*
Wiseman, David 1916- *43*
    Brief entry *40*
Wishinsky, Frieda 1948- *112*
    Earlier sketch in SATA *70*
Wisler, G(ary) Clifton 1950- *103*
    Brief entry *46*
    Earlier sketch in SATA *58*
    See McLennan, Will
Wismer, Donald (Richard) 1946- *59*
Wisner, Bill
    See Wisner, William L.
Wisner, William L. 1914(?)-1983 ....*42*
Wisnewski, David 1953-2002
    See Wisniewski, David
Wisniewski, David 1953-2002 ....*95*
    Obituary *139*
    See also CLR *51*
Wister, Owen 1860-1938 ....*62*
Witham, (Phillip) Ross 1917- *37*
Withers, Carl A. 1900-1970 ....*14*
Withrow, Sarah 1966- *124*
Witt, Dick 1948- *80*
Witt, Shirley Hill 1934- *17*
Wittanen, Etolin 1907- *55*
Wittels, Harriet Joan 1938- *31*
Wittig, Susan
    See Albert, Susan Wittig
Wittlinger, Ellen 1948- *122*
    Autobiography Feature *128*
    Earlier sketch in SATA *83*
Wittman, Sally (Anne Christensen)
    1941- *30*
Witty, Paul 1898-1976 ....*50*
    Obituary *30*
Wodehouse, P(elham) G(renville)
    1881-1975 ....*22*
Wodge, Dreary
    See Gorey, Edward (St. John)
Wohlberg, Meg 1905-1990 ....*41*
    Obituary *66*
Wohlrabe, Raymond A. 1900-1977 ....*4*

Wojciechowska, Maia (Teresa)
    1927-2002 ....*83*
    Autobiography Feature *104*
    Obituary *134*
    Earlier sketches in SATA *1, 28*
    See also CLR *1*
    See also SAAS *1*
Wojciechowski, Susan *126*
    Earlier sketch in SATA *78*
Wolcott, Patty 1929- *14*
Wold, Allen L. 1943- *64*
Wold, Jo Anne 1938- *30*
Woldin, Beth Weiner 1955- *34*
Wolf, Bernard 1930- *102*
    Brief entry *37*
Wolf, Gita 1956- *101*
Wolf, Janet 1957- *78*
Wolf, Sallie 1950- *80*
Wolfe, Art 1952- *76*
Wolfe, Burton H. 1932- *5*
Wolfe, Gene (Rodman) 1931- *118*
Wolfe, Louis 1905-1985 ....*8*
    Obituary *133*
Wolfe, Rinna (Evelyn) 1925- *38*
Wolfenden, George
    See Beardmore, George
Wolfer, Dianne 1961- *104*
    Autobiography Feature *117*
Wolff, Alexander (Nikolaus) 1957- *137*
    Earlier sketch in SATA *63*
Wolff, (Jenifer) Ashley 1956- *81*
    Earlier sketch in SATA *50*
Wolff, Diane 1945- *27*
Wolff, Ferida 1946- *79*
Wolff, Robert Jay 1905-1977 ....*10*
Wolff, Sonia
    See Levitin, Sonia (Wolff)
Wolff, Virginia Euwer 1937- *137*
    Earlier sketch in SATA *78*
    See also CLR *62*
Wolfman, Judy 1933- *138*
Wolfson, Evelyn 1937- *62*
Wolitzer, Hilma 1930- *31*
Wolkoff, Judie (Edwards) *93*
    Brief entry *37*
Wolkstein, Diane 1942- *138*
    Earlier sketches in SATA *7, 82*
Wolny, P.
    See Janeczko, Paul B(ryan)
Wolters, Richard A. 1920-1993 ....*35*
Wondriska, William 1931- *6*
Wong, Jade Snow 1922- *112*
Wong, Janet S. 1962- *98*
Wood, Addie Robinson
    See Wiggin, Eric E(llsworth)
Wood, Anne (Savage) 1937- *64*
Wood, Audrey *139*
    Brief entry *44*
    Earlier sketches in SATA *50, 81*
    See also CLR *26*
Wood, Catherine
    See Etchison, Birdie L(ee)
Wood, David 1944- *87*
Wood, Don 1945- *50*
    Brief entry *44*
    See also CLR *26*
Wood, Douglas (Eric) 1951- *132*
    Earlier sketch in SATA *81*
Wood, Edgar A(llardyce) 1907-1998 ....*14*
Wood, Esther
    See Brady, Esther Wood
Wood, Frances Elizabeth *34*
Wood, Frances M. 1951- *97*
Wood, James Playsted 1905- *1*
Wood, Jenny 1955- *88*
Wood, John Norris 1930- *85*
Wood, June Rae 1946- *120*
    Earlier sketch in SATA *79*
    See also CLR *82*
Wood, Kerry
    See Wood, Edgar A(llardyce)
Wood, Kim Marie *134*

Wood, Laura N.
    See Roper, Laura (Newbold) Wood
Wood, Linda C(arol) 1945- *59*
Wood, Marcia (Mae) 1956- *80*
Wood, Nancy 1936- *6*
Wood, Nuria
    See Nobisso, Josephine
Wood, Owen 1929- *64*
Wood, Phyllis Anderson 1923- *33*
    Brief entry *30*
Wood, Richard 1949- *110*
Wood, Tim(othy William Russell)
    1946- *88*
Woodard, Carol 1929- *14*
Woodburn, John Henry 1914- *11*
Woodbury, David Oakes 1896-1981 ....*62*
Woodford, Peggy 1937- *25*
Woodhouse, Barbara (Blackburn)
    1910-1988 ....*63*
Wooding, Sharon
    See Wooding, Sharon L(ouise)
Wooding, Sharon L(ouise) 1943- *66*
Woodman, Allen 1954- *76*
Woodrich, Mary Neville 1915- *2*
Woodruff, Elvira 1951- *106*
    Earlier sketch in SATA *70*
Woodruff, Joan Leslie 1953- *104*
Woodruff, Marian
    See Goudge, Eileen
Woodruff, Noah 1977- *86*
Woods, George A(llan) 1926-1988 ....*30*
    Obituary *57*
Woods, Geraldine 1948- *111*
    Brief entry *42*
    Earlier sketch in SATA *56*
Woods, Harold 1945- *56*
    Brief entry *42*
Woods, Lawrence
    See Lowndes, Robert A(ugustine) W(ard)
Woods, Margaret 1921- *2*
Woods, Nat
    See Stratemeyer, Edward L.
Woodson, Jack
    See Woodson, John Waddie Jr.
Woodson, Jacqueline (Amanda)
    1964- *139*
    Earlier sketch in SATA *94*
    See also CLR *49*
Woodson, John Waddie Jr. 1913- *10*
Woodtor, Dee
    See Woodtor, Delores Parmer
Woodtor, Dee Parmer 1945(?)-2002
    See Woodtor, Delores Parmer
Woodtor, Delores Parmer 1945-2002 ....*93*
Woodward, (Landon) Cleveland
    1900-1986 ....*10*
    Obituary *48*
Woodworth, Viki 1952- *127*
Woody, Regina Jones 1894-1983 ....*3*
Woog, Adam 1953- *125*
    Earlier sketch in SATA *84*
Wooldridge, Connie Nordhielm
    1950- *92*
Wooldridge, Frosty 1947- *140*
Wooldridge, Rhoda 1906-1988 ....*22*
Wooley, Susan Frelick 1945- *113*
Woolf, Paula 1950- *104*
Woolley, Catherine 1904- *3*
Woolman, Steven 1969- *90*
Woolsey, Janette 1904-1989 ....*3*
    Obituary *131*
Worcester, Donald E(mmet) 1915- *18*
Word, Reagan 1944- *103*
Work, Virginia 1946- *57*
    Brief entry *45*
Worline, Bonnie Bess 1914- *14*
Wormell, Christopher 1955- *103*
Wormell, Mary 1959- *96*
Wormser, Richard 1933-1977 ....*106*
    Autobiography Feature *118*
    See also SAAS *26*
Wormser, Sophie 1897-1979 ....*22*

Worth, Richard
    See Wiggin, Eric E(llsworth)
Worth, Richard 1945- 59
    Brief entry 46
Worth, Valerie -1994 70
    Earlier sketch in SATA 8
    See also CLR 21
    See Bahlke, Valerie Worth
Wortis, Avi 1937- 14
    See Avi
Wosmek, Frances 1917- 29
Woychuk, Denis 1953- 71
Wrede, Patricia C(ollins) 1953- 67
Wriggins, Sally Hovey 1922- 17
Wright, Alexandra 1979- 103
Wright, Betty Ren 109
    Brief entry 48
    Earlier sketch in SATA 63
Wright, Cliff 1963- 76
Wright, Courtni
    See Wright, Courtni C(rump)
Wright, Courtni C(rump) 1950- 84
Wright, Courtni Crump
    See Wright, Courtni C(rump)
Wright, Dare 1914(?)-2001 21
    Obituary 124
Wright, David K. 1943- 112
    Earlier sketch in SATA 73
Wright, Enid Meadowcroft (LaMonte)
    1898-1966 3
Wright, Esmond 1915- 10
Wright, Frances Fitzpatrick
    1897-1982 10
Wright, J. B.
    See Barkan, Joanne
Wright, Judith (Arundell) 1915-2000 ...14
    Obituary 121
Wright, Katrina
    See Gater, Dilys
Wright, Kenneth
    See del Rey, Lester
Wright, Kit 1944- 87
Wright, Leslie B(ailey) 1959- 91
Wright, Nancy Means 38
Wright, R(obert) H(amilton) 1906- 6
Wright, Rachel 134
Wright, Susan Kimmel 1950- 97
Wrightfrierson
    See Wright-Frierson, Virginia (Marguerite)
Wright-Frierson, Virginia (Marguerite)
    1949- 110
    Earlier sketch in SATA 58
Wrightson, (Alice) Patricia 1921- 112
    Earlier sketches in SATA 8, 66
    See also CLR 14
    See also SAAS 4
Wroble, Lisa A. 1963- 134
Wronker, Lili
    See Wronker, Lili Cassel
Wronker, Lili Cassel 1924- 10
Wryde, Dogear
    See Gorey, Edward (St. John)
Wu, Norbert 1961- 101
Wulffson, Don L. 1943- 88
    Earlier sketch in SATA 32
Wunderli, Stephen 1958- 79
Wunsch, Josephine (McLean) 1914- 64
Wuorio, Eva-Lis 1918- 34
    Brief entry 28
Wurts, Janny 1953- 98
Wyatt, B. D.
    See Robinson, Spider
Wyatt, Jane
    See Bradbury, Bianca (Ryley)
Wyeth, Betsy James 1921- 41
Wyeth, N(ewell) C(onvers)
    1882-1945 17
Wyler, Rose 1909-2000 18
    Obituary 121
Wylie, Betty Jane 48
Wylie, Laura
    See Matthews, Patricia (Anne)

Wylie, Laurie
    See Matthews, Patricia (Anne)
Wyllie, Stephen 86
Wyman, Andrea 75
Wyman, Carolyn 1956- 83
Wymer, Norman (George) 1911- 25
Wynard, Talbot
    See Hamilton, Charles (Harold St. John)
Wyndham, John
    See Harris, John (Wyndham Parkes Lucas) Beynon
Wyndham, Lee
    See Hyndman, Jane Andrews Lee
Wyndham, Robert
    See Hyndman, Robert Utley
Wynne-Jones, Tim(othy) 1948- 136
    Earlier sketches in SATA 67, 96
    See also CLR 58
Wynter, Edward (John) 1914- 14
Wynyard, Talbot
    See Hamilton, Charles (Harold St. John)
Wyss, Johann David Von 1743-1818 29
    Brief entry 27
Wyss, Thelma Hatch 1934- 140
    Earlier sketch in SATA 10

X

Xavier, Father
    See Hurwood, Bernhardt J.
Xuan, YongSheng 1952- 116
    Autobiography Feature 119

Y

Yaccarino, Dan 141
Yadin, (Rav-Aloof) Yigael
    1917-1984 55
Yaffe, Alan
    See Yorinks, Arthur
Yakovetic, (Joseph Sandy) 1952- 59
Yakovetic, Joe
    See Yakovetic, (Joseph Sandy)
Yamaguchi, Marianne (Illenberger)
    1936- 7
Yamaka, Sara 1978- 92
Yancey, Diane 1951- 138
    Earlier sketch in SATA 81
Yang, Jay 1941- 12
Yang, Mingyi 1943- 72
Yarbrough, Camille 1938- 79
    See also CLR 29
Yaroslava
    See Mills, Yaroslava Surmach
Yashima, Taro
    See CLR 4
    See Iwamatsu, Jun Atsushi
Yates, Elizabeth 1905-2001 68
    Obituary 128
    Earlier sketch in SATA 4
    See also SAAS 6
Yates, Janelle K(aye) 1957- 77
Yates, John 1939- 74
Yates, Philip 1956- 92
Yates, Raymond F(rancis) 1895-1966 31
Yaukey, Grace S(ydenstricker)
    1899-1994 80
    Earlier sketch in SATA 5
Ye, Ting-xing 1952- 106
Yeakley, Marjory Hall 1908- 21
Yeatman, Linda 1938- 42
Yee, Brenda Shannon 133
Yee, Paul (R.) 1956- 96
    Earlier sketch in SATA 67
    See also CLR 44
Yee, Wong Herbert 1953- 115
    Earlier sketch in SATA 78
Yeh, Chun-Chan 1914- 79

Yenawine, Philip 1942- 85
Yensid, Retlaw
    See Disney, Walt(er Elias)
Yeo, Wilma (Lethem) 1918-1994 81
    Earlier sketch in SATA 24
Yeoman, John 1934- 80
    Earlier sketch in SATA 28
    See also CLR 46
Yep, Laurence Michael 1948- 123
    Earlier sketches in SATA 7, 69
    See also CLR 54
Yepsen, Roger B(ennet), Jr. 1947- 59
Yerian, Cameron John 21
Yerian, Margaret A. 21
Yetska
    See Ironside, Jetske
Yoder, Dorothy Meenen 1921- 96
Yoder, Dot
    See Yoder, Dorothy Meenen
Yoder, Walter D. 1933- 88
Yolen, Jane (Hyatt) 1939- 112
    Autobiography Feature 111
    Earlier sketches in SATA 4, 40, 75
    See also CLR 44
    See also SAAS 1
Yonge, Charlotte (Mary) 1823-1901 17
Yorinks, Arthur 1953- 85
    Earlier sketches in SATA 33, 49
    See also CLR 20
York, Alison
    See Nicole, Christopher (Robin)
York, Andrew
    See Nicole, Christopher (Robin)
York, Carol Beach 1928- 77
    Earlier sketch in SATA 6
York, Rebecca
    See Buckholtz, Eileen (Garber)
    and Glick, Ruth (Burtnick)
York, Simon
    See Heinlein, Robert A(nson)
Yoshida, Toshi 1911- 77
Youd, C. S.
    See SAAS 6
    See Youd, (Christopher) Samuel
Youd, (Christopher) Samuel 1922- 135
    Brief entry 30
    Earlier sketch in SATA 47
    See Christopher, John
    and Youd, C. S.
Young, Bob
    See Young, Robert W(illiam)
    and Young, James Robert
Young, Carol 1945- 102
Young, Catherine
    See Olds, Helen Diehl
Young, Clarence 67
    Earlier sketch in SATA 1
    See Stratemeyer, Edward L.
Young, Collier
    See Bloch, Robert (Albert)
Young, Dan 1952- 126
Young, Dianne 1959- 88
Young, Dorothea Bennett 1924- 31
Young, Ed (Tse-chun) 1931- 122
    Earlier sketches in SATA 10, 74
    See also CLR 27
Young, Edward
    See Reinfeld, Fred
Young, Elaine L.
    See Schulte, Elaine L(ouise)
Young, James
    See Graham, Ian
Young, James
    See Graham, Ian
Young, Jan
    See Young, Janet Randall
Young, Janet Randall 1919-1994 3
Young, Jeff C. 1948- 132
Young, John
    See Macintosh, Brownie
Young, Judy (Elaine) Dockrey 1949- 72
Young, Karen Romano 1959- 116

Young, Ken 1956- 86
Young, Lois Horton 1911-1981 26
Young, Louise B. 1919- 64
Young, Margaret B(uckner) 1922- 2
Young, Mary 1940- 89
Young, Miriam 1913-1974 7
Young, Noela 1930- 89
Young, (Rodney Lee) Patrick (Jr.)
     1937- 22
Young, Percy M(arshall) 1912- 31
Young, Richard Alan 1946- 72
Young, Robert W(illiam) 1916-1969 3
Young, Ruth 1946- 67
Young, Scott A(lexander) 1918- 5
Young, Vivien
     See Gater, Dilys
Younger, Barbara 1954- 108
Youngs, Betty 1934-1985 53
     Obituary 42
Younkin, Paula 1942- 77
Yount, Lisa (Ann) 1944- 124
     Earlier sketch in SATA 74
Yount, Lisa (Ann) 1944- 124
Yuditskaya, Tatyana 1964- 75

Z

Zach, Cheryl (Byrd) 1947- 98
     Brief entry 51
     Earlier sketch in SATA 58
     See also SAAS 24
Zaffo, George J. (?)-1984 42
Zagwyn, Deborah Turney 1953- 138
     Earlier sketch in SATA 78
Zahn, Timothy 1951- 91
Zaid, Barry 1938- 51
Zaidenberg, Arthur 1908(?)-1990 34
     Obituary 66
Zalben, Jane Breskin 1950- 120
     Earlier sketches in SATA 7, 79
     See also CLR 84
Zallinger, Jean (Day) 1918- 115
     Earlier sketches in SATA 14, 80
Zallinger, Peter Franz 1943- 49
Zambreno, Mary Frances 1954- 140
     Earlier sketch in SATA 75
Zanderbergen, George
     See May, Julian
Zappler, Lisbeth 1930- 10
Zarchy, Harry 1912-1987 34
Zarin, Cynthia 1959- 108
Zaring, Jane (Thomas) 1936- 40
Zarins, Joyce Audy
     See dos Santos, Joyce Audy
Zaslavsky, Claudia 1917- 36

Zaugg, Sandra L. 1938- 118
Zaugg, Sandy
     See Zaugg, Sandra L.
Zaunders, Bo 1939- 137
Zawadzki, Marek 1958- 97
Zebra, A.
     See Scoltock, Jack
Zebrowski, George (T.) 1945- 67
Zeck, Gerald Anthony 1939- 40
Zeck, Gerry
     See Zeck, Gerald Anthony
Zed, Dr.
     See Penrose, Gordon
Zei, Alki 1925- 24
     See also CLR 6
Zeier, Joan T(heresa) 1931- 81
Zeinert, Karen 1942-2002 137
     Earlier sketch in SATA 79
Zelazny, Roger (Joseph) 1937-1995 57
     Brief entry 39
Zeldis, Malcah 1931- 86
Zelinsky, Paul O. 1953- 102
     Brief entry 33
     Earlier sketch in SATA 49
     See also CLR 55
Zellan, Audrey Penn 22
     See Penn, Audrey
Zemach, Harve 3
     See Fischtrom, Harvey
Zemach, Kaethe 1958- 49
     Brief entry 39
Zemach, Margot 1931-1989 70
     Obituary 59
     Earlier sketch in SATA 21
Zephaniah, Benjamin (Obadiah Iqbal)
     1958- 140
     Earlier sketch in SATA 86
Zerman, Melvyn Bernard 1930- 46
Zettner, Pat 1940- 70
Zhang, Christopher Zhong-Yuan
     1954- 91
Zhang, Song Nan 1942- 85
Ziefert, Harriet 1941- 101
Ziegler, Jack (Denmore) 1942- 60
Ziemienski, Dennis (Theodore)
     1947- 10
Ziliox, Marc
     See Fichter, George S.
Zillah
     See Macdonald, Zillah K(atherine)
Zim, Herbert S(pencer) 1909-1994 30
     Obituary 85
     Earlier sketch in SATA 1
     See also CLR 2
     See also SAAS 2
Zima, Gordon 1920- 90

Zimelman, Nathan 1921- 65
     Brief entry 37
Zimmer, Dirk 1943- 65
Zimmerman, Andrea Griffing 1950- 123
Zimmerman, H(einz) Werner 1951- 101
Zimmerman, Naoma 1914- 10
Zimmermann, Arnold E. 1909- 58
Zimmett, Debbie
     See Becker, Deborah Zimmett
Zimmy
     See Stratemeyer, Edward L.
Zimnik, Reiner 1930- 36
     See also CLR 3
Zindel, Bonnie 1943- 34
Zindel, Paul 1936-2003 102
     Earlier sketches in SATA 16, 58
     See also CLR 85
Ziner, Feenie
     See Ziner, Florence
Ziner, Florence 1921- 5
Zingara, Professor
     See Leeming, Joseph
Zion, Eugene 1913-1975 18
Zion, Gene
     See Zion, Eugene
Zolkowski, Cathy (A.) 1969- 121
Zolotow, Charlotte (Gertrude) S(hapiro)
     1915- 138
     Earlier sketches in SATA 1, 35, 78
     See also CLR 77
Zonderman, Jon 1957- 92
Zonia, Dhimitri 1921- 20
Zubrowski, Bernard 1939- 90
     Earlier sketch in SATA 35
Zubrowski, Bernie
     See Zubrowski, Bernard
Zucker, Miriam S.
     See Reichert, Miriam Zucker
Zudeck, Darryl 1961- 61
Zupa, G. Anthony
     See Zeck, Gerald Anthony
Zurbo, Matt(hew) 1967- 98
Zurhorst, Charles (Stewart, Jr.)
     1913-1989 12
Zuromskis, Diane
     See Stanley, Diane
Zuromskis, Diane Stanley
     See Stanley, Diane
Zwahlen, Diana 1947- 88
Zweifel, Frances W. 1931- 14
Zwerger, Lisbeth 1954- 130
     Earlier sketch in SATA 66
     See also CLR 46
     See also SAAS 13
Zwinger, Ann (H.) 1925- 46
Zymet, Cathy Alter 1965- 121

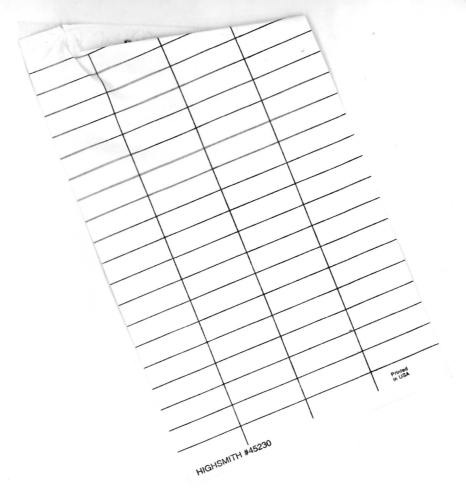

HIGHSMITH #45230

Printed
in USA